AMERICAN DESTINY

AMERICAN DESTINY
NARRATIVE OF A NATION

THIRD EDITION

MARK C. CARNES

Ann Whitney Olin Professor of History
Barnard College, Columbia University

JOHN A. GARRATY

Gouverneur Morris Professor of History, Emeritus
Columbia University

PEARSON
Longman

New York San Francisco Boston
London Toronto Sydney Tokyo Singapore Madrid
Mexico City Munich Paris Cape Town Hong Kong Montreal

Executive Editor: Michael Boezi
Assistant Development Manager: David B. Kear
Development Editor: Karen Helfrich
Executive Marketing Manager: Sue Westmoreland
Supplements Editor: Brian Belardi
Editorial Assistant: Vanessa Gennarelli
Production Manager: Ellen MacElree
Project Coordination, Text Design, and Electronic Page Makeup:
      Nesbitt Graphics, Inc.
Cover Design Manager: Wendy Ann Fredericks
Cover Designer: Susan Koski Zucker
Cover Photo: Milwaukee, WI © Michael DeFreitas
Photo Researcher: Linda Sykes
Senior Manufacturing Buyer: Dennis J. Para
Printer and Binder: Quebecor World/Taunton
Cover Printer: Phoenix Color Corps.

For permission to use copyrighted material, grateful acknowledgment is
made to the copyright holders on pp. C-1–C-5, which are hereby made
part of this copyright page.

Library of Congress Cataloging-in-Publication Data

Carnes, Mark C. (Mark Christopher)
American destiny: narrative of a nation / Mark C. Carnes, John A. Garraty
— 3rd ed.
v. cm.
Includes bibliographic references and index.
Contents: v. 1. To 1877 — v. 2. Since 1865.
ISBN 13: 978-0-205-56804-8 (Complete ed.)
           0-205-56804-1 (Complete ed.)
1. United States—History. I. Garraty, John Arthur, 1920– II. Title.
E178.6.C33 2008
973—dc22 2008040915

Please visit us at www.ablongman.com

ISBN 13: 978-0-205-56804-8 (Complete ed.)
ISBN 10:   0-205-56804-1 (Complete ed.)
ISBN 13: 978-0-321-51087-7 (Vol. 1)
ISBN 10:   0-321-51087-9 (Vol. 1)
ISBN 13: 978-0-321-51086-0 (Vol. 2)
ISBN 10:   0-321-51086-0 (Vol. 2)

1 2 3 4 5 6 7 8 9 10 —WCT— 10 09 08 07

To Our Children:

Stephanie and Kathy, Jack, and Sarah

Brief Contents

Detailed Contents ix
Maps and Graphs xix
Feature Essays xxi
Preface xxiii
Supplements for Instructors and Students xxvii
About the Authors xxx

PROLOGUE   Beginnings 1

CHAPTER 1   Alien Encounters: Europe in the Americas 17

CHAPTER 2   American Society in the Making 52

CHAPTER 3   America in the British Empire 86

CHAPTER 4   The American Revolution 126

CHAPTER 5   The Federalist Era: Nationalism Triumphant 162

CHAPTER 6   Jeffersonian Democracy 194

CHAPTER 7   National Growing Pains 218

CHAPTER 8   Toward a National Economy 250

CHAPTER 9   Jacksonian Democracy 276

CHAPTER 10   The Making of Middle-Class America 300

CHAPTER 11   Westward Expansion 328

CHAPTER 12   The Sections Go Their Ways 350

CHAPTER 13   The Coming of the Civil War 372

CHAPTER 14   The War to Save the Union 400

CHAPTER 15   Reconstruction and the South 435

CHAPTER 16   The Conquest of the West 460

CHAPTER 17   An Industrial Giant 482

CHAPTER 18   American Society in the Industrial Age 510

CHAPTER 19   Intellectual and Cultural Trends 535

CHAPTER 20   Politics: Local, State, and National 554

CHAPTER 21   The Age of Reform 581

CHAPTER 22   From Isolation to Empire 613

CHAPTER 23   Woodrow Wilson and the Great War 640

CHAPTER 24   Postwar Society and Culture: Change and Adjustment 670

CHAPTER 25   The New Era: 1921–1933 697

CHAPTER 26   The New Deal: 1933–1941 721

CHAPTER 27   War and Peace 753

CHAPTER 28   The American Century 780

CHAPTER 29   From Camelot to Watergate 810

CHAPTER 30   Society in Flux 840

CHAPTER 31   Running on Empty: The Nation Transformed 864

CHAPTER 32   Misdemeanors and High Crimes 890

Appendix A-1
Credits C-1
Index I-1

Detailed Contents

Maps and Graphs xix

Feature Essays xxi
  Re-Viewing the Past
  Debating the Past

Preface xxiii

Supplements for Instructors and Students xxvii

About the Authors xxx

PROLOGUE   Beginnings 1

First Peoples 2 ■ The Demise of the Big Mammals 2 ■ The Archaic
Period: A World Without Big Mammals 4 ■ The First Sedentary
Communities 5 ■ The Maize Revolution 7 ■ The Diffusion of Corn 9 ■
Population Growth After 800 9 ■ Cahokia: The Hub of Mississippian
Culture 10 ■ The Collapse of Urban Centers 12 ■ Eurasia and Africa 13 ■
Europe in Ferment 14

CHAPTER 1   Alien Encounters: Europe in the Americas 17

Sightings 18 ■ Columbus's Greatest Triumph—and Error 18 ■ Spain's
American Empire 21 ■ Extending Spain's Empire to the North 23 ■
Disease and Population Losses 25 ■ Ecological Imperialism 25 ■ Spain's
European Rivals 27 ■ The Protestant Reformation 28 ■ English
Beginnings in America 29 ■ The Settlement of Virginia 30 ■ "Purifying"
the Church of England 33 ■ Bradford and Plymouth Colony 35 ■
Winthrop and Massachusetts Bay Colony 36 ■ Troublemakers: Roger
Williams and Anne Hutchinson 39 ■ Other New England Colonies 41 ■
Pequot War and King Philip's War 41 ■ Maryland and the Carolinas 42 ■
French and Dutch Settlements 44 ■ The Middle Colonies 45 ■ Cultural
Collisions 47 ■ Cultural Fusions 49

CHAPTER 2   American Society in the Making 52

Settlement of New France 53 ■ Society in New Mexico, Texas, and
California 54 ■ The English Prevail on the Atlantic Seaboard 56 ■ The
Chesapeake Colonies 57 ■ The Lure of Land 57 ■ "Solving" the Labor
Shortage: Slavery 58 ■ Prosperity in a Pipe: Tobacco 59 ■ Bacon's
Rebellion 61 ■ The Carolinas 63 ■ Home and Family in the South 65 ■
Georgia and the Back Country 66 ■ Puritan New England 68 ■ Puritan
Women and Children 69 ■ Visible Puritan Saints and Others 70 ■

Democracies Without Democrats 71 ▪ The Dominion of New England 72
▪ Salem Bewitched 74 ▪ A Merchant's World 76 ▪ The Middle Colonies:
Economic Basis 77 ▪ The Middle Colonies: An Intermingling of Peoples
80 ▪ The Best Poor Man's Country 82 ▪ The Politics of Diversity 82 ▪
Becoming Americans 84

CHAPTER 3   America in the British Empire 86

The British Colonial System 87 ▪ Mercantilism 89 ▪ The Navigation Acts
90 ▪ The Effects of Mercantilism 92 ▪ The Great Awakening 93 ▪
The Rise and Fall of Jonathan Edwards 96 ▪ The Enlightenment in
America 97 ▪ Colonial Scientific Achievements 99 ▪ Repercussions of
Distant Wars 100 ▪ The Great War for the Empire 102 ▪ Britain
Victorious: The Peace of Paris 105 ▪ Burdens of an Expanded Empire 106
▪ Tightening Imperial Controls 108 ▪ The Sugar Act 110 ▪ American
Colonists Demand Rights 111 ▪ The Stamp Act: The Pot Set to Boiling 112
▪ Rioters or Rebels? 114 ▪ Taxation or Tyranny? 115 ▪ The Declaratory
Act 116 ▪ The Townshend Duties 117 ▪ The Boston Massacre 118 ▪
The Pot Spills Over 120 ▪ The Tea Act Crisis 121 ▪ From Resistance
to Revolution 122

CHAPTER 4   The American Revolution 126

The Shot Heard Round the World 127 ▪ The Second Continental Congress
129 ▪ The Battle of Bunker Hill 129 ▪ The Great Declaration 130 ▪ 1776:
The Balance of Forces 134 ▪ Loyalists 136 ▪ Early British Victories 137 ▪
Saratoga and the French Alliance 139 ▪ The War Moves South 142 ▪
Victory at Yorktown 143 ▪ Negotiating a Favorable Peace 145 ▪ National
Government Under the Articles of Confederation 147 ▪ Financing the War
150 ▪ State Republican Governments 152 ▪ Social Reform 153 ▪ Effects of
the Revolution on Women 155 ▪ Growth of a National Spirit 157 ▪ The
Great Land Ordinances 158 ▪ National Heroes 160

CHAPTER 5   The Federalist Era: Nationalism Triumphant 162

Inadequacies of the Articles of Confederation 163 ▪ Daniel Shays's "Little
Rebellion" 164 ▪ To Philadelphia, and the Constitution 165 ▪ The Great
Convention 166 ▪ The Compromises That Produced the Constitution 168
▪ Ratifying the Constitution 171 ▪ Washington as President 173 ▪
Congress Under Way 175 ▪ Hamilton and Financial Reform 176 ▪ The
Ohio Country: A Dark and Bloody Ground 180 ▪ Revolution in France 181
▪ Federalists and Republicans: The Rise of Political Parties 182 ▪ 1794:
Crisis and Resolution 183 ▪ Jay's Treaty 184 ▪ 1795: All's Well That Ends
Well 185 ▪ Washington's Farewell 186 ▪ The Election of 1796 187 ▪ The
XYZ Affair 189 ▪ The Alien and Sedition Acts 190 ▪ The Kentucky and
Virginia Resolves 191

CHAPTER 6 Jeffersonian Democracy 194

Jefferson Elected President 195 ■ The Federalist Contribution 196 ■
Thomas Jefferson: Political Theorist 197 ■ Jefferson as President 199 ■
Jefferson's Attack on the Judiciary 200 ■ The Barbary Pirates 201 ■ The
Louisiana Purchase 202 ■ The Federalists Discredited 206 ■ Lewis and
Clark 207 ■ The Burr Conspiracy 209 ■ Napoleon and the British 211 ■
The Impressment Controversy 212 ■ The Embargo Act 213 ■ Jeffersonian
Democracy 216

CHAPTER 7 National Growing Pains 218

Madison in Power 219 ■ Tecumseh and Indian Resistance 220 ■
Depression and Land Hunger 222 ■ Opponents of War 222 ■ The War of
1812 224 ■ Britain Assumes the Offensive 227 ■ "The Star Spangled
Banner" 228 ■ The Treaty of Ghent 230 ■ The Hartford Convention 231 ■
The Battle of New Orleans 232 ■ Victory Weakens the Federalists 233 ■
Anglo-American Rapprochement 234 ■ The Transcontinental Treaty 235 ■
The Monroe Doctrine 236 ■ The Era of Good Feelings 238 ■ New
Sectional Issues 240 ■ The Missouri Compromise 241 ■ The Election of
1824 244 ■ John Quincy Adams as President 246 ■ Calhoun's *Exposition
and Protest* 246 ■ The Meaning of Sectionalism 248

CHAPTER 8 Toward a National Economy 250

Gentility and the Consumer Revolution 251 ■ Birth of the Factory 252 ■
An Industrial Proletariat? 253 ■ Lowell's Waltham System: Women as
Factory Workers 255 ■ Irish and German Immigrants 256 ■ The
Persistence of the Household System 257 ■ Rise of Corporations 258 ■
Cotton Revolutionizes the South 258 ■ Revival of Slavery 261 ■ Roads to
Market 264 ■ Transportation and the Government 266 ■ Development of
Steamboats 267 ■ The Canal Boom 267 ■ New York City: Emporium of
the Western World 268 ■ The Marshall Court 270

CHAPTER 9 Jacksonian Democracy 276

"Democratizing" Politics 277 ■ 1828: The New Party System in Embryo 278
■ The Jacksonian Appeal 280 ■ The Spoils System 280 ■ President of All
the People 281 ■ Jackson: "The Bank . . . I Will Kill It!" 282 ■ Jackson's Bank
Veto 284 ■ Jackson Versus Calhoun 286 ■ Indian Removals 287 ■ The
Nullification Crisis 289 ■ Boom and Bust 292 ■ The Jacksonians 293 ■
Rise of the Whigs 294 ■ Martin Van Buren: Jacksonianism Without
Jackson 296 ■ The Log Cabin Campaign 297

CHAPTER 10 The Making of Middle-Class America 300

Tocqueville: Democracy in America 301 ■ The Family Recast 302 ■ The
Second Great Awakening 304 ■ Backwoods Utopias 306 ■ The Age of

Reform 309 ▪ "Demon Rum" 311 ▪ The Abolitionist Crusade 313 ▪
Women's Rights 316 ▪ The Romantic View of Life 318 ▪ Emerson and
Thoreau 319 ▪ Edgar Allan Poe 320 ▪ Nathaniel Hawthorne 321 ▪
Herman Melville 321 ▪ Walt Whitman 322 ▪ Education for Democracy
324 ▪ The State of the Colleges 325

CHAPTER 11   Westward Expansion 328

Tyler's Troubles 329 ▪ The Webster-Ashburton Treaty 330 ▪ The Texas
Question 330 ▪ Manifest Destiny 332 ▪ Life on the Trail 332 ▪ California
and Oregon 334 ▪ The Election of 1844 335 ▪ Polk as President 336 ▪
War with Mexico 337 ▪ To the Halls of Montezuma 338 ▪ The Treaty of
Guadalupe Hidalgo 340 ▪ The Fruits of Victory: Further Enlargement of
the United States 341 ▪ Slavery: The Storm Clouds Gather 342 ▪ The
Election of 1848 343 ▪ The Gold Rush 344 ▪ The Compromise of 1850 346

CHAPTER 12   The Sections Go Their Ways 350

The Economics of Slavery 351 ▪ The Sociology of Slavery 353 ▪
Psychological Effects of Slavery 356 ▪ Manufacturing in the South 358 ▪
The Northern Industrial Juggernaut 358 ▪ A Nation of Immigrants 360 ▪
How Wage Earners Lived 360 ▪ Foreign Commerce 362 ▪ Steam
Conquers the Atlantic 363 ▪ Canals and Railroads 364 ▪ Financing the
Railroads 365 ▪ Railroads and the Economy 366 ▪ Railroads and the
Sectional Conflict 369 ▪ The Economy on the Eve of Civil War 370

CHAPTER 13   The Coming of the Civil War 372

The Slave Power Comes North 373 ▪ *Uncle Tom's Cabin* 373 ▪ Diversions
Abroad: The "Young America" Movement 374 ▪ Stephen Douglas: "The
Little Giant" 376 ▪ The Kansas-Nebraska Act 377 ▪ Know-Nothings,
Republicans, and the Demise of the Two-Party System 379 ▪ "Bleeding
Kansas" 380 ▪ Senator Sumner Becomes a Martyr for Abolitionism 383 ▪
Buchanan Tries His Hand 384 ▪ The Dred Scott Decision 385 ▪ The
Proslavery Lecompton Constitution 387 ▪ The Emergence of Lincoln 388
▪ The Lincoln-Douglas Debates 389 ▪ John Brown's Raid 392 ▪ The
Election of 1860 393 ▪ The Secession Crisis 396

CHAPTER 14   The War to Save the Union 400

Lincoln's Cabinet 401 ▪ Fort Sumter: The First Shot 402 ▪ The Blue and
the Gray 402 ▪ The Test of Battle: Bull Run 405 ▪ Paying for the War 407
▪ Politics as Usual 407 ▪ Behind Confederate Lines 408 ▪ War in the
West: Shiloh 410 ▪ McClellan: The Reluctant Warrior 411 ▪ Lee
Counterattacks: Antietam 413 ▪ The Emancipation Proclamation 414 ▪
The Draft Riots 416 ▪ The Emancipated People 416 ▪ African American

Soldiers 417 ▪ Antietam to Gettysburg 418 ▪ Lincoln Finds His General: Grant at Vicksburg 422 ▪ Economic and Social Effects, North and South 423 ▪ Women in Wartime 424 ▪ Grant in the Wilderness 426 ▪ Sherman in Georgia 427 ▪ To Appomattox Court House 430 ▪ Winners, Losers, and the Future 430

CHAPTER 15 Reconstruction and the South 435

The Assassination of Lincoln 436 ▪ Presidential Reconstruction 436 ▪ Republican Radicals 439 ▪ Congress Rejects Johnsonian Reconstruction 440 ▪ The Fourteenth Amendment 441 ▪ The Reconstruction Acts 442 ▪ Congress Supreme 443 ▪ The Fifteenth Amendment 444 ▪ "Black Republican" Reconstruction: Scalawags and Carpetbaggers 445 ▪ The Ravaged Land 448 ▪ Sharecropping and the Crop-Lien System 450 ▪ The White Backlash 452 ▪ Grant as President 454 ▪ The Disputed Election of 1876 455 ▪ The Compromise of 1877 457

CHAPTER 16 The Conquest of the West 460

The West After the Civil War 461 ▪ The Plains Indians 462 ▪ Indian Wars 463 ▪ The Destruction of Tribal Life 466 ▪ The Lure of Gold and Silver in the West 468 ▪ Big Business and the Land Bonanza 471 ▪ Western Railroad Building 473 ▪ The Cattle Kingdom 476 ▪ Open-Range Ranching 477 ▪ Barbed-Wire Warfare 478

CHAPTER 17 An Industrial Giant 482

Essentials of Industrial Growth 483 ▪ Railroads: The First Big Business 484 ▪ Iron, Oil, and Electricity 486 ▪ Competition and Monopoly: The Railroads 489 ▪ Competition and Monopoly: Steel 491 ▪ Competition and Monopoly: Oil 493 ▪ American Ambivalence to Big Business 496 ▪ Reformers: George, Bellamy, Lloyd, and the Marxists 498 ▪ The Government Reacts to Big Business: Railroad Regulation 501 ▪ The Government Reacts to Big Business: The Sherman Antitrust Act 502 ▪ The Labor Union Movement 503 ▪ The American Federation of Labor 505 ▪ Labor Militancy Rebuffed 506 ▪ Whither America, Whither Democracy? 508

CHAPTER 18 American Society in the Industrial Age 510

Middle-Class Life 511 ▪ Skilled and Unskilled Workers 512 ▪ Working Women 513 ▪ Farmers 514 ▪ Working-Class Attitudes 516 ▪ Working Your Way Up 516 ▪ The "New" Immigration 518 ▪ New Immigrants Face New Nativism 520 ▪ The Expanding City and Its Problems 521 ▪ Teeming Tenements 523 ▪ The Cities Modernize 525 ▪ Leisure Activities: More Fun and Games 526 ▪ Christianity's Conscience and the Social Gospel 530 ▪ The Settlement Houses 531 ▪ Civilization and Its Discontents 533

CHAPTER 19   Intellectual and Cultural Trends 535

Colleges and Universities 536 ■ Revolution in the Social Sciences 539 ■ Progressive Education 540 ■ History 542 ■ Realism in Literature 542 ■ Mark Twain 544 ■ William Dean Howells 545 ■ Henry James 546 ■ The Pragmatic Approach 547 ■ The Knowledge Revolution 551

CHAPTER 20   Politics: Local, State, and National 554

Congress Ascendant 555 ■ The Recurrent Issues 557 ■ Party Politics: Sidestepping the Issue 559 ■ Lackluster Presidents: From Hayes to Harrison 559 ■ Blacks in the South After Reconstruction 564 ■ Booker T. Washington: A "Reasonable" Champion for Blacks 565 ■ City Bosses 567 ■ Crops and Complaints 569 ■ The Populist Movement 569 ■ Showdown on Silver 574 ■ The Depression of 1893 574 ■ The Election of 1896 577 ■ The Meaning of the Election 579

CHAPTER 21   The Age of Reform 581

Roots of Progressivism 582 ■ The Progressive Mind 584 ■ "Radical" Progressives: The Wave of the Future 586 ■ Political Reform: Cities First 586 ■ Political Reform: The States 587 ■ State Social Legislation 588 ■ Political Reform: The Woman Suffrage Movement 590 ■ Political Reform: Income Taxes and Popular Election of Senators 594 ■ Theodore Roosevelt: Cowboy in the White House 594 ■ Roosevelt and Big Business 596 ■ Roosevelt and the Coal Strike 596 ■ TR's Triumphs 598 ■ Roosevelt Tilts Left 600 ■ William Howard Taft: The Listless Progressive, or More Is Less 600 ■ Breakup of the Republican Party 602 ■ The Election of 1912 603 ■ Wilson: The New Freedom 605 ■ The Progressives and Minority Rights 607 ■ Black Militancy 608

CHAPTER 22   From Isolation to Empire 613

Origins of the Large Policy: Coveting Colonies 614 ■ Toward an Empire in the Pacific 616 ■ Toward an Empire in Latin America 619 ■ The Cuban Revolution 621 ■ The "Splendid Little" Spanish-American War 624 ■ Developing a Colonial Policy 627 ■ The Anti-Imperialists 627 ■ The Philippine Insurrection 629 ■ Cuba and the United States 630 ■ The United States in the Caribbean and Central America 631 ■ The Open Door Policy 633 ■ The Panama Canal 634 ■ Imperialism Without Colonies 638

CHAPTER 23   Woodrow Wilson and the Great War 640

Wilson's "Moral" Diplomacy 641 ■ Europe Explodes in War 642 ■ Freedom of the Seas 644 ■ The Election of 1916 646 ■ The Road to War 647 ■ Mobilizing the Economy 648 ■ Workers in Wartime 650 ■ Paying for the War 650 ■ Propaganda and Civil Liberties 651 ■ Wartime Reforms 652 ■ Women and Blacks in Wartime 653 ■ Americans: To the Trenches

and Over the Top 656 ▪ Preparing for Peace 657 ▪ The Paris Peace
Conference and the Versailles Treaty 660 ▪ The Senate Rejects the League
of Nations 662 ▪ The Red Scare 665 ▪ The Election of 1920 668

CHAPTER 24   Postwar Society and Culture:
Change and Adjustment 670

Closing the Gates to New Immigrants 671 ▪ New Urban Social Patterns
673 ▪ The Younger Generation 674 ▪ The "New" Woman 675 ▪ Popular
Culture: Movies and Radio 680 ▪ The Golden Age of Sports 682 ▪
Urban–Rural Conflicts: Fundamentalism 684 ▪ Urban–Rural Conflicts:
Prohibition 686 ▪ The Ku Klux Klan 686 ▪ Sacco and Vanzetti 688 ▪
Literary Trends 688 ▪ The "New Negro" 690 ▪ Economic Expansion 692
▪ The Age of the Consumer 692 ▪ Henry Ford 694 ▪ The Airplane 695

CHAPTER 25   The New Era: 1921–1933 697

Harding and "Normalcy" 698 ▪ "The Business of the United States Is
Business" 699 ▪ The Harding Scandals 700 ▪ Coolidge Prosperity 701 ▪
Peace Without a Sword 702 ▪ The Peace Movement 704 ▪ The Good
Neighbor Policy 704 ▪ The Totalitarian Challenge 705 ▪ War Debts and
Reparations 706 ▪ The Election of 1928 707 ▪ Economic Problems 709 ▪
The Stock Market Crash of 1929 710 ▪ Hoover and the Depression 711 ▪
The Economy Hits Bottom 714 ▪ The Depression and Its Victims 717 ▪
The Election of 1932 717

CHAPTER 26   The New Deal: 1933–1941 721

The Hundred Days 722 ▪ The National Recovery Administration (NRA) 723
▪ The Agricultural Adjustment Administration (AAA) 724 ▪ The Dust Bowl
725 ▪ The Tennessee Valley Authority (TVA) 726 ▪ The Unemployed 727
▪ Literature During the Depression 729 ▪ Three Extremists: Long,
Coughlin, and Townsend 729 ▪ The Second New Deal 734 ▪ The Election
of 1936 736 ▪ Roosevelt Tries to Undermine the Supreme Court 736 ▪ The
New Deal Winds Down 737 ▪ Significance of the New Deal 740 ▪ Women
as New Dealers: The Network 741 ▪ Blacks During the New Deal 742 ▪
A New Deal for Indians 743 ▪ The Role of Roosevelt 744 ▪ The Triumph
of Isolationism 746 ▪ War Again in Europe 747 ▪ A Third Term for FDR
749 ▪ The Undeclared War 750

CHAPTER 27   War and Peace 753

The Road to Pearl Harbor 754 ▪ Mobilizing the Home Front 755 ▪ The
War Economy 756 ▪ War and Social Change 757 ▪ Minorities in Time of
War: Blacks, Hispanics, and Indians 758 ▪ Internment of the Japanese 760
▪ Women's Contribution to the War Effort 761 ▪ Allied Strategy: Europe
First 763 ▪ Germany Overwhelmed 764 ▪ The Naval War in the Pacific 769

■ Island Hopping 771 ■ Building the Atom Bomb 772 ■ Wartime Diplomacy 775 ■ Allied Suspicion of Stalin 776 ■ Yalta and Potsdam 777

CHAPTER 28   The American Century 780

Truman Becomes President 781 ■ The Postwar Economy 781 ■ The Containment Policy 783 ■ A Turning Point in Greece 783 ■ The Marshall Plan and the Lesson of History 784 ■ The Election of 1948 787 ■ Containing Communism Abroad 789 ■ Hot War in Korea 790 ■ The Communist Issue at Home 794 ■ McCarthyism 795 ■ Dwight D. Eisenhower 796 ■ The Eisenhower-Dulles Foreign Policy 797 ■ McCarthy Self-Destructs 798 ■ Asian Policy After Korea 799 ■ Israel and the Middle East 802 ■ Eisenhower and Khrushchev 803 ■ Latin America Aroused 804 ■ The Politics of Civil Rights 805 ■ The Election of 1960 808

CHAPTER 29   From Camelot to Watergate 810

Kennedy in Camelot 811 ■ The Cuban Crises 811 ■ The Vietnam War 814 ■ "We Shall Overcome": The Civil Rights Movement 815 ■ Tragedy in Dallas: JFK Assassinated 818 ■ Lyndon Baines Johnson 819 ■ The Great Society 820 ■ Johnson Escalates the War 822 ■ Opposition to the War 823 ■ The Election of 1968 823 ■ Nixon as President: "Vietnamizing" the War 828 ■ The Cambodian "Incursion" 829 ■ Détente with Communism 830 ■ Nixon in Triumph 832 ■ Domestic Policy Under Nixon 832 ■ The Watergate Break-In 833 ■ More Troubles for Nixon 836 ■ The Judgment on Watergate: "Expletive Deleted" 836

CHAPTER 30   Society in Flux 840

A Society on the Move 841 ■ The Advent of Television 841 ■ At Home and Work 842 ■ The Growing Middle Class 844 ■ Religion in Changing Times 844 ■ The Perils of Progress 847 ■ New Racial Turmoil 848 ■ Native-Born Ethnics 850 ■ Rethinking Public Education 852 ■ Students in Revolt 854 ■ The Counterculture 856 ■ The Sexual Revolution 857 ■ Women's Liberation 860

CHAPTER 31   Running on Empty: The Nation Transformed 864

The Oil Crisis 865 ■ Ford as President 866 ■ The Fall of South Vietnam 867 ■ Ford Versus Carter 868 ■ The Carter Presidency 869 ■ A National Malaise 869 ■ Stagflation: The Weird Economy 870 ■ Families Under Stress: Defeat of the Equal Rights Ammendment 871 ■ Cold War or Détente? 873 ■ The Iran Crisis: Origins 874 ■ The Iran Crisis: Carter's Dilemma 874 ■ The Election of 1980 875 ■ Reagan as President 877 ■ Four More Years 878 ■ "The Reagan Revolution" 879 ■ Change and Uncertainty 880 ■ AIDS 882 ■ The New Merger Movement 884 ■ "A Job for Life": Layoffs Hit Home 884 ■ A "Bipolar" Economy, a Fractured Society 885 ■ The Iran-Contra Arms Deal 886

CHAPTER 32   Misdemeanors and High Crimes 890

The Election of 1988 891 ■ Crime and Punishment 892 ■ "Crack" and Urban Gangs 892 ■ George H. W. Bush as President 894 ■ The Collapse of Communism in Eastern Europe 894 ■ The War in the Persian Gulf 895 ■ The Deficit Worsens 898 ■ Enter Bill Clinton 898 ■ The Election of 1992 899 ■ Clinton as President 899 ■ Emergence of the Republican Majority 901 ■ The Election of 1996 901 ■ Clinton Impeached 902 ■ Clinton's Legacy 903 ■ A Racial Divide 904 ■ Violence and Popular Culture 905 ■ The Economic Boom and the Internet 907 ■ The 2000 Election: George W. Bush Wins by One Vote 908 ■ The New Terrorism Intensifies 909 ■ September 11, 2001 909 ■ America Fights Back: War in Afghanistan 911 ■ The Second Iraq War 912 ■ 2004: Bush Wins a Second Term 914 ■ More Trouble in Asia 915 ■ Concerns at Home 916 ■ Hurricane Katrina 918 ■ Iraq Insurgency Intensifies 920 ■ The Persistent Past and Imponderable Future 924

Appendix A-1
   The Declaration of Independence A-3
   The Constitution of the United States of America A-6
   Amendments to the Constitution A-14
   Supplementary Reading A-21
   Present-Day United States A-42
   Present-Day World A-44

Credits C-1
Index I-1

Maps and Graphs

MAPS	PAGE
Ancient Native American Communities	5
European Voyages of Discovery	20
The Great English Migration	38
Spain's North American Frontier	55
African Slave Trade, 1451–1870	59
English Colonies on the Atlantic Seaboard	67
Ethnic Groups in Eastern North America, 1750	81
British Successes, 1758–1763	105
European Claims in All of North America, 1763	107
Proclamation of 1763	109
New York and New Jersey Campaigns, 1776–1777	138
Saratoga Campaign, September 19–October 17, 1777	141
Campaign in the South, 1779–1781	144
The Yorktown Campaign, April–September 1781	145
The United States Under the Articles of Confederation, 1787	151
Ratification of the Constitution	174
The United States and Its Territories, 1787–1802	187
Exploring the Louisiana Purchase	208
The War of 1812	229
The United States, 1819	237
The Missouri Compromise, 1820	243
Canals and Roads, 1820–1850	271
Indian Removals	288
Trails West	335
The War with Mexico, 1846–1848	340
Compromise of 1850	348
Cotton and Slaves in the South, 1860	353
Railroads, 1860	365
Agriculture, 1860	368
"Bleeding Kansas"	383
Presidential Election, 1860	396
Secession of the South, 1860–1861	398
War in the West, 1862	411
War in the East, 1861–1862	413
Gettysburg Campaign, 1863	418
The Final Campaigns, 1864–1865	431

MAPS AND GRAPHS

xx

Return to the Union During Reconstruction	443
The Compromise of 1877	457
Loss of Indian Lands, 1850–2000	468
The West: Cattle, Railroads, and Mining, 1850–1893	477
The Forging of U.S. Steel	494
The Election of 1896	578
The Woman Suffrage Campaign, 1869–1919	593
The Election of 1912	604
The Course of Empire, 1867–1901	619
Spanish-American War, Caribbean Theater	626
The United States in the Caribbean and Central America	632
The U.S. Panama Canal	636
The Western Front, 1918	657
Europe Before the Great War	660
Europe After the Great War	661
The Tennessee Valley Authority	727
Japanese Relocation from the West Coast 1942–1945	760
The Liberation of Europe	765
World War II, Pacific Theater	771
Recipients of Marshall Plan, 1948–1952	785
Air Relief to Berlin, 1948–1949	786
North Korean Offensive, June–August 1950	792
Southeast Asia, 1954–1975	824
Failure of the Equal Rights Amendment, 1972–1982	872
The Collapse of Communism in Eastern Europe	895
The Middle East	896
Present-Day United States	A-42
Present-Day World	A-44

GRAPHS PAGE

Colonial Trade with England, 1700–1774	92
American Foreign Trade, 1790–1812	215
Cotton Production and Slave Population, 1800–1860	262
Prices for Cotton and for Slaves, 1802–1860	263
Rural Versus Urban Population, 1820–1860	301
Men Present for Service During the Civil War	403
Casualties of the Civil War	433
Southern Agriculture, 1850–1900	452
Immigration, 1860–1910	519
U-Boat Campaign, 1914–1918	648
Deaths of Armed Forces in the Great War	658
Unemployment and Federal Action, 1929–1941	728
High School and College Graduates, 1870–1983	853

Feature Essays

RE-VIEWING THE PAST   **PAGE**

The Crucible   78
The Patriot   148
Glory   420
Titanic   548
Chicago   678
Cinderella Man   730
Saving Private Ryan   766
Good Night, and Good Luck   800

DEBATING THE PAST   **PAGE**

Who—or What—Killed the Big Mammals?   3
How Many Indians Perished with European Settlement?   26
Were Puritan Communities Peaceable?   73
Was Economic Gain the Colonists' Main Motivation?   94
Was the American Revolution Rooted in Class Struggle?   132
What Ideas Shaped the Constitution?   168
Did Thomas Jefferson Father a Child by His Slave?   198
How Did Indians and Settlers Interact?   223
Did a "Market Revolution" Transform Early
    Nineteenth-Century America?   269
For Whom Did Jackson Fight?   295
Did Antebellum Reform Movements Improve Society?   310
Did the Frontier Change Women's Roles?   333
Did Slaves and Masters Form Emotional Bonds?   357
Was the Civil War Avoidable?   381
Why Did the South Lose the Civil War?   432
Were Reconstruction Governments Corrupt?   446
Was the Frontier Exceptionally Violent?   470
Were the Industrialists "Robber Barons" or Savvy Entrepreneurs?   500
Did Immigrants Assimilate?   524
Did the Frontier Engender Individualism and Democracy?   543
Were City Governments Corrupt and Incompetent?   568
Were the Progressives Forward-Looking?   597
Did the United States Acquire an Overseas Empire
    for Moral or Economic Reasons?   617
Did a Stroke Sway Wilson's Judgment?   666

Was the Decade of the 1920s One of Self-Absorption?   676
What Caused the Great Depression?   713
Did the New Deal Succeed?   739
Should the United States Have Used Atom Bombs Against Japan?   773
Did Truman Needlessly Exacerbate Relations with the Soviet Union?   791
Would JFK Have Sent a Half-Million American Troops to Vietnam?   825
Did Mass Culture Make Life Shallow?   858
Did Reagan End the Cold War?   881
Do Historians Ever Get It Right?   923

Preface

"AMERICAN DESTINY"—THESE WORDS, SO LADEN WITH PORTENT, may strike some readers as an unsuitable title for a sober work of history. Such words have been invoked on behalf of countless partisan causes and feverish enthusiasms: in John Louis O'Sullivan's 1845 editorial proclaiming it "our manifest destiny to overspread the continent allotted by Providence for the free development of our yearly multiplying millions"; in Daniel Webster's terse repudiation of the looming sectional crisis: "One country, one constitution, one destiny"; in Walt Whitman's celebration, after that crisis had erupted in civil war, of "one common indivisible destiny for ALL"; and in Franklin D. Roosevelt's reference during the Great Depression to his generation's "rendezvous with destiny." Modern politicians have found such expressions irresistible; Ronald Reagan—perhaps unwittingly—invoked puritan theology when he told a Republican gathering: "We will achieve our destiny to be a shining city on a hill for all mankind to see." George W. Bush, in his 2005 inaugural, reaffirmed the nation's commitment to freedom "by making every citizen an agent of his or her own destiny."

Even the nation's critics have been obliged to address the popular belief in an American destiny, if only to repudiate it. For instance, in 1853 Henry David Thoreau bristled that the American people might "go their way to their manifest destiny, a filibustering toward heaven by the great western route"; he intended to look in a different direction. In 1862 Frederick Douglass asserted that "the destiny of America" was also the destiny of black Americans. One hundred and one years later, Martin Luther King, Jr., writing from a jail in Birmingham, Alabama, resurrected Douglass's words: Insofar as "the goal of America is freedom," he declared, "our destiny is tied up with America's destiny." Suffragist Elizabeth Cady Stanton similarly feared for the nation unless it allowed each woman to become "arbiter of her own destiny."

But if most Americans have accepted the concept of a national purpose, they have endlessly debated where the nation was headed and the nature of the force impelling it there. Some have discerned the hand of God lifting the nation up—or perhaps hurling it down. Others have claimed that the nation's destiny was dictated by accident of geography or economics, by the "laws" of social evolution or the "spirit" of democratic liberalism, by the "patterns" of demography or "processes" of modernity, and so on. Our book, however, maintains that no single model explains the complexity of American history. Because historians are poor prophets, we make no attempt to peer into the future. For us, the concept of an American destiny describes a pervasive if inchoate longing that has exerted a powerful hold on the American imagination.

The subtitle—"Narrative of a Nation"—may also strike readers as provocative. Some historians contend that the diverse peoples of the United States cannot be encompassed within the analytical boundaries of a single nation. Consequently, we have not attempted a history of "the American people." Rather, we describe how the voices and actions of its many peoples have produced a particular political structure—the United States, a single nation—and how that nation has in turn influenced the lives of everyone.

Other historians object to the subjectivity of narrative history. But all history is subjective. Historians decide, quite arbitrarily, which stories to tell and how to tell them. Sources are incomplete and biased, our judgments more art than science. We have tried, by digging into the muck of the past, to haul out the bits that make sense, and to present them so as to tell a coherent story. Though some contend that the past is too murky to yield clear meanings, we persist because no one is satisfied with the mud.

But why bother? History, some say, is dead; let it rest in peace so that we can focus on our own lives.

This view is wrong. The past continuously radiates its influence on the present. To underscore this thesis, this edition of *American Destiny* includes a major new feature: Each chapter opens with a discussion of a contemporary issue and shows its relation to the themes of the chapter.

A few examples concern institutions that, though founded long ago, still influence our lives. The copyright provisions of the Constitution, debated over two centuries ago, prevent students from freely downloading songs on the Internet (Chapter 5). The emergence of global corporate behemoths like Wal-Mart, whose revenues exceed the gross national product of Saudi Arabia, was prefigured by the establishment and growth of great industrial corporations during the late nineteenth century (Chapter 17). Our paychecks are smaller because Franklin D. Roosevelt and Congress established Social Security to provide federal protection for the elderly and disabled during the Great Depression (Chapter 26).

Sometimes the past defines the hopes and prospects of entire peoples. The desperate poverty of reservation Indians, and their compensatory ownership of casinos, resulted from the destruction of tribal life during the last half of the nineteenth century (Chapter 16). The decision to use aptitude tests to select officers during World War II led to the Scholastic Aptitude Test (SAT), an obligatory rite of passage for many college students today (Chapter 28).

Sometimes insights about the present inform our thinking about the past. When harassed by telephone solicitors demanding payment of credit card bills, we better appreciate the personal struggles of debtors such as Thomas Jefferson and understand his antipathy to public debt (Chapter 6). Our own frustration with a political discourse that has been truncated into sound bites makes us long for the thoughtful deliberations of Lincoln and Douglas (Chapter 13).

Sometimes knowledge of the past alters our view of contemporary issues. An awareness of the fratricidal slaughter of the American Civil War helps make sense of the "senseless violence" among religious sects in post-Saddam Iraq (Chapter 14). Similarly, the fact that the United States wrested Texas and much of the Southwest from a young Mexican nation deepens our perspective on illegal Mexican immigration today (Chapter 11). We better comprehend the restrictions of freedoms entailed by the Patriot Act following September 11, 2001, in light of restrictions imposed during other wars (Chapter 23).

People have always looked to the past, whether chronicling a hunt for mammoth beasts in a cave painting, or recounting the foundation stories of their civilizations in the Bible or the Mahabharata. Our lives have grown out of the fertile soil of the past, many of whose elements cannot be readily analyzed or even discerned. For us, a less elusive element, but surely an important one, is the American nation, itself the product of the myriad actions, ideas, and forces described in the following pages. By considering its past, we better understand ourselves—and perhaps our own destiny.

New to This Edition

In addition to the new chapter introductions described above, this edition of *American Destiny* differs from its predecessors in several other ways:

- Each chapter has been revised to reflect new scholarship, to offer new perspectives, and to streamline and sharpen the prose. We have also restructured several chapters and compressed others to improve readability. Chapter 10, "The Making of Middle-Class America," combines coverage in the previous edition's Chapters 10 and 11, streamlining less essential detail to make the narrative more manageable for students. Subsequent chapters have been renumbered; in addition to the prologue, there are now 32 chapters, one fewer than in the previous edition. To sharpen the focus of Chapter 16, "The Conquest of the West," sections on post-reconstruction governments have been reorganized and moved to Chapter 20, "Politics: Local, State, and National." Chapter 32, "Misdemeanors and High Crimes," has been significantly updated.

- Archaeologists, anthropologists, and historians have literally unearthed a treasure of knowledge about the earliest inhabitants of what is now the United States. The prologue and first two chapters include vastly expanded sections on American Indians.

- This edition includes two new "Re-Viewing the Past" essays: *Cinderella Man*, a film starring Russell Crowe and Renée Zellweger, about a boxer's unlikely rise to become heavyweight champion during the Great Depression (Chapter 26), and *Good Night, and Good Luck*, a film starring George Clooney, depicting TV broadcaster Edward R. Murrow's confrontation with Wisconsin senator Joseph McCarthy in the 1950s (Chapter 28). We have also added questions for discussion in these features to spark class discussion or writing assignments.

Enduring Features

Debating the Past

Historians argue about nearly every aspect of the nation's complex past, and each chapter includes a "Debating the Past" essay on an important historiographical debate. Because such issues are hard to fix in memory, we have provided a photograph or picture to "trigger" the historiographical essay. For example, the question for Chapter 2—"Were Puritan Communities Peaceable?"—is prefaced by a contemporary painting of a seventeenth-century puritan village, with a river meandering through a nearby meadow. The question for Chapter 11—"Did the Frontier Change Women's Lives?"—commences with a photograph of a farm woman hauling buffalo chips in a wheelbarrow. Each essay concludes with a list of the major works cited. Our final debate—"Do Historians Ever Get It Right?" (Chapter 32)—poses a question that we hope will stimulate discussion.

Re-Viewing the Past

The "Re-Viewing the Past" feature shows how particular movies shape our understanding of history. Directors often spend scores of millions of dollars to show what the past looked like. For example, *The Crucible* (Chapter 2) provides a vivid evocation of puritan Salem, and *Saving Private Ryan* (Chapter 27) of the Normandy invasion of World War II. Yet moviemakers often alter people and events for dramatic purposes. We hope that these "Re-Viewing the Past" essays will provide guidance on which of Hollywood's stories contain some measure of truthfulness, which do not, and how viewers can tell the difference. The essays also serve as reminder that all historical narratives are interpretations, and all contain biases of selection, presentation, voice, and argument. When considering the past, people should be critical of what they see—and read.

Mark C. Carnes
John A. Garraty

Supplements for Instructors and Students

For Qualified College Adopters

Name of Supplement	Available in Print	Available Online	Instructor or Student Supplement	Description
Instructor's Resource Center (IRC)		✓	Instructor Supplement	Web site for downloading relevant supplements. Password protected. Please contact your local Pearson representative for an access code. *www.ablongman.com/irc*
MyHistoryLab		✓	Both	With the best of Longman's multimedia solutions for history in one easy-to-use place, MyHistoryLab offers students and instructors a state-of-the art interactive instructional solution for your U.S. history survey course. Built around a complete e-book version of this text, MyHistoryLab provides numerous study aids, review materials, and activities to make the study of history an enjoyable learning experience. Icons in the e-book link directly to relevant materials in context, many of which are assignable. MyHistoryLab includes several hundred primary source documents, videos, images, and maps, all with accompanying analysis questions. It also includes a History Bookshelf with 50 of the most commonly assigned books in U.S. history courses and a History Toolkit with guided tutorials and helpful links. MyHistoryLab is flexible and easy-to-use as a supplement to a traditional lecture course or to administer as a completely online course. *www.myhistorylab.com*
MyHistoryKit for American History		✓	Both	Online package of study materials, gradable quizzes and over 1,000 primary sources organized generically by typical American history themes to support your U.S. history survey text. Access code required. *www.myhistorykit.com*
American History Study Site		✓	Both	Online package of practice tests, Web links, and flashcards organized generically by major history topics to support your U.S. history survey text. Open access. *www.longmanamericanhistory.com*
Instructor's Manual	✓	✓	Instructor Supplement	Each chapter includes a chapter overview, lecture supplements, and questions for class discussion. Text specific.
Test Bank	✓	✓	Instructor Supplement	Contains thousands of conceptual, objective, and essay questions. Text specific.
Computerized Test Bank	✓	✓	Instructor Supplement	Includes all items in the printed test bank. Questions can be edited, and tests can be printed in several different formats. Text specific.

(continued)

For Qualified College Adopters

Name of Supplement	Available in Print	Available Online	Instructor or Student Supplement	Description
PowerPoint Presentation		✓	Instructor Supplement	Designed to accompany *The American Nation*, the comprehensive version of this text, these slides contain an outline of each chapter of the text and full-color images of maps and figures.
Digital Transparency Masters		✓	Instructor Supplement	Designed to accompany *The American Nation*, the comprehensive version of this text, these digital transparency masters are available exclusively on the Instructor's Resource Center. *www.ablongman.com/irc*
Comprehensive American History Digital Transparency Masters		✓	Instructor Supplement	Vast collection of American history transparency masters. Available exclusively on the Instructor's Resource Center. *www.ablongman.com/irc*
Discovering American History Through Maps and Views Digital Transparency Masters		✓	Instructor Supplement	Set of 140 full-color digital transparency masters includes cartographic and pictorial maps, views, photos; urban plans and building diagrams; and works of art. Available exclusively on the Instructor's Resource Center. *www.ablongman.com/irc*
History Digital Media Archive	CD		Instructor Supplement	Contains electronic images, interactive and static maps, and video. Available on CD only.
Visual Archives of American History, Updated Edition	CD		Instructor Supplement	Contains dozens of narrated vignettes and videos as well as hundreds of photos and illustrations. Available on CD only.
Study Guide	✓		Student Supplement	Contains chapter overviews, learning objectives, identifications, mapping exercises, multiple-choice and essay questions, and critical thinking exercises. Available in two volumes. Text specific.
Vango Notes		✓	Student Supplement	Downloadable MP3 audio topic reviews. Includes major themes, key terms, practice tests, and rapid reviews. *www.vangonotes.com*
Study Card for American History	✓		Student Supplement	Distills course information down to the basics, helping students quickly master the fundamentals and prepare for exams.
Research Navigator Guide	✓	✓	Student Supplement	A book that contains an access code to EBSCO ContentSelect, *The New York Times*, and "Best of the Web."
Longman American History Atlas	✓		Both	100 full-color maps.

For Qualified College Adopters

Name of Supplement	Available in Print	Available Online	Instructor or Student Supplement	Description
Mapping America: A Guide to Historical Geography	✓		Student Supplement	18 exercises explore the role of geography in history.
Voices of *The American Nation*	✓		Student Supplement	Two-volume collection of primary sources, organized to correspond to the table of contents of *American Destiny*.
America Through the Eyes of Its People	✓		Student Supplement	Two-volume comprehensive anthology of primary sources expertly balances social and political history and includes up-to-date narrative material.
American History Timeline	✓		Student Supplement	Gives students a chronological context to help them understand important political, social, economic, cultural, and technological events.
Sources of the African-American Past	✓		Student Supplement	This collection of primary sources covers key themes in the African-American experience.
Women and the National Experience	✓		Student Supplement	Primary source reader contains both classic and unusual documents describing the history of women in the United States.
Reading the American West	✓		Student Supplement	Primary sources in the history of the American West.
A Short Guide to Writing About History	✓		Student Supplement	Teaches students to write cogent history papers.
American History Firsthand: Working with Primary Sources	✓		Student Supplement	This two-volume collection of loose leaf reproduced primary sources exposes students to archival research.
Longman Penguin Putnam Inc. Value Packs	✓		Student Supplement	A variety of Penguin-Putnam texts are available at discounted prices when bundled with *American Destiny*. Complete list of available titles at *www.ablongman.com/penguin*.
Library of American Biography Series	✓		Student Supplement	Renowned series of biographies that focus on figures who had a significant impact on American history. Complete list at *www.ablongman.com/html/lab*.

About the Authors

© 1999 Joel Gordon

MARK C. CARNES received his undergraduate degree from Harvard and his Ph.D. in history from Columbia University, where he studied and trained with Professor John A. Garraty. The Ann Whitney Olin Professor of History at Barnard College, Columbia University, Professor Carnes has chaired both the departments of History and American Studies at Barnard. In addition to this textbook, Carnes and Garraty have co-authored *Mapping America's Past: A Historical Atlas* and are co-general editors of the 24-volume *American National Biography*, for which they were awarded the Waldo Leland Prize of the American Historical Association, the Darmouth Prize of the American Library Association, and the Hawkins Prize of the American Association of Publishers. In addition, Carnes has published numerous books in American social and cultural history, including *Past Imperfect: History According to the Movies* (1995), *Novel History: Historians and Novelists Confront America's Past (and Each Other)* (2001), and *Invisible Giants: 50 Americans That Shaped the Nation but Missed the History Books* (2002). Carnes also created "Reacting to the Past," which won the Theodore Hesburgh Award, sponsored by TIAA-CREF, as the outstanding pedagogical innovation of 2004.

"Garraty preaches a particular doctrine on historical writing, expounding on the details of a complex process whereby the murky abstractions of the past are distilled into clean, clear narrative. He insists that the writer's sole duty is to readers. This literary alchemy is all the more wondrous for being so devoid of artifice," Carnes observes.

© 1999 Joel Gordon

JOHN A. GARRATY holds a Ph.D. from Columbia University and an L.H.D. from Michigan State University, and is Gouverneur Morris Professor Emeritus of History at Columbia. He is the author, co-author, and editor of scores of books and articles, among them biographies of Silas Wright, Henry Cabot Lodge, Woodrow Wilson, George W. Perkins, and Theodore Roosevelt. Along with Mark Carnes, he is co-editor of the *American National Biography*. Garraty has also contributed a volume—*The New Commonwealth*—to the New American Nation series and edited *Quarrels That Shaped the Constitution*. He was a member of the Board of Directors of *American Heritage* magazine and served as both vice president and head of the teaching division of the American Historical Association. His areas of research interest include the Gilded Age, unemployment (in a historical sense), and the Great Depression of the 1930s. Of his collaboration with Carnes on *American Destiny*, Garraty says, "One of our favorite topics of discussion over these many years has been the craft of historical writing. We share a commitment to clarity and conciseness. We strive to avoid jargon and verbiage. We believe that while the political history of the nation provides a useful narrative framework, its people are what give the story meaning."

Beginnings

IN AUGUST 2005, HURRICANE KATRINA FORMED IN THE CARIBBEAN, swept north, gathered strength in the Gulf of Mexico, and slammed into the Gulf Coast, swamping New Orleans and the surrounding region. Nearly 1,500 people died. Property losses approached $100 billion.

Many blamed the intensity of the hurricane on global warming, a rise in temperatures that most scientists believe is aggravated by burning fossil fuels. They pointed out that hurricanes are fueled by the heat of tropical waters, and that during the 1990s ocean temperatures had increased a full degree Fahrenheit. During the summer of 2005, the hottest on record, the Gulf of Mexico was 5 degrees warmer than usual.

Others responded that evidence of man-made global warming is inconclusive and that any general trend in rising temperatures is part of a natural cycle. They noted that over the past three million years, the earth has experienced alternating cycles of warming and cooling, each cycle lasting about 100,000 years.[1] Many of these cycles predated even the earliest ancestors of man.

While scientists may argue over the causes of current rising temperatures, most agree that dramatic climate changes have altered history. We need only look to our past. The story of America in this sense commences over 100,000 years ago, after the last long period of global warming had ended. During that period, temperatures dropped and a prolonged ice age ensued. Ice sheets near the poles expanded. Some became nearly as broad as Australia and over 10,000 feet thick—the height of ten Empire State Buildings. Giant ice slabs entombed northern Europe and North America. As the slabs moved, they gouged deep holes in the earth's crust, forming the beds of the Great Lakes and Finger Lakes.

About 20,000 years ago the cooling cycle ended and the earth warmed. As the glaciers melted, they unloosed torrents of water that filled the beds of the Great

---

[1]What causes the cyclical shifts in global temperature is not known for sure. Some point to long-term shifts in the energy output of the sun, wobbles in the earth's orbit, and complicated convergences of other factors.

Lakes and Finger Lakes and scored the paths of the Mississippi, Missouri, Ohio, and Hudson rivers. The retreating glaciers also left behind huge deposits of rock; examples include Long Island and Staten Island.

Even before any humans had arrived in the Americas, climate had transformed the world they would inhabit. Climatic factors, too, determined who would first set foot in the hemisphere, where they would do so, and how they would survive.

First Peoples

The first human beings emerged in Africa more than two million years ago. Some devised stone tools, thus inaugurating the Paleolithic revolution, a life based on hunting and finding edible nuts, berries, and plants. The Paleolithic people who most resemble us in their aptitude for tools and facility with language appeared more recently, perhaps fewer than 40,000 years ago. They spread through much of Africa, Europe, and Asia, displacing those humans that had preceded them.

For thousands of years the frozen wasteland of Siberia remained impenetrable to these toolmaking humans. But as the supply of big mammals grew increasingly scarce elsewhere in Asia, hunters ventured farther north. What drew them especially were woolly mammoths. Weighing 16,000 pounds, about as much as a large elephant, a single mammoth provided enough meat to feed two dozen hunters nearly all winter. Its fur could be worn as clothing and its fat could be burned for heat. Its bones, when stretched with fur, functioned as simple tents. A woolly mammoth was a kind of movable mall, and hunters regarded it with the avidity of shoppers at a clearance sale. As mammoths moved deeper into the arctic tundra, so did their human predators.

Some of the hunters crossed what is now the Bering Strait to Alaska. What happened next is a matter of conjecture. Eventually these Paleo-Indians came upon lush grasslands, watered by the streams and lakes of the melting ice. Then they happened upon an astonishing scene: vast herds of large mammals. There were plenty of mammoths, but also equally enormous mastodons, with massive legs and stout feet; giant beavers the size of bears; 20-foot-long ground sloths weighing over 6,000 pounds; strange monsters such as glyptodonts, which resembled armadillos but weighed over a ton, and also countless camels, horses, cheetahs, caribou, and deer.

The Demise of the Big Mammals

With so much available game, the hunters' skills improved. They chiseled long stone blades especially designed to penetrate thick hides. Archaeologists have named these hunters after their ingenious blades, first found at Clovis, New Mexico.

WHO—OR WHAT—KILLED THE BIG MAMMALS?

Paul S. Martin (1984) estimated that Clovis peoples, numbering several hundred thousand at their peak, hunted to extinction some 93 billion pounds of animals throughout the western hemisphere. Critics of what has been dubbed the "overkill" hypothesis insisted that Martin's rendering of a swarm of human predators devouring entire species was far-fetched. Clovis "hunters" were mostly scavengers who rarely succeeded in killing woolly mammoths (see museum reconstruction below) and other huge beasts. The big mammals died off because the climate of North America grew far warmer and drier after 13,000 B.C.E. This damaged the ecosystem on which the big, furry mammals depended. Proponents of the "overkill" hypothesis responded that the big mammals had previously endured millions of years of climate fluctuations, some far more severe than the waning of the last Ice Age. That all these species would vanish during a climate shift that coincided with the arrival of human predators seems an improbable coincidence. And if the climate change was so extreme, why did it not result in the demise of species of birds and fish? Alfred Crosby (1986) also showed that the disappearance of many species of large mammals in Australia coincided with the

arrival of human beings to that continent. This debate has nevertheless raged for nearly a half century. It reminds us that history is not fixed; facts change, as does our way of looking at them.

Paul S. Martin and Richard G. Klein, eds., *Quaternary Extinctions* (1984), which includes Martin's essay and also those of supporters and critics; also Alfred Crosby, *Ecological Imperialism* (1986).

Loosed upon herds of unwary animals, these hunters seemingly slaughtered them almost at will, or stampeded them over cliffs. Archaeologists have found Clovis blades in nearly every state of the United States and even at the southern tip of South America.

And then the big mammals were gone. By about 8000 B.C.E.,[2] most of the large mammals of North America had become extinct, including the mammoths, mastodons, saber-toothed cats, giant beavers, bears, horses, and camels. Whether the hunters had killed off the big mammals or the warming climate caused the blubbery, heavily furred animals to become extinct is a source of debate. (See Debating the Past, "Who—or What—Killed the Big Mammals?" p. 3). What is beyond dispute is that the absence of large mammals profoundly influenced the subsequent course of American history.

The Archaic Period: A World Without Big Mammals

The loss of the big mammals marked the end of the Clovis culture. Descendants of Paleo-Indians had to find new sources of food, clothing, and shelter. The ensuing period, termed "archaic" and comprising about one hundred human generations, was characterized by scarcity. Prolonged droughts or severe winters resulted in starvation. Among the Indians north of Mexico, in what is now the United States, there was little if any population growth.

Eventually the Archaic Indians adapted to particular habitats. In woodland areas east of the Mississippi River, they learned to hunt small animals, like rabbits and beaver, that had previously not been worth the bother; or they learned to find stealthy animals like bear and caribou or to sneak up on skittish ones like elk and deer. On the Great Plains, Indians thrived on bison, which could be stampeded over cliffs.

Most Archaic bands searched for game continuously. They migrated from one place to another according to a seasonal schedule, often returning to the same campsites year after year. In the spring, when fish spawn, Archaic Indians moved to rivers and streams. In the summer, they hunted small animals. In the fall, they shifted to upland woods to gather protein-rich nuts, some of which they hid in caves for emergencies. In winter, they often migrated to forests in search of deer, bear, and caribou.

Often perilously hungry, they discovered that sunflower seeds and sumpweed (a type of spinach) were edible. Over 2,000 years ago, peoples in the Midwest planted sunflower and sumpweed seeds. They were the first inhabitants of what is now the United States to domesticate plants, although most Archaic peoples remained primarily hunters and foragers.

---

[2]B.C.E. *stands for "before the common era," and* C.E. *for "common era." These abbreviations are synonyms for* B.C. *and* A.D., *respectively. In this book dates not followed by* B.C.E. *refer to* C.E.

Ancient Native American Communities

The First Sedentary Communities

Some Archaic peoples happened on unusually rich habitats that could sustain them throughout the year. Indians living along the coast and rivers of the Pacific Northwest and Alaska found fish to be so plentiful that they could be scooped up in baskets. These people made nets and fishhooks. Eventually they built boats out of bark and animal skins. Those living along the New England coast discovered a seemingly inexhaustible supply of shellfish. But for even these people, survival was a full-time job.

As tribes remained longer in one area, they began to regard it as their own. They built more substantial habitations, developed pottery to carry water and cook food, and buried the dead with distinctive rituals in special places, often marked with mounds.

One of the earliest sedentary communities was located at what is now Poverty Point, on the Mississippi River floodplains north of Delhi, Louisiana. It was founded around 1500 B.C.E. Poverty Point Indians, like those of the Pacific Northwest, became adept at fishing with nets. They also supplemented their diet with bottle gourd seeds and squash.

Poverty Point peoples filled countless grass baskets with earth and dumped them onto enormous mounds. One mound, shaped like an octagon, had six terraced levels on which were built some 400 to 600 houses. Another was more than 700 feet long and 70 feet high. Viewed from above, it resembled a hawk. In all, the mounds consisted of over a million cubic yards of dirt.

The enormity of their construction projects reveals much about Poverty Point peoples. They could not have diverted so much time and energy to construction if they were not proficient at acquiring food. Moreover, while most Archaic bands were egalitarian, with little differentiation in status, the social structure of Poverty Point was hierarchical. Leaders conceived the plans and directed the labor to build the earthworks.

After about a thousand years, Poverty Point was abandoned. No one knows why. Several hundred years later, scores of smaller mound communities, known as Adena, sprouted in the Ohio and Mississippi river valleys. The inhabitants of these communities were also hunters and foragers who cultivated plants in their spare time. The Adena communities lasted several hundred years.

Around 200 B.C.E., another cluster of mound builders, known as Hopewell, flourished in Ohio and Illinois. Hopewell mounds were often shaped into squares, circles, and cones; some, viewed from above, resembled birds or serpents. Around 400 C.E., the Hopewell sites were abandoned.

An aerial view of the Great Serpent Mound in Locust Grove, Ohio, built by Mississippian peoples around 1100 C.E. Some Mississippian mounds were in the shape of squares, circles, or cones, but others resembled hawks or panthers, and still others, like this one, depicted a mythical creature or perhaps a snake devouring an egg. Scholars speculate that the shapes reflected religious beliefs or functioned as territorial markers for different clans.

The impermanence of these communities serves as a reminder that the transition from a nomadic existence of hunting and foraging to a settled life based on agriculture was slow and uneven. For the Archaic Indians living north of the Rio Grande, this was about to change. For people living in what is now Central America, it already had.

The Maize Revolution

Maize did not exist seven thousand years ago. But around 5000 B.C.E., perhaps far earlier, Indians in southern Mexico interbred various species of grasses, exploiting subtle changes and perhaps significant mutations. Eventually they created maize. A geneticist writing in *Science* in 2003 declared this to be "arguably man's first, and perhaps his greatest, feat of genetic engineering." The original ears were too small to provide much food value, but within several thousand years farmers in Central America had developed maize that resembled modern corn.

The Neolithic revolution—the transition from hunting and gathering to farming—had come to Central America. Within another thousand years or so, nearly every valley in central Mexico bristled with cornstalks. Population grew and cities emerged. Surplus corn allowed some people to specialize in activities unrelated to food production. By 100 C.E. Teotihuacan, 40 miles north of what is now Mexico City, had a population approaching 100,000 and featured miles of paved streets and a pyramid as large as those of Egypt. Mesoamerica was nearing its classical period, culminating in the great corn-growing civilizations of the Mayans, Aztecs, and Incas.

Eventually corn cultivation leapfrogged the deserts of northern Mexico and was adopted by the Indians of the Southwest: the Hohokam and Mogollon of

Scholars have failed to find any historical evidence of wild corn *(right)*. How, then, did it come to be? Some scientists believe that thousands of years ago Indian farmers somehow genetically engineered the transformation of teosinte *(left)*, a wild grass with tiny seeds, to evolve into maize.

Anasazi earthenware jars, from about 1200 C.E. The development of pottery was part of the ascent of a farming life. Corn could be stored in such jars, warding off starvation in lean winter months. Note the juxtaposition of straight lines and circles, an artistic pattern common among early American peoples.

Arizona and New Mexico; and the Anasazi of the Colorado Plateau. Abandoning their nomadic life, these Indians settled near rivers, built trenches and canals to channel water to the crops, dammed gullies to capture runoff from flash floods, and constructed homes near the cornfields.

Their culture revolved around corn. Sun and water became the focus of their religious beliefs, symbols of life and rebirth. Priest-astronomers carefully measured changes of the seasons. If corn was planted too early, it might shrivel before the late summer rains; if planted too late, it might be destroyed by frost. The centrality of corn to religious beliefs was underscored by the proximity of corn storage to sacred ceremonial pits, known as *kivas*. Corn Mother symbolism, suggesting a relationship between the fertility of the earth and of women, dominated religious practices. Control of the corn surplus was a key to political power.

Despite the aridity and blistering heat of the Southwest, the corn-cultivating peoples increased in number after 800 C.E. The Chaco Canyon, a 22-mile-long gorge in western New Mexico, witnessed the development of a most improbable human habitat. The Anasazi, who grew corn there, carved entire villages into the sandstone and shale cliffs. As population increased, the Anasazi built dozens of towns and villages linked by an elaborate system of roads. The largest of these cliff towns, Pueblo Bonito, had buildings more than five stories tall. The Hohokam constructed an irrigation canal system that spanned hundreds of miles and contained an intricate network of dams, sluices, and headgates. Snaketown, a Hohokam village 250 miles west of modern Phoenix, had a population of several thousand.

These communities were far smaller than those of their mightier neighbors to the south. But the triumph of the corn-growing Anasazi, Hohokam, and Mogollon is measured not by wealth and population figures but by the magnitude of the environmental challenges they overcame.

The Diffusion of Corn

Corn cultivation spread east and north. By 200 C.E., cornfields dotted the southern Mississippi River valley. Thereafter, the advance of corn slowed. Farther north, early cold snaps killed existing varieties of the plant. Moreover, corn cultivation required unremitting labor, and few Indians were eager to subject themselves to its incessant demands. Fields had to be cleared, usually by burning away the undergrowth. Then the soil was hoed using flat stones, clamshells, or the shoulder blades of large animals. After planting, the fields required constant weeding. Ripened corn had to be shucked and dried. Compared to the thrill of the hunt, the taste of game, and the varied tasks associated with a hunting and gathering, farming held little appeal. Males regarded it as a subsidiary activity, a task best relegated to women.

But over time many Indians learned that the alternative to agricultural labor was starvation. Fields farther north and east were cleared and planted with corn, beans, and squash. Old skeletons provide a precise means of tracking corn's advance. When corn is chewed, enzymes in the mouth convert its carbohydrates to sugar, a major cause of dental cavities. Radiocarbon dating of skeletons from the vicinity of what is now St. Louis first shows dental cavities around 700 and those from southern Wisconsin, around 900. By 1000 dental cavities appeared in skeletons throughout the Midwest and the East. Corn had become king.

Population Growth After 800

Corn stimulated population growth. An acre of woodlands fed two or three hunters or foragers; that same acre, planted in corn, provided for as many as 200 people. Hunting and foraging Indians usually found enough to eat in summer and fall, but in winter food sources might disappear. But dried corn, stored in glazed pots or sealed in underground pits, could sustain many people over a long period. Corn cultivators may not have had a particularly nutritious diet, but they could usually survive a long, hard winter.

Corn cultivators also had more children than hunting and gathering peoples. The high caloric corn diet caused women to menstruate at an earlier age, making it possible for them to have more children. Corn also promoted fertility by shortening the duration of breastfeeding. Even toothless infants could be fed a soft mush of boiled corn and could be weaned earlier; once mothers ceased breastfeeding, they were far more likely to become pregnant. Thus while hunter-gathering women would likely conceive no more frequently than once every four years, women who regularly ate corn were likely to have children twice as often.

A sedentary lifestyle promoted population growth in other ways. Infants and toddlers were a nuisance on the trail; some hunting and foraging Indians practiced abortion or even infanticide to ensure mobility and reduce the number of mouths to feed. But farming Indians nearly always could make use of additional hands, even young ones, to help with plowing, hoeing, weeding, and harvesting. Because farmers rarely moved, they built more permanent homes and more successfully sheltered infants from inclement weather and physical dangers.

As in the Southwest, the corn-cultivating peoples of the Mississippi Valley responded to increasing population by clearing more woodland and planting more corn. At first, corn cultivators and hunting-foraging peoples successfully cohabited within the same ecosystem: hunters traded for corn, essential for survival during winter, and corn cultivators traded for game, a source of complex protein. But over time the two groups often came into conflict, and when they did, the much more numerous corn cultivators prevailed.

The corn-cultivating societies expanded west into Dakota, east through the Carolinas, south into Florida, and north into Wisconsin. Their villages consisted of clusters of homes, surrounded by cornfields. They shared a constellation of beliefs and ritual practices. Like the Hopewell, they built burial mounds, but those of the corn cultivators were much larger. Some villages became towns and even small cities. Large temples and granaries and the homes of the governing elite were located on top of the mounds.

The most important and populous of these communities was located in the vicinity of St. Louis. Archaeologists call it Cahokia.

Cahokia: The Hub of Mississippian Culture

By 1000, Cahokia was a major center of trade, shops and crafts, and religious and political activities. It was the first true urban center in what is now the United States. By 1150, at the height of its development, it covered 6 square miles and had about 15,000 inhabitants.

The earthworks at Cahokia included some twenty huge mounds around a downtown plaza, with another 100 large mounds in the outlying areas. The largest mound was 110 feet high, covered 14 acres, and contained 20 million cubic yards of earth. It was probably the largest earthen structure in the Americas. Atop the mound was a 50-foot-high wood-framed temple.

Cahokian society was characterized by sharp class divisions. The elite lived in larger homes and consumed a better and more varied diet (their garbage pits included bones from the best cuts of meat). The corpse of one chieftain was buried upon a bed of 20,000 beaded shells; nearby was a long piece of shaped copper from Lake Superior, several bushels of bird and animal sculptures made of mica, and over 1,000 arrows, many with beautiful quartz or obsidian points.

That the Cahokia had enemies is suggested by the existence of a 3-mile-long wooden palisade surrounding the central core of the city. It consisted of 20,000

An artist's rendering of downtown Cahokia, around 1150 C.E. Cahokia was surrounded by a palisade, made of enormous tree trunks (*left*). On the great mounds within, the elite built homes and performed the ceremonial tasks of Mississippian culture. The open space in the center was probably filled with the stalls of craftspeople.

enormous tree trunks, pounded deep into the ground, interspersed with several dozen watchtowers from which defenders could unloose arrows upon besiegers.

Despite its daunting fortifications, or perhaps because of them, the elite did not command a large army. Its power derived chiefly from its ability to create a compelling religious worldview and express it in tangible symbols. Cahokia was a cultural and religious center rather than a fortress. In the central plaza, skilled workers carved religious figurines from quartz, mica, and galena. Others painted similar symbols on pottery or etched them in copper goods. Lesser chieftains brought corn and other foodstuffs into Cahokia, perhaps as tribute, while the Cahokia rulers reciprocated with gifts of figurines and copper or, in times of famine, grants of surplus corn. In Cahokia, too, priest-astronomers scrutinized the movements of the sun, moon, and stars.

Cahokia dominated a region of several hundred miles. Smaller mound-building communities emerged throughout the eastern woodlands and the Southeast. Two of the largest were Moundville, Alabama, and Etowah, Georgia. Cahokia also established (or perhaps inspired) distant satellite communities. Around 800, Mississippian Indians moved into southern Wisconsin and built Aztalan (in what is now Jefferson County), with similar corn storage depots and large ceremonial mounds surrounding a central plaza.

Like Cahokia, Aztalan erected a massive tree-trunk palisade with watchtowers. Archaeologists have found burned and butchered body parts throughout the ruins, evidence of warfare. Some speculate that the corn-growing Mississippians encroached on the Oneota, a hunting and gathering people, and that the communities long remained hostile.

The Mississippian elites did more than supervise construction of their own massive earthen tombs. They also solved complicated problems of political and social organization.

The Collapse of Urban Centers

Cahokia and Aztalan soon declined. By 1200, Cahokia's population had been reduced to several thousand people; by 1350, it was deserted. Etowah and Moundville went into decline somewhat later.

The major towns and villages of the Southwest civilizations faded as well. By 1200, the inhabitants of Chaco Canyon had vanished and nearly all of the pueblos of the Anasazi had been abandoned. Snaketown and dozens of towns of the Hohokam had become empty ruins, their canals choked with weeds.

What caused the collapse of these communities has long been a source of debate. Some scholars cite protracted droughts during the 1200s and 1300s. Others note that population growth harmed the environment. Slash-and-burn wood clearance thinned the eastern forests, and corn cultivation exhausted the soil. Archaeologists have determined that each Cahokian house required eighty large wooden posts—a half million for the entire city. The palisade at Cahokia consisted of thousands of the trunks of fully grown trees, and it was repeatedly rebuilt. Denuded of big trees, the watershed around Cahokia became susceptible to erosion and flooding, further depleting exhausted topsoils.

The farming Indians of the Southwest also stripped their lands of trees for fuel and for house and kiva construction. The wooden buildings at Chaco Canyon alone required nearly a quarter of a million trees. The irrigation system of the Hohokam harmed the environment in a different way. The canal networks distributed water from the Gila and (aptly named) Salt rivers, and in so doing deposited thousands of tons of mineral salts on cornfields. With little rainfall to leach the soils, the salt residues eventually reached toxic levels.

Crop yields declined as the demand for food in towns and villages was increasing. Studies of human skeletons in Mississippian burial mounds show higher incidences of disease and malnutrition after 1250. What happened next is unclear. Some archaeologists believe that many Mississippian Indians abandoned the cities and villages and quietly reverted to the hunting and foraging life of their Archaic forebears. Others argue that the end was calamitous. Late Mississippian skeletons were smaller and more likely to show signs of disease; they also had more broken bones; often arms, feet, and hands were dismembered. Recurrent famines and disease may have undermined the credibility of elites and the cultural system they supervised, weakening their control of poor urban people as well as chieftains in the hinterlands. The towering log palisades of the Mississippians and the impenetrable cliff dwellings of the Anasazi were manifestations of this collective insecurity.

Warfare became endemic among the corn-growing tribes of the Northeast. By 1300, the Iroquoian peoples of New York and Pennsylvania were building forts with defensive earthworks and palisades. Some tribes joined together to form military alliances. Soil exhaustion, perhaps aggravated by the droughts that had parched the cornfields of the Southwest, may have forced tribes to compete for land and resources. Some scholars propose that gender tensions may have exacerbated these conflicts. Men performed most of the hunting and foraging tasks, while women did most of the work in the cornfields. As corn supplanted game and fish as staples of the diet, women acquired more status and power. To reassert male dominance, men embarked on raids and warfare.

By 1500, nearly all of the large towns had been abandoned. New generations of Indians puzzled over who had inhabited the ruins, or who had erected the massive earthen mounds. The Navajo Indians referred to their predecessors as the "Anasazi," the "Ancient Ones."

The collapse of the cities disrupted trade networks. Some goods continued to move many, many miles, being passed from one tribe to another; but the flow of trade goods slowed to a trickle. Moreover, if the rise of powerful urban communities had forced earlier groups to band together, the demise of the urban communities encouraged the breakup of large groups and tribes. Hundreds, perhaps thousands of small bands lived in relative isolation.

To them, the great Aztec city of Tenochtitlán, beyond the Mexican desert, was only a rumor. Of Europe, Africa, and Asia, they knew nothing. That was about to change.

Eurasia and Africa

If the Neolithic revolution had made but fitful progress north of Mexico by 1500, its advance through Eurasia and Africa was nearly complete. Wheat, first domesticated in Southwest Asia after 9000 B.C.E., spread through the Nile Valley and the Mediterranean and eastward to India and China. Rice, domesticated in China much later, diffused throughout Eurasia. These lead crops were followed by others—oats, peas, olives, grapes, almonds, barley, oranges, lentils, and millet. Several thousand years later, farmers in Africa domesticated sorghum, palm oil, and yams.

The flow of people and crops between Eurasia and Africa was hindered after 4000 B.C.E., when the climate of Africa shifted and the Sahara broadened into a nearly impenetrable desert the size of the United States. The animals of Eurasia were as diverse as its crops. While few large mammals in the Americas survived the Clovis era, the ancient peoples of Eurasia learned how to domesticate horses, pigs, cows, goats, sheep, and oxen. In addition to protein-rich meat, cows and goats provided milk and dairy products such as cheese that could be stored for winter; horses and oxen dragged trees and boulders from fields, pulled ploughs through tough sod, and contributed manure for fertilizer. Eurasians greatly increased the power of oxen and horses by harnessing them to wheeled vehicles. Because of the diversity and nutritional value of its food sources, the Eurasian population increased rapidly.

To accommodate the growing demand for food, Eurasian farmers cut down forests, filled in marshlands, and terraced hillsides. Monarchs joined with merchants and bankers to build port facilities, canals, and fleets of ships to ensure the food supply to urban centers.

If cereal crops and animals dispersed throughout the vast Eurasian land-mass, so did new diseases. New strains of viruses and bacteria appeared in cows, pigs, goats, and sheep and readily spread to the humans that kept them. Diseases also spread readily in large cities, whose sanitation facilities were poor. Recurrent plagues swept across Eurasia. But those who survived acquired biological resistance.

West Africa evolved differently. The grassy savannah just south of the Sahara became the home for mostly herding peoples. Cities emerged in response to the growth of trans-Sahara trade: Finished goods, including cloth from North Africa, were traded for gold, salt, kola—a caffeine rich nut—and slaves. Warlords commanding horse-mounted troops vied for the control of the trade routes, and eventually founded the great kingdoms of Ghana, Mali, and Songhay. By 1500, Timbuktu, the capital of Mali, had become a major city, home to an important Islamic university and library.

Seldom did pastoral and trading empires penetrate far into the tropical regions farther south. The religion of Islam, which had spread through the grass-lands south of the Sahara, also made less progress among Africans on the tropical coast. There the tsetse fly, carrier of sleeping sickness, decimated horse and cattle herds. Malaria, too, discouraged potential invaders.

The village was the main unit of social organization of sub-Saharan Africa. Some villages merged into far-flung kinship networks and even small kingdoms, such as Benin and Congo. Relatively insulated from the imperial struggles farther north, these Africans mostly kept to themselves, growing crops and harvesting the lush vegetation of the forest. By 1500, the lives of these people, too, were about to change.

Europe in Ferment

During the 1400s, Europe's population increased by nearly a third; by 1500, population pressure was acute. When harvests were poor or grain shipments failed to arrive in towns, hunger riots destabilized the political order. Genoa, Italy, for example, was convulsed by fourteen revolutions from 1413 to 1453. Overpopulation was one reason why Jews, a vulnerable minority, were expelled from Spain and Portugal in 1492, and from Sicily in 1493.

Scarcity shook many peasants from the land and drove the urban poor from one city to another. Christoforo Colombo—or Columbus, as we call him—was among the restless youths who left home and took to the sea in search of a better life.

New ideas also unsettled European society. Movable type, which made the printing of books profitable, was perfected during the 1440s. By 1500, over 100 cities in Europe had at least one printing press and as many as 20 million volumes had been published. Books advanced new ideas and weakened the hold of traditional ones. Within a few decades, the treatises of Martin Luther and John Calvin initiated the Protestant Reformation. Books also excited the imagination and gave tangible expression to all manner of dreams and longings. (Columbus's restless curiosity had been stimulated by books on geography and navigation, especially Marco Polo's account of his journey to China.)

Incessant squabbles over land resulted in nearly constant warfare. The military arts advanced accordingly. Improvements in metallurgy made it possible to cast bronze and iron cannon capable of containing charges of gunpowder sufficient to hurl heavy balls great distances. By the early 1500s, cannons weighing a ton or more were mounted in sailing ships or upon carriages pulled by teams of horses. Warfare of this nature was expensive; the cost of constructing fleets, equipping armies, and building massive fortifications required the collective resources of many thousands. No longer an activity of rival cities or contending noblemen, warfare demanded the resources of entire nations.

A restless hunger for land, a population made resistant to biological pathogens, an explosion in communication and knowledge, a new technology and organization of warfare, and the emergence of powerful and contentious nation-states—all imparted a fateful dynamism to late fifteenth-century European society. Plainly, these Europeans had not solved their problems: Population growth exceeded available food sources; poverty undermined political order; and war loomed larger and more ominous. Equally plainly, the people of North America had failed to solve basic social problems: Nomadic Indians who practiced a hunting-gathering lifestyle were vulnerable to starvation as well as to encroachments by the more numerous peoples of the corn-farming tribes. Farming Indians, on the other hand, found it difficult to sustain even small urban communities over a long period. In the absence of writing systems and larger "national" political organizations, few could join in broad enterprises; none possessed military technologies comparable to the Europeans. And the peoples of the Americas lacked the immunity from infectious diseases that so many Europeans had acquired.

Separating these worlds was the impenetrable void of the Atlantic Ocean. Five hundred years earlier a Norseman, Leif Eriksson, had sailed along the coast of Greenland to the shores of Labrador, but little came of his expeditions. But toward the close of the fifteenth century, European sailors of a different type, adept at navigating through the open sea and willing to sail far from land, were about to venture across the expanses of the Atlantic. In so doing they would transform it into a bridge that would join these worlds, and the West African coast as well, bringing all three into fateful collision.

Milestones

c. 12,000 B.C.E. (perhaps earlier)	Humans from Asia cross Beringia to Alaska
c. 12,000–8000 B.C.E.	Humans diffuse throughout Americas
	Many species of large mammals become extinct in western hemisphere
	Clovis era ends
	Eurasians domesticate wheat
c. 4300 B.C.E.	Mesoamerican peoples cultivate corn and initiate Neolithic revolution
c. 2500 B.C.E.	Peoples of midwestern North America domesticate sunflowers and sumpweed
c. 1700 B.C.E.	First sedentary North American community is founded at today's Poverty Point, Louisiana
c. 1000 B.C.E.	Corn cultivation begins in the Southwest
c. 200 C.E.	Corn cultivation begins in the lower Mississippi Valley
c. 900 C.E.	Corn cultivation begins in Wisconsin
c. 1150 C.E.	Cahokia at its peak
c. 1200s–1300s	Protracted droughts in North America disrupt food supply; urban areas are abandoned

CHAPTER 1

Alien Encounters: Europe in the Americas

ON MARCH 16, 2003, A WEEK BEFORE THE UNITED STATES invaded Iraq, Vice President Richard Cheney told Tim Russert of NBC News, "My belief is we will, in fact, be greeted as liberators." By April 15, Saddam Hussein, the Iraqi dictator who was thought to possess weapons of mass destruction, had been driven from power. Now began the work of installing a democratic government. It did not go smoothly.

When U.S. diplomat Molly Phee was sent to Maysan province in southeastern Iraq to serve as its interim governor, she met with Sheik Rahim, a key Islamic cleric. After expressing his "delight" at being introduced to the leader of the transition government, Rahim proceeded to upbraid her: "This is a Muslim province and we prefer people to dress respectably. Can I please suggest that in future you cover your head?"

"I am a respectable woman," Phee replied in Arabic. "I am a Christian from another culture and in our culture respectable women do not cover their heads." Rahim glowered.

This conversation was symptomatic of the incomprehension that characterized the American-Iraqi encounter. Throughout Iraq, American soldiers were soon being attacked by the people they had come to liberate. Within months of Phee's arrival, mortar shells were peppering her compound nearly every night. During the next three years, as 3,000 American soldiers were killed by insurgents, it became apparent that many Iraqis did not regard the Americans as liberators.

If so wide a gap in understanding could appear in a world linked by Internet, cell phone, and television, how much more unfathomable was the cultural gap following the encounter of Europeans and American Indians five centuries ago, when neither group previously knew of the other's existence?

Christopher Columbus's fateful voyage brought alien worlds together, an encounter characterized by mutual incomprehension. In consequence, millions of American Indians perished, millions of Europeans emigrated to the Americas, and millions of Africans were sent there as slaves. The cultures of all peoples—food and diet, religious beliefs and practices, and modes of sustenance and social organization—changed in fundamental ways. During that fateful first century, American Indians, Europeans, and Africans interacted continuously—negotiating, fighting, trading, and intermarrying—without really understanding one another.

Sightings

At about two o'clock on the morning of October 12, 1492, a sailor named Roderigo de Triana, clinging in a gale to the mast of the *Pinta*, saw a gleam of white on the moonlit horizon and shouted: *"Tierra! Tierra!"* The land he had spied was an island in the West Indies called Guanahani by its inhabitants, a place distinguished neither for beauty nor size. Nevertheless, when Triana's master, Christopher Columbus, went ashore bearing the flag of Spain, he named it San Salvador, or Holy Savior. Columbus selected this imposing name for the island out of gratitude and wonder at having found it—he had sailed with three frail vessels more than 3,000 miles for 33 days without sighting land.

San Salvador was the gateway to two continents. Columbus did not know it, and he refused to accept the truth, but his voyage threw open to exploitation by the peoples of western Europe more than a quarter of all the land in the world, a region of more than 16 million square miles, an area lushly endowed with every imaginable resource. He made possible a mass movement into the New World from Europe—and later from Africa and other regions. By 1600, about 240,000 Spaniards had made their way to the Americas. Gathering force rapidly, this movement brought over 100 million persons from throughout the world to the Western Hemisphere.

Columbus's Great Triumph—and Error

Columbus was an intelligent as well as a dedicated and skillful mariner. He failed to grasp the significance of his accomplishment because he had no idea that he was on the edge of two huge continents previously unknown to Europeans. He was seeking a way to China and Japan and the Indies, the amazing countries described by the Venetian Marco Polo in the late thirteenth century.

Having read carefully Marco Polo's account of his adventures in the service of Kublai Khan, Columbus had decided that these rich lands could be reached by sailing directly west from Europe. The idea was not original, but while others merely talked about it, Columbus pursued it with dogged persistence.

If one could sail to Asia directly, the trading possibilities and the resulting profits would be limitless. Asian products were highly valued all over Europe. Spices such as pepper, cinnamon, ginger, nutmeg, and cloves were of primary importance, their role being not so much to titillate the palate as to disguise the taste of spoiled meats in regions that had little ice. Europeans also prized such tropical foods as rice, figs, and oranges, as well as perfumes (often used as a substitute for soap), silk and cotton, rugs, textiles such as muslin and damask, dyestuffs, fine steel products, precious stones, and various drugs.

But the cost of Asian products remained high. To transport spices from the Indies, silk from China, or rugs, cloth, and steel from the Middle East was extremely costly. The combined routes through central Asia were long and complicated. If the produce of eastern Asia could be carried to Europe by sea, the trip would be both cheaper and more comfortable. The goods would have to be loaded and unloaded only once. A small number of sailors could provide all the necessary labor, and the free wind would supply the power to move the cargo to its destination. By the fifteenth century, this idea was beginning to be transformed into action.

Christopher Columbus came to Portugal in 1476. Columbus was a weaver's son from Genoa, born in 1451. He had taken to the sea early, ranging widely in the Mediterranean. His arrival in Portugal was unplanned, since it resulted from the loss of his ship in a battle off the coast. For a time he worked as a chartmaker in Lisbon. He married a local woman. Then he was again at sea. He cruised northward, perhaps as far as Iceland, south to the equator, westward in the Atlantic to the Azores. Had his interest lain in that direction, he might well have been the first person to reach Asia by way of Africa, for in 1488 in Lisbon he met and talked with Bartholomeu Dias, just returned from his voyage around the southern tip of Africa, which had demonstrated that the way lay clear for a voyage eastward to the Indies.

But by this time Columbus had committed himself to reach China by sailing west into the Atlantic. There were doubters. Ancient Greek astronomers had estimated the earth's circumference at 24,000 miles. According to most estimates, the known world stretched about 14,000 miles from the Canary Islands in the west to Japan in the east. Therefore a ship sailing from the Canary Islands westward across the Atlantic would have to travel 10,000 miles before reaching Japan. But sailing ships of that time could not carry enough provisions for so long a journey. Columbus, however, estimated the earth's circumference at 18,000 miles: He believed he would have to sail only 4,000 miles across open sea—an audacious voyage, but not an impossible one.

When King John II refused to finance him, Columbus turned to the Spanish court, where, after many disappointments, he persuaded Queen Isabella to equip his expedition. In August 1492 he set out from the port of Palos with his tiny fleet, the *Santa Maria,* the *Pinta,* and the *Niña.* A little more than two months later, after a stopover in the Canary Islands, his lookout sighted land. According to his estimates, he was nearly on course, having traveled about 4,000 miles. But he was

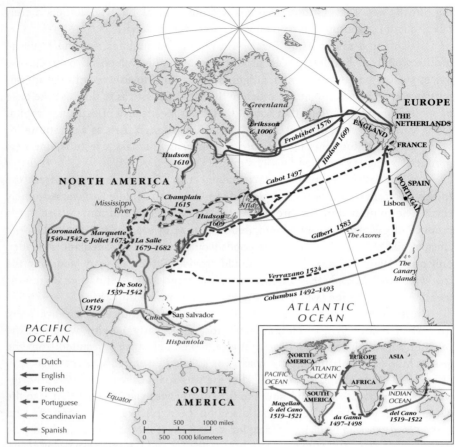

European Voyages of Discovery

nowhere near Japan or China. The ancient Greek astronomers were right and Columbus wrong. He had greatly underestimated the size of the earth.

Columbus refused to accept the plain evidence that this was not Asia, but an entirely new world. All about were strange plants, known neither to Europe nor to Asia. The copper-colored people who paddled out to inspect his fleet could no more follow the Arabic widely understood in the East than they could Spanish. Yet Columbus, consulting his charts, convinced himself that he had reached the Indies. That is why he called the natives Indians, a misnomer that became nearly universal and was increasingly used even by the native peoples themselves.

Searching for treasure, Columbus pushed on to Cuba. When he heard the native word *Cubanocan*, meaning "middle of Cuba," he mistook it for *El Gran Can* (Marco Polo's "Grand Khan") and sent emissaries on a fruitless search through the tropical jungle for the khan's palace. He finally returned to Spain relatively empty-handed but certain that he had explored the edge of Asia. Three later voyages failed to shake his conviction.

Spain's American Empire

Columbus died in 1506. By that time other captains had taken up the work, most of them more willing than he to accept what Europeans called the New World on its own terms. As early as 1493, Pope Alexander VI had divided the non-Christian world between Spain and Portugal. The next year, in the Treaty of Tordesillas, these powers negotiated an agreement about exploiting the new discoveries. In effect, Portugal continued to concentrate on Africa, leaving the New World, except for what eventually became Brazil, to the Spanish. Thereafter, from their base on Hispaniola (Santo Domingo), founded by Columbus, the Spaniards quickly fanned out through the Caribbean and then over large parts of the two continents that bordered it.

In 1513 Vasco Nuñez de Balboa crossed the Isthmus of Panama and discovered the Pacific Ocean. In 1519 Hernán Cortés landed an army in Mexico and overran the empire of the Aztecs, rich in gold and silver. That same year Ferdinand Magellan set out on his epic three-year voyage around the world. By discovering the strait at the southern tip of South America that bears his name, he gave the Spanish a clear idea of the size of the continent. In the 1530s Francisco Pizarro subdued the Inca empire in Peru, providing the Spaniards with still more treasure, drawn chiefly from the silver mines of Potosí.

The *conquistadores* were brave and imaginative men. It must not, however, be forgotten that they wrenched their empire from innocent hands; in an important sense, the settlement of the New World ranks among the most flagrant examples of unprovoked aggression in human history. When Columbus landed on San Salvador he planted a cross, "as a sign," he explained to Ferdinand and Isabella,

Horses (blindfolded) being loaded onto Spanish warships for shipment to the Americas. Native peoples had never seen horses (which had been extinct in the Americas for over ten thousand years). Nor had they seen enormous wooden warships powered by sails and carrying heavy cannons, nor warriors seated on horses and encased in armor.

"that your Highnesses held this land as your own." Of the Lucayans, the native inhabitants of San Salvador, Columbus wrote: "The people of this island . . . are artless and generous with what they have, to such a degree as no one would believe. . . . If it be asked for, they never say no, but rather invite the person to accept it, and show as much lovingness as though they would give their hearts."

Columbus also remarked of the Lucayans: "These people are very unskilled in arms . . . with fifty men they could all be subjected and made to do all that one wished." He and his compatriots tricked and cheated the Indians at every turn. Before entering a new area, Spanish generals customarily read a *Requerimiento* (requirement) to the inhabitants. This document recited a Spanish version of the history of the human race from the Creation to the division of the non-Christian world by Pope Alexander VI and then called on the Indians to recognize the sovereignty of the reigning Spanish monarch. If this demand was rejected, the Spanish promised: "We shall powerfully enter into your country, and . . . shall take you, your wives, and your children, and shall make slaves of them. . . . The death and losses which shall accrue from this are your fault." This arrogant harangue was read in Spanish and often out of earshot of the Indians. When they responded by fighting, the Spaniards decimated them, drove them from their lands, and held the broken survivors in contempt.

From the outset of the Europeans' invasion of the New World, sensitive observers had been appalled by their barbarity. Bartolomé de Las Casas, a Dominican missionary who arrived in Hispaniola nearly a decade after Columbus, compiled a passionate and grisly indictment:

> It was the general rule among Spaniards to be cruel; not just cruel, but extraordinarily cruel so that harsh and bitter treatment would prevent Indians from daring to think of themselves as human beings or having a minute to think at all. So they would cut an Indian's hands and leave them dangling by a shred of skin and they would send him on saying "Go now, spread the news to your chiefs." They would test their swords and their manly strength on captured Indians and place bets on the slicing off of heads or the cutting of bodies in half with one blow.

After stealing all the gold and silver they could find, the *conquistadores* sought alternative sources of wealth. They soon learned that land was worthless without labor to cultivate crops or extract precious metals. They therefore imposed the *encomienda* system, a kind of feudalism granting the first Spanish colonists control of conquered lands and obliging the Indians to provide forced labor and a fixed portion of their harvests. Because the conquerors' income was proportionate to the number of villagers under their authority, *conquistadores* concentrated on subjugating the heavily populated regions of Mexico: that is, those with the most extensive fields of maize. Cortés, for example, received such payments from 23,000 families in the fertile Oaxaca valley; their labor made him the wealthiest man in Spain.

Much of the work of implanting Spanish civilization was undertaken by Catholic missionaries. Like the *conquistadores*, Spanish friars built their first missions in the largest Indian villages and towns. In an effort to "love their neighbor," as Christ enjoined, they sought to save as many Indian souls as possible. But when some Indians held tight to their own gods and beliefs, missionaries destroyed *kivas* and temples, banned Indian dances and games, and outlawed polygamy. When Indians resisted, the friars called on Spanish soldiers to arrest the rebels.

By the 1570s the Spanish had founded about 200 cities and towns, each with a central plaza that included a town hall and church and precisely rectilinear street plans. They had also set up printing presses and published pamphlets and books, and established universities in Mexico City and Lima. With the help of Indian artisans, they had constructed and decorated lavishly a large number of impressive cathedrals.

Extending Spain's Empire to the North

Within two decades of Columbus's first voyage to the Americas, Spanish explorers had surveyed vast regions of what is now the United States. Juan Ponce de Léon, a shipmate of Columbus on the admiral's second voyage, made the first Spanish landing on the mainland of North America, exploring the east coast of Florida in 1513. In the 1520s Pánfilo de Narváez explored the Gulf Coast of North America westward from Florida, and after his death his lieutenant, Alvar Núñez Cabeza de Vaca, wandered for years in the region north of the Gulf. Finally, along with three companions, one a black slave named Esteban, Cabeza de Vaca made his way across what is now New Mexico and Arizona and then south to Mexico City. Between 1539 and 1543, Hernando de Soto traveled north from Florida to the Carolinas, then westward to the Mississippi River. During the same period Francisco Vásquez de Coronado ventured as far north as Kansas and west to the Grand Canyon. All sought to replicate Cortés's triumph; none succeeded; most treated the Indians barbarously.

By the early 1600s, Spanish explorers had reached Virginia, and in Florida a single Spanish military garrison remained at San Augustin—Saint Augustine. Years later the governor of Cuba, having failed to promote Spanish settlement of San Augustin, explained that "only hoodlums and the mischievous go there."

More consequential was the attempt to extend the Spanish empire beyond the Rio Grande into New Mexico. By the close of the sixteenth century, the Spaniards had learned that it was more profitable to acquire the crops and labor of Indian farmers than search for rumored cities of gold. In 1598, the viceroy of New Spain charged Don Juan de Onate with the task of subjugating the Indians of New Mexico and founding a colony in their midst. Onate led an expedition of 500 Spanish colonists and soldiers and a handful of Catholic missionaries across the Rio Grande into the territory of the Pueblo Indians, a farming people.

But the Pueblo were poor and their settlements meager; a Spanish soldier described New Mexico as "at the ends of the earth—remote beyond compare." When

Onate extorted maize, seized farmlands, and allowed cattle and pigs to plunder the fields, the Indians seethed. Eventually they ambushed a Spanish patrol, killing ten. Onate retaliated by butchering 800 Pueblo, including women and children, and arresting another 500. The captured males over 25 years of age were sold into slavery; to prevent them from running away, one of their feet was chopped off. Onate's methods generated no profits; in 1614 he was dismissed.

His successors found a surer source of wealth: capturing nomadic Indians, especially the Ute and Apache, and selling them as slaves to work in Mexican silver mines. Spanish soldiers forced Pueblo warriors to assist in slave raids; the Ute and Apache retaliated with furious attacks on Pueblo settlements.

Franciscan missionaries were given the task of Christianizing the Pueblo. They baptized thousands of mission Indians and instructed in the rudiments of the Catholic faith. They also taught Indians to use European tools, to grow wheat and other European crops, and to raise chickens and pigs and other barnyard animals. But the friars exacted a heavy price in labor from the people they presumed to enlighten and civilize. The Indians built and maintained the missions, tilled the surrounding fields, and served the every need of the friars and other Spanish colonists. For this they were paid little or nothing.

By the 1670s, after years of drought, the Pueblo became restive with these arrangements. They especially resented being coerced to take part in the slave raids. Shamans, too, increasingly called for a revival of the traditional religion. In 1675 the Spanish arrested forty-seven shamans; three were hanged and the remainder whipped as witches.

One of the latter, named Popé, secretly organized a general rebellion. In a swipe at the friars, he promised Pueblo warriors an additional wife for every Spanish soldier they killed. Without warning, some 17,000 Pueblo rose up against the Spanish, driving them out of towns and missions, destroying churches and killing priests, and plundering farms. The Spaniards fled to Santa Fe, escaping just before the Pueblo razed the town. The Pueblo drove the survivors all the way back to El Paso. Of the 1,000 Spanish in New Mexico, over 200 were killed.

In the mid-1690s the Spaniards regained control of most of the upper Rio Grande. Thereafter they maintained control with little difficulty. This was partly because the Spaniards had learned to deal less harshly with the Pueblo people. The Spaniards had also entered into complex trade with the nomadic Indians of the Great Plains and the foothills of the Rockies. Instead of themselves being the victims of slave raids, these Indians would capture more distant Indians and sell them to the Spaniards as slaves.

By the early 1700s Spain had become master of a huge American empire covering all of South America except Brazil, and also the southern fringe of North America, extending from California east to Florida. New Spain was ten times larger than Spain itself. The Spanish monarch ruled three times more Indian subjects than Spaniards.

But while Spain had founded a vast empire, one major and literally fatal problem remained. The Indian population was declining rapidly, and had done so from the start. Almost as soon as Europeans set foot on American soil, Indians began to die.

Disease and Population Losses

Of all the weapons the Europeans brought to the Americas, the most potent was one they could not see and of which they were mostly unaware: microorganisms that carried diseases such as smallpox, measles, bubonic plague, diphtheria, influenza, malaria, yellow fever, and typhoid. For centuries, these diseases had repeatedly ravaged Asia, Europe, and Africa. But American Indians had evolved over hundreds of generations without contact with these diseases. They lacked the biological defenses. Thus when these diseases first struck, many Indian villages were nearly wiped out. In 1585, for example, Sir Francis Drake, preparing for a raid against the Spanish, stopped at the Cape Verde Islands. There some of his men contracted a fever—probably typhus—but sailed for Florida undaunted by their discomfort. When they landed at St. Augustine, the disease spread to the Indians who, according to Drake, "died verie fast and said amongst themselves, it was the Englisshe God that made them die so faste."

Although infected Europeans transmitted new pathogens to the Indians, the diseases subsequently spread among Indians, rippling outward, far beyond the areas initially visited by the explorers. Soto's journey through the southeastern United States spread diseases throughout the region, virtually destroying the mound communities of Mississippian culture.

Indian losses from diseases were incalculable, although the lowest estimates begin in the millions. Scholars agree on only one fact concerning the population history of the North American Indians following the arrival of Columbus: The number of Indians declined precipitously. (See Debating the Past, "How Many Indians Perished with European Settlement?" p. 26.)

Ecological Imperialism

One reason why so many Indians succumbed to Eurasian microbes was that they were suffering from malnutrition. European plants and animals disrupted the native ecosystem. Pigs and cattle, brought in the first Spanish ships, were commonly set loose in the Americas. Unchallenged by the predators and microbes that had thinned animal populations in Europe and Asia, these big mammals reproduced rapidly, devouring maize, beans, and squash. Rats, stowaways on most European ships, also proliferated in the Americas, infesting Indian fields. When Europeans brought familiar plants, they unknowingly introduced

Debating the Past

HOW MANY INDIANS PERISHED WITH EUROPEAN SETTLEMENT?

In 1518 smallpox, long a scourge in Europe, ravaged the native peoples of the New World. This illustration shows Aztec victims being attended by a medicine man. "Those who did survive," reported Cortés's secretary, "having scratched themselves, were left in such a condition that they frightened the others with the many deep pits on their faces, hands, and bodies."

To calculate the magnitude of Indian losses, scholars had to determine the population at first contact with Europeans, a difficult task in the absence of Indian records. Early in the twentieth century, scholars gathered fragmentary population statistics as compiled by Catholic priests, Spanish officials, travelers, and soldiers. By aggregating this information for all tribes, including guesses where no data was available, scholars estimated an Indian population in the United States and Canada in the early sixteenth century of a little more than 1 million.

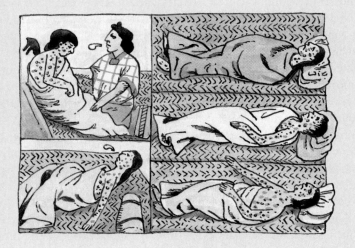

By the 1960s and 1970s, some thought this estimate far too low. They complained that it minimized both the achievements of Indian civilizations as well as the extent of the destruction wrought by European diseases and guns. Anthropologist Henry Dobyns (1983) found that when smallpox, measles, or tuberculosis struck some Indian villages, nineteen out of twenty Indians died. He thought this ratio characteristic of populations that lacked immunity to such diseases. He therefore multiplied the earlier population figures by twenty. After a few adjustments, he calculated the Indian population of the United States and Canada at 10 million to 12 million, and of the entire western hemisphere, at over 100 million.

Dobyns's methodology came under fire, but Thornton (1987) and others devised precontact estimates ranging from 4 million to 8 million. Since then, mathematicians have concluded that the data are so riddled with guesswork that no numerical estimates are reliable. But it is probably safe to conclude that Indian losses north of the Rio Grande numbered in the millions, and in the remainder of the western hemisphere, tens of millions.

Henry Dobyns, *Their Number Became Thinned: Native American Population Dynamics in Eastern North America* (1983), Russell Thornton, *American Indian Holocaust and Survival: A Population History Since 1492* (1987).

the seeds of hardy European weeds. Like the kudzu vines from Japan that have overrun much of the southeastern United States during the twentieth century, weeds from Europe choked Indian crops in the sixteenth century. Fewer ears of corn were harvested and Indians went hungry. When disease struck, many of them died.

The ships that brought Europeans to the Americas returned carrying more than gold and silver. European soldiers often contracted syphilis, a disease native to the Americas, and spread it to Europe and Asia. European ships also brought back maize and potato plants. These American crops yielded 50 percent more calories per acre than wheat, barley and oats, the major European grains. Hungry European peasants rapidly shifted to maize and potato cultivation; the population of Europe rose sharply. Manioc (cassava), another Indian plant with a high caloric yield, did not grow in the colder climate of Europe, but it transformed tropical Africa. Population levels soared. As declining Indian populations proved insufficient to exploit the seemingly inexhaustible lands of the western hemisphere, European conquerors imported African slaves to do more of the work.

Indians nevertheless benefited from some aspects of the ecological transformation of the western hemisphere. Horses originated in the Americas and passed into Asia during the great ice age; but after the Bering land bridge was flooded, horses became extinct in the Americas. Spanish *conquistadors* brought horses back to the Americas, and the horses thrived in the vast grasslands of North America. Plains Indians quickly used horses to hunt buffalo and to harass and evade encroaching Europeans. Farming Indians such as the Navaho profited from sheep cultivation by learning to weave fine woolen cloth.

The Columbian Exchange of plants and animals went both ways yet it remained unequal. The American Indians usually fared far worse than the Europeans. The best indicator is the shift in population: During the 300 years after Columbus, Europe's share of the world's population nearly doubled, increasing from about 11 percent to 20 percent. During the same period, the American Indians' share declined from about 7 percent to 1 percent.

Spain's European Rivals

Despite the staggering decline in Indian populations, Spanish colonization was a success by the one measure that most mattered in the sixteenth century: precious metals. By 1650, over 181 tons of gold and 16,000 tons of silver had been shipped from the Americas to New Spain. By 1585, a quarter of the empire's revenue came from American gold and silver.

At first, Spain's rivals did little to oppose Spanish colonization of the New World. In 1497 and 1498 King Henry VII of England sent Captain John Cabot to explore the New World. Cabot visited Newfoundland and the northeastern coast of the continent. His explorations formed the basis for later British claims in North America. In 1524 Giovanni da Verrazano made a similar voyage for France, coasting the continent from Carolina to Nova Scotia. Some ten years later the Frenchman Jacques Cartier explored the St. Lawrence River as far inland as present-day Montréal. During the sixteenth century, fishermen from France, Spain, Portugal, and England began exploiting the limitless supplies of cod and other fish they found in the cold waters off Newfoundland. They landed at many points along the mainland coast from Nova Scotia to Labrador to collect water and wood and to dry their catches, but they made no permanent settlements until the next century.

There were many reasons for this delay, the most important probably being the fact that Spain had achieved a large measure of internal tranquility by the sixteenth century, while France and England were still torn by serious religious and political conflicts. The Spanish also profited from having seized on those areas in America best suited to producing quick returns. Furthermore, in the first half of the sixteenth century, Spain, under Charles V, dominated Europe as well as America. Charles controlled the Low Countries, most of central Europe, and part of Italy. Reinforced by the treasure of the Aztecs and the Incas, Spain seemed too mighty to be challenged in either the New World or the Old World.

Under Philip II, who succeeded Charles in 1556, Spanish strength seemed at its peak, especially after Philip added Portugal to his domain in 1580. But beneath the pomp and splendor the great empire was in trouble. The corruption of the Spanish court had much to do with this. So did the ever-increasing dependence of Spain on the gold and silver of its colonies, which tended to undermine the local Spanish economy. Even more important was the disruption of the Catholic Church throughout Europe by the Protestant Reformation.

The Protestant Reformation

Many factors contributed to the Protestant Reformation. The spiritual lethargy and bureaucratic corruption besetting the Roman Catholic Church in the early sixteenth century made it a fit target for reform. The thriving business in the sale of indulgences, payments that were supposed to win for departed loved ones forgiveness for their earthly sins and thus release from purgatory, was a public scandal. The luxurious lifestyle of the popes and the papal court in Rome was another. Yet there had been countless earlier religious reform movements that had led to little or no change. The fact that the movement launched by Martin Luther in 1517 and carried forward by men like John Calvin addressed genuine shortcomings in the Roman Catholic Church does not entirely explain why it led so directly to the rupture of Christendom.

The charismatic leadership of Luther and the compelling brilliance of Calvin made their protests more effective than earlier efforts at reform. Probably more important, so did the political possibilities let loose by their challenge to Rome's spiritual authority. German princes seized on Luther's campaign against the sale of indulgences to stop all payments to Rome and to confiscate church property within their domains. Swiss cities like Geneva, where Calvin took up residence in 1536, and

Zurich joined the Protestant revolt for spiritual reasons, but also to establish their political independence from Catholic kings. Francis I of France remained a Catholic, but he took advantage of Rome's troubles to secure control over the clergy of his kingdom. The efforts of Spain to suppress Protestantism in the Low Countries only further stimulated nationalist movements there, especially among the Dutch.

The decision of Henry VIII of England in 1534 to break with Rome was at bottom a political one. The refusal of Pope Clement VII to agree to an annulment of Henry's marriage of 20 years to Catherine of Aragon, the daughter of Ferdinand and Isabella, provided the occasion. Catherine had given birth to six children, but only a daughter, Mary, survived childhood; Henry was without a male heir. By repudiating the pope's spiritual authority and declaring himself head of the English (Anglican) church, Henry freed himself to divorce Catherine and to marry whomever—and however often—he saw fit. By the time of his death five wives and 13 years later, England had become a Protestant nation. More important for our story, English colonies in America were mostly Protestant.

English Beginnings in America

The first English effort to plant European settlers in the New World was led by Sir Humphrey Gilbert, an Oxford educated soldier and courtier. English Queen Elizabeth I authorized him to explore and colonize "heathen lands not actually possessed by any Christian prince."

We know almost nothing about Gilbert's first attempt except that it occurred in 1578 and 1579; in 1583 he set sail again with five ships and over 200 settlers. He landed them on Newfoundland, then evidently decided to seek a more congenial site farther south. However, no colony was established, and on his way back to England his ship went down in a storm off the Azores.

Gilbert's half-brother, Sir Walter Raleigh, took up the work. Handsome, ambitious, and impulsive, Raleigh was a great favorite of Elizabeth. He sent a number of expeditions to explore the east coast of North America, a land he named Virginia in honor of his unmarried sovereign. In 1585 he settled about a hundred men on Roanoke Island, off the North Carolina coast, but these settlers returned home the next year. In 1587 Raleigh sent another group to Roanoke, including a number of women and children. Unfortunately, the supply ships sent to the colony in 1588 failed to arrive; when help did get there in 1590, not a soul could be found. The fate of the settlers has never been determined.

Experience had shown that the cost of planting settlements in a wilderness 3,000 miles from England was more than any individual purse could bear. (Raleigh lost about £40,000 in his overseas ventures; early in the game he began to advocate government support of colonization.) As early as 1584 Richard Hakluyt, England's foremost authority on the Americas and a talented propagandist for colonization, made a convincing case for royal aid. In his *Discourse on Western*

Elizabeth I, standing upon a map of England. This contemporary miniature (1592) might have struck viewers as ludicrous were it not for the fact that Queen Elizabeth was a consummate political strategist and formidable military foe. She built the fleet that destroyed the Spanish Armada in 1588.

Planting, Hakluyt stressed the military advantages of building "two or three strong fortes" along the Atlantic coast of North America. Ships operating from such bases would make life uncomfortable for "King Phillipe" by intercepting his treasure fleets—a matter, Hakluyt added coolly, "that toucheth him indeede to the quicke." Colonies in America would also spread the Protestant religion and enrich the parent country by expanding the market for English woolens, bringing in valuable tax revenues, and providing employment for the swarms of "lustie youthes that be turned to no provitable use" at home. From the great American forests would come the timber and naval stores needed to build a bigger navy and merchant marine.

Queen Elizabeth read Hakluyt's essay, but she was too cautious and too devious to act boldly on his suggestions. Only after her death in 1603 did full-scale efforts to found English colonies in America begin, and even then the organizing force came from merchant capitalists, not from the Crown.

The Settlement of Virginia

In September 1605 two groups of English merchants petitioned the new king, James I, for a license to colonize Virginia, as the whole area claimed by England was then named. This was granted the following April, and two joint-stock companies were organized, one controlled by London merchants, the other by a group from the area around Plymouth and Bristol.[1] Both were under the control of a Royal Council for Virginia, but James appointed prominent stockholders to the council, which meant that the companies had considerable independence.

This first charter revealed the commercial motivation of both king and company in the plainest terms. Although it spoke of spreading Christianity and bringing "the Infidels and Savages, living in those Parts, to human Civility," it stressed the right "to dig, mine, and search for all Manner of Mines of Gold, Silver, and Copper." On December 20, 1606, the London Company dispatched about a hundred settlers aboard the *Susan Constant, Discovery,* and *Godspeed.* This little band reached the Chesapeake Bay area in May 1607 and founded Jamestown, the first permanent English colony in the New World.

From the start everything seemed to go wrong. The immigrants established themselves in what was a mosquito-infested swamp simply because it appeared easily defensible against Indian attack. They failed to get a crop in the ground because of the lateness of the season and were soon almost without food. Their leaders, mere deputies of the London merchants, did not respond to the challenges of the wilderness. The settlers lacked the skills pioneers need. More than a third of them were "gentlemen" unused to manual labor, and many of the rest were the gentlemen's servants, almost equally unequipped for the task of colony building. During the first winter more than half of the settlers died.

The situation demanded people skilled in agriculture. But all the land belonged to the company, and aside from the gentlemen and their retainers, most of the settlers were only hired laborers who had contracted to work for it for seven years. They had little stake in establishing permanent farms. The merchant directors of the London Company, knowing little or nothing about Virginia, made matters worse. Instead of stressing farming and public improvements, they directed the energies of the colonists into such futile labors as searching for gold (the first supply ship devoted precious space to two goldsmiths and two "refiners"), glassblowing, silk raising, winemaking, and exploring the local rivers in hopes of finding a water route to the Pacific and the riches of China. Although the directors set up a council of settlers, they kept all real power in their own hands.

One colonist, Captain John Smith, tried to stop some of this foolishness. Smith had come to Virginia after a fantastic career as a soldier of fortune in eastern Europe, where he had fought many battles, been enslaved by a Turkish pasha, and triumphed in a variety of adventures, military and amorous. He quickly realized that building houses and raising food were essential to survival, and he soon became an expert forager and Indian trader. Smith was as eager as any seventeenth-century European to take advantage of the Indians and he had few compunctions about the methods employed in doing so. But he recognized both the limits of the colonists' power and the vast differences between Indian customs and values and

[1]The London Company was to colonize southern Virginia, while the Plymouth Company, the Plymouth-Bristol group of merchants, was granted northern Virginia.

his own. It was necessary, he insisted, to dominate the "proud Savages" yet to avoid bloodshed.

Smith pleaded with company officials in London to send over more people accustomed to working with their hands, such as farmers, fishermen, carpenters, masons, "diggers up of trees," and fewer gentlemen and "Tuftaffety humorists."[2] "A plaine soldier who can use a pickaxe and a spade is better than five knights," he said.

Whether Smith was actually rescued from death at the hands of the Indians by the princess Pocahontas is not certain, but there is little doubt that without his direction, the colony would have perished in the early days. However, he stayed in Virginia only two years.

Lacking intelligent leaders and faced with appalling hardships, the Jamestown colonists failed to develop a sufficient sense of common purpose. Each year they died in wholesale lots from disease, starvation (there was even a case of cannibalism among the desperate survivors), Indian attack, and, above all, ignorance and folly.

What saved the colonists was the gradual realization that they must produce their own food—cattle raising was especially important—and the cultivation of tobacco, which flourished there and could be sold profitably in England. Once the settlers discovered tobacco, no amount of company pressure could keep them at wasteful tasks like looking for gold.

John Rolfe, who is also famous for marrying Pocahontas, introduced West Indian tobacco—much milder than the local "weed" and thus more valuable—in 1612. With money earned from the sale of tobacco, the colonists could buy the manufactured articles they could not produce in a raw new country; this freed them from dependence on outside subsidies. It did not mean profit for the London Company, however, for by the time tobacco caught on, the surviving original colonists had served their seven years and were no longer hired hands. To attract more settlers, the company had permitted first tenancy and then outright ownership of farms. Thus the profits of tobacco went largely to the planters, not to the "adventurers" who had organized the colony.

The colonists erred grievously in mistreating the Powhatan Indians. It is quite likely that the settlement would not have survived if the Powhatan Indians had not given the colonists food in the first hard winters, taught them the ways of the forest, introduced them to valuable new crops such as corn and yams, and showed them how to clear dense timber by girdling the trees and burning them down after they were dead. The settlers accepted Indian aid, then took whatever else they wanted by force. English barbarities rivaled those of the Spaniards.

In 1610, for example, George Percy, an English officer, when ordered to punish a Powhatan chief for insolence, proudly described how his men marched into an Indian town, seized some of the natives, "putt some fiftene or sixtene to

---

[2]*Smith was referring to the gold tassels worn by titled students at Oxford and Cambridge at that time.*

This 1616 portrait depicts Pocahontas, daughter of Powhatan, the foremost chief of coastal Virginia. The colonists, in a dispute with Powhatan, took her hostage in 1613 and kept her in Jamestown. The next year she converted to Anglicanism, took the name "Lady Rebecca," and married John Rolfe, an alliance that helped defuse tensions between colonists and Indians. In 1616 the couple came to England with their infant son, where "Lady Rebecca" was received by King James I. She became celebrated as the "belle sauvage." She was the most prominent exemplar of those "intermediaries" who readily crossed the porous boundaries between colonist and Indian cultures.

the Sworde" and cut off their heads. Then he ordered his men to burn the houses and crops. When the expedition returned to its boats, his men complained that Percy had spared an Indian "quene and her Children." Percy relented, and threw the children overboard "shoteinge owtt their Braynes in the water." His men insisted that he burn the queen alive, but Percy, less cruel, stabbed her to death.

The Indians did not submit meekly to such treatment. They proved brave, skillful, and ferocious fighters once they understood that their very existence was at stake. When Powhatan Chief Openchancanough concluded that the English lust for land was inexhaustible, he made plans to wipe them out. To put the Virginians at ease, he sent presents of food to Jamestown. The next day his warriors attacked, killing 347 colonists. Most of the survivors fled to the fort. They remained there for months, neglecting the crops. When winter struck, hundreds more died of hunger.

Between 1606 and 1622 the London Company invested more than £160,000 in Virginia and sent over about 6,000 settlers. Yet no dividends were ever earned, and of this group, fewer than 1,500 were still alive in 1624. That year King James revoked the company's charter. Now a royal colony, Virginia was subject to direct control by the royal bureaucracy in London.

"Purifying" the Church of England

Although the prospect of a better material life brought most English settlers to America, for some, economic opportunity was not the only reason they abandoned what their contemporary William Shakespeare called "dear mother England." A profound unease with England's spiritual state—and therefore with their own while they remained there—explains why many colonists embarked on their "errand into the wilderness."

Despite the attempt of Henry VIII's older daughter, Queen Mary, to reinstate Catholicism during her brief reign (1553–1558), the Anglican Church became once and for all the official Church of England during the long reign of Elizabeth I (1558–1603). Like her father, Elizabeth took more interest in politics than in religion. So long as England had its own church, with her at its head, and with English rather than Latin as its official language, she was content. Aside from these changes, the Anglican Church under Elizabeth closely resembled the Catholic Church it had replaced.

This middle way satisfied most, but not all, of Elizabeth's subjects. Steadfast Catholics could not accept it. Some left England; the rest practiced their faith in private. At the other extreme, more radical Protestants, including a large percentage of England's university-trained clergy, insisted that Elizabeth had not gone far enough. The Anglican Church was still too much like the Church of Rome, they claimed. They objected to the richly decorated vestments worn by the clergy and to the use of candles, incense, and music in church services. They insisted that emphasis should be put on reading the Bible and analyzing the meaning of the Scriptures in order to encourage ordinary worshipers to understand their faith. Since they wanted to "purify" Anglicanism, these critics were called *puritans*. At first the name was a pejorative assigned to them by their opponents, but later it became a badge of honor.

Puritans objected to the way Elizabeth's bishops interpreted the Protestant doctrine of predestination. Their reading of the Book of Genesis convinced them that all human beings were properly damned by Adam's original sin and that what one did on earth had no effect on a person's fate after death. To believe otherwise was to limit God's power, which was precisely what the Catholic Church did in stressing its ability to forgive sins by granting indulgences. The Anglicans implied that while God had already decided whether or not a person was saved, an individual's efforts to lead a good life could somehow cause God to change His mind. The Anglican clergy did not come right out and say that good works could win a person admission to Heaven—that heresy was called Arminianism. But they encouraged people to hope that good works were something more than ends in themselves.

Puritans were also of two minds as to whether reform could be accomplished within the Anglican Church. During Elizabeth's reign, most hoped that it could. Whatever they did in their local churches, the puritans remained professed Anglicans. After James I succeeded Elizabeth I in 1603, however, their fears that the royal court might be backsliding into its old "popish" ways mounted. James was married to a Catholic, and the fact that he favored toleration for Catholics gave further substance to the rumor that he was himself a secret member of that church. This rumor proved to be false, but in his 22-year reign (1603–1625) James did little to advance the Protestant cause. His one contribution—which had a significance far beyond what he or anyone else anticipated—was to authorize a new translation of the Bible. The King James Version (1611) was both a monumental scholarly achievement and a literary masterpiece.

Bradford and Plymouth Colony

In 1606, worried about the future of their faith, members of the church in Scrooby, Nottinghamshire, "separated" from the Anglican Church, declaring it corrupt beyond salvage. In seventeenth-century England, Separatists had to go either underground or into exile. Since only the latter would permit them to practice their religious faith openly, exile it was. In 1608 some 125 of the group departed England for the Low Countries. They were led by their pastor, John Robinson; church elder William Brewster; and a 16-year-old youth, William Bradford. After a brief stay in Amsterdam, the group settled in the town of Leyden. In 1619, however, disheartened by the difficulties they had encountered in making a living, disappointed by the failure of others in England to join them, and distressed because their children were being "subjected to the great licentiousness of the youth" in Holland, these "Pilgrims" decided to move again—to seek "a place where they might have liberty and live comfortably."

The Pilgrims approached the Virginia Company about establishing a settlement near the mouth of the Hudson River on the northern boundary of the company's grant. The London Company, though unsympathetic to the religious views of the Pilgrims, agreed with their request. Since the Pilgrims were short of money, they formed a joint-stock company with other prospective emigrants and some optimistic investors who agreed to pay the expenses of the group in return for half the profits of the venture. In September 1620, about a hundred strong—only thirty-five of them Pilgrims from Leyden—they set out from Plymouth, England, on the *Mayflower*.

Had the *Mayflower* reached the passengers' intended destination, the Pilgrims might have been soon forgotten. Instead their ship touched America slightly to the north, on Cape Cod Bay. Unwilling to remain longer at the mercy of storm-tossed December seas, they decided to settle where they were. Since they were outside the jurisdiction of the London Company, some members of the group claimed to be

The story of the first 30 years of pilgrim life in Plymouth, Massachusetts, is preserved in Governor William Bradford's *Of Plymouth Plantation*. A glimpse of the first colony is shown in this reconstruction.

free of all governmental control. Therefore, before going ashore, the Pilgrims drew up the Mayflower Compact. "We whose names are underwritten," the Compact ran, "do by these Presents, solemnly and mutually in the presence of God and one another covenant and combine ourselves under into a civil Body Politick. . . and by Virtue hereof do enact. . . such just and equal laws. . . as shall be thought most meet and convenient for the general Good of the Colony."

Thus early in American history the idea was advanced that a society should be based on a set of rules chosen by its members. The Pilgrims chose William Bradford as their first governor. In this simple manner, ordinary people created a government that they hoped would enable them to cope with the unknown wilderness confronting them.

The story of the first 30 years of the Pilgrims' colony has been preserved in *Of Plymouth Plantation*, written by Bradford. Having landed on the bleak Massachusetts shore in December 1620 at a place they called Plymouth, the Pilgrims had to endure a winter of desperate hunger. About half of them died. But by great good luck there was an Indian in the area, named Tisquantum—Squanto—who spoke English! In addition to serving as an interpreter, he showed them the best places to fish and what to plant and how to cultivate it. They in turn worked hard, got their crops in the ground in good time, and after a bountiful harvest the following November, they treated themselves and their Indian neighbors to the first Thanksgiving feast.

Bradford prided himself on treating the Indians fairly. We "did not possess one foot of land in this Colony but what was fairly obtained by honest purchase of the Indian proprietors," Bradford boasted. But the Indians yielded the land readily because so many had died of smallpox, likely brought by settlers. And the Pilgrims, after hearing of the Powatan attack on Jamestown in 1622, ambushed a band of Massachusetts Indians, killing seven, and put the leader's head atop a post at the Plymouth fort.

Yet by 1650 there were still fewer than a thousand settlers, most of them living beyond the reach of the original church.

Winthrop and Massachusetts Bay Colony

The Pilgrims were not the first English colonists to inhabit the northern regions. The Plymouth Company had settled a group on the Kennebec River in 1607. These colonists gave up after a few months, but fishermen and traders continued to visit the area, which was christened New England by Captain John Smith after an expedition there in 1614.

In 1620 the Plymouth Company was reorganized as the Council for New England, which had among its principal stockholders Sir Ferdinando Gorges and his friend John Mason, former governor of an English settlement on Newfoundland. Their particular domain included a considerable part of what is now Maine and New Hampshire. More interested in real estate deals than in colonizing, the council disposed of a number of tracts in the area north of Cape Cod.

The most significant of these grants was a small one made to a group of puritans from Dorchester, who established a settlement at Salem in 1629.

Later that year these Dorchester puritans organized the Massachusetts Bay Company and obtained a royal grant to the area between the Charles and Merrimack rivers. The Massachusetts Bay Company was organized like any other commercial venture, but the puritans, acting with single-minded determination, made it a way of obtaining religious refuge in America.

Unlike the Separatists in Plymouth, most puritans had managed to satisfy both Crown and conscience while James I was king. The England of his son Charles I, who succeeded to the throne in 1625, posed a more serious challenge. Whereas James had been content to keep puritans at bay, Charles and his favorite Anglican cleric, William Laud, intended to bring them to heel. With the king's support, Laud proceeded to embellish the already elaborate Anglican ritual and to tighten the central control that the puritans found so distasteful. He removed ministers with puritan leanings from their pulpits and threatened church elders who harbored such ministers with imprisonment.

No longer able to remain within the Anglican fold in good conscience and now facing prison if they tried to worship in the way they believed right, many puritans decided to migrate to America. In the summer of 1630 nearly a thousand of them set out from England, carrying the charter of the Massachusetts Bay Company with them. By fall, they had founded Boston and several other towns.

The early settlements struggled. As in the South, the tasks of founding a new society in a strange land were more difficult than anyone had anticipated. Of the 1,000 English settlers who arrived in Massachusetts in the summer of 1630, 200 died during their first New England winter. Governor Winthrop himself lost eleven family servants. When ships arrived the following spring, they returned to England nearly filled with immigrants who had given up.

But they were replaced many times over. Continuing bad times in England and the persecution of puritans there led to the Great Migration of the 1630s. Within a decade, over 10,000 puritans had arrived in Massachusetts. This infusion of industrious, well-educated, and often prosperous colonists swiftly created a complex and distinct culture on the edge of what one of the pessimists among them called "a hideous and desolate wilderness, full of wild beasts and wild men."

The directors of the Massachusetts Bay Company believed their enterprise to be divinely inspired. Before leaving England, they elected John Winthrop, a 29-year-old Oxford-trained attorney, as governor of the colony. Throughout his 20 years of almost continuous service as governor, Winthrop spoke for the solid and sensible core of the puritans and their high-minded experiment. His lay sermon, "A Modelle of Christian Charity," delivered in mid-Atlantic on the deck of the *Arbella* in 1630, made clear his sense of the momentousness of that experiment:

> *Wee must Consider that wee shall be as a Citty upon a Hill, the eies of all people are upon us; soe that if wee shall deale falsely with our god in this worke wee have undertaken and soe cause him to withdrawe his present help from us, wee shall be*

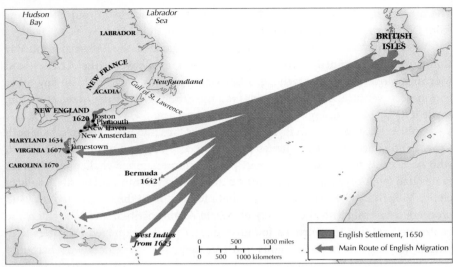

The Great English Migration

*made a story and a by-word through the world, wee shall open the mouthes of ene-
mies to speake evill of the wayes of god and all professours for Gods sake.*

The colonists created an elected legislature, the General Court. Their system
was not democratic in the modern sense because the right to vote and hold office
was limited to male church members, but this did not mean that the government
was run by clergymen or that it was not sensitive to the popular will. Clergymen
were influential, but since they were not allowed to hold public office, their authority was indirect and based on the respect of their parishioners, not on law or force.
At least until the mid-1640s, most families included at least one adult male church
member. Since these "freemen" soon secured the right to choose the governor and
elect the representatives ("deputies") to the General Court, a kind of practical
democracy existed.

The puritans had a clear sense of what their churches should be like. After getting permission from the General Court, a group of colonists who wished to form a
new church could select a minister and conduct their spiritual affairs as they saw
fit. Membership, however, was not open to everyone or even to all who led outwardly blameless lives. It was restricted to those who could present satisfactory evidence of their having experienced "saving grace," such as by a compelling recounting of some extraordinary emotional experience, some mystical sign of
intimate contact with God. This meant that full membership in the churches of
early Massachusetts was reserved for "visible saints." During the 1630s, however,
few applicants were denied membership. Having removed oneself from England
was considered in most cases sufficient proof of spiritual purity.

Troublemakers: Roger Williams and Anne Hutchinson

As Winthrop had on more than one occasion to lament, most of the colony's early troublemakers came not from those of doubtful spiritual condition but from its certified saints. The "godly and zealous" Roger Williams was a prime example. The Pilgrim leader William Bradford described Williams as possessed of "many precious parts, but very unsettled in judgment." Even by Plymouth's standards Williams was an extreme separatist. He was ready to bring down the wrath of Charles I on New England rather than accept the charters signed by him or his father, even if these documents provided the only legal basis for the governments of Plymouth and Massachusetts Bay.

Williams had arrived in Massachusetts in 1631. Following a short stay in Plymouth, he joined the church in Salem, which elected him minister in 1635. Well before then, however, his opposition to the alliance of church and civil government turned both ministers and magistrates against him. Part of his contrariness stemmed from his religious libertarianism. Magistrates should have no voice in spiritual matters, he insisted—"forced religion stinks in God's nostrils." He also offended property owners (which meant nearly everyone) by advancing the radical idea that it was "a Nationale sinne" for anyone, including the king, to take possession of any American land without buying it from the Indians.

Detail from the tombstone of a puritan cemetery in Boston. The grim reaper prods the skeletal man to his final destiny: Life is but a flickering flame, soon to be extinguished.

As long as Williams enjoyed the support of his Salem church, there was little the magistrates could do to silence him. But his refusal to heed those who counseled moderation—"all truths are not seasonable at all times," Governor Winthrop reminded him—swiftly eroded that support. In the fall of 1635, economic pressure put on the town of Salem by the General Court turned his congregation against him. The General Court then ordered him to leave the colony within six weeks.

Williams departed Massachusetts in January 1636, traveling south to the head of Narragansett Bay. There he worked out mutually acceptable arrangements with the local Indians and founded the town of Providence. In 1644, after obtaining a charter in England from Parliament, he established the colony of Rhode Island and Providence Plantations. The government was relatively democratic, all religions were tolerated, and church and state were rigidly separated. Whatever Williams's temperamental excesses, he was more than ready to practice what he preached when given the opportunity.

Anne Hutchinson, who arrived in Boston in 1631, was another "visible saint" who, in the judgment of the puritan establishment, went too far. Hutchinson was not to be taken lightly. According to Governor Winthrop, her husband William was "a man of mild temper and weak parts, wholly guided by his wife." (He was not so weak as to be unable to father Anne's fifteen children.) Duties as a midwife brought her into the homes of other Boston women, with whom she discussed and more than occasionally criticized the sermons of their minister, John Wilson.

The issue in dispute was whether God's saints could be confident of having truly received His gift of eternal life. Wilson and most of the ministers of the colony thought not. God's saints should ceaselessly monitor their thoughts and behavior. But Hutchinson thought this emphasis on behavior was similar to the Catholic belief that an individual's good deeds and penitence could bring God's salvation. Ministers should not demean God, Hutchinson declared, by suggesting that He would be impressed by human actions. She insisted that God's saints knew who they were; those presumed "saints" who had doubts on the matter were likely destined for eternal hell instead.

Hutchinson suggested that those possessed of God's grace were exempt from the rules of good behavior and even from the laws of the commonwealth. As her detractors pointed out, this was the conclusion some of the earliest German Protestants had reached, for which they were judged guilty of the heresy of antinomianism ("against the law") and burned at the stake.

In 1636 the General Court charged Hutchinson with defaming the clergy and brought her to trial. When her accusers quoted the Bible ("Honor thy father and thy mother") to make their case, she coolly announced that even the Ten Commandments must yield to one's own insights if these were directly inspired by God. When pressed for details, she acknowledged that she was a regular recipient of divine insights, communicated, as they were to Abraham, "by the voice of His own spirit in my soul." The General Court, on hearing this claim, banished her.

Hutchinson, together with her large family and a group of supporters, left Massachusetts in the spring of 1637 for Rhode Island, thereby adding to the reputation of that colony as the "sink" of New England. After her husband died in 1642, she and six of her children moved to the Dutch colony of New Netherland, where, the following year, she and all but her youngest daughter were killed by Indians.

The banishment of dissenters like Roger Williams and Anne Hutchinson did not endear the Massachusetts puritans to posterity. In both cases outspoken individualists seem to have been done in by frightened politicians and self-serving ministers. Yet Williams and Hutchinson posed genuine threats to the puritan community. Massachusetts was truly a social experiment. Could it accommodate such uncooperative spirits and remain intact? When forced to choose between the peace of the commonwealth and sending dissenters packing, Winthrop, the magistrates, and the ministers did not hesitate.

Other New England Colonies

From the successful Massachusetts Bay Colony, settlement radiated outward to other areas of New England, propelled by an expanding population and puritan intolerance. In 1629 Sir Ferdinando Gorges and John Mason divided their holdings, Gorges taking the Maine section (enlarged in 1639) and Mason, New Hampshire, but neither succeeded in making much of his claim. Massachusetts gradually took over these areas. The heirs of Gorges and Mason managed to regain legal possession briefly in the 1670s, but Massachusetts bought title to Maine for a pittance (£1250) in 1677. New Hampshire became a royal colony in 1680.

Meanwhile, beginning in 1635, a number of Massachusetts congregations had pushed southwestward into the fertile valley of the Connecticut River. A group headed by the Reverend Thomas Hooker founded Hartford in 1636. Hooker was influential in the drafting of the Fundamental Orders, a sort of constitution creating a government for the valley towns, in 1639. The Fundamental Orders resembled the Massachusetts system, except that they did not limit voting to church members. Other groups of puritans came directly from England to settle towns in and around New Haven in the 1630s. These were incorporated into Connecticut shortly after the Hooker colony obtained a royal charter in 1662.

Pequot War and King Philip's War

New England colonists repeatedly exploited disunity among Indians, who identified more with their hunting group, headed by a sachem, than with a particular tribe. Savvy English settlers could often turn one group against another. In both of the major Indian uprisings in New England during the seventeenth century, the colonists prevailed in part because they were assisted by Indian allies.

In the 1630s the Pequot Indians grew alarmed at the steady stream of English settlers to southeastern Connecticut. After several clashes in 1636, the colonists demanded that the Pequots surrender tribe members responsible for the attacks and pay tribute in wampum. When the Pequots refused, the governments of Massachusetts, Connecticut, and Plymouth declared war. In 1637 the New England armies, bolstered by warriors of the Narragansett and Mohegan tribes, traditional foes of the Pequots, attacked a Pequot village enclosed by a wooden palisade. When Pequots attempted to flee, the English set fire to the village, trapping the Indians and killing nearly all 400 inhabitants.

The Narragansett and Mohegan were aghast. They had intended to replace deceased relatives by adopting captured foes, especially women and children. The English way of fighting, they complained, was "too furious and slays too many people." Bradford, too, commented on the "fearful sight" of the trapped Pequots "thus frying in the fire," but he remembered to praise God for "so speedy a victory." The Pequots were crushed.

In the 1670s Metacom, a Wampanoag sachem, concluded that the only way to resist the English incursion was to drive them out by force of arms. By then, many Wampanoags had acquired flintlock muskets and learned to use them; warfare had become far more lethal. In 1675, after Plymouth colony had convicted and executed three Wampanoags, Metacom ignited an uprising against the New Englanders. Scores of sachems led attacks on more than half of the ninety puritan towns in New England, destroying twelve. About a thousand puritans were massacred; many more abandoned their farms.

The next year the colonists went on the offensive, bolstered by Mohawk allies. The New England militias destroyed Wampanoag villages and exhausted the Wampanoag's gunpowder. The Mohawks ambushed and killed Metacom, presenting his severed head to puritan authorities in Boston. The Wampanoag retreated into to the Great Swamp in Rhode Island and built a large fort. The colonists surrounded and burned the fort, massacred 300 Indians and destroyed the winter stores. In all, about 4,000 Wampanoags and their allies died in what was called "King Philip's" war—King Philip being the colonist's derisive name for Metacom.

Maryland and the Carolinas

The Virginia and New England colonies were essentially corporate ventures. Most of the other English colonies in America were founded by individuals or by a handful of partners who obtained charters from the ruling sovereign. It was becoming easier to establish settlements in America, for experience had taught the English a great deal about the colonization process. Settlers knew better what to bring with them and what to do after they arrived.

Numbers of influential Englishmen were eager to try their luck as colonizers. The grants they received made them "proprietors" of great estates, which were, at least in theory, their personal property. By granting land to settlers in return for a small annual rent, they hoped to obtain a steadily increasing income while holding a valuable speculative interest in all undeveloped land. At the same time, their political power, guaranteed by charter, would become increasingly important as their

In this 1670 illustration by the court painter for King Charles II, young Cecilius Calvert receives a map of Maryland from his grandfather, the second Lord Baltimore. The king's charter for Maryland provided that Cecilius's father and his heirs (first, Cecilius) were to hold the province as "true and absolute lords." The notion was as preposterous as Cecilius's aristocratic clothing. Cecilius died in 1682, before he could even attempt to rule Maryland like a feudal lord.

colonies expanded. In practice, however, the realities of life in America limited their freedom of action and their profits.

One of the first proprietary colonies was Maryland, granted by Charles I to George Calvert, Lord Baltimore. Calvert had a deep interest in America, being a member both of the London Company and of the Council for New England. He hoped to profit financially from Maryland, but, since he was a Catholic, he also intended the colony to be a haven for his co-religionists.

Calvert died shortly before Charles approved his charter, so the grant went to his son Cecilius. The first settlers arrived in 1634, founding St. Mary's, just north of the Potomac. The presence of the now well-established Virginia colony nearby greatly aided the Marylanders; they had little difficulty in getting started and in developing an economy based, like Virginia's, on tobacco. According to the Maryland charter, Lord Baltimore had the right to establish feudal manors, hold people in serfdom, make laws, and set up his own courts. He soon discovered, however, that to attract settlers he had to allow them to own their farms and that to maintain any political influence at all he had to give the settlers considerable say in local affairs. Other wise concessions marked his handling of the religious question. He would have preferred an exclusively Catholic colony, but while Catholics did go to Maryland, Protestants greatly outnumbered them. Baltimore dealt with this problem by agreeing to a Toleration Act (1649) that guaranteed freedom of religion to anyone "professing to believe in Jesus Christ." Though religious disputes persisted,

Calvert's compromise enabled Protestants to make a fortune and maintain an influence in Maryland until the Revolution.

The Carolina charter, like that of Maryland, accorded the proprietors wide authority. The first settlers arrived in 1670, most of them from the sugar plantations of Barbados, where slave labor was driving out small independent farmers. Charles Town (now Charleston) was founded in 1680. Another center of population sprang up in the Albemarle district, just south of Virginia, settled largely by individuals from that colony. Two quite different societies grew up in these areas. The Charleston colony, with an economy based on a thriving trade in furs and on the export of foodstuffs to the West Indies, was prosperous and cosmopolitan. The Albemarle settlement, where the soil was less fertile, was poorer and more primitive. Eventually, in 1712, the two were formally separated, becoming North and South Carolina.

French and Dutch Settlements

While the English were settling Virginia and New England, other Europeans were challenging Spain's monopoly elsewhere in the New World. Jacques Cartier attempted to found a French colony at Québec in the 1530s. Spain, initially alarmed by the French incursion, considered intervening; but the Spanish emperor thought it not worth the bother. Cartier soon concurred, as his settlement quickly succumbed to brutal winters, scurvy, and Indian attacks.

Not until the end of the century was another attempt made to colonize the region. Then some intrepid French traders initiated a trade with Indians for fur, which had become valuable in Europe. Europeans craved the soft, thick furs, especially beaver pelts, used for hats or to trim coats and dresses. Indians coveted the strength and sharpness of European metal knives and hatchets, the warmth and strength of European woolens, and—often enough—the intoxicating effects of alcohol.

Unlike the English, who occupied the Indian's land, or the Spanish, who subjugated Indians and exploited their labor, French traders viewed the Indians as essential trading partners. A handful of French traders, carrying their goods in canoes and small boats, made their way to Indian settlements along the St. Lawrence River and the shores of Lake Ontario and Lake Erie. But by 1650, there were only 700 French colonists in New France.

By then, France had perceived both the economic and military potential of North America and the vulnerability of its thinly populated string of settlements. To protect its toehold in North America, the French government built forts on key northern waterways and sent soldiers to protect the traders. French military expenditures helped sustain the fledgling colony. By 1700, about 15,000 French colonists lived in scattered settlements along an arc ranging from the mouth of the St. Lawrence in the northeast, through the Great Lakes, and down the Mississippi to the Gulf of Mexico.

By contrast, nearly a quarter of a million English settlers (and 34,000 Africans, most brought as slaves) had occupied the English colonies. As the English filled up the

Atlantic seaboard and pushed steadily westward, the French recruited the Algonquian Indians as military allies. The Algonquians were linguistically similar tribes who had been driven from the Atlantic seaboard into territory occupied by the Iroquois, a confederation of powerful tribes. English settlers commonly negotiated with the Iroquois.

Warfare ensued, usually French-Algonquian against English-Iroquois. But now that the Indians had guns and ammunition, warfare became bloodier, and all frontier settlements—Indian and colonist alike—became more vulnerable.

Complicating matters further was the Dutch settlement of New Netherland in the Hudson Valley. They based their claim to the region on the explorations of Henry Hudson in 1609. As early as 1624 they established an outpost, Fort Orange, on the site of present-day Albany. Two years later they founded New Amsterdam at the mouth of the Hudson River, and Peter Minuit, the director general of the West India Company, purchased Manhattan Island from the Indians for trading goods worth about 60 guilders.

The Dutch traded with the Indians for furs and plundered Spanish colonial commerce enthusiastically. Through the Charter of Privileges of Patroons, which authorized large grants of land to individuals who would bring over fifty settlers, they tried to encourage large-scale agriculture. Only one such estate—Rensselaerswyck, on the Hudson south of Fort Orange, owned by the rich Amsterdam merchant Kiliaen Van Rensselaer—was successful. Peter Minuit was removed from his post in New Amsterdam in 1631, but he organized a group of Swedish settlers several years later and founded the colony of New Sweden on the lower reaches of the Delaware River. New Sweden was in constant conflict with the Dutch, who finally overran it in 1655.

The Middle Colonies

Gradually it became clear that the English would dominate the entire coast between the St. Lawrence Valley and Florida. After 1660 only the Dutch challenged their monopoly. The two nations, once allies against Spain, had fallen out because of the fierce competition of their textile manufacturers and merchants. England's efforts to bar Dutch merchant vessels from its colonial trade also brought the two countries into conflict in America. Charles II precipitated a showdown by granting his brother James, Duke of York, the entire area between Connecticut and Maryland. This was tantamount to declaring war. In 1664 English forces captured New Amsterdam without a fight—there were only 1,500 people in the town—and soon the rest of the Dutch settlements capitulated. New Amsterdam became New York. The duke did not interfere much with the way of life of the Dutch settlers, and they were quickly reconciled to English rule. New York had no local assembly until the 1680s, but there had been no such body under the Dutch either.

In 1664, even before the capture of New Amsterdam, the Duke of York gave New Jersey, the region between the Hudson and the Delaware, to John, Lord Berkeley, and Sir George Carteret. To attract settlers, these proprietors offered land on easy terms and established freedom of religion and a democratic system of local government. A considerable number of puritans from New England and Long Island moved to the new province.

In 1674 Berkeley sold his interest in New Jersey to two Quakers. Quakers believed that they could communicate directly with their Maker; their religion required neither ritual nor ministers. Originally a sect emotional to the point of fanaticism, by the 1670s the Quakers had come to stress the doctrine of the Inner Light—the direct, mystical experience of religious truth—which they believed possible for all persons. They were at once humble and fiercely proud, pacifistic yet unwilling to bow before any person or to surrender their right to worship as they pleased. They distrusted the intellect in religious matters and, while ardent proselytizers of their own beliefs, they tolerated those of others cheerfully. When faced with opposition, they resorted to passive resistance, a tactic that embroiled them in grave difficulties in England and in most of the American colonies. In Massachusetts Bay, for example, four Quakers were executed when they refused either to conform to puritan ideas or to leave the colony.

The acquisition of New Jersey gave the Quakers a place where they could practice their religion in peace. The proprietors, in keeping with their principles, drafted an extremely liberal constitution for the colony, the Concessions and Agreements of 1677, which created an autonomous legislature and guaranteed settlers freedom of conscience, the right of trial by jury, and other civil rights.

Historian James Merrell notes several errors in Benjamin West's famous 1771 painting, *William Penn's Treaty with the Indians*. In 1682, when the treaty was negotiated, Penn was not yet so fat; the colonists' clothing and brick buildings resemble a scene in Philadelphia in the 1750s, not the 1680s; and the Indians are implausibly posed like Greek and Roman statues. Most important, the painting includes no translator, the one indispensable figure in the proceedings. All Indian and settler exchanges required "go-betweens" or "negotiators" to help each group explain itself to the other.

The main Quaker effort at colonization came in the region immediately west of New Jersey, a fertile area belonging to William Penn, the son of a wealthy English admiral. Penn had early rejected a life of ease and had become a Quaker missionary. As a result, he was twice jailed. Yet he possessed qualities that enabled him to hold the respect and friendship of people who found his religious ideas abhorrent. From his father, Penn had inherited a claim to £16,000 that the admiral had lent Charles II. The king, reluctant to part with that much cash, paid off the debt in 1681 by giving Penn the region north of Maryland and west of the Delaware River, insisting only that it be named Pennsylvania, in honor of the admiral. In 1682 Penn founded Philadelphia. The Duke of York then added Delaware, the region between Maryland and the Delaware Bay, to Penn's holdings.

William Penn considered his colony a "Holy Experiment." He treated the Indians fairly, buying title to their lands and trying to protect them in their dealings with settlers and traders. Anyone who believed in "one Almighty and Eternal God" was entitled to freedom of worship. Penn's political ideas were paternalistic rather than democratic; the assembly he established could only approve or reject laws proposed by the governor and council. But individual rights were as well protected in Pennsylvania as in New Jersey.

William Penn was neither a doctrinaire nor an ivory tower philosopher. He came to Pennsylvania himself when trouble developed between settlers and his representatives and agreed to adjustments in his first Frame of Government when he realized that local conditions demonstrated the need for change. His combination of toughness, liberality, and good salesmanship helped the colony to prosper and grow rapidly. Of course the presence of well-settled colonies on all sides and the richness of the soil had much to do with this happy state of affairs. By 1685 there were almost 9,000 settlers in Pennsylvania, and by 1700 twice that number, a heartening contrast to the early history of Virginia and Plymouth. Pennsylvania produced wheat, corn, rye, and other crops in abundance and found a ready market for its surpluses on the sugar plantations of the West Indies.

Cultural Collisions

Since the Indians did not worship the Christian God and indeed worshiped a large number of other gods, the Europeans dismissed them as contemptible heathens. Some insisted that the Indians were servants of Satan. "Probably the devil decoyed these miserable savages hither," one English colonist explained. Such colonists insisted that as minions of Satan, Indians were unworthy of becoming Christians. Other Europeans, such as the Spanish friars, did try to convert the Indians, and with considerable success; but as late as 1569, when Spain introduced the Inquisition into its colonies, the natives were exempted from its control on the ground that they were incapable of rational judgment and thus not responsible for their "heretical" religious beliefs.

Other troubles grew out of similar misunderstandings. European colonists assumed that Indian chiefs ruled with the same authority as their own kings. When Indians, whose loyalties were shaped by complex kinship relations more than by identification with any one leader, failed to honor commitments made by their chiefs, Europeans accused them of treachery. Conversely, Indians regarded treaty-making as an act of brotherhood, marked by rituals affirming mutual support. When settlers angrily blamed the Indians for violating the words on a scrap of paper, Indians were bewildered: Brothers would not treat each other so. Colonists compounded the confusion by describing their kings and governors as "fathers" to the Indians. But among Indians, who experienced childhood mostly among the kinfolk of mothers, fathers were regarded as indulgent and nonintrusive.

Indians who depended on hunting and fishing had little use for personal property that was not easily portable. They saw no reason to amass possessions, as individuals or as tribes. Even the Aztecs, with their treasures of gold and silver, valued the metals for their durability and the beautiful things that could be made with them rather than as objects of commerce.

Indians were puzzled that European men worked so hard in the fields; in many Indian societies, crop cultivation was women's work. Moreover, the bounty of the earth was such that no one needed to work all the time. The Europeans' ceaseless drudgery and relentless pursuit of material goods struck the Indians as perverse. In many Indian societies, sachems acquired power by giving away their goods. The Narragansett Indians even had a ritual in which they collected "almost all the riches they have to their gods"—kettles, hatchets, beads, knives—and burned them in a great fire.

This lack of concern for material things led Europeans to conclude that the native people of America were lazy and childlike. "[Indians] do but run over the grass, as do also foxes and wild beasts," an English settler wrote in 1622, "so it is lawful now to take a land, which none useth, and make use of it." In the sense that the Indians continuously interacted with nature, the first part of this statement contained a grain of truth, although of course the second did not follow from it logically.

That the Indians allowed their environment to remain pristine is a myth. Long before contact with the Europeans, Indians had cleared fields, burned the underbrush of forests, diverted rivers and streams, built roads and settlements, and deposited immense quantities of earth upon mounds.

But Europeans left a deeper imprint on the land. Their iron-tipped ploughs dug into the earth and made more of it accessible to cultivation, and their iron axes and saws enabled them to clear vast forests with relative ease. Pigs and cattle, too, ate their way through fields. Indians resented the intensity of English cultivation. After capturing several English farmers, some Algonquians buried them alive, all the while taunting them: "You English have grown exceedingly above the Ground. Let us now see how you will grow when planted into the ground."

The Europeans' inability to grasp the communal nature of land tenure among Indians also led to innumerable quarrels. Traditional tribal boundaries were neither spelled out in deeds or treaties nor marked by fences or any other sign of occupation. Often corn grown by a number of families was stored in a common bin and drawn on by all as needed. Such practices were utterly alien to the European mind.

Nowhere was the cultural chasm between Indians and Europeans more evident than in warfare. Indians did not seek to possess land, so they sought not to destroy an enemy but to display their valor, avenge an insult or perceived wrong, or acquire captives who could take the place of missing family members. The Indians preferred to ambush an opponent and seize the stragglers; when confronted by a superior force, they usually melted into the woods. The Europeans preferred to fight in heavily armed masses in order to obliterate the enemy.

Colonists denounced Indian perfidy for burning houses and towns; but they saw no inconsistency in burning Indian "nests," "wigwams," and "camps." Conversely, the Indians thought it within their rights to slaughter the cattle that devoured their crops and spoiled their hunting grounds. But when the Indians tortured the beasts in fury, the colonists regarded them as savages.

Cultural Fusions

Increase Mather, a puritan leader, worried that "Christians in this Land have become too like unto the Indians." Little wonder, he observed, that God had "afflicted us by them" through disease and other trials. Yet Mather's comments suggested that interaction between European settlers and the native peoples was characteristic of life in all the colonies. *Interaction* is the key word in this sentence. The so-called Columbian Exchange between Indian and European was a two-way street. The colonists learned a great deal about how to live in the American forest from the Indians: the names of plants and animals (hickory, pecan, raccoon, skunk, moose); what to eat in their new home and how to catch or grow it; what to wear (leather leggings and especially moccasins); how best to get from one place to another; how to fight; and in some respects how to think.

The colonists learned from the Indians how best to use many plants and animals for food and clothing, but they would probably have discovered most of these if the continent had been devoid of human life when they arrived. Corn, however, the staple of the diet of agricultural tribes, was something the Indians had domesticated. Its contribution to the success of English colonization was enormous.

The colonists also took advantage of that marvel of Indian technology, the birchbark canoe. An early explorer, Martin Pring, brought one back to England in 1603; it was 17 feet long and 4 feet wide and capable, according to Pring, of carrying nine full-grown men. Yet it weighed "not at the most above sixtie pounds," a thing, Pring added, "almost incredible in regard to the largenesse and capacitie thereof."

For their part, the Indians adopted European technology eagerly. All metal objects were indeed of great usefulness to them, although the products and tools that metals replaced were neither crude nor inefficient in most cases. (A bowman could get off six times as many shots in a given time as a seventeenth-century soldier armed with a firelock, and would probably hit the target more frequently.)

 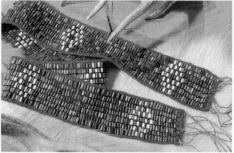

Indians were befuddled by the Europeans' craving for gold, such as these Spanish coins *(left)*. Europeans were similarly baffled by the Indians' attraction to wampum, seashells that were drilled, placed on a string, and formed into belts, such as this eighteenth-century Oneida belt *(right)*. No negotiations or trade with many Indian tribes could commence without gifts of wampum.

The fur trade illustrates the pervasiveness of Indian-European interaction. It was in some ways a perfect business arrangement. Both groups profited. The colonists got "valuable" furs for "cheap" European products, while the Indians got "priceless" tools, knives, and other trade goods in exchange for "cheap" beaver pelts and deerskins. The demand for furs caused the Indians to become more efficient hunters and trappers and even to absorb some of the settlers' ideas about private property and capitalist accumulation. Hunting parties became larger. Farming tribes shifted their villages in order to be nearer trade routes and waterways. In some cases tribal organization was altered: Small groups combined into confederations in order to control more territory when their hunting reduced the supplies of furs nearer home. Early in the seventeenth century, Huron Indians in the Great Lakes region, who had probably never seen a Frenchman, owned French products obtained from eastern tribes in exchange for Huron corn.

Europeans and Indians became interdependent. The colonists relied on Indian labor and products. Indians relied on European guns and metal tools. Some Indians became so enamored of European knives and metal tools that they forgot the stone-working skills of their Paleo-Indian ancestors. They now depended on Europeans for those products, much as the colonists themselves depended on Indian corn, potatoes, and other crops.

In sum, during the first 200-odd years that followed Columbus's first landfall in the Caribbean, a complex development had taken place in the Americas. Sometimes these alien encounters were amiable, as Indians and colonists exchanged ideas, skills, and goods; sometimes the encounters were hostile and bloody, with unimaginable cruelties inflicted by and on both sides. But the coming together of Indians and European settlers was mostly characterized by ambiguity and confusion, as markedly different peoples drew from their own traditions to make sense of a new world that little resembled what they knew. In time, their world would become our own.

EXPLORATION

c. 1000	Leif Eriksson reaches Newfoundland
1445–1488	Portuguese sailors explore west coast of Africa
1492	First voyage of Christopher Columbus
1497	John Cabot explores east coast of North America
1498	Vasco da Gama sails around Africa to India
1513	Ponce de Leon explores Florida
1519–1521	Hernán Cortés conquers Mexico
1519–1522	Ferdinand Magellan's crew circumnavigates globe
1539–1542	Hernando de Soto explores lower Mississippi River valley
1540–1542	Francisco Vasquez de Coronado explores Southwest
1579	Francis Drake explores coast of California
1609	Henry Hudson discovers Hudson River

SETTLEMENT

1493	Columbus founds La Navidad, Hispaniola
1494	Treaty of Tordesillas divides New World between Spain and Portugal
1576	Spanish settle St. Augustine
1587	English found "Lost Colony" of Roanoke Island
1607	English settle Jamestown
1608	French found Québec
1612	John Rolfe introduces tobacco cultivation in Virginia
1620	Pilgrims settle Plymouth, sign Mayflower Compact
1624	Dutch settle New Amsterdam
1630	English puritans settle Massachusetts Bay
1630–1640	Waves of English come to America during the Great Migration
1634	George Calvert, Lord Baltimore, founds Maryland as Catholic haven
1636	Roger Williams founds Rhode Island
	General Court of Massachusetts Bay Colony banishes Anne Hutchinson
1639	Thomas Hooker founds Connecticut
1642	French found Montréal
1664	English conquer Dutch New Amsterdam
1670	First settlers arrive in Carolina
1680	Charles Town (now Charleston) is settled
1682	William Penn founds Philadelphia

American Society in the Making

"WHAT IS AN AMERICAN?"

In 2006 a Purdue University survey asked this question of 1,500 U.S. citizens. More than 90 percent said that speaking and writing English well were important in defining American identity. Nearly as high a proportion equated American identity with a willingness to serve in the military and pledge allegiance to the nation. More than half reported that the "Christian faith" was also important in making someone an American, although nearly a third "strongly" disagreed.

But the roots of "American identity" extend deep into past, before most inhabitants of what is now the United States spoke English or worshiped in Christian churches, before the United States even existed as a nation. Indeed the question, "What is an American?" was posed in 1762 by Hector St. John de Crèvecoeur, a French settler in New York. His answer was both perceptive and prophetic: "The American," he declared, was a "new race of man," a "promiscuous" blending of English, Scotch, Irish, French, Dutch, Germans, and Swedes. Freed from the traditions and constraints of Europe, Americans were a composite people "whose labours and posterity will one day cause great changes in the world."

But Crèvecoeur neglected the idea, outlined in the previous chapter, that American identity also emerged from the encounter of Indian, European, and African peoples. Other factors also explain the distinctiveness of American identity. Land in what is now the United States was astoundingly plentiful and, by European standards, greatly underutilized; the labor to farm it and extract its wealth was scarce. Europeans, too, discovered that their institutions were often ill-adapted to American conditions; this encouraged innovation. Religious enthusiasts and educational reformers also learned that they had more scope to realize their visions.

Factors as material as the landscape encountered, as quantifiable as population patterns, as elusive as chance and calculation all shaped colonial social arrangements. Their cumulative impact did not at first produce anything like a uniform society. The "Americans" who evolved in what is now the United States were in many ways as different from each other as all were from their foreign cousins. The process by which these identities merged into an American nation remained incomplete. It was—and is—ongoing.

Settlement of New France

France's colonial enterprise in North America progressed slowly after 1700. The main problem, as before, was the difficulty in persuading French people to occupy isolated settlements in remote American frontiers. But some did come. Military garrisons built and occupied forts along the shores of the Great Lakes and at strategic positions overlooking the Mississippi, Illinois, and other rivers. Solitary French traders, paddling canoes laden with metal tools, cloth, and alcohol, ventured deep into the wilderness in search of increasingly scarce animal pelts. Jesuit missionaries endeavored to plant Christianity among the Indians in the region of Lake Michigan and the Illinois River. Missionaries founded Detroit in 1701, Kaskaskia, south of Cahokia, in 1703, and Fort de Chartres in 1720.

Attempts to anchor New France with a colony at the mouth of the Mississippi were frustrated by the region's maze of swamps, marshes, and meandering waterways which, though ideal for hiding pirates, discouraged settlement. One French missionary, unable to locate the mouth of the Mississippi, complained that the "coast changes shape at every moment." In 1712 France chartered a private company to build a colony in the region. It laid out a town, called New Orleans, at the site of a short portage between the Mississippi River and Lake Pontchartrain. The company granted tracts of land to settlers and transported several thousand of them to Louisiana. Some established farms, planting indigo, tobacco, rice and cotton; others acquired forest products, such as lumber, tar, and resin; still others traded for furs. The company established more settlements in the region, including one at Natchez, on a bluff above the Mississippi. But in 1729 the Natchez Indians wiped out this settlement and the company went bankrupt.

In 1731 the French government took control of Louisiana, with New Orleans as the administrative capital. Settlement lagged. The region was unsuited for farming, bemoaned one French official: "Now there is too much drought, now too much rain." By 1750 no more than 10,000 Europeans had colonized the region.

Few European women were among the immigrants to New France. In Louisiana, Frenchmen often married Indian women in Christian ceremonies, although the government tried to discourage the practice. Fur traders in the northern hinterlands also married Indians, whose knowledge of Indian languages, culture practices, and tribal relations proved helpful for business—and essential for survival. Children of mixed-blood were frequently seen throughout New France.

As beaver and other game became scarce, traders went still farther west. Eventually they came upon tribes that had been driven from Pennsylvania and

New York by the mighty Iroquois confederation. These Indians, fearful of the Iroquois, sought guns and ammunition. The traders complied, though not without misgivings. This escalation in armaments ensured that warfare among Indians would be more deadly, and that the isolated outposts of New France would be more vulnerable.

Society in New Mexico, Texas, and California

Once the Indians of the upper Mississippi acquired guns from French traders, the new weaponry quickly spread to the Indians of the Great Plains. Far earlier, the Apache and Comanche had become expert at riding European horses, which proliferated on the grasslands of the Great Plains. Now armed with light muskets, the Plains Indians became formidable foes; the Comanche were for several generations nearly invincible. Spanish raiders who had formerly seized Plains Indians for the slave trade now preyed upon less formidable nomadic tribes, such as the Ute, who lived in the foothills of the Rockies.

The Comanche, always adept as buffalo hunters, found it even easier with guns. As the number and size of their hunting bands increased, the Comanche encroached on Apache territory. Soon Comanche warriors, occasionally assisted by French traders and soldiers, raided remote Spanish and Pueblo settlements in New Mexico and Texas. "We do not have a single gun," declared one Spanish missionary in 1719, "while we see the French giving hundreds of arms to Indians."

The ascendancy of the Plains Indians endangered all of the new frontier missions and discouraged further settlement by Hispanics. In 1759 a Spanish commander of a *presidio* complained that the Comanche were "so superior in firearms as well as in numbers that our destruction seems probable." Only San Antonio, with 600 Hispanic settlers, amounted to much.

The trade in Indian slaves remained an enduring aspect of life along the sparsely populated northern rim of New Spain. Catholic missionaries usually prevented Spanish traders from enslaving Pueblo Indians, many of whom lived in mission towns and knew the rudiments of Catholicism. But no such arguments could protect the "wild" Indians such as the Ute of the foothills of the Rockies.

Indian slaves often had children by Hispanic fathers, who rarely acknowledged their paternity of such offspring. Known as *genizaros,* these children occupied the bottom rung of a social system largely based on the status of fathers. *Genizaros* learned Spanish and received training in Catholicism. In some towns, they comprised a third of the population. Females usually worked as household servants, males as indentured servants on ranches. Spanish officials, eager to increase the numbers of Spanish colonists, granted *genizaros* the right to own property. Many became ranchers and herders.

While the Comanche were imperiling the frontier of New Mexico and Texas, Spanish officials learned of a new threat in the 1760s: Britain and Russia were

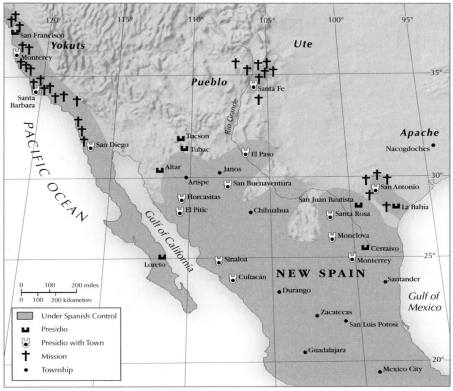

Under Spanish Control
Presidio
Presidio with Town
Mission
Township

Spain's North American Frontier

attempting to colonize the Northwest, the region that now comprises Oregon and Washington. This threatened Spain's claims to California, a remote wilderness inhabited by some 300,000 Indians. As in New Mexico, Spain, having failed to attract Hispanic settlers, invited Franciscan missionaries to *create* "Spanish" settlers by converting the Indians to Catholicism and Hispanicizing their language and culture. This would not prove easy. The Indians of California comprised over 300 tribes that spoke nearly 100 different languages.

In 1769 several score Jesuits and a detachment of Spanish soldiers established a *presidio* and mission in San Diego. Other missions followed at Monterey, Santa Barbara, and San Francisco; within several decades some twenty missions had been established in California.

The Jesuits monitored Indian life closely. They segregated all unmarried girls over the age of seven so as to prevent them from indulging in freer Indian sexual mores and to protect them from European rapists. The Jesuits also inculcated the discipline of work, overseeing the digging of irrigation ditches, the cultivation of crops, the tending of livestock, the manufacture of handicrafts, and the construction of churches, forts, and homes. The Indians received no wages, but instead were fed and cared for by the priests, whose first obligation was to God and the church. Because the California settlements were distant from New Spain, the missions survived chiefly by provisioning Spanish military garrisons.

Whatever success the Jesuits had in establishing the missions, however, was undone by disease. As had happened throughout the western hemisphere, the introduction of European pathogens among formerly isolated Indian populations resulted in catastrophic losses. European diseases hit all California Indians, not just those in the missions. By the close of the eighteenth century, Spain had failed in its effort to establish a strong Hispanic colony in California.

The English Prevail on the Atlantic Seaboard

By the mid-eighteenth century, England had successfully addressed the chief problem that bedeviled the French and Spanish colonial efforts: a dearth of colonists. By then, European settlers, most of them English, had taken possession of much of the Atlantic seaboard. But this basic fact overlooks the important differences among the colonies. Each of the Middle Colonies had distinctive histories and settlement patterns. Even the New England colonies, though originally founded for similar religious purposes, soon diverged.

The southern parts of English North America comprised three regions: the Chesapeake Bay, consisting of "tidewater" Virginia and Maryland; the "low country" of the Carolinas (and eventually Georgia); and the "back country," a vast territory that extended from the "fall line" in the foothills of the Appalachians, where

Mission San Diego de Alcalá, the oldest in California. Franciscan friars adapted Spanish conceptions to American building materials, chiefly adobe bricks cemented with wet clay. Because these materials could not bear much weight, the architects had to devise ingenious wall supports to create structures such as this mission church.

falls and rapids put an end to navigation on the tidal rivers, to the farthest point of western settlement. Not until well into the eighteenth century would the emergence of common features—export-oriented agricultural economies, a labor force in which black slaves figured prominently, the absence of towns of any size—prompt people to think of the "South" as a single region.

The Chesapeake Colonies

When the English philosopher Thomas Hobbes wrote in 1651 that human life tended to be "nasty, brutish, and short," he might well have had in mind the royal colony of Virginia. Although the colony grew from about 1,300 to nearly 5,000 in the decade after the Crown took it over in 1624, the death rate remained appalling. Since more than 9,000 immigrants had entered the colony, nearly half the population died during that decade.

Long after food shortages and Indian warfare had ceased to be serious problems, life in the Chesapeake remained precarious. Well into the 1700s a white male of 20 in Middlesex County, Virginia, could look forward only to about 25 more years of life. Across Chesapeake Bay, in Charles County, Maryland, life expectancy was even lower. The high death rate had important effects on family structure. Because relatively few people lived beyond their forties, more often than not children lost at least one of their parents before they reached maturity and in many instances both. Remarriage was a way of life. Apparently this situation did not cause drastic emotional problems for most people of the region. Men provided generously for their families in their wills, despite knowing that their wives would probably remarry quickly. Being brought up entirely by stepparents was so common that children tended to accept it almost as a matter of course.

Because of the persistent shortage of women in the Chesapeake region (men outnumbered women by three to two even in the early 1700s), widows easily found new husbands. Many men spent their entire lives alone or in the company of other men. Others married Indian women and became part of Indian society.

All Chesapeake settlers felt the psychological effects of their precarious and frustrating existence. Random mayhem and calculated violence posed a continuous threat to life and limb. Life was coarse at best and often as "brutish" as Hobbes had claimed, even allowing for the difficulties involved in carving out a community in the wilderness.

The Lure of Land

Agriculture was the bulwark of life for the Chesapeake settlers and the rest of the colonial South; the tragic experiences of the Jamestown settlement revealed this quickly enough. Jamestown also suggested that a colony could not succeed unless its inhabitants were allowed to own their own land. The first colonists had agreed to work for seven years in return for a share of the profits. When their contracts expired there were few profits. To satisfy these settlers and to attract new capital, the London Company declared a "dividend" of land, its only asset. The surviving colonists each received 100 acres. Thereafter, as prospects continued poor, the company relied more and more on grants of land to attract both capital and labor. A number of wealthy Englishmen were given immense tracts, some running to several hundred thousand acres. Lesser persons willing to settle in Virginia received more modest grants. Whether dangled before a great tycoon, a country squire, or a poor farmer, the offer of land had the effect of encouraging immigration to the colony. This was a much-desired end, for without the labor to develop it the land was worthless.

In the 1670s conflicts between Virginians who owned choice land and former servants on the outer edge of settlement brought the colony to the brink of class warfare. The costs of meeting the region's ever-growing need for labor with indentured servants were becoming prohibitive. Some other solution was needed.

"Solving" the Labor Shortage: Slavery

Probably the first African blacks brought to English North America arrived on a Dutch ship and were sold at Jamestown in 1619. Early records are vague and incomplete, so it is not possible to say whether these Africans were treated as slaves or freed after a period of years like indentured servants. What is certain is that by about 1640 *some* blacks were slaves (a few, with equal certainty, were free) and that by the 1660s local statutes had firmly established the institution in Virginia and Maryland.

Slavery soon spread throughout the colonies. As early as 1626 there were eleven slaves in New Netherland, and when the English conquered that colony in 1664 there were 700 slaves in a population of about 8,000. Relatively few blacks were imported until late in the seventeenth century, even in the southern colonies. In 1650 there were only 300 blacks in Virginia and as late as 1670 no more than 2,000.

White servants were much more highly prized. The African, after all, was almost entirely alien to both the European and the American ways of life. In a country starved for capital, the cost of slaves—roughly five times that of indentured servants—was another disadvantage. In 1664 the governor of Maryland informed Lord Baltimore that local planters would use more "neigros . . . if our purses would endure it." As long as white servants were available, few planters acquired slaves.

In the 1670s the flow of indentured servants slackened, the result of improving economic conditions in England and the competition of other colonies for servants. At the same time, the formation of the Royal African Company (1672) made slaves more readily available. By 1700, nearly 30,000 slaves lived in the English colonies.

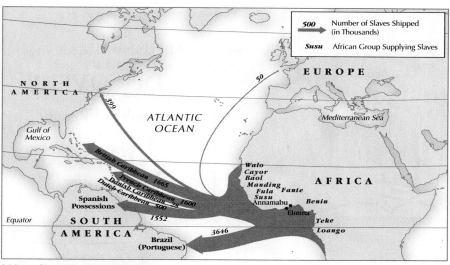

African Slave Trade, 1451–1870

Prosperity in a Pipe: Tobacco

Labor and land made agriculture possible, but it was necessary to find a market for American crops in the Old World if the colonists were to enjoy anything but the crudest sort of existence. They could not begin to manufacture all the articles they required; to obtain from England such items as plows and muskets and books and chinaware, they had to have cash crops, what their English creditors called "merchantable commodities." Here, at least, fortune favored the Chesapeake.

The founders of Virginia tried to produce all sorts of things that were needed in the old country: grapes and silk in particular, indigo, cotton, oranges, olives, sugar, and many other plants. But it was tobacco, unwanted, even strongly opposed at first, which became for farmers on both sides of Chesapeake Bay "their darling."

Tobacco was unknown in Europe until Spanish explorers brought it back from the West Indies. It was not common in England until the time of Sir Walter Raleigh. Then it quickly proved irresistible to thousands of devotees. At first the London Company discouraged its colonists from growing tobacco. Since it clearly contained some habit-forming drug, many people opposed its use. King James I wrote a pamphlet attacking the weed, in which, among other things, he anticipated the findings of modern cancer researchers by saying that smoking was a "vile and stinking" habit "dangerous to the Lungs." But English smokers and partakers of snuff ignored their king, and the Virginians ignored their company. By 1617 a pound of tobacco was worth more than 5 shillings in London. Company and Crown then changed their tune, granting the colonists a monopoly and encouraging them in every way.

PANACEA;
OR
The Universal Medicine,
BEING
A DISCOVERY
of the
Wonderfull Vertues
OF
Tobacco
Taken in a Pipe,
WITH
Its Operation and Use both in
Physick and *Chyrurgery.*

By Dr EVERARD, &c.

LONDON,
Printed for *Simon Miller* at the Star in Sr Pauls
Church-yard, near the West-end, 1659.

Tobacco companies advertised their product as far back as the seventeenth century. This 1659 advertisement lauds tobacco as a medical "panacea."

Unlike wheat, which required expensive plows and oxen to clear the land and prepare the soil, tobacco plants could be set on semicleared land and cultivated with a simple hoe. Although tobacco required lots of human labor, a single laborer working two or three acres could produce as much as 1,200 pounds of cured tobacco, which, in a good year, yielded a profit of more than 200 percent. This being the case, production in America leaped from 2,500 pounds in 1616 to nearly 30 million pounds in the late seventeenth century, or roughly 400 pounds of tobacco for every man, woman, and child in the Chesapeake colonies.

The tidewater region was blessed with many navigable rivers and the planters spread along their banks, giving the Chesapeake a shabby, helter-skelter character of rough habitations and growing tobacco, mostly planted in stump-littered fields, surrounded by fallow land and thickets interspersed with dense forest. There were no towns and almost no roads. English ships made their way up the rivers from farm to farm, gathering the tobacco at each planter's wharf. The vessels also served as general stores of a sort where planters could exchange tobacco for everything from cloth, shoes, tools, salt, and nails to such exotic items as tea, coffee, chocolate, and spices.

However, the tremendous increase in the production of tobacco caused the price to plummet in the late seventeenth century. This did not stop the expansion of the colonies, but it did alter the structure of their society. Small farmers found it more difficult to make a decent living. At the same time men with capital and individuals with political influence were amassing large tracts of land. If well-managed, a big plantation gave its owner important competitive advantages over the small farmer. Tobacco was notorious for the speed with which it exhausted the fertility of the soil. Growers with a lot of land could shift frequently to new fields within their holdings, allowing the old fields to lie fallow and thus maintain high yields, but the only option that small farmers had when their land gave out was to move to unsettled land on the frontier. To do that in the 1670s was to risk trouble with properly indignant Indians. It might also violate colonial laws designed to slow westward migration and limit tobacco production. Neither was about to stop settlement.

Bacon's Rebellion

Chesapeake settlers showed little respect for constituted authority, partly because most people lived on isolated plantations and partly because the London authorities were usually ignorant of their needs. The first Virginians often ignored directives of the London Company, while early Marylanders regularly disputed the right of the Calverts' agents to direct the affairs of the proprietorship. The most serious challenge took place in Virginia in 1676. Planters in the outlying counties heartily disliked the officials in Jamestown who ran the colony. The royal governor, Sir William Berkeley, and his "Green Spring" faction (the organization took its name from the governor's plantation) had ruled Virginia for more than 30 years. Outsiders resented the way Berkeley and his henchmen used their offices to line their pockets. They also resented their social pretensions, for Green Springers made no effort to conceal their opinion, which had considerable basis in fact, that western planters were a crude and vulgar lot.

Sir William Berkeley looks every inch the autocrat in this portrait, a copy of one painted by Sir Peter Lely. After Bacon's death, the governor took his revenge and had twenty-three rebels hanged. Said King Charles II: "The old fool has killed more people in that naked country than I have done for the murder of my father."

Early in 1676 planters on the western edge of settlement, always looking for excuses to grab land by doing away with the Indians who owned it, asked Berkeley to authorize an expedition against Indians who had been attacking nearby plantations. Berkeley refused. The planters then took matters into their own hands. Their leader, Nathaniel Bacon, was (and remains today) a controversial figure. His foes described him as extremely ambitious and possessed "of a most imperious and dangerous hidden Pride of heart." But even his sharpest critics conceded that he was "of an inviting aspect and powerful elocution" and well qualified "to lead a giddy and unthinking multitude."

When Berkeley refused to authorize him to attack the Indians, Bacon promptly showed himself only too willing to lead that multitude not only against Indians but against the governor. Without permission he raised an army of 500 men, described by the Berkeley faction as "rabble of the basest sort." Berkeley then declared him a traitor.

Several months of confusion followed during what is known as Bacon's Rebellion. Bacon murdered some peaceful Indians, marched on Jamestown and forced Berkeley to legitimize his authority, then headed west again to kill more Indians. In September he returned to Jamestown and burned it to the ground. Berkeley fled across Chesapeake Bay to the Eastern Shore. The Baconites plundered the estates of some of the Green Spring faction. But a few weeks later, Bacon came down with a "violent flux"—probably it was a bad case of dysentery—and he died. Soon thereafter an English naval squadron arrived with enough soldiers to restore order. Bacon's Rebellion came to an end.

On the surface, the uprising changed nothing. No sudden shift in political power occurred. Indeed, Bacon had not sought to change either the political system or the social and economic structure of the colony. But if the rebellion did not change anything, nothing was ever again quite the same after it ended. With seeming impartiality, the Baconites had warred against Indians and against other planters. But which was the real enemy? Surely the Baconite and Green Springer factions had no differences that could not be compromised. And their common interest extended beyond the question of how to deal with Indians. Both wanted cheap labor.

In the quarter-century following Bacon's Rebellion the Chesapeake region thus became committed to black slavery. And slave ownership resulted in large differences in the wealth and lifestyles of growers of tobacco. The few who succeeded in accumulating twenty or more slaves and enough land to keep them occupied grew richer. The majority either grew poorer or at best had to struggle to hold their own.

More important, however, Bacon's Rebellion sealed an implicit contract between the inhabitants of the "great houses" and those who lived in more modest lodgings: Southern whites might differ greatly in wealth and influence, but they stood as one and forever behind the principle that Africans must have neither. This was the basis—the price—of the harmony and prosperity achieved by those who survived "seasoning" in the Chesapeake colonies.

The Carolinas

The English and, after 1700, the Scots-Irish settlers of the tidewater parts of the Carolinas turned to agriculture as enthusiastically as had their Chesapeake neighbors. In substantial sections of what became North Carolina, tobacco flourished. In South Carolina, after two decades in which furs and cereals were the chief products, Madagascar rice was introduced in the low-lying coastal areas in 1696. It quickly proved its worth as a cash crop. By 1700 almost 100,000 pounds were being exported annually; by the eve of the Revolution rice exports from South Carolina and Georgia exceeded 65 million pounds a year.

Rice culture required water for flooding the fields. At first freshwater swamps were adapted to the crop, but by the middle of the eighteenth century the chief rice fields lay along the tidal rivers and inlets. Dikes and floodgates allowed fresh water to flow across the fields with the rising tide; when the tide fell, the gates closed automatically to keep the water in. The process was reversed when it was necessary to drain the land. Then the water ran out as the tide ebbed, and the pressure of the next flood pushed the gates shut.

In the 1740s another cash crop, indigo, was introduced in South Carolina by Eliza Lucas. Indigo did not compete with rice either for land or labor. It prospered on high ground and needed care in seasons when the slaves were not busy in the rice paddies. The British were delighted to have a new source of indigo because the blue dye was important in their woolens industry. Parliament quickly placed a bounty—a bonus—on it to stimulate production.

Their tobacco, rice, and indigo, along with furs and forest products, meant that the southern colonies had no difficulty in obtaining manufactured articles from abroad. Planters dealt with agents in England and Scotland, called factors, who managed the sale of their crops, filled their orders for manufactures, and supplied them with credit. This was a great convenience but not necessarily an advantage, for it prevented the development of a diversified economy. Throughout the colonial era, while small-scale manufacturing developed rapidly in the North, it was stillborn in the South.

On the South Carolina rice plantations, slave labor predominated from the beginning, for free workers would not submit to its backbreaking and unhealthy regimen. The first quarter of the eighteenth century saw an enormous influx of Africans into all the southern colonies. By 1730 roughly three out of every ten people south of Pennsylvania were black, and in South Carolina the blacks outnumbered the whites by two to one. "Carolina," remarked a newcomer in 1737, "looks more like a negro country than like a country settled by white people."

Given the existing race prejudice and the degrading impact of slavery, this demographic change had an enormous impact on life wherever African Americans were concentrated. In each colony regulations governing the behavior of blacks, both free and slave, increased in severity. The South Carolina Negro Act of 1740 denied slaves "freedom of movement, freedom of assembly, freedom to raise [their

Slaves on a South Carolina plantation, around 1790. Likely of Yoruba descent, they play west African instruments, such as the banjo, and also wear elaborate headgear, another Yoruba trait. But unlike their Yoruban contemporaries, who adorned faces and limbs with elaborate tattoos or scars, these slaves bear no evident body decorations. These people are African, indisputably, but also American.

own] food, to earn money, to learn to read English." The blacks had no civil rights under any of these codes, and punishments were sickeningly severe. For minor offenses, whipping was common, for serious crimes, death by hanging or by being burned alive. Slaves were sometimes castrated for sexual offenses—even for lewd talk about white women—or for repeated attempts to escape.

The "master" race sought to acculturate the slaves in order to make them more efficient workers. A slave who could understand English was easier to order about; one who could handle farm tools or wait on tables was more useful than one who could not; a carpenter or a mason was more valuable still. But acculturation increased the slave's independence and mobility, and this posed problems. Most field hands seldom tried to escape; they expressed their dissatisfactions by pilferage and petty sabotage, by laziness, or by feigning stupidity. Most runaways were artisans who hoped to "pass" as free in a nearby town. It was one of the many paradoxes of slavery that the more valuable a slave became, the harder that slave was to control.

Whites grossly exaggerated the danger of slave revolts. They pictured the black as a kind of malevolent ogre, powerful, bestial, and lascivious, a caldron of animal emotions that had to be restrained at any cost. Probably the characteristics they attributed to the blacks were really projections of their own passions. The most striking illustration was white fear that if blacks were free, they would breed with whites. Yet in practice, the interbreeding, which indeed took place, was almost exclusively the result of white men using their power as masters to have sexual relations with female slaves.

Thus the "peculiar institution" was fastened on America with economic, social, and psychic barbs. Ignorance and self-interest, lust for gold and for the flesh, primitive prejudices and complex social and legal ties, all combined to convince the whites that black slavery was not so much good as a fact of life. A few Quakers attacked the institution on the religious ground that all human beings are equal before God: "Christ dyed for all, both *Turks, Barbarians, Tartarians,* and *Ethyopians.*" Yet some Quakers owned slaves, and even the majority who did not usually succumbed to color prejudice. Blackness was a defect, but it was no justification for enslavement, they argued. But the Quaker view attracted little attention anywhere—none in areas where slavery was important.

Home and Family in the South

Life for all but the most affluent planters was by modern standards uncomfortable. Houses were mostly one- and two-room affairs, small, dark, and crowded. Furniture and utensils were sparse and crudely made. Chairs were rare; if a family possessed one it was reserved for the head of the house. People sat, slept, and ate on benches and planks. The typical dining table (the term itself was not in use) was made of two boards covered, if by anything, with a "board cloth." Toilets and plumbing of any kind were unknown; even chamber pots, which eliminated the nighttime trek to the privy, were beyond the reach of poorer families.

Clothes were equally crude and, since soap was expensive, rarely washed and therefore foul-smelling and often infested with vermin. Food was plentiful. Corn, served as bread, hominy, pancakes, and in various other forms, was the chief staple. But there was plenty of beef, pork, and game, usually boiled with various vegetables over an open fire.

White women (even indentured ones) rarely worked in the fields. Their responsibilities included tending to farm animals, making butter and cheese, pickling and preserving, spinning and sewing, and, of course, caring for children, which often involved orphans and stepchildren because of the fragility of life in the region. For exceptional women, the labor shortage created opportunities. Some managed large plantations; Eliza Lucas ran three in South Carolina for her absent father while still in her teens, and after the death of her husband, Charles Pinckney, she managed his extensive property holdings.

More well-to-do, "middling" planters had more comfortable lifestyles, but they still lived in relatively crowded quarters, having perhaps three rooms to house a family of four or five and a couple of servants. To sleep between sheets in a soft bed under blankets and quilts was luxury indeed in that world. Food in greater variety and abundance was another indication of a higher standard of living.

Until the early eighteenth century only a handful achieved real affluence. (The richest by far was Robert "King" Carter of Lancaster County, Virginia, who at the time of his death in 1732 owned 1,000 slaves and 300,000 acres.) Those fortunate few, masters of several plantations and many slaves, lived in solid, two-story houses of six or more rooms, furnished with English and other imported carpets, chairs, tables, wardrobes, chests, china, and silver. When the occasion warranted, the men wore fine broadcloth, the women the latest (or more likely the next-to-latest) fashions. Some even sent their children abroad for schooling. The founding of the College of William and Mary in Williamsburg, Virginia, in 1693 was an effort to provide the region with its own institution of higher learning, mainly in order to train clergymen. For decades, however, the College of William and Mary was not much more than a grammar school. Lawyers were relatively numerous, though rarely learned in the law. Doctors were so scarce that one sick planter wrote a letter to his brother in England describing his symptoms and asking him to consult a physician and let him know the diagnosis.

These large planters also held the commissions in the militia, the county judgeships, and the seats in the colonial legislatures. The control that these "leading families" exercised over their neighbors was not entirely unearned. They were, in general, responsible leaders. And they recognized the necessity of throwing open their houses and serving copious amounts of punch and rum to ordinary voters when election time rolled around. Such gatherings served to acknowledge the representative character of the system.

No matter what their station, southern families led relatively isolated lives. Churches, which might be expected to serve as centers of community life, were few and far between. By the middle of the eighteenth century the Anglican Church was the "established" religion, its ministers supported by public funds. The Virginia assembly had made attendance at Anglican services compulsory in 1619. In Maryland, Lord Baltimore's Toleration Act did not survive the settlement in the colony of large numbers of militant puritans. It was repealed in 1654, reenacted in 1657, then repealed again in 1692 when the Anglican Church was established.

Social events of any kind were great occasions. Births, marriages, and especially funerals called for much feasting; if there were neither heirs nor debts to satisfy, it was possible to "consume" the entire contents of a modest estate in celebrating the deceased's passing. (At one Maryland funeral the guests were provided with 55 gallons of an alcoholic concoction composed of brandy, cider, and sugar.)

Even the most successful planters were conserving types, not idle grandees chiefly concerned with conspicuous display. The vast, undeveloped country encouraged them to produce and then invest their savings in more production. William Byrd II (1674–1744), one of the richest men in Virginia, habitually rose before dawn. Besides his tobacco fields, he operated a sawmill and a grist mill, prospected for iron and coal, and engaged in the Indian trade.

Georgia and the Back Country

West of the fall line of the many rivers that irrigated tidewater Chesapeake and Carolina lay the back country. This region included the Great Valley of Virginia, the Piedmont, and what became the final English colony, Georgia, founded by a group of London philanthropists in 1733. These men were concerned over the plight of

English Colonies on the Atlantic Seaboard

honest persons imprisoned for debt, whom they intended to settle in the New World. (Many Europeans were still beguiled by the prospect of regenerating their society in the colonies. All told, about 50,000 British convicts were "transported" to America in the colonial period, partly to get rid of "undesirables," but partly for humane reasons.) The government, eager to create a buffer between South Carolina and the hostile Spanish in Florida, readily granted a charter (1732) to the group, whose members agreed to manage the colony without profit to themselves for a period of 21 years.

In 1733 their leader, James Oglethorpe, founded Savannah. Oglethorpe was a complicated person, vain, high-handed, and straitlaced, yet idealistic. He hoped to people the colony with sober and industrious yeoman farmers. Land grants were limited to 50 acres and made nontransferable. To ensure sobriety, rum and other "Spirits and Strong Waters" were banned. To guarantee that the colonists would have to work hard, the entry of "any Black . . . Negroe" was prohibited. Trade with Indians was to be strictly regulated in the interest of fair dealing.

Oglethorpe intended that silk, wine, and olive oil would be the main products—none of which, unfortunately, could be profitably produced in Georgia. His noble intentions came to naught. The settlers swiftly found ways to circumvent all restrictions. Rum flowed, slaves were imported, large land holdings amassed. Georgia developed an economy much like South Carolina's. In 1752 the founders, disillusioned, abandoned their responsibilities. Georgia then became a royal colony.

Now settlers penetrated the rest of the southern back country. So long as cheap land remained available closer to the coast and Indians along the frontier remained a threat, only the most daring and footloose hunters or fur traders lived far inland. But once settlement began, it came with a rush. Chief among those making the trek were Scots-Irish and German immigrants. By 1770 the back country contained about 250,000 settlers, 10 percent of the population of the colonies.

This internal migration did not proceed altogether peacefully. In 1771 frontiersmen in North Carolina calling themselves Regulators fought a pitched battle with 1,200 troops dispatched by the Carolina assembly, which was dominated by low-country interests. The Regulators were protesting their lack of representation in the assembly. They were crushed and their leaders executed. This was neither the last nor the bloodiest sectional conflict in American history.

Puritan New England

If survival in the Chesapeake required junking many European notions about social arrangements and submitting to the dictates of the wilderness, was this also true in Massachusetts and Connecticut? Ultimately it probably was, but at first puritan ideas certainly fought the New England reality to a draw.

Boston is located slightly more than 5° latitude north of Jamestown and almost 10° north of Charleston. Like other early New England towns and unlike these southern ones, Boston had a dependable water supply. The surrounding patchwork of forest, pond, dunes, and tide marsh was much more open than the malaria-infested terrain of the tidewater and low-country South. As a consequence New Englanders escaped "the agues and fevers" that beset settlers to the south, leaving them free to attend to their spiritual, economic, and social well-being. These differences alone made New England a much healthier habitat for settlers.

Puritan Women and Children

Dealings with neighbors and relatives and involvement in church activities marked the outer limits of the social range of most puritan women. Care of the children was a full-time occupation when broods of twelve or fourteen were more common than those of one or two. Fewer children died in New England than in the Chesapeake or in Europe, though few families escaped a miscarriage or a child's death along the way. Childbearing and motherhood, therefore, commonly extended over three decades of a woman's life. Meanwhile, she also functioned as the chief operating officer of the household. Cooking, baking, sewing, and supervising servants, as well as mastering such arcane knowledge as the chemistry needed to make cheese from milk, bacon from pork, bread from grain, and beer from malt, all fell to her.

As puritan social standards required husbands to rule over wives, so parents ruled over children. The virtue most insistently impressed on New England children was obedience; refusal to submit to parental direction was disturbing in itself and for what it implied about the child's eternal condition. Cotton Mather's advice, "better whipt, than damned," graced many a New England rod taken up by a parent in anger, from there to be rapidly transferred to the afterparts of misbehaving offspring. But household chores kept children out of mischief. By age six or seven girls did sewing and helped with housework and boys were put to work outdoors. Older children might be sent to live with another family to work as servants or apprentices.

Such practices, particularly when set beside portraits of early New England families that depict toddlers as somber-faced miniature adults wearing clothes indistinguishable from those of their parents, may convey the impression that puritans hustled their young through childhood with as little love as possible. New Englanders harbored no illusions. "Innocent vipers" is how one minister described children, having fourteen of his own to submit as evidence. Anne Bradstreet, mother of eight, characterized one as harboring "a perverse will, a love of what's

New England children like David, Joanna, and Abigail Mason (painted by an unknown artist around 1670) were expected to emulate adults in their chores and their appearance. Nevertheless, diaries and letters indicate that children were cherished by their parents in a way closer to modern family love than what their European contemporaries experienced.

forbid/a serpent's sting in pleasing face lay hid." Yet for all their acceptance of the doctrine of infant damnation, puritan parents were not indifferent to the fate of their children. "I do hope," Cotton Mather confessed at the burial of one of the eight children he lost before the age of two, "that when my children are gone they are not lost; but carried unto the Heavenly Feast with Abraham." Another minister assigned children who died in infancy "the easiest room in hell."

Visible Puritan Saints and Others

When it came to religion, puritans believed that church membership ought to be the joint decision of a would-be member and those already in the church. Those seeking admission would tell the congregation why they believed that they had received God's grace. Obvious sinners and those ignorant of Christian doctrine were rejected out of hand. But what of pious and God-fearing applicants who lacked compelling evidence of salvation? In the late 1630s, with the Great Migration in full swing and new arrivals clamoring for admission to the churches, such "merit-mongers" were excluded, thereby limiting church membership to the community's "visible saints." A decade later, the Great Migration over and applications down, some of the saints began to have second thoughts.

By the early 1650s fewer than half of all New England adults were church members, and so exacting had the examination for membership become, particularly in churches where the minister and elders outdid each other in the ferocity of their questioning, that most young people refused to submit themselves to it. How these growing numbers of nonmembers could be compelled to attend church services was a problem ministers could not long defer. Meanwhile, the magistrates found it harder to defend the policy of not letting taxpayers vote because they were not church members. But what really forced reconsideration of the membership policy were the concerns of nonmember parents about the souls of their children, who could not be baptized.

At first the churches permitted baptism of the children of church members. Later, some biblical purists came out against infant baptism altogether, but most puritans approved this practice, which allowed them the hope that a child who died after receiving baptism might at least be spared Hell's hottest precincts. Since most of the first generation were church members, nearly all the second-generation New Englanders were baptized, whether they became church members or not. The problem began with the third generation, the offspring of parents who had been baptized but who did not become church members. By the mid-1650s it was clear that if nothing were done, soon a majority of the people would be living in a state of original sin. If that happened, how could the churches remain the dominant force in New England life?

Fortunately, a way out was at hand. In 1657 an assembly of Massachusetts and Connecticut ministers recommended a form of intermediate church membership that would permit the baptism of people who were not visible saints. Five years later, some eighty ministers and laymen met at Boston's First Church to hammer out what came to be called the Half-Way Covenant. It provided limited (halfway) membership for any applicant not known to be a sinner who was willing to accept the provisions of the church covenant. They and their children could be baptized, but the sacrament of communion and a voice in church decision making were reserved for full members.

The General Court of Massachusetts endorsed the recommendations of the Half-Way Synod and urged all the churches of the Commonwealth to adopt them. Two years later it quietly extended the right to vote to halfway church members.

Opponents of the Half-Way Covenant argued that it reflected a slackening of religious fervor. Michael Wigglesworth gave poetic voice to these views in "God's Controversy with New England" and "The Day of Doom," both written in 1662. Perry Miller, a modern authority on puritan New England, argued that the early 1660s marked the beginning of the decline, or "declension," of the puritan experiment. Some loss of religious intensity there may have been, but the rise in church memberships, the continuing prestige accorded ministers, and the lessening of the intrachurch squabbling after the 1660s suggest that the secularization of New England society had a long way to go.

Democracies Without Democrats

Like the southern colonies, the New England colonies derived their authority from charters granted by the Crown or Parliament. Except for rare fits of meddling by London bureaucrats, they were largely left to their own devices where matters of purely local interest were concerned. This typically involved maintaining order by regulating how people behaved.

According to puritan theory, government was both a civil covenant, entered into by all who came within its jurisdiction, and the principal mechanism for policing the institutions on which the maintenance of the social order depended. When Massachusetts and Connecticut passed laws requiring church attendance, levying taxes for the support of the clergy, and banning Quakers from practicing their faith, they were acting as "shield of the churches." When they provided the death penalty both for adultery and for blaspheming a parent, they were defending the integrity of families. When they set the price a laborer might charge for his services or even the amount of gold braid that servants might wear on their jackets, they believed they were enforcing the puritan principle that people must accept their assigned stations in life. Puritan communities were, for a time, close-knit: murder, assault, and theft were rare. Disputes were adjudicated through an active court system.

But puritan civil authorities and ministers of the puritan (Congregational) church came under sharp attack from English Anglicans, Presbyterians, and Quakers. When the Massachusetts General Court hanged four stubborn Quakers who returned after being expelled from the colony, a royal order of 1662 forbade further executions.

Laws like these have prompted historians and Americans generally to characterize New England colonial legislation as socially repressive and personally invasive. Yet many of the laws remained in force through the colonial period without rousing much local opposition. Others, particularly those upholding religious discrimination or restricting economic activity, were repealed at the insistence of Parliament.

A healthy respect for the backsliding ways of humanity obliged New Englanders not to depend too much on provincial governments, whose jurisdiction extended over several thousand square miles. Almost of necessity, the primary responsibility for maintaining "Good Order and Peace" fell to the more than 500 towns of the region. These differed greatly in size and development. By the early eighteenth century the largest—Boston, Newport, and Portsmouth—were on their way toward becoming urban centers. This was before "frontier" towns like Amherst, Kent, and Hanover had even been founded. Nonetheless, town life gave New England the distinctiveness it has still not wholly lost.

The Dominion of New England

The most serious threat to these arrangements occurred in the 1680s. Following the execution of Charles I in 1649, England was ruled by one man, the Lord Protector, Oliver Cromwell, a puritan. Cromwell's death in 1658 led to the restoration of the Stuart monarchy in the person of Charles II (1660–1685). During his reign and the abbreviated one of his brother, James II (1685–1688), the government sought to bring the colonies under effective royal control.

Massachusetts seemed in particular need of supervision. Accordingly, in 1684 its charter was annulled and the colony, along with all those north of Pennsylvania, became part of the Dominion of New England, governed by Edmund Andros.

Andros arrived in Boston in late 1686 with orders to make the northern colonies behave like colonies, not like sovereign powers. He set out to abolish popular assemblies, to change the land-grant system so as to provide the king with quitrents, and to enforce religious toleration, particularly of Anglicans. Andros, being a professional soldier and administrator, scoffed at those who resisted his authority. "Knoweing no other government than their owne," he said, they "think it best, and are wedded to . . . it."

Fortunately for New Englanders so wedded, the Dominion fell victim two years later to yet another political turnabout in England, the Glorious Revolution. In 1688 Parliament decided it had had enough of the Catholic-leaning Stuarts and sent James II packing. In his place it installed James's daughter Mary and her resolutely Protestant Dutch husband, William of Orange. When news of these events

(text continues on page 74)

Debating the Past

WERE PURITAN COMMUNITIES PEACEABLE?

A smooth, quiet river flows past this eighteenth-century puritan town. A church spire rises, treelike, from its center. The painting is a composition in harmony. In *The Scarlet Letter* (1850), however, Nathaniel Hawthorne shattered this placid image: Puritan towns, he suggested, were plagued with envy, intolerance, and hypocrisy. Hawthorne's harsh assessment, which many historians shared, persisted into the twentieth century. This view changed with Perry Miller (1933), whose elegant analysis of puritan sermons and writings amply demonstrated "the majesty and coherence of Puritan thinking." The rise of atheistic communism in the Soviet Union after World War II further contributed to an appreciation of the nation's puritan roots. Daniel Boorstin (1958) wrote approvingly of the strong families, religious faith, and democratic governance of puritan towns. During the 1960s a new generation of historians examined the issue. They had been influenced by Fernand Braudel, a French scholar. Braudel encouraged historians to reconstruct the "total history" of particular communities, rather like anthropologists. The publication of four such studies in 1970 reinvigorated colonial social history. John Demos discovered that families in Plymouth, Massachusetts, were beset with psychological conflicts; Philip Greven and Kenneth Lockridge found that Dedham and Andover, Massachusetts, lost cohesion rapidly; Paul Zuckerman, on the other hand, concluded that his puritan towns most nearly resembled "peaceable kingdoms." Other studies complicated the picture further: Paul Boyer and Stephen Nissenbaum (1974) contended that Salem was wracked with class and religious tensions, while other scholars found increasingly cohesive puritan communities. Which description was more characteristic of the puritan pattern? In recent decades, historians David Hackett Fischer (1989) and Alan Taylor (2001) insisted that the puritans should be examined not in towns such as this one, but in relation to a much larger, even trans-Atlantic, context.

Perry Miller, *Orthodoxy in Massachusetts* (1933) and *The New England Mind* (1939), Daniel Boorstin, *The Colonial Experience* (1958), John Demos, *A Little Commonwealth* (1970), Philip J. Greven, *Four Generations* (1970), Kenneth Lockridge, *A New England Town* (1970), Michael Zuckerman, *Peaceable Kingdoms* (1970), Paul Boyer and Stephen Nissenbaum, *Salem Possessed* (1974), David Hackett Fischer, *Albion's Seed* (1989), Alan Taylor, *American Colonies* (2001).

reached Boston in the spring of 1689, a force of more than a thousand colonists led by a contingent of ministers seized Andros and lodged him in jail. Two years later Massachusetts was made a royal colony that also included Plymouth and Maine. As in all such colonies the governor was appointed by the king. The new General Court was elected by property owners; church membership was no longer a requirement for voting.

Salem Bewitched

In 1666, families living in the rural outback of the thriving town of Salem petitioned the General Court for the right to establish their own church. For political and economic reasons this was a questionable move, but in 1672 the General Court authorized the establishment of a separate parish. In so doing the Court put the 600-odd inhabitants of the village on their own politically as well.

Over the next 15 years three preachers came and went before, in 1689, one Samuel Parris became minister. Parris had spent 20 years in the Caribbean as a merchant and had taken up preaching only three years before coming to Salem. Accompanying him were his wife; a daughter, Betty; a niece, Abigail; and the family's West Indian slave, Tituba, who told fortunes and practiced magic on the side.

Parris proved as incapable of bringing peace to the feuding factions of Salem Village as had his predecessors. In January 1692 the church voted to dismiss him. At this point Betty and Abigail, now 9 and 11, along with Ann Putnam, a 12-year-old, started "uttering foolish, ridiculous speeches which neither they themselves nor any others could make sense of." A doctor diagnosed the girls' ravings as the work of the "Evil Hand" and declared them bewitched.

But who had done the bewitching? The first persons accused were three women whose unsavory reputations and frightening appearances made them likely candidates: Sarah Good, a pauper with a nasty tongue; Sarah Osborne, a bedridden widow; and the slave Tituba, who had brought suspicion on herself by volunteering to bake a "witch cake," made of rye meal and the girls' urine. The cake should be fed to a dog, Tituba said. If the girls were truly afflicted, the dog would show signs of bewitchment!

The three women were brought before the local deputies to the General Court. As each was questioned, the girls went into contortions: "their arms, necks and backs turned this way and that way . . . their mouths stopped, their throats choked, their limbs wracked and tormented." Tituba, likely impressed by the powers ascribed to her, promptly confessed to being a witch. Sarah Good and Sarah Osborne each claimed to be innocent, although Sarah Good expressed doubts about Sarah Osborne. All three were sent to jail on suspicion of practicing witchcraft.

These proceedings triggered new accusations. By the end of April 1692, twenty-four more people had been charged with practicing witchcraft. Officials in neighboring Andover, lacking their own "bewitched," called in the girls to help with their

Examination of a Witch. A stern puritan patriarch adjusts his glasses to better examine a beautiful—and partially disrobed—young woman. Ostensibly, he is looking for the "witch's teats" with which she suckled "black dogs" and other creatures of the Devil. Completed in 1853 by T. H. Matteson, this painting subtly indicts puritan men as lecherous hypocrites. In fact, most accused witches were in their forties or fifties. The painting thus reveals more about the nineteenth-century reaction against puritanism than about the puritans themselves.

investigations. By May the hunt had extended to Maine and Boston and up the social ladder to some of the colony's most prominent citizens, including Lady Mary Phips, whose husband, William, had just been appointed governor.

By June, when Governor Phips convened a special court consisting of members of his council, more than 150 persons (Lady Phips no longer among them) stood formally charged with practicing witchcraft. In the next four months the court convicted twenty-eight of them, most of them women. Five "confessed" and were spared; the rest were condemned to death. Several others escaped. But nineteen persons were hanged. The husband of a convicted witch refused to enter a plea when charged with being a "wizard." He was executed by having stones piled on him until he suffocated.

Anyone who spoke in defense of the accused was in danger of being charged with witchcraft, but some brave souls challenged both the procedures and the findings of the court. Finally, at the urging of the leading ministers of the Commonwealth, Governor Phips adjourned the court and forbade any further executions.

No one involved in these gruesome proceedings escaped with reputation intact, but those whose reputations suffered most were the ministers. Among the clergy only Increase Mather deserves any credit. He persuaded Phips to halt the executions, arguing that "it were better that ten witches should escape, than that one innocent person should be condemned." The behavior of his son Cotton defies apology. It was not that Cotton Mather accepted the existence of witches—at the time everyone did, which incidentally suggests that Tituba was not the only person in Salem who practiced witchcraft—or even that Mather took such pride in being the resident expert on demonology. It was rather his vindictiveness. He even stood at the foot of the gallows bullying hesitant hangmen into doing "their duty."

The episode also highlights the anxieties puritan men felt toward women. Many puritans believed that Satan worked his will especially through the allure of female sexuality. Moreover, many of the accused witches were widows of high status or older women who owned property; some of the women, like Tituba, had mastered herbal medicine and other suspiciously potent healing arts. Such women, especially those who lived apart from the daily guidance of men, potentially subverted the patriarchal authorities of church and state. (For more on this topic, see the feature essay, Re-Viewing the Past, "The Crucible," pp. 78–79.)

A Merchant's World

Prior experience (and the need to eat) turned the first New Englanders to farming. They grew barley (used to make beer), rye, oats, green vegetables, and also native crops such as potatoes, pumpkins, and, most important, Indian corn, or maize. Corn was easily cultivated. In the form of corn liquor, it was easy to store, to transport, and, in a pinch, to imbibe.

The colonists also had plenty of meat. They grazed cattle, sheep, and hogs on the common pastures or in the surrounding woodlands. Deer, along with turkey and other game birds, abounded. The Atlantic provided fish, especially cod, which was easily preserved by salting. In short, New Englanders ate an extremely nutritious diet. Abundant surpluses of firewood kept the winter cold from their doors. The combination contributed significantly to their good health and longevity.

But the shortness of the growing season, the rocky and often hilly terrain, and careless methods of cultivation, which exhausted the soil, meant that farmers did not produce large surpluses. Thus, while New Englanders could feed themselves without difficulty, they had relatively little to spare.

John Winthrop's generation of puritans accepted this economic marginality. They were to fasten their attention upon the next world rather than the one they occupied on earth.

But later generations did not share the anticommercial bias of the early puritans. At the beginning of the eighteenth century a Boston minister told his congregation of another minister who reminded his flock that "the main end of planting this wilderness" was religion. A prominent member of the congregation could not contain his disagreement. "Sir," he cried out, "you are mistaken. You think you are preaching to the people of the Bay; our main end was to catch fish."

Fish, caught offshore from Cape Cod to Newfoundland, provided merchants with their opening into the world of transatlantic commerce. In 1643 five New England vessels set out with their holds packed with fish that they sold in Spain and the Canary Islands; they took payment in sherry and madeira, for which a market existed in England. One of these ships also had the dubious distinction of initiating New England into the business of trafficking in human beings when its captain took payment in African slaves, whom he subsequently sold in the West Indies. This was the start of the famous triangular trade. Only occasionally was the pattern truly triangular; more often, intermediate legs gave it a polygonal character. So long as their ships ended up with something that could be exchanged for English goods needed at home, it did not matter what they started out with or how many things they bought and sold along the way.

So maritime trade and those who engaged in it became the driving force of the New England economy, important all out of proportion to the number of persons directly involved. Because those engaged congregated in Portsmouth, Salem, Boston, Newport, and New Haven, these towns soon differed greatly from towns in the interior. They were larger and faster growing, and a smaller percentage of their inhabitants was engaged in farming.

The largest and most thriving town was Boston, which by 1720 had become the commercial hub of the region. It had a population of more than 10,000; in the entire British Empire, only London and Bristol were larger. More than one-quarter of Boston's male adults had either invested in shipbuilding or were directly employed in maritime commerce. Ship captains and merchants held most of the public offices.

Beneath this emergent mercantile elite lived a stratum of artisans and small shopkeepers, and beneath these a substantial population of mariners, laborers, and "unattached" people with little or no property and still less political voice. In the 1670s, at least a dozen prostitutes plied their trade in Boston. By 1720 crime and poverty had become serious problems; public relief rolls frequently exceeded 200 souls, and dozens of criminals languished in the town jail. Boston bore little resemblance to what the first puritans had in mind when they planted their "Citty upon a Hill." But neither was it like any eighteenth-century European city. It stood there on Massachusetts Bay, midway between its Puritan origins and its American future.

The Middle Colonies: Economic Basis

New York, New Jersey, Pennsylvania, and Delaware owe their collective name, the Middle Colonies, to geography. Sandwiched between New England and the Chesapeake region, they often receive only passing notice in accounts of colonial America. The lack of a distinctive institution, such as slavery or the town meeting, explains part of this neglect.

Actually, both institutions existed there. Black slaves made up about 10 percent of the population; indeed, one New York county in the 1740s had proportionally more blacks than large sections of Virginia. And eastern Long Island was settled by people from Connecticut who brought the town meeting system with them.

This quality of "in-betweenness" extended to other economic and social arrangements. Like colonists elsewhere, most Middle Colonists became farmers.

(text continues on page 80)

The Crucible

Based on Arthur Miller's 1953 play, *The Crucible*, an interpretation of the Salem witch trials of 1692, this 1996 movie stars Winona Ryder, who plays Abigail Williams, consumed with desire for John Proctor (Daniel Day-Lewis), a married man. Proctor has broken off their affair and reconciled with his wife, Elizabeth (Joan Allen). As the movie begins, Abigail and some other girls have sneaked into the woods with Tituba, a slave who practices black magic. They ask about their future husbands, and some beg her to cast a spell on their favorites. Abigail whispers something to Tituba, who recoils in horror. Abigail's dark eyes, glowing with fury, inform the movie audience of her message: she wants John Proctor back and Elizabeth Proctor dead. Tituba slips into a trance and begins conjuring. Exhilarated by their illicit flouting of convention, and quivering with sexual energy, the girls throw off their clothes and dance wildly around a fire.

Then the minister happens onto the scene. The girls flee in terror. Some become hysterical. When confronted by church elders, Abigail, glancing furtively at the other girls, blurts out that Tituba was a witch who was trying to steal their souls. Tituba initially denies the charges, but after being whipped she confesses. Pressed further, she names two other women as accomplices in her sorcery. At the mention of their names, Abigail's face contorts with pain and she moans; tak-ing the cue, the other girls scream and writhe upon the floor. They supply the names of more witches. Alarmed by the enormity of Satan's plot in Salem, Massachusetts authorities initiate a thorough investigation.

The girls' hysterics intensify. Eventually over 100 suspected witches, most of them women, are arrested. The Proctors themselves come under suspicion. Asked to recite the Ten Commandments, John omits the injunction against adultery; the magistrate looks at him searchingly. When Abigail accuses Elizabeth of being a witch, John lashes out at the girl.

"She is a whore," he declares in court. "I have known her, sir."

"He is lying," she hisses. Suddenly her eyes widen, horror-stricken, and she screams that he, too, is in league with Satan. Her flawless histrionics again prevail: he is arrested, convicted, and sentenced to death. But his courage at the scaffold, and the deaths of others like him, cause the people of Massachusetts to end the witch hunt.

The movie vividly recreates a puritan world inhabited by palpable spirits. Contemporary viewers may snicker at scenes of adults scanning the night sky for flying witches and evil birds, but the puritans believed in such things. They regarded comets, meteors, and lightning as signals from God. When Cotton Mather lost the pages of some lecture, he concluded that "Spectres, or Agents in the invisible World, were the Robbers."

Episodes and language taken directly from trial records, though sometimes altered, infuse the movie with verisimilitude. For example, the Proctors were in fact interrogated on their biblical knowledge. Whereas in the movie John falters by omitting the commandment against adultery, in history, the fatal mistake was Elizabeth's. Asked to recite the Lord's Prayer, she substituted "hollowed be thy name" for "hallowed be thy name." The magistrates declared this to be a "depraving" act, for she had transformed the prayer into a curse—proof of satanic possession.

The movie's rendering of the girls' hysteria mostly corresponds with what we know from the historical record. A bewildered John

Winona Ryder as young puritan who accuses others of witchcraft.

Few portraits of single puritan women exist; their invisibility may help explain why some sought attention, perhaps by making witchcraft accusations. The young woman in this portrait became "visible" by becoming a mother.

his larger questions have long intrigued historians: Were the puritans sexually repressive? If so, did young people assent to puritan strictures or rebel against them?

Such questions cannot be answered with certainty. Few puritans left written accounts of their illicit thoughts and sexual behavior. Social historians have approached the matter from a different angle. Nearly all marriages and births in colonial New England (and most other places) were recorded. Scholars have scoured such records to determine how many brides gave birth to babies within six months of marriage; such women almost certainly had engaged in premarital intercourse.

This data for about a dozen communities in puritan New England indicate an extraordinarily low rate of premarital intercourse. This confirms that young puritan couples were watched closely. On the other hand, the low rate of premarital pregnancy might not signify puritan repression so much as young people's acceptance of puritan values.

When critics confronted Arthur Miller on his deviations from the historical record, and especially when they expressed skepticism over whether young Abigail Williams and the elderly John Proctor had an affair, Miller was unrepentant. "What's real?" he retorted. "We don't know what these people were like." Perhaps so, but one suspects that Winona Ryder's Abigail would have had a hard time of it in Salem in 1692. Could a bloom of such pungent and poisonous precocity have emerged through the stony soil of New England Puritanism, and if so, could it have survived the assiduous weeding of the puritans themselves?

Hale, a minister from Beverly, recorded that Abigail and her cousin were

> *bitten and pinched by invisible agents. Their arms, necks and backs turned this way and that way, and returned back again, so as it was impossible for them to do of themselves*

Historians still puzzle over the girls' behavior. Probably they were seeking attention, or venting anxiety over their fate as women in a patriarchal society; certainly their choice of victims suggests that they were voicing parental enmity toward neighbors. The movie alludes to such issues, but mostly attributes the girls' hysteria to sexual frustration, a consequence of puritan repression.

Ryder's Abigail symbolizes adolescent sexuality: her lust for John (and corresponding hatred of Elizabeth) precipitates the witch hunt. In point of fact, the real Abigail did accuse Elizabeth of witchcraft. The trial record reports that when Elizabeth denied the charge, Abigail raised her hand as if to strike her, but instead touched Elizabeth's hood "very lightly" and cried out, "My fingers! My fingers—burned!" Then Abigail swooned to the floor. But if these few details provide some basis for Abigail's conjectured affair with Elizabeth's husband, others call it into question, the most awkward being the gap in their ages: The real Abigail was 11 and Proctor, 60.

Whatever the merits of playwright Arthur Miller's speculation about Abigail and John,

---

Questions for Discussion

- What factors, apart from those mentioned in this essay, could explain why puritan brides rarely had babies within six months of their marriage? Was this a good measure of premarital chastity?
- How did puritan courtship differ from modern courtship?

But where northern farmers concentrated on producing crops for local consumption and southerners for export, Middle Colony farmers did both. In addition to raising foodstuffs and keeping livestock, they grew wheat, which the thin soil and shorter growing season of New England did not permit but for which there existed an expanding market in the densely settled Caribbean sugar islands.

Social arrangements differed more in degree than in kind from those in other colonies. Unlike New England settlers, who clustered together in agricultural villages, families in the Hudson Valley of New York and in southeastern Pennsylvania lived on the land they cultivated, often as spatially dispersed as the tobacco planters of the Chesapeake. In contrast with Virginia and Maryland, however, substantial numbers congregated in the seaport centers of New York City and Philadelphia. They also settled interior towns like Albany, an important center of the fur trade on the upper Hudson, and Germantown, an "urban village" northwest of Philadelphia where many people were engaged in trades like weaving and tailoring and flour milling.

The Middle Colonies: An Intermingling of Peoples

The Middle Colonists also possessed traits that later would be seen as distinctly "American." Their ethnic and religious heterogeneity is a case in point. In the 1640s, when New Amsterdam was only a village, one visitor claimed to have heard eighteen languages spoken there. Traveling through Pennsylvania a century later, the Swedish botanist Peter Kalm encountered "a very mixed company of different nations and religions." In addition to "Scots, English, Dutch, Germans, and Irish," he reported, "there were Roman Catholics, Presbyterians, Quakers, Methodists, Seventh day men, Moravians, Anabaptists, and one Jew." In New York City one embattled English resident complained: "Our chiefest unhappiness here is too great a mixture of nations, & English the least part."

Scandinavian and Dutch settlers outnumbered the English in New Jersey and Delaware even after the English took over these colonies. William Penn's first success in attracting colonists was with German Quakers and other persecuted religious sects, among them Mennonites and Moravians from the Rhine Valley. The first substantial influx of immigrants into New York after it became a royal colony consisted of French Huguenots.

Early in the eighteenth century, hordes of Scots-Irish settlers from northern Ireland and Scotland descended on Pennsylvania. These colonists spoke English but felt little loyalty to the English government, which had treated them badly back home, and less to the Anglican Church, since most of them were Presbyterians. Large numbers of them followed the valleys of the Appalachians south into the back country of Virginia and the Carolinas.

Why so few English in the Middle Colonies? Here, again, timing provides the best answer. The English economy was booming. There seemed to be work for all. Migration to North America, while never drying up, slowed to a trickle. The result was colonies in which English settlers were a minority.

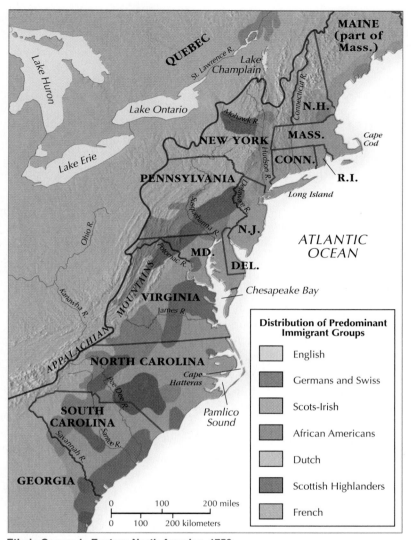

Ethnic Groups in Eastern North America, 1750

The intermingling of ethnic groups gave rise to many prejudices. Benjamin Franklin, though generally complimentary toward Pennsylvania's hardworking Germans, thought them clannish to a fault. The already cited French traveler Hector St. John de Crèvecoeur, while marveling at the adaptive qualities of "this promiscuous breed," complained that "the Irish . . . love to drink and to quarrel; they are litigious, and soon take to the gun, which is the ruin of everything." Yet by and large the various types managed to get along with each other successfully enough. Crèvecoeur attended a wedding in Pennsylvania where the groom's grandparents were English and Dutch and one of his uncles had married a

Frenchwoman. The groom and his three brothers, Crèvecoeur added with some amazement, "now have four wives of different nations."

The Best Poor Man's Country

Ethnic differences seldom caused conflict in the Middle Colonies because they seldom limited opportunity. The promise of prosperity (promotional pamphlets proclaimed Pennsylvania "the best poor man's country in the world") had attracted all in the first place, and achieving prosperity was relatively easy, even for those who came with only a willingness to work. From its founding, Pennsylvania granted upward of 500 acres of land to families on arrival, provided they would pay the proprietor an annual quitrent. Similar arrangements existed in New Jersey and Delaware. Soon travelers in the Middle Colonies were being struck by "a pleasing uniformity of decent competence.

New York was something of an exception to this favorable economic situation. When the English took over New York, they extended the Dutch patroon system by creating thirty manorial estates covering about 2 million acres. But ordinary New Yorkers never lacked ways of becoming landowners. A hundred acres along the Hudson River could be bought in 1730 for what an unskilled laborer could earn in three months. Even tenants on the manorial estates could obtain long-term leases that had most of the advantages of ownership but did not require the investment of any capital. "One may think oneself to be a great lord," one frustrated "lord" of a New York manor wrote a colleague, "but it does not amount to much, as you well know."

Mixed farming offered the most commonly trod path to prosperity in the Middle Colonies, but not the only one. Inland communities offered comfortable livelihoods for artisans. Farmers always needed barrels, candles, rope, horseshoes and nails, and dozens of other articles in everyday use. Countless opportunities awaited the ambitious settler in the shops, yards, and offices of New York and Philadelphia. Unlike Boston, New York and Philadelphia profited from navigable rivers that penetrated deep into the back country. Although founded half a century after New York and Boston, Philadelphia grew more rapidly than either. In the 1750s, when its population reached 15,000, it passed Boston to become the largest city in English America.

The Politics of Diversity

"Cannot more friendly and private courses be taken to set matters right in an infant province?" an exasperated William Penn asked the people of Pennsylvania in 1704. "For the love of God, me, and the poor country, be not so governmentish." However well-intentioned Penn's advice, however justified his annoyance, the Pennsylvanians ignored him. Instead, they and their fellows throughout the region constructed a political culture that diverged sharply from the patterns of New England and the South both in contentiousness and in the sophistication required of local politicians.

Superficially the governments of the Middle Colonies closely resembled those of earlier settlements. All had popularly elected representative assemblies, and most white male adults could vote. In Pennsylvania, where Penn had insisted that there be no religious test and where 50 acres constituted a freehold, something close to white universal manhood suffrage existed. In New York even non-property-holding white male residents voted in local elections, and rural tenants with lifetime leases enjoyed full voting rights.

In Pennsylvania and most of New York, representatives were elected by counties. In this they resembled Virginia and Maryland. But unlike the Southerners, voters did not tend to defer in politics to the landed gentry. In New York, in 1689, during the political vacuum following the abdication of King James II, Jacob Leisler, a disgruntled merchant and militia captain, seized control of the government. Leisler's Rebellion did not amount to much. He held power for less than two years before he was overthrown and sent to the gallows. Yet for two decades New York politics continued to be a struggle between the Leislerians, and other self-conscious "outs" who shared Leisler's dislike of English rule, and anti-Leislerians, who had in common only that they had opposed his takeover. Each group sought the support of a succession of ineffective governors, and the one that failed to get it invariably proceeded to make that poor man's tenure as miserable as possible.

New York lapsed into political tranquility during the governorship of Robert Hunter (1710–1719), but in the early 1730s conflict broke out over a claim for back salary by Governor William Cosby. When Lewis Morris, the chief justice of the supreme court, opposed Cosby's claim, the governor replaced him. Morris and his assembly allies responded by establishing the *New York Weekly Journal*. To edit the paper they hired an itinerant German printer, John Peter Zenger.

Governor Cosby might have tolerated the *Weekly Journal*'s front-page lectures on the right of the people to criticize their rulers had the back pages not contained advertisements referring to his supporters as spaniels and to him as a monkey. After submitting to two months of "open and implacable malice against me," he shut down the paper, arrested Zenger, and charged him with seditious libel.

What began as a squalid salary dispute became one of the most celebrated tests of freedom of the press in the history of journalism. At the trial Zenger's attorney, James Hamilton, argued that the truth of his client's criticisms of Cosby constituted a proper defense against seditious libel. This reasoning (though contrary to English law at the time) persuaded the jury to acquit Zenger.

Politics in Pennsylvania turned on conflict between two interest groups, one clustered around the proprietor, the other around the assembly, which was controlled by a coalition of Quaker representatives from Philadelphia and the German-speaking Pennsylvania Dutch.

Neither the proprietary party nor the Quaker party qualifies as a political party in the modern sense of being organized and maintained for the purpose of winning elections. Nor can they be categorized as standing for "democratic" or "aristocratic" interests. But their existence guaranteed that the political leaders had to take popular opinion into account. Moreover, having once appealed to public opinion, they had to be prepared to defer to it. Success turned as much on knowing how to follow as on knowing how to lead.

The 1763 uprising of the "Paxton Boys" of western Pennsylvania put this policy to a full test. The incident was triggered by eastern indifference to Indian attacks on the frontier—an indifference made possible by the fact that the east outnumbered the west in the assembly, 26 to 10. Fuming because they could obtain no help from Philadelphia against the Indians, a group of Scots-Irish from Lancaster county fell on a village of peaceful Conestoga Indians and murdered them in cold blood. Then these Paxton Boys marched on Philadelphia, several hundred strong.

Fortunately a delegation of burghers, headed by Benjamin Franklin, talked the Paxton Boys out of attacking the town by acknowledging the legitimacy of their grievances about representation and by promising to vote a bounty on Indian scalps! It was just such fancy footwork that established Franklin, the leader of the assembly party, as Pennsylvania's consummate politician. "Tell me, Mr. Franklin," a testy member of the proprietary party asked, "how is it that you are always with the majority?" Soon thereafter, the assembly sent Franklin to London to defend local interests against the British authorities, a situation in which he would definitely not be "with the majority."

Becoming Americans

In 1650, some 50,000 Europeans had come to North America. Most clung to the Atlantic coast, within easy reach of ships that could bring essential supplies, protection, and means of escape. Indians outnumbered Europeans by about 10 to 1; African slaves were still rare. French and Spanish colonization in what is now the United States was numerically even more inconsequential, with only about a thousand Hispanics and even fewer Frenchmen. From the Appalachian Mountains to the Pacific, most Indians had probably never seen a European.

By 1750 the Atlantic seaboard was occupied by nearly a million European settlers, the great majority of English background, with perhaps a quarter of a million African slaves. The Indians had not been entirely removed: scores of Indian villages had been enveloped by English settlement. Tens of thousands more Indians had retreated into coastal swamplands or the foothills of the Appalachians. But east of the Appalachian Mountains, English-speaking peoples had become masters of the land.

During the 100 years after 1650, New Spain and New France had also grown; but far fewer than 20,000 Hispanic and French-speaking people lived in those colonies. In most places west of the Appalachians, Indians feared other tribes far more than European interlopers.

By 1750 an immense sea of English-speaking peoples and African slaves had flooded into the eastern portion of the continent. Soon, they would spill beyond the Appalachian Mountains. By sheer force of their numbers, American identity would be strongly associated with the English language. Most, too, were farmers, united by a seemingly inexhaustible craving for land. But these enterprising immigrants also differed in fundamental ways. The cultures the immigrants brought with them varied according to the nationality, social status, and taste of the individual. The newcomers never lost their foreign heritage entirely, but they—and certainly their descendants—became something quite different from their relatives who remained in the Old World. They became what we call Americans.

But not right away.

Milestones		
	1619	First Africans are sold in Virginia
	1636	Puritans found Boston Latin School and Harvard College
	1657	Half-Way Covenant leads to rise in puritan church memberships
	1676	Western planters launch Bacon's Rebellion in Virginia
	1684–1688	Edmund Andros rules Dominion of New England
	1689	Leisler's Rebellion in New York seizes control of government
	1692	Salem village holds witchcraft trials
	1696	Virginia colonists found College of William and Mary
		Rice cultivation is introduced in South Carolina
	1701	Connecticut ministers found Yale College
	1733	George Oglethorpe leads settlement of Georgia

America in the British Empire

IN 2006 THE AVERAGE AMERICAN PAID ABOUT ONE-THIRD OF HIS or her income to the federal government. Polls show that most Americans believe their taxes are too high. Many cheat. According to a study by the Commerce Department, in 2005 Americans failed to report $1 trillion in income, depriving the government of over $300 billion in tax revenue. Many say that they pay taxes only because they are forced to do so.

Yet most Americans pay, and do so voluntarily. Of the 140 million Americans who owed federal taxes in 2005, 130 million filed returns. And while the tax code includes stern punishments for cheaters, criminal prosecutions are rare. In 2005 the IRS charged fewer than 500 Americans with criminal evasion of their taxes.

In the mid-1700s, by contrast, American colonists paid no more than one-twentieth of their income in taxes, far less than their relatives in England. Yet taxation provoked the colonists more than any other issue. John Adams, a Massachusetts lawyer whose opposition to taxes catapulted him to fame, blamed the American Revolution on England's "enormous taxes, burdensome taxes, oppressive, ruinous, intolerable taxes."

Colonial fury was partly due to a change in how London assessed and collected taxes. During the first half of the eighteenth century, most taxes were set by colonial assemblies and based on landholdings. But after 1763 the British government in London imposed new taxes on trade. When ships entered American ports, captains were required to pay taxes before the "enumerated" (taxable) cargos could be moved from the docks. Whenever Americans bought a bag of nails or a tin of tea, they were making indirect tax payments to London. Tax cheats avoided customs officials by smuggling goods into remote coves at night. But rather than evade the "intolerable" tax burden, colonists increasingly decided to eliminate it altogether.

Resistance to taxation was but one of the sources of ferment in mid-eighteenth-century America. The taxes themselves had been necessitated by war, always a destabilizing force in human affairs. Some people, too, experienced a "great awakening" in religious faith; others looked to the European Enlightenment and its enshrinement of reason and science. Traditional ideas and institutions were being scrutinized more closely. By the 1760s and 1770s, irritation over taxes was symptomatic of a more profound societal unease.

The British Colonial System

In the earliest days of any settlement, the need to rely on home authorities was so obvious that few questioned England's sovereignty. Thereafter, as the fledglings grew strong enough to think of using their own wings, distance and British political inefficiency combined to allow them a great deal of freedom. External affairs were controlled entirely by London, and royal representatives in America tried to direct colonial policy. But in practice the Crown generally yielded the initiative in local matters to the colonies while reserving the right to veto actions it deemed to be against the national interest.

Each colony had a governor. By the eighteenth century he was an appointed official, except in Rhode Island and Connecticut. Governors were chosen by the king in the case of the royal colonies and by the proprietors of Maryland, Delaware, and Pennsylvania. The governors' powers were much like those of the king in Great Britain. They executed the local laws, appointed many minor officials, summoned and dismissed the colonial assemblies, and proposed legislation to them. They possessed the right to veto colonial laws, but in most colonies, again like the king, they were financially dependent on their "subjects."

Each colony also had a legislature. Except in Pennsylvania, these assemblies consisted of two houses. The lower house, chosen by qualified voters, had general legislative powers, including control of the purse. In all the royal colonies members of the upper house, or council, were appointed by the king, except in Massachusetts, where they were elected by the General Court. The councils served primarily as advisors to the governors, but they also had some judicial and legislative powers. Judges were appointed by the king and served at his pleasure. Yet both councilors and judges were normally selected from among the leaders of the local communities; London had neither the time nor the will to investigate their political beliefs. The system therefore tended to strengthen the influence of the entrenched colonials.

Most colonial legislators were practical men. Knowing their own interests, they pursued them steadily, without much regard for political theories or the desires of the royal authorities. They extended their influence by slow accretion. They saw themselves as miniature Houses of Commons, steadily "nibbling" at the authority of the Crown. The king appointed their governors, but governors came and

Lewis Morris, a wealthy landowner, had extensive holdings in the Middle Colonies. He was named New Jersey's first governor when the colony became politically independent from New York in 1738. Honest but overbearing, Morris quarreled constantly with the state assembly over taxation, the militia, and land titles.

went. The lawmakers remained, accumulating experience, building on precedent, widening decade by decade their control over colonial affairs.

The official representatives of the Crown, whatever their powers, whatever their intentions, were prisoners of their surroundings. A royal governor lived thousands of miles from London, alone in a colonial world. Governors had no security of tenure; they served at the whim of the government in London. In their dealings with the assemblies they were often bound by rigid and impractical royal instructions. They had few jobs and favors to offer in their efforts to influence the legislators. Judges might interpret the law according to English precedents, but in local matters colonial juries had the final say. And juries were seldom awed by precedents that clashed with their own conceptions of justice.

Within the British government the king's Privy Council had the responsibility for formulating colonial policy. It could and did disallow (annul) specific colonial laws, but it did not proclaim constitutional principles to which all colonial legislatures must conform. It acted as a court of last appeal in colonial disputes and handled each case individually. One day the council might issue a set of instructions to the governor of Virginia, the next a different set to the governor of South Carolina. No one person or committee thought broadly about the administration of the overseas empire.

At times British authorities, uneasy over their lack of control of the colonies, attempted to create a more effective system. Whenever possible, broadly worded charters were revoked. In the 1680s James II brought New York, New Jersey, and all of New England under one administration, the Dominion of New England; he apparently planned to unify the southern colonies in a similar manner. But James's actions were deeply resented by the colonists, and after the Glorious Revolution and the collapse of the Dominion of New England, no further important efforts at unification were attempted. Instead, the tendency was in the other direction. Delaware was partially separated from Pennsylvania in 1704, and the two Carolinas formally split in 1712.

In 1696 colonial policy was effectively determined by a new Board of Trade, which nominated colonial governors and other high officials. It reviewed all the laws passed by the colonial legislatures, recommending the disallowance of those that seemed to conflict with imperial policy. The efficiency, assiduousness, and wisdom of the Board of Trade fluctuated over the years, but the Privy Council and the Crown nearly always accepted its recommendations.

Colonists naturally disliked having their laws disallowed, but London exercised this power with considerable restraint; only about 5 percent of the laws reviewed were rejected. Furthermore, the board served as an important intermediary for colonists seeking to influence king and Parliament. All the colonies in the eighteenth century maintained agents in London to present the colonial point of view before board members. The most famous colonial agent was Benjamin Franklin, who represented Pennsylvania, Georgia, New Jersey, and Massachusetts at various times during his long career. In general, however, colonial agents were seldom able to exert much influence on British policy.

The British never developed an effective, centralized government for the American colonies. By and large, their American "subjects" ran their own affairs. This fact more than any other explains our present federal system and the wide areas in which the state governments are sovereign and independent.

Mercantilism

The Board of Trade was concerned with commerce as well as colonial administration. According to prevailing European opinion, colonies were important for economic reasons, chiefly as a source of raw materials. To obtain these, British officials developed a number of loosely related policies that later economists called mercantilism. The most important raw materials in the eyes of mercantilists were gold and silver, since these metals, being universally valued and relatively rare, could be exchanged at any time for anything the owner desired or, being durable and compact, stored for future use. For these reasons, how much gold and silver ("treasure" according to mercantilists) a nation possessed was considered the best barometer of its prosperity and power.

Since gold and silver could not be mined in significant amounts in western Europe, every early colonist dreamed of finding "El Dorado." The Spanish were the winners in this search; from the mines of Mexico and South America a treasure in gold and silver poured into the Iberian peninsula. Failing to control the precious metals at the source, the other powers tried to obtain them by guile and warfare (witness the state-supported piracy of Francis Drake).

In the mid-seventeenth century another method, less hazardous and in the long run far more profitable, called itself to the attention of the statesmen of western Europe. If a country could make itself as self-sufficient as possible and also keep its citizens busy producing items sought in other lands, it could sell more goods abroad than it imported. This was known as having "a favorable balance of trade." A country with an unfavorable balance was obliged to make up the

Sea Captains Carousing in Surinam by John Greenwood, a late eighteenth-century oil painting that describes the effects of alcohol—one man guzzles his rum punch straight from the bowl, another vomits onto the floor, while a third pours his punch onto an insensate colleague. Greenwood implicitly denounces as well the trade in sugar (rum) and slaves in which these captains were engaged.

difference by "exporting" gold and silver. Mercantilists regarded colonies as a means of acquiring precious metals by helping the mother country generate a favorable trade balance. Colonists thus were to supply raw materials that would otherwise have to be purchased from foreign sources or colonists were to buy substantial amounts of manufactured goods produced in the mother country.

Of the English colonies in the New World, those in tropical and subtropical climes were valued for their raw materials. The more northerly ones were important as markets, but because they were small in the seventeenth century, in English eyes they took second place. In 1680 the sugar imported from the single West Indian island of Barbados was worth more than the goods sent to England by all the mainland colonies.

If the possession of gold and silver signified wealth, trade was the route that led to riches, and merchants were the captains who would pilot the ship of state to prosperity. "Trade is the Wealth of the World," Daniel Defoe wrote in 1728. One must, of course, have something to sell, so internal production must be stimulated. Parliament encouraged the British people to concentrate on manufacturing by placing tariffs—taxes on trade—on foreign manufactured goods and by subsidizing British-made textiles, iron, and other products.

The Navigation Acts

The nurture of commerce was fundamental. Toward this end Parliament enacted the Navigation Acts. These laws, put into effect over a period of half a century and more, were designed to bring gold and silver into the Royal Treasury, to develop the imperial merchant fleet, to channel the flow of colonial raw materials into England, and to keep foreign goods and vessels out of colonial ports.

The system originated in the 1650s in response to stiff commercial competition by the Dutch, whose sailors roamed the world's oceans in search of business. Before 1650 a large share of the produce of the English colonies in America reached Europe in Dutch vessels; the first slaves in Virginia, it will be recalled, arrived on a Dutch ship and were doubtless paid for in tobacco that was later burned in the clay pipes of the burghers of Amsterdam and Rotterdam.

The Navigation Act of 1660 reserved the entire trade of the colonies to English ships and required that the captain and three-quarters of his crew be English. (Colonists, of course, were English, and their ships were treated on the same terms as those sailing out of London or Liverpool.) The act also provided that certain colonial "enumerated articles"—sugar, tobacco, cotton, ginger, and dyes like indigo (purple) and fustic (yellow)—could not be "shipped, carried, conveyed or transported" outside the empire. Three years later Parliament required that with trifling exceptions all European products destined for the colonies be brought to England before being shipped across the Atlantic. Since trade between England and the colonies was reserved to English vessels, this meant that the goods would have to be unloaded and reloaded in England. Early in the eighteenth century the list of enumerated articles was expanded to include rice, molasses, naval stores, furs, and copper.

The English looked on the empire broadly; they envisioned the colonies as part of an economic unit, not as servile dependencies to be exploited for England's selfish benefit. The growing of tobacco in England was prohibited, and valuable bounties were paid to colonial producers of indigo and naval stores. A planned economy, England specializing in manufacturing and the colonies in the production of raw materials, was the grand design. By and large the system suited the realities of life in an underdeveloped country rich in raw materials and suffering from a chronic labor shortage.

Much has been made by some historians of the restrictions that the British placed on colonial manufacturing. The Wool Act of 1699 prohibited the export (but not the manufacture for local sale) of colonial woolen cloth. A similar law regarding hats was passed in 1732, and in 1750 an Iron Act outlawed the construction of new rolling and slitting mills in America. No other restrictions on manufacturing were imposed.

At most the Wool Act stifled a potential American industry; the law was directed chiefly at Irish woolens rather than American ones. The hat industry cannot be considered a major one. Iron, however, was important; by 1775 the industry was thriving in Virginia, Maryland, New Jersey, and Pennsylvania, and America was turning out one-seventh of the world supply. Yet the Iron Act was designed to steer the American iron industry in a certain direction, not to destroy it. Eager for iron to feed English mills, Parliament eliminated all duties on colonial pig and bar iron entering England, a great stimulus to the basic industry.

The Effects of Mercantilism

Colonists increasingly complained about mercantilism, but did it harm them? The chronic colonial shortage of hard money was superficially caused by the flow of specie—gold and silver—to England to meet the "unfavorable" balance of trade. The rapidly growing colonial economy consumed far more manufactured products than it could pay for out of current production. To be "in debt" to England really meant that the English were investing capital in America, a state of affairs that benefited lender and borrower alike.

Important colonial products for which no market existed in England (such as fish, wheat, and corn) were never enumerated and moved freely and directly to foreign ports. Most colonial manufacturing was untouched by English law. Shipbuilding benefited from the Navigation Acts, since many English merchants bought vessels built in the colonies. Between 1769 and 1771, Massachusetts, New Hampshire, and Rhode Island yards constructed perhaps 250 ships of 100 to 400 tons for transatlantic commerce and twice that many sloops and schooners for fishermen and coastal traders.

Two forces that worked in opposite directions must be considered before arriving at any judgment about English mercantilism. While the theory presupposed a general imperial interest above that of both colony and mother country, when conflicts of interest arose the latter nearly always predominated. Whenever Parliament or the Board of Trade resolved an Anglo-American disagreement, the colonists tended to lose.

Complementary interests conspired to keep conflicts at a minimum, but in the long run, as the American economy became more complex, the colonies would have been seriously hampered and much more trouble would have occurred had the system continued to operate.

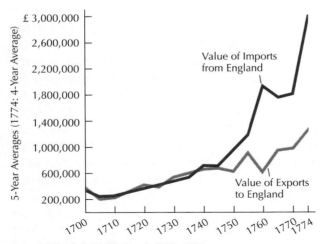

Colonial Trade with England, 1700–1774

On the other hand, the restrictions of English mercantilism were greatly lessened by inefficiency. The king and his ministers handed out government posts to win political favor or to repay political debts, regardless of the recipient's ability to perform the duties of the office.

Transported to remote America, this bumbling and cynical system scarcely functioned at all when local opinion resisted it. Smuggling became a respected profession, bribery of English officials standard practice. Despite a supposedly prohibitive duty of sixpence a gallon imposed by the Molasses Act of 1733, molasses from the French West Indies continued to be imported. The duty was seldom collected.

Mercantilist policies hurt some colonists such as the tobacco planters, who grew far more tobacco than British consumers could smoke. Tobacco planters wanted to ship directly to Dutch or French ports. But the policies helped others, and most people proved adept at getting around those aspects of the system that threatened them. In any case, the colonies enjoyed almost continuous prosperity, as even so dedicated a foe of mercantilist restrictions as Adam Smith admitted.

By the same token, England profited greatly from its overseas possessions. With all its inefficiencies, mercantilism worked. Prime Minister Sir Robert Walpole's famous policy of "salutary neglect," which involved looking the other way when Americans violated the Navigation Acts, was partly a bowing to the inevitable, partly the result of complacency. English manufactures were better and cheaper than those of other nations. This fact, together with ties of language and a common heritage, predisposed Americans toward doing business in England. All else followed naturally; the mercantilist laws merely steered the American economy in a direction it had already taken.

The Great Awakening

Although a majority of the settlers were of English, Scottish, or Scots-Irish descent, and their interests generally coincided with those of their cousins in the mother country, people in the colonies were beginning to recognize their common interests and character. Their loyalties were still predominantly local, but by 1750 the word *American*, used to describe something characteristic of all the British possessions in North America, had entered the language. Events in one part of America were beginning to have direct effects on other regions. One of the first of these developments was the so-called Great Awakening.

By the early eighteenth century, religious fervor had slackened in all the colonies. Prosperity turned many colonists away from their forebears' preoccupation with the rewards of the next world to the more tangible ones of this one. John Winthrop invested his faith in God and his own efforts in the task of creating a spiritual community; his grandsons invested in Connecticut real estate.

The proliferation of religious denominations made it impracticable to enforce laws requiring regular religious observances. Even in South Carolina, the colony that came closest to having an "Anglican Establishment," only a minority were

WAS ECONOMIC GAIN THE COLONISTS' MAIN MOTIVATION?

Debating the Past

This bustling New York farm scene was painted in 1732 on a wood plank. Were those who first placed it above their mantelpiece enshrining their prosperity or their family? Perhaps the first important account of the eighteenth century was by James Truslow Adams (1927), a Wall Street broker who amassed a fortune, retired at age 34, and turned to history. The colonists, he believed, were likewise consumed with acquiring better and more abundant food, clothing, furnishings, housing, and the status such goods signified. He doubted that they cared much about anything else. In the 1950s many scholars, flush with post–World War II patriotism, insisted that the colonists cared deeply about religious, political, and family values. Edmund Morgan (1958) best exemplified this viewpoint. But Adams's position resurfaced several decades later. James Lemon (1972) claimed that Pennsylvania attracted middle-class immigrants who quickly became profit-maximizing farmers. Jack Greene (1988) and Alan Kulikoff (1992) showed that farmers in the Chesapeake and the South had almost from the start been preoccupied with money and land. The studies of colonial towns during the 1970s transformed the debate. Philip Greven (1970) and others discovered that while nearly everyone craved land, they did so chiefly for their families. Parents sought enough land to give or bequeath to their many children, who otherwise, on attaining adulthood, would be forced to scatter. This focus on parents and family life also spotlighted the central role of women in colonial society, a theme that was developed by Linda Kerber (1980), Mary Beth Norton (1980), and many others.

James Truslow Adams, *Provincial Society* (1927), Edmund Morgan, *A Puritan Dilemma* (1958), James Lemon, *Best Poor Man's Country* (1972), Jack Greene, *Pursuits of Happiness* (1988), Alan Kulikoff, *Agrarian Origins of American Capitalism* (1992), Philip Greven, *Four Generations* (1970), Linda Kerber, *Women of the Republic* (1980), Mary Beth Norton, *Liberty's Daughters* (1980).

churchgoers. Settlers in frontier districts lived beyond the reach of church or clergy. The result was a large and growing number of "persons careless of all religion."

This state of affairs came to an abrupt end with the Great Awakening of the 1740s. The Awakening began in the Middle Colonies as the result of religious developments that originated in Europe. In the late 1720s two newly arrived ministers, Theodore Frelinghuysen, a Calvinist from Westphalia, and William Tennent, an Irish-born Presbyterian, sought to instill in their sleepy Pennsylvania and New Jersey congregations the evangelical zeal and spiritual enthusiasm they had witnessed among the Pietists in Germany and the Methodist followers of John Wesley in England. Their example inspired other clergymen, including Tennent's two sons.

In this painting evangelist George Whitefield appears to be cross-eyed. This is the fault of John Wollaston, the painter. Whitefield had eye problems; his detractors called him "Dr. Squintum." The woman's rapturous gaze is unaffected by Whitefield's own curious visage.

A more significant surge of religious enthusiasm followed the arrival in 1738 in Georgia of the Reverend George Whitefield, a young Oxford-trained Anglican minister. Whitefield was a marvelous pulpit orator and no mean actor. He played on the feelings of his audience the way a conductor directs a symphony. Whitefield undertook a series of fund-raising tours throughout the colonies. The most successful began in Philadelphia in 1739. Benjamin Franklin, not a very religious person and not easily moved by emotional appeals, heard one of these sermons. "I silently resolved he should get nothing from me," he later recalled.

> *I had in my Pocket a Handful of Copper Money, three or four silver Dollars, and five Pistoles in Gold. As he proceeded I began to soften and concluded to give the Coppers. Another Stroke of his Oratory . . . determin'd me to give the Silver; and he finish'd so admirably that I empty'd my Pocket wholly into the Collector's Dish.*

Whitefield's visit changed the "manners of our inhabitants," Franklin added.

Wherever Whitefield went he filled the churches. If no local clergyman offered his pulpit, he attracted thousands to meetings out of doors. During a three-day visit to Boston, 19,000 people (more than the population of the town) thronged to hear him. His oratorical brilliance aside, Whitefield succeeded in releasing an epidemic of religious emotionalism because his message was so well suited to American ears. By preaching a theology that one critic said was "scaled down to the comprehension of twelve-year-olds," he spared his audiences the rigors of hard thought. Though he usually began by chastising his listeners as sinners, "half animals and half devils," he invariably took care to leave them with the hope that eternal salvation could be theirs. While not denying the doctrine of predestination, he preached a God responsive to good intentions. He disregarded sectarian differences and encouraged his listeners to do the same. "God help us to forget party names and become Christians in deed and truth," he prayed.

Some churches split into factions. Those who supported the incumbent minister were called, among Congregationalists, "Old Lights," and among Presbyterians, "Old Sides," while those who favored revivalism were known as "New Lights" and "New Sides." These splits often ran along class lines. The richer, better-educated, and more influential members of the church tended to stay with the traditional arrangements.

But many were deeply moved by the new ideas. Persons chafing under the restraints of puritan authoritarianism, or feeling guilty over their preoccupation with material goods, now found release in religious ferment. For some the release was more than spiritual; Timothy Cutler, a conservative Anglican clergyman, complained that as a result of the Awakening "our presses are forever teeming with books and our women with bastards." Whether or not Cutler was correct, the Great Awakening helped some people to rid themselves of the idea that disobedience to authority entailed damnation. Anything that God justified, human law could not condemn. The Great Awakening did not entail opposition to British tax policies; but it did undermine traditional conceptions of authority.

Other institutions besides the churches were affected by the Great Awakening. In 1741 the president of Yale College criticized the theology of itinerant ministers who imitated Whitefield. One of these promptly retorted that a Yale faculty member had no more divine grace than a chair! Other revivalists called on the New Light churches of Connecticut to withdraw their support from Yale and endow a college of their own. The result was the College of New Jersey (now Princeton), founded in 1746 by New Side Presbyterians. Three other educational by-products of the Great Awakening followed: the College of Rhode Island (Brown), founded by Baptists in 1765; Queen's College (Rutgers), founded by Dutch Reformers in 1766; and Dartmouth, founded by New Light Congregationalists in 1769.

The Rise and Fall of Jonathan Edwards

Jonathan Edwards, the most famous native-born revivalist of the Great Awakening, was living proof that the evangelical temperament need not be hostile to learning. Edwards, though deeply pious, was passionately devoted to intellectual pursuits. But in 1725, four years after graduating from Yale, he was offered the position of assistant at his grandfather Solomon Stoddard's church in Northampton, Massachusetts. He accepted, and when Stoddard died two years later, Edwards became pastor.

During his six decades in Northampton, Stoddard had so dominated the ministers of the Connecticut Valley that some referred to him as "pope." His prominence came in part from the "open enrollment" admission policy he adopted for his own church. Evidence of saving grace was neither required nor expected of members: mere good behavior sufficed. As a result, the grandson inherited a congregation whose members were possessed of an "inordinate engagedness after this world." How ready they were to meet their Maker in the next was another question.

For all his learning and intellectual brilliance, Edwards did not stick at dramatizing what unconverted listeners had to look forward to. The heat of Hell's consuming fires and the stench of brimstone became palpable at his rendering. In his most famous sermon, "Sinners in the Hands of an Angry God," delivered at Enfield, Connecticut, in 1741, he pulled out all the stops, depicting a "dreadfully provoked" God holding the unconverted over the pit of Hell, "much as one holds a spider, or some loathsome insect." Later, on the off-chance that his listeners did not recognize themselves among the "insects" in God's hand, he declared that "this is the dismal case of every soul in this congregation that has not been born again, however moral and strict, sober and religious, they may otherwise be." A great moaning reverberated through the church. People cried out, "What must I do to be saved?"

Unfortunately for some church members, Edwards's warnings about the state of their souls caused much anxiety. One disconsolate member, Joseph Hawley, slit his throat. Edwards took the suicide calmly. "Satan seems to be in a great rage," he declared. But for some of Edwards's most prominent parishioners, Hawley's death roused doubts. They began to miss the forgiving God of Solomon Stoddard.

Rather than soften his message, Edwards persisted, and in 1749 his parishioners voted unanimously to dismiss him. He became a missionary to some Indians in Stockbridge, Massachusetts. In 1759 he was appointed president of Princeton, but he died of smallpox before he could take office.

By the early 1750s a reaction had set in against religious "enthusiasm" in all its forms. Except in the religion-starved South, where traveling New Side Presbyterians and Baptists continued their evangelizing efforts, the Great Awakening had run its course. Whitefield's tour of the colonies in 1754 attracted little notice.

Although it caused divisions, the Great Awakening also fostered religious toleration. If one group claimed the right to worship in its own way, how could it deny to other Protestant churches equal freedom? The Awakening was also the first truly national event in American history. It marks the time when the previously distinct histories of New England, the Middle Colonies, and the South began to intersect. Powerful links were being forged. As early as 1691 there was a rudimentary intercolonial postal system. In 1754, not long after the Awakening, the farsighted Benjamin Franklin advanced his Albany Plan for a colonial union to deal with common problems, such as defense against Indian attacks on the frontier. Thirteen once-isolated colonies, expanding to the north and south as well as westward, were merging.

The Enlightenment in America

The Great Awakening pointed ahead to an America marked by religious pluralism; by the 1740s many colonists were rejecting not only the stern Calvinism of Edwards but even the easy Arminianism of Solomon Stoddard in favor of a far less forbidding theology, one more in keeping with the ideas of the European Enlightenment.

The Enlightenment, whose proponents enshrined reason and scientific inquiry, had an enormous impact in America. The founders of the colonies were contemporaries of the astronomer Galileo Galilei (1564–1642), the philosopher-mathematician René Descartes (1596–1650), and Sir Isaac Newton (1642–1727), the genius who revealed to the world the workings of gravity and other laws of motion. American society developed amid the excitement generated by these great discoverers, who provided both a new understanding of the natural world and a mode of thought that implied that impersonal, scientific laws governed the behavior of all matter, animate and inanimate. Earth and the heavens, human beings and the lower animals—all seemed parts of an immense, intricate machine. God had set it all in motion and remained the master technician (the divine watchmaker) overseeing it, but He took fewer and fewer occasions to interfere with its immutable operation. If human reasoning powers and direct observation of natural phenomena rather than God's revelations provided the key to knowledge, it followed that knowledge of the laws of nature, by enabling people to understand the workings of the universe, would enable them to control their earthly destinies and to have at least a voice in their eternal destinies.

Most creative thinkers of the European Enlightenment realized that human beings were not entirely rational and that a complete understanding of the physical world was beyond their grasp. They did, however, believe that human beings were becoming more rational and would be able, by using their rational powers, to discover the laws governing the physical world. Their faith in these ideas produced the so-called Age of Reason. And while their confidence in human rationality now seems naive and the "laws" they formulated no longer appear so mechanically perfect (the universe is far less orderly than they imagined), they added immensely to knowledge.

Many churchgoing colonists, especially better educated ones, accepted the assumptions of the Age of Reason wholeheartedly. Some repudiated the doctrine of original sin and asserted the benevolence of God. Others came to doubt the divinity of Christ and eventually declared themselves Unitarians. Still others, among them Benjamin Franklin, embraced Deism, a faith that revered God for the marvels of His universe rather than for His power over humankind.

The impact of Enlightenment ideas went far beyond religion. The writings of John Locke and other political theorists found a receptive audience. So did the work of the Scottish philosophers Francis Hutcheson and David Hume and the French *philosophes,* particularly Montesquieu and Voltaire. Ideas generated in Europe often reached America with startling speed. No colonial political controversy really heated up in America until all involved had published pamphlets citing half a dozen European authorities. Radical ideas that in Europe were discussed only by an intellectual elite became almost commonplace in the colonies.

As the topics of learned discourse expanded, ministers lost their monopoly on intellectual life. By the 1750s, only a minority of Harvard and Yale graduates were becoming ministers. The College of Philadelphia (later the University of Pennsylvania), founded in 1751, and King's College (later Columbia), founded in New York in 1754, added two institutions to the growing ranks of American colleges, which were never primarily training grounds for clergymen.

Lawyers, who first appeared in any number in colonial towns in the 1740s, swiftly asserted their intellectual authority in public affairs. Physicians and the handful of professors of natural history declared themselves better able to make sense of the new scientific discoveries than clergymen. Yet because fields of knowledge were far less specialized than in modern times, self-educated amateurs could also make useful contributions.

The most famous instances of popular participation occurred in Philadelphia. It was there, in 1727, that 21-year-old Benjamin Franklin founded the Junto, a club at which he and other young artisans gathered on Friday evenings to discuss "any point of morals, politics, or natural philosophy." In 1743 Franklin established an expanded version of the Junto, the American Philosophical Society, which he hoped would "cultivate the finer arts and improve the common stock of knowledge."

Colonial Scientific Achievements

America produced no Galileo or Newton, but colonists contributed significantly to the collection of scientific knowledge. The unexplored continent provided a laboratory for the study of natural phenomena. The Philadelphia Quaker John Bartram, a "down right plain Country Man," ranged from Florida to the Great Lakes during the middle years of the eighteenth century, gathering and classifying hundreds of plants. Bartram also studied Indians closely, speculating about their origins and collecting information about their culture.

Benjamin Franklin is most often depicted as he looked in later life, with his own thinning hair rather than the wig that was de rigueur for an eighteenth-century man of good family. In this 1767 portrait, a younger Franklin follows the fashion.

Benjamin Franklin's far-ranging curiosity extended to science. "No one of the present age has made more important discoveries," Thomas Jefferson declared. Franklin's studies of electricity, which he capped in 1752 with his famous kite experiment, established him as a scientist of international stature. He also invented the lightning rod, the iron Franklin stove (a far more efficient way to heat a room than an open fireplace), bifocal spectacles, and several other ingenious devices. In addition he served 14 years (1751–1764) in the Pennsylvania assembly. He founded a circulating library and helped to get the first hospital in Philadelphia built. He came up with the idea of a lottery to raise money for public purposes. In his spare time he taught himself Latin, French, Spanish, and Italian.

Involvement at even the most marginal level in the intellectual affairs of Europe gave influential New Englanders, Middle Colonists, and Southerners a chance to get to know one another. Like the spread of evangelical religion, Enlightenment values created new forms of community in English America. Men who in 1750 were discussing botany, physics, and natural phenomena would also soon be exchanging ideas about governance.

Repercussions of Distant Wars

The British colonies were part of a great empire that was part of a still larger world. Seemingly isolated in their remote communities, scattered like a broken string of beads between the wide Atlantic and the trackless Appalachian forests, Americans were constantly affected by outside events both in the Old World and in the New. Under the spell of mercantilist logic, the western European nations competed fiercely for markets and colonial raw materials. War—hot and cold, declared and undeclared—was almost a permanent condition of seventeenth- and eighteenth-century life, and when the powers clashed they fought wherever they could get at one another, in America, in Europe, and elsewhere.

Although the American colonies were minor pieces in the game and were sometimes casually exchanged or sacrificed by the masterminds in London, Paris, and Madrid in pursuit of some supposedly more important objective, the colonists quickly generated their own international animosities. Frenchmen and Spaniards clashed savagely in Florida as early as the sixteenth century. Before the landing of the Pilgrims, Samuel Argall of Virginia was sacking French settlements in Maine and carrying off Jesuit priests into captivity at Jamestown. Instead of fostering tranquility and generosity, the abundance of America seemed to make the settlers belligerent and greedy.

The North Atlantic fisheries quickly became a source of trouble between Canadian and New England colonists, despite the fact that the waters of the Grand Banks teemed with cod and other fish. To dry and salt their catch the fishermen needed land bases, and French and English Americans struggled constantly over the harbors of Maine, Nova Scotia, and Newfoundland.

Even more troublesome was the fur trade. The yield of the forest was easily exhausted by indiscriminate slaughter, and traders contended bitterly to control valuable hunting grounds. The French in Canada conducted their fur trading through tribes such as the Algonquin and the Huron. This brought them into conflict with the Five Nations, the powerful Iroquois confederation of central New York. As early as 1609 the Five Nations were at war with the French and their Indian allies. For decades this struggle flared sporadically, the Iroquois more than holding their own both as fighters and as traders. The Iroquois brought quantities of beaver pelts to the Dutch at Albany, some obtained by their own trappers, others taken by ambushing the fur-laden canoes of their enemies. They preyed on and ultimately destroyed the Huron in the land north of Lake Ontario and dickered with Indian trappers in far-off Michigan. When the English took over the New Amsterdam colony they eagerly adopted the Iroquois as allies, buying their furs and supplying them with trading goods and guns.

By the last decade of the seventeenth century it had become clear that the Dutch lacked the strength to maintain a big empire and that Spain was fast declining. The future, especially in North America, belonged to England and France. In the wars of the next 125 years European alliances shifted dramatically, yet the English and what the Boston lawyer John Adams called "the turbulent Gallicks" were always on opposite sides.

In the first three of these conflicts colonists played only minor parts. The fighting in America consisted chiefly of sneak attacks on isolated outposts. In King William's War (1689–1697), the American phase of the War of the League of Augsburg, French forces raided Schenectady in New York and frontier settlements in New England. English colonists retaliated by capturing Port Royal, Nova Scotia, only to lose that outpost in a counterattack in 1691. The Peace of Ryswick in 1697 restored all captured territory in America to the original owners.

The next struggle was the War of the Spanish Succession (1702–1713), fought to prevent the union of Spain and France under the Bourbons. The Americans named this conflict Queen Anne's War. French-inspired Indians razed Deerfield, Massachusetts. A party of Carolinians burned St. Augustine in Spanish Florida. The New Englanders retook Port Royal. In the Treaty of Utrecht in 1713, France yielded Nova Scotia, Newfoundland, and the Hudson Bay region to Great Britain.

If the colonies were mere pawns in these wars, battle casualties were proportionately high and the civilian population of New England (and of Canada) paid heavily because of the fighting. Many frontier settlers were killed in the raids. Hundreds of townspeople died during the campaigns in Nova Scotia. Massachusetts taxes went up sharply and the colony issued large amounts of paper currency to pay its bills, causing an inflation that ate into the living standards of wage earners.

The American phase of the third Anglo-French conflict, the War of the Austrian Succession (1740–1748), was called King George's War. The usual Indian raids were launched in both directions across the lonely forests that separated the St. Lawrence settlements from the New York and New England frontier. A New England force captured the strategic fortress of Louisbourg on Cape Breton Island, guarding the entrance to the Gulf of St. Lawrence. The Treaty of Aix-la-Chapelle in 1748, however, required the return of Louisbourg, much to the chagrin of the New Englanders.

As this incident suggests, the colonial wars generated a certain amount of trouble between England and the colonies; matters that seemed unimportant in London might loom large in American eyes, and vice versa. But the conflicts were seldom serious. The wars did, however, increase the bad feelings between settlers north and south of the St. Lawrence. Every Indian raid was attributed to French provocateurs, although more often than not the English colonists themselves were responsible for the Indian troubles. Conflicting land claims further aggravated the situation. Massachusetts, Connecticut, and Virginia possessed overlapping claims to the Ohio Valley, and Pennsylvania and New York also had pretensions in the region. Yet the French, ranging broadly across the midcontinent, insisted that the Ohio country was exclusively theirs.

The Great War for the Empire

In this beautiful, almost untouched land, a handful of individuals determined the future of the continent. Over the years the French had established a chain of forts and trading posts running from Mackinac Island in northern Michigan to Kaskaskia on the Mississippi River and Vincennes on the Wabash River, and from Niagara in the east to the Bourbon River, near Lake Winnipeg, in the west. By the 1740s, however, Pennsylvania fur traders, led by George Croghan, a rugged Irishman, were setting up posts north of the Ohio River and bargaining with Miami and Huron Indians, who ordinarily sold their furs to the French. In 1748 Croghan built a fort at Pickawillany, deep in the Miami country, in what is now western Ohio. That same year agents of a group of Virginia land speculators who had recently organized what they called the Ohio Company reached this area.

With trifling exceptions, an insulating band of wilderness had always separated the French and English in America. Now the two powers came into contact. The immediate result was a showdown battle for control of North America, the "great war for the empire." Thoroughly alarmed by the presence of the English on land they had long considered their own, the French struck hard. Attacking suddenly in 1752, they wiped out Croghan's post at Pickawillany and drove his traders back into Pennsylvania. Then they built a string of barrier forts south from Lake Erie along the Pennsylvania line: Fort Presque Isle, Fort Le Boeuf, Fort Venango.

The Pennsylvania authorities chose to ignore this action, but Lieutenant Governor Robert Dinwiddie of Virginia (who was an investor in the Ohio Company) dispatched a 21-year-old surveyor named George Washington to warn the French that they were trespassing on Virginia territory.

Washington, a gangling, inarticulate, and intensely ambitious young planter, made his way northwest in the fall of 1753 and delivered Dinwiddie's message to the commandant at Fort Le Boeuf. It made no impression. "[The French] told me," Washington reported, "that it was their absolute Design to take Possession of the Ohio, and by G— they would do it." Governor Dinwiddie thereupon promoted Washington to lieutenant colonel and sent him back in the spring of 1754 with 150

This, the first portrait of George Washington, was done by Charles Willson Peale in 1772. Washington's right hand is inside his vest, a convention later associated with Napoleon; his left hand is behind his back. Perhaps this was to spare the painter of the trouble of rendering hands and fingers, always a challenge.

men to seize a strategic junction south of the new French forts, where the Allegheny and Monongahela rivers join to form the Ohio.

Eager but inexperienced in battle, young Washington botched his assignment. As his force labored painfully through the tangled mountain country southeast of the fork of the Ohio, he received word that the French had already occupied the position and were constructing a powerful post, Fort Duquesne. Outnumbered by perhaps four to one, Washington foolishly pushed on. He surprised and routed a French reconnaissance party, but this brought on him the main body of enemy troops.

Hastily he threw up a defensive position, aptly named Fort Necessity, but the ground was ill chosen; the French easily surrounded the fort and Washington had to surrender. After tricking the young officer, who could not read French, into signing an admission that he had "assassinated" the leader of the reconnaissance party, his captors, with the gateway to the Ohio country firmly in their hands, permitted him and his men to march off. Nevertheless, Washington returned to Virginia a hero, for although still undeclared, this was war, and he had struck the first blow against the hated French.

In the resulting conflict, which historians call the French and Indian War (to the colonists it was simply "the French War"), the English outnumbered the French by about 1.5 million to 90,000. But the English were divided and disorganized, the French disciplined and united. The French controlled the disputed territory, and most of the Indians took their side. As a colonial official wrote, together they made formidable forest fighters, "sometimes in our Front, sometimes in our Rear, and often on all sides of us, Hussar Fashion, taking the Advantage of every Tree and Bush." With an ignorance and arrogance typical of eighteenth-century colonial administration, the British mismanaged the war and failed to make effective use of local resources. For several years they stumbled from one defeat to another.

General Edward Braddock, a competent but uninspired soldier, was dispatched to Virginia to take command. In June 1755 he marched against Fort Duquesne with 1,400 Redcoats and a smaller number of colonials, only to be decisively defeated by a much smaller force of French and Indians. Braddock died bravely in battle, and only 500 of his men, led by Colonel Washington, who was serving as his aide-de-camp, made their way back to Virginia.

Elsewhere Anglo-American arms fared little better in the early years of the war. Expeditions against Fort Niagara, key to all French defenses in the west, and Crown Point, gateway to Montréal, bogged down. Meanwhile Indians, armed by the French, bathed the frontier in blood. Venting the frustration caused by 150 years of white advance, they attacked defenseless outposts with unrestrained brutality.

The most feared of the "French" Indians were the Delaware, a once-peaceful Pennsylvania tribe that had been harried from their homelands by English and Iroquois. General Braddock paid his Indian allies only £5 each for French scalps but offered £200 for the hair of Shinngass, the Delaware chieftain.

In 1756 the conflict spread to Europe to become the Seven Years' War. Prussia sided with Great Britain, Austria with the French. On the world stage, too, things went badly for the British. Finally, in 1758, as defeat succeeded defeat, King George II was forced to allow William Pitt, whom he detested, to take over leadership of the war effort. Pitt, grandson of "Diamond" Pitt, a nouveau riche East India merchant, was an unstable man who spent much of his life on the verge of madness, but he was a brilliant strategist and capable of inspiring the nation in its hour of trial.

Pitt recognized, as few contemporaries did, the potential value of North America. Instead of relying on the tightfisted and shortsighted colonial assemblies for men and money, he poured regiment after regiment of British regulars and the full resources of the British treasury into the contest, mortgaging the future recklessly to secure the prize. Grasping the importance of sea power in fighting a war on the other side of the Atlantic, he used the British navy to bottle up the enemy fleet and hamper French communications with Canada. He possessed a keen eye for military genius, and when he discovered it, he ignored seniority and the outraged feelings of mediocre generals and promoted talented young officers to top commands. (His greatest find was James Wolfe, whom he made a brigadier at age 31.)

In the winter of 1758, as Pitt's grand strategy matured, Fort Duquesne fell. It was appropriately renamed Fort Pitt, the present Pittsburgh. The following summer Fort Niagara was overrun. General Jeffrey Amherst took Crown Point, and Wolfe sailed up the St. Lawrence to Québec. There General Louis Joseph de Montcalm had prepared formidable defenses, but after months of probing and planning, Wolfe found and exploited a chink in the city's armor and captured it. Both he and Montcalm died in the battle. In 1760 Montréal fell and the French abandoned all Canada to the British. The British also won major victories against Spanish forces in Cuba and Manila, and against the French in the West Indies and India.

Britain Victorious: The Peace of Paris

Peace was restored in 1763 by the Treaty of Paris. Its terms were moderate considering the extent of the British triumph. France abandoned all claim to North America except for two small islands near Newfoundland; Great Britain took over Canada and the eastern half of the Mississippi Valley. Spain got back both the Philippine Islands and Cuba, but in exchange ceded East and West Florida to Great Britain. In a separate treaty, Spain also got New Orleans and the huge area of North America west of the Mississippi River.

"Half the continent," the historian Francis Parkman wrote, "had changed hands at the scratch of a pen." From the point of view of the English colonists in America, the victory was overwhelming. All threat to their frontiers seemed to have been swept away. Surely, they believed in the first happy moments of victory, their peaceful and prosperous expansion was ensured for countless generations.

No honest American could deny that the victory had been won chiefly by British troops and with British gold. Colonial militiamen fought well in defense of their homes or when some highly prized objective seemed ripe for the plucking; they lacked discipline and determination when required to fight far from home and under commanders they did not know. As one American official admitted, it was difficult to get New Englanders to enlist "unless assurances can be given that they shall not march to the southward of certain limits."

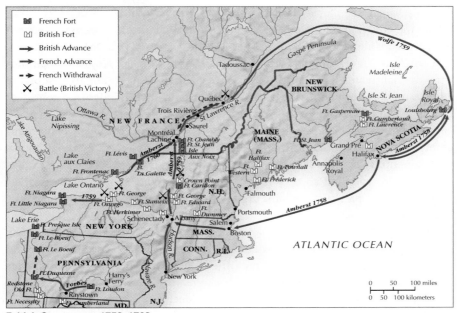

British Successes, 1758–1763

Colonials were delighted that scarlet-clad British regulars had borne the brunt of the fighting and happier still that the Crown had shouldered most of the financial burden of the long struggle. The local assemblies contributed to the cost, but except for Massachusetts and Virginia their outlays were trivial compared with the £82 million poured into the worldwide conflict by the British.

Little wonder that the great victory produced a burst of praise for king and mother country throughout America. Parades, cannonading, fireworks, banquets, the pealing of church bells—these were the order of the day in every colonial town. "Nothing," said Thomas Pownall, wartime governor of Massachusetts and a student of colonial administration, "can eradicate from [the colonists'] hearts their natural, almost mechanical affection to Great Britain." A young South Carolinian who had been educated in England claimed that the colonists were "more wrapped up in a king" than any people he had ever heard of.

Burdens of an Expanded Empire

In London peace proved a time for reassessment; that the empire of 1763 was not the same as the empire of 1754 was obvious. The new, far larger dominion would be much more expensive to maintain. Pitt had spent a huge sum winning and securing it, much of it borrowed money. Great Britain's national debt had doubled between 1754 and 1763. Now this debt must be serviced and repaid, and the strain that this would place on the economy was clear to all. Furthermore, the day-to-day cost of administering an empire that extended from the Hudson Bay to India was far larger than that which the already burdened British taxpayer could be expected to bear. Before the great war for the empire, Britain's North American possessions were administered for about £70,000 a year; after 1763 the cost was five times as much.

The American empire had also become far more complex. A system of administration that treated it as a string of separate plantations struggling to exist on the edge of the forest would no longer suffice. The war had been fought for control of the Ohio Valley. Now that the prize had been secured, ten thousand hands were eager to make off with it. The urge to expand was, despite the continent's enormous empty spaces, an old American drive. As early as the 1670s eastern stay-at-homes were lamenting the "insatiable desire after Land" that made people willing to "live like Heathen, only that so they might have Elbow-room enough in the world." Frontier warfare had frustrated this urge for seven long years. How best could it be satisfied now that peace had come?

Conflicting colonial claims, based on charters drafted by men who thought the Pacific lay over the next hill, threatened to make the Ohio valley a battleground once more. The Indians remained "unpacified." Rival land companies contested for charters, while fur traders strove to hold back the wave of settlement that must inevitably destroy the world of the beaver and the deer.

Apparently only Great Britain could deal with these problems and rivalries, for when Franklin had proposed a rudimentary form of colonial union—the Albany

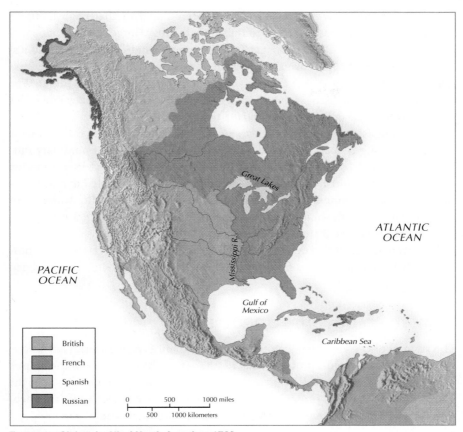

European Claims in All of North America, 1763

Plan of 1754—it was rejected by almost everyone. Unfortunately, the British government did not rise to the challenge. Perhaps this was to be expected. A handful of aristocrats (fewer than 150 peers were active in government affairs) dominated British politics, and they were more concerned with local offices and personal advantage than with large questions of policy. An American who spent some time in London in 1764 trying to obtain approval for a plan for the development of the West reported: "The people hear Spend thire time in Nothing but abuseing one Another and Striveing who shall be in power with a view to Serve themselves and Thire friends." King George III was not a tyrant, as once was commonly believed, but he was an inept politician and the victim of frequent bouts of illness.

Serene in their ignorance, most English leaders insisted that colonials were uncouth and generally inferior beings. During the French and Indian War, British commanders repeatedly expressed contempt for colonial militiamen, whom they considered fit only for "fatigue" duties such as digging trenches, chopping wood, and other noncombat tasks. General Wolfe characterized colonial troops as the "most contemptible cowardly dogs you can conceive," and another English officer, annoyed by their unsanitary habits, complained that they "infect the air with a disagreeable stink." The British officers failed to understand that colonial soldiers were volunteers who had formally contracted to serve under specific conditions. Lord Loudoun, the British commander-in-chief during the French and Indian War, was flabbergasted to discover that New England troops refused to obey one of his direct orders on the ground that it violated their contracts.

Many English people resented Americans simply because the colonies were rapidly becoming rich and powerful. They were growing at an extraordinary rate. Between 1750 and 1770 the population of British America increased from 1 million to more than 2 million. As early as 1751, Benjamin Franklin predicted that in a century "the greatest number of Englishmen will be on this Side of the Water." (His guess was nearly on the mark: in 1850 the population of Great Britain was 20.8 million, that of the United States 23.1 million, including some 4 million slaves and others who were not of British descent.) If the English did not say much about this possibility, they too considered it from time to time—without Franklin's complacency.

Tightening Imperial Controls

The attempt of the inefficient, ignorant, and indignant British government to deal with the intricate colonial problems that resulted from the great war for the empire led to the American Revolution. Trouble began when the British decided after the French and Indian War to intervene more actively in American affairs. Theoretically the colonies were entirely subordinate to Crown and Parliament, yet except for the disastrous attempt to centralize control of the colonies in the 1680s,

This engraving depicts Pontiac confronting Colonel Henry Bouquet. Pontiac had good reason to be angry. In a letter dated July 16, 1763, Sir Jeffrey Amherst, commander of British forces in North America, advised Bouquet to infect Pontiac's Indians with smallpox: "You will do well to try to Innoculate the Indians by means of Blanketts, as well as to try Every other method that can serve to Extirpate this Execrable Race." Bouquet responded a week later: "All your directions will be observed."

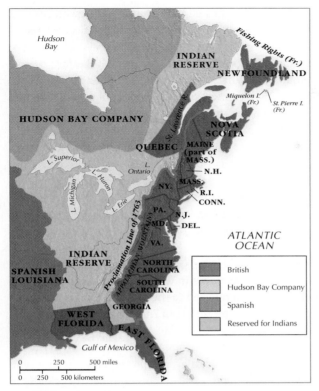

Proclamation of 1763

George III's Proclamation of 1763 in effect reserved for the Indians the vast area across the Appalachians (except for the new royal colonies of Québec, East Florida, and West Florida) as far west as Spanish Louisiana and as far north as the Hudson Bay Company preserve.

they had been allowed a remarkable degree of freedom to manage their own affairs. Of course they had come to expect this as their right.

Parliament had never attempted to tax American colonists. "Compelling the colonies to pay money without their consent would be rather like raising contributions in an enemy's country than taxing Englishmen for their own benefit," Benjamin Franklin wrote. Sir Robert Walpole, initiator of the policy of salutary neglect, recognized the colonial viewpoint. He responded to a suggestion that Parliament tax the colonies by saying: "I will leave that for some of my successors, who may have more courage than I have." Nevertheless, the *legality* of parliamentary taxation, or of other parliamentary intervention in colonial affairs, had not been seriously contested. During King George's War and again during the French and Indian War many British officials in America suggested that Parliament tax the colonies.

Despite the peace treaty of 1763, the American colonies continued to be a drain on the British treasury. Mostly this was due to the cost of fighting Indians. Freed of the restraint posed by French competition, Englishmen and colonists increased their pressure on the Indians. Fur traders cheated them outrageously, while callous military men hoped to exterminate them like vermin. One British officer expressed the wish that they could be hunted down with dogs.

Led by an Ottawa chief named Pontiac, the tribes made one last effort to drive the whites back across the mountains. What the whites called Pontiac's "Rebellion" caused much havoc, but it failed. By 1764 most of the western tribes had accepted the peace terms offered by a royal commissioner, Sir William Johnson, one of the few whites who understood and sympathized with them. The British government then placed fifteen regiments, some 6,000 soldiers, in posts along the entire arc of the frontier, as much to protect the Indians from the settlers as the settlers from the Indians. It proclaimed a new western policy: no settlers were to cross the Appalachian divide. Only licensed traders might do business with the Indians beyond that line. The purchase of Indian land was forbidden. In compensation, three new colonies—Québec, East Florida, and West Florida—were created, but they were not permitted to set up local assemblies.

This Proclamation of 1763 excited much indignation in America. The frustration of dozens of schemes for land development in the Ohio Valley angered many influential colonists. Colonel Washington referred to the proclamation contemptuously as "a temporary expedient to quiet the minds of Indians," and he continued to stake out claims to western lands.

Originally the British had intended the proclamation to be temporary. With the passage of time, however, checking westward expansion seemed a good way to save money, prevent trouble with the Indians, and keep the colonies tied closely to the mother country. The proclamation line, the Board of Trade declared, was "necessary for the preservation of the colonies in due subordination."[1] Naturally this attitude caused resentment in America. To close off the West temporarily in order to pacify the Indians made some sense; to keep it closed was like trying to contain a tidal wave.

The Sugar Act

Americans disliked the new western policy but realized that the problems were knotty and that no simple solution existed. Their protests were somewhat muted. Great Britain's effort to raise money in America to help support the increased cost of colonial administration caused far more vehement complaints. George Grenville, who became prime minister in 1763, was a fairly able man, although long-winded and rather narrow in outlook. His reputation as a financial expert was based chiefly on his eagerness to reduce government spending. Under his leadership Parliament passed, in April 1764, the so-called Sugar Act. This law placed tariffs on sugar, coffee,

---

[1]The British were particularly concerned about preserving the colonies as markets for their manufactures. They feared that the spread of population beyond the mountains would stimulate local manufacturing because the high cost of land transportation would make British goods prohibitively expensive.

wines, and other things imported into America in substantial amounts. At the same time, measures aimed at enforcing all the trade laws were put into effect. Those accused of violating the Sugar Act were to be tried before British naval officers in vice admiralty courts. Grenville was determined to end smuggling, corruption, and inefficiency. Soon the customs service was collecting each year fifteen times as much in duties as it had before the war.

More alarming was the nature of the Sugar Act and the manner of its passage. The Navigation Act duties had been intended to regulate commerce, and the sums collected had not cut deeply into profits. Indeed, the Navigation Acts might well be considered an instrument of imperial foreign policy, an area of government that everyone willingly conceded to London. Yet few Americans were willing to concede that Parliament had the right to tax them. As *Englishmen* they believed that no one should be deprived arbitrarily of property and that, as James Otis put it in his stirring pamphlet *The Rights of the British Colonies Asserted and Proved* (1764), everyone should be "free from all taxes but what he consents to in person, or by his representative." John Locke had made clear in his *Second Treatise on Government* (1690) that property ought never be taken from people without their consent, not because material values transcend all others but because human liberty can never be secure when arbitrary power of any kind exists. "If our Trade may be taxed why not our Lands?" the Boston town meeting asked when news of the Sugar Act reached America. "Why not the produce of our Lands and every Thing we possess or make use of?"

American Colonists Demand Rights

To most people in Great Britain the colonial protest against taxation without representation seemed a hypocritical quibble, and it is probably true that in 1764 many of the protesters had not thought the argument through. The distinction between tax laws and other types of legislation was artificial, the British reasoned. Either Parliament was sovereign in America or it was not, and only a fool or a traitor would argue that it was not. If the colonists were loyal subjects of George III, as they claimed, they should bear cheerfully their fair share of the cost of governing his widespread dominions. As to representation, the colonies *were* represented in Parliament; every member of that body stood for the interests of the entire empire. If Americans had no say in the election of members of Commons, neither did most English subjects.

This concept of "virtual" representation accurately described the British system. But it made no sense in America, where from the time of the first settlements members of the colonial assemblies had represented the people of the districts in which they stood for office. The confusion between virtual and actual (geographically based) representation revealed the extent to which colonial and British political practices had diverged over the years.

The British were correct in concluding that selfish motives influenced colonial objections to the Sugar Act. The colonists denounced taxation without representation, but an offer of a reasonable number of seats in Parliament would not have satisfied them. They would probably have complained about paying taxes to support imperial administration even if imposed by their own assemblies. American abundance and the simplicity of colonial life had enabled them to prosper without assuming any considerable tax burden. Now their maturing society was beginning to require communal rather than individual solutions to the problems of existence. Not many of them were prepared to face up to this hard truth.

Over the course of colonial history Americans had taken a narrow view of imperial concerns. They had avoided complying with the Navigation Acts whenever they could profit by doing so. Colonial militiamen had compiled a sorry record when asked to fight for Britain or even for the inhabitants of colonies other than their own. True, most Americans professed loyalty to the Crown, but not many would voluntarily open their purses except to benefit themselves. In short they were provincials, in attitude and in fact.

Although the colonists were opposed in principle to taxation without representation, they only failed to agree on a common plan of resistance. Many of the assemblies drafted protests, but these varied in force as well as in form. Merchant groups that tried to organize boycotts of products subject to the new taxes met with indifferent success. Then in 1765 Parliament provided the flux necessary for welding colonial opinion by passing the Stamp Act.

The Stamp Act: The Pot Set to Boiling

The Stamp Act placed stiff excise taxes on all kinds of printed matter. No one could sell newspapers or pamphlets, or convey licenses, diplomas, or legal papers without first buying special stamps and affixing them to the printed matter. Stamp duties were intended to be relatively painless to pay and cheap to collect; in England similar taxes brought in about £100,000 annually. Grenville hoped the Stamp Act would produce £60,000 a year in America, and the law provided that all revenue should be applied to "defraying the necessary expenses of defending, protecting, and securing, the . . . colonies."

Hardly a farthing was collected. As the Boston clergyman Jonathan Mayhew explained, "Almost every British American . . . considered it as an infraction of their rights, or their dearly purchased privileges." The Sugar Act had been related to Parliament's uncontested power to control colonial trade, but the Stamp Act was a direct tax. When Parliament ignored the politely phrased petitions of the colonial assemblies, more vigorous protests quickly followed.

Virginia took the lead. In late May 1765 Patrick Henry introduced resolutions asserting redundantly that the Burgesses possessed "the only and sole and exclusive right and power to lay taxes" on Virginians and suggesting that Parliament had no legal authority to tax the colonies at all. Henry spoke for what the royal governor called the "Young, hot and Giddy Members" of the legislature (most of whom, incidentally, had absented themselves from the meeting). The more extreme of Henry's resolutions were defeated, but the debate they occasioned attracted wide

By the mid-eighteenth century, tea had become a staple of the colonists' diet. (In 1766, for example, the residents of the Philadelphia poorhouse demanded that they be served Bohea tea rather than cheaper substitutes.) But colonial ceramics could not withstand boiling water. Thus tea cups and tea pots were manufactured in Staffordshire, England, which had perfected high-temperature ceramics. This "No Stamp Tax" teapot—ironically—was manufactured in England.

and favorable attention. On June 6 the Massachusetts assembly proposed an inter-colonial Stamp Act Congress, which, when it met in New York City in October, passed another series of resolutions of protest. The Stamp Act and other recent acts of Parliament were "burthensome and grievous," the delegates declared. "It is un-questionably essential to the freedom of a people . . . that no taxes be imposed on them but with their own consent."

During the summer irregular organizations known as Sons of Liberty began to agitate against the act. Far more than anyone realized, this marked the start of the revolution. For the first time extralegal organized resistance was taking place, dis-tinct from protest and argument conducted by constituted organs of government like the House of Burgesses and the Massachusetts General Court.

Although led by men of character and position, the "Liberty Boys" frequently resorted to violence to achieve their aims. In Boston they staged vicious riots, loot-ing and vandalizing the houses of the stamp master and his brother-in-law, Lieutenant Governor Thomas Hutchinson. In Connecticut stamp master Jared Ingersoll, a man of great courage and dignity, faced an angry mob demanding his resignation. When threatened with death if he refused, he coolly replied that he was prepared to die "perhaps as well now as another Time." Probably his life was not really in danger, but the size and determination of the crowd convinced him that resistance was useless, and he capitulated.

The stamps were printed in England and shipped to stamp masters (all Americans) in the colonies well in advance of November 1, 1765, the date the law was to go into effect. The New York stamp master had resigned, but the stamps were stored in the city under military guard. Radicals distributed placards reading: "The first Man that either distributes or makes use of Stampt Paper let him take care of his House, Person, and Effects. We dare." When Major Thomas James, the British officer who had charge of the stamps, promised that "the stamps would be crammed down New Yorkers' throats," a mob responded by breaking into his house, drinking all his wine, and smashing his furniture and china.

In some colonies the stamps were snatched by mobs and put to the torch amid rejoicing. Elsewhere they were locked up in secret by British officials or held on shipboard. For a time no business requiring stamped paper was transacted; then, gradually, people began to defy the law by issuing and accepting unstamped documents. Threatened by mob action should they resist, British officials stood by helplessly. The law was a dead letter.

The looting associated with this crisis alarmed many colonists, including some prominent opponents of the Stamp Act. "When the pot is set to boil," the lawyer John Adams remarked sadly, "the scum rises to the top." Another Bostonian called the vandalizing of Thomas Hutchinson's house a "flagrant instance of to what a pitch of infatuation an incensed populace can rise." Such people worried that the protests might be aimed at the wealthy and powerful in America as well as at British tyranny. This does not mean that they disapproved of crowd protests, or even the destruction of property during such protests, as distinct from stealing. Many such people took part in the rioting. "State-quakes," John Adams also said, this time complacently, were comparable to "earth-quakes" and other kinds of natural violence.

Rioters or Rebels?

That many of the poor resented the colonial elite goes without saying, as does the fact that in many instances the rioting got out of hand and took on a social as well as a political character. Times were hard, and the colonial elite, including most of the leading critics of British policy, had little compassion for the poor, whom they feared could be corrupted by anyone who offered them a square meal or a glass of rum. Once roused, laborers and artisans may well have directed their energies toward righting what they considered local wrongs.

Yet the mass of the people, being owners of property and capable of influencing political decisions, were not social revolutionaries. They might envy and resent the wealth and power of the great landowners and merchants, but there is little evidence that they wished to overthrow the established order.

The British were not surprised that Americans disliked the Stamp Act. They had not anticipated, however, that Americans would react so violently and so unanimously. Americans did so for many reasons. Business continued to be poor in

1765, and at a time when 3 shillings was a day's wage for an urban laborer, the stamp tax was 2 shillings for an advertisement in a newspaper, 5 shillings for a will, and 20 shillings for a license to sell liquor. The taxes would hurt the business of lawyers, merchants, newspaper editors, and tavernkeepers. Even clergymen dealt with papers requiring stamps. The protests of such influential and articulate people had a powerful impact on public opinion.

The greatest cause of concern to the colonists was Great Britain's flat rejection of the principle of no taxation without representation. This alarmed them for two closely related reasons. First of all, *as Americans* they objected to being taxed by a legislative body they had not been involved in choosing. To buy a stamp was to surrender all claim to self-government. Secondly, as *British subjects* they valued what they called "the rights of Englishmen." They saw the Stamp Act as only the worst in a series of arbitrary invasions of these rights.

Already Parliament had passed still another measure, the Quartering Act, requiring local legislatures to house and feed new British troops sent to the colonies. Besides being a form of indirect taxation, a standing army was universally deemed to be a threat to liberty. Why were Redcoats necessary in Boston and New York where there was no foreign enemy for thousands of miles in any direction? In hard times, soldiers were particularly unwelcome because, being miserably underpaid, they took any odd jobs they could get in their off hours, thus competing with unemployed colonists.

Reluctantly, many Americans were beginning to fear that the London authorities had organized a conspiracy to subvert the liberties of all British subjects.

Taxation or Tyranny?

In the eighteenth century the English were universally recognized to be the freest people in the world. In Mozart's opera, *The Abduction from the Seraglio* (1782), when the Turk Osmin tells the kidnapped Blonda that she is his slave, a "gift" from his master, she replies contemptuously: "A slave! I am an Englishwoman, born to freedom." Americans, like their English cousins, attributed their freedom to what they called their balanced government. In Britain power appeared to be shared by the Crown, the House of Lords (representing the aristocracy), and the House of Commons (representing the rest of the realm). The governors, councils, and assemblies seemed to play analogous roles in the colonies.

In reality this balance of separate forces never existed, either in Britain or in America. The apparent harmony of society was in both instances the product of a lack of seriously divisive issues, not of dynamic tension between rival forces. But the new laws seemed to Americans to threaten the balance, and this idea was reinforced by their observations of the corruption of English elections. Benjamin Franklin, being a colonial agent in London, knew British politics well. He complained that the entire country was "at market" and "might be bought . . . by the Devil himself" for about £12 million. A clique seeking unlimited power was trying to destroy balanced government in Britain and in America, or so many colonists thought.

There was no such conspiracy, yet no certain answer can be made to the question, Were American rights actually in danger? Grenville and his successors were English politicians, not tyrants. They looked down on bumptious colonials but surely had no wish to destroy them or their prosperity. The British attitude was like that of a parent making a recalcitrant youngster swallow a bitter medicine: protests were understandable, but in the patient's own interest they must be ignored. Franklin reported one high official in London as saying: "His Majesty's Instructions . . . are the LAW OF THE LAND; *they are*, the Law of the Land, and as such *ought to be* OBEYED."

At the same time, British leaders believed that the time had come to assert royal authority and centralize imperial power at the expense of colonial autonomy. The need to maintain a substantial British army in America to control the western Indians tempted the government to use some of the troops to "control" white Americans as well. This attitude probably had as much to do with the coming of the revolution as any specific act of Parliament because it flew in the face of the reality that the colonies had progressed beyond the "childhood" stage. They were no longer entirely dependent on "the mother country." This did not mean breaking away from the Empire. However, it surely meant dealing with Great Britain on terms approaching equality.

Besides refusing to use stamps, Americans responded to the Stamp Act by boycotting British goods. Nearly a thousand merchants signed nonimportation agreements. These struck British merchants hard in their pocketbooks, and they began to pressure Parliament for repeal. After a hot debate—Grenville, whose ministry had fallen over another issue, advocated using the army to enforce the act—the hated law was repealed in March 1766. In America there was jubilation at the news. The ban on British goods was lifted and the colonists congratulated themselves on having stood fast in defense of principle.

The Declaratory Act

The great controversy over the constitutional relationship of colony to mother country was only beginning. The same day that it repealed the Stamp Act, Parliament passed a Declaratory Act stating that the colonies were "subordinate" and that Parliament could enact any law it wished "to bind the colonies and people of America."

To most Americans this bald statement of parliamentary authority seemed unconstitutional—a flagrant violation of their understanding of how the British imperial system was supposed to work. Actually the Declaratory Act highlighted the degree to which British and American views of the system had drifted apart. The English and the colonials were using the same words but giving them different meanings. Their conflicting definitions of the word *representation* was a case in point. Another involved the word *constitution*, the term that James Otis had used in his attack on writs of assistance. To the British the Constitution meant the totality of laws, customs, and institutions that had developed over time and under which the nation functioned. In America, partly because governments were based on specific charters, the word meant a written document or contract spelling out, and thus limiting, the powers of government. If a law were unconstitutional, it simply had no force.

Even more basic were the differing meanings that English and Americans were giving to the word *sovereignty*. Eighteenth-century English political thinkers believed that sovereignty (ultimate political power) could not be divided. Government and law being based ultimately on force, some "final, unqualified, indivisible" authority had to exist if social order was to be preserved. The Glorious Revolution in England had settled the question of where sovereignty resided—in Parliament. The Declaratory Act, so obnoxious to Americans, seemed to the English the mere explication of the obvious. That colonial governments had passed local laws the English did not deny, but they had done so at the sufferance of the sovereign legislative power, Parliament.

Given these ideas and the long tradition out of which they had sprung, one can sympathize with the British failure to follow the colonists' reasoning (which had not yet evolved into a specific proposal for constitutional reform). But most responsible British officials refused even to listen to the American argument.

The Townshend Duties

Despite the repeal of the Stamp Act, the British did not abandon the policy of taxing the colonies. If direct taxes were inexpedient, indirect ones like the Sugar Act certainly were not. To persuade Parliament to repeal the Stamp Act, some Americans (most notably Benjamin Franklin) had claimed that the colonists objected only to direct taxes.

Therefore, in June 1767, the chancellor of the exchequer, Charles Townshend, introduced a series of levies on glass, lead, paints, paper, and tea imported into the colonies. Townshend was a charming man experienced in colonial administration, but he was something of a playboy (his nickname was Champagne Charlie), and he lacked both integrity and common sense. He liked to think of Americans as ungrateful children; he once said he would rather see the colonies turned into "Primitive Desarts" than treat them as equals.

By this time the colonists were thoroughly on guard, and they responded quickly to the Townshend levies with a new boycott of British goods. In addition they made elaborate efforts to stimulate colonial manufacturing. By the end of 1769 imports from the mother country had been almost halved. Meanwhile, administrative measures enacted along with the Townshend duties were creating more ill will. A Board of Customs Commissioners, with headquarters in Boston, took charge of enforcing the trade laws, and new vice admiralty courts were set up at Halifax, Boston, Philadelphia, and Charleston to handle violations. These courts operated without juries, and many colonists considered the new commissioners rapacious racketeers who systematically attempted to obtain judgments against honest merchants in order to collect the huge forfeitures—one-third of the value of ship and cargo—that were their share of all seizures.

The struggle forced Americans to do some deep thinking about both American and imperial political affairs. The colonies' common interests and growing economic and social interrelationships probably made some kind of union inevitable. Trouble with England speeded the process. In 1765 the Stamp Act Congress (another extralegal organization and thus a further step in the direction of revolution) had brought the delegates of nine colonies to New York. Now, in 1768, the Massachusetts General Court took the next step. It sent the legislatures of the other colonies a "Circular Letter" expressing the "humble opinion" that the Townshend Acts were "Infringements of their natural & constitutional Rights."

The question of the limits of British power in America was much debated, and this too was no doubt inevitable, again because of change and growth. Even in the late seventeenth century the assumptions that led Parliament to pass the Declaratory Act would have been unrealistic. By 1766 they were absurd.

After the passage of the Townshend Acts, John Dickinson, a Philadelphia lawyer, published "Letters from a Farmer in Pennsylvania to the Inhabitants of the British Colonies." Dickinson considered himself a loyal British subject trying to find a solution to colonial troubles. "Let us behave like dutiful children, who have received unmerited blows from a beloved parent," he wrote. Nevertheless, he stated plainly that Parliament had no right to tax the colonies. Another moderate Philadelphian, John Raynell, put it this way: "If the Americans are to be taxed by a Parliament where they are not . . . Represented, they are no longer Englishmen but Slaves."

Some Americans were much more radical than Dickinson. Samuel Adams of Boston, a genuine revolutionary agitator, believed by 1768 that Parliament had no right at all to legislate for the colonies. If few were ready to go that far, fewer still accepted the reasoning behind the Declaratory Act.

The British ignored American thinking. The Massachusetts Circular Letter had been framed in moderate language and clearly reflected the convictions of most of the people in the Bay Colony, yet when news of it reached England, the secretary of state for the colonies, Lord Hillsborough, ordered the governor to dissolve the legislature. Two regiments of British troops were transferred from the frontier to Boston, part of the aforementioned policy of bringing the army closer to the centers of colonial unrest.

The Boston Massacre

These acts convinced more Americans that the British were conspiring to destroy their liberties. Resentment was particularly strong in Boston, where the postwar depression had come on top of two decades of economic stagnation. Crowding 4,000

This portrait is from 1772, when Samuel Adams was furious over the Boston Massacre. The painter was John Singleton Copley. Although his parents were impoverished Irish immigrants, Copley had recently married the daughter of a rich Tory merchant. Did Copley side with his father-in-law, who detested Adams as a tribune of the "mob," or with Adams?

tough British soldiers into a town of 16,000 people, many of them as capable of taking care of themselves when challenged as any Redcoat, was a formula for disorder.

How many brawls and minor riots took place in the waterfront taverns and darkened alleys of the colonial ports that winter is lost to history. In January 1770 scuffles between Liberty Boys and Redcoats in the Golden Hill section of New York City resulted in a number of injuries. Then, in Boston on March 5, 1770, real trouble erupted. Late that afternoon a crowd of idlers began tossing snowballs at a company of Redcoats guarding the Custom House. Some of these missiles had been carefully wrapped around suitably sized rocks. Gradually the crowd increased in size and its mood grew meaner. The soldiers panicked and began firing their muskets. When the smoke cleared, five Bostonians lay dead and dying on the bloody ground.

This so-called Boston Massacre infuriated the populace. The violence played into the hands of radicals like Samuel Adams. But just as at the time of the Stamp Act riots, cooler heads prevailed. Announcing that he was "defending the rights of man and unconquerable truth," John Adams volunteered his services to make sure the soldiers got a fair trial. Most were acquitted; the rest were treated leniently by the standards of the day. In Great Britain, confrontation also gave way to adjustment. In April 1770 all the Townshend duties except a threepenny tax on tea were repealed. The tea tax was maintained as a matter of principle.

A kind of postmassacre truce settled over Boston and the rest of British America. During the next two years no serious crisis erupted. Imports of British goods were nearly 50 percent higher than before the nonimportation agreement. So long as the British continued to be conciliatory, the colonists seemed satisfied with their place in the empire.

The Bloody Massacre perpetrated in ... Street BOSTON on March 5th 1770 by a party of the 29th REGT.

This engraving of the Boston Massacre (1770) became the most reprinted depiction of the event, and probably the most inaccurate. It was done by Paul Revere, engraver, silversmith, and eventual patriot. The British soldiers did not form ranks and fire on command at the crowd. The judge at the subsequent trial of the British soldiers warned jurors not to be influenced by "the prints exhibited in our houses" that added "wings to fancy"—prints, specifically, such as this one. The jury of colonists acquitted all the British soldiers but two, who received mild punishments.

The Pot Spills Over

In 1772 this informal truce ended and new troubles broke out. The first was plainly the fault of the colonists involved. Early in June the British patrol boat *Gaspee* ran aground in Narragansett Bay, south of Providence, while pursuing a suspected smuggler. The *Gaspee*'s commander, Lieutenant Dudingston, had antagonized everyone in the area by his officiousness and zeal; that night a gang of local people boarded the helpless *Gaspee* and put it to the torch. This action was clearly criminal, but when the British attempted to bring the culprits to justice no one would testify against them. The British, frustrated and angry, were strengthened in their conviction that the colonists were utterly lawless.

Then Thomas Hutchinson, now governor of Massachusetts, announced that henceforth the Crown rather than the local legislature would pay his salary. Since control over the salaries of royal officials gave the legislature a powerful hold on them, this development was disturbing. Groups of radicals formed "committees of correspondence" and stepped up communications with one another, planning joint action in case of trouble. This was another monumental step along the road to revolution; an organized colony-wide resistance movement, lacking in any "legitimate" authority but ready to consult and act in the name of the public interest, was taking shape.

The Tea Act Crisis

In the spring of 1773 an entirely unrelated event precipitated the final crisis. The British East India Company held a monopoly of all trade between India and the rest of the empire. This monopoly had yielded fabulous returns, but decades of corruption and inefficiency together with heavy military expenses in recent years had weakened the company until it was almost bankrupt.

Among the assets of this venerable institution were some 17 million pounds of tea stored in English warehouses. The decline of the American market, a result first of the boycott and then of the smuggling of cheaper Dutch tea, partly accounted for the glut. Normally, East India Company tea was sold to English wholesalers. They in turn sold it to American wholesalers, who distributed it to local merchants for sale to the consumer. A substantial British tax was levied on the tea as well as the threepenny Townshend duty. Now Lord North, the new prime minister, decided to remit the British tax and to allow the company to sell directly in America through its own agents. The savings would permit a sharp reduction of the retail price and at the same time yield a nice profit to the company. The Townshend tax was retained, however, to preserve (as Lord North said when the East India Company directors suggested its repeal) the principle of Parliament's right to tax the colonies.

The company then shipped 1,700 chests of tea to colonial ports. Though the idea of high-quality tea offered at bargain prices was tempting, after a little thought nearly everyone in America appreciated the dangers involved in buying it. If Parliament could grant the East India Company a monopoly of the tea trade, it could parcel out all or any part of American commerce to whomever it pleased. More important, the act appeared utterly diabolical, a dastardly trick to trap them into paying the tea tax. The plot seemed obvious: the real price of Lord North's tea was American submission to parliamentary taxation.

Public indignation was so great in New York and Philadelphia that when the tea ships arrived, the authorities ordered them back to England without attempting to unload. The tea could be landed only "under the Protection of the Point of the Bayonet and Muzzle of the Cannon," the governor of New York reported. "Even then," he added, "I do not see how the Sales or Consumption could be effected."

The situation in Boston was different. The tea ship *Dartmouth* arrived on November 27. The radicals, marshaled by Sam Adams, were determined to prevent it from landing its cargo; Governor Hutchinson (who had managed to have two of his sons appointed to receive and sell the tea) was equally determined to collect the tax and enforce the law. For days the town seethed. Crowds milled in the streets, harangued by Adams and his friends, while the *Dartmouth* and two later arrivals swung with the tides on their moorings. Then, on the night of December 16, as Hutchinson was preparing to seize the tea for nonpayment of the duty, a band of colonists disguised as Indians rowed out to the ships and dumped the hated tea chests into the harbor.

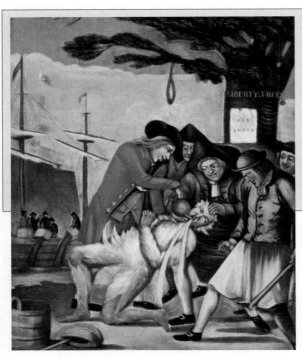

A noose hanging from a "Liberty Tree" reveals this artist's bias: the "tar-and-feathering" of a British official would doubtless culminate in greater violence. As historian Gordon Wood points out, however, the mob actions of the colonists often "grew out of folk festivals and traditional popular rites." A "tar-and-feathering," though painful and occasionally dangerous, was mostly a humiliation. By the early 1770s, though, the mockery was becoming tinged with violence.

The destruction of the tea was a serious crime and it was obvious that a solid majority of the people of Boston approved of it. The painted "Patriots" who jettisoned the chests were a veritable cross-section of society, and a huge crowd gathered at wharfside and cheered them on. The British burned with indignation when news of the "Tea Party" reached London. People talked (fortunately it was only talk) of flattening Boston with heavy artillery. Nearly everyone, even such a self-described British friend of the colonists as Edmund Burke, agreed that the colonists must be taught a lesson. George III himself said, "We must master them or totally leave them to themselves."

What particularly infuriated the British was the certain knowledge that no American jury would render a judgment against the criminals. The memory of the *Gaspee* affair was fresh in everyone's mind in England, as undoubtedly it was in the minds of those Bostonians who, wearing the thinnest of disguises, brazenly destroyed the tea.

From Resistance to Revolution

Parliament responded in the spring of 1774 by passing a series of acts known as the Coercive Acts. The Boston Port Act closed the harbor of Boston to all commerce until its citizens paid for the tea. The Administration of Justice Act provided for the transfer of cases to courts outside Massachusetts when the governor felt that an impartial trial could not be had within the colony. The Massachusetts Government Act revised the colony's charter drastically, strengthening the power of the governor, weakening that of the local town meetings, making the council appointive rather than elective, and changing the method by which juries were selected. These were unwise laws—they cost Great Britain an empire. All of them, and especially the Port Act, were unjust laws as well. Parliament was punishing the entire community for the crimes of individuals. Even more significant, they marked a drastic change in British policy—from legislation and strict administration to treating colonial protesters as criminals, from attempts to persuade and conciliate to coercion and punishment.

The Americans named the Coercive Acts the Intolerable Acts. That the British answer to the crisis was coercion the Americans found unendurable. Although neither the British nor the colonists yet realized it, the American Revolution had begun.

Step by step, in the course of a single decade, a group of separate political bodies, inhabited by people who (if we put aside the slaves who were outside the political system) were loyal subjects of Great Britain, had been forced by the logic of events—by new British policies and by a growing awareness of their common interests—to take political power into their own hands and to unite with one another to exercise that power effectively. Ordinary working people, not just merchants, lawyers, and other well-to-do people, played increasingly more prominent roles in public life as crisis after crisis roused their indignation. This did not yet mean that most Americans wanted to be free from British rule. Nearly every colonist was willing to see Great Britain continue to control, or at least regulate, such things as foreign relations, commercial policy, and other matters of general American interest. Parliament, however—and in the last analysis George III and most Britishers—insisted that their authority over the colonies was unlimited. Behind their stubbornness lay the arrogant psychology of the European: "*Colonists are inferior. . . . We own you.*"

Lord North directed the Coercive Acts at Massachusetts alone because he assumed that the other colonies, profiting from the discomfiture of Massachusetts, would not intervene, and because of the British tendency to think of the colonies as separate units connected only through London. His strategy failed because his assumption was incorrect: the colonies began at once to act in concert.

Extralegal political acts now became a matter of course. In June 1774 Massachusetts called for a meeting of delegates from all the colonies to consider common action. This First Continental Congress met at Philadelphia in September; only Georgia failed to send delegates. Many points of view were represented, but even the so-called conservative proposal, introduced by Joseph Galloway of Pennsylvania, called for a thorough overhaul of the empire. Galloway suggested an *American* government, consisting of a president general appointed by the king and a grand council chosen by the colonial assemblies, that would manage intercolonial affairs and possess a veto over parliamentary acts affecting the colonies.

This was not what the majority wanted. If taxation without representation was tyranny, so was all legislation. Therefore Parliament had no right to legislate in any way for the colonies. John Adams, while prepared to *allow* Parliament to regulate colonial trade, now believed that Parliament had no inherent right to control it. "The foundation . . . of all free government," he declared, "is a right in the people to participate in their legislative council." Americans "are entitled to a free and exclusive power of legislation in their several provincial legislatures."

Propelled by the reasoning of Adams and others, the Congress passed a declaration of grievances and resolves that amounted to a complete condemnation of Britain's actions since 1763. A Massachusetts proposal that the people take up arms to defend their rights was endorsed. The delegates also organized a "Continental Association" to boycott British goods and to stop all exports to the empire. To enforce this boycott, committees were appointed locally "to observe the conduct of all persons touching this association" and to expose violators to public scorn.

If the Continental Congress reflected the views of the majority—there is no reason to suspect that it did not—it is clear that the Americans had decided that drastic changes must be made. It was not merely a question of mutual defense against the threat of British power, not only (in Franklin's aphorism) a matter of hanging together lest they hang separately. A nation was being born.

Looking back many years later, one of the delegates to the First Continental Congress made just these points. He was John Adams of Massachusetts, and he said: "The revolution was complete, in the minds of the people, and the Union of the colonies, before the war commenced."

The furious American resistance to the new taxes baffled British officials. In 1774 Lord North declared that colonial opposition betrayed a "distempered state of turbulence." Some members of Parliament declared that the Americans had gone "stark staring mad" over taxes any reasonable person would pay willingly.

But what had begun as a dispute over taxes had shifted to a struggle over sovereignty. Colonists were not against taxes in principle—and their descendants would willingly (if not happily) pay taxes that most colonists would have regarded as base enslavement. The colonists insisted, however, that they also have a say in their governance. Their "madness," originally manifested in bitter opposition to trade taxes, would become a feverish commitment to war.

1650–1696	Parliament enacts Navigation Acts
1689–1697	King William's War (War of the League of Augsburg)
1699–1750	Parliament enacts laws regulating colonial manufacturing
1702–1713	Queen Anne's War (War of the Spanish Succession): France loses Nova Scotia, Newfoundland, and Hudson Bay to Britain
1733	Molasses Act's duty leads to smuggling
1738–1742	Religious enthusiasm surges during Great Awakening
1740–1748	King George's War (War of the Austrian Succession)
1743	Benjamin Franklin founds American Philosophical Society
1752	Franklin discovers nature of lightning
1754	Albany Congress paves way for Stamp Act Congress and Continental Congress
1754–1763	British and American Colonists fight French and Indians in French and Indian War (Seven Years' War)
1760	George III becomes king of England
1763	George III's Proclamation forbids settlement beyond Appalachians
1764	Sugar Act places tariffs on sugar, coffee, wines, and other imports
1765	Stamp Act places excise taxes on all printed matter, leads to Stamp Tax Congress
1766	Stamp Act is repealed; Declaratory Act asserts parliamentary authority over colonies
1767	Townshend Duties lead to Massachusetts Circular Letter
1770	Five American colonists die in Boston Massacre
1772	Colonists burn *Gaspee*
1773	Tea Act leads to Boston Tea Party
1774	Coercive Acts lead to First Continental Congress

The American Revolution

IN THE SPRING OF 2006, THE SAMUEL ADAMS BREWERY IN BOSTON announced its "Patriot Collection" of beers, each named for a Founding Father. "James Madison Dark Wheat" celebrated James Madison, who so loved beer that he "considered a proposal for a national brewery." "Ginger Honey Ale" was inspired by Thomas Jefferson and his wife, who together "brewed 15 gallons of ginger beer with fresh lemons and honey every two weeks." "George Washington Porter," a blend of aged and freshly brewed ales, honored the father of the nation's favorite beer. "Just as the founding fathers took America's destiny into their hands," the company declared, "so it was with their brewing."

The Founders are so deeply embedded in our culture that their names, in addition to appearing on beer bottles, can be spotted almost everywhere. "Washington" is the name of thirty-one counties and forty-two cities. Iowa and Indiana together have nearly a hundred "Washington" townships; California has twenty-eight "Washington Elementary Schools." After "Main Street," Washington is the most common street name in the United States. Schoolchildren relish his name: Since Washington's birthday was declared a national holiday in 1968, most states have chosen to honor him by keeping students home from school.

Indeed, the Founders now loom so large that it may seem they were invincible, their victory over the British empire a foregone conclusion. But in order for us to understand the American Revolution, we must examine it from the perspective of the past, before the names of the Founders adorned beer bottles and elementary schools, before the United States had become a mighty nation. The simple truth is that the American Revolution was accomplished by men and women who did not know whether they would succeed. At the outset, they did not even know whether they sought British concessions or independence, whether most colonists would side with them or remain loyal to His Majesty's government, whether foreign powers such as France could be enlisted to provide support, whether rebellion against political authority in London would undermine social order in America, or whether the many different peoples of the colonies could be knitted into a single nation. The revolutionaries did know, however, that if they failed they would likely face arrest, imprisonment, and even death.

As the colonial rebellion transformed into a full-scale war for independence, the colonists faced the challenges of creating and financing an army that could succeed against the Empire. In the midst of fighting, and in the wake of freedom from British rule, they faced an even greater challenge—the founding of a new nation, with a new government and a new national spirit.

The Shot Heard Round the World

The actions of the First Continental Congress led the British authorities to force a showdown with their bumptious colonial offspring. "The New England governments are in a state of rebellion," George III announced. "Blows must decide whether they are to be subject to this country or independent." General Thomas Gage, veteran of Braddock's ill-fated expedition against Fort Duquesne and now commander-in-chief of all British forces in North America, had already been appointed governor of Massachusetts. Some 4,000 Redcoats were concentrated in Boston, camped on the town common once peacefully reserved for the citizens' cows.

Parliament echoed with demands for a show of strength in America. After the Tea Party the general impression was that resistance to British rule was concentrated in Massachusetts. Based on the behavior of colonial militia in the French and Indian War, most Britishers did not think people in the other colonies would be inclined to fight outside their own region. General James Grant announced that with 1,000 men he "would undertake to go from one end of America to the other, and geld all the males, partly by force and partly by a little coaxing." Some opposed the idea of crushing the colonists, and others believed that it could not be easily managed, but they were a small minority. The House of Commons listened to Edmund Burke's magnificent speech on conciliating the colonies and then voted 270 to 78 against him.

The London government decided to use troops against Massachusetts in January 1775, but the order did not reach General Gage until April. In the interim both sides were active. Parliament voted new troop levies and declared Massachusetts to be in a state of rebellion. The Massachusetts Patriots, as they were now calling themselves, formed an extralegal provincial assembly, reorganized the militia, and began training "Minute Men" and other fighters. Soon companies armed with anything that would shoot were drilling on town commons throughout Massachusetts and in other colonies too.

When Gage received his orders on April 14, he acted swiftly. The Patriots had been accumulating arms at Concord, some 20 miles west of Boston. On the night of April 18, Gage dispatched 700 crack troops to seize these supplies. The Patriots were prepared. Paul Revere and other horsemen rode off to alert the countryside and warn John Hancock and Sam Adams, leaders of the provincial assembly, whose arrests had been ordered.

When the Redcoats reached Lexington early the next morning, they found the common occupied by about seventy Minute Men. After an argument, the Americans began to withdraw. Then someone fired a shot. There was a flurry of gunfire and the Minute Men fled, leaving eight of their number dead. The British then marched on to Concord, where they destroyed whatever supplies the Patriots had been unable to carry off.

But militiamen were pouring into the area from all sides. A hot skirmish at Concord's North Bridge forced the Redcoats to yield that position. Becoming alarmed, they began to march back to Boston. Soon they were being subjected to a withering fire from American irregulars along their line of march. A strange battle developed on a "field" 16 miles long and only a few hundred yards wide. Gage was obliged to send out an additional 1,500 soldiers, and total disaster was avoided only by deploying skirmishers to root out snipers hiding in barns and farmhouses along the road to Boston. When the first day of the Revolutionary War ended, the British had sustained 273 casualties, the Americans fewer than 100. "The Rebels are not the despicable rabble too many have supposed them to be," General Gage admitted.

For a brief moment of history tiny Massachusetts stood alone at arms against an empire that had humbled France and Spain. Yet Massachusetts assumed the offensive! The provincial government organized an expedition that captured Fort Ticonderoga and Crown Point, on Lake Champlain. The other colonies rallied quickly to the cause, sending reinforcements to Cambridge. When news of the battle reached Virginia, George Washington wrote sadly, "A brother's sword has been sheathed in a brother's breast and the once happy and peaceful plains of America are either to be drenched in blood or inhabited by a race of slaves." And then he added: "Can a virtuous man hesitate in his choice?"

Two weeks after the battle of Lexington and Concord, Ralph Earl, a colonial militiaman from Connecticut, was ordered to make sketches and paintings of what had transpired. Earl revisited the battlefield and interviewed those who had fought. He was an accurate painter. Note that each of the British formations, facing officers, contains exactly twenty-five men.

The Second Continental Congress

On May 10, 1775, the day Ticonderoga fell, the Second Continental Congress met in Philadelphia. It was a distinguished group, more radical than the First Congress. Besides John and Sam Adams, Patrick Henry and Richard Henry Lee of Virginia, and Christopher Gadsden of South Carolina, all holdovers from the First Congress, there was Thomas Jefferson, a lanky, sandy-haired young planter from Virginia. Jefferson had recently published "A Summary View of the Rights of British America," an essay criticizing the institution of monarchy and warning George III that "kings are the servants, not the proprietors of the people." The Virginia convention had also sent George Washington, who knew more than any other colonist about commanding men and who wore his buff-and-blue colonel's uniform, a not-too-subtle indication of his willingness to place this knowledge at the disposal of the Congress. The renowned Benjamin Franklin was a delegate, moving rapidly to the radical position.

The Boston merchant John Hancock was chosen president of the Congress, which, like the first, had no legal authority. Yet the delegates had to make agonizing decisions under the pressure of rapidly unfolding military events, with the future of every American depending on their actions. Delicate negotiations and honeyed words might yet persuade king and Parliament to change their ways, but precipitate, bold effort was essential to save Massachusetts.

In this predicament the Congress naturally dealt first with the military crisis. It organized the forces gathering around Boston into the so-called Continental Army and appointed George Washington commander-in-chief. After Washington and his staff left for Massachusetts on June 23, the Congress turned to the task of requisitioning men and supplies.

The Battle of Bunker Hill

Meanwhile, in Massachusetts, the first major battle of the war had been fought. The British position on the peninsula of Boston was impregnable to direct assault, but high ground north and south, at Charlestown and Dorchester Heights, could be used to pound the city with artillery. When the Continentals seized Bunker Hill and Breed's Hill at Charlestown and set up defenses on the latter, Gage determined at once to drive them off. This was accomplished on June 17. Twice the Redcoats marched in close ranks, bayonets fixed, up Breed's Hill, each time being driven back after suffering heavy losses. Stubbornly they came again, and this time they carried the redoubt, for the defenders had run out of ammunition.

The British then cleared the Charlestown peninsula, but the victory was really the Americans', for they had proved themselves against professional soldiers and had exacted a terrible toll. More than 1,000 Redcoats had fallen in a couple of hours, out of a force of some 2,500, while the Continentals lost only 400 men, most of them cut down by British bayonets after the hill was taken. "The day ended in glory," a British officer wrote, "but the loss was uncommon in officers for the number engaged."

The Battle of Bunker Hill, as it was called for no good reason, greatly reduced whatever hope remained for a negotiated settlement. The spilling of so much blood left each side determined to force the other's submission. The British recalled General Gage, replacing him with General William Howe, a respected veteran of the French and Indian War, and George III formally proclaimed the colonies to be "in open rebellion." The Continental Congress dispatched one last plea to the king (the Olive Branch Petition), but this was a sop to the moderates. Immediately thereafter it adopted the Declaration of the Causes and Necessity of Taking Up Arms, which condemned everything the British had done since 1763. Americans were "a people attacked by unprovoked enemies"; the time had come to choose between "submission" to "tyranny" and "resistance by force." The Congress then ordered an attack on Canada and created committees to seek foreign aid and to buy munitions abroad. It authorized the outfitting of a navy under Commodore Esek Hopkins of Rhode Island.

The Great Declaration

The Congress (and the majority of the people) still hung back from a break with the Crown. To declare for independence would be to burn the last bridge, to become traitors in the eyes of the mother country. Aside from the word's ugly associations, everyone knew what happened to traitors when their efforts failed. It was sobering to think of casting off everything that being English meant: love of king, the traditions of a great nation, pride in the power of a mighty empire. "Where shall we find another Britain?" John Dickinson had asked at the time of the Townshend Acts crisis. "Torn from the body to which we are united by religion, liberty, laws, affections, relation, language and commerce, we must bleed at every vein."

Then, too, rebellion might end in horrors worse than submission to British tyranny. The disturbances following the Stamp Act and the Tea Act had revealed an alarming fact about American society. The organizers of those protests, mostly persons of wealth and status, had thought in terms of "ordered resistance." They countenanced violence only as a means of forcing the British authorities to pay attention to their complaints. But protest meetings and mob actions had brought thousands of ordinary citizens into the struggle for local self-government. Some of the upper-class leaders among the Patriots, while eager to have their support, were concerned about what they would make of actual independence. In addition, not all the property that had been destroyed belonged to Loyalists and British officials. Too much exalted talk about "rights" and "liberties" might well give the poor (to say nothing of the slaves) an exaggerated impression of their importance.

Finally, in a world where every country had some kind of monarch, could common people *really* govern themselves? The most ardent defender of American rights might well hesitate after considering all the implications of independence.

Yet independence was probably inevitable by the end of 1775. The belief that George III had been misled by evil or stupid advisers on both sides of the Atlantic became progressively more difficult to sustain. Mistrust of Parliament—indeed, of the whole of British society—grew apace.

Two events in January 1776 pushed the colonies a long step toward a final break. First came the news that the British were sending hired Hessian soldiers to fight against them. Colonists associated mercenaries with looting and rape and feared that the German-speaking Hessians would run amok among them. Such callousness on the part of Britain made reconciliation seem out of the question.

The second decisive event was the publication of *Common Sense*. This tract was written by Thomas Paine, a one-time English corsetmaker and civil servant turned pamphleteer, a man who had been in America scarcely a year. *Common Sense* called boldly for complete independence. It attacked not only George III but the idea of monarchy itself. Paine applied the uncomplicated logic of the zealot to the recent history of America. Where the colonists had been humbly petitioning George III and swallowing their resentment when he ignored them, Paine called George a "Royal Brute" and "the hardened sullen-tempered Pharaoh of England." Many Americans had wanted to control their own affairs but feared the instability of un-tried republican government. To them Paine said: "We have it in our power to be-gin the world again." "A government of our own is our natural right," he insisted. "O! ye that love mankind! Ye that dare oppose not only tyranny but the tyrant, stand forth!"

The tone of the debate changed sharply as Paine's slashing attack took effect. In March 1776 the Congress unleashed privateers against British commerce; in April it opened American ports to foreign shipping; in May it urged the Patriots who had set up extralegal provincial conventions to frame constitutions and estab-lish state governments.

On June 7 Richard Henry Lee of Virginia introduced a resolution of the Virginia Convention:

> RESOLVED: *That these United Colonies are, and of right ought to be, free and in-dependent States, that they are absolved from all allegiance to the British Crown, and that all political connection between them and the State of Great Britain is, and ought to be, totally dissolved.*

This momentous resolution was not passed until July 2; the Congress first ap-pointed a committee consisting of Thomas Jefferson, Benjamin Franklin, John Adams, Roger Sherman, and Robert Livingston to frame a suitable justification of independence.

Thomas Jefferson was probably placed on the committee because politics re-quired that a Virginian be included and because of his literary skill and general in-telligence. Aside from writing *A Summary View of the Rights of British America*, he had done little to attract notice. At age 33 he was the youngest member of the Continental Congress and was only marginally interested in its deliberations. He had been slow to take his seat in the fall of 1775, and he had gone home to Virginia before Christmas. He put off returning several times and arrived in Philadelphia

Debating the Past

WAS THE AMERICAN REVOLUTION ROOTED IN CLASS STRUGGLE?

This 1795 engraving by John Trumbull of a Stamp Act protest delineates a class division. The three British Tories—one is suspended, the others are sprawled below—are wealthy. They wear wigs, stockings, and breeches; one has buckles on his shoes. The Patriots wear cloth hats, pants, and shoes with laces. Historian Carl Becker (1909) declared that the Revolution was fought "not only about home rule but also about who should rule at home." In his view, leaders of the Revolution sought not only to defeat the Crown in England but also the rabble in Boston and New York—the Patriots as depicted in the picture above. Arthur Schlesinger Sr. (1918) wrote that commercial elites "instigated" popular opposition to British policies, grew alarmed at the "engulfing tide of radicalism" that led to war, and then turned against the farmers and workers who did most of the fighting. Edmund Morgan (1956) rejected the notion that the Revolution grew out of class divisions. It did not constitute a victory of the rich over the poor, but "a union of three million cantankerous colonists into a new nation." Historians during the tumultuous 1960s underscored the divisions in American society. Gary B. Nash (1989) showed how declining opportunities had radicalized urban workers. Other social historians found yet other cleavages: Mary Beth Norton (1996) between men and women; Sylvia R. Frey (1991) between masters and slaves; Colin Calloway (1995) between colonists and Indians.

Carl Becker, *History of Political Parties in the Province of New York* (1909), Arthur M. Schlesinger Sr., *The Colonial Merchants and the American Revolution* (1918), Edmund Morgan, *The Birth of the Republic* (1956), Gary B. Nash, *The Urban Crucible* (1989), Mary Beth Norton, *Founding Mothers and Fathers* (1996), Sylvia R. Frey, *Water from the Rock* (1991), Colin Calloway, *American Revolution in Indian Country* (1995).

only on May 14. Had he delayed another month, someone else would have written the Declaration of Independence.

The committee asked Jefferson to prepare a draft. The result, with a few amendments made by Franklin and Adams and somewhat toned down by the whole Congress, was officially adopted by the delegates on July 4, 1776, two days after the delegates had voted for the decisive break with Great Britain.

Jefferson's Declaration of Independence (see the text of the document in the Appendix, pp. A-3–A-5) consisted of two parts. The first, introductory part justified the abstract right of any people to revolt and described the theory on which the Americans based their creation of a new, republican government. The second, much longer section was a list of the "injuries and usurpations" of George III, a bill of indictment explaining why the colonists felt driven to exercise the rights outlined in the first part of the document. Here Jefferson stressed the monarch's interference with the functioning of representative government in America, his harsh administration of colonial affairs, his restrictions on civil rights, and his maintenance of troops in the colonies without their consent.

Jefferson sought to marshal every possible evidence of British perfidy, and he made George III, rather than Parliament, the villain because the king was the personification of the nation against which America was rebelling. He held the monarch responsible for Parliament's efforts to tax the colonies and restrict their trade, for many actions by subordinates that George III had never deliberately authorized, and for some things that never happened. He even blamed the king for the existence of slavery in the colonies, a charge the Congress cut from the document not entirely because of its concern for accuracy. The long bill of particulars reads more like a lawyer's brief than a careful analysis, but it was intended to convince the world that the Americans had good reasons for exercising their right to form a government of their own.

This 1857 painting depicts the destruction of a statue of King George III during the Revolution. This rendering purges the "mob" action of its menacing violence: the arm gestures are celebratory rather than threatening, and the women and children are well-to-do. This is a middle-class view of the American Revolution, bloodless, public-spirited, and consensual.

Jefferson's general statement of the right of revolution has inspired oppressed peoples all over the world for more than 200 years:

> We hold these truths to be self-evident, that all men are created equal, that they are endowed by their Creator with certain unalienable Rights, that among these are Life, Liberty and the pursuit of Happiness. That to secure these rights, Governments are instituted among Men, deriving their just powers from the consent of the governed, That whenever any Form of Government becomes destructive of these ends, it is the Right of the People to alter or to abolish it, and to institute new Government. . . .

The Declaration was intended to influence foreign opinion, but its proclamation had little immediate effect outside Great Britain, and there it only made people angry and determined to subdue the rebels. A substantial number of European military men offered their services to the new nation, and a few of these might be called idealists, but most were adventurers and soldiers of fortune, thinking mostly of their own advantage. Why, then, has the Declaration had so much influence on modern history? Not because the thought was original with Jefferson. As John Adams later pointed out—Adams viewed his great contemporary with a mixture of affection, respect, and jealousy—the basic idea was commonplace among eighteenth-century liberals. "I did not consider it any part of my charge to invent new ideas," Jefferson explained, "but to place before mankind the common sense of the subject, in terms so plain and firm as to command their assent. . . . It was intended to be an expression of the American mind."

Revolution was not new, but the spectacle of a people solemnly explaining and justifying their right, in an orderly manner, to throw off their oppressors and establish a new system on their own authority was almost without precedent. Soon the French would be drawing on this example in their revolution, and rebels everywhere have since done likewise. And if Jefferson did not create the concept, he gave it a nearly perfect form.

1776: The Balance of Forces

A formal declaration of independence merely cleared the way for tackling the problems of founding a new nation. Lacking both traditions and authority based in law, the Congress had to create political institutions and a new national spirit, all in the midst of war.

Always the military situation took precedence, for a single disastrous setback might make everything else meaningless. At the start the Americans already possessed their lands (except for the few square miles occupied by British troops). Although thousands of colonists fought for George III, the British soon learned that to put down the American rebellion they would have to bring in men and supplies from bases on the other side of the Atlantic. This was a most formidable task.

Certain long-run factors operated in America's favor. Although His Majesty's soldiers were brave and well disciplined, the army was as inefficient and ill directed

A 1797 engraving of Deborah Sampson, the first woman to serve as a soldier in the Revolution. Born in 1760, Sampson in 1782 put on men's clothes and enlisted in the Massachusetts Militia under the name of Timothy Thayer. Her imposture was discovered and she was expelled. She then enlisted as Robert Shurtlieff in the Continental army. At a battle against Loyalists at Tarrytown, New York, she was wounded in the thigh. Rather than let a doctor treat her—and discover her gender—she extracted the musket ball herself. After the war, she continued to wear men's clothing until she married and had children.

as the rest of the British government. Whereas nearly everyone in Great Britain wanted to crack down on Boston after the Tea Party, many boggled at engaging in a full-scale war against all the colonies. Aside from a reluctance to spill so much blood, there was the question of expense. Finally, the idea of dispatching the cream of the British army to America while powerful enemies on the Continent still smarted from past defeats seemed risky. For all these reasons the British approached gingerly the task of subduing the rebellion. When Washington fortified Dorchester Heights overlooking Boston, General Howe withdrew his troops to Halifax rather than risk another Bunker Hill.

For a time, the initiative remained with the Americans. An expedition under General Richard Montgomery captured Montréal in November 1775, and another small force under Benedict Arnold advanced to the gates of Québec after a grueling march across the wilderness from Maine. Montgomery and Arnold attempted to storm the Québec defenses on December 31, 1775, but were repulsed with heavy losses. Even so, the British troops in Canada could not drive the remnants of the American army—perhaps 500 men in all—out of the province until reinforcements arrived in the spring.

Awareness of Britain's problems undoubtedly spurred the Continental Congress to the bold actions of the spring of 1776. However, on July 2, 1776, the same day that Congress voted for independence, General Howe was back on American soil, landing in force on Staten Island in New York harbor in preparation for an assault on the city. Soon Howe had at hand 32,000 well-equipped troops and a powerful fleet commanded by his brother, Richard, Lord Howe. If the British controlled New York City and the Hudson River, they could, as Washington realized, "stop intercourse between the northern and southern Colonies, upon which depends the Safety of America."

Suddenly the full strength of the empire seemed to have descended on the Americans. Superior British resources (a population of 9 million to the colonies' 2.5 million, large stocks of war materials and the industrial capacity to boost them further, mastery of the seas, a well-trained and experienced army, a highly centralized and, when necessary, ruthless government) were now all too evident.

The demonstration of British might in New York harbor accentuated American military and economic weaknesses: Both money and the tools of war were continually in short supply in a predominantly agricultural country. Many of Washington's soldiers were armed with weapons no more lethal than spears and tomahawks. Few had proper uniforms. Even the most patriotic resisted conforming to the conventions of military discipline; the men hated drilling and all parade-ground formality. And all these problems were complicated by the fact that Washington had to create an army organization out of whole cloth at the same time that he was fighting a war.

Supply problems were handled inefficiently and often corruptly. Few officers knew much about such mundane but vital matters as how to construct and maintain proper sanitary facilities when large numbers of soldiers were camped at one place for extended periods of time. What was inelegantly known as "the itch" afflicted soldiers throughout the war.

Loyalists

Behind the lines, the country was far from united. Whereas nearly all colonists had objected to British policies, many still hesitated to take up arms against the mother country. Even Massachusetts harbored many Loyalists, or Tories, as they were called; about a thousand Americans left Boston with General Howe, abandoning their homes rather than submit to the rebel army.

No one knows exactly how the colonists divided on the question of independence. John Adams's off-the-cuff estimate was that a third of the people were ardent Patriots, another third loyal to Great Britain, and the rest neutral or tending to favor whichever side seemed to be winning. This guess is probably as useful as any, although in keeping with Adams's character he may have understated the number who agreed with him and overstated those opposed to his position. Most historians think that about a fifth of the people were Loyalists and about two-fifths Patriots, but there are few hard figures to go by. What is certain is that large elements, perhaps a majority of the people, were more or less indifferent to the conflict or, in Tom Paine's famous phrase, were summer soldiers and sunshine patriots—they supported the Revolution when all was going well and lost their enthusiasm in difficult hours.

The divisions cut across geographical, social, and economic lines. A high proportion of those holding royal appointments and many Anglican clergymen remained loyal to King George, as did numbers of merchants with close connections in Britain. There were important pockets of Tory strength in rural sections of New

York, in the North Carolina backcountry, and among persons of non-English origin and other minority groups who tended to count on London for protection against the local majority.

The Tories lacked organization. While Patriot leaders worked closely together, many of the Tory "leaders" did not even know one another. They had no central committee to lay plans or coordinate their efforts. When the revolutionaries took over a colony, some Tories fled; others sought the protection of the British army; others took up arms; and still others accommodated themselves silently to the new regime.

If the differences separating Patriot from Loyalist are unclear, feelings were nonetheless bitter. Individual Loyalists were often set upon by mobs, tarred and feathered, and otherwise abused. Some were thrown into jail for no legitimate reason; others were exiled and their property confiscated. Battles between Tory units and the Continental Army were often exceptionally bloody. "Neighbor was against neighbor, father against son and son against father," one Connecticut Tory reported. "He that would not thrust his own blade through his brother's heart was called an infamous villain."

Early British Victories

General Howe's campaign against New York brought to light another American weakness—the lack of military experience. Washington, expecting Howe to attack New York, had moved south to meet the threat immediately after Howe had abandoned Boston. But both he and his men failed badly in this first major test. Late in August Howe crossed from Staten Island to Brooklyn. In the Battle of Long Island he easily outflanked and defeated Washington's army. Had he acted decisively, he could probably have ended the war on the spot, but Howe could not make up his mind whether to be a peacemaker or a conqueror. This hesitation in consolidating his gains permitted Washington to withdraw his troops to Manhattan Island.

Howe could still have trapped Washington simply by using his fleet to land troops on the northern end of Manhattan; instead he attacked New York City directly, leaving the Americans an escape route to the north. Again Patriot troops proved no match for British regulars. Although Washington threw his hat to the ground in a rage and threatened to shoot cowardly Connecticut soldiers as they fled the battlefield, he could not stop the rout and had to fall back on Harlem Heights in upper Manhattan. Yet once more Howe failed to pursue his advantage promptly.

Still, Washington refused to see the peril in remaining on an island while the enemy commanded the surrounding waters. Only when Howe shifted a powerful force to Westchester, directly threatening his rear, did Washington move north to the mainland. Finally, after several narrow escapes, he crossed the Hudson River and marched south to New Jersey, where the British could not use their naval superiority against him.

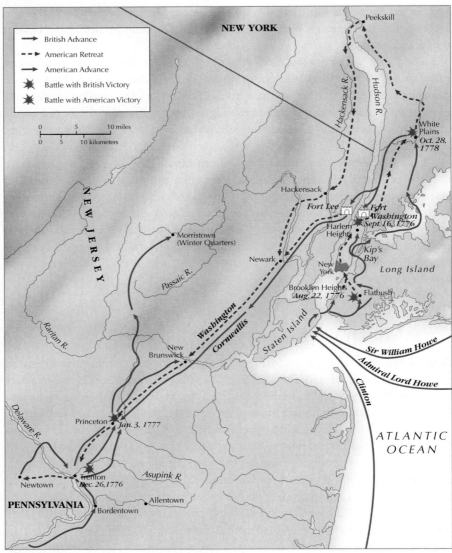

New York and New Jersey Campaigns, 1776–1777

The battles in and around New York City seemed to presage an easy British triumph. Yet somehow Washington salvaged a moral victory from these ignominious defeats. He learned rapidly; seldom thereafter did he place his troops in such vulnerable positions. And his men, in spite of repeated failure, had become an army. In November and December 1776 they retreated across New Jersey and into Pennsylvania. General Howe then abandoned the campaign, going into winter quarters in New York but posting garrisons at Trenton, Princeton, and other strategic points.

The troops at Trenton were hated Hessian mercenaries, and Washington decided to attack them. He crossed the ice-clogged Delaware River with 2,400 men on Christmas night during a wild storm. The little army then marched nine miles to Trenton, arriving at daybreak in the midst of a sleet storm. The Hessians were taken by surprise. Those who could fled in disorder; the rest—900 of them—surrendered.

The Hessians were first-class professional soldiers, probably the most competent troops in Europe at that time. The victory gave a boost to American morale. A few days later Washington outmaneuvered General Cornwallis, who had rushed to Trenton with reinforcements, and won another battle at Princeton. These engagements had little strategic importance, since both armies then went into winter quarters. Without them, however, there might not have been an army to resume the war in the spring.

Saratoga and the French Alliance

When spring reached New Jersey in April 1777, Washington had fewer than 5,000 men under arms. Great plans—far too many and too complicated, as it turned out—were afoot in the British camp. The strategy called for General John Burgoyne to lead a large army from Canada down Lake Champlain toward Albany while a smaller force under Lieutenant Colonel Barry St. Leger pushed eastward toward Albany from Fort Oswego on Lake Ontario. General Howe was to lead a third force north up the Hudson. The Patriots would be trapped and the New England states isolated from the rest.

As a venture in coordinated military tactics, the British campaign of 1777 was a fiasco. General Howe had spent the winter in New York wining and dining his officers and prominent local Loyalists and having a torrid affair with the wife of the

The British generals were criticized at home for their losses during the Revolutionary War. This 1779 cartoon shows a British commander in America relaxing in his command tent while his defeated colleagues surrender at Saratoga.

officer in charge of prisoners of war. He was less attentive to his responsibilities for the British army advancing south from Canada.

General "Gentleman Johnny" Burgoyne, a charming if somewhat bombastic character, part politician, part poet, part gambler, part ladies' man, yet also a brave soldier, had begun his march from Canada in mid-June. By early July his army, which consisted of 500 Indians, 650 Loyalists, and 6,000 regulars, had captured Fort Ticonderoga at the southern end of Lake Champlain. He quickly pushed beyond Lake George but then bogged down. Burdened by a huge baggage train that included 138 pieces of generally useless artillery, more than thirty carts laden with his personal wardrobe and supply of champagne, and his mistress, he could advance at but a snail's pace through the dense woods north of Saratoga.[1] Patriot militia impeded his way by felling trees across the forest trails.

St. Leger was also slow in carrying out his part of the grand design. He did not leave Fort Oswego until July 26, and when he stopped to besiege a Patriot force at Fort Stanwix, General Benedict Arnold had time to march west with 1,000 men from the army resisting Burgoyne and drive him back to Oswego.

Meanwhile, with magnificent disregard for the agreed-on plan, Howe wasted time trying to trap Washington into exposing his army in New Jersey. This enabled Washington to send some of his best troops to buttress the militia units opposing Burgoyne. Then, just when St. Leger was setting out for Albany, Howe took the bulk of his army off by sea to attack Philadelphia, leaving only a small force commanded by General Sir Henry Clinton to aid Burgoyne.

When Washington moved south to oppose Howe, the Britisher taught him a series of lessons in tactics, defeating him at the Battle of Brandywine, then luring him out of position and moving unopposed into Philadelphia. But by that time it was late September, and disaster was about to befall General Burgoyne.

The American forces under Philip Schuyler and later under Horatio Gates and Benedict Arnold had erected formidable defenses immediately south of Saratoga. Burgoyne struck at this position twice and was thrown back both times with heavy losses. Each day more local militia swelled the American forces. Soon Burgoyne was under siege, his troops pinned down by withering fire from every direction, unable even to bury their dead. The only hope was General Clinton, who had finally started up the Hudson from New York. Clinton got as far as Kingston, about 80 miles below Saratoga, but on October 16 he decided to return to New York for reinforcements. The next day, at Saratoga, Burgoyne surrendered. Some 5,700 British prisoners were marched off to Virginia.

This overwhelming triumph changed the course and character of the war. France would probably have entered the war in any case; the country had never reconciled itself to its losses in the Seven Years' War and for years had been build-

---

[1]*Many soldiers, enlisted men as well as officers, were accompanied by their wives or other women on campaigns. More than 2,000 accompanied the Burgoyne expedition. At one point Washington complained of "the multitude of women . . . especially those who are pregnant, or have children [that] clog upon every movement." Actually, women in eighteenth-century armies worked hard, doing most of the cooking, washing, and other "housekeeping" tasks.*

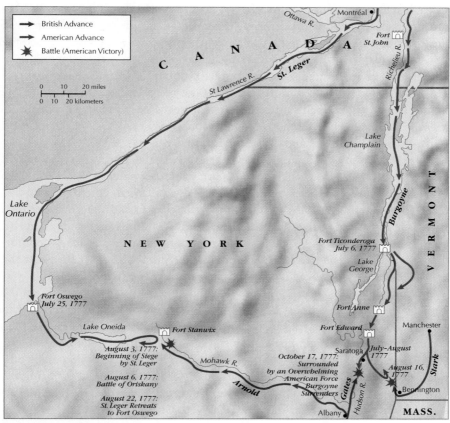

Legend:
- → British Advance
- → American Advance
- ✳ Battle (American Victory)

CANADA

Ottawa R.

Montréal

Fort St. John

Richelieu R.

St Lawrence R.

St. Leger

Lake Champlain

Burgoyne

Lake Ontario

VERMONT

NEW YORK

Fort Ticonderoga July 6, 1777

Lake George

Fort Oswego July 25, 1777

Fort Stanwix

Fort Anne

Fort Edward

Manchester

Lake Oneida

August 3, 1777: Beginning of Siege by St. Leger

Mohawk R.

Saratoga July–August 1777

Arnold

October 17, 1777: Surrounded by an Overwhelming American Force Burgoyne Surrenders

Gates

Hudson R.

Stark

August 16, 1777

Bennington

August 6, 1777: Battle of Oriskany

August 22, 1777: St. Leger Retreats to Fort Oswego

Albany

MASS.

Saratoga Campaign, September 19–October 17, 1777

ing a navy capable of taking on the British. Helping the Americans was simply another way of weakening their British enemy. As early as May 1776 the Comte de Vergennes, France's foreign minister, had persuaded Louis XVI to authorize the expenditure of 1 million livres for munitions for America, and more was added the next year. Spain also contributed, not out of sympathy for the Revolution but because of its desire to injure Great Britain. Soon vital supplies were being funneled secretly to the rebels through a dummy company, Roderigue Hortalez et Cie. When news of the victory at Saratoga reached Paris, the time seemed ripe and Louis XVI recognized the United States. Then Vergennes and three American commissioners in Paris, Benjamin Franklin, Arthur Lee, and Silas Deane, drafted a commercial treaty and a formal treaty of alliance. The two nations agreed to make "common cause and aid each other mutually" should war "break out" between France and Great Britain. Meanwhile, France guaranteed "the sovereignty and independence absolute and unlimited" of the United States. The help of Spain and France, Washington declared, "will not fail of establishing the Independence of America in a short time."

When the news of Saratoga reached England, Lord North realized that a Franco-American alliance was almost inevitable. To forestall it, he was ready to give in on all the issues that had agitated the colonies before 1775. Both the Coercive Acts and the Tea Act would be repealed; Parliament would pledge never to tax the colonies.

Instead of implementing this proposal promptly, Parliament delayed until March 1778. Royal peace commissioners did not reach Philadelphia until June, a month after Congress had ratified the French treaty. The British proposals were icily rejected, and while the peace commissioners were still in Philadelphia, war broke out between France and Great Britain.

The American Revolution, however, had yet to be won. After the loss of Philadelphia, Washington had settled his army for the winter at Valley Forge, 20 miles to the northwest. The army's supply system collapsed. Often the men had nothing to eat but "fire cake," a mixture of ground grain and water molded on a stick or in a pan and baked in a campfire. According to the Marquis de Lafayette, one of many Europeans who volunteered to fight on the American side, "the unfortunate soldiers . . . had neither coats, nor hats, nor shirts, nor shoes; their feet and legs froze till they grew black, and it was often necessary to amputate them."

To make matters worse, there was grumbling in Congress over Washington's failure to win victories and talk of replacing him as commander-in-chief with Horatio Gates, the "hero" of Saratoga. (In fact, Gates was an indifferent soldier, lacking in decisiveness and unable to instill confidence in his subordinates.)

As the winter dragged on, the Continental Army melted away. So many officers resigned that Washington was heard to say that he was afraid of "being left Alone with the Soldiers only." Since enlisted men could not legally resign, they deserted by the hundreds. Yet the army survived. Gradually the soldiers who remained became a tough, professional fighting force.

The War Moves South

Spring brought a revival of American hopes in the form of more supplies, new recruits, and, above all, word of the French alliance. In May 1778 the British replaced General Howe as commander with General Clinton, who decided to transfer his base back to New York. While Clinton was moving across New Jersey, Washington attacked him at Monmouth Court House. The fight was inconclusive, but the Americans held the field when the day ended and were able to claim a victory.

Thereafter British strategy changed. Fighting in the northern states degenerated into skirmishes and other small-unit clashes. Instead, relying on sea power, the supposed presence of many Tories in the South, and the possibility of obtaining the help of slaves, the British concentrated their efforts in South Carolina and Georgia. Savannah fell to them late in 1778, and most of the settled parts of Georgia were overrun during 1779. In 1780 Clinton led a massive expedition against Charleston. When the city surrendered in May, more than 3,000 soldiers were captured, the most overwhelming American defeat of the war. Leaving General Cornwallis and some 8,000 men to carry on the campaign, Clinton then sailed back to New York.

The Tories in South Carolina and Georgia came closer to meeting British expectations than in any other region, but the callous behavior of the British troops persuaded large numbers of hesitating citizens to join the Patriot cause. Guerrilla bands led by Francis Marion, the "Swamp Fox," Thomas Sumter, after whom Fort Sumter, famous in the Civil War, was named, and others like them provided a nucleus of resistance in areas that had supposedly been subdued.

But the tide soon turned. In 1779 the Spanish governor of Louisiana, José de Gálvez, administered a stinging defeat to British troops in Florida, and in 1780 and 1781 he captured the British-held Gulf ports of Pensacola and Mobile. More important, in June 1780 Congress placed Horatio Gates in charge of a southern army consisting of the irregular militia units and a hard core of Continentals transferred from Washington's command. Gates encountered Cornwallis at Camden, South Carolina. Foolishly, he entrusted a key sector of his line to untrained militiamen, who panicked when the British charged with fixed bayonets. Gates suffered heavy losses and had to fall back. Congress then recalled him, sensibly permitting Washington to replace him with General Nathanael Greene, a first-rate officer.

A band of militiamen had trapped a contingent of Tories at King's Mountain and forced its surrender. Greene, avoiding a major engagement with Cornwallis's superior numbers, divided his troops and staged a series of raids on scattered points. In January 1781, at the Battle of Cowpens in northwestern South Carolina, General Daniel Morgan inflicted a costly defeat on Colonel Banastre Tarleton, one of Cornwallis's most effective officers. Cornwallis pursued Morgan hotly, but the American rejoined Greene, and at Guilford Court House they again inflicted heavy losses on the British. Then Cornwallis withdrew to Wilmington, North Carolina, where he could rely on the fleet for support and reinforcements. Greene's Patriots quickly regained control of the Carolina backcountry.

Victory at Yorktown

Seeing no future in the Carolinas and unwilling to vegetate at Wilmington, Cornwallis marched north into Virginia, where he joined forces with troops under Benedict Arnold. (Disaffected by what he considered unjust criticism of his generalship, Arnold had sold out to the British in 1780. He intended to betray the bastion of West Point on the Hudson River. The scheme was foiled when incriminating papers were found on the person of a British spy, Major John André. Arnold fled to the British and André was hanged.) As in the Carolina campaign, the British had numerical superiority at first but lost it rapidly when local militia and Continental forces concentrated against them. Cornwallis soon discovered that Virginia Tories were of little help in such a situation. "When a Storm threatens, our friends disappear," he grumbled.

General Clinton ordered Cornwallis to establish a base at Yorktown, where he could be supplied by sea. It was a terrible mistake. The British navy in American waters far outnumbered American and French vessels, but the Atlantic is wide, and in those days communication was slow. The French had a fleet in the West Indies under Admiral François de Grasse and another squadron at Newport, Rhode Island,

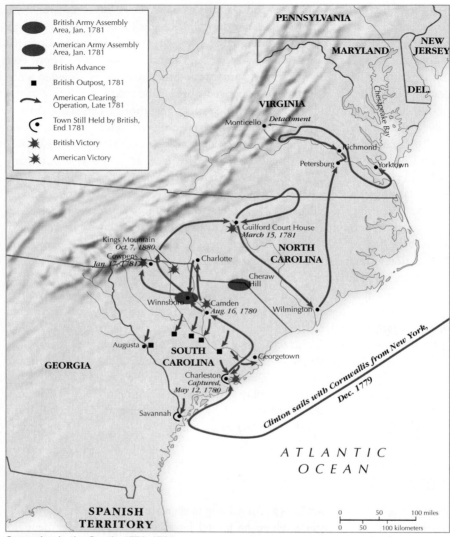

Legend
- British Army Assembly Area, Jan. 1781
- American Army Assembly Area, Jan. 1781
- British Advance
- British Outpost, 1781
- American Clearing Operation, Late 1781
- Town Still Held by British, End 1781
- British Victory
- American Victory

PENNSYLVANIA

MARYLAND

NEW JERSEY

DEL.

Chesapeake Bay

VIRGINIA

Monticello   *Detachment*

Richmond

Petersburg   Yorktown

Guilford Court House
March 15, 1781

Kings Mountain
Oct. 7, 1880

Cowpens
Jan. 17, 1781   Charlotte

NORTH CAROLINA

Cheraw Hill

Winnsboro   Camden
Aug. 16, 1780   Wilmington

Augusta

SOUTH CAROLINA

Georgetown

GEORGIA

Charleston
Captured, May 12, 1780

Savannah

Clinton sails with Cornwallis from New York, Dec. 1779

ATLANTIC OCEAN

SPANISH TERRITORY

0   50   100 miles
0   50   100 kilometers

Campaign in the South, 1779–1781

where a French army was stationed. In the summer of 1781 Washington, de Grasse, and the Comte de Rochambeau, commander of French land forces, designed and carried out with an efficiency unparalleled in eighteenth-century warfare a complex plan to bottle up Cornwallis.

The British navy in the West Indies and at New York might have forestalled this scheme had it moved promptly and in force. But Admiral Sir George Rodney sent only part of his Indies fleet. As a result, de Grasse, after a battle with a British fleet commanded by Admiral Thomas Graves, won control of the Chesapeake and cut Cornwallis off from the sea.

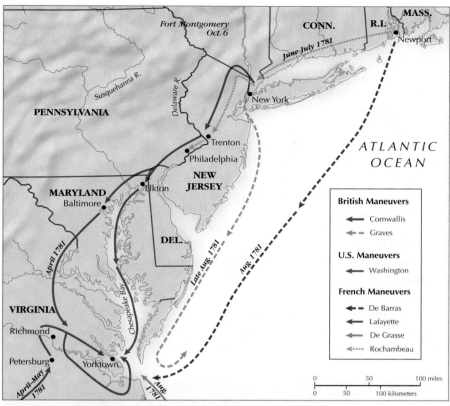

The Yorktown Campaign, April–September 1781

The next move was up to Washington, and this was his finest hour as a commander. He desperately wanted to attack the British base at New York, but at the urging of Rochambeau he agreed instead to strike at Yorktown. After tricking Clinton into thinking he was heading for New York, he pushed boldly south. In early September he reached Yorktown and joined up with an army commanded by Lafayette and troops from de Grasse's fleet. He soon had nearly 17,000 French and American veterans in position.

Cornwallis was helpless. He held out until October 17 and then asked for terms. Two days later more than 7,000 British soldiers marched out of their lines and laid down their arms. Then the jubilant Lafayette ordered his military band to play "Yankee Doodle."

Negotiating a Favorable Peace

The British gave up trying to suppress the rebellion after Yorktown, but the event that confirmed the existence of the United States as an independent nation was the signing of a peace treaty with Great Britain.

The Continental Congress appointed John Adams, Benjamin Franklin, John Jay, Thomas Jefferson, and Henry Laurens as a commission to conduct peace talks in Paris, France. Franklin and Jay did most of the actual negotiating. Congress, grateful for French aid during the Revolution, had instructed the commissioners to rely on the advice of the Comte de Vergennes. In Paris, however, the commissioners soon discovered that Vergennes was not the perfect friend of America that Congress believed him to be. He was, after all, a French official, and France had other interests far more important than concern for its American ally. Vergennes "means to keep his hand under our chin to prevent us from drowning," Adams complained, "but not to lift our head out of the water."

Franklin, whose fame as a scientist and sage had spread to Europe, was wined and dined by the cream of Paris and petted and fussed over by some of the city's most beautiful women. He did not press the American point of view as forcefully as he might have. But this was because he took the long view, which was to achieve a true reconciliation with the British, not simply to drive the hardest bargain possible. John Jay was somewhat more tough-minded. But on basic issues all the Americans were in agreement.

By the end of November 1782 a preliminary treaty had been signed. "His Britannic Majesty," Article 1 began, "acknowledges the said United States . . . to be free, sovereign and independent States." Other terms were equally in line with American hopes and objectives. The boundaries of the nation were set at the Great

The surrender of Cornwallis at Yorktown on October 19, 1781, painted by John Trumbull in 1820. In 1789 Trumbull, who had served as an aide to Washington, wrote to Thomas Jefferson that he wanted to make paintings "to preserve and diffuse the memory of the noblest series of actions which have e'er presented themselves to the history of man"—the American Revolution. The next year he went to London to study painting with Benjamin West; he was promptly arrested as an American spy. Fortunately, West had made connections with King George III and managed to spare Trumbull from the gallows.

Lakes, the Mississippi River, and 31° north latitude (roughly the northern boundary of Florida, which the British turned over to Spain).[2] Britain recognized the right of Americans to take fish on the Grand Banks off Newfoundland and, far more important, to dry and cure their catch on unsettled beaches in Labrador and Nova Scotia. The British agreed to withdraw their troops from American soil "with all convenient speed." On the touchy problem of Tory property seized during the Revolution, the Americans agreed only that Congress would "earnestly recommend" that the states "provide for the restitution of all estates, rights and properties which have been confiscated." They promised to prevent further property confiscation and prosecutions of Tories—certainly a wise as well as a humane policy—and they agreed not to impede the collection of debts owed British subjects. Vergennes was flabbergasted by the success of the Americans. "The English buy the peace more than they make it," he wrote. "Their concessions . . . exceed all that I should have thought possible."

The American commissioners obtained these favorable terms because they were shrewd diplomats and because of the rivalries that existed among the great European powers. In the last analysis, Britain preferred to have a weak nation of English-speaking people in command of the Mississippi Valley rather than France or Spain.

From their experience at the peace talks, the American leaders learned the importance of playing one power against another without committing themselves completely to any. This policy demanded constant contact with European affairs and skill at adjusting policies to changes in the European balance of power. It enabled the United States, a young and relatively feeble country, to grow and prosper.

National Government Under the Articles of Confederation

Independence was won on the battlefield and at the Paris Peace Conference, but it could not have been achieved without the work of the Continental Congress and the new state governments. The delegates recognized that the Congress was essentially a legislative body rather than a complete government and from the start they struggled to create a workable central authority. But their effort was handicapped by much confusion and bickering, and early military defeats sapped their energy and morale. In July 1776 John Dickinson prepared a draft national constitution, but it could not command much support. The larger states objected to equal representation of all the states, and the states with large western land claims refused to cede them to the central government. It was not until

(text continues on page 150)

---

[2]*Much of this vast region, of course, was controlled not by the British but by various Indian tribes.*

The Patriot

As the opening credits roll, Benjamin Martin (played by Mel Gibson) pries open a wooden box. It contains yellowing papers, a few medals and a tomahawk. He lifts the tomahawk, fingers its handle gingerly, and stares at the blade. "I had long feared that my sins would revisit me," a voice intones, "and the cost is more than I can bear." The viewer suspects—rightly, it turns out—that Martin's sins were violent, and that they had something to do with hacking people apart. But at the outset of *The Patriot*, Hollywood's $100-million blockbuster on the American Revolution, Martin is more pacifist than patriot. When the South Carolina legislature votes to go to war with Great Britain, he publicly declares that his chief obligation is to his family: "I will not fight."

He soon changes his mind after the British capture Charleston (1780), which brings onto the scene a villainous British cavalry officer, Colonel Tavington. Ordered by General Cornwallis to subdue the insurrection in the countryside, Tavington ransacks plantations, forces slaves into the King's service, and hounds the rebel militia. He also arrests Gabriel (Heath Ledger), Martin's oldest son, and orders the boy's execution as a spy. When Gabriel's younger brother tries to intervene, Tavington shoots the boy dead. Overcome with rage, Martin races to his room, grabs the hatchet, and proceeds to bury it—repeatedly—into the chests and skulls of countless British soldiers. He takes command of the militia, recruits more Patriots, and harries the British at every turn.

Mel Gibson as a Patriot leader with Jason Isaacs as Colonel Tavington, a barbarous British officer.

Tavington responds by intensifying his campaign against the rebels. His culminating barbarity is to round up the villagers of Wakefield (including Gabriel's fiancé), herd them into a church, and set it ablaze. All perish in unimaginable (and mercifully unfilmed) agony. Martin checks his rage long enough to plot the defeat of Cornwallis's army. This occurs at the Battle of Cowpens, where the militia holds its position despite being blasted by British artillery and decimated by repeated fusillades. When Tavington leads a cavalry charge, Martin's eyes widen and he reaches for the tomahawk. Tavington dies at Martin's hands, and Cornwallis is routed, too; the latter's subsequent surrender at Yorktown is now a foregone conclusion.

Historians have found much to criticize in the movie's retelling of the war in the South. There was no such person as Benjamin Martin, though elements of his story can be found in the exploits of guerrilla leaders such as Francis Marion ("the Swamp Fox"), Thomas Sumter, Andrew Pickens, and General Daniel Morgan, who commanded the Continentals at Cowpens. Although the British cavalry wear red uniforms in the movie, they were known as the Green Dragoons for a reason that seemingly eluded the filmmakers. The movie's version of the Battle of Cowpens featured a glorious display of fireworks, though neither army's artillery in South Carolina was capable of firing explosive shells. Cornwallis was not humiliated at Cowpens because he was not there. In the movie the British are caricatured as either evil geniuses or bungling twits; and the Patriots, as big-hearted rogues or pious patriarchs. The real combatants doubtless adhered less predictably to type. The most serious deviation from the historical record was the incineration of the occupied church: there is no record of any such event. "*The Patriot* is to history what Godzilla was to biology," declared historian David Hackett Fischer.

However, *The Patriot* raises and thoughtfully addresses an important historical issue: How can any society reconcile peaceable virtues—love for family, neighborliness, cooperation—with the violence of war? In *The Patriot*, the dilemma is symbolized by

148

Colonel Banastre Tarleton, on whom Tavington was based.

Martin's tomahawk. This weapon helps free his captured son and vanquish the evil Tavington; and yet it is also a manifestation of Martin's savage, even pathological, rage. Martin's secret shame, alluded to in the opening scene, was his dismembering corpses after a particularly brutal battle during the French and Indian War.

Eighteenth-century Europeans were in fact preoccupied with reconciling the violence of war with the need for social order. Their particular refinement of the military arts was the ordered massing of musket fire. The technology of warfare required intense discipline; and the new penchant for order imposed seeming coherence upon the chaos of the battlefield.

The Patriot provides a vivid rendering of this juxtaposition. Soldiers in beautifully colored uniforms march in straight, regular columns to the steady cadence of drums while officers bark precise commands: "Circle right. Face forward. Lift weapons . . ." These stately preliminaries, depicted on ripening fields beneath a summer sun, provide an unsettling backdrop for the ensuing violence: volleys of musket fire shatter the formations; low-velocity cannon balls decapitate soldiers; and bayonets pierce their chests.

Martin concludes that the British cannot be defeated in this type of battle. And they seldom were. Martin advocates guerrilla tactics, as did many southern Patriot militiamen. The British had good reason to doubt the legitimacy of this type of warfare. When men went wild on the battlefield, or fired shots and then hid among civilians, they were criminals, not soldiers. If such behavior were condoned, warfare would become barbarity.

The movie develops this point at considerable length. During a truce, Martin confers with Cornwallis, who complains that the

Patriot militia aimed at officers at the beginning of battles. Such behavior was inconsistent with "civilized warfare." The movie's debate over the nature of "civilized" warfare parallels an ongoing debate at the time. At the outset of the war, British officers took an oath affirming the British Articles of War, which protected citizens and soldiers who had surrendered. The American Congress also adopted the British Articles of War as the basis for discipline and military justice. But with the outbreak of guerrilla warfare in the South, both sides frequently ignored these rules.

"Colonel Tavington" was obviously based on Banastre Tarleton, the actual commander of the Green Dragoons. Tarleton became notorious after his soldiers raped three plantation women and killed several militiamen who had surrendered. This behavior worried Cornwallis, who sent a dispatch that, while commending his subordinate's courage and zeal, also included a warning: "Use your utmost endeavors to prevent the troops under your command from committing irregularities." In a subsequent engagement at Waxhaws, however, Tarleton again lost control of his men, who stabbed and slashed vanquished foes. An American officer discovered that the American corpses at Waxhaws had each received, on the average, sixteen wounds.

British and American officers sought to affirm that the war could be civilized. But such high-minded notions were repeatedly subverted during tomahawk-wielding guerrilla warfare and by excessively zealous commanders. The question then remained, as it does today, whether unchecked aggression is, among soldiers, a virtue or a vice. *The Patriot* raises these issues but does not resolve them. Martin, surely, should have kept his tomahawk in its locked box; but if he had, would the Patriots have won?

149

Questions for Discussion

- Do you think that the justice of a cause warrants the use of violence to attain it?
- Was guerrilla warfare in the South morally justified?
- In general, how can filmmakers contribute to understanding the past? How are they likely to alter the past to suit cinematic purposes?

November 1777 that the Articles of Confederation were submitted to the states for ratification. The approval of all the states was required before the Articles could go into effect. All acted fairly promptly but Maryland, which did not ratify the document until 1781.

The Articles merely provided a legal basis for authority that the Continental Congress had already been exercising. Each state, regardless of size, was to have but one vote; the union it created was only a "league of friendship." Article 2 defined the limit of national power: "Each state retains its sovereignty, freedom, and independence, and every Power, jurisdiction, and right, which is not by this confederation expressly delegated to the United States, in Congress assembled." Time proved this an inadequate arrangement, chiefly because the central government lacked the authority to impose taxes and had no way of enforcing the powers it did have.

Financing the War

In practice, Congress and the states carried on the war cooperatively. General officers were appointed by Congress, lesser ones locally. The Continental Army, the backbone of Washington's force, was supported by Congress. The states raised militia chiefly for short-term service. Militiamen fought well at times but often proved unreliable, especially when asked to fight at any great distance from their homes. Washington continually fretted about their "dirty mercenary spirit" and their "intractable" nature, yet he could not have won the war without them.

The fact that Congress's requisitions of money often went unhonored by the states does not mean that the states failed to contribute heavily to the war effort. Altogether they spent about $5.8 million in hard money, and they met Congress's demands for beef, corn, rum, fodder, and other military supplies. In addition, Congress raised large sums by borrowing. Americans bought bonds worth between $7 and $8 million during the war. Foreign governments lent another $8 million, most of this furnished by France. Congress also issued more than $240 million in paper money, the states over $200 million more. This currency fell rapidly in value, resulting in an inflation that caused hardship and grumbling. The people, in effect, paid much of the cost of the war through the depreciation of their savings, but it is hard to see how else the war could have been financed, given the prejudice of the populace against paying taxes to fight a war against British taxation.

At about the time the Articles of Confederation were ratified, Congress established Departments of Foreign Affairs, War, and Finance, with individual heads responsible to it. The most important of the new department heads was the superintendent of finance, Robert Morris, a Philadelphia merchant. When Morris took office, the Continental dollar was worthless, the system of supplying the army chaotic, the credit of the government exhausted. He set up an efficient method of obtaining food and uniforms for the army, persuaded Congress to

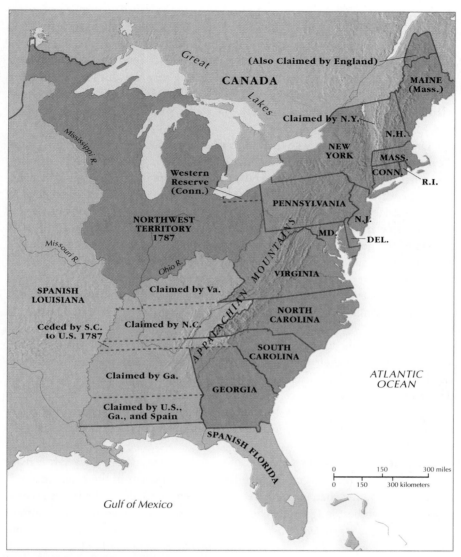

The United States Under the Articles of Confederation, 1787
New York and Virginia gave up their claims to the vast area that became the Northwest Territory and thus set a precedent for trans-Appalachian land policy. By 1802 the various state claims had been ceded to the national government. The original Northwest Territory (the Old Northwest) was bounded by the Ohio River, the Mississippi, and the Great Lakes.

charter a national Bank of North America, and aided by the slackening of military activity after Yorktown, got the country back on a hard money basis. New foreign loans were obtained, partly because Morris's efficiency and industry inspired confidence.

State Republican Governments

However crucial the role of Congress, in an important sense the real revolution occurred when the individual colonies broke their ties with Great Britain. Using their colonial charters as a basis, the states began framing new constitutions even before the Declaration of Independence. By early 1777 all but Connecticut and Rhode Island, which continued under their colonial charters well into the nineteenth century, had taken this decisive step.

On the surface the new governments were not drastically different from those they replaced. The most significant change was the removal of outside control, which had the effect of making the governments more responsive to public opinion. Gone were the times when a governor could be appointed and maintained in office by orders from London. The new constitutions varied in detail, but all provided for an elected legislature, an executive, and a system of courts. In general the powers of the governor and of judges were limited, the theory being that elected rulers no less than those appointed by kings were subject to the temptations of authority, that, as one Patriot put it, all men are "tyrants enough at heart." The typical governor had no voice in legislation and little in appointments. Pennsylvania went so far as to eliminate the office of governor, replacing it with an elected council of twelve.

Power was concentrated in the legislature, which the people had come to count on to defend their interests. In addition to the lawmaking authority exercised by the colonial assemblies, the state constitutions gave the legislatures the power to declare war, conduct foreign relations, control the courts, and perform many other essentially executive functions. While continuing to require that voters be property owners or taxpayers, the constitution makers remained suspicious even of the legislature.

They rejected the British concept of virtual representation. They saw legislators as representatives, that is, agents reflecting the interests of the voters of a particular district rather than superior persons chosen to decide public issues according to their own best judgment. Where political power was involved, the common American principle was every man for himself, but also everyone for the nation, the republic. People were no longer subjects, but citizens, *parts* of government, obedient to its laws, but not blindly subordinate to governmental authority epitomized in the monarch.

A majority of the constitutions contained bills of rights (such as the one George Mason wrote for Virginia) protecting the people's civil liberties against all branches of the government. In Britain such guarantees checked only the Crown; the Americans invoked them against their elected representatives as well.

The state governments combined the best of the British system, including its respect for status, fairness, and due process, with the uniquely American stress on individualism and a healthy dislike of too much authority. The idea of drafting written frames of government—contracts between the people and their representatives that carefully spelled out the powers and duties of the latter—grew out of the experience of the colonists after 1763, when the vagueness of the unwritten British constitution had caused so much controversy, and from the compact principle, the heart of republican government as described so eloquently in the Declaration of Independence. This constitutionalism represented one of the most important innovations of the Revolutionary era: a peaceful method for altering the political system. In the midst of violence, the states changed their frames of government in an orderly, legal manner—a truly remarkable achievement that became a beacon of hope to reformers all over the world. The states' example, the Reverend Simeon Howard of Massachusetts predicted, "will encourage the friends and rouse a spirit of liberty through other nations."

Social Reform

Many states seized the occasion of constitution making to introduce important political and social reforms. In Pennsylvania, Virginia, North Carolina, and other states the seats in the legislature were reapportioned in order to give the western districts their fair share. Primogeniture, entail (the right of an owner of property to prevent heirs from ever disposing of it), and quitrents were abolished wherever they had existed. Steps toward greater freedom of religion were taken, especially in states where the Anglican Church had enjoyed a privileged position. In Virginia the movement to separate church and state was given the force of law by Jefferson's Statute of Religious Liberty, enacted in 1786. "Our civil rights have no dependence on our religious opinions, any more than our opinions in physics or geometry," the statute declared. "Truth is great and will prevail if left to herself."

Many states continued to support religion; Massachusetts did not end public support of Congregational churches until the 1830s. But after the Revolution the states usually distributed the money roughly in accordance with the numerical strength of the various Protestant denominations.

A number of states moved tentatively against slavery. In attacking British policy after 1763, colonists had frequently claimed that Parliament was trying to make slaves of them. No less a personage than George Washington wrote in 1774: "We must assert our rights, or submit to every imposition, that can be heaped upon us, till custom and use shall make us tame and abject slaves." However exaggerated the language, such reasoning led to denunciations of slavery, often vague but significant in their effects on public opinion. The fact that practically every important thinker of the European Enlightenment (Montesquieu, Voltaire, Diderot, and Rousseau in France, David Hume, Samuel Johnson, and Adam Smith in England, to name the most important) had criticized slavery on moral and economic grounds also had an impact on educated opinion. Then, too, the forthright statements in the Declaration of Independence about liberty and equality seemed impossible to reconcile with slaveholding. "How is it," asked Dr. Johnson, who opposed independence vehemently, "that we hear the loudest yelps for liberty among the drivers of negroes?"

The war opened direct paths to freedom for some slaves. In November 1775 Lord Dunmore, the royal governor of Virginia, proclaimed that all slaves "able and willing to bear arms" for the British would be liberated. In fact, the British treated slaves as captured property, seizing them by the thousands in their campaigns in the South. The fate of these blacks is obscure. Some ended up in the West Indies, still slaves. Others were evacuated to Canada and liberated, and some of them settled the British colony of Sierra Leone in West Africa, founded in 1787. Probably many more escaped from bondage by running away during the confusion accompanying the British campaigns in the South.

About 5,000 blacks served in the Patriot army and navy. Most black soldiers were assigned noncombat duties, but there were some black soldiers in every major battle from Lexington to Yorktown.

Beginning with Pennsylvania in 1780, the northern states all did away with slavery. In most cases slaves born after a certain date were to become free on reaching maturity. Since New York did not pass a gradual emancipation law until 1799 and New Jersey not until 1804, there were numbers of slaves in the so-called free states well into the nineteenth century—more than 3,500 as late as 1830. But the institution was on its way toward extinction. All the states prohibited the importation of slaves from abroad, and except for Georgia and South Carolina, the southern states passed laws removing restrictions on the right of individual owners to free their slaves. The greatest success of voluntary emancipation came in Virginia, where, between 1782 and 1790, as many as 10,000 blacks were freed.

These advances encouraged foes of slavery to hope that the institution would soon disappear. But slavery died only where it was not economically important. Except for owners whose slaves were "carried off" by the British, only in Massachusetts, where the state supreme court ruled slavery unconstitutional in 1783, were owners deprived of existing slaves against their will.

Despite the continuing subordination of blacks, there is no question that the Revolution permanently changed the tone of American society. In the way they dressed, in their manner of speech, and in the way they dealt with one another in public places, Americans paid at least lip service to the idea of equality.

After the publication of Common Sense and the Declaration of Indepen- dence, with their excoriations of that "Royal Brute," King George III, it became fashionable to denounce the granting of titles of nobility, all "aristocrats," and any privilege based on birth. In 1783 a group of army officers founded a fraternal organization, the Society of Cincinnati. Although the revered George Washington was its president, many citizens found the mere existence of a club restricted to officers alarming; the fact that membership was to be hereditary, passing on the death of a member to his oldest son, caused a furor.

Nevertheless, little of the social and economic upheaval usually associated with revolutions occurred, before, during, or after 1776. At least part of the urban violence of the period (just how large a part is difficult to determine at this distance) had no social objective. America had its share of criminals, mischievous youths eager to flex their muscles, and other people unable to resist the temptation to break the law when it could be done without much risk of punishment. Certainly there was no wholesale proscription of any class, faith, or profession.

The property of Tories was frequently seized by the state governments, but almost never with the idea of redistributing wealth or providing the poor with land. While some large Tory estates were broken up and sold to small farmers, others passed intact to wealthy individuals or to groups of speculators. The war disrupted many traditional business relationships. Some merchants were unable to cope with the changes; others adapted well and grew rich. But the changes occurred without regard for the political beliefs or social values of either those who profited or those who lost.

During the war, conflicts erupted over economic issues involving land and taxation, yet no single class or interest triumphed in all the states or in the national government. In Pennsylvania, where the western radical element was strong, the constitution was extremely democratic; in Maryland and South Carolina the conservatives maintained control handily. Throughout the country, many great landowners were ardent Patriots, but others became Tories—and so did many small farmers.

Finally, the new governments became more responsive to public opinion, no matter what the particular shape of their political institutions. This was true principally because *Common Sense*, the Declaration of Independence, and the experience of participating in a revolution had made people conscious of their rights in a republic and of their power to enforce those rights. Conservatives swiftly discovered that state constitutions designed to insulate legislators and officials from popular pressures were ineffective when the populace felt strongly about any issue.

Effects of the Revolution on Women

In the late eighteenth century there was a trend in the Western world, barely perceptible at the time, toward increasing the legal rights of women. This movement was strengthened in America by the events leading up to the break with Great Britain and still more by the Declaration of Independence. When Americans began to think and talk about the rights of the individual and the evils of arbitrary rule, subtle effects on relations between the sexes followed. For example, it became somewhat easier for women to obtain divorces. In colonial times divorces were relatively rare, but easier for men to obtain than for women. After the Revolution the difference did not disappear, but it became considerably smaller. In Massachusetts, before the 1770s no woman is known to have obtained a divorce on the ground of her husband's adultery. Thereafter, successful suits by wives against errant husbands were not unusual. In 1791 a South Carolina judge went so far as to say that the law protecting "the absolute dominion" of husbands was "the offspring of a rude and barbarous age." The "progress of civilization," he continued, "has tended to ameliorate the condition of women, and to allow even to wives, something like personal identity."

As the tone of this "liberal" opinion indicates, the change in male attitudes that took place in America because of the Revolution was small. Courts in New York and Massachusetts refused to take action against Tory women whose husbands

Abigail Adams, in asking her husband John to "remember the ladies" when reforming society, was not advocating political rights for women. Rather, she wanted fairer treatment for women within the family. "Do not put such unlimited power into the hands of the husbands," she wrote him. "Remember all men would be tyrants if they could."

were Tories on the ground that it was the duty of women to obey their husbands, and when John Adams's wife Abigail warned him in 1776 that if he and his fellow rebels did not "remember the ladies" when reforming society, the women would "foment a Rebellion" of their own, he treated her remarks as a joke. Adams believed that voting (and as he wrote on another occasion, writing history) was "not the Province of the Ladies."[3]

However, the war effort increased the influence of women in several ways. With so many men in uniform, women took over the management of countless farms, shops, and businesses, and they became involved in the handling of other day-to-day matters that men had normally conducted. Their experiences made both them and in many cases their fathers and husbands more aware of their ability to take on all sorts of chores previously considered exclusively masculine in character. At the same time, women wanted to contribute to the winning of independence, and their efforts to do so made them conscious of their importance. Furthermore, the rhetoric of the Revolution, with its stress on liberty and equality, affected women in the same way that it caused many whites of both sexes to question the morality of slavery.

---

[3]*Adams's distaste for women historians may have been based on the fact that in his friend Mercy Otis Warren's History of the Rise, Progress, and Termination of the American Revolution (1805) Warren claimed that Adams sometimes allowed his "prejudices" to distort his judgment.*

Attitudes toward the education of women also changed because of the Revolution. According to the best estimates, at least half the white women in America could not read or write as late as the 1780s. In a land of opportunity like the United States, women seemed particularly important, not only because they themselves were citizens, but because of their role in training the next generation. "You distribute 'mental nourishment' along with physical," one orator told the women of America in 1795. "The reformation of the world is in your power. . . . The solidity and stability of your country rest with you." The idea of female education began to catch on. Schools for girls were founded, and the level of female literacy gradually rose.

Growth of a National Spirit

The growth of American nationalism was an important result of the Revolution. Most modern revolutions have been *caused* by nationalism and have *resulted* in independence. In the case of the American Revolution, the desire to be free antedated any intense national feeling. The colonies entered into a political union not because they felt an overwhelming desire to bring all Americans under one rule but because unity offered the only hope of winning a war against Great Britain. That they remained united after throwing off British rule reflects the degree to which nationalism had developed during the conflict.

By the middle of the eighteenth century the colonists had begun to think of themselves as a separate society distinct from Europe and even from Britain. Benjamin Franklin described himself not as a British subject but as "an American subject of the King," and in 1750 a Boston newspaper could urge its readers to drink "American" beer in order to free themselves from being "beholden to Foreigners" for their alcoholic beverages. Little political nationalism existed before the Revolution, however, in part because most people knew little about life outside their own colony. When a delegate to the first Continental Congress mentioned "Colonel Washington" to John Adams soon after the Congress met, Adams had to ask him who this "Colonel Washington" was. He had never heard the name before.

The new nationalism arose from a number of sources and expressed itself in different ways. Common sacrifices in war certainly played a part; the soldiers of the Continental Army fought in the summer heat of the Carolinas for the same cause that had led them to brave the ice floes of the Delaware in order to surprise the Hessians. Such men lost interest in state boundary lines; they became Americans.

The war caused many people to move from place to place. Soldiers traveled as the tide of war fluctuated; so too—far more than in earlier times—did prominent leaders. Members of Congress from every state had to travel to Philadelphia; in the process they saw much of the country and the people who inhabited it. Listening to their fellows and serving with them on committees almost inevitably broadened these men, most of them highly influential in their local communities.

With its thirteen stars and thirteen stripes representing the states, the American flag symbolized national unity and reflected the common feeling that such a symbol was necessary. Yet the flag had separate stars and stripes; local interests and local loyalties remained extremely strong, and these could be divisive when conflicts of interest arose.

Certain practical problems that demanded common solutions also drew the states together. No one seriously considered having thirteen postal systems or thirteen sets of diplomatic representatives abroad. Every new diplomatic appointment, every treaty of friendship or commerce signed, committed all to a common policy and thus bound them more closely together. And economic developments had a unifying effect. Deprived of English goods, Americans manufactured more things themselves, stimulating both interstate trade and national pride.

The Great Land Ordinances

The lands west of the Appalachians, initially a source of dispute, became a force for unity once they had been ceded to the national government. Everyone realized what a priceless national asset they were, and all now understood that no one state could determine the future of the West.

The politicians argued hotly about how these lands should be developed. Some advocated selling the land in township units in the traditional New England manner to groups or companies; others favored letting individual pioneers stake out farms in the helter-skelter manner common in the colonial South. The decision was a compromise. The Land Ordinance of 1785 provided for surveying western territories into 6-mile-square townships before sale. Every other township was to be further subdivided into thirty-six sections of 640 acres (1 square mile) each. The land was sold at auction at a minimum price of $1 an acre. The law favored speculative land-development companies, for even the 640-acre units were far too large and expensive for the typical frontier family. But the fact that the land was to be surveyed and sold by the central government was a nationalizing force. It ensured orderly development of the West and simplified the task of defending the frontier in the event of Indian attack. Congress set aside the sixteenth section of every township for the maintenance of schools, another farsighted decision.

Still more significant was the Northwest Ordinance of 1787, which established governments for the West. As early as 1775 settlers in frontier districts were petitioning Congress to allow them to enter the Union as independent states, and in 1780 Congress had resolved that all lands ceded to the nation by the existing states should be "formed into distinct republican States" with "the same rights of sovereignty, freedom and independence" as the original thirteen. In 1784 a committee headed by Thomas Jefferson worked out a plan for doing this, and in 1787 it was enacted into law. The area bounded by the Ohio, the Mississippi, and the Great Lakes was to be carved into not fewer than three or more than five territories. Until the adult male population of the entire area reached 5,000, it was to be ruled by a governor and three judges, all appointed by Congress. When 5,000 men of voting age had settled in the territory, the Ordinance authorized them to elect a legislature,

The Land Ordinance of 1785 called for surveying and dividing the Western Territories into one-mile square mile subdivisions—640 acres. These were further subdivided and sold as 40-acre tracts. Few pieces of legislation have left a more visible imprint upon the landscape. Nowadays the Midwest, as seen from an airplane, resembles a patchwork quilt of 40-acre squares, like this section of Kansas.

which could send a nonvoting delegate to Congress. Finally, when 60,000 persons had settled in any one of the political subdivisions, it was to become a state. It could draft a constitution and operate in any way it wished, save that the government had to be "republican" and that slavery was prohibited.

Seldom has a legislative body acted more wisely. That the western districts must become states everyone conceded from the start. The people had had their fill of colonialism under British rule, and the rebellious temper of frontier settlers made it impossible even to consider maintaining the West in a dependent status. (When North Carolina ceded its trans-Appalachian lands to the United States in 1784, the settlers there, uncertain how they would fare under federal rule, hastily organized an extralegal state of Franklin, and it was not until 1789 that the national government obtained control.) But it would have been unfair to turn the territories over to the firstcomers, who would have been unable to manage such large domains and would surely have taken advantage of their priority to dictate to later arrivals. A period of tutelage was necessary, a period when the "mother country" must guide and nourish its growing offspring.

The system worked well and was applied to nearly all the regions absorbed by the nation as it advanced westward. Together with the Ordinance of 1785, which branded its checkerboard pattern on the physical shape of the West, this law gave the growing country a unity essential to the growth of a national spirit.

National Heroes

The Revolution further fostered nationalism by giving the people their first commonly revered heroes. Benjamin Franklin was widely known before the break with Great Britain through his experiments with electricity, his immensely successful *Poor Richard's Almanack,* and his invention of the Franklin stove. His staunch support of the Patriot cause, his work in the Continental Congress, and his diplomatic successes in France, where he was extravagantly admired, added to his fame. Franklin demonstrated, to Europeans and to Americans themselves, that not all Americans need be ignorant rustics.

Washington, however, was "the chief human symbol of a common Americanism." Stern, cold, a man of few words, the great Virginian did not seem a likely candidate for hero worship. "My countenance never yet revealed my feelings," he himself admitted. Yet he had qualities that made people name babies after him and call him "the Father of His Country" long before the war was won: his personal sacrifices in the cause of independence, his integrity, and above all, perhaps, his obvious desire to retire to his Mount Vernon estate (for many Americans feared any powerful leader and worried lest Washington seek to become a dictator).

As a general, Washington was not a brilliant strategist like Napoleon. Neither was he a tactician of the quality of Caesar or Robert E. Lee. But he was a remarkable organizer and administrator—patient, thoughtful, conciliatory. In a way, his lack of genius made his achievements all the more impressive. He held his forces together in adversity, avoiding both useless slaughter and catastrophic defeat. People of all sections, from every walk of life, looked on Washington as the embodiment of American virtues: a man of deeds rather than words; a man of substance accustomed to luxury yet capable of enduring great hardships stoically and as much at home in the wilderness as an Indian; a bold Patriot, quick to take arms against British tyranny, yet eminently respectable. The Revolution might have been won without Washington, but it is unlikely that the free United States would have become so easily a true nation had he not been at its call.

1774	Thomas Jefferson writes *A Summary View of the Rights of British America*
	General Thomas Gage, commander-in-chief of British army in North America, is named governor of Massachusetts
1775	Colonists fight British in Battles of Lexington and Concord
	Second Continental Congress names George Washington commander-in-chief (of Continental Army)
	Gage is replaced as British commander by General Sir William Howe after Battle of Bunker Hill
1776	Thomas Paine publishes *Common Sense*
	Washington's troops occupy Boston
	Second Continental Congress issues Declaration of Independence
	Washington's troops are defeated in Battle of Long Island
	Washington evacuates New York City
	Washington's victory at Battle of Trenton boosts morale
1777	Washington's troops win Battle of Princeton
	American victory at Saratoga turns the tide and leads to alliance with France
	British occupy Philadelphia after Battle of Germantown
1777–1778	Continental Army winters at Valley Forge
1778	British capture Savannah
1780	British capture Charleston
1781	States ratify Articles of Confederation
	General Cornwallis surrenders at Yorktown
1783	Great Britain recognizes independence of United States by signing Peace of Paris
1785	Congress passes Land Ordinance of 1785
1787	Northwest Ordinance establishes governments for the West

The Federalist Era: Nationalism Triumphant

O N APRIL 3, 2003, THE PHONE RANG IN THE DORM ROOM OF JESSE Jordan, a freshman at Rensselaer Polytechnic Institute. Jordan had no idea that the Constitution of the United States was about to crash into his life. Jordan's dean was on the line. The nation's record companies, the dean explained, had filed a lawsuit against Jordan for copyright infringement. Jordan had illegally downloaded and shared files of Christina Aguilera's "Genie in a Bottle," Busta Rhymes's "Break Ya Neck," and hundreds of other songs. Because copyright law set fines of $150,000 or more for each infringement, Jordan owed the record companies $15 million, or so the lawsuit claimed.

That same day brought even worse news to Joseph Nievelt, a sophomore at Michigan Technological University. Because Nievelt had downloaded and shared thousands of songs, his fine was set at $97.8 billion. Jordan eventually turned over his life savings—$12,000—to settle the lawsuit. Nievelt paid $15,000.

If the Articles of Confederation had remained the law of the land, Jordan and Nievelt would have done nothing illegal. The Articles included no mention of copyright. In the 1780s, moreover, only a couple of states had made it illegal to copy an invention or print someone else's book. But James Madison observed that if inventors did not "own" their inventions, they would have little incentive to invent. Authors, too, could expect no profit if their books could be freely reprinted by others. The economy would suffer and knowledge would languish. Thomas Jefferson, on the other hand, observed that in England copyright laws allowed businesses to monopolize inventions and books. This drove prices up and restricted dissemination of ideas. He argued that ideas, once divulged, should swiftly and freely be made available to the public.

Eventually the framers reached a compromise and added it to the Constitution of the United States. Article 1, Section 8 empowered Congress to "promote the Progress of Science and the Useful Arts" by providing "authors and inventors" the "exclusive right" to their creations; however, this right would endure for a "limited" time only. Then the invention or book would become public property.

Although Jesse Jordan and Joseph Nievelt may not have been very happy with the Constitution on the particular point of copyright infringement, they, like most Americans today, appreciate the many important provisions of the Constitution, including the protection of the rights of individuals and the enumeration of the powers and responsibilities (and limitations) of the federal government. In the 1780s, however, many Americans were satisfied with the federal government under the Articles of Confederation. Whatever its weaknesses, it had negotiated the treaty ending the Revolutionary War, adopted humane and far-sighted land policies, and established a rudimentary bureaucracy to manage routine affairs. If, as Washington said, that government had moved "on crutches . . . tottering at every step," it moved forward nevertheless. Yet the country's evolution placed demands on the national government that its creators had not anticipated. Dissatisfaction with the Articles mounted; the Founders sought solutions that through a process of conflict and compromise would finally result in the Constitution.

Inadequacies of the Articles of Confederation

Following the Revolutionary War and the peace settlement at Paris, the United States faced new challenges. The new nation struggled to achieve control of its own territory, to define the nature of its trade relationships with Europe, and to overcome crippling economic depression and the specter of inflation. If the Articles had proved adequate in achieving victory in the war, they proved less so in addressing these new concerns.

Both Great Britain and Spain stood in the way of the United States winning control of its borders. Although the British kept their promise to withdraw their troops from American soil promptly, they refused to abandon seven military posts beyond the periphery of the original thirteen states. Pressing against America's exposed frontier like hot coals, these posts seared national pride. The inability to eject the British seemed a national disgrace. In 1784, moreover, the Spaniards had closed the lower Mississippi River to American commerce. This harmed settlers beyond the Appalachians who depended on the Mississippi and its network of tributaries to get their corn, tobacco, and other products to eastern and European markets. Many reasoned that a stronger central government might have dealt with Britain and Spain more forcefully and effectively.

Another key problem concerned trade. After hostilities had ended, British merchants, eager to regain markets closed to them during the Revolution, poured low-priced manufactured goods of all kinds into the United States. Americans, long deprived of British products, rushed to take advantage of the bargains. Soon imports of British goods were approaching the levels of the early 1770s, while exports to the empire reached no more than half their earlier volume.

The influx of British goods aggravated the situation just when the economy was suffering a dislocation as a result of the ending of the war. From 1784 to 1786 the country went through a period of bad times. The inability of Congress to find money to pay the nation's debts undermined public confidence. Veterans who had still not been paid, and private individuals and foreign governments that had lent the government money during the Revolution, were clamoring for their due. In some regions crop failures compounded the difficulties.

An obvious way of dealing with these problems would have been to place tariffs on British goods in order to limit British imports, but the Confederation lacked the authority to do this. When individual states erected tariff barriers, British merchants easily got around them by bringing their goods in through states that did not. That the central government lacked the power to control commerce disturbed merchants, other businessmen, and the ever-increasing number of national-minded citizens in every walk of life.

Thus a movement developed to give the Confederation the power to tax imports, and in 1781 Congress sought authority to levy a 5 percent tariff duty. This would enable Congress to pay off some of its obligations and also put pressure on the British to relax their restrictions on American trade with the West Indies. Every state but Rhode Island agreed, but the measure required the unanimous consent of the states and therefore failed.

Defeat of the tariff pointed to the need for revising the Articles of Confederation, for here was a case where a large percentage of the states were ready to increase the power of the national government yet were unable to do so. Although many individuals in every region were worried about creating a centralized monster that might gobble up the sovereignty of the states, the practical needs of the times convinced many others that this risk must be taken.

Daniel Shays's "Little Rebellion"

The Massachusetts legislature was determined to pay off the state debt and maintain a sound currency. Taxes amounting to almost £1.9 million were levied between 1780 and 1786, the burden falling most heavily on those of moderate income. The average Massachusetts farmer paid about a third of every year's income in taxes. Bad times and deflation led to many foreclosures, and the prisons were crowded with honest debtors. "Our Property is torn from us," one town complained, "our Gaols filled & still our Debts are not discharged."

This broadside lauds Daniel Shays *(left)*, who headed the armed rebellion against Massachusetts, which was cracking down on debtors. Shays is pictured in his Continental uniform. For his efforts at the Battle of Saratoga in 1777, Marquis de Lafayette had presented Shays with a ceremonial sword, pictured here. Shays sold the sword to pay off his debts.

In the summer of 1786 throngs of disgruntled farmers in the western communities began to stop foreclosures by forcibly preventing the courts from holding their sessions. Under the leadership of Daniel Shays, a veteran of Bunker Hill, Ticonderoga, and Saratoga, the "rebels" marched on Springfield and prevented the state supreme court from meeting. When the state government sent troops against them, the rebels attacked the Springfield arsenal. They were routed, and the uprising then collapsed. Shays fled to Vermont.

As Thomas Jefferson observed at safe remove from the trouble in Paris, where he was serving as minister to France, Shays's uprising was only "a *little* rebellion" and as such "a medicine necessary for the sound health of government." But Shays and his followers were genuinely exasperated by the refusal of the government even to try to provide relief for their troubles. By taking up arms they forced the authorities to heed them: At its next session the legislature made some concessions to their demands.

Unlike Jefferson, most well-to-do Americans considered Shays's uprising "Liberty run mad." "What, gracious God, is man! that there should be such inconsistency and perfidiousness in his conduct?" the usually unexcitable George Washington asked when news of the riots reached Virginia. "We are fast verging to anarchy and confusion!" During the crisis private persons had had to subscribe funds to put the rebels down, and when Massachusetts had appealed to Congress for help there was little Congress could legally do. The lessons seemed plain: Liberty must not become an excuse for license; greater authority must be vested in the central government.

To Philadelphia, and the Constitution

If most people wanted to increase the power of Congress, they were also afraid to shift the balance too far lest they destroy the sovereignty of the states and the rights of individuals. The machinery for change established in the Articles of Confederation, which required the unanimous consent of the states for all amendments, posed a particularly delicate problem. Experience had shown it unworkable, yet to bypass it would be revolutionary and therefore dangerous.

The first fumbling step toward reform was taken in March 1785 when representatives of Virginia and Maryland, meeting at the home of George Washington to settle a dispute over the improvement of navigation on the Potomac River, suggested a conference of all the states to discuss common problems of commerce.

Among the delegates was a young New York lawyer named Alexander Hamilton, a brilliant, imaginative, and daring man who was convinced that only drastic centralization would save the nation from disintegration. Hamilton described himself as a "nationalist." While the war still raged he contrasted the virtues of "a great Federal Republic" with the existing system of "petty states with the appearance only of union, jarring, jealous, and perverse." Instead of giving up, he proposed calling another convention to meet at Philadelphia to deal generally with constitutional reform. Delegates should be empowered to work out a broad plan for correcting "such defects as may be discovered to exist" in the Articles of Confederation.

The Annapolis group approved Hamilton's suggestion, and Congress reluctantly endorsed it. This time all the states but Rhode Island sent delegates. On May 25, 1787, the convention opened its proceedings at the State House in Philadelphia and unanimously elected George Washington its president. When it adjourned four months later, it had drafted the Constitution.

The Great Convention

Collectively the delegates possessed a rare combination of talents. Most of them had had considerable experience in politics, and the many lawyers among them were skilled in logic and debate. Furthermore, the times made them acutely aware of their opportunities. It was "a time when the greatest lawgivers of antiquity would have wished to live," an opportunity to "establish the wisest and happiest government that human wisdom can contrive," John Adams wrote. "We . . . decide for ever the fate of republican government," James Madison said during the deliberations.

If these remarks overstated the importance of their deliberations, they nonetheless represented the opinion of most of those present. They were boldly optimistic about their country. "We are laying the foundation of a great empire," Madison predicted. At the same time the delegates recognized the difficulties they faced. The ancient Roman republic was one model, and all knew that it had been overthrown by tyrants and eventually overrun by barbarians. The framers were also familiar with Enlightenment thinkers such as John Locke, Thomas Hobbes, and Montesquieu, and also with the ideas that swirled around the great disputes between Parliament and the Stuart monarchs during the seventeenth century.

Fortunately, they were nearly all of one mind on basic questions. That there should be a federal system, with both independent state governments and a national government with limited powers to handle matters of common interest, was accepted by all but one or two of them. Republican government, drawing its

Independence Hall in Philadelphia, where the Declaration of Independence was adopted (1776) and where the Constitution was drafted and signed (1787). Despite stifling heat, delegates kept the windows shut to keep their deliberations secret.

authority from the people and remaining responsible to them, was a universal assumption. A measure of democracy followed inevitably from this principle, for even the most aristocratic delegates agreed that ordinary citizens should share in the process of selecting those who were to make and execute the laws.

All agreed that no group within society, no matter how numerous, should have unrestricted authority. They looked on political power much as we today view nuclear energy: a force with tremendous potential value for humankind, but one easily misused and therefore dangerous to unleash. People meant well and had limitless possibilities, the constitution makers believed, but they were selfish by nature and could not be counted on to respect the interests of others. The ordinary people—small farmers, artisans, any taxpayer—should have a say in government in order to be able to protect themselves against those who would exploit their weakness, and the majority must somehow be prevented from plundering the rich, for property must be secure or no government could be stable. No single state or section must be allowed to predominate, nor should the legislature be supreme over the executive or the courts. Power, in short, must be divided, and the segments must be balanced one against the other.

At the outset the delegates decided to keep the proceedings secret. That way no one was tempted to play to the gallery or seek some personal political advantage at the expense of the common good. Next they agreed to go beyond their instructions to revise the Articles of Confederation and draft an entirely new form of government. This was a bold, perhaps illegal act, but it was in no way irresponsible

Debating the Past

WHAT IDEAS SHAPED THE CONSTITUTION?

In this 1788 cartoon, the angel "Concord" presents the Constitution to "Columbia"—an embodiment of the United States; a Greek temple sits in the background, its thirteen pillars representing the colonies. Were the people who drafted the Constitution inspired by classical antiquity? No, declared historian Charles A. Beard (1913). He argued that their chief concerns were to protect their property and business interests.

Few historians found much confirmation of Beard's thesis; but, what, then *were* the Founders thinking? Daniel Boorstin (1948) regarded the Founders as practical men who sought "a refuge from the diversity of ideas in the satisfying concreteness of experience." In 1967 Bernard Bailyn rejected this argument. His research revealed that the revolutionary leaders learned to cherish republican virtue and citizenship from ancient Roman philosophers such as Plutarch and Tacitus, from thinkers of the European Enlightenment, and from critics of eighteenth-century British monarchs. Joyce Appleby (1984) countered that if ideas were at the heart of the Constitution, they came from John Locke, a seventeenth-

century philosopher who enshrined property rights and the individual. The Constitution was a blueprint for capitalist development. Jack Rakove (1996) concluded that the Founders lacked any clear "original intent." They favored a government strong enough to protect people and promote their interests; they also favored individual rights and freedom. Which mattered more, they could not agree.

Charles A. Beard, *An Economic Interpretation of the Constitution of the United States* (1913), Daniel Boorstin, *The Lost World of Thomas Jefferson* (1948), Bernard Bailyn, *The Ideological Origins of the American Revolution* (1967), Gordon Wood, *The Creation of the American Republic* (1969), Joyce Appleby, *Capitalism and a New Social Order* (1984), Jack Rakove, *Original Meanings* (1996).

because nothing the convention might recommend was binding on anyone, and it was absolutely essential because under the Articles a single state could have prevented the adoption of any change. Alexander Hamilton captured the mood of the gathering when he said: "We can only propose and recommend—the power of ratifying or rejecting is still in the States. . . . We ought not to sacrifice the public Good to narrow Scruples."

The Compromises That Produced the Constitution

The delegates voted on May 30, 1787 that "a national Government ought to be established." They then set to work hammering out a specific plan. Furthermore, the delegates believed that the national government should have separate executive and judicial branches as well as a legislature. But two big questions had to be answered. The first—*What powers should this national government be granted?*—occasioned relatively little discussion. The right to levy taxes and to regulate interstate and foreign commerce was assigned to the central government almost without debate. So was the power to raise and maintain an army and navy and to summon the militia of the states to enforce national laws and suppress insurrections. With equal absence of argument, the states were deprived of their rights to issue money, to make treaties, and to tax either imports or exports without the permission of Congress. Thus, in summary fashion, was brought about a massive shift of power, a shift made necessary by the problems that had brought the delegates to Philadelphia and made practicable by the new nationalism of the 1780s.

The second major question—*Who shall control the national government?*—proved more difficult to answer in a manner satisfactory to all. Led by Virginia, the larger states pushed for representation in the national legislature based on population. The smaller states wished to maintain the existing system of equal representation for each state regardless of population. The large states rallied behind the Virginia Plan, drafted by James Madison and presented to the convention by Edmund Randolph, governor of the state. The small states supported the New Jersey Plan, prepared by William Paterson, a former attorney general of that state. The question was important; equal state representation would have been undemocratic, whereas a proportional system would have effectively destroyed the influence of all the states as states. But the delegates saw it in terms of combinations of large or small states, and this old-fashioned view was unrealistic: When the states combined, they did so on geographic, economic, or social grounds that seldom had anything to do with size. Nevertheless, the debate was long and heated, and for a time it threatened to disrupt the convention.

Day after day in the stifling heat of high summer, the weary delegates struggled to find a suitable compromise. Madison and a few others had to use every weapon in their arsenal of argument to hold the group together. (All told, during the 88 sessions of the convention, a total of 569 votes were taken.) July 2 was perhaps the most fateful day of the whole proceedings. "We are at full stop," said Roger Sherman of Connecticut, who had been one of the drafters of the Declaration of Independence. "If we do not concede on both sides," a North Carolina delegate warned, "our business must soon be at an end."

But the delegates did "concede on both sides," and the debates went on. Again on July 17 collapse threatened as the representatives of the larger states caucused to consider walking out of the convention. Fortunately they did not walk out, and finally the delegates adopted what is known as the Great Compromise. In the lower branch of the new legislature—the House of Representatives—places were to be assigned according to population and filled by popular vote. In the upper house— the Senate—each state was to have two members, elected by its legislature.

Then a complicated struggle took place between northern and southern delegates, occasioned by the institution of slavery and the differing economic interests of the regions. About one American in seven in the 1780s was a slave. Northerners contended that slaves should be counted in deciding each state's share of direct federal taxes. Southerners, of course, wanted to exclude slaves from the count. Yet Southerners wished to include slaves in determining each district's representation in the House of Representatives, although they had no intention of permitting the slaves to vote. In the Three-fifths Compromise it was agreed that "three-fifths of all other Persons" should be counted for both purposes. (As it turned out, the compromise was a victory for the Southerners, for direct taxes were only rarely levied by Congress before the Civil War.) Settlement of the knotty issue of the African slave trade was postponed by a clause making it illegal for Congress to outlaw the trade before 1808.

The final document (see the text of the Constitution in the Appendix, pp. A-6–A-13), signed on September 17, established a legislature of two houses; an executive branch, consisting of a president with wide powers and a vice president whose only function was to preside over the Senate; and a national judiciary consisting of a Supreme Court and such "inferior courts" as Congress might decide to create. The lower, popularly elected branch of the Congress was supposed to represent especially the mass of ordinary citizens. It was given the sole right to introduce bills for raising revenue. The twenty-six-member Senate was looked on by many as a sort of advisory council similar to the upper houses of the colonial legislatures. Its consent was required before any treaty could go into effect and for major presidential appointments. The Founders also intended the Senate to represent in Congress the interests not only of the separate states but of what Hamilton called "the rich and the well-born" as contrasted with "the great mass of the people."

The creation of a powerful president was the most drastic departure from past experience, and it is doubtful that the Founders would have gone so far had everyone not counted on Washington, a man universally esteemed for character, wis-

James Madison was a key figure at the Great Convention of 1787. He not only influenced the shaping of the Constitution but also kept the most complete record of the proceedings. "Every person," wrote one delegate, "seems to acknowledge his greatness."

dom, and impartiality, to be the first to occupy the office. Besides giving him general responsibility for executing the laws, the Constitution made the president commander-in-chief of the armed forces of the nation and general supervisor of its foreign relations. He was to appoint federal judges and other officials, and he might veto any law of Congress, although his veto could be overridden by a two-thirds majority of both houses. While not specifically ordered to submit a program of legislation to Congress, he was to deliver periodic reports on the "State of the Union" and recommend "such Measures as he shall judge necessary and expedient." Most modern presidents have interpreted this requirement as authorizing them to submit detailed legislative proposals and to use the full power and prestige of the office to get Congress to enact them.

Looking beyond Washington, whose choice was sure to come about under any system, the Constitution established a cumbersome method of electing presidents. Each state was to choose "electors" equal in number to its representation in Congress. The electors, meeting separately in their own states, were to vote for two persons for president. Supposedly the procedure would prevent anyone less universally admired than Washington from getting a majority in the "electoral college," in which case the House of Representatives would choose the president from among the leading candidates, each state having but one vote. However, the swift rise of national political parties prevented the expected fragmentation of the electors' votes, and only two elections have ever gone to the House for settlement.

The national court system was set up to adjudicate disputes under the laws and treaties of the United States. No such system had existed under the Articles, a major weakness. Although the Constitution did not specifically authorize the courts to declare laws void when they conflicted with the Constitution, the courts soon exercised this right of "judicial review" in cases involving both state and federal laws.

The Founders believed that since the new powers of government might easily be misused, each should be held within safe limits by some countervailing force. The Constitution is full of ingenious devices ("checks and balances") whereby one power controls and limits another without reducing it to impotence. "Let Congress Legislate, let others execute, let others judge," John Jay suggested. This separation of legislative, executive, and judicial functions is the fundamental example of the principle. Other examples are the president's veto; Congress's power of impeachment, cleverly divided between House and Senate; the Senate's power over treaties and appointments; and the balance between Congress's right to declare war and the president's control of the armed forces.

Ratifying the Constitution

Influenced by the widespread approval of the decision of Massachusetts to submit its state constitution of 1780 to the voters for ratification, the framers of the Constitution provided (Article VII) that their handiwork be ratified by special state conventions.

Such a complex and controversial document as the Constitution naturally excited argument throughout the country. Those who favored it called themselves Federalists, thereby avoiding the more accurate but politically unattractive label of Centralizers. Their opponents thus became the Anti-Federalists.

It is difficult to generalize about the members of these groups. The Federalists tended to be substantial individuals, members of the professions, well-to-do, active in commercial affairs, and somewhat alarmed by the changes wrought by the Revolution. They were more interested, perhaps, in orderly and efficient government than in safeguarding the maximum freedom of individual choice.

The Anti-Federalists were more often small farmers, debtors, and persons to whom free choice was more important than power and who resented those who sought and held power. "Lawyers and men of learning and money men . . . expect to be the managers of the Const[itution], and get all the power and all the money into their own hands," a Massachusetts Anti-Federalist complained. "Then they will swallow up all us little folks . . . just as the whale swallowed up *Jonah*." But many rich and worldly citizens opposed the Constitution, and many poor and obscure persons were for it. It seems likely that most did not support or oppose the new system for narrowly selfish reasons.

Very little of the opposition to the Constitution grew out of economic issues. Most people wanted the national debt paid off; nearly everyone opposed an unstable currency; most favored uniform trade policies; most were ready to give the new government a chance if they could be convinced that it would not destroy the states. When backers agreed to add amendments guaranteeing the civil liberties of the people against challenge by the national government and reserving all unmentioned power to the states, much of the opposition disappeared. Sam Adams ended up voting for the Constitution in the Massachusetts convention after the additions had been promised.

The Constitution met with remarkably little opposition in most of the state ratifying conventions, considering the importance of the changes it instituted. Delaware acted first, ratifying unanimously on December 7, 1787. Pennsylvania followed a few days later, voting for the document by a 2 to 1 majority. New Jersey approved unanimously on December 18; so did Georgia on January 2, 1788. A week later Connecticut fell in line, 128 to 40.

The Massachusetts convention provided the first close contest. Early in February, after an extensive debate, the delegates ratified by a vote of 187 to 168. In April, Maryland accepted the Constitution by nearly 6 to 1, and in May, South Carolina approved, 149 to 73. New Hampshire came along on June 21, voting 57 to 47 for the Constitution. This was the ninth state, making the Constitution legally operative.

Before the news from New Hampshire had spread throughout the country, the Virginia convention debated the issue. Virginia, the largest state and the home of so many prestigious figures, was absolutely essential if the Constitution was to succeed. With unquestioned patriots like Richard Henry Lee and Patrick Henry opposed, the result was not easy to predict. But when the vote came on June 25, Virginia ratified, 89 to 79. Aside from Rhode Island, this left only New York and North Carolina outside the Union.

New York politics presented a complex and baffling picture. Resistance to independence had been strong there in 1776 and remained a problem all through the war. Although New York was the third largest state, with a population rapidly approaching 340,000, it sided with the small states at Philadelphia, and two of its three delegates (Hamilton was the exception) walked out of the convention and took the lead in opposing ratification. A handful of great landowning and mercantile families dominated politics, but they were divided into shifting factions. In general, New York City, including most ordinary working people as well as the merchants, favored ratification and the rural areas were against it.

The Anti-Federalists, well organized and competently led in New York by Governor George Clinton, won 46 of the 65 seats at the ratifying convention. The New York Federalists had one great asset in the fact that so many states had already ratified and another in the person of Alexander Hamilton. Although contemptuous of the *weakness* of the Constitution, Hamilton supported it with all his energies as being incomparably stronger than the old government. Working with Madison and John Jay, he produced the *Federalist Papers,* a series of brilliant essays explaining and defending the new system. In his articles, Hamilton stressed the need for a strong federal executive, while Madison sought to allay fears that the new national government would have too much power by emphasizing the many checks and balances in the Constitution. The essays were published in the local press and later in book form. Although generations of judges and lawyers have treated them almost as parts of the Constitution, their impact on contemporary public opinion was probably slight. Open-minded members of the convention were undoubtedly influenced, but few delegates were open-minded.

Hamilton became a kind of one-man army in defense of the Constitution, plying hesitating delegates with dinners and drinks, facing obstinate ones with the threat that New York City would secede from the state if the Constitution were rejected. Once New Hampshire and Virginia had ratified, opposition in New York became a good deal less intransigent. In the end, by promising to support a call for a second national convention to consider amendments, the Federalists carried the day, 30 to 27. With New York in the fold, the new government was free to get under way. North Carolina finally ratified in November 1789, Rhode Island the following year, in May 1790.

Washington as President

Elections took place in the states during January and February 1789, and by early April enough congressmen had gathered in New York, the temporary national capital, to commence operation. The ballots of the presidential electors were officially counted in the Senate on April 6, Washington being the unanimous choice. John Adams, with 34 electoral votes, won the vice-presidency.

When he left Mount Vernon for the eight-day trip to New York for his inauguration, Washington's progress was a series of celebrations. In every town he was met by bands, honor guards, local dignitaries, and crowds of cheering citizens. The

Ratification of the Constitution

people were informally ratifying the decision to create a new and more powerful United States. On April 30 Washington took the oath of office at New York's Federal Hall.

Washington made a firm, dignified, conscientious, but cautious president. His acute sense of responsibility led him to face the task "with feelings not unlike those of a culprit who is going to the place of his execution." Each presidential action must of necessity establish a precedent. "The eyes of Argus are upon me," he complained, "and no slip will pass unnoticed." Hoping to make the presidency appear respectable in the eyes of the world, he saw to it that his carriage was drawn by six cream-colored horses, and when he rode (he was a magnificent horseman), it was on a great white charger, with the saddle of leopard skin and the cloth edged in gold. Twenty-one servants (seven of them slaves) attended his needs at the presidential mansion on Broadway.

Washington meticulously avoided treading on the toes of Congress, for he took seriously the principle of the separation of powers. Never would he speak for or against a candidate for Congress, nor did he think that the president should push or even propose legislation. When he knew a controversial question was to be discussed in Congress, he avoided the subject in his annual message. The veto, he believed, should be employed only when the president considered a bill unconstitutional.

Although the Constitution said nothing about a presidential Cabinet, Washington established the system of calling his department heads together for general advice, a practice that was followed by his successors. In selecting these department heads and other important administrators, he favored no particular faction. He insisted only that appointees be competent and "of known attachment to the Government we have chosen." He picked Hamilton for secretary of the treasury, Jefferson for secretary of state, General Henry Knox of Massachusetts for secretary of war, and Edmund Randolph for attorney general. He called on them for advice according to the logic of his particular needs and frequently without regard for their own specialties. Thus he sometimes consulted Jefferson about financial matters and Hamilton about foreign affairs. This system caused resentment and confusion, especially when rival factions began to coalesce around Hamilton and Jefferson.

Despite his respect for the opinions of others, Washington was a strong chief executive. As Hamilton put it, he "consulted much, pondered much, resolved slowly, resolved surely." His stress on the dignity of his office suited the needs of a new country whose people tended to be perhaps too informal. It was indeed important that the first president be particularly concerned about establishing precedents. His scrupulous care lest he overstep the bounds of presidential power helped erase the prejudices of those who feared that republican government must inevitably succumb to dictatorship and tyranny. When each step is an experiment, when foreign dangers loom at the end of every errant path, it is surely wise to go slowly. And no one should forget that Washington's devotion to duty did not always come easily. Occasionally he exploded. Thomas Jefferson has left us a graphic description of the president at a Cabinet meeting, in a rage because of some unfair criticism, swearing that "by god he had rather be on his farm than to be made emperor of the world."

Congress Under Way

By September 1789 Congress had created the State, Treasury, and War departments and passed a Judiciary Act establishing thirteen federal district courts and three circuit courts of appeal. The number of Supreme Court justices was set at six, and Washington named John Jay the chief justice.

True to Federalist promises—for a large majority of both houses were friendly to the Constitution—Congress prepared a list of a dozen amendments (ten were ratified) guaranteeing what Congressman James Madison, who drafted the amendments, called the "great rights of mankind." These amendments, known as the Bill of Rights (see Amendments to the Constitution in the Appendix, pp. A-14–A-20), provided that Congress should make no law infringing freedom of speech, the press, or religion. The right of trial by jury was reaffirmed, the right to bear arms guaranteed. No one was to be subject to "unreasonable" searches or seizures or compelled to testify against himself or herself in a criminal case. No one was to "be deprived of life, liberty, or property, without due process of law."

Despite Washington's reluctance to interfere with the activities of Congress, he urged acceptance of these amendments so that the "rights of freemen" would be "impregnably fortified." The Bill of Rights was unique; the English Bill of Rights of 1689 was much less broad-gauged and, being an act of Parliament, was subject to repeal by Parliament at any time. The Tenth Amendment—not, strictly speaking, a part of the Bill of Rights—was designed to mollify those who feared that the states would be destroyed by the new government. It provided that powers not delegated to the United States or denied specifically to the states by the Constitution were to reside either in the states or in the people.

As experts pointed out, the amendments were not logically necessary because the federal government had no authority to act in such matters to begin with. But many had wanted to be reassured. Experience has proved repeatedly that whatever the logic of the situation, the protection afforded individuals by the Bill of Rights has been anything but unnecessary.

The Bill of Rights did much to convince doubters that the new government would not become too powerful. More complex was the task of proving that it was powerful enough to deal with those national problems that the Confederation had not been able to solve: the threat to the West posed by the British, Spaniards, and Indians; the disruption of the pattern of American foreign commerce resulting from independence; and the collapse of the financial structure of the country.

Hamilton and Financial Reform

One of the first acts of Congress in 1789 was to employ its new power to tax. The simplest means of raising money seemed to be that first attempted by the British after 1763, a tariff on foreign imports. Congress levied a 5 percent duty on all foreign products entering the United States, applying higher rates to certain products, such as hemp, glass, and nails, as a measure of protection for American producers. The Tariff Act of 1789 also placed heavy tonnage duties on all foreign shipping, a mercantilist measure designed to stimulate the American merchant marine.

Raising money for current expenses was a small and relatively simple aspect of the financial problem faced by Washington's administration. The nation's debt was large, its credit shaky, its economic future uncertain. In October 1789

New Yorkers honor Hamilton during a parade marking ratification of the Constitution. That Hamilton stood on a ship was fitting, not only because he sought to strengthen the federal "ship of state" but also because New York merchants were among his staunchest backers.

Congress deposited on the slender shoulders of Secretary of the Treasury Hamilton the task of straightening out the fiscal mess and stimulating the country's economic development.

Hamilton at age 34 had already proved himself a remarkable man. Born in the British West Indies, the illegitimate son of a shiftless Scot who was little better than a beachcomber, and raised by his mother's family, he came to New York in 1773 to attend King's College. When the Revolution broke out, he joined the Continentals. At 22 he was a staff colonel, aide-de-camp to Washington. Later, at Yorktown, he led a line regiment, displaying a bravery approaching foolhardiness. He married the daughter of Philip Schuyler, a wealthy and influential New Yorker, and after the Revolution he practiced law in that state.

Hamilton was a bundle of contradictions. Witty, charming, possessed of a mind like a sharp knife, he was sometimes the soul of practicality, sometimes an incurable romantic. No more hardheaded realist ever lived, yet he was quick to resent any slight to his honor, even—tragically—ready to fight a duel though he abhorred the custom of dueling. A self-made man, he admired aristocracy and disparaged the abilities of the common run of mankind who, he said, "seldom judge or determine right." Although granting that Americans must be allowed to govern themselves, he was as apprehensive of the "turbulence" of the masses as a small boy passing a graveyard in the dark. "No popular government was ever without its

Catilines and its Caesars," he warned—a typical example of that generation's concern about the fate of the Roman republic.

The country, Hamilton insisted, needed a strong national government. "I acknowledge," he wrote in one of the *Federalist Papers*, "my aversion to every project that is calculated to disarm the government of a single weapon, which in any possible contingency might be usefully employed for the general defense and security." He avowed that government should be "a great Federal Republic," not "a number of petty states, with the appearance only of union, jarring, jealous, perverse, without any determined direction." He wished to reduce the states to mere administrative units, like English counties.

As secretary of the treasury, Hamilton proved to be a farsighted economic planner. The United States, a "Hercules in the cradle," needed capital to develop its untapped material and human resources. To persuade investors to commit their funds in America, the country would have to convince them that it would meet every obligation in full. His *Report on the Public Credit* outlined a plan for the federal government to borrow money to pay all of its debts as well as those of the states.

While most members of Congress agreed, albeit somewhat grudgingly, that the debt should be paid in full, they had misgivings as to who should get those payments. Many of the soldiers, farmers, and merchants who had been forced to accept government securities in lieu of cash for goods and services had sold their securities for a fraction of their face value to speculators; under Hamilton's proposal, the speculators—now paid for the full value of the securities—would make a killing. To the argument for divided payment, Hamilton answered coldly: "[The speculator] paid what the commodity was worth in the market, and took the risks. . . . He . . . ought to reap the benefit of his hazard."

Hamilton was essentially correct, and in the end Congress had to go along. After all, the speculators had not caused the securities to fall in value; indeed, as a group they had favored sound money and a strong government. The best way to restore the nation's credit was to convince investors that the government would honor all obligations in full. What infuriated his contemporaries and still attracts the scorn of many historians was Hamilton's motive. He deliberately intended his plan to give a special advantage to the rich. The government would be strong, he thought, only if well-to-do Americans enthusiastically supported it. What better way to win them over than to make it worth their while financially to do so?

In part, opposition to the funding plan was sectional, for citizens of the northern states held more than four-fifths of the national debt. The scheme for assuming the state debts aggravated the controversy, since most of the southern states had already paid off much of their Revolutionary War obligations. For months Congress was deadlocked. Finally, in July 1790, Hamilton worked out a compromise with Representative James Madison and Secretary of State Jefferson. The two Virginians swung a few southern votes, and Hamilton induced some of his followers to support the southern plan for locating the permanent capital of the Union on the Potomac River.

Jefferson later claimed that Hamilton had hoodwinked him. Having only recently returned from Europe, he said, "I was really a stranger to the whole subject." Hamilton had persuaded him to "rally around" by the false tale that "our Union" was threatened with dissolution. This was nonsense; Jefferson agreed to the compromise because he expected that Virginia and the rest of the South would profit from having the capital so near at hand.

The assumption bill passed, and the entire funding plan was a great success. Soon the United States had the highest possible credit rating in the world's financial centers. Foreign capital poured into the country.

Hamilton next proposed that Congress charter a national bank. Such an institution would provide safe storage for government funds and serve as an agent for the government in the collection, movement, and expenditure of tax money. Most important, because of its substantial resources a bank could finance new and expanding business enterprises, greatly speeding the economic growth of the nation. It would also be able to issue bank notes, thereby providing a vitally needed medium of exchange for the specie-starved economy. This Bank of the United States was to be partly owned by the government, but 80 percent of the $10 million stock issue was to be sold to private individuals.

The country had much to gain from such a bank, but again—Hamilton's cleverness was never more in evidence—the well-to-do commercial classes would gain still more. Government balances in the bank belonging to all the people would earn dividends for a handful of rich investors. Manufacturers and other capitalists would profit from the bank's credit facilities. Public funds would be invested in the bank, but control would remain in private hands, since the government would appoint only five of the twenty-five directors. Nevertheless, the bill creating the bank passed both houses of Congress with relative ease in February 1791.

President Washington, however, hesitated to sign it, for the bill's constitutionality had been questioned during the debate in Congress. Nowhere did the Constitution specifically authorize Congress to charter corporations or engage in the banking business. As was his wont when in doubt, Washington called on Jefferson and Hamilton for advice.

Hamilton defended the legality of the bank by enunciating the doctrine of "implied powers." If a logical connection existed between the purpose of the bill and powers clearly stated in the Constitution, he wrote, the bill was constitutional.

> If the end be clearly comprehended within any of the specified powers, and if the measure have an obvious relation to that end . . . it may safely be deemed to come within the compass of the national authority . . . . A bank has a natural relation to the power of collecting taxes—to that of regulating trade—to that of providing for the common defence.

Jefferson disagreed. Congress could only do what the Constitution specifically authorized, he said. The "elastic clause" granting it the right to pass "all Laws which shall be necessary and proper" to carry out the specified powers must be interpreted literally or Congress would "take possession of a boundless field of power, no longer susceptible to any definition." Because a bank was obviously not necessary, it was not authorized.

Although not entirely convinced, Washington accepted Hamilton's reasoning and signed the bill. He could just as easily have followed Jefferson, for the Constitution is not clear. If one stresses *proper* in the "necessary and proper" clause in Article I, Section 8 of the Constitution, one ends up a Hamiltonian; if one stresses *necessary*, then Jefferson's view is correct. Historically (and this is the important point) politicians have nearly always adopted the "loose" Hamiltonian "implied powers" interpretation when they favored a measure and the "strict" Jeffersonian one when they do not. Jefferson disliked the bank; therefore, he claimed it was unconstitutional. Had he approved, he doubtless would have taken a different tack.

In 1819 the Supreme Court officially sanctioned Hamilton's construction of the "necessary and proper" clause, and in general that interpretation has prevailed. Because the majority tends naturally toward an argument that increases its freedom of action, the pressure for this view has been continual and formidable. The Bank of the United States succeeded from the start. When its stock went on sale, investors snapped up every share in a matter of hours. People eagerly accepted its bank notes at face value. Business ventures of all kinds found it easier to raise new capital. Soon state-chartered banks entered the field. There were only three state banks in 1791; by 1801, there were thirty-two.

Hamilton had not finished. In December 1791 he submitted his *Report on Manufactures*, a bold call for economic planning. He called for government tariffs, subsidies, and awards to encourage American manufacturing. He hoped to change an essentially agricultural nation into one with a complex, self-sufficient economy. Once again business and commercial interests in particular would benefit. A majority of the Congress, however, balked at so broad-gauged a scheme. Hamilton's *Report* was set aside, although many of the specific tariffs he recommended were enacted into law in 1792.

Nevertheless, the secretary of the treasury had managed to transform the financial structure of the country and to prepare the ground for an economic revolution. The constitutional reforms of 1787 had made this possible, and Hamilton turned possibility into reality.

The Ohio Country: A Dark and Bloody Ground

Trouble came swiftly when white settlers moved onto the land north of the Ohio River in large numbers. The Indians, determined to hold this country at all costs, struck hard at the invaders. In 1790 the Miami chief Little Turtle, a gifted strategist, inflicted a double defeat on militia units commanded by General Josiah Harmar. The next year Little Turtle and his men defeated the forces of General Arthur St. Clair still more convincingly. Both Harmar and St. Clair resigned from the army, their careers ruined, but the defeats led Congress to authorize raising a regular army of 5,000 men.

By early 1792 the Indians had driven the whites into "beachheads" at Marietta and Cincinnati on the Ohio. Resentment of the federal government in the western counties of every state from New York to the Carolinas mounted, the people feeling that it was ignoring their interests. They were convinced that the British were inciting the Indians to attack them, yet the supposedly powerful national government seemed unable to force Great Britain to surrender its forts in the West.

Still worse, the Westerners believed, was the way the government was taxing them. In 1791, as part of his plan to take over the debts of the states, Hamilton had persuaded Congress to adopt an excise tax of 8 cents a gallon on American-made whiskey. Excise taxes were particularly disliked by most Americans. A duty on imported products was collected from merchants and passed on to consumers as part of the price, and it was by its nature imposed only on foreign-made products. People who did not want to pay it usually could find a domestic alternative. But the collection of excise taxes on American goods required hordes of tax collectors, armed with the power to snoop into one's affairs. Westerners, who were heavy drinkers and who turned much of their grain into whiskey in order to cope with the high cost of transportation, were especially angered by the tax on whiskey.

Knowing that the tax would be unpopular, Hamilton promised that the distillers would "be secured from every species of injury by the misconduct of the officers to be employed" in collecting it. But he was determined to enforce the law. To western complaints, he coolly suggested that farmers drank too much to begin with. If they found the tax oppressive, they should cut down on their consumption. Of course this did nothing to reduce western opposition to the tax. Resistance was especially intense in western Pennsylvania. When treasury agents tried to collect it there, they were forcibly prevented from doing so.

Revolution in France

Momentous events in Europe were also affecting the situation. In 1789 the French Revolution erupted, and four years later war broke out between France and Great Britain and most of the rest of Europe. With France fighting Great Britain and Spain, there arose the question of America's obligations under the Alliance of 1778. That treaty required the United States to defend the French West Indies "forever against all other powers." Suppose the British attacked Martinique; must America then go to war? Morally the United States was so obligated, but no responsible American statesman urged such a policy. With the British in Canada and Spanish forces to the west and south, the nation would be in serious danger if it entered the war. Instead, in April 1793, Washington issued a proclamation of neutrality committing the United States to be "friendly and impartial" toward both sides in the war.

Meanwhile the French had sent a special representative, Edmond Charles Genet, to the United States to seek support. Quickly concluding that the proclamation of neutrality was "a harmless little pleasantry designed to throw dust in the eyes of the British," he began, in plain violation of American law, to license

American vessels to operate as privateers against British shipping and to grant French military commissions to a number of Americans in order to mount expeditions against Spanish and British possessions in North America.

Washington received Genet coolly, and soon thereafter demanded that he stop his illegal activities. Genet, whose capacity for self-deception was monumental, appealed to public opinion over the president's head and continued to commission privateers. Washington then requested his recall.

The Genet affair was incidental to a far graver problem. Although the European war increased the foreign demand for American products, it also led to attacks on American shipping by both France and Great Britain. Each power captured American vessels headed for the other's ports whenever it could. In 1793 and 1794 about 600 United States ships were seized.

The British attacks caused far more damage, both physically and psychologically, because the British fleet was much larger than France's, and France at least professed to be America's friend and to favor freedom of trade for neutrals. Pouncing without warning, British warships captured about 250 American vessels and sent them off as prizes to British ports. The merchant marine, one American diplomat declared angrily, was being "kicked, cuffed, and plundered all over the Ocean."

The attacks roused a storm in America, reviving hatreds that had been smoldering since the Revolution. The continuing presence of British troops in the Northwest (in 1794 the British began to build a new fort in the Ohio country) and the restrictions imposed on American trade with the British West Indies raised tempers still further. To try to avoid a war, for he wisely believed that the United States should not become embroiled in the Anglo-French conflict, Washington sent Chief Justice John Jay to London to seek a settlement with the British.

Federalists and Republicans: The Rise of Political Parties

The furor over the violations of neutral rights focused attention on a new development, the formation of political parties. Why national political parties emerged after the ratification of a Constitution that made no provision for such organizations is a question that has long intrigued historians. Probably the main reason was the obvious one: By creating a strong central government the Constitution produced national issues and a focus for national discussion and settlement of these issues. Furthermore, by failing to create machinery for nominating candidates for federal offices, the Constitution left a vacuum, which informal party organizations filled. That the universally admired Washington headed the government was a force limiting partisanship, but his principal advisers, Hamilton and Jefferson, were in sharp disagreement, and they soon became the leaders around which parties coalesced.

In the spring of 1791 Jefferson and James Madison began to sound out other politicians about forming an informal political organization. Jefferson also appointed the poet Philip Freneau to a minor state department post and Freneau then began publishing a newspaper, the *National Gazette,* to disseminate the views of what became known as the Republican party. The *Gazette* was soon describing Jefferson as a "Colossus of Liberty" and flailing away editorially at Hamilton's policies. Hamilton hit back promptly, organizing his own followers in the Federalist party, the organ of which was John Fenno's *Gazette of the United States.*

At the start Hamilton had the ear of the president, and his allies controlled a majority in Congress. Jefferson, who disliked controversy, avoided a direct confrontation as long as he could. He went along with Hamilton's funding plan and traded the assumption of state debts for a capital on the Potomac. However, when Hamilton proposed the Bank of the United States, he dug in his heels. It seemed designed to benefit the northeastern commercial classes at the expense of southern and western farmers. He sensed a dastardly plot to milk the producing masses for the benefit of a few capitalists.

The growing controversy over the French Revolution and the resulting war between France and Great Britain widened the split between the parties. After the radicals in France executed Louis XVI and instituted the Reign of Terror, American conservatives were horrified. The Jeffersonians were also deeply shocked. However, they continued to defend the Revolution. Great southern landlords whose French counterparts were losing their estates—some their heads—extolled "the glorious successes of our Gallic brethren." In the same way the Federalists began to idealize the British, whom they considered the embodiment of the forces that were resisting French radicalism.

1794: Crisis and Resolution

During the summer of 1794 several superficially unrelated events brought the partisan conflicts of the period to a peak. For the better part of two years the government had been unable to collect Hamilton's whiskey tax in the West. In Pennsylvania, mobs had burned the homes of revenue agents, and several men had been killed. Late in July, 7,000 "rebels" converged on Pittsburgh, threatening to set fire to the town. They were turned away by the sight of federal artillery and the liberal dispensation of whiskey by the frightened inhabitants.

Early in August President Washington determined "to go to every length that the Constitution and laws would permit" to enforce the law. He mustered an enormous army of nearly 13,000 militiamen. This had the desired effect; when the troops arrived in western Pennsylvania, rebels were nowhere to be seen. The expected Whiskey Rebellion simply did not happen. Good sense had triumphed. Moderates in the region (not everyone, after all, was a distiller) agreed that even unpopular laws should be obeyed.

More important, perhaps, than the militia in pacifying the Pennsylvania frontier was another event that occurred while that army was being mobilized. This was the Battle of Fallen Timbers in Ohio near present-day Toledo, where the

In 1792 farmers in western Pennsylvania, outraged over Hamilton's tax on liquor, rose up in rebellion against tax collectors. Their banners included the slogan of the French revolutionaries: "Liberty, Equality, and Fraternity!" Washington crushed the rebellion in 1794.

regular army troops of Major General "Mad Anthony" Wayne won a decisive victory over the Indians. Wayne's victory opened the way for white settlement of the region. Some 2,000 of the whiskey tax rebels simply pulled up stakes and headed for Ohio after the effort to avoid the excise collapsed.

Jay's Treaty

Still more significant was the outcome of President Washington's decision to send John Jay to England to seek a treaty settling the conflicts that vexed relations between the two nations. The British genuinely wanted to reach an accommodation with the United States—as one minister quipped, the Americans "are so much in debt to this country that we scarcely dare to quarrel with them." Jay was received by both the King and Queen and wined and dined by the foreign secretary, the prime minister, and other officials. The British also feared that the two new republics, France and the United States, would draw together in a battle against Europe's monarchies. On the other hand, the British were riding the crest of a wave of important victories in the war in Europe and were not disposed to make concessions to the Americans simply to avoid trouble.

The treaty that Jay brought home did contain a number of concessions. The British agreed to evacuate the posts in the West. They also promised to compensate American shipowners for seizures in the West Indies and to open up their colonies in Asia to American ships. They conceded nothing, however, to American demands that the rights of neutrals on the high seas be respected; no one really expected them to do so in wartime. A provision opening the British West Indies to American commerce was so hedged with qualifications limiting the size of American vessels and the type of goods allowed that the United States refused to accept it.

Jay also committed the United States to paying pre-Revolutionary debts still owed British merchants, a slap in the face to many states whose courts had been impeding their collection. Yet nothing was said about the British paying for the slaves they had "abducted" during the fighting in the South.

Although Jay might have driven a harder bargain, this was a valuable treaty for the United States. But it was also a humiliating one. Most of what the United States gained already legally belonged to it, and the treaty sacrificed principles of importance to a nation dependent on foreign trade. When the terms became known, they raised a storm of popular protest. It seemed possible that President Washington would repudiate the treaty or that if he did not, the Senate would refuse to ratify it.

1795: All's Well That Ends Well

Washington did not repudiate Jay's Treaty and after long debate the Senate ratified it in June 1795. After a bitter debate, with most Republicans opposing the measure, the House passed the requisite funding resolution. The treaty marked an important step toward the regularization of Anglo-American relations, which in the long run was essential for both the economic and political security of the nation. And the evacuation of the British forts in the Northwest was of enormous immediate benefit.

Still another benefit was totally unplanned. Unexpectedly, Jay's Treaty enabled the United States to solve its problems on its southeastern frontier. During the early 1790s Spain had entered into alliances with the Cherokee, Creek, and other Indian tribes hostile to the Americans and built forts on territory ceded to the United States by Great Britain in the Treaty of Paris. In 1795, however, Spain intended to withdraw from the European war against France. Fearing a joint Anglo-American attack on Louisiana and its other American possessions, it decided to improve relations with the United States. Therefore the king's chief minister, Manuel de Godoy, known as "the Prince of Peace," offered the American envoy Thomas Pinckney a treaty that granted the United States the free navigation of the Mississippi River and the right of deposit at New Orleans that western Americans so urgently needed. This Treaty of San Lorenzo, popularly known as Pinckney's Treaty, also accepted the American version of the boundary between Spanish Florida and the United States.

The Senate ratified Jay's Treaty in June. Pinckney signed the Treaty of San Lorenzo in October that same year. These agreements put an end, at least temporarily, to European pressures in the trans-Appalachian region. Between the signings, in August 1795, as an aftermath of the Battle of Fallen Timbers, twelve tribes signed the Treaty of Greenville. The Indians surrendered huge sections of their lands, thus ending a struggle that had consumed a major portion of the government's revenues for years.

After the events of 1794 and 1795, settlers poured into the West as water bursts through a broken dike. "I believe scarcely anything short of a Chinese Wall or a line of Troops will restrain . . . the Incroachment of Settlers, upon the Indian Territory," President Washington explained in 1796. Kentucky had become a state in 1792; now, in 1796, Tennessee was admitted. Two years later the Mississippi Territory was organized, and at the end of the century, the Indiana Territory. The great westward flood reached full tide.

Washington's Farewell

Settlement of western problems did not, however, put an end to partisan strife. Even the sainted Washington was neither immune to attack nor entirely above the battle. On questions of finance and foreign policy he usually sided with Hamilton and thus increasingly incurred the anger of the Jeffersonians. But he was, after all, a Virginian. Only the most rabid partisan could think him a tool of northern commercial interests. He remained as he intended himself to be, a symbol of national unity. But he was determined to put away the cares of office at the end of his second term. In September 1796 he announced his retirement in a "Farewell Address" to the nation.

Washington found the acrimonious rivalry between Federalists and Republicans most disturbing. Hamilton advocated national unity, yet he seemed prepared to smash any individual or faction that disagreed with his vision of the country's future. Jefferson had risked his neck for independence, but he opposed the economic development needed to make America strong enough to defend that independence. Washington was less brilliant than either Hamilton or Jefferson but wiser. He appreciated how important it was that the new nation should remain at peace—with the rest of the world and with itself. In his farewell he deplored the "baneful effects of the spirit of party" that led honest people to use unscrupulous means to win a mean advantage over fellow Americans. He tried to show how the North benefited from the prosperity of the South, the South from that of the North, and the East and West also, in reciprocal fashion.

Washington urged the people to avoid both "inveterate antipathies" and "passionate attachments" to any foreign nation. Nothing had alarmed him more than the sight of Americans dividing into "French" and "English" factions. Furthermore, France had repeatedly interfered in American domestic affairs. "Against the insidious wiles of foreign influence," Washington now warned, "the jealousy of a free people ought to be constantly awake." America should develop its foreign trade but steer clear of foreign political connections as far as possible. "Permanent alliances" should be avoided, although "temporary alliances for extraordinary emergencies" might sometimes be useful.

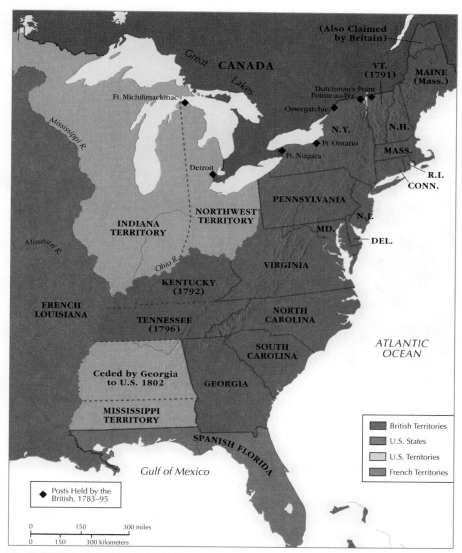

The United States and Its Territories, 1787–1802
In 1804 Georgia's cession became part of the Mississippi Territory. The seven British western forts were evacuated as a result of Jay's Treaty (1795).

The Election of 1796

Washington's Farewell Address was destined to have a long and important influence on American thinking, but its immediate impact was slight. He had intended it to cool political passions. Instead, in the words of Federalist congressman Fisher Ames, people took it as "a signal, like dropping a hat, for the party racers to start." By the time the 1796 presidential campaign had ended, many Federalists and Republicans were refusing to speak to one another.

This portrait of John Adams by William Winstanley was done in 1798. Jeffersonian newspapers referred to Adams derisively as "His Rotundity." Benjamin Bache, editor of the Philadelphia *Aurora*, described him as "blind, bald, toothless, querulous," which was three-quarters true but irrelevant.

Jefferson was the only Republican candidate seriously considered in 1796. The logical Federalist was Hamilton, but, as was to happen so often in American history with powerful leaders, he was not considered "available" because his controversial policies had made him many enemies. Gathering in caucus, the Federalists in Congress nominated Vice President John Adams for the top office and Thomas Pinckney of South Carolina, negotiator of the popular Spanish treaty, for vice president. In the election the Federalists were victorious.

Hamilton, hoping to run the new administration from the wings, preferred Pinckney to Adams. He arranged for some of the Federalist electors from South Carolina to vote only for Pinckney. (Pinckney, who was on the high seas at the time, did not even know he was running for vice president!) Catching wind of this, a number of New England electors retaliated by cutting Pinckney. As a result, Adams won in the electoral college, 71 to 68, over *Jefferson*, who thus became vice president. Pinckney got only 59 electoral votes.

That Adams would now be obliged to work with a vice president who led the opposition seemed to presage a decline in partisanship. Adams actually preferred the Virginian to Pinckney for the vice presidency, while Jefferson said that if Adams would "relinquish his bias to an English constitution," he might make a fine chief executive. The two had in common a distaste for Hamilton—a powerful bond.

However, the closeness of the election indicated a trend toward the Republicans, who were making constant and effective use of the charge that the

Federalists were "monocrats" (monarchists) determined to destroy American liberty. Without Washington to lead them, the Federalist politicians were already quarreling among themselves; honest, able, hardworking John Adams was too caustic and too scathingly frank to unite them. Everything seemed to indicate a Republican victory at the next election.

The XYZ Affair

At this point occurred one of the most remarkable reversals of public feeling in American history. French attacks on American shipping, begun out of irritation at the Jay Treaty and in order to influence the election, continued after Adams took office. Hoping to stop them, Adams appointed three commissioners (Charles Pinckney, U.S. minister to France, and elder brother of Thomas; John Marshall, a Virginia Federalist lawyer; and Elbridge Gerry of Massachusetts, who was not closely identified with either party) to try to negotiate a settlement. They were instructed to seek a moderate settlement, to "terminate our differences . . . without referring to the merits."

Their mission was a fiasco. Talleyrand, the French foreign minister, sent an agent later spoken of as X to demand "something for the pocket," a "gratification," (that is, a bribe) as the price of making a deal. Later two other Tallyrand agents, Y and Z, made the same demand. The Americans refused, more because they suspected Talleyrand's good faith than because of any particular distaste for bribery. "No, no, not a sixpence," Pinckney later told X. The talks broke up, and in April 1798 President Adams released the commissioners' reports.

They caused a sensation. Americans' sense of national honor, perhaps overly tender because the country was so young and insecure, was outraged. Pinckney's laconic refusal to pay a bribe was translated into the grandiose phrase "Millions for defense, but not one cent for tribute!" and broadcast throughout the land. John Adams, never a man with mass appeal, suddenly found himself a national hero. Federalist hotheads burned for a fight. Congress unilaterally abrogated the French Alliance, created a Navy Department, and appropriated enough money to build forty-odd warships and triple the size of the army. Washington came out of retirement to lead the forces, with Hamilton, now a general, as second in command. On the seas American privateers began to attack French shipping.

Adams did not much like the French and he could be extremely stubborn. A declaration of war would have been immensely popular. But perhaps—it is not an entirely illogical surmise about John Adams, who later in life described himself with some relish as "obnoxious, suspected, and unpopular"—the president did not want to be popular. Instead of calling for war, he contented himself with approving the buildup of the armed forces.

The Republicans, however, committed to friendship with France, did not appreciate Adams's moderation. Although angered by the XYZ Affair, they tried, one

William Russel Birch engraving of the construction of the twenty-eight-gun frigate *Philadelphia* in that city. The *Philadelphia* was one of the larger ships built during the heightened tensions with France after the XYZ affair.

Federalist complained, "to clog the wheels of government" by opposing the military appropriations. John Daly Burk of the New York *Time Piece* called Adams a "mock Monarch" surrounded by a "court composed of tories and speculators," which of course was a flat lie.

Many Federalists expected the Republicans to side with France if war broke out. Hysterical and near panic, they easily persuaded themselves that the danger of subversion was acute. The French Revolution and the resulting war were churning European society to the depths, stirring the hopes of liberals and striking fear in the hearts of conservatives. Refugees of both persuasions were flocking to the United States. Suddenly the presence of these foreigners seemed threatening to "native" Americans.

The Alien and Sedition Acts

Conservative Federalists saw in this situation a chance to smash the opposition. In June and July 1798 they pushed through Congress a series of repressive measures known as the Alien and Sedition Acts. The Alien Enemies Act gave the president the power to arrest or expel aliens in time of "declared war," but since the quasi-war with France was never declared, this measure had no practical importance. The

Alien Act authorized the president to expel all aliens whom he thought "dangerous to the peace and safety of the United States." (Adams never invoked this law, but a number of aliens left the country out of fear that he might.)

Finally, there was the Sedition Act. Its first section, making it a crime "to impede the operation of any law" or to attempt to instigate a riot or insurrection, was reasonable enough; but the act also made it illegal to publish, or even to utter, any "false, scandalous and malicious" criticism of high government officials. Although milder than British sedition laws, this proviso rested, as James Madison said, on "the exploded doctrine" that government officials "are the masters and not the servants of the people."

As the election of 1800 approached, the Federalists made a systematic attempt to silence the leading Republican newspapers. Twenty-five persons were prosecuted and ten convicted, all in patently unfair trials. In typical cases, the editor Thomas Cooper, an English-born radical, later president of the University of South Carolina, was sentenced to six months in jail and fined $400; the editor Charles Holt got three months and a $200 fine; and the editor James Callender got nine months and a $200 fine.

The Kentucky and Virginia Resolves

While Thomas Jefferson did not object to state sedition laws, he believed that the Alien and Sedition Acts violated the First Amendment's guarantees of freedom of speech and the press and were an invasion of the rights of the states. In 1798 he and Madison decided to draw up resolutions arguing that the laws were unconstitutional. Madison's draft was presented to the Virginia legislature and Jefferson's to the legislature of Kentucky.

Jefferson argued that since the Constitution was a compact made by sovereign states, each state had "an equal right to judge for itself" when the compact had been violated. Thus a state could declare a law of Congress unconstitutional. Madison's Virginia Resolves took an only slightly less forthright position.

Neither Kentucky nor Virginia tried to implement these resolves or to prevent the enforcement of the Alien and Sedition Acts. Jefferson and Madison were protesting Federalist high-handedness and firing the opening salvo of Jefferson's campaign for the presidency, not advancing a new constitutional theory of extreme states' rights. "Keep away all show of force," Jefferson advised his supporters.

This was sound advice, for events were again playing into the hands of the Republicans. Talleyrand had never wanted war with the United States. When he discovered how vehemently the Americans had reacted to his little attempt to replenish his personal fortune, he let Adams know that new negotiators would be properly received.

President Adams quickly grasped the importance of the French change of heart. Other leading Federalists, however, had lost their heads. By shouting about the French danger, they had roused the country against radicalism, and they did not intend to surrender this advantage tamely. Hamilton in particular wanted war at almost any price—if not against France, then against Spain. He saw himself at the head of the new American army sweeping first across Louisiana and the Floridas, then on to the South. "We ought to squint at South America," he suggested. "Tempting objects will be within our grasp."

But the Puritan John Adams was a specialist at resisting temptation. At this critical point his intelligence, his moderate political philosophy, and his stubborn integrity stood him in good stead. He would neither go to war merely to destroy the political opposition in America nor follow "the fools who were intriguing to plunge us into an alliance with England . . . and wild expeditions to South America." Instead he submitted to the Senate the name of a new minister plenipotentiary to France, and when the Federalists tried to block the appointment, he threatened to resign. That would have made Jefferson president! So the furious Federalists had to give in, although they forced Adams to send three men instead of one.

Napoleon had taken over France by the time the Americans arrived, and he drove a harder bargain than Talleyrand would have. But in the end he signed an agreement (the Convention of 1800) abrogating the Franco-American treaties of 1778. Nothing was said about the damage done to American shipping by the French, but the war scare was over.

The Kentucky and Virginia Resolves, however, had raised an issue that would loom large in the next century. If Congress passed laws that particular states thought to be unconstitutional, did states have the right to ignore those laws—or to withdraw from the Constitution altogether?

1781	States fail to approve Congress's tariff
1786	Rhode Island Supreme Court upholds state legal tender act (*Trevett* v. *Weeden*)
	Shays's Rebellion collapses in Springfield, Massachusetts
	Only five states send delegates to Annapolis Convention
1787	Delegates meet at Philadelphia Constitutional Convention
1787–1788	All states but North Carolina and Rhode Island ratify Constitution
1789	President Washington is inaugurated
	Storming of Bastille in Paris begins French Revolution
1790	Hamilton issues his *Report on Public Credit*
1791	Hamilton issues his *Report on Manufactures*
	First Ten Amendments (Bill of Rights) to the Constitution are ratified
	Republican and Federalist political parties are organized
	Philip Freneau's *National Gazette* and John Fenno's *Gazette of the United States* are founded
1793	French revolutionaries execute King Louis XVI
	Washington issues Declaration of Neutrality
1794	"Mad Anthony" Wayne's troops defeat Indians at Battle of Fallen Timbers
	Washington's militiamen thwart Whiskey Rebellion in Pennsylvania
1795	Senate ratifies humiliating Jay Treaty
1796	Washington announces his retirement in Farewell Address
	John Adams is elected president
1798	French demand bribe during XYZ Affair
	Congress passes Alien and Sedition Acts
1798–1799	Jefferson presents Kentucky Resolutions
	Madison presents Virginia Resolutions

Jeffersonian Democracy

DURING THEIR FIRST WEEK IN COLLEGE, FRESHMEN ON AVERAGE receive eight applications for credit cards. Credit card companies target college students because they have a lifetime to acquire debt—and pay it off. A recent government study showed that the average college senior had a credit card balance of $3,200. One in five college students had credit card debt between $3,000 and $7,000. Many cope with such debt by cutting expenses, taking jobs, or skipping school; some do not cope. A 2006 documentary film described the plight of two college students in Oklahoma who, awash in credit card debt, committed suicide.

Many college students incur debt responsibly, most often to pay for college. College graduates owe on the average $20,000 in student loans, but this usually pays off—literally: In 2004 college graduates on the average earned $51,500, while individuals with only a high school education earned $28,600.

Many of the Founders of the nation were also entangled in personal debt. In 1798 Robert Morris, the financier who had devised the funded debt to pay and equip George Washington's army, was imprisoned for personal debt. He languished in the Prune Street debtor's prison in Philadelphia for three years. Thomas Jefferson, on paper one of the richest men in Virginia, owner of thousands of acres of land and 200 slaves, was also plagued by debt. His financial woes mounted as he built additions to Monticello, his home, and acquired more books for his library, one of the finest in the nation. Creditors harassed him. "I am miserable till I shall owe not a shilling," he wrote in 1787. When he died, he was bankrupt. His slaves were sold to pay creditors.

Jefferson's antipathy to debt influenced his ideas about government. He opposed federal expenditures because they could lead to indebtedness. His parsimony left the nation vulnerable to foreigners, whether high-handed European rulers or pirate states in northern Africa. On a few occasions—such as the chance to acquire the Louisiana Territory—he splurged, but soon recanted. On leaving office he urged his successor to pay off the federal deficit.

Jefferson Elected President

Once the furor over war and subversion subsided, public attention focused on the presidential contest between Adams and Jefferson. Because of his stand for peace, Adams personally escaped the brunt of popular indignation against the Federalist party. His solid qualities had a strong appeal to conservatives, and fear that the Republicans would introduce radical "French" social reforms did not disappear when the danger of war with France ended. Many nationalist-minded voters worried that the Republicans, waving the banner of states' rights, would weaken the strong government established by the Federalists. The economic progress stimulated by Hamilton's financial reforms also seemed threatened. But when the electors' votes were counted in February 1801, the Republicans were discovered to have won narrowly, 73 to 65.

But which Republican was to be president? The Constitution did not distinguish between presidential and vice presidential candidates; it provided only that each elector vote for two candidates, the one with the most votes becoming president and the runner-up vice president. The development of national political parties made this system impractical. The vice presidential candidate of the Republicans was Aaron Burr of New York, a former senator and a rival of Hamilton in law and politics. But Republican party solidarity had been perfect; Jefferson and Burr received seventy-three votes each. Because of the tie, the Constitution required that the House of Representatives (voting by states) choose between them.

In the House the Republicans could control only eight of the sixteen state delegations. On the first ballot Jefferson got these eight votes, one short of election, while six states voted for Burr. Two state delegations, being evenly split, lost their votes. Through thirty-five ballots the deadlock persisted; the Federalist congressmen, fearful of Jefferson's supposed radicalism, voted solidly for Burr.

In the end, Alexander Hamilton decided who would be the next president. Although he considered Jefferson "too much in earnest in his democracy" and "not very mindful of truth," he detested Burr. He exerted his considerable influence on Federalist congressmen on Jefferson's behalf. Finally, on February 17, 1801, Jefferson was elected. Burr became vice president.

To make sure that this deadlock would never be repeated, the Twelfth Amendment was drafted, providing for separate balloting in the Electoral College for president and vice president. This change was ratified in 1804, shortly before the next election.

The Federalist Contribution

On March 4, 1801, in the raw new national capital on the Potomac River named in honor of George Washington, the Father of his Country, Thomas Jefferson took the presidential oath and delivered his inaugural address.[1] His goal was to recapture the simplicity and austerity—the "pure republicanism"—that had characterized "the spirit of '76." The new president believed that a revolution as important as that heralded by his immortal Declaration of Independence had occurred, and for once most of his political enemies agreed with him.

Certainly an era had ended. In the years between the Peace of Paris and Jay's Treaty, the Federalists had practically monopolized the political good sense of the nation. They were "right" in strengthening the federal government, in establishing a sound fiscal system, in trying to diversify the economy, in seeking an accommodation with Great Britain, and in refusing to be carried away with enthusiasm for France despite the bright dreams inspired by the French Revolution.

But the Federalists were unable to face up to defeat. When they saw the Republicans gathering strength by developing clever new techniques of party organization and propaganda, mouthing slogans about liberty, attacking "monocrats," glorifying both the past with its satisfying simplicity and the future with its promise of a glorious day when all men would be free, equal, and brothers, they panicked. Abandoning the sober wisdom of their great period, they fought to save themselves at any cost. The effort turned defeat into rout. The Republican victory, close in the Electoral College, approached landslide proportions in the congressional elections, where popular feeling expressed itself directly.

Jefferson erred, however, in calling this triumph a revolution. The real upheaval had been attempted in 1798; it was Federalist-inspired, and it failed. In 1800 the voters expressed a preference for the old over the new; that is, for individual freedom and limited national power. And Jefferson, despite Federalist fears that he would destroy the Constitution and establish a radical social order, presided instead over a regime that confirmed the great achievements of the Federalist era.

What was most significant about the election of 1800 was that it was *not* a revolution. After a bitter contest, the Jeffersonians took power and proceeded to change the policy of the government. They did so peacefully. Thus American republican government passed a crucial test: Control of its machinery had changed hands in a democratic and orderly way. And only slightly less significant, the informal party system had demonstrated its usefulness. The Jeffersonians had organized popular dissatisfaction with Federalist policies, formulated a platform of reform, chosen leaders to put their plans into effect, and elected those leaders to office.

---

[1] *In 1790, when Jefferson balked at having the federal government assume the obligation of paying state debts and creditors with claims on the Continental Congress, Hamilton agreed to place the national capital in Virginia.*

Thomas Jefferson: Political Theorist

Much as Jefferson worried that an indebted nation could become enslaved to its creditors, he feared banks because they too deprived debtors of true liberty. He believed *all* government a necessary evil at best, for by its nature it restricted the freedom of the individual. For this reason, he wanted the United States to remain a society of small independent farmers. Such a nation did not need much political organization.

Jefferson's main objection to Alexander Hamilton was that Hamilton wanted to commercialize and centralize the country; Hamilton embraced public debt so as to initiate public projects and promote investment. This Jefferson feared, for it would mean that financial speculators and creditors would acquire economic power. Moreover, a commercial economy would lead to the growth of cities, which would complicate society and hence require more regulation. "The mobs of great cities add just as much to the support of pure government," he said, "as sores do to the strength of the human body." Later in life he warned a nephew to avoid "populous cities" because, he said, in such places young men acquire "habits and partialities which do not contribute to the happiness of their afterlife." Like Hamilton, he believed that city workers were easy prey for demagogues. "I consider the class of artificers as the panderers of vice, and the instruments by which the liberties of a country are usually overturned," he said. "Those who labor in the earth," he also said, "are the chosen people of God, if ever He had a chosen people."

Jefferson objected to what he considered Hamilton's pro-British orientation. Despite his support of the American Revolution, Hamilton admired English society and the orderliness of the British government, and he modeled much of his financial program on the British example. To the author of the Declaration of Independence, these attitudes passed all understanding. Jefferson thought English society immoral and decadent, the British system of government fundamentally corrupt. Toward France, the two took opposite positions. Jefferson was in Paris when the French Revolution broke out; he was delighted to see another blow struck at tyranny. To Hamilton, the violence and social disruption caused by the French Revolution were anathema.

Like Hamilton, Jefferson thought human beings basically selfish. "Lions and tigers are mere lambs compared with men," he once said. Although he claimed to have some doubts about the subject, he suspected that blacks were "inferior to whites in the endowments both of body and mind." (Hamilton, who also owned slaves, stated flatly of blacks: "Their natural faculties are as good as ours.") Jefferson's pronouncements on race are yet more troubling in light of recent research, including DNA studies that point to the likelihood that he fathered one or more children by Sally Hemings, one of his slaves.

Yet like a good child of the Enlightenment, Jefferson believed that "no definite limits can be assigned to the improvability of the human race" and that unless people were free to follow the dictates of reason, the march of civilization would grind quickly to a halt. "To preserve the freedom of the human mind," he wrote, "every

Debating the Past

DID THOMAS JEFFERSON FATHER A CHILD BY HIS SLAVE?

The photo below *(left)* shows Thomas Jefferson's bedroom at Monticello. He designed the alcove to ensure privacy. A page from his farm accounts *(right)* in his own writing lists as slaves Sally Hemings and several of her children, including Madison, born in 1805, and Eston, born in 1808. In 1787, Sally Hemings, a young slave from the Jefferson plantation, was sent to Paris to serve Thomas Jefferson, U.S. minister to France, and his two daughters. Jefferson's wife had died five years earlier. After Jefferson was elected president in 1800, a newspaper claimed that he had fathered all of Hemings's children. Jefferson ignored the charges and his political allies denounced them as lies. In 1873 Madison Hemings told an Ohio reporter that his mother, Sally Hemings, had said that his father was Thomas Jefferson. Few took the story seriously. Jefferson scholar Merrill Peterson (1960) was the first to mention Madison Hemings's story, which he attributed to Federalists seeking to embarrass Jefferson and abolitionists seeking to discredit slavery. Dumas Malone (1948–1981), the preeminent Jefferson biographer, flatly

rejected the possibility of a Jefferson-Hemings liaison. Among scholars, Malone's views went mostly unchallenged for decades. But Annette Gordon-Reed (1997), a lawyer, accumulated considerable evidence in support of Madison Hemings's story, though she did not think it proven. The next year a forensic pathologist compared a DNA sample of a descendant of Field Jefferson, Thomas Jefferson's uncle, to that of a descendant of Eston Hemings. A genetic sequence matched. Eston had been fathered by a Jefferson. Some scholars pointed to Jefferson's younger brother, Randolph, as the father, but most Jefferson scholars concluded that Thomas Jefferson was the more likely father. No such revelations could diminish Jefferson's significance as statesman, but they further complicate our understanding of one of the nation's foremost apostles of freedom.

Merrill Peterson, *The Jefferson Image in the American Mind* (1960), Dumas Malone, *Jefferson and His Time*, 6 volumes (1948–1981), Annette Gordon-Reed, *Thomas Jefferson and Sally Hemings* (1997). See also Joseph Ellis, *American Sphinx* (1998).

spirit should be ready to devote itself to martyrdom." Democracy seemed to him not so much an ideal as a practical necessity. If people could not govern themselves, how could they be expected to govern their fellows? He had no patience with Hamilton's fondness for magnifying the virtues of the rich and the well-born. He believed that "genius" was a rare quality but one "which nature has shown as liberally among poor as rich." When a very old man he wrote:

"The mass of mankind has not been born with saddles on their backs, nor a favored few booted and spurred, ready to ride them legitimately, by the grace of God."

Jefferson as President

The novelty of the new administration lay in its style and its moderation. Jefferson saw to it that the whiskey tax and other Federalist excises were repealed, and he made sharp cuts in military and naval expenditures to keep the budget in balance. The Naturalization Act of 1798 was repealed, and the old five-year residence requirement for citizenship restored. The Sedition Act and the Alien Act expired of their own accord in 1801 and 1802.

The changes were not drastic. Jefferson made no effort to tear down the fiscal structure that Hamilton had erected. "We can pay off his debt," the new president confessed, "but we cannot get rid of his financial system." Nor did the author of the Kentucky Resolves try to alter the balance of federal-state power.

Yet there was a different tone to the new regime. Jefferson had no desire to surround himself with pomp and ceremony; the excessive formality of the Washington and Adams administrations had been distasteful to him. From the moment of his election, he played down the ceremonial aspects of the presidency. He asked that he be notified of his election by mail rather than by a committee, and he would have preferred to have taken the oath at Charlottesville, near Monticello, his home, rather than at Washington. After the inauguration, he returned to his boardinghouse on foot and took dinner in his usual seat at the common table.

In the White House he often wore a frayed coat and carpet slippers, even to receive the representatives of foreign powers when they arrived, resplendent with silk ribbons and a sense of their own importance, to present their credentials. At social affairs he paid little heed to the status and seniority of his guests. When dinner was announced, he offered his arm to whichever lady he was talking to at the moment and placed her at his right; other guests were free to sit wherever they found an empty chair. During business hours congressmen, friends, foreign officials, and plain citizens coming to call took their turn in the order of their arrival. "The principle of society with us," Jefferson explained, "is the equal rights of all. . . . Nobody shall be above you, nor you above anybody, *pell-mell* is our law."

Jefferson made effective use of his close supporters in Congress and of Cabinet members as well, in persuading Congress to go along with his proposals. His state papers were models of reason, minimizing conflicts, stressing areas where all honest people must agree. After all, as he indicated in his inaugural address, nearly all Americans believed in having both a federal government and a republican system. No great principle divided them into irreconcilable camps. Jefferson set out to bring them all into *his* camp, and he succeeded so well in four years that when he ran for reelection against Charles Pinckney, he got 162 of the 176 electoral votes cast. Eventually even John Quincy Adams, son of the second president, became a Jeffersonian.

At the same time, Jefferson was anything but nonpartisan in the sense that Washington had been. His Cabinet consisted exclusively of men of his own party. He exerted almost continuous pressure on Congress to make sure that his legislative program was enacted into law. He did not remove many Federalist officeholders, and at one point he remarked ruefully that government officials seldom died and never resigned. But when he could, he used his power of appointment to reward his friends and punish his enemies.

Jefferson's Attack on the Judiciary

Although notably open-minded and tolerant, Jefferson had a few stubborn prejudices. One was against kings, another against the British system of government. A third was against judges, or rather, against entrenched judicial power. While recognizing that judges must have a degree of independence, he feared what he called their "habit of going out of the question before them, to throw an anchor ahead, and grapple further hold for future advances of power." The biased behavior of Federalist judges during the trials under the Sedition Act had enormously increased this distrust, and it burst all bounds when the Federalist majority of the dying Congress rammed through the Judiciary Act of 1801.

The Judiciary Act created six new circuit courts, presided over by sixteen new federal judges and a small army of attorneys, marshals, and clerks. The expanding country needed the judges, but with the enthusiastic cooperation of President Adams, the Federalists made shameless use of the opportunity to fill all the new positions with conservative members of their own party. The new appointees were dubbed "midnight justices" because Adams had stayed up until midnight on March 3, his last day as president, feverishly signing their commissions.

The Republicans retaliated as soon as the new Congress met by repealing the Judiciary Act of 1801, but on taking office Jefferson had discovered that in the confusion of Adams's last hours, the commissions of a number of justices of the peace for the new District of Columbia had not been distributed. While these were small fry indeed, Jefferson was so angry that he ordered the commissions held up even though they had been signed by Adams.

One of the appointees, William Marbury, then petitioned the Supreme Court for a writ of mandamus (Latin for "we order") directing the new secretary of state, James Madison, to give him his commission.

The case of *Marbury* v. *Madison* (1803) placed Chief Justice John Marshall, one of Adams's "midnight" appointments, in an embarrassing position. Marbury had a strong claim; if Marshall refused to issue a mandamus, everyone would say he dared not stand up to Jefferson, and the prestige of the Court would suffer. If he issued the writ, however, he would place the Court in direct conflict with the executive. Jefferson particularly disliked Marshall. He would probably tell Madison to ignore the order, and in the prevailing state of public opinion nothing could be done about it. This would be a still more staggering blow to the judiciary. What should the chief justice do?

Marshall had studied law only briefly and had no previous judicial experience, but in this crisis he first displayed the genius that was to mark him as a great judge. By right Marbury should have his commission, he announced. However, the Court could not require Madison to give it to him. Marbury's request for a mandamus had been based on an ambiguous clause in the Judiciary Act of 1789. That clause was unconstitutional, Marshall declared, and therefore void. Congress could not legally give the Supreme Court the right to issue writs of mandamus in such circumstances.

With the skill and foresight of a chess grand master, Marshall turned what had looked like a trap into a triumph. By sacrificing the pawn, Marbury, he established the power of the Supreme Court to invalidate federal laws that conflicted with the Constitution. Jefferson could not check him because Marshall had *refused* power instead of throwing an anchor ahead, as Jefferson had feared. Yet he had certainly grappled a "further hold for future advances of power," and the president could do nothing to stop him.

The *Marbury* ruling made Jefferson more determined to strike at the Federalist-dominated courts. He decided to press for the impeachment of some of the more partisan judges. First he had the House of Representatives bring charges against District Judge John Pickering. Pickering was clearly deranged—he had frequently delivered profane and drunken harangues from the bench—and the Senate quickly voted to remove him. Then Jefferson went after a much larger fish, Samuel Chase, associate justice of the Supreme Court.

Chase had been prominent for decades, an early leader of the Sons of Liberty, a signer of the Declaration of Independence, active in the affairs of the Continental Congress. Washington had named him to the Supreme Court in 1796, and he had delivered a number of important opinions. But his handling of cases under the Sedition Act had been outrageously high-handed. Defense lawyers had become so exasperated as to throw down their briefs in disgust at some of his prejudiced rulings. However, the trial demonstrated that Chase's actions had not constituted the "high crimes and misdemeanors" required by the Constitution to remove a judge. Even Jefferson became disenchanted with the efforts of some of his more extreme followers and accepted Chase's acquittal with equanimity.

The Barbary Pirates

The North African Arab states of Morocco, Algiers, Tunis, and Tripoli had for decades made a business of piracy, seizing vessels all over the Mediterranean and holding crews and passengers for ransom. The European powers found it simpler to pay them annual protection money than to crush them. Under Washington and Adams, the United States joined in the payment of this tribute; while large, the sums were less than the increased costs of insurance for shippers when the protection was not purchased.

Such spinelessness ran against Jefferson's grain. "When this idea comes across my mind, my faculties are absolutely suspended between indignation and impatience," he said. When the pasha of Tripoli tried to raise the charges, he balked. Tripoli then declared war in May 1801, and Jefferson dispatched a squadron to the Mediterranean.

But the pirates were not overwhelmed, and a major American warship, the frigate *Philadelphia*, had to be destroyed after running aground off the Tripolitan coast. The payment of tribute continued until 1815. Just the same, America, though far removed from the pirate bases, was the only maritime nation that tried to resist the blackmail. Although the war failed to achieve Jefferson's purpose of ending the payments, the pasha agreed to a new treaty more favorable to the United States, and American sailors, led by Commodore Edward Preble, won valuable experience and a large portion of fame. The greatest hero was Lieutenant Stephen Decatur, who captured two pirate ships, led ten men in a daring raid on another in which he took on a gigantic sailor in a wild battle of cutlass against boarding pike, and snatched the stricken *Philadelphia* from the pirates by sneaking aboard and setting it afire.

The Louisiana Purchase

The major achievements of Jefferson's first term had to do with the American West, and the greatest by far was the acquisition of the huge area between the Mississippi River and the Rocky Mountains. In a sense the purchase of this region, called Louisiana, was fortuitous, an accidental by-product of European political adjustments and the whim of Napoleon Bonaparte. Certainly Jefferson had not planned it, for in his inaugural address he had expressed the opinion that the country already had all the land it would need "for a thousand generations." It was nonetheless the perfectly logical—one might almost say inevitable—result of a long series of events in the history of the Mississippi Valley.

Along with every other American who had even a superficial interest in the West, Jefferson understood that the United States must have access to the mouth of the Mississippi and the city of New Orleans or eventually lose everything beyond the Appalachians. "There is on the globe one single spot, the possessor of which is our natural and habitual enemy," he was soon to write. "It is New Orleans." Thus when he learned shortly after his inauguration that Spain had given Louisiana back to France, he was immediately on his guard. Control of Louisiana by Spain, a "feeble" country with "pacific dispositions," could be tolerated; control by a resurgent France dominated by Napoleon, the greatest military genius of the age, was entirely different. Did Napoleon have designs on Canada? Did he perhaps mean to resume the old Spanish and British game of encouraging the Indians to torment the American frontier? And what now would be the status of Pinckney's precious treaty?

Deeply worried, the president instructed his minister to France, Robert R. Livingston, to seek assurances that American rights in New Orleans would be respected and to negotiate the purchase of West Florida in case that region had also been turned over to France.

Jefferson's concern was well founded; France was indeed planning new imperial ventures in North America. Immediately after settling its difficulties with the United States through the Convention of 1800, France signed the secret Treaty of San Ildefonso with Spain, which returned Louisiana to France. Napoleon hoped to use this region as a breadbasket for the French West Indian sugar plantations, just as colonies like Pennsylvania and Massachusetts had fed the British sugar islands before the Revolution.

However, the most important French island, Saint Domingue (Hispaniola), at the time occupied entirely by the nation of Haiti, had slipped from French control. During the French Revolution, the slaves of the island had revolted. In 1793 they were granted personal freedom, but they fought on under the leadership of the "Black Napoleon," a self-taught genius named Toussaint Louverture, and by 1801 the island was entirely in their hands. The original Napoleon, taking advantage of the slackening of war in Europe, dispatched an army of 20,000 men under General Charles Leclerc to reconquer it.

When Jefferson learned of the Leclerc expedition, he had no trouble divining its relationship to Louisiana. His uneasiness became outright alarm. In April 1802 he again urged Minister Livingston to attempt the purchase of New Orleans and Florida or, as an alternative, to buy a tract of land near the mouth of the Mississippi where a new port could be constructed. Of necessity, the mild-mannered, idealistic president now became an aggressive realist. If the right of deposit could not be preserved through negotiation, it must be purchased with gunpowder, even if that meant acting in conjunction with the despised British. "The day that France takes possession of New Orleans," he warned, "we must marry ourselves to the British fleet and nation."

In October 1802 the Spanish, who had not yet actually turned Louisiana over to France, heightened the tension by suddenly revoking the right of deposit at New Orleans. We now know that the French had no hand in this action, but it was beyond reason to expect Jefferson or the American people to believe it at the time. With the West clamoring for relief, Jefferson appointed his friend and disciple James Monroe minister plenipotentiary and sent him to Paris with instructions to offer up to $10 million for New Orleans and Florida. If France refused, he and Livingston should open negotiations for a "closer connection" with the British.

The tension broke before Monroe even reached France. General Leclerc's Saint Domingue expedition ended in disaster. Although Toussaint surrendered, Haitian resistance continued. Yellow fever raged through the French army; Leclerc himself fell to the fever, which wiped out practically his entire force.

When news of this calamity reached Napoleon early in 1803, he began to have second thoughts about reviving French imperialism in the New World. Without Saint Domingue, the wilderness of Louisiana seemed of little value. Napoleon was

The 1790 slave rebellion in Haiti, led by Toussaint Louverture, caused thousands of French to flee the island; many settled in South Carolina. Their stories fueled fears of a slave uprising in the South.

preparing a new campaign in Europe. He could no longer spare troops to recapture a rebellious West Indian island or to hold Louisiana against a possible British attack, and he needed money.

For some weeks the commander of the most powerful army in the world mulled the question without consulting anyone. Then, with characteristic suddenness, he made up his mind. On April 10 he ordered Foreign Minister Talleyrand to offer not merely New Orleans but all of Louisiana to the Americans. The next day Talleyrand summoned Livingston to his office on the rue du Bac and dropped this bombshell. Livingston was almost struck speechless but quickly recovered his composure. When Talleyrand asked what the United States would give for the province, he suggested the French equivalent of about $5 million. Talleyrand pronounced the sum "too low" and urged Livingston to think about the subject for a day or two.

Livingston faced a situation that no modern diplomat would ever have to confront. His instructions said nothing about buying an area almost as large as the entire United States, and there was no time to write home for new instructions. The offer staggered the imagination. Luckily, Monroe arrived the next day to share the responsibility. The two Americans consulted, dickered with the French, and finally

New Orleans in 1803, when the city was acquired—along with much of the modern United States—in the Louisiana Purchase. It was known as the Crescent City because of the way it hugged a curved section of the Mississippi River. In 1803, its population was about 8,000, including 4,000 whites, 2,700 slaves, and about 1,300 free "persons of color."

agreed—they could scarcely have done otherwise—to accept the proposal. Early in May they signed a treaty. For 60 million francs—about $15 million—the United States was to have all of Louisiana.

No one knew exactly how large the region was or what it contained. When Livingston asked Talleyrand about the boundaries of the purchase, he replied: "I can give you no direction. You have made a noble bargain for yourselves, and I suppose you will make the most of it." Never, as the historian Henry Adams wrote, "did the United States government get so much for so little."

Napoleon's unexpected concession caused consternation in America, though there was never real doubt that the treaty would be ratified. Jefferson did not believe that the government had the power under the Constitution to add new territory or to grant American citizenship to the 50,000 residents of Louisiana by executive act, as the treaty required. He even drafted a constitutional amendment: "The province of Louisiana is incorporated with the United States and made part thereof," but his advisers convinced him that it would be dangerous to delay approval of the treaty until an amendment could be acted on by three-fourths of the states. Jefferson then suggested that the Senate ratify the treaty and submit an amendment afterward "confirming an act which the nation had not previously authorized." This idea was so obviously illogical that he quickly dropped it. Finally, he came to believe "that the less we say about constitutional difficulties the better." Since what he called "the good sense of our country" clearly wanted Louisiana, he decided to "acquiesce with satisfaction" while Congress overlooked the "metaphysical subtleties" of the problem and ratified the treaty.

It was ironic—and a man as perceptive as Hamilton must surely have recognized the irony—that the acquisition of Louisiana ensured Jefferson's reelection and further contributed to the downfall of the Federalists. The purchase was popular even in the New England bastions of that party. While the negotiations were progressing in Paris, Jefferson had written of partisan political affairs: "If we can settle happily the difficulties of the Mississippi, I think we may promise ourselves smooth seas during our time." These words turned out to be no more accurate than most political predictions, but the Louisiana Purchase drove another spike into the Federalists' coffin.

The Federalists Discredited

The West and South were solidly for Jefferson, and the North was rapidly succumbing to his charm. The addition of new western states would soon further reduce New England's power in national affairs. So complete did the Republican triumph seem that a handful of diehard Federalists in New England began to think of secession. Led by former secretary of state Timothy Pickering, a sour, implacable conservative, a group known as the Essex Junto organized in 1804 a scheme to break away from the Union and establish a "northern confederacy."

Even within the dwindling Federalist ranks the junto had little support. Nevertheless, Pickering and his friends pushed ahead, drafting a plan whereby, having captured political control of New York, they would take the entire Northeast out of the Union. Since they could not begin to win New York for anyone in their own ranks, they hit on the idea of supporting Vice President Aaron Burr, who was running against the "regular" Republican candidate for governor of New York. Although Burr did not promise to bring New York into their confederacy if elected, he encouraged them enough to win their backing. The foolishness of the plot was revealed in the April elections: Burr was overwhelmed by the regular Republican. The junto's scheme collapsed.

The incident, however, had a tragic aftermath. Hamilton had campaigned against Burr, whom he considered "an embryo Caesar." When he continued after the election to cast aspersions on Burr's character (not a very difficult assignment, since Burr, despite being a grandson of the preacher Jonathan Edwards, frequently violated both the political and sexual mores of the day), Burr challenged him to a duel. It was well known that Hamilton opposed dueling in principle, his own son having been slain in such an encounter, and he certainly had no need to prove his courage. But he believed that his honor was at stake. The two met with pistols on July 11, 1804, at Weehawken, New Jersey, across the Hudson River from New York City. Hamilton made no effort to hit the challenger, but Burr took careful aim. Hamilton fell, wounded; he died the next day. Thus a great, if enigmatic, man was

Pistols used in the duel between Aaron Burr and Alexander Hamilton. Before the duel Hamilton's lawyer drew up a contract specifying the terms: The duelists were to shoot from ten paces, and the barrels of the guns were to be no longer than 11 inches. Taking deadly aim, Burr fired a .54-caliber ball that hit Hamilton in the chest. It ricocheted off his rib, punctured his liver, and lodged in his backbone. He died the next day.

cut off in his prime. His work, in a sense, had been completed, and his philosophy of government was being everywhere rejected, yet the nation's loss was large.

Lewis and Clark

While the disgruntled Federalists dreamed of secession, Jefferson was planning the exploration of Louisiana and the region beyond. He especially hoped to find a water route to connect the upper Mississippi or its tributaries with the Pacific Ocean. Early in 1803 he got $2,500 from Congress and obtained the permission of the French to send his exploring party across Louisiana. To command the expedition he appointed his private secretary, Meriwether Lewis, a young Virginian who had seen considerable service with the army in the West and who possessed, according to Jefferson, "a great mass of accurate information on all the subjects of nature." Lewis chose as his companion officer William Clark, another soldier (he had served with General Anthony Wayne at the Battle of Fallen Timbers) who had much experience in negotiating with Indians.

Lewis and Clark gathered a group of forty-eight experienced men near St. Louis during the winter of 1803–1804. In the spring they made their way slowly up the Missouri River in a 55-foot keelboat and two dugout canoes, called pirogues. By late fall they had reached what is now North Dakota, where they built a small station, Fort Mandan, and spent the winter there. In April 1805, having shipped back to the president more than thirty boxes of plants, minerals, animal skins and bones, and Indian artifacts, they struck out again toward the mountains, accompanied by a Shoshone woman, Sacagawea, and her French-Canadian husband, Toussaint Charbonneau, who acted as interpreters and guides. They passed the Great Falls of the Missouri and then clambered over the Continental Divide at Lemhi Pass in

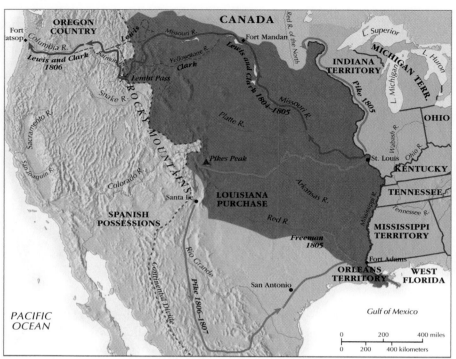

Exploring the Louisiana Purchase

southwestern Montana. Soon thereafter the going became easier, and they descended to the Pacific by way of the Clearwater and Columbia Rivers, reaching their destination in November. They had hoped to return by ship, but during the long, damp winter not a single vessel appeared. In the spring of 1806 they headed back by land, reaching St. Louis on September 23.

The country greeted the news of their return with delight. Besides locating several passes across the Rocky Mountains, Lewis and Clark had established friendly relations with a great many Indian tribes to whom they presented gifts, medals, American flags, and a sales talk designed to promote peace and the fur trade. They brought back a wealth of data about the country and its resources. The journals kept by members of the group were published and, along with their accurate maps, became major sources for scientists, students, and future explorers. To Jefferson's great personal satisfaction, Lewis provided him with many specimens of the local wildlife, including two grizzly bear cubs, which he kept for a time in a stone pit in the White House lawn.

The success of Lewis and Clark did not open the gates of Louisiana very wide. Other explorers sent out by Jefferson accomplished far less. Thomas Freeman, an Irish-born surveyor, led a small party up the Red River but ran into a powerful Spanish force near the present junction of Arkansas, Oklahoma, and Texas and was forced to retreat. Between 1805 and 1807 Lieutenant Zebulon Pike explored the upper Mississippi Valley and the Colorado region. (He discovered but failed to scale the peak south of Denver that bears his name.) Pike eventually made his way to

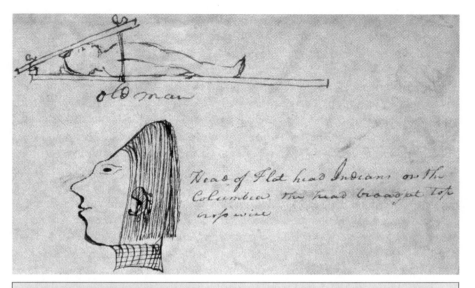

The "Flat Head" (Chinook) Indians acquired their name through shaping in infancy, as shown in a diagram from the Lewis and Clark journals. More remarkable to the explorers than the shape of the Indian heads was the tribeswomen's open sexuality. "The young females are fond of the attention of our men and appear to meet the sincere approbation of their friends and connections for thus obtaining their favors," Captain Clark confided in his diary.

Santa Fe and the upper reaches of the Rio Grande, but he was not nearly so careful and acute an observer as Lewis and Clark were and consequently brought back much less information. By 1808 fur traders based at St. Louis were beginning to invade the Rockies, and by 1812 there were 75,000 people in the southern section of the new territory, which was admitted to the Union that year as the state of Louisiana. The northern region lay almost untouched until much later.

The Burr Conspiracy

Republican virtue seemed to have triumphed. But Jefferson soon found himself in trouble at home and abroad.

In part his difficulties arose from the extent of the Republican victory. In 1805 his Federalist opponents had no useful ideas, no intelligent leadership, no effective numbers. They held only a quarter of the seats in Congress. As often happens in such situations, lack of opposition weakened party discipline and encouraged factionalism among the Republicans.

The Republican who caused Jefferson the most trouble was Aaron Burr, and the president was partly to blame for the difficulty. After their contest for the presidency in 1801, Jefferson pursued Burr vindictively, depriving him of federal patronage in New York and replacing him as the 1804 Republican vice presidential candidate with Governor George Clinton, Burr's chief rival in the state.

While still vice president, Burr began to flirt with treason. He approached Anthony Merry, the British minister in Washington, and offered to "effect a separation of the Western part of the United States." His price was £110,000 and the support of a British fleet off the mouth of the Mississippi. The British did not fall in with his scheme, but Burr went ahead nonetheless. Exactly what he had in mind has long been in dispute. Certainly he dreamed of acquiring a western empire for himself; whether he intended to wrest it from the United States or from Spanish territories beyond Louisiana is unclear. He joined forces with General James Wilkinson, whom Jefferson had appointed governor of the Louisiana Territory, who was secretly in the pay of Spain.

The opening of the Ohio and Mississippi valleys had not totally satisfied land-hungry Westerners. In 1806 Burr and Wilkinson had no difficulty raising a small force at a place called Blennerhassett Island, in the Ohio River. Some six dozen men began to move downriver toward New Orleans under Burr's command. Whether the objective was New Orleans or some part of Mexico, the scheme was clearly illegal. For some reason, however—possibly because he was incapable of loyalty to anyone[2]—Wilkinson betrayed Burr to Jefferson at the last moment. Burr tried to escape to Spanish Florida but was captured in February 1807, brought to Richmond, Virginia, under guard, and charged with high treason.

Any president will deal summarily with traitors, but Jefferson's attitude during Burr's trial reveals the depth of his hatred. He "made himself a party to the prosecution," personally sending evidence to the U.S. attorney who was handling the case and offering blanket pardons to associates of Burr who would agree to turn state's evidence. In stark contrast, Chief Justice Marshall, presiding at the trial in his capacity as judge of the circuit court, repeatedly showed favoritism to the prisoner.

In this contest between two great men at their worst, Jefferson as a vindictive executive and Marshall as a prejudiced judge, the victory went to the judge. Organizing "a military assemblage," Marshall declared on his charge to the jury, "was not a levying of war." To "advise or procure treason" was not in itself treason. Unless two independent witnesses testified to an overt act of treason as thus defined, the accused should be declared innocent. The jury, deliberating only 25 minutes, found Burr not guilty.

Throughout the trial, Burr never lost his self-possession. He seemed to view the proceedings with amiable cynicism. Then, since he was wanted either for murder or for treason in six states, he went into exile in Europe. Some years later he returned to New York, where he spent an unregenerate old age, fathering two illegitimate children in his seventies and being divorced by his second wife on grounds of adultery at 80.

The Burr affair was a blow to Jefferson's prestige; it left him more embittered against Marshall and the federal judiciary, and it added nothing to his reputation as a statesman.

---

[2]John Randolph said of him: "Wilkinson is the only man that I ever saw who was from the bark to the very core a villain."

The Battle of Trafalgar, by Nicholas Pocock (1808), showing two flotillas of English ships attacking a combined fleet of French and Spanish ships (1805). Seventeen French and Spanish ships surrendered or were sunk; the English fleet lost no ships, although its commander, Admiral Nelson, died in the battle.

Napoleon and the British

Jefferson's difficulties with Burr may be traced at least in part to the purchase of Louisiana, which, empty and unknown, excited the greed of men like Burr and Wilkinson. But problems infinitely more serious were also related to Louisiana.

Napoleon had jettisoned Louisiana to clear the decks before resuming the battle for control of Europe. This war had the effect of stimulating the American economy, for the warring powers needed American goods and American vessels. Shipbuilding boomed; foreign trade, which had quintupled since 1793, nearly doubled again between 1803 and 1805. By the summer of 1807, however, the situation had changed: a most unusual stalemate had developed in the war.

In October 1805 Britain's Horatio Nelson demolished the combined Spanish and French fleets in the Battle of Trafalgar, off the coast of Spain. Napoleon, now at the summit of his powers, quickly redressed the balance, smashing army after army thrown against him by Great Britain's continental allies. By 1807 he was master of Europe, while the British controlled the seas around the Continent. Neither nation could strike directly at the other.

They therefore resorted to commercial warfare, striving to disrupt each other's economy. Napoleon struck first with his Berlin Decree (November 1806), which made "all commerce and correspondence" with Great Britain illegal. The British retaliated with a series of edicts called Orders in Council, blockading most continental ports and barring from them all foreign vessels unless they first stopped at a British port and paid customs duties. Napoleon then issued his Milan Decree (December 1807), declaring any vessel that submitted to the British rules "to have become English property" and thus subject to seizure.

When war first broke out between Britain and France in 1792, the colonial trade of both sides had fallen largely into American hands because the danger of capture drove many belligerent merchant vessels from the seas. This commerce had engaged Americans in some devious practices. For example, American merchants carried sugar from the French colony of Martinique first to the United States, a legal peacetime voyage under French mercantilism. Then they reshipped it to France as American sugar. Since the United States was a neutral nation and sugar was not contraband of war, the Americans expected the British to let their ships pass with impunity. Continental products likewise reached the French West Indies by way of United States ports, and the American government encouraged the traffic in both directions by refunding customs duties on foreign products reshipped within a year. Between 1803 and 1806 the annual value of foreign products reexported from the United States jumped from $13 million to $60 million! In 1806 the United States exported 47 million pounds of coffee—none, of course, of local origin.

This underhanded commerce irritated the British. In the cases of the *Essex* and the *William* (1805–1806), a British judge, Sir William Grant, decreed that American ships could no longer rely on "mere voluntary *ceremonies*" to circumvent the Rule of 1756. Thus just when Britain and France were cracking down on direct trade by neutrals, Britain determined to halt the American reexport trade, thereby gravely threatening American prosperity.

The Impressment Controversy

More dismaying were the cruel indignities being visited on American seamen by the British practice of impressment. Under British law any able-bodied subject could be drafted for service in the Royal Navy in an emergency. Normally, when the commander of a warship found himself shorthanded, he put into a British port and sent a "press gang" ashore to round up the necessary men in harborside pubs. When far from home waters, he might hail any passing British merchant ship and commandeer the necessary men, though this practice was understandably unpopular in British maritime circles. He might also stop a *neutral* merchant vessel on the high seas and remove any British subject. Since the United States owned by far the largest merchant fleet among the neutrals, its vessels bore the brunt of this practice.

Impressment had been a cause of Anglo-American conflict for many years; American pride suffered every time a vessel carrying the flag of the United States was forced to heave to at the command of a British man-of-war. Still more galling was the contemptuous behavior of British officers when they boarded American ships. In 1796 an American captain named Figsby was stopped twice by British warships while carrying a cargo of poultry and other livestock to Guadeloupe. First a privateer, the *Sea Nymph*, impressed two of his crew, confiscated most of his chickens, "abused" him, and stole his ship's flag. Two days later HMS *Unicorn* took another of Figsby's men, the rest of his poultry, four sheep, and three hogs.

Many British captains made little effort to be sure they were impressing British subjects; any likely looking lad might be taken when the need was great. Furthermore, there were legal questions in dispute. When did an English immigrant become an American? When he was naturalized, the United States claimed. Never, the British retorted; "once an Englishman, always an Englishman."

The Jefferson administration conceded the right of the British to impress their own subjects from American merchant ships. When naturalized Americans were impressed, however, the administration was irritated, and when native-born Americans were taken, it became incensed. Impressment, Secretary of State Madison said in 1807, was "anomalous in principle . . . grievous in practice, and . . . abominable in abuse." Between 1803 and 1812 at least 5,000 sailors were snatched from the decks of U.S. vessels and forced to serve in the Royal Navy. Most of them—estimates run as high as three out of every four—were Americans.

The British did not claim the right to impress native-born Americans, and when it could be proved that boarding officers had done so, the men in question were released by higher authority. During the course of the controversy, the British authorities freed 3,800 impressed Americans, which suggests that many more were seized. However, the British refused to abandon impressment.

The combination of impressment, British interference with the reexport trade, and the general harassment of neutral commerce instituted by both Great Britain and France would have perplexed the most informed and hardheaded of leaders, and in dealing with these problems Jefferson was neither informed nor hardheaded. He believed it much wiser to stand up for one's rights than to compromise, yet he hated the very thought of war. Instead of building a navy that other nations would have to respect, he relied on a tiny fleet of frigates and a swarm of gunboats that were useless against the Royal Navy—"a macabre-monument," in the words of one historian, "to his hasty, ill-digested ideas" about defense.[3]

The Embargo Act

The frailty of Jefferson's policy became obvious once the warring powers began to attack neutral shipping in earnest. Between 1803 and 1807 the British seized more than 500 American ships, Napoleon more than 200 more. The United States, with only a handful of large ships, could do nothing.

The ultimate in frustration came on June 22, 1807, off Norfolk, Virginia. The American 46-gun frigate *Chesapeake* had just left port for patrol duty in the Mediterranean. Among its crew were a British sailor who had deserted from HMS *Halifax* and three Americans who had been illegally impressed by the captain of

[3]*The gunboats had performed effectively against the Barbary pirates, but Jefferson was enamored of them mainly because they were cheap. A gunboat cost about $10,000 to build, a big frigate over $300,000.*

The Ograbme ("embargo" spelled backward), a unique snapping turtle created by cartoonist Alexander Anderson, effectively frustrates an American tobacco smuggler.

HMS *Melampus* and had later escaped. The *Chesapeake* was barely out of sight of land when the 56-gun HMS *Leopard* approached and signaled the *Chesapeake* to heave to. Thinking that *Leopard* wanted to make some routine communication, Captain James Barron did so. A British officer came aboard and demanded that the four "deserters" be handed over to him. Barron refused, whereupon as soon as the officer was back on board, *Leopard* opened fire on the unsuspecting American ship, killing three sailors. Barron had to surrender. The "deserters" were seized, and then the crippled *Chesapeake* was allowed to limp back to port.

The attack was in violation of international law, for no nation claimed the right to impress sailors from warships. The British government admitted this, though it delayed making restitution for years. The American press clamored for war, but the country had nothing to fight with. Jefferson contented himself with ordering British warships out of American territorial waters. However, he was determined to put a stop to the indignities being heaped on the flag by Great Britain and France. The result was the Embargo Act.

The Embargo Act prohibited all exports. American vessels could not clear for any foreign port, and foreign vessels could do so only if empty. Importing was not forbidden, but few foreign ships would come to the United States if they had to return without a cargo. Although the law was sure to injure the American economy, Jefferson hoped that it would work in two ways to benefit the nation. By keeping U.S. merchant ships off the seas, it would end all chance of injury to them and to the national honor. By cutting off American goods and markets, it would put great economic pressure on Britain and France to moderate policies toward American shipping. The fact that boycotts had repeatedly wrested concessions from the British during the crises preceding the Revolution was certainly in Jefferson's mind when he devised the embargo.

Seldom has a law been so bitterly resented and resisted by a large segment of the public. It demanded of the maritime interests far greater sacrifices than they could reasonably be expected to make. Massachusetts-owned ships alone were

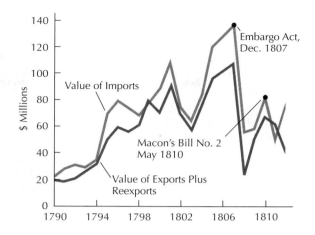

American Foreign Trade, 1790–1812

The embargo's effects are shown graphically here. The space between the upper (import) and the lower (export) line indicates a persistent foreign-trade deficit.

earning over $15 million a year in freight charges by 1807, and Bay State merchants were making far larger gains from the buying and selling of goods. Foreign commerce was the most expansive force in the economy, the chief reason for the nation's prosperity. As John Randolph remarked in a typical sally, the administration was trying "to cure the corns by cutting off the toes."

The Embargo Act had catastrophic effects. Exports fell from $108 million in 1807 to $22 million in 1808, imports from $138 million to less than $57 million. Prices of farm products and manufactured goods reacted violently; seamen were thrown out of work; merchants found their businesses disrupted.

Surely the embargo was a mistake. The United States ought either to have suffered the indignities heaped on its vessels for the sake of profits or, by constructing a powerful navy, made it dangerous for the belligerents to treat its merchant ships so roughly. Jefferson was too proud to choose the former alternative, too frugal to choose the latter. Instead he applied harsher and harsher regulations in a futile effort to accomplish his purpose. Militiamen patrolled the Canadian border; revenuers searched out smuggled goods without proper warrants. The illegal trade continued, and in his last months as president Jefferson simply gave up. Even then he would not admit that the embargo was a fiasco and urge its repeal. Only in Jefferson's last week in office did a leaderless Congress finally abolish it, substituting the Non-Intercourse Act, which forbade trade only with Great Britain and France and authorized the president to end the boycott against either power by proclamation when and if it stopped violating the rights of Americans.

Thus Jefferson's political career ended on a sour note. Several weeks after he had left office and returned to Monticello, he privately advised his successor, James Madison, to trust his own judgment to govern because the people readily succumbed to "the floating lies of the day."

Jeffersonian Democracy

Yet, Jefferson completed the construction of the political institution known as the Republican party and the philosophy of government known as Jeffersonian democracy. From what sort of materials had he built this polity? In part Jefferson's success was a matter of personality; in the march of American democracy he stood halfway, temperamentally, between Washington and Andrew Jackson, perfectly in tune with the thinking of his times.

Jefferson's marvelous talents as a writer help explain his success. He expounded his ideas in language that few people could resist. He had a remarkable facility for discovering practical arguments to justify his beliefs—as when he suggested that by letting everyone vote, elections would be made more honest because with large numbers going to the polls, bribery would become prohibitively expensive.

Jefferson prepared the country for democracy by proving that a democrat could establish and maintain a stable regime. The Federalist tyranny of 1798 was compounded of selfishness and stupidity, but it was also based in part on honest fears that an egalitarian regime would not protect the fabric of society from hotheads and crackpots.

Jefferson calmed these fears. "Pell-mell" might scandalize the British and Spanish ministers and a few locals, but it was scarcely revolutionary. The most partisan Federalist was hard put to see a Robespierre, leader during the Reign of Terror in France, in the amiable president scratching out state papers at his desk or chatting with a Kentucky congressman at a "republican" dinner party. Furthermore, Jefferson accepted Federalist ideas on public finance, even learning to live with Hamilton's bank. As a good democrat, he drew a nice distinction between his own opinions and the wishes of the majority, which he felt must always take priority. Even in his first inaugural he admitted that manufacturing and commerce were, along with agriculture, the "pillars of our prosperity," and while believing that these activities would thrive best when "left most free to individual enterprise," he accepted the principle that the government should protect them when necessary from "casual embarrassments." During his term the country grew and prospered, the commercial classes sharing in the bounty along with the farmers so close to Jefferson's heart. Blithely he set out to win the support of all who could vote. "It is material to the safety of Republicanism," he wrote in 1803, "to detach the mercantile interests from its enemies and incorporate them into the body of its friends."

Thus Jefferson undermined the Federalists all along the line. They had said that the country must pay a stiff price for prosperity and orderly government, and they demanded prompt payment in full, both in cash (taxes) and in the form of limitations on human liberty. Under Jefferson these much-desired goals had been achieved cheaply and without sacrificing freedom. A land whose riches could only be guessed at had been obtained without firing a shot and without burdening the people with new taxes. "What farmer, what mechanic, what laborer, ever sees a tax-gatherer of the United States?" the president could ask in 1805, without a single Federalist rising to challenge him. Order without discipline, security without a large military establishment, prosperity without regulatory legislation, freedom without license—truly the Sage of Monticello appeared to have led his fellow Americans into a golden age.

Jefferson insisted that one of his chief accomplishments had been to reduce the national debt from $83 million to $57 million. Writing from Monticello shortly after leaving office, he urged his successors to eliminate the remainder. "The discharge of the public debt," he warned Treasury Secretary Gallatin, "is vital to the destinies of our government."

Yet Jefferson had also learned the perils of an inadequately funded government. His unwillingness to build a real navy had rendered the nation vulnerable to foreign states. Conversely, he had exulted in the purchase of Louisiana, and he backed modest proposals for spending federal money on roads, canals, and other projects that, according to his political philosophy, ought to have been left to the states and private individuals. Jefferson had even learned to live with Hamilton's bank. Debt, Jefferson accepted, was sometimes good policy.

Milestones

1800	Jefferson is elected president (Revolution of 1800)
1801	Judiciary Act of 1801 allows Adams to appoint many Federalist judges
1801–1805	United States wages war against Barbary pirates in North Africa
1803	Supreme Court declares part of Judiciary Act of 1789 unconstitutional (*Marbury* v. *Madison*)
	Jefferson negotiates Louisiana Purchase with France
1804	Aaron Burr kills Alexander Hamilton in duel
	Jefferson is reelected
1804–1806	Lewis and Clark explore West
1806	Aaron Burr schemes to take land in West during Burr Conspiracy
1806–1807	Napoleon issues Berlin and Milan decrees in order to disrupt British shipping and economy
1807	HMS *Leopard* attacks USS *Chesapeake*
	Embargo Act prohibits all exports
1809	Non-Intercourse Act forbids trade with Great Britain and France

National Growing Pains

IN RECENT YEARS, THE STICKER PRICE OF BICYCLES SOLD IN THE United States has been inflated by about $5 to cover the import tax—tariff—on foreign-made bicycles. In 2005, 99 percent of the 20 million bikes sold in the United States were manufactured abroad and thus subject to the tariff. (Of these, over 90 percent were made in China.)

Tariffs protect domestic manufacturers from foreign competition and generate revenue for the federal government. In 2005, for example, the bicycle tariff yielded $100 million; federal income from all tariffs approached $23 billion. But this was a mere drop in the mighty stream of federal revenue, which in that year exceeded $2.1 trillion. Of this sum, nearly $1 trillion came from individual income taxes, $280 billion from corporate income taxes, and $800 billion from payments to the Social Security system.

It was different 200 years ago. In 1809, the total revenue of the U.S. Treasury fell short of $8 million.[1] Of that, more than $7 million was generated by the tariff. The sale of public lands and of postage stamps provided most of the balance.

Without income from the tariff, the federal government could have done little more than deliver the mail. Tariff taxes, by raising the cost of cloth and metal goods produced by large British factories, protected American manufacturers of those goods. But this meant that farmers would pay more for clothing and farm implements. Worse, Britain and other foreign nations could retaliate against high American tariffs by setting their own tariffs on American imports to *their* countries—chiefly tobacco, cotton, wheat, and other foodstuffs mostly grown in the South and West.

---

[1]*The revenue figures for 1809 and those for 2005 are not adjusted for inflation. That is because the nature of most goods has changed so much that comparison is meaningless.*

The tariff pitted one section of the nation against another. The North, increasingly a manufacturing region, supported high tariffs, while the South, chiefly an exporter of farm products, opposed them. The West was divided on the matter, opposing higher prices for manufactured goods but requiring federal help for economic development and defense.

From 1809 to 1828, Americans repeatedly decided to expand the role of the federal government. Armies and navies were raised to subdue the Indians and defend the nation from European predators; highways were built to encourage trade and promote settlement of the Louisiana territories. The federal budget tripled. As costs went up, so did the tariff. The 1828 "Tariff of Abominations" was the highest to that time. That year, of the total revenue, more than 90 percent came from the tariff. The growth of the nation—and of the national government—came at a price.

Madison in Power

It is a measure of Jefferson's popularity and of the political ineptitude of the Federalists that the Republicans won the election of 1808 handily despite the embargo. James Madison got 122 of the 173 electoral votes for the presidency, and the party carried both houses of Congress, although by reduced majorities.

In his inaugural address, Madison observed that the "present situation" of the United States was "full of difficulties" and that war continued to rage among European powers. Yet he assumed the presidency, he said, "with no other discouragement than what springs from my own inadequacy." The content of the speech was as modest as its delivery; virtually no one could hear it.

Madison was a small, neat, rather precise person, narrower in his interests than Jefferson but in many ways a deeper thinker. He was more conscientious in the performance of his duties and more consistent in adhering to his principles. Ideologically, however, they were as close as two active and intelligent people could be. Madison had no better solution to offer for the problem of the hour than had Jefferson. The Non-Intercourse Act proved difficult to enforce—once an American ship left port, there was no way to prevent the skipper from steering for England or France—and it exerted little economic pressure on the British, who continued to seize American vessels.

Because prudent captains remained in port, trade stagnated. Federal revenue declined. In 1809, Secretary of the Treasury Albert Gallatin was alarmed by the growing federal deficit. He urged Representative Nathaniel Macon of North Carolina to introduce legislation to remove all restrictions on commerce with France and Britain. Known as Macon's Bill No. 2, it authorized the president to reapply the principle of nonintercourse to either of the major powers if the other should "cease to violate the neutral commerce of the United States." This bill became law in May 1810.

The volume of United States commerce with the British Isles swiftly zoomed to pre-embargo levels. The mighty British fleet controlled the seas. Napoleon therefore announced that he had repealed his decrees against neutral shipping.

Madison, seeking concessions from Britain, closed American ports to British ships and goods. Napoleon, despite his announcement to the contrary, continued to seize American ships and cargoes whenever it suited him to do so.

The British grimly refused to modify the Orders in Council. Madison could not afford either to admit that Napoleon had deceived him or to reverse American policy still another time. Reluctantly he came to the conclusion that unless Britain repealed the Orders, the United States must declare war.

Tecumseh and Indian Resistance

There were other reasons for fighting besides British violations of neutral rights. The Indians were again restive, and western farmers believed that the British in Canada were egging them on. This had been true in the past but was no longer the case in 1811 and 1812. American domination of the southern Great Lakes region was no longer in question.

American political leaders tended to believe that Indians should be encouraged to become farmers and to copy the "civilized" ways of whites. However, no government had been able to control the frontiersmen, who by bribery, trickery, and force were driving the tribes back year after year from the rich lands of the Ohio Valley. General William Henry Harrison, governor of the Indiana Territory, a tough, relentless soldier, kept constant pressure on them. He wrested land from one tribe by promising it aid against a traditional enemy, from another as a penalty for having murdered a white man, from others by corrupting a few chiefs. Harrison justified his sordid behavior by citing the end in view—that "one of the fairest portions of the globe" be secured as "the seat of civilization, of science, and of true religion." The "wretched savages" should not be allowed to stand in the path of this worthy objective. As early as 1805 it was clear that unless something drastic was done, Harrison's aggressiveness, together with the corroding effects of white civilization, would soon obliterate the tribes.

At this point the Shawnee chief, Tecumseh, made a bold and imaginative effort to reverse the trend by binding all the tribes east of the Mississippi into a great confederation. Traveling from the Wisconsin country to the Floridas, he persuaded tribe after tribe to join him. "Let the white race perish," Tecumseh declared. "They seize your land; they corrupt your women. . . . Back whence they came, upon a trail of blood, they must be driven!"

To Tecumseh's political movement his brother Tenskwatawa, known as "The Prophet," added the force of a moral crusade. Instead of copying white customs, the Prophet said, Indians must give up white ways, white clothes, and white liquor and reinvigorate their own culture. Ceding lands to the whites must stop because the Great Spirit intended that the land be used in common by all.

The Prophet was a fanatic who saw visions and claimed to be able to control the movement of heavenly bodies. Tecumseh, however, possessed true genius. A powerful orator and a great organizer, he had deep insight into the needs of his people. Harrison himself said of Tecumseh: "He is one of those uncommon

As a young man Tecumseh *(left)* was a superb hunter and warrior; his younger brother, Tenskwatawa *(right)* was awkward and inept with weapons; he accidentally gouged out his right eye with an arrow. In 1805 he had a religious vision, became known as "The Prophet," and inspired Tecumseh's warriors.

geniuses which spring up occasionally to produce revolutions and overturn the established order of things." The two brothers made a formidable team. By 1811 thousands of Indians were organizing to drive the whites off their lands. Alarm swept through the West.

With about a thousand soldiers, General Harrison marched boldly against the brothers' camp at Prophetstown, where Tippecanoe Creek joins the Wabash River, in Indiana. Tecumseh was away recruiting men, and the Prophet recklessly ordered an assault on Harrison's camp outside the village on November 7, 1811. When the white soldiers held their ground despite the Prophet's magic, the Indians lost confidence and fell back. Harrison then destroyed Prophetstown.

While the Battle of Tippecanoe was pretty much a draw, it disillusioned the Indians and shattered their confederation. Frontier warfare continued, but in the disorganized manner of former times. Like all such fighting it was brutal and bloody.

Unwilling as usual to admit that their own excesses were the chief cause of the trouble, the settlers directed their resentment at the British in Canada. "This combination headed by the Shawanese prophet is a British scheme," a resolution adopted by the citizens of Vincennes, Indiana, proclaimed. As a result, the cry for war with Great Britain rang along the frontier.

Depression and Land Hunger

Some Westerners pressed for war because they were suffering an agricultural depression. The prices they received for their wheat, tobacco, and other products in the markets of New Orleans were falling, and they attributed the decline to the loss of foreign markets and to plunder by the British. American commercial restrictions had more to do with the western depression than the British, and in any case the slow and cumbersome transportation and distribution system that western farmers were saddled with was the major cause of their difficulties. But the farmers were no more inclined to accept these explanations than they were to absolve the British from responsibility for the Indian difficulties. If only the seas were free, they reasoned, costs would go down, prices would rise, and prosperity would return.

To some extent western expansionism also heightened the war fever. The West contained immense tracts of virgin land, but Westerners wanted more. Canada would surely fall to American arms in the event of war, the frontiersmen believed. So, apparently, would Florida, for Spain was now Britain's ally. Florida in itself provided no cause for a war, for it was sure to fall into American hands before long. In 1810 Madison had snapped up the extreme western section without eliciting any effective response from Spain.

But Westerners, and many Easterners too, were more patriots than imperialists or merchants in 1811 and 1812. When the "War Hawks" (their young leaders in Congress) called for war against Great Britain, they did so because they saw no other way to defend the national honor and force repeal of the Orders in Council. The choice seemed to lie between war and surrender of true independence. As Madison put it, to bow to British policy would be to "recolonize" American foreign commerce.

Opponents of War

Large numbers of people, however, thought that a war against Great Britain would be a national calamity. Some Federalists would have resisted anything the administration proposed; Congressman Josiah Quincy of Massachusetts declared that he "could not be kicked" into the war, which he considered a cowardly, futile, and unconstitutional business designed primarily to ensure the reelection of Madison. According to Quincy the War Hawks were "backwoodsmen" willing to wage a "cruel, wanton, senseless and wicked" war in order to swallow up Canada.

But other people based their objections on economics and a healthy realism. No shipowner could view with equanimity the idea of taking on the largest navy in the world. Such persons complained sincerely enough about impressment and the Orders in Council, but war seemed worse to them by far. Self-interest led them to urge patience.

Such a policy would have been wise, for Great Britain did not represent a real threat to the United States. British naval officers were high-handed, officials in London complacent, British diplomats in Washington second-rate and obtuse. Yet

Debating the Past

HOW DID INDIANS AND SETTLERS INTERACT?

Two Indians *(below)* gaze at a frontier settlement. In 1893 historian Frederick Jackson Turner, the most important historian of his era, credited the frontier for the individualistic ethos that made the United States distinctive. In his view, the frontier had not been a particular zone or region, but "the outer edge of the wave—the meeting point between savagery and civilization." The nature of the interaction between Indians and settlers was one-sided: the Indians fell back. But in recent decades, historians have challenged this concept not only because it disparaged Indian societies and cultures, but also because it ignored the many ways in which Indians and settlers interacted. Abandoning the concept of an Indian-settler frontier, Richard White (1991) described a "middle ground" and James Merrell (1999) the "edge of the woods," a region where Indians and settlers resolved disputes, traded goods, and exchanged ideas. The concept of a "middle ground" put Indians and settlers on equal footing. But that also may be its chief difficulty. Daniel K. Richter (2001) and Jane T. Merritt (2003) showed that while

Indians preferred to co-exist with the settlers rather than fight them, by the eighteenth century raw power prevailed—as did, usually, the settlers.

Frederick Jackson Turner, "The Significance of the Frontier in American History" (1893), Patricia Nelson Limerick, *The Legacy of Conquest* (1987), Richard White, *The Middle Ground* (1991), James Merrell, *Into the Woods* (1999), Daniel K. Richter, *Facing East from Indian Country* (2001), Jane T. Merritt, *At the Crossroads* (2003).

language, culture, and strong economic ties bound the two countries. Napoleon, on the other hand, represented a tremendous potential danger. He had offhandedly turned over Louisiana, but even Jefferson, the chief beneficiary of his largesse, hated everything he stood for. Jefferson called Napoleon "an unprincipled tyrant who is deluging the continent of Europe with blood."

What made the situation even more unfortunate was the fact that by 1812 conditions had changed in England in a way that made a softening of British maritime policy likely. A depression caused chiefly by the increasing effectiveness of Napoleon's Continental System was plaguing the country. (The Continental System, based on Napoleon's Berlin and Milan decrees, forbade neutral countries or French allies from trading with Britain or its colonies.) Manufacturers, blaming the slump on the loss of American markets, were urging repeal of Britain's Orders in Council. Gradually, though with exasperating slowness, the British government prepared to yield. On June 23, after a change of ministries, the new foreign secretary, Lord Castlereagh, suspended the Orders. Five days earlier, alas, the United States had declared war.

The War of 1812

The illogic of the War Hawks in pressing for a fight was exceeded only by their ineffectiveness in planning and managing the struggle. By what possible strategy could the ostensible objective of the war be achieved? To construct a navy capable of challenging the British fleet would have been the work of many years and a more expensive proposition than the War Hawks were willing to consider. So hopeless was that prospect that Congress failed to undertake any new construction in the first year of the conflict. Several hundred merchant ships lashed a few cannon to their decks and sailed off as privateers to attack British commerce. The navy's seven modern frigates, built during the war scare after the XYZ affair, put to sea. But these forces could make no pretense of disputing Britain's mastery of the Atlantic.

For a brief moment the American frigates held center stage, for they were faster, tougher, larger, and more powerfully armed than their British counterparts. Barely two months after the declaration of war, Captain Isaac Hull in USS *Constitution* chanced upon HMS *Guerrière* in mid-Atlantic, outmaneuvered *Guerrière* brilliantly, brought down its mizzenmast with his first volley, and then gunned it into submission, a hopeless wreck. In October USS *United States*, captained by Stephen Decatur, hero of the war against the Barbary pirates, caught HMS *Macedonian* off the Madeiras, pounded it unmercifully at long range, and forced the British ship to surrender. *Macedonian* was taken into New London as a prize; over a third of the 300-man crew were casualties, while American losses were but a dozen. Then, in December, *Constitution*, now under Captain William Bainbridge, took on the British frigate *Java* off Brazil. "Old Ironsides" shot away *Java's* mainmast and reduced it to a hulk too battered for salvage.

These victories had little influence on the outcome of the war. The Royal Navy had thirty-four frigates, seven more powerful ships of the line, and dozens of smaller vessels. As soon as these forces could concentrate against them, the American frigates were immobilized, forced to spend the war gathering barnacles at their moorings while powerful British squadrons ranged offshore. The privateering merchantmen were more effective because they were so numerous; they captured more than 1,300 British vessels during the war. The best of them—vessels like *America* and *True-Blooded Yankee*—were redesigned, given more sail to increase their speed, and formidably armed. *America* captured twenty-six prizes valued at more than a million dollars. *True-Blooded Yankee* took twenty-seven vessels and destroyed seven more in a Scottish harbor.

Great Britain's one weak spot seemed to be Canada. The colony had but half a million inhabitants to oppose 7.5 million Americans. Only 2,257 British regulars guarded the long border from Montréal to Detroit. The Canadian militia was feeble, and many of its members, being American-born, sympathized with the "invaders." According to the War Hawk congressman Henry Clay of Kentucky, the West was one solid horde of ferocious frontiersmen, armed to the teeth and thirsting for Canadian blood. Yet such talk was mostly brag and bluster; when Congress authorized increasing the army by 25,000 men, Kentucky produced 400 enlistments.

With a few exceptions, American forces in the War of 1812 were ill-trained and ill-led, and poor strategy resulted in several disgraceful defeats. Here, a resplendently dressed militia officer consults a map.

American military leadership proved extremely disappointing. Madison showed poor judgment by relying on officers who had served with distinction in the Revolution. Instead of a concentrated strike against Canada's St. Lawrence River lifeline, which would have isolated Upper Canada, the generals planned a complicated three-pronged attack. It failed dismally. In July 1812 General William Hull, veteran of the battles of Trenton, Saratoga, and Monmouth and now governor of the Michigan Territory, marched forth with 2,200 men against the Canadian positions facing Detroit. Hoping that the Canadian militia would desert, he delayed his assault, only to find his communications threatened by hostile Indians led by Tecumseh. Hastily he retreated to Detroit, and when the Canadians, under General Isaac Brock, pursued him, he surrendered the fort without firing a shot! In October another force attempted to invade Canada from Fort Niagara. After an initial success it was crushed by superior numbers, while a large contingent of New York militiamen watched from the east bank of the Niagara River, unwilling to fight outside their own state.

The third arm of the American "attack" was equally unsuccessful. Major General Henry Dearborn, who had fought honorably in the Revolution from Bunker Hill to Yorktown, but who had now grown so fat that he needed a specially designed cart to get from place to place, set out from Plattsburgh, New York, at the head of an army of militiamen. Their objective was Montréal, but when they reached the border, the troops refused to cross. Dearborn meekly marched them back to Plattsburgh.

Meanwhile, the British had captured Fort Michilimackinac in northern Michigan, and the Indians had taken Fort Dearborn (now Chicago), massacring 85 captives. Instead of sweeping triumphantly through Canada, the Americans found themselves trying desperately to keep the Canadians out of Ohio.

Stirred by these disasters, Westerners rallied somewhat in 1813. General Harrison, the victor of Tippecanoe, headed an army of Kentuckians in a series of inconclusive battles against British troops and Indians led by Tecumseh. He found it impossible to recapture Detroit because a British squadron controlling Lake Erie threatened his communications. President Madison therefore assigned Captain Oliver Hazard Perry to the task of building a fleet to challenge this force. In September 1813, at Put-in-Bay near the western end of the lake, Perry destroyed the British vessels in a bloody battle in which 85 of the 103 men on Perry's flagship were casualties. "We have met the enemy and they are ours," he reported. About a quarter of Perry's 400 men were blacks, which led him to remark that "the color of a man's skin" was no more an indication of his worth than "the cut and trimmings" of his coat. With the Americans in control of Lake Erie, Detroit became untenable for the British, and when they fell back, Harrison gave chase and defeated them at the Thames River, some 60 miles northeast of Detroit. Although little more than a skirmish, this battle had large repercussions. Tecumseh was among the dead (an eccentric American colonel, Richard Mentor Johnson, was to base a long and successful political career, culminating in his election as vice president of the United States in 1836, on his claim of having personally done in the great chief), and without him the Indians lost heart. But American attempts to win control of Lake Ontario and to invade Canada in the

In the heat of the Battle of Lake Erie, Perry had to abandon his flagship, the *Lawrence*, which had been shot to pieces by enemy fire. (Over three-fourths of the ship's crew were killed or wounded.) He was rowed to the Niagara, from which he directed the rest of the engagement.

Niagara region were again thrown back. Late in 1813 the British captured Fort Niagara and burned the town of Buffalo. The conquest of Canada was as far from realization as ever.

Britain Assumes the Offensive

Until 1814 the British put relatively little effort into the American war, being concerned primarily with the struggle against Napoleon. However, in 1812 Napoleon had invaded Russia and been thrown back; thereafter, one by one, his European satellites rose against him. Gradually he relinquished his conquests; the Allies—his enemies—marched into France, Paris fell, and in April 1814 the emperor abdicated. Then the British, free to strike hard at the United States, dispatched some 14,000 veterans to Canada.

By the spring of 1814 British strategists had devised a master plan for crushing the United States. One army, 11,000 strong, was to march from Montréal, tracing the route that General Burgoyne had followed to disaster in the Revolution. A smaller amphibious force was to make a feint at the Chesapeake Bay area, destroying coastal towns and threatening Washington and Baltimore. A third army was to assemble at Jamaica and sail to attack New Orleans and bottle up the West.

It is necessary, in considering the War of 1812, to remind oneself repeatedly that in the course of the conflict many brave young men lost their lives. Without this sobering reflection it would be easy to dismiss the conflict as a great farce compounded of stupidity, incompetence, and brag. The British, despite their years of experience against Napoleon, were scarcely more effective than the Americans when they assumed the offensive. They achieved significant success only in the diversionary attack in the Chesapeake Bay area.

While the main British army was assembling in Canada, some 4,000 veterans under General Robert Ross sailed from Bermuda for the Chesapeake. After making a rendezvous with a fleet commanded by Vice Admiral Sir Alexander Cochrane and Rear Admiral Sir George Cockburn, which had been terrorizing the coast, they landed in Maryland at the mouth of the Patuxent River, southeast of Washington. A squadron of gunboats "protecting" the capital promptly withdrew upstream; when the British pursued, their commander ordered them blown up to keep them from being captured.

The British troops marched rapidly toward Washington. At Bladensburg, on the outskirts of the city, they came upon an army twice their number, commanded by General William H. Winder, a Baltimore lawyer who had already been captured and released by the British in the Canadian fighting. While President Madison and other officials watched, the British charged—and Winder's army turned tail almost without firing a shot. The British swarmed into the capital and put most public buildings to the torch. Before personally setting fire to the White House, Admiral Cockburn took one of the president's hats and a cushion from Dolley Madison's chair as souvenirs, and, finding the table set for dinner, derisively drank a toast to "Jemmy's health," adding, an observer coyly recalled, "pleasantries too vulgar for me to repeat."

This was the sum of the British success. When they attempted to take Baltimore, they were stopped by a formidable line of defenses devised by General Samuel Smith, a militia officer. General Ross fell in the attack. The fleet then moved up the Patapsco River and pounded Fort McHenry with its cannon, raining 1,800 shells upon it in a 25-hour bombardment on September 13 and 14.

"The Star Spangled Banner"

While this attack was in progress, an American civilian, Francis Scott Key, who had been temporarily detained on one of the British ships, watched anxiously through the night. Key had boarded the vessel before the attack in an effort to obtain the release of an American doctor who had been taken into custody in Washington. As twilight faded, Key had seen the Stars and Stripes flying proudly over the battered fort. During the night the glare of rockets and bursting of bombs gave proof that the defenders were holding out. Then, by the first light of the new day, Key saw again the flag, still waving over Fort McHenry. Drawing an old letter from his pocket, he dashed off the words to "The Star Spangled Banner," which, when set to music, was to become the national anthem of the United States.

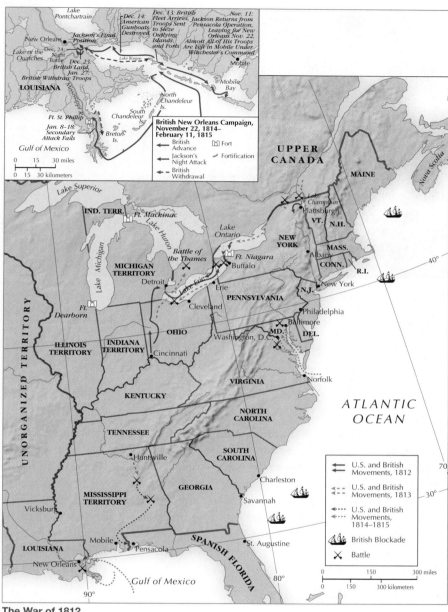

The War of 1812

To Key that dawn seemed a turning point in the war. He was roughly correct, for in those last weeks of the summer of 1814 the struggle began to move toward resolution. Unable to crack the defenses of Baltimore, the British withdrew to their ships; shortly after, they sailed to Jamaica to join the forces preparing to attack New Orleans.

The destruction of Washington had been a profound shock. Thousands came forward to enlist in the army. The new determination and spirit were strengthened

The Bombardment of Fort McHenry by John Bower, with the Stars and Stripes flying over the fort *(center)*. The British fleet fired 1,800 bombs and red-glaring incendiary rockets. The fort did not return fire because the British ships were beyond the range of its cannon. Although "The Star Spangled Banner" celebrates the "home of the brave," the defenders of Fort McHenry sensibly fled the ramparts and took cover below during the bombardment; they sustained only thirty casualties.

by news from the northern front, where General Sir George Prevost had been leading the main British invasion force south from Montréal. At Plattsburgh, on the western shore of Lake Champlain, his 1,000 Redcoats came up against a well-designed defense line manned by 3,300 Americans under General Alexander Macomb. Prevost called up his supporting fleet of four ships and a dozen gunboats. An American fleet of roughly similar strength under Captain Thomas Macdonough, a youthful officer who had served with Decatur against the Barbary pirates, came forward to oppose the British. On September 11, in a brutal battle at point-blank range, Macdonough destroyed the British ships and drove off the gunboats. With the Americans now threatening his flank, Prevost lost heart and retreated to Canada.

The Treaty of Ghent

The war might as well have ended with the battles of Plattsburgh, Washington, and Baltimore, for later military developments had no effect on the outcome. Earlier in 1814 both sides had agreed to discuss peace terms. Commissioners were appointed and negotiations begun during the summer at Ghent, in Belgium. The British were in no hurry to sign a treaty, believing that their three-pronged offensive in 1814 would swing the balance in their favor. But news of the defeat at Plattsburgh modified their ambitions, and when the Duke of Wellington advised that from a military point of view they had no case for territorial concessions so long as the United States controlled the Great Lakes, they agreed to settle for *status quo ante bellum,* to leave things as they were before the war. The other issues, everyone suddenly realized, had simply evaporated. The mighty war triggered by the French Revolution seemed finally over. The seas were free to all ships, and the Royal Navy no longer had need to snatch sailors from the vessels of the United States or of any other power. On Christmas Eve 1814 the treaty, which merely ended the state of hostilities, was signed. Although, like other members of his family, he was not noted for tact, John Quincy Adams rose to the spirit of the occasion. "I hope," he said, "it will be the last treaty of peace between Great Britain and the United States." And so it was.

The Hartford Convention

Before news of the treaty could cross the Atlantic, two events took place that had important effects but that would not have occurred had the news reached America more rapidly. The first was the Hartford Convention, a meeting of New England Federalists held in December 1814 and January 1815 to protest the war and to plan for a convention of the states to revise the Constitution.

Sentiment in New England had opposed the war from the beginning. The governor of Massachusetts titled his annual address in 1813 "On the Present Unhappy War," and the General Court went on record calling the conflict "impolitic, improper, and unjust." The Federalist party had been quick to employ the discontent to revive its fortunes. Federalist-controlled state administrations refused to provide militia to aid in the fight and discouraged individuals and banks from lending money to the hard-pressed national government.

Their attitude toward the war made the Federalists even more unpopular with the rest of the country, and this in turn encouraged extremists to talk of seceding from the Union. After Massachusetts summoned the meeting of the Hartford Convention, the fear was widespread that the delegates would propose a New England Confederacy, thereby striking at the Union in a moment of great trial.

Luckily for the country, moderate Federalists controlled the convention. They approved a statement that in case of "deliberate, dangerous and palpable infractions of the Constitution" a state has the right "to interpose its authority" to protect itself. This concept, similar to that expressed in the Kentucky and Virginia resolutions by the Republicans when they were in the minority, was accompanied by a list of proposed constitutional amendments designed to make the national government conform more closely to the New England ideal. These would have (1) repealed the Three-fifths Compromise on representation and direct taxes, which favored the slaveholding states; (2) required a two-thirds vote of Congress for the admission of new states and for declaring war; (3) reduced Congress's power to restrict trade by measures such as an embargo; (4) limited presidents to a single term; and (5) made it illegal for naturalized citizens to hold national office.

Nothing formally proposed at Hartford was treasonable, but the proceedings were kept secret, and rumors of impending secession were rife. In this atmosphere came the news from Ghent of an honorable peace. The Federalists had been denouncing the war and predicting a British triumph; now they were discredited.

The Battle of New Orleans

Still more discrediting to Federalists was the second event that would not have happened had communications been more rapid: the Battle of New Orleans. During the fall of 1814 the British had gathered an army at Negril Bay in Jamaica, commanded by Major General Sir Edward Pakenham, brother-in-law of the Duke of Wellington. Late in November an armada of sixty ships set out for New Orleans with 11,000 soldiers. Instead of sailing directly up from the mouth of the Mississippi as the Americans expected, Pakenham approached the city by way of Lake Borgne, to the east. Proceeding through a maze of swamps and bayous, he advanced close to the city's gates before being detected. Early on the afternoon of December 23, three mud-spattered local planters burst into the headquarters of General Andrew Jackson, commanding the defenses of New Orleans, with the news.

For once in this war of error and incompetence the United States had the right man in the right place at the right time. After his Revolutionary War experiences, Jackson had studied law, then moved West, settling in Nashville, Tennessee. He served briefly in both houses of Congress and was active in Tennessee affairs. Jackson was a hard man and fierce-tempered, frequently involved in brawls and duels, but honest and, by western standards, a good public servant. When the war broke out, he was named major general of volunteers. Almost alone among non-professional troops during the conflict, his men won impressive victories, savagely crushing the Creek Indians in a series of battles in Alabama.

Jackson's success was due to his toughness and determination. Discipline based on fear, respect, and their awareness of his genuine concern for their well-being made his individualistic frontier militiamen into an army. His men called Jackson Old Hickory; the Indians called him Sharp Knife.

Following these victories, Jackson was assigned the job of defending the Gulf Coast against the expected British strike. Although he had misjudged Pakenham's destination, he was ready when the news of the British arrival reached him. "By the Eternal," he vowed, "they shall not sleep on our soil." "Gentlemen," he told his staff officers, "the British are below, we must fight them tonight."

While the British rested and awaited reinforcements, planning to take the city the next morning, Jackson rushed up men and guns. At 7:30 P.M. on December 23 he struck hard, taking the British by surprise. But Pakenham's veterans rallied quickly, and the battle was inconclusive. With Redcoats pouring in from the fleet, Jackson fell back to a point 5 miles below New Orleans and dug in.

He chose his position wisely. On his right was the Mississippi, on his left an impenetrable swamp, to the front an open field. On the day before Christmas (while the commissioners in Ghent were signing the peace treaty), Jackson's army, which included a segregated unit of free black militiamen, erected an earthen parapet about 10 yards behind a dry canal bed. Here the Americans would make their stand.

For two weeks Pakenham probed the American line. Jackson strengthened his defenses daily. At night, patrols of silent Tennesseans slipped out with knife and tomahawk to stalk British sentries. They called this grim business "going hunting." On January 8, 1815, Pakenham ordered an all-out frontal assault. The American position was formidable, but these were men who had defeated Napoleon. At dawn, through the lowland mists, the Redcoats moved forward with fixed bayonets. Pakenham assumed that the undisciplined Americans—about 4,500 strong— would run at the sight of bare steel.

The Americans did not run. Perhaps they feared the wrath of their commander more than enemy bayonets. Artillery raked the advancing British, and when the range closed to about 150 yards, the riflemen opened up. Jackson had formed his men in three ranks behind the parapet. One rank fired, then stepped down as another took its place. By the time the third had loosed its volley, the first had reloaded and was ready to fire again. Nothing could stand against this rain of lead. General Pakenham was wounded twice, then killed by a shell fragment while calling up his last reserves. During the battle a single brave British officer reached the top of the parapet. When retreat was finally sounded, the British had suffered almost 2,100 casualties, including nearly 300 killed. Thirteen Americans lost their lives, and fifty-eight more were wounded or missing.

Victory Weakens the Federalists

Word of Jackson's magnificent triumph reached Washington almost simultaneously with the good news from Ghent. People found it easy to confuse the chronology and consider the war a victory won on the battlefield below New Orleans instead of the standoff it had been. Jackson became the "Hero of New Orleans"; his proud fellow citizens rated his military abilities superior to those of the Duke of Wellington. The nation rejoiced. One sour Republican complained that the Federalists of Massachusetts had fired off more powder and wounded more men celebrating the victory than they had during the whole course of the conflict. The Senate ratified the peace treaty unanimously, and the frustrations and failures of the past few years were forgotten.

The nation had suffered relatively few casualties and little economic loss, except to the shipping interests. The Indians were the main losers in the contest.

When Jackson defeated the Creeks, for example, he forced them to surrender 23 million acres, constituting three-fifths of what is now Alabama and one-fifth of Georgia.

The war completed the destruction of the Federalist party. It soon disappeared even in New England, swamped beneath a wave of patriotism that flooded the land.

The chief reason for the happy results of the war had little to do with American events. After 1815 Europe settled down to what was to be a century of relative peace. With peace came an end to serious foreign threats to America and a revival of commerce. European emigration to the United States, long held back by the troubled times, spurted ahead, providing the expanding country with its most valuable asset—strong, willing hands to do the work of developing the land. The mood of Jefferson's first term, when democracy had reigned amid peace and plenty, returned with a rush. And the nation, having had its fill of international complications, turned in on itself as Jefferson had wished. The politicians, ever sensitive to public attitudes, had learned what seemed at the time a valuable lesson. Foreign affairs were a potent cause of domestic conflict. The volatile character of sectional politics was thus another reason why America should escape from involvement in European affairs.

Anglo-American Rapprochement

There remained a few matters to straighten out with Great Britain, Spain, and Europe generally. Since no territory had changed hands at Ghent, neither signatory had reason to harbor a grudge. There was no sudden flowering of Anglo-American friendship. Yet for years no serious trouble marred Anglo-American relations. The war had taught the British to respect Americans, if not to love them.

In this atmosphere the two countries worked out peaceful solutions to a number of old problems. American trade was becoming ever more important to the British, that of the sugar islands less so. In July 1815 they therefore signed a commercial convention ending discriminatory duties and making other adjustments favorable to trade. Boundary difficulties also moved toward resolution. At Ghent the diplomats had created several joint commissions to settle the disputed boundary between the United States and Canada. Many years were to pass before the line was finally drawn, but establishing the principle of defining the border by negotiation was important. In time, a line extending over 3,000 miles was agreed to without the firing of a single shot.

Immediately after the war the British reinforced their garrisons in Canada and began to rebuild their shattered Great Lakes fleet. The United States took similar steps. But both nations found the cost of rearming more than they cared to bear. When the United States suggested demilitarizing the lakes, the British agreed. The Rush-Bagot Agreement of 1817 limited each country to one 100-ton vessel armed with a single 18-pounder on Lake Champlain and another on Lake Ontario. They were to have two each for all the other Great Lakes.

The Kingsley plantation, on Ford George Island in Jacksonville, Florida. Zephaniah Kingsley, the owner, bought Anta, a 13-year-old slave, in 1806. Although they never had a legal marriage ceremony, Zephaniah described Anta—now Anna—as his wife. He freed her and all five of her children, whom he recognized as his heirs. Anna managed the plantation until 1821, when Spain finally transferred Florida to the United States. Unwilling to live under the harsh slave laws that prevailed in the South, Kingsley emigrated to Haiti with Anna and their children. The slave quarters are on the right.

Gradually, as an outgrowth of this decision, the entire border was demilitarized, a remarkable achievement. In the Convention of 1818 the two countries agreed to the 49th parallel as the northern boundary of the Louisiana Territory between the Lake of the Woods and the Rocky Mountains, and to the joint control of the Oregon country for ten years.

The Transcontinental Treaty

The acquisition of Spanish Florida and the settlement of the western boundary of Louisiana were also accomplished as an aftermath of the War of 1812, but in a far different spirit. Spain's control of the Floridas was feeble. West Florida had passed into American hands by 1813, and frontiersmen in Georgia were eyeing East Florida greedily. Indians struck frequently into Georgia from Florida, then fled to sanctuary across the line. American slaves who escaped across the border could not be recovered. In 1818 James Monroe, who had been elected president in 1816, ordered General Andrew Jackson to clear raiding Seminole Indians from American soil and to pursue them into Florida if necessary. Seizing on these instructions, Jackson marched into Florida and easily captured two Spanish forts.

Although Jackson eventually withdrew from Florida, the impotence of the Spanish government made it obvious even in Madrid that if nothing were done, the United States would soon fill the power vacuum by seizing the territory. The Spanish minister to the United States, Luis de Onís, undertook to negotiate a treaty

with Monroe's Secretary of State John Quincy Adams. Adams pressed Onís merci-
lessly on the question of Louisiana's western boundary, and eventually the minister
agreed to accept a boundary that followed the Sabine, Red, and Arkansas Rivers to
the Continental Divide and the 42nd parallel to the Pacific, thus abandoning Spain's
claim to a huge area beyond the Rockies that had no connection at all with the
Louisiana Purchase. The United States obtained Florida in return for a mere $5 mil-
lion, and that paid not to Spain but to Americans who held claims against the
Spanish government.

This "Transcontinental Treaty," also known as the Adams-Onís Treaty, was
signed in 1819, although ratification was delayed until 1821. Most Americans at the
time thought the acquisition of Florida the most important part of the treaty, but
Adams, whose vision of America's future was truly continental, knew better. "The
acquisition of a definite line of boundary to the [Pacific] forms a great epoch in our
history," he recorded in his diary.

The Monroe Doctrine

Concern with defining the boundaries of the United States did not reflect a desire
to limit expansion; rather, the feeling was that there should be no more quibbling
and quarreling with foreign powers that might distract the people from the great
task of national development. The classic enunciation of this point of view, the
completion of America's withdrawal from Europe, was the Monroe Doctrine.

Two separate strands met in this pronouncement. The first led from Moscow to
Alaska and down the Pacific Coast to the Oregon country. Beginning with the explorations of Vitus Bering in 1741, the Russians had maintained an interest in fishing
and fur trading along the northwest coast of North America. In 1821 the Russian czar
extended his claim south to the 51st parallel and forbade the ships of other powers to
enter coastal waters north of that point. This announcement was disturbing.

The second strand ran from the courts of the European monarchs to Latin
America. Between 1817 and 1822 practically the entire region from the Rio Grande
to the Strait of Magellan had won its independence. Spain, former master of all the
area except Brazil, was too weak to win it back by force, but Austria, Prussia, France,
and Russia decided at the Congress of Verona in 1822 to try to regain the area for
Spain in the interests of "legitimacy." There was talk of sending a large French
army to South America. This possibility also caused grave concern in Washington.

To the Russian threat, Monroe and Secretary of State Adams responded
with a terse warning: "The American continents are no longer subjects for any
new European colonial establishments." This statement did not impress the
Russians, but they had no intention of colonizing the region. In 1824 they signed
a treaty with the United States abandoning all claims below the present southern limit of Alaska (54° 40' north latitude) and removing their restrictions on foreign shipping.

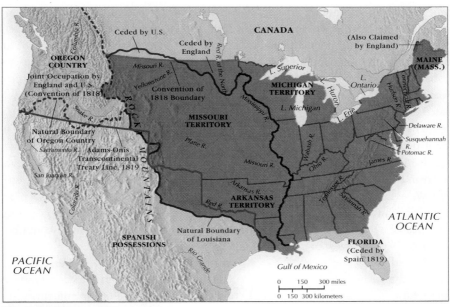

The United States, 1819

The Latin American problem was more complex. In 1823 the British foreign minister, George Canning, suggested to the American minister in London that the United States and Britain issue a joint statement opposing any French interference in South America, pledging that they themselves would never annex any part of Spain's old empire, and saying nothing about recognition of the new republics that were emerging in Latin America. This proposal of joint action with the British was flattering to the United States but scarcely in its best interests. The United States had already recognized the new republics, and it had no desire to help Great Britain retain its South American trade. As Secretary Adams pointed out, to agree to the proposal would be to abandon the possibility of someday adding Cuba or any other part of Latin America to the United States. America should act independently, Adams urged. "It would be more candid, as well as more dignified, to avow our principles explicitly . . . than to come in as a cockboat in the wake of the British man-of-war."

Monroe heartily endorsed Adams's argument and decided to include a statement of American policy in his annual message to Congress in December 1823. "The American continents," he wrote, "by the free and independent condition which they have assumed and maintain, are henceforth not to be considered as subjects for future colonization by any European powers." Europe's political system was "essentially different" from that developing in the New World, and the two should not be mixed. The United States would not interfere with existing European colonies in North or South America and would avoid involvement in strictly European affairs, but any attempt to extend European control to countries in the hemisphere that had already won their independence would be considered, Monroe warned, "the manifestation of an unfriendly disposition toward the United States" and consequently a threat to the nation's "peace and safety."

This policy statement—it was not dignified with the title Monroe Doctrine until decades later—attracted little notice in Europe or Latin America and not much more at home. Obviously the United States, whose own capital had been overrun by a mere raiding party less than ten years before, could not police the entire Western Hemisphere. European statesmen dismissed Monroe's message as "arrogant" and "blustering," worthy only of "the most profound contempt." Latin Americans, while appreciating the intent behind it, knew better than to count on American aid in case of attack.

Nevertheless, the principles laid down by President Monroe so perfectly expressed the wishes of the people of the United States that when the country grew powerful enough to enforce them, there was little need to alter or embellish his pronouncement. However understood at the time, the doctrine may be seen as the final stage in the evolution of American independence.

From this perspective, the famous Declaration of 1776 merely began a process of separation and self-determination. The peace treaty ending the Revolutionary War was a further step, and Washington's Declaration of Neutrality in 1793 was another, demonstrating as it did the capacity of the United States to determine its own best interests despite the treaty of alliance with France. The removal of British troops from the northwest forts, achieved by the otherwise ignominious Jay Treaty, marked the next stage. Then the Louisiana Purchase made a further advance toward true independence by ensuring that the Mississippi River could not be closed to the commerce so vital to the development of the western territories.

The standoff War of 1812 ended any lingering British hope of regaining control of America, the Latin American revolutions further weakened colonialism in the Western Hemisphere, and the Transcontinental Treaty pushed the last European power from the path of westward expansion. Monroe's "doctrine" was a kind of public announcement that the sovereign United States had completed its independence and wanted nothing more than to be left alone to concentrate on its own development. Better yet if Europe could be made to allow the entire hemisphere to follow its own path.

The Era of Good Feelings

The person who gave his name to the so-called doctrine was an unusually lucky man. James Monroe lived a long life in good health and saw at close hand most of the great events in the history of the young republic. At the age of 18 he shed his blood for liberty at the Battle of Trenton. He was twice governor of Virginia, a United States senator, and a Cabinet member. He was at various times the nation's representative in Paris, Madrid, and London. Elected president in 1816, his good fortune continued. The world was finally at peace, the country united and prosperous. A person of good feeling who would keep a steady hand on the helm and hold to the present course seemed called for, and Monroe possessed exactly the qualities that the times required. "He is a man whose soul might be turned wrongside outwards, without discovering a blemish," Jefferson said, and John Quincy Adams, a harsh critic of public figures, praised Monroe's courtesy, sincerity, and sound judgment.

Courtesy and purity of soul do not always suffice to make a good president. In more troubled times Monroe might well have brought disaster, for he was neither an outstanding intellect nor a forceful leader. He blazed few paths, organized no personal machine. The Monroe Doctrine, by far the most significant achievement of his administration, was as much the work of Secretary of State Adams as his own. No one ever claimed that Monroe was much better than second-rate, yet when his first term ended, he was reelected without organized opposition.

By 1817 the divisive issues of earlier days had vanished. Monroe dramatized their disappearance by beginning his first term with a goodwill tour of New England, heartland of the opposition. The tour was a triumph. Everywhere the president was greeted with tremendous enthusiasm. After he visited Boston, once the headquarters and now the graveyard of Federalism, a Federalist newspaper, the *Columbian Centinel*, gave the age its name. Pointing out that the celebrations attending Monroe's visit had brought together in friendly intercourse many persons "whom party politics had long severed," it dubbed the times the "Era of Good Feelings."

The Jeffersonian balance between individual liberty and responsible government, having survived both bad management and war, had justified itself to the opposition. The new unity was symbolized by the restored friendship of Jefferson and John Adams. In 1801 Adams had slipped sulkily out of Washington without waiting to attend his successor's inauguration, but after ten years of icy silence, the two old collaborators effected a reconciliation. Although they continued to disagree vigorously about matters of philosophy and government, the bitterness between them disappeared entirely. By Monroe's day, Jefferson was writing long letters to "my dear friend," ranging over such subjects as theology, the proper reading of the classics, and agricultural improvements, and receiving equally warm and voluminous replies. "Whether you or I were right," Adams wrote amiably to Jefferson, "Posterity must judge."

When political divisions appeared again, as they soon did, it was not because the old balance had been shaky. Few of the new controversies challenged Republican principles or revived old issues. Instead, these controversies were children of the present and the future, products of the continuing growth of the country. From 1790 to 1820, the area of the United States doubled, but very little of the Louisiana Purchase had been settled. More significant, the population of the nation had more than doubled, from 4 million to 9.6 million. The pace of the westward movement had also quickened; by 1820 the moving edge of the frontier ran in a long, irregular curve from Michigan to Arkansas.

New Sectional Issues

Sectional tensions led to many disputes over the tariff, banking, federal land policy, and internal improvements. Overshadowing all of these was the debate over slavery.

The War of 1812 and the depression that struck the country in 1819 had shaped many of the controversies. The tariff question was affected by both. To meet the added expenses occasioned by the War of 1812, Congress doubled all tariffs. In 1816, when the revenue was no longer needed, a new act kept duties close to wartime levels to protect the nation's infant industries, especially textiles, from foreign competitors.

Initially there was backing for high duties in every section except New England, which had suffered little from foreign competition and therefore supported free trade. But with the passage of time the South rejected protection almost completely. Industry failed to develop, and since Southerners exported most of their cotton and tobacco, they soon concluded that besides increasing the cost of nearly everything they bought, high duties on imports would limit the foreign market for southern staples by inhibiting international exchange. As this fact became clear, the West tended to divide on the tariff question: the Northwest and much of Kentucky, which had a special interest in protecting its considerable hemp production, favored high duties; the Southwest, where cotton was the major crop, favored low duties.

National banking policy was another important political issue affected by the war and the depression. Presidents Jefferson and Madison had managed to live with the Bank of the United States despite its dubious constitutionality, but its charter was not renewed when it expired in 1811. Aside from the constitutional question, the major opposition to recharter came from state banks eager to take over the business of the Bank for themselves. The fact that English investors owned most of the Bank's stock was also used as an argument against recharter.

Many more state banks were created after 1811, and most extended credit recklessly. When the British raid on Washington and Baltimore in 1814 sent panicky depositors scurrying to convert their deposits into gold or silver, the overextended financiers could not oblige them. All banks outside New England suspended specie payments; that is, they stopped exchanging their bank notes for hard money on demand. Paper money immediately fell in value; a paper dollar was soon worth only 85 cents in coin in Philadelphia, less in Baltimore. Government business also suffered from the absence of a national bank. In October 1814 Secretary of the Treasury Alexander J. Dallas submitted a plan for a second Bank of the United States, and after considerable wrangling over its precise form, the institution was authorized in April 1816.

Capitalized at $35 million, the new Bank was much larger than its predecessor. However, unlike Hamilton's creation, the second Bank was badly managed at the start. But the appointment in 1819 of Langdon Cheves of South Carolina as president of the Bank restored the bank's reputation. Cheves restricted credit, issuing far fewer loans than his predecessor. This infuriated many borrowers. "The Bank was saved," the contemporary economist William Gouge wrote somewhat hyperbolically, "and the people were ruined." Indeed, the bank reached a low point in public favor. Irresponsible state banks resented it, as did the advocates of hard money.

Regional lines were less sharply drawn on the Bank issue than on the tariff. Northern congressmen voted against the Bank 53 to 44 in 1816—many of them because they objected to the particular proposal, not because they were against any national bank. Those from other sections favored it, 58 to 30. The economic depression of the Panic of 1819 produced further opposition to the institution in the West.

Land policy in the West also caused sectional controversy. No one wished to eliminate the system of survey and sale, but there was continuous pressure to reduce the price of public land and the minimum unit offered for sale. Sectional attitudes toward the public lands were fairly straightforward. The West wanted cheap land; the North and South tended to look on the national domain as an asset that should be converted into as much cash as possible. Northern manufacturers feared that cheap land in the West would drain off surplus labor and force wages up, while Southern planters were concerned about the competition that would develop when new lands in the Southwest were put to the plow to grow cotton. The West, however, was ready to fight to the last line of defense over land policy, while the other regions would usually compromise on the issue to gain support for their own vital interests.

Sectional alignments on the question of internal improvements were similar to those on land policy, but this issue, soon to become very important, had not greatly agitated national affairs before 1820. The only significant federal internal improvement project undertaken before that date was the National Road.

The most divisive sectional issue was slavery. After the compromises affecting the "peculiar institution" made at the Constitutional Convention, it caused remarkably little conflict in national politics before 1819. Although the importation of blacks rose in the 1790s, Congress abolished the African slave trade in 1808 without major incident. As the nation expanded, free and slave states were added to the Union in equal numbers—free states of Ohio, Indiana, and Illinois being balanced by the slave states of Louisiana, Mississippi, and Alabama. In 1819 there were twenty-two states, eleven slave and eleven free. The expansion of slavery occasioned by the cotton boom led Southerners to support it more aggressively, which tended to irritate many Northerners, but most persons considered slavery mainly a local issue. To the extent that it was a national question, the North opposed it and the South defended it ardently. The West leaned toward the southern point of view, for in addition to the southwestern slave states, the Northwest was sympathetic, partly because much of its produce was sold on southern plantations and partly because at least half of its early settlers came from Virginia, Kentucky, and other slave states.

The Missouri Compromise

The sectional concerns of the 1820s repeatedly influenced politics. The depression of 1819 to 1822 increased people's tensions over the issues of the day. For example, manufacturers who wanted high tariffs in 1816 were more vehemently in favor of protection in 1820 when their business fell off. Even when economic conditions improved, geographic alignments on key issues tended to solidify.

One of the first and most critical of the sectional questions concerned the admission of Missouri as a slave state. When Louisiana entered the Union in 1812, the rest of the Louisiana Purchase was organized as the Missouri Territory. Building on a nucleus of Spanish and French inhabitants, the region west and north of St. Louis grew rapidly, and in 1817 the Missourians petitioned for statehood. A large percentage of the settlers—the population exceeded 60,000 by 1818—were Southerners who had moved into the valleys of the Arkansas and Missouri rivers. Since many of them owned slaves, Missouri would become a slave state.

The admission of new states had always been a routine matter, in keeping with the pattern established by the Northwest Ordinance. But during the debate on the Missouri Enabling Act in February 1819, Congressman James Tallmadge of New York introduced an amendment prohibiting "the further introduction of slavery" and providing that all slaves born in Missouri after the territory became a state should be freed at age 25.

While Tallmadge was merely seeking to apply in the territory the pattern of race relations that had developed in the states immediately east of Missouri, his amendment represented, at least in spirit, something of a revolution. The Northwest Ordinance had prohibited slavery in the land between the Mississippi and the Ohio, but that area had only a handful of slaveowners in 1787 and little prospect of attracting more. Elsewhere no effort to restrict the movement of slaves into new territory had been attempted. If one assumed (as whites always had) that the slaves themselves should have no say in the matter, it appeared democratic to let the settlers of Missouri decide the slavery question for themselves. Nevertheless, the Tallmadge amendment passed the House, the vote following sectional lines closely. The Senate, however, resoundingly rejected it. The less populous southern part of Missouri was then organized separately as the Arkansas Territory, and an attempt to bar slavery there was stifled. The Missouri Enabling Act failed to pass before Congress adjourned.

When the next Congress met in December 1819, the Missouri issue came up at once. The vote on Tallmadge's amendment had shown that the rapidly growing North controlled the House of Representatives. It was vital, Southerners felt, to preserve a balance in the Senate. Yet Northerners objected to the fact that Missouri extended hundreds of miles north of the Ohio River, which they considered slavery's natural boundary. Angry debate raged in Congress for months.

The debate did not turn on the morality of slavery or the rights of blacks. Northerners objected to adding new slave states because under the Three-fifths Compromise these states would be overrepresented in Congress (60 percent of their slaves would be counted in determining the size of the states' delegations in the House of Representatives) and because they did not relish competing with slave labor. Since the question was political influence rather than the rights and wrongs of slavery, a compromise was worked out in 1820. Missouri entered the

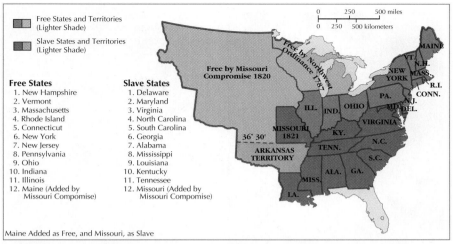

Free States and Territories
(Lighter Shade)

Slave States and Territories
(Lighter Shade)

Free States
1. New Hampshire
2. Vermont
3. Massachusetts
4. Rhode Island
5. Connecticut
6. New York
7. New Jersey
8. Pennsylvania
9. Ohio
10. Indiana
11. Illinois
12. Maine (Added by
    Missouri Compomise)

Slave States
1. Delaware
2. Maryland
3. Virginia
4. North Carolina
5. South Carolina
6. Georgia
7. Alabama
8. Mississippi
9. Louisiana
10. Kentucky
11. Tennessee
12. Missouri (Added by
    Missouri Compromise)

Maine Added as Free, and Missouri, as Slave

The Missouri Compromise, 1820

The Missouri Compromise temporarily put aside the congressional debate over slavery, with the slave states (12) and free states (12) being in perfect balance. This meant, of course, that the Senate was evenly divided as well. But what would happen when other parts of the Missouri Territory sought admission to the Union as states?

Union as a slave state and Maine, having been separated from Massachusetts, was admitted as a free state to preserve the balance in the Senate.

To prevent further conflict, Congress adopted the proposal of Senator Jesse B. Thomas of Illinois, which "forever prohibited" slavery in all other parts of the Louisiana Purchase north of 36° 30' latitude, the westward extension of Missouri's southern boundary. Although this division would keep slavery out of most of the territory, Southerners accepted it cheerfully. The land south of the line, the present states of Arkansas and Oklahoma, seemed ideally suited for the expanded plantation economy, and most persons considered the treeless northern regions little better than a desert. One northern senator, decrying the division, contemptuously described the land north and west of Missouri, today one of the world's richest agricultural regions, as "a prairie without food or water."

The Missouri Compromise did not end the crisis. When Missouri submitted its constitution for approval by Congress (the final step in the admission process), the document, besides authorizing slavery and prohibiting the emancipation of any slave without the consent of the owner, required the state legislature to pass a law barring free blacks and mulattos from entering the state "under any pretext whatever." This provision plainly violated Article IV, Section 2, of the U.S. Constitution: "The Citizens of each State shall be entitled to all Privileges and Immunities of Citizens in the several States." It did not, however, represent any more of a break with established racial patterns, North or South, than the Tallmadge amendment; many states east of Missouri barred free blacks without regard for the Constitution.

Nevertheless, northern congressmen hypocritically refused to accept the Missouri constitution. Once more the debate raged. Again, since few Northerners cared to defend the rights of blacks, the issue was compromised. In March 1821

Henry Clay of Kentucky. "Life itself is but a compromise between death and life," Clay said, a principle he applied to politics.

Congressman Henry Clay of Kentucky found a face-saving formula: Out of respect for the "supreme law of the land," Congress accepted the Missouri constitution with the notation that no law passed in conformity to it should be construed as violating Article IV, Section 2 of the U.S. Constitution.

Every thinking person recognized the political dynamite inherent in the Missouri controversy. The sectional lineup had been terrifyingly compact. What meant the Union if so trivial a matter as one new state could so divide the people? Moreover, despite the timidity and hypocrisy of the North, everyone realized that the rights and wrongs of slavery lay at the heart of the conflict. "We have the wolf by the ears, and we can neither safely hold him, nor safely let him go," Jefferson wrote a month after Missouri became a state. The dispute, he said, "like a fire bell in the night, awakened and filled me with terror." Jefferson knew that the compromise had not quenched the flames ignited by the Missouri debates. "This is a reprieve only," he said. John Quincy Adams called it the "title page to a great tragic volume." Yet one could still hope that the fire bell was only a false alarm, that Adams's tragic volume would remain unread.

The Election of 1824

Other controversies that aroused strong feelings did not seem to divide the country so deeply. The question of federal internal improvements caused endless debate that split the country on geographical lines. In 1816 the nationalist-minded Congressman John C. Calhoun of South Carolina had pressed a plan to set up a $1.5 million fund for roads and canals. Congress approved this despite strong opposi-

Eyes like "anthracite furnaces," the English historian Thomas Carlyle remarked of Daniel Webster; this is the "Black Dan" portrait by Francis Alexander (1835).

tion in New England and a divided South. In 1822 a bill providing money for the upkeep of the National Road caused another sectional split. Both measures were vetoed, but in 1824 Monroe approved a differently worded internal improvement act. Such proposals excited intense reactions. Congressman John Randolph of Virginia, opposing the 1824 bill with his usual ferocity, threatened to employ "every . . . means short of actual insurrection" to defeat it. Yet no one—not even Randolph, it will be noted—threatened the Union on this issue.

The tariff continued to divide the country. When a new, still higher tariff was enacted in 1824, the slave states voted almost unanimously against it, the North and Northwest in favor, and New England remained of two minds. Daniel Webster of Massachusetts (after conducting a poll of business leaders before deciding how to vote) made a powerful speech against the act, but the measure passed without creating a major storm.

The presidential fight was waged on personal grounds, although the heat generated by the contest began the process of reenergizing party politics. Besides Calhoun the candidates were Andrew Jackson, hero of the Battle of New Orleans, William Crawford of Georgia, John Quincy Adams, and Henry Clay of Kentucky. The maneuvering among them was complex, the infighting savage. In March 1824, Calhoun, who was young enough to wait for the White House, withdrew and declared for the vice presidency, which he won easily. Crawford, who had the support of many congressional leaders, seemed the likely winner, but he suffered a series of paralytic strokes that gravely injured his chances.

Despite the bitterness of the contest, it attracted relatively little public interest; barely a quarter of those eligible took the trouble to vote. In the Electoral College Jackson led with 99, Adams had 84, Crawford 41, and Clay 37. Since no one had a majority, the contest was thrown into the House of Representatives, which, under the Constitution, had to choose from among the three leaders, each state delegation having one vote. By employing his great influence in the House, Clay swung the balance. Not wishing to advance the fortunes of a rival Westerner like Jackson and feeling, with reason, that Crawford's health made him unavailable, Clay gave his support to Adams, who was thereupon elected.

John Quincy Adams as President

Adams, who took a Hamiltonian view of the future of the country, hoped to use the national authority to foster all sorts of useful projects. He asked Congress for a federal program of internal improvements so vast that even Clay boggled when he realized its scope. He came out for aid to manufacturing and agriculture, for a national university, and even for a government astronomical observatory. For a nationalist of unchallengeable Jeffersonian origins like Clay or Calhoun to have pressed for so extensive a program would have been politically risky. For the son of John Adams to do so was disastrous; every doubter remembered his Federalist background and decided that he was trying to overturn the glorious "Revolution of 1800."

Adams proved to be his own worst enemy, for he was an inept politician. Although capable on occasion of turning a phrase—in his first annual message to Congress he described astronomical observatories as "light-houses of the skies"— his general style of public utterance was bumbling and cumbersome. Knowing that many citizens considered things like observatories impractical extravagances, he urged Congress not to be "palsied by the will of our constituents." To persuade Americans, who were almost pathological on the subject of monarchy, to support his road building program, he cited with approval the work being done abroad by "the nations of Europe and . . . their rulers," which revived fears that all Adamses were royalists at heart. He was insensitive to the ebb and flow of public feeling; even when he wanted to move with the tide, he seldom managed to dramatize and publicize his stand effectively. There was wide support in the country for a federal bankruptcy law, but instead of describing himself in plain language as a friend of poor debtors, Adams called for the "amelioration" of the "often oppressive codes relating to insolvency" and buried the recommendation at the tail end of a dull state paper.

Calhoun's *Exposition and Protest*

The tariff question added to the president's troubles. High duties, increasingly more repulsive to the export-conscious South, attracted more and more favor in the North and West. Besides manufacturers, lead miners in Missouri, hemp raisers in Kentucky, wool growers in New York, and many other interests demanded protection against foreign competition. The absence of party discipline provided an

This striking portrait of John C. Calhoun was painted sometime between 1818 and 1825, probably by Charles Bird King. Calhoun was in his thirties.

ideal climate for "logrolling" in Congress. Legislators found themselves under pressure from their constituents to raise the duties on products of local importance; to satisfy these demands, they traded votes with other congressmen similarly situated. In this way massive "support" for protection was generated.

In 1828 a new tariff was hammered into shape by the House Committee on Manufactures. Northern and western agricultural interests were in command; they wrote into the bill extremely high duties on raw wool, hemp, flax, fur, and liquor. New England manufacturers protested vociferously, for although their products were protected, the proposed law would increase the cost of their raw materials. This gave Southerners, now hopelessly in the minority on the tariff question, a chance to block the bill. When the New Englanders proposed amendments lowering the duties on raw materials, the Southerners voted nay, hoping to force them to reject the measure on the final vote. This desperate strategy failed. New England had by this time committed its future to manufacturing, a change signaled by the somersault of Webster, who, ever responsive to local pressures, now voted for protection. After winning some minor concessions in the Senate, largely through the intervention of Martin Van Buren of New York, enough New Englanders accepted the so-called Tariff of Abominations to ensure its passage.

Vice President Calhoun believed that the new tariff would impoverish the South. He warned Jackson that relief from high import taxes must soon be provided or the Union would be shaken to its foundations. Then he returned to his South Carolina plantation and wrote an essay, *The South Carolina Exposition and Protest*, repudiating the nationalist philosophy he had previously championed.

The South Carolina legislature released this document to the country in December 1828, along with eight resolutions denouncing the protective tariff as unfair and unconstitutional. The theorist Calhoun, however, was not content with outlining the case against the tariff. His *Exposition* provided an ingenious defense of the right of the people of a state to reject a law of Congress. Starting with John Locke's revered concept of government as a contractual relationship, he argued that since the states had created the Union, logic dictated that they be the final arbiters of the meaning of the Constitution. If a special state convention, representing the sovereignty of the people, decided that an act of Congress violated the Constitution, it could interpose its authority and "nullify" the law within its boundaries. Calhoun did not seek to implement this theory in 1828, for he hoped that the next administration would lower the tariff and make nullification unnecessary.

The Meaning of Sectionalism

The sectional issues that occupied the energies of politicians and strained the ties between the people of the different regions were produced by powerful forces that actually bound the sections together. Growth caused differences that sometimes led to conflict, but growth itself was the product of prosperity. People were drawn to the West by the expectation that life would be better there, as more often than not it was, at least in the long run. Henry Clay proclaimed his support for an "American System" where each section of the nation would specialize economically, thus benefiting the nation as a whole. He argued plausibly that western farmers would profit by selling their crops to eastern city dwellers and that spending public money on building roads and other internal improvements would make transportation and communication less expensive and thus benefit everyone.

Another force unifying the nation was patriotism; the increasing size and prosperity of the nation made people proud to be part of a growing, dynamic society. Still another was the uniqueness of the American system of government and the people's knowledge that their immediate ancestors had created it. John Adams and Thomas Jefferson died on the same day, July 4, 1826, the fiftieth anniversary of the signing of the Declaration of Independence. People took this not as a remarkable coincidence, but as a sign from the heavens, an indication that God looked with favor on the American experiment.

1808	James Madison is elected president
1810	Macon's Bill No. 2 removes all restrictions on commerce with Britain and France
1811	Battle of Tippecanoe shatters Indian confederation
1812	James Madison is reelected president
	Congress declares war on Great Britain
	USS *Constitution* and *United States* win naval victories
1813	Oliver Hazard Perry destroys British fleet in Battle of Lake Erie
	William Henry Harrison defeats British in Battle of the Thames
	Tecumseh dies at Battle of the Thames
1814	British burn Washington, D.C.
	Francis Scott Key writes "The Star Spangled Banner" during bombardment of Fort McHenry
	New England Federalists meet at Hartford Convention
	Treaty of Ghent officially ends war of 1812
1815	Andrew Jackson defeats British at Battle of New Orleans
1816	James Monroe is elected president
1817	Rush-Bagot Agreement limits American and British forces on Lake Champlain and Great Lakes
1819	United States signs Transcontinental Treaty with Spain
1819–1822	United States experiences economic depression
1820	James Monroe is reelected president
1820–1821	Missouri Compromise closes Missouri Territory to slavery, but opens Arkansas Territory to slavery
1820–1850	Cities and manufacturing grow rapidly
1823	Monroe Doctrine says U.S. will consider future European colonization in western hemisphere a threat to America
1824–1825	House of Representatives decides election of 1824 in favor of John Quincy Adams
1828	Congress passes Tariff of Abominations
	South Carolina legislature releases Calhoun's *Exposition and Protest*, leading to debate over nullification

Toward a National Economy

THE PURSUIT OF HAPPYNESS (2006), A MOVIE STARRING WILL Smith, tells the story of Chris Gardner, a struggling salesman who dreams of a better life. Early in the film, while musing about Thomas Jefferson and the Declaration of Independence, Gardner raises the theme of the movie's (misspelled) title: "The passage about our right to life, liberty, and the pursuit of happiness—How did he know to put the pursuit part in there? That happiness?"

Gardner covets wealth. His heart flutters when he sees a Porsche. To own such a car would be happiness. Then, after losing both his job and wife, he careens into abject poverty. He and his young son sleep on the floors of public bathrooms; sometimes they go hungry. Gardner takes a job as an unpaid intern; once he reports for work without shoes. Happiness now means a plateful of food, a warm bed, and decent clothing. The movie ends happily; as in real life, Gardner gets a job with the brokerage, rises to the top, and makes a fortune.

Gardner's insight about Jefferson and the pursuit of happiness was on target. The Founding Fathers did not regard political rights merely as abstract philosophies but as a means to satisfy human desires. And in terms of food, clothing, and shelter, most Americans in the early 1800s were far better off than their counterparts in Europe. But Americans wanted more. During the early decades of the nineteenth century, they initiated the dynamic transformation of the economy. They built factories and devised machines to produce more goods at a lower cost. They recruited immigrants, women, and children to take low-paying jobs and they bought more slaves. They imposed new forms of discipline on all workers. They constructed turnpikes and canals. They built cities to distribute the wealth of the regions. They concocted legal structures to protect corporations and channel wealth into productive enterprises.

Did the booming economy generate happiness? By the mid-1800s, many observers had doubts. "I have never thought America a happy country," Thomas Law Nichols, a physician and health reformer, wrote at midcentury. "Every little ragged boy dreams of being a John Jacob Astor" (a reference to perhaps the wealthiest man in New York). "The dream may be a pleasant one while it lasts, but what of the excited, restless, feverish life spent in the pursuit of phantoms?"

Gentility and the Consumer Revolution

The democratic revolution was accompanied by widespread emulation of aristocratic behavior. On his trip to Paris in 1778 on behalf of the Continental Congress, John Adams denounced the splendor of the houses, furniture, and clothing. "I cannot help suspecting that the more Elegance, the less Virtue," he concluded. Yet despite the constraints of war, Adams purchased a lavish carriage. On returning to America, he bought a three-story mansion and furnished it with Louis XV chairs and, among other extravagances, an ornate wine cooler from Vincennes, France.

Among aristocratic circles in Europe, gentility was the product of ancestry and cultivated style; but in America it was largely defined by possession of material goods. Houses with parlors, dining rooms, and hallways bulged with countless articles of consumption: porcelain plates, silver tea services, woolen carpets, walnut tables. By the mid-eighteenth century the "refinement of America" had touched the homes of some southern planters and urban merchants; but a half century later porcelain plates made by English craftsman Josiah Wedgwood and mahogany washstands by Thomas Chippendale were appearing even in frontier communities. Americans were demanding more goods than such craftsmen could turn out. Everywhere producers sought to expand their workshops, hire and train more artisans, and acquire large stocks of materials and labor-saving machines.

Americans enshrined the simple life and a homespun equality; yet they coveted the cultural markers of aristocracy, such as imported porcelain tea services. This one, made in France, was given to Alexander Hamilton. Gentility spread, historian Richard Bushman writes, "because people longed to be associated with the 'best society.'"

But first they had to locate the requisite capital, find ways to supervise large numbers of workers, and discover how to get raw materials to factories and products to customers. The solutions to these problems, taken together, constituted the "market revolution" of the early nineteenth century. The "industrial revolution" came on its heels.

Birth of the Factory

By the 1770s British manufacturers, especially those in textiles, had made astonishing progress in mechanizing their operations, bringing workers together in buildings called factories where waterpower, and later steam, supplied the force to run new spinning and weaving devices that increased productivity and reduced labor costs.

Because machine-spun cotton was cheaper and of better quality than that spun by hand, producers in other countries were eager to adopt British methods. Americans had depended on Great Britain for such products until the Revolution cut off supplies; then the new spirit of nationalism gave impetus to the development of local industry. A number of state legislatures offered bounties to anyone who would introduce the new machinery. The British, however, guarded their secrets vigilantly. It was illegal to export any of the new machines or to send their plans abroad. Workers skilled in their construction and use were forbidden to leave the country. These restrictions were effective for a time; the principles on which the new machines were based were simple enough, but to construct workable models without plans was another matter. Although a number of persons tried to do so, it was not until Samuel Slater installed his machines in Pawtucket, Rhode Island, that a successful factory was constructed.

Slater, born in England, was more than a skilled mechanic. Attracted by stories of the rewards offered in the United States, he slipped out of England in 1789. Not daring to carry any plans, he depended on his memory and his mechanical sense for the complicated specifications of the necessary machines. Moses Brown brought Slater to Rhode Island to help run his textile-manufacturing operation. Slater insisted on scrapping the crude machinery Brown's company had assembled. Then, working in secrecy with a carpenter who was "under bond not to steal the patterns nor disclose the nature of the work," Slater built and installed his machinery. In December 1790 the first American factory began production.

It was a humble beginning indeed. Slater's machines made only cotton thread, which Brown's company sold in its Providence store and "put out" to individual artisans, who, working for wages, wove it into cloth in their homes. The machines were tended by a labor force of nine children, for the work was simple and the pace slow. The young operatives' pay ranged from 33 to 67 cents a week, about what a youngster could earn in other occupations.[1]

---

[1]This labor pattern persisted for several decades. In 1813 a cotton manufacturer placed the following advertisement in the Utica (N.Y.) Patriot: "A few sober and industrious families of at least five children each, over the age of eight years are wanted at the Cotton Factory. Widows with large families would do well to attend this notice."

The factory was profitable from the start. Slater soon branched out on his own, and others trained by him opened their own establishments. By 1800 seven mills possessing 2,000 spindles were in operation; by 1815, after production had been stimulated by the War of 1812, there were 130,000 spindles turning in 213 factories. Many of the new factories were inefficient, but the well-managed ones earned large profits. Slater began with almost nothing. When he died in 1835 he owned mill properties in Rhode Island, Massachusetts, Connecticut, and New Hampshire in addition to other interests. By the standards of the day he was a rich man.

Before long the Boston Associates, a group of merchants headed by Francis Cabot Lowell, added a new dimension to factory production. Beginning at Waltham, Massachusetts, where the Charles River provided the necessary water-power, between 1813 and 1850 they revolutionized textile production. Some early factory owners had set up hand looms in their plants, but the weavers could not keep pace with the whirring spinning jennies. Lowell, after an extensive study of British mills, smuggled the plans for an efficient power loom into America. His Boston Manufacturing Company at Waltham, capitalized at $300,000, combined machine production, large-scale operation, efficient management, and centralized marketing procedures. It concentrated on the mass production of a standardized product.

Lowell's cloth, though plain and rather coarse, was durable and cheap. His profits averaged almost 20 percent a year during the Era of Good Feelings. In 1823 the Boston Associates began to harness the power of the Merrimack River, setting up a new $600,000 corporation at the sleepy village of East Chelmsford, Massachusetts (population 300), where there was a fall of 32 feet in the river. Within three years the town, appropriately renamed Lowell, had 2,000 inhabitants.

An Industrial Proletariat?

As machines displaced skilled labor, the ability of laborers to influence working conditions declined. If skilled, they either became employers and developed entrepreneurial and managerial skills, or they descended into the mass of wage earners. Simultaneously, the changing structure of production widened the gap between owners and workers and blurred the distinction between skilled and unskilled labor.

These trends might have been expected to generate hostility between workers and employers. To some extent they did. There were strikes for higher wages and to protest work speedups throughout the 1830s and again in the 1850s. Efforts to found unions and to create political organizations dedicated to advancing the interests of workers were also undertaken. But well into the 1850s Americans displayed less evidence of the class solidarity common among European workers.

Why America did not produce a self-conscious working class is a question that has long intrigued historians. As with most such large questions, no single answer has been forthcoming. Some historians argue that the existence of the frontier siphoned off displaced and dissatisfied workers. The number of urban laborers who went West could not have been large, but the fact that the expanding economy created many opportunities for laborers to rise out of the working class was surely another reason why so few of them developed strong class feelings.

Other historians believe that ethnic and racial differences kept workers from seeing themselves as a distinct class with common needs and common enemies. The influx of needy immigrants willing to accept almost any wage was certainly resented by native-born workers. The growing number of free blacks in northern cities—between 1800 and 1830 the number tripled in Philadelphia and quadrupled in New York—also inhibited the development of a self-identified working class.

These answers help explain the relative absence of class conflict during the early stages of the industrial revolution in America, but so does the fact that conditions in the early shops and factories represented an improvement for the people who worked in them. This was the case with nearly all European immigrants, though less so for urban free blacks, since in the South many found work in the skilled trades.

Most workers in the early textile factories were drawn from outside the regular labor market. Relatively few artisan spinners and weavers became factory workers; indeed, some of them continued to work as they had, for it was many years before the factories could even begin to satisfy the ever-increasing demand for cloth. Nor did immigrants attend the new machines. Instead, the mill owners relied chiefly on women and children. They did so because machines lessened the need for skill and strength and because the labor shortage made it necessary to tap unexploited sources. By the early 1820s about half the cotton textile workers in the factories were under 16 years of age.

Most people of that generation considered this a good thing. They reasoned that the work was easy and that it kept youngsters busy at useful tasks while providing their families with extra income. Roxanna Foote, whose daughter, Harriet Beecher Stowe, wrote *Uncle Tom's Cabin*, came from a solid middle-class family in Guilford, Connecticut. Nevertheless, she worked full-time before her marriage in her grandfather's small spinning mill. "This spinning-mill was a favorite spot," a relative recalled many years later. "Here the girls often received visitors, or read or chatted while they spun." Roxanna explained her daily regimen as a mill girl matter-of-factly: "I generally rise with the sun, and, after breakfast, take my wheel, which is my daily companion, and the evening is generally devoted to reading, writing, and knitting."

This seems an idealized picture, or perhaps working for one's grandfather made a difference. Another young girl, Emily Chubbock, later a well-known writer, had a less pleasant recollection of her experience as an 11-year-old factory hand earning $1.25 a week. "My principal recollections . . . are of noise and filth, bleeding hands and aching feet, and a very sad heart." In any case, a society accustomed to seeing the children of fairly well-to-do farmers working full-time in the fields was not shocked by the sight of children working all day in mills. In factories where laborers were hired in family units, no member earned very much, but with a couple of adolescent daughters and perhaps a son of 9 or 10 helping out, a family could take home enough to live decently. For most working Americans, then as now, that was success enough.

The first mill operations performed only the task of spinning wool, cotton, and other fibers into thread; soon weaving was also mechanized, so that fabric ready to be cut and sewn was manufactured. Note the child at left, working under the spindles where an adult could not stand.

Lowell's Waltham System: Women as Factory Workers

Instead of hiring children, the Boston Associates developed the "Waltham System" of employing young, unmarried women in their new textile mills. For a generation after the opening of the Merrimack Manufacturing Company in 1823, the thriving factory towns of Lowell, Chicopee, and Manchester provided the background for a remarkable industrial idyll. Young women came from farms all over New England to work for a year or two in the mills. They were lodged in company boardinghouses, which, like college dormitories, became centers of social life. Unlike modern college dormitories, the boardinghouses were strictly supervised; straitlaced New Englanders did not hesitate to permit their daughters to live in them. The regulations laid down by one company, for example, required that all employees "show that they are penetrated by a laudable love of temperance and virtue." "Ardent spirits" were banished from company property, "games of hazard and cards" prohibited. A 10 P.M. curfew was strictly enforced.

The women earned between $2.50 and $3.25 a week, about half of which went for room and board. Some of the remainder they sent home, the rest (what there was of it) they could spend as they wished.

Most of these young women did not have to support themselves. They worked to save up for their marriage, to help educate a younger brother, or simply for the experience and excitement of meeting new people and escaping the confining environment of the farm. "The feeling that at this new work, the few hours they had of every-day leisure was entirely their own was a satisfaction to them," one Lowell worker recalled. Anything but an industrial proletariat, they filled the windows of the factories with flowering plants, organized sewing circles, edited their own literary periodicals, and attended lectures on edifying subjects. That such activity was possible on top of a 70-hour work week is a commentary on both the resiliency of youth and the leisurely pace of these early factories. The English novelist Charles Dickens, though scarcely enchanted by other American ways, was impressed by his visit to Lowell, which he compared most favorably to "those great haunts of misery," the English manufacturing towns. "They were all well dressed," he wrote of the workers. "They were healthy in appearance, many of them remarkably so, and had the manners and deportment of young women. . . . The rooms in which they worked were as well ordered as themselves."

Life in the mills was not all it might have been. Although they made up 85 percent of the workforce, women were kept out of supervisory positions. In 1834 workers in several mills "turned out" to protest cuts in their wages and a hike in what they paid for board. This work stoppage did not force a reversal of management policy. Another strike two years later in response to a work speedup was somewhat more successful. But when a drop in prices in the 1840s led the owners to introduce new rules designed to increase production, workers lacked the organizational strength to block them. By then young women of the kind that had flocked to the mills in the 1820s and 1830s were beginning to find work as schoolteachers and clerks. Mill owners turned increasingly to Irish immigrants to operate their machines.

Irish and German Immigrants

Between 1790 and 1820 the population of the United States had more than doubled to 9.6 million. The most remarkable feature of this growth was that it resulted almost entirely from natural increase. The birthrate in the early nineteenth century exceeded 50 per 1,000 population, a rate as high as that of any country in the world today. Fewer than 250,000 immigrants entered the United States between 1790 and 1820. European wars, the ending of the slave trade, and doubts about the viability of the new republic slowed the flow of humanity across the Atlantic to a trickle.

But soon after the final defeat of Napoleon in 1815, immigration picked up. In the 1820s, some 150,000 European immigrants arrived; in the 1830s, 600,000; in the 1840s, 1.7 million. The 1850 census, the first to make the distinction, estimated that of the nation's population of 23 million, more than 10 percent were foreign-born. In the Northeast the proportion exceeded 15 percent.

Most of this human tide came from Germany and Ireland, but substantial numbers also came from Great Britain and the Scandinavian countries. As with earlier immigrants, most were drawn to America by what are called "pull" factors:

the prospect of abundant land, good wages, and economic opportunity generally, or by the promise of political and religious freedom. But many came because of "push" factors: to stay where they were meant to face starvation. This was particularly true of those from Ireland, where a potato blight triggered the flight of tens of thousands. This Irish exodus continued; by the end of the century there were more people of Irish origin in America than in Ireland.

Once ashore in New York, Boston, or Philadelphia, most relatively prosperous immigrants pushed directly westward. Others found work in the new factory towns along the route of the Erie Canal, in the lower Delaware Valley southeast of Philadelphia, or along the Merrimack River north of Boston. But most of the Irish immigrants, "the poorest and most wretched population that can be found in the world," one of their priests called them, lacked the means to go West. Aside from the cost of transportation, starting a farm required far more capital than they could raise. Like it or not, they had to settle in the eastern cities.

Viewed in historical perspective, this massive wave of immigration stimulated the American economy. In the short run, the influx of the 1830s and 1840s depressed living standards and strained the social fabric. For the first time the nation had acquired a culturally distinctive, citybound, and propertyless class. The poor Irish immigrants had to accept whatever wages employers offered them. By doing so they caused resentment among native workers, resentment exacerbated by the unfamiliarity of the Irish with city ways and by their Roman Catholic faith, which the Protestant majority associated with European authoritarianism and corruption.

The Persistence of the Household System

Since technology affected American industry unevenly, contemporaries found the changes difficult to evaluate. Interchangeable firing pins for rifles did not lead at once even to matching pairs of shoes. More than 15 years passed after John Fitch built and launched the world's first regularly scheduled steamboat in 1790 before it was widely accepted. Few people in the 1820s appreciated how profound the impact of the factory system would be. The city of Lowell seemed remarkable and important but not necessarily a herald of future trends.

Yet in nearly every field apparently minor changes were being made. Beginning around 1815, small improvements in the design of waterwheels, such as the use of leather transmission belts and metal gears, made possible larger and more efficient machinery in mills and factories. The woolen industry gradually became as mechanized as the cotton. Iron production advanced beyond the stage of the blacksmith's forge and the small foundry only slowly; nevertheless, by 1810 machines were stamping out nails at a third of the cost of the hand-forged type, and a few years later sheet iron, formerly hammered out laboriously by hand, was being produced in efficient rolling mills. At about this time the puddling process for refining pig iron made it possible to use coal for fuel instead of expensive charcoal.

Key improvements were made soon after the War of 1812 in the manufacture of paper, glass, and pottery. The commercial canning of sterilized foods in airtight containers began about 1820. The invention in that year of a machine for cutting ice, which reduced the cost by over 50 percent, had equally important effects on urban eating habits.

Rise of Corporations

Mechanization required substantial capital investment, and capital was chronically in short supply. The modern method of organizing large enterprises, the corporation, was slow to develop. Between 1781 and 1801 only 326 corporations were chartered by the states, and only a few of them were engaged in manufacturing.

The general opinion was that only quasi-public projects, such as roads and waterworks, were entitled to the privilege of incorporation. Anyone interested in organizing a corporation had to obtain a special act of a state legislature. And even among businessmen there was a tendency to associate corporations with monopoly, with corruption, and with the undermining of individual enterprise.

While the growth of industry did not suddenly revolutionize American life, it reshaped society in various ways. For a time it lessened the importance of foreign commerce. Some relative decline from the lush years immediately preceding Jefferson's embargo was no doubt inevitable, especially in the fabulously profitable reexport trade. But American industrial growth reduced the need for foreign products and thus the business of merchants. Only in the 1850s, when the wealth and population of the United States were more than three times what they had been in the first years of the century, did the value of American exports climb back to the levels of 1807. As the country moved closer to self-sufficiency (a point it never reached), nationalistic and isolationist sentiments were subtly augmented. During the embargo and the War of 1812 a great deal of capital had been transferred from commerce to industry; afterward new capital continued to prefer industry, attracted by the high profits and growing prestige of manufacturing. The rise of manufacturing affected farmers too, for as cities grew in size and number, the need to feed the populace caused commercial agriculture to flourish. Dairy farming, truck gardening, and fruit growing began to thrive around every manufacturing center.

Cotton Revolutionizes the South

By far the most important indirect effect of industrialization occurred in the South, which soon began to produce cotton to supply the new textile factories of Great Britain and New England. The possibility of growing large amounts of this crop in America had not been seriously considered in colonial times, but by the 1780s the demand for raw cotton to feed the voracious British mills was causing many

American farmers to experiment with the crop. Most of the world's cotton at this time came from Egypt, India, and the East Indies. The plant was considered tropical, most varieties being unable to survive the slightest frost. Alexander Hamilton, who missed nothing that related to the economic growth of the country, reported: "It has been observed . . . that the nearer the place of growth to the equator, the better the quality of the cotton."

Beginning in 1786, "sea-island" cotton was grown successfully in the mild, humid lowlands and offshore islands along the coasts of Georgia and South Carolina. This was a high-quality cotton, silky and long-fibered like the Egyptian. But its susceptibility to frost severely limited the area of its cultivation. Elsewhere in the South, "green-seed," or upland, cotton flourished, but this plant had little commercial value because the seeds could not be easily separated from the lint. When sea-island cotton was passed between two rollers, its shiny black seeds simply popped out; with upland cotton the seeds were pulled through with the lint and crushed, the oils and broken bits destroying the value of the fiber. To remove the seeds by hand was laborious; a slave working all day could clean scarcely a pound of the white fluff. This made it an uneconomical crop. In 1791 the usually optimistic Hamilton admitted in his *Report on Manufactures* that "the extensive cultivation of cotton can, perhaps, hardly be expected."

This was the situation in the spring of 1793, when Eli Whitney was a guest at Mulberry Grove, the plantation of Catherine Greene, widow of General Nathanael Greene, some dozen miles from Savannah.[2] Whitney had accepted a position as private tutor at 100 guineas a year with a nearby family and had stopped to visit a friend, Phineas Miller, who was overseer of the Greene plantation. While at Mulberry Grove, Whitney, who had never seen a cotton plant before, met a number of the local landowners.

> I heard [he wrote his father] much of the extreme difficulty of ginning Cotton, that is, separating it from its seed. There were a number of very respectable Gentlemen at Mrs. Greene's who all agreed that if a machine could be invented that would clean the Cotton with expedition, it would be a great thing both to the Country and to the inventor.

Whitney thought about the problem for a few days and then "struck out a plan of a machine." He described it to Miller, who enthusiastically offered to finance the invention. Since Whitney had just learned that his job as tutor would pay only 50 guineas, he accepted Miller's proposal.

Within ten days he had solved the problem that had baffled the planters. His gin (engine) consisted of a cylinder covered with rows of wire teeth rotating in a box filled with cotton. As the cylinder turned, the teeth passed through narrow slits in a metal grating. Cotton fibers were caught by the teeth and pulled through the

---

[2]The property, formerly owned by a prominent Georgia Tory, had been given to Greene by the state in gratitude for his having driven out the British during the Revolution.

Eli Whitney's cotton gin made it easier to process cotton; this stimulated cotton production and greatly increased the demand for slaves to farm and collect it, as the picture suggests.

slits. The seeds, too thick to pass through the openings, were left behind. A second cylinder, with brushes rotating in the opposite direction to sweep the cotton from the wires, prevented matting and clogging.

This "absurdly simple contrivance" almost instantly transformed southern agriculture. With a gin a slave could clean fifty times as much cotton as by hand; soon larger models driven by mules and horses were available. The machines were so easy to construct (once the basic idea was understood) that Whitney and Miller were never able to enforce their patent rights effectively. Rival manufacturers shamelessly pirated their work, and countless farmers built gins of their own. Cotton production increased from 3,000 bales in 1790 to well over 400,000 bales a year in the early 1820s. The South boomed.

Upland cotton would grow wherever there were 200 consecutive days without frost and 24 inches of rain. The crop engulfed Georgia and South Carolina and spread north into parts of Virginia. After Andrew Jackson smashed the southwestern Indians during the War of 1812, the rich "Black Belt" area of central Alabama and northern Mississippi and the delta region along the lower Mississippi River were rapidly taken over by the fluffy white staple. In 1821 Alabama alone raised 40,000 bales. Central Tennessee also became important cotton country.

Cotton stimulated the economy of the rest of the nation as well. Most of it was exported, the sale paying for much-needed European products. The transportation, insurance, and final disposition of the crop fell largely into the hands of northern merchants, who profited accordingly. And the surplus corn and hogs of western farmers helped feed the slaves of the new cotton plantations. Cotton was the major force in the economy for a generation, beginning about 1815.

Revival of Slavery

Amid the national rejoicing over this prosperity, one aspect both sad and ominous was easily overlooked. Slavery, a declining or at worst stagnant institution in the decade of the Revolution, was revitalized in the following years.

Libertarian beliefs inspired by the Revolution ran into the roadblock of race prejudice as soon as some of the practical aspects of freedom for blacks became apparent. As disciples of John Locke, the Revolutionary generation had a deep respect for property rights; in the last analysis most white Americans placed these rights ahead of the personal liberty of black Americans. Forced abolition of slavery therefore attracted few recruits. Moreover, the rhetoric of the Revolution had raised the aspirations of blacks. Increasing signs of rebelliousness appeared among them, especially after the slave uprising in Saint Domingue, which culminated, after a great bloodbath, in the establishment of the black Republic of Haiti in 1804. This example of a successful slave revolt filled white Americans with apprehension. Their fears were irrational (Haitian blacks outnumbered whites and mulattos combined by seven to one) but nonetheless real. And fear led to repression; the exposure in 1801 of a plot to revolt in Virginia, led by the slave Gabriel, resulted in some three dozen executions even though no actual uprising had occurred.

The mood of the Revolutionary decade had led a substantial number of masters to free their slaves. Unfortunately this led many other whites to have second thoughts about ending slavery. "If the blacks see all of their color slaves, it will seem to them a disposition of Providence, and they will be content," a Virginia legislator, apparently something of an amateur psychologist, claimed. "But if they see others like themselves free . . . they will repine." As the number of free blacks rose, restrictions on them were everywhere tightened.

In the 1780s many opponents of slavery began to think of solving the "Negro problem" by colonizing freed slaves in some distant region—in the western districts or perhaps in Africa. The colonization movement had two aspects. One, a manifestation of an embryonic black nationalism, reflected the disgust of black Americans with local racial attitudes and their interest in African civilization. Paul Cuffe, a Massachusetts Quaker, managed to finance the emigration of thirty-eight of his fellow blacks to British Sierra Leone in 1815, but few others followed. Most influential northern blacks, the most conspicuous among them the Reverend Richard Allen, bishop of the African Methodist Church, opposed the idea vigorously.

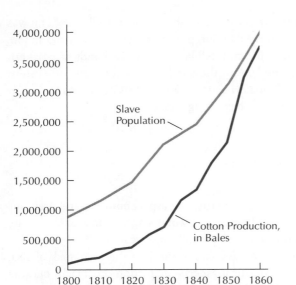

Cotton Production and Slave Population, 1800–1860

Slave Population

Cotton Production, in Bales

4,000,000
3,500,000
3,000,000
2,500,000
2,000,000
1,500,000
1,000,000
500,000
0

1800 1810 1820 1830 1840 1850 1860

The other colonization movement, led by whites, was paternalistic. Some white colonizationists genuinely abhorred slavery. Others could not stomach living with free blacks; to them colonization was merely a polite word for deportation. Most white colonizationists were conservatives who considered themselves realists.

The colonization idea became popular in Virginia in the 1790s, but nothing was achieved until after the founding of the American Colonization Society in 1817. The society purchased African land and established the Republic of Liberia. However, despite the cooperation of a handful of black nationalists and the patronage of many important white Southerners, including Presidents Madison and Monroe and Chief Justice Marshall, it accomplished little. Although some white colonizationists expected former slaves to go to Africa as Christian missionaries to convert and "civilize" the natives, few blacks wished to migrate to a land so alien to their own experience. Only about 12,000 went to Liberia, and the toll taken among them by tropical diseases was large. As late as 1850 the black American population of Liberia was only 6,000.

The cotton boom of the early nineteenth century acted as a brake on the colonization movement. As cotton production expanded, the need for labor in the South grew apace. The price of slaves doubled between 1795 and 1804. As it rose, the inclination of even the most kindhearted masters to free their slaves began to falter. Although the importation of slaves from abroad had been outlawed by all the states, perhaps 25,000 were smuggled into the country in the 1790s. In 1804 South Carolina reopened the trade, and between that date and 1808, when the constitutional prohibition of importation became effective, some 40,000 were brought in. Thereafter the miserable traffic in human beings continued clandestinely, though on a lesser scale.

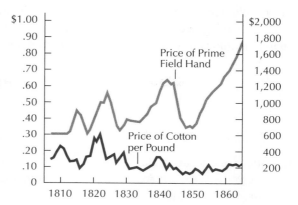

Prices for Cotton and for Slaves, 1802–1860
The vertical axis on the left shows cents, and the curve for the price of cotton should be read against it; the right vertical axis shows dollars, and the price of slaves should be read against it. These prices are from New Orleans records. The rising trend of slave prices (and a growing slave population) shows the continuing profitability and viability of slavery up to 1860.

The cotton boom triggered an internal trade in slaves that frequently ripped black families apart. While it had always been legal for owners to transport their own slaves to a new state if they were settling there, many states forbade, or at least severely restricted, interstate commercial transactions in human flesh. A Virginia law of 1778, for example, prohibited the importation of slaves for purposes of sale, and persons entering the state with slaves had to swear that they did not intend to sell them. Once cotton became important, these laws were either repealed or systematically evaded. There was a surplus of slaves in one part of the United States and an acute shortage in another. A migration from the upper South to the cotton lands quickly sprang up. Slaves from "free" New York and New Jersey and even from New England began to appear on the auction blocks of Savannah and Charleston. Early in the Era of Good Feelings, newspapers in New Orleans were carrying reports such as: "Jersey negroes appear to be particularly adapted to this market. . . . We have the right to calculate on large importations in the future, from the success which hitherto attended the sale."

By about 1820 the letter of the law began to be changed. Soon the slave trade became an organized business, cruel and shameful, frowned on by the "best" people of the South, managed by the depraved and the greedy, yet patronized by nearly anyone who needed labor. "The native land of Washington, Jefferson, and Madison," one disgusted Virginian told a French visitor, "[has] become the Guinea of the United States."

The lot of African Americans in the northern states was almost as bad as that of southern free blacks. Except in New England, where there were few blacks to begin with, most were denied the vote, either directly or by extralegal pressures. They could not testify in court, intermarry with whites, obtain decent jobs or housing, or get even a rudimentary education. Most states segregated blacks in theaters, hospitals, and churches and on public transportation facilities. They were barred from hotels and restaurants patronized by whites.

Northern blacks could at least protest and try to convince the white majority of the injustice of their treatment. These rights were denied their southern brethren.

They could and did publish newspapers and pamphlets, organize for political action, petition legislatures and the Congress for redress of grievance—in short, they applied methods of peaceful persuasion in an effort to improve their position in society.

Roads to Market

Inventions and technological improvements were extremely important in the settlement of the West. On superficial examination, this may not seem to have been the case, for the hordes of settlers who struggled across the mountains immediately after the War of 1812 were no better equipped than their ancestors who had pushed up the eastern slopes in previous generations. Many plodded on foot over hundreds of miles, dragging crude carts laden with their meager possessions. More fortunate pioneers traveled on horseback or in heavy, cumbersome wagons, the best known being the canvas-topped Conestoga "covered wagons," pulled by horses or oxen.

In many cases the pioneers followed trails and roads no better than those of colonial days—quagmires in wet weather, rutted and pitted with potholes a good part of the year. When they settled down, their way of life was no more advanced than that of the Pilgrims. At first they were creatures of the forest, feeding on its abundance, building their homes and simple furniture with its wood, clothing themselves in the furs of forest animals. They usually planted the first crop in a natural glade; thereafter, year by year, they pushed back the trees with ax and saw and fire until the land was cleared. Any source of power more complicated than an ox was beyond their ken. Until the population of the territory had grown large enough to support town life, settlers were as dependent on crude household manufacturers as any earlier pioneer.

The spread of settlement into the Mississippi Valley created challenges that required technological advances if they were to be met. In the social climate of that age in the United States, these advances were not slow in coming. Most were related to transportation, the major problem for Westerners. Without economical means of getting their produce to market, they were condemned to lives of crude self-sufficiency. Everyone recognized that an efficient transportation network would increase land values, stimulate domestic and foreign trade, and strengthen the entire economy.

The Mississippi River and its tributaries provided a natural highway for western commerce and communication, but it was one that had grave disadvantages. Farm products could be floated down to New Orleans on rafts and flatboats, but the descent along the Ohio River from Pittsburgh to the Mississippi took at least a month. Transportation upstream was out of the question for anything but the lightest and most valuable products, and even for them it was extremely expensive. In any case, the natural flow of trade was be-

This stagecoach, having just passed over a solid road of made of tree trunks, must now make its way across an all-dirt road. Already its wheels have sunk several inches into the mud.

tween East and West. That is why, from early in the westward movement, much attention was given to building roads linking the Mississippi Valley to the eastern seaboard.

Constructing decent roads over the rugged Appalachians was a formidable task. The steepest grades had to be reduced by cutting through hills and filling in low places, all without modern blasting and earth-moving equipment. Streams had to be bridged. Drainage ditches were essential if the roads were not to be washed out by the first rains, and a firm foundation of stones, topped with a well-crowned gravel dressing, had to be provided if they were to stand up under the pounding of heavy wagons. The skills required for building roads of this quality had been developed in Great Britain and France, and the earliest American examples, constructed in the 1790s, were similar to good European highways. The first such road, connecting Philadelphia and Lancaster, Pennsylvania, opened to traffic in 1794.

In heavily populated sections the volume of traffic made good roads worth their cost, which ran to as much as $13,000 a mile where the terrain was difficult, though the average was perhaps half that figure. In some cases good roads ran into fairly remote areas. In New York, always a leading state in the movement for improved transportation, an excellent road had been built all the way from Albany to Lake Erie by the time of the War of 1812, and by 1821 the state had some 4,000 miles of good roads.

Transportation and the Government

Most of the improved highways and many bridges were built as business ventures by private interests. Promoters charged tolls, the rates being set by the states. Tolls were collected at gates along the way; hinged poles suspended across the road were turned back by a guard after receipt of the toll. Hence these thoroughfares were known as turnpikes, or simply pikes.

The profits earned by a few early turnpikes, such as the one between Philadelphia and Lancaster, caused the boom in private road building, but even the most fortunate of the turnpike companies did not make much money. Maintenance was expensive, traffic spotty.

Despite much talk about individual self-reliance and free enterprise, local, state, and national governments contributed heavily to the development of what in the jargon of the day were called "internal improvements." They served as "primary entrepreneurs," supplying capital for risky but socially desirable enterprises, with the result that a fascinating mixture of private and public energy went into the building of these institutions. At the federal level even the parsimonious Jeffersonians became deeply involved.

Logically, the major highways, especially those over the mountains, should have been built by the national government. Strategic military requirements alone would have justified such a program. One major artery, the Old National Road, running from Cumberland, Maryland, to Wheeling, in western Virginia, was constructed by the United States between 1811 and 1818. In time it was extended as far west as Vandalia, Illinois. However, further federal road building was hampered by political squabbles in Congress, usually phrased in constitutional terms but in fact based on sectional rivalries and other economic conflicts. Thus no comprehensive highway program was undertaken in the nineteenth century.

While the National Road, the New York Pike, and other, rougher trails such as the Wilderness Road into the Kentucky country were adequate for the movement of settlers, they did not begin to answer the West's need for cheap and efficient transportation. Wagon freight rates averaged at least 30 cents a ton-mile around 1815. At such rates, to transport a ton of oats from Buffalo to New York would have cost twelve times the value of the oats! To put the problem another way, four horses could haul a ton and a half of oats about 18 or 20 miles a day over a good road. If they could obtain half their feed by grazing, the horses would still consume about 50 pounds of oats a day. It requires little mathematics to figure out how much oats would be left in the wagon when it reached New York City, almost 400 miles away.

Until the coming of the railroad, which was just being introduced in England in 1825, the cost of shipping bulky goods by land over the great distances common in America was prohibitive. Businessmen and inventors concentrated instead on improving water transport, first by designing better boats and then by developing artificial waterways.

Development of Steamboats

Rafts and flatboats were adequate for downstream travel, but the only practical so-lution to upstream travel was the steamboat. One early enthusiast was John Stevens, a wealthy New Jerseyite, who designed an improved steam boiler for which he received one of the first patents issued by the United States. Stevens got his brother-in-law, Robert R. Livingston, interested in the problem, and the latter used his political influence to obtain an exclusive charter to operate steamboats on New York waters. In 1802, while in France trying to buy New Orleans from Napoleon, Livingston got to know Robert Fulton, a young American artist and en-gineer who was experimenting with steam navigation, and agreed to finance his work. In 1807, after returning to New York, Fulton constructed the *North River Steam Boat*, famous to history as the *Clermont*.

The *Clermont* was 142 feet long, 18 feet abeam, and drew 7 feet of water. With its towering stack belching black smoke, its side wheels could push it along at a steady 5 miles an hour. Nothing about it was radically new, but Fulton brought the essentials—engine, boiler, paddle wheels, and hull—into proper balance and thereby produced an efficient vessel.

No one could patent a steamboat; soon the new vessels were plying the waters of every navigable river from the Mississippi east. After 1815 steamers were making the run from New Orleans as far as Ohio. By 1820 at least sixty vessels were operat-ing between New Orleans and Louisville, and by the end of the decade there were more than 200 steamers on the Mississippi.

The day of the steamboat had dawned, and although the following generation would experience its high noon, even in the 1820s its major effects were clear. The great Mississippi Valley, in the full tide of its development, was immensely en-riched. Produce poured down to New Orleans, which soon ranked with New York and Liverpool among the world's great ports. Only 80,000 tons of freight reached New Orleans from the interior in 1816 and 1817, more than 542,000 tons in 1840 and 1841. Upriver traffic was affected even more spectacularly. Freight charges plummeted, in some cases to a tenth of what they had been after the War of 1812. Around 1818 coffee cost 16 cents a pound more in Cincinnati than in New Orleans, a decade later less than 3 cents more. The Northwest emerged from self-suffi-ciency with a rush and became part of the national market.

The Canal Boom

While the steamboat was conquering western rivers, canals were being con-structed that further improved the transportation network. Since the midwestern rivers all emptied into the Gulf of Mexico, they did not provide a direct link with the eastern seaboard. If an artificial waterway could be cut between the great cen-tral valley and some navigable stream flowing into the Atlantic, all sections would profit immensely.

Canals were more expensive than roads, but so long as the motive power used in overland transportation was the humble horse, they offered enormous economic advantages to shippers. Because there is less friction to overcome, a team plodding along a towpath could pull a canal barge with a 100-ton load and make better time over long distances than it could pulling a single ton in a wagon on the finest road.

Although canals were as old as Egypt, only about 100 miles of them existed in the United States as late as 1816. Construction costs aside, in a rough and mountainous country canals presented formidable engineering problems. To link the Mississippi Valley and the Atlantic meant somehow circumventing the Appalachian Mountains. Most people thought this impossible.

Mayor DeWitt Clinton of New York believed that such a project was feasible in New York State. In 1810, while serving as state canal commissioner, he traveled across central New York and convinced himself that it would be practicable to dig a canal from Buffalo, on Lake Erie, to the Hudson River. The Mohawk Valley cuts through the Appalachian chain just north of Albany, and at no point along the route to Buffalo does the land rise more than 570 feet above the level of the Hudson. Marshaling a mass of technical, financial, and commercial information (and making effective use of his political influence), Clinton placed his proposal before the New York legislature.

In 1817 New York State began construction along a route 363 miles long, most of it across densely forested wilderness. At the time the longest canal in the United States ran less than 28 miles!

The Erie, completed in 1825, was an immediate financial success. Together with the companion Champlain Canal, which linked Lake Champlain and the Hudson, it brought in over half a million dollars in tolls in its first year. Soon its entire $7 million cost had been recovered, and it was earning profits of about $3 million a year. The effect of this prosperity on New York State was enormous. Buffalo, Rochester, Syracuse, and half a dozen lesser towns along the canal flourished.

New York City: Emporium of the Western World

The Erie Canal cemented New York's position as the national metropolis. Most European-manufactured goods destined for the Mississippi Valley entered the country at New York and passed on to the West over the canal. The success of the Erie also sparked a nationwide canal-building boom. Most canals were constructed either by the states, as in the case of the Erie, or as "mixed enterprises" that combined public and private energies.

No state profited as much from this construction as New York, for none possessed New York's geographic advantages. The rocky hills of New England discouraged all but fanatics. Canals were built connecting Worcester and Northampton, Massachusetts, with the coast, but they were financial failures. The Delaware and Hudson Canal, running from northeastern Pennsylvania across northern New Jersey and lower New York to the Hudson, was completed by private interests in

DID A "MARKET REVOLUTION" TRANSFORM EARLY NINETEENTH-CENTURY AMERICA?

In this 1847 painting by George Caleb Bingham, a steamboat in the distance has run aground. The men in the flatboat are considering, perhaps, whether to help lighten its load. Their faces brim with satisfaction. *They* are not soot-begrimed wage slaves who shovel coal into smoke-belching machines. *They* work when and where they wish, moved only by the pull of the current and the sweat of their muscles. And yet the viewer senses that their satisfaction will be fleeting. The steamboat will get going again. George Rogers Taylor (1951) proposed that the key factor in the transformation of the economy during the early nineteenth century was a "transportation revolution," the development of a system of canals, steamboats, and railroads. But in the 1990s other scholars suggested that the "transportation revolution" was merely a component of a larger and more powerful process: a "market revolution." The thesis was proposed by Charles Sellers (1991), Harry Watson (1990), and others. They argued that early in the nineteenth century some well-connected entrepreneurs used public funds to establish banks

and corporations and to construct the nation's transportation infrastructure. This transformed craftsmen into factory workers and subsistence farmers into petty capitalists. In the frenzy to make money, such people turned their backs on family and community. The "market revolution" thesis has provoked many debates, not the least of which is whether it was a good thing. Sellers was sure that its effects were harmful. "Capitalism commodifies and exploits all life," he declared. But the only judgment that matters was that of the people such as those depicted above. If the steamboat captain had offered them higher wages and steady work, would they have accepted?

George Rogers Taylor, *The Transportation Revolution* (1951), Charles Sellers, *The Market Revolution* (1991), Harry Watson, *Liberty and Power* (1990).

A view of New York's Broadway in 1835. The broad avenue was home to many of the large, modern stores that helped make New York City the commercial center of the nation.

1828. It managed to earn respectable dividends by barging coal to the eastern seaboard, but it made no attempt to compete with the Erie for the western trade. Pennsylvania, desperate to keep up with New York, engaged in an orgy of construction. In 1834 it completed a complicated system, part canal and part railroad, over the mountains to Pittsburgh. This Mainline Canal cost a staggering sum for that day. With its 177 locks and cumbersome "inclined-plane railroad" it was slow and expensive to operate and never competed effectively with the Erie. Efforts of Maryland to link Baltimore with the West by water failed utterly.

Beyond the mountains there was even greater zeal for canal construction in the 1820s and still more in the 1830s. Once the Erie opened the way across New York, farmers in the Ohio country demanded that links be built between the Ohio River and the Great Lakes so that they could ship their produce by water directly to the East. Local feeder canals seemed equally necessary; with corn worth 20 cents a bushel at Columbus selling for 50 cents at Marietta, on the Ohio, the value of cheap transportation became obvious to Ohio farmers.

Even before the completion of the Erie, Ohio had begun construction of the Ohio and Erie Canal running from the Ohio River to Cleveland. Another, from Toledo to Cincinnati, was begun in 1832. Meanwhile, Indiana had undertaken the 450-mile Wabash and Erie Canal. These canals were well conceived, but the western states overextended themselves building dozens of feeder lines, trying, it sometimes seemed, to supply all farmers west of the Appalachians with water connections from their barns to the New York docks. Politics made such programs almost inevitable, for in order to win support for their pet projects, legislators had to

Canals and Roads, 1820–1850

back the schemes of their fellows. The result was frequently financial disaster. There was not enough traffic to pay for all the waterways that were dug. By 1844, $60 million in state "improvement" bonds were in default. Nevertheless, the canals benefited both western farmers and the national economy.

The Marshall Court

The most important legal advantages bestowed on business in the period were the gift of Chief Justice John Marshall. Historians have tended to forget that Chief Justice John Marshall had six colleagues on the Supreme Court, and that is easy to understand. Marshall's particular combination of charm, logic, and forcefulness made the Court during his long reign, if not a rubber stamp, remarkably submissive to his view of the Constitution. Marshall's belief in a powerful central government explains his tendency to hand down decisions favorable to manufacturing and business interests. He also thought that "the business community was the agent of order and progress" and tended to interpret the Constitution in a way that would advance its interests.

Many important cases came before the Court between 1819 and 1824, and in each one Marshall's decision was applauded by most of the business community. The cases involved two major principles: the "sanctity" of contracts and the supremacy of federal legislation over the laws of the states. Marshall shared the conviction of the Revolutionary generation that property had to be protected against arbitrary seizure if liberty was to be preserved. Contracts between private individuals and between individuals and the government must be strictly enforced, he believed, or chaos would result. He therefore gave the widest possible application to the constitutional provision that no state could pass any law "impairing the Obligation of Contracts."

In *Dartmouth College* v. *Woodward* (1819), which involved an attempt by New Hampshire to alter the charter granted to Dartmouth by King George III in 1769, Marshall held that such a charter was a contract and might not be canceled or altered without the consent of both parties. The state had sought not to destroy the college but to change it from a private to a public institution, yet Marshall held that to do so would violate the contract clause.

Marshall's decisions concerning the division of power between the federal government and the states were even more important. The question of the constitutionality of a national bank, first debated by Hamilton and Jefferson, had not been submitted to the courts during the life of the first Bank of the United States. By the time of the second Bank there were many state banks, and some of them felt that their interests were threatened by the national institution. Responding to pressure from local banks, the Maryland legislature placed an annual tax of $15,000 on "foreign" banks, including the Bank of the United States! The Maryland branch of the Bank of the United States refused to pay, whereupon the state brought suit against its cashier, John W. McCulloch. *McCulloch* v. *Maryland* was crucial to the Bank, for five other states had levied taxes on its branches, and others would surely follow suit if the Maryland law were upheld.

Marshall extinguished the threat. The Bank of the United States was constitutional, he announced in phrases taken almost verbatim from Hamilton's 1791 memorandum to Washington on the subject; its legality was implied in many of the powers specifically granted to Congress. Full "discretion" must be allowed Congress in deciding exactly how its powers "are to be carried into execution." Since the Bank was legal, the Maryland tax was unconstitutional. Marshall found a "plain repugnance" in the thought of "conferring on one government a power to control the constitutional measures of another." He put this idea in the simplest possible language: "The power to tax involves the power to destroy . . . the power to destroy may defeat and render useless the power to create." The long-range significance of the decision lay in its strengthening of the implied powers of Congress and its con-

The artist Chester Harding painted John Marshall in 1828, during the Chief Justice's twenty-seventh year on the Supreme Court. "The unpretentious dignity [and] the sober factualism" of Harding's style (as art historian Oliver Larkin describes it) was well suited to Marshall's character.

firmation of the Hamiltonian or "loose" interpretation of the Constitution. By establishing the legality of the Bank, it also aided the growth of the economy.

In 1824 Marshall handed down an important decision involving the regulation of interstate commerce. This was the "steamboat case," *Gibbons* v. *Ogden*. In 1815 Aaron Ogden, former United States senator and governor of New Jersey, had purchased the right to operate a ferry between Elizabeth Point, New Jersey, and New York City from Robert Fulton's backer, Robert R. Livingston, who held a New York monopoly of steamboat navigation on the Hudson. When Thomas Gibbons, who held a federal coasting license, set up a competing line, Ogden sued him. Ogden argued in effect that Gibbons could operate his boat (whose captain was Cornelius Vanderbilt, later a famous railroad magnate) on the New Jersey side of the Hudson but had no right to cross into New York waters. After complicated litigation in the lower courts, the case reached the Supreme Court on appeal. Marshall decided in favor of Gibbons, effectively destroying the New York monopoly. A state can regulate commerce which begins and ends in its own territory but not when the transaction involves crossing a state line; then the national authority takes precedence. "The act of Congress," he said, "is supreme; and the law of the state . . . must yield to it."

This decision threw open the interstate steamboat business to all comers, and since an adequate 100-ton vessel could be built for as little as $7,000, dozens of small operators were soon engaged in it. Their competition tended to keep rates low and service efficient, to the great advantage of the country. More important in the long run was the fact that in order to include the ferry business within the federal government's power to regulate interstate commerce, Marshall had given the word the widest possible meaning. "Commerce, undoubtedly, is traffic, but it is something more,—it is intercourse." By construing the "commerce" clause so broadly, he made it easy for future generations of judges to extend its coverage to include the control of interstate electric power lines and even radio and television transmission.

Many of Marshall's decisions aided the economic development of the country in specific ways, but his chief contribution lay in his broadly national view of economic affairs. When he tried consciously to favor business by making contracts inviolable, his influence was important but limited—and, as it worked out, impermanent. In the steamboat case and in *McCulloch* v. *Maryland,* where he was really deciding between rival property interests, his work was more truly judicial in spirit and far more lasting. In such matters his nationalism enabled him to add form and substance to Hamilton's vision of the economic future of the United States.

Marshall and his colleagues firmly established the principle of judicial limitation on the power of legislatures and made the Supreme Court a vital part of the American system of government. In an age plagued by narrow sectional jealousies, Marshall's contribution was of immense influence and significance, and on it rests his claim to greatness.

John Marshall died in 1835. Two years later, in the *Charles River Bridge* case, the court handed down another decision that aided economic development. The state of Massachusetts had built a bridge across the Charles River between Boston and Cambridge that drew traffic from an older, privately owned toll bridge nearby. Since no tolls were collected from users of the state bridge after construction costs were recovered, owners of the older bridge sued for damages on the ground that the free bridge made the stock in their company worthless. They argued that in building the bridge, Massachusetts had violated the contract clause of the Constitution.

The Court, however, now speaking through the new Chief Justice, Roger B. Taney, decided otherwise. The state had a right to place "the comfort and convenience" of the whole community over that of a particular company, Taney declared. "Improvements" that add to public "wealth and property" take precedence. How John Marshall would have voted in this case, in which he would have had to choose between his Dartmouth College and steamboat case arguments, will never be known. But like most of the decisions of the Court that were made while Marshall was Chief Justice, the Charles River Bridge case advanced the interests of those who favored economic development. Whether they were pursuing political advantage or economic, the Americans of the early nineteenth century seemed committed to a policy of compromise and accommodation.

1790	Samuel Slater sets up first American factory
1793	Eli Whitney invents cotton gin
1794	Philadelphia–Lancaster turnpike is built
1807	Robert Fulton constructs *North River Steam Boat (Clermont)*
1808	Constitutional prohibition of importation of slaves goes into effect
1813	Boston Manufacturing Company opens in Waltham, Massachusetts
1816	Second Bank of the United States is created
1817	American Colonization Society is founded in order to establish republic of Liberia for freed slaves
1819	Chief Justice John Marshall asserts "sanctity" of contracts in *Dartmouth College* v. *Woodward*
	Chief Justice Marshall strengthens implied powers of Congress in *McCulloch* v. *Maryland* (Bank of United States)
1824	Chief Justice Marshall defends supremacy of federal government over states in *Gibbons* v. *Ogden* (steamboat case)
1825	Erie Canal is completed
1837	Chief Justice Roger B. Taney rules in favor of the whole community over a particular company in *Charles River Bridge* v. *Warren Bridge*

9 CHAPTER

Jacksonian Democracy

PUNDITS COMPLAIN OF THE POLITICAL APATHY OF AMERICANS, AND of young people in particular. The critics point to the fact that even in the hotly contested 2004 presidential campaign, only 58 percent of the eligible voting-age population went to the polls.

Such criticisms assume that it was different in the days of the Founding Fathers. But this is not true. During the early 1800s, a much lower proportion of eligible voters went to the polls. In the 1824 presidential election, for example, only 27 percent of the eligible voters cast ballots, a total of 350,000; the vote was divided among four candidates.

But this apathy evaporated during the heated campaign leading to the 1828 presidential election. Andrew Jackson transformed his supporters—called Jacksonians— into the Democratic party, built a rudimentary bureaucracy to manage its affairs, and appealed directly—and effectively—to voters. That year, a total of 1.1 million votes were cast, 58 percent of the eligible voters.

Jackson won in a landslide. During the next few decades, his opponents had little choice but to emulate his strategy and build a rival party. The American political system emerged in consequence. Its central features included a consistent turnout of over half the electorate, at least during presidential elections, and a two-party culture that inhibited formation of additional parties.

Almost from the start, however, Jackson's more inclusive politics encountered new challenges and obstacles. Victorious campaign workers clamored for government jobs. Energized voters, seeking cheap land, ignored the plight of the Indians, not to mention legal rights secured by treaties. As more people voted, too, politicians were obliged to "represent" a vast electorate, which made it difficult to broker deals. Sectional tensions intensified; campaigns acquired a new stridency occasionally tinged with demagoguery. The new politics of democratic engagement were not without costs; within several decades, these would include civil war.

"Democratizing" Politics

At 11 A.M. on March 4, 1829, a bright sunny day, Andrew Jackson, hatless and dressed severely in black, left his quarters at Gadsby's Hotel. Accompanied by a few close associates, he walked up Pennsylvania Avenue to the Capitol. At a few minutes after noon he emerged on the East Portico with the justices of the Supreme Court and other dignitaries. Before a throng of more than 15,000 people he delivered an almost inaudible and thoroughly commonplace inaugural address and then took the presidential oath. The first man to congratulate him was Chief Justice Marshall, who had administered the oath. The second was "Honest George" Kremer, a Pennsylvania congressman best known for the leopardskin coat that he affected, who led the cheering crowd that brushed past the barricade and scrambled up the Capitol steps to wring the new president's hand.

Jackson shouldered his way through the crush, mounted a splendid white horse, and rode off to the White House. A reception had been announced, to which "the officially and socially eligible as defined by precedent" had been invited. The day was unseasonably warm after a hard winter, and the streets of Washington were muddy. As Jackson rode down Pennsylvania Avenue, the crowds that had turned out to see the Hero of New Orleans followed-on horseback, in rickety wagons, and on foot. Nothing could keep them out of the executive mansion, and the result was chaos. Long tables laden with cakes, ice cream, and orange punch had been set up in the East Room, but these scarcely deflected the well-wishers. Jackson was pressed back helplessly as men tracked mud across valuable rugs and clambered up on delicate chairs to catch a glimpse of him. The White House shook with their shouts. Glassware splintered, furniture was overturned, women fainted.

Jackson was a thin old man despite his toughness, and soon he was in danger. Fortunately, friends formed a cordon and managed to extricate him through a rear door. The new president spent his first night in office at Gadsby's hotel.

Only a generation earlier Jefferson had felt obliged to introduce pell-mell to encourage informality in the White House (see p. 199). Now a man whom John Quincy Adams called "a barbarian" held Jefferson's office, and, as one Supreme Court justice complained, "The reign of King 'Mob' seemed triumphant."

Jackson's inauguration, and especially this celebration in the White House, symbolized the triumph of "democracy," the achievement of place and station by "the common man." Having been taught by Jefferson that all men are created equal, the Americans of Jackson's day (conveniently ignoring males with black skins, to say nothing of women, regardless of color) found it easy to believe that every person was as competent and as politically important as his neighbor.

The difference between Jacksonian democracy and the Jefferson variety was more one of attitude than of practice. Jefferson had believed that ordinary citizens could be educated to determine what was right. Jackson insisted that they knew what was right by instinct. Jefferson's pell-mell encouraged the average citizen to hold up his head; by the time of Jackson, the "common man" gloried in ordinariness and made mediocrity a virtue. The slightest hint of distinctiveness or servility became suspect. That President Washington required his footmen to wear uniforms was taken as a matter of course in the 1790s, but the British minister in Jackson's day found it next to impossible to find Americans willing to don his splendid livery. While most middle-class families could still hire people to do their cooking and housework, the word *servant* itself fell out of fashion, replaced by the egalitarian *help*.

Even the presidency, designed to be removed from direct public control by the Electoral College, felt the impact of the new thinking. By Jackson's time only two states, Delaware and South Carolina, still provided for the choice of presidential electors by the legislature; in all others they were selected by popular vote. The system of permitting the congressional caucus to name the candidates for the presidency came to an end before 1828. Jackson and Adams were put forward by state legislatures, and soon thereafter the still more democratic system of nomination by national party conventions was adopted. Officeholders began to stress the fact that they were *representatives* as well as leaders and to appeal more openly and much more intensively for votes. The public responded. At each succeeding presidential election, more people went to the polls. Eight times as many people voted in 1840 as in 1824.

As voting became more important, so did competition among candidates, and this led to changes in the role and structure of political parties. Running campaigns and getting out the vote required money, people, and organized effort. Party managers, often holders of relatively minor offices, held rallies, staged parades, dreamed up catchy slogans, and printed broadsides, party newspapers, and ballots containing the names of the party's nominees for distribution to their supporters. Parties became powerful institutions that instilled loyalty among adherents.

1828: The New Party System in Embryo

The new system could scarcely have been imagined in 1825 while John Quincy Adams ruled over the White House; Adams was not well equipped either to lead King Mob or to hold it in check. Indeed, it was the battle to succeed Adams that caused the system to develop. The campaign began almost on the day of his selection by the House of Representatives. Jackson felt that he, the man who had received the largest number of votes, had been cheated of the presidency in 1824 by "the corrupt bargain" that he believed Adams had made with Henry Clay, and he sought vindication.

Relying heavily on his military reputation and on Adams's talent for making enemies, Jackson avoided taking a stand on issues and on questions where his

Rachel Jackson, wife of Andrew Jackson. At 17 she had married Lewis Robards, but theirs was a tempestuous marriage. After two years she returned to her family in Natchez, Mississippi. Robards sued for divorce in Virginia on grounds of desertion. Several months later she married Jackson in Mississippi. But, unbeknownst to Jackson, Robards would not finalize the divorce until a year after Rachel's marriage to Jackson. In defending Rachel's honor from a charge of bigamy, Jackson killed a man in a duel. During the 1824 and 1828 presidential campaigns, critics denounced their marriage as immoral. Rachel died in December 1828, weeks before her husband was inaugurated.

views might displease one or another faction. The political situation thus became chaotic, one side unable to marshal support for its policies, the other unwilling to adopt policies for fear of losing support.

The campaign was disgraced by character assassination and lies of the worst sort. Administration supporters denounced Jackson as a bloodthirsty military tyrant, a drunkard, and a gambler. His wife Rachel, ailing and shy, was dragged into the campaign by an Adams pamphleteer who branded her a "convicted adultress." (See picture above.)

Furious, the Jacksonians (now calling themselves Democrats) replied in kind. They charged that while serving as American minister to Russia, Adams had supplied a beautiful American virgin for the delectation of the czar. Discovering that Adams had purchased a chess set and a billiard table for the White House, they accused him of squandering public money on gambling devices. They translated his long and distinguished public service into the statistic that he had received over the years a sum equal to $16 for every day of his life in government pay. The great questions of the day were largely ignored.

All this was inexcusable, and both sides must share the blame. But as the politicians noticed when the votes were counted, their efforts had certainly brought out the electorate. *Each* candidate received far more votes than all four candidates had received in the preceding presidential election.

When inauguration day arrived, Adams refused to attend the ceremonies because Jackson had failed to pay the traditional pre-inaugural courtesy call on him at the White House, but the Old Puritan may have been equally, if unconsciously, motivated by shame at tactics he had countenanced during the campaign. Jackson felt vindication, not shame, but in any case, deep personal feelings were uppermost in everyone's mind at the formal changing of the guard. The real issues, however, remained. Andrew Jackson would now have to deal with them.

The Jacksonian Appeal

Although Jackson's supporters liked to cast him as the political heir of Jefferson, he was in many ways like the conservative Washington: a soldier first, an inveterate speculator in western lands, the owner of a fine plantation and of many slaves, a man with few intellectual interests and only sketchily educated.

Nor was Jackson quite the rough-hewn frontier character he sometimes seemed. True, he could not spell (again, like Washington), he possessed the unsavory habits of the tobacco chewer, and he had a violent temper. But his manners and lifestyle were those of a southern planter. Jackson's judgment was intuitive yet usually sound; his frequent rages were often feigned, designed to accomplish some carefully thought-out purpose.

Whatever his personal convictions, Jackson stood as the symbol for a new, democratically oriented generation. That he was both a great hero and in many ways a most extraordinary person helps explain his mass appeal. He had defeated a mighty British army and killed hosts of Indians, but he acted on hunches and not always consistently, shouted and pounded his fist when angry, put loyalty to old comrades above efficiency when making appointments, distrusted "aristocrats" and all special privilege. Perhaps he was rich, perhaps conservative, but he was a man of the people, born in a frontier cabin, familiar with the problems of the average citizen.

Jackson epitomized many American ideals. He was intensely patriotic, generous to a fault, natural and democratic in manner (at home alike in the forest and in the ballroom of a fine mansion). He admired good horseflesh and beautiful women, yet no sterner moralist ever lived; he was a fighter, a relentless foe, but a gentleman in the best American sense. That some special providence watched over him (as over the United States) appeared beyond argument to those who had followed his career. He seemed, in short, both an average and an ideal American, one the people could identify with and still revere.

For these reasons Jackson drew support from every section and every social class: western farmers and southern planters, urban workers and bankers and merchants. In this sense he was profoundly democratic—and in the sense, too, that whatever his position on public issues, he believed in equality of opportunity, distrusted entrenched status of every sort, and rejected no free American because of humble origins or inadequate education.

The Spoils System

Jackson took office with the firm intention of punishing the "vile wretches" who had attacked him so viciously during the campaign. (Rachel Jackson died shortly after the election, and her devoted husband was convinced that the indignities heaped on her by Adams partisans had hastened her decline.) The new concept of political office as a reward for victory seemed to justify a housecleaning in Washington.

Eager for the "spoils," an army of politicians invaded Washington. There was nothing especially innovative about this invasion, for the principle of filling offices with one's partisans was almost as old as the republic. However, the long lapse of time since the last real political shift, and the recent untypical example of John Quincy Adams, who rarely removed or appointed anyone for political reasons, made Jackson's policy appear revolutionary. His removals were not entirely unjustified, for many government workers had grown senile and others corrupt. A number of officials were found to be short in their accounts; a few were hopeless drunks. Jackson was determined to root out the thieves. Even Adams admitted that some of those Jackson dismissed deserved their fate.

Aside from going along with the spoils system and eliminating crooks and incompetents, Jackson advanced another reason for turning experienced government employees out of their jobs: the principle of rotation. "No man has any more intrinsic right to official station than another," he said. Those who hold government jobs for a long time "are apt to acquire a habit of looking with indifference upon the public interests and of tolerating conduct from which an unpracticed man would revolt." By "rotating" jobholders periodically, more citizens could participate in the tasks of government, and the danger of creating an entrenched bureaucracy would be eliminated. The problem was that the constant replacing of trained workers by novices was not likely to increase the efficiency of the government. Jackson's response to this argument was typical: "The duties of all public officers are . . . so plain and simple that men of intelligence may readily qualify themselves for their performance."

Contempt for expert knowledge and the belief that ordinary Americans can do anything they set their minds to became fundamental tenets of Jacksonian democracy. To apply them to present-day government would be to court disaster, but in the early nineteenth century it was not so preposterous, because the role that government played in American life was simple and nontechnical.

Spoilsmen roamed the capital in force during the spring of 1829, seeking, as the forthright Jackson said, "a tit to suck the treasury pap." Their philosophy was well summarized by a New Yorker: "No d——d rascal who made use of his office . . . for the purpose of keeping Mr. Adams in, and Genl. Jackson out of power is entitled to the least lenity or mercy. . . . Whether or not I shall get anything in the general scramble for plunder, remains to be proven, but I rather guess I shall."

President of All the People

More than any earlier president, Jackson conceived of himself as the direct representative of all the people and therefore the embodiment of national power. From Washington to John Quincy Adams, his predecessors together had vetoed only

This painting of Jackson is by Ralph E. W. Earl (1833), whose father, a soldier, had been assigned to do accurate paintings of the battles of Lexington and Concord. The son married a niece of Andrew Jackson and completed this imposing portrait.

nine bills, all on the ground that they believed the measures unconstitutional. Jackson vetoed a dozen, some simply because he thought the legislation inexpedient. Yet he had no ambition to expand the scope of federal authority at the expense of the states. Basically he was a Jeffersonian; he favored a "frugal," constitutionally limited national government. Furthermore, he was a poor administrator, given to penny-pinching and lacking in imagination. His strong prejudices and his contempt for expert advice, even in fields such as banking where his ignorance was almost total, did him no credit and the country considerable harm.

Jackson's great success (not merely his popularity) was primarily the result of his personality. A shrewd French observer, Michel Chevalier, after commenting on "his chivalric character, his lofty integrity, and his ardent patriotism," pointed out what was probably the central element in Jackson's appeal. "His tactic in politics, as well as in war," Chevalier wrote in 1824, "is to throw himself forward with the cry of *Comrades, follow me!*" Sometimes he might be wrong, but always he was a leader.

Jackson: "The Bank . . . I Will Kill It!"

In the fall of 1832 Jackson was reelected president, handily defeating Henry Clay. The main issue in this election, aside from Jackson's personal popularity, was the president's determination to destroy the second Bank of the United States. In this "Bank war," Jackson won a complete victory, yet the effects of his triumph were anything but beneficial to the country.

After *McCulloch* v. *Maryland* had presumably established its legality and the conservative Langdon Cheves had gotten it on a sound footing, the Bank of the

United States had flourished. In 1823 Cheves was replaced as president by Nicholas Biddle, who managed it brilliantly. A talented Philadelphian, only 37 when he took over the Bank, Biddle was experienced in literature, the law, and diplomacy as well as in finance. Almost alone in the United States, Biddle realized that his institution could act as a rudimentary central bank, regulating the availability of credit throughout the nation by controlling the lending policies of the state banks. Small banks, possessing limited amounts of gold and silver, sometimes overextended themselves in making large amounts of bank notes available to borrowers in order to earn interest. All this paper money was legally convertible into hard cash on demand, but in the ordinary run of business people seldom bothered to convert their notes so long as they thought the issuing bank was sound.

Bank notes passed freely from hand to hand and from bank to bank in every section of the country. Eventually much of the paper money of the local banks came across the counter of one or another of the twenty-two branches of the Bank of the United States. By collecting these notes and presenting them for conversion into coin, Biddle could compel the local banks to maintain adequate reserves of gold and silver—in other words, make them hold their lending policies within bounds. "The Bank of the United States," he explained, "has succeeded in keeping in check many institutions which might otherwise have been tempted into extravagant and ruinous excesses."

Biddle's policies in the 1820s were good for the Bank of the United States, which earned substantial profits, for the state banks, and probably for the country. Pressures on local bankers to make loans were enormous. The nation had an insatiable need for capital, and the general mood of the people was optimistic. Everyone wanted to borrow, and everyone expected values to rise, as in general they did. But by making liberal loans to produce merchants, for example, rural bankers indirectly stimulated farmers to expand their output beyond current demand, which eventually led to a decline in prices and an agricultural depression. In every field of economic activity, reckless lending caused inflation and greatly exaggerated the ups and downs of the business cycle. It can be argued, however, that by restricting the lending of state banks, Biddle was slowing the rate of economic growth and that in a predominantly agricultural society an occasional slump was not a large price to pay for rapid economic development.

Biddle's policies acted to stabilize the economy, and many interests, including a substantial percentage of state bankers, supported them. They also provoked a great deal of opposition. In part the opposition originated in pure ignorance: Distrust of paper money did not disappear, and people who disliked all paper saw the Bank as merely the largest (and thus the worst) of many bad institutions. At the other extreme, some bankers chafed under Biddle's restraints because by discouraging them from lending freely, he was limiting their profits. Few financiers realized what Biddle was trying to accomplish. What was "sound" banking practice? Honest people disagreed, and many turned against the ideas of Nicholas Biddle.

Jackson's Bank Veto

Opposition to the Bank was diffuse and unorganized until Andrew Jackson brought it together. When he did, the Bank was quickly destroyed. Jackson can be included among the ignorant enemies of the institution, a hard-money man suspicious of all commercial banking. "I think it right to be perfectly frank with you," he told Biddle in 1829. "I do not dislike your Bank any more than all banks. But ever since I read the history of the South Sea Bubble I have been afraid of banks."

Jackson's attitude dismayed Biddle. It also mystified him, since the Bank was the country's best defense against a speculative mania like the eighteenth-century South Sea Bubble, in which hundreds of naive British investors had been fleeced. Almost against his will, Biddle found himself gravitating toward Clay and the new National Republican party, offering advantageous loans and retainers to politicians and newspaper editors in order to build up a following. Thereafter, events moved inevitably toward a showdown, for the president's combative instincts were easily aroused. "The Bank," he told Van Buren, "is trying to kill me, *but I will kill it!*"

Henry Clay, Daniel Webster, and other prominent National Republicans hoped to use the Bank controversy against Jackson. They reasoned that the institution was so important to the country that Jackson's opposition to it would undermine his popularity. They therefore urged Biddle to ask Congress to renew the Bank's charter. The charter would not expire until 1836, but by pressing the issue before the 1832 presidential election, they could force Jackson either to approve the recharter bill or to veto it (which would give candidate Clay a lively issue in the campaign). The banker yielded to this strategy and a recharter bill passed Congress early in July 1832. Jackson promptly vetoed it.

Jackson's message explaining why he had rejected the bill was immensely popular, but it adds nothing to his reputation as a statesman. Being a good Jeffersonian—and no friend of John Marshall—he insisted that the Bank was unconstitutional. (*McCulloch* v. *Maryland* he brushed aside, saying that as president he had sworn to uphold the Constitution as *he* understood it.) The Bank was inexpedient, he argued. A dangerous private monopoly that allowed a handful of rich men to accumulate "many millions" of dollars, the Bank was making "the rich richer and the potent more powerful." Furthermore, many of its stockholders were foreigners: "If we must have a bank . . . it should be *purely American*.".[1]

Biddle considered Jackson's veto "a manifesto of anarchy," its tone like "the fury of a chained panther biting the bars of his cage." A large majority of the voters, however, approved of Jackson's hard-hitting attack.

Buttressed by his election triumph, Jackson acted swiftly. "Until I can strangle this hydra of corruption, the Bank, I will not shrink from my duty," he said. Shortly after the start of his second term, he decided to withdraw the government funds deposited in its vaults. Under the law only the secretary of the treasury could re-

---

[1] *The country needed all the foreign capital it could attract. Foreigners owned only $8 million of the $35 million stock, and in any case they could not vote their shares.*

move the deposits. When Secretary Louis McLane refused to do so, believing that the alternative depositories, the state banks, were less safe, Jackson promptly "promoted" him to secretary of state and appointed William J. Duane, a Pennsylvania lawyer, to the treasury post. Foolishly, he failed to ask Duane his views on the issue before appointing him. Too late he discovered that the new secretary agreed with McLane! It would not be "prudent" to entrust the government's money to "local and irresponsible" banks, Duane said.

Believing that Cabinet officers should obey the president as automatically as a colonel obeys a general, Jackson dismissed Duane, replacing him with Attorney General Roger B. Taney, who had been advising the president closely on Bank affairs. Taney carried out the order by depositing new federal receipts in seven state banks in eastern cities while continuing to meet government expenses with drafts on the Bank of the United States.

The situation was confused and slightly unethical. Set on winning the Bank war, Jackson lost sight of his fear of unsound paper money. Taney, however, knew exactly what he was doing. One of the state banks receiving federal funds was the Union Bank of Baltimore. Taney owned stock in this institution, and its president was his close friend. Little wonder that Jackson's enemies were soon calling the favored state banks "pet" banks. This charge was not entirely fair because Taney took pains to see that the deposits were placed in financially sound institutions.

"King Andrew the First," standing atop the U.S. Constitution—a scepter in one hand, and a veto in another. Compare this drawing to the one of Queen Elizabeth on page 30.

Furthermore, by 1836 the government's funds had been spread out reasonably equitably in about ninety banks. But neither was the charge entirely unfair; the administration certainly favored institutions whose directors were politically sympathetic to it.

When Taney began to remove the deposits, the government had $9,868,000 to its credit in the Bank of the United States; within three months the figure fell to about $4 million. Faced with the withdrawal of so much cash, Biddle had to contract his operations. He decided to exaggerate the contraction, pressing the state banks hard by presenting all their notes and checks that came across his counter for conversion into specie and drastically limiting his own bank's business loans. He hoped that the resulting shortage of credit would be blamed on Jackson and that it would force the president to return the deposits. "Nothing but the evidence of suffering . . . will produce any effect," he reasoned.

For a time the strategy appeared to be working. Paper money became scarce, specie almost unobtainable. A serious panic threatened. New York banks were soon refusing to make any loans at all. "Nobody buys; nobody can sell," a French visitor to the city observed. Memorials and petitions poured in on Congress. Worried and indignant delegations of businessmen began trooping to Washington seeking "relief." Clay, Webster, and John C. Calhoun thundered against Jackson in the Senate.

The president would not budge. "I am fixed in my course as firm as the Rockey Mountain," he wrote Vice President Van Buren. No "frail mortals" who worshiped "the golden calf" could change his mind. To others he swore he would sooner cut off his right arm and "undergo the torture of ten Spanish inquisitions" than restore the deposits. When delegations came to him, he roared: "Go to Nicholas Biddle. . . . Biddle has all the money!" And in the end—because he was right—business leaders began to take the old general's advice. Pressure on Biddle mounted swiftly, and in July 1834 he suddenly reversed his policy and began to lend money freely. The artificial crisis ended.

Jackson Versus Calhoun

Although southern-born, Jackson had devoted too much of his life to fighting for the entire United States to countenance disunion. Therefore, in April 1830, when the states' rights faction invited him to a dinner to celebrate the anniversary of Jefferson's birth, he came prepared. The evening reverberated with speeches and toasts of a states' rights tenor, but when the president was called on to volunteer a toast, he raised his glass, fixed his eyes on John C. Calhoun, and said: "Our *Federal Union: It must be preserved!*" Calhoun took up the challenge at once. "The Union," he retorted, "next to our liberty, most dear!"

It is difficult to measure the importance of the animosity between Jackson and Calhoun in the crisis to which this clash was a prelude. Calhoun wanted very much to be president. He had failed to inherit the office from John Quincy Adams and had accepted the vice presidency again under Jackson in the hope of succeeding him at the end of one term, if not sooner, for Jackson's health was known to be frail. Yet Old Hickory showed no sign of passing on or retiring. Jackson also seemed to place special confidence in the shrewd Van Buren, who, as secretary of state, also had claim to the succession.

A silly social fracas in which Calhoun's wife appeared to take the lead in the systematic snubbing of Peggy Eaton, wife of the secretary of war, had estranged Jackson and Calhoun. (Peggy was supposed to have had an affair with Eaton while she was still married to another man, and Jackson, undoubtedly sympathetic because of the attacks he and Rachel had endured, stoutly defended her good name.) Then, shortly after the Jefferson Day dinner, Jackson discovered that in 1818, when he had invaded Florida, Calhoun, then secretary of war, had recommended to President Monroe that Jackson be summoned before a court of inquiry and charged with disobeying orders. Since Calhoun had repeatedly led Jackson to believe that he had supported him at the time, the revelation convinced the president that Calhoun was not a man of honor.

The personal difficulties are worth stressing because Jackson and Calhoun were not far apart ideologically except on the ultimate issue of the right of a state to overrule federal authority. Jackson was a strong president, but he did not believe that the area of national power was large or that it should be expanded. His interests in government economy, in the distribution of federal surpluses to the states, and in interpreting the powers of Congress narrowly were all similar to Calhoun's. Like most Westerners, he favored internal improvements, but he preferred that local projects be left to the states. In 1830 he vetoed a bill providing aid for the construction of the Maysville Road because the route was wholly within Kentucky. There were political reasons for this veto, which was a slap at Kentucky's hero, Henry Clay, but it could not fail to please Calhoun.

Indian Removals

The president also took a states' rights position in the controversy that arose between the Cherokee Indians and Georgia. Jackson subscribed to the theory, advanced by Jefferson, that Indians were "savage" because they roamed wild in a trackless wilderness. The "original inhabitants of our forests" were "incapable of self-government," Jackson claimed, ignoring the fact that the Cherokee lived settled lives and had governed themselves without trouble before the whites arrived.

The Cherokee inhabited a region coveted by whites because it was suitable for growing cotton. Since most Indians preferred to maintain their tribal ways, Jackson pursued a policy of removing them from the path of white settlement. This policy seems heartless to modern critics, but since few Indians were willing to adopt the white way of life, most contemporary whites considered removal the only humane solution if the nation was to continue to expand. Jackson insisted that the Indians receive fair prices for their lands and that the government bear the expense of resettling them. He believed that moving them beyond the Mississippi River would

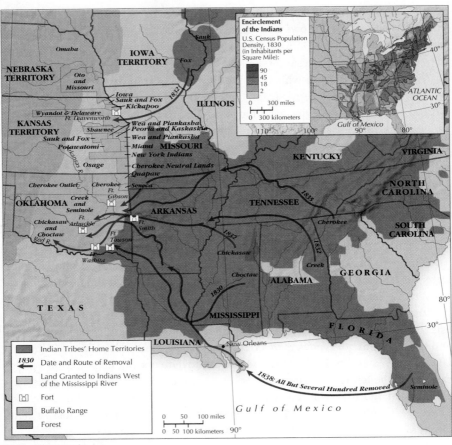

Indian Removals

protect them from the "degradation and destruction to which they were rapidly hastening . . . in the States."

Many tribes resigned themselves to removal without argument. Between 1831 and 1833, some 15,000 Choctaw migrated from their lands in Mississippi to the region west of the Arkansas Territory.

In *Democracy in America*, the Frenchman Alexis de Tocqueville described "the frightful sufferings that attend these forced migrations," and he added sadly that the migrants "have no longer a country, and soon will not be a people." He vividly described a group of Choctaw crossing the Mississippi River at Memphis in the dead of winter:

> *The cold was unusually severe; the snow had frozen hard upon the ground, and the river was drifting huge masses of ice. The Indians had their families with them, and they brought in their train the wounded and the sick, with children newly born and old men upon the verge of death. They possessed neither tents nor wagons, but only*

their arms and some provisions. I saw them embark to pass the mighty river, and never will that solemn spectacle fade from my remembrance. No cry, no sob, was heard among the assembled crowd; all were silent.

Tocqueville was particularly moved by the sight of an old woman whom he described in a letter to his mother. She was "naked save for a covering which left visible, at a thousand places, the most emaciated figure imaginable. . . . To leave one's country at that age to seek one's fortune in a foreign land, what misery!"

A few tribes, such as Black Hawk's Sauk and Fox in Illinois and Osceola's Seminole in Florida, resisted removal and were subdued by troops. One Indian nation, the Cherokee, sought to hold on to their lands by adjusting to white ways. They took up farming and cattle raising, developed a written language, drafted a constitution, and tried to establish a state within a state in northwestern Georgia. Several treaties with the United States seemed to establish the legality of their government. But Georgia would not recognize the Cherokee Nation. It passed a law in 1828 declaring all Cherokee laws void and the region part of Georgia.

The Indians challenged this law in the Supreme Court. When a Cherokee named Corn Tassel, convicted in a Georgia court of the murder of another Indian, appealed on the ground that the crime had taken place in Cherokee territory, Chief Justice John Marshall agreed and declared the Georgia action unconstitutional.

Jackson backed Georgia's position. No independent nation could exist within the United States, he insisted. Georgia thereupon hanged Corn Tassel. In 1838, after Jackson had left the White House, the United States forced 15,000 Cherokee to leave Georgia for Oklahoma. At least 4,000 of them died on the way; the route has been aptly named the Trail of Tears.

Jackson's willingness to allow Georgia to ignore decisions of the U.S. Supreme Court persuaded extreme southern states' righters that he would not oppose the doctrine of nullification should it be formally applied to a law of Congress. They deceived themselves egregiously. Jackson did not challenge Georgia because he approved of the state's position. He spoke of "the poor deluded . . . Cherokees" and called William Wirt, the distinguished lawyer who defended their cause, a "truly wicked" man. Jackson was not one to worry about being inconsistent. When South Carolina revived the talk of nullification in 1832, he acted in quite a different manner.

The Nullification Crisis

The proposed alliance of South and West to reduce the tariff and the price of land had not materialized, partly because Webster had discredited the South in the eyes of western patriots and partly because the planters of South Carolina and Georgia, fearing the competition of fertile new cotton lands in Alabama and Mississippi, opposed the rapid exploitation of the West almost as vociferously as northern manufacturers did. When a new tariff law was passed in 1832, it lowered duties much less than the Southerners desired. At once talk of nullifying it began to be heard in South Carolina.

In addition to the economic woes of the up-country cotton planters, the great planter-aristocrats of the rice-growing Tidewater, though relatively prosperous, were troubled by northern criticisms of slavery. In the rice region, blacks outnumbered whites two to one; it was the densest concentration of blacks in the United States. Thousands of these slaves were African-born, brought in during the burst of importations before Congress outlawed the trade in 1808. Controlled usually by overseers of the worst sort, the slaves seemed to their masters like savage beasts straining to rise up against their oppressors. In 1822 the exposure in Charleston of a planned revolt organized by Denmark Vesey, who had bought his freedom with money won in a lottery, had alarmed many whites. News of a far more serious uprising in Virginia led by the slave Nat Turner in 1831, just as the tariff controversy was coming to a head, added to popular concern. Radical South Carolinians saw protective tariffs and agitation against slavery as the two sides of one coin; against both aspects of what appeared to them the tyranny of the majority, nullification seemed the logical defense. Yield on the tariff, editor Henry L. Pinckney of the influential *Charleston Mercury* warned, and "abolition will become the order of the day."

President Jackson brushed aside Calhoun's mental gymnastics; intuitively he realized the central reality: If a state could nullify a law of Congress, the Union could not exist. "Tell . . . the Nullifiers from me that they can talk and write resolutions and print threats to their hearts' content," he warned a South Carolina representative when Congress adjourned in July 1832. "But if one drop of blood be shed there in defiance of the laws of the United States, I will hang the first man of them I can get my hands on to the first tree I can find."

The warning was not taken seriously in South Carolina. In October the state legislature provided for the election of a special convention, which, when it met, contained a solid majority of nullifiers. On November 24, 1832, the convention passed an ordinance of nullification prohibiting the collection of tariff duties in the state after February 1, 1833. The legislature then authorized the raising of an army and appropriated money to supply it with weapons.

Jackson quickly began military preparations of his own, telling friends that he would have 50,000 men ready to move in a little over a month. He also made a statesmanlike effort to end the crisis peaceably. First he suggested to Congress that it lower the tariff further. On December 10 he delivered a "Proclamation to the People of South Carolina." Nullification could only lead to the destruction of the Union, he said. "The laws of the United States must be executed. I have no discretionary power on the subject. . . . Those who told you that you might peaceably prevent their execution deceived you." Old Hickory added sternly: "Disunion by armed force is *treason*. Are you really ready to incur its guilt?" Jackson's reasoning profoundly shocked even opponents of nullification. If South Carolina did not back down, the president's threat to use force would mean civil war and possibly the destruction of the Union he claimed to be defending.

Calhoun sought desperately to control the crisis. By prearrangement with Senator Hayne, he resigned as vice president and was appointed to replace Hayne in the Senate, where he led the search for a peaceful solution. Having been de-

A South Carolina belle sewing—albeit languorously—a palmetto (a stylized palm leaf) onto a "nullification hat."

feated in his campaign for the presidency, Clay was a willing ally. In addition, many who admired Jackson nonetheless, as Van Buren later wrote, "distrusted his prudence," fearing that he would "commit some rash act." They believed in dealing with the controversy by discussion and compromise.

As a result, administration leaders introduced both a new tariff bill and a Force Bill granting the president additional authority to execute the revenue laws. Jackson was perfectly willing to see the tariff reduced but insisted that he was determined to enforce the law. As the February 1 deadline approached, he claimed that he could raise 200,000 men if needed to suppress resistance. "Union men, fear not," he said. "*The Union will be preserved.*"

Jackson's determination sobered the South Carolina radicals. Their appeal for the support of other southern states fell on deaf ears: All rejected the idea of nullification. The unionist minority in South Carolina added to the radicals' difficulties by threatening civil war if federal authority were defied. Calhoun, though a brave man, was alarmed for his own safety, for Jackson had threatened to "hang him as high as Haman" if nullification were attempted. Observers described him as "excessively uneasy." He was suddenly eager to avoid a showdown.

Ten days before the deadline, South Carolina postponed nullification pending the outcome of the tariff debate. Then, in March 1833, Calhoun and Clay pushed a compromise tariff through Congress. As part of the agreement Congress also passed the Force Bill, mostly as a face-saving device for the president.

And so the Union weathered the storm. Having stepped to the brink of civil war, the nation had drawn hastily back. The South Carolina legislature professed to be satisfied with the new tariff (in fact it made few immediate reductions, providing for a gradual lowering of rates over a ten-year period) and repealed the Nullification Ordinance, saving face by nullifying the Force Act, which was now a dead letter. But the radical South Carolina planters were becoming convinced that only secession would protect slavery. The nullification fiasco had proved that they could not succeed without the support of other slave states. Thereafter they devoted themselves ceaselessly to obtaining it.

Boom and Bust

During 1833 and 1834 Secretary of the Treasury Taney insisted that the pet banks maintain large reserves. But other state banks began to offer credit on easy terms, aided by a large increase in their reserves of gold and silver resulting from causes unconnected with the policies of either the government or Biddle's Bank. A decline in the Chinese demand for Mexican silver led to increased exports of the metal to the United States, and the rise of American interest rates attracted English capital into the country. Heavy English purchases of American cotton at high prices also increased the flow of specie into American banks. These developments caused bank notes in circulation to jump from $82 million in January 1835 to $120 million in December 1836. Bank deposits rose even more rapidly.

Much of the new money flowed into speculation in land; a mania to invest in property swept the country. The increased volume of currency caused prices to soar 15 percent in six months, buoying investors' spirits and making them ever more optimistic about the future. By the summer of 1835 one observer estimated that in New York City, which had about 250,000 residents, enough house lots had been laid out and sold to support a population of 2 million. Chicago at this time had only 2,000 to 3,000 inhabitants, yet most of the land for 25 miles around had been sold and resold in small lots by speculators anticipating the growth of the area. Throughout the West farmers borrowed money from local banks by mortgaging their land, used the money to buy more land from the government, and then borrowed still more money from the banks on the strength of their new deeds.

So long as prices rose, the process could be repeated endlessly. In 1832, while the Bank of the United States still regulated the money supply, federal income from the sale of land was $2.6 million. In 1834 it was $4.9 million; in 1835, $14.8 million. In 1836 it rose to $24.9 million, and the government found itself totally free of debt and with a surplus of $20 million!

Finally Jackson became alarmed by the speculative mania. In the summer of 1836 he issued the Specie Circular, which provided that purchasers must henceforth pay for public land in gold or silver. At once the rush to buy land came to a halt. As demand slackened, prices sagged. Speculators, unable to dispose of lands mortgaged to the banks, had to abandon them to the banks, but the banks could not realize enough on the foreclosed property to recover their loans. Suddenly the public mood changed. Commodity prices tumbled 30 percent between February and May.

Hordes of depositors sought to withdraw their money in the form of specie, and soon the banks exhausted their supplies. Panic swept the country in the spring of 1837 as every bank in the nation was forced to suspend specie payments. The boom was over.

Major swings in the business cycle can never be attributed to the actions of a single person, however powerful, but there is no doubt that Jackson's war against the Bank exaggerated the swings of the economic pendulum, not so much by its direct effects as by the impact of the president's ill-considered policies on popular thinking. His Specie Circular did not prevent speculators from buying land—at most it caused purchasers to pay a premium for gold or silver. But it convinced potential buyers that the boom was going to end and led them to make decisions that in fact ended it. Old Hickory's combination of impetuousness, combativeness, arrogance, and ignorance rendered the nation he loved so dearly a serious disservice.

The Jacksonians

Jackson's personality had a large impact on the shape and tone of American politics and thus with the development of the second party system. When he came to office, nearly everyone professed to be a follower of Jefferson. By 1836 being a Jeffersonian no longer meant much; what mattered was how one felt about Andrew Jackson. He had ridden to power at the head of a diverse political army, but he left behind him an organization with a fairly cohesive, if not necessarily consistent, body of ideas. This Democratic party contained rich citizens and poor, Easterners and Westerners, abolitionists as well as slaveholders. It was not yet a close-knit national organization, but—always allowing for individual exceptions— the Jacksonians agreed on certain underlying principles. These included suspicion of special privilege and large business corporations, both typified by the Bank of the United States; freedom of economic opportunity, unfettered by private or governmental restrictions; absolute political freedom, at least for white males; and the conviction that any ordinary man is capable of performing the duties of most public offices.

Jackson's ability to reconcile his belief in the supremacy of the Union with his conviction that national authority should be held within narrow limits tended to make the Democrats the party of those who believed that the powers of the states should not be diminished. Tocqueville caught this aspect of Jackson's philosophy perfectly: "Far from wishing to extend Federal power," he wrote, "the president belongs to the party that wishes to limit that power."

Although the radical Locofoco[2] wing of the party championed the idea, nearly all Jacksonians, like their leader, favored giving the small man his chance—by supporting public education, for example, and by refusing to place much weight on a

---

[2]A locofoco was a type of friction match. The name was first applied in politics when a group of New York Jacksonians used these matches to light candles when a conservative faction tried to break up their meeting by turning off the gaslights.

person's origin, dress, or manners. "One individual is as good as another" (for accuracy we must insert the adjective *white*) was their axiom. This attitude helps explain why immigrants, Catholics, and other minority groups usually voted Democratic. However, the Jacksonians showed no tendency either to penalize the wealthy or to intervene in economic affairs to aid the underprivileged. The motto "That government is best which governs least" graced the masthead of the chief Jacksonian newspaper, the *Washington Globe*, throughout the era.

Rise of the Whigs

The opposition to Jackson was far less cohesive. Henry Clay's National Republican party provided a nucleus, but Clay never dominated that party as Jackson dominated the Democrats. Its orientation was basically anti-Jackson. It was as though the American people were a great block of granite from which some sculptor had just fashioned a statue of Jackson, the chips scattered about the floor of the studio representing the opposition.

While Jackson was president, the impact of his personality delayed the formation of a true two-party system, but as soon as he surrendered power, the opposition, taking heart, began to coalesce. Many Democrats could not accept the odd logic of Jacksonian finance. As early as 1834 they, together with the Clay element, the extreme states' righters who followed Calhoun, and other dissident groups, were calling themselves Whigs. The name harkened back to the Revolution. It implied patriotic distaste for too-powerful executives, expressed specifically as resistance to the tyranny of "King Andrew."

This coalition possessed great resources of wealth and talent. Anyone who understood banking was almost obliged to become a Whig unless he was connected with one of Jackson's "pets." Those spiritual descendants of Hamilton who rejected the administration's refusal to approach economic problems from a broadly national perspective also joined in large numbers. Those who found the coarseness and "pushiness" of the Jacksonians offensive were another element in the new party. The anti-intellectual and antiscientific bias of the administration (Jackson rejected proposals for a national university, an observatory, and a scientific and literary institute) drove many ministers, lawyers, doctors, and other well-educated people into the Whig fold.

The philosopher Ralph Waldo Emerson was no doubt thinking of these types when he described the Whigs as "the enterprizing, intelligent, well-meaning and wealthy part of the people," but Whig arguments also appealed to ordinary voters who were predisposed to favor strong governments that would check the "excesses" of unrestricted individualism.

The Whigs were slow to develop effective party organization. They had too many generals and not enough troops. The issues that defined the Whigs varied from one state to another. For the most part, the sole unifying principle was oppo-

Debating the Past

FOR WHOM DID JACKSON FIGHT?

In 1837, his last year as president, Jackson here distributes hunks of a 1,400-pound cheese, a gift from New York farmers. They thought it the best present the "farming class" could give to someone who so forcefully had represented "their interest." In 1855 historian George Bancroft maintained that Jackson himself embodied America, for he "shared and possessed all the creative ideas of his country and his time." (This is the sort of twaddle that gives nineteenth-century historians a bad name.) In 1945 Arthur M. Schlesinger Jr.—son of the progressive historian—praised Jackson for battling on behalf of farmers and workers against big business. Jackson approached politics in terms of class rather than geography, and in that sense anticipated Franklin Delano Roosevelt. In both eras, Schlesinger observed, "the business community" had brought "national affairs to a state of crisis." Richard Hofstadter (1948) conceded that Jackson's fight against business had "many superficial points in common" with Roosevelt's. But Jackson had been no friend of the "common man," for he had consistently promoted the interests of well-to-do farmers and local entrepreneurs. This point received some confirmation from Edward Pessen's (1969) study

of wealth accumulation during the Jacksonian era, which showed that the rich grew richer and the poor, poorer. Robert Remini (1984), on the other hand, argued that Jackson adhered to republican ideals: he did what was good for the nation as a whole. Whatever the reality, many different people *believed* that Jackson represented them. Note that at the public reception shown above, some wore formal attire and others, work clothes. But all got cheese.

George Bancroft, *Literary and Historical Miscellanies* (1855), Arthur M. Schlesinger Jr., *Age of Jackson* (1945), Richard Hofstadter, *The American Political Tradition* (1948), Edward Pessen, *Jacksonian America* (1969), Lee Benson, *The Concept of Jacksonian Democracy* (1961), Robert Remini, *Andrew Jackson and the Course of American Democracy* (1984).

sition to Jackson. Furthermore, they stood in conflict with the major trend of the age: the glorification of the common man.

Lacking a dominant leader in 1836, the Whigs relied on "favorite sons," hoping to throw the presidential election into the House of Representatives. Daniel Webster ran in New England. For the West and South, Hugh Lawson White of Tennessee, a former friend who had broken with Jackson, was counted on to carry the fight. General William Henry Harrison was supposed to win in the Northwest and to draw support everywhere from those who liked to vote for military heroes. This sorry strategy failed; Jackson's handpicked candidate, Martin Van Buren, won a majority of both the popular and the electoral votes.

Martin Van Buren: Jacksonianism Without Jackson

Van Buren's brilliance as a political manipulator—the Red Fox, the Little Magician—has tended to obscure his statesmanlike qualities and his engaging personality. He made a powerful argument, for example, that political parties were a force for unity, not for partisan bickering. In addition, high office sobered him, and improved his judgment. He fought the Bank of the United States as a monopoly, but he also opposed irresponsible state banks. Van Buren believed in public construction of internal improvements, but he favored state rather than national programs, and he urged a rational approach: Each project must stand on its own as a useful and profitable public utility.

He continued to equivocate spectacularly on the tariff—in his *Autobiography* he described two of his supporters walking home after listening to him talk on the tariff, each convinced that it had been a brilliant speech, but neither having obtained the slightest idea as to where Van Buren stood on the subject—but he was never in the pocket of any special interest group or tariff lobbyist. He accounted himself a good Jeffersonian, tending to prefer state action to federal, but he was by no means doctrinaire. Basically he approached most questions rationally and pragmatically.

Van Buren had outmaneuvered Calhoun easily in the struggle to succeed Jackson, winning the old hero's confidence and serving him well. In 1832 he was elected vice president and thereafter was conceded to be the "heir apparent." In 1835 the Democratic National Convention unanimously nominated him for president.

Van Buren took office just as the Panic of 1837 struck the country. Its effects were frightening but short-lived. When the banks stopped converting paper money into gold and silver, they outraged conservatives but in effect eased the pressure on the money market: Interest rates declined and business loans again became relatively easy to obtain. In 1836, at the height of the boom in land sales, Congress had voted to "distribute" the new treasury surplus to the states, and this flow of money, which the states promptly spent, also stimulated the revival. Late in 1838 the banks resumed specie payments.

But in 1839 a bumper crop caused a sharp decline in the price of cotton. Then a number of state governments that had overextended themselves in road- and canal-building projects were forced to default on their debts. This discouraged investors, particularly foreigners. A general economic depression ensued that lasted until 1843.

Van Buren was not responsible for the panic or the depression, but his manner of dealing with economic issues was scarcely helpful. He saw his role as being concerned only with problems plaguing the government, ignoring the economy as a whole. "The less government interferes with private pursuits the better for the general prosperity," he pontificated. As Daniel Webster scornfully pointed out, Van Buren was following a policy of "leaving the people to shift for themselves," one that many Whigs rejected.

Van Buren's chief goal was finding a substitute for the state banks as a place to keep federal funds. The depression and the suspension of specie payments embarrassed the government along with private depositors. He soon settled on the idea of "divorcing" the government from all banking activities. His independent treasury bill called for the construction of government-owned vaults where federal revenues could be stored until needed. To ensure absolute safety, all payments to the government were to be made in hard cash. After a battle that lasted until the summer of 1840, the Independent Treasury Act passed both the House and the Senate.

Opposition to the Independent Treasury Act had been bitter, and not all of it was partisan. Bankers and businessmen objected to the government's withholding so much specie from the banks, which needed all the hard money they could get to support loans that were the lifeblood of economic growth. It seemed irresponsible for the federal government to turn its back on the banks, which so obviously performed a semipublic function. These criticisms made good sense, but through a lucky combination of circumstances, the system worked reasonably well for many years.

By creating suspicion in the public mind, officially stated distrust of banks acted as a damper on their tendency to overexpand. No acute shortage of specie developed because heavy agricultural exports and the investment of much European capital in American railroads beginning in the mid-1840s brought in large amounts of new gold and silver. After 1849 the discovery of gold in California added another important source of specie. The supply of money and bank credit kept pace roughly with the growth of the economy, but through no fault of the government. "Wildcat" banks proliferated. Fraud and counterfeiting were common, and the operation of everyday business affairs was inconvenienced in countless ways. The disordered state of the currency remained a grave problem until corrected by Civil War banking legislation.

The Log Cabin Campaign

It was not his financial policy that led to Van Buren's defeat in 1840. The depression naturally hurt the Democrats, and the Whigs were far better organized than in 1836. The Whigs also adopted a different strategy. The Jacksonians had come to power on

The 1840 presidential campaign was the first to use circus hoopla and the techniques of mass appeal that came to characterize political contests in the United States. This photograph is of a log cabin with a "hard cider" keg that was carried on a pole at rallies for William Henry Harrison.

the coattails of a popular general whose views on public questions they concealed or ignored. They had maintained themselves by shouting the praises of the common man. Now the Whigs seized on these techniques and carried them to their logical—or illogical—conclusion. Not even bothering to draft a program, and passing over Clay and Webster, whose views were known and therefore controversial, they nominated General William Henry Harrison for president. The "Hero of Tippecanoe" was counted on to conquer the party created in the image of the Hero of New Orleans. To "balance" the ticket, the Whigs chose a former Democrat, John Tyler of Virginia, an ardent supporter of states' rights, as their vice presidential candidate.

Harrison came from a distinguished family, being the son of Benjamin Harrison, a signer of the Declaration of Independence and a former governor of Virginia. He was well educated and in at least comfortable financial circumstances. The Whigs ignored these facts. The log cabin and the cider barrel became their symbols, which every political meeting saw reproduced in a dozen forms. The leading Whig campaign newspaper, edited by a vigorous New Englander named Horace Greeley, was called the *Log Cabin*. Cartoons, doggerel, slogans, and souvenirs were everywhere substituted for argument.

The Democrats used the same methods as the Whigs and were equally well organized, but they had little heart for the fight. The best they could come up with was the fact that their vice presidential candidate, Richard Mentor Johnson, had killed Tecumseh, not merely defeated him. Van Buren tried to focus public attention on issues, but his voice could not be heard above the huzzahs of the Whigs. When the Whigs chanted "Tippecanoe and Tyler too!" and "Van, Van, is a used-up man" and rolled out another barrel of hard cider, the best the Democrats could come up with was:

Rumpsey, Dumpsey,
Colonel Johnson
Killed Tecumseh.

A huge turnout (four-fifths of the eligible voters) carried Harrison to victory by a margin of almost 150,000. The electoral vote was 234 to 60.

The Democrats had been blown up by their own bomb. In 1828 they had portrayed John Quincy Adams as a bloated aristocrat and Jackson as a simple farmer. The lurid talk of Van Buren dining off golden plates was no different from the stories that made Adams out to be a passionate gambler. If Van Buren was a lesser man than Adams, Harrison was a pale imitation indeed of Andrew Jackson.

The Whigs continued to repeat history by rushing to gather the spoils of victory. Washington was again flooded by office seekers; the political confusion was monumental. Harrison had no ambition to be an aggressive leader. He believed that Jackson had misused the veto and professed to put as much emphasis as had Washington on the principle of the separation of legislative and executive powers. This delighted the Whig leaders in Congress, who had had their fill of the "executive usurpation" of Jackson. Either Clay or Webster seemed destined to be the real ruler of the new administration, and soon the two were squabbling over their old general like sparrows over a crust.

At the height of their squabble, less than a month after his inauguration, Harrison fell gravely ill. Pneumonia developed, and on April 4 he died. John Tyler of Virginia, honest and conscientious but doctrinaire, became president of the United States. The political climate of the country was changed dramatically. Events began to march in a new direction.

Milestones

1828	Andrew Jackson is elected president
1829	Crowds cause chaos at Jackson's White House inaugural reception
1830	Jackson vetoes the Maysville Road Bill
1831	Nat Turner leads slave rebellion in Virginia
1831–1838	Southern Indians are removed to Oklahoma
1832	South Carolina defends states' rights in Ordinance of Nullification
	Force Bill grants president authority to execute revenue laws
	Jackson vetoes Bank Recharter Bill
	Jackson is reelected president
1833	Treasury Secretary Roger B. Taney orders Treasury funds removed from Bank of the United States
	Calhoun and Clay push through Compromise Tariff
1836	Jackson issues Specie Circular to control speculation
	Martin Van Buren is elected president
1837–1838	Panic sweeps nation, ending economic boom
1838	4,000 Cherokee die on Trail of Tears to Oklahoma
1840	Independent Treasury Act divorces federal government from all banking activities
	"Log Cabin" Campaign is first to use "hoopla"
	William Henry Harrison is elected president
1841	Harrison dies one month after inauguration; John Tyler becomes president

10 CHAPTER

The Making of Middle-Class America

"THE AMERICAN FAMILY IS IN A STATE OF CRISIS"—THE PHRASE IS trumpeted by countless politicians and pollsters. The statistics seem to prove them right. Today, nearly a third of all children are born to unwed mothers; half of all marriages end in divorce; a third of all families are headed by a single parent; more than half of all single mothers with children younger than six work outside the home. Only a fourth of all households fit the "traditional" conception of family: a husband, a wife who does not work outside the home, and children.

But complaints about a "crisis" in the family have provoked cries of alarm for over a century, when divorce rates first began to rise. If ever the traditional "ideal" prevailed in America, it was during decades after 1820. In 1830 divorce was rare; the overwhelming majority of families had two parents; only one in fifteen women worked outside the home, and when these women married they almost always quit their jobs. With the exception of slave families, the traditional family structure had become normative.

Whether such families were "happier" or "stronger" than now is a different matter. Divorce was rare partly because it was hard to attain. South Carolina recognized no legal grounds for divorce. Many other states granted divorce only if a spouse committed adultery. Many couples thus endured loveless, unhappy marriages.

But after 1820, the family was perceived as a new and dynamic force in American society. Middle-class women, especially those freed from the drudgery of farm chores, were especially influential. Sarah Hale, the leading female journalist of the era, pronounced women to be "God's appointed agents of morality." Such women organized religious revivals, spearheaded efforts to improve prisons and mental asylums, and campaigned for temperance, abolitionism, and women's rights. Young middle-class women, too, were avid readers, and their patronage stimulated publication of books and magazines. These women shaped society and culture even more directly by serving as teachers in the common schools that extended public education to much of the nation.

The reformers of the era decried the pessimism of their Calvinist forebears and enshrined human sensibilities. Romanticism in the arts and literature was the cultural expression of a spirit affirming that Americans and their institutions could—and would—grow and change for the better.

Tocqueville: Democracy in America

On May 12, 1831, two French aristocrats, Alexis de Tocqueville and Gustave de Beaumont, arrived in New York City from Le Havre on the packet *President*. Their official purpose was to make a study of American prisons for the French government. But they really came, as Tocqueville explained, "to see what a great republic is like."

Tocqueville and Beaumont believed that Europe was passing from its aristocratic past into a democratic future. How better to prepare for the change, they believed, than by studying the United States, where democracy was already the "enduring and normal state" of the land. The visit provided the material for Tocqueville's classic *De la Démocratie en Amérique,* published in France in 1835 and a year later in an English translation. *Democracy in America* has been the starting point for virtually all subsequent writers who have tried to describe what Tocqueville called "the creative elements" of American institutions.

The gist of *Democracy in America* is contained in the book's first sentence: "No novelty in the United States struck me more vividly during my stay there than the equality of conditions." Tocqueville meant not that Americans lived in a state of total equality, but that the inequalities that did exist among white Americans were

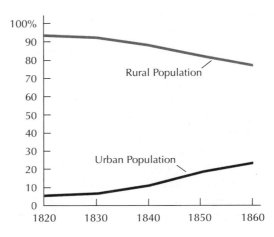

Rural Versus Urban Population, 1820–1860

As the balance of rural and urban population began to shift during the years from 1820 to 1860, the number of cities with populations over 100,000 grew from one in 1820—New York—to nine in 1870, including southern and western cities like New Orleans and San Francisco.

not enforced by institutions or supported by public opinion. Moreover, the inequalities paled when compared with those of Europe. "In America," he concluded, "men are nearer equality than in any other country in the world." The circumstances of one's birth meant little, one's education less, and one's intelligence scarcely anything. Economic differences, while real and certainly "paraded" by those who enjoyed "a pre-eminence of wealth," were transitory. "Such wealth," Tocqueville assured his readers, "is within reach of all."

Despite a blindness to the growing gap between rich and poor, Tocqueville realized that America was undergoing some fundamental social changes. These changes, he wrote, were being made by "an innumerable crowd who are . . . not exactly rich nor yet quite poor [and who] have enough property to want order and not enough to excite envy." In his notes he put it even more succinctly: "The whole society seems to have turned into one middle class."

The Family Recast

Tocqueville was particularly struck by the character of the family. Americans, he wrote, showed an "equal regard" for husbands and wives, but defined their roles differently. This was made possible by the growth of the market economy, which undermined the home and family as the basic unit of economic production. More and more people did their work in shops, in offices, or on factory floors. Whether a job was skilled or unskilled, white-collar or blue-collar, or strictly professional, it took the family breadwinner out of the house during working hours six days a week. This did not mean that the family necessarily ceased to be an economic unit. But the labor of the father and any children with jobs came home in the form of cash, thus at least initially in the custody of the individual earners. The social consequences of this change were enormous for the traditional "head of the family" and for his wife and children.

Because he was away so much, the husband had to surrender to his wife some of the power in the family that he had formerly exercised, if for no other reason than that she was always there. Noah Webster explained that the ideal father's authority was "like the mild dominion of a limited monarch, and not the iron rule of an austere tyrant." It certainly explains why Tocqueville concluded that "a sort of equality reigns around the domestic hearth" in America.

The new power and prestige that wives and mothers enjoyed were not obtained without cost. Since they were exercising day-to-day control over household affairs, they were expected to tend only to those affairs. Expanding their interest to other fields of human endeavor was frowned on. Where the typical wife had formerly been a partner in a family enterprise, she now left earning a living entirely to her husband. She was certainly not encouraged to have an independent career as, say, a lawyer or doctor. Time spent away from home or devoted to matters unrelated to the care of husband and family was, according to the new normative doctrine of "separate spheres," time misappropriated.

Joseph Moore and His Family (1839), by Erastus Salisbury Field, reflects the emerging middle-class family. Although the painting is named after the father, the mother is carefully placed in a precisely equivalent position; each child has a space of his or her own.

This trend widened the gap between the middle and lower classes. For a middle-class wife and mother to take a job or, still worse, to devote herself to any "frivolous" activity outside the home was considered a dereliction of duty. Such an attitude could not possibly develop in lower-class families where everyone had to work simply to keep food on the table.

Some women objected to making a cult out of "womanhood": by placing an ideal on so high a pedestal, all real women would fall short. Others escaped its more suffocating aspects by forming close friendships with other women. But most women, including such forceful proponents of women's rights as Hale and the educator Catharine Beecher, subscribed to the view that a woman's place was in the home. "The formation of the moral and intellectual character of the young is committed mainly to the female hand," Beecher wrote in *A Treatise on Domestic Economy for the Use of Young Ladies* (1841). "The mother forms the character of the future man."

Another reason for the shift in domestic influence from husbands to wives was that women began to have fewer children. Here again, the change happened earliest and was most pronounced among families in the rapidly urbanizing Northeast. On the frontier, where middle-class norms lagged behind, couples generally had larger families. But the birthrate gradually declined all over the country. People married later than in earlier periods. Long courtships and broken engagements were common, probably because prospective marriage partners were becoming more selective. On average, women began having their children two or three years later than their mothers had, and they stopped two or three years sooner. Apparently many middle-class couples made a conscious effort to limit family size, even when doing so required sexual abstinence.

Having fewer children led parents to value children more highly, or so it would seem from the additional time and affection lavished on them. Here again, the mother provided most of both. Child rearing fell within her "sphere" and occupied the time that earlier generations of mothers had devoted to such tasks as weaving, sewing, and farm chores. Not the least of these new responsibilities was overseeing the children's education, both secular and religious.

The Second Great Awakening

The inclination to set aside other Calvinist tenets, such as predestination, became more pronounced as a new wave of revivalism took shape in the 1790s. This Second Great Awakening began as a counteroffensive to the deistic thinking and other forms of "infidelity" that New England Congregationalists and southern Methodists alike identified with the French Revolution. Prominent New England ministers, who considered themselves traditionalists but also revivalists, men such as Yale's president, Timothy Dwight, and Dwight's student, the Reverend Lyman Beecher, placed less stress in their sermons on God's arbitrary power over mortals, more on the promise of the salvation of sinners because of God's mercy and "disinterested benevolence." When another of Dwight's students, Horace Bushnell, declared in a sermon on "Christian nurture" in 1844 that Christian parents should prepare their children "for the skies," he meant that parents could contribute to their children's salvation.

Calvinism came under more direct assault from Charles Grandison Finney, probably the most effective of a number of charismatic evangelists who brought the Second Great Awakening to its crest. In 1821 Finney abandoned a promising career as a lawyer and became an itinerant preacher. His most spectacular successes occurred during a series of revivals conducted in towns along the Erie Canal, a region Finney called "the burned-over district" because it had been the site of so many revivals before his own. From Utica, where his revival began in 1826, to Rochester, where it climaxed in 1831, he exhorted his listeners to take their salvation into their own hands. He insisted that people could control their own fate. He dismissed Calvinism as a "theological fiction." Salvation was available to anyone. But the day of judgment was just around the corner; there was little time to waste.

During and after Finney's efforts in Utica, conversions increased sharply. In Rochester, church membership doubled in six months. Elsewhere in the country, churches capitalized on the efforts of other evangelists to fill their pews. In 1831 alone, church membership grew by 100,000, an increase, according to a New England minister, "unparalleled in the history of the church." The success of the evangelists of the Second Great Awakening stemmed from the timeliness of their

Religious revivals stirred passions, as this rendering of an 1839 camp meeting suggests: people are gesticulating, swooning, and writhing on the ground. Finney endorsed such "excitements" as essential for conversion. But some doubted the wisdom of eliciting passions so as to persuade people to exercise more restraint and sin less often.

assault on Calvinist doctrine and even more from their methods. Finney, for example, consciously set out to be entertaining as well as edifying. The singing of hymns and the solicitation of personal testimonies provided his meetings with emotional release and human interest. Prominent among his innovations was the "anxious bench," where leading members of the community awaited the final prompting from within before coming forward to declare themselves saved.

Women, and especially the wives of the business leaders of the community, felt particularly responsible for the Christian education of their children, which fell within their separate sphere. Many women had servants and thus had time and energy to devote to their own and their offsprings' salvation.

Paradoxically, this caused many of them to venture out of that sphere—and out of the shadow of their husbands. They founded the Oneida County Female Missionary Society, an association that did most of the organizing and a good deal of the financing of the climactic years of the Second Awakening. The Female Missionary Society raised more than $1,000 a year (no small sum at that time) to support the revival in Utica, in its environs, and throughout the burned-over district. Apparently without consciously intending to do so, women challenged the authority of the paternalistic, authoritarian churches they so fervently embraced. Then, by mixtures of exhortation, example, and affection, they set out to save the souls of their loved ones, first their children and ultimately their husbands too.

The Shakers segregated the sexes and enforced celibacy. Pent-up sexual tensions were released in religious ecstasy expressed through church dances, as the lines of men and women approached each other—but never touched.

Backwoods Utopias

Rather than save individual souls, some Americans sought to reform society or, more venturesome, withdraw from workaday American society and establish experimental communities. The first communitarians were religious reformers. In a sense the Pilgrims fall into this category, along with a number of other groups in colonial times, but only in the nineteenth century did the idea flourish.

One of the most influential of the earlier communities were the Shakers, founded by Ann Lee, an Englishwoman who came to America in 1774. Mother Ann, as she was called, saw visions that convinced her that Christ would come to earth again as a woman and that she was that woman. With a handful of followers she founded a community near Albany, New York. The group grew rapidly, and after Ann Lee's death in 1784 her movement continued to expand. By the 1830s her followers had established about twenty successful communities.

The Shakers practiced celibacy; believing that the millennium was imminent, they saw no reason for perpetuating the human race. Each group lived in a large Family House, the sexes strictly segregated. Property was held in common but controlled by a ruling hierarchy. So much stress was placed on equality of labor and reward and on voluntary acceptance of the rules, however, that the system does not seem to have been oppressive.

The Shaker religion, joyful and fervent, was marked by much group singing and dancing, which provided the members with emotional release from their tightly controlled regimen. An industrious, skillful people, they made a special virtue of simplicity; some of their designs for buildings and, especially, furniture achieved a classic beauty seldom equaled among untutored artisans. Despite their customs, the Shakers were universally tolerated and even admired.

There were many other religious colonies, such as the Amana Community, which flourished in New York and Iowa in the 1840s and 1850s, and John Humphrey Noyes's Oneida Community, where the members practiced "complex" marriage—a form of promiscuity based on the principle that every man in the group was married to every woman. They prospered by developing a number of manufacturing skills.

The most important of the religious communitarians were the Mormons. A remarkable Vermont farm boy, Joseph Smith, founded the religion in western New York in the 1820s. Smith saw visions; he claimed to have discovered and translated an ancient text, the Book of Mormon, written in hieroglyphics on plates of gold, which described the adventures of a tribe of Israelites that had populated America from biblical times until their destruction in a great war in 400 C.E. With a small band of followers, Smith established a community in Ohio in 1831. The Mormons' dedication and economic efficiency attracted large numbers of converts, but their unorthodox religious views and their exclusivism, a product of their sense of being a chosen people, caused some non-Mormons to resent and persecute Smith and his followers. The Mormons were forced to move first to Missouri and then back to Illinois, where in 1839 they founded the town of Nauvoo.

Nauvoo flourished—by 1844 it was the largest city in the state, with a population of 15,000—but once again the Mormons ran into local trouble. They quarreled among themselves, especially after Smith secretly authorized polygamy (he called it "celestial marriage") and a number of other unusual rites for members of the "Holy Order," the top leaders of the church.[1] They created a paramilitary organization, the Nauvoo Legion, headed by Smith, envisaging themselves as a semi-independent state within the Union. Smith announced that he was a candidate for president of the United States. Rumors circulated that the Mormons intended to take over the entire Northwest for their "empire." Once again local "gentiles" rose against them. Smith was arrested, then murdered by a mob.

Under a new leader, Brigham Young, the Mormons sought a haven beyond the frontier. In 1847 they marched westward, pressing through the mountains until they reached the desolate wilderness on the shores of the Great Salt Lake. There, at last, they established their Zion and began to make their truly significant impact on American history. Irrigation made the desert flourish, precious water wisely being treated as a community asset. Hard, cooperative, intelligently directed effort

---

[1]One justification of polygamy, paradoxically, was that marriage was a sacred, eternal state. If a man remarried after his wife's death, eventually he would have two wives in Heaven. Therefore why not on earth?

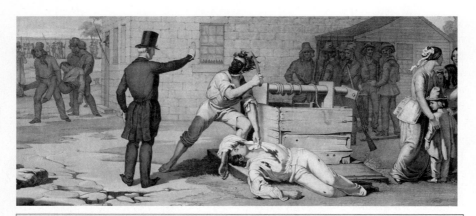

Persecution forced the Mormons to move from New York to Ohio to Missouri, before settling for a time in Nauvoo, Illinois. There, in 1844 Joseph Smith, the Mormon leader, announced his candidacy for president of the United States. Smith and his brother Hyrum were arrested by local authorities and murdered in their jail cell by a hostile mob.

spelled growth and prosperity; more than 11,000 people were living in the area when it became part of the Utah Territory in 1850. In time the communal Mormon settlement broke down, but the religion has remained—known as the Church of Latter-Day Saints, a major force in the shaping of the West. The Mormon Church is still by far the most powerful single influence in Utah and is a thriving organization in many other parts of the United States and in Europe.

Despite their many common characteristics, the religious communities varied enormously; subordination of the individual to the group did not destroy group individualism. Their sexual practices, for example, ranged from the "complex marriage" of the Oneidans through Mormon polygamy and ordinary monogamy to the reluctant acceptance of sexual intercourse by the Amana Community and the celibacy of the Shakers. The communities are significant as reflections of the urgent reform spirit of the age.

The communities had some influence on reformers who wished to experiment with social organization. When Robert Owen, a British utopian socialist who believed in economic as well as political equality and who considered competition debasing, decided to create an ideal community in America, he purchased the Rappite settlement at New Harmony, Indiana. Owen's advocacy of free love and "enlightened atheism" did not add to the stability of his group or to its popularity among outsiders. The colony was a costly failure.

The American followers of Charles Fourier, a French utopian socialist who proposed that society should be organized in cooperative units called phalanxes, fared better. Fourierism did not seek to tamper with sexual and religious mores. Its advocates included important journalists such as Horace Greeley of the *New York Tribune* and Parke Godwin of the *New York Evening Post*. In the 1840s several dozen Fourierist colonies were established in the northern and western states. Members worked at whatever tasks they wished and only as much as they wished. Wages were paid according to the "repulsiveness" of the tasks performed; the person who "chose" to clean out a cesspool would receive more than someone hoeing corn or mending a fence or engaging in some task requiring complex skills. As might be expected, none of the communities lasted very long.

The Age of Reform

The communitarians were the most colorful of the reformers, their proposals the most spectacular. More effective, however, were the many individuals who took on themselves responsibility for caring for the physically and mentally disabled and for the rehabilitation of criminals. The work of Thomas Gallaudet in developing methods for educating deaf people reflects the spirit of the times. Gallaudet's school in Hartford, Connecticut, opened its doors in 1817; by 1851 similar schools for the deaf had been established in fourteen states.

Dr. Samuel Gridley Howe did similar work with the blind, devising means for making books with raised letters (Louis Braille's system of raised dots was not introduced until later in the century) that the blind could "read" with their fingers. Howe headed a school for the blind in Boston, the pioneering Perkins Institution, which opened in 1832. Of all that Charles Dickens observed in America, nothing so favorably impressed him as Howe's success in educating 12-year-old Laura Bridgman, who was deaf, mute, and blind. Howe was also interested in trying to educate the mentally disabled and in other causes, including antislavery. "Every creature in human shape should command our respect," he insisted. "The strong should help the weak, so that the whole should advance as a band of brethren."

One of the most striking aspects of the reform movement was the emphasis reformers placed on establishing special institutions for dealing with social problems. In the colonial period, orphans, indigent persons, the insane, and the feeble-minded were usually cared for by members of their own families or boarded in a neighboring household. They remained part of the community. Even criminals were seldom "locked away" for extended jail terms; punishment commonly consisted of whipping, being placed in stocks in the town square, or (for serious crimes) execution. But once persuaded that people were primarily shaped by their surroundings, reformers demanded that deviant and dependent members of the community be taken from their present corrupting circumstances and placed in specialized institutions where they could be trained or rehabilitated. Almshouses, orphanages, reformatories, prisons, and "lunatic asylums" sprang up throughout the United States.

The rationale for this movement was scientific; elaborate statistical reports attested to the benefits that such institutions would bring to both inmates and society as a whole. The motivating spirit of the founders of these asylums was humane, although many of the institutions seem anything but humane to the modern eye.

DID ANTEBELLUM REFORM MOVEMENTS IMPROVE SOCIETY?

The Eastern State Penitentiary in Philadelphia was built in the 1820s. The lithograph *(below left)* was done by Samuel Cowperthwaite, Convict # 2954. Eastern State consisted of seven rows of cells radiating out from the central tower. The design ensured continuous supervision and isolation. The reformers who conceived of the prison thought it would teach an inmate to "listen to the reproaches of his conscience." The dessert plate *(below right)* commemorating the jail is proof that some people believed in its mission. After visiting the prison, however, Charles Dickens described its system of confinement as "rigid, strict and hopeless." In *Madness and Civilization* (1961) and *Discipline and Punish* (1975), the French philosopher Michel Foucault similarly regarded such institutions as part of the process whereby modern societies squelched individuality. Those who refused to accept the discipline of teachers, employers, and government officials were labeled "deviants" and sent to institutions that would "reform" them through the imposition of order, a thesis that David J. Rothman (1971) applied to antebellum

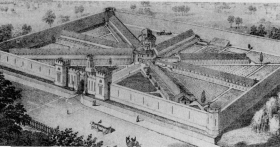

penitentiaries and asylums. Before Foucault, most scholars had endorsed antebellum reforms. Now these reforms were reassessed more critically. Michael B. Katz (1968) and Stanley K. Schultz (1973) argued that the public schools were means for preparing the young for industrial labor by instilling discipline and regimentation. Movements to promote temperance and suppress prostitution, similarly, were increasingly viewed as unwarranted intrusions on private matters. But in the 1980s women's historians altered this debate. Mary Ryan (1981) and others showed that women dominated nearly all antebellum reform movements, and for good reason. The child who could not attend a school was often subjected to the ceaseless drudgery of farm or factory. The exuberant individualist who tarried at the tavern sometimes beat his wife on returning home. The Eastern State Penitentiary and the antebellum insane asylums were fearsome places, but would their inmates have been better off on the streets? Excessive discipline erodes individuality; excessive individuality erodes social cohesion.

Michel Foucault, *Madness and Civilization* (1961) and *Discipline and Punish* (1975), Michael B. Katz, *The Irony of Early School Reform* (1968), Stanley K. Schultz, *The Culture Factory* (1973), David J. Rothman, *The Discovery of the Asylum* (1971), Mary Ryan, *Cradle of the Middle Class* (1981).

The highly regarded Philadelphia prison system was based on strict solitary confinement, which was supposed to lead culprits to reflect on their sins and then reform their ways. The prison was literally a penitentiary, a place to repent. In fact, the system drove some inmates mad, and soon a rival Auburn system was introduced in New York State, which allowed for some social contact among prisoners and for work in shops and stone quarries. Absolute silence was required at all times. The prisoners were herded about in lockstep and punished by flogging for the slightest infraction of the rules. Regular "moral and religious instruction" was provided, which the authorities believed would lead inmates to reform their lives. Tocqueville and Beaumont, in their report on American prisons, concluded that the Philadelphia system produced "the deepest impression on the soul of the convict," while the Auburn system made the convict "more conformable to the habits of man in society." (See also Debating the Past, p. 310)

The hospitals for mental patients were intended to cure inmates, not merely to confine them. The emphasis was on isolating them from the pressures of society; on order, quiet, routine; on control but not on punishment. The unfortunates were seen as *deranged*; the task was to *arrange* their lives in a rational manner. In practice, shortages of trained personnel, niggardly legislative appropriations, and the inherent difficulty of managing violent and irrational patients often produced deplorable conditions in the asylums.

This situation led Dorothea Dix, a woman of almost saintlike selflessness, to devote thirty years of her life to a campaign to improve the care of the insane. She traveled to every state in the Union, and as far afield as Turkey and Japan, inspecting asylums and poorhouses. Insane persons in Massachusetts, she wrote in a memorial intended to shock state legislators into action, were being kept in cages and closets, "*chained, naked, beaten with rods, and lashed into obedience!*" Her reports led to some improvement in conditions in Massachusetts and other states, but in the long run the bright hopes of the reformers were never realized. Institutions founded to uplift the deviant and dependent all too soon became places where society's "misfits" might safely be kept out of sight.

"Demon Rum"

Women did much of the work in all antebellum reforms, but they were especially active in the temperance movement. The husband who squandered his earnings on booze, or who came home drunk and debauched, imperiled the family. Thus middle-class women who believed that a woman's place was in the home were obliged to take on a public role to protect the family.

Alcohol—"demon rum"—was perhaps foremost among those threats. By the 1820s Americans were consuming prodigious amounts of alcohol, more than ever before or since. Not that the colonists had been teetotalers. Liquor, mostly in the form of rum or hard apple cider, was cheap and everywhere available; taverns were an integral part of colonial society. There were alcoholics in colonial America, but because neither political nor religious leaders considered drinking dangerous, there was no alcohol "problem." Most doctors recommended the regular consumption of alcohol as healthy. John Adams, certainly the soul of propriety, drank a tankard of hard cider every day for breakfast. Dr. Benjamin Rush's *Inquiry into the Effects of Ardent Spirits* (1784), which questioned the medicinal benefits of alcohol, fell on deaf ears.

However, alcohol consumption increased markedly in the early years of the new republic, thanks primarily to the availability of cheap corn and rye whiskey distilled in the new states of Kentucky and Tennessee. In the 1820s the per capita consumption of hard liquor reached 5 gallons, well over twice what it is today. Since small children and many grown people did not drink that much, others obviously drank a great deal more. Many women drank, if mostly at home; and reports of carousing among 14-year-old college freshmen show that youngsters did too. But the bulk of the heavy drinking occurred when men got together, at taverns or grogshops and at work. Many prominent politicians, including Clay and Webster, were heavy consumers. Webster is said to have kept several thousand bottles of wine, whiskey, and other alcoholic beverages in his cellar.

Artisans and common laborers regarded their twice-daily "dram" of whiskey as part of their wages. In workshops, masters were expected to halt production periodically to drink with their apprentices and journeymen. Trips to the neighborhood grogshop also figured into the workaday routine. In 1829 Secretary of War John Eaton estimated that three-quarters of the nation's laborers drank at least 4 ounces of distilled spirits a day.

The foundation of the American Temperance Union in 1826 signaled the start of a national crusade against drunkenness. Employing lectures, pamphlets, rallies, essay contests, and other techniques, the union set out to persuade people to "sign the pledge" not to drink liquor. Primitive sociological studies of the effects of drunkenness (reformers were able to show a high statistical correlation between alcohol consumption and crime) added to the effectiveness of the campaign.

In 1840 an organization of reformed alcoholics, the Washingtonians, set out to reclaim alcoholics. One of the most effective Washingtonians was John B. Gough, rescued by the organization after seven years in the gutter. "Crawl from the slimy ooze, ye drowned drunkards," Gough would shout, "and with suffocation's blue and livid lips speak out against the drink!"

Revivalist ministers like Charles Grandison Finney argued that alcohol was one of the great barriers to conversion, which helps explain why Utica, a town of fewer than 13,000 residents in 1840, supported four separate temperance societies in that year. Employers all over the country also signed on, declaring their businesses henceforward to be "cold-water" enterprises. Soon the temperance movement claimed a million members.

The temperance people aroused bitter opposition, particularly after they moved beyond calls for restraint to demands for prohibition of all alcohol. German and Irish immigrants, for the most part Catholics, and also members of Protestant sects that used wine in their religious services, objected to being told by reformers that their drinking would have to stop. But by the early 1840s the reformers had secured legislation in many states that imposed strict licensing systems and heavy liquor taxes. Local option laws permitted towns and counties to ban the sale of alcohol altogether.

In 1851 Maine passed the first effective law prohibiting the manufacture and sale of alcoholic beverages. The leader of the campaign was Mayor Neal Dow of Portland, a businessman who became a prohibitionist after seeing the damage done by drunkenness among workers in his tannery. By 1855 a dozen other states had passed laws based on the Maine statute, and the nation's per capita consumption of alcohol had plummeted to 2 gallons a year.

The Abolitionist Crusade

No reform movement of this era was more significant, more ambiguous, or more provocative of later historical investigation than the drive to abolish slavery. That slavery should have been a cause of indignation to reform-minded Americans was inevitable. Humanitarians were outraged by the master's whip and by the practice of disrupting families. Democrats protested the denial of political and civil rights to slaves. Perfectionists of all stripes deplored the fact that slaves had no chance to improve themselves. However, well into the 1820s, the abolitionist cause attracted few followers because there seemed to be no way of getting rid of slavery short of revolution. While a few theorists argued that the Fifth Amendment, which provides that no one may be "deprived of life, liberty, or property, without due process of law," could be interpreted to mean that the Constitution outlawed slavery, the great majority believed that the institution was not subject to federal control.

Particularly in the wake of the Missouri Compromise, antislavery Northerners neatly compartmentalized their thinking. Slavery was wrong; they would not tolerate it in their own communities. But since the Constitution obliged them to tolerate it in states where it existed, they felt no responsibility to fight it. The issue was explosive enough even when limited to the question of the expansion of slavery into the territories. People who advocated any kind of forced abolition in states where it was legal were judged irresponsible in the extreme.

More provocative and less accommodating to local sensibilities were people such as William Lloyd Garrison of Massachusetts, who called for "immediate" abolition. When his extreme position made continued residence in Baltimore impossible, he returned to Boston, where in 1831 he established his own newspaper, *The Liberator*. "I am in earnest," he announced in the first issue. "I will not equivocate— I will not excuse—I will not retreat a single inch—and I will be heard."

Garrison's position, and that espoused by the New England Anti-Slavery Society, which he organized in 1831, was absolutely unyielding: Slaves must be freed immediately and treated as equals; compensated emancipation was unacceptable, colonization unthinkable. Because the U.S. government countenanced slavery, Garrison refused to engage in political activity to achieve his ends. Burning a copy of the Constitution—that "agreement with hell"—became a regular feature at Society-sponsored public lectures.

Few white Americans found Garrison's line of argument convincing, and many were outraged by his confrontational tactics. Whenever he spoke in public, he risked being mobbed by what newspaper accounts approvingly described as "gentlemen of property and standing." In 1833 a Garrison meeting in New York City was broken up by colonizationists. Two years later a mob dragged Garrison through the streets of his own Boston. That same day a mob broke up the convention of the New York Anti-Slavery Society in Utica.

In the wake of this violence some of Garrison's backers had second thoughts about his call for an immediate end to slavery. The wealthy New York businessmen Arthur and Lewis Tappan, who had subsidized *The Liberator,* turned instead to Theodore Dwight Weld, a young minister who was part of Charles Grandison Finney's "holy band" of revivalists. Weld and his followers spoke of "immediate" emancipation "gradually" achieved, and they were willing to engage in political activity to achieve that goal.

In 1840 the Tappans and Weld broke with Garrison over the issue of involvement in politics and the participation of female abolitionists as public lecturers. Garrison, mindful of women's central role in other reforms, supported the women. "The destiny of the slaves is in the hands of American women," he had declared in 1833. Weld thought women lecturers would needlessly antagonize would-be supporters.

Many blacks were abolitionists long before the white movement began to attract attention. In 1830 some fifty black antislavery societies existed, and thereafter these groups grew in size and importance, being generally associated with the Garrisonian wing. White abolitionists eagerly sought out black speakers, especially runaway slaves, whose heartrending accounts of their experiences aroused sympathies and who, merely by speaking clearly and with conviction, stood as living proof that blacks were neither animals nor fools.

The first prominent black abolitionist was David Walker, whose powerful *Appeal to the Coloured Citizens of the World* (1829) is now considered one of the roots of the modern black nationalist movement. Walker was born free and had experienced American racism extensively in both the South and the North. He denounced white talk of democracy and freedom as pure hypocrisy and predicted that when God finally brought justice to America white "tyrants will wish they were never born!"

Frederick Douglass, a former slave who had escaped from Maryland, was one of the most remarkable Americans of his generation. While a bondsman he had received a full portion of beatings and other indignities, but he had been allowed to learn to read and write and to master a trade, opportunities denied the vast majority of slaves. Settling in Boston, he became an agent of the Massachusetts Anti-Slavery Society and a featured speaker at its public meetings.

Frederick Douglass in 1847, having escaped from slavery nine years earlier. He attracted large audiences as an antislavery lecturer, though his white supporters worried that he neither looked nor sounded like a former slave. Lest audiences think him an imposter, William Lloyd Garrison counseled him to not sound too "learned." Another thought it would be better if he had "a little of the plantation in his speech." Douglass rejected such suggestions.

Douglass was a tall, majestically handsome man who radiated determination and indignation. Slavery, he told white audiences, "brands your republicanism as a sham, your humanity as a base pretense, your Christianity as a lie." In 1845 he published his *Narrative of the Life of Frederick Douglass,* one of the most gripping autobiographical accounts of a slave's life ever written. Douglass insisted that freedom for blacks required not merely emancipation but full equality, social and economic as well as political. Not many white Northerners accepted his reasoning, but few who heard him or read his works could afterward maintain the illusion that all blacks were dull-witted or resigned to inferior status.

At first Douglass was, in his own words, "a faithful disciple" of Garrison, prepared to tear up the Constitution and destroy the Union to gain his ends. In the late 1840s, however, he changed his mind, deciding that the Constitution, created to "establish Justice, insure domestic Tranquility . . . and secure the Blessings of Liberty," as its preamble states, "could not well have been designed at the same time to maintain and perpetuate a system of rapine and murder like slavery." Thereafter he fought slavery and race prejudice from within the system, something Garrison was never willing to do.

Garrison's importance cannot be measured by the number of his followers, which was never large. Unlike more moderately inclined enemies of slavery, he recognized that abolitionism was a revolutionary movement, not merely one more middle-class reform. He also understood that achieving racial equality, not merely "freeing" the slaves, was the only way to reach the abolitionists' professed objective: full justice for blacks. And he saw clearly that few whites, even among abolitionists, believed that blacks were their equals.

Women's Rights

The question of slavery was related to another major reform movement of the era, the crusade for women's rights. The relationship was personal and ideological, direct and indirect, simple and profound. Superficially, the connection can be explained in this way: Women were as likely as men to find slavery offensive and to protest against it. When they did so, they ran into even more adamant resistance, the prejudices of those who objected to abolitionists being reinforced by their feelings that women should not speak in public or participate in political affairs. Thus female abolitionists, driven by the urgencies of conscience, were almost forced to become advocates of women's rights. "We have good cause to be grateful to the slave," the feminist Abby Kelley wrote. "In striving to strike his irons off, we found most surely, that we were manacled ourselves."

At a more profound level, the reference that abolitionists made to the Declaration of Independence to justify their attack on slavery radicalized women with regard to their own place in society. Were only all men created equal and endowed by God with unalienable rights? For many women the question was a consciousness-raising experience; they began to believe that, like blacks, they were imprisoned from birth in a caste system, legally subordinated and assigned menial social and economic roles that prevented them from developing their full potentialities. Such women considered themselves in a sense worse off than blacks, who had at least the psychological advantage of confronting an openly hostile and repressive society rather than one concealed behind the cloying rhetoric of romantic love.

With the major exception of Margaret Fuller, whose book *Women in the Nineteenth Century* (1844) made a frontal assault on all forms of sexual discrimination, the leading advocates of equal rights for women began their public careers in the abolitionist movement. Among the first were Sarah and Angelina Grimké, South Carolinians who abandoned their native state and the domestic sphere to devote themselves to speaking out against slavery. (In 1841 Angelina married Theodore Dwight Weld.) Male objections to the Grimkés' activities soon made them advocates of women's rights. Similarly, the refusal of delegates to the World Anti-Slavery Convention held in London in 1840 to let women participate in their debates precipitated the decision of two American abolitionists, Lucretia Mott and Elizabeth Cady Stanton, to turn their attention to the women's rights movement.

Slavery aside, there were other aspects of feminist consciousness-raising. Some women rejected the idea that they should confine themselves to a sphere of activity consisting mostly of child rearing and housekeeping. The very effort to enforce this kind of specialization made women aware of their second-class citizenship and thus more likely to be dissatisfied. They lacked not merely the right to vote, of which they did not make a major issue, but if married, the right to own property or to make a will. Lydia Maria Child, a popular novelist, found this last restriction particularly offensive. It excited her "towering indignation" that her husband had to sign her will.

The subordination of women was as old as most civilizations. The attack on it came not because of any new discrimination but for the same reasons that moti-

Anna Elizabeth Klumpke's portrait of Elizabeth Cady Stanton (1887). In 1848 Stanton helped draft the Declaration of Sentiments, spelling out the injustices of man to woman. The conclusion: "He has endeavored, in every way he could, to destroy her confidence in her own powers, to lessen her self-respect, and to make her willing to lead a dependent and abject life."

vated reformers against other forms of injustice: belief in progress, a sense of personal responsibility, and the conviction that institutions could be changed and that the time for changing them was limited.

When women sought to involve themselves in reform, they became aware of perhaps the most serious handicap that society imposed on them—the conflict between their roles as wives and mothers and their urge to participate in the affairs of the larger world. Elizabeth Cady Stanton has left a striking description of this dilemma. She lived in the 1840s in Seneca Falls, a small town in central New York. Her husband was frequently away on business; she had a brood of growing children and little domestic help. When, stimulated by her interest in abolition and women's rights, she sought to become active in the movements, her family responsibilities made it almost impossible even to read about them.

"I now fully understood the practical difficulties most women had to contend with," she recalled in her autobiography, *Eighty Years and More* (1898):

> *The general discontent I felt with woman's portion as wife, mother, housekeeper, physician, and spiritual guide, the chaotic condition into which everything fell without her constant supervision, and the wearied, anxious look of the majority of women, impressed me with the strong feeling that some active measures should be taken.*

Active measures she took. Together with Lucretia Mott and a few others of like mind, she organized a meeting, the Seneca Falls Convention (July 1848), and drafted a Declaration of Sentiments patterned on the Declaration of Independence. "We hold these truths to be self-evident: that all men and women are created equal," it stated, and it went on to list the "injuries and usurpations" of men, just as Jefferson had outlined those of George III.

From this seed the movement grew. During the 1850s a series of national conventions was held, and more and more reformers, including William Lloyd Garrison, joined the cause. Of the recruits, Susan B. Anthony was the most influential, for she was the first to see the need for thorough organization if effective pressure was to be brought to bear on male-dominated society. Her first campaign, mounted in 1854 and 1855 in behalf of a petition to the New York legislature calling for reform of the property and divorce laws, accumulated 6,000 signatures. But the petition did not persuade the legislature to act. Indeed, the feminists achieved very few practical results during the Age of Reform. Their leaders, however, were persevering types, most of them extraordinarily long-lived. Their major efforts lay in the future.

The Romantic View of Life

The spreading belief that human institutions were improving had a profound effect on the arts and literature. In the Western world, it gave rise to romanticism, a revolt against the bloodless logic of the Age of Reason. It was a noticeable if unnamed point of view in Germany, France, and England as early as the 1780s and in America a generation later; by the second quarter of the nineteenth century, few intellectuals were unmarked by it. "Romantics" believed that change and growth were the essence of life, for individuals and for institutions. They valued feeling and intuition over pure thought, and they stressed the differences between individuals and societies rather than the similarities. Ardent love of country characterized the movement; individualism, optimism, ingenuousness, and emotion were its bywords. Romanticism, too, drew much from the religious sensibilities of mothers. Children were innately good; pernicious influences led to their corruption.

The romantic way of thinking found its greatest American expression in transcendentalism, a New England creation that is difficult to describe because it emphasized the indefinable and the unknowable. It was a mystical, intuitive way of looking at life that subordinated facts to feelings. Its literal meaning was "to go beyond the world of the senses," by which the transcendentalists meant the material and observable world. To the transcendentalists, human beings were truly divine because they were part of nature, itself the essence of divinity. Their intellectual capacities did not define their capabilities, for they could "transcend" reason by having faith in themselves and in the fundamental benevolence of the universe. Transcendentalists were complete individualists, seeing the social whole as no more than the sum of its parts. Organized religion, indeed all institutions were unimportant if not counterproductive; what mattered was the single person and that people aspire, stretch *beyond* their known capabilities. Failure resulted only from lack of effort. The expression "Hitch your wagon to a star" is of transcendentalist origin.

Emerson and Thoreau

The leading transcendentalist thinker was Ralph Waldo Emerson. Born in 1803 and educated at Harvard, Emerson became a minister, but in 1832 he gave up his pulpit, deciding that "the profession is antiquated." After traveling in Europe he settled in Concord, Massachusetts, where he had a long career as an essayist, lecturer, and sage.

Emerson's philosophy was at once buoyantly optimistic and rigorously intellectual, self-confident, and conscientious. In "The American Scholar," a notable address he delivered at Harvard in 1837, he urged Americans to put aside their devotion to things European and seek inspiration in their immediate surroundings. Emerson saw himself as pitting "spiritual powers" against "the mechanical powers and the mechanical philosophy of this time." The new industrial society of New England disturbed him profoundly.

Because he put so much emphasis on self-reliance, Emerson disliked powerful governments. "The less government we have the better," he said. In a sense he was the prototype of some modern alienated intellectuals, so repelled by the world as it was that he would not actively try to change it. Nevertheless he thought strong leadership essential. Emerson also had a strong practical streak. He made his living by lecturing, tracking tirelessly across the country, talking before every type of audience for fees ranging from $50 to several hundreds.

Closely identified with Emerson was his Concord neighbor Henry David Thoreau. After graduating from Harvard in 1837, Thoreau taught school for a time and helped out in a small pencil-making business run by his family. He was a strange man, gentle, a dreamer, content to absorb the beauties of nature almost intuitively, yet stubborn and individualistic to the point of selfishness. The hectic scramble for wealth that Thoreau saw all about him he found disgusting—and alarming, for he believed it was destroying both the natural and the human resources of the country.

Like Emerson, Thoreau objected to many of society's restrictions on the individual. "That government is best which governs not at all," he said, going both Emerson and the Jeffersonians one better. He was perfectly prepared to see himself as a majority of one. "When were the good and the brave ever in a majority?" Thoreau asked. "If a man does not keep pace with his companions," he wrote on another occasion, "perhaps it is because he hears a different drummer."

In 1845 Thoreau decided to put to the test his theory that a person need not depend on society for a satisfying existence. He built a cabin at Walden Pond on some property owned by Emerson and lived there alone for two years. The best fruit of this period was that extraordinary book *Walden* (1854). Superficially, *Walden* is the story of Thoreau's experiment, movingly and beautifully written. It is also an acid indictment of the social behavior of the average American, an attack on unthinking conformity, on subordinating one's own judgment to that of the herd.

The most graphic illustration of Thoreau's confidence in his own values occurred while he was living at Walden. At that time the Mexican War was raging.

Thoreau considered the war immoral because it advanced the cause of slavery. To protest, he refused to pay his Massachusetts poll tax. For this he was arrested and lodged in jail, although only for one night because an aunt promptly paid the tax for him. His essay "Civil Disobedience," explaining his view of the proper relation between the individual and the state, resulted from this experience. Like Emerson, however, Thoreau refused to participate in practical reform movements. "I love Henry," one of his friends said, "but I cannot like him; and as for taking his arm, I should as soon think of taking the arm of an elm tree."

Edgar Allan Poe

The work of all the imaginative writers of the period reveals romantic influences, and it is possibly an indication of the affinity of the romantic approach to American conditions that a number of excellent writers of poetry and fiction first appeared in the 1830s and 1840s. Edgar Allan Poe, one of the most remarkable, seems almost a caricature of the romantic image of the tortured genius. Poe was born in Boston in 1809, the son of poor actors who died before he was three years old. He was raised by a wealthy Virginian, John Allan.

Few persons as neurotic as Poe have been able to produce first-rate work. In college he ran up debts of $2,500 in less than a year and had to withdraw. He won an appointment to West Point but was discharged after a few months for disobedience and "gross neglect of duty." He was a lifelong alcoholic and an occasional taker of drugs. He married a child of 13.

Poe was obsessed with death. Once he attempted to poison himself; repeatedly he was down and out, even to the verge of starvation. He was haunted by melancho-

In 1845 Edgar Allan Poe, impoverished and an alcoholic, was living in the "greatest wretchedness." His young wife was dying of tuberculosis. That same year he wrote "The Raven," a poem about an ill-omened bird that intrudes on a young man's grief over the death of his beloved. "Take thy beak from out of my heart" the man screams. Quoth the raven—famously— "Nevermore."

lia and hallucinations. Yet he was an excellent magazine editor, a penetrating critic, a poet of unique if somewhat narrow talents, and a fine short story writer. Although he died at age 40, he turned out a large volume of serious, highly original work.

Poe responded strongly to the lure of romanticism. His works abound with examples of wild imagination and fascination with mystery, fright, and the occult. If he did not invent the detective story, he perfected it; his tales "The Murders in the Rue Morgue" and "The Purloined Letter" stressed the thought processes of a clever detective in solving a mystery by reasoning from evidence.

Although dissolute in his personal life, when Poe touched pen to paper, he became a disciplined craftsman. The most fantastic passages in his works are the result of careful, reasoned selection; not a word, he believed, could be removed without damage to the whole. And despite his rejection of most of the values prized by middle-class America, Poe was widely read in his own day. His poem "The Raven" won instantaneous popularity when it was published in 1845. Had he been a little more stable, he might have made a good living with his pen—but in that case he might not have written as he did.

Nathaniel Hawthorne

Another product of the prevailing romanticism was Nathaniel Hawthorne, born in 1804 in Salem, Massachusetts. When Hawthorne was a small child, his father died and his grief-stricken mother became a recluse. Left largely to his own devices, he grew to be a lonely, introspective person. Wandering about New England by himself in summertime, he soaked up local lore, which he drew on in writing short stories.

Hawthorne's early stories, originally published in magazines, were brought together in *Twice-Told Tales* (1837). They made excellent use of New England culture and history for background but were concerned chiefly with the struggles of individuals with sin, guilt, and especially the pride and isolation that often afflict those who place too much reliance on their own judgment. His greatest works were two novels written after the Whigs turned him out of his government job in 1849. *The Scarlet Letter* (1850), a grim yet sympathetic analysis of adultery, condemned not the woman, Hester Prynne, but the people who presumed to judge her. *The House of the Seven Gables* (1851) was a gripping account of the decay of an old New England family brought on by the guilt feelings of the current owners of the house, caused by the way their ancestors had cheated the original owners of the property.

Herman Melville

In 1850, while Hawthorne was writing *The House of the Seven Gables*, his publisher introduced him to another writer who was in the midst of a novel. The writer was Herman Melville; the book, *Moby Dick*. Hawthorne and Melville became good friends at once, for despite their dissimilar backgrounds, they had a great deal in common. Melville was a New Yorker, born in 1819, one of eight children of a merchant of distinguished lineage. His father, however, lost all his money and died when the boy was 12. Herman left school at 15, worked briefly as a bank clerk, and in 1837 went to sea. For 18 months, in 1841 and 1842, he was crewman on the whaler *Acushnet*. Then he jumped ship in the South Seas. For a time he lived among a tribe of cannibals in the Marquesas; later he made his way to Tahiti, where he idled away nearly a year. After another year at sea he returned to America in the fall of 1844.

Although he had never before attempted serious writing, in 1846 he published *Typee*, an account of his life in the Marquesas. The book was a great success, for Melville had visited a part of the world almost unknown to Americans, and his descriptions of his bizarre experiences suited the taste of a romantic age. Success inspired him to write a sequel, *Omoo* (1847); other books followed quickly.

Experience made Melville too aware of the evil in the world to be a transcendentalist. His dark view of human nature culminated in *Moby Dick* (1851). This book, Melville said, was "broiled in hellfire." Against the background of a whaling voyage (no better account of whaling has ever been written), he dealt subtly and symbolically with the problems of good and evil, of courage and cowardice, of faith, stubbornness, pride. In Captain Ahab, driven relentlessly to hunt down the huge white whale Moby Dick, which had destroyed his leg, Melville created one of the great figures of literature; in the book as a whole, he produced one of the finest novels written by an American, comparable to the best in any language.

As Melville's work became more profound, it lost its appeal to the average reader, and its originality and symbolic meaning escaped most critics. *Moby Dick*, his masterpiece, received little attention and most of that unfavorable. He kept on writing until his death in 1891 but was virtually ignored. Only in the 1920s did the critics rediscover him and give him his merited place in the history of American literature. His "Billy Budd, Foretopman," now considered one of his best stories, was not published until 1924.

Walt Whitman

Walt Whitman, whose *Leaves of Grass* (1855) was the last of the great literary works of this brief outpouring of genius, was the most romantic and by far the most distinctly American writer of his age. He was born on Long Island, outside New York City, in 1819. At 13 he left school and worked for a printer; thereafter he held a succession of newspaper jobs in the metropolitan area.

Although genuinely a "common man," thoroughly at home among tradesmen and laborers, he was surely not an ordinary man. Deeply introspective, he read omnivorously, if in a rather disorganized fashion, while working out a new, intensely personal mode of expression. During the early 1850s, while employed as a carpenter and composing the poems that made up *Leaves of Grass*, he regularly carried a book of Emerson in his lunch box. "I was simmering, simmering, simmering," he later recalled. "Emerson brought me to a boil." The transcendental

Some scholars regard Walt Whitman as the poet of nature, and others, of the body—a reference to erotic lines such as: "Without shame the man I like knows and avows the deliciousness of his sex, / Without shame the woman I like knows and avows hers." Whitman's *Leaves of Grass* had every leaf in nature, complained critic E. P. Whipple, except the fig leaf.

idea that inspiration and aspiration are at the heart of all achievement captivated him. Poets could best express themselves, he believed, by relying uncritically on their natural inclinations without regard for rigid metrical forms.

Leaves of Grass consisted of a preface, in which Whitman made the extraordinary statement that Americans had "probably the fullest poetical nature" of any people in history, and twelve poems in free verse: rambling, uneven, appearing to most readers shocking both in the commonplace nature of the subject matter and the coarseness of the language. Emerson, Thoreau, and a few others saw a fresh talent in these poems, but most readers and reviewers found them offensive. Indeed, the work was so undisciplined and so much of it had no obvious meaning that it was easy to miss the many passages of great beauty and originality.

Whitman's work was more authentically American than that of any contemporary. His egoism—he titled one of his finest poems "Song of Myself"—was tempered by his belief that he was typical of all humanity:

> I celebrate myself and sing myself
> And what I assume you shall assume,
> For every atom belonging to me as good belongs to you.

He had a remarkable ear for rendering common speech poetically, for employing slang, for catching the breezy informality of Americans and their faith in themselves:

> Earth! you seem to look for something at my hands,
> Say, old top-knot, what do you want?
> I bequeath myself to the dirt to grow from the grass I love,
> If you want me again look for me under your boot-soles.

Because of these qualities and because in his later work, especially during the Civil War, he occasionally struck a popular chord, Whitman was never as neglected as Melville. When he died in 1892, he was, if not entirely understood, at least widely appreciated.

Education for Democracy

The literary flowering of the mid-nineteenth century did not reach a broad audience; apart from Whitman, none of the great writers of the day found a large reading audience. But although few Americans aspired to the intellectual refinement found among some European elites, literacy was expanding markedly in the United States.

Except on the edge of the frontier and in the South, most youngsters between the ages of five and ten attended a school for at least a couple of months of the year. These schools, however, were privately run and charged fees. Attendance was not required and fell off sharply once children learned to read and do their sums well enough to get along in day-to-day life. The teachers were usually young men waiting for something better to turn up.

All this changed with the rise of the common school movement. At the heart of the movement was the belief, widely expressed in the first days of the republic, that a government based on democratic rule must provide the means, as Jefferson put it, to "diffuse knowledge throughout the mass of the people." This meant free tax-supported schools, which all children were expected to attend. It also came to mean that such an educational system should be administered on a statewide basis and that teaching should become a profession that required formal training.

The two most effective leaders of the common school movement were Henry Barnard and Horace Mann. Both were New Englanders, Whigs, trained in the law, and in other ways conservative types. They shared an unquenchable faith in the improvability of the human race through education. Mann drafted the 1837 Massachusetts law creating a state school board and then became its first secretary. Over the next decade Mann's annual reports carried the case for common schools to every corner of the land. Seldom given to understatement, Mann called common schools "the greatest discovery ever made by man." He encouraged young women to become teachers while commending them to school boards by claiming that they could get along on lower salaries than men.

Young women adhered to the call. By 1860, women comprised 78 percent of the common school teachers in Massachusetts, a trend that prefigured developments elsewhere. The influx of young women invigorated the common schools and brought missionary zeal to the enterprise. Harriet Beecher Stowe, who once taught at the Hartford Seminary, explained that male teachers lacked the "patience, the long-suffering, and gentleness necessary to superintend the formation of character."

By the 1850s every state outside the South provided free elementary schools and supported institutions for training teachers. Many extended public education to include high schools, and Michigan and Iowa even established publicly supported colleges.

In addition to common schools, thousands of female seminaries were built between 1820 and 1850, many of them by evangelical denominations. During the Revolutionary Era, it was thought that half as many women were literate as men; but the Census of 1850 revealed that women's literacy equaled that of men.

The State of the Colleges

Unlike common schools, with their democratic overtones, private colleges had at best a precarious place in Jacksonian America. For one thing, there were too many of them. Any town with pretensions of becoming a regional center felt it had to have a college. Ohio had twenty-five in the 1850s, Tennessee sixteen. Many of these institutions were short-lived. Of the fourteen colleges founded in Kentucky between 1800 and 1850, only half were still operating in 1860.

The problem of supply was compounded by a demand problem—too few students. Enrollment at the largest, Yale, never topped 400 until the mid-1840s. On the eve of the Civil War the largest state university, North Carolina, had fewer than 500. Higher education was beyond the means of the average family. Although most colleges charged less than half the $55 tuition required by Harvard, that was still too much for most families, wages being what they were. So desperate was the shortage that colleges accepted applicants as young as 11 and 12 and as old as 30.

Once enrolled, students had little worry about making the grade, not least because grades were not given. Since students were hard to come by and classwork was considered relatively unimportant, discipline was lax. Official authority was frequently challenged, and rioting was known to break out over such weighty matters as the quality of meals. A father who visited his son's college dormitory in 1818 found it inhabited by "half a dozen loungers in a state of oriental lethargy, each stretched out upon two or three chairs, with scarce any indication of life in them [other] than the feeble effort to keep up the fire of their cigars."

The typical college curriculum, dominated by the study of Latin and Greek, had almost no practical relevance except for future clergymen. The Yale faculty, most of them ministers, defended the classics as admirably providing for both "the discipline and the furniture of the mind," but these subjects commended themselves to college officials chiefly because they did not require costly equipment or a faculty that knew anything else. Professors spent most of their time in and out of the classroom trying to maintain a semblance of order, "to the exclusion of any great literary undertakings to which their choice might lead them," one explained. "Our country is yet too young for old professors," a Bostonian informed a foreign visitor in the 1830s, "and, besides, they are too poorly paid to induce first rate men to devote themselves to the business of lecturing. . . . We consider professors as secondary men."

Fortunately for the future of higher education, some college officials recognized the need for a drastic overhaul of their institutions. President Francis Wayland of Brown University used his 1842 address, "On the Present Collegiate System," to call for a thorough revamping of the curriculum to make it responsive to the economic realities of American society. This meant more courses in science, economics (where Wayland's own *Elements of Political Economy* might be used), modern history, and applied mathematics; fewer in Hebrew, biblical studies, Greek, and ancient history.

Yale established a separate school of science in 1847, which it hoped would attract serious-minded students and research-minded professors. At Harvard, which also opened a scientific school, students were allowed to choose some of their courses and were compelled to earn grades as a stimulus to study. Colleges in the West and the South began to offer mechanical and agricultural subjects relevant to their regional economies. Oberlin enrolled four female students in 1837, and the first women's college, the Georgia Female College, opened its doors in 1839.

These reforms slowed the downward spiral of colleges; they did not restore them to the honored place they had enjoyed in the Revolutionary era. Of the first six presidents of the United States, only Washington did not graduate from college. Beginning in 1829, seven of the next eleven did not. In this presidents Jackson, Van Buren, Harrison, Taylor, Fillmore, Lincoln, and Johnson were like 98 of every 100 white males, all blacks and Indians, and all but a handful of white women in mid-nineteenth-century America. Going to college had yet, in Wayland's words, to "commend itself to the good sense and patriotism of the American people."

Milestones

1774	Mother Ann Lee founds first Shaker community
1784	Dr. Benjamin Rush's *Inquiry into the Effects of Ardent Spirits* questions alcohol's benefits
1826	American Temperance Union begins campaign against drunkenness
1829	Black abolitionist David Walker publishes *Appeal to the Coloured Citizens of the World*
1830s	Second Great Awakening stresses promise of salvation
	Prison reformers debate Auburn versus Philadelphia system
1830–1850	Utopian communities flourish
1830	Joseph Smith shares his "vision" in *Book of Mormon*
1831	Abolitionist William Lloyd Garrison founds *The Liberator* and the New England Anti-Slavery Society
1831–1832	Alexis de Tocqueville and Gustave de Beaumont tour America
1832	Perkins Institution for the Blind opens in Boston
1837	Illinois abolitionist Elijah Lovejoy is murdered
	Ralph Waldo Emerson delivers "The American Scholar" at Harvard
	Horace Mann and Henry Barnard call for common schools
1843	Dorothea Dix exposes treatment of the insane in *Memorial to the Legislature of Massachusetts*
1844	Margaret Fuller condemns sexual discrimination in *Women in the Nineteenth Century*
	Nauvoo mob murders Joseph Smith
1845	Frederick Douglass describes slave life in *Narrative of the Life of Frederick Douglass*
1847	Brigham Young leads Mormon migration to Great Salt Lake
1848	Elizabeth Cady Stanton and Lucretia Mott organize Seneca Falls Convention and draft Declaration of Sentiments
1850	Nathaniel Hawthorne publishes *The Scarlet Letter*
1851	Maine bans alcoholic beverages
	Herman Melville publishes *Moby Dick*
1854	Henry David Thoreau attacks conformity in *Walden*
1854–1855	Susan B. Anthony leads petition campaign against New York property and divorce laws
1855–1892	Walt Whitman publishes *Leaves of Grass* (various editions)

Westward Expansion

IN OCTOBER 2006, PRESIDENT GEORGE W. BUSH SIGNED THE Secure Fence Act, which provided for construction of a 700-mile fence stretching from Brownsville, Texas, to a western point near San Diego, California. "We must keep our borders secure," Bush explained. Every year since 2000, nearly a half million Mexicans entered the United States illegally. By 2007, the number of illegal aliens in the United States exceeded 11 million. "Ours is a nation of immigrants," Bush added, "but we're also a nation of laws." Congress concurred; the Secure Fence Act passed in the House of Representatives by a margin of 101 votes.

But throughout the debate, several historical facts went virtually unnoticed. Most ironic was the fact that the fence was to be built to prevent Mexicans from passing into lands that had once belonged to Mexico. The American Southwest, of course, had previously been occupied by Indians and their ancestors, a region that was subsequently claimed by Spain. In 1821 Mexico secured independence from Spain and claimed ownership of all of New Spain. By then, however, American settlers were flocking into the Southwest, especially Texas. In 1830, the Mexican government outlawed further American immigration into the region.

Initially the Mexican government ignored the flood of American immigrants; but by the mid-1830s it stepped up border patrols and sent an army to drive illegal immigrants from Texas. This led to clashes that culminated in war. Mexico's defeat caused a shift in boundaries. Now the Southwest belonged to the United States. Mexicans who entered the region were trespassing; in time, they would become illegal immigrants.

The Mexican War was just one of the unintended consequences of the settlement of the West. Another concerned slavery. As the United States acquired more territory and created more states, would slavery expand as well? Would the "peculiar institution" eventually stretch from the Atlantic to the Pacific and span the entire continent? The prospect disquieted many.

Tyler's Troubles

John Tyler, who became president in 1841 after the death of William Henry Harrison, was a thin, rather delicate-appearing man with pale blue eyes and a long nose. Courteous, tactful, soft-spoken, he gave the impression of being weak, an impression reinforced by his professed belief that the president should defer to Congress in the formulation of policy. This was a false impression; John Tyler was stubborn and proud, and these characteristics combined with an almost total lack of imagination to make him worship consistency, as so many second-raters do. He had turned away from Jackson because of the aggressive way the president had used his powers of appointment and the veto, but he also disagreed with Henry Clay and the northern Whigs about the Bank, protection, and federal internal improvements. Being a states' rights Southerner, he considered such measures unconstitutional. Nevertheless, he was prepared to cooperate with Clay as the leader of what he called the "more immediate representatives" of the people, the members of Congress. But he was not prepared to be Clay's puppet. He asked all of Harrison's Cabinet to remain in office.

Tyler and Clay did not get along, and for this Clay was chiefly to blame. He behaved in an overbearing manner that was out of keeping with his nature, probably because he resented having been passed over by the Whigs in 1840. In Congress, Clay announced a comprehensive program that ignored Tyler's states' rights view of the Constitution. Most important was his plan to set up a new Bank of the United States. A bill to repeal the Independent Treasury Act caused no difficulty, but when Congress passed a new Bank bill, Tyler vetoed it. The entire Cabinet except Secretary of State Daniel Webster thereupon resigned in protest.

John Tyler posed for a daguerreotypist about 1850, after he had retired from public life. Never fully committed to the cause of the party that put him in power, he proved to be an ineffective president.

Abandoned by the Whigs, Tyler attempted to build a party of his own. He failed to do so, and for the remainder of his term the political squabbling in Washington was continuous.

The Webster-Ashburton Treaty

Webster's decision to remain in the Cabinet was motivated in part by his desire to settle the boundary between Maine and New Brunswick. The intent of the peace treaty of 1783 had been to award the United States all land in the area drained by rivers flowing into the Atlantic rather than into the St. Lawrence, but the wording was obscure and the old maps conflicting. In 1842 the British sent a new minister, Lord Ashburton, to the United States to try to settle all outstanding disputes. Ashburton and Webster easily worked out a compromise boundary. Lord Ashburton, gratified by having obtained a portion of the disputed lands to build a military road, made concessions elsewhere along the Canadian and American border. British dependence on foreign foodstuffs was increasing; America's need for British capital was rising. War, or even unsettled affairs, would have injured vital business relations and produced no compensating gains.

The Texas Question

The settlement with Great Britain won support in every section of the United States, but the same could not be said for Tyler's attempt to annex the Republic of Texas, for this involved the question of slavery. In the Transcontinental Treaty of 1819 with Spain, the boundary of the United States had been drawn in such a way as to exclude Texas. This seemed unimportant at the time, yet within months of the treaty's ratification in February 1821, Americans led by Stephen F. Austin had begun to settle in the area. Almost simultaneously Mexico threw off the last vestiges of Spanish rule.

Cotton flourished on the fertile Texas plains, and for a time, the new Mexican authorities offered free land and something approaching local autonomy to groups of settlers from the United States. By 1830 there were some 20,000 white Americans in Texas, about 2,000 slaves, and only a few thousand Mexicans.

As soon as the Mexican government began to restrict them, the Texans began to seek independence. In 1835 a series of skirmishes escalated into a full-scale rebellion. The Mexican president, Antonio López de Santa Anna, marched north with 6,000 soldiers to subdue the rebels. Late in February 1836 he reached San Antonio.

A force of 187 men under Colonel William B. Travis held the city. They took refuge behind the stout walls of a former mission called the Alamo. For ten days they beat off Santa Anna's assaults, inflicting terrible casualties on the attackers. Finally, on March 6, the Mexicans breached and scaled the walls. Once inside they killed everyone, even the wounded. Among the dead were the legendary Davy Crockett and Jim Bowie, inventor of the Bowie knife.

After the Alamo and a similar slaughter at another garrison at Goliad, southeast of San Antonio, peaceful settlement of the dispute between Texas and Mexico was impossible. Meanwhile, on March 2, 1836, Texas had declared its independence. Sam Houston, a former congressman and governor of Tennessee and an experienced Indian fighter, was placed in charge of the rebel army. For a time Houston retreated before Santa Anna's troops, who greatly outnumbered his own. At the San Jacinto River he took a stand. On April 21, 1836, shouting "Forward! Charge! Remember the Alamo! Remember Goliad!" his troops routed the Mexican army, which soon retreated across the Rio Grande. In October, Houston was elected president of the Republic of Texas, and a month later a plebiscite revealed that an overwhelming majority favored annexation by the United States.

President Jackson hesitated. To take Texas might lead to war with Mexico. Assuredly it would stir up the slavery controversy. On his last day in office he recognized the republic, but he made no move to accept it into the Union, nor did his successor, Van Buren. Texas thereupon went its own way, which involved developing friendly ties with Great Britain. An independent Texas suited British tastes perfectly, for it could provide an alternative supply of raw cotton and a market for manufactures unfettered by tariffs.

These events caused alarm in the United States, especially among Southerners, who dreaded the possibility that a Texas dominated by Great Britain might abolish slavery. As a Southerner, Tyler shared these feelings; as a beleaguered politician, spurned by the Whigs and held in contempt by most Democrats, he saw in annexation a chance to revive his fortunes. When Webster resigned as secretary of state in 1843, Tyler replaced him with a fellow Virginian, Abel P. Upshur, whom he ordered to seek a treaty of annexation. The South was eager to take Texas, and in the West and even the Northeast the patriotic urge to add such a magnificent new territory to the national domain was great. Counting noses, Upshur convinced himself that the Senate would approve annexation by the necessary two-thirds majority. He negotiated a treaty in February 1844, but before he could sign it he was killed by the accidental explosion of a cannon on the USS *Princeton* during a weapons demonstration.

To ensure the winning of Texas, Tyler appointed John C. Calhoun secretary of state. This was a blunder; by then Calhoun was so closely associated with the South and with slavery that his appointment alienated thousands of Northerners who might otherwise have welcomed annexation. Suddenly Texas became a hot political issue. Clay and Van Buren, who seemed assured of the 1844 Whig and Democratic presidential nominations, promptly announced that they opposed annexation, chiefly on the ground that it would probably lead to war with Mexico. With a national election in the offing, northern and western senators refused to vote for annexation, and in June the Senate rejected the treaty, 35 to 16. The Texans were angry and embarrassed, the British eager again to take advantage of the situation.

Manifest Destiny

The Senate, Clay, and Van Buren had all misinterpreted public opinion. Where pioneers had once stood in awe before the majesty of the Blue Ridge, then hesitated to venture from the protective shadows of the forest into the open prairies of Illinois, they now shrugged their shoulders at great deserts and began to talk of the Rocky Mountains as "mere molehills" along the road to the Pacific. After 200 years of westward expansion had brought them as far as Missouri and Iowa, Americans perceived their destined goal. *The whole continent was to be theirs!* Theirs to exploit, and theirs to make into one mighty nation, a land of opportunity, a showcase to display the virtues of democratic institutions, living proof that Americans were indeed God's chosen people. A New York journalist, John L. O'Sullivan, captured the new mood in a sentence. Nothing must interfere, he wrote in 1845, with "the fulfillment of our *manifest destiny* to overspread the continent allotted by Providence for the free development of our yearly multiplying millions."

The expansion, stimulated by the natural growth of the population and by a revived flood of immigration, was going on in every section and with little regard for political boundaries. New settlers rolled westward in hordes. Between 1830 and 1835, some 10,000 entered "foreign" Texas, and this was a trickle compared to what the early 1840s were to bring. The politicians did not sense the new mood in 1844; even Calhoun, who saw the acquisition of Texas as part of a broader program, was thinking of balancing sectional interests rather than of national expansion.

Life on the Trail

The romantic myths attached by later generations to this mighty human tide have obscured the adjustments forced on the pioneers and focused attention on the least significant of the dangers they faced and the hardships they endured. For example, Indians could of course be deadly enemies, but pioneers were more likely to complain that the Indians they encountered were dirty, lazy, and pitiably poor than to worry about the danger of Indian attack. Women tended to fear their strangeness, not their actual behavior. One reported that Indian men were commonly "guiltless of clothing."

The greater dangers were accidents on the trail, particularly to children, and also unsanitary conditions and exposure to the elements. "Going west" had always been laborious, but in the 1840s the distances covered were longer by far and the comforts and conveniences of "civilization" that had to be left behind, being more extensive than those available to earlier generations, tended to be more painful to surrender.

Travel on the plains west of the Mississippi was especially taxing for women. Some assumed tasks traditionally performed by men. "I keep close to my gun and dog," a woman from Illinois wrote in her diary. But most found the experience disillusioning. Guidebooks promised them that "regular exercise, in the open air . . .

DID THE FRONTIER CHANGE WOMEN'S ROLES?

Debating the Past

Ada McColl here gathers buffalo chips to be burned for fuel. She and all other frontier women were missing from Frederick Jackson Turner's famous argument (1893) on the centrality of the frontier to American history. Subsequent scholars provided some anecdotal accounts of women on the frontier, but it was not until the 1970s, when feminism moved to the center of national debate, that scholars flocked to the subject. In a study of letters and diaries, John Mack Faragher (1979) concluded that women on the overland trail had not experienced feminist liberation but had instead been exploited. The men's tasks of herding animals and overcoming streams and boulders allowed occasional respites, but women worked ceaselessly—preparing meals, caring for children, cleaning clothes—in nearly impossible conditions. That same year Julie Roy Jeffrey drew a similar picture. Although women were "co-partners in the frontier adventure," husbands still made the "major decisions." Equally important, frontier women themselves endorsed the "cult of true womanhood": the woman's role was to elevate human affairs. Such women sought to civilize the frontier. Sandra L. Myres (1982), on the other hand, argued that while frontier women accepted traditional women's roles, they also sought to "enlarge the scope of women's place" and in so doing undermined traditions. Research in the 1990s has altered this picture. On the frontier, land was power. Elaine Lindgren (1991) and Katherine Harris (1993) have shown that women often acquired land and managed it effectively.

Frederick Jackson Turner, "The Significance of the Frontier in American History" (1893), John Mack Faragher, *Women and Men on the Overland Trail* (1979), Julie Roy Jeffrey, *Frontier Women* (1979), Sandra L. Myres, *Westering Women and the Frontier Experience* (1982), Elaine Lindgren, *Land in Her Own Name* (1991), Katherine Harris, *Long Vistas* (1993).

gives additional vigor and strength." But the books did not prepare women for collecting dried buffalo dung for fuel, for the heat and choking dust of summer, for the monotony, the dirt, the cramped quarters. Caring for an infant or a two-year-old in a wagon could be torture week after week on the trail.

In their letters and journals pioneer women mostly complained of being bone weary. "It is impossible to keep anything clean," one recorded. "Oh dear," another wrote in her journal, "I do so want to get there, it is now almost four months since we have slept in a house." What sort of a house a pioneer family would actually sleep in when they reached their destination is a question this woman did not record, which was probably fortunate for her peace of mind.

California and Oregon

By 1840 many Americans had settled far to the west in California, which was unmistakably Mexican territory, and in the Oregon country, jointly claimed by the United States and Great Britain; and it was to these distant regions that the pioneers were going in increasing numbers as the decade progressed. California was a sparsely settled land of some 7,000 Spanish-speaking ranchers and a handful of "Anglo" settlers from the United States. Until the 1830s, when their estates were broken up by the anticlerical Mexican government, twenty-one Catholic missions, stretching north from San Diego to San Francisco, controlled more than 30,000 Indian converts, who were little better off than slaves.

Oregon, a vaguely defined area between California and Russian Alaska, proved still more alluring to Americans. Captain Robert Gray had sailed up the Columbia River in 1792, and Lewis and Clark had visited the region on their great expedition. In 1811 John Jacob Astor's Pacific Fur Company had established trading posts on the Columbia. Two decades later Methodist, Presbyterian, and Catholic missionaries began to find their way into the Willamette Valley, a green land of rich soil, mild climate, and tall forests teeming with game. Gradually a small number of settlers followed, until by 1840 there were about 500 Americans in the Willamette area.

In the early 1840s, fired by the spirit of manifest destiny, the country suddenly burned with "Oregon fever." In dozens upon dozens of towns, societies were founded to collect information and organize groups to make the march to the Pacific. Land hunger (stimulated by glowing reports from the scene) drew the new migrants most powerfully, but the patriotic concept of manifest destiny gave the trek across the 2,000 miles of wilderness separating Oregon from the western edge of American settlement in Missouri the character of a crusade. In 1843 nearly 1,000 pioneers made the long trip.

The Oregon Trail began at the western border of Missouri and followed the Kansas River and the perverse, muddy Platte ("a mile wide and six inches deep") past Fort Laramie to the Rockies. It crossed the Continental Divide by the relatively easy South Pass, veered south to Fort Bridger, on Mexican soil, and then ran north and west through the valley of the Snake River and eventually, by way of the Columbia, to Fort Vancouver, a British post guarding the entrance to the Willamette Valley.

Over this tortuous path wound the canvas-covered caravans with their scouts and their accompanying herds. Each group became a self-governing community on the march, with regulations democratically agreed on "for the purpose of keeping good order and promoting civil and military discipline." Most of the travelers consisted of young families, some from as far away as the east coast cities, more from towns and farms in the Ohio Valley. Few could be classified as poor because the cost of the trip for a family of four was about $600, no small sum at that time. (The faster and less fatiguing trip by ship around South America cost about $600 per person.)

For large groups Indians posed no great threat (though constant vigilance was necessary), but the five-month trip was full of labor, discomfort, and uncertainty. "It became so monotonous after a while that I would have welcomed an Indian fight if

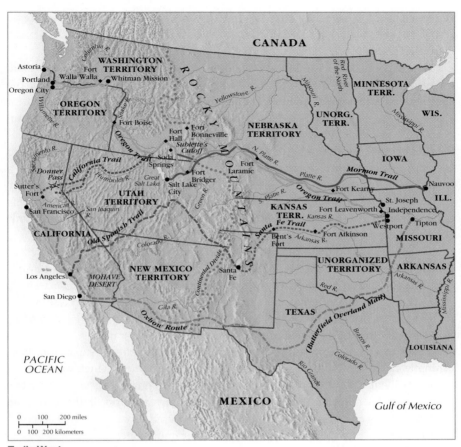

Trails West

The Old Spanish Trail was the earliest of the trails west. Part of it was mapped in 1776 by a Franciscan missionary. The Santa Fe Trail came into use after 1823. The Oregon Trail was pioneered by trappers and missionaries. The Mormon Trail was first traversed in 1847, while the Oxbow Route, developed under a federal mail contract, was used from 1858 to 1861.

awake," one man wrote. And at the end lay the regular tasks of pioneering. The spirit of the trailblazers is caught in an entry from the diary of James Nesmith:

> *Friday, October 27.—Arrived at Oregon City at the falls of the Willamette.*
> *Saturday, October 28.—Went to work.*

The Election of 1844

In the spring of 1844 expansion did not seem likely to affect the presidential election. The Whigs nominated Clay unanimously and ignored Texas in their party platform. When the Democrats gathered in convention at Baltimore in May, Van

Buren appeared to have the nomination in his pocket. He too wanted to keep Texas out of the campaign. John C. Calhoun, however, was determined to make Texas a campaign issue.

That a politician of Van Buren's caliber, controlling the party machinery, could be upset at a national convention seemed unthinkable. But upset he was, for the southern delegates rallied round the Calhoun policy of taking Texas to save it for slavery. "I can beat Clay and Van Buren put together on this issue," Calhoun boasted. "They are behind the age." With the aid of a few northern expansionists the Southerners forced through a rule requiring that a candidate must be approved by a two-thirds majority. Van Buren could not muster that much support. After a brief deadlock, a "dark horse," James K. Polk of Tennessee, swept the convention.

Polk was a good Jacksonian; his supporters called him "Young Hickory." He opposed high tariffs and was dead set against establishing another national bank. But he believed in taking Texas, and he favored expansion generally.

Texas was now in the campaign. When Clay sensed the new expansionist sentiment of the voters, he tried to hedge on his opposition to annexation, but by doing so he probably lost as many votes as he gained. The election was extremely close. The campaign followed the pattern established in 1840, with stress on parades, mass meetings, and slogans. Polk carried the country by only 38,000 of 2.7 million votes. In the Electoral College the vote was 170 to 105.

Polk's narrow victory was nevertheless taken as a mandate for expansion. Tyler promptly called on Congress to take Texas by joint resolution, which would avoid the necessity of obtaining a two-thirds majority in the Senate. This was done a few days before Tyler left the White House. Under the resolution, if the new state agreed, as many as four new states might be carved from its territory. Polk accepted this arrangement, and in December 1845 Texas became a state.

Polk as President

President Polk, a slightly built, erect man with grave, steel-gray eyes, was approaching 50 years of age. His mind was not of the first order, for he was too tense and calculating to allow his intellect free rein, but he was an efficient, hard worker with a strong will and a tough skin, qualities that stood him in good stead in the White House, and he made politics his whole life.

Oregon was the first order of business. In his inaugural address Polk stated the American claim to the entire region in the plainest terms, but he informed the British minister in Washington, Richard Pakenham, that he would accept a boundary following the 49th parallel to the Pacific. Pakenham rejected this proposal without submitting it to London, and Polk thereupon decided to insist again on the whole area. When Congress met in December 1845, he asked for authority to give the necessary one year's notice for abrogating the 1818 treaty of joint occupation. "The only way to treat John Bull," he told one congressman, "was to look him straight in the eye." Following considerable discussion, Congress complied and in May 1846 Polk notified Great Britain that he intended to terminate the joint occupation.

The British then decided to compromise. Officials of the Hudson's Bay Company had become alarmed by the rapid growth of the American settlement in the Willamette Valley. By 1845 there were some 5,000 people there, whereas the country north of the Columbia contained no more than 750 British subjects. A clash between the groups could have but one result. The company decided to shift its base from the Columbia to Vancouver Island. And British experts outside the company reported that the Oregon country could not possibly be defended in case of war. Thus, when Polk accompanied the one-year notice with a hint that he would again consider a compromise, the British foreign secretary, Lord Aberdeen, hastily suggested Polk's earlier proposal, dividing the Oregon territory along the 49th parallel. Polk, abandoning his belligerent attitude, agreed. The treaty followed that line from the Rockies to Puget Sound, but Vancouver Island, which extends below the line, was left entirely to the British, so that both nations retained free use of the Strait of Juan de Fuca. Although some northern Democrats accused Polk of treachery because he had failed to fight for all of Oregon, the treaty so obviously accorded with the national interest that the Senate approved it by a large majority in June 1846. Polk was then free to take up the Texas question in earnest.

War with Mexico

One reason for the popularity of the Oregon compromise was that the country was already at war with Mexico and wanted no trouble with Great Britain. The war had broken out in large measure because of the expansionist spirit, and the confidence born of its overwhelming advantages of size and wealth certainly encouraged the United States to bully Mexico. In addition, Mexico had defaulted on debts owed the United States, which caused some people to suggest using force to obtain the money. But Mexican pride was also involved. Texas had been independent for the better part of a decade, and Mexico had made no serious effort to reconquer it; nevertheless, Mexico never recognized its independence and promptly broke off diplomatic relations when the United States annexed the republic.

Polk then ordered General Zachary Taylor into Texas to defend the border. However, the location of that border was in dispute. Texas claimed the Rio Grande; Mexico insisted that the boundary was the Nueces River, which emptied into the Gulf of Mexico about 150 miles to the north. Taylor reached the Nueces in July 1845 with about 1,500 troops and crossed into the disputed territory. He stopped on the southern bank at Corpus Christi, not wishing to provoke the Mexicans by marching to the Rio Grande.

Polk had already ordered Taylor to advance to the Rio Grande. By late March 1846 the army, swelled to about 4,000, had taken up positions near the Mexican town of Matamoros. The Mexicans crossed the river on April 25 and attacked an American mounted patrol. They were driven back easily, but when news of the fighting reached Washington, Polk asked Congress to declare war. He treated the matter as a *fait accompli*: "War exists," he stated flatly. Congress accepted this reasoning and without actually declaring war voted to raise and supply an additional 50,000 troops.

From the first battle, the outcome of the Mexican War was never in doubt. At Palo Alto, north of the Rio Grande, 2,300 Americans scattered a Mexican force more than twice their number. Then, hotly pursuing, 1,700 Americans routed 7,500 Mexicans at Resaca de la Palma. Fewer than fifty U.S. soldiers lost their lives in these engagements, while Mexican losses in killed, wounded, and captured exceeded 1,000. Within a week of the outbreak of hostilities, the Mexicans had been driven across the Rio Grande and General Taylor had his troops firmly established on the southern bank.

To the Halls of Montezuma

President Polk insisted not only on directing grand strategy (he displayed real ability as a military planner) but on supervising hundreds of petty details, down to the purchase of mules and the promotion of enlisted men. But he allowed party considerations to control his choice of generals. This partisanship caused unnecessary turmoil in army ranks. He wanted, as Thomas Hart Benton said, "a small war, just large enough to require a treaty of peace, and not large enough to make military reputations dangerous for the presidency."

Unfortunately for Polk, both Taylor and Winfield Scott, the commanding general in Washington, were Whigs. Polk, who tended to suspect the motives of anyone who disagreed with him, feared that one or the other would make political capital of his popularity as a military leader. The examples of his hero, Jackson, and of General Harrison loomed large in Polk's thinking.

The dust had barely settled on the field of Buena Vista when Whig politicians began to pay Taylor court. "Great expectations and great consequences rest upon

This 1846 daguerreotype is the earliest known American war photograph. U.S. General John E. Wood poses with his staff in Saltillo, Mexico.

you," a Kentucky politician explained to him. "People everywhere begin to talk of converting you into a political leader, when the War is done."

Polk's concern was heightened because domestic opposition to the war was growing. Many Northerners feared that the war would lead to the expansion of slavery. Others—among them an obscure Illinois congressman named Abraham Lincoln—felt that Polk had misled Congress about the original outbreak of fighting and that the United States was the aggressor. The farther from the Rio Grande one went in the United States, the less popular "Mr. Polk's war" became; in New England opposition was almost as widespread as it had been to "Mr. Madison's war" in 1812.

Polk's design for prosecuting the war consisted of three parts. First, he would clear the Mexicans from Texas and occupy the northern provinces of Mexico. Second, he would take possession of California and New Mexico. Finally, he would march on Mexico City. Proceeding west from the Rio Grande, Taylor swiftly overran Mexico's northern provinces. In June 1846, American settlers in the Sacramento Valley seized Sonoma and raised the Bear Flag of the Republic of California. Another group, headed by Captain John C. Frémont, leader of an American exploring party that happened to be in the area, clashed with the Mexican authorities around Monterey, California, and then joined with the Sonoma rebels. A naval squadron under Commodore John D. Sloat captured Monterey and San Francisco in July 1846, and a squadron of cavalry joined the other American units in mopping-up operations around San Diego and Los Angeles. By February 1847 the United States had won control of nearly all of Mexico north of the capital city.

The campaign against Mexico City was the most difficult of the war. Fearful of Taylor's growing popularity and entertaining certain honest misgivings about his ability to oversee a complicated campaign, Polk put Winfield Scott in charge of the offensive.

Scott landed his army south of Vera Cruz, Mexico, on March 9, 1847, laid siege to the city, and obtained its surrender in less than three weeks with the loss of only a handful of his 10,000 men. Marching westward through hostile country, he maintained effective discipline, avoiding atrocities that might have inflamed the countryside against him. Finding his way blocked by well-placed artillery and a large army at Cerro Gordo, where the National Road rose steeply toward the central highlands, Scott outflanked the Mexican position and then carried it by storm, capturing more than 3,000 prisoners and much equipment. By mid-May he had advanced to Puebla, only 80 miles southeast of Mexico City.

After delaying until August for the arrival of reinforcements, he pressed on, won two hard-fought victories at the outskirts of the capital, and on September 14 hammered his way into the city. In every engagement the American troops had been outnumbered, yet they always exacted a far heavier toll from the defenders than they themselves were forced to pay. In the fighting on the edge of Mexico City, for example, Scott's army sustained about 1,000 casualties, for the Mexicans defended their capital bravely. But 4,000 Mexicans were killed or wounded in the

The War with Mexico, 1846–1848

engagements, and 3,000 (including eight generals, two of them former presidents of the republic) were taken prisoner. No less an authority than the Duke of Wellington, the conqueror of Napoleon, called Scott's campaign the most brilliant of modern times.

The Treaty of Guadalupe Hidalgo

The Mexicans were thoroughly beaten, but they refused to accept the situation. Early in February the Treaty of Guadalupe Hidalgo was completed. By its terms Mexico accepted the Rio Grande as the boundary of Texas and ceded New Mexico and Upper California to the United States. In return the United States agreed to pay Mexico $15 million and to take on the claims of American citizens against Mexico, which by that time amounted to another $3.25 million.

The relatively easy military victory made some people ashamed that their country was crushing a weaker neighbor. Abolitionists, led by William Lloyd Garrison, called it an "invasion . . . waged solely for the detestable and horrible purpose of extending and perpetuating American slavery." The Senate, subject to the same pressures as the president, ratified the agreement by a vote of 38 to 14.

The Fruits of Victory: Further Enlargement of the United States

The Mexican War, won quickly and at relatively small cost in lives and money, brought huge territorial gains. The Pacific coast from south of San Diego to the 49th parallel and all the land between the coast and the Continental Divide had become the property of the American people. Immense amounts of labor and capital would have to be invested before this new territory could be made to yield its bounty, but the country clearly had the capacity to accomplish the job.

PLUCKED :
OR,

THE MEXICAN EAGLE BEFORE THE WAR!   THE MEXICAN EAGLE AFTER THE WAR!

An 1847 cartoon chortling over Mexico's defeat. Sam Houston captured the jingoistic sentiment of the moment: "The Mexicans, are no better than Indians," he said, "and I see no reason why we should not go on in the same course now, and take their land."

In this atmosphere came what seemed a sign from the heavens. In January 1848, while Scott's veterans rested on their victorious arms in Mexico City, a mechanic named James W. Marshall was building a sawmill on the American River in the Sacramento Valley east of San Francisco. One day, while supervising the deepening of the millrace, he noticed a few flecks of yellow in the bed of the stream. These he gathered up and tested. They were pure gold.

Other strikes had been made in California and been treated skeptically or as matters of local curiosity; since the days of Jamestown, too many pioneers had run fruitlessly in search of El Dorado, and too much fool's gold had been passed off as the real thing. Yet this discovery produced an international sensation. The gold was real and plentiful—$200 million of it was extracted in four years—but equally important was the fact that everyone was ready to believe the news. The gold rush reflected the heady confidence inspired by Guadalupe Hidalgo; it seemed the ultimate justification of manifest destiny. Surely an era of continental prosperity and harmony had dawned.

Slavery: The Storm Clouds Gather

Prosperity came in full measure but harmony did not, for once again expansion brought the nation face to face with the divisive question of slavery. This giant chunk of North America, most of it vacant, its future soon to be determined—should it be slave or free? The question, in one sense, seems hardly worth the national crisis it provoked. Slavery appeared to have little future in New Mexico and California, none in Oregon. Why did the South fight so hard for the right to bring slaves into a region that seemed so poorly suited to their exploitation?

Narrow partisanship provides part of the explanation. In districts where slavery was entrenched, a congressman who zealously defended the institution against the most trivial slight usually found himself a popular hero. In the northern states, the representatives who were vigilant in what they might describe as "freedom's cause" seldom regretted it on election day. But slavery raised a moral question. Most Americans tried to avoid confronting this truth; as patriots they assumed that any sectional issue could be solved by compromise. However, while the majority of whites had little respect for blacks, slave or free, few persons, northern or southern, could look upon the ownership of one human being by another as simply an alternative form of economic organization and argue its merits as they would those of the protective tariff or a national bank. Twist the facts as they might, slavery was either right or it was wrong; being on the whole honest and moral, they could not, having faced that truth, stand by unconcerned while the question was debated.

The question could come up in Congress only indirectly, for the Constitution did not give the federal government any control over slavery in the states. But Congress had complete control in the territories. Therefore the fact that slavery had no future in the Mexican cession was unimportant—in fact, for the foes of slavery, it was an advantage. By attacking slavery where it did not and probably never could exist, they could conceal from the slaveholders—and perhaps even from themselves—their hope ultimately to extinguish the institution.

Slavery had complicated the Texas problem from the start, and it beclouded the future of the Southwest even before the Mexican flag had been stripped from the staffs at Santa Fe and Los Angeles. On August 8, 1846, during the debate on a bill appropriating money for the conduct of the war, Democratic Congressman David Wilmot of Pennsylvania introduced an amendment that provided "as an express and fundamental condition to the acquisition of any territory from the Republic of Mexico" that "neither slavery nor involuntary servitude shall ever exist in any part of said territory".

Southerners found the Wilmot Proviso particularly insulting. Nevertheless, it passed the House, where northern congressmen outnumbered southern. But it was defeated in the Senate, where Southerners held the balance. To counter the Proviso, Calhoun, once again serving as senator from South Carolina, introduced resolutions in 1846 arguing that Congress had no right to bar slavery from any territory; because territories belonged to all the states, slave and free, all should have equal rights in them. From this position it was only a step (soon taken) to demanding that Congress guarantee the right of slave owners to bring slaves into the territories and establish federal slave codes in the territories. Most Northerners considered this proposal as repulsive as Southerners found the Wilmot Proviso.

Calhoun's resolutions could never pass the House of Representatives, and Wilmot's Proviso had no chance in the Senate. Yet their very existence threatened the Union; as Senator Benton remarked, they were like the blades of a pair of scissors, ineffective separately, an efficient cutting tool taken together.

To resolve the territorial problem, two compromises were offered. One, eventually backed by President Polk, would extend the Missouri Compromise line to the Pacific. The majority of Southerners were willing to go along with this scheme, but most Northerners would no longer agree to the reservation of *any* new territory for slavery. The other possibility, advocated by Senator Lewis Cass of Michigan, called for organizing new territories without mention of slavery, thus leaving it to local settlers, through their territorial legislatures, to determine their own institutions. Cass's "popular sovereignty," known more vulgarly as "squatter sovereignty," had the superficial merit of appearing to be democratic. Its virtue for the members of Congress, however, was that it allowed them to escape the responsibility of deciding the question themselves.

The Election of 1848

Plainly the time had come, in a democracy, to go to the people. The coming presidential election seemed to provide an ideal opportunity.

The opportunity was missed. The politicians of the parties hedged, fearful of losing votes in one section or another. With the issues blurred, voters had no real choice. That the Whigs should behave in such a manner was perhaps to be expected of the party of "Tippecanoe and Tyler Too," but in 1848 they outdid even their 1840 performance, nominating Zachary Taylor for president. They chose the general despite his lack of political sophistication and after he had flatly refused to state his opinion on any current subject. The party offered no platform. Taylor was a brave man and a fine general; the Democrats had mistreated him; he was a common, ordinary fellow, unpretentious and warmhearted. Such was the Whig "argument." Taylor's contribution to the campaign was so naive as to be pathetic. "I am a Whig, *but not an ultra Whig*. . . . If elected . . . I should feel bound to administer the government untrammeled by party schemes."

The Democratic nominee was Lewis Cass, the father of popular sovereignty, but the party did not endorse that or any other solution to the territorial question. Cass was at least an experienced politician, having been governor of the Michigan Territory, secretary of war, minister to France, and senator.

The Van Buren wing of the Democratic party was known as the Barnburners to call attention to their radicalism—supposedly they would burn down the barn to get rid of the rats. The Barnburners could not stomach Cass's willingness to countenance the extension of slavery into new territories. Combining with the antislavery Liberty party, they formed the Free Soil party and nominated Van Buren.

Van Buren knew he could not be elected, but he believed the time had come to take a stand. "The minds of nearly all mankind have been penetrated by a conviction of the evils of slavery," the onetime "Fox" and "Magician" declared. The Free Soil party polled nearly 300,000 votes, about 10 percent of the total, in a very dull campaign. Offered a choice between the honest ignorance of Taylor and the cynical opportunism of Cass, the voters—by a narrow margin—chose the former, Taylor receiving 1.36 million votes to Cass's 1.22 million. Taylor carried eight of the fifteen slave states and seven of the fifteen free states, proof that the sectional issue had been avoided. The chief significance of the election was the growing strength of the antislavery forces; in the next decade, this would bring about the collapse of the second party system.

The Gold Rush

The question of slavery in the territories could no longer be deferred. The discovery of gold had brought an army of prospectors into California. By the summer of 1848 San Francisco had become almost a ghost town, and an estimated two-thirds of the adult males of Oregon had hastened south to the gold fields. After President Polk confirmed the "extraordinary character" of the strike in his annual message of December 1848, there was no containing the gold seekers. During 1849, some 25,000 Americans made their way to California from the East by ship; more than 55,000 others crossed the continent by overland routes. About 8,000 Mexicans, 5,000 South Americans, and numbers of Europeans joined the rush.

The rough limits of the gold country had been quickly marked out. For 150 miles and more along the western slope of the Sierra stretched the great mother lode. Along the expanse any stream or canyon, any ancient gravel bed might conceal a treasure in nuggets, flakes, or dust. Armed with pickaxes and shovels, with washing pans, even with knives and spoons, eager prospectors hacked and dug and sifted, each accumulating a hoard, some great, some small, of gleaming yellow metal.

The impact on the region was enormous. Between 1849 and 1860 about 200,000 people, nearly all of them males, crossed the Rockies to California and thousands more reached California by ship via Cape Horn. Almost overnight the Spanish American population was reduced to the status of a minority. Disregarding justice and reason alike, the newcomers from the East, as one observer noted, "regarded every man but a native [North] American as an interloper." They referred to people of Latin American origin as "greasers" and sought by law and by violence to keep them from mining for gold. Even the local Californians (now American citizens) were discriminated against. The few free blacks in California and the several thousand more who came in search of gold were treated no better. As for the far larger Indian population, it was almost wiped out. There were about 150,000 Indians in California in the mid-1840s but only 35,000 in 1860.

The ethnic conflict was only part of the problem. Rough, hard men, separated from women, lusting for gold in a strange wild country where fortunes could be made in a day, gambled away in an hour, or stolen in an instant—the situation demanded the establishment of a territorial government. President Taylor appreciated this, and in his gruff, simple-hearted way he suggested an uncomplicated answer: admit California directly as a state, letting the Californians decide for themselves about slavery. The rest of the Mexican cession could be formed into another state. No need for Congress, with its angry rivalries, to meddle at all, he believed. In this way the nation could avoid the divisive effects of sectional debate.

The Californians reacted favorably to Taylor's proposal. They were overwhelmingly opposed to slavery, though not for humanitarian reasons. On the contrary, they tended to look on blacks as they did Mexicans and feared that if slavery were permitted, white gold seekers would be disadvantaged. "They would be unable," one delegate to the California constitutional convention predicted, "to compete with the bands of negroes who would be set to work under the direction of capitalists. It would become a monopoly." By October 1849 they had drawn up a constitution that outlawed slavery, and by December the new state government was functioning.

Taylor was the owner of a large plantation and more than 100 slaves; Southerners had assumed (without bothering to ask) that he would fight to keep the territories open to slavery. But being a military man, he was above all a nationalist; he disliked the divisiveness that partisan discussion of the issue was producing. Southerners were horrified by the president's reasoning. To admit California

Gold prospectors used a "long Tom" to wash gold from gravel in a stream. The California gold rush brought mostly men—along with a few women—west in search of their fortunes.

would destroy the balance between free and slave states in the Senate; to allow all the new land to become free would doom the South to wither in a corner of the country, surrounded by hostile free states. Should that happen, how long could slavery sustain itself, even in South Carolina? Radicals were already saying that the South would have to choose between secession and surrender. Taylor's plan played into the hands of extremists.

The Compromise of 1850

This was no longer a squabble over territorial governments. With the Union itself at stake, Henry Clay rose to save the day. He had been as angry and frustrated when the Whigs nominated Taylor as he had been when they passed him over for Harrison. Now, well beyond age 70 and in ill health, he put away his ambition and his resentment and for the last time concentrated his remarkable vision on a great, multifaceted national problem. California must be free and soon admitted to the Union, but the South must have some compensation. For that matter, why not seize the opportunity to settle every outstanding sectional conflict related to slavery? Clay wondered long and hard, drew up a plan, then consulted his old Whig rival Webster and obtained his general approval. On January 29, 1850, he laid his proposal, "founded upon mutual forbearance," before the Senate. A few days later he defended it on the floor of the Senate in the last great speech of his life.

California should be brought directly into the Union as a free state, he argued. The rest of the Southwest should be organized as a territory without mention of slavery: The Southerners would retain the right to bring slaves there, while in fact none would do so. "You have got what is worth more than a thousand Wilmot Provisos," Clay pointed out to his northern colleagues. "You have nature on your side." Empty lands in dispute along the Texas border should be assigned to the New Mexico Territory, Clay continued, but in exchange the United States should take over Texas's preannexation debts. The slave trade should be abolished in the District of Columbia (but not slavery itself), and a more effective federal fugitive slave law should be enacted and strictly enforced in the North.

Clay's proposals occasioned one of the most magnificent debates in the history of the Senate. Every important member had his say. Calhoun, perhaps even more than Clay, realized that the future of the nation was at stake and that his own days were numbered (he died four weeks later). He was so feeble that he could not deliver his speech himself. He sat impassive, wrapped in a great cloak, gripping the arms of his chair, while Senator James M. Mason of Virginia read it to the crowded Senate. Calhoun thought his plan would save the Union, but his speech was an argument for secession; he demanded that the North yield completely on every point, ceasing even to discuss the question of slavery. Clay's compromise was unsatisfactory; he himself had no other to offer. If you will not yield, he said to the northern senators, "let the States . . . agree to separate and part in peace. If you are unwilling we should part in peace, tell us so, and we shall know what to do."

Three days later, on March 7, Daniel Webster took the floor. He too had begun to fail. Years of heavy drinking and other forms of self-indulgence had taken their toll. The brilliant volubility and the thunder were gone, and when he spoke his face was bathed in sweat and there were strange pauses in his delivery. But his argument was lucid. Clay's proposals should be adopted. Since the future of all the territories had already been fixed by geographic and economic factors, the Wilmot Proviso was unnecessary. The North's constitutional obligation to yield fugitive slaves, he said, braving the wrath of New England abolitionists, was "binding in honor and conscience." (A cynic might say that once again Webster was placing property rights above human rights.) The Union, he continued, could not be sundered without bloodshed. At the thought of that dread possibility, the old fire flared: "Peaceable secession!" Webster exclaimed, "Heaven forbid! Where is the flag of the republic to remain? Where is the eagle still to tower?" The debate did not end with the aging giants. Every possible viewpoint was presented, argued, rebutted, rehashed. Senator William H. Seward of New York, a new Whig leader, close to Taylor's ear, caused a stir while arguing against concessions to the slave interests by saying that despite the constitutional obligation to return fugitive slaves, a "higher law" than the Constitution, the law of God, forbade anything that countenanced the evil of slavery.

The majority clearly favored some compromise, but nothing could have been accomplished without the death of President Taylor on July 9, 1850. Obstinate,

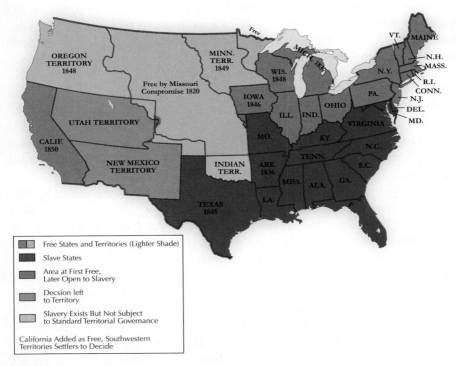

Free States and Territories (Lighter Shade)

Slave States

Area at First Free,
Later Open to Slavery

Decsion left
to Territory

Slavery Exists But Not Subject
to Standard Territorial Governance

California Added as Free, Southwestern
Territories Settlers to Decide

Compromise of 1850

probably resentful because few people paid him half the heed they paid Clay and other prominent members of Congress, the president had insisted on his own plan to bring both California and New Mexico directly into the Union. When Vice President Millard Fillmore, who was a politician, not an ideologue, succeeded Taylor, the deadlock between the White House and Capitol Hill was broken.

In the Senate and then in the House, tangled combinations pushed through the separate measures, one by one. California became the thirty-first state. The rest of the Mexican cession was divided into two territories, New Mexico and Utah, each to be admitted to the Union when qualified, "with or without slavery as [its] constitution may prescribe." Texas received $10 million to pay off its debt in return for accepting a narrower western boundary. The slave trade in the District of Columbia was abolished as of January 1, 1851. The Fugitive Slave Act of 1793 was amended to provide for the appointment of federal commissioners with authority to issue warrants, summon posses, and compel citizens under pain of fine or imprisonment to assist in the capture of fugitives. Commissioners who decided that an accused person was a runaway received a larger fee than if they declared the person legally free. The accused could not testify in their own defense. They were to be returned to the South without jury trial merely on the submission of an affidavit by their "owner."

In this piecemeal fashion the Union was preserved. The credit belongs mostly to Clay, whose original conceptualization of the compromise enabled lesser minds to understand what they must do.

Everywhere sober and conservative citizens sighed with relief. Mass meetings throughout the country "ratified" the result. Hundreds of newspapers gave the compromise editorial approval. In Washington patriotic harmony reigned. "You would suppose that nobody had ever thought of disunion," Webster wrote. "All say they always meant to stand by the Union to the last." When Congress met again in December it seemed that party discord had been buried forever. "I have determined never to make another speech on the slavery question," Senator Douglas told his colleagues. "Let us cease agitating, stop the debate, and drop the subject." If this were done, he predicted, the compromise would be accepted as a "final settlement." With this bit of wishful thinking the year 1850 passed into history.

Milestones

1835	Alamo falls to Santa Anna's Mexican army
1836	Sam Houston routs Santa Anna at Battle of San Jacinto
1837	U.S. recognizes Republic of Texas
1841	William Henry Harrison is elected president
	William Henry Harrison dies; Vice President John Tyler becomes president
1842	Webster-Ashburton Treaty determines Maine boundary
1843	Oregon Trail opens
1844	James K. Polk is elected president
1845	U.S. annexes Texas
	John L. O'Sullivan coins the expression *manifest destiny*
1846	U.S. and Britain settle Oregon boundary dispute
1846–1848	U.S. wages "Mr. Polk's War" with Mexico
1846	House of Representatives adopts Wilmot Proviso prohibiting slavery in Mexican cession, but Senate defeats it
1847	General Winfield Scott captures Mexico City
1848	James W. Marshall discovers gold at Sutter's Mill, California
	Treaty of Guadalupe Hidalgo brings U.S. huge territorial gains
	Zachary Taylor is elected president
1850	Taylor dies; Vice President Millard Fillmore becomes president
	Henry Clay's Compromise of 1850 preserves Union

The Sections Go Their Ways

DEARBORN, MICHIGAN, HEADQUARTERS OF THE FORD MOTOR Company, is in many ways the prototypical American city. Yet nearly a third of its 100,000 residents are Arab-speaking immigrants from Lebanon, Iraq, Yemen, and Palestine.

Lowell, Massachusetts, whose textile mills employed young women from New England farms during the 1820s and 1830s, is now the home to some 20,000 Cambodians, refugees from the regime of Pol Pot, a Communist dictator who killed 2 million of his people.

About 10,000 Sudanese, refugees from a genocidal war in Africa, have flocked to Omaha, Nebraska, to work in its meatpacking plants. Nearly as many Bosnians, refugees from a civil war in the Balkans, have settled in Boise, Idaho.

The United States, long a nation of immigrants, remains so. And while some immigrant groups still settle together in tightly knit local communities, they are not concentrated primarily in port cities or border towns as many new immigrants were in the early nineteenth century. Immigrants today move throughout the United States, following opportunity. Although recent Hispanic immigrants constitute a large proportion of the workforce in much of the South and Southwest, they have settled throughout the nation. Even in Maine and Utah, people of Hispanic origin constitute the largest minority.

But during the first half of the nineteenth century, each section of the nation had a distinctive workforce. Immigrants who sought work in factories generally settled in the Northeast, while those interested in farming were drawn to the West. The culture of the South was in large part shaped by its unwilling immigrants, the slaves.

Improvements in transportation after 1830 reduced the differences among the sections. The Northeast and the West became economically interdependent. The

South, whose transportation infrastructure lagged, nevertheless benefited from the development of the steamship, which greatly reduced the cost of shipping to Europe. By the 1850s the nation remained divided—chiefly between the slave economy of the South and the nominally "free" labor of the North. But as the nation was knit together more tightly, the incompatibility of those systems could no longer be ignored.

The Economics of Slavery

The increased importance of cotton in the South strengthened the hold of slavery on the region. The price of slaves rose until by the 1850s a prime field hand was worth as much as $1,800, roughly three times the cost in the 1820s. While the prestige value of owning this kind of property affected prices, the rise chiefly reflected the increasing value of the South's agricultural output. "Crop value per slave" jumped from less than $15 early in the century to more than $125 in 1859.

In the cotton fields of the Deep South slaves brought several hundred dollars per head more than in the older regions; thus the tendency to sell them "down the river" continued. Mississippi took in some 10,000 slaves a year throughout the period; by 1830 the black population of the state exceeded the white. The westward shift of cotton cultivation was accompanied by the forcible transfer of more than a million African American slaves from the seaboard states to the dark, rich soil of

Price, Birch & Company of Virginia, "dealers in Slaves." Such companies not only sold slaves but also arranged for them to work in nearby shops and factories.

regions watered by the Mississippi and Arkansas rivers and their tributaries. This "second great migration" of blacks greatly surpassed the original uprooting of blacks from Africa to the United States.

Slave trading became a big business. In the 1850s there were about fifty dealers in Charleston and 200 in New Orleans. The largest traders were Isaac Franklin and John Armfield, who collected slaves from Virginia and Maryland at their "model jail" in Alexandria and shipped them by land and sea to a depot near Natchez. Each of the partners cleared half a million dollars before retiring, and some smaller operators did proportionately well.

The impact of the trade on the slaves was frequently disastrous. Husbands were often separated from wives, parents from children. This was somewhat less likely to happen on large, well-managed plantations than on small farms, but it was common enough everywhere. According to one study, one-third of all slave first "marriages" in the upper South were broken by forced separation and nearly half of all children were separated from at least one parent. Families were torn apart less frequently in the lower South, where far more slaves were bought than sold.

Because the business was so profitable, the prejudice against slave traders abated as the price of slaves rose. Men of high social status became traders, and persons of humble origin who had prospered in the trade had little difficulty in buying land and setting up as respectable planters.

As blacks became more expensive, the ownership of slaves became more concentrated. In 1860 only about 46,000 of the 8 million white residents of the slave states had as many as twenty slaves. When one calculates the cost of twenty slaves and the land to keep them profitably occupied, it is easy to understand why this figure is so small. The most efficient size of a plantation worked by gangs of slaves ranged between 1,000 and 2,000 acres. In every part of the South the majority of farmers cultivated no more than 200 acres, in many sections fewer than 100 acres. On the eve of the Civil War only one white family in four in the South owned any slaves at all. A few large plantations and many small farms—this was the pattern.

There were few genuine economies of scale in southern agriculture. Small farmers grew the staple crops; and many of them owned a few slaves, often working beside them in the fields. These yeomen farmers were hardworking, self-reliant, and moderately prosperous, quite unlike the poor whites of the pine barrens and the remote valleys of the Appalachians who scratched a meager subsistence from substandard soils and lived in ignorance and squalor.

Well-managed plantations yielded annual profits of 10 percent and more, and, in general, money invested in southern agriculture earned at least a modest return. Considering the way the workforce was exploited, this is hardly surprising. Recent estimates indicate that after allowing for the cost of land and capital, the average plantation slave "earned" cotton worth $78.78 in 1859. It cost masters about $32 a year to feed, clothe, and house a slave. In other words, almost 60 percent of the product of slave labor was expropriated by the masters.

Foreign observers in New England frequently noted the alertness and industriousness of ordinary laborers and attributed this, justifiably, to the high level of literacy. Nearly everyone in New England could read and write. Correspondingly, the stagnation and inefficiency of southern labor could be attributed in part to the high degree of illiteracy, for over 20 percent of *white* Southerners could not read or write, another tragic squandering of human resources.

The Sociology of Slavery

It is difficult to generalize about slavery because so much depended on the individual master's behavior. Although some former slaves told of masters who refused to whip them, Bennet Barrow of Louisiana, a harsh master, averaged one whipping a month. "The great secret of our success," another planter recalled years later, "was the great motive power contained in that little instrument." Overseers were commonly instructed to give twenty lashes for ordinary offenses, such as shirking work or stealing, and thirty-nine for more serious offenses, such as running away. Sometimes slaves were whipped to death; however, by 1821, all southern states had

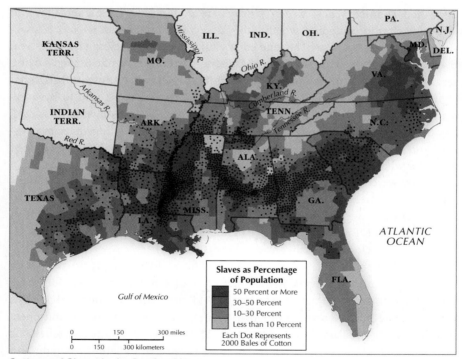

Cotton and Slaves in the South, 1860

Not surprisingly, the areas of greatest cotton production were also the areas with the highest proportion of slaves in the population. Note the concentrations of both in the Piedmont, the Alabama Black Belt, and the lower Mississippi Valley, and the relative absence of both in the Appalachian Mountains.

passed laws allowing a master to be charged with murder if he caused a slave's death from excessive punishment. Conviction normally resulted in a fine. In 1840 a South Carolina woman convicted of killing a slave was fined $214.28.

Most owners provided adequate clothing, housing, and food for their slaves. Only a fool or a sadist would fail to take care of such valuable property. However, vital statistics indicate that infant mortality among slaves was twice the white rate, life expectancy at least five years less.

On balance, it is significant that the United States was the only nation in the Western Hemisphere where the slave population grew by natural increase. After the ending of the slave trade in 1808, the black population increased at nearly the same rate as the white. Put differently, during the entire period from the founding of Jamestown to the Civil War, only a little more than half a million slaves were imported into the country, about 5 percent of the number of Africans carried by slavers to the New World. Yet in 1860 there were about 4 million blacks in the United States.

Most owners felt responsibilities toward their slaves, and slaves were dependent on and in some ways imitative of white values. However, powerful fears and resentments, not always recognized, existed on both sides. The plantation environment forced the two races to live in close proximity. From this circumstance could arise every sort of human relationship. One planter, using the appropriate pseudonym Clod Thumper, could write: "Africans are nothing but brutes, and they will love you better for whipping, whether they deserve it or not." Another, describing a slave named Bug, could say: "No one knows but myself what feeling I have for him. Black as he is we were raised together." One southern white woman tended a dying servant with "the kindest and most unremitting attention." Another, discovered crying after the death of a slave she had repeatedly abused, is said to have explained her grief by complaining that she "didn't have nobody to whip no more."

Such diametrically conflicting sentiments often existed within the same person. And almost no white Southerners had any difficulty exploiting the labor of slaves for whom they felt genuine affection.

Slaves were without rights; they developed a distinctive way of life by attempting to resist oppression and injustice while accommodating themselves to the system. Their marriages had no legal status, but their partnerships seem to have been loving and stable. Even families whose members were sold to different masters often maintained close ties over considerable distances.

Slave religion, on the surface an untutored form of Christianity tinctured with some African survivals, seemed to most slave owners a useful instrument for teaching meekness and resignation and for providing harmless emotional release, which it sometimes was and did. However, religious meetings, secret and open, provided slaves with the opportunity to organize, which led at times to rebellions and more often to less drastic ways of resisting white domination. Religion also sustained the slaves' sense of their own worth as beings made in the image of God, and it taught them, therefore, that while human beings can be enslaved in body, their spirits cannot be enslaved without their consent.

Observing that slaves often seemed happy and were only rarely overtly rebellious, whites persuaded themselves that most blacks accepted the system without resentment and indeed preferred slavery to the uncertainties of freedom. There was much talk about "loyal and faithful servants." The Civil War, when slaves flocked to the Union lines once assured of freedom and fair treatment, would disabuse them of this illusion.

As the price of slaves rose and as northern opposition to the institution grew more vocal, the system hardened perceptibly. White Southerners made much of the danger of insurrection. When a plot was uncovered or a revolt took place, instant and savage reprisals resulted. In 1822, after the conspiracy of Denmark Vesey was exposed by informers, thirty-seven slaves were executed and another thirty-odd deported, although no overt act of rebellion had occurred. After an uprising in Louisiana, sixteen blacks were decapitated, their heads left to rot on poles along the Mississippi as a grim warning.

The Nat Turner revolt in Virginia in 1831 was the most sensational of the slave uprisings; fifty-seven whites lost their lives before it was suppressed. White Southerners treated runaways almost as brutally as rebels, although they posed no real threat to whites. The authorities tracked down fugitives with bloodhounds and subjected captives to merciless lashings.

After the Nat Turner revolt, interest in doing away with slavery vanished in the white South. The southern states made it increasingly difficult for masters to free their slaves; during 1859 only about 3,000 in a slave population of nearly 4 million were given their freedom.

Slavery did not flourish in urban settings, and cities did not flourish in societies where slavery was important. Most southern cities were small, and within them, slaves made up a small fraction of the labor force. The existence of slavery goes a long way toward explaining why the South was so rural and why it had so little industry. Blacks were much harder to supervise and control in urban settings. Individual slaves were successfully employed in southern manufacturing plants, but they made up only an insignificant fraction of the South's small industrial labor supply.

Southern whites considered the existence of free blacks undesirable, no matter where they lived. The mere fact that they could support themselves disproved the notion that blacks were by nature childlike and shiftless, unable to work efficiently without white guidance. From the whites' point of view, free blacks set a bad example for slaves. In a petition calling for the expulsion of free blacks from the state, a group of South Carolinians noted that slaves

> continualy have before their eyes, persons of the same color . . . freed from the control of masters, working where they please, going where they please, and expending their money how they please.

At a minimum, as another Southerner said, the sight of "a vile and lazy free negro lolling in the sun-shine" might make slaves envious. Still worse, it might encourage them to try to escape, and worst of all, the free blacks might help them do so.

Many southern states passed laws aimed at forcing free blacks to emigrate, but these laws were not well enforced. There is ample evidence that the white people of, say, Maryland, would have liked to get rid of the state's large free black population. Free blacks were barred from occupations in which they might cause trouble—no free black could be the captain of a ship, for example—and they were required by law to find a "respectable" white person who would testify as to their "good conduct and character." But whites, who needed slave labor, did not try very hard to expel them.

Psychological Effects of Slavery

The injustice of slavery needs no proof; less obvious is the fact that it had a corrosive effect on the personalities of Southerners, slave and free alike. By "the making of a human being an animal without hope," the system bore heavily on all slaves' sense of their own worth. Some found the condition absolutely unbearable. They became the habitual runaways who collected whip scars like medals, the "loyal" servants who struck out in rage against a master knowing that the result would be certain death, and the leaders of slave revolts.

Denmark Vesey of South Carolina, even after buying his freedom, could not stomach the subservience demanded of slaves by the system. When he saw Charleston slaves step into the gutter to make way for whites, he taunted them: "You deserve to remain slaves!" For years he preached resistance to his fellows, drawing his texts from the Declaration of Independence and the Bible and promising help from black Haiti. So vehemently did he argue that some of his followers claimed they feared Vesey more than their masters, even more than God. He planned his uprising for five years, patiently working out the details, only to see it aborted at the last moment when a few of his recruits lost their nerve and betrayed him. For Denmark Vesey, death was probably preferable to living with such rage as his soul contained.

Yet Veseys were rare. Most slaves appeared at least resigned to their fate. Many seemed even to accept the whites' evaluation of their inherent abilities and place in society. Of course in most instances it is impossible to know whether this apparent subservience was feigned in order to avoid trouble.

Slaves had strong family and group attachments and a complex culture of their own, maintained, so to speak, under the noses of their masters. By a mixture of subterfuge, accommodation, and passive resistance, they erected subtle defenses against exploitation, achieving a sense of community that helped sustain the psychic integrity of individuals. But slavery discouraged, if it did not extinguish, independent judgment and self-reliance. These qualities are difficult enough to develop in human beings under the best of circumstances; when every element in white society encouraged slaves to let others do their thinking for them, to avoid questioning the status quo, to lead a simple life, many did so willingly enough. Was this not slavery's greatest shame?

Whites, too, were harmed by the slave system. Associating working for others with servility discouraged many poor white Southerners from hiring out to earn a

Debating the Past

DID SLAVES AND MASTERS FORM EMOTIONAL BONDS?

Slavery, Ulrich Bonnell Phillips (1918) declared, was a benign institution. "Severity was clearly the exception, and kindliness the rule," he remarked. Kenneth Stampp (1956), writing as the civil rights movement of the 1950s was gaining momentum, repudiated Phillips's thesis. Slavery ripped apart families, reduced human beings to chattel, and eroded the slave's sense of self. The kindness of some slave masters was that of a father toward a "fawning dependent," he argued. Stanley Elkins (1959) went further still, comparing southern slavery to the subjugation of inmates in Nazi concentration camps. Slavery was so absolute that the psyche of African Americans was crushed for generations. Two major works in the 1970s challenged this rendering of slavery but in different ways. Eugene D. Genovese (1974) argued that masters and slaves were locked in a system of mutual dependence. Slaves were bound to their owners "in an organic relationship so complex and ambivalent that neither could express the simplest human feelings without reference to each other." Their emotional ties, however complicated, were real. Herbert Gutman (1976) insisted that slaves did not bond with their masters. Slave parents, children, and other relatives formed lasting ties that endured. Because it is hard to know what people really felt, the issue resists historical analysis: Did the slave girl in this photograph know for sure how she felt about the child in her arms?

Ulrich Bonnell Phillips, *American Negro Slavery* (1918), Kenneth Stampp, *The Peculiar Institution* (1956), Stanley Elkins, *Slavery* (1959), Eugene D. Genovese, *Roll, Jordan, Roll* (1974), Herbert Gutman, *The Black Family in Slavery and Freedom* (1976).

stake. Slavery provided the weak, the shiftless, and the unsuccessful with a scapegoat that made their own miserable state easier to bear but harder to escape.

More subtly, the patriarchal nature of the slave system reinforced the already existing tendency toward male dominance over wives and children typical of the larger society. For men of exceptional character, the responsibilities of ownership could be ennobling, but for hotheads, alcoholics, or others with psychological problems, the power could be brutalizing, with terrible effects on the whole plantation community, whites and blacks alike.

Aside from its fundamental immorality, slavery caused basically decent people to commit countless petty cruelties. "I feel badly, got very angry and whipped Lavinia," one Louisiana woman wrote in her diary. "O! for government over my temper." But for slavery, she would surely have had better self-control. The finest white Southerners were often warped by the institution. Even those who abhorred slavery sometimes let it corrupt their thinking: "I consider the labor of a breeding woman as no object, and that a child raised every 2 years is of more profit than the crop of the best laboring man." This cold calculation came from the pen of Thomas Jefferson, author of the Declaration of Independence, a man who, it now seems likely, fathered at least one child by a slave.

Manufacturing in the South

Although the temper of southern society discouraged business and commercial activities, considerable manufacturing developed. Small flour and lumber mills flourished. There were important rope-making plants in Kentucky and commercial cotton presses, used to compact cotton into 500-pound bales, in many southern cities. Iron and coal were mined in Virginia, Kentucky, and Tennessee. In the 1850s the Tredegar Iron Works in Richmond did an annual business of about $1 million.

Less than 15 percent of all the goods manufactured in the United States in 1860 came from the South; the region did not really develop an industrial society. Its textile manufacturers depended on the North for machinery, for skilled workers and technicians, for financing, and for insurance. When the English geologist Charles Lyell visited New Orleans in 1846, he was astounded to discover that the thriving city supported not a single book publisher. Even a local guidebook that he purchased bore a New York imprint.

The Northern Industrial Juggernaut

The most obvious change in the North in the decades before the Civil War was the rapid growth of industry. The best estimates suggest that immediately after the War of 1812 the United States was manufacturing less than $200 million worth of goods annually. In 1859 the northeastern states alone produced $1.27 billion of the national total of almost $2 billion.

Manufacturing expanded in so many directions that it is difficult to portray or to summarize its evolution. The factory system made great strides. The development of rich anthracite coal fields in Pennsylvania was particularly important in this connection. The coal could be floated cheaply on canals to convenient sites and used to produce both heat for smelting and metalworking and steam power to drive machinery. Steam permitted greater flexibility in locating factories and in organizing work within them, and since waterpower was already being used to capacity, steam was essential for the expansion of output.

American industry displayed a remarkable receptivity to technological change. The list of inventions and processes developed between 1825 and 1850 included—besides such obviously important items as the sewing machine, the vulcanization of rubber, and the cylinder press—the screw-making machine, the friction match, the lead pencil, and an apparatus for making soda water.

In the 1820s a foreign visitor noted: "Everything new is quickly introduced here, and all the latest inventions. . . . The moment an American hears the word 'invention' he pricks up his ears." Twenty years later a Frenchman wrote: "If they continue to work with the same ardor, they will soon have nothing more to desire or to do. All the mountains will be flattened, the valleys filled, all matter rendered productive." By 1850 the United States led the world in the manufacture of goods that required the use of precision instruments, and in certain industries the country was well on the way toward modern mass production methods. American clocks, pistols, rifles, and locks were outstanding.

In the 1850s the earlier prejudice against the corporation began to break down; by the end of the decade the northern and northwestern states had all passed general incorporation laws. Of course, the corporate device made possible larger accumulations of capital. While the federal government did not charter business corporations, two actions of Congress illustrate the shift in public attitudes. In 1840 a group of scientists sought a federal charter for a National Institution for the Promotion of Science. They were turned down on constitutional grounds; if Congress "went on erecting corporations in this way," one legislator said, "they would come, at last, to have corporations for everything." In 1863, however, the bill creating the National Academy of Science passed both houses without debate.

Industrial growth led to a great increase in the demand for labor. The effects, however, were mixed. Skilled artisans, technicians, and toolmakers earned good wages and found it relatively easy to set themselves up first as independent craftsmen, later as small manufacturers. The expanding frontier drained off much agricultural labor that might otherwise have been attracted to industry, and the thriving new towns of the West absorbed large numbers of eastern artisans of every kind. At the same time, the pay of an unskilled worker was never enough to support a family decently, and the new machines weakened the bargaining power of artisans by making skill less important.

Many other forces acted to stimulate the growth of manufacturing. Immigration increased rapidly in the 1830s and 1840s. An avalanche of strong backs, willing hands, and keen minds descended on the country from Europe. European investors poured large sums into the booming American economy, and the savings of millions of Americans and the great hoard of new California gold added to the supply of capital. Improvements in transportation, population growth, the absence of internal tariff barriers, and the relatively high per capita wealth all meant an ever-expanding market for manufactured goods.

A Nation of Immigrants

Rapid industrialization influenced American life in countless ways, none more significant than its effect on the character of the workforce and consequently on the structure of society. The jobs created by industrial expansion attracted European immigrants by the tens of thousands. It is a truism that America is a nation of immigrants—recall that even the ancestors of the Indians came to the New World from Asia. But only with the development of nationalism, that is, with the establishment of the independent United States, did the word *immigrant,* meaning a foreign-born resident, come into existence.

The "native" population (native in this case meaning those whose ancestors had come from Europe rather than Native Americans, the Indians) tended to look down on immigrants, and many of the immigrants, in turn, developed prejudices of their own. The Irish, for example, disliked blacks, with whom they often competed for work. One Irish leader in the old country, Daniel O'Connell, admitted that the American Irish were "among the worst enemies of the colored race." And of course blacks responded with equal bitterness. "Every hour sees us elbowed out of some employment to make room for some newly arrived emigrant from the Emerald Isle, whose hunger and color entitle him to special favor," one of them complained. Antiblack prejudice was less noticeable among other immigrant groups but by no means absent; most immigrants adopted the views of the local majority, which was often unfriendly to African Americans.

Social and racial rivalries aside, unskilled immigrants caused serious disruptions of economic patterns wherever they appeared. Their absorption into the factories of New England speeded the disintegration of the system of hiring young farm women. Already competition and technical advances in the textile industry were increasing the pace of the machines and reducing the number of skilled workers needed to run them. Fewer young farm women were willing to work under these conditions. Recent immigrants, who required less "coddling" and who seemed to provide the mills with a "permanent" working force, replaced the women in large numbers. By 1860 Irish immigrants alone made up more than 50 percent of the labor force in the New England mills.

How Wage Earners Lived

In the early factory towns, most working families maintained small vegetable gardens and a few chickens; low wage rates did not necessarily reflect a low standard of living. But in the new industrial slums even a blade of grass was unusual. In 1851 the editor Horace Greeley's *New York Tribune* published a minimum weekly budget for a family of five. The budget, which allowed nothing for savings, medical bills, recreation, or other amenities (Greeley did include 12 cents a week for newspapers), came to $10.37. Since the weekly pay of a factory hand seldom reached $5, the wives and children of most male factory workers also had to labor in the factories merely

A strike by 800 women shoemakers in Lynn, Massachusetts, 1860. In 1851 a Lynn shoemaker had adapted a Howe sewing machine so that it could pierce and sew leather, work normally performed by married women in their homes. Because these large machines required employees to leave home and children and work at the shoe-stitching factories, few married women would do so; here they are protesting their displacement.

to survive. And child labor in the 1850s differed fundamentally from child labor in the 1820s. The pace of the machines had become much faster by then, and the working environment more depressing.

Relatively few workers belonged to unions, but federations of craft unions sprang up in some cities, and during the boom that preceded the Panic of 1837, a National Trades Union representing a few northeastern cities managed to hold conventions. Early in the Jackson era, "workingmen's" political parties enjoyed a brief popularity, occasionally electing a few local officials. These organizations were made up mostly of skilled craftsmen, professional reformers, and even businessmen. They soon expired, destroyed by internal bickering over questions that had little or nothing to do with working conditions.

The flush times of the early 1850s caused the union movement to revive. Many strikes occurred, and a few new national organizations appeared. However, most unions were local institutions, weak and with little control over their membership. The Panic of 1857 dealt the labor movement another body blow. Thus there was no trend toward the general unionization of labor between 1820 and the Civil War.

This republican value system, along with the fluidity of society, the influx of job-hungry immigrants, and the widespread employment of women and children in unskilled jobs made labor organization difficult. The assumption was that nearly anyone who was willing to work could eventually escape from the wage-earning class. "If any continue through life in the condition of the hired laborer," Abraham Lincoln declared in 1859, "it is . . . because of either a dependent nature which prefers it, or improvidence, folly, or singular misfortune."

Foreign Commerce

Changes in the pattern of foreign commerce were less noticeable than those in manufacturing but were nevertheless significant. After increasing erratically during the 1820s and 1830s, both imports and exports leapt forward in the next 20 years. The nation remained primarily an exporter of raw materials and an importer of manufactured goods, and in most years it imported more than it exported. Cotton continued to be the most valuable export, in 1860 accounting for a record $191 million of total exports of $333 million. Despite America's own thriving industry, textiles still held the lead among imports, with iron products second. As in earlier days, Great Britain was both the best customer of the United States and its leading supplier.

The success of sailing packets, those "square-riggers on schedule," greatly facilitated the movement of passengers and freight. Fifty-two packets were operating between New York and Europe by 1845, and many more plied between New York and other American ports. The packets accelerated the tendency for trade to concentrate in New York and to a lesser extent in Philadelphia, Baltimore, and New Orleans. The commerce of Boston and smaller New England towns like Providence and New Haven, which had flourished in earlier days, now languished.

New Bedford and a few other southern New England towns shrewdly saved their prosperity by concentrating on whaling, which boomed between 1830 and 1860. The supply of whales seemed unlimited—as indeed it was, given the primitive hunting techniques of the age of sail. By the mid-1850s, with sperm oil selling at more than $1.75 a gallon and the country exporting an average of $2.7 million worth of whale oil and whalebone a year, New Bedford boasted a whaling fleet of well over 300 vessels and a population approaching 25,000.

The increase in the volume and value of trade and its concentration at larger ports had a marked effect on the construction of ships. By the 1850s the average vessel was three times the size of those built 30 years earlier. Startling improvements in design, culminating in the long, sleek, white-winged clipper ships, made possible speeds previously undreamed of. Appearing just in time to supply the need for fast transportation to the California gold fields, the clippers cut sailing time around Cape Horn to San Francisco from five or six months to three, the record of 89 days being held jointly by the *Andrew Jackson* and Donald McKay's famous *Flying Cloud*. Another McKay-designed clipper, *Champion of the Seas*, once logged 465 nautical miles in 24 hours, far in excess of the best efforts of modern yachts. To achieve such speeds, cargo capacity had to be sacrificed, making clippers uneconomical for carrying the bulky produce that was the mainstay of commerce. But for specialty goods, in their brief heyday the clippers were unsurpassed. Hong Kong merchants, never known for extravagance, willingly paid 75 cents a cubic foot to ship tea by clipper to London even though slower vessels charged only 28 cents. In the early 1850s clippers sold for as much as $150,000; with decent luck a ship might earn its full cost in a voyage or two.

Steam Conquers the Atlantic

The reign of the clipper ship was short. Like so many other things, ocean commerce was being mechanized. Steamships conquered the high seas more slowly than the rivers because early models were unsafe in rough waters and uneconomical. A riverboat could take on fuel along its route, whereas an Atlantic steamer had to carry tons of coal across the ocean, thereby reducing its capacity for cargo. However, by the late 1840s, steamships were capturing most of the passenger traffic, mail contracts, and first-class freight. These vessels could not keep up with the clippers in a heavy breeze, but their average speed was far greater, especially on the westward voyage against the prevailing winds. Steamers were soon crossing the Atlantic in less than ten days. Nevertheless, for very long voyages, such as the 15,000-mile haul around South America to California, fast sailing ships held their own for many years.

The combination of competition, government subsidy, and technological advance drove down shipping rates. Between the mid-1820s and the mid-1850s the cost of moving a pound of cotton from New York to Liverpool fell from 1 cent to about a third of a cent. Transatlantic passengers could obtain the best accommoda-

Giant Steamboats on the Levee at New Orleans (1853), a painting by Hippolyte Sebron, a Frenchman. A picture of stately elegance, these boats required unusually powerful engines to make way against the strong currents of the Mississippi. Improvements in engine design and iron casting helped boats meet the river's challenge.

tions on the fastest ships for under $200, good accommodations on slower packets for as little as $75.

Rates were especially low for European emigrants willing to travel to America on cargo vessels. By the 1840s at least 4,000 ships were engaged in carrying bulky American cotton and Canadian lumber to Europe. On their return trips with manufactured goods they had much unoccupied space, which they converted into rough quarters for passengers. Conditions on these ships were crowded, gloomy, and foul. Frequently epidemics took a fearful toll among steerage passengers. On one crossing of the ship *Lark*, 158 of 440 passengers died of typhus.

Yet without this cheap means of transportation, thousands of poor immigrants would simply have remained at home. Bargain freight rates also help explain the clamor of American manufacturers for high tariffs, for transportation costs added relatively little to the price of European goods.

Canals and Railroads

Another dramatic change was the shift in the direction of the nation's internal commerce and its immense increase. From the time of the first settlers in the Mississippi Valley, the Great River had controlled the flow of goods from farm to market. The completion of the Erie Canal in 1825 heralded a shift, speeded by the feverish canal construction of the following decade. In 1830 there were 1,277 miles of canal in the United States; by 1840 there were 3,326 miles.

Each year saw more western produce moving to market through the canals. In 1845 the Erie Canal was still drawing over two-thirds of its west-east traffic from within New York, but by 1847, despite the fact that this local business held steady, more than half of its traffic came from west of Buffalo, and by 1851 more than two-thirds. The volume of western commerce over the Erie Canal in 1851 amounted to more than twenty times what it had been in 1836, while the value of western goods reaching New Orleans in this period increased only two and a half times.

The first railroads did not compete with the canals for intersectional traffic. The through connections needed to move goods economically over great distances materialized slowly. Of the 6,000 miles of track operating in 1848, nearly all lay east of the Appalachians, and little of it had been coordinated into railroad systems. The intention of most early builders had been to monopolize the trade of surrounding districts, not to establish connections with competing centers. Frequently, railroads used tracks of different widths deliberately to prevent other lines from tying into their tracks.

Between 1848 and 1852 railroad mileage nearly doubled. Three years later it had doubled again, and by 1860 the nation had 30,636 miles of track. During this extraordinary burst of activity, four companies drove lines of gleaming iron from the Atlantic seaboard to the great interior valley. In 1851 the Erie Railroad, longest road in the world with 537 miles of track, linked the Hudson River north of New York City with Dunkirk on Lake Erie. Late the next year the Baltimore and Ohio reached the Ohio River at Wheeling, and in 1853 a banker named Erastus Corning

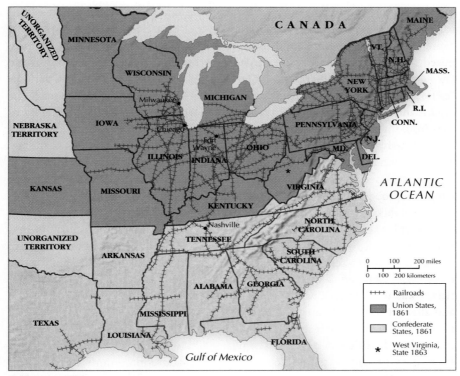

Railroads, 1860
This map shows trunk lines (lines carrying through-traffic) in operation in 1860. Certain towns and cities owed their spectacularly rapid growth to the railroad, Chicago being an outstanding example. The map suggests the strong influence of the railroads on the expansion and economic prosperity of smaller cities such as Fort Wayne, Milwaukee, and Nashville. At the outbreak of the Civil War in 1861, the relative lack of railroads in the South was a major disadvantage for the Confederacy.

consolidated eight short lines connecting Albany and Buffalo to form the New York Central Railroad. Finally, in 1858 the Pennsylvania Railroad completed a line across the mountains from Philadelphia to Pittsburgh.

In the states beyond the Appalachians, building went on at an even more feverish pace. By 1855 passengers could travel from Chicago or St. Louis to the east coast at a cost of $20 to $30, the trip taking, with luck, less than 48 hours. A generation earlier such a trip had required two to three weeks. Construction was slower in the South: Mississippi laid about 800 miles of track, Alabama 600.

Financing the Railroads

Railroad building required immense amounts of labor and capital at a time when many other demands for these resources existed. Immigrants or (in the South) slaves did most of the heavy work. Raising the necessary money proved a more complex task.

Private investors supplied about three-quarters of the money invested in railroads before 1860, more than $800 million in the 1850s alone. Much of this capital came from local merchants and businessmen and from farmers along the proposed rights-of-way. Funds were easy to raise because subscribers seldom had to lay out the full price of their stock at one time; instead they were subject to periodic "calls" for a percentage of their commitment as construction progressed. If the road made money, much of the additional mileage could be paid for out of earnings from the first sections built.

But many railroads that failed to find enough investors sought public money. Towns, counties, and the states themselves lent money to railroads and invested in their stock. Special privileges, such as exemption from taxation and the right to condemn property, were often granted, and in a few cases states built and operated roads as public corporations.

As with earlier internal improvement proposals, federal financial aid to railroads was usually blocked in Congress by a combination of eastern and southern votes. But in 1850 a scheme for granting federal lands to the states to build a line from Lake Michigan to the Gulf of Mexico passed both houses. The main beneficiary was the Illinois Central Railroad, which received a 200-foot right-of-way and alternate strips of land along the track 1 mile wide and 6 miles deep, a total of almost 2.6 million acres. By mortgaging this land and by selling portions of it to farmers, the Illinois Central raised nearly all the $23.4 million it spent on construction. The success of this operation led to additional grants of almost 20 million acres in the 1850s, benefiting more than forty railroads. Far larger federal grants were made after the Civil War, when the transcontinental lines were built.

Railroads and the Economy

The effects of so much railroad construction were profound. Although the main reason that farmers put more land under the plow was an increase in the price of agricultural products, the railroad helped determine just what land was used and how profitably it could be farmed. Much of the fertile prairie through which the Illinois Central ran had been available for settlement for many years before 1850, but development had been slow because it was remote from navigable waters and had no timber. In 1840 the three counties immediately northeast of Springfield had a population of about 8,500. They produced about 59,000 bushels of wheat and 690,000 bushels of corn. In the next decade the region grew slowly by the standards of that day: The three counties had about 14,000 people in 1850 and produced 71,000 bushels of wheat and 2.2 million bushels of corn. Then came the railroad and with it an agricultural revolution. By 1860 the population of the three counties had soared to over 38,000, wheat production had topped 550,000 bushels, and corn 5.7 million bushels. "Land-grant" railroads such as the Illinois Central stimulated agricultural expansion by advertising their lands widely and selling farm sites at low rates on liberal terms.

"OUR FIELD IS THE WORLD."

LIGHT DRAFT. SUPERIOR DESIGN.

CLEAN AND RAPID CUTTER.

McCORMICK N°.2 IRON MOWER

McCormick Harvesting Machine Co., Chicago.

ESTABLISHED 1831.

An advertisement for the McCormick Reaper, so light that it could be pulled quickly by two horses.

Access to world markets gave the farmers of the upper Mississippi Valley an incentive to increase output. Land was plentiful and cheap, but farm labor was scarce; consequently agricultural wages rose sharply, especially after 1850. New tools and machines appeared in time to ease the labor shortage. First came the steel plowshare, invented by John Deere, a Vermont-born blacksmith who had moved to Illinois in 1837. The prairie sod was tough and sticky, but Deere's smooth metal plows cut through it easily. In 1839 Deere turned out ten such plows in his little shop in Moline, Illinois. By 1857 he was selling 10,000 a year.

Still more important was the perfection of the mechanical reaper, for wheat production was limited more by the amount that farmers could handle during the brief harvest season than by the acreage they could plant and cultivate. The major figure in the development of the reaper was Cyrus Hall McCormick. McCormick's horse-drawn reaper bent the grain against the cutting knife and then deposited it neatly on a platform, whence it could easily be raked into windrows. With this machine, two workers could cut fourteen times as much wheat as with scythes.

McCormick prospered, but despite his patents, he could not keep other manufacturers out of the business. Competition led to continual improvement of the machines and kept prices within the reach of most farmers. Installment selling

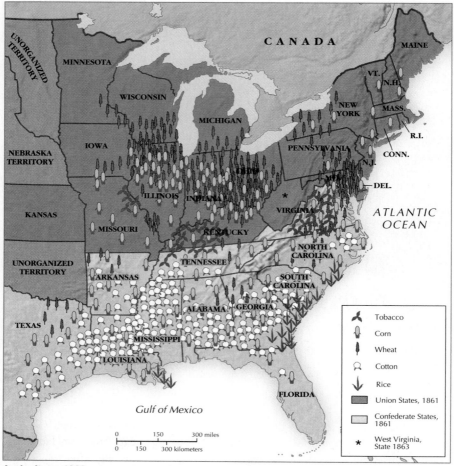

Agriculture, 1860

added to demand. By 1860 nearly 80,000 reapers had been sold; their efficiency helps explain why wheat output rose by nearly 75 percent in the 1850s.

The railroad had an equally powerful impact on American cities. The eastern seaports benefited, and so did countless intermediate centers, such as Buffalo and Cincinnati. But no city was affected more profoundly by railroads than Chicago.

In 1850 not a single line had reached there; five years later it was a terminal for 2,200 miles of track and controlled the commerce of an imperial domain. By extending half a dozen lines west to the Mississippi, it drained off nearly all the river traffic north of St. Louis. The Illinois Central sucked the expanding output of the prairies into Chicago as well. Most of this freight went eastward over the new railroads or on the Great Lakes and the Erie Canal. Nearly 350,000 tons of shipping plied the lakes by 1855.

The railroads, like the textile industry, stimulated other kinds of economic activity. They transformed agriculture, both real estate values and the buying and selling of land increased whenever the iron horse puffed into a new district. The railroads spurred regional concentration of industry and an increase in the size of business units. Their insatiable need for capital stimulated the growth of investment banking. Their massive size required the creation of complex structures and the employment of salaried managers.

The railroads consumed nearly half the nation's output of bar and sheet iron in 1860. Probably more labor and more capital were occupied in economic activities resulting from the development of railroads than in the roads themselves—another way of saying that the railroads were immensely valuable internal improvements.

The proliferation of trunk lines and the competition of the canal system (for many products the slowness of canal transportation was not a serious handicap) led to a sharp decline in freight and passenger rates. Cheap transportation had a revolutionary effect on western agriculture. Farmers in Iowa could now raise grain to feed the factory workers of Lowell and even of Manchester, England. Two-thirds of the meat consumed in New York City was soon arriving by rail from beyond the Appalachians. The center of American wheat production shifted westward to Illinois, Wisconsin, and Indiana. When the Crimean War (1853–1856) and European crop failures increased foreign demand, these regions boomed. Success bred success for farmers and for the railroads. Profits earned from carrying wheat enabled the roads to build feeder lines that opened up still-wider areas to commercial agriculture and made it easy to bring in lumber, farm machinery, household furnishings, and the settlers themselves at low cost.

Railroads and the Sectional Conflict

Increased production and cheap transportation boosted the western farmer's income and standard of living. The days of isolation and self-sufficiency, even for the family on the edge of the frontier, rapidly disappeared. Pioneers quickly became operators of businesses and, to a far greater extent than their forebears, consumers, buying all sorts of manufactured articles that their ancestors had made for themselves or done without. These changes had their costs. Like southern planters, they now became dependent on middlemen and lost some of their feeling of self-reliance. Overproduction became a problem. Buying a farm began to require more capital, for as profits increased, so did the price of land. Machinery was an additional expense. The proportion of farm laborers and tenants increased.

The linking of East and West had fateful effects on politics. The increased ease of movement from section to section and the ever more complex social and economic integration of East and West stimulated nationalism and thus became a force for the preservation of the Union. Without the railroads and canals, Illinois and Iowa would scarcely have dared to side against the South in 1861. When the

Mississippi ceased to be essential to them, citizens of the upper valley could afford to be more hostile to slavery and especially to its westward extension. Economic ties with the Northeast reinforced cultural connections.

The South might have preserved its influence in the Northwest if it had pressed forward its own railroad-building program. It failed to do so. There were many southern lines but nothing like a southern system. As late as 1856 one could get from Memphis to Richmond or Charleston only by very indirect routes. As late as 1859 the land-grant road extending the Illinois Central to Mobile, Alabama, was not complete, nor did any economical connection exist between Chicago and New Orleans.

This state of affairs could be accounted for in part by the scattered population of the South, the paucity of passenger traffic, the seasonal nature of much of the freight business, and the absence of large cities. Southerners placed too much reliance on the Mississippi: The fact that traffic on the river continued to be heavy throughout the 1850s blinded them to the precipitous rate at which their relative share of the nation's trade was declining. But the fundamental cause of the South's backwardness in railroad construction was the attitude of its leaders. Southerners of means were no more interested in commerce than in industry; their capital found other outlets.

The Economy on the Eve of Civil War

Between the mid-1840s and the mid-1850s the United States experienced one of the most remarkable periods of growth in the history of the world. Every economic indicator surged forward: manufacturing, grain and cotton production, population, railroad mileage, gold production, sales of public land. The building of the railroads stimulated business, and by making transportation cheaper, the completed lines energized the nation's economy. The American System that Henry Clay had dreamed of arrived with a rush just as Clay was passing from the scene.

Inevitably, this growth caused dislocations that were aggravated by the boom psychology that once again infected the popular mind. In 1857 there was a serious collapse. The return of Russian wheat to the world market after the Crimean War caused grain prices to fall. This checked agricultural expansion, which hurt the railroads and cut down on the demand for manufactures. Unemployment increased. Frightened depositors started runs on banks, most of which had to suspend specie payments.

People called this abrupt downturn the Panic of 1857. Yet the vigor of the economy was such that the bad times did not last long. The upper Mississippi Valley suffered most, for so much new land had been opened up that supplies of farm produce greatly exceeded demand. Elsewhere conditions improved rapidly.

The South, somewhat out of the hectic rush to begin with, was affected very little by the collapse of 1857, for cotton prices continued to be high. This gave planters the false impression that their economy was immune to such violent downturns. Some began to argue that the South would be better off out of the Union.

Before a new national upward swing could become well established, however, the sectional crisis between North and South shook people's confidence in the future. Then the war came, and a new set of forces shaped economic development.

Milestones		
	1808	Congress bans further importation of slaves
	1822	Thirty-seven slaves are executed when Denmark Vesey's "conspiracy" is exposed
	1825	Erie Canal is completed, connecting East and Midwest
	1830	Baltimore and Ohio railroad begins operation
	1831	Nat Turner's slave uprising results in death of 57 whites
	1837	Cyrus Hall McCormick invents reaper to harvest wheat
	1839	John Deere begins manufacturing steel plows
	1840–1857	Economy surges during boom in manufacturing, railroad construction, and foreign commerce
	1846	Elias Howe invents sewing machine
	1850	Congress grants land to aid construction of Illinois Central Railroad
	1854	Clipper ship *Flying Cloud* sails from New York to San Francisco in 89 days
	1857	Brief economic depression (Panic of 1857) collapses economy

13 CHAPTER

The Coming of the Civil War

Two-thirds of Americans indicate that television is their main source of information about national politics. Around election time, 30-second television ads are the most ubiquitous (and dubious) source of information. (Such ads consumed most of the $1.2 billion cost of the 2004 presidential campaign.) Network news stories also inform voters about campaign issues, but over the past two decades such coverage has been condensed. In 1968, the average length of a quotation from a candidate on the evening news was 42 seconds; by 2000, such quotes had been reduced to 7 seconds. The term "sound bite" entered the political lexicon.

Televised debates provide a more sustained consideration of political issues. But the proportion of Americans who follow the debates has declined. In 1960, 77 percent of Americans watched the first televised debate between John F. Kennedy and Richard Nixon; even more tuned in to the 1980 debate between Ronald Reagan and Jimmy Carter. But during the 1996, 2000, and 2004 campaigns, fewer than one-third of Americans on the average watched the presidential debates.

We do not know precisely how many Americans gathered in the courthouse squares to listen to speeches and debates in the nineteenth century, yet we do know that politics then required a substantial investment of time. Unlike the visual medium of television, the spoken word takes time to digest. "Speak slowly," Lincoln advised a supporter who was to read a speech on his behalf. The seven influential debates between Abraham Lincoln and Stephen A. Douglas in 1858 each lasted over three hours.

During the 1850s the drumbeat of words grew faster and louder: Southern appeals for enforcement of the Fugitive Slave Act; Harriet Beecher Stowe's heartrending description of slavery in *Uncle Tom's Cabin*; the impassioned debates over "bleeding Kansas"; the Supreme Court's inflammatory decision in the Dred Scott case; the invective both for and against the manic crusade of John Brown. The din culminated in the superheated rhetoric of the 1860 presidential campaign. Then the words would be drowned out by the roar of cannon.

The Slave Power Comes North

The political settlement between North and South that Henry Clay designed in 1850 lasted only four years. One specific event wrecked it, but it was probably doomed in any case. Americans continued to migrate westward by the thousands, and as long as slaveholders could carry their human property into federally controlled territories, northern resentment would smolder. Slaves continued to seek freedom in the North, and the federal Fugitive Slave Act of 1850, which imposed fines for hiding or rescuing fugitive slaves, could not guarantee their capture and return. Abolitionists intensified their propaganda.

The new fugitive slave law encouraged more white Southerners to try to recover escaped slaves. Something approaching panic reigned in the black communities of northern cities when slave hunters arrived to seize former slaves. Thousands of blacks, not all of them fugitive slaves, fled to Canada, but many remained, and Northerners frequently refused to stand aside when such people were dragged off in chains.

Shortly after the passage of the act, James Hamlet was seized in New York City, convicted, and returned to slavery in Maryland without even being allowed to communicate with his wife and children. The New York black community was outraged, and with help from white neighbors it swiftly raised $800 to buy his freedom. Early in 1851 a Virginia agent captured Frederick "Shadrach" Jenkins, a waiter in a Boston coffeehouse. While Jenkins was being held for deportation, a mob of African Americans broke into the courthouse and hustled him off to Canada. That October a slave named Jerry, who had escaped from Missouri, was arrested in Syracuse, New York. Within minutes the whole town had the news. Crowds surged through the streets, and when night fell, a mob smashed into the building where Jerry was being held and spirited him away to safety in Canada.

Such incidents exacerbated sectional feelings. White Southerners accused the North of reneging on one of the main promises made in the Compromise of 1850, while the sight of harmless human beings being hustled off to a life of slavery disturbed many Northerners who were not abolitionists.

However, most white Northerners were not prepared to interfere with the enforcement of the Fugitive Slave Act themselves. Of the 332 blacks put on trial under the law, about 300 were returned to slavery, most without incident.

Uncle Tom's Cabin

Tremendously important in increasing sectional tensions and bringing home the evils of slavery to still more people in the North was Harriet Beecher Stowe's novel *Uncle Tom's Cabin* (1852). Stowe was neither a professional writer nor an abolitionist, and she had almost no firsthand knowledge of slavery. But her conscience had been roused by the Fugitive Slave Act. In gathering material for the book, she depended heavily on abolitionist writers, many of whom she knew. She dashed it off quickly; as she later recalled, it seemed to write itself. Nevertheless, *Uncle Tom's Cabin* was an enormous success: 10,000 copies were sold in a week; 300,000 in a year. It was translated into dozens of languages. Dramatized versions were staged in countries throughout the world.

Harriet Beecher Stowe was hardly a distinguished writer; it was her approach to the subject that explains the book's success. Her tale of the pious, patient slave Uncle Tom, the saintly white child Eva, and the callous slave driver Simon Legree appealed to an audience far wider than that reached by the abolitionists. She avoided the self-righteous, accusatory tone of most abolitionist tracts and did not seek to convert readers to belief in racial equality. Many of her southern white characters were fine, sensitive people, while the cruel Simon Legree was a transplanted Connecticut Yankee. There were many heart-rending scenes of pain, self-sacrifice, and heroism. The story proved especially effective on the stage: The slave Eliza crossing the frozen Ohio River to freedom, the death of Little Eva, Eva and Tom ascending to Heaven—these scenes left audiences in tears.

Southern critics pointed out, correctly enough, that Stowe's picture of plantation life was distorted, her slaves atypical. They called her a "coarse, ugly, long-tongued woman" and accused her of trying to "awaken rancorous hatred and malignant jealousies" that would undermine national unity. Most Northerners, having little basis on which to judge the accuracy of the book, tended to discount southern criticism as biased. In any case, *Uncle Tom's Cabin* raised questions that transcended the issue of accuracy. Did it matter if every slave was not as kindly as Uncle Tom, as determined as George Harris? What if only one white master was as evil as Simon Legree? No earlier white American writer had looked at slaves as people.

Uncle Tom's Cabin touched the hearts of millions. Some became abolitionists; others, still hesitating to step forward, asked themselves as they put the book down: Is slavery just?

Diversions Abroad: The "Young America" Movement

Clearly a distraction was needed to help keep the lid on sectional troubles. Some people hoped to find one in foreign affairs. The spirit of manifest destiny explains this in large part; once the United States had reached the Pacific, expansionists began to think of transmitting the dynamic, democratic U.S. spirit to other countries by aiding local revolutionaries, opening new markets, perhaps even annexing foreign lands. This became known as the "Young America" movement, whose

A poster advertising *Uncle Tom's Cabin* in 1852, the year of its publication. The following year, Harriet Beecher Stowe published *A Key to Uncle Tom's Cabin,* intended to provide documentary evidence in support of disputed details of her indictment of slavery.

adherents were confident that democracy would triumph everywhere, even if by conquest.

Some looked to Central America. The rapid development of California created a need for improved communication with the West Coast. A canal across Central America would cut weeks from the sailing time between New York and San Francisco. In 1850 Secretary of State John M. Clayton and the British minister to the United States, Henry Lytton Bulwer, negotiated a treaty providing for the demilitarization and joint Anglo-American control of any canal across the isthmus.

As this area assumed strategic importance to the United States, the desire to obtain Cuba grew stronger. In 1854 President Franklin Pierce instructed his minister to Spain to offer $130 million for the island. The State Department prepared a confidential dispatch suggesting that if Spain refused to sell Cuba, "the great law of self-preservation" might justify "wresting" it from Spain by force.

News of the dispatch—known as the Ostend Manifesto—leaked out, and it had to be published. Northern opinion was outraged by this "slaveholders' plot." Europeans claimed to be shocked by such "dishonorable" and "clandestine" diplomacy. The government had to disavow the manifesto, and any hope of obtaining Cuba or any other territory in the Caribbean vanished.

Stephen Douglas: "The Little Giant"

The most prominent spokesman of the Young America movement was Stephen A. Douglas. The senator from Illinois was the Henry Clay of his generation. Like Clay at his best, Douglas was able to see the needs of the nation in the broadest perspective. He held a succession of state offices before being elected to Congress in 1842 at the age of 29. After only two terms in the House, he was chosen U.S. senator.

The foundations of Douglas's politics were expansion and popular sovereignty. He had been willing to fight for all of Oregon in 1846, and he supported the Mexican War to the hilt, in sharp contrast to his one-term Illinois colleague in Congress, Abraham Lincoln. That local settlers should determine their own institutions was, to his way of thinking, axiomatic. Arguments over the future of slavery in the territories he believed a foolish waste of energy and time since he was convinced that natural conditions would keep the institution out of the West.

The main thing, he insisted, was to get on with the development of the United States. Let the nation build railroads, acquire new territory, expand its trade. He believed slavery "a curse beyond computation" for both blacks and whites, but he refused to admit that any moral issue was involved. He cared not, he boasted, whether slavery was voted up or voted down. This was not really true, but the question was interfering with the rapid exploitation of the continent. Douglas wanted it settled so that the country could concentrate on more important matters.

Douglas's success in steering the Compromise of 1850 through Congress added to his reputation. In 1851, he set out to win the Democratic presidential nomination, reasoning that since he was the brightest, most imaginative, and hardest-working Democrat around, he had every right to press his claim.

This brash aggressiveness proved his undoing. He expressed open contempt for James Buchanan and said of his other chief rival, Lewis Cass, who had won considerable fame while serving as minister to France, that his "reputation was beyond the C."

Stephen A. Douglas, dubbed the "Little Giant" for his height—he was 5 feet 4 inches tall—and his pugnacity. John Quincy Adams observed that during a debate Douglas worked himself into "such a heat that if his body had been made of combustible matter it would have burnt out."

At the 1852 Democratic convention Douglas had no chance. Cass and Buchanan killed each other off, and the delegates finally chose a dark horse, Franklin Pierce of New Hampshire. The Whigs, rejecting the colorless Fillmore, nominated General Winfield Scott, who was known as "Old Fuss and Feathers" because of his "punctiliousness in dress and decorum." In the campaign both sides supported the Compromise of 1850. The Democrats won an easy victory, 254 electoral votes to 42.

So handsome a triumph seemed to ensure stability, but in fact it was a prelude to political chaos. The Whig party was crumbling fast. The shifting amalgam of ethnic and cultural issues that held the party together at the local level dissolved as the slavery debate became more heated. The "Cotton" Whigs of the South, alienated by the antislavery sentiments of their northern brethren, were flocking into the Democratic fold. In the North the Whigs, divided between an antislavery wing ("Conscience Whigs") and another that was undisturbed by slavery, found themselves more and more at odds with each other. Congress fell overwhelmingly into the hands of proslavery southern Democrats, a development profoundly disturbing to northern Democrats as well as to Whigs.

The Kansas-Nebraska Act

Franklin Pierce was a youthful-appearing 48 years old when he took office. He was generally well liked by politicians. His career had included service in both houses of Congress. Alcohol had become a problem for him in Washington, however, and in 1842 he had resigned from the Senate and returned home to try to best the bottle, a struggle in which he was successful. His law practice boomed, and he added to his reputation by serving as a brigadier general during the Mexican War. Although his nomination for president came as a surprise, once made, it had appeared perfectly reasonable. Great things were expected of his administration, especially after he surrounded himself with men of all factions: To balance his appointment of a radical states' rights Mississippian, Jefferson Davis, as secretary of war, for example, he named a conservative Northerner, William L. Marcy of New York, as secretary of state.

Only a strong leader, however, can manage a ministry of all talents, and that President Pierce was not. The ship of state was soon drifting; Pierce seemed incapable of holding firm the helm.

This was the situation in January 1854 when Senator Douglas, chairman of the Committee on Territories, introduced what looked like a routine bill organizing the land west of Missouri and Iowa as the Nebraska Territory. Since settlers were beginning to trickle into the area, the time had arrived to set up a civil administration. The powerful southern faction in Congress would not go along with Douglas's proposal as it stood. Nebraska would presumably become a free state, for it lay north of latitude 36°30' in a district from which slavery had been excluded by the Missouri Compromise. Under pressure from the Southerners, led by Senator David R. Atchison of Missouri, Douglas agreed first to divide the region into two territories, Kansas and Nebraska, and then—a fateful concession—to repeal the part of the Missouri Compromise that excluded slavery from land north of 36°30'. Whether the new territories should become slave or free, he argued, should be left to the decision of the settlers in accordance with the democratic principle of popular sovereignty. The fact that he might advance his presidential ambitions by making concessions to the South must have influenced Douglas too, as must the local political situation in Missouri, where slaveholders feared being "surrounded" on three sides by free states.

Douglas's miscalculation of northern sentiment was monumental. It was one thing to apply popular sovereignty to the new territories in the Southwest, quite another to apply it to a region that had been part of the United States for half a century and free soil for 34 years. Word that the area was to be opened to slavery caused an indignant outcry; many moderate opponents of slavery were radicalized. A group of abolitionist congressmen issued what they called their "Appeal of the Independent Democrats" (actually, all were Free Soilers and Whigs) denouncing the Kansas-Nebraska bill as "a gross violation of a sacred pledge" and calling for a campaign of letter writing, petitions, and public meetings to prevent its passage. The unanimity and force of the northern public's reaction was like nothing in America since the days of the Stamp Act and the Intolerable Acts.

But protests could not defeat the bill. Southerners in both houses backed it regardless of party. Douglas, at his best when under attack, pushed it with all his power. The authors of the "Appeal," he charged, were "the pure unadulterated representatives of Abolitionism, Free Soilism, [and] Niggerism." President Pierce added whatever force the administration could muster. As a result, the northern Democrats split and the bill became law late in May 1854. In this manner the nation took the greatest single step in its march toward the abyss of secession and civil war.

KIDNAPPING
AGAIN!!
A MAN WAS STOLEN LAST NIGHT BY THE
Fugitive Slave Bill COMMISSIONER!
HE WILL HAVE HIS
MOCK TRIAL
ON SATURDAY, MAY 27, AT 9 O'CLOCK,
In the Kidnapper's 'Court,' before the Hon. Slave Bill Commissioner,
AT THE COURT HOUSE, IN COURT SQUARE.
SHALL BOSTON STEAL ANOTHER MAN?
Thursday, May 25, 1854.

Anthony Burns, the subject of this Boston poster, was the third runaway slave to be seized and returned to the South under the hated Fugitive Slave Act of 1850. The Burns case galvanized public opinion just when Congress was debating the Kansas-Nebraska Act. The passage of that bill further outraged Northerners.

The repeal of the Missouri Compromise struck the North like a slap in the face—at once shameful and challenging. Presumably the question of slavery in the territories had been settled forever; now, seemingly without justification, it had been reopened. On May 24, two days after the Kansas-Nebraska bill passed the House of Representatives, Anthony Burns, a slave who had escaped from Virginia by stowing away on a ship, was arrested in Boston. Massachusetts abolitionists brought suit against Burns's former master, charging false arrest. They also organized a protest meeting at which they inflamed the crowd into attacking the court-house where Burns was being held. The mob broke into the building and a guard was killed, but federal marshals drove off the attackers.

President Pierce ordered the Boston district attorney to "incur any expense" to enforce the law. He also sent a revenue cutter to Boston to carry Burns back to Virginia. Thus Burns was returned to his master, but it required two companies of soldiers and 1,000 police and marines to get him aboard ship. As the grim parade marched past buildings festooned with black crepe, the crowd screamed "Kidnappers! Kidnappers!" at the soldiers. Estimates of the cost of returning this single slave to his owner ran as high as $100,000. A few months later, northern sympathizers bought Burns his freedom—for a few hundred dollars.

In previous cases Boston's conservative leaders, Whig to a man, had tended to hold back; after the Burns incident, they were thoroughly radicalized. "We went to bed one night old fashioned . . . Whigs," one of them explained, "and waked up stark mad Abolitionists."

Know-Nothings, Republicans, and the Demise of the Two-Party System

There were ninety-one free-state Democrats in the House of Representatives when the Kansas-Nebraska Act was passed, only twenty-five after the next election. With the Whig party already moribund, dissidents flocked to two new parties.

One was the American, or "Know-Nothing," party, so called because it grew out of a secret society whose members used the password "I don't know." The Know-Nothings were primarily nativists—immigration was soaring in the early 1850s, and the influx of poor foreigners was causing genuine social problems. Crime was on the rise in the cities along with drunkenness and other "diseases of poverty."

Several emotion-charged issues related to the fact that a large percentage of the immigrants were Irish and German Catholics also troubled the Know-Nothings. Questions such as public financing of parochial schools, lay control of church policies, the prohibition of alcoholic beverages, and increasing the time before an immigrant could apply for citizenship (the Know-Nothings favored 21 years) were matters of major importance to them. Since these were divisive issues, the established political parties tried to avoid them; hence the development of the new party.

The American party was important in the South as well as in the North, and while most Know-Nothings disliked blacks and considered them inherently inferior beings, they tended to adopt the dominant view of slavery in whichever section they were located. In the North most opposed the Kansas-Nebraska Act.

Operating often in tacit alliance with the antislavery forces (dislike of slavery did not prevent many abolitionists from being prejudiced against Catholics and immigrants), the northern Know-Nothings won a string of local victories in 1854 and elected more than forty congressmen.

Far more significant in the long run was the formation of the Republican party, which was made up of former Free Soilers, Conscience Whigs, and "Anti-Nebraska" Democrats. The American party was a national organization, but the Republican party was purely sectional. It sprang up spontaneously throughout the Old Northwest and caught on with a rush in New England.

Republicans presented themselves as the party of freedom. They were not abolitionists (though most abolitionists were soon voting Republican), but they insisted that slavery be kept out of the territories. They believed that if America was to remain a land of opportunity, free white labor must have exclusive access to the West. Thus the party appealed not only to voters who disapproved of slavery, but also to those who wished to keep blacks—free or slave—out of their states. In 1854 the Republicans won more than a hundred seats in the House of Representatives and control of many state governments.

The Whig party had almost disappeared in the northern states and the Democratic party had been gravely weakened, but it was unclear how these two new parties would fare. The Know-Nothing party had the superficial advantage of being a nationwide organization, but where slavery was concerned, this was anything but advantageous. And many Northerners who disliked slavery were troubled by the harsh Know-Nothing policies toward immigrants and Catholics. If the Know-Nothings were in control, said former Whig congressman Abraham Lincoln in 1855, the Declaration of Independence would read "all men are created equal, except negroes, *and foreigners, and catholics.*"

"Bleeding Kansas"

The furor over slavery might have died down if settlement of the new territories had proceeded in an orderly manner. Almost none of the settlers who flocked to Kansas owned slaves and relatively few of them were primarily interested in the slavery question.

When Congress opened the gates to settlement in May 1854, none of the land in the territory was available for sale. Treaties extinguishing Indian titles had yet to be ratified, and public lands had not been surveyed. In July Congress authorized squatters to occupy unsurveyed federal lands, but much of this property was far to the west of the frontier and practically inaccessible. The situation led to confusion over property boundaries, to graft and speculation, and to gen-

WAS THE CIVIL WAR AVOIDABLE?

Debating the Past

In 1855 Senator William H. Seward, New York's most prominent Whig, declared from the steps of the capitol in Albany that his party was dead. He advised supporters to join the new Republican party, which opposed slavery. Three years later Seward, a Republican, declared that conflict between the North and South was "irrepressible." Charles and Mary Beard used the term *irrepressible conflict* as a chapter title in their 1927 history text, arguing that antithetical economic systems—one based on free labor and the other on slavery—could not coexist. The argument was fleshed out by Arthur Cole in *The Irrepressible Conflict* (1934), who added that slavery was both outmoded and immoral. War had been inevitable, as was the South's defeat. In *The Repressible Conflict* (1939), Avery Craven dismissed Cole's book as a "belated abolitionist tract." War arose, Craven insisted, when northern "fanatics" whipped up sentiment against the South and southern politicians responded with equal vituperation. The "molders of public opinion" divided the nation by creating "the fiction of two distinct peoples." James G. Randall (1942) similarly saw no differences between the

North and South of sufficient magnitude to rip the nation apart. The leaders of both sides—he called them a "bungling generation"—should not have allowed overheated passions to ignite a civil war. In the 1970s and 1980s historians who embraced the "new political history," which focused on statistical analyses of voting behavior rather than the rhetoric of politicians, argued that war might have been avoided if the Whig party had not disintegrated. William Gienapp (1987) and Michael Holt (1999) credited the two-party system of the Whigs and Democrats with holding the nation together during difficult times; local coalitions on issues such as temperance and immigration had forestalled the divisive reckoning over slavery. It was the emergence of the Republican party in these contexts, not the economic tension between the sections, that made war "irrepressible."

Charles and Mary Beard, *The Rise of American Civilization* (1927), Arthur Cole, *The Irrepressible Conflict* (1934), Avery Craven, *The Repressible Conflict* (1939), James G. Randall, *The Coming of the Civil War* (1942), William Gienapp, *The Origins of the Republican Party* (1987), Michael Holt, *The Rise and Fall of the American Whig Party* (1999).

eral uncertainty, thereby exacerbating the difficulty of establishing an orderly government.

The legal status of slavery in Kansas became the focus of all these conflicts. Both northern abolitionists and southern defenders of slavery were determined to have Kansas. The New England Emigrant Aid Society was formed, with grandiose plans for transporting antislavery settlers to the area. The society transported only a handful of New Englanders to Kansas. Yet the New Englanders were very conspicuous, and the society helped many midwestern antislavery settlers to make the move.

Doing so stirred white Southerners to action. The proslavery forces enjoyed several advantages in this struggle. The first inhabitants in frontier regions nearly always came from lands immediately to the east. In this case they were proslavery Missourians. When word spread that "foreigners" from New England were seeking to "steal" Kansas, many Missourians rushed to protect their "rights." "If we win we carry slavery to the Pacific Ocean," Senator Atchison boasted.

In November 1854 an election was held in Kansas to pick a territorial delegate to Congress. A large band of Missourians crossed over specifically to vote for a proslavery candidate and elected him easily. In March 1855 some 5,000 "border ruffians" again descended on Kansas and elected a territorial legislature. A census had recorded 2,905 eligible voters, but 6,307 votes were cast. The legislature promptly enacted a slave code and laws prohibiting abolitionist agitation. Antislavery settlers refused to recognize this regime and held elections of their own. By January 1856 two governments existed in Kansas, one based on fraud, the other extralegal.

By denouncing the free-state government located at Topeka, President Pierce encouraged the proslavery settlers to assume the offensive. In May, 800 of them sacked the antislavery town of Lawrence. An extremist named John Brown then took the law into his own hands in retaliation. By his reckoning, five Free Soilers had been killed by proslavery forces. In May 1856, together with six companions (four of them his sons), Brown stole into a settlement on Pottawatomie Creek in the dead of night. They dragged five unsuspecting men from their rude cabins and murdered them. This slaughter brought men on both sides to arms by the hundreds. Marauding bands came to blows and terrorized homesteads, first attempting to ascertain the inhabitants' position on slavery.

Brown and his followers escaped capture and were never indicted for the murders, but pressure from federal troops eventually forced him to go into hiding. He finally left Kansas in October 1856. By that time some 200 persons had lost their lives.

A certain amount of violence was normal in any frontier community, but it suited the political interests of the Republicans to make the situation in Kansas seem worse than it was. Exaggerated accounts of "bleeding Kansas" filled the pages of northern newspapers. The Democrats were also partly to blame, for although residents of nearby states often tried to influence elections in new territories, the actions of the border ruffians made a mockery of the democratic process.

However, the main responsibility for the Kansas tragedy must be borne by the Pierce administration. Under popular sovereignty the national government was supposed to see that elections were orderly and honest. Instead, the president acted as a partisan. When the first governor of the territory objected to the manner in which the proslavery legislature had been elected, Pierce replaced him with a man who backed the southern group without question.

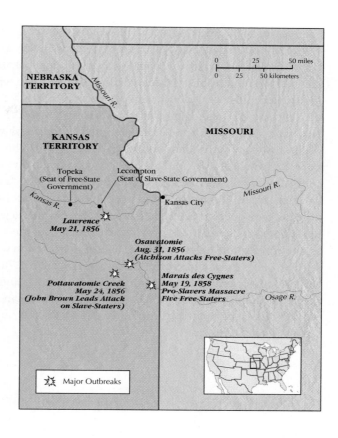

Senator Sumner Becomes a Martyr for Abolitionism

As counterpoint to the fighting in Kansas there arose an almost continuous clamor in the halls of Congress. Red-faced legislators traded insults and threats. Epithets like "liar" were freely tossed about. Prominent in these angry outbursts was a new senator, Charles Sumner of Massachusetts. In the Kansas debates Sumner displayed an icy disdain for his foes. Colleagues threatened him with assassination, called him a "filthy reptile" and a "leper." He was impervious to such hostility. In the spring of 1856 he loosed a dreadful blast titled "The Crime Against Kansas." Characterizing administration policy as tyrannical, imbecilic, absurd, and infamous, he demanded that Kansas be admitted to the Union at once as a free state. Then he began a long and intemperate attack on both Douglas and the elderly Senator Andrew P. Butler of South Carolina, who was not present to defend himself.

Sumner described Butler as a "Don Quixote" who had taken "the harlot, slavery" as his mistress, and he spoke scornfully of "the loose expectoration" of Butler's speech. This was an inexcusable reference to the uncontrollable drooling to which the elderly senator was subject. While he was still talking, Douglas, who shrugged off most political name-calling as part of the game, was heard to mutter, "That damn fool will get himself killed by some other damn fool."

Such a "fool" quickly materialized in the person of Congressman Preston S. Brooks of South Carolina, a nephew of Senator Butler. Since Butler was absent from Washington, Brooks, who was probably as mentally unbalanced as Sumner, assumed the responsibility of defending his kinsman's honor. A southern romantic par excellence, he decided that caning Sumner would reflect his contempt more effectively than challenging him to a duel. Two days after the speech, Brooks entered the Senate as it adjourned. Sumner remained at his desk writing. Waiting until a talkative woman in the lobby had left so that she would be spared the sight of violence, Brooks then walked up to Sumner and rained blows on his head with a cane until Sumner fell, unconscious and bloody, to the floor. "I . . . gave him about 30 first-rate stripes," Brooks later boasted. "Towards the last he bellowed like a calf. I wore my cane out completely but saved the head which is gold." The physical damage suffered by Sumner was not life-threatening, but the incident so affected him psychologically that he was unable to return to his seat in Congress until 1859.

Both sides made much of this disgraceful incident. When the House censured him, Brooks resigned, returned to his home district, and was triumphantly reelected. A number of well-wishers sent him souvenir canes. Northerners viewed the affair as illustrating the brutalizing effect of slavery on southern whites and made a hero of Sumner.

Buchanan Tries His Hand

Such was the atmosphere surrounding the 1856 presidential election. The Republican party now dominated much of the North. It nominated John C. Frémont, "the Pathfinder," one of the heroes of the conquest of California during the war with Mexico. Frémont fit the Whig tradition of presidential candidates: a popular military man with almost no political experience. Unlike Taylor and Scott, however, he was articulate on the issue of slavery in the territories. Although citizens of diverse interests had joined the party, Republicans expressed their objectives in one simple slogan: "Free soil, free speech, and Frémont."

The Democrats cast aside the ineffectual Pierce, but they did not dare nominate Douglas because he had raised such a storm in the North. They settled on James Buchanan, chiefly because he had been out of the country serving as minister to Great Britain during the long debate over Kansas! The American party nominated former president Millard Fillmore, a choice the remnants of the Whigs endorsed.

In the campaign, the Democrats concentrated on denouncing the Republicans as a sectional party that threatened to destroy the Union. On this issue they carried the day. Buchanan won only a minority of the popular vote, but he had strength in every section. He got 174 electoral votes to Frémont's 114 and Fillmore's 8. The significant contest took place in the populous states just north of slave territory— Pennsylvania, Ohio, Indiana, and Illinois. Of these, Buchanan carried all but Ohio, although by narrow margins.

Personally, Buchanan was a bundle of contradictions. Dignified in bearing and by nature cautious, he could consume enormous amounts of liquor without showing the slightest sign of inebriation. A big, heavy man, he was nonetheless remarkably graceful and light on his tiny feet, of which he was inordinately proud. He wore a very high collar to conceal a scarred neck, and because of an eye defect he habitually carried his head to one side and slightly forward, which gave him, as his biographer says, "a perpetual attitude of courteous deference and attentive interest" that sometimes led individuals to believe they had won a greater share of his attention and support than was actually the case. In fact he was extremely stubborn and sometimes vindictive.

The Dred Scott Decision

Before Buchanan could fairly take the Kansas problem in hand, an event occurred that drove another deep wedge between North and South. Back in 1834 Dr. John Emerson of St. Louis joined the army as a surgeon and was assigned to duty at Rock Island, Illinois. Later he was transferred to Fort Snelling, in the Wisconsin Territory. In 1838 he returned to Missouri. Accompanying him on these travels was his body servant, Dred Scott, a slave. In 1846, after Emerson's death, Scott and his wife Harriet, whom he had married while in Wisconsin, with the help of a friendly lawyer brought suit in the Missouri courts for their liberty. They claimed that residence in Illinois, where slavery was barred under the Northwest Ordinance, and in the Wisconsin Territory, where the Missouri Compromise outlawed it, had made them free.

The future of Dred and Harriet Scott mattered not at all to the country or the courts; at issue was the question of whether Congress or the local legislatures had the power to outlaw slavery in the territories. After many years of litigation, the case reached the Supreme Court of the United States. On March 6, 1857, two days after Buchanan's inauguration, the high tribunal acted. Free or slave, the Court declared, blacks were not citizens; therefore, Scott could not sue in a federal court. This was dubious legal logic because many blacks were accepted as citizens in some states when the Constitution was drafted and ratified, and Article IV, Section 2, says that "the citizens of each state shall be entitled to all privileges and immunities of citizens in the several states." But the decision settled Scott's fate.

However, the Court went further. Since the plaintiff had returned to Missouri, the laws of Illinois no longer applied to him. His residence in the Wisconsin Territory—this was the most controversial part of the decision—did not make him free because the Missouri Compromise was unconstitutional. According to the Bill of Rights (the Fifth Amendment), the federal government cannot deprive any person of life, liberty, or property without due process of law.[1] Therefore, Chief Justice Roger

---

[1]*Some state constitutions had similar provisions, but the slave states obviously did not.*

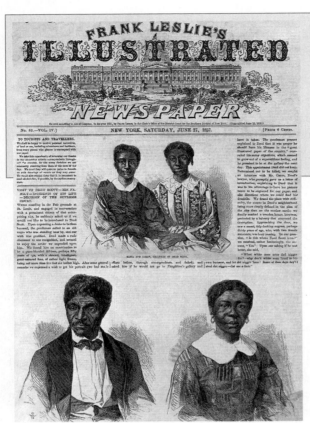

Dred Scott and his wife and children, featured on the cover of *Frank Leslie's Illustrated Newspaper*. Historian Joshua Brown argues in *Beyond the Lines* (2002) that this publication was the precursor to today's popular newsmagazines. Its plentiful pictures were made possible by the new technology of mass-produced wood engraving.

B. Taney reasoned, "an Act of Congress which deprives a person . . . of his liberty or property merely because he came himself or brought his property into a particular Territory . . . could hardly be dignified with the name of due process of law."

In addition to invalidating the already repealed Missouri Compromise, the decision threatened Douglas's principle of popular sovereignty, for if Congress could not exclude slaves from a territory, how could a mere territorial legislature do so? Until statehood was granted, slavery seemed as inviolate as freedom of religion or speech or any other civil liberty guaranteed by the Constitution. Where formerly freedom (as guaranteed in the Bill of Rights) was a national institution and slavery a local one, now, according to the Court, slavery was nationwide, excluded only where states had specifically abolished it.

The irony of employing the Bill of Rights to keep blacks in chains did not escape northern critics. Now slaves could be brought into the Minnesota Territory, even into Oregon. In his inaugural address Buchanan had sanctimoniously urged the people to accept the forthcoming ruling, "whatever this may be," as a final settlement. Many assumed (indeed, it was true) that he had put pressure on the Court to act as it did and that he knew in advance of his speech what the decision would be. If this "greatest crime in the judicial annals of the Republic" was allowed to stand, Northerners argued, the Republican party would have no reason to exist: Its program had been declared unconstitutional! The Dred Scott decision convinced thousands that the South was engaged in an aggressive attempt to extend the peculiar institution so far that it could no longer be considered peculiar.

The Proslavery Lecompton Constitution

Kansas soon provided a test for northern suspicions. Initially Buchanan handled the problem of Kansas well by appointing Robert J. Walker as governor. Although he was from Mississippi, Walker had no desire to foist slavery on the territory against the will of its inhabitants. He was a small man, only five feet tall, but he had more political stature by far than any previous governor of the territory. A former senator and Cabinet member, he was also courageous, patriotic, and tough-minded, much like Douglas in temperament and belief.

The proslavery leaders in Kansas had managed to convene a constitutional convention at Lecompton, but the Free Soil forces boycotted the election of delegates. When this rump body drafted a proslavery constitution and then refused to submit it to a fair vote of all the settlers, Walker denounced its work and hurried back to Washington to explain the situation to Buchanan.

The president refused to face reality. His prosouthern advisers were clamoring for him to "save" Kansas. Instead of rejecting the Lecompton constitution, he asked Congress to admit Kansas to the Union with this document as its frame of government.

Buchanan's decision brought him head-on against Stephen A. Douglas, and the repercussions of their clash shattered the Democratic party. Principle and self-interest (an irresistible combination) forced Douglas to oppose the leader of his party. If he stood aside while Congress admitted Kansas, he not only would be abandoning popular sovereignty, but he would be committing political suicide as well. He was up for reelection to the Senate in 1858. All but one of the fifty-six newspapers in Illinois had declared editorially against the Lecompton constitution; if Douglas supported it, his defeat was certain. In a dramatic confrontation at the White House, he and Buchanan argued the question at length, tempers rising. Finally, the president tried to force him into line. "Mr. Douglas," he said, "I desire you to remember that no Democrat ever yet differed from an Administration of his own choice without being crushed." "Mr. President," Douglas replied contemptuously, "I wish you to remember that General Jackson is dead!" And he stalked out of the room.

Buchanan then compounded his error by putting tremendous political pressure on Douglas, cutting off his Illinois patronage on the eve of his reelection campaign. Of course Douglas persisted, openly joining the Republicans in the fight. Congress rejected the Lecompton bill.

Meanwhile, the extent of the fraud perpetrated at Lecompton became clear. In October 1857 a new legislature had been chosen in Kansas, antislavery voters participating in the balloting. It ordered a referendum on the Lecompton constitution in January 1858. This time the proslavery settlers boycotted the vote and the constitution was overwhelmingly rejected. When Buchanan persisted in pressing Congress to admit Kansas under the Lecompton constitution, Congress ordered another referendum. Kansans rejected it by a huge margin.

The Emergence of Lincoln

These were dark days. During the Panic of 1857 Northerners put the blame for the hard times on the southern-dominated Congress, which had just reduced tariff duties to the lowest levels in nearly half a century. As prices plummeted and unemployment rose, they attributed the collapse to foreign competition and accused the South of having sacrificed the prosperity of the rest of the nation for its selfish advantage. The South in turn read in its relative immunity from the depression proof of the superiority of the slave system, which further stimulated the running sectional debate about the relative merits of free and slave labor.

Dissolution threatened the Union. To many Americans, Stephen A. Douglas seemed to offer the best hope of preserving it. For this reason unusual attention was focused on his campaign for reelection to the Senate in 1858. The importance of the contest and Douglas's national prestige put great pressure on the Republicans of Illinois to nominate someone who would make a good showing against him. The man they chose was Abraham Lincoln.

After a towering figure has passed from the stage, it is always difficult to discover what he was like before his rise to prominence. This is especially true of Lincoln, who changed greatly when power, responsibility, and fame came to him. Lincoln was not unknown in 1858, but his public career had not been distinguished. He was born in Kentucky in 1809, and the story of his early life can be condensed, as he once said himself, into a single line from Thomas Gray's *Elegy:* "The short and simple annals of the poor." His illiterate father, Thomas Lincoln, was a typical frontier wanderer. When Abraham was seven years old, the family moved to Indiana. In 1830 they pushed west again into southern Illinois. The boy received almost no formal schooling.

However, Lincoln had a good mind, and he was extremely ambitious.[2] He cut loose from his family, made a trip to New Orleans, and for a time managed a general store in New Salem, Illinois. In 1834, when barely 25, he won a seat in the Illinois legislature as a Whig. Meanwhile, he studied law and was admitted to the bar in 1836.

---

[2]*His law partner, William Herndon, said that Lincoln's ambition was "a little engine that knows no rest."*

Lincoln remained in the legislature until 1842, displaying a perfect willingness to adopt the Whig position on all issues. In 1846 he was elected to Congress. While not engaged in politics he worked at the law, maintaining an office in Springfield and following the circuit, taking a variety of cases, few of much importance. He earned a decent but by no means sumptuous living. After one term in Congress, marked by his partisan opposition to Polk's Mexican policy, his political career petered out. He seemed fated to pass his remaining years as a small-town lawyer.

The revival of the slavery controversy in 1854 stirred Lincoln deeply. No abolitionist, he had tried to take a "realistic" view of the problem. The Kansas-Nebraska bill led him to see the moral issue more clearly. "If slavery is not wrong, nothing is wrong," he stated with the directness and simplicity of expression for which he later became famous. Compromises made in the past for the sake of sectional harmony had always sought to preserve as much territory as possible for freedom. Yet unlike most Free Soilers, he did not blame the Southerners for slavery. "They are just what we would be in their situation," he confessed.

Thus Lincoln was at once compassionate toward the slave owner and stern toward the institution. "A house divided against itself cannot stand," he warned. "I believe this government cannot endure permanently half slave and half free." Without minimizing the difficulties or urging a hasty or ill-considered solution, Lincoln demanded that the people look toward a day, however remote, when not only Kansas but the entire country would be free.

The Lincoln-Douglas Debates

As Lincoln developed these ideas his reputation grew. In 1855 he almost won the Whig nomination for senator. He became a Republican shortly thereafter, and in June 1856, at the first Republican National Convention, he received 110 votes for the vice presidential nomination. He seemed the logical man to pit against Douglas in 1858.

In July, Lincoln challenged Douglas to a series of seven debates. The senator accepted. The debates were well attended and widely reported, for the idea of a direct confrontation between candidates for an important office captured the popular imagination.

The choice of the next senator lay, of course, in the hands of the Illinois legislature. Technically, Douglas and Lincoln were campaigning for candidates for the legislature who were pledged to support them for the Senate seat. The two employed different political styles, each calculated to project a particular image. Douglas epitomized efficiency and success. He dressed in the latest fashion, favoring flashy vests and the finest broadcloth. He was a glad-hander and a heavy drinker—he apparently died of cirrhosis of the liver. Ordinarily he arrived in town in a private railroad car, to be met by a brass band, then to ride at the head of a parade to the appointed place.

How Lincoln aged during his term of office is evident in comparing Alexander Hesler's portrait, taken on June 3, 1860, with one by an unnamed photographer, taken April 10, 1865.

Lincoln appeared before the voters as a man of the people. He wore ill-fitting black suits and a stovepipe hat—repository for letters, bills, scribbled notes, and other scraps—that exaggerated his great height. He presented a worn and rumpled appearance, partly because he traveled from place to place on day coaches, accompanied by only a few advisers. When local supporters came to meet him at the station, he preferred to walk with them through the streets to the scene of the debate.

Douglas's strategy was to make Lincoln look like an abolitionist. He accused the Republicans of favoring racial equality and refusing to abide by the decision of the Supreme Court in the Dred Scott case. Himself he pictured as a heroic champion of democracy, attacked on one side by the "black" Republicans and on the other by Buchanan supporters, yet ready to fight to his last breath for popular sovereignty.

Lincoln tried to picture Douglas as proslavery and a defender of the Dred Scott decision. "Slavery is an unqualified evil to the negro, to the white man, to the soil, and to the State," he said. "Judge Douglas," he also said, "is blowing out the moral lights around us, when he contends that whoever wants slaves has a right to hold them."

However, Lincoln often weakened the impact of his arguments, being perhaps too eager to demonstrate his conservatism. "All men are created equal," he would say on the authority of the Declaration of Independence, only to add: "I am not, nor ever have been, in favor of bringing about in any way the social and political equality of the white and black races." He opposed allowing blacks to vote, to sit on juries, to marry whites, even to be citizens. He predicted the "ultimate extinction" of slavery, but when pressed he predicted that it would not occur "in less than a hundred years at the least." He took a fence-sitting position on the question of abolition in the District of Columbia and stated flatly that he did not favor repeal of the Fugitive Slave Act.

In the debate at Freeport, a town northwest of Chicago near the Wisconsin line, Lincoln asked Douglas if, considering the Dred Scott decision, the people of a territory could exclude slavery before the territory became a state. Unhesitatingly Douglas replied that they could, simply by not passing the local laws essential for holding blacks in bondage. "It matters not what way the Supreme Court may hereafter decide as to the abstract question," Douglas said. "The people have the lawful means to introduce or exclude it as they please, for the reason that slavery cannot exist . . . unless it is supported by local police regulations."

This argument saved Douglas in Illinois. The Democrats carried the legislature by a narrow margin, whereas it is almost certain that if Douglas had accepted the Dred Scott decision outright, the balance would have swung to the Republicans. But the so-called Freeport Doctrine cost him heavily two years later when he made his bid for the Democratic presidential nomination. "It matters not what way the Supreme Court may hereafter decide"—southern extremists would not accept a man who suggested that the Dred Scott decision could be circumvented, although in fact Douglas had only stated the obvious.

The campaign of 1858 marked Douglas's last triumph, Lincoln's last defeat. Elsewhere the elections in the North went heavily to the Republicans. When the old Congress reconvened in December, northern-sponsored economic measures (a higher tariff, the transcontinental railroad, river and harbor improvements, a free homestead bill) were all blocked by southern votes.

Whether the South could continue to prevent the passage of this legislation in the new Congress was problematical. In early 1859 even many moderate Southerners were uneasy about the future. The radicals, made panicky by Republican victories and their own failure to win in Kansas, spoke openly of secession if a Republican was elected president in 1860. Lincoln's "house divided" speech was quoted out of context, while Douglas's Freeport Doctrine added to southern woes. When Senator William H. Seward of New York spoke of an "irrepressible conflict" between freedom and slavery, white Southerners became still more alarmed.

Naturally they struck back. Led by such self-described "fire-eaters" as William L. Yancey of Alabama and Senators Jefferson Davis of Mississippi, John Slidell of Louisiana, and James H. Hammond of South Carolina, they demanded a federal slave code for the territories and talked of annexing Cuba and reviving the African slave trade.

John Brown's Raid

In October 1859, John Brown, the scourge of Kansas, made his second contribution to the unfolding sectional drama. Gathering a group of eighteen followers, white and black, he staged an attack on Harpers Ferry, Virginia, a town on the Potomac River upstream from Washington. Having boned up on guerrilla tactics, he planned to seize the federal arsenal there; arm the slaves, whom he thought would flock to his side; and then establish a black republic in the mountains of Virginia.

Simply by overpowering a few night watchmen, Brown and his men occupied the arsenal and a nearby rifle factory. They captured several hostages, one of them Colonel Lewis Washington, a great-grandnephew of George Washington. But no slaves came forward to join them. Federal troops commanded by Robert E. Lee soon trapped Brown's men in an engine house of the Baltimore and Ohio Railroad. After a two-day siege in which the attackers picked off ten of his men, Brown was captured.

No incident so well illustrates the role of emotion and irrationality in the sectional crisis as does John Brown's raid. After his ghastly Pottawatomie murders it should have been obvious to anyone that he was both a fanatic and mentally unstable: Some of the victims were hacked to bits with a broadsword. Yet numbers of high-minded Northerners, including Emerson and Thoreau, had supported Brown and his antislavery "work" after 1856. Some—among them Franklin B. Sanborn, a teacher; Thomas Wentworth Higginson, a clergyman; and the merchant George L. Stearns—contributed knowingly to his Harpers Ferry enterprise.

White Southerners reacted to Harpers Ferry with equal irrationality, some with a rage similar to Brown's. Dozens of hapless Northerners in the southern states were arrested, beaten, or driven off. One, falsely suspected of being an accomplice of Brown, was lynched.

Brown's fate lay in the hands of the Virginia authorities. Ignoring his obvious derangement, they charged him with treason, conspiracy, and murder. He was speedily convicted and sentenced to death by hanging.

Yet "Old Brown" had still one more contribution to make to the developing sectional tragedy. Despite the furor he had created, cool heads everywhere called for calm and denounced his attack. Most Republican politicians repudiated him. Even execution would probably not have made a martyr of Brown had he behaved like a madman after his capture. Instead, an enormous dignity descended on him as he lay in his Virginia jail awaiting death. Whatever his faults, he truly believed in racial equality. He addressed blacks who worked for him as "Mister" and arranged for them to eat at his table and sit with his family in church.

This conviction served him well in his last days. "If it is deemed necessary that I should forfeit my life for the furtherance of the ends of justice, and mingle my blood further with the blood of . . . millions in this slave country whose rights are

After John Brown's capture, Emerson called him "a martyr" who would "make the gallows as glorious as the cross." Brown's principled radicalism found favor during the Depression decade of the 1930s. John Stewart Curry's mural, completed in 1943, depicted the demented Brown in the pose of Christ on the cross. The image offended the Kansas legislature, which had commissioned Curry to portray Kansas history in a "sane and sensible manner."

disregarded by wicked, cruel, and unjust enactments," he said before the judge pronounced sentence, "I say, let it be done."

This John Brown, with his patriarchal beard and sad eyes, so apparently incompatible with the bloody terrorist of Pottawatomie and Harpers Ferry, led thousands in the North to ignore his past and treat him almost as a saint.

And so Brown, hanged on December 2, 1859, became to the North a hero and to the South a symbol of northern ruthlessness. Soon, as the popular song had it, Brown's body lay "a-mouldering in the grave," and the memory of his bloody act did indeed go "marching on."

The Election of 1860

By 1860 the nation was teetering on the brink of disunion. Radicals North and South were heedlessly provoking one another. Stephen A. Douglas was probably the last hope of avoiding a rupture between North and South. But when the Democrats met at Charleston, South Carolina, in April 1860 to choose a presidential candidate, the southern delegates would not support him unless he promised not to disturb slavery in the territories. Indeed, they went further in their demands. The North, William L. Yancey of Alabama insisted, must accept the proposition that slavery was not merely tolerable but right. Of course the Northerners would not go so far. "Gentlemen of the South," said Senator George E. Pugh of Ohio in replying to Yancey, "you mistake us—you mistake us! We will not do it!" When southern proposals were voted down, most of the delegates from the deep South walked out and the convention adjourned without naming a candidate.

In June the Democrats reconvened at Baltimore. Again they failed to reach agreement. The two wings then met separately, the Northerners nominating Douglas, the Southerners John C. Breckenridge of Kentucky, Buchanan's vice president. On the question of slavery in the territories, the Northerners promised to "abide by the decision of the Supreme Court," which meant, in effect, that they stood for Douglas's Freeport Doctrine. The Southerners announced their belief that neither Congress nor any territorial government could prevent citizens from settling "with their property" in any territory.

Meanwhile, the Republicans, who met in Chicago in mid-May, had drafted a platform attractive to all classes and all sections of the northern and western states. For manufacturers they proposed a high tariff, for farmers a homestead law providing free land for settlers. Internal improvements "of a National character," notably a railroad to the Pacific, should receive federal aid. No restrictions should be placed on immigration. As to slavery in the territories, the Republicans did not equivocate: "The normal condition of all the territory of the United States is that of freedom." Neither Congress nor a local legislature could "give legal existence to Slavery in any Territory."

In choosing a presidential candidate the Republicans displayed equally shrewd political judgment. Senator Seward was the front-runner, but he had taken too extreme a stand and appeared unlikely to carry the crucial states of Pennsylvania, Indiana, and Illinois. He led on the first ballot but could not get a majority. Then the delegates began to look closely at Abraham Lincoln. His thoughtful and moderate views on the main issue of the times and his formidable debating skills attracted many, and so did his political personality. "Honest Abe," the "Railsplitter," a man of humble origins (born in a log cabin), self-educated, self-made, a common man but by no means an ordinary man—the combination seemed unbeatable.

It also helped that Lincoln was from a crucial state and had an excellent team of convention managers. Taking advantage of the fact that the convention was meeting in Lincoln's home state, they packed the gallery with leather-lunged Chicago ward heelers who were assigned the task of shouting for their man. They also made a series of deals with the leaders of other state delegations to win additional votes. "I authorize no bargains and will be bound by none," Lincoln telegraphed the convention. "Lincoln ain't here and don't know what we have to meet," one of his managers remarked—and proceeded to trade off two Cabinet posts for the votes of key states.

On the second ballot Lincoln drew shoulder to shoulder with Seward, on the third he was within two votes of victory. Before the roll could be called again, dele-

THE UNDECIDED POLITICAL PRIZE FIGHT.

Modern scholars of the media have found that most news reporting of political campaigns focuses not on issues but on the contest itself. This cartoon, depicting Abraham Lincoln and Stephen A. Douglas as boxers during the 1860 presidential campaign, shows that Americans have long been attuned to the competitive aspects of politics.

gates began to switch their votes, and in a landslide, soon made unanimous, Lincoln was nominated.

A few days earlier the remnants of the American and Whig parties had formed the Constitutional Union party and nominated John Bell of Tennessee for president. "It is both the part of patriotism and of duty," they resolved, "to recognize no political principle other than the Constitution of the country, the union of the states, and the enforcement of the laws." Ostrichlike, the Constitutional Unionists ignored the conflicts rending the nation. Only in the border states, where the consequences of disunion were sure to be most tragic, did they have any following.

With four candidates in the field, no one could win a popular majority, but it soon became clear that Lincoln was going to be elected. Breckenridge had most of the slave states in his pocket and Bell would run strong in the border regions, but the populous northern and western states had a majority of the electoral votes, and there the choice lay between the Republicans and the Douglas Democrats. In such a contest the Republicans, with their attractive economic program and their strong stand against slavery in the territories, were sure to come out on top.

Lincoln avoided campaigning and made no public statements. Douglas, recognizing the certainty of Lincoln's victory, accepted his fate and for the first time in his career rose above ambition. "We must try to save the Union," he said. "I will go South."

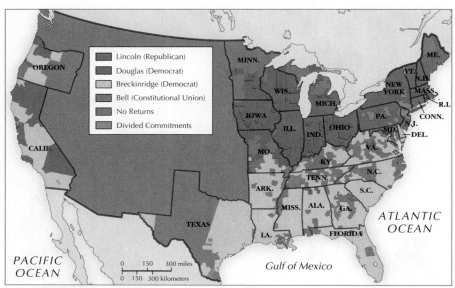

Presidential Election, 1860

In the heart of the Cotton Kingdom, he appealed to the voters to stand by the Union regardless of who was elected. He was the only candidate to do so; the others refused to remind the people that their election might result in secession and civil war.

When the votes were counted, Lincoln had 1.866 million, almost a million fewer than the combined total of his three opponents, but he swept the North and West, which gave him 180 electoral votes and the presidency. Douglas received 1.383 million votes, so distributed that he carried only Missouri and part of New Jersey. Breckenridge, with 848,000 popular votes, won most of the South; Bell, with 593,000, carried Virginia, Tennessee, and Kentucky. Lincoln was thus a minority president, but his title to the office was unquestionable. Even if his opponents could have combined their popular votes in each state, Lincoln would have won.

The Secession Crisis

Only days after Lincoln's victory, the South Carolina legislature ordered an election of delegates to a convention to decide the state's future course. On December 20 the convention voted unanimously to secede, basing its action on the logic of Calhoun. "The State of South Carolina has resumed her position among the nations of the world," the delegates announced. By February 1, 1861, the six other states of the lower South had followed suit. A week later, at Montgomery, Alabama, a provisional government of the Confederate States of America was established. Virginia, Tennessee, North Carolina, and Arkansas did not leave the Union but announced that if the federal government attempted to use force against the Confederacy, they too would secede.

Why were white Southerners willing to wreck the Union their forebears had put together with so much love and labor? No simple explanation is possible. The danger that the expanding North would overwhelm them was for neither today nor tomorrow. Lincoln had assured them that he would respect slavery where it existed. The Democrats had retained control of Congress in the election; the Supreme Court was firmly in their hands as well. If the North did try to destroy slavery, secession would perhaps be a logical tactic, but why not wait until the threat materialized? To leave the Union meant abandoning the very objectives for which the South had been contending for over a decade: a share of the federal territories and an enforceable fugitive slave law.

One reason why the South rejected this line of thinking was the tremendous economic energy generated in the North, which seemed to threaten the South's independence. As one Southerner complained at a commercial convention in 1855:

> From the rattle with which the nurse tickles the ear of the child born in the South to the shroud which covers the cold form of the dead, everything comes from the North. We rise from between sheets made in Northern looms, and pillows of Northern feathers, to wash in basins made in the North. . . . We eat from Northern plates and dishes; our rooms are swept with Northern brooms, our gardens dug with Northern spades . . . and the very wood which feeds our fires is cut with Northern axes, helved with hickory brought from Connecticut and New York.

Secession, white Southerners argued, would "liberate" the South and produce the kind of balanced economy that was proving so successful in the North. Moreover, the mere possibility of emancipation was a powerful force for secession. "We must either submit to degradation, and to the loss of property worth four billions," the Mississippi convention declared, "or we must secede."

The years of sectional conflict, the growing northern criticism of slavery, perhaps even an unconscious awareness that this criticism was well founded, had undermined and in many cases destroyed the patriotic feelings of white Southerners. Because of the constant clamor set up by New England antislavery groups, the South tended to identify all Northerners as "Yankee abolitionists" and to resent them with increasing passion. "I look upon the whole New England race as a troublesome unquiet set of meddlers," one Georgian wrote. In addition, a Republican president would not need the consent of Congress to flood the South with unfriendly federal officials-abolitionists and perhaps even blacks. Such a possibility most white Southerners found unsupportable. Fear approaching panic swept the region.

Although states' rights provided the rationale for leaving the Union, and Southerners expounded the strict constructionist interpretation of the Constitution with great ingenuity, the economic and emotional factors were far more basic. The lower South decided to go ahead with secession regardless of the cost. "Let the consequences be what they may," an Atlanta newspaper proclaimed. "Whether the

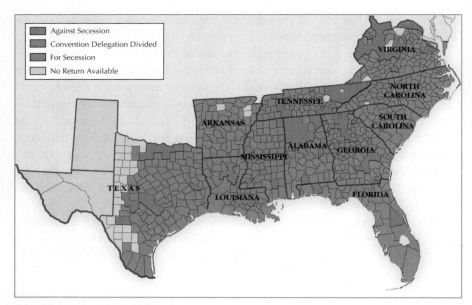

Secession of the South, 1860–1861

A comparison of this map with the one on page 353 shows the minimal support for secession in the mainly nonslave mountain areas of the Appalachians. The strong antisecession sentiment in the mountainous areas of Virginia eventually led several counties there to break from Virginia in 1863 and form the new state of West Virginia.

Potomac is crimsoned in human gore, and Pennsylvania Avenue is paved ten fathoms in depth with mangled bodies . . . the South will never submit."

Not every slave owner could contemplate secession with such bloodthirsty equanimity. Some believed that the risks of war and slave insurrection were too great. Others retained a profound loyalty to the United States. Many accepted secession only after the deepest examination of conscience. Lieutenant Colonel Robert E. Lee of Virginia was typical of thousands. "I see only that a fearful calamity is upon us," he wrote during the secession crisis. "There is no sacrifice I am not ready to make for the preservation of the Union save that of honour. If a disruption takes place, I shall go back in sorrow to my people & share the misery of my native state."

In the North there was a foolish but understandable reluctance to believe that the South really intended to break away. President-elect Lincoln was inclined to write off secession as a bluff designed to win concessions he was determined not to make. He also showed lamentable political caution in refusing to announce his plans or to cooperate with the outgoing Democratic administration before his inauguration.

The new southern Confederacy set vigorously to work drafting a constitution, choosing Jefferson Davis as provisional president, seizing arsenals and other federal property within its boundaries, and preparing to dispatch diplomatic representatives to enlist the support of foreign powers. Buchanan bumbled helplessly in Washington. And out in Illinois, Abraham Lincoln juggled Cabinet posts and grew a beard.

1850	Compromise of 1850 preserves Union
	U.S. and Great Britain sign Clayton-Bulwer Treaty on interoceanic travel
1851–1860	Northerners resist enforcement of Fugitive Slave Act
1852	Harriet Beecher Stowe publishes *Uncle Tom's Cabin*, a novel depicting slavery
	Franklin Pierce is elected president
1854	U.S. disavows secret Ostend Manifesto on Cuba
	Kansas-Nebraska Act repeals Missouri Compromise
1856–1858	Proslavery forces oppose Free Soilers in "Bleeding Kansas" Territory
1856	John Brown and followers murder five proslavery men in Pottawatomie Massacre
	South Carolina's Preston Brooks canes Senator Charles Sumner of Massachusetts on Senate floor
	James Buchanan is elected president
1857	U.S. Supreme Court issues decision in Dred Scott case, declaring slaves are not citizens
	Panic of 1857 collapses economy
1858	Abraham Lincoln loses Senate race to Stephen Douglas after Lincoln-Douglas debates, but wins national attention
1859	John Brown raids Harpers Ferry, Virginia, arsenal
1860	Abraham Lincoln is elected president
	South Carolina secedes from Union
1861	Seven southern states establish Confederate States of America

CHAPTER

The War to Save
the Union

ON FEBRUARY 22, 2006, SUNNI INSURGENTS OVERWHELMED THE caretaker and staff of the Mosque of the Golden Dome in Samarra, 60 miles north of Baghdad, Iraq. The mosque was among the most revered Shiite shrines in the Middle East, visited by more than a million Muslims each year. The attackers placed explosive devices at the base of the dome and left the building. Moments later, an explosion collapsed the dome, shattering its 72,000 golden tiles.

If the purpose of the bombing were to ignite a civil war between Sunni and Shiite Muslims, it succeeded spectacularly. By sunset, Shiite militiamen bent on revenge had destroyed twenty-seven Sunni mosques, killed three imams—Islamic holy men—and assaulted hundreds of Sunnis. Over the next 12 months, the cycle of violence escalated, resulting in the deaths of over 34,000 Iraqi civilians. (This accounting is provided by the United Nations; other estimates are higher.) "The gates of hell are open in Iraq," declared Amr Moussa, head of the Arab League.

Americans have been baffled by such acts of "senseless violence"—the phrase used by President Bush after the attack on the Golden Dome. "Why do Sunnis kill Shiites?" asked Trent Lott, a Republican senator from Mississippi. "Why do they hate each other?" Bill O'Reilly, a TV commentator, provided a characteristically blunt answer: "There are so many nuts in the country—so many crazies." Why else would Iraqi kill Iraqi, and Muslim kill Muslim?

The reasons for any civil war are not so simple, as Americans were to learn in 1861. Brother fought brother; men intent on destroying each other prayed to the same God.

The U.S. Civil War moved forward, as wars do, impelled by its own terrible momentum. The first inconclusive battle led to others. More men were called to arms, often against their will. Farms and factories were diverted to the war effort. Lincoln emancipated slaves as a measure to weaken the South. The strains of the war fractured the political consensus. When the guns at last fell silent, a half million men lay dead.

President Abraham Lincoln, while touring the hospital wards after yet another gruesome battle, despaired at the horror of it all: "If there is a worse place than hell, I am in it."

Lincoln's Cabinet

The nomination of Lincoln had succeeded brilliantly for the Republicans, but was his election a good thing for the country? As the inauguration approached, many Americans had doubts. Honest Abe was a clever politician who had spoken well about the central issue of the times, but would he act decisively in this crisis? His behavior as president-elect was not reassuring. He spent much time closeted with politicians. Was he too obtuse to understand the grave threat to the Union posed by secession? People remembered uneasily that he had never held executive office, that his congressional career had been short and undistinguished. When he finally uprooted himself from Springfield in February 1861, his occasional speeches en route to Washington were vague, almost flippant. He kissed babies, shook hands, mouthed platitudes. Some people thought it downright cowardly that he let himself be spirited in the dead of night through Baltimore, where feeling against him ran high.

Everyone waited tensely to see whether Lincoln would oppose secession with force, but Lincoln seemed concerned only with organizing his Cabinet. William H. Seward, the secretary of state, was the ablest and best known of the appointees. Despite his reputation for radicalism, the hawk-nosed, chinless, tousle-haired Seward hoped to conciliate the South and was thus in bad odor with the radical wing of the Republican party. In time Seward proved himself Lincoln's strong right arm. Senator Salmon P. Chase, a bald, square-jawed, antislavery leader from Ohio, whom Lincoln named secretary of the treasury, represented the radicals. Chase was humorless and vain but able; he detested Seward. Many of the president's other selections worried thoughtful people.

Lincoln's inaugural address was conciliatory but firm. Southern institutions were in no danger from his administration. Secession, however, was illegal, the Union "perpetual." "A husband and wife may be divorced," Lincoln said, employing one of his homely and unconsciously risqué metaphors, "but the different parts of our country cannot . . . . Intercourse, either amicable or hostile, must continue between them." His tone was calm and warm. His concluding words catch the spirit of the inaugural perfectly:

> I am loath to close. We are not enemies, but friends. We must not be enemies.
> Though passion may have strained, it must not break, our bonds of affection. The
> mystic chords of memory, stretching from every battlefield and patriot grave to every
> living heart . . . will yet swell the chorus of the Union when again touched, as surely
> they will be, by the better angels of our nature.

Fort Sumter: The First Shot

While denying the legality of secession, Lincoln had taken a temporizing position. The Confederates had seized most federal property in the Deep South. Lincoln admitted frankly that he would not attempt to reclaim this property. However, two strongholds, Fort Sumter, on an island in Charleston harbor, and Fort Pickens, at Pensacola, Florida, were still in loyal Union hands. Most Republicans did not want to surrender them without a show of resistance. To do so, one wrote, would be to convert the American eagle into a "debilitated chicken."

Yet to reinforce the forts might mean bloodshed that would make reconciliation impossible. After weeks of indecision, Lincoln took the moderate step of sending a naval expedition to supply the beleaguered Sumter garrison with food. Unwilling to permit this, the Confederates opened fire on the fort on April 12 before the supply ships arrived. After holding out for 34 hours, Major Robert Anderson and his men surrendered.

The attack precipitated an outburst of patriotic indignation in the North. Lincoln issued a call for 75,000 volunteers; his request prompted Virginia, North Carolina, Arkansas, and Tennessee to secede. After years of crises and compromises, the nation chose to settle the great quarrel between the sections by force of arms.

The Southerners were seeking to exercise what a later generation would call the right of self-determination. How, they asked, could the North square its professed belief in democracy with its refusal to permit the southern states to leave the Union when a majority of their citizens wished to do so?

Lincoln took the position that secession was a rejection of democracy. If the South could refuse to abide by the result of an election in which it had freely participated, then everything that monarchists and other conservatives had said about the instability of republican governments would be proved true. "The central idea of secession is the essence of anarchy," he said. The United States must "demonstrate to the world" that "when ballots have been fairly and constitutionally decided, there can be no successful appeal except to ballots themselves, at succeeding elections."

Although abolition was to be one of the major results of the Civil War, the war was fought for nationalistic reasons, not to destroy slavery. Lincoln made this plain when he wrote in response to an editorial by Horace Greeley urging immediate emancipation: "I would save the Union. . . . If I could save the Union without freeing any slave, I would do it; and if I could save it by freeing all the slaves, I would do it; and if I could do it by freeing some and leaving others alone, I would also do that." He added, however, "I intend no modification of my oft-expressed personal wish that all men, everywhere, could be free."

The Blue and the Gray

In any test between the United States and the Confederacy, the former possessed tremendous advantages. There were more than 20 million people in the northern states (excluding Kentucky and Missouri, where opinion was divided) but only 9

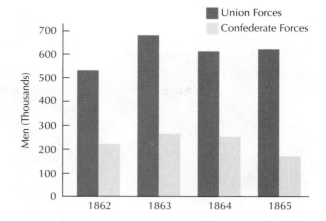

Men Present for Service During the Civil War

403

million in the South, including 3.5 million slaves whom the whites hesitated to trust with arms. The North's economic capacity to wage war was even more preponderant. It was manufacturing nine times as much as the Confederacy (including 97 percent of the nation's firearms) and had a far larger and more efficient railroad system than the South. Northern control of the merchant marine and the navy made possible a blockade of the Confederacy, a particularly potent threat to a region so dependent on foreign markets.

The Confederates discounted these advantages. Many doubted that public opinion in the North would sustain Lincoln if he attempted to meet secession with force. Northern manufacturers needed southern markets, and merchants depended heavily on southern business. Many western farmers still sent their produce down the Mississippi. War would threaten the prosperity of all these groups, Southerners maintained. Should the North try to cut Europe off from southern cotton, the European powers, particularly Great Britain, would descend on the land in their might, force open southern ports, and provide the Confederacy with the means of defending itself forever. Moreover, the South provided nearly three-fourths of the world's cotton, essential for most textile mills. "You do not dare to make war on cotton," Senator Hammond of South Carolina had taunted his northern colleagues in 1858. "No power on earth dares to make war upon it. Cotton is king."

The Confederacy also counted on certain military advantages. The new nation need only hold what it had; it could fight a defensive war, less costly in men and material and of great importance in maintaining morale and winning outside sympathy. Southerners would be defending not only their social institutions but also their homes and families.

Luck played a part too; the Confederacy quickly found a great commander, while many of the northern generals in the early stages of the war proved either bungling or indecisive. In battle after battle Union armies were defeated by forces of equal or smaller size.

Young volunteers of the First Virginia Militia, in 1861. Why did they join the Confederate army? "It is better to spend our all in defending our country than to be subjugated and have it taken away from us," one explained, a sentiment that appeared often in the letters of Confederate soldiers. Soldiers on both sides believed that their cause was righteous.

There was little to distinguish the enlisted men of the two sides. Both, conscious of their forefathers of 1776, fought for liberty, though they interpreted the concept in opposite ways.

Both sides faced massive difficulties in organizing for a war long feared but never properly anticipated. After southern defections, the regular Union army consisted of only 13,000 officers and enlisted men, far too few to absorb the 186,000 who had joined the colors by early summer, much less the additional 450,000 who had volunteered by the end of the year. Recruiting was left to the states, each being assigned a quota; there was little central organization. Natty companies of "Fire Zouaves" and "Garibaldi Guards" in gorgeous uniforms rubbed shoulders with slovenly units composed of toughs and criminals and with regiments of farm boys from Iowa, Illinois, and Michigan. Unlike later conflicts in which men from all parts of the country were mixed in each regiment, Civil War units were recruited locally. Men in each company tended to have known one another or had friends in common in civilian life. But few knew even the rudiments of soldiering. The hastily composed high command, headed by the elderly Winfield Scott, debated grand strategy endlessly while regimental commanders lacked decent maps of Virginia.

The Confederacy faced far greater problems than the North, for it had to create an entire administration under pressure of war, with the additional handicap of the states' rights philosophy to which it was committed. The Confederate constitution explicitly recognized the sovereignty of the states and contained no broad authorization for laws designed to advance the general welfare. State governments repeatedly defied the central administration, located at Richmond after Virginia seceded, even with regard to military affairs.

The call to arms produced a turnout in the Confederacy perhaps even more impressive than that in the North; by July 1861 about 112,000 men were under arms. As in the North, men of every type enlisted, and morale was high. Some

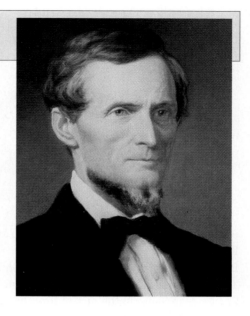

Jefferson Davis sat for this portrait in 1863 in his mansion in Richmond. It is the only wartime portrait from the life of the Confederate president.

wealthy recruits brought slave servants with them to care for their needs in camp, cavalrymen supplied their own horses, and many men arrived with their own shotguns and hunting rifles. Ordinary militia companies sporting names like Tallapoosa Thrashers, Cherokee Lincoln Killers, and Chickasaw Desperadoes marched in step with troops of "character, blood, and social position" bearing names like Richmond Howitzers and Louisiana Zouaves. ("Zouave" mania swept both North and South, prospective soldiers evidently considering broad sashes and baggy breeches the embodiment of military splendor.)

President Jefferson Davis represented the best type of southern planter, noted for his humane treatment of his slaves. In politics he had pursued a somewhat unusual course. While senator from Mississippi, he opposed the Compromise of 1850 and became a leader of the southern radicals. After Franklin Pierce appointed him secretary of war, however, he took a more nationalistic position, one close to that of Stephen Douglas. Davis supported the building of a transcontinental railroad and spoke in favor of the annexation of Cuba and other Caribbean areas. He rejected Douglas's position during the Kansas controversy but tried to close the breach in Democratic ranks opened by the Kansas debacle. After the 1860 election he supported secession only reluctantly, preferring to give Lincoln a chance to prove that he meant the South no harm.

The Test of Battle: Bull Run

"Forward to Richmond!" "On to Washington!" Such shouts propelled the armies into battle long before either was properly trained. On July 21 at Manassas Junction, Virginia, some 20 miles below Washington, on a branch of the Potomac called Bull

A dead young soldier. Eighteen-year-olds were the largest age group in the first year of the war in both armies. Soldiers were universally called "the boys"; and officers, even in their thirties, were called "old men." One of the most popular war songs was "Just Before the Battle, Mother."

Run, 30,000 Union soldiers under General Irvin McDowell attacked a roughly equal force of Confederates commanded by the "Napoleon of the South," Pierre G. T. Beauregard. McDowell swept back the Confederate left flank. Victory seemed sure. Then a Virginia brigade under Thomas J. Jackson rushed to the field by rail from the Shenandoah Valley in the nick of time, held doggedly to a key hill, and checked the advance. (A South Carolina general, seeking to rally his own men, pointed to the hill and shouted: "Look, there is Jackson with his Virginians, standing like a stone wall against the enemy." Thus "Stonewall" Jackson received his nickname.)

The Southerners then counterattacked, driving the Union soldiers back. As often happens with green troops, retreat quickly turned to rout. McDowell's men fled toward the defenses of Washington, abandoning their weapons, stumbling through lines of supply wagons, trampling foolish sightseers who had come out to watch the battle. Panic engulfed Washington. Richmond exulted. Both sides expected the northern capital to fall within hours.

The inexperienced southern troops were too disorganized to follow up their victory. Casualties on both sides were light, and the battle had little direct effect on anything but morale. Southern confidence soared, while the North began to realize how immense the task of subduing the Confederacy would be.

After Bull Run, Lincoln devised a broader, more systematic strategy for winning the war. The navy would clamp a tight blockade on all southern ports. In the West operations designed to gain control of the Mississippi would be undertaken. (This was part of General Scott's "Anaconda Plan," designed to starve the South into submission.) More important, a new army would be mustered at Washington to invade Virginia. Congress promptly authorized the enlistment of 500,000 three-year volunteers. To lead this army and—after General Scott's retirement in November—to command the Union forces, Lincoln appointed a 34-year-old major general, George B. McClellan.

McClellan was the North's first military hero. Units under his command had driven the Confederates from the pro-Union western counties of Virginia, clearing the way for the admission of West Virginia as a separate state in 1863. The fighting had been on a small scale, but McClellan, an incurable romantic and something of an egomaniac, managed to inflate its importance. "You have annihilated two armies," he proclaimed in a widely publicized message to his troops. Few Northerners noticed that they had "annihilated" only about 250 Confederates.

Paying for the War

After Bull Run, McClellan concentrated on training his troops and preparing them for a major offensive. By the fall of 1861 a real army was taking shape along the Potomac: disciplined, confident, adequately supplied. Northern shops and factories were producing guns, ammunition, wagons, uniforms, shoes, and the countless other supplies needed to fight a great war. Most manufacturers operated on a small scale, but with the armed forces soon wearing out 3 million pairs of shoes and 1.5 million uniforms a year and with men leaving their jobs by the hundreds of thousands to fight, the tendency of industry to mechanize and to increase the size of the average manufacturing unit became ever more pronounced.

At the beginning of the war Secretary of the Treasury Salmon P. Chase underestimated how much it would cost. He learned quickly. In August 1861 Congress passed an income tax law (3 percent on incomes over $800, which effectively exempted ordinary wage earners) and assessed a direct tax on the states. Loans amounting to $140 million were authorized. As the war dragged on and expenses mounted, new excise taxes on every imaginable product and service were passed, and still further borrowing was necessary. In 1863 the banking system was overhauled.

During the war the federal government borrowed a total of $2.2 billion and collected $667 million in taxes, slightly over 20 percent of its total expenditures. These unprecedented large sums proved inadequate. Some obligations were met by printing paper money unredeemable in coin. About $431 million in "greenbacks"—the term distinguished this fiat money from the redeemable yellowback bills—were issued during the conflict. Public confidence in all paper money vacillated with each change in the fortunes of the Union armies, but by the end of the war the cost of living in the North had doubled.

On balance, the heavy emphasis on borrowing and currency inflation was expensive but not irresponsible. In a country still chiefly agricultural, people had relatively low cash incomes and therefore could not easily bear a heavy tax load. Many Americans considered it reasonable to expect future generations to pay part of the dollar cost of saving the Union when theirs was contributing so heavily in labor and blood.

Politics as Usual

Partisan politics was altered by the war but not suspended. The secession of the southern states left the Republicans with large majorities in both houses of Congress. Most Democrats supported measures necessary for the conduct of the war but objected to the way the Lincoln administration was conducting it. The sharpest conflicts came when slavery and race relations were under discussion. The

Democrats adopted a conservative stance, as reflected in the slogan "The Constitution as it is; the Union as it was; the Negroes where they are." The Republicans divided into Moderate and Radical wings. Political divisions on economic issues such as tariffs and land policy tended to cut across party lines and, so far as the Republicans were concerned, to bear little relation to slavery and race. As the war progressed, the Radical faction became increasingly influential.

In 1861 the most prominent Radical senator was Charles Sumner, finally recovered from his caning by Preston Brooks and brimful of hatred for slaveholders. In the House, Thaddeus Stevens of Pennsylvania was the rising power. Sumner and Stevens were uncompromising on all questions relating to slaves; they insisted not merely on abolition but on granting full political and civil rights to blacks. Moderate Republicans objected vehemently to treating blacks as equals and opposed making abolition a war aim, and even many of the so-called Radicals disagreed with Sumner and Stevens on race relations.

At the other end of the political spectrum stood the so-called Peace Democrats. These "Copperheads" (apparently the reference was not to the poisonous snake but to an earlier time when some hard-money Democrats wore copper pennies around their necks) opposed all measures in support of the war. They hoped to win control of Congress and force a negotiated peace. Few were actually disloyal, but their activities at a time when thousands of men were risking their lives in battle infuriated many Northerners.

Lincoln treated dissenters with a curious mixture of repression and tolerance. He suspended the writ of habeas corpus in critical areas and applied martial law freely. Over 13,000 persons were arrested and held without trial, many, as it later turned out, unjustly. The president argued that the government dared not stand on ceremony in a national emergency. His object, he insisted, was not to punish but to prevent. Arbitrary arrests were rarely, if ever, made for purely political purposes, and free elections were held as scheduled throughout the war.

The most notorious domestic foe of the administration was the Peace Democrat Congressman Clement L. Vallandigham of Ohio, who was sent to prison by a military court. There were two rebellions in progress, Vallandigham claimed, "the Secessionist Rebellion" and "the Abolitionist Rebellion." "I am against both," he added. But Lincoln ordered him released and banished to the Confederacy. Once at liberty Vallandigham moved to Canada, from which refuge he ran unsuccessfully for governor of Ohio.

"Perish offices," he once said, "perish life itself, but do the thing that is right." In 1864 he returned to Ohio. Although he campaigned against Lincoln in the presidential election, he was not arrested. Lincoln was no dictator.

Behind Confederate Lines

The South also revised its strategy after Bull Run. Although it might have been wiser to risk everything on a bold invasion of the North, President Davis relied primarily on a strong defense to wear down the Union's will to fight. In 1862 the

Confederate Congress passed a conscription act that permitted the hiring of substitutes and exempted many classes of people (including college professors, druggists, and mail carriers) whose work could hardly have been deemed essential. A provision deferring one slave owner or overseer for every plantation of twenty or more slaves led many to grumble about "a rich man's war and a poor man's fight."

Finance was the Confederacy's most vexing problem. The blockade made it impossible to raise much money through tariffs. The Confederate Congress passed an income tax together with many excise taxes but all told they covered only 2 percent of its needs by taxation. The most effective levy was a tax in kind, amounting to one-tenth of each farmer's production. The South borrowed as much as it could ($712 million), even mortgaging cotton undeliverable because of the blockade, in order to gain European credits. But it relied mainly on printing paper currency; over $1.5 billion poured from the presses during the war. Considering the amount issued, this currency held its value well until late in the war, when the military fortunes of the Confederacy began to decline. Then the bottom fell out, and by early 1865 the Confederate dollar was worth less than 2 cents in gold.

Outfitting the army strained southern resources to the limit. Large supplies of small arms (some 600,000 weapons during the entire war) came from Europe through the blockade, along with other valuable matériel. As the blockade became more efficient, however, it became increasingly difficult to obtain European goods. The Confederates did manage to build a number of munitions plants, and they captured huge amounts of northern arms. No battle was lost because of a lack of guns or other military equipment, although shortages of shoes and uniforms handicapped the Confederate forces on some occasions.

Foreign policy loomed large in Confederate thinking, for the "cotton is king" theory presupposed that the great European powers would break any northern blockade to get cotton for their textile mills. Southern expectations were not realized, however. The European nations would have been delighted to see the United States broken up, but none was prepared to support the Confederacy directly. The attitude of Great Britain was decisive. The cutting off of cotton did not hit the British as hard as the South had hoped. They had a large supply on hand when the war broke out, and when that was exhausted, alternative sources in India and Egypt took up part of the slack.

Several times the Union and Great Britain came to the brink of war. In 1862 two powerful cruisers, the *Florida* and the *Alabama*, were built for the Confederates in English shipyards under the most transparent of subterfuges. Despite American protests, they were permitted to put to sea and were soon wreaking havoc among northern merchant ships. When two ironclad "rams" were also built in Britain for the Confederates, the United States made it clear that it would declare war if the ships were delivered. The British government then confiscated the vessels, avoiding a showdown.

Charles Francis Adams, the American minister in London, ably handled the many vexing problems that arose. However, the military situation determined

British policy; once the North obtained a clear superiority on the battlefield, the possibility of intervention vanished.

War in the West: Shiloh

After Bull Run no battles were fought until early 1862. Then, while McClellan continued his deliberate preparations to attack Richmond, important fighting occurred far to the west. Most of the Plains Indians sided with the Confederacy, principally because of their resentment of the federal government's policies toward them. White settlers from Colorado to California were mostly Unionists. In March 1862 a Texas army advancing beyond Santa Fe clashed with a Union force in the Battle of Glorieta Pass. The battle was indecisive, but a Union unit destroyed the Texans' supply train. The Texans felt compelled to retreat to the Rio Grande, thus ending the Confederate threat to the Far West.

Meanwhile, far larger Union forces, led by a shabby, cigar-smoking West Pointer named Ulysses S. Grant, had invaded Tennessee from a base at Cairo, Illinois. Making effective use of armored gunboats, Grant captured Fort Henry and Fort Donelson, strongholds on the Tennessee and Cumberland rivers, taking 14,000 prisoners. Next he marched toward Corinth, Mississippi, an important railroad junction.

To check Grant's advance, the Confederates massed 40,000 men under Albert Sidney Johnston. On April 6, while Grant slowly concentrated his forces, Johnston struck suddenly at Shiloh, 20 miles north of Corinth. Some Union soldiers were caught half-dressed, others in the midst of brewing their morning coffee. A few died in their blankets. "We were more than surprised," one Illinois officer later admitted. "We were astonished." However, Grant's men stood their ground. At the end of a day of ghastly carnage the Confederates held the advantage, but fresh Union troops poured in during the night, and on the second day of battle the tide turned. The Confederates fell back toward Corinth, exhausted and demoralized.

Grant, shaken by the unexpected attack and appalled by his losses, allowed the enemy to escape. This cost him the fine reputation he had won in capturing Fort Henry and Fort Donelson. He was relieved of his command. Although Corinth eventually fell and New Orleans was captured by a naval force under the command of Captain David Farragut, Vicksburg, key to control of the Mississippi, remained firmly in Confederate hands. A great opportunity had been lost.

Shiloh had other results. The staggering casualties shook the confidence of both belligerents. More Americans fell there in two days than in all the battles of the Revolution, the War of 1812, and the Mexican War combined. Union losses exceeded 13,000 out of 63,000 engaged; the Confederates lost 10,699, including General Johnston. Technology in the shape of more accurate guns that could be fired far more rapidly than the muskets of earlier times and more powerful artillery were responsible for the carnage. Gradually the generals began to reconsider their tactics and to experiment with field fortifications and other defensive measures.

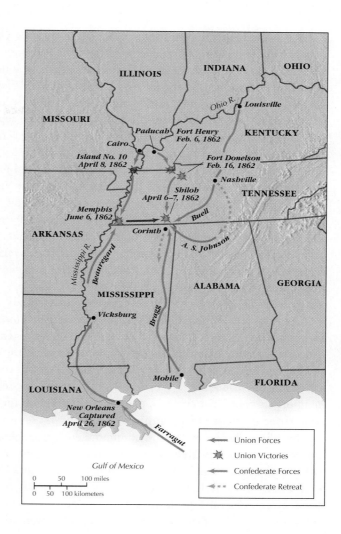

War in the West, 1862
Although Union forces ultimately took Shiloh in April 1862, the city of Vicksburg, and thus control of the Mississippi, remained in southern hands.

And the people, North and South, stopped thinking of the war as a romantic test of courage and military guile.

McClellan: The Reluctant Warrior

In Virginia, General McClellan, after unaccountable delays, was finally moving against Richmond. Instead of trying to advance across the difficult terrain of northern Virginia, he transported his army by water to the tip of the peninsula formed by the York and James rivers in order to attack Richmond from the southeast. After the famous battle on March 9, 1862, between the USS *Monitor* and the Confederate *Merrimack*, the first fight in history between armored warships, control of these waters was securely in northern hands.

McClellan began the Peninsula campaign in mid-March. Proceeding deliberately, he floated an army of 112,000 men down the Potomac and by May 14 had established a base at White House Landing, less than 25 miles from Richmond. A swift thrust might have ended the war quickly, but McClellan delayed, despite the fact that he had 80,000 men in striking position and large reserves. As he pushed forward slowly, the Confederates caught part of his force separated from the main body by the rain-swollen Chickahominy River and attacked. The Battle of Seven Pines was indecisive yet resulted in more than 10,000 casualties.

At Seven Pines the Confederate commander, General Joseph E. Johnston, was severely wounded; leadership of the Army of Northern Virginia then passed to Robert E. Lee. Although a reluctant supporter of secession, Lee was a superb soldier. During the Mexican War his gallantry under fire inspired General Scott to call him the bravest man in the army; another officer rhapsodized over his "daring reconnaissances pushed up to the cannon's mouth." He also had displayed an almost instinctive mastery of tactics. Admiral Raphael Semmes, who accompanied Scott's army on the march to Mexico City, recalled in 1851 that Lee "seemed to receive impressions intuitively, which it cost other men much labor to acquire."

Lee was McClellan's antithesis. McClellan seemed almost deliberately to avoid understanding his foes, acting as though every southern general was a genius. Lee, a master psychologist on the battlefield, took the measure of each Union general and devised his tactics accordingly. Where McClellan was complex, egotistical, perhaps even unbalanced, Lee was courtly, tactful, and entirely without McClellan's vainglorious belief that he was a man of destiny. Yet on the battlefield Lee's boldness skirted the edge of foolhardiness.

To relieve the pressure on Richmond, Lee sent General "Stonewall" Jackson, soon to be his most trusted lieutenant, on a diversionary raid in the Shenandoah Valley, west of Richmond and Washington. Jackson struck hard and swiftly at scattered Union forces in the region, winning a number of battles and capturing vast stores of equipment. Lincoln dispatched 20,000 reserves to the Shenandoah to check him—to the dismay of McClellan, who wanted the troops to attack Richmond from the north. But after Seven Pines, Lee ordered Jackson back to Richmond. While Union armies streamed toward the valley, Jackson slipped stealthily between them. On June 25 he reached Ashland, directly north of the Confederate capital.

Before that date McClellan had possessed clear numerical superiority yet had only inched ahead; now the advantage lay with Lee, and the very next day he attacked. For seven days the battle raged. Lee's plan was brilliant but too complicated for an army yet untested: The full weight of his force never hit the northern army at any one time. Nevertheless, the shock was formidable. McClellan, who excelled in defense, fell back, his lines intact, exacting a fearful toll. Under difficult conditions he managed to transfer his troops to a new base on the James River at Harrison's Landing, where the guns of the navy could shield his position. Again the loss of life was terrible: Northern casualties totaled 15,800; those of the South nearly 20,000 in the Seven Days' Battle for Richmond.

Lee Counterattacks: Antietam

McClellan was still within striking distance of Richmond, in an impregnable position with secure supply lines and 86,000 soldiers ready to resume battle. Lee had absorbed heavy losses without winning any significant advantage. Yet Lincoln was exasperated with McClellan for having surrendered the initiative and, after much deliberation, reduced his authority by placing him under General Henry W. Halleck. Halleck called off the Peninsula campaign and ordered McClellan to move his army from the James to the Potomac, near Washington. He was to join General John Pope, who was gathering a new army between Washington and Richmond.

To allow Halleck to pull back the troops was a bad mistake. When they withdrew, Lee seized the initiative. With typical decisiveness and daring, he marched rapidly north. Late in August his Confederates drove General Pope's confused troops from the same ground, Bull Run, where the first major engagement of the war had been fought.

Thirteen months had passed since the first failure at Bull Run, and despite the expenditure of thousands of lives, the Union army stood as far from Richmond as ever. Dismayed by Pope's incompetence, Lincoln turned in desperation back to

War in the East, 1861–1862

After the first battle at Bull Run, in July 1861, there was little action until the following spring, when McClellan launched his Peninsula campaign. The Battle of Antietam was the culmination of the fighting in the summer of 1862.

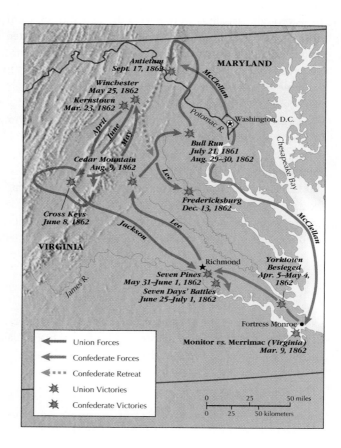

McClellan. When his secretary protested that McClellan had expressed contempt for the president, Lincoln replied gently: "We must use what tools we have."

While McClellan was regrouping the shaken Union Army, Lee once again took the offensive. He realized that no number of individual southern triumphs could destroy the enormous material advantages of the North. Unless some dramatic blow, delivered on northern soil, persuaded the people of the United States that military victory was impossible, the South would surely be crushed in the long run by the weight of superior resources. Lee therefore marched rapidly northwest around the defenses of Washington.

Acting with even more than his usual boldness, Lee divided his army of 60,000 into a number of units. One, under Stonewall Jackson, descended on weakly defended Harpers Ferry, capturing more than 11,000 prisoners. Another pressed as far north as Hagerstown, Maryland, nearly to the Pennsylvania line. McClellan pursued with his usual deliberation until a captured dispatch revealed to him Lee's dispositions. Then he moved a bit more swiftly, forcing Lee to stand and fight on September 17 at Sharpsburg, Maryland, between the Potomac and Antietam Creek.[1] On a field that offered Lee no room to maneuver, 70,000 Union soldiers clashed with 40,000 Confederates. When darkness fell, more than 22,000 lay dead or wounded on the bloody field.

Although casualties were evenly divided and the Confederate lines remained intact, Lee's position was perilous. His men were exhausted. McClellan had not yet thrown in his reserves, and new federal units were arriving hourly. A bold northern general would have continued the fight without respite through the night. One of ordinary aggressiveness would have waited for first light and then struck with every soldier who could hold a rifle, for with the Potomac at his back, Lee could not retreat under fire without inviting disaster. McClellan, however, did nothing. For an entire day, while Lee scanned the field in futile search of some weakness in the Union lines, he held his fire. That night the Confederates slipped back across the Potomac into Virginia.

Lee's invasion had failed; his army had been badly mauled; the gravest threat to the Union in the war had been checked. But McClellan had let victory slip through his fingers. Soon Lee was back behind the defenses of Richmond, rebuilding his army.

Once again, this time finally, Lincoln dismissed McClellan from his command.

The Emancipation Proclamation

As the war progressed, the Radical faction in Congress gradually chipped away at slavery. In April 1862 the Radicals pushed through a bill abolishing slavery in the District of Columbia; two months later another measure outlawed it in the territo-

---

[1]*Southerners tended to identify battles by nearby towns, northerners by bodies of water. Thus Manassas and Bull Run, Sharpsburg and Antietam, Murfreesboro and Stone's River, and so on.*

ries; in July the Confiscation Act "freed" all slaves owned by persons in rebellion against the United States. Lincoln had resisted emancipation because he feared it would divide the country and injure the war effort, not because he personally disapproved. Indeed, he frequently cited Radical pressure as an excuse for doing what he wished to do on his own.

By the summer of 1862, however, he was convinced that for military reasons and to win the support of liberal opinion in Europe, the government should make abolition a war aim. "We must free the slaves or be ourselves subdued," he explained to a member of his Cabinet. The "victory" at Antietam Creek gave him his opportunity, and on September 22 he made public the Emancipation Proclamation. After January 1, 1863, it said, all slaves in areas in rebellion against the United States "shall be then, thenceforward, and forever free."

No single slave was freed directly by Lincoln's announcement, which did not apply to the border states or to those sections of the Confederacy, like New Orleans and Norfolk, Virginia, already controlled by federal troops. The proclamation differed in philosophy, however, from the Confiscation Act in striking at the institution, not at the property of rebels. Henceforth every Union victory would speed the destruction of slavery without regard for the attitudes of individual masters.

Southerners considered the Emancipation Proclamation an incitement to slave rebellion—as one of them put it, an "infamous attempt to . . . convert the quiet, ignorant, and dependent black son of toil into a savage incendiary and brutal murderer." Most antislavery groups thought it did not go far enough. Lincoln "is only stopping on the edge of Niagara, to pick up a few chips," one abolitionist declared. "He and they will go over together." Foreign opinion was mixed: Liberals tended to applaud, conservatives to react with alarm or contempt.

As Lincoln anticipated, the proclamation had a subtle but continuing impact in the North. Its immediate effect was to aggravate racial prejudices. Millions of whites disapproved of slavery yet abhorred the idea of equality for blacks. David Wilmot, for example, insisted that his famous proviso was designed to preserve the territories for whites rather than to weaken slavery, and as late as 1857 the people of Iowa rejected black suffrage by a vote of 49,000 to 8,000.

The Democrats spared no effort to make political capital of these fears and prejudices even before Lincoln's Emancipation Proclamation, and they made large gains in the 1862 election, especially in the Northwest. So strong was antiblack feeling that most of the Republican politicians who defended emancipation did so with racist arguments. Far from encouraging southern blacks to move north, they claimed, the ending of slavery would lead to a mass migration of northern blacks to the South.

When the Emancipation Proclamation began actually to free slaves, the government pursued a policy of "containment," that is, of keeping the former slaves in the South. Panicky fears of an inundation of blacks subsided in the North. Nevertheless, emancipation remained a cause of social discontent. In March 1863, volunteering having fallen off, Congress passed the Conscription Act. The law applied to all men between ages 20 and 45, but it allowed draftees to hire substitutes and even to buy exemption for $300, provisions that were patently unfair to the poor. During the remainder of the war 46,000 men were actually drafted, whereas 118,000 hired substitutes, and another 161,000 "failed to report." Conscription represented an enormous expansion of national authority, since in effect it gave the government the power of life and death over individual citizens.

The Draft Riots

After the passage of the Conscription Act, draft riots erupted in a number of cities. By far the most serious disturbance occurred in New York City in July 1863. Many workers resented conscription in principle and were embittered by the $300 exemption fee (which represented a year's wages). The idea of being forced to risk their lives to free slaves who would then, they believed, compete with them for jobs infuriated them. On July 13 a mob attacked the office where the names of conscripts were being drawn. Most of the rioters were poor Irish Catholic laborers who resented both the blacks and the middle-class Protestant whites who seemed to them responsible for the special attention blacks were suddenly receiving. For four days the city was an inferno. Public buildings, shops, and private residences were put to the torch. What began as a protest against the draft became an assault on blacks and the well-to-do. It took federal troops and the temporary suspension of the draft in the city to put an end to the rioting. By the time order was restored more than a hundred people (most of them rioters) had lost their lives.

Most white Northerners did not surrender their comforting belief in black inferiority, and Lincoln was no exception. Yet Lincoln was evolving. He talked about deporting freed slaves to the tropics, but he did not send any there. And he began to receive black leaders in the White House and to allow black groups to hold meetings on the grounds.

Many other Americans were changing too. The brutality of the New York riots horrified many white citizens. Over $40,000 was swiftly raised to aid the victims, and some conservatives were so appalled by the Irish rioters that they began to talk of giving blacks the vote. The influential *Atlantic Monthly* commented: "It is impossible to name any standard . . . that will give a vote to the Celt [the Irish] and exclude the negro."

The Emancipated People

To blacks, both slave and free, the Emancipation Proclamation served as a beacon. Even if it failed immediately to liberate one slave or to lift the burdens of prejudice from one black back, it stood as a promise of future improvement. "I took the proclamation for a little more than it purported," Frederick Douglass recalled in his autobiography, "and saw in its spirit a life and power far beyond its letter." Lincoln was by modern standards a racist, but his most militant black contemporaries respected him deeply. The *Anglo-African,* an uncompromising black newspaper (the position of which is revealed in an 1862 editorial that asked: "Poor, chicken-hearted, semi-barbarous Caucasians, when will you learn that 'the earth was made for MAN?'"), referred in 1864 to Lincoln's "many noble acts" and urged his reelection. Douglass said of him: "Lincoln was not . . . either our man or our model. In his interests, in his association, in his habits of thought and in his prejudices, he was a white man." Nevertheless, Douglass described Lincoln as "one whom I could love, honor, and trust without reserve or doubt."

As for the slaves of the South, after January 1, 1863, whenever the "Army of Freedom" approached, they laid down their plows and hoes and flocked to the Union lines in droves. Instead of referring to their workers as "servants" or "my black family," many owners began to describe them as "slaves" or "niggers."

African American Soldiers

A revolutionary shift occurred in white thinking about using black men as soldiers. Although they had fought in the Revolution and in the Battle of New Orleans during the War of 1812, a law of 1792 barred blacks from the army. During the early stages of the rebellion, despite the eagerness of thousands of free blacks to enlist, the prohibition remained in force. By 1862, however, the need for manpower was creating pressure for change. In August Secretary of War Edwin M. Stanton authorized the military government of the captured South Carolina Sea Islands to enlist slaves in the area. After the Emancipation Proclamation specifically authorized the enlistment of blacks, the governor of Massachusetts moved to organize a black regiment, the famous Massachusetts 54th. Swiftly thereafter, other states began to recruit black soldiers, and in May 1863 the federal government established a Bureau of Colored Troops to supervise their enlistment. By the end of the war one soldier in eight in the Union army was black.

Enlisting so many black soldiers changed the war from a struggle to save the Union to a kind of revolution. "Let the black man . . . get an eagle on his button and a musket on his shoulder," wrote Frederick Douglass, "and there is no power on earth which can deny that he has won the right to citizenship."

At first black soldiers received only $7 a month, about half what white soldiers were paid. But they soon proved themselves in battle; of the 178,000 who served in the Union army, 37,000 were killed, a rate of loss about 40 percent higher than that among white troops. The Congressional Medal of Honor was awarded to twenty-one blacks.

The higher death rates among black soldiers were partly due to the fury of Confederate soldiers. Many black captives were killed on the spot. After overrunning the garrison of Fort Pillow on the Mississippi River, the Confederates massacred several dozen black soldiers, along with their white commander. Lincoln was tempted to order reprisals, but he and his advisers realized that to do so would have been both morally wrong (two wrongs never make a right) and likely to lead to still more atrocities. "Blood can not restore blood," Lincoln said in his usual direct way.

Antietam to Gettysburg

It was well that Lincoln seized on Antietam to release his proclamation; had he waited for a more impressive victory, he would have waited nearly a year. To replace McClellan, he chose General Ambrose E. Burnside, best known to history for his magnificent side-whiskers (originally called burnsides, later, at first jokingly, sideburns). Unlike McClellan, Burnside was aggressive—too aggressive. He planned to ford the Rappahannock River at Fredericksburg. Supply problems and bad weather delayed him until mid-December, giving Lee time to concentrate his army in impregnable positions behind the town. Although he had more than 120,000 men against Lee's 75,000, Burnside should have called off the attack when he saw Lee's advantage; instead he ordered the troops forward. Crossing the river over pontoon bridges, his divisions occupied Fredericksburg. Then, in wave after wave, they charged the Confederate defense line while Lee's artillery riddled them from nearby Marye's Heights. Watching the battle from his command post on the heights, General Lee was deeply moved. Turning to General James Longstreet, he said: "It is well that war is so terrible—we should grow too fond of it!"

On December 14, the day following this futile assault, General Burnside, tears streaming down his cheeks, ordered the evacuation of Fredericksburg. Shortly thereafter General Joseph Hooker replaced him.

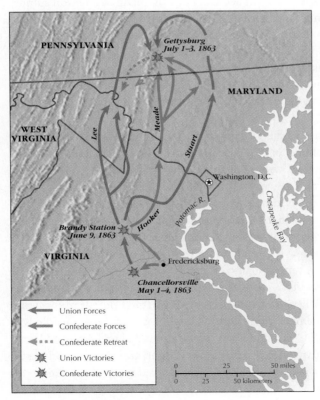

Gettysburg Campaign, 1863

Gettysburg, in July 1863, marked the turning point of the war; after this battle the South never again tried to invade the North.

Unlike Burnside, "Fighting Joe" Hooker was ill-tempered, vindictive, and devious. He proved no better than his predecessor, but his failings were more like McClellan's than Burnside's. By the spring of 1863 he had 125,000 men ready for action. Late in April he forded the Rappahannock and quickly concentrated at Chancellorsville, about 10 miles west of Fredericksburg. His army outnumbered the Confederates by more than two to one; he should have forced a battle at once. Instead he delayed, and while he did, Lee sent Stonewall Jackson's corps of 28,000 men across tangled countryside to a position directly athwart Hooker's unsuspecting flank. At 6 P.M. on May 2, Jackson attacked.

Completely surprised, the Union right crumbled, brigade after brigade overrun before it could wheel to meet Jackson's charge. At the first sound of firing, Lee had struck along the entire front to impede Union troop movements. If the battle had begun earlier in the day, the Confederates might have won a decisive victory; as it happened, nightfall brought a lull, and the next day the Union troops rallied and held their ground. Heavy fighting continued until May 5, when Hooker abandoned the field and retreated in good order behind the Rappahannock.

Chancellorsville cost the Confederates dearly, for their losses, in excess of 12,000, were almost as heavy as the North's and harder to replace. They also lost Stonewall Jackson, struck down by the bullets of his own men while returning from a reconnaissance. Nevertheless, the Union army had suffered another fearful blow to its morale.

Lee knew that time was still on the side of the North; to defend Richmond was not enough. Already federal troops in the West were closing in on Vicksburg, threatening to cut Confederate communications with Arkansas and Texas. Now was the time to strike, while the morale of the North was at low ebb. With 75,000 soldiers he crossed the Potomac again, a larger Union force dogging his right flank. By late June his army had fanned out across southern Pennsylvania in a 50-mile arc from Chambersburg to the Susquehanna. Gray-clad soldiers ranged 50 miles *northwest* of Baltimore, within 10 miles of Harrisburg, Pennsylvania.

As Union soldiers had been doing in Virginia, Lee's men destroyed property and commandeered food, horses, and clothing wherever they could find them. They even seized a number of blacks and sent them south to be sold as slaves. On July 1 a Confederate division looking for shoes in the town of Gettysburg clashed with two brigades of Union cavalry northwest of the town. Both sides sent out calls for reinforcements. Like iron filings drawn to a magnet, the two armies converged. The Confederates won control of the town, but the Union army, now commanded by General George G. Meade, took a strong position on Cemetery Ridge, a hook-shaped stretch of high ground just to the south. Lee's men occupied Seminary Ridge, a parallel position.

On this field the fate of the Union was probably decided. For two days the Confederates attacked Cemetery Ridge, pounding it with the heaviest artillery barrage ever seen in America and sweeping bravely up its flanks in repeated assaults. During General George E. Pickett's famous charge, a handful of his men actually reached the Union lines, but reserves drove them back. By nightfall on July 3 the Confederate army was spent, the Union lines unbroken.

Glory

Glory (1989) tells the story of the 54th Massachusetts Volunteer Infantry, a black regiment, from its establishment in the fall of 1862 through its attack on Fort Wagner, South Carolina, on July 18, 1863.

"Historical accuracy," director Edward Zwick declared, was "the goal of everyone involved in the production." Filmmakers make such assertions, but Zwick proved that he had attended to the historical record. The peak of Shaw's cap was dyed the exact shade of medium green used by officers of the Massachusetts 54th; and when shoes were distributed to the recruits, there were no "lefts" or "rights": shoes were to shape themselves to either foot from wear. Few viewers could be expected to take note of such historical details, but Zwick included them nevertheless.

Zwick's evident commitment to history makes his deviations all the more interesting. Consider the opening scenes. The movie begins with a panoramic shot of rolling hills, dotted with tents. Fog blankets the valley and softens the morning light. The camera moves closer, focusing on Union soldiers around a campfire. Then the quiet is shattered by explosions: soldiers hasten to form ranks, trot toward a battlefield, and charge across it, a young officer in the vanguard. (He is Captain Robert Gould Shaw, played by Matthew Broderick.) The attackers are decimated. When Shaw turns to rally his troops, he sees that they are fleeing in terror. Then he is hit and loses consciousness.

Shaw is sent home to Boston to convalesce. At a reception, Governor Andrew offers the young officer command of the Massachusetts 54th, a black regiment being raised in Boston. Shaw hesitates for a moment. Then he confers privately with another officer, who is appalled.

"I knew how much you'd like to be a colonel, but a colored regiment?"

"I'm gonna do it," Shaw replies.

"You're not serious."

"Yeah."

These scenes contain truths without being entirely truthful. Governor Andrew did offer the commission and Shaw accepted it. But at the time Shaw was in Virginia. Andrew, in Boston, conveyed it through Shaw's father and young Shaw initially refused. Zwick has compressed the story chronologically, squeezing weeks into minutes; and he has rearranged it geographically to enable Andrew and young Shaw to meet. Such modifications are common in "reel history," and these do not impair historical understanding.

But *Glory* deviates from the historical record in more significant ways. It suggests, for example, that the Massachusetts 54th was composed mostly of former slaves whose hatred of slavery was based on personal experience. In truth, the Massachusetts 54th was recruited from blacks in northern states: Most had been born free.

The fiction that they had been slaves, however, made it possible for Zwick to examine a larger truth. Of the 178,000 blacks who served in the Union army, fewer than one-fifth were from the North; the great majority *were* former slaves. Nearly 100,000 were recruited from Louisiana, Mississippi, or Tennessee. *Glory* thus merges the story of the free blacks of the Massachusetts 54th with that of former slaves who were recruited from the Deep South.

Zwick exploited the dramatic potential of the latter groups. How did slaves respond when, having just received their freedom, they were placed under the absolute power of white officers?

Glory develops the question chiefly through the character of Trip (Denzel Washington), a former slave who hates all whites, including Shaw. Shaw illuminates the other side of the question. An inveterate abolitionist, he reluctantly decides that former slaves must be whipped (literally) into shape. When Trip sneaks off one night and is captured for desertion, Shaw orders him flogged. When Trip's back is bared, Shaw sees that it is laced with scars from whippings by slave masters. During the flogging, Trip fixes Shaw with a hateful stare, a powerful scene that underscores the movie's central irony: To end slavery, Shaw has superseded the plantation master while Trip has again become a slave.

Matthew Broderick, as Robert Gould Shaw in the movie *Glory,* and Robert Gould Shaw, Commander of the Massachusetts 54th.

Private Charles Arnum, a free black volunteer from Springfield, Massachusetts, and Denzel Washington as the former slave recruit Trip, in the movie *Glory.*

Whatever its dramatic merits, the scene is unhistorical. In 1861 Congress had outlawed flogging in the military. Disobedient soldiers were tied in a crouched position, or they were suspended by their thumbs, toes just touching the ground.

Physical punishment was one of the chief sources of contention between ex-slave soldiers and white officers. "I am no slave to be driven," one black recruit informed a brutish commander. When an officer of the 38th Colored Infantry tied a black recruit up by the thumbs, his friends cut him down and forced the officers back with bayonets: "No white son of a bitch can tie a man up here," they declared. The blacks were charged with mutiny and several were executed, an incident that shows that former slaves did not willingly submit to army discipline tainted with racism. Though African Americans constituted only 8 percent of the Union army, 80 percent of those executed for mutiny were black. Many white officers, as the movie suggests, did assert that former slaves must be treated like slaves. "I no longer wonder why slave drivers were cruel. I am," one white officer confided in a letter.

Could such soldiers—black recruits and white officers alike—have been good ones? The movie answers the question by recreating the actual attack on Fort Wagner. It shows the blacks of the Massachusetts 54th marching to the front of the line and forming up along a narrow beach. On Shaw's command, they charge forward. Unlike the white troops in the opening scene, the blacks follow him to the ramparts; when he falls, they continue onward until they are wiped out.

Were the soldiers of the Massachusetts 54th as courageous as those in the movie?

Shortly after the battle, Lieutenant Iredell Jones, a Confederate officer, reported: "The negroes fought gallantly, and were headed by as brave a colonel as ever lived." Of the 600 members of the 54th Massachusetts, 40 percent were casualties on that day, an extraordinarily high ratio. Did ex-slaves fight as courageously as the free blacks of the 54th? The answer to this question came not at Fort Wagner, but at other, less publicized battles. A few weeks earlier, for example, several companies of the Louisiana (Colored) Infantry, composed of former slaves who had been in the army only for several weeks, fought off a furious Confederate assault at Milliken's Bend near Vicksburg. The Confederate general was astonished when whites in the Union army fled but the blacks held their ground despite sustaining staggering casualties—45 percent—the highest of any single battle in the war.

Thus while *Glory* is a fictional composite—of free black and ex-slave recruits, and of the assault on Fort Wagner and Milliken's Bend—it conveys a broader truth about black soldiers. Howell Cobb, a Confederate senator from Georgia, declared: "If the black can make a good soldier, our whole system of government is wrong." *Glory* shows that although white officers and black recruits did not form a harmonious team, they together proved that slavery was doomed.

421

Questions for Discussion
- Was conscription during the Civil War a form of slavery?
- Would free blacks or former slaves more likely have been the better soldiers?

The following day was the Fourth of July. The two weary forces rested on their arms. Had the Union army attacked in force, the Confederates might have been crushed, but just as McClellan had hesitated after Antietam, Meade let opportunity pass. On July 5 Lee retreated to safety. For the first time he had been clearly bested on the field of battle.

Lincoln Finds His General: Grant at Vicksburg

On Independence Day, a day after Gettysburg, federal troops won another great victory far to the west. When General Halleck was called east in July 1862, Ulysses S. Grant resumed command of the Union troops. Grant was one of the most controversial officers in the army. At West Point he had compiled an indifferent record, ranking twenty-first in a class of thirty-nine. During the Mexican War he served well, but when he was later assigned to a lonely post in the West, he took to drink and was forced to resign his commission. Thereafter he was by turns a farmer, a real estate agent, and a clerk in a leather goods store. In 1861, approaching age 40, he seemed well into a life of frustration and mediocrity.

The war gave him a second chance. Back in service, however, his reputation as a ne'er-do-well and his unmilitary bearing worked against him, as did the heavy casualties suffered by his troops at Shiloh. Yet the fact that he knew how to manage a large army and win battles did not escape Lincoln. According to tradition, when a gossip tried to poison the president against Grant by referring to his drinking, Lincoln retorted that if he knew what brand Grant favored, he would send a barrel of it to some of his other generals.[2] Grant never used alcohol as a substitute for courage. "Old Ulysses," one of his soldiers said, "he don't scare worth a damn."

Grant's major aim was to capture Vicksburg, a city of tremendous strategic importance. Together with Port Hudson, a bastion north of Baton Rouge, Louisiana, it guarded a 150-mile stretch of the Mississippi. The river between these points was inaccessible to federal gunboats. So long as Vicksburg remained in southern hands, the trans-Mississippi region could send men and supplies to the rest of the Confederacy.

Vicksburg sits on a bluff overlooking a sharp bend in the river. When it proved unapproachable from either the west or the north, Grant devised an audacious scheme for getting at it from the east. He descended the Mississippi from Memphis to a point a few miles north of the city. Then, leaving part of his force behind to create the impression that he planned to attack from the north, he crossed the west bank and slipped quickly southward. Recrossing the river below Vicksburg, he abandoned his communications and supply lines and struck at Jackson, the capital of Mississippi. In a series of swift engagements his troops captured Jackson, cutting off

---

[2]*Lincoln denied having said this, pointing out that it was a version of a remark about General James Wolfe attributed to King George II. When a critic remarked that Wolfe was a madman, the King is said to have replied: "I wish he would bite some of the others."*

the army of General John C. Pemberton, defending Vicksburg, from other Confederate units. Turning next on Pemberton, Grant defeated him in two decisive battles, Champion's Hill and Big Black River, and drove him inside the Vicksburg fortifications. By mid-May the city was under siege. Grant applied relentless pressure, and on July 4 Pemberton surrendered. With Vicksburg in Union hands, federal gunboats could range the entire length of the Mississippi.[3] Texas and Arkansas were for all practical purposes lost to the Confederacy.

Lincoln had disliked Grant's plan for capturing Vicksburg. Now he generously confessed his error and placed Grant in command of all federal troops west of the Appalachians. Grant promptly took charge of the fighting around Chattanooga, Tennessee, where Confederate advances, beginning with the Battle of Chickamauga (September 19–20), were threatening to develop into a major disaster for the North. Shifting corps commanders and bringing up fresh units, he won another decisive victory at Chattanooga in a series of battles ending on November 25, 1863. This cleared the way for an invasion of Georgia. Suddenly this unkempt, stubby little man, who looked more like a tramp than a general, emerged as the military leader the North had been so desperately seeking. In March 1864 Lincoln summoned him to Washington, named him lieutenant general, and gave him supreme command of the armies of the United States.

Economic and Social Effects, North and South

Although much blood would yet be spilled, by the end of 1863 the Confederacy was on the road to defeat. Northern military pressure, gradually increasing, was eroding the South's most precious resource: manpower. An ever-tightening naval blockade was reducing its economic strength. Shortages developed that, combined with the flood of currency pouring from the presses, led to drastic inflation. By 1864 an officer's coat cost $2,000 in Confederate money, cigars sold for $10 each, butter was $25 a pound, and flour went for $275 a barrel. Wages rose too, but not nearly as rapidly.

The southern railroad network was gradually wearing out, the major lines maintaining operations only by cannibalizing less vital roads. Imported products such as coffee disappeared; even salt became scarce. Efforts to increase manufacturing were only moderately successful because of the shortage of labor, capital, and technical knowledge.

In the North, after a brief depression in 1861 caused by the uncertainties of the situation and the loss of southern business, the economy flourished. Government purchases greatly stimulated certain lines of manufacturing, the railroads operated at close to capacity and with increasing efficiency, the farm machinery business boomed because so many farmers left their fields to serve in the army, and bad harvests in Europe boosted agricultural prices.

---

[3]*Port Hudson, isolated by Vicksburg's fall, surrendered on July 9.*

Congress passed a number of economic measures long desired but held up in the past by southern opposition. The Homestead Act (1862) gave 160 acres to any settler who would farm the land for five years. The Morrill Land Grant Act of the same year provided the states with land at the rate of 30,000 acres for each member of Congress to support state agricultural colleges. Various tariff acts raised the duties on manufactured goods to an average rate of 47 percent in order to protect domestic manufacturers from foreign competition. The Pacific Railway Act (1862) authorized subsidies in land and money for the construction of a transcontinental railroad. And the National Banking Act of 1863 gave the country, at last, a uniform currency.

All these laws stimulated the economy. Whether the overall economic effect of the Civil War on the Union was beneficial is less clear. Since it was fought mostly with rifles, light cannon, horses, and wagons, it had much less effect on heavy industry than later wars would have. Although the economy grew, it did so more slowly during the 1860s than in the decades preceding and following. Prices soared beginning in 1862, averaging about 80 percent over the 1860 level by the end of the war. As in the South, wages did not keep pace. This did not make for a healthy economy; nor did the fact that there were chronic shortages of labor in many fields, shortages aggravated by a sharp drop in the number of immigrants.

As the war dragged on and the continuing inflation eroded purchasing power, resentment on the part of workers deepened. During the 1850s iron molders, cigar makers, and some other skilled workers had formed national unions. This trend continued through the war years. There were many strikes. Inflation and shortages encouraged speculation and fostered a selfish, materialistic attitude toward life. Many contractors took advantage of wartime confusion to sell the government shoddy goods. By 1864 cotton was worth $1.90 a pound in New England. It could be had for 20 cents a pound in the South. Although it was illegal to traffic in the staple across the lines, unscrupulous operators did so and made huge profits.

Yet the war undoubtedly hastened industrialization and laid the basis for many other aspects of modern civilization. It posed problems of organization and planning, both military and civilian, that challenged the talents of creative persons and thus led to a more complex and efficient economy. The mechanization of production, the growth of large corporations, the creation of a better banking system, and the emergence of business leaders attuned to these conditions would surely have occurred in any case, for industrialization was underway long before the South seceded. Nevertheless, the war greatly speeded all these changes.

Women in Wartime

Many southern women took over the management of farms and small plantations when their menfolk went off to war. Others became volunteer nurses, and after an initial period of resistance, the Confederate army began to enlist women in the medical corps. At least two female nurses, Captain Sally Tompkins and Kate

Women in the South playing croquet during the war, preserving the amenities of plantation life. By 1864 southern leaders were complaining that many southern women had lost their zeal for the Cause. Poor women engaged in bread riots; and well-to-do women held "incessant parties and balls." Through such actions, women registered their discontent with the war—and with the paternalist ethos of southern chivalry, which had manifestly failed to protect and defend southern womanhood.

Cumming, left records of their experiences that throw much light on how the wounded were treated during the war. Other southern women worked as clerks in newly organized government departments.

Southern "ladyhood" more generally was yet another casualty of the war. The absence or death of husbands or other male relations changed attitudes toward gender roles. When her husband obeyed a military order to abandon Atlanta to the advancing Union armies, Julia Davidson, about to give birth, denounced the "men of Atlanta" for having "run and left Atlanta" and their homes. Such women learned to fend for themselves. "Necessity," Davidson later wrote her husband, would "make a different woman of me."

Large numbers of women also contributed to the northern war effort. As in the South, farm women went out into fields to plant and harvest crops, aided in many instances by new farm machinery. Many others took jobs in textile factories; in establishments making shoes, uniforms, and other supplies for the army; and in government agencies. But as was usually the case, the low wages traditionally paid women acted as a brake on wage increases for their male colleagues.

Besides working in factories and shops and on farms, northern women, again like their southern counterparts, aided the war effort more directly. Elizabeth Blackwell, the first American woman doctor of medicine, had already founded the New York Infirmary for Women and Children. After war broke out she helped set

A family of a soldier in the 31st Philadelphia Infantry, camped near Washington, D.C. Although both armies discouraged women from following soldier-husbands, the practice was fairly common. Women proved indispensable as laundresses and cooks. Although women were initially excluded from army hospitals, the policy quickly changed and camp women often worked as nurses during battles.

up what became the U.S. Sanitary Commission, an organization of women similar to the Christian Commission dedicated to improving sanitary conditions at army camps, supplying hospitals with volunteer nurses, and raising money for medical supplies. Many thousands of women volunteers took part in Sanitary Commission and related programs.

An additional 3,000-odd women served as regular army nurses during the conflict. At the start the high command of both armies resisted the efforts of women to help, but necessity and a grudging recognition of the competence of these women gradually brought the generals around. Clara Barton, a schoolteacher and government clerk, was among the first women to dress wounds at forward stations on the battlefield. After she ran out of bandages at Antietam, she dressed wounds with green corn leaves. The chief surgeon declared her to be "the angel of the battlefield." The "proper sphere" of American woman was expanding, another illustration of the modernizing effect of the war.

Grant in the Wilderness

Grant's strategy as supreme commander was simple, logical, and ruthless. He would attack Lee and try to capture Richmond, Virginia. General William Tecumseh Sherman would drive from Chattanooga toward Atlanta, Georgia. Like a lobster's claw, the two armies could then close to crush all resistance. Early in May 1864 Grant and Sherman commenced operations, each with more than 100,000 men.

Grant marched the Army of the Potomac directly into the tangled wilderness area south of the Rappahannock, where Hooker had been routed a year earlier. Lee, having only 60,000 men, forced the battle in the roughest possible country, where Grant found it difficult to make efficient use of his larger force. For two days (May 5–6) the Battle of the Wilderness raged. When it was over, the North had sustained another 18,000 casualties, far more than the Confederates. But unlike his predecessors, Grant did not fall back after being checked, nor did he expose his army to the kind of devastating counterattack at which Lee was so expert. Instead he shifted his troops to the southeast, attempting to outflank the Confederates. Divining his intent, Lee rushed his divisions southeastward and disposed them behind hastily erected earthworks in well-placed positions around Spotsylvania Court House. Grant attacked. After five more days, at a cost to the Union army of another 12,000 men, the Confederate lines were still intact.

Grant had grasped the fundamental truth that the war could be won only by grinding the South down beneath the weight of numbers. His own losses of men and equipment could be replaced; Lee's could not. When critics complained of the cost, he replied doggedly that he intended to fight on in the same manner if it took all summer. Once more he pressed southeastward in an effort to outflank the enemy. At Cold Harbor, 9 miles from Richmond, he found the Confederates once more in strong defenses. He attacked. It was a battle as foolish and nearly as one-sided as General Pakenham's assault on Jackson's line outside New Orleans in 1815. "At Cold Harbor," the forthright Grant confessed in his memoirs, "no advantage whatever was gained to compensate for the heavy losses we sustained."

Sixty thousand casualties in less than a month! The news sent a wave of dismay through the North. There were demands that "Butcher" Grant be removed from command. Lincoln, however, stood firm. Although the price was fearfully high, Grant was gaining his objective. At Cold Harbor, Lee had to fight without a single regiment in general reserve while Grant's army was larger than at the start of the offensive. When Grant next swung around his flank, striking south of the James River toward Petersburg, Lee had to rush his troops to that city to hold him.

As the Confederates dug in, Grant put Petersburg under siege. Soon both armies had constructed complicated lines of breastworks and trenches, running for miles in a great arc south of Petersburg, much like the fortifications that would be used in France in World War I. Methodically the Union forces extended their lines, seeking to weaken the Confederates and cut the rail connections supplying Lee's troops and the city of Richmond. Grant could not overwhelm him, but by late June, Lee was pinned to earth. Moving again would mean having to abandon Richmond—tantamount, in southern eyes, to surrender.

Sherman in Georgia

The summer of 1864 saw the North submerged in pessimism. The Army of the Potomac held Lee at bay but appeared powerless to defeat him. In Georgia, General Sherman inched forward methodically against the wily Joseph E. Johnston, but

Ulysses S. Grant, shown at City Point, Virginia, during the siege of Petersburg. An 8.5-ton siege gun, mounted on a railroad flatcar, hurled 200-pound bombs onto Confederate positions during the siege. Trench warfare ensued, a chilling harbinger of World War I in early twentieth-century Europe.

when he tried a direct assault at Kennesaw Mountain on June 27, he was thrown back with heavy casualties. In July Confederate raiders under General Jubal Early dashed suddenly across the Potomac from the Shenandoah Valley to within five miles of Washington before being turned back. A draft call for 500,000 additional men did not improve the public temper. Huge losses and the absence of a decisive victory were taxing the northern will to continue the fight.

In June, Lincoln had been renominated on a National Union ticket, with the Tennessee Unionist Andrew Johnson, a former Democrat, as his running mate. He was under attack not only from the Democrats, who nominated General McClellan and came out for a policy that might almost be characterized as peace at any price, but also from the Radical Republicans, many of whom had wished to dump him in favor of Secretary of the Treasury Chase.

Then, almost overnight, the whole atmosphere changed. On September 2, General Sherman's army fought its way into Atlanta. When the Confederates coun-

Although Sherman's 100,000 Union soldiers marched to Atlanta, his men were supplied by sixteen railway trains from Chattanooga, Tennessee. After taking Atlanta late in the summer of 1864, Sherman pulled up the railway line and burned the depots. On his march to the sea, he destroyed several hundred miles of railroads.

tered with an offensive northward toward Tennessee,[4] Sherman did not follow. Instead he abandoned his communications with Chattanooga and marched unopposed through Georgia, "from Atlanta to the sea."

The march through Georgia had many objectives besides conquering territory. One obvious one was economic, the destruction of southern resources. "[We] must make old and young, rich and poor feel the hard hand of war," Sherman said. Before taking Atlanta he wrote his wife: "We have devoured the land. . . . All the people retire before us and desolation is behind. To realize what war is one should follow our tracks."

Another object of Sherman's march was psychological. "If the North can march an army right through the South," he told General Grant, Southerners will take it "as proof positive that the North can prevail." This was certainly true of Georgia's blacks, who flocked to the invaders by the thousands, women and children as well as men, all cheering mightily when the soldiers put their former masters' homes to the torch. "They pray and shout and mix up my name with Moses," Sherman explained.

Sherman's victories staggered the Confederacy and the anti-Lincoln forces in the North. In November the president was easily reelected, 212 electoral votes to 21. The country was determined to carry on the struggle.

---

[4]*This force was crushed before Nashville in December by a Union army under General George Thomas.*

At last the South's will to resist began to crack. Sherman entered Savannah on December 22, having denuded a strip of Georgia 60 miles wide. Early in January 1865 he marched northward, leaving behind "a broad black streak of ruin and desolation—the fences all gone; lonesome smoke-stacks, surrounded by dark heaps of ashes and cinders, marking the spots where human habitations had stood." In February his troops captured Columbia, South Carolina. Soon they were in North Carolina, advancing relentlessly. In Virginia, Grant's vise grew tighter day by day while the Confederate lines became thinner and more ragged.

To Appomattox Court House

On March 4 Lincoln took the presidential oath and delivered his second inaugural address. Photographs taken at about this time show how four years of war had marked him. Somehow he had become both gentle and steel-tough, both haggard and inwardly calm. With victory sure, he spoke for tolerance, mercy, and reconstruction. "Let us judge not," he said after stating again his personal dislike of slavery, "that we be not judged." He urged all Americans to turn without malice to the task of mending the damage and to make a just and lasting peace between the sections.

Now the Confederate troops around Petersburg could no longer withstand the federal pressure. Desperately Lee tried to pull his forces back to the Richmond and Danville Railroad at Lynchburg, but the swift wings of Grant's army enveloped them. Richmond fell on April 3. With fewer than 30,000 men to oppose Grant's 115,000, Lee recognized the futility of further resistance. On April 9 he and Grant met by prearrangement at Appomattox Court House.

It was a scene at once pathetic and inspiring. Lee was noble in defeat; Grant, despite his rough-hewn exterior, sensitive and magnanimous in victory. "I met you once before, General Lee, while we were serving in Mexico," Grant said after they had shaken hands. "I have always remembered your appearance, and I think I should have recognized you anywhere." They talked briefly of that earlier war, and then, acting on Lincoln's instructions, Grant outlined his terms. All that would be required was that the Confederate soldiers lay down their arms. They could return to their homes in peace. When Lee hinted (he was too proud to ask outright for the concession) that his men would profit greatly if allowed to retain possession of their horses, Grant agreed to let them do so.

Winners, Losers, and the Future

And so the war ended in 1865. It had cost the nation more than 600,000 lives, nearly as many as in all other American wars combined. The story of one of the lost thousands must stand for all, Union and Confederate. Jones Budbury, a tall, 19-

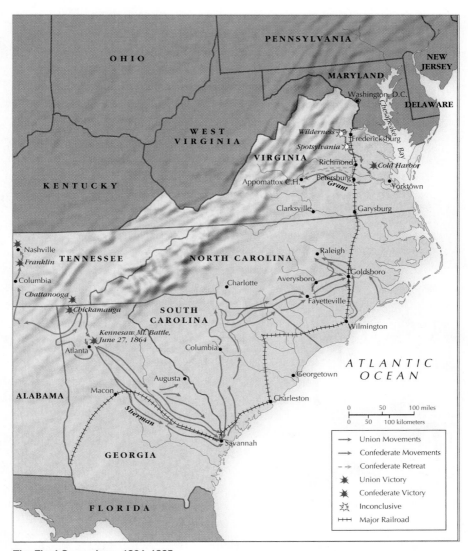

The Final Campaigns, 1864–1865
Grant's repeated and costly (60,000 casualties the first month) attempts to outflank Lee are detailed here. At Five Forks the long siege of Petersburg was broken; Richmond was evacuated. A week later, Lee surrendered. Sherman's campaign in Georgia and the Carolinas is also depicted.

year-old redhead, was working in a Pennsylvania textile mill when the war broke out, and he enlisted at once. His regiment first saw action at Bull Run. He took part in McClellan's Peninsula campaign. He fought at Second Bull Run, at Chancellorsville, and at Gettysburg. A few months after Gettysburg he was wounded in the foot and spent some time in an army hospital. By the spring of 1864 he had risen through the ranks to first sergeant and his hair had turned gray. In June he was captured and sent to Andersonville military prison, near Macon,

Debating the Past

WHY DID THE SOUTH LOSE THE CIVIL WAR?

The answer to this question had long been answered with numbers: The South had too few people and factories. But many have rebutted this point by noting that the South nearly *did* win. Moreover, while southern commanders were plagued with shortages, they lost no battles because they ran out of bullets or shells. In a study of industrial output, Emory Thomas (1979) concluded that southern leadership "outdid its northern counterpart in mobilizing for total war." The South's chief deficiency was, surprisingly, in food production. Frank L. Owsley (1925) blamed the South's defeat on "state's rights jealousy and particularism." Confederate states failed to coordinate financing and production and thus made the South's defeat "inevitable." Jeffrey Hummel (1996), however, has advanced the opposite argument: Jefferson Davis's centralization of power strangled the South with bureaucratic inefficiency and deprived it of ideological coherence. David Eicher (2006) adds that Davis interfered with generals and promoted incompetents. Folklore holds that the genius of southern generals, especially Robert E. Lee, overcame all southern deficiencies. But in *Attack and Die* (1982), a book

whose thesis is contained in its title, Grady McWhiney and Perry D. Jamieson insisted that Lee's audacity, and that of other southern generals, was ill-suited to the military technology of the day. Rifles were particularly effective at cutting down attacking armies. Detailed statistical analysis, however, has challenged this thesis: the North and South initiated attacks with nearly equal frequency and losses. Edward Channing (1925) proposed that the South was defeated because by 1865 Confederates "lost the will to fight." This is rather like saying that the South stopped fighting because it decided to stop fighting—an instance of circular reasoning. But many historians have found the argument, restated more subtly, to be persuasive. Herman Hattaway and Archer Jones (1986) proposed that while the Confederacy could field and equip an effective army for most of the war, "an insufficient nationalism" failed to "survive the strains imposed by lengthy hostilities." The scene above is of Richmond in April 1865.

Emory Thomas, *The Confederate Nation* (1979), Frank L. Owsley, *State Rights in the Confederacy* (1925), Grady McWhiney and Perry D. Jamieson, *Attack and Die* (1982), Edward Channing, *History of the United States* (1925), Herman Hattaway and Archer Jones, *How the North Won* (1986), Jeffrey Hummel, *Emancipating Slaves, Enslaving Free Men* (1996), David Eicher, *Dixie Betrayed* (2006).

Casualties of the Civil War

The Union death rate was 23 percent, the Confederate 24 percent. In general, twice as many soldiers were killed by disease as were killed by bullets.

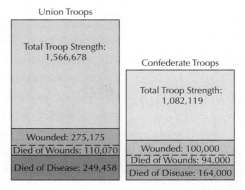

Union Troops

Total Troop Strength: 1,566,678

Wounded: 275,175
Died of Wounds: 110,070
Died of Disease: 249,458

Confederate Troops

Total Troop Strength: 1,082,119

Wounded: 100,000
Died of Wounds: 94,000
Died of Disease: 164,000

Georgia, but he fell ill and the Confederates released him. In March 1865 he was back with his regiment in the lines besieging Richmond. On April 6, three days before Lee's surrender, Jones Budbury was killed while pursuing Confederate units near Sailor's Creek, Virginia.

The war also caused enormous property losses, especially in the Confederacy. All the human and material destruction explains the eroding hatred and bitterness that the war implanted in millions of hearts. The corruption, the gross materialism, and the selfishness generated by wartime conditions were other disagreeable by-products of the conflict. Such sores fester in any society, but the Civil War bred conditions that inflamed and multiplied them. The war produced many examples of charity, self-sacrifice, and devotion to duty as well, yet if the general moral atmosphere of the postwar generation can be said to have resulted from the experiences of 1861 to 1865, the effect overall was bad.

What had been obtained at this price? Slavery was dead. Paradoxically, while the war had been fought to preserve the Union, after 1865 the people tended to see the United States not as a union of states but as a nation. After Appomattox, secession was almost literally inconceivable. In a strictly political sense, as Lincoln had predicted from the start, the northern victory heartened friends of republican government and democracy throughout the world. A better-integrated society and a more technically advanced and productive economic system also resulted from the war.

The Americans of 1865 estimated the balance between cost and profit according to their individual fortunes and prejudices. Only the wisest realized that no final accounting could be made until the people had decided what to do with the fruits of victory. That the physical damage would be repaired no one could reasonably doubt; that even the loss of human resources would be restored in short order was equally apparent. But would the nation make good use of the opportunities the war had made available? What would the former slaves do with freedom? How would whites, northern and southern, react to emancipation? To what end would the new technology and social efficiency be directed? Would the people be able to forget the recent past and fulfill the hopes for which so many brave soldiers had given their "last full measure of devotion"?

Milestones

1861	Confederates attack Fort Sumter; Lincoln calls for 75,000 volunteers
	First Battle of Bull Run (Virginia) boosts Confederate morale
	Lincoln appoints George B. McClellan Union commander
1862	Confederate Congress passes Conscription Act
	Battle of Glorieta Pass ends Confederate threat to Far West
	USS *Monitor* defeats Confederate *Merrimack* in battle of ironclads
	Robert E. Lee assumes command of Confederate Army of Northern Virginia
	Lee and Stonewall Jackson defeat huge Union army at Seven Days' Battle for Richmond
	Lee and Jackson defeat Union army at Second Battle of Bull Run
	Lee's northern advance is stopped at Battle of Antietam; 22,000 die
	Emancipation Proclamation frees slaves in 'areas of rebellion'
	Congress passes Homestead, Morrill Land Grant, and Pacific Railway acts
1863	Congress passes Conscription and National Banking acts
	Federal troops subdue draft riots in New York City
	Union army defeats Confederates at Gettysburg
	Union siege and capture of Vicksburg, Mississippi, gives Union control of entire Mississippi River
1864	Grant pushes deep into Virginia in costly battles of the Wilderness, Spotsylvania Court House, and Cold Harbor
	Sherman captures Atlanta, Georgia; marches to sea; captures Savannah
	Lincoln is reelected president
1864–1865	Grant takes Petersburg, Virginia, after 10-month siege
1865	Sherman captures Columbia, South Carolina
	Lee surrenders to Grant at Appomattox Court House, Virginia

CHAPTER 15

Reconstruction and the South

IN JANUARY 2007, CONGRESSMAN JOHN CONYERS OF MICHIGAN introduced a bill that would require the federal government to reimburse African Americans for the harm done to them by slavery and its aftermath. "It is a fact that slavery flourished in the United States and constituted an immoral and inhumane deprivation of African slaves' lives, liberty and cultural heritage," Conyers declared.

Why, doubters asked, should the nation make reparations to the *descendants* of slaves? Conyers responded that the legacy of slavery continued to inflict "great injustices" on "millions of African Americans today."

Although Conyers' bill (which he has submitted every year since 1989[1]) has yet to be passed by Congress, it encouraged Deadria Farmer-Paellman, a law school student, to file a lawsuit in 2002 against twenty railroad, tobacco, insurance, and textile companies. "These companies have amassed enormous wealth off the backs of enslaved Africans," Farmer-Paellman insisted. She held that they should be forced to make restitution to black Americans.

The lawsuits provided statistics on the unequal economic status of white and black Americans. In 2002, the median household income was $47,000 for whites and $29,000 for blacks. About one-fourth of all black households fell below the poverty line, twice as high a proportion as among whites. The median net worth for white households was $72,000, and for black households, $10,000.

Was the legacy of slavery responsible for these disparities? Conyers believed so. He had assigned his bill the number 40—a reference to General William Sherman's promise during the Civil War to provide free slaves with "40 acres and a mule."

---

[1] *Conyers, who is black, was responding to a law passed by Congress in 1988 to make a lump sum payment of $20,000 to those who had suffered during the internment of Japanese by the United States during World War II.*

But the promise after the Civil War went unfulfilled. At first, Radical Republicans in Congress did everything to elevate the ex-slaves (and to keep down former Confederates). For a time, Andrew Johnson, Lincoln's successor, stoutly resisted the Republican initiative—for which he was impeached and nearly removed from office. The Republican-dominated Congress then embarked on one of the most ambitious experiments in social engineering ever devised, an attempt to confer on ex-slaves political power over their former masters. Despite some major accomplishments, Reconstruction was undone by racial intransigence and violence, Republican mistakes, and persistent economic obstacles. In 1877, the experiment came to an end. Deprived of federal assistance, former slaves were obliged to make do on their own.

The Assassination of Lincoln

On April 5, 1865, Abraham Lincoln visited Richmond, Virginia. The fallen Confederate capital lay in ruins, sections blackened by fire, but the president was able to walk the streets unmolested and almost unattended. Everywhere black people crowded around him worshipfully; some fell to their knees as he passed, crying "Glory, Hallelujah," hailing him as a messiah. Even white townspeople seemed to have accepted defeat without resentment.

A few days later, in Washington, Lincoln delivered an important speech on Reconstruction, urging compassion and open-mindedness. On April 14 he held a Cabinet meeting at which postwar readjustment was considered at length. That evening, while Lincoln was watching a performance of the play *Our American Cousin* at Ford's Theater, a half-mad actor, John Wilkes Booth, slipped into the president's box and shot him in the back of the head with a small pistol. Early the next morning, without having regained consciousness, Lincoln died.

The murder was part of a complicated plot organized by die-hard pro-Southerners. Seldom have fanatics displayed so little understanding of their own interests, for with Lincoln perished the South's best hope for a mild peace. After his body had been taken home to Illinois, the national mood hardened; apparently the awesome drama was still unfolding—retribution and a final humbling of the South were inevitable.

Presidential Reconstruction

Despite its bloodiness, the Civil War had caused less intersectional hatred than might have been expected. Although civilian property was often seized or destroyed, the invading armies treated the southern population with forbearance, both during the war and after Appomattox. While confederate President Davis was ensconced in Richmond behind Lee's army, Northerners boasted that they would "hang Jeff Davis to a sour apple tree," and when he was captured in Georgia in May

1865, he was at once clapped into irons preparatory to being tried for treason and murder. But feeling against Davis subsided quickly. In 1867 the military turned him over to the civil courts, which released him on bail. He was never brought to trial. A few other Confederate officials spent short periods behind bars, but the only Southerner executed for war crimes was Major Henry Wirz, the commandant of Andersonville military prison.

The legal questions related to bringing the defeated states back into the Union were extremely complex. Since Southerners believed that secession was legal, logic should have compelled them to argue that they were out of the Union and would thus have to be formally readmitted. Northerners should have taken the contrary position, for they had fought to prove that secession was illegal. Yet the people of both sections did just the opposite. Senator Charles Sumner and Congressman Thaddeus Stevens, in 1861 uncompromising expounders of the theory that the Union was indissoluble, now insisted that the Confederate states had "committed suicide" and should be treated like "conquered provinces." Lincoln believed the issue a "pernicious abstraction" and tried to ignore it.

The process of readmission began in 1862, when Lincoln reappointed provisional governors for those parts of the South that had been occupied by federal troops. On December 8, 1863, he issued a proclamation setting forth a general policy. With the exception of high Confederate officials and a few other special groups, all Southerners could reinstate themselves as United States citizens by taking a simple loyalty oath. When, in any state, a number equal to 10 percent of those voting in the 1860 election had taken this oath, they could set up state government. Such governments had to be republican in form, must recognize the "permanent freedom" of the slaves, and must provide for education for blacks. The plan, however, did not require that blacks be given the right to vote.

The "Ten Percent Plan" reflected Lincoln's lack of vindictiveness and his political wisdom. He realized that any government based on such a small minority of the population would be, as he put it, merely "a tangible nucleus which the remainder . . . may rally around as fast as it can," a sort of puppet regime, like the paper government established in those sections of Virginia under federal control.[2] The regimes established under this plan in Tennessee, Louisiana, and Arkansas bore, in the president's mind, the same relation to finally reconstructed states that an egg bears to a chicken. "We shall sooner have the fowl by hatching it than by smashing it," he remarked. He knew that eventually representatives of the southern states would again be sitting in Congress, and he wished to lay the groundwork for a strong Republican party in the section. Yet he realized that Congress had no intention of seating representatives from the "10 percent" states at once.

The Radicals in Congress disliked the Ten Percent Plan, partly because of its moderation and partly because it enabled Lincoln to determine Union policy toward the recaptured regions. In July 1864 they passed the Wade-Davis bill, which

---

[2]*By approving the separation of the western counties that had refused to secede, this government provided a legal pretext for the creation of West Virginia.*

provided for constitutional conventions only after a majority of the others in a southern state had taken a loyalty oath. Confederate officials and anyone who had "voluntarily borne arms against the United States" were barred from voting in the election or serving at the convention. Besides prohibiting slavery, the new state constitutions would have to repudiate Confederate debts. Lincoln disposed of the Wade-Davis bill with a pocket veto and there matters stood when Andrew Johnson became president following the assassination.

Lincoln had picked Johnson for a running mate in 1864 because he was a border-state Unionist Democrat and something of a hero as a result of his courageous service as military governor of Tennessee. His political strength came from the poor whites and yeomen farmers of eastern Tennessee, and he was fond of extolling the common man and attacking "stuck-up aristocrats."

Thaddeus Stevens called Johnson a "rank demagogue" and a "damned scoundrel," and it is true that Johnson was a masterful rabble-rouser. But few men of his generation labored so consistently on behalf of small farmers. Free homesteads, public education, absolute social equality—such were his objectives. The father of communism, Karl Marx, a close observer of American affairs at this time, wrote approvingly of Johnson's "deadly hatred of the oligarchy."

Johnson was a Democrat, but because of his record and his reassuring penchant for excoriating southern aristocrats, the Republicans in Congress were ready to cooperate with him. "Johnson, we have faith in you," said Senator Ben Wade, author of the Wade-Davis bill, the day after Lincoln's death. "By the gods, there will be no trouble now in running the government!"

Johnson's reply, "Treason must be made infamous," delighted the Radicals, but the president proved temperamentally unable to work with them. Opposition was his specialty; he soon alienated every powerful Republican in Washington.

Radical Republicans listened to Johnson's diatribes against secessionists and the great planters and assumed that he was anti-southern. Nothing could have been further from the truth. He had great respect for states' rights and he shared most of his poor white Tennessee constituents' contempt of blacks. "Damn the negroes, I am fighting these traitorous aristocrats, their masters," he told a friend during the war. "I wish to God," he said on another occasion, "every head of a family in the United States had one slave to take the drudgery and menial service off his family."

The new president did not want to injure or humiliate all white Southerners. He issued an amnesty proclamation only slightly more rigorous than Lincoln's. It assumed, correctly enough, that with the war over most southern voters would freely take the loyalty oath; thus it contained no 10 percent clause. More classes of Confederates, including those who owned taxable property in excess of $20,000, were excluded from the general pardon. By the time Congress convened in December 1865, all the southern states had organized governments, ratified the Thirteenth Amendment abolishing slavery, and elected senators and representa-

A portrait of Andrew Johnson as president (1866), painted by Frank Buchser.

tives. Johnson promptly recommended these new governments to the attention of Congress.

Republican Radicals

Johnson's proposal had no chance in Congress. The Thirteenth Amendment had the effect of increasing the representation of the southern states in Congress because it made the Three-fifths Compromise meaningless. Henceforth those who had been slaves would be counted as whole persons in apportioning seats in the House of Representatives. If Congress seated the Southerners, the balance of power might swing to the Democrats. To expect the Republicans to surrender power in such a fashion was unrealistic. Former Copperheads gushing with extravagant praise for Johnson put them instantly on guard.

Southern voters had provoked northern resentment by their choice of congressmen. Georgia elected Alexander H. Stephens, vice president of the Confederacy, to the Senate, although he was still in a federal prison awaiting trial for treason! Several dozen men who had served in the Confederate Congress had been elected to either the House or the Senate, together with four generals and many other high officials. The southern people understandably selected locally respected and experienced leaders, but it was equally reasonable that these choices would sit poorly with Northerners.

Finally, the so-called Black Codes enacted by southern governments to control former slaves alarmed the North. These varied in severity from state to state, but all, as one planter admitted, set out to keep the blacks "as near to a state of bondage as possible." Blacks could not bear arms, be employed in occupations other than farming and domestic service, or leave their jobs without forfeiting back pay. The Mississippi code required them to sign labor contracts for the year in January, and, in addition, drunkards, vagrants, beggars, "common night-walkers," and even "mischief makers" and persons who "misspend what they earn" and who could not pay the stiff fines assessed for such misbehavior were to be "hired out . . . at public outcry" to the white persons who would take them for the shortest period in return for paying the fines. Such laws, apparently designed to get around the Thirteenth Amendment, outraged Northerners.

Congress Rejects Johnsonian Reconstruction

President Johnson's attitude speeded the swing toward the Radical position. Congress passed a bill expanding and extending the Freedmen's Bureau, which had been established in March 1865 to care for refugees. The bureau, a branch of the War Department, was already exercising considerable coercive and supervisory power in the South. Now Congress sought to add to its authority in order to protect the black population. Although the bill had wide support, Johnson vetoed it, arguing that it was an unconstitutional extension of military authority in peacetime. Congress then passed a Civil Rights Act that, besides declaring specifically that blacks were citizens of the United States, denied the states the power to restrict their rights to testify in court, to make contracts for their labor, and to hold property. In other words, it put teeth in the Thirteenth Amendment.

Once again the president refused to go along, although his veto was sure to drive more moderates into the arms of the Radicals. On April 9, 1866, Congress repassed the Civil Rights Act by a two-thirds majority, the first time in American history that a major piece of legislation became law over the veto of a president. This event marked a revolution in the history of Reconstruction. Thereafter Congress, not President Johnson, had the upper hand.

The president misread northern opinion. He believed that Congress had no right to pass laws affecting the South before southern representatives had been readmitted to Congress. However, in the light of the refusal of most southern whites to grant any real power or responsibility to the freedmen (an attitude that Johnson did not condemn), the public would not accept this point of view. Johnson placed his own judgment over that of the overwhelming majority of northern voters, and this was a great error, morally and tactically. By encouraging white Southerners to resist efforts to improve the lot of blacks, Johnson played into the hands of the Radicals.

The Radicals encountered grave problems in fighting for their program. Northerners might object to the Black Codes and to seating "rebels" in Congress, but few believed in racial equality. Between 1865 and 1868, Wisconsin, Minnesota,

Connecticut, Nebraska, New Jersey, Ohio, Michigan, and Pennsylvania all rejected bills granting blacks the vote.

Thus, while the Radicals sought partisan advantage in their battle with Johnson and sometimes played on war-bred passions in achieving their ends, they were taking large political risks in defense of genuinely held principles. One historian has aptly called them the "moral trustees" of the Civil War.

The Fourteenth Amendment

In June 1866 Congress submitted to the states a new amendment to the Constitution. The Fourteenth Amendment was, in the context of the times, a truly radical measure. Never before had newly freed slaves been granted significant political rights. For example, in the British Caribbean sugar islands, where slavery had been abolished in the 1830s, stiff property qualifications and poll taxes kept freedmen from voting. The Fourteenth Amendment was also a milestone along the road to the centralization of political power in the United States because it reduced the power of all the states. In this sense it confirmed the great change wrought by the Civil War: the growth of a more complex, more closely integrated social and economic structure requiring closer national supervision. Few people understood this aspect of the amendment at the time.

First the amendment supplied a broad definition of American citizenship: "All persons born or naturalized in the United States, and subject to the jurisdiction thereof, are citizens of the United States and of the State wherein they reside." Obviously this included blacks. Then it struck at discriminatory legislation like the Black Codes: "No State shall make or enforce any law which shall abridge the privileges or immunities of citizens of the United States; nor shall any State deprive any person of life, liberty, or property, without due process of law." The next section attempted to force the southern states to permit blacks to vote. If a state denied the vote to any class of its adult male citizens, its representation was to be reduced proportionately. Under another clause, former federal officials who had served the Confederacy were barred from holding either state or federal office unless specifically pardoned by a two-thirds vote of Congress. Finally, the Confederate debt was repudiated.

While the amendment did not specifically outlaw segregation or prevent a state from disenfranchising blacks, the southern states would have none of it. Without them the necessary three-fourths majority of the states could not be obtained.

President Johnson vowed to make the choice between the Fourteenth Amendment and his own policy the main issue of the 1866 congressional elections. He embarked on "a swing around the circle" to rally the public to his cause. He failed dismally. Northern women objected to the implication in the amendment that black men were more fit to vote than white women, but a large majority of northern voters was determined that African Americans must have at least formal legal equality. The Republicans won better than two-thirds of the seats in both houses, together with control of all the northern state governments. Johnson emerged from the campaign discredited, the Radicals stronger and determined to have their way. The southern states, Congressman James A. Garfield of Ohio said in February 1867, have "flung back into our teeth the magnanimous offer of a generous nation. It is now our turn to act."

The Reconstruction Acts

Had the southern states been willing to accept the Fourteenth Amendment, coercive measures might have been avoided. Their recalcitrance and continuing indications that local authorities were persecuting blacks finally led to the passage, on March 2, 1867, of the First Reconstruction Act. This law divided the former Confederacy—exclusive of Tennessee, which had ratified the Fourteenth Amendment—into five military districts, each controlled by a major general. It gave these officers almost dictatorial power to protect the civil rights of "all persons," maintain order, and supervise the administration of justice. To rid themselves of military rule, the former states were required to adopt new state constitutions guaranteeing blacks the right to vote and disenfranchising broad classes of ex-Confederates. If the new constitutions proved satisfactory to Congress, and if the new governments ratified the Fourteenth Amendment, their representatives would be admitted to Congress and military rule ended. Johnson's veto of the act was easily overridden.

Although drastic, the Reconstruction Act was so vague that it proved unworkable. Military control was easily established. But in deference to moderate Republican views, the law had not spelled out the process by which the new constitutions were to be drawn up. Southern whites preferred the status quo, even under army control, to enfranchising blacks and retiring their own respected leaders. They made no effort to follow the steps laid down in the law. Congress therefore passed a second act, requiring the military authorities to register voters and supervise the election of delegates to constitutional conventions. A third act further clarified procedures.

Still white Southerners resisted. The laws required that the constitutions be approved by a majority of the registered voters. Simply by staying away from the polls, whites prevented ratification in state after state. At last, in March 1868, a full year after the First Reconstruction Act, Congress changed the rules again. The constitutions were to be ratified by a majority of the voters. In June 1868 Arkansas, having fulfilled the requirements, was readmitted to the Union, and by July a sufficient number of states had ratified the Fourteenth Amendment to make it part of the Constitution. But it was not until July 1870 that the last southern state, Georgia, qualified to the satisfaction of Congress.

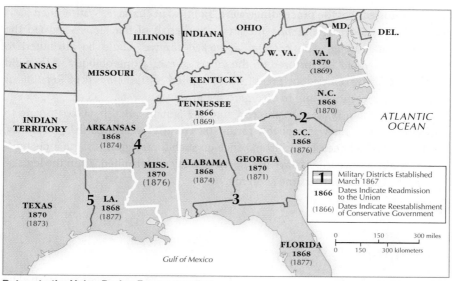

Return to the Union During Reconstruction

Map legend:
- **1** Military Districts Established March 1867
- **1866** Dates Indicate Readmission to the Union
- **(1866)** Dates Indicate Reestablishment of Conservative Government

0   150   300 miles
0   150   300 kilometers

Congress Supreme

To carry out this program in the face of determined southern resistance required a degree of single-mindedness over a long period seldom demonstrated by an American legislature. A series of measures passed between 1866 and 1868 increased the authority of Congress over the army, over the process of amending the Constitution, and over Cabinet members and lesser appointive officers. Even the Supreme Court was affected. Its size was reduced and its jurisdiction over civil rights cases limited. Finally, in a showdown caused by emotion more than by practical considerations, the Republicans attempted to remove President Johnson from office.

The chief issue was the Tenure of Office Act of 1867, which prohibited the president from removing officials who had been appointed with the consent of the Senate without first obtaining Senate approval. In February 1868 Johnson "violated" this act by dismissing Secretary of War Edwin M. Stanton, who had been openly in sympathy with the Radicals for some time. The House, acting under the procedure set up in the Constitution for removing the president, promptly impeached him before the bar of the Senate, Chief Justice Salmon P. Chase presiding.

In the trial, Johnson's lawyers easily established that he had removed Stanton only in an effort to prove the Tenure of Office Act unconstitutional. They demonstrated that the act did not protect Stanton to begin with, since it gave Cabinet members tenure "during the term of the President by whom they may have been appointed," and Stanton had been appointed in 1862, during Lincoln's first term!

Nevertheless the Radicals pressed the charges (eleven separate articles) relentlessly. To the argument that Johnson had committed no crime, the learned Senator

Sumner retorted that the proceedings were "political in character" rather than judicial. Thaddeus Stevens, directing the attack on behalf of the House, warned the senators that although "no corrupt or wicked motive" could be attributed to Johnson, they would "be tortured on the gibbet of everlasting obloquy" if they did not convict him. Tremendous pressure was applied to the handful of Republican senators who were unwilling to disregard the evidence.

Seven of them resisted to the end, and the Senate failed by a single vote to convict Johnson. This was probably fortunate. The trial weakened the presidency, but if Johnson had been forced from office on such flimsy grounds, the independence of the executive might have been permanently undermined. Then the legislative branch would have become supreme.

The Fifteenth Amendment

The failure of the impeachment did not affect the course of Reconstruction. The president was acquitted on May 16, 1868. A few days later, the Republican National Convention nominated General Ulysses S. Grant for the presidency. At the Democratic convention Johnson had considerable support, but the delegates nominated Horatio Seymour, a former governor of New York. In November Grant won an easy victory in the Electoral College, 214 to 80, but the popular vote was close: 3 million to 2.7 million. Although he would probably have carried the Electoral College in any case, Grant's margin in the popular vote was supplied by southern blacks enfranchised under the Reconstruction acts, about 450,000 of whom supported him. On the other hand, Grant had carried Indiana by fewer than 10,000 votes and lost New York by a similar number. If blacks in these and other closely divided states had voted, Republican strength would have been greatly enhanced.

Suddenly Congress blossomed with suffrage amendments. After considerable bickering over details, the Fifteenth Amendment was sent to the states for ratification in February 1869. It forbade all the states to deny the vote to anyone "on account of race, color, or previous condition of servitude." Once again nothing was said about denial of the vote on the basis of sex, which caused feminists, such as Elizabeth Cady Stanton, to be even more outraged than they had been by the Fourteenth Amendment.

Most southern states, still under federal pressure, ratified the amendment swiftly. The same was true in most of New England and in some western states. Bitter battles were waged in Connecticut, New York, Pennsylvania, and the states immediately north of the Ohio River, but by March 1870 most of them had ratified the amendment and it became part of the Constitution.

The debates occasioned by these conventions show that partisan advantage was not the only reason why voters approved black suffrage at last. The unfairness of a double standard of voting, North and South, the contribution of black soldiers during the war, and the hope that by passing the amendment the strife of Reconstruction could finally be ended all played a part.

When the Fifteenth Amendment went into effect, President Grant called it "the greatest civil change and . . . the most important event that has occurred since the nation came to life." The American Anti-Slavery Society formally dissolved itself, its work apparently completed. "The Fifteenth Amendment confers upon the African race the care of its own destiny," Radical Congressman James A. Garfield wrote proudly after the amendment was ratified. "It places their fortunes in their own hands."

"Black Republican" Reconstruction: Scalawags and Carpetbaggers

The Radicals had at last succeeded in imposing their will on the South. Throughout the region former slaves had real political influence; they voted, held office, and exercised the "privileges" and enjoyed the "immunities" guaranteed them by the Fourteenth Amendment. Almost to a man they voted Republican.

The spectacle of blacks not five years removed from slavery in positions of power and responsibility attracted much attention at the time and has since been examined exhaustively by historians. But the real rulers of the "black Republican" governments were white: the "scalawags"—Southerners willing to cooperate with the Republicans because they accepted the results of the war and wished to advance their own interests—and the "carpetbaggers"—Northerners who went to the South as idealists to help the freed slaves, as employees of the federal government, or more commonly as settlers hoping to improve themselves.

The scalawags were by far the more numerous. A few were prewar politicians or well-to-do planters, men such as the Mississippi planter John L. Alcorn and Joseph E. Brown, the Confederate governor of Georgia. General James Longstreet, one of Lee's most important lieutenants, was another prominent Southerner who cooperated with the Republicans. But most were people who had supported the Whig party before the secession crisis and who saw the Republicans as the logical successors of the Whigs.

The carpetbaggers were a particularly varied lot. Most had mixed motives for coming south and personal gain was certainly among them. But so were opposition to slavery and the belief that blacks deserved to be treated decently and given a chance to get ahead in the world.

Many northern blacks became carpetbaggers: former Union soldiers, missionaries from northern black churches, and also teachers, lawyers, and other members of the small northern black professional class. Many of these became officeholders, but like southern black politicians their influence was limited.

Debating the Past

WERE RECONSTRUCTION GOVERNMENTS CORRUPT?

Racist depictions of Reconstruction were common. This one by Thomas Nast was entitled "Colored Rule in a Reconstructed (?) State" and appeared in the influential *Harper's Weekly* (1874). The harsh assessment of Reconstruction persisted. In 1902 Columbia historian William A. Dunning declared that free slaves were mere children, incapable of holding office. Such views informed D. W. Griffith's 1915 film, *The Birth of a Nation*. In 1910 W. E. B. Du Bois, an African American scholar, was the first to applaud Reconstruction for broadening educational opportunities and democratizing government, but few historians concurred. In the 1960s, as the civil rights movement was gaining momentum, more scholars came out in support of Reconstruction. Kenneth Stampp (1965) emphasized the Reconstruction governments' attempts to protect freedmen; that same year, Joel Williamson turned Dunning's thesis on its head and endorsed nearly all aspects of Reconstruction. More recent scholars have generally taken a moderate position: Reconstruction may have failed, but its accomplishments under difficult circumstances of white opposition were substantial; see, for example, Eric Foner (1988). Certain facts are beyond argument. Black officeholders during Reconstruction were neither numerous nor inordinately influential. None was ever elected governor of a state; fewer than a dozen and a half during the entire period served in Congress. Blacks held many minor offices and were influential in southern legislatures, although (except in South Carolina) they never made up the majority.

William A. Dunning, *Reconstruction and the Constitution* (1902), W. E. B. Du Bois, *Black Reconstruction in America* (1935), Kenneth Stampp, *The Peculiar Institution* (1965), Joel Williamson, *After Slavery* (1965), Eric Foner, *Reconstruction* (1988).

During Reconstruction, fourteen blacks won election to the House of Representatives and two, Hiram Revels and Blanche K. Bruce, served in the Senate. Revels, at far left, won the Mississippi Senate seat that Jefferson Davis had once held. He later became president of Alcorn University. Congressman R. Brown Elliot, at far right, had been educated at Eton in England.

In South Carolina and elsewhere, blacks proved in the main able and conscientious public servants: able because the best tended to rise to the top in such a fluid situation and conscientious because most of those who achieved importance sought eagerly to demonstrate the capacity of their race for self-government. Even at the local level, where the quality of officials was usually poor, there was little difference in the degree of competence displayed by white and black officeholders. In power, the blacks were not vindictive; by and large they did not seek to restrict the rights of ex-Confederates.

Not all black legislators and administrators were paragons of virtue. In South Carolina, despite their control of the legislature, they broke up into factions repeatedly and failed to press for laws that would improve the lot of poor black farm workers. And waste and corruption were common during Reconstruction governments, whether the politicians were black or white.

In fact, the Radical southern governments accomplished a great deal. They spent money freely but not entirely wastefully. Tax rates zoomed, but the money financed the repair and expansion of the South's dilapidated railroad network, rebuilt crumbling levees, and expanded social services. Before the Civil War, southern planters possessed a disproportionate share of political as well as economic power, and they spent relatively little public money on education and public services of all kinds.

During Reconstruction an enormous gap had to be filled, and it took money to fill it. The Freedmen's Bureau made a major contribution. Northern religious and philanthropic organizations also did important work. Eventually, however, the state governments established and supported hospitals, asylums, and systems of free public education that, while segregated, greatly benefited everyone, whites as well as blacks. Much state money was also spent on economic development: land reclamation, repairing and expanding the war-ravaged railroads, maintaining levees.

The former slaves grasped eagerly at the opportunities to learn. Schools and other institutions were supported chiefly by property taxes, and these, of course, hit well-to-do planters hard. Hence much of the complaining about the "extravagance" of Reconstruction governments concealed traditional selfish objections to paying for public projects. Eventually the benefits of expanded government services to the entire population became clear, and when white supremacy was reestablished, most of the new services remained in force, and the corruption and inefficiency inherited from the carpetbagger governments continued.

The Ravaged Land

The South's grave economic problems complicated the rebuilding of its political system. The section had never been as prosperous as the North, and wartime destruction left it desperately poor by any standard. In the long run the abolition of slavery released immeasurable quantities of human energy previously stifled, but the immediate effect was to create confusion. Freedom to move without a pass, to "see the world," was one of the former slaves' most cherished benefits of emancipation. Understandably, many at first equated legal freedom with freedom from having to earn a living, a tendency reinforced for a time by the willingness of the Freedmen's Bureau to provide rations and other forms of relief in war-devastated areas. Most, however, soon accepted the fact that they must earn a living; a small plot of land of their own ("40 acres and a mule") would complete their independence.

This objective was forcefully supported by the relentless Congressman Thaddeus Stevens, whose hatred of the planter class was pathological. "The property of the chief rebels should be seized," he stated. If the lands of the richest "70,000 proud, bloated and defiant rebels" were confiscated, the federal government would obtain 394 million acres. Every adult male ex-slave could easily be supplied with 40 acres. The beauty of his scheme, Stevens insisted, was that "nine-tenths of the [southern] people would remain untouched." Dispossessing the great planters would make the South "a safe republic," its lands cultivated by "the free labor of intelligent citizens." If the plan drove the planters into exile, "all the better."

Aside from its vindictiveness, the proposals of Stevens and other extremists were simplistic. Land without tools, seed, and other necessities would have done the freedmen little good. Congress did throw open 46 million acres of poor-quality federal land in the South to blacks under the Homestead Act, but few settled on it.

The Freedmen's Bureau built 4,329 schools, attended by some 250,000 former slaves, in the postwar South. Many of the teachers in these schools were abolitionists or missionaries from New England. The schools drew African Americans of all ages, from children to grandparents, who were eager for the advantages offered by education.

Establishing former slaves on small farms with adequate financial aid would have been of incalculable benefit to them. This would have been practicable, but extremely expensive. It was not done.

The former slaves therefore had either to agree to work for their former owners or strike out on their own. White planters, influenced by the precipitous decline of sugar production in Jamaica and other Caribbean islands that had followed the abolition of slavery there, expected freed blacks to be incapable of self-directed effort. If allowed to become independent farmers, they would either starve to death or descend into barbarism. Of course the blacks did neither. True, the output of cotton and other southern staples declined precipitously after slavery was abolished. Observers soon came to the conclusion that a free black produced much less than a slave had produced. "You can't get only about two-thirds as much out of 'em now as you could when they were slaves," an Arkansas planter complained.

However, the decline in productivity was not caused by the inability of free blacks to work independently. They simply chose no longer to work like slaves. They let their children play instead of forcing them into the fields. Mothers devoted more time to childcare and housework, less to farm labor. Elderly blacks worked less.

The family life of former slaves was changed in other ways. Male authority increased when husbands became true heads of families. (Under slavery the ultimate responsibility for providing for women and children was the master's.) When blacks became citizens, the men acquired rights and powers denied to all women, such as the right to hold public office and serve on juries. Similarly, black women became more like white women, devoting themselves to separate "spheres" where their lives revolved around housekeeping and child rearing.

Sharecropping and the Crop-Lien System

Quite swiftly, a new agricultural system known as sharecropping emerged. Instead of cultivating the land by gang labor as in antebellum times, planters broke up their estates into small units and established on each unit a black family. The planter provided housing, agricultural implements, draft animals, seed, and other supplies, and the family provided labor. The crop was divided between planter and laborer, usually on a fifty-fifty basis. If the landlord supplied only land and housing, the laborer got a larger share. This was called share tenancy.

Sharecropping gave blacks the day-to-day control of their lives that they craved and the hope of earning enough to buy a small farm. But few blacks succeeded in this goal. As late as 1880 blacks owned less than 10 percent of the agricultural land in the South, although they made up more than half of the region's farm population. Mississippi actually prohibited the purchase of farmland by blacks.

Many white farmers in the South were also trapped by the sharecropping system and by white efforts to keep blacks in a subordinate position. New fencing laws kept them from grazing livestock on undeveloped land, a practice common before the Civil War. But the main cause of southern rural poverty for whites as well as for blacks was the lack of enough capital to finance the sharecropping system. Like their colonial ancestors, the landowners had to borrow against October's harvest to pay for April's seed. Thus the crop-lien system developed.

Under the crop-lien system, both landowner and sharecropper depended on credit supplied by local bankers, merchants, and storekeepers for everything from seed, tools, and fertilizer to overalls, coffee, and salt. Crossroads stores proliferated, and a new class of small merchants appeared. The prices of goods sold on credit were high, adding to the burden borne by the rural population. The small southern merchants were almost equally victimized by the system, for they also lacked capital, bought goods on credit, and had to pay high interest rates.

Seen in broad perspective, the situation is not difficult to understand. The South, drained of every resource by the war, was competing for funds with the North and West, both vigorous and expanding and therefore voracious consumers of capital. Reconstruction, in the literal sense of the word, was accomplished chiefly at the expense of the standard of living of the producing classes. The crop-lien system and the small storekeeper were only agents of an economic process dictated by national, perhaps even worldwide, conditions.

Compared with the rest of the country, progress in the South was slow. Just before the Civil War cotton harvests averaged about 4 million bales. During the con-

After the Civil War, most blacks worked as sharecroppers on land owned by whites. In this photograph, black sharecroppers pick cotton, a major cash crop of the South with the owner of the land getting a share of the crop (crop-lien). The crop-lien system injured everyone. Diversified farming would have reduced the farmers' need for cash, preserved the fertility of the soil, and, by placing a premium on imagination and shrewdness, aided the best of them to rise in the world. Because the price for cotton remained low, sharecroppers often fell into debt and were tied to the land almost as tightly as under slavery.

flict, output fell to about half a million, and the former Confederate states did not enjoy a 4-million-bale year again until 1870. In contrast, national wheat production in 1859 was 175 million bushels and in 1878, 449 million. About 7,000 miles of railroad were built in the South between 1865 and 1879; in the rest of the nation nearly 45,000 miles of track were laid.

But in the late 1870s, cotton production revived. It soon regained, and thereafter long retained, its title as "king" of the southern economy. This was true in large measure because of the crop-lien system.

The South made important gains in manufacturing after the war. The tobacco industry, stimulated by the sudden popularity of the cigarette, expanded rapidly. Virginia and North Carolina tobacco towns like Richmond, Lynchburg, and Durham flourished. The exploitation of the coal and iron deposits of northeastern Alabama in the early 1870s made a boomtown of Birmingham. The manufacture of cotton cloth increased, productive capacity nearly doubling between 1865 and 1880. Yet the mills of Massachusetts alone had eight times the capacity of the entire South in 1880. Despite the increases, the South's share of the national output of manufactured goods declined sharply during the Reconstruction era.

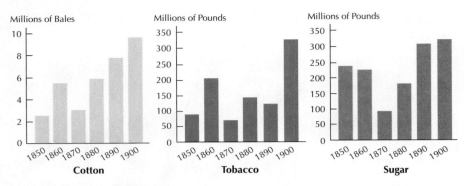

Southern Agriculture, 1850–1900
Cotton production recovered to its prewar level by 1880, but tobacco and sugar production lagged. Not until 1900 did tobacco growers have a better year than they had in 1860. The years following 1870 saw a general downward trend in wholesale prices for farm commodities. (Statistics are for the eleven states of the Confederacy.)

The White Backlash

Radical southern governments could sustain themselves only as long as they had the support of a significant proportion of the white population, for except in South Carolina and Louisiana, the blacks were not numerous enough to win elections alone. The key to survival lay in the hands of the wealthy merchants and planters, mostly former Whigs. People of this sort had nothing to fear from black economic competition. Taking a broad view, they could see that improving the lot of the former slaves would benefit all classes.

Southern white Republicans used the Union League of America, a patriotic club founded during the war, to control the black vote. Employing secret rituals, exotic symbols, and other paraphernalia calculated to impress unsophisticated people, they enrolled the freedmen in droves and marched them to the polls en masse.

Powerless to check the League by open methods, dissident Southerners established a number of secret terrorist societies, bearing such names as the Ku Klux Klan, the Knights of the White Camelia, and the Pale Faces. The most notorious of these organizations was the Klan, which originated in Tennessee in 1866. At first it was purely a social club, but by 1868 it had been taken over by vigilante types dedicated to driving blacks out of politics, and it was spreading rapidly across the South. Sheet-clad nightriders roamed the countryside, frightening the impressionable and chastising the defiant. Klansmen, using a weird mumbo jumbo and claiming to be the ghosts of Confederate soldiers, spread horrendous rumors and published broadsides designed to persuade the freedmen that it was unhealthy for them to participate in politics.

When intimidation failed, the Klansmen resorted to force. After being whipped by one group in Tennessee, a recently elected justice of the peace reported: "They said they had nothing particular against me . . . but they did not intend any nigger to hold office." In hundreds of cases the KKK murdered their opponents, often in the most gruesome manner.

Congress struck at the Klan with three Force Acts (1870–1871), which placed elections under federal jurisdiction and imposed fines and prison sentences on persons convicted of interfering with any citizen's exercise of the franchise. Troops were dispatched to areas where the Klan was strong, and by 1872 the federal authorities had arrested enough Klansmen to break up the organization.

Nevertheless the Klan contributed substantially to the destruction of Radical regimes in the South. Its depredations weakened the will of white Republicans (few of whom really believed in racial equality), and it intimidated many blacks. The fact that the army had to be called in to suppress it was a glaring illustration of the weakness of the Reconstruction governments.

Gradually it became respectable to intimidate black voters. Beginning in Mississippi in 1874, terrorism spread through the South. Instead of hiding behind masks and operating in the dark, these terrorists donned red shirts, organized into military companies, and paraded openly. Mississippi redshirts seized militant blacks and whipped them publicly. Killings were frequent. When blacks dared to fight back, heavily armed whites put them to rout. In other states similar results followed.

Before long the blacks learned to stay home on election day. One by one, "Conservative" parties—Democratic in national affairs—took over southern state governments. Intimidation was only a partial explanation of this development. The increasing solidarity of whites, northern and southern, was equally significant.

The North had subjected the South to control from Washington while preserving state sovereignty in the North itself. In the long run this discrimination proved unworkable. Many Northerners had supported the Radical policy only out of irritation with President Johnson. After his retirement their enthusiasm waned. The war was fading into the past and with it the worst of the anger it had generated.

Northern voters could still be stirred by references to the sacrifices Republicans had made to save the Union and by reminders that the Democratic party was the organization of rebels, Copperheads, and the Ku Klux Klan. "If the Devil himself were at the helm of the ship of state," wrote the novelist Lydia Maria Child in 1872, "my conscience would not allow me to aid in removing him to make room for the Democratic party." Yet emotional appeals could not convince Northerners that it was still necessary to maintain a large army in the South. In 1869 the occupying forces were down to 11,000 men. After Klan disruption and intimidation had made a farce of the 1874 elections in Mississippi, Governor Ames appealed to Washington for help. President Grant's attorney general, Edwards Pierrepont, refused to act. "The whole public are tired out with these autumnal outbreaks in the South," he told Ames. "Preserve the peace by the forces of your own state."

Nationalism was reasserting itself. Had not Washington and Jefferson been Virginians? Was not Andrew Jackson Carolina-born? Since most Northerners had little real love or respect for blacks, their interest in racial equality flagged once they felt reasonably certain that blacks would not be re-enslaved if left to their own devices in the South.

Another, much subtler force was also at work. The prewar Republican party had stressed the common interest of workers, manufacturers, and farmers in a free and mobile society, a land of equal opportunity where all could work in harmony. Southern whites had insisted that laborers must be disciplined if large enterprises were to be run efficiently. By the 1870s, as large industrial enterprises developed in the northern states, the thinking of business leaders changed—the southern argument began to make sense to them, and they became more sympathetic to the southern demand for more control over "their" labor force.

Grant as President

Other matters occupied the attention of northern voters. The expansion of industry and the rapid development of the West, stimulated by a new wave of railroad building, loomed more important to many than the fortunes of the former slaves. Beginning in 1873, when a stock market panic struck at public confidence, economic difficulties plagued the country. Heated controversies arose over tariff policy, with western agricultural interests seeking to force reductions from the high levels established during the war, and over the handling of the wartime greenback paper money, with debtor groups and many manufacturers favoring further expansion of the supply of dollars and conservative merchants and bankers arguing for retiring the greenbacks in order to return to a "sound" currency.

More damaging to the Republicans was the failure of Ulysses S. Grant to live up to expectations as president. His most serious weakness as president was his failure to deal effectively with economic and social problems, but the one that injured him and the Republicans most was his inability to cope with government corruption. The worst of the scandals—such as the Whiskey Ring affair, which implicated Grant's private secretary, Orville E. Babcock, and cost the government millions in tax revenue, and the corruption of Secretary of War William W. Belknap in the management of Indian affairs—did not become public knowledge during Grant's first term. However, in 1872 Republican reformers, alarmed by rumors of corruption and disappointed by Grant's failure to press for civil service reform, organized the Liberal Republican party and nominated Horace Greeley, the able but eccentric editor of the *New York Tribune,* for president.

The Liberal Republicans were mostly well-educated, socially prominent types— editors, college presidents, economists, along with a sprinkling of businessmen and politicians. Their liberalism was of the laissez-faire variety; they were for low tariffs and sound money, and against what they called "class legislation," meaning measures benefiting particular groups, whether labor unions or railroad companies or farm organizations. Nearly all had supported Reconstruction at the start, but by the early 1870s most were including southern blacks among the special interests that ought to be left to their own devices. Their observation of urban corruption and of unrestricted immigration led them to disparage universal suffrage, which, one of them said, "can only mean in plain English the government of ignorance and vice."

An 1872 Grant campaign poster of "Our Three Great Presidents." The poster was about two-thirds right.

The Democrats also nominated Greeley in 1872, although he had devoted his political life to flailing the Democratic party in the *Tribune*. That surrender to expediency, together with Greeley's temperamental unsuitability for the presidency, made the campaign a fiasco for the reformers. Grant triumphed easily, with a popular majority of nearly 800,000.

Nevertheless, the defection of the Liberal Republicans hurt the Republican party in Congress. In the 1874 elections, no longer hampered as in the presidential contest by Greeley's notoriety and Grant's fame, the Democrats carried the House of Representatives. It was clear that the days of military rule in the South were ending. By the end of 1875 only three southern states—South Carolina, Florida, and Louisiana—were still under Republican control.

The Republican party in the South was "dead as a doornail," a reporter noted. He reflected the opinion of thousands when he added: "We ought to have a sound sensible republican . . . for the next President as a measure of safety; but only on the condition of absolute noninterference in Southern local affairs, for which there is no further need or excuse."

The Disputed Election of 1876

Against this background the presidential election of 1876 took place. Since corruption in government was the most widely discussed issue, the Republicans passed over their most attractive political personality, the dynamic James G. Blaine, Speaker of the House of Representatives, who had been connected with some chicanery involving railroad securities. Instead they nominated Governor Rutherford B. Hayes of Ohio, a former general with an untarnished reputation. The Democrats picked Governor Samuel J. Tilden of New York, a wealthy lawyer who had attracted national attention for his part in breaking up the Tweed Ring in New York City.

In November early returns indicated that Tilden had carried New York, New Jersey, Connecticut, Indiana, and all the southern states, including Louisiana, South Carolina, and Florida, where Republican regimes were still in control. This seemed to give him 203 electoral votes to Hayes's 165, and a popular plurality in the neighborhood of 250,000 out of more than 8 million votes cast. However, Republican leaders had anticipated the possible loss of Florida, South Carolina, and Louisiana and were prepared to use their control of the election machinery in those states to throw out sufficient Democratic ballots to alter the results if doing so would change the national outcome. Realizing that the electoral votes of those states were exactly enough to elect their man, they telegraphed their henchmen on the scene, ordering them to go into action. The local Republicans then invalidated Democratic ballots in wholesale lots and filed returns showing Hayes the winner. Naturally the local Democrats protested vigorously and filed their own returns.

The Constitution provides (Article II, Section 1) that presidential electors must meet in their respective states to vote and forward the results to "the Seat of the Government." There, it adds, "the President of the Senate shall, in the Presence of the Senate and House of Representatives, open all the Certificates, and the Votes shall then be counted." But who was to do the counting? The House was Democratic, the Senate Republican; neither would agree to allow the other to do the job. On January 29, 1877, scarcely a month before inauguration day, Congress created a 15-member electoral commission to decide the disputed cases, The "neutral" vote was to be provided by Justice Joseph Bradley of New Jersey, a Republican.

Evidence presented before the commission revealed a disgraceful picture of election shenanigans. On the one hand, in all three disputed states Democrats had clearly cast a majority of the votes; on the other, it was unquestionable that many blacks had been forcibly prevented from voting.

In truth, both sides were shamefully corrupt. The governor of Louisiana was reported willing to sell his state's electoral votes for $200,000. The Florida election board was supposed to have offered itself to Tilden for the same price. "That seems to be the standard figure," Tilden remarked ruefully.

The Democrats had some hopes that Justice Bradley would be sympathetic to their case, for he was known to be opposed to harsh Reconstruction policies. On the eve of the commission's decision in the Florida controversy, he was apparently ready to vote in favor of Tilden. But the Republicans subjected him to tremendous political pressure. When he read his opinion on February 8, it was for Hayes. Thus, by a vote of 8 to 7, the commission awarded Florida's electoral votes to the Republicans.

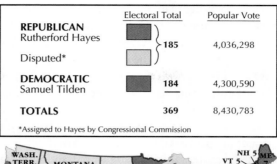

	Electoral Total	Popular Vote
REPUBLICAN Rutherford Hayes	} 185	4,036,298
Disputed*		
DEMOCRATIC Samuel Tilden	184	4,300,590
TOTALS	369	8,430,783

*Assigned to Hayes by Congressional Commission

The rest of the proceedings was routine. The commission assigned all the disputed electoral votes (including one in Oregon where the Democratic governor had seized on a technicality to replace a single Republican elector with a Democrat) to Hayes.

Democratic institutions, shaken by the South's refusal to go along with the majority in 1860 and by the suppression of civil rights during the rebellion, and further weakened by military intervention and the intimidation of blacks in the South during Reconstruction, seemed now a farce. According to Tilden's campaign manager, angry Democrats in fifteen states, chiefly war veterans, were readying themselves to march on Washington to force the inauguration of Tilden. Tempers flared in Congress, where some spoke ominously of a filibuster that would prevent the recording of the electoral vote and leave the country, on March 4, with no president at all.

The Compromise of 1877

Forces for compromise had been at work behind the scenes in Washington for some time. Although northern Democrats threatened to fight to the last ditch, many southern Democrats were willing to accept Hayes if he would promise to remove the troops and allow the southern states to manage their internal affairs by themselves. Ex-Whig planters and merchants who had reluctantly abandoned the carpetbag governments and who sympathized with Republican economic policies hoped that by supporting Hayes they might contribute to the restoration of the two-party system that had been destroyed in the South during the 1850s. Ohio Congressman James A. Garfield urged Hayes to find "some discreet way" of showing these Southerners that he favored "internal improvements." Hayes replied: "Your views are so nearly the same as mine that I need not say a word."

Tradition has it that a great compromise between the sections was worked out during a dramatic meeting at the Wormley Hotel[3] in Washington on February 26. Actually the negotiations were drawn out and informal, and the Wormley conference was but one of many. With the tacit support of many Democrats, the electoral vote was counted by the president of the Senate on March 2, and Hayes was declared elected, 185 votes to 184.

Like all compromises, this agreement was not entirely satisfactory; like most, it was not honored in every detail. Hayes recalled the last troops from South Carolina and Louisiana in April. He appointed a former Confederate general, David M. Key of Tennessee, postmaster general and delegated to him the congenial task of finding Southerners willing to serve their country as officials of a Republican administration. But the alliance of ex-Whigs and northern Republicans did not flourish; the South remained solidly Democratic. The major significance of the compromise, one of the great intersectional political accommodations of American history, was that it ended Reconstruction and inaugurated a new political order in the South. More than the Constitutional amendments and federal statutes, this new regime would shape the destinies of the four million freedmen.

For most, this future was to be bleak. Forgotten in the North, manipulated and then callously rejected by the South, rebuffed by the Supreme Court, voiceless in national affairs, they and their descendants were condemned in the interests of sectional harmony to lives of poverty, indignity, and little hope. Meanwhile, the rest of the United States continued its golden march toward wealth and power.

---

[3]Ironically, the hotel was owned by James Wormley, reputedly the wealthiest black in Washington.

1863	Lincoln announces "Ten Percent Plan" for Reconstruction
1865	Federal government sets up Freedmen's Bureau
	Lee surrenders at Appomattox Court House
	Lincoln is assassinated; Andrew Johnson becomes president
	Johnson issues amnesty proclamation
	States ratify Thirteenth Amendment abolishing slavery
1865–1866	Southern states enact Black Codes
1866	Civil Rights Act passes over Johnson's veto
	Johnson campaigns for his Reconstruction policy
1867	First Reconstruction Act puts former Confederacy under military rule
	Tenure of Office Act protects Senate appointees
1868	House of Representatives impeaches Johnson
	Fourth Reconstruction Act requires a majority of Southern voters to ratify state consititutions
	Senate acquits Johnson
	States ratify Fourteenth Amendment extending rights to freed slaves
	Ulysses S. Grant is elected president
	Ku Klux Klan uses intimidation and force throughout South
1870	States ratify Fifteenth Amendment granting black suffrage
1870–1871	Force (Ku Klux Klan) Act destroys Klan
1872	Liberal Republican party nominates Horace Greeley for president
	Grant is reelected president
1876	Rutherford B. Hayes runs against Samuel Tilden in disputed presidential election
1877	Electoral Commission awards disputed votes to Rutherford B. Hayes, who becomes president
	Hayes agrees to Compromise of 1877

The Conquest of the West

ACCORDING TO THE 2000 CENSUS, FOUR OF THE FIVE POOREST counties in the nation contained Indian reservations. Buffalo County, South Dakota, with 57 percent of its households below the poverty level, was the poorest in the nation; it encompassed the Crow Creek Indian Reservation. The Pine Ridge Indian Reservation (South Dakota), Gila River Reservation (Arizona), and Rosebud Reservations (South Dakota) were nearly as poor, with over half their households living in poverty.

Other census statistics further detail the extent of the poverty on Indian reservations. Nearly a third of Navajo and over a quarter of Hopi homes lack indoor plumbing. A third of the Indians living on the Navajo, Pine Ridge, and San Carlos (Arizona) reservations are unemployed, nearly six times the national average. Among Indians as a whole, nearly a fourth live in poverty, about twice the national average.

In 1988, to combat such dire poverty, Congress enacted the Indian Gaming Regulatory Act. It allowed tribes to own casinos and other gambling operations. Within two decades, over 200 tribes—well over a third of the total—had built 360 casinos and gaming establishments. By 2007, annual revenue from Indian casinos exceeded $22 billion, more than the combined income of the NBA, NFL, and Major League Baseball.

But casino revenue is distributed unevenly. Foxwoods in Connecticut, the largest casino in the United States, generates about $1 billion, a windfall for the Mashantucket Pequot Tribe. On the other hand, the Little Big Horn Casino, located in southeastern Montana near the battlefield where Custer fell, yielded a profit of only $100 a month during its first year of operation. Half of all reservation Indians live in Montana, Nevada, North and South Dakota, and Oklahoma, far from potential throngs of gamblers; these Indians receive less than 3 percent of casino proceeds, or about $400 per person.

The plight of western Indians today was determined by events during the decades after 1865. Ranchers and farmers seized more Indian land. Railroad construction destabilized the habitat that sutained Indian life, especially the grazing lands of the buffalo, and brought still more settlers. The federal government pushed Indians onto reservations, often on land unsuitable for cultivation, and sent troops to harrass those who refused to abandon a nomadic life. (See maps "Loss of Indian Lands, 1850–2000," p. 468.) By the turn of the twentieth century, the economic foundations of tribal life had been destroyed; relief, when it finally arrived many decades later, came in the form of slot machines.

The West After the Civil War

Although the image of the West as the land of great open spaces is accurate enough, the region contained several bustling cities. San Francisco, with a population approaching 250,000 in the late 1870s, had long outgrown its role as a rickety boomtown where the forty-niners bought supplies and squandered whatever wealth they had sifted from the streams of the Sierras. Though still an important warehouse and supply center, the city had become the commercial and financial heart of the Pacific Coast and a center of light manufacturing, food processing, and machine shops. Denver, San Antonio, and Salt Lake City were far smaller, but growing rapidly and equally "urban."

There was no one West, no typical Westerner. If the economy was predominantly agricultural and extractive, it was also commercial and entering the early stages of industrial development. The seeds of such large enterprises as Wells Fargo, Levi Strauss, and half a dozen important department store empires were sown in the immediate postwar decades.

Beginning in the mid-1850s a steady flow of Chinese migrated to the United States, most of them to the west coast. About four or five thousand came each year, until the negotiation of the Burlingame Treaty of 1868, the purpose of which was to provide cheap labor for railroad construction crews. Thereafter the annual influx more than doubled, although before 1882 it exceeded 20,000 only twice. When the railroads were completed and the Chinese began to compete with native workers, a great cry of resentment went up on the west coast. Riots broke out in San Francisco in 1877. Chinese workers were called "groveling worms," "more slavish and brutish than the beasts that roam the fields." The California constitution of 1879 denied the right to vote to any "native of China" along with idiots, the insane, and persons convicted of "any infamous crime."

When Chinese immigration increased in 1882 to nearly 40,000, the protests reached such a peak that Congress passed the Chinese Exclusion Act, prohibiting all Chinese immigration for ten years. Later legislation extended the ban indefinitely.

Nevertheless, many parts of the West had as large a percentage of foreign-born residents as the populous eastern states—nearly a third of all Californians were foreign-born, as were more than 40 percent of Nevadans and more than half the residents of Idaho and Arizona. There were, of course, large populations of Spanish-speaking Americans of Mexican origin all over the Southwest. Chinese and Irish laborers were pouring into California by the thousands, and there were substantial numbers of Germans in Texas. Germans, Scandinavians, and other Europeans were also numerous on the High Plains east of the Rockies.

The Plains Indians

For 250 years the Indians had been driven back steadily, yet on the eve of the Civil War they still inhabited roughly half the United States. By 1877 the survivors of most of the eastern tribes were living peacefully in Indian Territory, what is now Oklahoma. In California the forty-niners had made short work of the local tribes. Elsewhere in the West—in the deserts of the Great Basin between the Sierras and the Rockies, in the mountains themselves, and on the semiarid, grass-covered plains between the Rockies and the edge of white civilization in eastern Kansas and Nebraska—nearly a quarter of a million Indians dominated the land.

By far the most important lived on the High Plains. From the Blackfoot of southwestern Canada and the Sioux of Minnesota and the Dakotas to the Cheyenne of Colorado and Wyoming and the Comanche of northern Texas, the Plains tribes possessed a generally uniform culture. All lived by hunting the hulking American bison, or buffalo, which ranged over the Plains by the millions. The buffalo provided the Indians with food, clothing, and even shelter, for the famous Indian tepee was covered with hides. On the treeless Plains, dried buffalo dung was used for fuel. The buffalo was also an important symbol in Indian religion.

Although they seemed the epitome of freedom, pride, and self-reliance, the Plains Indians had begun to fall under the sway of white power. They eagerly adopted the products of the more technically advanced culture—cloth, metal tools, weapons, cheap decorations. However, the most important thing the whites gave them had nothing to do with technology: It was the horse.

After the start of the gold rush the need to link the East with California meant that the tribes were pushed aside. Deliberately the government in Washington prepared the way. In 1851 Thomas Fitzpatrick—an experienced mountain man, a founder of the Rocky Mountain Fur Company, scout for the first large group of settlers to Oregon in 1841 and for American soldiers in California during the Mexican War, and now an Indian agent—summoned a great "council" of the tribes. About 10,000 Indians, representing nearly all the Plains tribes, gathered that September at Horse Creek, 37 miles east of Fort Laramie, in what is now Wyoming.

The Indians respected Fitzpatrick, who had recently married a woman who was half Indian. At Horse Creek he persuaded each tribe to accept definite limits to its hunting grounds. For example, the Sioux nations were to stay north of the Platte

River, and the Cheyenne and Arapaho were to confine themselves to the Colorado foothills. In return the Indians were promised gifts and annual payments. This policy, known as "concentration," was designed to cut down on intertribal warfare and—far more important—to enable the government to negotiate separately with each tribe. It was the classic strategy of divide and conquer.

Although it made a mockery of diplomacy to treat Indian tribes as though they were European powers, the United States maintained that each tribe was a sovereign nation, to be dealt with as an equal in solemn treaties. Both sides knew that this was not the case. When Indians agreed to meet in council, they were tacitly admitting defeat. They seldom drove hard bargains or broke off negotiations. Moreover, tribal chiefs had only limited power; young braves frequently refused to respect agreements made by their elders.

Indian Wars

The government showed little interest in honoring agreements with Indians. No sooner had the Kansas-Nebraska bill become law than the Kansas, Omaha, Pawnee, and Yankton Sioux tribes began to feel pressure for further concessions of territory. A gold rush into Colorado in 1859 sent thousands of greedy prospectors across the Plains to drive the Cheyenne and Arapaho from land guaranteed them in 1851. By 1860 most of Kansas and Nebraska had been cleared. Other trouble developed in the Sioux country. Thus it happened that in 1862, after federal troops had been pulled out of the West for service against the Confederacy, most of the Plains Indians rose up against the whites. For five years intermittent but bloody clashes kept the entire area in a state of alarm.

This was guerrilla warfare, with all its horror and treachery. In 1864 a party of Colorado militia under the command of Colonel J. M. Chivington fell on an unsuspecting Cheyenne community at Sand Creek and killed several hundred. A white observer described the scene: "They were scalped, their brains knocked out; the men used their knives, ripped open women, clubbed little children, knocked them in the head with their guns, beat their brains out, mutilated their bodies in every sense of the word."

In turn the Indians slaughtered dozens of isolated white families, ambushed small parties, and fought many successful skirmishes against troops and militia. They achieved their most notable triumph in December 1866, when the Oglala Sioux, under their great chief Red Cloud, wiped out a party of eighty-two soldiers under Captain W. J. Fetterman. Red Cloud fought ruthlessly, but only when goaded by the construction of the Bozeman Trail, a road through the heart of the Sioux hunting grounds in southern Montana.[1]

---

[1]Fetterman had boasted that with eighty caualrymen he could ride the entire length of the Bozeman Trail. When he tried, however, he blundered into an ambush.

Robert Lindneux's *The Battle of Sand Creek, 1864*. Lindneux, born in 1871, did not witness what transpired at Sand Creek, Colorado. But although he used "battle" in the title of his painting, he depicted a massacre. "Kill and scalp all, big and little," Colonel J. M. Chivington, a minister in private life, told his men. The American flag *(center-right)* was doubtless meant as irony.

In 1867 the government tried a new strategy. The "concentration" policy had evidently not gone far enough. All the Plains Indians would be confined to two small reservations, one in the Black Hills of the Dakota Territory, the other in Oklahoma, and forced to become farmers. At two great conclaves held in 1867 and 1868 at Medicine Lodge Creek and Fort Laramie, the principal chiefs yielded to the government's demands.

Many Indians refused to abide by these agreements. With their whole way of life at stake, they raged across the Plains like a prairie fire—and were almost as destructive.

That a relative handful of "savages," without central leadership, could hold off the cream of the army, battle-hardened in the Civil War, can be explained by the fact that the U.S. Army, usually with fewer than 20,000 soldiers, had to operate over a million square miles. Few Indian leaders were capable of organizing a campaign or following up an advantage. But the Indians made superb guerrillas. Every observer called them the best cavalry soldiers in the world. Armed with stubby, powerful bows capable of driving an arrow clear through a bull buffalo, they were a fair match for troops equipped with carbines and Colt revolvers. Expertly they led pursuers into ambushes, swept down on unsuspecting supply details, stole up on small parties the way a mountain lion stalks a grazing lamb. They could sometimes be rounded up, as when General Philip Sheridan herded the tribes of the Southwest into Indian Territory in 1869. But once the troops withdrew, braves began to melt away into the emptiness of the surrounding grasslands. The distinction between "treaty" Indians, who had agreed to live on the new reservations, and the "non-treaty" variety shifted almost from day to day. Trouble flared here one week, next week somewhere else, perhaps 500 miles away. No less an authority than General William Tecumseh Sherman testified that a mere fifty Indians could often "checkmate" 3,000 soldiers.

If one concedes that no one could reverse the direction of history or stop the invasion of Indian lands, then some version of the "small reservation" policy would probably have been best for the Indians. Had they been guaranteed a reasonable amount of land and adequate subsidies and allowed to maintain their way of life, they might have accepted the situation and ceased to harry the whites.

Whatever chance that policy had was weakened by the government's poor administration of Indian affairs. In dealing with Indians, nineteenth-century Americans displayed a grave insensitivity. After 1849 the Department of the Interior supposedly had charge of tribal affairs. Most of its agents systematically cheated the Indians. One, heavily involved in mining operations on the side, diverted goods intended for his charges to his private ventures. When an inspector looked into his records, he sold him shares in a mine. That worthy in turn protected himself by sharing some of the loot with the son of the commissioner of Indian affairs. Army officers squabbled frequently with Indian agents over policy, and an "Indian Ring" in the Department of the Interior system typically stole funds and supplies intended for the reservation Indians. "No branch of the national government is so spotted with fraud, so tainted with corruption . . . as this Indian Bureau," Congressman Garfield charged in 1869.

President Grant wished to place the reservations under army control, but the Indians opposed this. They fared no better around army camps than on the reservations. In 1869 Congress created a nonpolitical Board of Indian Commissioners to oversee Indian affairs, but the bureaucrats in Washington stymied the commissioners at every turn.

In 1874 gold was discovered in the Black Hills Indian reservation. By the next winter thousands of miners had invaded the reserved area. Already alarmed by the approach of crews building the Northern Pacific Railroad, the Sioux once again went on the warpath. Joining with nontreaty tribes to the west, they concentrated in the region of the Bighorn River, in southern Montana Territory.

The summer of 1876 saw three columns of troops in the field against them. The commander of one column, General Alfred H. Terry, sent ahead a small detachment of the Seventh Cavalry under Colonel George A. Custer with orders to locate the Indians' camp and then block their escape route into the inaccessible Bighorn Mountains. Custer was vain and rash, and vanity and rashness were grave handicaps when fighting Indians. Grossly underestimating the number of the Indians, he decided to attack directly with his tiny force of 264 men. At the Little Bighorn late in June he found himself surrounded by 2,500 Sioux under Rain-in-the-Face, Crazy Horse, and Sitting Bull. He and all his men died on the field.

Because it was so one-sided, "Custer's Last Stand" was not a typical battle, although it may be taken as symbolic of the Indian warfare of the period in the sense that it was characterized by bravery, foolhardiness, and a tragic waste of life. The battle greatly heartened the Indians, but it did not gain them their cause. That autumn, short of rations and hard-pressed by overwhelming numbers of soldiers, they surrendered and returned to the reservation.

The Destruction of Tribal Life

After Little Bighorn, the fighting slackened. Two factors were chiefly responsible: the building of transcontinental railroads and the destruction of the buffalo. An estimated 13 to 15 million head of buffalo had roamed the Plains in the mid-1860s. Then the slaughter began. Thousands were butchered to feed the gangs of laborers engaged in building the Union Pacific Railroad. Thousands more fell before the guns of sportsmen. Buffalo hunting became a fad, and a brisk demand developed for buffalo rugs and mounted buffalo heads. Railroads made the Army a far more efficient force. Troops and supplies could be moved swiftly when trouble with the tribes erupted. The railroads also contributed to the decimation of the buffalo by running excursion trains for hunters; even the shameful practice of gunning down the beasts directly from railroad cars was allowed.

The discovery in 1871 of a way to make commercial use of buffalo hides completed the tragedy. In the next three years about 9 million head were killed; after another decade the animals were almost extinct. No more efficient way could have been found for destroying the Plains Indians. The disappearance of the bison left them starving and homeless.

By 1887 the tribes of the mountains and deserts beyond the Plains had also given up the fight. Typical of the heartlessness of the government's treatment of these peoples was that afforded the Nez Percé of Oregon and Idaho, who were led by the remarkable Chief Joseph. After outwitting federal troops in a campaign across more than a thousand miles of rough country, Joseph finally surrendered in October 1877. The Nez Percé were then settled on "the malarial bottoms of the Indian Territory" in far-off Oklahoma.

The last Indians to abandon the unequal battle were the relentless Apache of the Southwest, who finally yielded on the capture of their leader, Geronimo, in 1886.

By the 1880s, the advance of whites into the Plains had become, in the words of one congressman, as irresistible "as that of Sherman's to the sea." Greed for land lay behind the pressure, but large numbers of disinterested people, including most of those who deplored the way the Indians had been treated in the past, believed that the only practical way to solve the "Indian problem" was to persuade the Indians to abandon their tribal culture and live on family farms. The "wild" Indian must be changed into a "civilized" member of "American" society.

To accomplish this goal Congress passed the Dawes Severalty Act of 1887. Tribal lands were to be split up into individual allotments. To keep speculators

A mound of buffalo skulls. In 1870 an estimated 15 million buffalo roamed the Plains; by 1900, there were fewer than 1,000. During an eight-month period between 1867 and 1868, William F. Cody (Buffalo Bill) killed 4,280 buffalo, which fed construction crews for the Union Pacific railroad. Tourists also took up buffalo hunting, often shooting them from trains. The depletion of the buffalo, which provided the Plains Indians with meat and hides, was a major source of conflict with whites.

from wresting the allotments from the Indians while they were adjusting to their new way of life, the land could not be disposed of for 25 years. Funds were to be appropriated for educating and training the Indians, and those who accepted allotments, took up residence "separate from any tribe," and "adopted the habits of civilized life" were to be granted U.S. citizenship.

The sponsors of the Severalty Act thought they were effecting a fine humanitarian reform. "We must throw some protection over [the Indian]," Senator Henry L. Dawes declared. "We must hold up his hand." But no one expected all the Indians to accept allotments at once, and for some years little pressure was put on any to do so. The law was a statement of policy rather than a set of specific rules and orders. "Too great haste . . . should be avoided," Indian Commissioner John Atkins explained. "Character, habits, and antecedents cannot be changed by enactment."

The Dawes Act had disastrous results in the long run. It assumed that Indians could be transformed into small agricultural capitalists by an act of Congress. It shattered what was left of the Indians' culture without enabling them to adapt to white ways. Moreover, unscrupulous white men systematically tricked many Indians into leasing their allotments for a pittance, and local authorities often

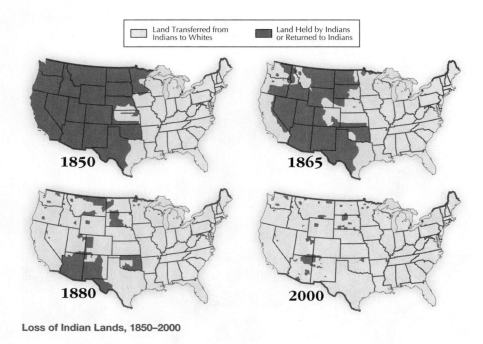

Land Transferred from Indians to Whites Land Held by Indians or Returned to Indians

1850 1865

1880 2000

Loss of Indian Lands, 1850–2000

taxed Indian lands at excessive rates. In 1934, after about 86 million of the 138 million acres assigned under the Dawes Act had passed into white hands, the government returned to a policy of encouraging tribal ownership of Indian lands.

The Lure of Gold and Silver in the West

The natural resources of the nation were exploited in these decades even more ruthlessly and thoughtlessly than were its human resources. Americans had long regarded the West as a limitless treasure to be grasped as rapidly as possible, and after 1865 they engrossed its riches still faster and in a wider variety of ways. From the mid-1850s to the mid-1870s thousands of gold-crazed prospectors fanned out through the Rockies, panning every stream and hacking furiously at every likely outcropping from the Fraser River country of British Columbia to Tucson in southern Arizona, from the eastern slopes of the Sierras to the Great Plains.

Gold and silver were scattered throughout the area, though usually too thinly to make mining profitable. Whenever anyone made a "strike," prospectors, the vast majority utterly without previous experience but driven by what a mining journal of the period called an "unhealthy desire" for sudden wealth, flocked to the site, drawn by rumors of stream beds gleaming with gold-rich gravel and of nuggets the size of men's fists. For a few months the area teemed with activity. Towns of 5,000 or more sprang up overnight; improvised roads were crowded with people and supply wagons. Claims were staked out along every stream and gully. Then, usually, expectations faded in the light of reality: high prices, low yields, hardship, violence, and deception. The boom collapsed and the towns died as quickly as they had risen. A few would have found wealth, the rest only backbreaking labor and disappointment—until tales of another strike sent them dashing feverishly across the land on another golden chase.

In the spring of 1858 it was on the Fraser River in Canada that the horde descended, 30,000 Californians in the vanguard. The following spring, Pikes Peak in Colorado attracted the pack, experienced California prospectors ("yonder siders") mixing with "greenhorns" from every corner of the globe. In June 1859 came the finds in Nevada, where the famous Comstock Lode yielded ores worth nearly $4,000 a ton. In 1861, while men in the settled areas were laying down their tools to take up arms, the miners were racing to the Idaho panhandle, hoping to become millionaires overnight. The next year the rush was to the Snake River valley, then in 1863 and 1864 to Montana. In 1874 to 1876 the Black Hills in the heart of the Sioux lands were inundated.

The sudden prosperity of the mining towns attracted every kind of shady character—according to one forty-niner "rascals from Oregon, pickpockets from New York, accomplished gentlemen from Europe, interlopers from Lima and Chile, Mexican thieves, gamblers from no particular spot, and assassins manufactured in Hell." Gambling dens, dance halls, saloons, and brothels mushroomed wherever precious metal was found.

Law enforcement was a constant problem. Much of the difficulty lay in the antisocial attitudes of the miners themselves. Gold and silver dominated people's thoughts and dreams, and few paid much attention to the means employed in accumulating this wealth. Storekeepers charged outrageous prices; claim holders "salted" worthless properties with nuggets in order to swindle gullible investors. Ostentation characterized the successful, braggadocio those who failed. During the administration of President Grant, Virginia City, Nevada, was at the peak of its vulgar prosperity, producing an average of $12 million a year in ore. Built on the richness of the Comstock Lode ($306 million in gold and silver was extracted from the Comstock in 20 years), it had 25 saloons before it had 4,000 people. By the 1870s its mountainside site was disfigured by ugly, ornate mansions where successful mine operators ate from fine china and swilled champagne as though it were water.

In 1873, after the discovery of the Big Bonanza, a seam of rich ore more than 50 feet thick, the future of Virginia City seemed boundless. Other discoveries shortly thereafter indicated to optimists that the mining boom in the West would continue indefinitely. The finds in the Black Hills district in 1875 and 1876, heralding deposits yielding eventually $100 million, led to the mushroom growth of Deadwood, home of Wild Bill Hickok, Deadwood Dick, Calamity Jane, and such lesser-known characters as California Jack and Poker Alice. The West continued to yield much gold and silver, especially silver, but big corporations produced nearly all of it. The mines around Deadwood were soon controlled by one large company, Homestake Mining. Butte, Montana, was similarly dominated by Anaconda Mining.

CHAPTER 16

WAS THE FRONTIER EXCEPTIONALLY VIOLENT?

In 1882 the *New York Daily Graphic* described Jesse James *(left)* as "the most renowned murderer and robber of his age." Here he is shown with members of his gang, each holding a rifle and wearing a holster and pistol, a stereotypical image of gun violence in the frontier West.

Several decades ago historians challenged the notion that the western frontier was exceptionally violent. Robert Dykstra observed that most of the frontier was devoted to agriculture and that such communities were peaceable. John Unruh Jr., and John Reid were struck by how few crimes occurred during the difficult, long months of the overland trail.

Some historians have approached this issue by compiling comparative statistics of homicides per 100,000 population (the standard way that federal crime statistics are now expressed). In 1985, when Miami had a homicide rate of 33, the highest in the nation, Roger D. McGrath found that a California mining camp in the 1870s had a rate of 116. John Boessenecker discovered that in 1851 Los Angeles County had a staggering rate of 1,240. Clare McKenna Jr., arrived at a similar conclusion based on crime statistics for rural California.

Critics, however, rejected the methodology. They note that in a frontier town of 100 people, a single murder generates a fearful homicide rate of 1,000. Little wonder that Jesse James was perceived as a one-gang crime wave.

Robert R. Dykstra, *The Cattle Towns* (1968), John Unruh Jr., *The Plains Across* (1979), John Reid, *Law for the Elephant* (1980), Roger D. McGrath, *Gunfighters, Highwaymen & Vigilantes* (1985), John Boessenecker, *Gold Dust and Gunsmoke* (1999), Clare V. McKenna Jr., *Race and Homicide in Nineteenth-Century California* (2002). McKenna found that most homicides were somehow bound up with alcohol, while David Courtwright, *Violent Land* (1996), believed that high levels of violence were due to the relative absence of the restraining hand of women in frontier communities. See also David Peterson del Mar, *Beaten Down: A History of Interpersonal Violence in the West* (2002).

This is the culminating irony of the history of the mining frontier: Shoestring prospectors, independent and enterprising, made the key discoveries. They established local institutions and supplied the West with much of its color and folklore. But the stockholders of large corporations, many of whom had never seen a mine, made off with the lion's share of the wealth. Those whose worship of gold was direct and incessant, the prospectors who peopled the mining towns and gave the frontier its character, mostly died poor, still seeking a prize as elusive if not as illusory as the pot of gold at the end of the rainbow.

Though marked by violence, fraud, greed, and lost hopes, the gold rushes had valuable results. The most obvious was the new metal itself, which bolstered the financial position of the United States during and after the Civil War. Quantities of European goods needed for the war effort and for postwar economic development were paid for with the yield of the new mines. Gold and silver also caused a great increase of interest in the West. A valuable literature appeared, part imaginative, part reportorial, describing the mining camps and the life of the prospectors. These works fascinated contemporaries (as they have continued to fascinate succeeding generations when adapted to the motion picture and to television). Mark Twain's *Roughing It* (1872), based in part on his experiences in the Nevada mining country, is the most famous example of this literature.

Each new strike and rush, no matter how fleeting, brought permanent settlers along with the prospectors: farmers, cattlemen, storekeepers, teamsters, lawyers, and ministers. The boomtowns had to import everything from bread, meat, and liquor to building materials and tools of every sort. Without the well-worn trails blazed by earlier hunters and migrants headed for Oregon and California, and of freighting companies equipped to haul heavy loads over long distances, the towns could not have existed. Some of the gold seekers saw from the start that a better living could be made supplying the needs of prospectors than looking for the elusive metal. Others, failing to find mineral wealth, took up whatever occupation they could rather than starve or return home empty-handed. In every mining town—along with the saloons and brothels—schools, churches, and newspaper offices sprang up.

The mines also speeded the political organization of the West. Colorado and Nevada became territories in 1861, Arizona and Idaho in 1863, Montana in 1864. Although Nevada was admitted to the Union before it had 60,000 residents (in 1864, to ratify the Thirteenth Amendment and help reelect Lincoln), most of these territories did not become states for decades. But because of the miners, the framework for future development was early established.

Big Business and the Land Bonanza

While the miners were engrossing the mineral wealth of the West, other interests were snapping up the region's choice farmland. Presumably the Homestead Act of

1862 had ended the reign of the speculator and the large landholder. An early amendment to the act even prevented husbands and wives from filing separate claims. The West, land reformers had assumed, would soon be dotted with 160-acre family farms.

These reformers were doomed to disappointment. Most landless Americans were too poor to become farmers even when they could obtain land without cost. The expense of moving a family to the ever-receding frontier exceeded the means of many, and the cost of a plow, hoes and scythes, draft animals, a wagon, a well, fencing, and of building the simplest house might come to $1,000—a formidable barrier. As for the industrial workers for whom the free land was supposed to provide a "safety valve," they had neither the skills nor the inclination to become farmers. Homesteaders usually came from districts not far removed from frontier conditions. And despite the intent of the law, speculators often managed to obtain large tracts. They hired men to stake out claims, falsely swear that they had fulfilled the conditions laid down in the law for obtaining legal title, and then deed the land over to their employers.

Even if the land laws been better drafted and more honestly enforced, the policy of granting free land to small homesteaders would likely have failed. Aside from the built-in difficulties faced by small-scale agriculturalists in the West, too many people in every section were eager to exploit the nation's land for their own profit. Immediately after the Civil War, Congress reserved 47.7 million acres of public land in the South for homesteaders, stopping all cash sales in the region. But in 1876 this policy was reversed and the land thrown open. Speculators flocked to the feast in such numbers that the Illinois Central Railroad ran special trains from Chicago to Mississippi and Louisiana. Between 1877 and 1888 over 5.6 million acres were sold; much of the land was covered with valuable pine and cypress.

However they attained their acres, frontier farmers of the 1870s and 1880s grappled with novel problems as they pushed across the Plains with their families. The soil was rich, but the climate, especially in the semiarid regions beyond 98° longitude, made agriculture frequently difficult and often impossible. Blizzards, floods, grasshopper plagues, and prairie fires caused repeated heartaches, but periodic drought and searing summer heat were the worst hazards, destroying the hopes and fortunes of thousands.

Despite the hazards of Plains agriculture, the region became the breadbasket of America in the decades following the Civil War. By 1889 Minnesota topped the nation in wheat production, and ten years later four of the five leading wheat states lay west of the Mississippi. The Plains also accounted for heavy percentages of the nation's other cereal crops, together with immense quantities of beef, pork, and mutton.

Like other exploiters of the nation's resources, farmers took whatever they could from the soil with little heed for preserving its fertility and preventing erosion. The consequent national loss was less apparent because it was diffuse and slow to assume drastic proportions, but it was nonetheless real.

Western Railroad Building

Further exploitation of land resources by private interests resulted from the government's policy of subsidizing western railroads. Here was a clear illustration of the conflict between the idea of the West as a national heritage to be disposed of to deserving citizens and the concept of the region as a cornucopia pouring forth riches to be gathered up and carted off by anyone powerful and determined enough to take them. When it came to a choice between giving a particular tract to railroads or to homesteaders, the homesteaders nearly always lost out. On the other hand, the swift development of western railroads was essential if farmers, miners, and cattle ranchers were to prosper.

Unless the government had been willing to build the transcontinental lines itself—and this was unthinkable in an age dominated by belief in individual exploitation—some system of subsidy was essential. Private investors would not hazard the huge sums needed to lay tracks across hundreds of miles of rugged, empty country when traffic over the road could not possibly profit for many years. It might appear that subsidizing construction by direct outlays of public funds would have been adopted, but that idea had few supporters. Most voters were wary of entrusting the dispensing of large sums to politicians. Grants of land seemed a sensible way of financing construction. The method avoided direct outlays of public funds, for the companies could pledge the land as security for bond issues or sell it directly for cash.

Federal land grants to railroads began in 1850 with those allotted to the Illinois Central. Over the next two decades about 49 million acres were given to various lines indirectly in the form of grants to the states, but the most lavish gifts of the public domain were those made directly to builders of intersectional trunk lines. These roads received more than 155 million acres, although about 25 million acres reverted to the government because some companies failed to lay the required miles of track. About 75 percent of this land went to aid the construction of four transcontinental railroads: the Union Pacific-Central Pacific line, running from Nebraska to San Francisco, completed in 1869; the Atchison, Topeka and Santa Fe, running from Kansas City to Los Angeles by way of Santa Fe and Albuquerque, completed in 1883; the Southern Pacific, running from San Francisco to New Orleans by way of Yuma and El Paso, completed in 1883; and the Northern Pacific, running from Duluth, Minnesota, to Portland, Oregon, completed in 1883.

The Pacific Railway Act of 1862 established the pattern for these grants. It gave the builders of the Union Pacific and Central Pacific railroads 5 square miles of public land on each side of their right-of-way for each mile of track laid. The land was allotted in alternate sections, forming a pattern like a checkerboard, the squares of one color representing railroad property, the other government property. Presumably this arrangement benefited the entire nation since half the land close to the railroad remained in public hands.

Historians have argued at length about the fairness of the land-grant system. No railroad corporation grew wealthy directly from the sale of its lands, which were sold at prices averaging between $2 and $5 an acre. Collectively the roads took in between $400 million and $500 million from this source, but only over the course of a century. Land-grant lines encouraged the growth of the West by advertising their property widely and by providing cheap transportation for prospective settlers and efficient shipping services for farmers. They were required by law to carry troops and handle government business free or at reduced rates, which saved the government millions over the years. At the same time the system imposed no effective restraints on how the railroads used the funds raised with federal aid. Being able to lay track with money obtained from land grants, the operators tended to be extravagant and often downright corrupt.

The construction of the Central Pacific in the 1860s illustrates how the system encouraged extravagance. The line was controlled by four businessmen: Collis P. Huntington ("scrupulously dishonest" but an excellent manager); Leland Stanford, a Sacramento grocer and politician; Mark Hopkins, a hardware merchant; and Charles Crocker, a hulking, relentless driver of men who had come to California during the gold rush and made a small fortune as a merchant. The Central Pacific and the Union Pacific were given, in addition to their land grants, loans in the form of government bonds—from $16,000 to $48,000 for each mile of track laid, depending on the difficulty of the terrain. The two lines competed with each other for the subsidies, the Central Pacific building eastward from Sacramento, the Union Pacific westward from Nebraska. They put huge crews to work grading and laying track, bringing up supplies over the already completed road. The Union Pacific employed Civil War veterans and Irish immigrants; the Central, Chinese immigrants.

This plan favored the Union Pacific. While the Central Pacific was inching up the gorges and granite of the mighty Sierras, the Union Pacific was racing across the level plains laying 540 miles of track between 1865 and 1867. Once beyond the Sierras, the Central Pacific would have easy going across the Nevada-Utah plateau country, but by then it might be too late to prevent the Union Pacific from making off with most of the government aid.

Crocker managed the Central Pacific construction crews. He wasted huge sums by working through the winter in the High Sierras. Often the men labored in tunnels dug through 40-foot snowdrifts to get at the frozen ground. To speed construction of the Summit Tunnel, Crocker had a shaft cut down from above so that crews could work out from the middle as well as in from each end. In 1866, over the most difficult terrain, he laid 28 miles of track, at a cost of more than $280,000 a mile. Experts later estimated that 70 percent of this sum could have been saved had speed not been a factor. Such wastefulness made economic sense to Huntington, Stanford, Hopkins, and Crocker because of the profits they were making through the Central Pacific's construction company and because of the gains they could count on once they reached the flat country beyond the Sierras, where costs would amount to only half the federal aid.

Crocker's herculean efforts paid off. The mountains were conquered, and then the crews raced across the Great Basin to Salt Lake City and beyond. The meeting of the rails—the occasion of a national celebration—took place at Promontory,

Chinese railway workers in the Far West. "Without them," Leland Stanford, president of the Central Pacific Railroad said, "it would be impossible to complete the western portion of this great national highway." Some Chinese were drawn from the gold fields farther north, and others were imported from China, under five-year contracts with the railroads in which they were paid $10 or $12 a month.

north of Ogden, Utah, on May 10, 1869. Leland Stanford drove the final ceremonial golden spike with a silver hammer.[2] The Union Pacific had built 1,086 miles of track, the Central 689 miles.

In the long run the wasteful way in which the Central Pacific was built hurt the railroad severely. It was ill constructed, over grades too steep and around curves too sharp, and burdened with debts that were too large. Steep grades meant that heavier, more expensive locomotives burning more coal were needed to pull

---

[2] *A mysterious "San Francisco jeweler" passed among the onlookers, taking orders for souvenir watch chains that he proposed to make from the spike at $5 each.*

lighter loads—a sure way to lower profits. Such was the fate of nearly all the railroads constructed with the help of government subsidies.

The only transcontinental railroad built without land grants was the Great Northern, running from St. Paul, Minnesota, to the Pacific. Spending private capital, its guiding genius, James J. Hill, was compelled to build economically and to plan carefully. As a result, his was the only transcontinental line to weather the depression of the 1890s without going into bankruptcy.

The Cattle Kingdom

While miners were digging out the mineral wealth of the West and railroaders were taking possession of much of its land, another group was exploiting endless acres of its grass. For 20 years after the Civil War cattlemen and sheep raisers dominated huge areas of the High Plains, making millions of dollars by grazing their herds on lands they did not own.

Columbus brought the first cattle to the New World in 1493, on his second voyage, and later conquistadores took them to every corner of Spain's American empire. Mexico proved to be so well suited to cattle raising that many were allowed to roam loose. They multiplied rapidly, and by the late eighteenth century what is now southern Texas harbored enormous herds. The beasts interbred with nondescript "English" cattle, brought into the area by settlers from the United States, to produce the Texas longhorn. Hardy, wiry, ill-tempered, and fleet, with horns often attaining a spread of 6 feet, these animals were far from ideal as beef cattle and almost as hard to capture as wild horses, but they existed in southern Texas by the millions, most of them unowned.

The lack of markets and transportation explains why Texas cattle were lightly regarded. But conditions were changing. Industrial growth in the East was causing an increase in the urban population and a consequent rise in the demand for food. At the same time, the expansion of the railroad network made it possible to move cattle cheaply over long distances. As the iron rails inched across the Plains, astute cattlemen began to do some elementary figuring. Longhorns could be had locally for $3 and $4 a head. In the northern cities they would bring ten times that much, perhaps even more. Why not round them up and herd them northward to the railroads, allowing them to feed along the way on the abundant grasses of the Plains? The land was unoccupied and owned by the federal government. Anyone could drive cattle across it without paying a fee or asking anyone's permission. The grass the cattle ate on the way swiftly renewed itself.

In 1866 a number of Texans drove large herds northward toward Sedalia, Missouri, railhead of the Missouri Pacific. This route took the herds through wooded and settled country and across Indian reservations, which provoked many difficulties. At the same time Charles Goodnight and Oliver Loving successfully drove 2,000 head in a great arc west to the New Mexico Territory and then north to Colorado.

The next year the drovers, inspired by a clever young Illinois cattle dealer named Joseph G. McCoy and other entrepreneurs, led their herds north by a more westerly route, across unsettled grasslands, to the Kansas Pacific line at Abilene,

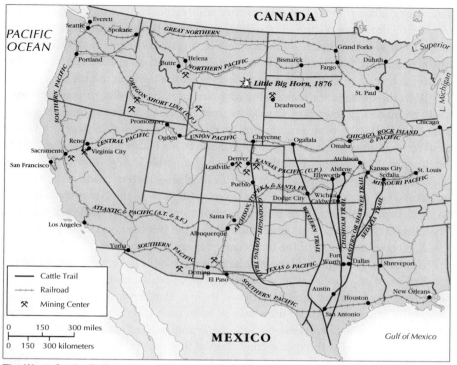

The West: Cattle, Railroads, and Mining, 1850–1893

Kansas, which McCoy described as "a very small, dead place, consisting of about one dozen log huts." They earned excellent profits, and during the next five years about 1.5 million head made the "long drive" over the Chisholm Trail to Abilene, where they were sold to ranchers, feedlot operators, and the agents of eastern meatpackers. Other shipping points sprang up as the railroads pushed westward. According to the best estimates 10 million head were driven north before the practice ended in the mid-1880s.

Open-Range Ranching

Soon cattlemen discovered that the hardy Texas stock could survive the winters of the northern Plains. Attracted by the apparently limitless forage, they began to bring up herds to stock the vast regions where the buffalo had so recently roamed. Introducing pedigreed Hereford bulls, they improved the stock without weakening its resistance to harsh conditions. By 1880 some 4.5 million head had spread across the sea of grass that ran from Kansas to Montana and west to the Rockies.

The prairie grasses offered ranchers a bonanza almost as valuable as the gold mines. Open-range ranching required actual ownership of no more than a few acres along some watercourse. In this semiarid region, control of water enabled a rancher to dominate all the surrounding area back to the divide separating his range from the next stream without investing a cent in the purchase of land. His cattle, wandering freely on the public domain, fattened on grass owned by all the people, to be turned into beefsteak and leather for the profit of the rancher.

With the demand for meat rising and transportation cheap, princely fortunes could be made in a few years. Capitalists from the East and from Europe began to pour funds into the business. Eastern "dudes" like Theodore Roosevelt, a young New York assemblyman who sank over $50,000 in his Elkhorn Ranch in the Dakota Territory in 1883, bought up cattle as a sort of profitable hobby. (Roosevelt, clad in buckskin and bearing a small armory of rifles and six-shooters, made quite a splash in Dakota, but not as a rancher.) Soon large outfits such as the Nebraska Land and Cattle Company, controlled by British investors, and the Union Cattle Company of Wyoming, a $3 million corporation, dominated the business, just as large companies had taken over most of the important gold and silver mines.

Unlike other exploiters of the West's resources, cattle ranchers did not at first injure or reduce any public resource. Grass eaten by their stock annually renewed itself; droppings from the animals enriched the soil. Furthermore, ranchers poached on the public domain because there was no reasonable way for them to obtain legal possession of the large areas necessary to raise cattle on the Plains. Federal land laws made no allowance for the special conditions of the semiarid West.

A system to take account for those conditions was soon devised by Major John Wesley Powell, later the director of the U.S. Geological Survey. His *Report on the Lands of the Arid Region of the United States* (1879) suggested that western lands be divided into three classes: irrigable lands, timberlands, and "pasturage" lands. On the pasturage lands the "farm unit" ought to be at least 2,560 acres (four sections), Powell urged. Groups of these units should be organized into "pasturage districts" in which the ranchers "should have the right to make their own regulations for the division of lands, the use of the water . . . and for the pasturage of lands in common or in severalty."

Barbed-Wire Warfare

Congress refused to change the land laws in any basic way, and this had two harmful effects. First, it encouraged fraud: Those who could not get title to enough land honestly turned to subterfuge. The Desert Land Act (1877) allowed anyone to obtain 640 acres in the arid states for $1.25 an acre provided the owner irrigated part of it within three years. Since the original claimant could transfer the holding, the ranchers set their cowboys and other hands to filing claims, which were then signed over to them. Over 2.6 million acres were taken up under the act, and according to the best estimate, 95 percent of the claims were fraudulent—no sincere effort was made to irrigate the land.

In 1885 masked Nebraskans seeking access to water posed for photographer S. D. Butcher, who captioned the picture "Settlers taking the law into their own hands: Cutting 15 miles of the Brighton Ranch fence."

Second, overcrowding became a problem that led to serious conflicts, even killings, because no one had uncontestable title to the land. The leading ranchers banded together in cattlemen's associations to deal with overcrowding and with such problems as quarantine regulations, water rights, and thievery. In most cases these associations devised effective and sensible rules, but their functions would better have been performed by the government, as such matters usually are.

To keep other ranchers' cattle from those sections of the public domain they considered their own, the associations and many individuals began to fence huge areas. This was possible only because of the invention in 1874 of barbed wire by Joseph F. Glidden, an Illinois farmer. By the 1880s thousands of miles of the new fencing had been strung across the Plains, often across roads and in a few cases around entire communities. "Barbed-wire wars" resulted, fought by rancher against rancher, cattleman against sheepman, herder against farmer. The associations tried to police their fences and to punish anyone who cut their wire. Posted signs gave dire warnings to trespassers. "The Son of a Bitch who opens this fence had better look out for his scalp," one such sign announced, another fine statement of the philosophy of the age.

By stringing so much wire the cattlemen were unwittingly destroying their own way of doing business. On a truly open range, cattle could fend for themselves, instinctively finding water during droughts, drifting safely downwind before blizzards. Barbed wire prevented their free movement. During winter storms these slender strands became as lethal as high-tension wires: the drifting cattle piled up against them and died by the thousands.

The boom times were ending. Overproduction was driving down the price of beef; expenses were on the rise; many sections of the range were badly overgrazed.

The dry summer of 1886 left the stock in such poor condition as winter approached that the *Rocky Mountain Husbandman* urged its readers to sell their cattle despite the prevailing low prices rather than "endanger the whole herd by having the range overstocked."

Some ranchers took this advice; those who did not made a fatal error. Winter that year arrived early and with unparalleled fury. Blizzards raged and temperatures plummeted far below zero. Cattle crowded into low places only to be engulfed in giant snowdrifts; barbed wire took a fearful toll. When spring finally came, the streams were choked with rotting carcasses. Between 80 and 90 percent of all cattle on the range were dead. "We have had a perfect smashup all through the cattle country," Theodore Roosevelt wrote sadly in April 1887 from Elkhorn Ranch.

That cruel winter finished open-range cattle-raising. The large companies were bankrupt; many independent operators, Roosevelt among them, became discouraged and sold out. When the industry revived, it was on a smaller, more efficiently organized scale. The fencing movement continued, but now ranchers enclosed only the land they actually owned. It then became possible to bring in pedigreed bulls to improve the breed. Cattle-raising, like mining before it, ceased to be an adventure in rollicking individualism and became a business.

By the late 1880s the bonanza days of the West were over. No previous frontier had caught the imagination of Americans so completely as the Great West, with its heroic size, its awesome emptiness, its massive, sculptured beauty. Most of what Walter Prescott Webb, author of the classic study *The Great Plains* (1931) called the "primary windfalls" of the region—the furs, the precious metals, the forests, the cattle, and the grass—had been snatched up by first comers and by individuals already wealthy. Big companies were taking over all the West's resources. The frontier was no more.

But the frontier never existed except as an intellectual construction among white settlers and those who wrote about them. To the Indians, the land was simply home. The "conquest of the frontier" was thus an appealing evasion: it transformed the harmful actions and policies of the nation into an expression of human progress, the march westward of "civilization."

"Civilization," though, was changing. The nation was becoming more powerful, richer, and larger, and its economic structure more complex and diversified as the West yielded its treasures. But the East, and especially eastern industrialists and financiers, was increasingly dominating the economy of the entire nation.

1859	Discovery of the Comstock Lode lures miners west
1864	Chivington massacre of Cheyenne
1869	Union Pacific Railroad completed
	Board of Indian Commissioners established
1876	Sioux slaughter Custer's cavalry at Battle of Little Bighorn
1877	Desert Land Act favors ranchers
1879	Major Powell's *Report on the Lands of the Arid Region* suggests division of West
1882	Chinese Exclusion Act bans Chinese immigrant workers for 10 years
1886–1887	Blizzards end open-range ranching
1887	Dawes Severalty Act splits tribal lands

An Industrial Giant

IN 2006, WAL-MART, WITH 1.8 MILLION EMPLOYEES, BECAME THE biggest corporation in the history of the world. Nearly one in every five retail sales in the United States took place at a Wal-Mart cash register. Its revenues of $351 billion exceeded the gross national product of Saudi Arabia.

Wal-Mart's clout was such that it became a frequent target of popular satire. In 2004 the TV cartoon *South Park* lampooned "Wall-Mart," an evil discount retailer that turned South Park into a ghost town. In 2006 *Saturday Night Live* ran a satirical advertisement for "Sale-Mart," a big-box store that was "all about low prices." Toothless employees expressed satisfaction with the company's dental plan. The announcer told shoppers to hurry to the pharmacy, "where generic prescription drugs are two handfuls for a dollar."

Real-world critics of Wal-Mart leveled similar charges. A labor union Web site described Wal-Mart as a "death star" that "destroys all other economic activity in its path." Others noted that many Wal-Mart workers in the United States qualified for public assistance while Cambodians working for Wal-Mart suppliers earned 17 cents an hour.

Defenders of Wal-Mart, whose motto is "Always Low Prices," pointed out that its relentless efforts at cost-cutting have saved U.S. consumers as much as $200 billion a year, nearly $2,000 per household. A retailer helps society best, they insisted, by lowering prices.

This debate echoes that which accompanied the rise of powerful industrial combinations during the last third of the nineteenth century, when far-flung railroad companies imposed their will on local communities. Industrial corporations followed suit, especially in steel, iron, oil, and electricity. Reformers and labor leaders denounced this concentration of wealth and power. Some advocated regulation while others called for revolution. Then, as now, defenders of big business pointed out its benefits: new products, more efficient production, reduced prices.

But the question remains: Does the economic efficiency generated by economic concentration justify its threat to democratic institutions?

Essentials of Industrial Growth

When the Civil War began, the country's industrial output, while important and increasing, did not approach that of major European powers. By the end of the century the United States had become far and away the colossus among world manufacturers, dwarfing the production of Great Britain and Germany. The world had never seen such a remarkable example of rapid economic growth. The value of American manufactured products rose from $1.8 billion in 1859 to over $13 billion in 1899.

American manufacturing flourished for many reasons. New natural resources were discovered and exploited steadily, thereby increasing opportunities. These opportunities, in turn, attracted the brightest and most energetic of a vigorous and expanding population. The growth of the country added constantly to the size of the national market, and protective tariffs shielded that market from foreign competition. Foreign capital, however, entered the market freely, in part because tariffs kept out so many foreign goods.

The dominant spirit of the time encouraged businessmen to maximum effort by emphasizing progress, yet it also produced a generation of Robber Barons. The energetic search for wealth led to corrupt business practices such as stock manipulation, bribery, and cutthroat competition and ultimately to "combinations in restraint of trade," a kind of American euphemism for monopoly. European immigrants provided the additional labor needed by expanding industry; 2.5 million arrived in the 1870s, twice that number in the 1880s. These immigrants saw America as a land of opportunity, and for many, probably most, it was that indeed. But for others, emigrating to the United States meant a constant struggle for survival; dreary, often unhealthy living conditions; and grinding poverty.

It was a period of rapid advance in basic science, and technicians created a bountiful harvest of new machines, processes, and power sources that increased productivity in many industries and created new industries as well. In agriculture there were what one contemporary expert called "an endless variety of cultivators," better harvesters and binding machines, and combines capable of threshing and bagging 450 pounds of grain a minute. An 1886 report of the Illinois Bureau of Labor Statistics claimed that "new machinery has displaced fully 50 percent of the muscular labor formerly required to do a given amount of work in the manufacture of agricultural implements." Of course that also meant that many farm families were "displaced" from their homes and livelihoods, and it made farmers dependent on the vagaries of distant markets and powerful economic forces they could not control.

As a result of improvements in the milling of grain, packaged cereals appeared on the American breakfast table. The commercial canning of food, spurred by the "automatic line" canning factory, expanded so rapidly that by 1887 a writer in *Good Housekeeping* could say: "Housekeeping is getting to be ready made, as well as clothing." The Bonsack cigarette-rolling machine created a new industry that changed the habits of millions. George B. Eastman created still another with his development of mass-produced, roll photographic film and the simple but efficient Kodak camera. The perfection of the typewriter by the Remington company in the 1880s revolutionized the way office work was performed. But even some of these inventions were mixed blessings. The harm done by the popularity of cigarettes, for example, needs no explanation.

Railroads: The First Big Business

Railroads were important first as an industry in themselves. Fewer than 35,000 miles of track existed when Lee laid down his sword at Appomattox in 1865. Ten years later railroad mileage exceeded 74,000 and the skeleton of the network was complete. Over the next two decades the skeleton was fleshed out. In 1890 the mature but still-growing system took in over $1 billion in passenger and freight revenues. (The federal government's income in 1890 was only $403 million.) The value of railroad properties and equipment was more than $8.7 billion. The national railroad debt of $5.1 billion was almost five times the national debt of $1.1 billion! By 1900 the nation had 193,000 miles of track.

The emphasis in railroad construction after 1865 was on organizing integrated systems. The lines had high fixed costs: taxes, interest on their bonds, maintenance of track and rolling stock, and salaries of office personnel. A short train with half-empty cars required almost as many workers and as much fuel to operate as a long one jammed with freight or passengers. To earn profits the railroads had to carry as much traffic as possible. They therefore spread out feeder lines to draw business to their main lines the way the root network of a tree draws water into its trunk.

Before the Civil War, passengers and freight could travel by rail from beyond Chicago and St. Louis to the Atlantic coast, but only after the war did true interregional trunk lines appear. In 1861, for example, the New York Central ran from Albany to Buffalo. One could proceed from Buffalo to Chicago, but on a different company's trains. In 1867 the New York Central passed into the hands of "Commodore" Cornelius Vanderbilt, who had made a large fortune in the shipping business. Vanderbilt already controlled lines running from Albany to New York City; now he merged these properties with the New York Central. In 1873 he integrated the Lake Shore and Michigan Southern into his empire and two years later the Michigan Central. At his death in 1877 the New York Central operated a network of over 4,500 miles of track between New York City and most of the principal cities of the Midwest.

While Vanderbilt was putting together the New York Central complex, Thomas A. Scott was fusing roads to Cincinnati, Indianapolis, St. Louis, and Chicago to his Pennsylvania Railroad, which linked Pittsburgh and Philadelphia. In 1871 the Pennsylvania line obtained access to New York; soon it reached Baltimore and Washington. By 1869 another important system, the Erie, extended from New York to Cleveland, Cincinnati, and St. Louis. Soon thereafter it too tapped the markets of

The Union Railroad Station in Montgomery, Alabama, designed by Henry Hobson Richardson, the nation's foremost architect of the era. Richardson borrowed ideas from the past—the arches evoked the early Middle Ages—but adapted them to contemporary purposes. This building's massiveness and horizontal lines hinted at the power and reach of the railroads.

Chicago and other cities. In 1874 the Baltimore and Ohio rail line also obtained access to Chicago.

The transcontinental railroads were trunk lines from the start; the emptiness of the western country would have made short lines unprofitable, and builders quickly grasped the need for direct connections to eastern markets and thorough integration of feeder lines.

The dominant system builder of the Southwest was Jay Gould, a soft-spoken, unostentatious-looking man who was in fact ruthless, cynical, and aggressive. Another railroad president once called Gould a "perfect eel." Gould took over the Kansas Pacific, running from Denver to Kansas City, and consolidated it with the Union Pacific and the Missouri Pacific, a line from Kansas City to St. Louis. Often he put together such properties merely to unload them on other railroads at a profit, but his grasp of the importance of integration was sound.

In the Northwest, Henry Villard, a German-born former newspaperman, constructed another great complex based on his control of the Northern Pacific. James J. Hill controlled the Great Northern system, still another western network.

The Civil War had highlighted the need for thorough railroad connections in the South. Shortly after the conflict the Chesapeake and Ohio opened a direct line from Norfolk, Virginia, to Cincinnati. By the late 1880s, the Richmond and West Point Terminal Company controlled an 8,558-mile network. Like other southern trunk lines such as the Louisville and Nashville and the Atlantic Coast Line, this system was controlled by northern capitalists.

The trunk lines interconnected and thus had to standardize many of their activities. This in turn led to the standardization of other aspects of life. The present system of time zones was developed in 1883 by the railroads. The standard track gauge (4 feet 8½ inches) was established in 1886. Standardized car coupling and braking mechanisms, standard signal systems, even standard methods of accounting were essential to the effective functioning of the network.

The lines sought to work out fixed rates for carrying different types of freight, charging more for valuable manufactured goods than for bulky products like coal or wheat, and they agreed to permit rate concessions to shippers when necessary to avoid hauling empty cars. In other words, they charged what the traffic would bear. However, by the 1880s the men who ran the railroads had come to recognize the advantages of cooperating with one another to avoid "senseless" competition. Railroad management was becoming a kind of profession, with certain standard ways of doing things, even with its own professional journals and with regional organizations such as the Eastern Trunk Line Association and the Western Traffic Association.

To speed the settlement of new regions, the land-grant railroads sold land cheaply and on easy terms, for sales meant future business as well as current income. They offered reduced rates to travelers interested in buying farms and set up "bureaus of immigration" that distributed brochures describing the wonders of the new country. Their agents greeted immigrants at the eastern ports and tried to steer them to railroad property. They sent agents who were usually themselves immigrants—often ministers—all over Europe to recruit prospective settlers.

Technological advances in railroading accelerated economic development in complex ways. In 1869 George Westinghouse invented the air brake. By enabling an engineer to apply the brakes to all cars simultaneously (formerly each car had to be braked separately by its own conductor or brakeman), this invention made possible revolutionary increases in the size of trains and the speed at which they could safely operate. The sleeping car, invented in 1864 by George Pullman, now came into its own.

To pull the heavier trains, more powerful locomotives were needed. They in turn produced a call for stronger and more durable rails to bear the additional weight. Steel, itself reduced in cost because of technological developments, supplied the answer, for steel rails outlasted iron by many years despite the use of much heavier equipment.

A close tie developed between the railroads and the nation's telegraph network, dominated by the Western Union Company. Commonly the railroads allowed Western Union to string wires along their rights-of-way, and they transported telegraphers and their equipment without charge. In return they received free telegraphic service, important for efficiency and safety.

Iron, Oil, and Electricity

The transformation of iron manufacturing affected the nation almost as much as railroad development. Output rose from 920,000 tons in 1860 to 10.3 million tons in 1900, but the big change came in the development of ways to mass-produce steel. In its pure form (wrought iron) the metal is tough but relatively soft. Ordinary cast iron, which contains large amounts of carbon and other impurities, is hard but brittle. Steel, which contains 1 or 2 percent carbon, combines the hardness of cast iron with the toughness of wrought iron. For nearly every purpose—structural girders for bridges and buildings, railroad track, machine tools, boiler plate, barbed wire—steel is immensely superior to other kinds of iron.

But steel was so expensive to manufacture that it could not be used for bulky products until the invention in the 1850s of the Bessemer process, perfected independently by Henry Bessemer, an Englishman, and William Kelly of Kentucky. Bessemer and Kelly discovered that a stream of air directed into a mass of molten iron caused the carbon and other impurities to combine with oxygen and burn off. When measured amounts of carbon, silicon, and manganese were then added, the brew became steel. What had been a rare metal could now be produced by the hundreds and thousands of tons. The Bessemer process and the open-hearth method, a slower but more precise technique that enabled producers to sample the molten mass and thus control quality closely, were introduced commercially in the 1860s. In 1870, 77,000 tons of steel were manufactured; by 1890, that had expanded to nearly 5 million tons. Such growth would have been impossible without the huge supplies of iron ore in the United States and the coal necessary to fire the furnaces that refined it. In the 1870s the great iron fields rimming Lake Superior began to yield their treasures. The enormous iron concentrations of the Mesabi region made a compass needle spin like a top. Mesabi ores could be mined with steam shovels, almost like gravel.

Pittsburgh, surrounded by vast coal deposits, became the iron and steel capital of the country, the Minnesota ores reaching it by way of steamers on the Great Lakes and rail lines from Cleveland. Other cities in Pennsylvania and Ohio were important producers, and a separate complex, centering on Birmingham, Alabama, developed to exploit local iron and coal fields.

The petroleum industry expanded even more spectacularly than iron and steel. Edwin L. Drake drilled the first successful well in Pennsylvania in 1859. During the Civil War, production ranged between 2 million and 3 million barrels a year. By 1890 the figure had leaped to about 50 million barrels.

Before the invention of the gasoline engine and the automobile, the most important petroleum product was kerosene, which was burned in lamps. Refiners heated crude oil in large kettles and, after the volatile elements had escaped, condensed the kerosene in coils cooled by water. The heavier petroleum tars were discarded.

Technological advances came rapidly. By the early 1870s, refiners had learned how to "crack" petroleum by applying high temperatures to the crude oil in order to rearrange its molecular structure, thereby increasing the percentage of kerosene yielded. By-products such as naphtha, gasoline (used in vaporized form as an illuminating gas), rhigolene (a local anesthetic), cymogene (a coolant for refrigerating machines), and many lubricants and waxes began to appear on the market. At the same time a great increase in the supply of crude oil—especially after the German-born chemist Herman Frasch perfected a method for removing sulfur from low-quality petroleum—drove prices down.

These circumstances put a premium on refining efficiency. Larger plants using expensive machinery and employing skilled technicians became more important. In the mid-1860s only three refineries in the country could process 2,000 barrels of crude oil a week; a decade later plants capable of handling 1,000 barrels a day were common.

Two other important new industries were the telephone and electric light businesses. Both were typical of the period, being products of technical advances and intimately related to the growth of a high-speed, urban civilization that put great stress on communication. The telephone was invented in 1876 by Alexander Graham Bell, who had been led to the study of acoustics through his interest in the education of the deaf. The invention soon proved its value. By 1900 there were almost 800,000 telephones in the country, twice the total for all Europe. The American Telephone and Telegraph Company, a consolidation of over 100 local systems, dominated the business.

When Western Union realized the importance of the telephone, it tried for a time to compete with Bell by developing a machine of its own. The man it commissioned to devise this machine was Thomas A. Edison, but Bell's patents proved unassailable. Edison had already made a number of contributions toward solving what he called the "mysteries of electrical force," including a multiplex telegraph capable of sending four messages over a single wire at the same time. At Menlo Park, New Jersey, he built the prototype of the modern research laboratory, where specific problems could be attacked on a mass scale by a team of trained specialists. During his lifetime he took out more than 1,000 patents, dealing with machines as varied as the phonograph, the motion-picture projector, the storage battery, and the mimeograph.

Edison's most significant achievement was the incandescent lamp, or electric lightbulb. Others before him had experimented with the idea of producing light by passing electricity through a filament in a vacuum. Always, however, the filaments quickly burned out. Edison tried hundreds of fibers before producing, in 1879, a carbonized filament that would glow brightly in a vacuum tube for as long as 170 hours without crumbling. At Christmastime he decorated the grounds about his laboratory with a few dozen of the new lights. People flocked by the thousands to see this miracle of the "Wizard of Menlo Park." The inventor boasted that soon he would be able to illuminate entire towns, even great cities like New York.

He was true to his promise. In 1882 his Edison Illuminating Company opened a power station in New York City and began to supply current for lighting to eighty five consumers, including the *New York Times* and the banking house of J. P. Morgan and Company. Soon central stations were springing up everywhere until, by 1898, there were about 3,000 in the country.

The substitution of electric for steam power in factories was as liberating as that of steam for waterpower before the Civil War. Small, safe electric motors replaced dangerous and cumbersome mazes of belts and wheels. The electric power industry expanded rapidly. By the early years of the twentieth century almost 6 billion kilowatt-hours of electricity were being produced annually. Yet this was only the beginning.

"A sneeze captured on film"—the first copyrighted movie (1894). In 1889 Thomas A. Edison conceived of a machine that would do for the eye what the phonograph did for the ear. Over the next two years, Edison invented two separate devices—a camera to take a rapid sequence of pictures and a machine to view them called a Kinetoscope. In 1893 he developed reliable film for his camera. The motion picture industry was born.

Competition and Monopoly: The Railroads

During the post–Civil War era, expansion in industry went hand in hand with concentration. The principal cause of this trend, aside from the obvious economies resulting from large-scale production and the growing importance of expensive machinery, was the downward trend of prices after 1873. The deflation, which resulted mainly from the failure of the money supply to keep pace with the rapid increase in the volume of goods produced, affected agricultural goods as well as manufactures, and it lasted until 1896 or 1897.

Contemporaries believed that they were living through a "great depression." That label is misleading, for output expanded almost continuously, and at a rapid rate, until 1893, when production slumped and a true depression struck the country. Falling prices, however, kept a steady pressure on profit margins, and this led to increased production and thus to intense competition for markets.

According to the classical economists, competition advanced the public interest by keeping prices low and ensuring the most efficient producer the largest profit. Up to a point it accomplished these purposes in the years after 1865, but it also caused side effects that injured both the economy and society as a whole. Railroad managers, for instance, found it impossible to enforce "official" rate schedules and maintain their regional associations once competitive pressures mounted. In 1865 it had cost from 96 cents to $2.15 per 100 pounds, depending on the class of freight, to ship goods from New York to Chicago. In 1888 rates ranged from 35 cents to 75 cents.

Competition cut deeply into railroad profits, causing the lines to seek desperately to increase volume. They did so chiefly by reducing rates still more, on a selective basis. They gave rebates (secret reductions below the published rates) to large shippers in order to capture their business. Giving discounts to those who shipped in volume made economic sense: It was easier to handle freight in carload lots than in smaller units. So intense was the battle for business, however, that the railroads often made concessions to big customers far beyond what the economics of bulk shipment justified. In the 1870s the New York Central regularly reduced the rates charged important shippers by 50 to 80 percent. One large Utica dry-goods merchant received a rate of 9 cents while others paid 33 cents. Two big New York City grain merchants paid so little that they soon controlled the grain business of the entire city.

Railroad officials disliked rebating but found no way to avoid the practice. "Notwithstanding my horror of rebates," the president of a New England trunk line told one of his executives in discussing the case of a brick manufacturer, "bill at the usual rate, and rebate Mr. Cole 25 cents a thousand." In extreme cases the railroads even gave large shippers drawbacks, which were rebates on the business of the shippers' competitors. (For example, the same New England trunk line not only made Cole's competitiors pay higher freight rates but also returned a percentage of the income from those rates to Mr. Cole!) Besides rebating, railroads issued passes to favored shippers, built sidings at the plants of important companies without charge, and gave freely of their landholdings to attract businesses to their territory. "The force of competition," a railroad man explained, "is one that no carrying corporation can withstand and before which the managing officers of a corporation are helpless." James F. Joy of the Chicago, Burlington, and Quincy made the same point more bluntly: "Unless you prepare to defend yourselves," he advised the president of the Michigan Central, "you will be boarded by pirates in all quarters."

To make up for losses forced on them by competitive pressures, railroads charged higher rates at waypoints along their tracks where no competition existed. Frequently it cost more to ship a product a short distance than a longer one. Rochester, New York, was served only by the New York Central. In the 1870s it cost 30 cents to transport a barrel of flour from Rochester to New York City, a distance of 350 miles. At the same time flour could be shipped from Minneapolis to New York, a distance of well over 1,000 miles, for only 20 cents a barrel. One Rochester businessman told a state investigating committee that he could save 18 cents a hundredweight by sending goods to St. Louis by way of New York, where several carriers competed for the traffic, even though, in fact, the goods might come back through Rochester over the same tracks on the way to St. Louis!

Although cheap transportation stimulated the economy, few people benefited from cutthroat competition. Small shippers—and all businessmen in cities and towns with limited rail outlets—suffered; railroad discrimination speeded the concentration of industry in large corporations located in major centers. The instability of rates even troubled interests like the Midwestern flour millers who benefited from the competitive situation, for it hampered planning. Nor could manufacturers who received rebates be entirely happy, since few could be sure that some other producer was not getting a larger reduction.

Probably the worst sufferers were the railroads themselves. The loss of revenue resulting from rate cutting, combined with inflated debts, put most of them in grave difficulty when faced with a downturn in the business cycle. In 1876 two-fifths of all railroad bonds were in default; three years later sixty-five lines were bankrupt. Wits called Samuel J. Tilden, the 1876 Democratic presidential candidate, "the Great Forecloser" because of his work reorganizing bankrupt railroads at this time. Since the public would not countenance bankrupt railroads going out of business, these companies were placed in the hands of court-appointed receivers. The receivers, however, seldom provided efficient management and had no funds at their disposal for new equipment.

During the 1880s the major railroads responded to these pressures by building or buying lines in order to create interregional systems. These were the first giant corporations, capitalized in the hundreds of millions of dollars. Their enormous cost led to another wave of bankruptcies when a true depression struck in the 1890s.

The consequent reorganizations brought most of the big systems under the control of financiers, notably J. Pierpont Morgan and such other private bankers as Kuhn, Loeb of New York and Lee, Higginson of Boston.

Critics called the reorganizations "Morganizations." Representatives of the bankers sat on the board of every line they saved and their influence was predominant. They consistently opposed rate wars, rebating, and other competitive practices. In effect, control of the railroad network became centralized, even though the companies maintained their separate existences and operated in a seemingly independent manner. When Morgan died in 1913, "Morgan men" dominated the boards of the New York Central; the Erie; the New York, New Haven, and Hartford; the Southern; the Pere Marquette; the Atchison, Topeka and Santa Fe; and many other lines.

Competition and Monopoly: Steel

The iron and steel industry was also intensely competitive. Despite the trend toward higher production, demand varied erratically from year to year, even from month to month. In good times producers built new facilities, only to suffer heavy losses when demand declined. The forward rush of technology put a tremendous emphasis on efficiency; expensive plants quickly became obsolete. Improved transportation facilities allowed manufacturers in widely separated places to compete with one another.

The kingpin of the industry was Andrew Carnegie. Carnegie was born in Scotland and came to the United States in 1848 at the age of 12. His first job, as a bobbin boy in a cotton mill, brought him $1.20 a week, but his talents perfectly fitted the times and he rose rapidly: to Western Union messenger boy, to telegrapher, to private secretary, to railroad manager. He saved his money, made some shrewd investments, and by 1868 had an income of $50,000 a year.

At about this time he decided to specialize in the iron business. Carnegie possessed great talent as a salesman, boundless faith in the future of the country, an uncanny knack of choosing topflight subordinates, and enough ruthlessness to survive in the iron and steel jungle. Where other steelmen built new plants in good times, he preferred to expand in bad times, when it cost far less to do so. During the 1870s, he later recalled, "many of my friends needed money. . . . I bought out five or six of them. That is what gave me my leading interest in this steel business."

Carnegie grasped the importance of technological improvements. Slightly skeptical of the Bessemer process at first, once he became convinced of its practicality he adopted it enthusiastically. In 1875 he built the J. Edgar Thomson Steel Works, named after a president of the Pennsylvania Railroad, his biggest customer. He employed chemists and other specialists and was soon making steel from iron oxides that other manufacturers had discarded as waste. He was a merciless competitor. When a plant manager announced: "We broke all records for making steel last week," Carnegie replied: "Congratulations! Why not do it every week?" Carnegie sold rails by paying "commissions" to railroad purchasing agents, and he was not above reneging on a contract if he thought it profitable and safe to do so.

By 1890 the Carnegie Steel Company dominated the industry, and its output increased nearly tenfold during the next decade. Profits soared. Alarmed by his increasing control of the industry, the makers of finished steel products such as barbed wire and tubing considered pooling their resources and making steel themselves. Carnegie, his competitive temper aroused, threatened to manufacture wire, pipes, and other finished products. A colossal steel war seemed imminent.

However, Carnegie longed to retire in order to devote himself to philanthropic work. He believed that great wealth entailed social responsibilities and that it was a disgrace to die rich. When J. P. Morgan approached him through an intermediary with an offer to buy him out, he assented readily. In 1901 Morgan put together United States Steel, the "world's first billion-dollar corporation." This combination included all the Carnegie properties, the Federal Steel Company (Carnegie's largest competitor), and such important fabricators of finished products as the American Steel and Wire Company, the American Tin Plate Company, and the National Tube Company. Vast reserves of Minnesota iron ore and a fleet of Great Lakes ore steamers were also included. U.S. Steel was capitalized at $1.4 billion, about twice the value of its component properties but not necessarily an overestimation of its profit-earning capacity. The owners of Carnegie Steel received $492 million, of which $250 million went to Carnegie himself.

Competition and Monopoly: Oil

The pattern of fierce competition leading to combination and monopoly is well illustrated by the history of the petroleum industry. Irresistible pressures pushed the refiners into a brutal struggle to dominate the business. Production of crude oil, subject to the uncertainties of prospecting and drilling, fluctuated constantly and without regard for need. In general, output surged far ahead of demand.

By the 1870s the chief oil-refining centers were Cleveland, Pittsburgh, Baltimore, and the New York City area. Of these Cleveland was the fastest growing, chiefly because the New York Central and Erie railroads competed fiercely for its oil trade and the Erie Canal offered an alternative route.

The Standard Oil Company of Cleveland, founded in 1870 by a 31-year-old merchant named John D. Rockefeller, emerged as the giant among the refiners. Rockefeller exploited every possible technical advance and employed fair means and foul to persuade competitors either to sell out or to join forces. By 1879 he controlled 90 percent of the nation's oil-refining capacity along with a network of oil pipelines and large reserves of petroleum in the ground.

Standard Oil emerged victorious from the competitive wars because Rockefeller and his associates were the toughest and most imaginative fighters as well as the most efficient refiners in the business. In addition to obtaining from the railroads a 10 percent rebate and drawbacks on its competitors' shipments, Standard Oil cut prices locally to force small independents to sell out or face ruin. Since kerosene was sold in grocery stores, Standard supplied its own outlets with meat, sugar, and other products at artificially low prices to help crush the stores that handled other brands of kerosene. The company employed spies to track down the customers of independents and offer them oil at bargain prices. Bribery was also a Standard practice; the reformer Henry Demarest Lloyd quipped that the company had done everything to the Pennsylvania legislature except refine it.

Although a bold planner and a daring taker of necessary risks, Rockefeller was far too orderly and astute to enjoy the free-swinging battles that plagued his industry. Born in an upstate New York village in 1839, he settled in Cleveland in 1855 and became a produce merchant. During the Civil War he invested in a local refinery and by 1865 was engaged full time in the oil business.

Like Carnegie, Rockefeller was an organizer; he knew little about the technology of petroleum. His forte was meticulous attention to detail: stories are told of his ordering the number of drops of solder used to seal oil cans reduced from 40 to 39 and of his insisting that the manager of one of his refineries account for 750 missing barrel bungs. Not miserliness but a profound grasp of the economies of large-scale production explain this behavior.

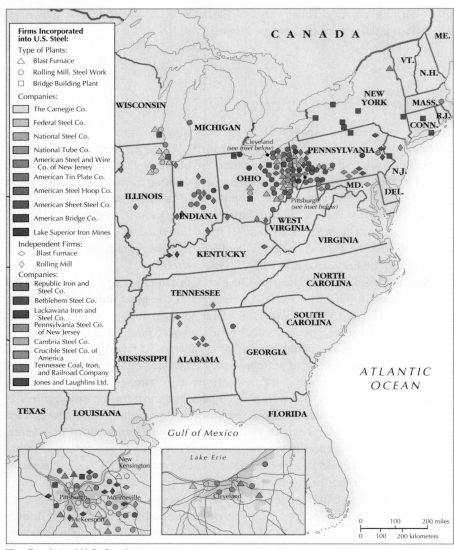

The Forging of U.S. Steel

Legend:

Firms Incorporated into U.S. Steel:

Type of Plants:
△ Blast Furnace
○ Rolling Mill, Steel Work
□ Bridge Building Plant

Companies:
The Carnegie Co.
Federal Steel Co.
National Steel Co.
National Tube Co.
American Steel and Wire Co. of New Jersey
American Tin Plate Co.
American Steel Hoop Co.
American Sheet Steel Co.
American Bridge Co.
Lake Superior Iron Mines

Independent Firms:
◇ Blast Furnace
◇ Rolling Mill

Companies:
Republic Iron and Steel Co.
Bethlehem Steel Co.
Lackawana Iron and Steel Co.
Pennsylvania Steel Co. of New Jersey
Cambria Steel Co.
Crucible Steel Co. of America
Tennessee Coal, Iron, and Railroad Company
Jones and Laughlins Ltd.

Rockefeller competed ruthlessly not primarily to crush other refiners but to persuade them to join with him, to share the business peaceably and rationally so that all could profit. Competition was obsolescent, he argued, though no more effective competitor than he ever lived.

Having achieved his monopoly, Rockefeller stabilized and structured it by creating a new type of business organization, the trust. Standard Oil was an Ohio corporation, prohibited by local law from owning plants in other states or holding stock in out-of-state corporations. As Rockefeller and his associates took over dozens of companies with facilities scattered across the country, serious legal and

A regally attired John D. Rockefeller, astride a barrel from his Standard Oil refinery, his crown encircled by the railroads he controlled. His actual attire was considerably less conspicuous.

managerial difficulties arose. How could these many organizations be integrated with Standard Oil of Ohio?

A rotund, genial little Pennsylvania lawyer named Samuel C. T. Dodd came up with an answer to this question in 1879.[1] The stock of Standard of Ohio and of all the other companies that the Rockefeller interests had swallowed up was turned over to nine trustees, who were empowered to "exercise general supervision" over all the properties. In exchange, stockholders received trust certificates, on which dividends were paid. This seemingly simple device brought order to the petroleum business. Competition almost disappeared; prices steadied; profits skyrocketed. By 1892 John D. Rockefeller was worth over $800 million.

The Standard Oil Trust was not a corporation. It had no charter, indeed no legal existence at all. For many years few people outside the organization knew that it existed. The form they chose persuaded Rockefeller and other Standard Oil officials that without violating their consciences, they could deny under oath that Standard Oil of Ohio owned or controlled other corporations "directly or indirectly

---

[1]*The trust formula was not "perfected" until 1882.*

through its officers or agents." The trustees controlled these organizations—and Standard of Ohio too!

After Standard Oil's duplicity was revealed during a New York investigation in 1888, the word *trust*, formerly signifying a fiduciary arrangement for the protection of the interests of individuals incompetent or unwilling to guard them themselves, became a synonym for monopoly. However, from the company's point of view, monopoly was not the purpose of the trust—that had been achieved before the device was invented. Centralization of the management of diverse and far-flung operations in the interest of efficiency was its chief function. Standard Oil headquarters in New York became the brain of a complex network where information from salaried managers in the field was collected and digested, where top managerial decisions were made, and whence orders went out to armies of drillers, refiners, scientists, and salesmen.

The pattern of competition leading to dominance by a few great companies was repeated in many businesses. In life insurance an immense expansion took place after the Civil War, stimulated by the development of a new type of group policy, the "tontine," by Henry B. Hyde of the Equitable Life Company.[2] High-pressure salesmanship prevailed; agents gave rebates to customers by shaving their own commissions; companies stole crack agents from their rivals and raided new territories. They sometimes invested as much as 96 percent of the first year's premiums in obtaining new business. By 1900, after three decades of fierce competition, three giants dominated the industry—Equitable, New York Life, and Mutual Life, each with approximately $1 billion of insurance in force.

In retailing, the period saw the growth of urban department stores. In 1862 Alexander T. Stewart had built an eight-story emporium in New York City that covered an entire block and employed 2,000 persons. John Wanamaker in Philadelphia and Marshall Field in Chicago headed similar establishments by the 1880s, and there were others. These department stores advertised heavily, stressing low prices, efficient service, and money-back guarantees. High volume made for large profits. Here is how one of Field's biographers described his methods:

> His was a one-price store, with the price plainly marked on the merchandise. Goods were not misrepresented, and a reputation for quality merchandise and for fair and honest dealing was built up. . . . Courtesy toward customers was an unfailing rule.

American Ambivalence to Big Business

The expansion of industry and its concentration in fewer and fewer hands changed the way many people felt about the role of government in economic and social affairs. On the one hand, they professed to believe strongly in a government policy of

---

[2]A tontine policy paid no dividends for a stated period of years. The heirs of the policyholder who died received the face value but no dividends. At the end of the tontine period, survivors collected not only their own dividends but those of the unfortunates who had died or permitted their policies to lapse. This was psychologically appealing, since it stressed living rather than dying and added an element of gambling to insurance.

noninterference, or laissez-faire. "'Things regulate themselves' . . . means, of course, that God regulates them by his general laws," Professor Francis Bowen of Harvard wrote in his *American Political Economy* (1870).

Certain intellectual currents encouraged this type of thinking. Charles Darwin's *The Origin of Species* was published in 1859, and by the 1870s his theory of evolution was beginning to influence opinion in the United States. That nature had ordained a kind of inevitable progress, governed by the natural selection of those individual organisms best adapted to survive in a particular environment, seemed eminently reasonable to most Americans, for it fit well with their own experiences. "Let the buyer beware; that covers the whole business," the sugar magnate Henry O. Havemeyer explained to an investigating committee. "You cannot wet-nurse people from the time they are born until the time they die. They have to wade and get stuck, and that is the way men are educated."

This reasoning was similar to that of the classical economists and was thus at least as old as Adam Smith's *Wealth of Nations* (1776). But it appeared to supply a hard scientific substitute for Smith's "invisible hand" as an explanation of why free competition advanced the common good.

Yale professor William Graham Sumner sometimes used the survival-of-the-fittest analogy in teaching undergraduates. "Professor," one student asked Sumner, "don't you believe in any government aid to industries?" "No!" Sumner replied, "It's root, hog, or die." The student persisted: "Suppose some professor of political science came along and took your job away from you. Wouldn't you be sore?" "Any other professor is welcome to try," Sumner answered promptly. "If he gets my job, it is my fault. My business is to teach the subject so well that no one can take the job away from me." Sumner's argument described what came to be known as *social Darwinism*, the belief that the activities of people, that is, their business and social relationships, were governed by the Darwinian principle that "the fittest" will always "survive" if allowed to exercise their capacities without restriction.

But the fact that Americans disliked powerful governments in general and strict regulation of the economy in particular had never meant that they objected to all government activity in the economic sphere. Banking laws, tariffs, internal-improvement legislation, and the granting of public land to railroads are only the most obvious of the economic regulations enforced in the nineteenth century by both the federal government and the states. Americans saw no contradiction between government activities of this type and the free enterprise philosophy, for such laws were intended to release human energy and thus increase the area in which freedom could operate. Tariffs stimulated industry and created new jobs, railroad grants opened up new regions for development, and so on.

The growth of huge industrial and financial organizations and the increasing complexity of economic relations frightened people yet made them at the same time greedy for more of the goods and services the new society was turning out. To many, the great new corporations and trusts resembled Frankenstein's monster—marvelous and powerful but a grave threat to society.

To some extent public fear of the industrial giants reflected concern about monopoly. If Standard Oil dominated oil refining, it might raise prices inordinately at vast cost to consumers. Charles Francis Adams Jr., expressed this feeling in the 1870s: "In the minds of the great majority, and not without reason, the idea of any industrial combination is closely connected with that of monopoly, and monopoly with extortion."

Although in isolated cases monopolists did raise prices unreasonably, generally they did not. On the contrary, prices tended to fall until by the 1890s a veritable "consumer's millennium" had arrived. Far more important in causing resentment was the fear that the monopolists were destroying economic opportunity and threatening democratic institutions. It was not the wealth of tycoons like Carnegie and Rockefeller and Morgan so much as their influence that worried people. In the face of the growing disparity between rich and poor, could republican institutions survive? "The belief is common," wrote Charles Francis Adams's brother Henry as early as 1870, "that the day is at hand when corporations . . . will ultimately succeed in directing government itself."

As criticism mounted, business leaders rose to their own defense. Rockefeller described in graphic terms the chaotic conditions that plagued the oil industry before the rise of Standard Oil: "It seemed absolutely necessary to extend the market for oil . . . and also greatly improve the process of refining so that oil could be made and sold cheaply, yet with a profit. We proceeded to buy the largest and best refining concerns and centralized the administration of them with a view to securing greater economy and efficiency." Carnegie, in an essay published in 1889, insisted that the concentration of wealth was necessary if humanity was to progress, softening this "Gospel of Wealth" by insisting that the rich must use their money "in the manner which . . . is best calculated to produce the most beneficial results for the community." The rich man was merely a trustee for his "poorer brethren," Carnegie said, "bringing to their service his superior wisdom, experience, and ability to administer." Lesser tycoons echoed these arguments.

The voices of the critics were louder if not necessarily more influential. Many clergymen denounced unrestrained competition, which they considered un-Christian. The new class of professional economists (the American Economic Association was founded in 1885) tended to repudiate laissez-faire. State aid, Richard T. Ely of Johns Hopkins University wrote, "is an indispensable condition of human progress."

Reformers: George, Bellamy, Lloyd, and the Marxists

The popularity of a number of radical theorists reflects public feeling in the period. In 1879 Henry George, a California journalist, published *Progress and Poverty*, a forthright attack on the uneven distribution of wealth in the United States. George argued that labor was the true and only source of capital. Observing the speculative fever of the West, which enabled landowners to reap profits merely by holding property while population increased, George proposed a property tax that would confiscate this "unearned increment." The value of land depended on society and should belong to society; allowing individuals to keep this wealth was the major cause of the growing disparity between rich and poor, George believed.

George's "single tax," as others called it, would bring in so much money that no other taxes would be necessary, and the government would have plenty of funds to establish new schools, museums, theaters, and other badly needed social and cultural services. While the single tax on property was never adopted, George's ideas attracted enthusiastic attention. Single tax clubs sprang up throughout the nation, and *Progress and Poverty* became a best-seller.

Even more spectacular was the reception afforded *Looking Backward, 2000–1887*, a utopian novel written in 1888 by Edward Bellamy. This book, which sold over a million copies in its first few years, described a future America that was completely socialized, all economic activity carefully planned. Bellamy compared nineteenth-century society to a lumbering stagecoach upon which the favored few rode in comfort while the mass of the people hauled them along life's route. Occasionally one of the toilers managed to fight his way onto the coach; whenever a rider fell from it, he had to join the multitude dragging it along.

Such, Bellamy wrote, was the working of the vaunted American competitive system. He suggested that the ideal socialist state, in which all citizens shared equally, would arrive without revolution or violence. The trend toward consolidation would continue, he predicted, until one monster trust controlled all economic activity. At this point everyone would realize that nationalization was essential.

A third influential attack on monopoly came from Henry Demarest Lloyd, whose *Wealth Against Commonwealth* appeared in 1894. Lloyd, a journalist of independent means, devoted years to preparing a denunciation of the Standard Oil Company. Marshaling masses of facts and vivid examples of Standard's evildoing, he assaulted the trust at every point. Although in his zeal Lloyd sometimes distorted and exaggerated the evidence to make his indictment more effective— "Every important man in the oil, coal and many other trusts ought today to be in some one of our penitentiaries," he wrote in a typical overstatement—as a polemic his book was peerless. His forceful but uncomplicated arguments and his copious references to official documents made *Wealth Against Commonwealth* utterly convincing to thousands. The book was more than an attack on Standard Oil. Lloyd denounced the application of Darwin's concept of survival of the fittest to economic and social affairs, and he condemned laissez-faire policies as leading directly to monopoly.

The popularity of these books indicates that the trend toward monopoly in the United States worried many. But despite the drastic changes suggested in their pages, none of these writers questioned the underlying values of the middle-class majority. They insisted that reform could be accomplished without serious inconvenience to any individual or class. In *Looking Backward* Bellamy pictured the so-

WERE THE INDUSTRIALISTS "ROBBER BARONS" OR SAVVY ENTREPRENEURS?

The Biltmore Estate in Asheville, North Carolina *(left)*, was completed in 1895 by George Vanderbilt; it required 1,000 workers to build the house.

Such wealth caused consternation at the time, and a later generation of historians picked up on the issue. In 1934 biographer Matthew Josephson, writing during the nation's worst depression, blamed the late nineteenth-century industrialists—robber barons, in his words—for the evident flaws in the economy. But in 1942, when the United States was at war and its industries were out-producing Nazi Germany and Japan, historians Thomas C. Cochran and William Miller contended that the late-nineteenth-century industrialists had exhibited skill and daring.

Historians subsequently shifted focus from the character of the entrepreneurs to the systems they built. In the early 1960s Alfred D. Chandler Jr. argued that the great industrialists, in response to the demands of burgeoning urban markets, created the requisite large-scale industrial enterprises.

Other historians countered that much of the nation's industrial growth was achieved not by the huge corporations and their famous owners, but by small firms (John N. Ingham, 1991) or by midlevel managers (Oliver Zunz, 1990).

Most historians concede that the industrialists often put their fortunes to good use. The critics of Andrew Carnegie, for example, may have studied in one of the scores of libraries he donated to communities, such as that in Tuskegee, Alabama *(right)*.

Matthew Josephson, *The Robber Barons* (1934), Thomas C. Cochran and William Miller, *The Age of Enterprise* (1942), Alfred D. Chandler Jr., *Strategy and Structure* (1962), John N. Ingham, *Making Iron and Steel* (1991), Oliver Zunz, *Making America Corporate* (1990).

cialists of the future gathered around a radiolike gadget in a well-furnished parlor listening to a minister delivering an inspiring sermon.

Nor did most of their millions of readers seriously consider trying to apply the reformers' ideas. Henry George ran for mayor of New York City in 1886 and lost narrowly to Abram S. Hewitt, a wealthy iron manufacturer, but even if he had won, he would have been powerless to apply the single tax to metropolitan property. The national discontent was apparently not as profound as the popularity of these works might suggest. If John D. Rockefeller became the bogeyman of American industry because of Lloyd's attack, no one prevented him from also becoming the richest man in the United States.

By the 1870s the ideas of European socialists were beginning to penetrate the United States, and in 1877 a Socialist Labor party was founded. The first serious attempt to explain the ideas of German political philosopher Karl Marx to Americans was Laurence Gronlund's *The Cooperative Commonwealth*, which was published in 1884, two years before Marx's *Das Kapital* was translated into English.

Capitalism, Gronlund claimed, contained the seeds of its own destruction. The state ought to own all the means of production. Competition was "Established Anarchy," middlemen were "parasites," speculators "vampires." "Capital and Labor," he wrote in one of the rare humorous lines in his book, "are just as harmonious as roast beef and a hungry stomach." Yet like other harsh critics of that day, Gronlund expected the millennium to arrive in a peaceful, indeed orderly manner. The red flag of socialism, he said, "has no relation to blood." The movement could accommodate "representatives of all classes," even "thoughtful" middleman parasites.

The Government Reacts to Big Business: Railroad Regulation

Political action related to the growth of big business came first on the state level and dealt chiefly with the regulation of railroads. Even before the Civil War, a number of New England states established railroad commissions to supervise lines within their borders; by the end of the century, twenty-eight states had such boards.

Strict regulation was largely the result of agitation by the National Grange of the Patrons of Husbandry. The Grange, founded in 1867 by Oliver H. Kelley, was created to provide social and cultural benefits for isolated rural communities. As it spread and grew in influence—fourteen states had Granges by 1872 and membership reached 800,000 in 1874—the movement became political too. "Granger" candidates, often not themselves farmers (many local businessmen resented such railroad practices as rebating), won control of a number of state legislatures in the West and South. Granger-controlled legislatures established "reasonable" maximum rates and outlawed "unjust" discrimination. The legislature also set up a commission to enforce the laws and punish violators.

The railroads protested, insisting that they were being deprived of property without due process of law. In *Munn v. Illinois* (1877), a case that involved a grain elevator whose owner had refused to comply with a state warehouse act, the Supreme Court upheld the constitutionality of this kind of act. Any business that served a public interest, such as a railroad or a grain warehouse, was subject to state control, the justices ruled. Legislatures might fix maximum charges; if the charges seemed unreasonable to the parties concerned, they should direct their complaints to the legislatures or to the voters, not to the courts.

Regulation of the railroad network by the individual states was inefficient, and in some cases the commissions were incompetent and even corrupt. To alleviate such abuses, Congress in 1877 passed the Interstate Commerce Act. All charges made by railroads "shall be reasonable and just," the act stated. Rebates, drawbacks, the long-and-short-haul evil, and other competitive practices were declared unlawful, and so were their monopolistic counterparts—pools and traffic-sharing agreements. Railroads were required to publish schedules of rates and forbidden to change them without due public notice. Most important, the law established an Interstate Commerce Commission (ICC), the first federal regulatory board, to supervise the affairs of railroads, investigate complaints, and issue cease and desist orders when the roads acted illegally.

The Interstate Commerce Act broke new ground, yet it was neither a radical nor a particularly effective measure. Its terms contradicted one another, some being designed to stimulate, others to penalize, competition. The new commission had less power than the law seemed to give it. It could not fix rates, only bring the railroads to court when it considered rates unreasonably high. Such cases could be extremely complicated; applying the law "was like cutting a path through a jungle." With the truth so hard to determine and the burden of proof on the commission, the courts in nearly every instance decided in favor of the railroads.

Nevertheless, by describing so clearly the right of Congress to regulate private corporations engaged in interstate commerce, the Interstate Commerce Act challenged the philosophy of laissez-faire. Later legislation made the commission more effective. The commission also served as the model for a host of similar federal administrative authorities, such as the Federal Communications Commission (1934).

The Government Reacts to Big Business: The Sherman Antitrust Act

As with railroad legislation, the first antitrust laws originated in the states, but they were southern and western states with relatively little industry, and most of the statutes were vaguely worded and ill-enforced. Federal action came in 1890 with the passage of the Sherman Antitrust Act. Any combination "in the form of trust or otherwise" that was "in restraint of trade or commerce among the several states, or with foreign nations" was declared illegal. Persons forming such combinations were subject to fines of $5,000 and a year in jail. Individuals and businesses suffering losses because of actions that violated the law were authorized to sue in the federal courts for triple damages.

Where the Interstate Commerce Act sought to outlaw the excesses of competition, the Sherman Act was supposed to restore competition. If businessmen joined together to "restrain" (monopolize) trade in a particular field, they should be punished and their deeds undone. "The great thing this bill does," Senator George Frisbie Hoar of Massachusetts explained, "is to extend the common-law principle . . . to international and interstate commerce." This was important because the states ran into legal difficulties when they tried to use the common law to restrict corporations engaged in interstate activities.

In fact, the Supreme Court quickly weakened the Sherman Act. In *United States v. E. C. Knight Company* (1895) it held that the American Sugar Refining Company had not violated the law by taking over a number of important competitors. Although the Sugar Trust now controlled about 98 percent of all sugar refining in the United States, it was not restraining trade. "Doubtless the power to control the manufacture of a given thing involves in a certain sense the control of its disposition," the Court said in one of the greatest feats of judicial understatement of all time. "Although the exercise of that power may result in bringing the operation of commerce into play, it does not control it, and affects it only incidentally and indirectly."

If the creation of the Sugar Trust did not violate the Sherman Act, it seemed unlikely that any other combination of manufacturers could be convicted under the law. However, in several cases in 1898 and 1899 the Supreme Court ruled that agreements to fix prices or divide markets did violate the Sherman Act. These decisions precipitated a wave of outright mergers in which a handful of large companies swallowed up hundreds of smaller ones. Presumably mergers were not illegal. When, some years after his retirement, Andrew Carnegie was asked by a committee of the House of Representatives to explain how he had dared participate in the formation of the U.S. Steel Corporation, he replied: "Nobody ever mentioned the Sherman Act to me that I remember."

The Labor Union Movement

At the time of the Civil War only a small percentage of the American workforce was organized, and most union members were cigarmakers, printers, carpenters, and other skilled artisans, not factory hands. Aside from ironworkers, railroad workers, and miners, few industrial laborers belonged to unions. Nevertheless the union was the workers' response to the big corporation: a combination designed to eliminate competition for jobs and to provide efficient organization for labor.

After 1865 the growth of national craft unions, which had been stimulated by labor dissatisfaction during the Civil War, quickened perceptibly. In 1866 a federation of these organizations, the National Labor Union, was founded and by the early 1870s many new trades, notably in railroading, had been unionized.

Most of the leaders of these unions were visionaries who were out of touch with the practical needs and aspirations of workers. They opposed the wage system, strikes, and anything that increased the laborers' sense of being members of the working class. A major objective was the formation of worker-owned cooperatives.

Far more remarkable was the Knights of Labor, a curious organization founded in 1869 by a group of Philadelphia garment workers headed by Uriah S. Stephens. Like so many labor organizers of the period, Stephens was a reformer of wide interests rather than a man dedicated to the specific problems of industrial workers. He, his successor Terence V. Powderly, and many other leaders of the

Here Jay Gould, perhaps the most vilified of the "robber barons," is depicted as a spider amidst a web of control bound by the telegraph lines of Western Union. Alfred Chandler, Jr., as noted in the feature Debating the Past on page 500, took a more positive look at the nation's industrialists. He credited Gould with salvaging the Union Pacific Railroad, building his own railroad company (Missouri Pacific), and rationalizing the nation's communications system.

Knights would have been thoroughly at home in the labor organizations of the Jacksonian era. Like the Jacksonians, they supported political objectives that had no direct connection with working conditions, such as currency reform and the curbing of land speculation. They rejected the idea that workers must resign themselves to remaining wage earners. By pooling their resources, working people could advance up the economic ladder and enter the capitalist class. "There is no good reason," Powderly wrote in his autobiography, *The Path I Trod*, "why labor cannot, through cooperation, own and operate mines, factories, and railroads." The leading Knights saw no contradiction between their denunciation of "soulless" monopolies and "drones" like bankers and lawyers and their talk of "combining all branches of trade in one common brotherhood." Such muddled thinking led the Knights to attack the wage system and to frown on strikes as "acts of private warfare."

Under Powderly, secrecy was discarded. Between 1882 and 1886 successful strikes by local "assemblies" against western railroads, including one against the hated Jay Gould's Missouri Pacific, brought recruits by the thousands. The membership passed 42,000 in 1882, 110,000 in 1885, and in 1886 it soared beyond the 700,000 mark. Alas, sudden prosperity was too much for the Knights. Its national leadership was unable to control local groups. A number of poorly planned strikes failed dismally, and the public was alienated by sporadic acts of violence and intimidation. Disillusioned recruits began to drift away.

Circumstances largely fortuitous caused the collapse of the organization. By 1886 the movement for the eight-hour day had gained wide support among workers, including many who did not belong to unions. Several hundred thousand (estimates vary) were on strike in various parts of the country by May of that year. In Chicago, a center of the eight-hour movement, about 80,000 workers were involved, and a small group of anarchists was trying to take advantage of the excitement to win support.

When a striker was killed in a fracas at the McCormick Harvesting Machine Company, the anarchists called a protest meeting on May 4, at Haymarket Square. Police intervened to break up the meeting, and someone—his identity was never established—hurled a bomb into their ranks. Seven policemen were killed and many others injured.

The American Federation of Labor

Although the anarchists were the immediate victims of the resulting public indignation and hysteria—seven were condemned to death and four eventually executed—organized labor, especially the Knights, suffered heavily. No tie between the Knights and the bombing could be established, but the union had been closely connected with the eight-hour agitation, and the public tended to associate it with violence and radicalism. Its membership declined as suddenly as it had risen, and soon it ceased to exist as a force in the labor movement.

The Knights' place was taken by the American Federation of Labor (AFL), a combination of national craft unions established in 1886. In a sense the AFL was a reactionary organization. Its principal leaders, Adolph Strasser and Samuel Gompers of the Cigarmakers Union, were, like the founders of the Knights of Labor, originally interested in utopian social reforms. They even toyed with the idea of forming a workers' political party. Experience, however, soon led them to concentrate on organizing skilled workers and fighting for "bread-and-butter" issues such as higher wages and shorter hours. "Our organization does not consist of idealists," Strasser explained to a congressional committee. "We do not control the production of the world. That is controlled by the employers. . . . I look first to cigars."

The AFL accepted the fact that most workers would remain wage earners all their lives and tried to develop in them a sense of common purpose and pride in their skills and station. Strasser and Gompers paid great attention to building a strong organization of dues-paying members committed to unionism as a way of improving their lot. Rank-and-file AFL members were naturally eager to win wage increases and other benefits, but most also valued their unions for the companionship they provided, the sense of belonging to a group. In other words, despite statements such as Strasser's, unions, in and out of the AFL, were a kind of club as well as a means of defending and advancing their members' material interests.

The chief weapon of the federation was the strike, which it used to win concessions from employers and to attract recruits. Gompers, president of the AFL almost continuously from 1886 until his death in 1924, encouraged workers to make "intelligent use of the ballot" in order to advance their interests. The federation worked for such things as eight-hour days, employers' liability, and mine-safety laws, but it avoided direct involvement in politics. "I have my own philosophy and my own dreams," Gompers once told a left-wing French politician, "but first and

This rendering of the Haymarket Riot in Chicago in 1886 depicted an uprising tantamount to the toppling of the monarchy during the French Revolution. Its exaggerations, so characteristic of the journalism of the day, contributed to the demand for harsh prosecutions.

foremost I want to increase the workingman's welfare year by year. . . . The French workers waste their economic force by their political divisions."

Gompers's approach to labor problems produced solid, if unspectacular, growth for the AFL. Unions with a total of about 150,000 members formed the federation in 1886. By 1892 the membership had reached 250,000, and in 1901 it passed the million mark.

Labor Militancy Rebuffed

The stress of the AFL on the strike weapon reflected rather than caused the increasing militancy of labor. Workers felt themselves threatened from all sides: the growing size and power of their corporate employers; the substitution of machines for human skills; the invasion of foreign workers willing to accept substandard wages. At the same time they had tasted some of the material benefits of industrialization and had learned the advantages of concerted action.

The average employer behaved like a tyrant when dealing with his workers. He discharged them arbitrarily when they tried to organize unions; he hired scabs to replace strikers; he frequently failed to provide the most rudimentary protection against injury on the job. Some employers, Carnegie for example, professed to approve of unions, but almost none would bargain with labor collectively. To do so, they argued, would be to deprive workers of their freedom to contract for their own labor in any way they saw fit.

The industrialists of the period were not all ogres; they were as alarmed by the rapid changes of the times as their workers, and since they had more at stake materially, they were probably more frightened by the uncertainties. Deflation, technological change, and intense competition kept even the most successful under constant pressure.

Thus capital and labor were often spoiling for a fight, frequently without fully understanding why. When labor troubles developed, they tended to be bitter, even violent. In 1877 a great railroad strike convulsed much of the nation. It began on the Baltimore and Ohio system in response to a wage cut and spread to other eastern lines and then throughout the West until about two-thirds of the railroad mileage of the country had been shut down. Violence broke out, rail yards were put to the torch, dismayed and frightened businessmen formed militia companies to patrol the streets of Chicago and other cities. Eventually President Hayes sent federal troops to the trouble spots to restore order, and the strike collapsed. There had been no real danger of revolution, but the violence and destruction of the strike had been without precedent in America.

The disturbances of 1877 were a response to a business slump, those of the next decade a response to good times. Twice as many strikes occurred in 1886 as in any previous year. Even before the Haymarket bombing centered the country's attention on labor problems, the situation had become so disturbing that President Grover Cleveland, in the first presidential message devoted to labor problems, had urged Congress to create a voluntary arbitration board to aid in settling labor disputes—a remarkable suggestion for a man of Cleveland's conservative, laissez-faire approach to economic issues.

In 1892 a violent strike broke out among silver miners at Coeur d'Alene, Idaho, and a far more important clash shook Andrew Carnegie's Homestead steel plant near Pittsburgh when strikers attacked 300 private guards brought in to protect strikebreakers. Seven guards were killed at Homestead and the rest forced to "surrender" and march off ignominiously. The Homestead affair was part of a struggle between capital and labor in the steel industry. Steel producers insisted that the workers were holding back progress by resisting technological advances, while the workers believed that the company was refusing to share the fruits of more efficient operation fairly. The strike was precipitated by the decision of company officials to crush the union at all costs. The final defeat, after a five-month walkout, of the 24,000-member Amalgamated Association of Iron and Steel Workers, one of the most important elements in the AFL, destroyed unionism as an effective force in the steel industry and set back the progress of organized labor all over the country.

As in the case of the Haymarket bombing, the activities of radicals on the fringe of the dispute turned the public against the steelworkers. The boss of

Homestead was Henry Clay Frick, a tough-minded foe of unions who was determined to "teach our employees a lesson." Frick made the decision to bring in strikebreakers and to employ Pinkerton detectives to protect them. During the course of the strike, Alexander Berkman, an anarchist, burst into Frick's office and attempted to assassinate him. Frick was only slightly wounded, but the attack brought him much sympathy and unjustly discredited the strikers.

The most important strike of the period took place in 1894. It began when the workers at George Pullman's Palace Car factory outside Chicago walked out in protest against wage cuts. (While reducing wages, Pullman insisted on holding the line on rents in the company town of Pullman; when a delegation called on him to remonstrate, he refused to give in and had three of the leaders fired.) Some Pullman workers belonged to the American Railway Union, headed by Eugene V. Debs. After the strike had dragged along for weeks, the union voted to refuse to handle trains with Pullman cars. The union was perfectly willing to handle mail trains, but the owners refused to run trains unless they were made up of a full complement of cars.

When Pullman cars were added to mail trains, the workers refused to move them. The resulting railroad strike tied up trunk lines running in and out of Chicago. The railroad owners appealed to President Cleveland to send troops to preserve order. On the pretext that the soldiers were needed to ensure the movement of the mails, Cleveland agreed. When Debs defied a federal injunction to end the walkout, he was jailed for contempt and the strike was broken.

Whither America, Whither Democracy?

Each year more of the nation's wealth and power seemed to fall into fewer hands. As with the railroads, other industries were being influenced, if not completely dominated, by bankers. The firm of J. P. Morgan and Company controlled many railroads; the largest steel, electrical, agricultural machinery, rubber, and shipping companies; two life insurance companies; and a number of banks. By 1913 Morgan and the Rockefeller National City Bank group between them could name 341 directors to 112 corporations worth over $22.2 billion. The "Money Trust," a loose but potent fraternity of financiers, seemed fated to become the ultimate monopoly.

Centralization unquestionably increased efficiency, at least in industries that used a great deal of expensive machinery to turn out goods for the mass market, and in those where close coordination of output, distribution, and sales was important. The public benefited immensely from the productive efficiency of the new empires. Living standards rose.

But the trend toward giantism raised doubts. With ownership falling into fewer hands, what would be the ultimate effect of big business on American democracy? What did it mean for ordinary people when a few tycoons possessed huge fortunes and commanded such influence even on Congress and the courts?

The crushing of the Pullman strike demonstrated the power of the courts to break strikes by issuing injunctions. And the courts seemed only concerned with protecting the interests of the rich and powerful. Particularly ominous for organized labor was the fact that the federal government based its request for the injunction that broke the strike on the Sherman Antitrust Act, arguing that the American Railway Union was a combination in restraint of trade. An indirect result of the Pullman strike was that while serving his sentence for contempt, Eugene Debs was visited by a number of prominent socialists who sought to convert him to their cause. One gave him a copy of Karl Marx's *Capital,* which he found too dull to finish, but he did read *Looking Backward* and *Wealth Against Commonwealth.* In 1897 he became a socialist.

Milestones

1859	First oil well is drilled in Pennsylvania
	Charles Darwin publishes *The Origin of Species*
1868	Carnegie Steel Company is formed
1869	George Westinghouse invents air brake
	Garment workers found Knights of Labor
1870–1890	Railroad trunk lines are completed
1876	Alexander Graham Bell invents telephone
1877	Great railroad strike convulses nation
	Munn v. *Illinois* upholds state regulatory laws
1879	Thomas Edison invents electric light bulb
	Reformer Henry George publishes *Progress and Poverty*
1884	Marxist Laurence Gronlund publishes *The Cooperative Commonwealth*
1886	Anarchists clash with police in Chicago's Haymarket bombing
	Craft unions found American Federation of Labor (AFL)
1887	Interstate Commerce Act regulates railroads
1888	Edward Bellamy publishes utopian novel *Looking Backward*
1889	Philanthropist Andrew Carnegie publishes "Gospel of Wealth"
1890	Sherman Antitrust Act outlaws monopolies
1892	Seven Pinkerton guards are killed in Homestead steel strike
1894	Eugene V. Debs leads American Railway Union in Pullman strike
	Henry Demarest Lloyd condemns laissez-faire in *Wealth Against Commonwealth*
1895	*U.S.* v. *E.C. Knight Company* weakens Sherman Antitrust Act
1901	J. P. Morgan forms U.S. Steel, "world's first billion-dollar corporation"

American Society in the Industrial Age

T HE MALL OF AMERICA OUTSIDE MINNEAPOLIS, MINNESOTA, IS THE largest enclosed mall in the United States. It is also the nation's most popular tourist destination, visited by 100,000 people every day. This mall, like many others, was also once a popular hangout for young people. On Friday and Saturday nights, as many as 10,000 teenagers would gather there. But this practice ended in 1996, when the Mall of America instituted a 6:00 P.M. weekend curfew on teenagers under 16 unless accompanied by an adult. Since then, hundreds of malls have adopted similar curfews.

Teenagers, who on the average spend 3.5 hours a week in malls, howled in protest. "We just want to be able to hang out at the mall," complained Kimberly Flanagan, 16, of Charlotte, North Carolina. Kary Ross, an attorney for the American Civil Liberties Union, sided with the teenagers: "We're opposed to curfews that treat all minors as if they're criminals."

Malls insist that as privately owned enterprises, they are exempt from First Amendment protections, such as freedom of speech and the right to assemble. Malls are not public property. Yet recent malls have been designed to evoke the public spaces of the nineteenth-century city. The Mall of America includes an exhibition gallery, amusement park, wedding chapel, assembly hall, school, medical clinic, and a central "Rotunda" for staging "public events" ranging from gardening shows to Hulk Hogan wrestling matches.

In the late nineteenth century, city life was played out in spaces that really were public. Factory hands walked to work along crowded streets or jammed into streetcars or subways. Courting couples strolled through shopping districts or public parks. Children played in streets. "Little Italy" or "Chinatown" provided exotic attractions for all. Amusement parks and sporting events drew huge throngs. In New

York City, a journalist explained in 1883, a "huge conglomerate mass" came together in public spaces to form a "vague and vast harmony."

But city life was not for all. In 1900, 50 percent more Americans lived in rural areas than in urban areas—even when "urban" was generously defined as holding more than 2,500 people. Why, asked sociologist Henry Fletcher in 1895, do "large masses of people, apparently against their own interests," abandon the nation's healthful and sociable rural areas and crowd into the nation's insalubrious and anonymous cities?

Nineteenth-century cities, though noisy, chaotic, and often ill-governed, exerted a peculiar fascination. There workers, even immigrants and young women, could more easily find jobs. Housing, for all its limitations, was cheap. Urban problems were daunting, but the immense aggregation of peoples constituted a limitless potential for uplift and reform. City life was a great spectacle, played out mostly in public spaces.

Middle-Class Life

"This middle-class country had got a middle-class president, at last," Ralph Waldo Emerson had noted with satisfaction when Lincoln took office in 1861. Emerson did not endorse an economic class so much as a set of values that were, pointedly, antithetical to those of the antebellum South. Middle-class culture took the best aspects of romanticism—the enshrinement of human potential, the restless striving for personal betterment, the zest for competition and excitement—and tempered them with a passion for self-control and regularity.

But the Civil War sapped middle-class culture of its reforming zeal. The vital energy that had spawned antebellum reforms became transmuted into greater mass; the fervor of the individual was channeled into institutions. American society and culture underwent a process of "incorporation," as the predominant form of the business world seeped deep into the American consciousness.

Historians had long claimed that family relations were stiff and, in matters pertaining to sexuality, downright prudish. One witless historian imagined that intercourse occurred "in a dark bedroom into which the husband would creep to create his offspring in silence while the wife endured the connection in a coma." But diaries and letters provide ample proof that many couples experienced emotionally intense and sexually fulfilling relationships. Elaborate and protracted courtship rituals, which doubtless proved frustrating, intensified the expression of love by delaying its gratification. Middle-class mothers at the end of the century had two or three children, four or five fewer than their grandmothers. Their families were smaller mostly because they married later in life and practiced abstinence, though during the last half of the century contraceptive devices were both more reliable and more commercially available.

The children in middle-class families, while much treasured, were carefully supervised. Upwardly striving parents were much concerned about the status and prospects of their children's marriage partners, but it was no longer considered proper to interfere with "the course of true love" for any materialistic or purely social reason.

While most women remained home to supervise their children, men worked away from home, in shops and offices. Members of the professions and the large and diffuse groups of shopkeepers, small manufacturers, skilled craftsmen, and established farmers that made up the middle class lived in varying degrees of comfort. A family with an annual income of $1,000 in the 1880s would have no need to skimp on food, clothing, or shelter. When Professor Woodrow Wilson moved with his family to Wesleyan University in 1888, he was able to rent a large house and employ two full-time servants on his salary of $2,500 a year. Indeed, at this time, about a quarter of all urban families employed at least one servant.

Skilled and Unskilled Workers

Wage earners felt the full force of the industrial tide, being affected in countless ways—some beneficial, others unfortunate. As manufacturing and mining became more important, the number of workers in these fields multiplied rapidly: from 885,000 in 1860 to more than 3.2 million in 1890. While workers lacked much sense of solidarity, they exerted a far larger influence on society at the turn of the century than they had in the years before the Civil War.

More efficient methods of production enabled them to increase their output, making possible a rise in their standard of living. The working day still tended to approximate the hours of daylight, but it was shortening perceptibly by the 1880s, at least in many occupations. In 1860 the average workday had been 11 hours, but by 1880 only one worker in four labored more than 10 hours and radicals were beginning to talk about 8 hours as a fair day's work.

This generalization, however, conceals some important differences. Skilled industrial workers—such types as railroad engineers and conductors, machinists, and iron molders—were relatively well off in most cases. But it was still true that unskilled laborers could not earn enough to maintain a family decently by their own efforts alone.

Industrialization created problems for workers beyond the obvious one of earning enough money to support themselves. By and large, skilled workers improved their positions relatively, despite the increased use of machinery. Furthermore, when machines took the place of human skills, jobs became monotonous. Mechanization undermined both the artisans' pride and their bargaining power with their employers. As expensive machinery became more important, the worker seemed less important. Machines more than workers controlled the pace of work and its duration. The time clock regulated the labor force more rigidly than the most exacting foreman. The length of the workday may have declined, but the pace of work and the danger involved in working around heavy, high-speed machinery increased accordingly.

As businesses grew larger, personal contact between employer and hired hand tended to disappear. Relations between them became less human, more businesslike, and ruthless. On the other hand, large enterprises usually employed a higher percentage of managerial and clerical workers than smaller companies, thus providing opportunities for more "blue-collar" workers to rise in the industrial hierarchy. But the trend toward bigness made it more difficult for workers to rise from the ranks of labor to become manufacturers themselves, as Andrew Carnegie, for example, had done during the Civil War era.

Another problem for workers was that industrialization tended to accentuate swings of the business cycle. On the upswing something approaching full employment existed, but in periods of depression unemployment became a problem that affected workers without regard for their individual abilities. It is significant that the word *unemployment* (though not, of course, the condition itself) was a late-nineteenth-century invention.

Working Women

Women continued to supply a significant part of the industrial working force. But now many more of them were working outside their homes; the factory had almost completely replaced the household as the seat of manufacturing.[1] Textile mills and "the sewing trades" absorbed a large percentage of women, but in all fields women were paid substantially lower wages than men.

Women found many new types of work in these years, a fact commented on by the *New York Times* as early as 1869. They made up the overwhelming majority of salespersons and cashiers in the big new department stores. Store managers considered women more polite, easier to control, and more honest than male workers, all qualities especially valuable in the huge emporiums. Over half of the more than 1,700 employees in A. T. Stewart's New York store were women.

Educated, middle-class women also dominated the new profession of nursing that developed alongside the expanding medical profession and the establishment of large urban hospitals. To nearly all doctors, to most men, and indeed to many women of that day, nursing seemed the perfect female profession since it required the same characteristics that women were thought to have by nature: selflessness, cleanliness, kindliness, tact, sensitivity, and submissiveness to male control.

Middle-class women did replace men as teachers in most of the nation's grade schools, and they also replaced men as clerks and secretaries and operators of the new typewriters in government departments and in business offices. Most men with the knowledge of spelling and grammar that these positions required had better opportunities and were uninterested in office work, so women high school graduates, of whom there was an increasing number, filled the gap.

---

[1]*However, at least half of all working women were domestic servants.*

The glove counter at Rike's Department Store in Dayton, Ohio (1893). Shopping was an excuse for middle-class women to venture from the home into public. Rike's department store was decorated much like the Victorian home: potted ferns, stuffed animals, and carpeted stairways. The salesgirl *(far right)* was obliged to leave the home to work. She spent much of her income to "keep up appearances" to enable her to mix with middle-class shoppers.

Both department store clerks and "typewriters" (as they were called) earned more money than unskilled factory workers, and working conditions were more pleasant. Opportunities for promotion for women, however, were rare; managerial posts in these fields remained almost exclusively in the hands of men.

Farmers

Long the backbone of American society, independent farmers and the agricultural way of life were rapidly being left behind in the race for wealth and status. The number of farmers and the volume of agricultural production continued to rise, but agriculture's relative place in the national economy was declining. Between 1860 and 1890 the number of farms rose from 2 million to 4.5 million; wheat output leaped from 173 million bushels to 449 million, cotton from 5.3 million bales to 8.5 million. The rural population increased from 25 million to 40.8 million. Yet industry was expanding far faster, and the urban population, quadrupling in the period, would soon overtake and pass that of the countryside.

Farmers were not all affected by economic developments in the same way. Because of the steady decline of the price level, those in newly settled regions were

A sod house in North Dakota, 1896. Individual "bricks" of sod were hewn from the ground and stacked in layers to build such houses. The roof was made of timber packed with branches, twigs, straw, and more sod. This house was expanded with a room made of planed lumber *(right)*. Sod houses were quite cool in summer and warm in winter, although excess moisture was always a problem.

usually worse off than those in older areas since they had to borrow money to get started and were therefore burdened with fixed interest charges that became harder to meet each year. In the 1870s farmers in Illinois and Iowa suffered most—which accounts for the strength of the Granger movement in that region. Except as a purely social organization, the Grange had little importance in eastern states, where rapidly expanding urban markets made farmers relatively prosperous. A typical eastern farm family raising wheat and other grains and perhaps some livestock worked hard but made a good living. Such a family might employ a neighbor's daughter to help with housework, milking, and similar chores and a "hired hand" whose work was mainly in the fields.

By the late 1880s farmers in the old Middle West had also become better established. Even when prices dipped and a general depression gripped the country, they were able to weather the bad times nicely by taking advantage of lower transportation costs, better farm machinery, and new fertilizers and insecticides to increase output and by shifting from wheat to the production of corn, oats, hogs, and cattle, which had not declined so drastically in price.

On the agricultural frontier from Texas to the Dakotas, and through the states of the old Confederacy, farmers were less fortunate. The burdens of the crop-lien system kept thousands of southern farmers in poverty, while on the Plains life was a succession of hardships. The first settlers in western Kansas, Nebraska, and the Dakotas took up land along the rivers and creeks, where they found enough timber for home building, fuel, and fencing. Later arrivals had to build houses of the tough prairie sod and depend on hay, sunflower stalks, and buffalo dung for fuel.

Frontier farm families had always had to work hard and endure the hazards of storm, drought, and insect plagues, along with isolation and loneliness. But all these burdens were magnified on the prairies and the High Plains. Life was particularly hard for farm women, who, in addition to childcare and housework, performed endless farm chores—milking cows, feeding livestock, raising vegetables, and so on. "I . . . am set and running every morning at half-past four o'clock, and run all day, often until half-past eleven P.M.," one farm woman explained. "Is it any wonder I have become slightly demoralized?"

Working-Class Attitudes

Social workers and government officials made many efforts in the 1880s and 1890s to find out how working people felt about all sorts of matters connected with their jobs. Their reports reveal a wide spectrum of opinion. To the question, asked of two Wisconsin carpenters, "What new laws, in your opinion, ought to be enacted?" one replied: "Keep down strikes and rioters. Let every man attend to his own business." But the other answered: "Complete nationalization of land and all ways of transportation. Burn all government bonds. A graduated income tax. . . . Abolish child labor and [pass] any other act that capitalists say is wrong."

Every variation of opinion between these extremes was expressed by working people in many sections and in many kinds of work. In 1881 a female textile worker in Lawrence, Massachusetts, said to an interviewer: "If you will stand by the mill, and see the people coming out, you will be surprised to see the happy, contented look they all have."

Despite such remarks and the general improvement in living standards, it is clear, if only from the large number of bitter strikes of the period, that there was a considerable dissatisfaction among industrial workers. Writing in 1885, the labor leader Terence V. Powderly reported that "a deep-rooted feeling of discontent pervades the masses."

The discontent had many causes. For some, poverty was still the chief problem, but for others, rising aspirations triggered discontent. Workers were confused about their destiny; the tradition that no one of ability need remain a hired hand died hard. They wanted to believe their bosses and the politicians when those worthies voiced the old slogans about a classless society and the community of interest of capital and labor. "Our men," William Vanderbilt of the New York Central Railroad said in 1877, "feel that, although I . . . may have my millions and they the rewards of their daily toil, still we are about equal in the end. If they suffer, I suffer, and if I suffer, they cannot escape."

Working Your Way Up

To study mobility in a large industrial country is extraordinarily difficult. Americans in the late nineteenth century believed their society offered great opportunities for individual advancement, and to prove it they pointed to men like Andrew Carnegie and to other poor boys who accumulated large fortunes. How general was the rise from rags to riches (or even to modest comfort) is another question.

Americans had been on the move, mostly, of course, in a westward direction, since the colonial period, but studies of census records show that there was considerable geographic mobility in urban areas throughout the last half of the nineteenth century and into the twentieth. Most investigations reveal that only about half the people recorded in one census were still in the same place ten years later. The nation had a vast reservoir of rootless people. For many, the way to move up in the world was to move on.

In most of the cities studied, mobility was accompanied by some economic and social improvement. On the average, about a quarter of the manual laborers traced rose to middle-class status during their lifetimes, and the sons of manual laborers were still more likely to improve their place in society. In New York City about a third of the Italian and Jewish immigrants of the 1890s had risen from unskilled to skilled jobs a decade later. Even in Newburyport, Massachusetts, a town that was something of an economic backwater, most laborers made some progress, though far fewer rose to skilled or white-collar positions than in more prosperous cities.

Such progress was primarily the result of the economic growth the nation was experiencing and of the energy and ambition of the people, native-born and immigrant alike, who were pouring into the cities in such numbers. The public education system gave an additional boost to the upwardly mobile.

The history of American education after about 1870 reflects the impact of social and economic change. Although Horace Mann, Henry Barnard, and others had laid the foundations for state-supported school systems, most of these systems became compulsory only after the Civil War, when the growth of cities provided the concentration of population and financial resources necessary for economical mass education. In the 1860s about half the children in the country were getting some formal education, but this did not mean that half the children were attending school at any one time.

Thereafter, steady growth and improvement took place. Attendance in the public schools increased from 6.8 million in 1870 to 15.5 million in 1900, a remarkable expansion even when allowance is made for the growth of the population. More remarkable still, during a time when prices were declining steadily, public expenditures for education nearly quadrupled. A typical elementary school graduate, at least in the cities, could count on having studied, besides the traditional "Three Rs," history, geography, a bit of science, drawing, and physical training.

Industrialization created many demands for vocational and technical training; both employers and unskilled workers quickly grasped the possibilities. Science courses were taught in some of the new high schools, but secondary education was still assumed to be only for those with special abilities and youths whose families did not require that they immediately become breadwinners. As late as 1890 fewer than 300,000 of the 14.3 million children attending public and private schools had progressed beyond the eighth grade and nearly a third of these were attending private institutions.

Education certainly helped young people to rise in the world, but progress from rags to real riches was far from common. Carnegies were rare. A study of the family backgrounds of 200 late-nineteenth-century business leaders revealed that nearly all of them grew up in well-to-do middle-class families. They were far better educated than the general run, and most were members of one or another Protestant church.

The unrealistic expectations inspired by the rags-to-riches myth more than the absence of real opportunity probably explains why so many workers, even when expressing dissatisfaction with life as it was, continued to subscribe to such middle-class values as hard work and thrift—that is, they continued to hope.

The "New" Immigration

Industrial expansion increased the need for labor, and this in turn powerfully stimulated immigration. Between 1866 and 1915 about 25 million foreigners entered the United States. Industrial growth alone does not explain the influx. The launching in 1858 of the English liner *Great Eastern*, which was nearly 700 feet from stem to stern and weighed about 19,000 tons, opened a new era in transatlantic travel. Although most immigrants traveled in steerage, which was cramped and almost totally lacking in anything that could be considered an amenity, the Atlantic crossing, once so hazardous, became safe and speedy with the perfection of the steamship. Competition between the great packet lines such as Cunard, North German Lloyd, and Holland-America drove down the cost of the passage, and advertising by the lines further stimulated traffic.

"Push" pressures as well as these "pull" factors had much to do with the new patterns of immigration. Improvements in transportation produced unexpected and disruptive changes in the economies of many European countries. Cheap wheat from the United States, Russia, and other parts of the world poured into Europe, bringing disaster to farmers throughout Europe. The spreading industrial revolution and the increased use of farm machinery led to the collapse of the peasant economy of central and southern Europe. For rural inhabitants this meant the loss of self-sufficiency, the fragmentation of landholdings, unemployment, and for many the decision to make a new start in the New World.

Political and religious persecutions pushed still others into the migrating stream, but the main reason for immigration remained the desire for economic betterment. "In America," a British immigrant reported, "you get pies and puddings."

While immigrants continued to people the farms of America, industry absorbed an ever-increasing number of the newcomers. In 1870 one industrial worker in three was foreign-born. When congressional investigators examined twenty-one major industries early in the new century, they discovered that well over half of the labor force had not been born in the United States.

Before 1882, when—in addition to the Chinese—criminals, and persons adjudged mentally defective or liable to become public charges were excluded, entry

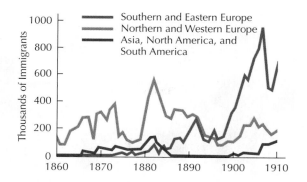

Immigration, 1860–1910

In this graph, Germany is counted as a part of northern and western Europe. Note the new immigration from southern and eastern Europe in the early 1900s.

into the United States was almost unrestricted. Indeed, until 1891 the Atlantic coast states, not the federal government, exercised whatever controls were imposed on newcomers. Even when federally imposed, medical inspection was perfunctory. Public health officials boasted that with "one glance" at each arrival, the inspectors could "take in six details, namely the scalp, face, neck, hands, gait and general condition, both mental and physical." Only those who failed this "test" were examined more closely. On average, only one immigrant in fifty was ultimately rejected.

Private agencies, philanthropic and commercial, served as a link between the new arrivals and employers looking for labor. Until the Foran Act of 1885 outlawed the practice, a few companies brought in skilled workers under contract, advancing them passage money and collecting it in installments from their paychecks, a system somewhat like the indentured servitude of colonial times. Numerous nationality groups assisted (and sometimes exploited) their compatriots by organizing "immigrant banks" that recruited labor in the old country, arranged transportation, and then housed the newcomers in boardinghouses in the United States while finding them jobs. The *padrone* system of the Italians and Greeks was typical. The *padrone,* a sort of contractor who agreed to supply gangs of unskilled workers to companies for a lump sum, usually signed on immigrants unfamiliar with American wage levels at rates that ensured him a healthy profit.

Beginning in the 1880s, the spreading effects of industrialization in Europe caused a shift in the sources of American immigration from northern and western to southern and eastern sections of the Continent. In 1882, 789,000 immigrants entered the United States; more than 350,000 came from Great Britain and Germany, only 32,000 from Italy, and fewer than 17,000 from Russia. In 1907—the all-time peak year, with 1,285,000 immigrants—Great Britain and Germany supplied fewer than half as many as they had 25 years earlier, while Russia and Italy were supplying eleven times as many as then. Up to 1880, only about 200,000 southern and eastern Europeans had migrated to America. Between 1880 and 1910, approximately 8.4 million arrived.

THE "NEW" IMMIGRATION

519

An 1891 cartoon blaming immigrants for the ills of American society: anarchy, socialism, mayhem, and organized crime.

New Immigrants Face New Nativism

The "new" immigrants, like the "old" Irish of the 1840s and 1850s, were mostly peasants. They also seemed more than ordinarily clannish; southern Italians typically called all people outside their families *forestieri,* "foreigners." Old-stock Americans thought them harder to assimilate, and in fact many were. Some Italian immigrants, for example, were unmarried men who had come to the United States to earn enough money to buy a farm back home. Such people made hard and willing workers but were not much concerned with being part of an American community.

These "birds of passage" were a substantial minority, but the immigrant who saved in order to bring his wife and children or his younger brothers and sisters to America was more typical. In addition, thousands of immigrants came as family groups and intended to remain. Some, like the eastern European Jewish migrants, were refugees who were almost desperately eager to become Americans, although of course they retained and nurtured much of their traditional culture.

Many "older" Americans concluded, wrongly but understandably, that the new immigrants were incapable of becoming good citizens and should be kept out. During the 1880s, large numbers of social workers, economists, and church leaders, worried by the problems that arose when so many poor immigrants flocked into cities already bursting at the seams, began to believe that some restriction should be placed on the incoming human tide. The directors of charitable organizations, which bore the burden of aiding the most unfortunate immigrants, complained that their resources were being exhausted by the needs of the flood.

Social Darwinists and people obsessed with pseudoscientific ideas about "racial purity" also found the new immigration alarming. Misunderstanding the findings of the new science of genetics, they attributed the social problems associated with mass immigration to supposed physiological characteristics of the newcomers. Forgetting that earlier Americans had accused pre–Civil War Irish and German immigrants of similar deficiencies, they decided that the peoples of southern and eastern Europe were racially (and therefore permanently) inferior to "Nordic" and "Anglo-Saxon" types and ought to be kept out.

Workers, fearing the competition of people with low living standards and no bargaining power, spoke out against the "enticing of penniless and unapprised immigrants . . . to undermine our wages and social welfare." In 1883 the president of the Amalgamated Iron and Steel Workers told a Senate committee that Hungarian, Polish, Italian, and other immigrants "can live where I think a decent man would die; they can live on . . . food that other men would not touch." A Wisconsin iron worker put it this way: "Immigrants work for almost nothing and seem to be able to live on wind—something I can not do."

After the Exclusion Act of 1882 and the almost meaningless 1885 ban on importing contract labor, no further restrictions were imposed on immigration until the twentieth century. Strong support for a literacy test for admission developed in the 1890s, pushed by a new organization, the Immigration Restriction League. Since there was much more illiteracy in the southeastern quarter of Europe than in the northwestern, such a test would discriminate without seeming to do so on national or racial grounds. A literacy test bill passed both houses of Congress in 1897, but President Cleveland vetoed it. Such a "radical departure" from the "generous and free-handed policy" of the past, Cleveland said, was unjustified. He added, perhaps with tongue in cheek, that a literacy requirement would not keep out "unruly agitators," who were only too adept at reading and writing.

The Expanding City and Its Problems

Americans who favored restricting immigration made much of the fact that so many of the newcomers crowded into the cities, aggravating problems of housing, public health, crime, and immorality. Immigrants concentrated in the cities because the jobs created by expanding industry were located there. So, of course, did native-born Americans; the proportion of urban dwellers had been steadily increasing since about 1820.

Industrialization does not entirely explain the growth of nineteenth-century cities. All the large American cities began as commercial centers, and the development of huge metropolises like New York and Chicago would have been impossible without the national transportation network. But by the final decades of the century, the expansion of industry had become the chief cause of city growth. Thus the urban concentration continued; in 1890 one person in three lived in a city, by 1910 nearly one in two.

Impoverished immigrant families, like the one in this 1889 Jacob Riis photograph, often lived in tiny windowless rooms in crowded tenement districts. Riis devised a "flash bulb" for indoor photographs in poorly illuminated rooms like this one.

A steadily increasing proportion of the urban population was made up of immigrants. In 1890 the foreign-born population of Chicago almost equaled the total population of Chicago in 1880; a third of all Bostonians and a quarter of all Philadelphians were immigrants; and four out of five residents of New York City were either foreign-born or the children of immigrants.

After 1890 the immigrant concentration became even more dense. The migrants from eastern and southern Europe lacked the resources to travel to the agriculturally developing regions (to say nothing of the sums necessary to acquire land and farm equipment). As the concentration progressed it fed upon itself, for all the eastern cities developed many ethnic neighborhoods, in each of which immigrants of one nationality congregated. Lonely, confused, often unable to speak English, the Italians, the Greeks, the Polish and Russian Jews, and other immigrants tended to settle where their predecessors had settled.

Most newcomers intended to become U.S. citizens, to be absorbed in the famous American "melting pot." But they also wanted to maintain their traditional culture. They supported "national" churches and schools. Newspapers in their native languages flourished, as did social organizations of all sorts. Each great American city became a Europe in microcosm. New York City, the great *entrepôt,* had a Little Italy; Polish, Greek, Jewish, and Bohemian quarters; and even a Chinatown.

Observing the immigrants' attachment to "foreign" values and institutions, numbers of "natives" accused the newcomers of resisting Americanization and blamed them for urban problems. The immigrants were involved in these problems, but the rapidity of urban expansion explains the troubles associated with city life far more fully than the high percentage of foreigners.

Teeming Tenements

The cities were suffering from growing pains. Sewer and water facilities frequently could not keep pace with skyrocketing needs. By the 1890s the tremendous growth of Chicago had put such a strain on its sanitation system that the Chicago River had become virtually an open sewer, and the city's drinking water contained such a high concentration of germ-killing chemicals that it tasted like creosote. In the 1880s all the sewers of Baltimore emptied into the sluggish Back Basin, and according to the journalist H. L. Mencken, every summer the city smelled "like a billion polecats." Fire protection became less and less adequate; garbage piled up in the streets faster than it could be carted away; and the streets themselves crumbled beneath the pounding of heavy traffic. Urban growth proceeded with such speed that new streets were laid out more rapidly than they could be paved. Chicago had more than 1,400 miles of dirt streets in 1890.

People poured into the great cities faster than housing could be built to accommodate them. The influx into areas already densely packed in the 1840s became unbearable as rising property values and the absence of zoning laws conspired to make builders use every possible foot of space, squeezing out light and air ruthlessly in order to wedge in a few additional family units.

Substandard living quarters aggravated other evils such as disease and the disintegration of family life, with its attendant mental anguish, crime, and juvenile delinquency. The bloody New York City riots of 1863, though sparked by dislike of the Civil War draft and of blacks, reflected the bitterness and frustration of thousands jammed together amid filth and threatened by disease. A citizens' committee seeking to discover the causes of the riots expressed its amazement after visiting the slums "that so much misery, disease, and wretchedness can be huddled together and hidden . . . unvisited and unthought of, so near our own abodes."

New York City created a Metropolitan Health Board in 1866, and a state tenement house law the following year made a feeble beginning at regulating city housing. Another law in 1879 placed a limit on the percentage of lot space that could be covered by new construction and established minimal standards of plumbing and ventilation. The magazine *Plumber and Sanitary Engineer* sponsored a contest to pick the best design for a tenement that met these specifications. The winner of the competition was James E. Ware, whose plan for a "dumbbell" apartment house managed to crowd from twenty-four to thirty-two four-room apartments on a plot of ground only 25 by 100 feet.

Despite these efforts in 1890 more than 1.4 million persons were living on Manhattan Island, and in some sections the population density exceeded 900 persons per acre. The unhealthiness of the tenements was notorious. No one knows

DID IMMIGRANTS ASSIMILATE?

In this 1909 photograph, immigrant children at Ellis Island hold American flags as they share a ride in an "Uncle Sam" wagon. Did they and their parents readily adjust to life in the United States?

In 1951 historian Oscar Handlin thought not. He asserted that immigrants were "uprooted" from the lives they had known and "replanted" in "strange ground, among strangers, where strange manners prevailed." Many were shattered by the experience, which accounted for rampant crime, ruptured families, and social disorder in tenement districts.

But subsequent studies found that many immigrants adapted well. John Bodnar (1985) pointedly described immigrants as "transplanted" rather than "uprooted." When challenged by new situations, they "forged a culture, a constellation of behavioral and thought patterns which would offer them explanations, order, and a prescription for how to live with their lives." Sometimes they modified traditional institutions to serve new purposes; sometimes they created new ones, such as ethnic clubs and parochial schools. The diversity of immigrant experi-

ences was reflected in the *Harvard Encyclopedia of American Ethnic Groups* (1980), edited by Handlin and Stephen Thernstrom. The trend toward specialized studies of different groups prompted Arthur M. Schlesinger Jr. (1992) to bemoan his profession's role in the "disuniting of America."

In short, each child in "Uncle Sam's" wagon experienced life in his or her own way; but they were in for the ride together.

Oscar Handlin, *The Uprooted*, 1951, John Bodnar, *The Transplanted* (1985), Arthur M. Schlesinger Jr., *The Disuniting of America* (1992). Other studies anticipating Bodnar's thesis are Francis G. Courvares, *The Remaking of Pittsburgh* (1984), Humbert S. Nelli, *Italians in Chicago* (1970), Alan Dawley, *Class and Community* (1976), and Virginia Yans-McLaughlin, *Family and Community: Italian Immigrants in Buffalo* (1977). Ronald Takaki, *A Different Mirror* (1993) endorses the multiculturalist approach. See also Roger Daniels, *Guarding the Golden Door: American Immigration Policy and Immigrants since 1882* (2004).

exactly, but as late as 1900 about three quarters of the residents of New York City's Lower East Side lacked indoor toilets and had to use backyard outhouses to relieve themselves. One noxious corner became known as the "lung block" because of the prevalence of tuberculosis among its inhabitants. In 1900 three out of five babies born in one poor district of Chicago died before their first birthday.

Slums bred criminals—the wonder was that they did not breed more. They also drove well-to-do residents into exclusive sections and to the suburbs. From Boston's Beacon Hill and Back Bay to San Francisco's Nob Hill, the rich retired into their cluttered mansions and ignored conditions in the poorer parts of town.

The Cities Modernize

As American cities grew larger and more crowded, thereby aggravating a host of social problems, practical forces operated to bring about improvements. Once the relationship between polluted water and disease was fully understood, everyone saw the need for decent water and sewage systems. While some businessmen profited from corrupt dealings with the city machines, more of them wanted efficient and honest government in order to reduce their tax bills. City dwellers of all classes resented dirt, noise, and ugliness, and in many communities public-spirited groups formed societies to plant trees, clean up littered areas, and develop recreational facilities. When one city undertook improvements, others tended to follow suit, spurred on by local pride and the booster spirit.

Gradually the basic facilities of urban living were improved. Streets were paved, first with cobblestones and wood blocks and then with smoother, quieter asphalt. Gaslight, then electric arc lights, and finally Edison's incandescent lamps brightened the cities after dark, making law enforcement easier, stimulating night life, and permitting factories and shops to operate after sunset.

Urban transportation underwent enormous changes. Until the 1880s, horse-drawn cars running on tracks set flush with the street were the main means of urban public transportation. In 1860 New York City's horsecars were carrying about 100,000 passengers a day. But horsecars had serious drawbacks. Enormous numbers of horses were needed, and feeding and stabling the animals was costly. Their droppings (10 pounds per day per horse) became a major source of urban pollution. That is why the invention of the electric trolley car in the 1880s put an end to horsecar transportation. Trolleys were cheaper and less unsightly than horsecars and quieter than steam-powered trains.

A retired naval officer, Frank J. Sprague, installed the first practical electric trolley line in Richmond, Virginia, in 1887–1888. At once other cities seized on the trolley. Lines soon radiated outward from the city centers, bringing commuters and shoppers from the residential districts to the business district. Without them the big-city department stores could not have flourished as they did. By 1895 some 850 lines were busily hauling city dwellers over 10,000 miles of track, and mileage tripled in the following decade. As with other new enterprises, ownership of street railways quickly became centralized until a few big operators controlled the trolleys of more than 100 eastern cities and towns.

Streetcars changed the character of big-city life. Before their introduction urban communities were limited by the distances people could conveniently walk to work. The "walking city" could not easily extend more than 2½ miles from its center. Streetcars increased this radius to 6 miles or more, which meant that the area of the city expanded enormously. Dramatic population shifts resulted as the better-off moved away from the center in search of air and space, abandoning the crumbling, jam-packed older neighborhoods to the poor. Thus economic segregation speeded the growth of ghettos. Older peripheral towns that had maintained some of the self-contained qualities of village life were swallowed up, becoming metropolitan centers.

As time passed, each new area, originally peopled by rising economic groups, tended to become crowded and then to deteriorate. By extending their tracks beyond the developed areas, the streetcar companies further speeded suburban growth because they assured developers, bankers, builders, and middle-class home buyers of efficient transport to the center of town. By keeping fares low (5 cents a ride was standard) the lines enabled poor people to "escape" to the countryside on holidays.

Advances in bridge design, notably the perfection of the steel-cable suspension bridge by John A. Roebling, aided the ebb and flow of metropolitan populations. The Brooklyn Bridge described by a poet as "a weird metallic Apparition . . . the cables, like divine messages from above . . . cutting and dividing into innumerable musical spaces the nude immensity of the sky," was Roebling's triumph. Completed in 1883 at a cost of $15 million, it was soon carrying more than 33 million passengers a year over the East River between Manhattan and Brooklyn.

Efforts to relieve the congestion in slum districts made little headway. In Brooklyn Alfred T. White established Home Buildings, a 40-family model tenement in 1877; eventually he expanded the experiment to include 267 apartments. Each unit had plenty of light and air and contained its own sink and toilet. Ellen Collins developed a smaller project in Manhattan's Fourth Ward in the 1890s. These model tenements were self-sustaining, but of necessity they yielded only modest returns. The landlords were essentially philanthropists; their work had no significant impact on urban housing in the nineteenth century.

Leisure Activities: More Fun and Games

By bringing together large numbers of people, cities made possible many kinds of social activity difficult or impossible to maintain in rural areas. Cities remained unsurpassed as centers of artistic and intellectual life. New York was the outstanding example, as seen in its many theaters and in the founding of the American Museum of Natural History (1870), the Metropolitan Museum of Art (1870), and the Metropolitan Opera (1883), but other cities were equally hospitable to such endeav-

On Sundays in the late nineteenth century, city people crowded into streetcars and thronged to the countryside. Enticed by this taste of bucolic splendor, many chose to live in the suburbs and take the streetcars to work downtown. Soon the population density of the suburbs resembled that of the cities.

ors. Boston's Museum of Fine Arts, for example, was founded in 1870 and the Boston Symphony in 1881.

Of course less sophisticated forms of recreation also flourished in the urban environment. From 1865 to 1885 the number of breweries in Massachusetts quadrupled. It is only a slight exaggeration to say that in crowded urban centers there was a saloon on every corner; during the last third of the century the number of saloons in the country tripled. Saloons were strictly male working-class institutions, usually decorated with pictures and other mementos of sports heroes, the bar perhaps under the charge of a retired pugilist.

For workingmen the saloon was a kind of club, a place to meet friends, exchange news and gossip, gamble, and eat, as well as to drink beer and whiskey. Saloons also flourished because factory owners and other employers of large numbers of workers tended to forbid the consumption of alcohol on their premises. In addition, the gradual reduction of the workday left men with more free time, which may explain why vaudeville and burlesques, the latter described by one straightlaced critic as a "disgraceful spectacle of padded legs juggling and tight-laced wriggling," also proliferated.

Calvinist-inspired opposition to sports as a frivolous waste of valuable time was steadily evaporating, replaced among the upper and middle classes by the realization that games like golf and tennis were "healthy occupation[s] for mind and body." Bicycling became a fad, both as a means of getting from place to place in the ever-expanding cities and as a form of exercise and recreation.

Many of the new streetcar companies built picnic grounds and amusement parks at their outer limits. In good weather thousands seeking to relax after a hard day's work flocked to these "trolley parks" to enjoy a fresh-air meal or patronize the shooting galleries, merry-go-rounds, and "freak shows."

The postwar era also saw the first important development of spectator sports, again because cities provided the concentrations of population necessary to support them. Curious relationships developed between upper- and working-class interests and between competitive sports as pure enjoyment for players and spectators and sports as something to bet on. Horse racing had strictly upper-class origins, but racetracks attracted huge crowds of ordinary people more intent on picking a winner than on improving the breed.

Professional boxing offers an even better example. It was in a sense a hobby of the rich, who sponsored favorite gladiators, offered prizes, and often wagered large sums on the matches. But the audiences were made up overwhelmingly of young working-class males, from whose ranks most of the fighters emerged. The gambling and also the brutality of the bloody, bare-knuckle character of the fights caused many communities to outlaw boxing, a fact that added to the appeal of the sport for some.

The first widely popular pugilist was the legendary "Boston Strong Boy," John L. Sullivan, who became heavyweight champion in 1882 by disposing of one Paddy Ryan in nine rounds. Sullivan was an immensely powerful man whose idea of fighting, according to his biographer, "was simply to hammer his opponent into unconsciousness," something he did repeatedly during his ten-year reign. Sullivan became an international celebrity and made and lost large sums during this period. He was also the beneficiary of patronage in such forms as a diamond belt worth $10,000 presented to him by some of his admirers. Yet boxing remained a raffish, clandestine occupation. One of Sullivan's important fights took place in France, on the estate of Baron Rothschild, yet when it ended both he and his opponent were arrested.

Three major team games—baseball, football, and basketball—developed in something approaching their modern form during the last quarter of the century. Various forms of what became baseball were played long before that time. Organized teams, in most cases made up of upper-class amateurs, first emerged in the 1840s, but the game only became truly popular during the Civil War, when it was a major form of camp recreation for the troops.

After the war professional teams began to appear (the first, the Cincinnati Red Stockings, paid players between $800 and $1,400 for the season), and in 1876 teams in eight cities formed the National League. The American League followed in 1901. After a brief period of rivalry, the two leagues made peace in 1903, the year of the first World Series.

Organized play led to codification of the rules and improvements in technique and strategy, for example, the development of "minor" leagues; impartial umpires calling balls and strikes and ruling on close plays; the use of catcher's masks and

Luna Park at Coney Island was a vast living theater, in which the strollers were both spectators and actors. At night, a quarter million electric lights turned Luna Park into what its designer, Frederic Thompson, called "a different world—a dream world, perhaps a nightmare world—where all is bizarre and fantastic."

padded gloves; the invention of various kinds of curves and other erratic pitches (often enhanced by "doctoring" the ball). As early as the 1870s, baseball was being called "the national game" and losing all upper-class connotations. Important games attracted crowds in the tens of thousands; betting became a problem. Despite its urban origins, its broad green fields and dusty base paths gave the game a rural character that only recently has begun to fade away.

Nobody "invented" baseball, but both football and basketball owe their present form to individuals. James Naismith's invention of basketball is undisputed. In 1891, while a student at a YMCA school, he attached peach baskets to the edge of an elevated running track in the gymnasium and drew up what are still the basic rules of the game. The first basketball was a soccer ball. The game was popular from the start, but because it was played indoors it was not an important spectator sport until much later.

Football was not created by one person in the way that basketball was; it evolved out of English rugby. For many decades it remained almost entirely a college sport (and thus played almost entirely by upper- and middle-class types). Organized collegiate sports dated back to before the Civil War; the first intercollegiate matches were rowing races between Harvard and Yale students. The first intercollege football game occurred when Princeton defeated Rutgers in 1869, and by the 1880s college football had become extremely popular.

Spectator sports had little appeal to women at this time and indeed for decades thereafter. And few women participated in organized athletics. Sports were "manly" activities; a woman might ride a bicycle, play croquet and perhaps a little tennis, but to display any concentrated interest in excelling in a sport was considered unfeminine.

Christianity's Conscience and the Social Gospel

The modernization of the great cities was not solving most of the social problems of the slums. As this fact became clear, a number of urban religious leaders began to take a hard look at the situation. Traditionally, American churchmen had insisted that where sin was concerned there were no extenuating circumstances. To the well-to-do they preached the virtues of thrift and hard work; to the poor they extended the possibility of a better existence in the next world; to all they stressed one's responsibility for one's own behavior—and thus for one's own salvation. Such a point of view brought meager comfort to residents of slums. Consequently, the churches lost influence in the poorer sections. Furthermore, as better-off citizens followed the streetcar lines out from the city centers, their church leaders followed them.

An increasing proportion of the residents of the blighted districts were Catholics, and the Roman church devoted much effort to distributing alms, maintaining homes for orphans and old people, and other forms of social welfare. But church leaders seemed unconcerned with the social causes of the blight; they were deeply committed to the idea that sin and vice were personal, poverty an act of God. They deplored the rising tide of crime, disease, and destitution among their coreligionists, yet they failed to see the connection between these evils and the squalor of the slums. "Intemperance is the great evil we have to overcome," wrote the president of the leading Catholic charitable organization, the Society of St. Vincent de Paul. "It is the source of the misery for at least three-fourths of the families we are called upon to visit and relieve."

The conservatism of most Protestant and Catholic clergymen did not prevent some earnest preachers from working directly to improve the lot of the city poor. Some followed the path blazed by Dwight L. Moody, a lay evangelist who became famous throughout America and Great Britain in the 1870s. A gargantuan figure weighing nearly 300 pounds, Moody conducted a vigorous campaign to persuade the denizens of the slums to cast aside their sinful ways. He went among them full of enthusiasm and God's love and made an impact no less powerful than that of George Whitefield during the Great Awakening of the eighteenth century or Charles Grandison Finney in the first part of the nineteenth. The evangelists founded mission schools in the slums and tried to provide spiritual and recreational facilities for the unfortunate. They were prominent in the establishment of American branches of the YMCA (1851) and the Salvation Army (1880).

However, many evangelists paid little heed to the causes of urban poverty and vice, believing that faith in God would enable the poor to transcend the material difficulties of life. For a number of Protestant clergymen who had become familiar with the slums, a different approach seemed called for. Slum conditions caused the sins and crimes of the cities; the wretched human beings who committed them could not be blamed, these ministers argued. They began to preach a "Social Gospel" that focused on improving living conditions rather than on saving souls. If people were to lead pure lives, they must have enough to eat, decent homes, and opportunities to develop their talents. Social Gospelers advocated civil service reform, child labor legislation, regulation of big corporations, and heavy taxes on incomes and inheritances.

The most influential preacher of the Social Gospel was probably Washington Gladden. At first, Gladden, who was raised on a Massachusetts farm, had opposed all government interference in social and economic affairs, but his experiences as a minister in Springfield, Massachusetts, and Columbus, Ohio, exposed him to the realities of life in industrial cities, and his views changed. In *Applied Christianity* (1886) and in other works he defended labor's right to organize and strike and denounced the idea that supply and demand should control wage rates. He favored factory inspection laws, strict regulation of public utilities, and other reforms.

Gladden never questioned the basic values of capitalism. But by the 1890s a number of ministers had gone all the way to socialism. The Reverend William D. P. Bliss of Boston, for example, believed in the kind of welfare state envisioned by Edward Bellamy in *Looking Backward*. He founded the Society of Christian Socialists (1889) and edited a radical journal, *The Dawn*. In addition to nationalizing industry, Bliss and other Christian Socialists advocated government unemployment relief programs, public housing and slum clearance projects, and other measures designed to aid the city poor.

Nothing so well reveals the receptivity of the public to the Social Gospel as the popularity of Charles M. Sheldon's novel *In His Steps* (1896), one of America's all-time best-sellers. Sheldon, a minister in Topeka, Kansas, described what happened in the mythical city of Raymond when a group of leading citizens decided to live truly Christian lives, asking themselves "What would Jesus do?" before adopting any course of action. Naturally the tone of Raymond's society was immensely improved, but basic social reforms followed quickly. The Rectangle, a terrible slum area, "too dirty, too coarse, too sinful, too awful for close contact," became the center of a great reform effort. One of Raymond's "leading society heiresses" undertook a slum clearance project, and a concerted attack was made on drunkenness and immorality. The moral regeneration of the entire community was soon accomplished.

The Settlement Houses

Although millions read *In His Steps*, its effect, and that of other Social Gospel literature, was merely inspirational. On the practical level, a number of earnest souls began to grapple with slum problems by organizing what were known as settlement houses. These were community centers located in poor districts that provided guidance and

This portrait of Jane Addams was completed in 1896 by Alice Kellog Tyler, who worked as an artist at Hull House.

services to all who would use them. The settlement workers, most of them idealistic, well-to-do young people, lived in the houses and were active in neighborhood affairs.

The prototype of the settlement house was London's Toynbee Hall, founded in the early 1880s; the first American example was the Neighborhood Guild, opened on the Lower East Side of New York in 1886 by Dr. Stanton Coit. By the turn of the century 100 had been established, the most famous being Jane Addams's Hull House in Chicago (1889), Robert A. Woods's South End House in Boston (1892), and Lillian Wald's Henry Street Settlement in New York (1893).

While some men were active in the movement, the most important settlement house workers were women fresh from college—the first generation of young women to experience the trauma of having developed their capacities only to find that society offered them few opportunities to use them. The settlements provided an outlet for their hopes and energies, and they seized upon the work avidly.

The settlement workers tried to interpret American ways to the new immigrants and to create a community spirit in order to teach, in the words of one of them, "right living through social relations." Unlike most charity workers, who acted out of a sense of upper-class responsibility toward the unfortunate, they expected to benefit morally and intellectually themselves by experiencing a way of life far different from their own and by obtaining "the first-hand knowledge the college classroom cannot give."

In Boston Robert A. Woods organized clubs to get the youngsters of the South End off the streets, helped establish a restaurant where a meal could be had for 5 cents, acted as an arbitrator in labor disputes, and lobbied for laws tightening up the franchises of public utility companies. In Chicago Jane Addams developed an outstanding cultural program that included classes in music and art and an excellent "little theater" group. Hull House soon boasted a gymnasium, a day nursery, and several social clubs. Addams also worked tirelessly and effectively for improved public services and for social legislation of all kinds. She even got herself appointed garbage inspector in her ward and hounded local landlords and the garbage contractor until something approaching decent service was established.

A few critics considered the settlement houses mere devices to socialize the unruly poor by teaching them the "punctilios of upper-class propriety," but almost everyone appreciated their virtues. By the end of the century the Catholics, laggard in entering the arena of practical social reform, were joining the movement, partly because they were losing many communicants to socially minded Protestant churches. The first Catholic-run settlement house was founded in 1898 in an Italian district of New York. Two years later Brownson House in Los Angeles, catering chiefly to Mexican immigrants, threw open its doors.

With all their accomplishments, the settlement houses seemed to be fighting a losing battle. "Private beneficence," Jane Addams wrote of Hull House, "is totally inadequate to deal with the vast numbers of the city's disinherited." Much as a tropical forest grows faster than a handful of men armed with machetes can cut it down, so the slums, fed by an annual influx of hundreds of thousands, blighted new areas more rapidly than settlement house workers could clean up old ones. It became increasingly apparent that the wealth and authority of the state must be brought to bear in order to keep abreast of the problem.

Civilization and Its Discontents

As the nineteenth century died, the majority of the American people, especially those comfortably well-off, the residents of small towns, the shopkeepers, and some farmers and skilled workers, remained confirmed optimists and uncritical admirers of their civilization. However, blacks, immigrants, and others who failed to share equitably in the good things of life, along with a growing number of humanitarian reformers, found little to cheer about and much to lament in their increasingly industrialized society. Giant monopolies flourished despite federal restrictions. The gap between rich and poor appeared to be widening, while the slum spread its poison and the materially successful made a god of their success. Human values seemed in grave danger of being crushed by impersonal forces typified by the great corporations.

In 1871 Walt Whitman, usually so full of extravagant praise for everything American, had called his fellow countrymen the "most materialistic and money-making people ever known":

> I say we had best look our times and lands searchingly in the face, like a physician diagnosing some deep disease. Never was there, perhaps, more hollowness of heart than at present, and here in the United States.

Harvard professor Henry Adams was critical of the way his contemporaries had become moneygrubbers. "All one's friends," he complained, along with church and university leaders and other educated people, "had joined the banks to force submission to capitalism."

Of course intellectuals often tend to be critical of the world they live in, whatever its nature; Thoreau denounced materialism and the worship of progress in the 1840s as vigorously as any late nineteenth-century prophet of gloom. But the voices of the dissatisfied were rising. Despite the many benefits that industrialization had made possible, it was by no means clear around 1900 that the American people were really better off under the new dispensation.

That the United States was fast becoming a modern nation no one disputed. Physician George M. Beard contended that "modern civilization" overloaded the human nervous system the way burning too many of Thomas Edison's lightbulbs overloaded an electrical circuit. On the other hand, Edward Bellamy saw the future as a "paradise of order, equity, and felicity." Most Americans took a more balanced view, believing that the modern world encompassed new possibilities as well as perils. The future beckoned, and yet it also menaced.

Milestones

1858	English launch transatlantic liner *Great Eastern*
1870	Metropolitan Museum of Art and American Museum of Natural History open in New York City
1876	Eight teams form National Baseball League
1880	American branch of Salvation Army is founded
1880s	"New" immigration begins
1882	John L. Sullivan wins heavyweight boxing championship
	Exclusion Act bans Chinese immigrants
1883	Roebling completes Brooklyn Bridge
1885	Foran Act outlaws importing contract skilled labor
1888	Richmond, Virginia, opens first urban electric streetcar system
1889	Jane Addams founds Hull House
1896	Charles M. Sheldon asks "What would Jesus do?" in best-selling *In His Steps*
1897	Cleveland vetoes Congress's literacy test bill

CHAPTER 19

Intellectual and Cultural Trends

IN JANUARY 2007, THE UNIVERSITY OF ALABAMA HIRED NICK SABAN, formerly coach of the Miami Dolphins, as head football coach. Saban would receive $32 million over eight years, a salary eight times greater than the president of the University of Alabama, who earned $500,000 a year. In fact, the average annual salary of the 119 coaches of Division 1-A college football was nearly $1 million, more than that of only a handful of university presidents.

This dismayed many. "The message to the athletes," observed Peter Roby, former basketball coach at Harvard, "is that [the universities] are willing to do anything in order to win." Such words echoed the phrase that Vince Lombardi, legendary football coach of the Green Bay Packers, made famous: "Winning isn't everything: it's the only thing."

This insistence on winning football originated in the late nineteenth century. At that time, a few colleges paid coaches, recruited star prep school athletes, and charged spectators to watch the games. Action became faster and rougher. Soon the spectacle attracted huge audiences. Action often got out of hand and, lacking satisfactory protective equipment, many football players sustained serious injuries; each year, some were killed.

In 1892, William Rainey Harper, president of the University of Chicago, defended the high cost of winning football. "If the world can afford to sacrifice lives for commercial gain"—a reference to the victims of industrial accidents—"it can more easily afford to make similar sacrifices on the altar of vigorous and unsullied manhood." In 1896 Massachusetts Senator Henry Cabot Lodge told Harvard students that "the injuries incurred on the playing-field are part of the price which the English-speaking race has paid for being world-conquerors."

The rise of football in the 1890s symbolized a profound transformation in cultural and intellectual life. The religious sensibilities and gentlemanly precepts of an earlier age were yielding to a tougher mind-set. Life was a struggle, Darwin had proclaimed, in which the fittest prevailed and the losers vanished. Power trounced sentiment. Ideas were valuable not because they espoused truths or evinced beauty, but because they could leave a mark on the world. Art and literature functioned not to transcend life or prettify it but to lay bare its grim reality. This stern ethos unsettled many but also invigorated those who yearned to confront the world as it was.

Colleges and Universities

Industrialization altered the way Americans thought at the same time that it transformed their ways of making a living. Technological advances revolutionized the communication of ideas more drastically than they did the transportation of goods or the manufacture of steel. The materialism that permeated American attitudes toward business also affected contemporary education and literature, while Charles Darwin's theory of evolution influenced American philosophers, lawyers, and historians profoundly. This was especially true of the nation's institutions of higher education.

Between 1878 and 1898, the number of colleges rose from about 350 to 500, and the student body roughly tripled. Despite this growth, less than 2 percent of the college-age population attended college, but the aspirations of the nation's youth were rising, and more and more parents had the financial means necessary for fulfilling them.

More significant than the expansion of the colleges were the alterations in their curricula and in the atmosphere permeating the average campus. In 1870 most colleges remained what they had been in the 1830s: small, limited in their offerings, intellectually stagnant. The ill-paid professors were seldom scholars of stature. Thereafter, change came like a flood tide. State universities proliferated; the federal government's land-grant program in support of training in "agriculture and the mechanic arts," established under the Morrill Act of 1862, came into its own; wealthy philanthropists poured fortunes into old institutions and founded new ones; educators introduced new courses and adopted new teaching methods; professional schools of law, medicine, education, business, journalism, and other specialties increased in number.

In the forefront of reform was Harvard, the oldest and most prestigious college in the country. In the 1860s it possessed an excellent faculty, but teaching methods were antiquated and the curriculum had remained almost unchanged since the colonial period. In 1869, however, a dynamic president, the chemist Charles W. Eliot, undertook a transformation of the college. Eliot introduced the elective system, gradually eliminating required courses and expanding offerings in such areas as modern languages, economics, and the laboratory sciences. For the first time, students were allowed to borrow books from the library!

An even more important development in higher education was the founding of Johns Hopkins in 1876. This university was one of many established in the period by wealthy industrialists; its benefactor, the Baltimore merchant Johns Hopkins, had made his fortune in the Baltimore and Ohio Railroad. Its distinctiveness, however, was due to the vision of Daniel Coit Gilman, its first president.

Gilman modeled Johns Hopkins on the German universities, where meticulous research and freedom of inquiry were the guiding principles. In staffing the institution, he sought scholars of the highest reputation, scouring Europe as well as America in his search for talent and offering outstanding men high salaries for that time—up to $5,000 for a professor, roughly ten times the income of a skilled artisan. Johns Hopkins specialized in graduate education. In the generation after its founding, it turned out a remarkable percentage of the most important scholars in the nation, including Woodrow Wilson in political science, John Dewey in philosophy, Frederick Jackson Turner in history, and John R. Commons in economics.

The example of Johns Hopkins encouraged other wealthy individuals to endow universities offering advanced work. Clark University in Worcester, Massachusetts, founded by Jonas Clark, a merchant and real estate speculator, opened its doors in 1889. Its president, G. Stanley Hall, had been a professor of psychology at Hopkins, and he built the new university in that institution's image. More important was John D. Rockefeller's creation, the University of Chicago (1892), whose first president, William Rainey Harper, was a brilliant biblical scholar—he received his Ph.D. from Yale at the age of 18—an imaginative administrator, and a

Gilman Hall, the first academic building at Johns Hopkins University; it remains a hub of student life.

Advances in women's higher education opened up new fields of study for women. Here, a group of Smith College students with picks and hammers sets out for a geology field trip in the 1880s.

football enthusiast, as noted at the outset of this chapter. The new university, he told Rockefeller, should be designed "with the example of Johns Hopkins before our eyes." Chicago soon offered first-class graduate and undergraduate education. During its first year there were 120 instructors for fewer than 600 students, and despite fears that the mighty tycoon Rockefeller would force his social and economic views on the institution, academic freedom was the rule.

State and federal aid to higher education expanded rapidly. The Morrill Act, granting land to each state at a rate of 30,000 acres for each senator and representative, provided the endowments that gave many important modern universities, such as Illinois, Michigan State, and Ohio State, their start. While the federal assistance was earmarked for specific subjects, the land-grant colleges offered a full range of courses, and all received additional state funds. The land-grant universities adopted new ideas quickly. They were coeducational from the start, and most developed professional schools and experimented with extension work and summer programs.

Typical of the better state institutions was the University of Michigan, which reached the top rank among the nation's universities during the presidency of James B. Angell (1871–1909). Like Eliot at Harvard, Angell expanded the undergraduate curriculum and strengthened the law and medical schools. He encouraged graduate studies, seeking to make Michigan "part of the great world of scholars," and sought ways in which the university could serve the general community.

Important advances were made in women's higher education. Beginning with Vassar College, which opened its doors to 300 women students in 1865, the opportunity for young women to pursue serious academic work gradually expanded. Wellesley and Smith, both founded in 1875, completed the so-called Big Three women's colleges. Together with the already established Mount Holyoke, and with Bryn Mawr (1885), Barnard (1889), and Radcliffe (1893), they became known as the Seven Sisters.

The only professional careers easily available to women were nursing, teaching, and the new area called social work. Nevertheless, the remarkable women that these institutions trained were conscious of their uniqueness and determined to demonstrate their capabilities. They provided most of the leaders of the early twentieth-century drive for equal rights for women.

Not all the changes in higher education were beneficial. The elective system led to superficiality; students gained a smattering of knowledge of many subjects and mastered none. For example, 55 percent of the Harvard class of 1898 took elementary courses and no others during their four years of study. Intensive graduate work often produced narrowness of outlook and research monographs on trivial subjects. Attempts to apply the scientific method in fields such as history and economics often enticed students into making smug (and preposterous) claims to objectivity and definitiveness.

The gifts of rich industrialists sometimes came with strings, and college boards of trustees tended to be dominated by businessmen who sometimes attempted to impose their own social and economic beliefs on faculty members. Although few professors lost their positions because their views offended trustees, at many institutions trustees exerted constant nagging pressures that limited academic freedom and scholarly objectivity. At state colleges, politicians often interfered in academic affairs, even treating professorships as part of the patronage system.

Thorstein Veblen pointed out in his caustic study *The Higher Learning in America* (1918) that "the intrusion of businesslike ideals, aims and methods" harmed the universities in countless subtle ways. Size alone—the verbose Veblen called it "an executive weakness for spectacular magnitude"—became an end in itself, and the practical values of education were exalted over the humanistic. When universities grew bigger, administration became more complicated and the prestige of administrators rose inordinately. At many institutions professors came to be regarded as mere employees of the governing boards. In 1893 the members of the faculty of Stanford University were officially classified as personal servants of Mrs. Leland Stanford, widow of the founder. This was done in good cause—the Stanford estate was tied up in probate court and the ruling made it possible to pay professors out of Mrs. Stanford's allowance for household expenses—but that such a procedure was even conceivable must have appalled the scholarly world.

Thus higher education reflected American values, with all their strengths and weaknesses. A complex society required a more professional and specialized education for its youth; the coarseness and the rampant materialism and competitiveness of the era inevitably found expression in the colleges and universities.

Revolution in the Social Sciences

In the social sciences a close connection existed between the practical issues of the age and the achievements of the leading thinkers. The application of the theory of evolution to every aspect of human relations, the impact of industrialization on

CHAPTER 19 INTELLECTUAL AND CULTURAL TRENDS

540

society—such topics were of intense concern to American economists, sociologists, and historians. An understanding of Darwin increased the already strong interest in studying the development of institutions and their interactions with one another. Controversies over trusts, slum conditions, and other problems drew scholars out of their towers and into practical affairs.

Social scientists were impressed by the progress being made in the physical and biological sciences. They eagerly applied the scientific method to their own specialties, hoping thereby to arrive at objective truths in fields that by nature were essentially subjective.

Among the economists something approaching a revolution took place in the 1880s. The classical school, which maintained that immutable natural laws governed all human behavior and which used the insights of Darwin only to justify unrestrained competition and laissez-faire, was challenged by a group of young economists who argued that as times changed, economic theories and laws must be modified in order to remain relevant. Richard T. Ely, another of the scholars who made Johns Hopkins a font of new ideas in the 1880s, summarized the thinking of this group in 1885. "The state [is] an educational and ethical agency whose positive aid is an indispensable condition of human progress," Ely proclaimed. Laissez-faire was outmoded and dangerous. Economic problems were basically moral problems; their solution required "the united efforts of Church, state and science." The proper way to study these problems was by analyzing actual conditions, not by applying abstract laws or principles.

A similar revolution struck sociology in the mid-1880s. Prevailing opinion up to that time rejected the idea of government interference with the organization of society. The influence of the English social Darwinist Herbert Spencer, who objected even to public schools and the postal system, was immense. Spencer and his American disciples, among them Edward L. Youmans, editor of *Popular Science Monthly*, twisted the ideas of Darwin to mean that society could be changed only by the force of evolution, which moved with cosmic slowness. "You and I can do nothing at all," Youmans told the reformer Henry George. "It's all a matter of evolution. Perhaps in four or five thousand years evolution may have carried men beyond this state of things."

Progressive Education

Traditionally, American teachers had emphasized the three Rs and relied on strict discipline and rote learning. Typical of the pedagogues of the period was the Chicago teacher, described by a reformer in the 1890s, who told her students firmly: "Don't stop to think, tell me what you know!" Yet new ideas were attracting attention. According to a German educator, Johann Friedrich Herbart, teachers could best arouse the interest of their students by relating new information to what they already knew; good teaching called for professional training, psychological insight, enthusiasm, and imagination, not merely facts and a birch rod. At the same time, evolutionists were pressing for a kind of education that would help children to "survive" by adapting to the demands of their rapidly changing urban environment.

Forward-looking educators seized on these ideas because dynamic social changes were making the old system increasingly inadequate. Settlement house workers discovered that slum children needed training in handicrafts, good citizenship, and personal hygiene as much as in reading and writing. They were appalled by the local schools, which suffered from the same diseases—filth, overcrowding, rickety construction—that plagued the tenements, and by school systems that were controlled by machine politicians who doled out teaching positions to party hacks and other untrained persons. They argued that school playgrounds, nurseries, kindergartens, and adult education programs were essential in communities where most women worked and many people lacked much formal education. "We are impatient with the schools which lay all stress on reading and writing," Jane Addams declared. This type of education "fails to give the child any clew to the life about him." The philosopher who summarized and gave direction to these forces was John Dewey, a professor at the University of Chicago. Dewey was concerned with the implications of evolution—indeed, of all science—for education.

"Education," Dewey insisted in *The School and Society* (1899), a work in which he described and defended his theories, was "the fundamental method of social progress and reform." To seek to improve conditions merely by passing laws was "futile." Moreover, in an industrial society the family no longer performed many of the educational functions it had carried out in an agrarian society. Farm children learn about nature, about work, about human character in countless ways denied to children in cities. The school can fill the gap by becoming "an embryonic community . . . with types of occupations that reflect the life of the larger society." At the same time, education should center on the child, and new information should be related to what the child already knows. Children's imagination, energy, and curiosity are tools for broadening their outlook and increasing their store of information. Finally, the school should become an instrument for social reform, "saturating [the child] with the spirit of service" and helping to produce a "society which is worthy, lovely, and harmonious." Education, in other words, ought to build character and teach good citizenship as well as transmit knowledge.

The School and Society created a stir, and Dewey immediately assumed leadership of what in the next generation was called progressive education. Although the gains made in public education before 1900 were more quantitative than qualitative and the philosophy dominant in most schools was not very different at the end of the century from that prevailing in Horace Mann's day, change was in the air. The best educators of the period were full of optimism, convinced that the future was theirs.

History

Evolution, too, influenced the study of history. Many scholars of the origins and evolution of political institutions concluded, after much "scientific" study of old charters and law codes, that the roots of democracy were to be found in the customs of the ancient tribes of northern Europe. This theory of the "Teutonic origins" of democracy, which has since been thoroughly discredited, fitted well with the prejudices of people of British stock, and it provided ammunition for those who favored restricting immigration and for those who argued that blacks were inferior beings.

Out of this work, however, came an essentially democratic concept, the frontier thesis of Frederick Jackson Turner, still another scholar trained at Johns Hopkins. Turner's essay "The Significance of the Frontier in American History" (1893) argued that the frontier experience, through which every section of the country had passed, had affected the thinking of the people and the shape of American institutions. The isolation of the frontier and the need during each successive westward advance to create civilization anew, Turner wrote, account for the individualism of Americans and the democratic character of their society. Nearly everything unique in our culture could be traced to the existence of the frontier, he claimed.

Turner, and still more his many disciples, made too much of his basic insights. Life on the frontier was not as democratic as Turner believed, and it certainly does not "explain" American development as completely as he said it did. Nevertheless, his work showed how important it was to investigate the evolution of institutions, and it encouraged historians to study social and economic, as well as purely political, subjects. If the claims of the new historians to objectivity and definitiveness were absurdly overstated, their emphasis on thoroughness, exactitude, and impartiality did much to raise standards in the profession. Perhaps the finest product of the new scientific school, a happy combination of meticulous scholarship and literary artistry, was Henry Adams's nine-volume *History of the United States During the Administrations of Jefferson and Madison.*

Realism in Literature

When what Mark Twain called the Gilded Age began, American literature was dominated by the romantic mood. All the important writers of the 1840s and 1850s except Hawthorne, Thoreau, and Poe were still living. Longfellow stood at the height of his fame, and the lachrymose Susan Warner—"tears on almost every page"—continued to turn out stories in the style of her popular *The Wide, Wide World.* Romanticism, however, had lost its creative force; most writing in the decade after 1865 was sentimental trash pandering to the preconceptions of middle-class readers. Magazines like the *Atlantic Monthly* overflowed with stories about fair ladies worshiped from afar by stainless heroes, women coping selflessly with drunken husbands, and poor but honest youths rising through various combinations of virtue and diligence to

DID THE FRONTIER ENGENDER INDIVIDUALISM AND DEMOCRACY?

This 1887 photograph depicts a family in Custer County, Nebraska. Their optimism is indicated by the fact that they have begun to build a house *(center)*; yet their isolation suggests their vulnerability, as does the dugout *(upper left)* they now live in. Were such people self-reliant individualists or needy dependents?

In 1893 historian Frederick Jackson Turner argued that the boundless expanses of the frontier gave rise to democracy, individualism and "withal that buoyancy and exuberance which comes with freedom." Insofar as the frontier was then receding before the advance of urbanization and industrialization, Turner's readers had cause for alarm. Historians adopting Turner's analysis—and there were many—were generally pessimistic about the prospects for American democracy.

Philosopher John Dewey (1922) was among those who dissented. He argued that rather than promoting democracy, the frontier had a "depressing effect upon the free life of inquiry and criticism." Other scholars insisted that democracy flourished not in the West but in urban and industrial areas. In subsequent decades scholars challenged Turner's assertions that frontier peoples were self-sufficient and their democratic institutions vital.

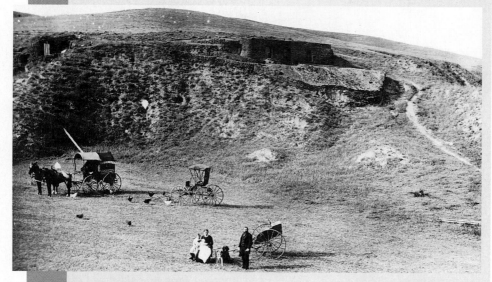

Richard White (1991) insisted that the West, more so than any other region, had been "historically a dependency of the federal government." Donald Worster (1992) contended that its predominant economy—cattle raising and irrigation agriculture—was developed mostly by large corporations.

And even if the frontier promoted democratic sensibilities, this came at the cost of dispossessing the Indians—missing from the photograph—who had previously ranged over this land.

Donald Worster, *Under Western Skies* (1992), Richard White, *"It's Your Misfortune and None of My Own"* (1991), Peggy Pascoe, *Relations of Rescue: The Search for Female Moral Authority in the American West, 1874–1939* (1990), Patricia Limerick, *Legacy of Conquest* (1988), and Elliot West, *The Contested Plains* (1998).

positions of wealth and influence. Most writers of fiction tended to ignore the eternal conflicts inherent in human nature and the social problems of the age; polite entertainment and pious moralizing appeared to be their only objectives.

The patent unreality, even dishonesty, of contemporary fiction eventually caused a reaction. The most important forces giving rise to the Age of Realism were those that were transforming every other aspect of American life: industrialism, with its associated complexities and social problems; the theory of evolution, which made people more aware of the force of the environment and the basic conflicts of existence; the new science, which taught dispassionate, empirical observation. Novelists undertook the examination of social problems such as slum life, the conflict between capital and labor, and political corruption. They created multidimensional characters, depicted persons of every social class, used dialect and slang to capture the flavor of particular types, and fashioned painstaking descriptions of the surroundings into which they placed their subjects. The romantic novel did not disappear. General Lew Wallace's *Ben Hur* (1880) and Frances Hodgson Burnett's *Little Lord Fauntleroy* (1886) were best-sellers. But by 1880 realism was the point of view of the finest literary talents in the country.

Mark Twain

While it was easy to romanticize the West, that region lent itself to the realistic approach. Almost of necessity, novelists writing about the West described coarse characters from the lower levels of society and dealt with crime and violence. It would have been difficult indeed to write a genteel romance about a mining camp. The outstanding figure of western literature, the first great American realist, was Mark Twain.

Twain, whose real name was Samuel L. Clemens, was born in 1835. He grew up in Hannibal, Missouri, on the banks of the Mississippi. After mastering the printer's trade and working as a riverboat pilot, he went west to Nevada in 1861. The wild, rough life of Virginia City fascinated him, but prospecting got him nowhere, and he became a reporter for the *Territorial Enterprise*. Soon he was publishing humorous stories about the local life under the nom de plume Mark Twain. In 1865, while working in California, he wrote "The Celebrated Jumping Frog of Calaveras County," a story that brought him national recognition. A tour of Europe and the Holy Land in 1867 to 1868 led to *The Innocents Abroad* (1869), which made him famous.

Twain's greatness stemmed from his keen reportorial eye and ear, his eagerness to live life to the full, his marvelous sense of humor, and his ability to be at once in society and outside it, to love humanity yet be repelled by human vanity and perversity. He epitomized the zest and adaptability of his age and also its materialism. No contemporary pursued the almighty dollar more zealously. An inveterate speculator, he made a fortune with his pen and lost it in foolish business ventures. Twain died a dark pessimist, surrounded by adulation yet alone, an alien and a stranger in the land he loved and knew so well.

Twain exceeded every contemporary in the portrayal of character. In *Huckleberry Finn* (1884), his masterpiece, his portrait of the slave Jim, loyal, patient, naive, yet withal a man, is unforgettable. When Huck takes advantage of Jim's credulity merely for his own amusement, the slave turns from him coldly and says: "Dat truck dah is trash; en trash is what people is dat puts dirt on de head er dey fren's en makes 'em ashamed." And there is Huck Finn himself, full of devilry, romantic, amoral—up to a point—and at bottom the complete realist. When Miss Watson tells him he can get anything he wants by praying for it, he makes the effort, is disillusioned, and concludes: "If a body can get anything they pray for, why don't Deacon Winn get back the money he lost on pork? . . . Why can't Miss Watson fat up? No, I says to myself, there ain't nothing in it."

Whether directly, as in *The Innocents Abroad* and in his fascinating account of the world of the river pilot, *Life on the Mississippi* (1883), or when transformed by his imagination in works of fiction such as *Tom Sawyer* (1876) and *A Connecticut Yankee in King Arthur's Court* (1889), Mark Twain always put much of his own experience and feeling into his work. A story, he told a fellow author, "must be written with the blood out of a man's heart." Twain's achievement was magnificent. Rough and uneven like the man himself, his works catch more of the spirit of the age he named than those of any other writer.

William Dean Howells

Twain's realism was far less self-conscious than that of his longtime friend William Dean Howells. Like Twain, Howells, who was born in Ohio in 1837, had little formal education. He learned the printer's trade from his father and became a reporter for the *Ohio State Journal*. After the Civil War he worked briefly for *The Nation* in New York and then moved to Boston, where he became editor of the *Atlantic Monthly*. In 1886 he returned to New York as editor of *Harper's*.

A long series of novels and much literary criticism poured from Howells's pen over the next 30 years. While he insisted on treating his material honestly, he was not at first a critic of society, being content to write about what he called "the smiling aspects" of life. Realism to Howells meant concern for the complexities of individual personalities and faithful description of the genteel, middle-class world he knew best.

Besides a sharp eye and an open mind, Howells had a real social conscience. Gradually he became aware of the problems that industrialization had created. In 1885, in *The Rise of Silas Lapham*, he dealt with some of the ethical conflicts faced by businessmen in a competitive society. The harsh public reaction to the Haymarket bombing in 1886 stirred him, and he threw himself into a futile campaign to prevent the execution of the anarchist suspects. Thereafter he moved rapidly toward the left. In *A Hazard of New Fortunes* (1890), he attempted to portray the whole range of metropolitan life, weaving the destinies of a dozen interesting personalities from diverse sections and social classes. The book represents a triumph of realism in its careful descriptions of various sections of New York and the ways of life of rich and poor, in the intricacy of its characters, and in its rejection of sentimentality and romantic love.

His own works were widely read, and Howells was also the most influential critic of his time. He helped bring the best contemporary foreign writers, including Tolstoy, Dostoevsky, Ibsen, and Zola, to the attention of readers in the United States, and he encouraged many important young American novelists, among them Stephen Crane, Theodore Dreiser, Frank Norris, and Hamlin Garland.

Some of these writers went far beyond Howells's realism to what they called naturalism. Many, like Twain and Howells, began as newspaper reporters. Working for a big-city daily in the 1890s was sure to teach anyone a great deal about the dark side of life. Naturalist writers believed that the human being was essentially an animal, a helpless creature whose fate was determined by environment. Their world was Darwin's world—mindless, without mercy or justice. They wrote chiefly about the most primitive emotions—lust, hate, greed. In *Maggie, A Girl of the Streets* (1893), Stephen Crane described the seduction, degradation, and eventual suicide of a young woman, all set against the background of a sordid slum; in *The Red Badge of Courage* (1895), he captured the pain and humor of war. In *McTeague* (1899), Frank Norris told the story of a brutal, dull-witted dentist who murdered his greed-crazed wife with his bare fists.

Henry James

Henry James was very different in spirit and background from the tempestuous naturalists. Born to wealth, reared in a cosmopolitan atmosphere, twisted in some strange way while still a child and unable to achieve satisfactory relationships with women, James spent most of his mature life in Europe, writing novels, short stories, plays, and volumes of criticism. Although far removed from the world of practical affairs, he was preeminently a realist, determined, as he once said, "to leave a multitude of pictures of my time" for the future to contemplate.

Although he preferred living in the cultivated surroundings of London high society, James yearned for the recognition of his fellow Americans almost as avidly as Mark Twain. However, he was incapable of modifying his rarefied, overly subtle manner of writing. Most serious writers of the time admired his books, and he received many honors, but he never achieved widespread popularity. His major theme was the clash of American and European cultures, his primary interest the close-up examination of wealthy, sensitive, yet often corrupt persons in a cultivated but far from polite society.

James's reputation, greater today than in his lifetime, rests more on his highly refined accounts of the interactions of individuals and their environment and his masterful commentaries on the novel as a literary form than on his ability as a storyteller. Few major writers have been more long-winded, more prone to circumlocution. Yet few have been so dedicated to their art, possessed of such psychological penetration, or so successful in producing a large body of important work.

Henry James *(left)*, a novelist of exquisite perception, withdrew from America to Europe; his brother, William *(right)* shook off a bout of depression in his twenties, propounded pragmatism, a philosophy that eschewed abstraction, and criticized aesthetes such as his brother: "There is no more contemptible type of human character than that of the nerveless sentimentalist and dreamer, who spends his life in a weltering sea of sensibility and emotion, but who never does a manly concrete deed."

The Pragmatic Approach

It would have been remarkable indeed if the intellectual ferment of the late nineteenth century had not affected contemporary ideas about the meaning of life, the truth of revealed religion, moral values, and similar fundamental problems. In particular the theory of evolution, so important in altering contemporary views of science, history, and social relations, produced significant changes in American thinking about religious and philosophical questions.

Evolution posed an immediate challenge to religion: If Darwin was correct, the biblical account of the creation was apparently untrue and the idea that the human race had been formed in God's image was highly unlikely. A bitter controversy erupted, described by President Andrew D. White of Cornell in *The Warfare of Science with Theology in Christendom* (1896). While millions continued to believe in the literal truth of the Bible, among intellectuals, lay and clerical, victory went to the evolutionists because, in addition to the arguments of the geologists and the biologists, scholars were throwing light on the historical origins of the Bible, showing that its words were of human rather than divine inspiration.

The effects of Darwinism on philosophy were less dramatic but in the end more significant. Fixed systems and eternal truths were difficult to justify in a world that was constantly evolving. By the early 1870s a few philosophers had begun to reason that ideas and theories mattered little except when applied to specifics.

(text continues on page 550)

Titanic

James Cameron's *Titanic* (1997) was a blockbuster. He made audiences feel what it was like to be on the ship. When the deck tilted to the right, viewers leaned to the left; many gasped as the ship plunged into the icy depths. What sent a shiver down the spine was the knowledge that real people had experienced what was being depicted on the screen.

Cameron well understood the audience's craving to relive a true story. The movie opens with footage of the actual HMS *Titanic* on the floor of the Atlantic, fish gliding silently through its barnacle-encrusted wreckage. Cameron also spent scores of millions of dollars devising computer-enhanced techniques to ensure that his *Titanic* looked like the one that went down in the North Atlantic on the night of April 14–15, 1912.

But Cameron's *Titanic* was more than a disaster movie. It was also the story of two young people who fall in love. The romance begins when Jack (Leonardo DiCaprio), a struggling artist, spots Rose (Kate Winslet), a wealthy socialite, climbing over the railing and peering despondently into the water below. Obliged to marry a contemptuous (and contemptible) snob, she is miserable. Jack, from a lower deck, scrambles up and persuades her to forgo the plunge.

As a reward for saving Rose, Jack is invited to dine with Rose's table. At dinner, Rose appraises Jack more carefully—and is impressed. He looks good in a tuxedo, displays plenty of moxie, and possesses artistic talent ("Jack, you see things!"). She proposes that she pose for him in the nude. A few hours later they venture below decks and, in anticipation of the courtship rituals of future decades, locate an automobile, climb inside, and rip off each other's clothes. Soon the car is bouncing. The windows steam up, and a hand leaves an imprint, fingers outstretched in ecstasy.

Minutes later they are cooled off when the ship has its close encounter of the icy kind. Jack—young, vital, alive—perishes in the frigid waters; but he has imparted to Rose a gift of love, and thus of life. This tale of young lovers, held apart by society, is a nauti-cal "Romeo and Juliet," a brief, pure instant of love, tragically ended by death.

If Cameron's *Titanic* is a love story for the ages, it was also frozen in a particular place and in a particular time. Much as Cameron spent millions to show the ship as it really was, he took similar pains to give a convincing rendering of New York society, especially its clothing, silverware, and social conventions.

Of the latter, the most significant for the story are the elaborate rituals of Victorian courtship. Rose seeks to break free from her impending marriage partly because she despises her fiancé, but also because marriage to him constitutes the final, irreversible step into the gilded cage of a society lady. Jack's presence at dinner with the "best" of society underscores the shallow materialism of this upper crust and its preoccupation with wealth, its disdain for those who lack both, its absurd rules of etiquette, and its repressive attitudes toward sexuality. Viewers of the movie, looking through Rose's eyes, may wonder how such rituals ever came to be.

Some had existed for centuries. The idealization of courtly love and pure womanhood was a commonplace of medieval literature; in the early nineteenth century novelist Jane Austen described the subtle interplay of money and romance in England. But the rituals of New York society in the Gilded Age were characterized by sumptuous and public displays of wealth—glittering balls and extravagant "Grand Tours" of Europe.

This new mode of courtship was largely the creation of Mrs. John Jacob Astor, wife of one of New York's wealthiest businessmen, and her friends. After the Civil War, industrialization and urbanization were generating new wealth and destroying the old at a dizzying pace. While prominent businessmen and investment bankers were devising institutions to impose order on industrial chaos, their wives were regularizing its social elite. They endeavored to determine who should be admitted to New York's "best" families—and who should not.

548

Leonardo DiCaprio and Kate Winslet as lovers on the *Titanic*.

A young society couple courting in New York, about 1914.

By controlling entrance into society, women such as Mrs. Astor (and her imitators in nearly every city in the nation) also determined the disposition, through marriage and inheritance, of the nation's largest fortunes. Society women possessed immense power.

Although the system was created and supervised by mature women, it demanded the compliance of adolescent girls. The process began when a wealthy mother took her daughter on a round of visits to society women, to whom they would present their "calling cards." If mother and daughter were judged suitable, they would be invited in for tea; if the girl behaved with decorum (and if her father's assets proved sound), she would be invited to balls and other formal events. At or near her sixteenth birthday, her parents would hold a ball in her honor—in New York the event usually took place at Delmonico's restaurant—marking her "debut" into society. She wore a white gown symbolizing her virginity. A male relative presented her formally to the prominent women. Now she could accept male suitors from "society."

This highly stylized—almost tribal—ritual brought young women to the threshold of womanhood. Marriage awaited beyond the door. Many eagerly anticipated the acquisition of adult status and the social power it entailed. Others regarded this rite with terror. (Novelist Edith Wharton remembered her debut as a "long cold agony of shyness.") In the early twentieth century, some young women began to rebel. Elsie Clews, daughter of a Wall Street banker, refused to wear corsets. When her mother wasn't looking, she took off her veil and white gloves. She subsequently scandalized Newport—the fashionable Rhode Island summer resort for society's

wealthy—by going swimming with a young man without a chaperone (but not without a bathing suit). To her mother's dismay, Clews delayed marriage and went to Barnard College; eventually she became a respected anthropologist (Elsie Clews Parsons).

Kate Winslet's "Rose" was, like Elsie Clews, a prematurely "modern" woman. But Clews tore off only her veil and white gloves, not all her clothes; she dispensed with the rituals of courtship, not its substance. Even in the waning years of the Victorian era, few wealthy young women succumbed to impoverished men, however earnest and appealing.

Victorian courtship was necessarily protracted. Young women did not unburden themselves to strangers; and even to friends, especially of the opposite sex, the process of revealing one's inner feelings unfolded slowly, often after a series of tests and trials. Letters and diaries show that, over time, these personal revelations often led to sexual intimacies.

Cameron's *Titanic* looked like the past; but the heart of the movie is Jack and Rose's whirlwind romance. While Rose's story addresses some of the anxieties of young society women, it more closely resembles the courtship patterns of Hollywood today than the experiences of young people at the beginning of the last century.

Questions for Discussion

- Jack and Rose "hooked up," to use modern slang. Why was such behavior improbable among young women of wealthy families in the late nineteenth century?
- What other behaviors in the film seem anachronistic?

"Nothing justifies the development of abstract principles but their utility in enlarging our concrete knowledge of nature," wrote Chauncey Wright, secretary of the American Academy of Arts and Sciences. In "How to Make Our Ideas Clear" (1878), Wright's friend Charles S. Peirce, an amazingly versatile and talented albeit obscure thinker, argued that concepts could be fairly understood only in terms of their practical effects. Once the mind accepted the truth of evolution, Peirce believed, logic required that it accept the impermanence even of scientific laws. There was, he wrote, "an element of indeterminacy, spontaneity, or absolute chance in nature."

This startling philosophy, which Peirce called pragmatism, was presented in more understandable language by William James, brother of the novelist. James was one of the most remarkable persons of his generation. Educated in London, Paris, Bonn, and Geneva—as well as at Harvard—he studied painting, participated in a zoological expedition to South America, earned a medical degree, and was professor at Harvard successively of comparative anatomy, psychology, and finally philosophy. His *Principles of Psychology* (1890) may be said to have established that discipline as a modern science. His *Varieties of Religious Experience* (1902), which treated the subject from both psychological and philosophical points of view, helped thousands of readers reconcile their religious faith with their increasing knowledge of psychology and the physical universe.

Although he was less rigorous a logician than Peirce, James's wide range and his verve and imagination as a writer made him by far the most influential philosopher of his time. He rejected the deterministic interpretation of Darwinism and all other one-idea explanations of existence. Belief in free will was one of his axioms; environment might influence survival, but so did the *desire* to survive, which existed independent of surrounding circumstances. Even truth was relative; it did not exist in the abstract but *happened* under particular circumstances. What a person thought helped to make thought occur, or come true. The mind, James wrote in a typically vivid phrase, has "a vote" in determining truth. Religion was true, for example, because people were religious.

The pragmatic approach inspired much of the reform spirit of the late nineteenth century and even more of that of the early twentieth. James's hammer blows shattered the laissez-faire extremism of Herbert Spencer. In "Great Men and Their Environment" (1880) James argued that social changes were brought about by the actions of geniuses whom society had selected and raised to positions of power, rather than by the impersonal force of the environment. Such reasoning fitted the preconceptions of rugged individualists yet encouraged those dissatisfied with society to work for change. Educational reformers like John Dewey, the institutionalist school of economists, settlement house workers, and other reformers adopted pragmatism eagerly. James's philosophy did much to revive the buoyant optimism that had characterized the pre–Civil War reform movement.

Yet pragmatism brought Americans face-to-face with somber problems. While relativism made them optimistic, it also bred insecurity, for there could be no certainty, no comforting reliance on any eternal value in the absence of absolute truth.

Pragmatism also seemed to suggest that the end justified the means, that what worked was more important than what ought to be. At the time of James's death in 1910, the *Commercial and Financial Chronicle* pointed out that the pragmatic philosophy was helpful to businessmen in making decisions. By emphasizing practice at the expense of theory, the new philosophy encouraged materialism, anti-intellectualism, and other unlovely aspects of the American character. And what place had conventional morality in such a system? Perhaps pragmatism placed too much reliance on the free will of human beings, ignoring their capacity for selfishness and self-delusion.

The people of the new century found pragmatism a heady wine. They would quaff it freely and enthusiastically—down to the bitter dregs.

The Knowledge Revolution

Improvements in public education and the needs of an increasingly complex society for every type of intellectual skill caused a veritable revolution in how knowledge was discovered, disseminated, and put to use. Millions profited from the proliferation of public libraries. By the end of the century nearly all the states supported libraries. Private donors, led by the steel industrialist Andrew Carnegie, contributed millions to the cause. In 1900 over 1,700 libraries in the United States had collections of more than 5,000 volumes.

Newspapers were an even more important means of disseminating information and educating the masses. Here new technology supplied the major incentive for change. The development by Richard Hoe and Stephen Tucker of

The first commercially successful typewriter, manufactured in quantity beginning in 1874. It used the QWERTY keyboard found on later typewriters— and eventually on computer keyboards.

the web press (1871), which printed simultaneously on both sides of paper fed into it from large rolls, and Ottmar Mergenthaler's linotype machine (1886), which cast rows of type as needed directly from molten metal, cut printing costs dramatically. Machines for making paper out of wood pulp reduced the cost of newsprint to a quarter of what it had been in the 1860s. By 1895 machines were printing, cutting, and folding 32-page newspapers at a rate of 24,000 an hour.

The telegraph and transoceanic cables wrought a similar transformation in the gathering of news. Press associations, led by the New York Associated Press, flourished; the syndicated article appeared; and a few publishers—Edward W. Scripps was the first—began to acquire chains of newspapers.

Publishers tended to be conservative, but reaching the masses meant lowering intellectual and cultural standards, appealing to emotions, and adopting popular, sometimes radical, causes. Cheap, mass-circulation papers had first appeared in the 1830s and 1840s, the most successful being the *Sun,* the *Herald,* and the *Tribune* in New York, the *Philadelphia Public Ledger,* and the *Baltimore Sun.* None of them much exceeded a circulation of 50,000 before the Civil War. The first publisher to reach a truly massive audience was Joseph Pulitzer, a Hungarian-born immigrant who made a first-rate paper of the *St. Louis Post-Dispatch.* In 1883 Pulitzer bought the *New York World,* a sheet with a circulation of perhaps 20,000. Within a year he was selling 100,000 copies daily, and by the late 1890s the *World's* circulation regularly exceeded 1 million.

"The *World* is the people's newspaper," Pulitzer boasted, and in the sense that it appealed to men and women of every sort, he was correct. Pulitzer's methods were quickly copied by competitors, especially William Randolph Hearst, who purchased the *New York Journal* in 1895 and soon outdid the *World* in sensationalism. But no other newspaperman of the era approached Pulitzer in originality, boldness, and the knack of reaching the masses without abandoning seriousness of purpose and basic integrity.

Growth and ferment also characterized the magazine world. In 1865 there were about 700 magazines in the country, by the turn of the century more than 5,000. Until the mid-1880s, few of the new magazines were in any way unusual. A handful of serious periodicals, such as the *Atlantic Monthly, Harper's,* and *The Century,* dominated the field. They were staid in tone and conservative in politics. Although they had great influence, none approached mass circulation because of the limited size of the upper-middle-class audience they aimed at.

1862	Morrill Act establishes land-grant colleges
1865	Vassar College is founded for women
1869	Charles W. Eliot becomes Harvard's president, undertakes transformation of college by introducing elective system and expanding offerings
1876	Johns Hopkins University is founded to specialize in graduate education
1883	Joseph Pulitzer purchases *New York World*
1884	Mark Twain publishes *Huckleberry Finn*
1886	Ottmar Mergenthaler invents linotype machine
	William Dean Howells becomes editor of *Harper's*
1890	William James publishes *Principles of Psychology*
1893	Frederick Jackson Turner publishes "Significance of the Frontier in American History"
1895	William Randolph Hearst purchases the *New York Journal*
1899	John Dewey publishes *The School and Society*

Politics: Local, State, and National

NEWSPAPER READERSHIP HAS BEEN DECLINING DURING THE PAST quarter century. In 1970, 62 million newspapers were sold every day. Although the nation's population has increased by nearly 50 percent since then, daily newspaper circulation has fallen 15 percent. Twice as many people get their news from television as from newspapers, and the Internet has cut into newspaper readership still further.

In the late nineteenth century, however, the newspaper served as an indispensable guide for daily living. Demand was so great that even small cities supported a half-dozen newspapers. In 1830, the combined daily circulation of all newspapers in New York City was 16,000; but by 1899, it had soared to nearly 3 million. During the three decades after 1880, newspaper circulation nationwide increased from 3.6 million to over 24 million.

The growth of newspaper circulation corresponded to a sharp intensification in political involvement. While today about half of eligible voters go to the polls in presidential election years, from 1876 to 1896, over three-fourths of the eligible voters did so—the highest rates in the nation's history.

This puzzles scholars, because the issues of that time seem so tepid: the "patriotism" of elderly Democrats; soldiers' pensions; the tariff; paper money; civil service reform. Perhaps the most volatile issue—the plight of former slaves—was assiduously evaded; the other key issue—the modest role of the federal government—went without saying and, being unsaid, generated no controversy.

Why, then, did people vote so diligently?

Part of the explanation is that many cared passionately about their town or city. This interest fueled the rise of the newspaper, and newspapers in turn sharpened the focus on local matters. Urban corruption—a recurrent source of newspaper headlines—brought out the voters. Then, during the 1890s, a nationwide industrial depression crushed many local manufacturing firms, just as an agricultural crisis was sweeping through the midsection of the nation.

Because the nation had become more tightly integrated, these great economic upheavals jolted nearly every community. National policy and local issues converged on the front pages of nearly every newspaper, culminating in the extraordinary election of 1896, which brought over 80 percent of the electorate to the polls. In Illinois, Indiana, Iowa, Michigan, and Ohio, important farm states, over 95 percent of those eligible to vote did so. Not until the Great Depression, some 30 years hence, would Americans again believe that the fate of their community depended on the outcome of a presidential campaign.

Congress Ascendant

A succession of weak executives presided over the White House during the last quarter of the nineteenth century. Although the impeachment proceedings against Andrew Johnson had failed, Congress dominated the government. Within Congress, the Senate generally overshadowed the House of Representatives. In his novel *Democracy* (1880), the cynical Henry Adams wrote that the United States had a "government of the people, by the people, for the benefit of Senators." Critics called the Senate a "rich man's club," and it did contain many millionaires, among them Leland Stanford, founder of the Central Pacific Railroad; the mining tycoon James G. "Bonanza" Fair of Nevada; Philetus Sawyer, a self-made Wisconsin lumberman; and Nelson Aldrich of Rhode Island, whose wealth derived from banking and a host of corporate connections. However, the true sources of the Senate's influence lay in the long tenure of many of its members (which enabled them to master the craft of politics), in the fact that it was small enough to encourage real debate, and in its long-established reputation for wisdom, intelligence, and statesmanship.

The House of Representatives, on the other hand, was one of the most disorderly and inefficient legislative bodies in the world. "As I make my notes," a reporter wrote in 1882 while sitting in the House gallery,

> I see a dozen men reading newspapers with their feet on their desks. . . . "Pig Iron"
> Kelley of Pennsylvania has dropped his newspaper and is paring his fingernails. . . .
> The vile odor of . . . tobacco . . . rises from the two-for-five-cents cigars in the
> mouths of the so-called gentlemen below. . . . They chew, too! Every desk has a spit-
> toon of pink and gold china beside it to catch the filth from the statesman's mouth.

The great political parties professed undying enmity to each other, but they seldom took clearly opposing positions on the questions of the day. Democrats were separated from Republicans more by accidents of geography, religious affiliation, ethnic background, and emotion than by economic issues. Questions

An 1887 cartoon indicting the Senate for closely attending to the Big (read, fat) Trusts rather than to the needs of the public (whose "entrance" to the Senate is "closed"). Drawn by Joseph Keppler, a caricaturist who was born and trained in Germany, this type of grotesque satire greatly influenced late nineteenth-century American comic arts.

of state and local importance, unrelated to national politics, often determined the outcome of congressional elections and thus who controlled the federal government.

The fundamental division between Democrats and Republicans was sectional, a result of the Civil War. The South, after the political rights of blacks had been drastically circumscribed, became heavily Democratic. Most of New England was solidly Republican. Elsewhere the two parties stood in fair balance, although the Republicans tended to have the advantage. A preponderance of the well-to-do, cultured Northerners were Republicans. Perhaps in reaction to this concentration, immigrants, Catholics, and other minority groups—except for blacks—tended to vote Democratic. But the numerous exceptions weakened the applicability of these generalizations. German and Scandinavian immigrants usually voted Republican; many powerful business leaders supported the Democrats.

The bulk of the people—farmers, laborers, shopkeepers, white-collar workers—distributed their ballots fairly evenly between the two parties in most elections; the balance of political power after 1876 was almost perfect. Between 1856 and 1912 the Democrats elected a president only twice (1884 and 1892), but most contests were extremely close. Majorities in both the Senate and the House fluctuated continually. Between 1876 and 1896 the "dominant" Republican party controlled both houses of Congress and the presidency at the same time for only a single two-year period.

The Recurrent Issues

Four questions obsessed politicians in these years. One was the "bloody shirt." The term, which became part of the language after a Massachusetts congressman dramatically displayed to his colleagues in the House the bloodstained shirt of an Ohio carpetbagger who had been flogged by terrorists in Mississippi, referred to the tactic of reminding the electorate of the northern states that the men who had precipitated the Civil War had been Democrats. Should Democrats regain power, former rebels would run the government and undo all the work accomplished at such sacrifice during the war. "Every man that endeavored to tear down the old flag," a Republican orator proclaimed in 1876, "was a Democrat. Every man that tried to destroy this nation was a Democrat. . . . The man that assassinated Abraham Lincoln was a Democrat. . . . Soldiers, every scar you have on your heroic bodies was given you by a Democrat." And every scoundrel or incompetent who sought office under the Republican banner waved the bloody shirt in order to divert the attention of northern voters from his own shortcomings. The technique worked so well that many decent candidates could not resist the temptation to employ it in close races. Nothing, of course, so effectively obscured the real issues of the day.

Waving the bloody shirt was related intimately to the issue of the rights of blacks. Throughout this period Republicans vacillated between trying to build up their organization in the South by appealing to black voters—which required them to make sure that blacks in the South could vote—and trying to win conservative white support by stressing economic issues such as the tariff. When the former strategy seemed wise, they waved the bloody shirt with vigor; in the latter case, they piously announced that the blacks' future was "as safe in the hands of one party as it is in the other."

The question of veterans' pensions also bore a close relationship to the bloody shirt. Following the Civil War, Union soldiers founded the Grand Army of the Republic (GAR). By 1890 the organization had a membership of 409,000. The GAR put immense pressure on Congress, first for aid to veterans with service-connected disabilities, then for those with any disability, and eventually for all former Union soldiers. Republican politicians played on the emotions of the former soldiers by waving the bloody shirt, but the tough-minded leaders of the GAR demanded that they prove their sincerity by treating in openhanded fashion the warriors whose blood had stained the shirt.

The tariff was another perennial issue. Despite considerable loose talk about free trade, almost no one in the United States except for a handful of professional economists, most of them college professors, believed in eliminating duties on imports. Manufacturers desired protective tariffs to keep out competing products, and a majority of their workers were convinced that wage levels would fall if goods produced by cheap foreign labor entered the United States untaxed. Many farmers supported protection, although almost no competing agricultural products were being imported. Congressman William McKinley of Ohio, who reputedly could make reciting a tariff schedule sound like poetry, stated the majority opinion in the clearest terms: high tariffs foster the growth of industry and thus create jobs. "Reduce the tariff and labor is the first to suffer," he said.

A third political question was currency reform. During the Civil War, the government, faced with obligations it could not meet by taxing or borrowing, suspended specie payments and issued about $450 million in paper money. The greenbacks did not command the full confidence of a people accustomed to money readily convertible into gold or silver. Greenbacks seemed to threaten inflation, for how could one trust the government not to issue them in wholesale lots to avoid passing unpopular tax laws? Thus, when the war ended, strong sentiment developed for withdrawing the greenbacks from circulation and returning to a bullion standard.

In fact, beginning during Reconstruction, prices declined sharply. The deflation increased the real income of bondholders and other creditors but injured debtors. Farmers were particularly hard hit, for many of them had borrowed heavily during the wartime boom to finance expansion.

Here was a question of real significance. Many groups supported some kind of currency inflation. A National Greenback party nominated Peter Cooper, an iron manufacturer, for president in 1876. Cooper received only 81,000 votes, but a new Greenback Labor party polled over a million in 1878, electing fourteen congressmen. However, the major parties refused to confront each other over the currency question. While Republicans professed to be the party of sound money, most western Republicans favored expansion of the currency. And while one wing of the Democrats flirted with the Greenbackers, the conservative, or "Bourbon," Democrats favored deflation as much as Republicans did. Under various administrations steps were taken to increase or decrease the amount of money in circulation, but the net effect on the economy was not significant.

The final major political issue was civil service reform. That the federal bureaucracy needed overhauling nearly everyone agreed. As American society grew larger and more complex, the government necessarily took on more functions. The need for professional administration increased. The number of federal employees rose from 53,000 in 1871 to 256,000 at the end of the century. Corruption flourished; waste and inefficiency were the normal state of affairs. The collection of tariff duties offered perhaps the greatest opportunity for venality. The New York Custom House, one observer wrote in 1872, teemed with "corrupting merchants and their clerks and runners, who think that all men can be bought, and . . . corrupt swarms [of clerks], who shamelessly seek their price."

With a succession of relatively ineffective presidents and a Congress that squandered its energies on private bills, pork-barrel projects, and other trivia, the administration of the government was strikingly inefficient.

Every honest observer could see the need for reform, but the politicians refused to surrender the power of dispensing government jobs to their lieutenants without regard for qualifications. They argued that patronage was the lifeblood of politics, that parties could not function without armies of loyal political workers, and that the workers expected and deserved the rewards of office when their efforts were crowned with victory at the polls. Typical was the attitude of the New York assemblyman who, according to Theodore Roosevelt, had "the same idea about Public Life and the Civil Service that a vulture has of a dead sheep." When reformers suggested establishing the most modest kind of professional, nonpartisan civil service, politicians of both parties subjected them to every kind of insult and ridicule even though both the Democratic and Republican parties regularly wrote civil service reform planks into their platforms.

Party Politics: Sidestepping the Issues

With the Democrats invincible in the South and the Republicans predominant in New England and most of the states beyond the Mississippi, the outcome of presidential elections was usually determined in a handful of populous states: New York (together with its satellites, New Jersey and Connecticut), Ohio, Indiana, and Illinois. The fact that opinion in these states on important questions such as the tariff and monetary policy was divided and that every imaginable religious and ethnic interest was represented in the electorate goes far to explain why the parties hesitated to commit themselves on issues. In every presidential election, Democrats and Republicans concentrated their heaviest guns on these states. Of the eighteen Democrats and Republicans nominated for president in the nine elections between 1868 and 1900, only three were not from New York, Ohio, Indiana, or Illinois, and all three lost.

The level of political morality was abysmal. Mudslinging, character assassination, and plain lying were standard practice; bribery was routine. Drifters and other dissolute citizens were paid in cash—or more often in free drinks—to vote the party ticket. The names of persons long dead were solemnly inscribed in voting registers, their suffrages exercised by impostors. During the 1880 campaign the Democratic national chairman, hearing that the Republicans were planning to transport Kentuckians into Indiana to vote illegally in that crucial state, urged Indiana Democrats to "check this outrageous fraud." Then, perhaps seeking an easier solution to the problem, he added: "If necessary . . . keep even with them."

Lackluster Presidents: From Hayes to Harrison

The leading statesmen of the period were disinterested in important contemporary questions, powerless to influence them, or content with things are they were. Consider the presidents.

Rutherford B. Hayes, president from 1877 to 1881, came to office with a distinguished record. He attended Kenyon College and Harvard Law School before settling down to practice in Cincinnati. Although he had a family to support, he volunteered for service in the Union army within weeks after the first shell fell on Fort Sumter. Hayes was wounded at South Mountain on the eve of Antietam and later served under Sheridan in the Shenandoah Valley campaign of 1864. Entering the army as a major, he emerged a major general. In 1864 he was elected to Congress; four years later he became governor of Ohio, serving three terms altogether. The Republicans nominated him for president in 1876 because of his reputation for honesty and moderation, and his election, made possible by the Compromise of 1877, seemed to presage an era of sectional harmony and political probity.

Outwardly Hayes had a sunny disposition; inwardly, in his own words, he was sometimes "nervous to the point of disaster." Despite his geniality, he was utterly without political glamour. He accounted himself a civil service reformer, being opposed to the collection of political contributions from federal officeholders. Hayes complained about the South's failure to treat blacks decently after the withdrawal of federal troops, but he took no action. He worked harder for civil service reform, yet failed to achieve the "thorough, rapid, and complete" change he had promised. In most matters, he was content to "let the record show that he had made the requests."

Hayes's successor, James A. Garfield, elected president in 1880, was cut down by an assassin's bullet just four months after his inauguration. During the war Garfield fought at Shiloh and later at Chickamauga. In two years he rose from lieutenant colonel to major general. In 1863 he won a seat in Congress, where his oratorical and managerial skills brought him to prominence in the affairs of the Republican party.

Garfield had been a compromise choice at the 1880 Republican convention. His election precipitated a great battle over patronage, the new president standing in a sort of no-man's land between contending factions within the party. In July 1881 an unbalanced office-seeker named Charles J. Guiteau shot Garfield in the Washington railroad station. After lingering for weeks, the president died on September 19.

The assassination of Garfield elevated Chester A. Arthur to the presidency. A New York lawyer and abolitionist, Arthur became an early convert to the Republican party and rose rapidly in its local councils. In 1871 Grant gave him the juiciest political plum in the country, the collectorship of the Port of New York, which he held until removed by Hayes in 1878 for refusing to keep his hands out of party politics.

The vice presidency was the only elective position that Arthur had ever held. Before Garfield's death, he had paid little attention to questions like the tariff and monetary policy, being content to take in fees ranging upward of $50,000 a year as collector of the port and to oversee the operations of the New York customs office, with its hordes of clerks and laborers. (During Arthur's tenure, the novelist Herman Melville was employed as an "outdoor inspector" by the custom house.) Of course, Arthur was an unblushing defender of the spoils system, though in fairness it must be said that he was personally honest and an excellent administrator.

The tragic circumstances of his elevation to the presidency sobered Arthur considerably. Although he was a genial, convivial man, perhaps overly fond of good food and flashy clothes, he comported himself with dignity as president. He handled patronage matters with restraint, and he gave at least nominal support to the movement for civil service reform, which had been strengthened by the public's

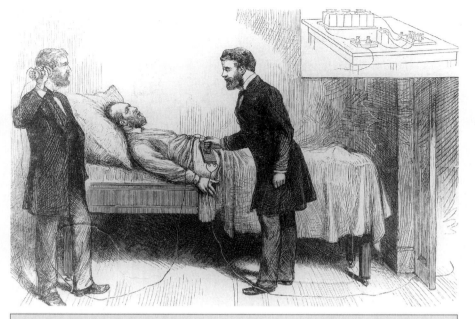

James A. Garfield, mortally wounded. After failing to locate the bullet, surgeons called in Alexander Graham Bell, the famous inventor. Bell conceived of a device, pictured here, that anticipated the mine detector. Bell's machine failed to locate the bullet, however, perhaps because the metal bed springs interfered with its operation. Garfield died, either from the bullet or the surgeon's unsuccessful attempts to extricate it.

indignation at the assassination of Garfield. In 1883 Congress passed the Pendleton Act, "classifying" about 10 percent of all government jobs and creating the bipartisan Civil Service Commission to administer competitive examinations for these positions. The law made it illegal to force officeholders to make political contributions and empowered the president to expand the list of classified positions at his discretion.

As an administrator Arthur was systematic, thoughtful, businesslike, and at the same time cheerful and considerate. Just the same, he too was a political failure. He made relatively little effort to push his program through Congress. He did not seek a second term in 1884.

The election of 1884 brought the Democrat Grover Cleveland to the White House. Cleveland grew up in western New York. After studying law, he settled in Buffalo. Although somewhat lacking in the social graces and in intellectual pretensions, he had a basic integrity that everyone recognized; when a group of reformers sought a candidate for mayor in 1881, he was a natural choice. His success in Buffalo led to his election as governor of New York in 1882.

In the governor's chair his no-nonsense attitude toward public administration endeared him to civil service reformers at the same time that his basic conservatism pleased businessmen. When he vetoed a popular bill to force a reduction of the fares charged by the New York City elevated railway on the ground that it was an unconstitutional violation of the company's franchise, his reputation soared. Here was a man who cared more for principle than for the adulation of the multitude, a man who was courageous, honest, hardworking, and eminently sound. The Democrats nominated him for president in 1884.

The election revolved around personal issues, for the platforms of the parties were almost identical. On the one hand, the Republican candidate, the dynamic James G. Blaine, had an immense following, but his reputation had been soiled by the publication of the "Mulligan letters," which connected him with the corrupt granting of congressional favors to the Little Rock and Fort Smith Railroad. On the other hand, it came out during the campaign that Cleveland, a bachelor, had fathered an illegitimate child. Instead of debating public issues, the Republicans chanted the ditty

Ma! Ma! Where's my pa?
Gone to the White House,
Ha! Ha! Ha!

to which the Democrats countered

Blaine, Blaine, James G. Blaine,
The continental liar from the State of Maine.

Blaine lost more heavily in the mudslinging than Cleveland, whose quiet courage in saying, "Tell the truth" when his past was brought to light contrasted favorably with Blaine's glib and unconvincing denials. A significant group of eastern Republicans, known as mugwumps, campaigned for the Democrats.[1] However, Blaine ran a strong race against a general pro-Democratic trend; Cleveland won the election by fewer than 25,000 votes. The change of 600 ballots in New York would have given that state, and the presidency, to his opponent.

As a Democrat, Cleveland had no stomach for refighting the Civil War. Civil service reformers overestimated his commitment to their cause, for he believed in rotation in office. He would not summarily dismiss Republicans, but he thought that when they had served four years, they "should as a rule give way to good men of our party." He did, however, insist on honesty and efficiency regardless of party. As a result, he made few poor appointments.

Toward the end of his term Cleveland bestirred himself and tried to provide constructive leadership on the tariff question. The government was embarrassed by a large revenue surplus, which Cleveland hoped to reduce by cutting the duties on necessities and on raw materials used in manufacturing. He devoted his entire annual message of December 1887 to the tariff, thereby focusing public attention on the subject. When worried Democrats reminded him that an election was com-

---

[1]*The mugwumps considered themselves reformers, but on social and economic questions nearly all of them were very conservative. They were sound-money proponents and advocates of laissez-faire. Reform to them consisted almost entirely of doing away with corruption and making the government more efficient.*

President Grover Cleveland and Frances Folsom in 1888. The couple had married two years earlier; he was 48, and she, 21, the youngest First Lady. Her popularity blunted criticisms that Cleveland, a bachelor, had earlier fathered an illegitimate child. When he lost the 1888 election, his wife predicted that she would return as First Lady. Four years later, she did.

The THREAD THAT BINDS THE UNION.

ing up and that the tariff might cause a rift in the organization, he replied simply: "What is the use of being elected or re-elected, unless you stand for something?"

In that contest, Cleveland obtained a plurality of the popular vote, but his opponent, Benjamin Harrison, grandson of President William Henry Harrison, carried most of the key northeastern industrial states by narrow margins, thereby obtaining a comfortable majority in the Electoral College, 233 to 168.

Although intelligent and able, Harrison was too reserved to make a good politician. One observer called him a "human iceberg." During the Civil War he fought under Sherman at Atlanta and won a reputation as a stern, effective disciplinarian. In 1876 he ran unsuccessfully for governor of Indiana but in 1881 was elected to the Senate.

Harrison believed ardently in protective tariffs, and no more flamboyant waver of the bloody shirt existed. Harrison professed to favor civil service reform, but fashioned an unimpressive record on the question. He appointed the vigorous young reformer Theodore Roosevelt to the Civil Service Commission and then proceeded to undercut him systematically. Before long the frustrated Roosevelt was calling the president a "cold blooded, narrow minded, prejudiced, obstinate, timid old psalm-singing Indianapolis politician."

Under Harrison, Congress distinguished itself by expending, for the first time in a period of peace, more than $1 billion in a single session. It raised the tariff to an all-time high. The Sherman Antitrust Act was also passed.

Harrison had little to do with the fate of any of these measures. The Republicans lost control of Congress in 1890, and two years later Grover Cleveland swept back into power, defeating Harrison by more than 350,000 votes.

Blacks in the South After Reconstruction

Perhaps the most important issue of the last quarter of the nineteenth century was the fate of the former slaves after the withdrawal of federal troops from the South. Shortly after his inauguration in 1877, President Hayes made a goodwill tour of the South and he urged blacks to trust southern whites. A new Era of Good Feelings had dawned, he announced. Some southern leaders made earnest attempts to respect the civil rights of African Americans. That same year Governor Wade Hampton of South Carolina proposed to "secure to every citizen, the lowest as well as the highest, black as well as white, full and equal protection in the enjoyment of all his rights under the Constitution."

But the pledge was not kept. By December, Hayes was sadly disillusioned. "By state legislation, by frauds, by intimidation, and by violence of the most atrocious character, colored citizens have been deprived of the right of suffrage," he wrote in his diary. However, he did nothing to remedy the situation. Frederick Douglass called Hayes's policy "sickly conciliation."

Hayes's successors in the 1880s did no better. "Time is the only cure," President Garfield said, thereby confessing that he had no policy at all. President Arthur gave federal patronage to antiblack groups in an effort to split the Democratic South. In President Cleveland's day African Americans had scarcely a friend in high places, North or South. In 1887 Cleveland explained to a correspondent why he opposed "mixed schools." Expert opinion, the president said, held "that separate schools were of much more benefit for the colored people." Hayes, Garfield, and Arthur were Republicans, Cleveland a Democrat; party made little difference. Both parties subscribed to hypocritical statements about equality and constitutional rights, and neither did anything to implement them.

For a time blacks were not totally disenfranchised in the South. Rival white factions tried to manipulate them, and corruption flourished as widely as in the machine-dominated wards of the northern cities. In the 1890s, however, the southern states, led by Mississippi, began to deprive blacks of the vote despite the Fifteenth Amendment. Poll taxes raised a formidable economic barrier, one that also disenfranchised many poor whites. Literacy tests completed the work; a number of states provided a loophole for illiterate whites by including an "understanding" clause whereby an illiterate person could qualify by demonstrating an ability to explain the meaning of a section of the state constitution when an election official read it to him. Blacks who attempted to take the test were uniformly declared to have failed it.

In *Plessy* v. *Ferguson* (1896), the Court ruled that even in places of public accommodation, such as railroads and, by implication, schools, segregation was legal as long as facilities of equal quality were provided. "If one race be inferior to the other socially, the Constitution of the United States cannot put them upon the same plane." In a noble dissent in the *Plessy* case, Justice John Marshall Harlan protested this line of argument. "Our Constitution is color-blind," he said. "The arbitrary separation of citizens, on the basis of race . . . is a badge of servitude wholly inconsistent with civil freedom. . . . The two races in this country are indissolubly linked together, and the interests of both require that the common government of all shall not permit the seeds of race hatred to be planted under the sanction of law."

More than half a century was to pass before the Court came around to Harlan's reasoning and reversed the *Plessy* decision. Meanwhile, total segregation was imposed throughout the South. Separate schools, prisons, hospitals, recreational facilities, and even cemeteries were provided for blacks, and these were almost never equal to those available to whites.

Most Northerners supported the government and the Court. Newspapers presented a stereotyped, derogatory picture of blacks, no matter what the circumstances. Northern magazines, even high-quality publications such as *Harper's*, *Scribner's*, and *The Century*, repeatedly made blacks the butt of crude jokes.

The southern insistence on segregating the public schools, buttressed by the separate but equal decision of the Supreme Court in *Plessy* v. *Ferguson*, imposed a crushing financial burden on poor, sparsely settled communities, and the dominant opinion that blacks were not really educable did not encourage these communities to make special efforts in their behalf.

Booker T. Washington: A "Reasonable" Champion for Blacks

Southern blacks reacted to this deplorable situation in a variety of ways. Some sought redress in racial pride and what would later be called black nationalism. Some became so disaffected that they tried to revive the African colonization movement. "Africa is our home," insisted Bishop Henry M. Turner, a huge, plain-spoken man who had served as an army chaplain during the war and as a member of the Georgia legislature during Reconstruction. Another militant, T. Thomas Fortune, editor of the *New York Age* and founder of the Afro-American League (1887), called on blacks to demand full civil rights, better schools, and fair wages and to fight against discrimination of every sort. "Let us stand up like men in our own organization," he urged. "If others use . . . violence to combat our peaceful arguments, it is not for us to run away from violence."

For a time, militancy and black separatism won few adherents among southern blacks. For one thing, life was better than it had been under slavery. Segregation actually helped southern blacks who became barbers, undertakers, restaurateurs, and shopkeepers because whites were reluctant to supply such services to blacks. Even when whites competed with black businesses, the resentment caused by segregation led blacks to patronize establishments run by people of their

George Washington Carver, second from right, teaching in a chemistry laboratory at Tuskegee Institute (1906). As Director of Agriculture at the Institute, Carver taught crop rotation, which revolutionized southern agriculture.

own race. According to the most conservative estimates, the living standard of the average southern black more than doubled between 1865 and 1900. But this only made many southern whites more angry and vindictive.

This helps explain the tactics of Booker T. Washington, one of the most extraordinary Americans of that generation. Washington had been born a slave in Virginia in 1856. Laboriously he obtained an education, supporting himself while a student by working as a janitor. In 1881, with the financial help of northern philanthropists, he founded Tuskegee Institute in Alabama. His experiences convinced Washington that blacks must lift themselves up by their own bootstraps but that they must also accommodate themselves to white prejudices. A persuasive speaker and a brilliant fund-raiser, he soon developed a national reputation as a "reasonable" champion of his race. (In 1891 Harvard awarded him an honorary degree.)

In 1895 Washington made a now-famous speech to a mixed audience at the Cotton States International Exposition in Atlanta. To the blacks he said: "Cast down your bucket where you are," by which he meant stop fighting segregation and second-class citizenship and concentrate on learning useful skills. "Dignify and glorify common labor," he urged. "Agitation of questions of racial equality is the extremest folly." Progress up the social and economic ladder would come not from "artificial forcing" but from self-improvement. "There is as much dignity in tilling a field as in writing a poem."

Washington asked the whites of what he called "our beloved South" to lend the blacks a hand in their efforts to advance themselves. If you will do so, he promised, you will be "surrounded by the most patient, faithful, law-abiding, and unresentful people that the world has seen."

This "Atlanta Compromise" delighted white Southerners and won Washington financial support in every section of the country. He became one of the most powerful men in the United States, consulted by presidents, in close touch with business and philanthropic leaders, and capable of influencing in countless unobtrusive ways the fate of millions of blacks.

Blacks responded to the compromise with mixed feelings. Accepting Washington's approach might relieve them of many burdens and dangers. Being obsequious might, like discretion, be the better part of valor. But Washington was asking them to give up specific rights in return for vague promises of future help. The cost was high in surrendered personal dignity and lost hopes of obtaining real justice.

Washington's career illustrates the terrible dilemma that American blacks have always faced: the choice between confrontation and accommodation. This choice was particularly difficult in the late nineteenth century.

City Bosses

Outside of the South, the main issue concerned municipal government. This was complicated by the religious and ethnic character of the inhabitants and by the special problems of late-nineteenth-century urban life: rapid, helter-skelter growth; the influx of European immigrants; the need to develop costly transportation, sanitation, and other public utility systems; and the crime and corruption that the size, confusion, and anonymity incidental to urban existence fostered.

The immigrants who flocked into American cities in the 1880s and early 1890s were largely of peasant stock, and having come from societies unacquainted with democracy, they had no experience with representative government. The tendency of urban workers to move frequently in search of better jobs further lessened the likelihood that they would develop political influence independently.

Furthermore, the difficulties of life in the slums bewildered and often overwhelmed newcomers, both native- and foreign-born. Hopeful, but passive and naive, they could hardly be expected to take a broad view of social problems when so beset by personal ones. This enabled shrewd urban politicians—most of them in this period of Irish origin, the Irish being the first-comers among the migrants and, according to mobility studies, more likely to stay put—to take command of the city masses and march them in obedient phalanxes to the polls.

Most city machines were loose-knit neighborhood organizations headed by ward bosses, not tightly geared hierarchical bureaucracies ruled by a single leader. Timothy "Big Tim" Sullivan of New York's Lower East Side and Michael "Hinky Dink" Kenna of Chicago's First Ward were typical of the breed. Sullivan, Kenna, and others like them performed many useful services for people they liked to think of as their constituents. They found jobs for new arrivals and distributed food and other help to all in bad times. Anyone in trouble with the law could obtain at least a hearing from the ward boss, and often, if the crime was minor or due to ignorance,

WERE CITY GOVERNMENTS CORRUPT AND INCOMPETENT?

This 1871 cartoon lampoons "Boss Tweed" for crushing a helpless New York City.

James Bryce (1888), a British observer, described municipal government as "the one conspicuous failure of the United States." Two years later Andrew D. White, president of Cornell, called American city governments "the worst in Christendom—the most expensive, the most inefficient, and the most corrupt." In 1904 journalist Lincoln Steffens's *The Shame of the Cities* offered a searing denunciation of municipal corruption throughout the nation, a view with which most historians long concurred. As late as 1974, Ernest S. Griffith characterized nineteenth-century municipal governments as cesspools of corruption and inefficiency.

But by then, other scholars were considering the nineteenth-century city governments in a more favorable light. During the 1960s many cities were plagued by race riots and beset with financial woes. They struggled merely to maintain the hospitals, museums, orphanages, waterworks, and sewage and transit systems

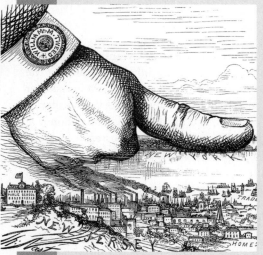

that had been built by presumably incompetent municipal governments during the Gilded Age. In *The Unheralded Triumph* (1984), a book whose thesis is carried in its title, Jon C. Teaford applauded municipal leaders of the late nineteenth century for building the complex infrastructure of rapidly growing cities. Historians such as John Buenker (1973) also observed that while the bosses often pilfered public monies, they also provided essential services for needy immigrants.

Corrupt bosses like Tweed stuck their hands deep into city coffers; but their thumbs failed to keep down those who did the work of building the great cities.

James Bryce, *The American Commonwealth* (1888), Jon C. Teaford, *The Unheralded Triumph: City Government in America, 1860–1900* (1984), Ernest S. Griffith, *A History of American City Government* (1974), John Buenker, *Urban Liberalism and Progressive Reform* (1973).

the difficulty was quietly "fixed" and the culprit was sent off with a word of caution. Sullivan provided turkey dinners for 5,000 or more homeless people each Christmas, distributed new shoes to the poor children of his district on his birthday, and arranged summer boat rides and picnics for young and old alike. At any time of year the victim of some sudden disaster could turn to the local clubhouse for help. Informally, probably without consciously intending to do so, the bosses educated the immigrants in the complexities of American civilization, helping them to leap the gulf between the almost medieval society of their origins and the modern industrial world.

The price of such aid—the bosses were not altruists—was unquestioning political support, which the bosses converted into cash. In New York, Sullivan levied tribute on gambling, had a hand in the liquor business, and controlled the issuance of peddlers' licenses. When he died in 1913, he was reputedly worth $1 million. Yet he and others like him were immensely popular; 25,000 grieving constituents followed Big Tim's coffin on its way to the grave.

The more visible and better-known city bosses played even less socially justifiable roles than the ward bosses. Their principal technique for extracting money from the public till was the kickback. To get city contracts, suppliers were made to pad their bills and, when paid for their work with funds from the city treasury, turn over the excess to the politicians. Similarly, operators of streetcar lines, gas and electricity companies, and other public utilities were compelled to pay huge bribes to obtain favorable franchises.

The most notorious of the nineteenth-century city bosses was William Marcy Tweed, whose "Tweed Ring" extracted tens of millions of dollars from New York City during the brief period 1869 to 1871. Tweed was swiftly jailed. More typical was Richard Croker, who ruled New York's Tammany Hall organization from the mid-1880s to the end of the century. Croker held a number of local offices, but his power rested on his position as chairman of the Tammany Hall finance committee. Although more concerned than Tweed with the social and economic services that machines provided, Croker was primarily a corrupt political manipulator; he accumulated a large fortune and owned a mansion and a stable of racehorses, one of which was good enough to win the English Derby.

Despite their welfare work and their popularity, most bosses were essentially thieves. Efforts to romanticize them as the Robin Hoods of industrial society grossly distort the facts. However, the system developed and survived because too many middle-class city dwellers were indifferent to the fate of the poor. Except during occasional reform waves, few tried to check the politicos' greed.

Many substantial citizens shared at least indirectly in the corruption. The owners of tenements were interested in crowding as many rent payers as possible into their buildings. Utility companies seeking franchises preferred a system that enabled them to buy favors. Honest citizens who had no selfish stake in the system and who were repelled by the sordidness of city government were seldom sufficiently concerned to do anything about it. When young Theodore Roosevelt decided to seek a political career in 1880, his New York socialite friends laughed in his face. They told him, Roosevelt wrote in his autobiography, "that politics were 'low'; that the organizations were not controlled by 'gentlemen'; that I would find them run by saloonkeepers, horse-car conductors, and the like."

Crops and Complaints

The emptiness of American politics may well have stemmed from the complacency of the middle-class majority. The country was growing; no foreign enemy threatened it; the poor were mostly recent immigrants, blacks, and others with little influence who were easily ignored by those in comfortable circumstances. However, one important group in society suffered increasingly as the years rolled by: the farmers. Out of their travail came the force that finally, in the 1890s, brought American politics face to face with the problems of the age.

After the Civil War, farmers did well. Harvests were bountiful and wheat prices high, with wheat selling at over a dollar a bushel in the early 1870s. Well into the 1880s farmers on the Plains experienced boom conditions. In that decade the population of Kansas increased by 43 percent, that of Nebraska by 134 percent, that of the Dakotas by 278 percent. Land prices rose and farmers borrowed money to expand their farms.

In the 1890s disaster struck. First came a succession of dry years and poor harvests. Then farmers in Australia, Canada, Russia, and Argentina took advantage of improvements in transportation to sell their produce in European markets that had relied on American foodstuffs. The price of wheat fell to about 60 cents a bushel. Cotton, the great southern staple, which sold for more than 30 cents a pound in 1866 and 15 cents in the early 1870s, at times in the 1890s fell below 6 cents.

The tariff on manufactured goods appeared to aggravate the farmers' predicament and so did the domestic marketing system, which enabled a multitude of middlemen to gobble up a large share of the profits of agriculture. The shortage of credit, particularly in the South, was an additional burden.

The downward swing of the business cycle in the early 1890s completed the devastation. Settlers who had paid more for their lands than they were worth and borrowed money at high interest rates to do so found themselves squeezed relentlessly. Thousands lost their farms and returned eastward, penniless and dispirited. The population of Nebraska increased by fewer than 4,000 persons in the entire decade of the 1890s.

The Populist Movement

The agricultural depression triggered a new outburst of farm radicalism, the Alliance movement. Alliances were organizations of farmers' clubs, most of which had sprung up during the bad times of the late 1870s. The first Knights of Reliance group was founded in 1877 in Lampasas County, Texas. As the Farmers Alliance, this organization gradually expanded in northeastern Texas, and after 1885 it spread rapidly throughout the cotton states. Alliance leaders stressed cooperation. Their co-ops bought fertilizer and other supplies in bulk and sold them at fair prices to members. They sought to market their crops cooperatively but could not raise the necessary capital from banks, with the result that some of them began to question the workings of the American financial and monetary system. They became economic and social radicals in the process. A similar though less influential Alliance movement developed in the North.

The alliances adopted somewhat differing policies, but all agreed that agricultural prices were too low, that transportation costs were too high, and that some-

Mary Elizabeth Lease was a prominent Populist, noted for her rallying cry to "raise less corn and more hell."

thing was radically wrong with the nation's financial system. "There are three great crops raised in Nebraska," an angry rural editor proclaimed in 1890. "One is a crop of corn, one is a crop of freight rates, and one a crop of interest. One is produced by farmers who by sweat and toil farm the land. The other two are produced by men who sit in their offices and behind their bank counters and farm the farmers." All agreed on the need for political action if the lot of the agriculturalist was to be improved.

Although the state alliances of the Dakotas and Kansas joined the Southern Alliance in 1889, for a time local prejudices and conflicting interests prevented the formation of a single national organization. Northern farmers mostly voted Republican, Southerners Democratic, and resentments created during the Civil War lingered in all sections. Cotton-producing Southerners opposed the protective tariff; most Northerners, fearing the competition of foreign grain producers, favored it. Railroad regulation and federal land policy seemed vital questions to Northerners; financial reform loomed most important in southern eyes. Northerners were receptive to the idea of forming a third party, while Southerners, wedded to the one-party system, preferred working to capture local Democratic machines.

The farm groups entered local politics in the 1890 elections. Convinced of the righteousness of their cause, they campaigned with tremendous fervor. The results were encouraging. In the South, Alliance-sponsored gubernatorial candidates won in Georgia, Tennessee, South Carolina, and Texas; eight southern legislatures fell under Alliance control, and forty-four representatives and three senators committed to Alliance objectives were sent to Washington. In the West, Alliance candidates swept Kansas and captured a majority in the Nebraska legislature and enough seats in Minnesota and South Dakota to hold the balance of power between the major parties.

Such success, coupled with the reluctance of the Republicans and Democrats to make concessions to their demands, encouraged Alliance leaders to create a new national party. By uniting southern and western farmers, they succeeded in breaking the sectional barrier erected by the Civil War. If they could recruit industrial workers, perhaps a real political revolution could be accomplished. In February 1892, farm leaders, representatives of the Knights of Labor, and various professional reformers, some 800 in all, met at St. Louis. They organized the People's, or Populist, party, and issued a call for a national convention to meet at Omaha in July.

That convention nominated General James B. Weaver of Iowa for president (with a one-legged Confederate veteran as his running mate) and drafted a platform that called for a graduated income tax and national ownership of railroads and the telegraph and telephone systems. It also advocated a "subtreasury" plan that would permit farmers to keep nonperishable crops off the market when prices were low. Under this proposal the government would make loans in the form of greenbacks to farmers, secured by crops held in storage in federal warehouses. When prices rose, the farmers could sell their crops and repay the loans. To combat deflation further, the platform demanded the unlimited coinage of silver and an increase in the money supply "to no less than $50 per capita."

To make the government more responsive to public opinion, the Populists urged the adoption of the initiative and referendum procedures and the election of U.S. senators by popular vote. To win the support of industrial workers, their platform denounced the use of Pinkerton detectives in labor disputes and backed the eight-hour day and the restriction of "undesirable" immigration.

The appearance of the new party was the most exciting and significant aspect of the presidential campaign of 1892, which saw Harrison and Cleveland refighting the election of 1888. The Populists put forth a host of colorful spellbinders: Tom Watson, a Georgia congressman whose temper was such that on one occasion he administered a beating to a local planter with the man's own riding crop; William A. Peffer, a senator from Kansas whose long beard and grave demeanor gave him the look of a Hebrew prophet; "Sockless Jerry" Simpson of Kansas, unlettered but full of grassroots shrewdness and wit, a former Greenbacker, and an admirer of the single tax doctrine of Henry George; Ignatius Donnelly, the "Minnesota Sage," who claimed to be an authority on science, economics, and Shakespeare (he believed that Francis Bacon wrote the plays) and whose widely read novel, *Caesar's Column* (1891), pictured an America of the future wherein a handful of plutocrats tyrannized masses of downtrodden workers and serfs.

In the one-party South, Populist strategists sought to wean black farmers away from the ruling Democratic organization. Southern black farmers had their own Colored Alliance, and even before 1892 their leaders had worked closely with the

In Kansas in 1893 a Populist governor and a Populist-controlled Senate invalidated the election of some Republicans in the Kansas House of Representatives, giving the Populists control of that body, too. The displaced Republicans, denied seats, smashed their way into the capitol building with this sledgehammer and ousted the Populists, who decided to meet in a separate building. Each proclaimed itself to be the true legislature of Congress and passed its own laws. Eventually the Kansas Supreme Court decided in favor of the Republican legislature and disbanded the Populist gathering.

white alliances. Nearly 100 black delegates had attended the Populist convention at St. Louis. Of course, the blacks would be useless to the party if they could not vote; therefore, white Populist leaders opposed the southern trend toward disfranchising African Americans and called for full civil rights for all.

In the Northwest, the Populists assailed the "bankers' conspiracy" in unbridled terms. Donnelly, running for governor of Minnesota, made 150 speeches, vowing to make the campaign "the liveliest ever seen" in the state.

The results proved disappointing. Tom Watson lost his seat in Congress, and Donnelly ran a poor third in the Minnesota gubernatorial race. The Populists did sweep Kansas. They elected numbers of local officials in other western states and cast over a million votes for General Weaver. But the effort to unite white and black farmers in the South failed miserably. Conservative Democrats, while continuing with considerable success to attract black voters, played on racial fears cruelly, insisting that the Populists sought to undermine white supremacy. Since most white Populists saw the alliance with blacks as at best a marriage of convenience, this argument had a deadly effect. Elsewhere, even in the old centers of the Granger movement, the party made no significant impression. Urban workers remained aloof.

By standing firmly for conservative financial policies, Cleveland attracted considerable Republican support and won a solid victory over Harrison in the electoral college, 277 to 145. Weaver's electoral vote was 22.

Showdown on Silver

One conclusion that politicians reached after analyzing the 1892 election was that the money question, particularly the controversy over the coinage of silver, was of paramount interest to the voters. Despite the wide-ranging appeal of the Populist platform, most of Weaver's strength came from the silver-mining states.

In truth, the issue of gold versus silver was superficial; the important question was what, if anything, should be done to check the deflationary spiral. The declining price level benefited people with fixed incomes and injured most others. Industrial workers profited from deflation except when depression caused unemployment.

By the early 1890s, discussion of federal monetary policy revolved around the coinage of silver. Traditionally, the United States had been on a bimetallic standard. Both gold and silver were coined, the number of grains of each in the dollar being adjusted periodically to reflect the commercial value of the two metals. The discovery of numerous gold mines in California in the 1840s and 1850s depressed the price of gold relative to silver. By 1861, a silver dollar could be melted down and sold for $1.03. No miner took silver to the mint to be stamped into coin. In a short time, silver dollars were withdrawn and only gold dollars circulated. However, an avalanche of silver from the mines of Nevada and Colorado gradually depressed the price until, around 1874, it again became profitable for miners to coin their bullion. Alas, when they tried to do so, they discovered that the Coinage Act of 1873, taking account of the fact that no silver had been presented to the mint in years, had demonetized the metal.

Silver miners denounced this "Crime of '73." Inflationists joined them in demanding a return to bimetallism. They knew that if more dollars were put into circulation, the value of each dollar would decline; that is, prices and wages would rise. Conservatives, still fighting the battle against inflationary greenback paper money, resisted strongly. The result was a series of compromises. In 1878 the Bland-Allison Silver Purchase Act authorized the buying of between $2 and $4 million of silver a month at the market price, but this had little inflationary effect because the government consistently purchased the minimum amount. The commercial price of silver continued to fall. In 1890 the Sherman Silver Purchase Act required the government to buy 4.5 million *ounces* of silver monthly, but in the face of increasing supplies the price of silver fell still further. By 1894, a silver coin weighed 32 times more than a gold one.

The compromises satisfied no one. Silver miners grumbled because their bullion brought in only half what it had in the early 1870s. Debtors noted angrily that because of the general decline in prices, the dollars they used to meet their obligations were worth more than twice as much as in 1865. Advocates of the gold standard feared that unlimited silver coinage would be authorized, "destroying the value of the dollar."

The Depression of 1893

Both the silverites and "gold bugs" warned of economic disaster if their policies were not followed. Then, in 1893, after the London banking house of Baring Brothers collapsed, a financial panic precipitated a worldwide industrial depression. In the

United States hundreds of cotton mills and iron foundries closed, never to reopen. During the harsh winter of 1893–1894, millions were without jobs. Discontented industrial workers added their voices to the complaints of the Midwestern farmers.

President Cleveland believed that the controversy over silver had caused the depression by shaking the confidence of the business community and that all would be well if the country returned to a single gold standard. He summoned a special session of Congress, and by exerting immense political pressure he obtained the repeal of the Sherman Silver Purchase Act in October 1893. All that this accomplished was to split the Democratic party, its southern and western wings deserting him almost to a man.

During 1894 and 1895, while the nation floundered in the worst depression it had ever experienced, a series of events further undermined public confidence. In the spring of 1894 several "armies" of the unemployed, the most imposing led by Jacob S. Coxey, an eccentric Ohio businessman, marched on Washington to demand relief. Coxey wanted the government to undertake a program of federal public works and to authorize local communities to exchange non-interest-bearing bonds with the Treasury for $500 million in paper money, the funds to be used to hire unemployed workers to build roads. The scheme, Coxey claimed, would pump money into the economy, provide work for the jobless, and benefit the entire nation by improving transportation facilities.

When Coxey's group of demonstrators, perhaps 500 in all, reached Washington, he and two other leaders were arrested for trespassing on the grounds of the Capitol. Their followers were dispersed by club-wielding policemen. This callous treatment convinced many Americans that the government had little interest in the suffering of the people, an opinion strengthened when Cleveland, in July 1894, used federal troops to crush the Pullman strike.

The next year the Supreme Court handed down several reactionary decisions. In *United States* v. *E. C. Knight Company* it refused to employ the Sherman Antitrust Act to break up the Sugar Trust. In *Pollock* v. *Farmers' Loan and Trust Company* it invalidated a federal income tax law despite the fact that a similar measure levied during the Civil War had been upheld by the Court in *Springer* v. *United States* (1881). Throughout 1894 the Treasury's supply of gold dwindled as worried citizens exchanged greenbacks (now convertible into gold) for hard money and foreign investors cashed in large amounts of American securities. The government tried to sell bonds for gold to bolster the reserve, but the gold reserve continued to melt away. Early in 1895 it touched a low point of $41 million.

At this juncture a syndicate of bankers headed by J. P. Morgan turned the tide by underwriting a $62 million bond issue, guaranteeing that half the gold would come from Europe. This caused a great public outcry; the spectacle of the nation being saved from bankruptcy by a private banker infuriated millions.

These events, together with the continuing depression, discredited the Cleveland administration. As the presidential election of 1896 approached, with the Populists demanding unlimited coinage of silver, the major parties found it impossible to continue straddling the money question. The Populist vote had increased by 42 percent in the 1894 congressional elections. Southern and western Democratic leaders feared that they would lose their following unless Cleveland was repudiated. Western

William Jennings Bryan's "Cross of Gold" speech inspired this cartoonist's caricature of it as "plagiarized from the Bible." Bryan's speech in favor of bimetallism was, in fact, studded with religious references. He described the unlimited coinage of silver and gold as a "holy cause" supported by those who built churches "where they praise their Creator."

Republicans, led by Senator Henry M. Teller of Colorado, were threatening to bolt to the Populists unless their party came out for silver coinage. After a generation of political equivocation, the major parties had to face an important issue squarely.

The Republicans, meeting to choose a candidate at St. Louis in June 1896, announced for the gold standard. "We are unalterably opposed to every measure calculated to debase our currency or impair the credit of our country," the platform declared. "We are therefore opposed to the free coinage of silver. . . . The existing gold standard must be maintained." The party then nominated Ohio's William McKinley for president. McKinley, best known for his staunch advocacy of the protective tariff yet highly regarded by labor, was expected to run strongly in the Midwest and the East.

The Democratic convention met in July at Chicago. The pro-gold Cleveland element made a hard fight, but the silverites swept them aside. The high point came when a youthful Nebraskan named William Jennings Bryan spoke for silver against gold, for western farmers against the industrial East. Bryan's every sentence provoked ear-shattering applause. He ended with a marvelous figure of speech that set the tone for the coming campaign. "You shall not press down upon the brow of labor this crown of thorns," he warned, bringing his hands down suggestively to his temples. "You shall not crucify mankind upon a cross of gold!" Dramatically, he extended his arms to the side, the very figure of the crucified Christ.

The convention promptly adopted a platform calling for "the free and unlimited coinage of both silver and gold at the present legal ratio of 16 to 1" and went on to nominate Bryan, who was barely 36 years old, for president.

This action put tremendous pressure on the Populists. If they supported the Democrat Bryan, they risked losing their party identity; if they nominated another candidate, they would ensure McKinley's election. In part because the delegates could not find a person of stature willing to become a candidate against Bryan, the Populist convention nominated him, seeking to preserve the party identity by substituting Watson for the Democratic vice-presidential nominee, Arthur Sewall of Maine.

The Election of 1896

Never did a presidential campaign raise such intense emotions. The Republicans from the silver-mining states swung solidly behind Bryan. But many solid-money Democrats, especially in the Northeast, refused to accept the decision of the Chicago convention. Cleveland professed to be "so dazed by the political situation that I am in no condition for speech or thought on the subject." Many others adopted the policy of Governor David B. Hill of New York, who said, "I am a Democrat still—very still."

At the start the Republicans seemed to have everything in their favor. Bryan's youth and relative lack of political experience—two terms in the House—contrasted unfavorably with McKinley's distinguished war record, his long service in Congress and as governor of Ohio, and his reputation for honesty and good judgment. The severe depression operated in favor of the party out of power, although by repudiating Cleveland the Democrats escaped much of the burden of explaining away his errors. The newspapers came out almost unanimously for the Republicans. Important Democratic papers such as the *New York World*, the *Boston Herald*, the *Baltimore Sun*, the *Chicago Chronicle*, and the *Richmond Times* supported McKinley editorially and even slanted news stories against the Democrats. The Democrats had very little money and few well-known speakers to fight the campaign.

But Bryan proved a formidable opponent. Casting aside tradition, he took to the stump personally, traveling 18,000 miles and making over 600 speeches. He was one of the greatest of orators. A big, handsome man with a voice capable of carrying without strain to the far corners of a great hall yet equally effective before a cluster of listeners at a rural crossroads, he projected an image of absolute sincerity without appearing fanatical or argumentative. At every major stop on his tour, huge crowds assembled.

McKinley's campaign was managed by a new type of politician, Marcus Alonzo Hanna, an Ohio businessman. In a sense Hanna was a product of the Pendleton Civil Service Act. When deprived of the contributions of officeholders, the parties turned to business for funds, and Hanna was one of the first leaders with a foot in both camps. Politics fascinated him, and despite his wealth and wide interests, he was willing to labor endlessly at the routine work of political organization.

Hanna aspired to be a kingmaker and early fastened on McKinley, whose charm he found irresistible, as the vehicle for satisfying his ambition. He spent

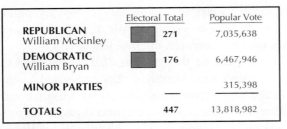

The Election of 1896

	Electoral Total	Popular Vote
REPUBLICAN William McKinley	271	7,035,638
DEMOCRATIC William Bryan	176	6,467,946
MINOR PARTIES	—	315,398
TOTALS	447	13,818,982

about $100,000 of his own money on the preconvention campaign. His attitude toward the candidate, one mutual friend observed, was "that of a big, bashful boy toward the girl he loves."

Before most Republicans realized how effective Bryan was on the stump, Hanna perceived the danger and sprang into action. Since the late 1880s the character of political organization had been changing. The Civil Service Act was also cutting down on the number of jobs available to reward campaign workers. At the same time, the new mass circulation newspapers and the nationwide press associations were increasing the pressure on candidates to speak openly and often on national issues. This trend put a premium on party organization and consistency—the old political trick of speaking out of one side of the mouth to one audience and out the other to a different audience no longer worked very well.

Hanna, who was certain that money was the key to political power, raised an enormous campaign fund. When businessmen hesitated to contribute, he used a combination of persuasiveness and intimidation to pry open their purses. Banks and insurance companies were "assessed" a percentage of their assets, big corporations a share of their receipts, until some $3.5 million had been collected.

Hanna disbursed these funds with efficiency and imagination. He sent 1500 speakers into the doubtful districts and blanketed the land with 250 million pieces of campaign literature, printed in a dozen languages. "He has advertised McKinley as if he were a patent medicine," Theodore Roosevelt, never at a loss for words, exclaimed.

Incapable of competing with Bryan as a swayer of mass audiences, McKinley conducted a "front-porch campaign." Superficially the proceedings were delightfully informal. From every corner of the land, groups representing various regions, occupations, and interests descended on McKinley's unpretentious frame house in Canton, Ohio. Gathering on the lawn—the grass was soon reduced to mud, the fence stripped of pickets by souvenir hunters—the visitors paid their compliments to the candidate and heard him deliver a brief speech, while beside him on the porch his aged mother and adoring invalid wife listened with rapt attention. Then there was a small reception, during which the delegates were given an opportunity to shake their host's hand.

Despite the air of informality, these performances were carefully staged. The delegations arrived on a tightly coordinated schedule worked out by McKinley's staff and the railroads, which operated cut-rate excursion trains to Canton from all over the nation. McKinley was fully briefed on the special interests and attitudes of each group, and the speeches of delegation leaders were submitted in advance. Often his secretary amended these remarks, and on occasion McKinley wrote the visitors' speeches himself. His own talks were carefully prepared, each calculated to make a particular point. All were reported fully in the newspapers. Thus without moving from his doorstep, McKinley met thousands of people from every section of the country.

These tactics worked admirably. On election day McKinley collected 271 electoral votes to Bryan's 176, the popular vote being 7,036,000 to 6,468,000.

The Meaning of the Election

During the campaign, some frightened Republicans had laid plans for fleeing the country if Bryan were elected, and belligerent ones, such as Theodore Roosevelt, then police commissioner of New York City, readied themselves to meet the "social revolutionaries" on the battlefield. McKinley's victory sent such people into transports of joy. Most conservatives concluded that the way of life they so fervently admired had been saved for all time.

However heartfelt, such sentiments were not founded on fact. With workers standing beside capitalists and with the farm vote split, it cannot be said that the election divided the nation class against class or that McKinley's victory saved the country from revolution.

Far from representing a triumph for the status quo, the election marked the coming of age of modern America. The battle between gold and silver, which everyone had considered so vital, had little real significance. The inflationists seemed to have been beaten, but new discoveries of gold in Alaska and South Africa and improved methods of extracting gold from low-grade ores soon led to a great expansion of the money supply. In any case, within two decades the system of basing the volume of currency on bullion had been abandoned. Bryan and the "political" Populists who supported him, supposedly the advance agents of revolution, were oriented more toward the past than the future; their ideal was the rural America of Jefferson and Jackson.

McKinley, for all his innate conservatism, was capable of looking ahead toward the new century. His approach was national where Bryan's was basically parochial.

Though never daring and seldom imaginative, McKinley was able to deal pragmatically with current problems. Before long, as the United States became increasingly an exporter of manufactures, he would even modify his position on the tariff. And no one better reflected the spirit of the age than Mark Hanna, the outstanding political realist of his generation. Far from preventing change, the outcome of the election of 1896 made possible still greater changes as the United States moved into the twentieth century.

Milestones

1873	Congress suspends the coining of silver ("Crime of '73")
1876	Rutherford B. Hayes is elected president
1877	Farmers Alliance movement is founded
1878	Bland-Allison Act authorizes government silver purchases
1879	Specie payments resume
1880	James Garfield is elected president
1881	Garfield is assassinated; Grover Cleveland becomes president
	Booker T. Washington founds Tuskegee Institute for blacks
1883	Pendleton Act creates Civil Service Commission
1884	"Mugwump" Republicans support Democratic candidate Cleveland in 1884 presidential campaign
	Grover Cleveland is elected president
1887	Cleveland delivers tariff message
1888	Benjamin Harrison is elected president
1890	Sherman Silver Purchase Act requires government silver purchase
1890–1900	Blacks are deprived of the vote in the South
1892	People's (Populist) Party is founded
	Cleveland is elected president a second time
1893	Sherman Silver Purchase Act is repealed
1893	Panic of 1893 causes industrial depression
1894	Coxey's Army marches to Washington to demand relief
1895	Supreme Court declares federal income tax unconstitutional (Pollock v. Farmers' Loan and Trust Company)
	Booker T. Washington urges self-improvement in Atlanta Compromise speech
	J. P. Morgan raises $62 million in gold for the U.S. Treasury
1896	William Jennings Bryan delivers "Cross of Gold" speech
	William McKinley is elected president
	Supreme Court upholds "separate but equal" facilities in Plessy v. Ferguson

CHAPTER 21

The Age of Reform

Many People Say That Young Americans Are Politically apathetic. Critics note, for example, that in 2004 only 42 percent of those aged 18 to 24 voted, while 61 percent of those over age 24 went to the polls. The next year a survey of a quarter of a million college freshmen revealed that nearly two-thirds did not think it "important to keep up to date with political affairs."

But such numbers are misleading. Closer analysis reveals a huge schism among young adults. Of those between ages 18 and 24 who had attended college, 67 percent voted in 2004; but for those in that age group without college experience, half as many voted. College-educated young people were thus among the most politically active demographic groups. Their numbers would have been higher still if more states explicitly allowed students to declare their college address as their voting residence. As of 2006, only Colorado, Iowa, Louisiana, North Carolina, and Wisconsin had such laws.

Moreover, although many college students do not bother to follow politics or go to the polls, many participate in public affairs in other ways. A major survey in 2006 found that 42 percent of current college students had done volunteer work during the previous six months. Over 20 percent had raised money for charity, many by participating in sponsored races or other events. About the same proportion had been actively working on community problems.

Young people who have attended college are demonstrably not apathetic. In this sense, they resemble their counterparts during the "age of reform" early in the twentieth century. Then, large numbers of young adults worked to improve society through community-based activism or political activity. They investigated tenements, factories, schools, municipal governments, and consumer goods. They joined political movements to fight city bosses and to restrain the excessive influence of corporations on state, local, and federal governments. They promoted legislation to protect women and children from exploitative employers and to secure voting rights for women. They advocated conservation of natural resources. They swelled the ranks of the Socialist party, the Progressive party, and of more radical movements. In response to this sea change among younger voters, the Republican and Democrat parties embraced some reforms that earlier generations had regarded as wild-eyed radicalism.

Roots of Progressivism

The progressives were never a single group seeking a single objective. The movement sprang from many sources. One was the fight against corruption and inefficiency in government, which began with the Liberal Republicans of the Grant era and was continued by the mugwumps of the 1880s. The struggle for civil service reform was only the first skirmish in this battle; the continuing power of corrupt political machines and the growing influence of large corporations and their lobbyists on municipal and state governments outraged thousands of citizens and led them to seek ways of purifying politics and making the machinery of government at all levels responsive to the majority rather than to special-interest groups.

Progressivism also had roots in the effort to regulate and control big business, which characterized the Granger and Populist agitation of the 1870s and 1890s. The failure of the Interstate Commerce Act to end railroad abuses and of the Sherman Antitrust Act to check the growth of large corporations became increasingly apparent after 1900. The return of prosperity after the depression of the 1890s encouraged reformers by removing the inhibiting fear, so influential in the 1896 presidential campaign, that an assault on the industrial giants might lead to the collapse of the economy.

Between 1897 and 1904 the trend toward concentration in industry accelerated. Such new giants as Amalgamated Copper (1899), U.S. Steel (1901), and International Harvester (1902) attracted most of the attention, but even more alarming were the overall statistics. In a single year (1899) more than 1,200 firms were absorbed in mergers, the resulting combinations being capitalized at $2.2 billion. By 1904 there were 318 industrial combinations in the country with an aggregate capital of $7.5 billion. People who considered bigness inherently evil demanded that the huge new "trusts" be broken up or at least strictly controlled.

Settlement house workers and other reformers concerned about the welfare of the urban poor made up a third battalion in the progressive army. This was an area in which women made the most important contributions. The working and living conditions of slum dwellers remained abominable, and the child labor problem was particularly acute; in 1900 about 1.7 million children under the age of 16 were working full time—more than the membership of the American Federation of Labor. In addition, laws regulating the hours and working conditions of women in industry were far from adequate, and almost nothing had been done, despite the increased use of dangerous machinery in the factories, to enforce safety rules or to provide compensation or insurance for workers injured on the job. As the number of professionally competent social workers grew, the movement for social welfare legislation gained momentum.

Orchard Street, a tenement district in lower Manhattan, in New York City. The unpaved street, ankle deep in mud, is lined with garbage. The sidewalks are packed with makeshift stalls and wagons, loaded with food, clothing, and other commodities for sale. Reformers worried that the congestion and filth of such streets constituted a health hazard. But many people who lived there enjoyed the sociability of the crowded streets; note that the man at the lower left is smiling.

America was becoming more urban, more industrial, more mechanized, more centralized—in short, more complex. This trend put a premium on efficiency and cooperation. It seemed obvious to the progressives that people must become more socially minded, the economy more carefully organized.

By attracting additional thousands of sympathizers to the general cause of reform, the return of prosperity after 1896 fueled the progressive movement. Good times made people more tolerant and generous. As long as profits were on the rise, the average employer did not object if labor improved its position too. Middle-class Americans who had been prepared to go to the barricades in the event of a Bryan victory in 1896 became conscience-stricken when they compared their own comfortable circumstances with those of the "huddled masses" of immigrants and native-born poor.

Giant industrial and commercial corporations undermined not so much the economic well-being as the ambitions and sense of importance of the middle class. What owner of a small mill or shop could now hope to rise to the heights attained by Carnegie or merchants like John Wanamaker and Marshall Field? The growth of large labor organizations worried such types. In general, character and moral values seemed less influential; organizations—cold, impersonal, heartless—were coming to control business, politics, and too many other aspects of life.

Protestant pastors accustomed to the respect and deference of their flocks found their moral leadership challenged by materialistic congregations who did not even pay them decent salaries. College professors worried about their institutions falling under the sway of wealthy trustees who had little interest in or respect for learning. Lawyers had been "the aristocracy of the United States," James Bryce recalled in 1905; they were now merely "a part of the great organized system of industrial and financial enterprise."

The middle classes could support reform measures without feeling that they were being very radical because they were resisting change and because the intellectual currents of the time harmonized with their ideas of social improvement and the welfare state. The new doctrines of the social scientists, the Social Gospel religious leaders, and the philosophers of pragmatism provided a favorable climate for progressivism.

As the diffuse progressive army gradually formed its battalions, a new journalistic fad brought the movement into focus. For many years magazines had been publishing articles discussing current political, social, and economic problems. Henry Demarest Lloyd's first blast at the Standard Oil monopoly appeared in the *Atlantic Monthly* in 1881. Over the years the tempo and forcefulness of this type of literature increased. Then, in the fall of 1902, *McClure's* began two particularly hard-hitting series of articles, one on Standard Oil by Ida Tarbell, the other on big-city political machines by Lincoln Steffens. These articles provoked much comment; soon many were clamoring to get copies of the magazine.

Other editors jumped to adopt the McClure formula. A small army of professional writers soon flooded the periodical press with denunciations of the insurance business, the drug business, college athletics, prostitution, sweatshop labor, political corruption, and dozens of other subjects. This type of article inspired Theodore Roosevelt, with his gift for vivid language, to compare the journalists to "the Man with the Muck-Rake" in John Bunyan's *Pilgrim's Progress,* whose attention was so fixed on the filth at his feet that he could not notice the "celestial crown" that was offered him in exchange. Roosevelt's characterization grossly misrepresented the literature of exposure, but the label *muckraking* was thereafter affixed to the type. Despite its literal connotations, *muckraker* became a term of honor.

The Progressive Mind

Progressives sought to arouse the conscience of "the people" in order to "purify" American life. They believed that the source of society's evils lay in the structure of its institutions, not in the weaknesses or sinfulness of individuals. Therefore, local, state, and national government must be made more responsive to the will of citizens who stood for the traditional virtues.

When government had been thus reformed, then it must act; whatever its virtues, laissez-faire was obsolete. Businessmen, especially big businessmen, must be compelled to behave fairly, their acquisitive drives curbed in the interests of jus-

New York artist George Luks's portrayal of the various corporate monopolies and franchises that preyed on New York City in 1900. Luks was one of the so-called Ashcan School artists who turned to city streets and the people of the slums for their subjects. Though individualists, the artists supported political and social reform and were part of the progressive movement.

tice and equal opportunity for all. The weaker elements in society—women, children, the poor, the infirm—must be protected against unscrupulous power.

Many progressives who desired to improve the living standards of industrial workers rejected the proposition that workers could help themselves best by organizing powerful national unions. They found it difficult to cooperate with actual working people, who seemed to them unrefined and narrow-minded. Union leaders favored government action to outlaw child labor and restrict immigration but adopted a laissez-faire attitude toward wages-and-hours legislation; they preferred to win these objectives through collective bargaining, thereby justifying their own existence. Many who favored "municipal socialism" (public ownership of streetcar lines, waterworks, and other local utilities) adamantly opposed national ownership of railroads. Progressives stressed individual freedom yet gave strong backing to the drive to deprive the public of its right to drink alcoholic beverages.

The progressives never challenged the fundamental principles of capitalism, nor did they attempt a basic reorganization of society. They would have little to do with the socialist brand of reform. Wisconsin was the most progressive of states, but its leaders never cooperated with the Socialist party of Milwaukee. When socialists threatened to win control of Los Angeles in 1911, California progressives made common cause with reactionary groups in order to defeat them. Many progressives were anti-immigrant, and only a handful had anything to offer blacks, surely the most exploited group in American society.

"Radical" Progressives: The Wave of the Future

Some people espoused more radical views. The hard times of the 1890s and the callous reactions of conservatives to the victims of that depression pushed many toward Marxist socialism. In 1900 the labor leader Eugene V. Debs ran for president on the Socialist ticket. He polled fewer than 100,000 votes. When he ran again in 1904 he got more than 400,000, and in later elections still more. Labor leaders hoping to organize unskilled workers in heavy industry were increasingly frustrated by the craft orientation of the American Federation of Labor, and some saw in socialism a way to win rank-and-file backing.

In 1905 Debs, William "Big Bill" Haywood of the Western Federation of Miners, Mary Harris "Mother" Jones—a former organizer for the United Mine Workers, Daniel De Leon of the Socialist Labor party, and a few others organized a new union: the Industrial Workers of the World (IWW). The IWW was openly anticapitalist. The preamble to its constitution began: "The working class and the employing class have nothing in common."

But the IWW never attracted many ordinary workers. Haywood, its most prominent leader, was usually a general in search of an army. His forte was attracting attention to spontaneous strikes by unorganized workers, not the patient recruiting of workers and the pursuit of practical goals. Shortly after the founding of the IWW, he was charged with complicity in the murder of an antiunion governor of Idaho after an earlier strike but was acquitted. In 1912 he was closely involved in a bitter and at times bloody strike of textile workers in Lawrence, Massachusetts, which was settled with some benefit to the strikers, and in a strike the following winter and spring by silk workers in Paterson, New Jersey, which was a failure.

Political Reform: Cities First

Beginning in the late 1890s progressives mounted a massive assault on dishonest and inefficient urban governments. In San Francisco a group headed by Fremont Older, a newspaperman, and Rudolph Spreckels, a wealthy sugar manufacturer, broke the machine of Mayor Abe Ruef, one of the most powerful bosses in the nation; Ruef ended up in jail. In Toledo, Ohio, Samuel M. "Golden Rule" Jones was elected mayor in 1897 and succeeded in arousing the citizenry against the corrupt officials. Other important progressive mayors were Tom L. Johnson of Cleveland, whose administration Lincoln Steffens called the best in the United States; Seth Low and later John P. Mitchell of New York; and Hazen S. Pingree of Detroit.

City reformers could seldom destroy the machines without changing urban political institutions. Some cities obtained "home rule" charters that gave them greater freedom from state control in dealing with local matters. Many created research bureaus that investigated government problems in a scientific and nonpartisan manner. A number of middle-sized communities (Galveston, Texas, was the prototype) experimented with a system that integrated executive and legislative powers in the hands of a small elected commission, thereby concentrating responsibility and making it easier to coordinate complex activities. Out of this experiment came the city manager system, under which the commissioners appointed a professional manager to administer city affairs on a nonpartisan basis. Dayton, Ohio, which adopted the plan after a flood devastated the town in 1913, offers the best illustration of the city manager system in the progressive era.

Once the political system had been made responsive to the desires of the people, the progressives hoped to use it to improve society itself. Many cities experimented with "gas and water socialism," taking over public utility companies and operating them as departments of the municipal government. Under "Golden Rule" Jones, Toledo established a minimum wage for city employees, built playgrounds and golf courses, and moderated its harsh penal code. Mayor Seth Low improved New York's public transportation system and obtained passage of the tenement house law of 1901. Mayor Tom Johnson forced a fare cut to 3 cents on the Cleveland street railways.

Political Reform: The States

To carry out this kind of change required the support of state legislatures since all municipal government depends on the authority of a sovereign state. Such approval was often difficult to obtain—local bosses were usually entrenched in powerful state machines, and rural majorities insensitive to urban needs controlled most legislatures. Therefore the progressives had to strike at inefficiency and corruption at the state level too.

During the first decade of the new century, Robert M. La Follette, one of the most remarkable figures of the age, transformed Wisconsin, the progressive state par excellence. La Follette was born in Primrose, Wisconsin, in 1855. He had served three terms as a Republican congressman (1885–1891) and developed a reputation as an uncompromising foe of corruption before being elected governor in 1900. That the people would always do the right thing if properly informed and inspired was the fundamental article of his political faith. "Machine control is based upon misrepresentation and ignorance," La Follette said. "Democracy is based upon knowledge." His own career seemed to prove his point, for in his repeated clashes with the conservative Wisconsin Republican machine, he won battle after battle by vigorous grassroots campaigning.

Despite the opposition of railroad and lumber interests, as governor La Follette secured passage of a direct primary system for nominating candidates, a corrupt practices act, and laws limiting campaign expenditures and lobbying activities. In power he became something of a boss himself. He made ruthless use of patronage, demanded absolute loyalty of his subordinates, and often stretched, or at least oversimplified, the truth when presenting complex issues to the voters.

Reform administrations swept into office in Iowa and Arkansas (1901); Oregon (1902); Minnesota, Kansas, and Mississippi (1904); New York and Georgia (1906);

Nebraska (1909); and New Jersey and Colorado (1910). In some cases the reformers were Republicans, in others Democrats, but in all the example of Wisconsin was influential. By 1910, fifteen states had established legislative reference services, most of them staffed by personnel trained in Wisconsin. The direct primary system became almost universal.

Some states went beyond Wisconsin in striving to make their governments responsive to the popular will. In 1902 Oregon began to experiment with the initiative, a system by which a bill could be forced on the attention of the legislature by popular petition, and the referendum, a method for allowing the electorate to approve measures rejected by their representatives and to repeal measures that the legislature had passed. Eleven states, most of them in the West, legalized these devices by 1914.

State Social Legislation

The first state laws aimed at social problems long preceded the progressive era, but most were either so imprecise as to be unenforceable or, like the Georgia law "limiting" textile workers to eleven hours a day, so weak as to be ineffective. In 1874 Massachusetts restricted the working hours of women and children to ten per day, and by the 1890s many other states, mostly in the East and Midwest, had followed suit. Illinois passed an eight-hour law for women workers in 1893. A New York law of 1882 struck at the sweatshops of the slums by prohibiting the manufacture of cigars on premises "occupied as a house or residence."

As part of this trend, some states established special rules for workers in hazardous industries. But before 1900 the collective impact of such legislation was not impressive. Powerful manufacturers and landlords often succeeded in defeating the bills or rendering them innocuous. The federal system further complicated the task of obtaining effective legislation.

The Fourteenth Amendment to the Constitution, although enacted to protect the civil rights of blacks, imposed a revolutionary restriction on the states by forbidding them to "deprive any person of life, liberty, or property without due process of law." Since much state social legislation represented new uses of coercive power that conservative judges considered dangerous and unwise, the Fourteenth Amendment gave such judges an excuse to overturn the laws on the grounds that they deprived employers of the "liberty" to choose how long their employees should work or the conditions of the workplace.

As stricter and more far-reaching laws were enacted, many judges, sensing what they took to be a trend toward socialism and regimentation, adopted an increasingly narrow interpretation of state authority to regulate business. In 1905 the U.S. Supreme Court declared in the case of *Lochner* v. *New York* that a New York ten-hour act for bakers deprived the bakers of the liberty of working as long as they wished and thus violated the Fourteenth Amendment. Justice Oliver Wendell Holmes Jr. wrote a famous dissenting opinion in this case. If the people of New

Orphans on the steps of an orphanage, 1911. From 1854 to 1929, nearly 200,000 orphans or abandoned children from eastern cities were sent on "orphan trains" to live with farming families in the Midwest. Billy the Kid was one of the less successful "orphan train" placements.

York believed that the public health was endangered by bakers working long hours, he reasoned, it was not the Court's job to overrule them.

Nevertheless, the progressives continued to battle for legislation to use state power against business. Women played a particularly important part in these struggles. Sparked by the National Child Labor Committee, organized in 1904, reformers over the next ten years obtained laws in nearly every state banning the employment of young children and limiting the hours of older ones. Many of these laws were poorly enforced, yet when Congress passed a federal child labor law in 1916, the Supreme Court declared it unconstitutional.[1]

By 1917 nearly all the states had placed limitations on the hours of women industrial workers, and about ten had set minimum wage standards for women. But once again federal action that would have extended such regulation to the entire country did not materialize. A minimum wage law for women in the District of Columbia was overturned by the Court in *Adkins* v. *Children's Hospital* (1923).

Laws protecting workers against on-the-job accidents were also enacted by many states. Disasters like the 1911 fire in New York City, in which nearly 150 women perished because the Triangle shirtwaist factory had no fire escapes, led to the passage of stricter municipal building codes and factory inspection acts. By 1910 most states had modified the common-law principle that a worker accepted the risk of accident as a condition of employment and was not entitled to compensation if injured unless it could be proved that the employer had been negligent. Gradually the states adopted accident insurance plans, and some began to grant

[1]*A second child labor law, passed in 1919, was also thrown out by the Court, and a child labor amendment, submitted in 1924, failed to achieve ratification by the necessary three-quarters of the states.*

pensions to widows with small children. Most manufacturers favored such measures, if for no other reason than that they regularized procedures and avoided costly lawsuits.

The passage of so much state social legislation sent conservatives scurrying to the Supreme Court for redress. Such persons believed that no government had the power to deprive either workers or employers of the right to negotiate any kind of labor contract they wished. The decision of the Supreme Court in *Lochner* v. *New York* seemed to indicate that the justices would adopt this point of view. When an Oregon law limiting women laundry workers to ten hours a day was challenged in *Muller* v. *Oregon* (1908), Florence Kelley and Josephine Goldmark of the Consumers' League persuaded Louis D. Brandeis to defend the statute before the Court.

The Consumers' League, whose slogan was "investigate, agitate, legislate," was probably the most effective of the many women's reform organizations of the period. With the aid of league researchers, Brandeis prepared a remarkable brief stuffed with economic and sociological evidence indicating that long hours damaged both the health of individual women and the health of society. This nonlegal evidence greatly impressed the justices, who upheld the constitutionality of the Oregon law. "Woman's physical structure, and the functions she performs in consequence thereof, justify special legislation," they concluded. After 1908 the right of states to protect women, children, and workers performing dangerous and unhealthy tasks by special legislation was widely accepted. The use of the "Brandeis brief" technique to demonstrate the need for such legislation became standard practice.

Progressives also launched a massive if ill-coordinated attack on problems related to monopoly. The variety of regulatory legislation passed by the states between 1900 and 1917 was almost infinite. Wisconsin enacted a graduated personal income tax, forced corporations to bear a larger share of the cost of government, created an industrial commission to enforce the state's labor and factory legislation, and established a conservation commission, headed by Charles R. Van Hise, president of the University of Wisconsin.

A similar spate of legislation characterized the brief reign of Woodrow Wilson as governor of New Jersey (1911–1913). Urged on by the relentless Wilson, the legislature created a commission to fix rates and set standards for railroad, gas, electric, and telephone corporations, enacted storage and food inspection laws, and passed seven bills (the "Seven Sisters" laws) tightening the state's loose controls over corporations. Economic reforms in other states were less spectacular but impressive in the mass. However, piecemeal state regulation failed to solve the problems of an ever more complex economy. The most significant battles for economic reform were fought in Congress.

Political Reform: The Woman Suffrage Movement

On the national level the progressive era saw the culmination of the struggle for woman suffrage. The shock occasioned by the failure of the Fourteenth and

A banner in a 1911 woman suffrage parade carries one of the longest-standing arguments in favor of women getting the vote.

Fifteenth Amendments to give women the vote after the Civil War continued to embitter most leaders of the movement. But it resulted in a split among feminists. One group, the American Woman Suffrage Association (AWSA), focused on the vote question alone. The more radical National Woman Suffrage Association (NWSA), led by Elizabeth Cady Stanton and Susan B. Anthony, concerned itself with many issues of importance to women as well as suffrage. The NWSA put the immediate interests of women ahead of everything else. It was deeply involved in efforts to unionize women workers, yet it did not hesitate to urge women to be strikebreakers if they could get better jobs by doing so.

Aside from their lack of unity, feminists were handicapped in the late nineteenth century by Victorian sexual inhibitions, which most of their leaders shared. Even under the best of circumstances, dislike of male-dominated society is hard enough to separate from dislike of men. At a time when sex was an unmentionable topic in polite society, some of the most militant advocates of women's rights probably did not understand their own feelings. Most feminists, for example, opposed contraception, insisting that birth control by any means other than abstinence would encourage what they called masculine lust. The Victorian idealization of female "purity" and the popular image of women as the revered guardians of home and family further confused many reformers. And the trend of nineteenth-century scientific thinking influenced by the Darwinian concept of biological adaptation led to the conclusion that the female personality was different from that of the male and that the differences were inherent, not culturally determined.

These ideas and prejudices enticed feminists into a logical trap. If women were morally superior to men—a tempting conclusion—giving women the vote would improve the character of the electorate. Society would benefit because politics would become less corrupt, war a thing of the past. "City housekeeping has failed," said Jane Addams of Hull House in arguing for the reform of municipal government, "partly because women, the traditional housekeepers, have not been consulted."

The trouble with this argument (aside from the fact that opponents could easily demonstrate that in states where women did vote, governments were no better or worse than elsewhere) was that it surrendered the principle of equality. In the long run this was to have serious consequences for the women's movement, although the immediate effect of the purity argument was probably to advance the suffragists' cause.

By the early twentieth century there were signs of progress. In 1890 the two major women's groups combined as the National American Woman Suffrage Association (NAWSA). Stanton and Anthony were the first two presidents of the association. The NAWSA made winning the right to vote its main objective and concentrated on a state-by-state approach. Wyoming gave women the vote in 1869, and Utah, Colorado, and Idaho had been won over to woman suffrage by 1896. The 1911 election in California was crucial. Fifteen years earlier, California voters had rejected the measure. But in 1911, despite determined opposition from saloonkeepers, the proposal passed, though just barely. Within three years, most other western states fell into line. For the first time, large numbers of working-class women began to agitate for the vote. In 1917, bosses at New York City's Tammany Hall, who had engineered the defeat of woman suffrage in that state two years earlier, concluded that passage was inevitable and threw their support to the measure, which passed.

The suffragists then shifted the campaign back to the national level, the lead taken by a new organization, the Congressional Union, headed by Alice Paul and the wealthy reformer Alva Belmont. When President Wilson refused to support the idea of a constitutional amendment granting women the vote, militant women picketed the White House. A number of them, including the daughter of Thomas Bayard, a former senator and secretary of state, were arrested and sentenced to sixty days in the workhouse. This roused a storm of criticism, and Wilson quickly pardoned the picketers. After some hesitation the NAWSA stopped concentrating on the state-by-state approach and began to campaign for a constitutional amendment. Pressure on Congress mounted steadily. The amendment finally won congressional approval in 1919. By 1920 the necessary three-quarters of the states had ratified the Nineteenth Amendment; the long fight was over.

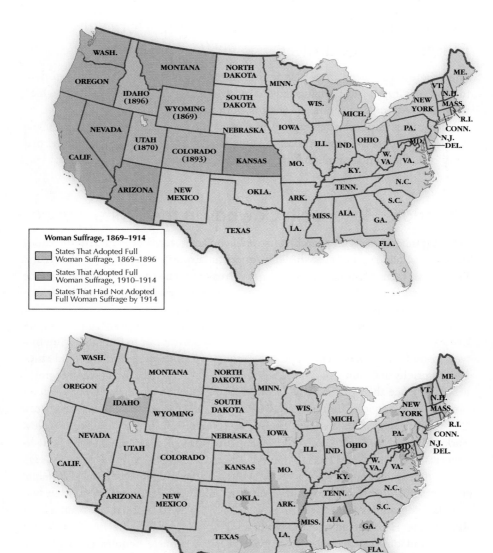

Woman Suffrage, 1869–1914

- States That Adopted Full Woman Suffrage, 1869–1896
- States That Adopted Full Woman Suffrage, 1910–1914
- States That Had Not Adopted Full Woman Suffrage by 1914

Woman Suffrage Resolution May 21, 1919, House of Representatives

- Yes
- No
- Not Voting

The Woman Suffrage Campaign, 1869–1919

In 1869 Wyoming, while still a territory, voted to give women the vote. The next year, after Mormon leader Brigham Young endorsed woman suffrage, Utah followed. Then came Colorado (1893) and Idaho (1896), frontier states that sought to attract women settlers. In 1911, by a margin of 3,587 votes, California endorsed woman suffrage, and within three years the remainder of the western states had done so too. World War I stimulated support for the Woman Suffrage (Nineteenth) Amendment. The May 21, 1919 vote in the House of Representatives shows that most of the opposing votes came from southern congressmen who believed that woman suffrage would be the first step in securing the vote for blacks.

Political Reform: Income Taxes and Popular Election of Senators

The progressive reform drive also found expression in the Sixteenth Amendment to the Constitution, authorizing federal income taxes, and the Seventeenth, which required the popular election of senators, both ratified in 1913.

No other important alterations of the national political system were made during the progressive era. Although some twenty states passed presidential primary laws, the cumbersome method of electing presidents was not changed.

Theodore Roosevelt: Cowboy in the White House

On September 6, 1901, an anarchist named Leon Czolgosz shot President McKinley during a public reception at the Pan-American Exposition at Buffalo, New York. Eight days later McKinley died and Vice President Theodore Roosevelt became president of the United States. His ascension to the presidency marked the beginning of a new era in national politics.

Although only forty-two years old, by far the youngest president in the nation's history up to that time, Roosevelt brought solid qualifications to the office. Son of a well-to-do New York merchant, he had graduated from Harvard in 1880 and studied law briefly at Columbia, though he did not obtain a degree. In addition to political experience that included three terms in the New York assembly, six years on the U.S. Civil Service Commission, two years as police commissioner of New York City, another as assistant secretary of the navy, and a term as governor of New York, he had been a rancher in the Dakota Territory and a soldier in the Spanish-American War. He was also a well-known historian: His *Naval War of 1812* (1882), begun during his undergraduate days at Harvard, and his four-volume *Winning of the West* (1889–1896) were valuable works of scholarship, and he had written two popular biographies and other books as well. Politically, he had always been a loyal Republican. He rejected the mugwump heresy in 1884, despite his distaste for Blaine, and during the tempestuous 1890s he vigorously denounced populism, Bryanism, and "labor agitators."

Nevertheless, Roosevelt's elevation to the presidency alarmed many conservatives, and not without reason. He did not fit their conception, based on a composite image of the chief executives from Hayes to McKinley, of what a president should be like. He seemed too undignified, too energetic, too outspoken, too unconventional. It was one thing to have operated a cattle ranch, another to have captured a gang of rustlers at gunpoint; one thing to have run a metropolitan police force, another to have roamed New York slums in the small hours to catch patrolmen fraternizing with thieves and prostitutes; one thing to have commanded a regiment, another to have killed a Spaniard personally.

Roosevelt had been a sickly child, plagued by asthma and poor eyesight, and he seems to have spent much of his adult life compensating for the sense of in-

The original stuffed bear, introduced as a toy in 1903. About the same time president "Teddy" Roosevelt, a big game hunter, refrained from shooting a bear cub. A cartoon rendering of that cub resembled the new toy, which people began referring to as "Teddy's Bears"—soon shortened to "Teddy Bears."

adequacy that these troubles bred in him. He repeatedly carried his displays of physical stamina and personal courage and his love of athletics and big-game hunting to preternatural lengths. Henry Adams, who watched Roosevelt's development over the years with a mixture of fear and amusement, said that he was "pure act."

Had Roosevelt been the impetuous hothead that conservatives feared, he would have plunged ahead without regard for their feelings and influence. Instead he moved slowly and often got what he wanted by using his executive power rather than by persuading Congress to pass new laws. His domestic program included some measure of control of big corporations, more power for the Interstate Commerce Commission (ICC), and the conservation of natural resources. By consulting congressional leaders and following their advice not to bring up controversial matters like the tariff and currency reform, he obtained a modest budget of new laws.

The Newlands Act (1902) funneled the proceeds from land sales in the West into federal irrigation projects. The Department of Commerce and Labor, which was to include a Bureau of Corporations with authority to investigate industrial combines and issue reports, was established. The Elkins Railroad Act of 1903 strengthened the ICC's hand against the railroads by making the receiving as well as the granting of rebates illegal and by forbidding the roads to deviate in any way from their published rates.

Roosevelt and Big Business

Roosevelt soon became known as a trustbuster, and in the sense that he considered the monopoly problem the most pressing issue of the times, this was accurate to an extent. But he did not believe in breaking up big corporations indiscriminately. Regulation seemed the best way to deal with large corporations because, he said, industrial giantism "could not be eliminated unless we were willing to turn back the wheels of modern progress."

With Congress unwilling to pass a stiff regulatory law, Roosevelt resorted to the Sherman Act to get at the problem. Although the Supreme Court decision in the Sugar Trust case seemed to have emasculated that law, in 1902 he ordered the Justice Department to bring suit against the Northern Securities Company.

The announcement of the suit caused consternation in the business world. Attorney General Philander C. Knox pressed the case vigorously, and in 1904 the Supreme Court ordered the dissolution of the Northern Securities Company.

Roosevelt then ordered suits against the meat packers, the Standard Oil Trust, and the American Tobacco Company. His stock among progressives rose, yet he had not embarrassed the conservatives in Congress by demanding new antitrust legislation.

The president went out of his way to assure cooperative corporation magnates that he was not against size per se. At a White House conference in 1905, Roosevelt and Elbert H. Gary, chairman of the board of U.S. Steel, reached a "gentlemen's agreement" whereby Gary promised "to cooperate with the Government in every possible way." The Bureau of Corporations would conduct an investigation of U.S. Steel, Gary allowing it full access to company records. Roosevelt in turn promised that if the investigation revealed any corporate malpractices, he would allow Gary to set matters right voluntarily, thereby avoiding an antitrust suit. He reached a similar agreement with the International Harvester Company two years later.

Roosevelt and the Coal Strike

Roosevelt made remarkable use of his executive power during the anthracite coal strike of 1902. In June the United Mine Workers (UMW), led by John Mitchell, laid down their picks and demanded higher wages, an eight-hour day, and recognition of the union. Most of the anthracite mines were owned by railroads. Two years earlier the miners had won a 10 percent wage increase in a similar strike, chiefly because the owners feared that labor unrest might endanger the election of McKinley. Now the coal companies were dead set against further concessions; when the men walked out, they shut down the mines and prepared to starve the strikers into submission.

The strike dragged on through summer and early fall. The miners conducted themselves with great restraint, avoiding violence and offering to submit their claims to arbitration. As the price of anthracite soared with the approach of winter, sentiment in their behalf mounted.

WERE THE PROGRESSIVES FORWARD-LOOKING?

Debating the Past

"Jack and the Wall Street Giants" shows a diminutive Teddy Roosevelt taking on the titans of Wall Street, among them railroad barons James J. Hill and Jay Gould and financier J. P. Morgan. The cartoon anticipates the familiar argument—that the progressives sought genuine change. But it also suggests that the prospects for victory were poor. Note that TR stands alone. By the 1930s, when the nation was mired in depression, many blamed the progressives. In 1932 John Chamberlain published a "Farewell to Reform" that excoriated progressive leaders for failing to check the power of the trusts. That failure, Richard Hofstadter (1955) declared, was rooted in their psychology. The progressives, mostly members of the middle class and the declining old elites, felt threatened by the increasing power and status of the new tycoons, many of them coarse, domineering, and fond of vulgar display. The antics of machine politicians who made a mockery of the traditions of duty, service, and patriotism associated with statesmanship also troubled them.

Progressives sought to restore "familiar and traditional ideals," and their nostrums were as old-fashioned as their goals. Revisionist historians such as Gabriel Kolko (1963) pushed Hofstadter's argument still further: the progressives never sought meaningful reform in the first place. They endorsed government regulation to prevent anarchic economic competition, and they hoped to ameliorate the plight of workers to forestall revolution. Their "progressivism" was in fact the "triumph of conservatism." Daniel Rodgers (1998) was among the many who insisted that this portrait was overdrawn. The progressives in the United States were not much different from reformers at that time in Europe. All shared a dynamic rhetoric; all sought to counteract the increasing concentration of industrial power; none met with great success. In the cartoon TR is armed only with the sword of "Public Service." Did he mean to preach to the giants or slay them?

John Chamberlain, *Farewell to Reform* (1932), Richard Hofstadter, *The Age of Reform* (1955), Gabriel Kolko, *The Triumph of Conservatism* (1963), Allen Weinstein, *The Decline of Socialism in America* (1967), Robert Wiebe, *The Search for Order* (1967), Daniel Rodgers, *Atlantic Crossings* (1998).

The owners' spokesman, George F. Baer of the Reading Railroad, proved particularly inept at public relations. Baer stated categorically that God was on the side of management, but when someone suggested asking an important Roman Catholic prelate to arbitrate the dispute, he replied icily: "Anthracite mining is a business and not a religious, sentimental or academic proposition."

Roosevelt shared the public's sympathy for the miners, and the threat of a coal shortage alarmed him. Early in October he summoned both sides to a conference in Washington and urged them as patriotic Americans to sacrifice any "personal consideration" for the "general good." His action enraged the coal operators, for they believed he was trying to force them to recognize the union. They refused even to speak to the UMW representatives at the conference and demanded that Roosevelt end the strike by force and bring suit against the union under the Sherman Act. Mitchell, aware of the immense prestige that Roosevelt had conferred on the union by calling the conference, cooperated fully with the president.

The attitudes of management and of the union further strengthened public support for the miners. Encouraged by this state of affairs, Roosevelt took a bold step: He announced that unless a settlement was reached promptly, he would order federal troops into the anthracite regions, not to break the strike but to seize and operate the mines.

The threat of government intervention brought the owners to terms. The miners would return to the pits and all issues between them and the coal companies would be submitted for settlement to a commission appointed by Roosevelt. Both sides accepted the arrangement, and the men went back to work. In March 1903 the commission granted the miners a 10 percent wage increase and a nine-hour workday.

To the public the incident seemed a perfect illustration of the progressive spirit—in Roosevelt's words, everyone had received a "Square Deal." In fact the results were by no means so clear-cut. The miners gained relatively little and the companies lost still less, for they were not required to recognize the UMW and the commission also recommended a 10 percent increase in the price of coal, ample compensation for the increased wage costs. The president was the main winner. The public acclaimed him as a fearless, imaginative, public-spirited leader. Without calling on Congress for support, he had expanded his own authority and hence that of the federal government. His action marked a major forward step in the evolution of the modern presidency.

TR's Triumphs

By reviving the Sherman Act, settling the coal strike, and pushing moderate reforms through Congress, Roosevelt ensured that he would be reelected president in 1904. Progressives, if not captivated, were at least pleased by his performance. Conservative Republicans offered no serious objection. Sensing that Roosevelt had won over the liberals, the Democrats nominated a conservative, Judge Alton B. Parker of New York, and bid for the support of eastern industrialists.

This strategy failed, for businessmen continued to eye the party of Bryan with intense suspicion. They preferred, as the *New York Sun* put it, "the impulsive candidate of the party of conservatism to the conservative candidate of the party which the business interests regard as permanently and dangerously impulsive." Despite his resentment at Roosevelt's attack on the Northern Securities Company, J. P. Morgan contributed $150,000 to the Republican campaign. Other tycoons gave with equal generosity. Roosevelt swept the country, carrying even the normally Democratic border states of Maryland and Missouri.

Encouraged by the landslide and the increasing militancy of progressives, Roosevelt pressed for more reform legislation. His most imaginative proposal was a plan to make the District of Columbia a model progressive community. He suggested child labor and factory inspection laws and a slum clearance program, but Congress refused to act. Likewise, his request for a minimum wage for railroad workers was rejected.

He had greater success when he proposed still another increase in the power of the Interstate Commerce Commission. Rebating remained a serious problem. With progressive state governors demanding federal action and farmers and manufacturers, especially in the Midwest, clamoring for relief against discriminatory rates, Roosevelt was ready by 1905 to make railroad legislation his major objective. The ICC should be empowered to fix rates, not merely to challenge unreasonable ones. It should have the right to inspect the private records of the railroads since fair rates could not be determined unless the true financial condition of the roads was known.

Because these proposals struck at rights that businessmen considered sacrosanct, many congressmen balked. But Roosevelt applied presidential pressure, and in June 1906 the Hepburn bill became law. It gave the commission the power to inspect the books of railroad companies, to set maximum rates (once a complaint had been filed by a shipper), and to control sleeping car companies, owners of oil pipelines, and other firms engaged in transportation. In all, the Hepburn Act made the ICC a more powerful and more active body.

Congress also passed meat inspection and pure food and drug legislation. In 1906 Upton Sinclair published *The Jungle,* a devastating exposé of the filthy conditions in the Chicago slaughterhouses. Sinclair was more interested in writing a socialist tract than he was in meat inspection, but his book, a best-seller, raised a storm against the packers. After Roosevelt read *The Jungle* he sent two officials to Chicago to investigate. Their report was so shocking, he said, that its publication would "be well-nigh ruinous to our export trade in meat." He threatened to release the report, however, unless Congress acted. After a hot fight, the meat inspection bill passed. The Pure Food and Drug Act, forbidding the manufacture and sale of adulterated and fraudulently labeled products, rode through Congress on the coattails of this measure.

Roosevelt has probably received more credit than he deserves for these laws. He compromised with opponents of meat inspection cheerfully, despite his loud denunciations of the evils under attack. "As now carried on the [meat-packing] business is both a menace to health and an outrage on decency," he said: "No legislation that is not drastic and thoroughgoing will be of avail." Yet he went along with the packers' demand that the government pay the costs of inspection, though he believed that "the only way to secure efficiency is by the imposition upon the packers of a fee." Nevertheless, the end results were positive and in line with his conception of the public good.

To advanced liberals Roosevelt's achievements seemed limited when placed beside his professed objectives and his smug evaluations of what he had done. How could he be a reformer and a defender of established interests at the same time? Roosevelt found no difficulty in holding such a position.

Roosevelt Tilts Left

As the progressive movement advanced, Roosevelt advanced with it. He never accepted all the ideas of what he called its "lunatic fringe," but he took steadily more liberal positions. He always insisted that he was not hostile to business interests, but when those interests sought to exploit the national domain, they had no more implacable foe. Conservation of natural resources was dear to his heart and probably his most significant achievement as president. He placed some 150 million acres of forest lands in federal reserves, and he strictly enforced the laws governing grazing, mining, and lumbering.

In 1908 Roosevelt came out in favor of federal income and inheritance taxes, stricter regulation of interstate corporations, and reforms designed to help industrial workers. He denounced "the speculative folly and the flagrant dishonesty" of "malefactors of great wealth," further alienating conservative, or Old Guard, Republicans, who resented the attacks on their integrity implicit in Roosevelt's statements. When the president began criticizing the courts, the last bastion of conservatism, he lost all chance of obtaining further reform legislation. As he said himself, during his last months in office "stagnation continued to rage with uninterrupted violence."

William Howard Taft: The Listless Progressive, or More Is Less

But Roosevelt remained popular and politically powerful; before his term ended, he chose William Howard Taft, his secretary of war, to succeed him and easily obtained Taft's nomination. William Jennings Bryan was again the Democratic candidate. Campaigning on Roosevelt's record, Taft carried the country by well over a million votes, defeating Bryan 321 to 162 in the Electoral College.

Taft was intelligent, experienced, and public spirited; he seemed ideally suited to carry out Roosevelt's policies. Born in Cincinnati in 1857, educated at Yale, he had served as an Ohio judge, as solicitor general of the United States under Benjamin Harrison, and then as a federal circuit court judge before accepting McKinley's assignment to head the Philippine Commission in 1900. His success as civil governor of the Philippines led Roosevelt to make him secretary of war in 1904.

Taft supported the Square Deal loyally. This, together with his mentor's ardent endorsement, won him the backing of most progressive Republicans. Yet the Old Guard liked him too; although outgoing, he had none of the Roosevelt impetuosity and aggressiveness. His genial personality and his obvious desire to avoid conflict appealed to moderates.

However, Taft lacked the physical and mental stamina required of a modern chief executive. Although not lazy, he weighed over 300 pounds and needed to rest this vast bulk more than the job allowed. He liked to eat in leisurely fashion, to idle away mornings on the golf course, to take an afternoon nap. Campaigning bored him; speech making seemed a useless chore. He supported many progressive measures, but he never absorbed the progressive spirit.

A hapless Taft is entangled in governmental yarn, while a disapproving Roosevelt looks on. "Goodness gracious! I must have been dozing," reads the caption, a reference to Taft's penchant for naps.

Taft honestly wanted to carry out most of Roosevelt's policies. He enforced the Sherman Act vigorously and continued to expand the national forest reserves. He signed the Mann-Elkins Act of 1910, which empowered the ICC to suspend rate increases without waiting for a shipper to complain and established the Commerce Court to speed the settlement of railroad rate cases. An eight-hour day for all persons engaged in work on government contracts, mine safety legislation, and several other reform measures received his approval. He even summoned Congress into special session specifically to reduce tariff duties—something that Roosevelt had not dared to attempt.

But Taft had been disturbed by Roosevelt's sweeping use of executive power. "We have got to work out our problems on the basis of law," he insisted. Whereas Roosevelt had excelled at maneuvering around congressional opposition and at finding ways to accomplish his objectives without waiting for Congress to act, Taft adamantly refused to use such tactics. His restraint was in many ways admirable, but it reduced his effectiveness.

In 1910 Taft got into difficulty with conservationists. Although he believed in husbanding natural resources carefully, he did not like the way Roosevelt had circumvented Congress in adding to the forest reserves. He demanded, and eventually obtained, specific legislation to accomplish this purpose. The issue that aroused the conservationists concerned the integrity of his secretary of the interior, Richard A. Ballinger. A less than ardent conservationist, Ballinger returned to the public domain certain waterpower sites that the Roosevelt administration had withdrawn on the legally questionable ground that they were to become ranger stations. Ballinger's action alarmed Chief Forester Gifford Pinchot, the darling of the conservationists. When Pinchot learned that Ballinger intended to validate the shaky claim of mining interests to a large tract of coal-rich land in Alaska, he launched an intemperate attack on the secretary.

In the Ballinger-Pinchot controversy Taft felt obliged to support his own man. The coal lands dispute was complex, and Pinchot's charges were exaggerated. It was certainly unfair to call Ballinger "the most effective opponent the conservation policies have yet had." When Pinchot, whose own motives were partly political, persisted in criticizing Ballinger, Taft dismissed the chief forester. He had no choice under the circumstances, but a more adept politician might have found some way of avoiding a showdown.

Breakup of the Republican Party

One ominous aspect of the Ballinger-Pinchot affair was that Pinchot was a close friend of Theodore Roosevelt. After Taft's inauguration, Roosevelt had gone off to hunt big game in Africa, bearing in his baggage an autographed photograph of his protégé and a touching letter of appreciation, in which the new president said: "I can never forget that the power I now exercise was a voluntary transfer from you to me." For months, as he trudged across Africa, guns blazing, Roosevelt was out of touch with affairs in the United States. As soon as he emerged from the wilderness in March 1910, bearing more than 3,000 trophies, including nine lions, five elephants, and thirteen rhinos, he was caught up in the squabble between the progressive members of his party and its titular head. Pinchot met him in Italy, laden with injured innocence and a packet of angry letters from various progressives. TR's intimate friend Senator Henry Cabot Lodge, essentially a conservative, barraged him with messages, the gist of which was that Taft was lazy and inept and that Roosevelt should prepare to become the "Moses" who would guide the party "out of the wilderness of doubt and discontent" into which Taft had led it.

Roosevelt hoped to steer a middle course, but Pinchot's complaints impressed him. Taft had decided to strike out on his own, he concluded. "No man must render such a service as that I rendered Taft and expect the individual . . . not in the end to become uncomfortable and resentful," he wrote Lodge sadly. Taft sensed the former president's coolness and was offended.

Perhaps the resulting rupture was inevitable. The Republican party was dividing into two factions, the progressives and the Old Guard. Forced to choose between them, Taft threw in his lot with the Old Guard. Roosevelt backed the progressives. Speaking at Osawatomie, Kansas, in August 1910, he came out for a comprehensive program of social legislation, which he called the New Nationalism. Besides attacking "special privilege" and the "unfair money-getting" practices of "lawbreakers of great wealth," he called for a broad expansion of federal power. "The betterment we seek must be accomplished," he said, "mainly through the National Government."

The final break came in October 1911, when the president ordered an antitrust suit against U.S. Steel. Roosevelt opposed breaking up large corporations. "The effort at prohibiting all combination has substantially failed," Taft said. "The way out lies . . . in completely controlling them." He was prepared to enforce the Sherman Act "or die in the attempt." But what angered Roosevelt was Taft's emphasis in the suit on U.S. Steel's absorption of the Tennessee Coal and Iron Company, which Roosevelt had unofficially authorized during the panic of 1907. The government's antitrust brief made Roosevelt appear to have been either an abettor of monopoly or, far worse, a fool who had been duped by the steel corporation. Early in 1912 he declared himself a candidate for the Republican presidential nomination.

Roosevelt plunged into the preconvention campaign with typical energy. He was almost uniformly victorious in states that held presidential primaries, carrying even Ohio, Taft's home state. However, the president controlled the party machinery and entered the national convention with a small majority of the delegates. Since some Taft delegates had been chosen under questionable circumstances, the Roosevelt forces challenged the right of 254 of them to their seats. The Taft-controlled credentials committee, paying little attention to the evidence, gave all but a few of the disputed seats to the president, who then won the nomination on the first ballot.

Roosevelt was understandably outraged by the ruthless manner in which the Taft "steamroller" had overridden his forces. When his leading supporters urged him to organize a third party, and when two of them, George W. Perkins, formerly a partner of the banker J. P. Morgan, and the publisher Frank Munsey, offered to finance the campaign, Roosevelt agreed to make the race.

In August, amid scenes of hysterical enthusiasm, the first convention of the Progressive party met at Chicago and nominated him for president. Announcing that he felt "as strong as a bull moose," Roosevelt delivered a stirring "confession of faith," calling for strict regulation of corporations, a tariff commission, national presidential primaries, minimum wage and workers' compensation laws, the elimination of child labor, and many other reforms.

The Election of 1912

The Democrats made the most of the opportunity offered by the Republican schism. Had they nominated a conservative or allowed Bryan a fourth chance, they would probably have ensured Roosevelt's election. Instead, after battling through forty-six ballots at their convention in Baltimore, they nominated Woodrow Wilson, who had achieved a remarkable liberal record as governor of New Jersey. Incidentally, Wilson was one of three southern candidates for the nomination, further evidence that the sectional conflicts of Reconstruction had been forgotten.

Although as a political scientist Wilson had criticized the status quo and taken a pragmatic approach to the idea of government regulation of the economy, he had objected strongly to Bryan's brand of politics. In 1896 he voted for the Gold Democratic party candidate instead of Bryan. But by 1912, influenced partly by

		Electoral Total	Popular Vote
DEMOCRATIC Woodrow Wilson		435	6,286,820
PROGRESSIVE (BULL MOOSE) Theodore Roosevelt		88	4,126,020
REPUBLICAN William Taft		8	3,483,922
SOCIALIST Eugene V. Debs			897,011
TOTALS		531	14,793,773

The Election of 1912
The fourth-largest vote getter in the election of 1912 was Eugene V. Debs of the Socialist party, who gained nearly 900,000 popular votes (or approximately 6 percent of the total popular vote) but no electoral votes.

ambition and partly by the spirit of the times, he had been converted to progressivism. He called his brand of reform the New Freedom.

The federal government could best advance the cause of social justice, Wilson reasoned, by eradicating the special privileges that enabled the "interests" to flourish. Where Roosevelt had lost faith in competition as a way of protecting the public against monopolies, Wilson insisted that competition could be restored. The government must break up the great trusts, establish fair rules for doing business, and subject violators to stiff punishments. Thereafter, the free enterprise system would protect the public from exploitation without destroying individual initiative and opportunity.

Roosevelt's reasoning was perhaps theoretically more sound. He called for a New Nationalism. Laissez-faire made less sense than it had in earlier times. The complexities of the modern world seemed to call for a positive approach, a plan, the close application of human intelligence to social and economic problems.

To choose between the New Nationalism and the New Freedom, between the dynamic Roosevelt and the idealistic Wilson, was indeed difficult. Thousands grappled with this problem before going to the polls, but partisan politics determined the outcome of the election. Taft got the hard-core Republican vote but lost the progressive wing of the party to Roosevelt. Wilson had the solid support of both conservative and liberal Democrats. As a result, Wilson won an easy victory in the Electoral College, receiving 435 votes to Roosevelt's 88 and Taft's 8. The popular vote was Wilson, 6,286,000; Roosevelt, 4,126,000; and Taft, 3,484,000.

If partisan politics had determined the winner, the election was nonetheless an overwhelming endorsement of progressivism. The temper of the times was shown by the 897,000 votes for Eugene Debs, who was again the Socialist candidate. Altogether, professed liberals amassed over 11 million of the 15 million ballots cast. Wilson was a minority president, but he took office with a clear mandate to press forward with further reforms.

Wilson: The New Freedom

No one ever rose more suddenly or spectacularly in American politics than Woodrow Wilson. In the spring of 1910 he was president of Princeton University; he had never held or even run for public office. In the fall of 1912 he was president-elect of the United States. Yet if his rise was meteoric, in a very real sense he had devoted his life to preparing for it. He was born in Staunton, Virginia, in 1856, the son of a Presbyterian minister. As a student he became interested in political theory, dreaming of representing his state in the Senate. He studied law solely because he thought it the best avenue to public office, and when he discovered that he did not like legal work, he took a doctorate at Johns Hopkins in political science.

For years Wilson's political ambitions appeared doomed to frustration. He taught at Bryn Mawr, then at Wesleyan, finally at his alma mater, Princeton. He wrote several influential books, among them *Congressional Government* and *The State,* and achieved an outstanding reputation as a teacher and lecturer. In 1902 he was chosen president of Princeton and soon won a place among the nation's leading educators. He revised the curriculum, introducing many new subjects and insisting that students pursue an organized and integrated course of study. He insti-

Woodrow Wilson, presiding over the 1906 Princeton commencement, with steel magnate and educational philanthropist Andrew Carnegie firmly in tow.

tuted the preceptorial system, which placed the students in close intellectual and social contact with their teachers. He attracted outstanding young scholars to the Princeton faculty.

Wilson was an immediate success as president. Since Roosevelt's last year in office Congress had been almost continually at war with the executive branch and with itself. Legislative achievements had been few. Now a small avalanche of important measures received the approval of the lawmakers. In October 1913 the Underwood Tariff brought the first significant reduction of duties since before the Civil War. To compensate for the expected loss of revenue, the act provided for a graduated tax on personal incomes.

Two months later the Federal Reserve Act gave the country a central banking system for the first time since Jackson destroyed the Bank of the United States. The measure divided the nation into twelve banking districts, each under the supervision of a Federal Reserve bank, a sort of bank for bankers. All national banks in each district and any state banks that wished to participate had to invest 6 percent of their capital and surplus in the reserve bank, which was empowered to exchange (the technical term is *rediscount*) paper money, called Federal Reserve notes, for the commercial and agricultural paper that member banks took in as security from borrowers. The volume of currency was no longer at the mercy of the supply of gold or any other particular commodity.

The crown and nerve center of the system was the Federal Reserve Board in Washington, which appointed a majority of the directors of the Federal Reserve banks and had some control over rediscount rates (the commission charged by the reserve banks for performing the rediscounting function). The board provided a modicum of public control over the banks, but the effort to weaken the power of the great New York banks by decentralizing the system proved ineffective. Nevertheless, a true central banking system was created.

When inflation threatened, the reserve banks could raise the rediscount rate, discouraging borrowing and thus reducing the amount of money in circulation. In bad times it could lower the rate, making it easier to borrow and injecting new dollars into the economy. Much remained to be learned about the proper management of the money supply, but the nation finally had a flexible yet safe currency.

In 1914 Congress passed two important laws affecting corporations. One created the Federal Trade Commission (FTC) to replace Roosevelt's Bureau of Corporations. In addition to investigating corporations and publishing reports, this nonpartisan board could issue cease-and-desist orders against "unfair" trade practices brought to light through its research. The law did not define the term *unfair*, and the commission's rulings could be taken on appeal to the federal courts, but the FTC was nonetheless a powerful instrument for protecting the public against the trusts.

The second measure, the Clayton Antitrust Act, made certain specific business practices illegal, including price discrimination that tended to foster monopolies; "tying" agreements, which forbade retailers from handling the products of a firm's competitors; and the creation of interlocking directorates as a means of controlling competing companies. The officers of corporations could be held individually responsible if their companies violated the antitrust laws.

The Democrats controlled both houses of Congress for the first time since 1890 and were eager to make a good record, but Wilson's imaginative and aggressive use of presidential power was decisive. He called the legislators into special session in April 1913 and appeared before them to lay out his program; he was the first president to address Congress in person since John Adams. Then he followed the course of administration bills closely. He had a private telephone line installed between the Capitol and the White House. Administration representatives haunted the cloakrooms and lobbies of both houses. Cooperative congressmen began to receive notes of praise and encouragement, recalcitrant ones stern demands for support, often pecked out on the president's own portable typewriter.

There were limits to Wilson's progressivism, limits imposed partly by his temperament and partly by his philosophy. He objected as strenuously to laws granting special favors to farmers and workers as to those benefiting the tycoons. When a bill was introduced in 1914 making low-interest loans available to farmers, he refused to support it. "It is unwise and unjustifiable to extend the credit of the Government to a single class of the community," he said. He considered the provision exempting unions from the antitrust laws equally unsound. Nor would he push for a federal law prohibiting child labor; such a measure would be unconstitutional, he believed. He also refused to back the constitutional amendment giving the vote to women.

By the end of 1914 Wilson's record, on balance, was positive but distinctly limited. The president believed that the major progressive goals had been achieved; he had no plans for further reform. Many other progressives thought that a great deal more remained to be done.

The Progressives and Minority Rights

On one important issue, race relations, Wilson was distinctly reactionary. With a mere handful of exceptions, the progressives exhibited strong prejudices against people of color and against certain categories of whites as well. Many were as unsympathetic to immigrants from Asia and eastern and southern Europe as any of the "conservative" opponents of immigration in the 1880s and 1890s. The Gentlemen's Agreement excluding Japanese immigrants was reached in 1907 at the height of the progressive movement.

American Indians were also affected by the progressives' racial attitudes. Where the sponsors of the Dawes Act (1887) had assumed that Indians were inherently capable of adopting the ways of "civilized" people, in the progressive period the tendency was to write Indians off as fundamentally inferior and to assume that they would make second-class citizens at best. A leading muckraker, Ray Stannard Baker, who was far more sympathetic to blacks than most progressives, dismissed Indians as pathetic beings, "eating, sleeping, idling, with no more thought of the future than a white man's child." In 1902 Congress passed the Dead Indian Land Act, which made it easier for Indians to sell allotments that they had inherited, and in 1906 another law further relaxed restrictions on land sales. Efforts to improve the education of Indian children continued, but most progressives assumed that only vocational training would help them. Theodore Roosevelt knew from his experiences as a rancher in the Dakota Territory that Indians could be as energetic and capable as whites, but he considered these "exceptional." As for the rest, it would be many generations before they could be expected to "move forward" enough to become "ordinary citizens," Roosevelt believed.

To say that African Americans did not fare well at the hands of progressives would be a gross understatement. Populist efforts to unite white and black farmers in the southern states had led to the imposition of further repressive measures. Segregation became more rigid, white opposition to black voting more monolithic. In 1900 the body of a Mississippi black was dug up by order of the state legislature and reburied in a segregated cemetery; in Virginia in 1902 the daughter of Robert E. Lee was arrested for riding in the black section of a railroad car. "Insult is being added to injury continually," a black journalist in Alabama complained. "Have those in power forgotten that there is a God?"

Many progressive women, still smarting from the insult to their sex entailed in the Fourteenth and Fifteenth Amendments and eager to attract southern support for their campaign for the vote, adopted racist arguments. They contrasted the supposed corruption and incompetence of black voters with their own "purity" and intelligence. Southern progressives of both sexes argued that disfranchising blacks would reduce corruption by removing from unscrupulous white politicians the temptation to purchase black votes!

The typical southern attitude toward the education of blacks was summed up in a folk proverb: "When you educate a Negro, you spoil a good field hand." In 1910 only about 8,000 black children in the entire South were attending high schools. Despite the almost total suppression of black rights, lynchings continued to occur; between 1900 and 1914 more than 1,100 blacks were murdered by mobs, most (but not all) in the southern states. In the rare cases in which local prosecutors brought the lynchers to trial, juries almost without exception brought in verdicts of not guilty.

Booker T. Washington was shaken by this trend, but he could find no way to combat it. The times were passing him by. He appealed to his white southern "friends" for help but got nowhere. Increasingly he talked about the virtues of rural life, the evils of big cities, and the uselessness of higher education for black people. By the turn of the century a number of young, well-educated blacks, most of them Northerners, were breaking away from his accommodationist leadership.

Black Militancy

William E. B. Du Bois was the most prominent of the militants. Du Bois was born in Great Barrington, Massachusetts, in 1868. His father, a restless wanderer of

Negro and French Huguenot stock, abandoned the family, and young William grew up on the edge of poverty. Neither accepted nor openly rejected by the overwhelmingly white community, he devoted himself to his studies, showing such brilliance that his future education was ensured by scholarships: to Fisk University, then to Harvard, then to the University of Berlin. In 1895 Du Bois became the first American black to earn a Ph.D. in history from Harvard; his dissertation was *The Suppression of the African Slave Trade* (1896).

Personal success and "acceptance" by whites did not make the proud and sensitive Du Bois complacent. Outraged by white racism and the willingness of many blacks to settle for second-class citizenship, he set out to make American blacks proud of their color—"Beauty is black," he said—and of their African origins and culture.

Like Washington, Du Bois wanted blacks to lift themselves up by their own bootstraps. They must establish their own businesses, run their own newspapers and colleges, write their own literature; they must preserve their identity rather than seek to amalgamate themselves into a society that offered them only crumbs and contempt. At first he cooperated with Washington, but in 1903, in the essay "Of Mr. Booker T. Washington and Others," he subjected Washington's "attitude of adjustment and submission" to polite but searching criticism. Washington had asked blacks to give up political power, civil rights, and the hope of higher education, not realizing that "voting is necessary to modern manhood, that . . . discrimination is barbarism, and that black boys need education as well as white boys." Washington "apologizes for injustice," Du Bois charged. "He belittles the emasculating effects

A striking likeness of W. E. B. Du Bois drawn by Winold Reiss when Du Bois was in his fifties.

of caste distinctions, and opposes the higher training and ambitions of our brightest minds." Du Bois deemed this totally wrong. "The way for a people to gain their reasonable rights is not by voluntarily throwing them away."

Du Bois was not an uncritical admirer of the ordinary American black. He believed that "immorality, crime, and laziness" were common vices. Quite properly he blamed the weaknesses of blacks on the treatment afforded them by whites, but his approach to the solution of racial problems was frankly elitist. "The Negro race," he wrote, "is going to be saved by its exceptional men," what he called the "talented tenth" of the black population. After describing in vivid detail how white mistreatment had corrupted his people, Du Bois added loftily: "A saving remnant continually survives and persists, continually aspires, continually shows itself in thrift and ability and character."

Whatever his prejudices, Du Bois exposed both the weaknesses of Washington's strategy and the callousness of white American attitudes. Accommodation was not working. Washington was praised, even lionized by prominent southern whites, yet when Theodore Roosevelt invited him to a meal at the White House they exploded with indignation, and Roosevelt, although not personally prejudiced, meekly backtracked, never repeating his "mistake." He defended his record by saying, "I have stood as valiantly for the rights of the negro as any president since Lincoln." That, sad to relate, was true enough.

Not mere impatience but despair led Du Bois and a few like-minded blacks to meet at Niagara Falls in July 1905 and to issue a stirring list of demands: the unrestricted right to vote, an end to every kind of segregation, equality of economic opportunity, higher education for the talented, equal justice in the courts, and an end to trade-union discrimination. This Niagara movement did not attract mass support, but it did stir the consciences of some whites, many of them the descendants of abolitionists, who were also becoming disenchanted by the failure of accommodation to provide blacks with real opportunity.

In 1909, the centennial of the birth of Abraham Lincoln, a group of these liberals, including the newspaperman Oswald Garrison Villard (grandson of William Lloyd Garrison), the social worker Jane Addams, the philosopher John Dewey, and the novelist William Dean Howells, founded the National Association for the Advancement of Colored People (NAACP). The organization was dedicated to the eradication of racial discrimination. Its leadership was predominantly white in the early years, but Du Bois became a national officer and the editor of its journal, *The Crisis*.

A turning point had been reached. After 1909 virtually every important leader, white and black alike, rejected the Washington approach. More and more, blacks turned to the study of their past in an effort to stimulate pride in their heritage.

This militancy produced few results in the Progressive Era. Theodore Roosevelt behaved no differently than earlier Republican presidents; he courted blacks when he thought it advantageous, turned his back when he did not. When he ran for president on the Progressive ticket in 1912, he pursued a "lily-white" policy, hoping to break the Democrats' monopoly in the South. By trusting in "[white] men of justice and of vision," Roosevelt argued in the face of decades of experience to the contrary, "the colored men of the South will ultimately get justice."

The southern-born Wilson was actively hostile to blacks. During the 1912 campaign he appealed to them for support and promised to "assist in advancing the interest of their race" in every possible way. Once elected, he refused even to appoint a privately financed commission to study the race problem. Southerners dominated his administration and Congress; as a result, blacks were further degraded. No fewer than thirty-five blacks in the Atlanta post office lost their jobs. In Washington employees in many government offices were rigidly segregated, and those who objected were summarily discharged.

Du Bois, who had supported Wilson in 1912, attacked administration policy in *The Crisis*. In November 1914 the militant editor of the *Boston Guardian*, William Monroe Trotter, a classmate of Du Bois at Harvard and a far more caustic critic of the Washington approach, led a delegation to the White House to protest the segregation policy of the government. When Wilson accused him of blackmail, Trotter lost his temper, and an ugly confrontation resulted. The mood of black leaders had changed completely.

By this time the Great War had broken out in Europe. Soon every American would feel its effects, blacks perhaps more than any other group. In November 1915, a year almost to the day after Trotter's clash with Wilson, Booker T. Washington died. One era had ended; a new one was beginning. Many of the young Americans who had participated in the various crusades of the "age of reform" would soon embark on another crusade—but one of a very different character.

Milestones

1890	American Woman Suffrage Association and National Woman Suffrage Association unite to form National American Woman Suffrage Association (NAWSA)
1900	Robert La Follette is elected governor of Wisconsin
1901	McKinley is assassinated; Theodore Roosevelt becomes president
1902	Roosevelt helps settle anthracite coal strike
	Oregon adopts initiative system for proposing legislation
1904	Northern Securities case revives Sherman Antitrust Act
	National Child Labor Committee is established
	Theodore Roosevelt is elected president
1905	Anticapitalist Industrial Workers of the World (IWW) is founded
1906	Hepburn Act strengthens Interstate Commerce Commission
	Upton Sinclair exposes Chicago slaughterhouses in *The Jungle*
1907	U.S. Steel absorbs Tennessee Coal and Iron Company
1908	*Muller v. Oregon* upholds law limiting women's work hours
	William Howard Taft is elected president
1909	National Association for the Advancement of Colored People (NAACP) is founded
1910	Ballinger-Pinchot controversy deepens Roosevelt-Taft rift
1911	Roosevelt delivers speech outlining his New Nationalism program
1912	Roosevelt runs for president on Progressive ticket
	Democrat Woodrow Wilson is elected president
1913	Sixteenth Amendment authorizes federal income taxes
	Seventeenth Amendment provides direct election of U.S. senators
	Underwood Tariff reduces duties
	Federal Reserve Act creates a central banking system
1914	Federal Trade Commission (FTC) is created to protect against trusts
	Clayton Antitrust Act regulates business
1920	Nineteenth Amendment guarantees women the right to vote

CHAPTER 22

From Isolation to Empire

DURING THE PRESIDENTIAL CAMPAIGN OF 2000, REPUBLICAN candidate George W. Bush chastised Al Gore, the Democratic candidate and then-vice president, for the Clinton administration's use of American troops in Haiti and the Balkans during the late 1990s. "If we don't stop extending our troops all around the world in nation-building missions," he declared, "then we're going to have a serious problem coming down the road." Gore countered that the United States "must reject the new isolationism that says 'Don't help anywhere because we cannot help everywhere.'"

A Gallup/*USA Today* poll that year showed that Americans were evenly divided on the issue of isolationism, half supporting—and disagreeing with—the statement: "The U.S. should mind its own business internationally and let other countries get along as best they can on their own."

Few on either side of the issue could have imagined that within two years, tens of thousands of American troops would be patrolling the high mountains of the Hindu Kush, fighting enemies at places named Tora Bora and Mazar-e Sharif, and working to install a new government in Afghanistan. A National Geographic Society survey found that while nearly half of Americans aged 18 to 24 knew that the fictional island for the *Survivor* TV series was located in the South Pacific, only one in six could find Afghanistan on a map—even after the United States had invaded the country.

In the decades following the Civil War, Americans gave little thought to foreign affairs. During the 1888 presidential campaign, Benjamin Harrison reflected a widely held belief when he said that the United States was "an apart nation" and so it should remain. James Bryce, a British political theorist, made the same point in *The American Commonwealth*. "Happy America," he wrote, stood "apart in a world of her own . . . safe even from menace."

But sentiment was shifting. More Americans endorsed a "large policy" of colonial acquisitions, expanded trade and influence in Central and Latin America, and intervention in the Cuban war for independence from Spain.

In 1898 tens of thousands of American troops were dispatched to Cuba and, within a year, to the Philippines as well. And for years thereafter, Americans at home struggled to locate on globes and atlases battle sites in places such as Balangiga and Pulang Lupa.

Origins of the Large Policy: Coveting Colonies

The nation's interests in the world gradually increased. During the Civil War, France had established a protectorate over Mexico, installing the Archduke Maximilian of Austria as emperor. In 1866 Secretary of State William H. Seward demanded that the French withdraw, and the United States moved 50,000 soldiers to the Rio Grande. While fear of American intervention was only one of many reasons for their action, the French pulled their troops out of Mexico during the winter of 1866–1867. Mexican nationalists promptly seized and executed Maximilian. In 1867, at the instigation of Seward, the United States purchased Alaska from Russia for $7.2 million, thereby ridding the continent of another foreign power.

In 1867 the aggressive Seward acquired the Midway Islands in the western Pacific, which had been discovered in 1859 by an American naval officer, N. C. Brooks. Seward also made overtures toward annexing the Hawaiian Islands, and he looked longingly at Cuba. In 1870 President Grant submitted to the Senate a treaty annexing the Dominican Republic. He applied tremendous pressure in an effort to obtain ratification, thus forcing a "great debate" on extracontinental expansion. Expansionists stressed the wealth and resources of the country, the markets it would provide, even its "salubrious climate." But the arguments of the opposition proved more persuasive. The distance of the Dominican Republic from the continent and its crowded, dark-skinned population of what one congressman called "semi-civilized, semi-barbarous men who cannot speak our language" made annexation unattractive. The treaty was rejected. Seward had to admit that there was no significant support in the country for his expansionist plans.

The internal growth that preoccupied Americans eventually led them to look outward. By the late 1880s the country was exporting a steadily increasing share of its agricultural and industrial output. Exports, only $450 million in 1870, passed the billion-dollar mark early in the 1890s. Imports increased at a rate only slightly less spectacular.

The character of foreign trade was also changing: Manufactures loomed ever more important among exports until in 1898 the country shipped abroad more manufactured goods than it imported. By this time American steelmakers could compete with producers anywhere in the world. In 1900 one American firm received a large order for steel plates from a Glasgow shipbuilder, and another won contracts for structural steel to be used in constructing bridges for the Uganda

Railroad in British East Africa. When a member of Parliament questioned the colonial secretary about the latter deal, the secretary replied: "Tenders [bids] were invited in the United Kingdom. . . [but] one of the American tenders was found to be considerably the lowest in every respect and was therefore accepted." When American industrialists became conscious of their ability to compete with Europeans in far-off markets, they took more interest in world affairs, particularly during periods of depression, when domestic consumption fell.

Shifting intellectual currents further altered the attitudes of Americans. Darwin's theories, applicable by analogy to international relations, gave the concept of manifest destiny a new plausibility. Darwinists like the historian John Fiske argued that the American democratic system of government was so clearly the world's "fittest" that it was destined to spread peacefully over "every land on the earth's surface." In *Our Country* (1885) Josiah Strong found racist and religious justifications for American expansionism, again based on the theory of evolution. The Anglo-Saxon race, centered now in the United States, possessed "an instinct or genius for colonization," Strong claimed. "God, with infinite wisdom and skill is training the Anglo-Saxon race for . . . the final competition of races." Soon American civilization would "move down upon" Mexico and all Latin America and "out upon the islands of the sea, over upon Africa and beyond." "Can anyone doubt," Strong asked, "that the result of this . . . will be 'the survival of the fittest'?"[1]

The completion of the conquest of the American West encouraged Americans to consider expansion beyond the seas. "For nearly 300 years the dominant fact in American life has been expansion," declared Frederick Jackson Turner, propounder of the frontier thesis. "That these energies of expansion will no longer operate would be a rash prediction." Turner and writers who advanced other expansionist arguments were much influenced by foreign thinking.

Finally, military and strategic arguments were advanced to justify adopting a "large" policy. The powerful Union army had been demobilized rapidly after Appomattox; in the 1880s only about 25,000 men were under arms, their chief occupation fighting Indians in the West.

Half the navy, too, had been scrapped after the war, and the remaining ships were obsolete. While other nations were building steam-powered iron warships, the United States still depended on wooden sailing vessels. In 1867 a British naval publication accurately described the American fleet as "hapless, broken-down, tattered [and] forlorn."

Although no foreign power menaced the country, the decrepit state of the navy vexed many of its officers and led one of them, Captain Alfred Thayer Mahan, to develop a startling theory about the importance of sea power. He explained his theory in two important books, *The Influence of Sea Power Upon History* (1890) and *The Influence of Sea Power Upon the French Revolution and Empire* (1892). According to Mahan, history proved that a nation with a powerful navy and the overseas bases necessary to maintain it would be invulnerable in war and prosperous in time of

---

[1] In later writings Strong insisted that by "fittest" he meant "social efficiency," not "mere strength."

peace. Applied to the current American situation, this meant that in addition to building a modern fleet, the United States should obtain a string of coaling stations and bases in the Caribbean, annex the Hawaiian Islands, and cut a canal across Central America.

Writing at a time when the imperialist-minded European nations showed signs of extending their influence in South America and the Pacific islands, Mahan attracted many influential disciples. One was Congressman Henry Cabot Lodge of Massachusetts, a prominent member of the Naval Affairs Committee. Lodge had married into a navy family and was close with the head of the new Naval War College, Commodore Stephen B. Luce. In 1883 he helped push through Congress an act authorizing the building of three steel warships, and he consistently advocated expanding and modernizing the fleet. Elected to the Senate in 1893, Lodge pressed for expansionist policies, basing his arguments on Mahan's strategic concepts. "Sea power," Lodge proclaimed, "is essential to the greatness of every splendid people." Lodge's friend Theodore Roosevelt was another ardent supporter of the "large" policy, but he had little influence until McKinley appointed him assistant secretary of the navy in 1897.

Toward an Empire in the Pacific

The interest of the United States in the Pacific and East Asia began in the late eighteenth century, when the first American merchant ship dropped anchor in the harbor of Canton, China. After the Treaty of Wanghia (1844), American merchants in China enjoyed many privileges and trade expanded rapidly. Missionaries began to flock into the country—in the late 1880s, over 500 were living there.

The Hawaiian Islands were an important way station on the route to China, and by 1820 merchants and missionaries were making contacts there. As early as 1854 a movement to annex the islands to the United States existed, although it foundered because Hawaii insisted on being admitted to the Union as a state. Commodore Matthew Perry's expedition to Japan led to the signing of a commercial treaty (1858) that opened several Japanese ports to American traders.

The United States pursued a policy of cooperating with the European powers in expanding commercial opportunities in East Asia. In Hawaii the tendency was to claim a special position but to accept the fact that Europeans also had interests in the islands. This state of affairs did not change radically following the Civil War. Despite Chinese protests over the exclusion of their nationals from the United States after 1882, American commercial privileges in China were not disturbed.

American influence in Hawaii increased steadily; the descendants of missionary families, most of them engaged in raising sugar, dominated the Hawaiian monarchy. While they made no overt effort to make the islands an American colony, all the expansionist ideas of the era—manifest destiny, Darwinism, Josiah Strong's racist and religious assumptions, and the relentless force of American commercial interests—pointed them in that direction. In 1875 a reciprocity treaty admitted Hawaiian sugar to the United States free of duty in return for a promise to yield no territory to a

DID THE UNITED STATES ACQUIRE AN OVERSEAS EMPIRE FOR MORAL OR ECONOMIC REASONS?

The American flag, second from left, flies over a warehouse in Guangzhou on the south coast of China in the late nineteenth century. The second photo, dated 1898, is of a family of Presbyterian missionaries in Beijing, attended by Chinese servants. In an influential work, diplomat and historian George F. Kennan (1951) contended that expansionist policies during these years were animated by excessive morality and idealism. McKinley went to war with Spain over the injustice of its colonial rule in Cuba, and he claimed to colonize the Philippines to "educate the Filipinos, and uplift and Christianize them."

During the 1960s and 1970s, however, revisionist historians argued that expansionist schemes were not in the least motivated by idealism. William A. Williams (1972) claimed that American policymakers sought profitable economic penetration of underdeveloped areas. Their subsidiary aim was to encourage these countries to "modernize," that is, to remake themselves in the image of the United States. The Open Door policy, in Williams's view, was not unrealistic and by no means a failure—indeed, it was too successful. He criticized American policy because of its harmful effects on underdeveloped countries. The policy, Williams contended, was "tragic" rather than evil, because its creators were not evil but possessed only limited vision. They did not recognize the contradictions in their ideas and values. They saw American expansion as beneficial to all concerned—and not exclusively in materialistic terms. They genuinely believed that they were exporting democracy along with capitalism and industrialization. Yet while U.S. statesmen abroad certainly sought to fill the warehouses, records show that they spent most of their time speaking with American missionaries and attending to their problems. Religious and moral considerations did matter. Emily S. Rosenberg (1999) showed how cultural and economic forces intersected to promote expansionism.

George F. Kennan, *American Diplomacy* (1951), William Appleman Williams, *The Tragedy of American Diplomacy* (1972), Emily S. Roserberg, *Financial Missionaries to the World* (1999).

foreign power. When this treaty was renewed in 1887, the United States obtained the right to establish a naval base at Pearl Harbor. In addition to occupying Midway, America obtained a foothold in the Samoan Islands in the South Pacific.

During the 1890s American interest in the Pacific area steadily intensified. Conditions in Hawaii had much to do with this. The McKinley Tariff Act of 1890, discontinuing the duty on raw sugar and compensating American producers of cane and beet sugar by granting them a bounty of 2 cents a pound, struck Hawaiian sugar growers hard, for it destroyed the advantage they had gained in the reciprocity treaty.

The following year the death of the complaisant King Kalakaua brought Queen Liliuokalani, a determined nationalist, to the throne. Placing herself at the head of a "Hawaii for the Hawaiians" movement, she abolished the existing constitution under which the white minority had pretty much controlled the islands and attempted to rule as an absolute monarch. The resident Americans then staged a coup. In January 1893, with the connivance of the U.S. minister, John L. Stevens, who ordered 150 marines from the cruiser *Boston* into Honolulu, they deposed Queen Liliuokalani and set up a provisional government. Stevens recognized their regime at once, and the new government sent a delegation to Washington to seek a treaty of annexation.

In the closing days of the Harrison administration such a treaty was negotiated and sent to the Senate, but when Cleveland took office in March, he withdrew it. The new president disapproved of the way American troops had been used to overthrow the monarchy. He sent a special commissioner, James H. Blount, to Hawaii to investigate. When Blount reported that the Hawaiians opposed annexation, the president dismissed Stevens and attempted to restore Queen Liliuokalani. Since the provisional government was by that time firmly entrenched, this could

A sugarcane field on the island of Maui, Hawaii. In 1899, the value of sugar crops of Louisiana, Georgia, Alabama, Texas, Mississippi, and Florida—the major sugar-producing states— barely exceeded that for Hawaii alone. Congressmen from those states almost all voted against annexation of Hawaii.

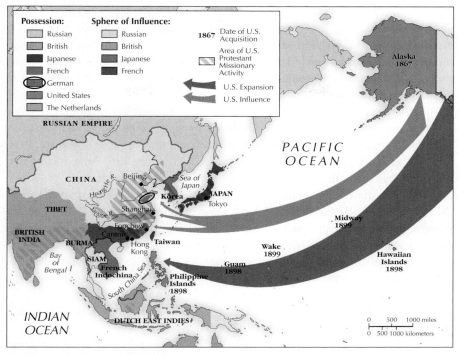

Possession:

Russian	
British	
Japanese	
French	
German	
United States	
The Netherlands	

Sphere of Influence:

Russian	
British	
Japanese	
French	

1867 Date of U.S. Acquisition

Area of U.S. Protestant Missionary Activity

U.S. Expansion

U.S. Influence

RUSSIAN EMPIRE

PACIFIC OCEAN

Alaska 1867

CHINA — Beijing — Sea of Japan — JAPAN — Tokyo

Huang He R. — Yangtze R. — Shanghai — Korea

TIBET

Foochow

BRITISH INDIA — BURMA — Canton — Hong Kong — Taiwan

Bay of Bengal — SIAM — French Indochina

South China Sea

Guam 1898

Wake 1899

Midway 1899

Hawaiian Islands 1898

Philippine Islands 1898

INDIAN OCEAN

DUTCH EAST INDIES

0   500   1000 miles
0   500 1000 kilometers

The Course of Empire, 1867–1901

not be accomplished peacefully. Because Cleveland was unwilling to use force against the Americans in the islands, however much he objected to their actions, he found himself unable to do anything. The revolutionary government of Hawaii remained in power, independent yet eager to be annexed.

The Hawaiian debate continued sporadically over the next four years. It provided a thorough airing of the question of overseas expansion. Fears that another power—Great Britain or perhaps Japan—might step into the void created by Cleveland's refusal to act alarmed those who favored annexation. When the Republicans returned to power in 1897, a new annexation treaty was negotiated, but domestic sugar producers now threw their weight against it, and the McKinley administration could not obtain the necessary two-thirds majority in the Senate. Finally, in July 1898, after the outbreak of the Spanish-American War, Congress annexed the islands by joint resolution, a procedure requiring only a simple majority vote.

Toward an Empire in Latin America

As early as 1869 President Grant had come out for an American-owned canal across the isthmus of Panama, in spite of the fact that the United States had agreed in the Clayton-Bulwer Treaty with Great Britain (1850) that neither nation would "obtain or maintain for itself any exclusive control" over an interoceanic canal. In 1880, when the French engineer Ferdinand de Lesseps organized a company to build a canal across the isthmus, President Hayes announced that the United States would not permit a European power to control such a waterway. "The policy of the country is a canal under American control," he announced, another blithe disregard of the Clayton-Bulwer agreement.

When Cleveland returned to power in 1893, the possibility of trouble in Latin America seemed remote, for he had always opposed imperialistic ventures. Yet scarcely two years later the United States was again on the verge of war in South America as a result of a crisis in Venezuela, and before this issue was settled Cleveland had made the most powerful claim to American hegemony in the hemisphere ever uttered. The tangled borderland between Venezuela and British Guiana (present-day Guyana) had long been in dispute, Venezuela demanding more of the region than it was entitled to and Great Britain making exaggerated claims and imperiously refusing to submit the question to arbitration.

There was considerable latent anti-British feeling in the United States. By taking the Venezuelan side in the boundary dispute, Cleveland would be defending a weak neighbor against a great power, a position certain to evoke a popular response. "Turn this Venezuela question up or down, North, South, East or West, and it is a winner" one Democrat advised the president.

Cleveland did not resist the temptation to intervene. In July 1895 he ordered Secretary of State Richard Olney to send a near ultimatum to the British. By occupying the disputed territory, Olney insisted, Great Britain was invading Venezuela and violating the Monroe Doctrine. Quite gratuitously, he went on to boast: "Today the United States is practically sovereign on this continent, and its fiat is law upon the subjects to which it confines its interposition." Unless Great Britain responded promptly by agreeing to arbitration, the president would call the question to the attention of Congress.

The note threatened war, but the British ignored it for months. They did not take the United States seriously as a world power, and with reason, for the American navy, although expanding, could not hope to stand up against the British, who had fifty battleships, twenty-five armored cruisers, and many smaller vessels. When Lord Salisbury, the prime minister and foreign secretary, finally replied, he rejected outright the argument that the Monroe Doctrine had any status under international law and refused to arbitrate what he called the "exaggerated pretensions" of the Venezuelans.

While Olney's note had been belligerent, Salisbury's reply was supercilious and caustic. Cleveland was furious. On December 17, 1895, he asked Congress for authority to appoint an American commission to determine the correct line between British Guiana and Venezuela. When that had been done, he added, the United States should "resist by every means in its power" the appropriation by Great Britain of any territory "we have determined of right belongs to Venezuela." Congress responded at once, unanimously appropriating $100,000 for the boundary commission. Popular approval was almost universal.

Great Britain agreed to arbitrate the boundary. The war scare subsided; soon Olney was talking about "our inborn and instinctive English sympathies" and offering "to stand side by side and shoulder to shoulder with England in . . . the defense of human rights." When the boundary tribunal awarded nearly all the disputed region to Great Britain, whatever ill feeling the surrender may have occasioned in that country faded away. Instead of leading to war, the affair marked the beginning of an era of Anglo-American friendship. It had the unfortunate effect, however, of adding to the long-held American conviction that the nation could get what it wanted in international affairs by threat and bluster—a dangerous illusion.

The Cuban Revolution

On February 10, 1896, scarcely a week after Venezuela and Great Britain had signed the treaty ending their dispute, General Valeriano Weyler arrived in Havana from Spain to take up his duties as governor of Cuba. His assignment to this post was occasioned by the guerrilla warfare that Cuban nationalist rebels had been waging for almost a year. Weyler, a tough and ruthless soldier, set out to administer Cuba with "a salutary rigor." He began herding the rural population into wretched "reconcentration" camps to deprive the rebels of food and recruits. Resistance in Cuba hardened.

Public sympathy in the United States went to the Cubans, who seemed to be fighting for liberty and democracy against an autocratic Old World power. Most newspapers supported the rebels; labor unions, veterans' organizations, many Protestant clergymen, a great majority of American blacks, and important politicians in both major parties demanded that the United States aid their cause. Rapidly increasing American investments in Cuban sugar plantations, now approaching $50 million, were endangered by the fighting and by the social chaos sweeping across the island.

Cuban propagandists in the United States played on American sentiments cleverly. When reports, often exaggerated, of the cruelty of "Butcher" Weyler and the horrors of his reconcentration camps filtered into America, the cry for action intensified. In April 1896 Congress adopted a resolution suggesting that the revolutionaries be granted the rights of belligerents. Since this would have been akin to formal recognition, Cleveland would not go that far, but he did exert diplomatic pressure on Spain to remove the causes of the rebels' complaints, and he offered the services of his government as mediator. The Spanish rejected the suggestion. For a time the issue subsided. The election of 1896 deflected American attention from Cuba, and then McKinley refused to take any action that might disturb Spanish-American relations. Business interests—except those with holdings in Cuba—backed McKinley, for they feared that a crisis would upset the economy, which was just beginning to pick up after the depression. In Cuba General Weyler made some progress toward stifling rebel resistance.

An 1898 German cartoon poking fun at Uncle Sam for coming to the "aid" of a mermaid—Cuba.

American expansionists, however, continued to demand intervention, and the press, especially Joseph Pulitzer's *New York World* and William Randolph Hearst's *New York Journal,* competing fiercely to increase circulation, kept resentment alive with tales of Spanish atrocities. McKinley remained adamant. Although he warned Spain that Cuba must be pacified, and soon, his tone was friendly and he issued no ultimatum. A new government in Spain relieved the situation by recalling Weyler and promising partial self-government to the Cubans.

In a message to Congress in December 1897, McKinley urged that Spain be given "a reasonable chance to realize her expectations" in the island.

His hopes were doomed, primarily because Spain failed to "realize her expectations." The fighting in Cuba continued. When riots broke out in Havana in January 1898, McKinley ordered the battleship *Maine* to Havana harbor to protect American citizens.

Shortly thereafter Hearst's *New York Journal* printed a letter written to a friend in Cuba by the Spanish minister in Washington, Dupuy de Lôme. The letter had been stolen by a spy. De Lôme, an experienced but arrogant diplomat, failed to appreciate McKinley's efforts to avoid intervening in Cuba. In the letter he characterized the president as a *politicastro,* or "small-time politician," which was a gross error, and a "bidder for the admiration of the crowd," which was equally insulting though somewhat closer to the truth. Americans were outraged, and de Lôme's hasty resignation did little to soothe their feelings.

Then, on February 15, the *Maine* exploded and sank in Havana harbor, 260 of the crew perishing in the disaster. Interventionists in the United States accused Spain of having destroyed the ship and clamored for war. The willingness of Americans to blame Spain indicates the extent of anti-Spanish opinion in the United States by 1898. No one has ever discovered what actually happened. A naval

The explosion of the *Maine* in Havana harbor, killing 260 men, caused much speculation in the newspapers and across the nation as to its cause. Many Americans pointed the finger at Spain, a reaction that typified American sentiment toward the Spanish in 1898. What really caused the explosion remains unknown. Each of the colors for this chromolithograph, by Louis Kurz and Alexander Allison, was produced from a different lithographer stone.

court of inquiry decided that the vessel had been sunk by a submarine mine, but it now seems more likely that an internal explosion destroyed the *Maine.* The Spanish government could hardly have been foolish enough to commit an act that would probably bring American troops into Cuba.

With admirable courage, McKinley refused to panic; but he could not resist the wishes of millions of citizens that something be done to stop the fighting and allow the Cubans to determine their own fate: Spanish pride and Cuban patriotism had taken the issue of peace or war out of the president's hands. Spain could not put down the rebellion, and it would not yield to the nationalists' increasingly extreme demands. To have granted independence to Cuba might have caused the Madrid government to fall, might even have led to the collapse of the monarchy, for the Spanish public was in no mood to surrender. The Cubans, sensing that the continuing bloodshed aided their cause, refused to give the Spanish regime room to maneuver. After the *Maine* disaster, Spain might have agreed to an armistice had the rebels asked for one, and in the resulting negotiations it might well have given up the island. The rebels refused to make the first move. The fighting continued, bringing the United States every day closer to intervention.

The president faced a dilemma. Most of the business interests of the country, to which he was particularly sensitive, opposed intervention. His personal feelings were equally firm. "I have been through one war," he told a friend. "I have seen the dead piled up, and I do not want to see another." Congress, however, seemed determined to act. When he submitted a restrained report on the sinking of the *Maine*, the Democrats in Congress, even most of those who had supported Cleveland's policies, gleefully accused him of timidity.

McKinley spent a succession of sleepless nights; sedatives brought him no repose. Finally, early in April, the president drafted a message asking for authority to use the armed forces "to secure a full and final termination of hostilities" in Cuba.

At the last moment the Spanish government seemed to yield; it ordered its troops in Cuba to cease hostilities. McKinley passed this information on to Congress along with his war message, but he gave it no emphasis and did not try to check the march toward war. To seek further delay would have been courageous but not necessarily wiser. Merely to stop fighting was not enough. The Cuban nationalists now insisted on full independence, and the Spanish politicians were unprepared to abandon the last remnant of their once-great American empire. If the United States took Cuba by force, the Spanish leaders might save their political skins; if they meekly surrendered the island, they were done for.

The "Splendid Little" Spanish-American War

On April 20, 1898, Congress, by joint resolution, recognized the independence of Cuba and authorized the use of the armed forces to drive out the Spanish. An amendment proposed by Senator Henry M. Teller disclaiming any intention of adding Cuban territory to the United States passed without opposition. Four days later Spain declared war on the United States.

The Spanish-American War was fought to free Cuba, but the first action took place on the other side of the globe, in the Philippine Islands. Weeks earlier, Theodore Roosevelt, at the time assistant secretary of the navy, had alerted Commodore George Dewey, who was in command of the United States Asiatic Squadron located at Hong Kong, to move against the Spanish base at Manila if war came. Dewey had acted promptly, drilling his gun crews, taking on supplies, giving his gleaming white ships a coat of battle-gray paint, and establishing secret contacts with the Filipino nationalist leader, Emilio Aguinaldo. When word of the declaration of war reached him, Dewey steamed from Hong Kong across the South China Sea with four cruisers and two gunboats. On the night of April 30 he entered Manila Bay, and at daybreak he opened fire on the Spanish fleet at 5,000 yards. His squadron made five passes, each time reducing the range; when the smoke had cleared, all ten of Admiral Montojo's ships had been destroyed. Not a single American was killed in the engagement.

Dewey immediately asked for troops to take and hold Manila, for now that war had been declared, he could not return to Hong Kong or put in at any other neutral port. McKinley took the fateful step of dispatching some 11,000 soldiers and additional naval support. On August 13 these forces, assisted by Filipino irregulars under Aguinaldo, captured Manila.

Sailors on the U.S.S. *Oregon* watching the destruction of the Spanish cruiser, *Cristobal Colon*, during the Battle of Santiago, Cuba, July 3, 1898.

Meanwhile, in Cuba, the United States had won a swift and total victory, though more because of the weakness of the Spanish armed forces than because of the power or efficiency of the American. When the war began, the U.S. regular army consisted of about 28,000 men. This tiny force was bolstered by 200,000 hastily enlisted volunteers. In May an expeditionary force gathered at Tampa, Florida. That hamlet was inundated by the masses of men and supplies that descended upon it. Entire regiments sat without uniforms or weapons while hundreds of freight cars jammed with equipment lay forgotten on sidings. Army management was abominable, rivalry between commanders a serious problem. Aggressive units like the regiment of "Rough Riders" raised by Theodore Roosevelt, who had resigned his navy department post to become a lieutenant colonel of volunteers, scrambled for space and supplies, shouldering aside other units to get what they needed. "No words could describe . . . the confusion and lack of system and the general mismanagement of affairs here," the angry Roosevelt complained.

Since a Spanish fleet under Admiral Pascual Cervera was known to be in Caribbean waters, no invading army could safely embark until the fleet could be located. On May 29 American ships found Cervera at Santiago harbor, on the eastern end of Cuba, and established a blockade. In June a 17,000-man expeditionary force commanded by General William Shafter landed at Daiquiri, east of Santiago, and pressed quickly toward the city, handicapped more by its own bad staff work than by the enemy, though the Spanish troops resisted bravely. The Americans sweated through Cuba's torrid summer in heavy wool winter uniforms, ate "embalmed beef" out of cans, and fought mostly with old-fashioned rifles using black powder cartridges that marked the position of each soldier with a puff of smoke whenever he pulled the trigger. On July 1 they broke through undermanned Spanish defenses and stormed San Juan Hill, the intrepid Roosevelt at the forefront. ("Are you afraid to stand up while I am on horseback?" Roosevelt demanded of one soldier.)

With Santiago harbor in range of American artillery, Admiral Cervera had to run the blockade. On July 3 his black-hulled ships, flags proudly flying, steamed

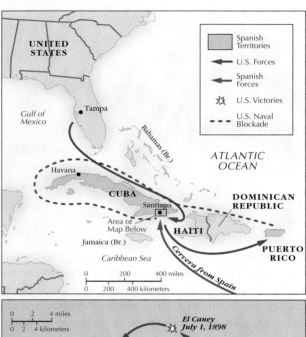

**Spanish-American War,
Caribbean Theater**

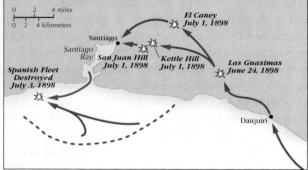

forth from the harbor and fled westward along the coast. Like hounds after rabbits, five American battleships and two cruisers, commanded by Rear Admiral William T. Sampson and Commodore Winfield Scott Schley, ran them down. In four hours the entire Spanish force was destroyed by a hail of 8-inch and 13-inch projectiles (the size of artillery shells refers to their diameter). Damage to the American ships was superficial; only one American seaman lost his life in the engagement.

The end then came abruptly. Santiago surrendered on July 17. A few days later, other U.S. troops completed the occupation of Puerto Rico. On August 12, one day before the fall of Manila, Spain agreed to get out of Cuba and to cede Puerto Rico and an island in the Marianas (Guam) to the United States. The future of the Philippines was to be settled at a formal peace conference, convening in Paris on October 1.

Developing a Colonial Policy

Although the Spanish resisted surrendering the Philippines at Paris, they had been so thoroughly defeated that they had no choice. The decision hung rather on the outcome of a conflict over policy within the United States. The war, won at so little cost militarily, produced problems far larger than those it solved.[2] The nation had become a great power in the world's eyes. The annexation of Hawaii and other overseas bases intensified the conviction of European leaders that the United States was determined to become a major force in international affairs.

But were the American people determined to exercise that force? The debate over taking the Philippine Islands throws much light on their attitudes. The imagination of Americans had been captured by the trappings of empire, not by its essence. It was titillating to think of a world map liberally sprinkled with American flags and of the economic benefits that colonies might bring, but most citizens were not prepared to join in a worldwide struggle for power and influence. They entered blithely on adventures in far-off regions without facing the implications of their decision.

Since the United States (in the Teller Amendment) had renounced any claim to Cuba, even though the island had long been desired by expansionists, logic dictated that a similar policy be applied to the Philippines, a remote land few Americans had ever thought about before 1898. But expansionists were eager to annex the entire archipelago. Even before he had learned to spell the name, Senator Lodge was saying that "the Phillipines [sic] mean a vast future trade and wealth and power," offering the nation a greater opportunity "than anything that has happened . . . since the annexation of Louisiana."

President McKinley adopted a more cautious stance, but he too favored "the general principle of holding on to what we can get." A speaking tour of the Midwest in October 1898, during which he experimented with varying degrees of commitment to expansionism, convinced him that the public wanted the islands. Business opinion had shifted dramatically during the war. Business leaders were now calling the Philippines the gateway to the markets of East Asia.

The Anti-Imperialists

The war had produced a wave of unifying patriotic feeling. It greatly furthered reconciliation between the North and the South; two major generals, for example, were Confederate veterans. But victory raised new divisive questions. An important minority objected strongly to the U.S. acquisition of overseas possessions. Persons as different in interest and philosophy as the tycoon Andrew Carnegie and the labor leader Samuel Gompers, as the venerable Republican Senator George Frisbie Hoar of Massachusetts and "Pitchfork Ben" Tillman, the southern Democratic fire-

THE ANTI-IMPERIALISTS

627

---

[2]More than 5,000 Americans died as a result of the conflict, but fewer than 400 fell in combat. The others were mostly victims of yellow fever, typhoid, and other diseases.

brand, together with the writers Mark Twain and William Dean Howells, the reformers Lincoln Steffens and Jane Addams, and the educators Charles W. Eliot of Harvard and David Starr Jordan of Stanford united in opposing annexation of the Philippines.

The anti-imperialists insisted that since no one would consider statehood for the Philippines, it would be unconstitutional to annex them. It was a violation of the spirit of the Declaration of Independence to govern a foreign territory without the consent of its inhabitants, Senator Hoar argued; by taking over "vassal states" in "barbarous archipelagoes" the United States was "trampling . . . on our own great Charter, which recognizes alike the liberty and the dignity of individual manhood."

McKinley was not insensitive to this appeal to idealism and tradition, which was the fundamental element in the anti-imperialist argument. But he rejected it. Labor leaders particularly feared the competition of "the Chinese, the Negritos, and the Malays" who presumably would flood into the United States if the Philippines were taken. More compelling to McKinley was the absence of any practical alternative to annexation. Public opinion would not sanction restoring Spanish authority in the Philippines or allowing some other power to have them. That the Filipinos were sufficiently advanced and united socially to form a stable government if granted independence seemed unlikely. Senator Hoar believed that "for years and for generations, and perhaps for centuries, there would have been turbulence, disorder and revolution" in the islands if they were left to their own devices.

Strangely—for he was a kind and gentle man—Hoar faced this possibility with equanimity. McKinley was unable to do so. The president searched the depths of his soul and could find no solution but annexation. Of course the state of public feeling made the decision easier, and he probably found the idea of presiding over an empire appealing. Certainly the commercial possibilities did not escape him. In the end it was with a heavy sense of responsibility that he ordered the American peace commissioners to insist on acquiring the Philippines. To salve the feelings of the Spanish the United States agreed to pay $20 million for the archipelago, but it was a forced sale, accepted by Spain under duress.

The peace treaty faced a hard battle in the U.S. Senate, where a combination of partisan politics and anticolonialism made it difficult to amass the two-thirds majority necessary for ratification. McKinley had shrewdly appointed three senators, including one Democrat, to the peace commission. This predisposed many members of the upper house to approve the treaty, but the vote was close. William Jennings Bryan, titular head of the Democratic party, could probably have prevented ratification had he urged his supporters to vote nay. The question should be decided, Bryan said, "not by a minority of the Senate but by a majority of the people" at the next presidential election. Perplexed by Bryan's stand, a number of Democrats allowed themselves to be persuaded by the expansionists' arguments and by McKinley's judicious use of patronage; the treaty was ratified in February 1899 by a vote of 57 to 27.

The Philippine Insurrection

The national referendum that Bryan had hoped for never materialized. Bryan himself confused the issue in 1900 by making free silver a major plank in his platform, thereby driving conservative anti-imperialists into McKinley's arms. Moreover, early in 1899 the Filipino nationalists under Aguinaldo, furious because the United States would not withdraw, took up arms. A savage guerrilla war resulted, one that cost far more in lives and money than the "splendid little" Spanish-American conflict.

Like all conflicts waged in tangled country chiefly by small, isolated units surrounded by a hostile civilian population, neither side displayed much regard for the "rules" of war. Goaded by sneak attacks and instances of cruelty to captives, American soldiers, most of whom had little respect for Filipinos to begin with, responded in kind. Civilians were rounded up, prisoners tortured, property destroyed. Horrifying tales of rape, arson, and murder by U.S. troops filtered into the country, providing ammunition for the anti-imperialists. "You seem to have about finished your work of civilizing the Filipinos," Andrew Carnegie wrote angrily to one of the American peace commissioners. "About 8,000 of them have been completely civilized and sent to Heaven. I hope you like it." In fact, far more than 8,000 Filipinos lost their lives during the conflict, which raged for three years. More than 70,000 American soldiers had to be sent to the islands before the resistance was crushed, and about as many of them lost their lives as had perished in the Cuban conflict.

Emilio Aguinaldo, shown here with his young son, commanded Filipino insurgents who worked with Commodore Dewey to help overthrow Spanish rule of the Philippines in 1898. He later took up arms against the United States in a brutal three-year struggle when President McKinley opposed granting independence to the islands.

A commission that had been sent to the Philippines by McKinley in 1899 before the fighting started to study the problem attributed the insurrection to the ambitions of the nationalist leaders and recommended that the Philippines be granted independence at an indefinite future date. In 1900 McKinley sent another commission, this one headed by William Howard Taft, a federal judge, to establish a government. Taft, a warmhearted, affable man, took an instant liking to the Filipinos, and his policy of encouraging them to participate in the territorial government attracted many converts. In July 1901 he became the first civilian governor of the Philippines.

Actually, McKinley's reelection in 1900 settled the Philippine question so far as most Americans were concerned. Anti-imperialists still claimed that it was unconstitutional to take over territories without the consent of the local population. Their reasoning, while certainly not unsound, was unhistorical. No American government had seriously considered the wishes of the American Indians, the French and Spanish settlers in Louisiana, the Eskimos of Alaska, or the people of Hawaii when it had seemed in the national interest to annex new lands.

Cuba and the United States

Nevertheless, grave constitutional questions arose as a result of the acquisitions that followed the Spanish-American War. McKinley acted with remarkable independence in handling the problems involved in expansion. He set up military governments in Cuba, Puerto Rico, and the Philippines without specific congressional authority. But eventually both Congress and the Supreme Court took a hand in shaping colonial policy. In 1900 Congress passed the Foraker Act, establishing a civil government for Puerto Rico. It did not give the Puerto Ricans either American citizenship or full local self-government, and it placed a tariff on Puerto Rican products imported into the United States.

While the most heated arguments raged over Philippine policy, the most difficult colonial problems concerned the relationship between the United States and Cuba, for there idealism and self-interest clashed painfully. Despite the desire of most Americans to get out of Cuba, an independent government could not easily be created. Order and prosperity did not automatically appear when the red and gold ensigns of Spain were hauled down from the flagstaffs of Havana and Santiago.

The insurgent government was feeble, corrupt, and oligarchic, the Cuban economy in a state of collapse, life chaotic. The first Americans entering Havana found the streets littered with garbage and the corpses of horses and dogs. All public services were at a standstill; it seemed essential for the United States, as McKinley said, to give "aid and direction" until "tranquillity" could be restored.

When McKinley established a military government for Cuba late in 1898, it was soon embroiled with local leaders. Then an eager horde of American promoters descended on Cuba in search of profitable franchises and concessions. Congress put a stop to this exploitation by forbidding all such grants as long as the occupation continued.

In the end the United States did withdraw, after doing a great deal to modernize sugar production, improve sanitary conditions, establish schools, and restore orderly administration. In November 1900 a Cuban constitutional convention met at Havana and proceeded without substantial American interference or direction to draft a frame of government. The chief restrictions imposed by this document on Cuba's freedom concerned foreign relations; at the insistence of the United States, it authorized American intervention whenever necessary "for the preservation of Cuban independence" and "the maintenance of a government adequate for the protection of life, property, and individual liberty." Cuba had to promise to make no treaty with a foreign power compromising its independence and to grant naval bases on its soil to the United States.

The Cubans, after some grumbling, accepted this arrangement, known as the Platt Amendment. It had the support of most American opponents of imperialism. The amendment was a true compromise: it safeguarded American interests while granting to the Cubans real self-government on internal matters. In May 1902 the United States turned over the reins of government to the new republic. The next year the two countries signed a reciprocity treaty tightening the economic bonds between them.

True friendship did not result. Although American troops occupied Cuba only once more, in 1906, and then at the specific request of Cuban authorities, the United States repeatedly used the threat of intervention to coerce the Cuban government. American economic penetration proceeded rapidly and without regard for the well-being of the Cuban peasants, many of whom lived in a state of peonage on great sugar plantations. Nor did the Americans' good intentions make up for their tendency to consider themselves innately superior to the Cubans and to overlook the fact that Cubans did not always wish to adopt American customs and culture.

The United States in the Caribbean and Central America

If the purpose of the Spanish-American War had been to bring peace and order to Cuba, the Platt Amendment was a logical step. The same purpose soon necesstated a further extension of the principle, for once the United States accepted the role of protector and stabilizer in parts of the Caribbean and Central America, it seemed desirable, for the same economic, strategic, and humanitarian reasons, to supervise the entire region.

The Caribbean and Central American countries were economically underdeveloped, socially backward, politically unstable, and desperately poor. Everywhere a few families owned most of the land and dominated social and political life. Most of the people were uneducated peasants, many of whom were little better off than slaves. Rival cliques of wealthy families struggled for power, force being the usual method of effecting a change in government. Most of the meager income of the average Caribbean state was swallowed up by the military or diverted into the pockets of the current rulers.

In 1903, after Theodore Roosevelt had become president, the Dominican Republic defaulted on bonds totaling some $40 million. When European investors urged their governments to intervene, Roosevelt announced that under the Monroe Doctrine the United States could not permit foreign nations to intervene in Latin America. But, he added, Latin American nations should not be allowed to escape their obligations. "If we intend to say 'Hands off'. . . sooner or later we must keep order ourselves," he told Secretary of War Elihu Root.

The president did not want to make a colony of the Dominican Republic. "I have about the same desire to annex it as a gorged boa constrictor might have to swallow a porcupine wrong-end-to," he said. He therefore arranged for the United States to take charge of the Dominican customs service—the one reliable source of revenue in that poverty-stricken country. Fifty-five percent of the customs duties would be devoted to debt payment, the remainder turned over to the Dominican government to care for its internal needs. Roosevelt defined his policy, known as the Roosevelt Corollary to the Monroe Doctrine, in a message to Congress in December 1904. "Chronic wrongdoing" in Latin America, he stated with his typical disregard for the subtleties of complex affairs, might require outside intervention. Since, under the Monroe Doctrine, no other nation could step in, the United States must "exercise . . . an international police power."

In the short run this policy worked. Dominican customs were honestly collected for the first time and the country's finances put in order. The presence of American warships in the area provided a needed measure of political stability. In

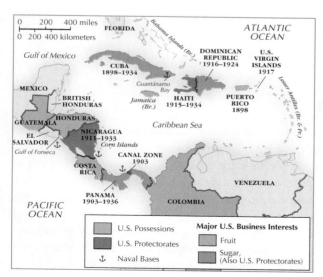

The United States in the Caribbean and Central America

Puerto Rico was ceded by Spain to the United States after the Spanish-American War; the Virgin Islands were bought from Denmark; the Canal Zone was leased from Panama. The ranges of dates following Cuba, the Dominican Republic, Haiti, Nicaragua, and Panama cover those years during which the United States either had troops in occupation or in some other way (such as financial) had a protectorate relationship with that country.

the long run, however, the Roosevelt Corollary caused a great deal of resentment in Latin America, for it added to nationalist fears that the United States wished to exploit the region for its own benefit.

The Open Door Policy

Coincidental with the Cuban rebellion of the 1890s, a far greater upheaval had convulsed the ancient empire of China. In 1894–1895 Japan easily defeated China in a war over Korea. Alarmed by Japan's aggressiveness, the European powers hastened to carve out for themselves new spheres of influence along China's coast. After the annexation of the Philippines, McKinley's secretary of state, John Hay, urged on by business leaders fearful of losing out in the scramble to exploit the Chinese market, tried to prevent the further absorption of China by the great powers.

For the United States to join in the dismemberment of China was politically impossible because of anti-imperialist feeling, so Hay sought to protect American interests by clever diplomacy. In a series of "Open Door" notes (1899) he asked the powers to agree to respect the trading rights of all countries and to impose no discriminatory duties within their spheres of influence. Chinese tariffs should continue to be collected in these areas and by Chinese officials.

The replies to the Open Door notes were at best noncommittal, yet Hay blandly announced in March 1900 that the powers had "accepted" his suggestions! Thus he could claim to have prevented the breakup of the Chinese empire and protected the right of Americans to do business freely in its territories. In reality nothing had been accomplished; the imperialist nations did not extend their political control of China only because they feared that by doing so they might precipitate a major war among themselves. Nevertheless, Hay's action marked a revolutionary departure from the traditional American policy of isolation, a bold advance into the complicated and dangerous world of international power politics.

Within a few months of Hay's announcement the Open Door policy was put to the test. Chinese nationalists, angered by the spreading influence of foreign governments, launched the so-called Boxer Rebellion. They swarmed into Beijing and drove foreigners behind the walls of their legations, which were placed under siege. For weeks, until an international rescue expedition (which included 2,500 American soldiers) broke through to free them, the fate of the foreigners was unknown. Fearing that the Europeans would use the rebellion as a pretext for further expropriations, Hay sent off another round of Open Door notes announcing that the United States believed in the preservation of "Chinese territorial and administrative entity" and in "the principle of equal and impartial trade with all parts of the Chinese Empire." This broadened the Open Door policy to include all China, not merely the European spheres of influence.

In time the United States would pay a heavy price for this unrealistic attitude, but in the decade following 1900 its policy of diplomatic meddling unbacked by bayonets worked fairly well. Japan attacked Russia in a quarrel over Manchuria, smashing the Russian fleet in 1905 and winning a series of battles on the mainland. Japan was not prepared for a long war, however, and suggested to President Roosevelt that an American offer to mediate would be favorably received.

Eager to preserve the nice balance in East Asia, which enabled the United States to exert influence without any significant commitment of force, Roosevelt accepted the hint. In June 1905 he invited the belligerents to a conference at Portsmouth, New Hampshire. At the conference the Japanese won title to Russia's sphere around Port Arthur and a free hand in Korea, but when they demanded Sakhalin Island and a large money indemnity, the Russians balked. Unwilling to resume the war, the Japanese settled for half of Sakhalin and no money.

The Treaty of Portsmouth was unpopular in Japan, and the government managed to place the blame on Roosevelt, who had supported the compromise. Ill feeling against Americans increased in 1906 when the San Francisco school board, responding to local opposition to the influx of cheap labor from Japan, instituted a policy of segregating Asian children in a special school. Japan protested, and President Roosevelt persuaded the San Franciscans to abandon segregation in exchange for his pledge to cut off further Japanese immigration. He accomplished this through a "Gentlemen's Agreement" (1907) in which the Japanese promised not to issue passports to laborers seeking to come to America. Discriminatory legislation based specifically on race was thus avoided. However, the atmosphere between the two countries remained charged. Japanese resentment at American racial prejudice was great; many Americans talked fearfully of the "yellow peril."

Theodore Roosevelt was preeminently a realist in foreign relations. "Don't bluster," he once said. "Don't flourish a revolver, and never draw unless you intend to shoot." In East Asia he failed to follow his own advice. He considered the situation in that part of the world fraught with peril. The Philippines, he said, were "our heel of Achilles," indefensible in case of a Japanese attack. He suggested privately that the United States ought to "be prepared for giving the islands independence . . . much sooner than I think advisable from their own standpoint."

Yet while Roosevelt did not appreciably increase American naval and military strength in East Asia, neither did he stop trying to influence the course of events in the area, and he took no step toward withdrawing from the Philippines. He sent the fleet on a world cruise to demonstrate its might to Japan but knew well that this was mere bluff. "The 'Open Door' policy," he advised his successor, "completely disappears as soon as a powerful nation determines to disregard it." Nevertheless he allowed the belief to persist in the United States that the nation could influence the course of East Asian history without risk or real involvement.

The Panama Canal

In the Caribbean region American policy centered on building an interoceanic canal across Central America. Expanding interests in Latin America and East Asia made a canal necessary, a truth pointed up during the war with Spain by the two-month voyage of USS *Oregon* from California waters around South America to participate in the action against Admiral Cervera's fleet at Santiago. The first step was to get rid of the old Clayton-Bulwer Treaty with Great Britain, which barred the United States from building a canal on its own. In 1901 Lord Pauncefote, the British ambassador, and Secretary of State John Hay negotiated an agreement abolishing the Clayton-Bulwer pact and giving the United States the right to build and, by implication, fortify a waterway across the isthmus. The United States agreed in turn to maintain any such canal "free and open to the vessels of commerce and of war of all nations."

One possible canal route lay across the Colombian province of Panama, where the French-controlled New Panama Canal Company had taken over the franchise of the old De Lesseps company. Although only fifty miles separated the oceans in Panama, the terrain there was rugged and the climate unhealthy. While the French company had sunk much money into the project, it had little to show for its efforts aside from some rough excavations. A second possible route ran across Nicaragua. This route was about 200 miles long but was relatively easy since much of it traversed Lake Nicaragua and other natural waterways.

President McKinley appointed a commission to study the alternatives. It reported that the Panamanian route was technically superior, but recommended building in Nicaragua because the New Panama Canal Company was asking $109 million for its assets, which the commission valued at only $40 million. Lacking another potential purchaser, the French company lowered its price to $40 million, and after a great deal of clever propagandizing by Philippe Bunau-Varilla, a French engineer with heavy investments in the company, President Roosevelt settled on the Panamanian route.

In January 1903 Secretary of State Hay negotiated a treaty with Tomás Herrán, the Colombian chargé d'affaires in Washington. In return for a 99-year lease on a zone across Panama 6 miles wide, the United States agreed to pay Colombia $10 million and an annual rent of $250,000. The Colombian senate, however, unanimously rejected this treaty, in part because it did not adequately protect Colombian sovereignty over Panama and in part because it hardly seemed fair that the New Panama Canal Company should receive $40 million for its frozen assets and Colombia only $10 million. The government demanded $15 million directly from the United States, plus $10 million of the company's share.

A little more patience might have produced a mutually satisfactory settlement, but Roosevelt looked on the Colombians as highwaymen who were "mad to get hold of the $40,000,000 of the Frenchmen." ("You could no more make an agreement with the Colombian rulers," Roosevelt later remarked, "than you could nail currant jelly to a wall.") When Panamanians, egged on by the French company, staged a revolution in November 1903, Roosevelt ordered the cruiser *Nashville* to Panama. Colombian government forces found themselves looking down the barrels of the guns of the *Nashville* and shortly thereafter eight other American warships. The revolution succeeded.

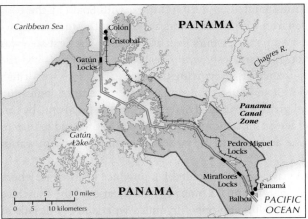

The U.S. Panama Canal

Following many negotiations, construction on the Panama Canal began in 1904. After many delays and hardships, it was completed in 1914.

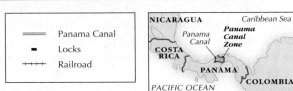

Roosevelt instantly recognized the new Republic of Panama. Secretary Hay and the new "Panamanian" minister, Bunau-Varilla, then negotiated a treaty granting the United States a zone 10 miles wide in perpetuity, on the same terms as those rejected by Colombia. Within the Canal Zone the United States could act as "the sovereign of the territory . . . to the entire exclusion of . . . the Republic of Panama." The United States guaranteed the independence of the republic. The New Panama Canal Company then received its $40 million, including a substantial share for Bunau-Varilla.

Historians have condemned Roosevelt for his actions in this shabby affair, and with good reason. It was not that he fomented the revolution, for he did not. Separated from the government at Bogotá by an impenetrable jungle, the people of Panama province had long wanted to be free of Colombian rule. Since an American-built canal would bring a flood of dollars and jobs to the area, they were prepared to take any necessary steps to avoid having the United States shift to the Nicaraguan route. Nor was it that Roosevelt prevented Colombia from suppressing the revolution. He sinned, rather, in his disregard of Latin American sensibilities. He referred to the Colombians as "dagoes" and insisted smugly that he was defending "the interests of collective civilization" when he overrode their opposition to his plans. "They cut their own throats," he said. "They tried to hold us up; and too late they have discovered their criminal error."

If uncharitable, Roosevelt's analysis was not entirely inaccurate, yet it did not justify his haste in taking Panama under his wing. "Have I defended myself?" Roosevelt asked Secretary of War Root. "You certainly have, Mr. President," Root

The Culebra cut—a mountain containing some 100 million cubic yards of rock that had been removed for the Panama Canal.

retorted. "You were accused of seduction and you have conclusively proved that you were guilty of rape." Throughout Latin America, especially as nationalist sentiments grew stronger, Roosevelt's intolerance and aggressiveness in the canal incident bred resentment and fear.

In 1921 the United States made amends by giving Colombia $25 million. Colombia in turn recognized the independence of the Republic of Panama, but Panama was independent only in name because the United States controlled the canal. Meanwhile, the first vessels passed through the canal in 1914—and American hegemony in the Caribbean expanded. Yet even in that strategically vital area there was more show than substance to American strength. The navy ruled Caribbean waters largely by default, for it lacked adequate bases in the region. In 1903, as authorized by the Cuban constitution, the United States obtained an excellent site for a base at Guantanamo Bay, but before 1914 Congress appropriated only $89,000 to develop it.

Roosevelt's successor, William Howard Taft, tried to influence events in the Caribbean without intervening militarily. He called this policy "dollar diplomacy," reasoning that economic penetration would bring stability to underdeveloped areas and power and profit to the United States without the government's having to commit troops or spend public funds.

When Nicaragua defaulted on its foreign debt in 1911, the U.S. State Department arranged for American bankers to reorganize Nicaraguan finances and manage the customs service. Although the government truthfully insisted that it did not "cover an inch of territory south of the Rio Grande," dollar diplomacy provoked further apprehension in Latin America. Efforts to establish similar arrangements in Honduras, Costa Rica, and Guatemala all failed. In Nicaragua orderly administration of the finances did not bring internal peace. In 1912, 2,500 American marines and sailors were sent to Nicaragua to put down a revolution.

U.S. economic penetration proceeded briskly. American investments in Cuba reached $500 million by 1920, and smaller but significant investments were made in the Dominican Republic and in Haiti. In Central America the United Fruit Company accumulated large holdings in banana plantations, railroads, and other ventures. Other firms plunged heavily into Mexico's rich mineral resources.

Imperialism Without Colonies

The United States deserves fair marks for effort in its foreign relations following the Spanish-American War, barely passable marks for performance, and failing marks for results. If imperialism is defined narrowly as a policy of occupying and governing foreign lands, American imperialism lasted for a very short time. With trivial exceptions, all the American colonies—Hawaii, the Philippines, Guam, Puerto Rico, the Guantanamo base, and the Canal Zone—were obtained between 1898 and 1903. Both the U.S. government and American businessmen showed little interest in finding out what the people of Cuba wanted from life. They assumed that the Cubans wanted what everybody (read "Americans") wanted and, if by some strange chance this was not the case, that it was best to give it to them anyway. Dollar diplomacy had two main objectives, the avoidance of violence and the economic development of Latin America; it paid small heed to how peace was maintained and how the fruits of development were distributed. The policy was self-defeating, for in the long run stability depended on the support of local people, and this was seldom forthcoming.

By the eve of World War I the United States had become a world power and had assumed what it saw as a duty to guide the development of many countries with traditions far different from its own. The American people, however, did not understand what world power involved. While they stood ready to extend their influence into distant lands, they did so with little awareness of the implications of their behavior for themselves or for other peoples. The national psychology, if such a term has any meaning, remained fundamentally isolationist. Americans understood that their wealth and numbers made their nation strong and that geography made it virtually invulnerable. Thus they proceeded to do what they wanted to do in foreign affairs, limited more by their humanly flexible consciences than by any rational analysis of the probable consequences. This policy seemed safe enough—in 1914.

1850	Britain and United States sign Clayton-Bulwer Treaty concerning interoceanic canal
1858	Commercial treaty with Japan opens several ports to American trade
1867	United States buys Alaska from Russia
1875	Reciprocity treaty increases U.S. influence in Hawaii
1885	Josiah Strong justifies expansionism in *Our Country*
1890	Alfred T. Mahan fuels American imperialism in *The Influence of Sea Power*
1893	United States helps sugar planters depose Queen Liliuokalani of Hawaii
1895	United States supports Venezuela in European border dispute over British Guiana
1898	*Maine* explodes in Havana harbor
	Spanish-American war breaks out
	Dewey defeats Spanish fleet at Battle of Manila Bay
	Theodore Roosevelt leads Rough Riders at the Battle of San Juan Hill
	United States annexes Hawaii
1899	Hays's Open Door notes safeguard U.S. access to China trade
1900	Platt Amendment gives United States naval stations and right to intervene in Cuba
1901	Hay-Pauncefote agreement gives United States rights to build interoceanic canal
1902	Europeans accept Monroe Doctrine during Venezuela bond dispute
1904	Roosevelt Corollary to Monroe Doctrine gives United States "international police power"
1907	"Gentlemen's Agreement" curtails Japanese immigration

Woodrow Wilson and the Great War

"TONIGHT," PRESIDENT GEORGE W. BUSH DECLARED ON September 21, 2001, ten days after terrorists had killed 3,000 people on American soil, "we will come together to give law enforcement the additional tools it needs to track down terror here at home."

Over the next few weeks, the Bush administration proposed a sweeping legislative package entitled "Uniting and Strengthening America by Providing Appropriate Tools Required to Intercept and Obstruct Terrorism." (The bill's title generated the acronym, USA PATRIOT.) The Patriot Act gave the FBI and other law enforcement agencies wide powers to conduct secret searches, initiate phone and Internet surveillance, and access personal records with minimal judicial oversight. It also permitted noncitizens to be jailed or denied readmission to the United States on the basis of suspicious words and statements. It swept through Congress with only a couple of dissenting votes.

During the next two months, nearly 1,200 were arrested under Patriot Act provisions. Several hundred were incarcerated at the American military base at Guantanamo Bay in Cuba, which, because it was located on foreign soil, did not entitle prisoners to constitutional protections, or so the administration claimed. Many were held for years without being indicted of a crime.

Critics as well as defenders of the Patriot Act pointed to its historical precursors during World War I. At President Wilson's urging, Congress passed the Espionage Act (1917) and the Sedition Act (1918); both sharply curtailed constitutional freedoms during time of war.

Supporters of the Patriot Act noted that all presidents—even ostensible liberals such as Wilson—have restricted civil liberties during wartime; the Patriot Act, they added, was far milder than Wilson's measures. Critics of the Patriot Act countered that wartime restrictions on civil liberties, including those proposed by Wilson, seldom bear close scrutiny after hostilities cease.

Wilson had hoped to stay out of the bloody vortex that was the Great War; but once war came, in addition to stamping out dissent, he recruited workers, farmers, financiers, and manufacturers for the war effort. He also sought to take advantage of the transformations wrought by the war to promote various reforms—including creation of an international body to mediate future conflicts. The tragedy of the Wilson years was that none of it turned out quite as he had imagined.

Wilson's "Moral" Diplomacy

Wilson set out to raise the moral tone of American foreign policy by denouncing dollar diplomacy. Encouraging bankers to lend money to countries like China, he said, implied the possibility of "forcible interference" if the loans were not repaid, and that would be "obnoxious to the principles upon which the government of our people rests." To seek special economic concessions in Latin America was "unfair" and "degrading." The United States would deal with Latin American nations "upon terms of equality and honor."

In certain small matters Wilson succeeded in conducting American diplomacy on this idealistic basis. When the Japanese attempted in the notorious Twenty-One Demands (1915) to reduce China almost to the status of a Japanese protectorate, he persuaded them to modify their conditions slightly.

Where more important interests were concerned, Wilson sometimes failed to live up to his promises. Because of the strategic importance of the Panama Canal, he was unwilling to tolerate "unrest" anywhere in the Caribbean. Within months of his inauguration he was pursuing the same tactics circumstances had forced on Roosevelt and Taft. The Bryan-Chamorro Treaty of 1914, which gave the United States an option to build a canal across Nicaragua, made that country virtually an American protectorate and served to maintain in power an unpopular dictator, Adolfo Díaz.

An example of missionary diplomacy with much more serious results occurred in Mexico. In 1911 a liberal coalition overthrew the dictator Porfirio Díaz and Francisco Madero became president. Soon thereafter one of Madero's generals, Victoriano Huerta, seized power and had his former chief murdered. Most European states recognized Huerta's new government, but Wilson, appalled by Madero's murder, refused to do so. "I will not recognize a government of butchers," he declared.

Wilson brought enormous pressure to bear against Huerta. He demanded that Huerta hold free elections as the price of American mediation in the continuing civil war. Huerta would not yield an inch.

The tense situation exploded in April 1914, when a small party of American sailors was arrested in the port of Tampico, Mexico. When the Mexican government refused to supply the apology demanded by the sailors' commander, Wilson fastened on the affair as an excuse for sending troops into Mexico.

The invasion took place at Veracruz, whence Winfield Scott had launched the assault on Mexico City in 1847. Instead of meekly surrendering the city, the Mexicans resisted tenaciously, suffering 400 casualties before falling back. This bloodshed caused dismay throughout Latin America. Huerta, hard-pressed by Mexican opponents, abdicated. On August 20, 1914, General Venustiano Carranza entered Mexico City in triumph.

Carranza favored representative government, but he proved scarcely more successful than the tyrant Huerta in controlling the country. One of his own generals, Francisco "Pancho" Villa, rose against him and seized control of Mexico City.

Wilson now made a monumental blunder. Villa professed to be willing to cooperate with the United States, and Wilson, taking him at his word, gave him his support. However, Villa was little more than an ambitious bandit with no other objective than personal power. Carranza, though no radical, was committed to social reform. Fighting back, Carranza drove Villa's forces into the northern provinces.

Wilson finally realized the extent of Carranza's influence in Mexico, and in October 1915 he recognized the Carranza government. Still his Mexican troubles were not over. Early in 1916, Villa, seeking to undermine Carranza by forcing the United States to intervene, stopped a train in northern Mexico and killed sixteen American passengers in cold blood. Then he crossed into New Mexico and burned the town of Columbus, killing nineteen. Having learned his lesson, Wilson would have preferred to bear even this assault in silence, but public opinion forced him to send American troops under General John J. Pershing across the border in pursuit of Villa.

Villa proved impossible to catch. Cleverly he drew Pershing deeper and deeper into Mexico, and this alarmed Carranza, who insisted that the Americans withdraw. Several clashes occurred between Pershing's men and Mexican regulars, and for a brief period in June 1916 war seemed imminent. Wilson now acted bravely and wisely. Early in 1917 he recalled Pershing's force, leaving the Mexicans to work out their own destiny.

Missionary diplomacy in Mexico had produced mixed but in the long run beneficial results. By opposing Huerta, Wilson had surrendered to his prejudices, yet he had also helped the real revolutionaries even though they opposed his acts. His bungling bred anti-Americanism in Mexico, but by his later restraint in the face of stinging provocations, he permitted the constitutionalists to consolidate their power.

Europe Explodes in War

On June 28, 1914, in the Austro-Hungarian provincial capital of Sarajevo, Gavrilo Princip, a young student, assassinated the Archduke Franz Ferdinand, heir to the imperial throne. Princip was a member of the Black Hand, a Serbian terrorist organization. He was seeking to further the cause of Serbian nationalism. Instead his

During World War I, advancing armies unloosed ferocious artillery barrages to destroy deeply entrenched enemy positions. Before the Third Battle of Ypres, the British fired four and a half million shells at German defenses, pulverizing the landscape. But as the British moved forward they became mired in mud (*above*); they lost 300,000 men in the action. Few Americans perceived the special horrors of this type of warfare.

rash act precipitated a general European war. Within little more than a month, following a complex series of diplomatic challenges and responses, two great coalitions, the Central Powers (chiefly Germany, Austria-Hungary, and Ottoman Turkey) and the Allied Powers (chiefly Great Britain, France, and Russia), were locked in a brutal struggle that brought one era in world history to a close and inaugurated another.

There were good reasons why the United States sought to remain neutral in this conflict, which contemporaries were soon to call the Great War. Over a third of the 92 million U.S. inhabitants were either European-born or the children of European immigrants. Sentimental ties bound them to the lands of their ancestors. American involvement would create new internal stresses in a society already strained by the task of assimilating so many diverse groups. War was also an affront to the prevailing progressive spirit, which assumed that human beings were reasonable, high-minded, and capable of settling disputes peaceably. Along with the traditional American fear of entanglement in European affairs, these were ample reasons for remaining aloof.

Although most Americans hoped to keep out of the war, nearly everyone was partial to one side or the other. People of German or Austrian descent, about 8 million in number, and the nation's 4.5 million Irish Americans, motivated chiefly by hatred of the British, sympathized with the Central Powers. The majority of the people, however, influenced by bonds of language and culture, preferred an Allied victory, and when the Germans launched a mighty assault across neutral Belgium in an effort to outflank the French armies, many Americans were outraged.

As the war progressed, the Allies cleverly exploited American prejudices by such devices as publishing exaggerated tales of German atrocities against Belgian civilians. A supposedly impartial study of these charges by the widely respected James Bryce, author of *The American Commonwealth*, portrayed the Germans as ruthless barbarians. The Germans also conducted a propaganda campaign in the United States, but they labored under severe handicaps and won few converts.

Freedom of the Seas

Propaganda did not basically alter American attitudes; far more important were questions arising out of trade and commerce. Under international law, neutrals could trade freely with any belligerent. Americans were prepared to do so, but because the British fleet dominated the North Atlantic, they could not. The situation was similar to the one that had prevailed during the Napoleonic Wars. The British declared nearly all commodities, even foodstuffs, to be contraband of war. They forced neutral merchant ships into British or French ports in order to search them for goods headed for the enemy. Many cargoes were confiscated, often without payment. American firms that traded with the Central Powers were "blacklisted," which meant that no British subject could deal with them. When Americans protested, the British answered that in a battle for survival, they dared not adhere to old-fashioned rules of international law.

Although British tactics frequently exasperated Wilson, they did not result in the loss of innocent lives. He never considered taking as drastic a step as an embargo. To allow the British to make the rules meant siding against the Central Powers. Yet to insist on the old rules (which had never been strictly obeyed in wartime) meant siding against the Allies because that would have deprived them of much of the value of their naval superiority. *Nothing* the United States might do would be truly impartial.

Wilson's own sentiments made it doubly difficult for him to object strenuously to British practices. No American admired British institutions and culture more extravagantly. "Everything I love most in the world is at stake," he confessed privately to the British ambassador. A German victory "would be fatal to our form of Government and American ideals."

The immense expansion of American trade with the Allies made an embargo unthinkable. While commerce with the Central Powers fell to a trickle, that with the Allies soared from $825 million in 1914 to over $3.2 billion in 1916. An attempt to limit this commerce would have raised a storm; to have eliminated it would have caused a catastrophe. Munitions makers and other businessmen did not want the United States to enter the war. Neutrality suited their purposes admirably.

Britain and France soon exhausted their ready cash, and by early 1917 they had borrowed well over $2 billion. Although these loans violated no principle of international law, they fastened the United States more closely to the Allies' cause.

Three weeks before the *Lusitania* was torpedoed, this notice appeared in the classified sections of Washington newspapers.

NOTICE!

TRAVELLERS intending to embark on the Atlantic voyage are reminded that a state of war exists between Germany and her allies and Great Britain and her allies; that the zone of war includes the waters adjacent to the British Isles; that, in accordance with formal notice given by the Imperial German Government, vessels flying the flag of Great Britain, or of any of her allies, are liable to destruction in those waters and that travellers sailing in the war zone on ships of Great Britain or her allies do so at their own risk.

IMPERIAL GERMAN EMBASSY

WASHINGTON, D. C., APRIL 22, 1915.

During the first months of the Great War, the Germans were not especially concerned about neutral trade or American goods because they expected to crush the Allied armies quickly. When their first swift thrust into France was blunted along the Marne River, only twenty miles from Paris, and the war became a bloody stalemate, they began to challenge the Allies' control of the seas. Unwilling to risk their battleships and cruisers against the much larger British fleet, they resorted to a new weapon, the submarine, commonly known as the U-boat (for *Unterseeboot*). German submarines played a role in World War I not unlike that of American privateers in the Revolution and the War of 1812: They ranged the seas stealthily in search of merchant ships. However, submarines could not operate under the ordinary rules of war, which required that a raider stop its prey, examine its papers and cargo, and give the crew and passengers time to get off in lifeboats before sending it to the bottom. When surfaced, U-boats were vulnerable to the deck guns that many merchant ships carried; they could even be sunk by ramming, once they had stopped and put out a boarding party. Therefore, they commonly launched their torpedoes from below the surface without warning, often resulting in a heavy loss of life.

In February 1915 the Germans declared the waters surrounding the British Isles a zone of war and announced that they would sink without warning all enemy merchant ships encountered in the area. Since Allied vessels sometimes flew neutral flags to disguise their identity, neutral ships entering the zone would do so at their own risk. This statement was largely bluff, for the Germans had only a handful of submarines at sea; but they were feverishly building more.

Wilson—perhaps too hurriedly, considering the importance of the question—warned the Germans that he would hold them to "strict accountability" for any loss of American life or property resulting from violations of "acknowledged [neutral] rights on the high seas." He did not distinguish clearly between losses incurred through the destruction of *American* ships and those resulting from the sinking of other vessels. The issue acquired significance on May 7, 1915, when the submarine *U–20* sank the British liner *Lusitania* off the Irish coast. Nearly 1,200 persons, including 128 Americans, lost their lives.

The torpedoing of the *Lusitania* caused as profound and emotional a reaction in the United States as that following the destruction of the *Maine* in Havana harbor. Wilson, like McKinley in 1898, was shocked, but he kept his head. He demanded that Germany disavow the sinking, indemnify the victims, and promise to stop attacking passenger vessels. When the Germans quibbled about these points, he responded with further diplomatic correspondence rather than with an ultimatum.

In one sense, this was sound policy. It would have been difficult for the German government to back down before a U.S. ultimatum. In addition, if Wilson had forced a showdown, he would have alienated a large segment of American opinion. After dragging out the controversy for nearly a year, the German government apologized and agreed to pay an indemnity.

In November 1915 Wilson at last began to press for increased military and naval expenditures. Nevertheless, he continued to vacillate. He dispatched a sharp note protesting Allied blacklisting of American firms, and to his confidant, Colonel Edward M. House, he called the British "poor boobs!"

The Election of 1916

Part of Wilson's hesitation in 1916 resulted from the political difficulties he faced in his fight for reelection. He had won the presidency in 1912 only because the Republican party had split in two. Now Theodore Roosevelt, the chief defector, had become so incensed by Wilson's refusal to commit the United States to the Allied cause that he was ready to support almost any Republican in order to guarantee the president's defeat. At the same time, many progressives were complaining about Wilson's unwillingness to work for further domestic reforms. Unless he could find additional support, he seemed likely to be defeated. He attacked the problem by wooing the progressives. In January 1916 he appointed Louis D. Brandeis to the

Supreme Court. In addition to being an advanced progressive, Brandeis was the first Jewish American appointed to the Court. Wilson's action won him many friends among people who favored fair treatment for minority groups. In July he bid for the farm vote by signing the Farm Loan Act to provide low-cost loans based on agricultural credit. Shortly thereafter, he approved the Keating-Owen Child Labor Act barring goods manufactured by the labor of children under sixteen from interstate commerce, and a workers' compensation act for federal employees.

The key issue in the campaign was American policy toward the warring powers. Wilson intended to stress preparedness, which he was now wholeheartedly supporting. However, during the Democratic convention, the delegates shook the hall with cheers whenever orators referred to the president's success in keeping the country out of the war. "He Kept Us Out of War" became the Democratic slogan.

To his credit, Wilson made no promises. "I can't keep the country out of war," he told one member of his Cabinet. "Any little German lieutenant can put us into the war at any time by some calculated outrage." His attitude undoubtedly cost him the votes of extremists on both sides, but it won the backing of thousands of moderates.

The combination of progressivism and the peace issue placed the Democrats on substantially equal terms with the Republicans, who nominated Charles Evans Hughes. Thereafter, personal factors probably tipped the balance. Hughes was very stiff (Theodore Roosevelt called him a bearded Woodrow Wilson) and an ineffective speaker; he offended a number of important politicians, especially in crucial California, where he inadvertently snubbed the popular progressive governor, Hiram Johnson; and he equivocated on a number of issues. Nevertheless, on election night he appeared to have won, having carried nearly all the East and Midwest. Late returns gave Wilson California, however, and with it victory by the narrow margin of 277 to 254 in the Electoral College. He led Hughes in the popular vote, 9.1 million to 8.5 million.

The Road to War

Encouraged by his triumph, appalled by the continuing slaughter on the battlefields, fearful that the United States would be dragged into the conflagration, Wilson made one last effort to end the war by negotiation. In 1915 and again in 1916 he had sent his friend Colonel House on secret missions to London, Paris, and Berlin to try to mediate among the belligerents. Each mission had proved fruitless, but after another long season of bloodshed, perhaps the powers would listen to reason.

Wilson, on January 22, 1917, delivered a moving speech aimed at "the people of the countries now at war" more than at their governments. Any settlement imposed by a victor, he declared, would breed hatred and more wars. There must be "peace without victory," based on the principles that all nations were equal and that every nationality should determine its own form of government. He mentioned,

U-Boat Campaign, 1914–1918

albeit vaguely, disarmament and freedom of the seas, and he suggested the creation of some kind of international organization to preserve world peace. "There must be not a balance of power, but a community of power," he said, and he added, "I am speaking for the silent mass of mankind everywhere."

This noble appeal met a tragic fate. The Germans had already decided to unleash their submarines against all vessels headed for Allied ports. After February 1, any ship in the war zone would be attacked without warning. Possessed now of more than 100 U-boats, the German military leaders had convinced themselves that they could starve the British people into submission and reduce the Allied armies to impotence by cutting off the flow of American supplies. The United States would probably declare war, but the Germans believed that they could overwhelm the Allies before the Americans could get to the battlefields in force. In 1917, after the German military leaders had made this decision, events moved relentlessly, almost uninfluenced by the actors who presumably controlled the fate of the world. In February and March, German U-boats sank more ships, including several passenger liners. On April 2, Wilson asked Congress to declare war. Germany, he said, was guilty of "throwing to the winds all scruples of humanity." "The world must be made safe for democracy." Two days later, Congress declared war by a vote of 82–6 in the Senate, and 373–50 in the House.

Mobilizing the Economy

America's entry into the Great War determined its outcome. The Allies were running out of money and supplies; their troops, decimated by nearly three years in the trenches, were exhausted, disheartened, and rebellious. In February and March 1917, U-boats sent over a million tons of Allied shipping to the bottom of the Atlantic. The outbreak of the Russian Revolution in March 1917, at first lifting the spirits of the Western democracies, led to the Bolshevik takeover under Lenin. The Russian armies collapsed; by December 1917 Russia was out of the war and the

Germans were moving masses of men and equipment from the eastern front to France. Without the aid of the United States, it is likely that the war would have ended in 1918 on terms dictated from Berlin. Instead American men and supplies helped contain the Germans' last drives and then push them back to final defeat.

Still, it was a close Allied victory, for the United States entered the war little better prepared to fight than it had been in 1898. The conversion of American industry to war production had to be organized and carried out without prearrangement. Confusion and waste resulted. The hurriedly designed shipbuilding program was an almost total fiasco. The big guns that backed up American soldiers in 1918 were made in France and Great Britain; of the 8.8 million rounds of artillery ammunition fired by American troops, a mere 8,000 were manufactured in the United States. Congress authorized the manufacture of 20,000 airplanes, but only a handful, mostly British-designed planes made in America, got to France.

The problem of mobilization was complicated. It took Congress six weeks of hot debate merely to decide on conscription. Only in September 1917, nearly six months after the declaration of war, did the first draftees reach the training camps, and it is hard to see how Wilson could have speeded this process appreciably. He wisely supported the professional soldiers, who insisted that he resist the appeals of politicians who wanted to raise volunteer units, even rejecting, at considerable political cost, Theodore Roosevelt's offer to raise an entire army division.

Wilson was a forceful and inspiring war leader once he grasped what needed to be done. He displayed both determination and unfailing patience in the face of frustration and criticism. Raising an army was only a small part of the job. The Allies had to be supplied with food and munitions, and immense amounts of money had to be collected.

After several false starts, Wilson placed the task in the hands of the War Industries Board (WIB). The board was given almost dictatorial power to allocate scarce materials, standardize production, fix prices, and coordinate American and Allied purchasing. Evaluating the mobilization effort raises interesting historical questions. The antitrust laws were suspended and producers were encouraged, even compelled, to cooperate with one another. Government regulation went far beyond what the New Nationalists had envisaged in 1912.

As for the New Freedom variety of laissez-faire, it had no place in a wartime economy. The nation's railroads, strained by immensely increased traffic, became progressively less efficient. A monumental tie-up in December and January 1917–1918 finally persuaded Wilson to appoint Secretary of the Treasury William G. McAdoo director-general of the railroads, with power to run the roads as a single system. McAdoo's Railroad Administration pooled all railroad equipment, centralized purchasing, standardized accounting practices, and raised wages and passenger rates.

Wilson accepted the kind of government-industry agreement developed under Theodore Roosevelt that he had denounced in 1912. Prices were set by the WIB at levels that allowed large profits—U.S. Steel, for example, despite high taxes, cleared over half a billion dollars in two years. It is at least arguable that producers would have turned out just as much even if compelled to charge lower prices.

The history of industrial mobilization was the history of the entire home front effort in microcosm: marvels were performed, but the task was so gigantic and unprecedented that a full year passed before an efficient system had been devised, and many unforeseen results occurred.

The problem of mobilizing agricultural resources was solved more quickly, and this was fortunate because in April 1917 the British had on hand only a six-week supply of food. As food administrator Wilson appointed Herbert Hoover, a mining engineer who had headed the Belgian Relief Commission earlier in the war. Acting under powers granted by the Lever Act of 1917, Hoover set the price of wheat at $2.20 a bushel in order to encourage production. He established a government corporation to purchase the entire American and Cuban sugar crop, which he then doled out to American and British refiners. To avoid rationing he organized a campaign to persuade consumers to conserve food voluntarily. One slogan ran "If U fast U beat U boats"; another, "Serve beans by all means." "Wheatless Mondays" and "meatless Tuesdays" were the rule, and although no law compelled their observance, the public responded patriotically.

Without subjecting its own citizens to serious inconvenience, the United States increased food exports from 12.3 million tons to 18.6 million tons. Farmers, of course, profited greatly. Their real income went up nearly 30 percent between 1915 and 1918.

Workers in Wartime

With the army siphoning so many men from the labor market and with immigration reduced to a trickle, unemployment disappeared and wages rose. Although the cost of living soared, imposing hardships on people with fixed incomes, the boom produced unprecedented opportunities.

The War Labor Policies Board, chaired by Felix Frankfurter of the Harvard Law School, set wages-and-hours standards for each major war industry. Since these were determined in consultation with employers and representatives of labor, they speeded the unionization of workers by compelling management, even in antiunion industries like steel, to deal with labor leaders. Union membership rose by 2.3 million during the war.

Trends in the steel industry reflected the improvement of wartime labor earnings. Wages of unskilled steelworkers more than doubled. Thousands of southern blacks, attracted by jobs in big-city factories, flocked into the steel towns. Union organizers made inroads in many plants, and by the summer of 1918 they were preparing an all-out effort to unionize the industry. If the world was to be made safe for democracy, they argued, there must be "economic democracy [along] with political democracy."

Paying for the War

Wilson managed the task of financing the war effectively. The struggle cost the United States about $33.5 billion, not counting pensions and other postwar expenses. About $7 billion of this was lent to the Allies,[1] but since this money was spent largely in America, it contributed to the national prosperity.

Over two-thirds of the cost of the war was met by borrowing. Five Liberty and Victory Loan drives, spurred by advertising, parades, and other appeals to patriotism, persuaded people to open their purses. Industrialists, eager to instill in their employees a sense of personal involvement in the war effort, conducted campaigns in their plants. Some went so far as to threaten "A Bond or Your Job," but more typical was the appeal of the managers of the Gary, Indiana, plant of U.S. Steel, who published bond advertisements in six languages in order to reach their immigrant workers.

In addition to borrowing, the government collected about $10.5 billion in taxes during the war. A steeply graduated income tax took more than 75 percent of the incomes of the wealthiest citizens. A 65 percent excess-profits tax and a 25 percent inheritance tax were also enacted. Thus although many individuals made fortunes from the war, its cost was distributed far more equitably than during the Civil War.

Propaganda and Civil Liberties

Wilson was preeminently a teacher and preacher, a specialist in the transmission of ideas and ideals. He excelled at mobilizing public opinion and inspiring Americans to work for the better world he hoped would emerge from the war. In April 1917 he created the Committee on Public Information (CPI), headed by the journalist George Creel. Soon 75,000 speakers were deluging the country with propaganda prepared by hundreds of CPI writers. They pictured the war as a crusade for freedom and democracy, the Germans as a bestial people bent on world domination.

A large majority of the nation supported the war enthusiastically. But thousands of persons—German Americans and Irish Americans, for example; people of pacifist leanings such as Jane Addams, the founder of Hull House; and some who thought both sides in the war were wrong—still opposed American involvement. Creel's committee and a number of unofficial "patriotic" groups allowed their enthusiasm for the conversion of the hesitant to become suppression of dissent.

Although Wilson spoke in defense of free speech, his actions opposed it. He signed the Espionage Act of 1917, which imposed fines of up to $10,000 and jail sentences ranging to twenty years on persons convicted of aiding the enemy or obstructing recruiting, and he authorized the postmaster general to ban from the mails any material that seemed treasonable or seditious.

In May 1918, again with Wilson's approval, Congress passed the Sedition Act, which made "saying anything" to discourage the purchase of war bonds a crime, with the proviso that investment counselors could still offer "bona fide and not disloyal advice" to clients. The law also made it illegal to "utter, print, write, or publish any dis-

---

[1]In 1914 Americans owed foreigners about $3.8 billion. By 1919 Americans were owed $12.5 billion by Europeans alone.

These members of the Woman's Peace party urge Wilson to find a way to stay out of the war in Europe. They are carrying fans to reinforce their message.

loyal, profane, scurrilous, or abusive language" about the government, the Constitution, or the uniform of the army or navy. Socialist periodicals such as *The Masses* were suppressed, and Eugene V. Debs, formerly a candidate for president, was sentenced to ten years in prison for making an antiwar speech. Ricardo Flores Magón, an anarchist, was sentenced to twenty years in jail for publishing a statement criticizing Wilson's Mexican policy, an issue that had nothing to do with the war.

These laws went far beyond what was necessary to protect the national interest. Citizens were jailed for suggesting that the draft law was unconstitutional and for criticizing private organizations like the Red Cross and the YMCA. One woman was sent to prison for writing, "I am for the people, and the government is for the profiteers."

The Supreme Court upheld the constitutionality of the Espionage Act in *Schenck* v. *United States* (1919), a case involving a man who had mailed circulars to draftees urging them to refuse to report for induction into the army. Free speech has its limits, Justice Oliver Wendell Holmes Jr., explained. No one has the right to cry, "Fire!" in a crowded theater. When there is a "clear and present danger" that a particular statement would threaten the national interest, it can be repressed by law. In peacetime Schenck's circulars would be permissible, but not in time of war.

Wartime Reforms

The American mobilization experience was part and product of the progressive era. The work of the progressives at the national and state levels in expanding government functions in order to deal with social and economic problems provided precedents and conditioned the people for the all-out effort of 1917 and 1918. Social and economic planning and the management of huge business operations by public boards and committees got their first practical tests. College professors, technicians, and others with complex skills entered government service en masse. The federal government for the first time actively entered such fields as housing and labor relations.

Many progressives believed that the war was creating the sense of common purpose that would stimulate the people to act unselfishly to benefit the poor and to eradicate social evils. Patriotism and public service seemed at last united. Secretary of War Newton D. Baker, a prewar urban reformer, expressed this attitude in supporting a federal child labor law: "We cannot afford, when we are losing boys in France, to lose children in the United States."

Men and women of this sort worked for a dozen causes only remotely related to the war effort. The woman suffrage movement was brought to fruition, as was the campaign against alcohol. Both the Eighteenth Amendment, outlawing the manufacture, sale, import, and export of alcoholic beverages, and the Nineteenth, giving women the vote, were adopted at least in part because of the war. Reformers began to talk about health insurance. The progressive campaign against prostitution and venereal disease gained strength, winning the enthusiastic support both of persons worried about inexperienced local girls being seduced by the soldiers and of those concerned lest prostitutes lead innocent soldiers astray. One of the latter type claimed to have persuaded "over 1,000 fallen women" to promise not to go near any army camps.

Women and Blacks in Wartime

Although a number of prominent feminists were pacifists, most supported the war enthusiastically, moved by patriotism and the belief that opposition to the war would doom their hopes of gaining the vote. They also expected that the war would open up many kinds of high-paying jobs to women. To some extent it did; about a million women replaced men in uniform, but the numbers actually engaged in war industries were small (about 6,000 found jobs making airplanes, for example), and the gains were fleeting. When the war ended, most women who were engaged in industrial work either left their jobs voluntarily or were fired to make room for returning veterans. Some women went overseas as nurses, and a few served as ambulance drivers and YMCA workers.

Most unions were unsympathetic to the idea of enrolling women, and the government did little to encourage women to do more for the war effort than prepare bandages, knit warm clothing for soldiers, participate in food conservation programs, and encourage people to buy war bonds. There was a Women in Industry Service in the Department of Labor and a Woman's Committee of the Council of National Defense, but both served primarily as window dressing for the Wilson administration. The final report of another wartime agency, issued in 1919, admitted that few women war workers had been paid as much as men and that

Women workers at the Dupont factory in Old Hickory, Tennessee, in 1917. They are forming smokeless gunpowder into long strips, which will then be cut to be used in artillery shells and other armaments.

women had been promoted more slowly than men, were not accepted by unions, and were discharged promptly when the war ended.

The wartime "great migration" of southern blacks to northern cities where jobs were available brought them important economic benefits. Actually, the emigration of blacks from the former slave states began with emancipation, but the mass exodus that many people had expected was slow to materialize. Between 1870 and 1890 only about 80,000 blacks moved to northern cities. Compared with the influx from Europe and from northern farms, this number was inconsequential. The black proportion of the population of New York City, for example, fell from over 10 percent in 1800 to under 2 percent in 1900.

Around the turn of the century, as the first postslavery generation reached maturity and as southern repression increased, the northward movement quickened—about 200,000 blacks migrated between 1890 and 1910. Then, after 1914, the war boom drew blacks north in a flood. The African American population of New York City rose from 92,000 to 152,000; that of Chicago from 44,000 to 109,000; that of Detroit from 5,700 to 41,000.

Life for the newcomers was difficult; many whites resented them; workers feared them as potential strikebreakers yet refused to admit them into their unions. In East St. Louis, Illinois, where employers had brought in large numbers of blacks in an attempt to discourage local unions from striking for higher wages, a bloody riot erupted during the summer of 1917 in which nine whites and an unde-

A recruiting poster for the "True Sons of Freedom," which encouraged African Americans to enlist. In fact, some 350,000 black Americans served in segregated units during the Great War. Several such units fought alongside French units, and 171 African Americans were awarded the French Legion of Honor, an award for courageous military service.

termined number of blacks were killed. As in peacetime, the Wilson administration was at worst antagonistic and at best indifferent to blacks' needs and aspirations.

There were two black regiments in the regular army and a number of black national guard units when the war began, and once these outfits were brought up to combat strength, no more volunteers were accepted. Indeed, at first no blacks were conscripted; Southerners in particular found the thought of giving large numbers of guns to blacks and teaching them how to use them most disturbing. However, blacks were soon drafted, and once they were, a larger proportion of them than whites were taken. One Georgia draft board exempted more than 500 of 815 white registrants and only 6 of the 202 blacks in its jurisdiction before its members were relieved of their duties. After a riot in Texas in which black soldiers killed seventeen white civilians, black recruits were dispersed among many camps for training to lessen the possibility of trouble.

In the military service, all blacks were placed in segregated units. Only a handful were commissioned as officers. Despite the valor displayed by black soldiers in the Civil War and the large role they played in the Spanish-American War, where five blacks had won the Congressional Medal of Honor, most blacks, even those sent overseas, were assigned to labor battalions, working as stevedores and common laborers. But many fought and died for their country. Altogether about 200,000 served overseas. There were black Red Cross nurses in France, and some blacks held relatively high posts in government agencies in Washington, the most important being Emmett J. Scott, who was special assistant for Negro affairs in the War Department.

W. E. B. Du Bois supported the war wholeheartedly. He praised Wilson for making, at last, a strong statement against lynching, which had increased to a shocking extent during the previous decade. He even went along with the fact that the handful of black officer candidates were trained in a segregated camp. "Let us," he wrote in *The Crisis*, "while the war lasts, forget our special grievances and close ranks shoulder to shoulder with our fellow citizens and the allied nations that are fighting for democracy."

Many blacks condemned Du Bois's accommodationism (which he promptly abandoned when the war ended), but most saw the war as an opportunity to demonstrate their patriotism and prove their worth. For the moment the prevailing mood was one of optimism. "We may expect to see the walls of prejudice gradually crumble"—this was the common attitude of blacks in 1917 and 1918. If winning the war would make the world safe for democracy, surely blacks in the United States would be better off when it was won. Whether or not this turned out to be so was (and still is) a matter of opinion.

Americans: To the Trenches and Over the Top

All activity on the home front had one ultimate objective: defeating the Central Powers on the battlefield. This was accomplished. The navy performed with special distinction. In April 1917, German submarines sank more than 870,000 tons of Allied shipping; after April 1918, monthly losses never reached 300,000 tons. The decision to send merchant ships across the Atlantic in convoys screened by destroyers made the reduction possible. Checking the U-boats was essential because of the need to transport American troops to Europe. Slightly more than 2 million soldiers made the voyage safely.

The first units of the American Expeditionary Force (AEF), elements of the regular army commanded by General John J. Pershing, reached Paris on Independence Day, 1917. They took up positions on the front near Verdun in October. Not until the spring of 1918, however, did the American "doughboys" play a significant role in the fighting, though their mere presence boosted French and British morale.

Pershing insisted on maintaining his troops as independent units; he would not allow them to be filtered into the Allied armies as reinforcements. This was part of a perhaps unfortunate general policy that reflected America's isolationism. (Wilson always referred to the other nations fighting Germany as "associates," not as "allies.")

In March 1918 the Germans launched a great spring offensive, their armies strengthened by thousands of veterans from the Russian front. By late May they had reached a point on the Marne River near the town of Château-Thierry, only fifty miles from Paris. Early in June the AEF fought its first major engagements, driving the Germans back from Château-Thierry and Belleau Wood.

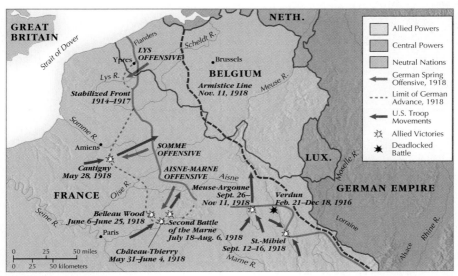

The Western Front, 1918

In this fighting only about 27,500 Americans saw action, and they suffered appalling losses. Nevertheless, when the Germans advanced again in the direction of the Marne in mid-July, 85,000 Americans were in the lines that withstood their charge. Then, in the major turning point of the war, the Allied armies counterattacked. Some 270,000 Americans participated, helping to flatten the German bulge between Reims and Soissons. By late August the American First Army, 500,000 strong, was poised before the Saint-Mihiel salient, a deep extension of the German lines southeast of Verdun. On September 12 this army, buttressed by French troops, struck and in two days wiped out the salient.

Late in September began the greatest American engagement of the war. No fewer than 1.2 million doughboys plunged into the Argonne Forest. For over a month of indescribable horror they inched ahead through the tangle of the Argonne and the formidable defenses of the Hindenburg line, while to the west, French and British armies staged similar drives. In this one offensive the AEF suffered 120,000 casualties. Finally, on November 1, they broke the German center and raced toward the vital Sedan-Mézières railroad. On November 11, with Allied armies advancing on all fronts, the Germans signed the armistice, ending the fighting.

Preparing for Peace

The fighting ended on November 11, 1918, but the shape of the postwar world remained to be determined. European society had been shaken to its foundations. Confusion reigned. People wanted peace yet burned for revenge. Millions faced starvation. Other millions were disillusioned by the seemingly purposeless sacri-

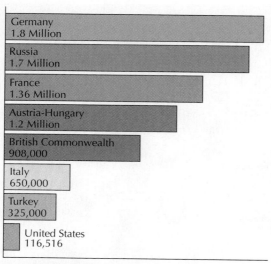

Deaths of Armed Forces in the Great War

fices of four years of horrible war. Communism—to some an idealistic promise of human betterment, to others a commitment to rational economic and social planning, to still others a danger to individual freedom, toleration, and democracy—having conquered Russia, threatened to envelop Germany and much of the defunct Austro-Hungarian Empire, perhaps even the victorious Allies. How could stability be restored? How could victory be made worth its enormous cost?

Woodrow Wilson had grasped the significance of the war while most statesmen still thought that triumph on the battlefield would settle everything automatically. As early as January 1917 he had realized that victory would be wasted if the winners permitted themselves the luxury of vengeance. Such a policy would disrupt the balance of power and lead to economic and social chaos. The victors must build a better society, not punish those they believed had destroyed the old.

In a speech to Congress on January 8, 1918, Wilson outlined a plan, known as the Fourteen Points, designed to make the world "fit and safe to live in." The peace treaty should be negotiated in full view of world opinion, not in secret. It should guarantee the freedom of the seas to all nations, in war as in peacetime. It should tear down barriers to international trade, provide for a drastic reduction of armaments, and establish a colonial system that would take proper account of the interests of the native peoples concerned. European boundaries should be redrawn so that no substantial group would have to live under a government not of its own choosing.

Wilson's Fourteen Points for a fair peace lifted the hopes of people everywhere. After the guns fell silent, however, the vagueness and inconsistencies in his list became apparent. Complete national self-determination was impossible in Europe; there were too many regions of mixed population for every group to be satisfied. Self-determination, like the war itself, also fostered the spirit of nationalism that

Wilson's dream of international organization, a league of nations, was designed to de-emphasize. Furthermore, the Allies had made territorial commitments to one another in secret treaties that ran counter to the principle of self-determination, and they were not ready to give up all claims to Germany's colonies. Freedom of the seas in wartime posed another problem; the British flatly refused to accept the idea. In every Allied country, millions rejected the idea of a peace without indemnities. They expected to make the enemy pay for the war, hoping, as Sir Eric Geddes, first lord of the Admiralty, said, to squeeze Germany "as a lemon is squeezed—until the pips squeak."

Wilson assumed that the practical benefits of his program would compel opponents to fall in line. He had the immense advantage of seeking nothing for his own country and the additional strength of being leader of the one important nation to emerge from the war richer and more powerful than it had been in 1914.

Yet this combination of altruism, idealism, and power was his undoing; it intensified his tendency to be overbearing and undermined his judgment. He had never found it easy to compromise. Once, when he was president of Princeton, he got into an argument over some abstract question with a professor while shooting a game of pool. To avoid acrimony, the professor finally said: "Well, Doctor Wilson, there are two sides to every question." "Yes," Wilson answered, "a right side and a wrong side." Now, believing that the fate of humanity hung on his actions, he was unyielding. Always a preacher, he became in his own mind a prophet—almost, one fears, a kind of god.

Wilson then came to a daring decision: He would personally attend the conference as a member of the United States Peace Commission. This was a precedent-shattering step, for no president had ever left American territory while in office. (Taft, who had a summer home on the St. Lawrence River in Canada, never vacationed there during his term, believing that to do so would be unconstitutional.)

Wilson probably erred in going to Paris, but not because of the novelty or possible illegality of the act. By going, he was turning his back on obvious domestic problems. Western farmers believed that they had been discriminated against during the war, since wheat prices had been controlled while southern cotton had been allowed to rise unchecked from seven cents a pound in 1914 to thirty-five cents in 1919. The administration's drastic tax program had angered many businessmen. Labor, despite its gains, was restive in the face of reconversion to peacetime conditions.

Wilson had increased his political difficulties by making a partisan appeal for the election of a Democratic Congress in 1918. Republicans, who had in many instances supported his war program more loyally than the Democrats, considered the action a gross affront. The appeal failed; the Republicans won majorities in both houses. Wilson appeared to have been repudiated at home at the very moment that he set forth to represent the nation abroad. Most important, Wilson intended to break with the isolationist tradition and bring the United States into a league of nations. Such a revolutionary change would require explanation; he should have undertaken a major campaign to convince the American people of the wisdom of this step.

Europe Before the Great War

The Paris Peace Conference and the Versailles Treaty

Wilson arrived in Europe a world hero. He toured England, France, and Italy briefly and was greeted ecstatically almost everywhere. The reception tended to increase his sense of mission and to convince him, in the fashion of a typical progressive, that whatever the European politicians might say about it, "the people" were behind his program.

When the conference settled down to its work, control quickly fell into the hands of the so-called Big Four: Wilson, Prime Minister David Lloyd George of Great Britain, Premier Georges Clemenceau of France, and Prime Minister Vittorio Orlando of Italy. Wilson stood out in this group but did not dominate it. His principal advantage in the negotiations was his untiring industry. He alone of the leaders tried to master all the complex details of the task.

The 78-year-old Clemenceau cared only for one thing: French security. He viewed Wilson cynically, saying that since mankind had been unable to keep God's Ten Commandments, it was unlikely to do better with Wilson's Fourteen Points. Lloyd George's approach was pragmatic and almost cavalier. He sympathized with much that Wilson was trying to accomplish but found the president's frequent sermonettes about "right being more important than might, and justice being more eternal than

Europe After the Great War

force" incomprehensible. "If you want to succeed in politics," Lloyd George advised a British statesman, "you must keep your conscience well under control." Orlando, clever, cultured, a believer in international cooperation but inflexible where Italian national interests were concerned, was not the equal of his three colleagues in influence. He left the conference in a huff when they failed to meet all his demands.

The conference labored from January to May 1919 and finally brought forth the Versailles Treaty. American liberals whose hopes had soared at the thought of a peace based on the Fourteen Points found the document abysmally disappointing.

The peace settlement failed to carry out the principle of self-determination completely. It gave Italy a large section of the Austrian Tyrol, though the area contained 200,000 people who considered themselves Austrians. Other German-speaking groups were incorporated into the new states of Poland and Czechoslovakia.

The victors forced Germany to accept responsibility for having caused the war—an act of senseless vindictiveness as well as a gross oversimplification—and to sign a "blank check," agreeing to pay for all damage to civilian properties and even future pensions and other indirect war costs. This reparations bill, as finally determined, amounted to $33 billion. Instead of attacking imperialism, the treaty attacked German imperialism; instead of seeking a new international social order based on liberty and democracy, it created a great-power entente designed to crush

Germany and to exclude Bolshevik Russia from the family of nations. It said nothing about freedom of the seas, the reduction of tariffs, or disarmament.

Wilson himself backtracked on his pledge to honor the right of self-determination. For example, Point 12 of the Fourteen Points called for the "autonomous development" of Arab peoples who had lived under Ottoman rule. But Wilson had second thoughts about their self-determination. Secretary of State Lansing worried about the "danger of putting such ideas into the minds of certain races," particularly the "Mohammedans of Syria and Palestine." Wilson reluctantly deleted explicit references to self-determination from the postwar settlements. Arab leaders seethed. Similarly, Ho Chi Minh, a young Vietnamese nationalist, was embittered by the failure at Versailles to deliver his people from French colonial rule. He decided to become a communist revolutionary. The repercussions of Arab and Vietnamese discontent, though far removed from American interests at the time, would be felt in full force much later.

Wilson expected the League of Nations to make up for all the inadequacies of the Versailles Treaty. Once the League had begun to function, problems like freedom of the seas and disarmament would solve themselves, he argued, and the relaxation of trade barriers would surely follow. The League would arbitrate international disputes, act as a central body for registering treaties, and employ military and economic sanctions against aggressor nations. Each member promised (Article 10) to protect the "territorial integrity" and "political independence" of all other members. No nation could be made to go to war against its will, but Wilson emphasized that all were *morally* obligated to carry out League decisions. By any standard, Wilson had achieved a remarkably moderate peace, one full of hope for the future. Except for the war guilt clause and the heavy reparations imposed on Germany, he could be justly proud of his work.

The Senate Rejects the League of Nations

When Wilson returned from France, he finally directed his attention to the task of winning public approval of his handiwork. A large majority of the people probably favored the League of Nations in principle, though few understood all its implications or were entirely happy with every detail. Wilson had persuaded the Allies to accept certain changes in the original draft to mollify American opposition. No nation could be forced to accept a colonial mandate, and "domestic questions" such as tariffs and the control of immigration and the Monroe Doctrine were excluded from League control.

Many senators found these modifications insufficient. Even before the peace conference ended, thirty-seven Republican senators signed a manifesto, devised by Henry Cabot Lodge of Massachusetts, opposing Wilson's League and demanding that the question of an international organization be put off until "the urgent business of negotiating peace terms with Germany" had been completed. Wilson rejected this suggestion icily. Further alterations were out of the question. "Anyone who opposes me . . . I'll crush!" he told one Democratic senator. "I shall consent to nothing. The Senate must take its medicine." Thus the stage was set for a monumental test of strength between the president and the Republican majority in the Senate.

Partisanship, principle, and prejudice clashed mightily in this contest. A presidential election loomed. Should the League prove a success, the Republicans wanted to be able to claim a share of the credit, but Wilson refused to allow them to participate in drafting the document. Alarm at the possible sacrifice of American sovereignty to an international authority led many Republicans to urge modification of the League covenant. Personal dislike of Wilson and his high-handed methods motivated others to oppose the League. The intense desire of the people to secure an end to the long war made Republican leaders hesitate before voting down the Versailles Treaty, but they could not reject the League without rejecting the treaty.

Wilson could count on the Democratic senators almost to a man, but he had to win over many Republicans to obtain the two-thirds majority necessary for ratification. Republican opinion divided roughly into three segments. At one extreme were some dozen "irreconcilables," led by the shaggy-browed William E. Borah of Idaho, an able and kindly person of progressive leanings but an uncompromising isolationist. Borah claimed that he would vote against the League even if Jesus Christ returned to earth to argue in its behalf, and most of his followers were equally inflexible. At the other extreme stood another dozen "mild" reservationists who were in favor of the League but who hoped to alter it in minor ways, chiefly for political purposes. In the middle were the "strong" reservationists, senators willing to go along with the League only if American sovereignty were fully protected and if it were made clear that their party had played a major role in fashioning the final document.

Senator Lodge, the leader of the Republican opposition, was a haughty, rather cynical, intensely partisan individual. He possessed a keen intelligence, a mastery of parliamentary procedure, and, as chairman of the Senate Foreign Relations Committee, a great deal of power. Although not an isolationist, he had little faith in

Despite Wilson's serving as mother hen, the League of Nations never hatched—at least as far as the United States was concerned.

the League. He also had a profound distrust of Democrats, especially Wilson, whom he considered a hypocrite and a coward. The president's pious idealism left him cold.

Lodge belonged to the strong reservationist faction. His own proposals, known as the Lodge Reservations, fourteen in number to match Wilson's Fourteen Points, limited U.S. obligations to the League and stated in unmistakable terms the right of Congress to decide when to honor these obligations. The most important reservation applied to Article 10 of the League covenant, which committed signatories to protect the political independence and territorial integrity of all member nations. Wilson had rightly called Article 10 "the heart of the Covenant." One of Lodge's reservations made it inoperable so far as the United States was concerned "unless in any particular case the Congress . . . shall by act or joint resolution so provide."

Lodge performed brilliantly, if somewhat unscrupulously, in uniting the three Republican factions behind his reservations. He got the irreconcilables to agree to them by conceding their right to vote against the final version in any event, and he held the mild reservationists in line by modifying some of his demands and stressing the importance of party unity. Reservations—as distinct from amendments— would not have to win the formal approval of other League members. In addition, the Lodge proposals dealt forthrightly with the problem of reconciling traditional concepts of national sovereignty with the new idea of world cooperation. Supporters of the League could accept them without sacrifice of principle. Wilson, however, refused to agree. "Accept the Treaty with the Lodge reservations?" the president snorted when a friendly senator warned him that he must accept a compromise. "Never! Never!"

This foolish intransigence seems almost incomprehensible in a man of Wilson's intelligence and political experience. In part his hatred of Lodge accounts for it, in part his faith in his League. His physical condition in 1919 also played a role. At Paris he had suffered a violent attack of indigestion that was probably a symptom of a minor stroke. Thereafter, many observers noted small changes in his personality, particularly increased stubbornness and a loss of good judgment. Instead of making concessions, the president set out early in September on a nationwide speaking crusade to rally support for the League. In three weeks, Wilson traveled some 10,000 miles by train and gave forty speeches, some of them brilliant. But they had little effect on senatorial opinion, and the effort drained his last physical reserves. On September 25, after an address in Pueblo, Colorado, he collapsed. The rest of the trip had to be canceled. A few days later, in Washington, he suffered a severe stroke that partially paralyzed his left side.

For nearly two months the president was almost totally cut off from affairs of state, leaving supporters of the League leaderless while Lodge maneuvered the reservations through the Senate. Gradually, popular attitudes toward the League shifted. The arguments of the irreconcilables persuaded many citizens that Wilson had made too sharp a break with America's isolationist past and that the Lodge Reservations were therefore necessary. Other issues connected with the reconversion of society to a peacetime basis increasingly occupied the public mind.

A coalition of Democratic and moderate Republican senators could easily have carried the treaty. That no such coalition was organized was Wilson's fault. Lodge obtained the simple majority necessary to add his reservations to the treaty merely by keeping his own party united. When the time came for the final roll call on November 19, Wilson, bitter and emotionally distraught, urged the Democrats to vote for rejection. "Better a thousand times to go down fighting than to dip your colors to dishonorable compromise," he explained to his wife. Thus the amended treaty failed, thirty-five to fifty-five, the irreconcilables and the Democrats voting against it. Lodge then allowed the original draft without his reservations to come to a vote. Again the result was defeat, thirty-eight to fifty-three. Only one Republican cast a ballot for ratification.

Dismayed but not yet crushed, friends of the League in both parties forced reconsideration of the treaty early in 1920. Neither Lodge nor Wilson would yield an inch. Lodge, who had little confidence in the effectiveness of any league of nations, was under no compulsion to compromise. Wilson, who believed that the League was the world's best hope, did have such a compulsion. Yet he would not compromise either, and this ensured the Treaty's defeat.

Wilson's behavior is further evidence of his physical and mental decline. Had he died or stepped down, the treaty, with reservations, would almost certainly have been ratified. When the Senate balloted again in March, half the Democrats voted for the treaty with the Lodge Reservations. The others, mostly southern party regulars, joined the irreconcilables. Together they mustered thirty-five votes, seven more than the one-third that meant defeat.

The Red Scare

Everyone wanted peace, but wartime tensions did not subside; apparently people continued to need some release for the aggressive drives they had formerly focused on the Germans. Most Americans drew invidious comparisons between the lot of the unemployed soldier who had risked his life for a dollar a day and that of the striker who had drawn fat wages during the war in perfect safety.

The activities of radicals in the labor movement led millions of citizens to associate unionism and strikes with the new threat of communist world revolution. Although there were only a relative handful of communists in the United States, Russia's experience persuaded many people that a tiny minority of ruthless revolutionaries could take over a nation of millions if conditions were right. Communists appointed themselves the champions of workers; labor unrest attracted them magnetically. When strikes broke out, some accompanied by violence, many people interpreted them as communist-inspired preludes to revolution.

Organized labor in America had seldom been truly radical. The Industrial Workers of the World (IWW) had made little impression in most industries. But some labor leaders had been attracted to socialism, and many Americans failed to distinguish between the common ends sought by communists and socialists and the entirely different methods by which they proposed to achieve those ends.

DID A STROKE SWAY WILSON'S JUDGMENT?

Debating the Past

Wilson's refusal to accept some of Lodge's reservations to the League of Nations ensured its defeat; and without the participation of the young new superpower, the League was likely doomed to failure. Was Wilson's refusal motivated by principle or personal pique?

Historians such as Arthur Link (1957) maintained that Lodge's reservations would have emasculated the League. Because "half a League" was worse than none at all, Wilson was right to have stood firm. Wilson's critics described his actions as little more than a temper tantrum, like a child who destroys a favorite toy. George Kennan (1951) thought Wilson's judgment was beclouded by foolish and impractical moral imperatives.

These pictures suggest another interpretation. The first shows Wilson at his inauguration in 1912; the second, at his last cabinet meeting in 1919, after he had suffered a major stroke. Edwin Weinstein (1981), a physician, found that Wilson's stroke had been more debilitating than had been reported. His impaired physical condition had probably contributed to Wilson's obdurate refusal to compromise.

Arthur Link, *Wilson the Diplomatist* (1957), George Kennan, *American Diplomacy* (1951), Edwin Weinstein, *A Medical and Psychological Biography* (1981).

When a general strike paralyzed Seattle in February 1919, the fact that a procommunist had helped organize it sent shivers down countless conservative spines. When the radical William Z. Foster began a drive to organize the steel industry at about this time, the fears became more intense. In September 1919 a total of 343,000 steelworkers walked off their jobs, and in the same month the Boston police went on strike. Violence marked the steel strike, and the suspension of police protection in Boston led to looting and fighting that ended only when Governor Calvin Coolidge (who might have prevented the strike had he acted earlier) called out the National Guard.

During the same period a handful of terrorists caused widespread alarm by attempting to murder various prominent persons, including John D. Rockefeller,

Justice Oliver Wendell Holmes Jr., and Attorney General A. Mitchell Palmer. Although the terrorists were anarchists and anarchism had little in common with communism, many citizens lumped all extremists together and associated them with a monstrous assault on society.

What aroused the public even more was the fact that most radicals were not American citizens. Wartime fear of alien saboteurs easily transformed itself into peacetime terror of foreign radicals. In place of Germany, the enemy became the lowly immigrant, usually an Italian or a Jew or a Slav and usually an industrial worker. In this muddled way, radicalism, unionism, and questions of racial and national origins combined to make many Americans believe that their way of life was in imminent danger. Thus the "red scare" was born.

Attorney General Palmer was the key figure in the resulting purge. He had been a typical progressive, a supporter of the League of Nations and such reforms as woman suffrage and child labor legislation. But pressure from Congress and his growing conviction that the communists really were a menace led him to join the "red hunt." Soon he was saying of the radicals: "Out of the sly and crafty eyes of many of them leap cupidity, cruelty, insanity, and crime; from their lopsided faces, sloping brows, and misshapen features may be recognized the unmistakable criminal type."

In August 1919, Palmer established within the Department of Justice the General Intelligence Division, headed by J. Edgar Hoover, to collect information about clandestine radical activities. In November, Justice Department agents in a dozen cities swooped down on the meeting places of an anarchist organization known as the Union of Russian Workers. More than 650 persons, many of them

The "red scare" that followed the Great War caused panic and new racial violence throughout the nation. Paranoid delusions of "dangerous aliens" and "foreign subversives" were prevalent, as this cartoon demonstrates.

unconnected with the union, were arrested but in only forty-three cases could evidence be found to justify deportation.

Nevertheless, the public reacted so favorably that Palmer, thinking now of winning the 1920 Democratic presidential nomination, planned an immense roundup of communists. He obtained 3,000 warrants, and on January 2, 1920, his agents, reinforced by local police and self-appointed vigilantes, struck simultaneously in thirty-three cities.

About 6,000 persons were taken into custody, many of them citizens and therefore not subject to the deportation laws, many others unconnected with any radical cause. Some were held incommunicado for weeks while the authorities searched for evidence against them. In a number of cases, individuals who went to visit prisoners were themselves thrown behind bars on the theory that they too must be communists. Hundreds of suspects were jammed into filthy "bullpens," beaten, and forced to sign "confessions."

The public tolerated these wholesale violations of civil liberties because of the supposed menace of communism. Gradually, however, protests began to be heard, first from lawyers and liberal magazines, then from a wider segment of the population. No revolutionary outbreak had taken place. Of 6,000 seized in the Palmer raids, only 556 proved liable to deportation. The widespread ransacking of communists' homes and meeting places produced mountains of inflammatory literature but only three pistols. Within a few months, the red scare subsided.

The Election of 1920

Wilson still hoped for vindication at the polls in the presidential election, which he sought to make a "great and solemn referendum" on the League. He would have liked to run for a third term, but in his enfeebled condition he attracted no support among Democratic leaders. The party nominated James M. Cox of Ohio.

Cox favored joining the League, but the election did not produce the referendum on the new organization that Wilson desired. The Republicans, whose candidate was another Ohioan, Senator Warren G. Harding, equivocated shamelessly on the issue. The election turned on other matters, largely emotional. Disillusioned by the results of the war, many Americans had had their fill of idealism. They wanted, apparently, to end the long period of moral uplift and reform agitation that had begun under Theodore Roosevelt and return to what Harding called "normalcy."

To the extent that the voters were expressing opinions on Wilson's League, their response was overwhelmingly negative. Senator Harding, a strong reservationist, swept the country, winning over 16.1 million votes to Cox's 9.1 million. In July 1921, Congress formally ended the war with the Central Powers by passing a joint resolution.

The defeat of the League was a tragedy both for Wilson, whose crusade for a world order based on peace and justice ended in failure, and for the world, which was condemned to endure another, still more horrible and costly war. Perhaps this dreadful outcome could not have been avoided. Had Wilson compromised and Lodge behaved like a statesman instead of a politician, the United States would have joined the League, but it might well have failed to respond when called on to meet its obligations. As events soon demonstrated, the League powers acted timidly and even dishonorably when challenged by aggressor nations.

Yet it might have been different had the Senate ratified the Versailles Treaty. What was lost when the treaty failed was not peace but the possibility of peace, a tragic loss indeed.

Milestones

1914	United States invades Veracruz, Mexico
	Great War begins in Europe
1915	German U-boat torpedoes *Lusitania*
	United States recognizes Carranza government in Mexico
1916	Wilson appoints Louis D. Brandeis to Supreme Court
	"Pancho" Villa burns Columbus, New Mexico
	Wilson is reelected president
1917	Russian Revolution begins
	United States declares war on Central Powers
	Herbert Hoover is named food administrator
1918	Sedition Act limits freedom of speech
	Wilson announces Fourteen Points
	Republicans gain control of both houses of Congress
	Armistice ends the Great War
1919	Steel workers strike
	Red Scare culminates in Palmer raids
	Big Four meet at Paris Peace Conference
	Senate rejects Versailles Treaty and League of Nations
	Wilson suffers massive stroke
1920	Senate again rejects Versailles Treaty and League of Nations
	Warren Harding is elected president

Postwar Society and Culture: Change and Adjustment

MANY COLLEGE STUDENTS DRINK—A LOT. EXACTLY HOW MUCH was the subject of a decade-long study, completed in 2007, by the National Center on Addiction and Substance Abuse (CASA) at Columbia University. It found that in 2005, 40 percent of full-time college students had recently engaged in binge-drinking, and that nearly 25 percent met the medical criteria for substance abuse. The study further determined that 1,717 college students died from alcohol-related injuries (most involving traffic accidents) in 2001, the most recent year for which data had been scrutinized. That same year, some 97,000 students were victims of alcohol-related sexual assault or date rape.

"It's time to get the 'high' out of higher education," declared Joseph A. Califano, president of CASA and former U.S. Secretary of Health, Education, and Welfare. He blamed college administrators for condoning a "college culture of abuse." Campaigns to promote responsible drinking accomplished little, he noted. The only effective strategy to reduce drinking was campus-wide prohibition.

But many bristled at this. A professor at the University of Hawaii declared that a proposal to ban alcohol on campus was reminiscent of prohibition, the Eighteenth Amendment, which in 1919 outlawed the manufacture and sale of alcohol—and which was widely ignored. "You cannot root out the drinking of alcohol by outlawing it," he added. Beer representatives similarly invoked the lessons of history when Florida State University proposed legislation in 2005 to prevent local bars from offering free drinks to women. "Problems cannot be legislated out of existence," the beer makers declared in a letter to university officials. "That was tried over 80 years ago with Prohibition."

The Eighteenth Amendment was passed in response to what many perceived to be increasingly dissolute lifestyles during the "Jazz Age." But other changes were nearly as disturbing to many Americans. The recent flood of immigration had strained the nation's social fabric, especially in cities. Young women were challenging traditional gender roles. Blacks were becoming more militant in demanding equality. Gays were becoming visible—at least to each other. Movies and radio, and even artists and writers, stimulated a rebellious youth culture. Advertising encouraged people to lose themselves in the delights of consumption.

These transformations also elicited opposition. The federal government curtailed immigration and cracked down on foreign-born radicals. The Ku Klux Klan reemerged to intimidate immigrants and blacks. Traditionalists inveighed against the enticements of popular culture and decline in faith. Prohibition generated the most headlines, but it was only the most visible expression of a reaction to broad social and cultural change.

Closing the Gates to New Immigrants

The ending of the red scare did not herald the disappearance of xenophobia. It was perhaps inevitable and possibly wise that some limitation be placed on the entry of immigrants into the United States after the war. An immense backlog of prospective migrants had piled up during the conflict, and the desperate postwar economic condition of Europe led hundreds of thousands to seek better circumstances in the United States. Immigration increased from 110,000 in 1919 to 430,000 in 1920 and to 805,000 in 1921, with every prospect of continuing to rise.

In 1921 Congress, reflecting a widespread prejudice against eastern and southern Europeans, passed an emergency act establishing a quota system. Each year 3 percent of the number of foreign-born residents of the United States in 1910 (about 350,000 persons) might enter the country. Each country's quota was based on the number of its nationals in the United States in 1910. This meant that only a relative handful of the total would be from southern and eastern Europe. In 1924 the quota was reduced to 2 percent and the base year shifted to 1890, thereby lowering further the proportion of southern and eastern Europeans admitted.

In 1929 Congress established a system that allowed only 150,000 immigrants a year to enter the country. (In recent years, that annual number of legal immigrants has been increased to 700,000.) Each national quota was based on the supposed origins of the entire white population of the United States in 1920, not merely on the foreign-born. Here is an example of how the system worked:

"Give me your tired, your poor, your huddled masses yearning to breathe free, the wretched refuse of your teeming shore"—these words of Emma Lazarus, inscribed at the base of the Statue of Liberty, tell only part of the story. Most immigrants were young and hopeful, like this family at Ellis Island; many were resolute and ambitious. The restriction of immigration during the 1920s, conceived to exclude misfits, also deprived the nation of such as these.

$$\frac{\text{Italian quota}}{150,000} = \frac{\text{Italian-origin population, 1920}}{\text{White population, 1920}}$$

$$\frac{\text{Italian quota}}{150,000} = \frac{3,800,000}{95,500,000}$$

$$\text{Italian quota} = 6,000 \text{ (approximately)}$$

The system was complicated and unscientific, for no one could determine with accuracy the "origins" of millions of citizens. More seriously, it ignored America's long history of constantly changing ethnic heterogeneity. The motto *E Pluribus Unum,* conceived to represent the unity of the original thirteen states, applied even more appropriately to the blending of different cultures into one nationality. The new law sought to freeze the mix, to turn the American melting pot into a kind of gigantic ice cube.

The United States had closed the gates. The National Origins Act caused the foreign-born percentage of the population to fall from about 13 percent in 1920 to 4.7 percent in 1970. (In comparison, in 2005 over 11 percent of the population was foreign born.) Instead of an open, cosmopolitan society eager to accept, in Emma Lazarus's stirring line, the "huddled masses yearning to breathe free," America now became committed to preserving a homogeneous, "Anglo-Saxon" population.

Distaste for the "new" immigrants from eastern Europe, many of whom were Jewish, expanded into a more general anti-Semitism in the 1920s. American Jews, whether foreign-born or native, were subjected to increasing discrimination, not because they were slow in adopting American ways but because (being ambitious and hardworking, as immigrants were supposed to be) many of them were getting ahead in the world somewhat more rapidly than expected. Prestigious colleges like Harvard, Yale, and Columbia that had in the past admitted Jews based on their academic records now imposed unofficial but effective quotas. Medical schools also established quotas, and no matter how talented, most young Jewish lawyers and bankers could find places only in so-called Jewish firms.

New Urban Social Patterns

The census of 1920 revealed that for the first time a majority of Americans (54 million in a population of 106 million) lived in "urban" rather than "rural" places. These figures are somewhat misleading when applied to the study of social attitudes because the census classified anyone in a community of 2,500 or more as urban. Of the 54 million "urban" residents in 1920, over 16 million lived in villages and towns of fewer than 25,000 persons and the evidence suggests strongly that a large majority of them held ideas and values more like those of rural citizens than like those of city dwellers. But the truly urban Americans, the one person in four who lived in a city of 100,000 or more—and particularly the nearly 16.4 million who lived in metropolises of at least half a million—were increasing steadily in number and influence. More than 19 million persons moved from farms to cities in the 1920s, and the population living in centers of 100,000 or more increased by about a third.

Earlier differences between working-class and middle-class family structures persisted. In 1920 about a quarter of the American women who were working were married, but less than 10 percent of all married women were working. Middle-class married women who worked were nearly all either childless or highly paid professionals who were able to employ servants. Most male skilled workers now earned enough to support a family in modest comfort so long as they could work steadily, but an unskilled laborer still could not. Wives in most such families helped out, usually by taking in laundry or doing piecework sewing for jobbers.

By the 1920s the idea of intrafamily democracy had emerged. In such families, husbands and wives would deal with each other as equals, which given existing conditions meant sharing housework and childcare, downplaying male authority, and stressing mutual satisfaction in sexual and other matters. On the one hand, they should be friends and lovers, not merely housekeepers, earners of money, and producers of children. On the other hand, advocates of these companionate relationships believed that there was nothing particularly sacred about marriage; divorce should be made easier for couples who did not get along, provided they did not have children.

The growth of large cities further loosened social constraints on sexuality. Amid the sea of people who surged down the streets or into the subways, the solitary individual acquired a freedom derived from anonymity. (For further perspective on urban life, see the Re-Viewing the Past essay "Chicago," pp. 678–679.) Homosexuals, in particular, developed a set of identifying signals and fashioned a distinctive culture in parks, cafeterias, nightclubs, and rooming houses of big cities. Because most others wrongly assumed that male homosexuality was characterized by effeminacy, they were unaware of the extent of the emerging gay culture.

The Younger Generation

The Great War profoundly affected the generation born around the turn of the century. It had raised, and its outcome dashed, their hopes for the future. Now the narrowness and prudery of so many of their elders and the stuffy conservatism of nearly all politicians seemed not merely old-fashioned but ludicrous. The actions of red-baiters and reactionaries led them to exaggerate the importance of their right to express themselves in bizarre ways. Their models and indeed some of their leaders were the prewar Greenwich Village bohemians.

The 1920s has been described as the Jazz Age, the era of "flaming youth," when young people danced to syncopated "African" rhythms, careened about the countryside in automobiles in search of pleasure and forgetfulness, and made gods of movie stars and professional athletes. This view of the period bears a superficial resemblance to reality. "Younger people," one observer noted in 1922, were attempting "to create a way of life free from the bondage of an authority that has lost all meaning." But if they differed from their parents and grandparents, it was primarily because young people were adjusting to more profound and more rapid changes in their world than their grandparents could have imagined.

For young people during the 1920s relations between the sexes were becoming more relaxed and uninhibited. Respectable young women smoked cigarettes, something previously done in public only by prostitutes and bohemian types. They cast off heavy corsets, wore lipstick and "exotic" perfumes, and shortened both their hair and their skirts, the latter rising steadily from instep to ankle to calf to knee and beyond as the decade progressed. For decades female dressmakers and beauty salon proprietors had sold their own beauty products and potions. By 1920, however, new cosmetic corporations, managed primarily by men, appropriated the products and marketing strategies of local women entrepreneurs and catered to national mass markets.

Conservatives bemoaned what they described as the breakdown of moral standards, the fragmentation of the family, and the decline of parental authority—all with some reason. Nevertheless, society was not collapsing. Much of the rebelliousness of the young, like their particular style of dress, was faddish in nature, in a sense a kind of youthful conformity. This was particularly true of college students. Elaborate rituals governed every aspect of their extracurricular life, which was consuming a steadily larger share of most students' time and energy. Fraternity and sorority initiations, "proms," attendance at Saturday afternoon football games, styles of dress, and college slang, seemingly aspects of independence and free choice, were nearly everywhere shaped and controlled by peer pressure.

But young people's new ways of relating to one another, while influenced by the desire to conform, were not mere fads and were not confined to people under 30. This can be seen most clearly in the birth control movement, the drive to legalize the use of contraceptives.

The "New" Woman

The young people of the 1920s were more open about sex and perhaps more sexually precocious than the young had been before the war. This does not mean that most of them engaged in sexual intercourse before marriage or that they tended to marry earlier. Single young people might "believe in" birth control, but relatively few (at least by modern standards) had occasion to practice it. Contraception was a concern of married people, and particularly of married women.

The leading American proponent of birth control in the 1920s, actually the person who coined the term, was Margaret Sanger, one of the less self-centered Greenwich Village bohemians. Before the war she was a political radical, a friend of Eugene Debs, "Big Bill" Haywood, and the anarchist Emma Goldman. Gradually, however, her attention focused on the plight of the poor women she encountered while working as a nurse; many of these women, burdened by large numbers of children, knew nothing about contraception. Sanger began to write articles and pamphlets designed to enlighten them, but when she did so she ran afoul of the Comstock Act of 1873, an antiobscenity law that banned the distribution of information about contraception from the mails. She was frequently in trouble with the law, but she was persistent to the edge of fanaticism. In 1921 she founded the American Birth Control League and two years later a research center.

The medical profession, though wary of the issue, gave some support to the birth control movement, as did the eugenicists, who claimed that unless the fecundity of "unfit" types (people others might describe simply as poor) was curbed, "race suicide" would result. Sanger accepted support wherever it could be found; by the end of the decade she was no longer on the cutting edge of the movement or even a very radical feminist. But by that time resistance to the use of contraception was crumbling.

Other gender-based restrictions and limitations of particular importance to women also seemed to be breaking down. The divorce laws had been modified in most states. More women were taking jobs, attracted by the expanding demand for clerks, typists, salespeople, receptionists, telephone operators, and similar service-oriented occupations. Over 10.6 million women were working by the end of the decade, in contrast with 8.4 million in 1920. The Department of Labor's Women's Bureau, outgrowth of a wartime agency, was founded in 1920 and was soon conducting investigations of the working conditions women faced in different industries and how various laws affected them.

WAS THE DECADE OF THE 1920S ONE OF SELF-ABSORPTION?

This magazine cover is a stereotypical expression of the Roaring Twenties: a chic young woman, knee exposed, smoking, drinking, and cavorting with a gin-toting cad in a roadster.

The decade was scarcely over when Frederick Lewis Allen indicted it in *Only Yesterday* (1931), an immediate best-seller. In his view young people believed that "life was futile and nothing much mattered." So they occupied themselves with "tremendous trifles" such as mah-jongg, jazz, and illicit booze. Of the wider world, they cared little. In 1937 Samuel Eliot Morison and Henry Steele Commager added a political gloss to Allen's cultural pessimism. Because people were "weary of reform and disillusioned by the crusade of democracy," they drifted toward conservatism.

Two important works were published in 1955. John Higham referred to the "tribal twenties" as a time when Americans attempted to "close the gates" of immigration, and Richard Hofstadter derided the decade as an insignificant "entr'acte" bracketed by the more consequential eras of progressivism and New Deal reform.

William Leuchtenburg (1958) sought to balance these assessments: there was much more to the decade than "raccoon coats and bathtub gin." While conceding that politicians had failed to solve problems of state authority, industrial concentration, and mass culture, they had not done much worse than the progressives. (Recall Debating the Past, p. 597.)

In later decades leftist scholars such as Roland Marchand (1985) associated the 1920s with the triumph of advertising and consumption, part of a "cultural hegemony" that promoted sales to ensure corporate profits. On the other hand, Kathy Peiss (1998) was among a group of scholars who insisted that consumption could add depth and richness to life. She found, for example, that in purchasing cosmetics women partook of the "pleasures of fantasy and desire."

George Chauncey (1994) championed the self-absorption—self-expression?—of gays who, left mostly to themselves, exulted in a remarkably open homosexual culture in the big cities.

Frederick Lewis Allen, *Only Yesterday* (1931), Samuel Eliot Morison and Henry Steele Commager, *The Growth of the American Republic* (1937), John Higham, *Strangers in the Land* (1955), Richard Hofstadter, *The Age of Reform* (1955), William Leuchtenburg, *The Perils of Prosperity* (1958), Roland Marchand, *Advertising the American Dream* (1985), T. J. Jackson Lears, *Fables of Abundance* (1995), Warren I. Susman, *Culture as History* (1984), Kathy Peiss, *Hope in a Jar* (1998), George Chauncey, *Gay New York* (1994).

This photograph of Margaret Sanger was taken during her trial in January 1917. Having opened the nation's first birth control clinic in Brooklyn, New York, she was convicted of disseminating information on contraception and served 30 days in prison. Friends had advised Sanger to dress conservatively and affect a "Madonna type" persona. Despite her demure clothing, her eyes express her characteristic assertiveness.

But most of these gains were illusory. Relaxation of the strict standards of sexual morality did not eliminate the double standard. More women worked, but most of the jobs they held were still menial or of a kind that few men wanted: domestic service, elementary school teaching, clerical work, selling behind a counter. One of the worst blows fell in 1923 when in the case of *Adkins* v. *Children's Hospital*, the Supreme Court declared a federal law that limited the hours of work for women in the District of Columbia unconstitutional. This rendered women ineligible for many higher-level professional jobs, such as medical internships and positions in law firms.

When they competed for jobs with men, women usually received much lower wages. Efforts to get the American Federation of Labor to take up the issue failed; few of the unions in the federation admitted women.

The 1920s proved disillusioning to feminists, who now paid a price for their single-minded pursuit of the right to vote in the progressive era. After the ratification of the Nineteenth Amendment, Carrie Chapman Catt was exultant: "We are no longer petitioners," she announced, "but free and equal citizens." Many activists, assuming the battle won, lost interest in agitating for change. They believed that the suffrage amendment had given them the one weapon needed to achieve whatever women still lacked. In fact, it soon became apparent that women did not vote as a bloc. Many married women voted for the candidates their husbands supported.

Chicago

Chicago (2003) is a tale of illicit sex, booze, and "all that jazz." The characters played by Renée Zellweger and Catherine Zeta-Jones aspire to cabaret stardom. Each is married, each is having an affair, each is jilted, and each shoots her wayward lover because "he had it coming." The newspapers gleefully promote their stories. From prison, while awaiting trial for murder, the women compete to garner the most headlines, courting the fame that will boost their careers. Richard Gere, who plays their celebrity lawyer, "razzle dazzles" all Chicago (including both juries) and gets the women acquitted. *Chicago* is a musical. It does not claim to be history. The movie, however, is based on a true story; and both the movie and the story illuminate important aspects of the Roaring Twenties.

On March 11, 1924, Walter Law, an automobile salesman, was found slumped against the steering wheel of a car in downtown Chicago. He was dead from a gunshot wound to the head. A pistol and an empty bottle of gin were on the floor. The car was registered to Belva Gaertner, a twice-divorced cabaret singer known as Belle Brown. Police hurried to her rooming house and peppered her with questions.

"We went driving, Mr. Law and I," she told them. She explained that they had stopped at the Bingham "café," bought a bottle of gin (illegally, since this was during Prohibition), and

Catherine Zeta-Jones and Renée Zellweger.

drove around town. "I don't know what happened next," she declared. During the interrogation Gaertner paced nervously, perhaps for good reason: Her clothes were soaked with blood. She was charged with murder.

On April 3, police received a phone call that a man had attempted to rape a young married woman and that she had shot him. The woman was Beulah Annan, who worked at a laundry. At her apartment, police found Harry Kalstedt dead from a gunshot wound. Annan insisted that she had acted in self-defense, and her husband supported her story. But police hammered away at the fact that Kalstedt had worked at the same laundry as Annan, and that he had been shot in the back. Annan eventually confessed that the two had been having an affair and that, when he threatened to dump her, she shot him. For two hours, as he lay dying, she drank cocktails and listened to a recording of "Hula Lou," a foxtrot about a Hawaiian girl "with more sweeties than a dog has fleas."

Maurine Watkins, a young reporter, covered both stories for the *Chicago Tribune*. Murder had long been a staple of local journalism, but Watkins recognized the extraordinary appeal of this story: jazz, booze, and two comely "lady murderesses," as Watkins termed them. While awaiting trial in prison, the women provided Watkins with delicious quotes.

Gaertner told Watkins that she was innocent. "No woman can love a man enough to kill him," she explained. "There are always plenty more." She added: "Gin and guns—either one is bad enough, but together they get you in a dickens of a mess." When the grand jury ruled that she could be tried for murder, Gaertner was irritated. "That was bum," she snapped. She called the jurors "narrow-minded old birds—bet they never heard a jazz band in their lives. Now, if I'm tried, I want worldly men, broad-minded men, men who know what it is to get out a bit. Why, no one like that would convict me!"

During the trial, Annan's attorney pointed to "this frail little girl, struggling with a drunken brute." On May 25, after deliberating less than two hours, the all-male jury acquit-

Belva Gaertner and Beulah Annan, "lady murderesses."

ted her of the crime. (Justice in those days was swift; in Illinois, too, it was devoid of women, who did not gain the right to serve on juries until 1939.) Two weeks after Annan's trial, Gaertner was also found not guilty. "Another pretty woman gone free," muttered the prosecutor. Watkins noted that four other women remained on death row, but none were as "stylish" or "pretty" as Gaertner and Annan.

Unlike the movie's "lady murderesses," Annan and Gaertner did not team up in a cabaret act. Annan had a nervous breakdown, was institutionalized, and died in 1928. Of Gaertner's subsequent life, little is known. Watkins abandoned journalism and entered Yale drama school. In 1926 she wrote *Chicago*, a comedy derived from the Gaertner and Annan trials, and it ran on Broadway for 172 performances. The next year Cecil B. De Mille adapted the play as a silent movie. In 1975 director Bob Fosse bought the rights to *Chicago* and created the Broadway musical on which the 2003 movie was based.

The "lady murderesses" became part of the lore of the Roaring Twenties; the story seemed to confirm the fears of traditionalists. One minister warned about jazz's "wriggling movement and sensuous stimulation" of the body's "sensory center." Short, bobbed, or marcelled hair was similarly worrisome, because it signified a young woman's break from convention. Silk stockings, skirts that exposed knees, and straight dresses that de-emphasized the waist further suggested that women's bodies were not meant solely for

childbirth. The movie makes all of these points with suitable salaciousness.

The movie also reiterates widespread concerns about city life. Several months after the acquittal of Gaertner and Annan, *Literary Digest* warned "country girls" of the moral dangers of large cities. Such fears echoed the judgments of sociologists, especially those of "the Chicago school" headed by Robert Park of the University of Chicago. The Chicago sociologists contended that large cities shattered traditional bonds of family and community and fostered crime and deviance.

Scholars now recognize that the portrait of urban city life as propounded by "the Chicago school"—and by movies such as *Chicago*—was overdrawn. Urbanization did not shatter family and ethnic ties. Neighborliness and community persisted even in blighted tenement districts. Few people cast off social conventions, much less succumbed to murderous impulses. In short, Belva Gaertner and Beulah Annan were good copy, and stories such as theirs helped make that celebrated decade roar, but most folks painted the town less vividly, if at all.

Questions for Discussion

■ Does the film photograph of Catherine Zeta-Jones and Renée Zellweger resemble Beulah Annan and Belva Gaertner? Why would Hollywood take pains to depict the visual aspects of the past accurately?

When radical feminists discovered that voting did not automatically bring true equality, they founded the National Woman's Party (NWP) and began campaigning for an equal rights amendment. Their dynamic leader, Alice Paul, disdained specific goals such as disarmament, ending child labor, and liberalized birth control. Total equality for women was the one objective. The party considered protective legislation governing the hours and working conditions of women discriminatory. This caused the so-called social feminists, who believed that children and working women needed the protection provided by such laws, to break away.

The NWP never attracted a wide following, but only partly because of the split with the social feminists. Many of the younger radical women, like the bohemians of the progressive era, were primarily concerned with their personal freedom to behave as they wished; politics did not interest them. But a more important reason was that nearly all the radicals failed to see that questions of gender—the attitudes that men and women *were taught* to take toward each other, not immutable physical or psychological differences—stood in the way of sexual equality. Many more women joined the more moderate League of Women Voters, which attempted to mobilize support for a broad spectrum of reforms, some of which had no specific connection to the interests of women as such. The entire women's movement lost momentum. The battle for the equal rights amendment persisted through the 1930s, but it was lost. By the end of that decade the movement was moribund.

Popular Culture: Movies and Radio

The postwar decade saw immense changes in popular culture. Unlike the literary flowering of the era (see pages 688–690), these changes seemed in tune with the times, not a reaction against them. This was true in part because they were products as much of technology as of human imagination.

The first motion pictures were made around 1900, but the medium only came into its own after the Great War. The early films, such as the eight-minute epic *The Great Train Robbery* (1903), were brief, action-packed, and unpretentious. Professional actors and most educated people viewed them with amused contempt. But their success was instantaneous with recent immigrants and many other slum dwellers. In 1912 there were nearly 13,000 movie houses in the United States, more than 500 in New York City alone. Many of these places were converted stores called nickelodeons because the admission charge was only 5 cents.

In the beginning the mere recording of movement seemed to satisfy the public, but success led to rapid technical and artistic improvements and consequently to more cultivated audiences. D. W. Griffith's 12-reel *Birth of a Nation* (1915) was a particularly important breakthrough in both areas, although Griffith's sympathetic treatment of the Ku Klux Klan of Reconstruction days angered blacks and white liberals.

By the mid-1920s the movie industry, centered in Hollywood, California, was the fourth largest in the nation in capital investment. Films moved from the nickelodeons to converted theaters. So large was the audience that movie "palaces" seating several thousand people sprang up in the major cities. *Daily* ticket sales averaged more than 10 million. With the introduction of talking movies, *The Jazz*

Would women believe the claims of cosmetics advertisements? "Kissproof" promised to make a woman's lips "pulsate with the very spirit of reckless, irrepressible youth." In a 1927 survey of housewives in Columbus, Ohio, Pond's Company found that two-thirds of the women could not even recall the company's advertisements. Younger women, however, were more impressionable. When the J. Walter Thompson advertising agency asked Vassar students to describe cosmetics, they unconsciously used the exact phrases from advertising copy—proof of its power.

Singer (1927) being the first of significance, and color films a few years later, the motion picture reached technological maturity. Costs and profits mounted; by the 1930s million-dollar productions were common.

Charlie Chaplin was the greatest film star of the era. His characterization of the sad-eyed little tramp with his toothbrush moustache and his cane, tight frock coat, and baggy trousers became famous throughout the world. Chaplin's films were superficially unpretentious; they seemed even in the 1920s old-fashioned, aimed at the lower-class audiences that had first found the movies magical. But his work proved both universally popular and enduring; he was perhaps the greatest comic artist of all time. The animated cartoon, perfected by Walt Disney in the 1930s, was a lesser but significant cinematic achievement; Mickey Mouse, Donald Duck, and other Disney cartoon characters gave endless delight to millions of children.

Even more pervasive than the movies in its effects on the American people was radio. Wireless transmission of sound was developed in the late nineteenth century by many scientists in Europe and the United States. During the war radio was put to important military uses and was strictly controlled, but immediately thereafter the airwaves were thrown open to everybody.

Radio was briefly the domain of hobbyists, thousands of "hams" broadcasting in indiscriminate fashion. Even under these conditions, the manufacture of radio equipment became a big business. In 1920 the first commercial station (KDKA in Pittsburgh) began broadcasting, and by the end of 1922 over 500 stations were in operation. In 1926 the National Broadcasting Company, the first continentwide network, was created.

It took little time for broadcasters to discover the power of the new medium. When one pioneer interrupted a music program to ask listeners to phone in requests, the station received 3,000 calls in an hour. The immediacy of radio explained its tremendous impact. As a means of communicating the latest news, it had no peer; beginning with the broadcast of the 1924 presidential nominating conventions, all major public events were covered live. Advertisers seized on radio too; it proved to be as effective a way to sell soap as to transmit news.

In 1927 Congress limited the number of stations and parceled out wavelengths to prevent interference. Further legislation in 1934 established the Federal Communications Commission (FCC), with power to revoke the licenses of stations that failed to operate in the public interest. But the FCC placed no effective controls on programming or on advertising practices.

The Golden Age of Sports

The extraordinary popularity of sports in the postwar period can be explained in a number of ways. People had more money to spend and more free time to fill. Radio was bringing suspenseful, play-by-play accounts of sports contests into millions of homes, thus encouraging tens of thousands to want to see similar events with their own eyes. New means of persuasion developed by advertisers to sell lipstick, breakfast cereal, and refrigerators were applied with equal success to sporting events and to the athletes who participated in them.

There had been great athletes before; indeed probably the greatest all-around athlete of the twentieth century was Jim Thorpe, a Sac and Fox Indian who won both the pentathlon and the decathlon at the 1912 Olympic Games, made Walter Camp's All-American football team in 1912 and 1913, then played major league baseball for several years before becoming a pioneer founder and player in the National Football League. But what truly made the 1920s a golden age was a coincidence—the emergence in a few short years of a remarkable collection of what today would be called superstars.

In football there was the University of Illinois's Harold "Red" Grange, who averaged over 10 yards a carry during his college career and who in one incredible quarter during the 1924 game between Illinois and Michigan carried the ball four times and scored a touchdown each time, gaining in the process 263 yards. In prize fighting, heavyweight champion Jack Dempsey, the "Manassas Mauler," knocked out a succession of challengers in bloody battles only to be deposed in 1927 by "Gentleman Gene" Tunney, who gave him a 15-round boxing lesson and then, according to Tunney's own account, celebrated by consuming "several pots of tea."

During the same years William "Big Bill" Tilden dominated tennis, winning the national singles title every year from 1920 to 1925 along with nearly every other tournament he entered. Beginning in 1923, Robert T. "Bobby" Jones ruled over the world of golf with equal authority, his climactic achievement being his capture of

Newly built Yankee Stadium, on opening day of the 1923 baseball season. Babe Ruth hit his first home run and soon Yankee Stadium was dubbed "the House that Ruth Built." That year, perhaps his best, Ruth hit forty-one home runs, batted .393, and drew 170 walks. He got on base more than half the times he appeared at the plate. Ruth's feats matched the colossal appearance of Yankee Stadium, whose arches evoked the imperial grandeur of ancient Rome.

the amateur and open championships of both the United States and Great Britain in 1930.

A few women athletes dominated their sports during this Golden Age in similar fashion. In tennis Helen Wills was three times United States singles champion and the winner of the women's singles at Wimbledon eight times in the late 1920s and early 1930s. The swimmer Gertrude Ederle, holder of eighteen world records by the time she was 17, swam the English Channel on her second attempt, in 1926. She was not only the first woman to do so, but she did it faster than any of the four men who had previously made it across.

However, the sports star among stars was "the Sultan of Swat," baseball's Babe Ruth.[1] Ruth not only dominated baseball, he changed it from a game ruled by pitchers and low scores to one in which hitting was more greatly admired. Originally himself a brilliant pitcher, his incredible hitting ability made him more valuable in the outfield, where he could play every day. Before Ruth, John "Home Run" Baker was the most famous slugger; his greatest annual home run total was twelve, achieved shortly before the Great War. Ruth hit twenty-nine in 1919 and fifty-four in 1920, his first year with the New York Yankees. By 1923 he was so feared that pitchers intentionally walked him more than half the times he appeared at the plate.

The achievements of these and other outstanding athletes had a cumulative effect. New stadiums were built, and they were filled by "the largest crowds that ever witnessed athletic sports since the fall of Rome." Record crowds paying unprecedented sums attended all sorts of events.

---

[1]His full name was George Herman Ruth, but the nickname Babe, given to him early in his career, was what everyone called him.

Urban–Rural Conflicts: Fundamentalism

These were buoyant times for people in tune with the times—the young, the devil-may-care, factory workers with money in their pockets, many different types. But nearly all of them were city people. However, the tensions and hostilities of the 1920s exaggerated an older rift in American society—the conflict between urban and rural ways of life. To many among the scattered millions who tilled the soil and among the millions who lived in towns and small cities, the new city-oriented culture seemed sinful, overly materialistic, and unhealthy. To them change was something to be resented and resisted.

Yet there was no denying its fascination. Made even more aware of the appeal of the city by radio and the automobile, farmers and townspeople coveted the comfort and excitement of city life at the same time that they condemned its vices. Rural society proclaimed the superiority of its ways at least in part to protect itself from temptation. Change, omnipresent in the postwar world, must be resisted even at the cost of individualism and freedom.

One expression of this resistance was a resurgence of religious fundamentalism. Although it was especially prevalent among Baptists and Methodists, fundamentalism was primarily an attitude of mind, profoundly conservative, rather than a religious idea. Fundamentalists rejected the theory of evolution as well as advanced hypotheses on the origins of the universe.

What made crusaders of the fundamentalists was their resentment of modern urban culture. Although in some cases they harassed liberal ministers, their religious attitudes had little public significance; their efforts to impose their views on public education were another matter. The teaching of evolution must be prohibited, they insisted. Throughout the 1920s they campaigned vigorously for laws banning discussion of Darwin's theory in textbooks and classrooms. By 1929 five southern states had passed laws prohibiting the teaching of evolution in the public schools.

The fundamentalists won a minor victory in 1925, when Tennessee passed a law forbidding instructors in the state's schools and colleges to teach "any theory that denies the story of the Divine Creation of man as taught in the Bible." Although the bill passed both houses by big majorities, most legislators voted aye only because they dared not expose themselves to charges that they disbelieved the Bible. Educators in the state, hoping to obtain larger school appropriations from the legislature, hesitated to protest.

On learning of the passage of this act, the American Civil Liberties Union announced that it would finance a test case challenging its constitutionality if a Tennessee teacher would deliberately violate the statute. Urged on by friends, John T. Scopes, a young biology teacher in Dayton, reluctantly agreed to do so. He was arrested. A battery of nationally known lawyers came forward to defend him, and the state obtained the services of William Jennings Bryan. The "Monkey Trial" became an overnight sensation.

Clarence Darrow, chief counsel for the defendant, stated the issue clearly. "Scopes isn't on trial," he said, "civilization is on trial. The prosecution is opening

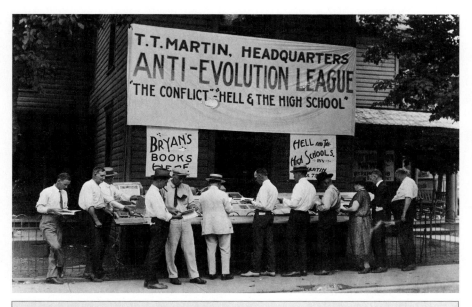

At the Scopes Monkey Trial, this open-air stall offers anti-evolution books, such as those by William Jennings Bryan and another title, "Hell & the High School."

the doors for a reign of bigotry equal to anything in the Middle Ages. No man's belief will be safe if they win." The comic aspects of the trial obscured this issue. Big-city reporters like H. L. Mencken of the *Baltimore Evening Sun* flocked to Dayton to make sport of the fundamentalists. Scopes's conviction was a foregone conclusion; after the jury rendered its verdict, the judge fined him $100.

Nevertheless the trial exposed the danger of the fundamentalist position. The high point came when Bryan agreed to testify as an expert witness on the Bible. In a sweltering courtroom, both men in shirtsleeves, the lanky, rough-hewn Darrow cross-examined the aging champion of fundamentalism, exposing his childlike faith and his disdain for the science of the day. Bryan admitted to believing that Eve had been created from Adam's rib and that a whale had swallowed Jonah. "I believe in a God that can make a whale and can make a man and make both do what He pleases," he explained.

The Monkey Trial ended badly for nearly everyone concerned. Scopes moved away from Dayton; the judge, John Raulston, was defeated when he sought reelection; Bryan died in his sleep a few days after the trial. But fundamentalism continued to flourish, not only in the nation's backwaters but also in many cities, brought there by rural people in search of work. In retrospect, even the heroes of the Scopes trial—science and freedom of thought—seem somewhat less stainless than they did to liberals at the time. The account of evolution in the textbook used by Scopes was hopelessly deficient and laced with bigotry, yet it was advanced as unassailable fact. In a section on the "Races of Man," for example, it described Caucasians as "the highest type of all . . . represented by the civilized white inhabitants of Europe and America."

Urban–Rural Conflicts: Prohibition

The conflict between the countryside and the city was fought on many fronts, and in one sector the rural forces achieved a quick victory. This was the Eighteenth Amendment, ratified in 1919, which prohibited the manufacture, transportation, and sale of alcoholic beverages. Although there were some big-city advocates of prohibition, the Eighteenth Amendment, in the words of one historian marked a triumph of the "Corn Belt over the conveyor belt."

This "experiment noble in purpose," as Herbert Hoover called it, achieved a number of socially desirable results. It reduced the annual national consumption of alcohol from 2.6 gallons per capita in the period just before the war to less than 1 gallon in the early 1930s. Arrests for drunkenness fell off sharply, as did deaths from alcoholism. Fewer workers squandered their wages on drink. If the drys had been willing to legalize beer and wine, the experiment might have worked. Instead, by insisting on total abstinence, they drove thousands of moderates to violate the law. Strict enforcement became impossible, especially in the cities.

In areas where sentiment favored prohibition strongly, liquor remained difficult to find. Elsewhere, anyone with sufficient money could obtain it easily. Smuggling became a major business, *bootlegger* a household word. Private individuals busied themselves learning how to manufacture "bathtub gin." Many druggists issued prescriptions for alcohol with a free hand. The manufacture of wine for religious ceremonies was legal, and consumption of sacramental wine jumped by 800,000 gallons during the first two years of prohibition. The saloon disappeared, replaced by the speakeasy, a supposedly secret bar or club, operating under the benevolent eye of the local police.

That the law was often violated does not mean that it was ineffective, any more than violations of laws against theft and murder mean that those laws are ineffective. Although gangsters such as Alphonse "Scarface Al" Capone of Chicago were engaged in the liquor traffic, their "organizations" existed before the passage of the Eighteenth Amendment. But prohibition widened already serious rifts in the social fabric of the country. Organized crime became more powerful. Besides undermining public morality by encouraging hypocrisy, prohibition almost destroyed the Democratic party as a national organization. Democratic immigrants in the cities hated it, but southern Democrats sang its praises, often while continuing to drink (the humorist Will Rogers quipped that Mississippi would vote dry "as long as the voters could stagger to the polls").

The Ku Klux Klan

The most horrible manifestation of the social malaise of the 1920s was the revival of the Ku Klux Klan. This new Klan, founded in 1915 by William J. Simmons, a former preacher, admitted only native-born white Protestants. The distrust of foreigners, blacks, Catholics, and Jews implicit in this regulation explains why it flourished

A Ku Klux Klan initiation ceremony photographed in Kansas in the 1920s. During its peak influence at mid-decade, Klan endorsement was essential to political candidates in many areas of the West and Midwest. Campaigning for reelection in 1934, an Indiana congressman testified, "I was told to join the Klan, or else."

in the social climate that spawned religious fundamentalism, immigration restriction, and prohibition. In 1920 two unscrupulous publicity agents, Edward Y. Clarke and Elizabeth Tyler, got control of the movement and organized a massive membership drive, diverting a major share of the initiation fees into their own pockets. In a little over a year they enrolled 100,000 recruits, and by 1923 they claimed the astonishing total of 5 million.

The Klan had relatively little appeal in the Northeast or in metropolitan centers in other parts of the country, but it found many members in middle-sized cities and in the small towns and villages of midwestern and western states like Indiana and Oregon. The scapegoats in such regions were immigrants, Jews, and especially Catholics. The rationale was an urge to return to an older, supposedly finer America and to stamp out all varieties of nonconformity. Klansmen "watched everybody," themselves safe from observation behind their masks and robes. They persecuted gamblers, "loose" women, violators of the prohibition laws, and anyone who happened to differ from them on religious questions or who belonged to a "foreign race."

The very success of the Klan led to its undoing. Factionalism sprang up, and rival leaders squabbled over the large sums that had been collected from the membership. The cruel and outrageous behavior of the organization roused both liberals and conservatives in every part of the country. And of course its victims joined forces against their tormentors. When the powerful leader of the Indiana Klan, a middle-aged reprobate named David C. Stephenson, was convicted of assaulting and causing the death of a young woman, the rank and file abandoned the organization in droves. The Klan remained influential for a number of years, contributing to the defeat of the Catholic Alfred E. Smith in the 1928 presidential election, but it ceased to be a dynamic force after 1924. By 1930 it had only some 9,000 members.

Sacco and Vanzetti

The excesses of the fundamentalists, the xenophobes, the Klan, the red-baiters, and the prohibitionists disturbed American intellectuals profoundly. More and more they became alienated, bitter, and contemptuous of those who appeared to control the country. Yet their alienation came at the very time that society was subjected to complex economic, political, and technological challenges that required the attention of people with brains and sophistication. This compounded the confusion and disillusionment characteristic of the period.

Nothing demonstrates this fact as clearly as the Sacco-Vanzetti case. In April 1920 two men in South Braintree, Massachusetts, killed a paymaster and a guard in a daring daylight robbery of a shoe factory. Shortly thereafter Nicola Sacco and Bartolomeo Vanzetti were charged with the crime, and in 1921 they were convicted of murder. Sacco and Vanzetti were anarchists and Italian immigrants. Their trial was a travesty of justice. The presiding judge, Webster Thayer, conducted the proceedings like a prosecuting attorney; privately he referred to the defendants as "those anarchist bastards."

The case became a cause célèbre. Prominent persons throughout the world protested, and for years Sacco and Vanzetti were kept alive by efforts to obtain a new trial. Vanzetti's quiet dignity and courage in the face of death wrung the hearts of millions. "You see me before you, not trembling," he told the court. "I never commit a crime in my life." When, in August 1927, the two were at last electrocuted, the disillusionment of American intellectuals with prevailing values was profound. Some historians, impressed by modern ballistic studies of Sacco's gun, now suspect that he, at least, may have been guilty. Nevertheless, the truth and the shame remain: Sacco and Vanzetti paid with their lives for being radicals and aliens, not for any crime.

Literary Trends

The literature of the 1920s reflects the disillusionment of the intellectuals. The prewar period had been an age of hopeful experimentation in the world of letters. But the progressive era writers, along with most other intellectuals, were beginning to abandon this view by about 1912. The wasteful horrors of the Great War and then the antics of the fundamentalists and the cruelty of the red-baiters and the Klan turned them into critics of society. After the war the poet Ezra Pound dropped his talk of an American Renaissance and wrote instead of a "botched civilization."

The symbol of what some called the "lost generation," in his own mind as well as to his contemporaries and to later critics, was F. Scott Fitzgerald. Born to modest wealth in St. Paul, Minnesota, in 1896, Fitzgerald attended Princeton and served in the army during the Great War. He rose to sudden fame in 1920 when he published *This Side of Paradise*, a somewhat sophomoric novel that appealed powerfully to college students and captured the fears and confusions of the lost generation. In *The Great Gatsby* (1925), a more mature work, Fitzgerald dissected a modern millionaire—coarse, unscrupulous, jaded, in love with another man's wife. Gatsby's tragedy lay in his dedication to a woman who, Fitzgerald made clear, did not merit his passion. He lived in "the service of a vast, vulgar, meretricious beauty," and in the end he understood this himself.

The tragedy of *The Great Gatsby* was related to Fitzgerald's own. Pleasure-loving and extravagant, he squandered the money earned by *This Side of Paradise*. He descended into the despair of alcoholism and ended his days as a Hollywood scriptwriter.

Many young American writers and artists became expatriates in the 1920s. They flocked to Rome, Berlin, and especially Paris, where they could live cheaply and escape what seemed to them the "conspiracy against the individual" prevalent in their own country. Ernest Hemingway was the most talented of the expatriates. He had served in the Italian army during the war and been grievously wounded (in spirit as well as in body). He settled in Paris in 1922 to write. His first novel, *The Sun Also Rises* (1926), portrayed the café world of the expatriate and the rootless desperation, amorality, and sense of outrage at life's meaninglessness that obsessed so many in those years. In *A Farewell to Arms* (1929) he drew on his military experiences to describe the confusion and horror of war.

Hemingway's books were best-sellers and he became a legend in his own time, but his style rather than his ideas explains his towering reputation. Few novelists have been as capable of suggesting powerful emotions and action in so few words. Mark Twain and Stephen Crane were his models; Gertrude Stein, a writer and revolutionary genius, his teacher. But his style was his own, direct, simple, taut, sparse.

Edith Wharton was of the New York aristocracy. She was educated by tutors and governesses and never went to college. To counteract what she called "the creeping darkness of neurasthenia," she traveled frequently to Europe, eventually chose to live there, and took up writing. In Paris at the outset of the Great War, she threw herself into war-related charities. But after the war, she retreated from the jangling energy of postwar life and culture. "I am steeping myself in the nineteenth century," she explained to a friend, "like taking refuge in a mighty temple." The product of her retreat, *The Age of Innocence* (1920), offered a penetrating portrait of an unsettlingly serene if vanished world. *The Nation* remarked that Wharton had described the wealthy of old New York "as familiarly as if she loved them and as lucidly as if she hated them." Though the younger novelists of the decade often dismissed her work as uninventive and dowdy, and she theirs as unformed and thin, her judgment has proven the more enduring.

Sinclair Lewis was probably the most popular American novelist of the 1920s. Like Fitzgerald, his first major work brought him instant fame and notoriety—and for the same reason. *Main Street* (1920) portrayed the smug ignorance and bigotry of the American small town so accurately that even Lewis's victims recognized themselves; his title became a symbol for provinciality and middle-class meanness of spirit. In *Babbitt* (1922), he created what many people considered the typical businessman of the 1920s, gregarious, a "booster," blindly orthodox in his political and social opinions, a slave to every cliché, and full of loud self-confidence but under the surface a bumbling, rather timid fellow who would have liked to be better than he was but dared not try.

The "New Negro"

The postwar reaction brought despair for many blacks. Aside from the barbarities of the Klan, they suffered from the postwar middle-class hostility to labor (and from the persistent reluctance of organized labor to admit black workers into its ranks). The increasing presence of southern blacks in northern cities also caused conflict. Some 393,000 settled in New York, Pennsylvania, and Illinois in the 1920s, most of them in New York City, Philadelphia, and Chicago. The black population of New York City more than doubled between 1920 and 1930.

In earlier periods blacks in northern cities had tended to live together, but in small neighborhoods scattered over large areas. Now the tendency was toward concentration in what came to be called ghettos.

Coming after the hopes inspired by wartime gains, the disappointments of the 1920s produced a new militancy among many blacks. In 1919 W. E. B. Du Bois wrote in *The Crisis*: "We are cowards and jackasses if . . . we do not marshal every ounce of our brain and brawn to fight . . . against the forces of hell in our own land." He increased his commitment to black nationalism, organizing a series of Pan African Conferences in an effort—futile, as it turned out—to create an international black movement.

Du Bois never made up his mind whether to work for integration or black separatism. Such ambivalence never troubled Marcus Garvey, a West Indian whose Universal Negro Improvement Association attracted hundreds of thousands of followers in the early 1920s. Garvey had nothing but contempt for whites, for light-skinned blacks like Du Bois, and for organizations such as the NAACP, which sought to bring whites and blacks together to fight segregation and other forms of prejudice. "Back to Africa" was his slogan; the black man must "work out his salvation in his motherland." (Paradoxically, Garvey's ideas won the enthusiastic support of the Ku Klux Klan and other white racist groups.)

Garvey's message was naive, but it served to build racial pride among the masses of poor and unschooled blacks. He dressed in elaborate braided uniforms, wore a plumed hat, drove about in a limousine. Both God and Christ were black, he insisted. He organized black businesses of many sorts, including a company that manufactured black dolls. He established a corps of Black Cross nurses and a Black Star Line Steamship Company to transport blacks back to Africa.

The ghettos produced compensating advantages for blacks. One effect, not fully utilized until later, was to increase their political power by enabling them to elect representatives to state legislatures and to Congress and to exert considerable influence in closely contested elections. More immediately, city life stimulated self-confidence; despite their horrors, the ghettos offered economic opportunity, political rights, and freedom from the everyday debasements of life in the South. The ghetto was a black world where black men and women could be themselves.

Black separatist Marcus Garvey and his followers were one of many factions of the black movement during the 1920s and 1930s. Other groups, such as the NAACP, worked to bring blacks and whites together, rather than segregating them further.

Black writers, musicians, and artists found in the ghettos both an audience and the "spiritual emancipation" that unleashed their capacities. Jazz, the great popular music of the age, was largely the creation of black musicians working in New Orleans before the turn of the century. By the 1920s it had spread throughout the country and to most of the rest of the world. White musicians and white audiences took it up—in a way it became a force for racial tolerance and understanding.

Jazz meant improvisation, and both players and audiences experienced in it a kind of liberation. Jazz was the music of the 1920s in part because it expressed the desire of so many people to break with tradition and throw off conventional restraints. Surely this helps to explain why it was so important to blacks.

Harlem, the largest black community in the world, became in the 1920s a cultural capital, center of the "Harlem Renaissance." Black newspapers and magazines flourished along with theatrical companies and libraries. Du Bois opened *The Crisis* to young writers and artists, and a dozen "little" magazines sprang up. Langston Hughes, one of the best poets of the era, described the exhilaration of his first arrival in this city within a city, a magnet for every black intellectual and artist. "Harlem! I . . . dropped my bags, took a deep breath, and felt happy again."

With some exceptions, African American writers like Hughes did not share in the disillusionment that afflicted so many white intellectuals. The persistence of prejudice angered them and made them militant. But to be militant, one must be at some level hopeful. Sociologists and psychologists (for whom the ghettos were indispensable social laboratories) were demonstrating that environment rather than heredity was preventing black economic progress. Together with the achievements of creative blacks, which for the first time were being appreciated by large numbers of white intellectuals, these discoveries seemed to herald the eventual disappearance of racial prejudice.

Economic Expansion

Despite the turmoil of the times and the dissatisfactions expressed by some of the nation's best minds, the 1920s was an exceptionally prosperous decade. Business boomed, real wages rose, unemployment declined. The United States was as rich as all Europe; perhaps 40 percent of the world's total wealth lay in American hands. Little wonder that business leaders and other conservatives described the period as a "new era."

The prosperity rested on many bases, one of which was the friendly, hands-off attitude of the federal government, which bolstered the confidence of the business community. The Federal Reserve Board kept interest rates low, a further stimulus to economic growth. Pent-up wartime demand helped to power the boom; the construction business in particular profited from a series of extremely busy years. The continuing mechanization and rationalization of industry provided a more fundamental stimulus to the economy. From heavy road-grading equipment and concrete mixers to devices for making cigars and glass tubes, from pneumatic tools to the dial telephone, machinery was replacing human hands at an ever more rapid rate. Industrial output almost doubled between 1921 and 1929 without any substantial increase in the industrial labor force. Greater use of power, especially of electricity, also encouraged expansion—by 1929 the United States was producing more electricity than the rest of the world combined.

The Age of the Consumer

The growing ability of manufacturers to produce goods meant that great effort had to be made to create new consumer demands. Advertising and salesmanship were raised almost to the status of fine arts. Bruce Barton, one of the advertising "geniuses" of the era, wrote a best-selling book, *The Man Nobody Knows* (1925), in which he described Jesus as the "founder of modern business," the man who "picked up twelve men from the bottom ranks . . . and forged them into an organization that conquered the world."

Producers concentrated on making their goods more attractive and on changing models frequently to entice buyers into the market. The practice of selling goods on the installment plan helped bring expensive items within the reach of the

This 1925 magazine advertisement for a Cadillac Coach shows how twentieth-century businesses sought to link nineteenth-century symbols of wealth (horseback riding, the coat-of-arms of nobility, flower gardens) with symbolic expressions of modernity, encapsulated by the independence of short-haired, fashionably dressed young women.

The Human Desire to Own the Best   Suggests *the* Cadillac

Own the Car You Long Have Wanted

Value more remarkable than that of this fine Cadillac Coach is simply not to be had in the motor car market.

For Cadillac has built—not merely a closed car at open car price—but a closed car in which outstanding value, quality and beauty go hand in hand.

Those who have viewed the Coach, who have observed the elegance and comfort of its large five-passenger body and experienced the powerful, vibrationless performance of the V-63 eight-cylinder chassis, tell us that the car confers new meaning upon Coach design.

And so, in steadily increasing numbers, discriminating purchasers are acquiring this fine Cadillac Coach, fulfilling their desire to own the best.

$3185
f. o. b. Detroit

CADILLAC MOTOR CAR COMPANY, DETROIT, MICHIGAN
Division of General Motors Corporation

C A D I L L A C   C O A C H

masses. Inventions and technological advances created new or improved products: radios, automobiles, electric appliances such as vacuum cleaners and refrigerators, gadgets like cigarette lighters, and new forms of entertainment like motion pictures. These influences interacted much as the textile industry in the early nineteenth century and the railroad industry after the Civil War had been the "multipliers" of their times.

Undoubtedly the automobile had the single most important impact on the nation's economy in the 1920s. Although well over a million cars a year were being regularly produced by 1916, the real expansion of the industry came after 1921. Output reached 3.6 million in 1923 and fell below that figure only twice during the remainder of the decade. By 1929, 23 million private cars clogged the highways, an average of nearly one per family.

The auto industry created industries that manufactured tires and spark plugs and other products. It consumed immense quantities of rubber, paint, glass, nickel, and petroleum products. It triggered a gigantic road-building program: there were 387,000 miles of paved roads in the United States in 1921, 662,000 miles in 1929. Thousands of persons found employment in filling stations, roadside stands, and other businesses catering to the motoring public. The tourist industry profited, and the shift of population from the cities to the suburbs was accelerated.

The automobile made life more mobile yet also more encapsulated. It changed recreational patterns and family life. It created a generation of tinkerers and amateur mechanics and explorers. In addition, it profoundly affected the way

Americans thought. It gave them a freedom never before imagined. The owner of the most rickety jalopy could travel further, faster, and far more comfortably than a monarch of old with his pureblooded steeds and gilded coaches.

These benefits were real and priceless. But cars became important symbols. They gave their owners the feeling of power and status that a horse gave to a medieval knight. According to some authorities the typical American cared more about owning an automobile than a house.

In time there were undesirable, even dangerous results of the automotive revolution: roadside scenery disfigured by billboards, gas stations, and other enterprises aimed at satisfying the traveler's needs; horrendous traffic jams; soaring accident rates; air pollution; the neglect of public transportation, which was an important cause of the deterioration of inner cities. All these disadvantages were noticed during the 1920s, but in the springtime of the new industry they were discounted. The automobile seemed an unalloyed blessing—part toy, part tool, part symbol of American freedom, prosperity, and individualism.

Henry Ford

The person most responsible for the growth of the automobile industry was Henry Ford, a self-taught mechanic from Greenfield, Michigan. Ford was neither a great inventor nor one of the true automobile pioneers. He was not even the first person to manufacture a good low-priced car (that being the achievement of Ransom E. Olds, producer of the "Merry Oldsmobile"). Ford's first brilliant insight was to "get the prices down to the buying power." Through mass production, cars could be made cheaply enough to put them within reach of the ordinary citizen. In 1908 he designed the Model T Ford, a simple, tough box on wheels. In a year he proved his point by selling 11,000 Model T's. Relentlessly cutting costs and increasing efficiency with the assembly line system, he expanded production at an unbelievable rate. By 1925 he was turning out more than 9,000 cars a day, one approximately every 10 seconds, and the price of the Model T had been reduced below $300.

Ford's second insight was the importance of high wages in stimulating output (and selling more automobiles). The assembly line simplified the laborer's task and increased the pace of work; at the same time it made each worker much more productive. Jobs became boring and fatiguing, absenteeism and labor turnover serious problems. To combat this difficulty, in 1914 Ford established the $5 day, an increase of about $2 over prevailing wages. The rate of turnover in his plant fell 90 percent, and although critics charged that he recaptured his additional labor costs by speeding up the line, his policy had a revolutionary effect on wage rates. Later he raised the minimum to $6 and then to $7 a day.

Ford's profits soared along with sales; since he owned the entire company, he became a billionaire. He also became an authentic folk hero: his homespun style, his dislike of bankers and sophisticated society, and his intense individualism endeared him to millions. He stood as a symbol of the wonders of the American system—he had given the nation a marvelous convenience at a low price, at the same time enriching himself and raising the living standards of his thousands of employees.

Success made Ford stubborn. The Model T remained essentially unchanged for nearly 20 years. Other companies, notably General Motors, were soon turning out better vehicles for very little more money. Customers, increasingly affluent and style-conscious, began to shift to Chevrolets and Chryslers. Finally, in 1927, Ford shut down all operations for 18 months in order to retool for the Model A. His competitors rushed in during this period to fill the vacuum. Although his company continued to make a great deal of money, Ford never regained the dominant position he had held for so long.

Ford was enormously uninformed, yet—because of his success and the praise the world heaped on him—he did not hesitate to speak out on subjects far outside his area of competence, from the evils of drink and tobacco to medicine and international affairs. He developed political ambitions and published virulent anti-Semitic propaganda. He said he would not give 5 cents for all the art in the world.

The Airplane

Henry Ford was also an early manufacturer of airplanes, and while the airplane industry was not economically important in the 1920s, its development in that decade laid the basis for changes in lifestyles and attitudes at least as momentous as those produced by the automobile. The invention of the internal combustion gasoline engine, with its extremely high ratio of power to weight, made the airplane possible, which explains why the early experiments with "flying machines" took place at about the same time that the prototypes of the modern automobile were being manufactured. Wilbur and Orville Wright made their famous flight at Kitty Hawk, North Carolina, in 1903, five years before Ford produced his Model T. Another pair of brothers, Malcolm and Haimes Lockheed, built their Model G, one of the earliest commercial planes (commercial in the sense that they used it to take passengers up at $5 a ride) in 1913.

The Great War speeded the advance of airplane technology, and most of the planes built in the 1920s were intended for military use. Practical commercial air travel was long delayed. Aerial acrobats, parachute jumpers, wing walkers, and other daredevils who put on shows at county fairs and similar places where crowds gathered were the principal civilian aviators of the 1920s. They "barnstormed" from town to town, living the same kind of inbred, encapsulated lives that circus people did, their chief rewards being the sense of independence and pride that the successful performance of their highly skilled but risky trade provided.

The great event of the decade for aviation, still an achievement that must strike awe in the hearts of reflective persons, was Charles A. Lindbergh's nonstop flight from New York to Paris in May 1927. It took more than 33 hours for Lindbergh's single-engine *Spirit of St. Louis* to cross the Atlantic, a formidable physical achievement for the pilot as well as an example of skill and courage. When the public learned that the intrepid "Lucky Lindy" was handsome, modest, uninterested in converting his new fame into cash, and a model of propriety (he neither drank nor smoked), his role as American hero was ensured. It was a role Lindbergh detested—one biographer has described him as "by nature solitary"—but could not avoid.

Lindbergh's flight enormously increased public interest in flying, but it was a landmark in aviation technology as well. The day of routine passenger flights was at last about to dawn. In July 1927, a mere two months after the *Spirit of St. Louis* touched down at Le Bourget Field in France, William E. Boeing of Boeing Air Transport began flying passengers and mail between San Francisco and Chicago, using the M–40, a plane of his own design and manufacture. Early in 1928 he changed the company name to United Aircraft and Transport. Two years later Boeing produced the first all-metal low-wing plane and, in 1933, the twin-engine 247, a prototype for many others.

In retrospect the postwar era seems even more a period of transition than it appeared to most people at the time. Rarely had change come so swiftly, and rarely had old and new existed side by side in such profusion. Creativity and reaction, hope and despair, freedom and repression—the modern world in all its unfathomable complexity was emerging.

Milestones

1903	Wright brothers fly at Kitty Hawk, N.C.
1908	Henry Ford designs Model T automobile
1914	Ford establishes $5 day for autoworkers
1919	Eighteenth Amendment outlaws alcoholic beverages (Prohibition)
	Nineteenth Amendment gives women right to vote
1920	Sinclair Lewis publishes *Main Street*
	First commercial radio station, KDKA, Pittsburgh, begins broadcasting
1920s	Black culture flourishes in Harlem Renaissance
1921	Margaret Sanger founds American Birth Control League
1923	Supreme Court overturns law limiting women's work hours (*Adkins v. Children's Hospital*)
1924	Ku Klux Klan membership peaks
1925	Scopes is convicted for teaching evolution
	F. Scott Fitzgerald publishes *The Great Gatsby*
1926	Gertrude Ederle swims English Channel
	Ernest Hemingway publishes *The Sun Also Rises*
	Charles Lindbergh flies solo across Atlantic
	Sacco and Vanzetti are executed
	The Jazz Singer, the first motion picture with sound, is released
	Jack Dempsey loses heavyweight boxing title to Gene Tunney

CHAPTER 25

The New Era: 1921–1933

O N DECEMBER 5, 2005, GREG HOGAN JR., PRESIDENT OF THE Lehigh University Class of 2008, walked into a Wachovia Bank and gave the teller a note saying that he had a gun and wanted cash. She looked at him searchingly. He managed a menacing stare. Then she pushed a tray of money toward him. He stuffed a sheaf of bills—$2,871, it turned out—into a backpack and fled. Within hours he was arrested for bank robbery. Later he was convicted and sent to Graterford maximum security prison to serve a 22-month term.

Hogan stole the money to feed his addiction: an online poker game called Texas Hold'em. Hogan's addiction, though extreme, is by no means unusual. Online casinos target college students, nearly all of whom have credit cards and ready access to the Internet. An ad in CollegeHumor.com shows pictures of students playing online poker during a lecture. The caption reads: "Gambling while in class. Who doesn't think that wireless Internet is the greatest invention ever?"

The strategy has paid off. The Annenberg Public Policy Center at the University of Pennsylvania estimated that nearly one-tenth of college students gamble online. A survey by the University of Connecticut Health Center found that one-fourth of online college bettors fit the clinical definition of a pathological gambler. Although federal officials say that all online gambling in the United States is illegal, online gambling has increased exponentially since 2003, when Chris Moneymaker won the 2003 World Series of Poker—and $2.5 million.

During the 1920s, all forms of gambling were illegal in the United States. But in that decade another form of betting swept the nation: investing in the stock market, often on borrowed money. "We have become a nation of gamblers," declared a Columbia economist, "betting recklessly on stocks." The stock market collapse in 1929 triggered the Great Depression. A government study concluded that the "feverish and exciting atmosphere" of the stock market had "kindled and magnified the urge for gambling."

The Great Depression came as a shock. In 1924 Commerce Secretary Herbert Hoover had proclaimed "a new era" in which cutthroat competition was being superseded by cooperative associations of producers. This heralded "infinite possibilities of moral progress." Such words perhaps sounded hollow, coming in the wake of a Harding administration disgraced by scandal. By 1924 Calvin Coolidge was president, to be succeeded by Hoover in 1929; both presided over a nation that basked in the dawn of a prosperous new era, shadowed only by the threat of another European war. Many Americans, giddy over their stock market winnings, placed more and more bets on Wall Street. When it all went bust, many found themselves mired in the depths of the Great Depression.

Harding and "Normalcy"

Warren G. Harding was a newspaperman by trade, publisher of the *Marion Star*, with previous political experience as a legislator and lieutenant governor in his home state, Ohio, and as a U.S. senator. No president, before or since, looked more like a statesman; few were less suited for running the country.

Harding won the 1920 Republican nomination because the party convention could not decide between General Leonard Wood, who represented the Theodore Roosevelt progressives, and Frank Lowden, governor of Illinois. Harding's genial

Warren G. Harding looked presidential, and his voice was suitably deep and resonant. Yet he lacked mental agility and discipline. Republican Senator Frank Brandegee explained Harding's nomination by proclaiming him "the best of the second-raters," and thus the natural compromise between contending factions in the party.

nature and lack of strong convictions made him attractive to many of the politicos after eight years of the headstrong Wilson. During the campaign he exasperated sophisticates by his ignorance and imprecision. He coined the famous vulgarism *normalcy* as a substitute for the word *normality*; referred, during a speech before a group of actors, to Shakespeare's play "Charles the Fifth," and committed numerous other blunders. "Why does he not get a private secretary who can clothe . . . his 'ideas' in the language customarily used by educated men?" one Boston gentleman demanded of Senator Lodge, who was strongly supporting Harding. Lodge, ordinarily a stickler for linguistic exactitude, replied acidly that he found Harding a paragon by comparison with Wilson, "a man who wrote English very well without ever saying anything." A large majority of the voters, untroubled by the candidate's lack of erudition, shared Lodge's confidence that Harding would be a vast improvement over Wilson.

As president, Harding tuned the most important government departments over to efficient administrators of impeccable reputation: Charles Evans Hughes as Secretary of State, Herbert Hoover as Secretary of Commerce, Andrew Mellon as Secretary of the Treasury, and Henry C. Wallace as Secretary of Agriculture. He kept track of what these men did but seldom initiated policy in their areas. However, Harding gave many other offices, including some of major importance, to the unsavory "Ohio Gang" headed by Harry M. Daugherty, whom he named Attorney General.

The president was too kindly, too well-intentioned, and too unambitious to be dishonest. He appointed corrupt officials like Daugherty, Secretary of the Interior Albert B. Fall, Director of the Mint "Ed" Scobey, and Charles R. Forbes, head of the new Veterans Bureau, out of a sense of personal obligation or because they were old friends who shared his taste for poker and liquor. Before 1921 he had enjoyed officeholding; but in the White House he found only misery. "The White House is a prison," he complained. "I can't get away from the men who dog my footsteps. I am in jail."

"The Business of the United States Is Business"

Secretary of the Treasury Mellon, multimillionaire banker and master of the aluminum industry, dominated the administration's domestic policy. Mellon set out to lower the taxes of the rich, reverse the low-tariff policies of the Wilson period, return to the laissez-faire philosophy of McKinley, and reduce the national debt by cutting expenses and administrating the government more efficiently.

In principle his program had considerable merit, yet Mellon carried his policies to unreasonable extremes. He proposed eliminating inheritance taxes and reducing the tax on high incomes by two-thirds, but he opposed lower rates for taxpayers earning less than $66,000 a year, apparently not realizing that economic expansion required greater mass consumption as well. Freeing the rich from "oppressive" taxation, he argued, would enable them to invest more in potentially productive enterprises, the success of which would create jobs for ordinary people.

Mellon's tax and tariff program ran into stiff opposition from midwestern Republicans and southern Democrats, who combined to form the so-called farm bloc. The farm bloc represented a kind of conservative populism, economic grievances combining with a general prejudice against "Wall Street financiers" and rich industrialists to unite agriculture against "the interests." Mellon epitomized everything the farm bloc disliked and their representatives in Congress pared back most of his proposals.

Mellon nevertheless succeeded in balancing the budget and reducing the national debt by an average of over $500 million a year. So committed were the Republican leaders to retrenchment that they even resisted the demands of veterans, organized in the politically potent American Legion, for an "adjusted compensation" bonus.

That the business community heartily approved the policies of Harding and Coolidge is not surprising. Both presidents were uncritical advocates of the business point of view. "We want less government in business and more business in government," Harding pontificated, to which Coolidge added, "The business of the United States is business." Harding and Coolidge used their power of appointment to convert regulatory bodies like the Interstate Commerce Commission (ICC) and the Federal Reserve Board into probusiness agencies that ceased almost entirely to restrict the activities of the industries they were supposed to be controlling.

The Harding Scandals

At least Mellon was honest. That could not be said of Daugherty and the Ohio Gang. The worst scandal involved Secretary of the Interior Fall, a former senator. In 1921 Fall arranged with the complaisant Secretary of the Navy Edwin Denby for the transfer to the Interior Department of government oil reserves being held for the future use of the navy. He then leased these properties to private oil companies. Edward L. Doheny's Pan-American Petroleum Company got the Elk Hills reserve in California; the Teapot Dome reserve in Wyoming was turned over to Harry F. Sinclair's Mammoth Oil Company. When critics protested, Fall explained that it was necessary to develop the Elk Hills and Teapot Dome properties because adjoining private drillers were draining off the navy's oil. Nevertheless, in 1923 the Senate ordered a full-scale investigation, conducted by Senator Thomas J. Walsh of Montana. It soon came out that Doheny had "lent" Fall $100,000 in hard cash, handed over secretly in a "little black bag." Sinclair had given Fall over $300,000 in cash and negotiable securities.

Although the three culprits escaped conviction on the charge of conspiring to defraud the government, Sinclair was sentenced to nine months in jail for contempt of the Senate and for tampering with a jury, and Fall was fined $100,000 and given a year in prison for accepting a bribe. In 1927 the Supreme Court revoked the leases and the two reserves were returned to the government.

The public still knew little of the scandals when, in June 1923, Harding left Washington on a speaking tour that included a visit to Alaska. His health was poor and his spirits low, for he had begun to understand how his "Goddamn friends" had betrayed him. On the return trip from Alaska, he came down with what his physician, an incompetent crony whom he had made surgeon general of the United States, diagnosed as ptomaine poisoning resulting from his having eaten a tainted Japanese crab. In fact the president had suffered a heart attack. He died in San Francisco on August 2.

Few presidents have been more deeply mourned by the people at the moment of their passing. Harding's kindly nature, his very ordinariness, increased his human appeal. Three million people viewed his coffin as it passed across the country. When the scandals came to light, sadness turned to scorn and contempt.

Coolidge Prosperity

Had he lived, Harding might well have been defeated in 1924 because of the scandals. Vice President Coolidge, unconnected with the troubles and not the type to surround himself with cronies of any kind, seemed the ideal person to clean out the corrupt officials. Coolidge was a taciturn, extremely conservative New Englander with a long record in Massachusetts politics climaxed by his inept but much admired suppression of the Boston police strike while governor. Harding had referred to him as "that little fellow from Massachusetts." Coolidge preferred to follow public opinion and hope for the best.

Coolidge defused his predecessor's scandals by replacing Harding's Attorney General Daugherty with Harlan Fiske Stone, dean of the Columbia University Law

Calvin Coolidge's quiet presidential style was a sharp contrast to the outspoken Warren Harding. When Coolidge died in 1933, humorist Dorothy Parker remarked, "How could they tell?"

School. Soon Coolidge became the darling of the conservatives. His admiration for businessmen and his devotion to laissez-faire knew no limit. "The man who builds a factory builds a temple," he said in all seriousness. "The Government can do more to remedy the economic ills of the people by a system of rigid economy in public expenditures than can be accomplished through any other action." Andrew Mellon, whom he kept on as secretary of the treasury, became his mentor in economic affairs.

Coolidge won the 1924 Republican nomination easily. The Democrats, badly split, required 103 ballots to choose a candidate. The southern wing, dry, anti-immigrant, pro-Klan, had fixed on William G. McAdoo, Wilson's secretary of the treasury. The eastern, urban, wet element supported Governor Alfred E. Smith of New York, child of the slums, a Catholic who had compiled a distinguished record in social welfare legislation. After days of futile politicking, the party compromised on John W. Davis, a conservative corporation lawyer closely allied with the Morgan banking interests.

Dismayed by the conservatism of Coolidge and Davis, Robert M. La Follette, backed by the farm bloc, the Socialist party, the American Federation of Labor, and numbers of intellectuals, entered the race as the candidate of a new Progressive party. The Progressives adopted a neopopulist platform calling for the nationalization of railroads, the direct election of the president, the protection of labor's right to bargain collectively, and other reforms.

The situation was almost exactly the opposite of 1912, when one conservative had run against two liberals and had been swamped. But times had changed. Coolidge received 15.7 million votes, Davis 8.4 million, La Follette 4.8 million. Conservatism was clearly the dominant mood of the country.

While Coolidge reigned, complacency was the order of the day. "Mr. Coolidge's genius for inactivity is developed to a very high point," the correspondent Walter Lippmann wrote. "It is a grim, determined, alert inactivity, which keeps Mr. Coolidge occupied constantly."[1] "The country," the president reported to Congress in 1928, "can regard the present with satisfaction, and anticipate the future with optimism."

Peace Without a Sword

Presidents Harding and Coolidge handled foreign relations in much the same way they managed domestic affairs. Harding deferred to senatorial prejudice against executive domination in the area and let Secretary of State Charles Evans Hughes make policy. Coolidge adopted a similar course. In directing foreign relations, they faced the obstacle of a resurgent isolationism. The carnage and apparent senselessness of the Great War convinced millions that the only way to be

---

[1]*Coolidge was physically delicate, being plagued by chronic stomach trouble. He required 10 or 11 hours of sleep a day.*

sure it would not happen again was to "steer clear" of "entanglements." That these famous words had been used by Washington and Jefferson in vastly different contexts did not deter the isolationists of the 1920s from attributing to them the same authority they gave to Scripture. On the other hand, far-flung American economic interests, the need for both raw materials for industry and foreign markets for America's growing surpluses of agricultural and manufactured goods, made close attention to and involvement in developments all over the world unavoidable.

Isolationist sentiments, therefore, did not deter the government from seeking to advance American interests abroad. The Open Door concept remained predominant; the State Department worked to obtain opportunities in underdeveloped countries for exporters and investors, hoping both to stimulate the American economy and to bring stability to "backward" nations. Although this policy sometimes roused local resentments because of the tendency of the United States to support entrenched elites while the mass of peasants and city workers lived in poverty, it also resulted in a further retreat from active interventionism.

The first important diplomatic event of the period revealed a great deal about American foreign policy after the Great War. During the war, Japan had greatly increased its influence in the Far East, especially in Manchuria, the northeastern province of warlord-dominated China. To maintain the Open Door in China, it would be necessary to check Japanese expansion. But there was little hope of restoring the old spheres of influence, which the mass of Chinese people bitterly resented. In addition, Japan, the United States, and Great Britain were engaged in expensive naval building programs, a competition none of them really wanted but from which each dared not withdraw.

In November 1921, hoping to reach a general agreement with China, Japan, and the Europeans that would keep China open to the commerce of all and slow the armaments race, Secretary of State Hughes convened a conference in Washington. By the following February the Washington Conference had drafted three major treaties and a number of lesser agreements: the Five-Power Treaty, the Four-Power Treaty, and the Nine-Power Treaty. These treaties committed major nations—including the United States—to refrain from aggression and excessive military buildups. But the treaties were uniformly toothless. The signers of the Four-Power Treaty—the United States, Great Britain, Japan, and France—agreed only to consult in case of aggression in the Pacific; they made no promises to help one another or to restrict their own freedom of action. As President Harding assured the Senate, "there [was] no commitment to armed force, no alliance, no written or moral obligation to join in defense."

The United States entered into all these agreements without realizing their full implications and not really prepared to play an active part in Far Eastern affairs. "We have no favorites in the present dog fight in China," the head of the Far Eastern division of the State Department wrote of the civil war going on there in 1924. "They all look alike to us." The Japanese soon realized that the United States would not do much to defend its interests in China.

The Peace Movement

The Americans of the 1920s wanted peace but would neither surrender their prejudices and dislikes nor build the defenses necessary to make it safe to indulge these passions. "The people have had all the war, all the taxation, and all the military service that they want," President Coolidge announced in 1925.

Peace societies flourished, among them the Carnegie Endowment for International Peace, designed "to hasten the abolition of war, the foulest blot upon our civilization," and the Woodrow Wilson Foundation, aimed at helping "the liberal forces of mankind throughout the world . . . who intend to promote peace by the means of justice." In 1923 Edward W. Bok, retired editor of the *Ladies' Home Journal*, offered a prize of $100,000 for the best workable plan for preserving international peace. He was flooded with suggestions.

The culmination of this illusory faith in preventing war by criticizing it came with the signing of the Kellogg-Briand Pact in 1928. The treaty was born in the fertile brain of French Foreign Minister Aristide Briand, who was eager to collect allies against possible attack by a resurgent Germany. In 1927 Briand proposed to Secretary of State Frank B. Kellogg that their countries agree never to go to war with each other. Kellogg found the idea as repugnant as any conventional alliance, but American isolationists and pacifists found the suggestion fascinating. They plagued Kellogg with demands that he negotiate such a treaty.

To extricate himself from this situation, Kellogg suggested that the pact be broadened to include all nations. Now Briand was angry. Like Kellogg, he saw how meaningless such a treaty would be, especially when Kellogg insisted that it be hedged with a proviso that "every nation is free at all times . . . to defend its territory from attack and it alone is competent to decide when circumstances require war in self-defense." Nevertheless, Briand too found public pressures irresistible. In August 1928, at Paris, diplomats from fifteen nations bestowed upon one another an "international kiss," condemning "recourse to war for the solution of international controversies" and renouncing war "as an instrument of national policy." Seldom has so unrealistic a promise been made by so many intelligent people. Yet most Americans considered the Kellogg-Briand Pact a milestone in the history of civilization: The Senate, habitually so suspicious of international commitments, ratified it 85 to 1.

The Good Neighbor Policy

The conflict between the desire to avoid foreign entanglements and the desire to advance American economic interests is well illustrated by events in Latin America. In dealing with this part of the world, Harding and Coolidge performed neither better nor worse than Wilson had. In the face of continued radicalism and instability in Mexico, which caused Americans with interests in land and oil rights to suffer heavy losses, President Coolidge acted with forbearance. The Mexicans were able to complete their social and economic revolution in the 1920s without significant interference by the United States.

Under Coolidge's successor, Herbert Hoover, the United States began at last to treat Latin American nations as equals. Hoover reversed Wilson's policy of trying to teach them "to elect good men." The Clark Memorandum (1930), written by Undersecretary of State J. Reuben Clark, disassociated the right of intervention in Latin America from the Roosevelt Corollary. The corollary had been an improper extension of the Monroe Doctrine, Clark declared. The right of the United States to intervene depended rather on "the doctrine of self-preservation."

The distinction seemed slight to Latin Americans, but since it seemed unlikely that the existence of the United States could be threatened in the area, it was important. By 1934 the marines who had been occupying Nicaragua, Haiti, and the Dominican Republic had all been withdrawn and the United States had renounced the right to intervene in Cuban affairs, thereby abrogating the Platt Amendment to the Cuban constitution. Instead of functioning as the policeman for the region, the United States would be its "good neighbor." Unfortunately, the United States did little to try to improve social and economic conditions in the Caribbean region, so the underlying envy and resentment of "rich Uncle Sam" did not disappear.

The Totalitarian Challenge

The futility and danger of isolationism were exposed in September 1931 when the Japanese, long dominant in Chinese Manchuria, marched in an army and converted the province into a puppet state named Manchukuo. This action violated both the Kellogg-Briand and Nine-Power pacts. China, now controlled by General Chiang Kai-shek, appealed to the League of Nations and to the United States for help. Neither would intervene. When League officials asked about the possibility of

Japanese troops advance through the ruins of the Chinese city of Shanghai in March 1932, a year after Japan had seized Manchuria. Five years later, Japan embarked on the conquest of all of China.

American cooperation in some kind of police action, President Hoover refused to consider either economic or military reprisals. The United States was not a world policeman, he said. The Nine-Power and Kellogg-Briand treaties were "solely moral instruments."

The League sent a commission to Manchuria to investigate. Henry L. Stimson, Hoover's secretary of state, announced (the Stimson Doctrine) that the United States would never recognize the legality of seizures made in violation of American treaty rights. This proclamation served only to irritate the Japanese.

In January 1932 Japan attacked Shanghai, the bloody battle marked by the indiscriminate bombing of residential districts. When the League at last officially condemned their aggressions, the Japanese withdrew from the organization and extended their control of northern China. The lesson of Manchuria was not lost on Adolf Hitler, who became chancellor of Germany on January 30, 1933.

War Debts and Reparations

The democracies did not take a strong stand against Japan in part because they were quarreling about other matters. Particularly divisive was the controversy over war debts—those of Germany to the Allies and those of the Allies to the United States. The United States had lent more than $10 billion to its comrades in arms. Since most of this money had been spent on weapons and other supplies in the United States, it might well have been considered part of America's contribution to the war effort. The public, however, demanded full repayment—with interest. "These were loans, not contributions," Secretary of the Treasury Mellon firmly declared.

Repayment of such a sum was virtually impossible. In the first place, the money had not been put to productive use. Dollars lent to build factories or roads might be expected to earn profits for the borrower, but those devoted to the purchase of shells only destroyed wealth. Furthermore, the American protective tariff reduced the ability of the Allies to earn the dollars needed to pay the debts.

The Allies tried to load their obligations to the United States, along with the other costs of the war, on the backs of the Germans. They demanded that the Germans pay reparations amounting to $33 billion. If this sum were collected, they declared, they could rebuild their economies and obtain the international exchange needed to pay their debts to the United States. But Germany was reluctant even to try to pay such huge reparations, and when Germany defaulted, so did the Allies.

Everyone shared the blame: the Germans because they resorted to a runaway inflation that reduced the mark to less than one trillionth of its prewar value, at least in part in hopes of avoiding their international obligations; the Americans because they refused to recognize the connection between the tariff and the debt question; the Allies because they made little effort to pay even a reasonable proportion of their obligations.

Because of hyperinflation, German bank notes were worth little more than the paper they were printed on. These German boys use them to make a kite.

In 1924 an international agreement, the Dawes Plan, provided Germany with a $200 million loan designed to stabilize its currency. Germany agreed to pay about $250 million a year in reparations. In 1929 the Young Plan further scaled down the reparations bill. In practice, the Allies paid the United States about what they collected from Germany. Since Germany got the money largely from private American loans, the United States would have served itself and the rest of the world far better had it written off the war debts at the start. In any case, in the late 1920s Americans stopped lending money to Germany, the Great Depression struck, Germany defaulted on its reparations payments, and the Allies then gave up all pretense of meeting their obligations to the United States. The last token payments were made in 1933. All that remained was a heritage of mistrust and hostility.

The Election of 1928

Meanwhile, dramatic changes had occurred in the United States. The climax of Coolidge prosperity came in 1928. The president—somewhat cryptically, as was his wont—decided not to run again, and Secretary of Commerce Hoover, whom he detested, easily won the Republican nomination. Hoover was the intellectual leader, almost the philosopher, of the New Era. American capitalists, he believed, had learned to curb their selfish instincts. Voluntary trade associations could create "codes of business practice and ethics that would eliminate abuses and make for higher standards."

Herbert Hoover relaxes during the 1928 presidential campaign. "That man has been offering me advice for the last five years," President Coolidge said of his secretary of commerce, "all of it bad."

Although stiff and uncommunicative and entirely without experience in elective office, Hoover made an admirable candidate in 1928. His roots in the Midwest and West (Iowa-born, he was raised in Oregon and educated at Stanford University in California) neatly balanced his outstanding reputation among eastern business tycoons. He took a "modern" approach to both capital and labor; businessmen should cooperate with one another and with their workers too. He opposed both union busting and trustbusting. His career as a mining engineer had given him a wide knowledge of the world, yet he had become highly critical of Europe—which disarmed the isolationists, who might otherwise have suspected that his long years abroad had made him an effete cosmopolite.

The Democrats, having had their fill of factionalism in 1924, could no longer deny the nomination to Governor Al Smith. Superficially, Smith was Hoover's antithesis. Born and raised in New York's Lower East Side slums, affable, witty, determinedly casual of manner, he had been schooled in machine politics by Tammany Hall. He was a Catholic, Hoover a Quaker, a wet where Hoover supported prohibition; he dealt easily with people of every race and nationality, while Hoover had little interest in and less knowledge of blacks and immigrants. However, like Hoover, Smith managed to combine a basic conservatism with humanitarian concern for the underprivileged. As adept in administration as Hoover, he was equally uncritical of the American capitalist system.

In the election Hoover won a smashing triumph, 444 to 87 in the Electoral College, 21.4 million to 14 million in the popular vote. All the usually Democratic border states and even North Carolina, Florida, and Texas went to the Republicans, along with the entire West and the Northeast save for Massachusetts and Rhode Island.

After this defeat the Democratic party appeared on the verge of extinction. Nothing could have been further from the truth. The religious question and his big-city roots had hurt Smith, but the chief reason he lost was prosperity—and the good times were soon to end. Hoover's overwhelming victory also concealed a political realignment that was taking place. Working-class voters in the cities, largely Catholic and unimpressed by Coolidge prosperity, had swung heavily to the Democrats. In 1924 the twelve largest cities had been solidly Republican; in 1928 all went Democratic. In agricultural states like Iowa, Smith ran far better than Davis had in 1924, for Coolidge's vetoes of bills designed to raise farm prices had caused considerable resentment. A new coalition of urban workers and dissatisfied farmers was in the making.

Economic Problems

The American economic system of the 1920s had grave flaws. Certain industries did not share in the good times. The coal business, suffering from the competition of petroleum, entered a period of decline. Cotton and woolen textiles also lagged because of the competition of new synthetics, principally rayon. Industry began to be plagued by falling profit margins and chronic unemployment.

The movement toward consolidation in industry, somewhat checked during the latter part of the progressive era, resumed; by 1929, 200 corporations controlled nearly half the nation's corporate assets. General Motors, Ford, and Chrysler turned out nearly 90 percent of all American cars and trucks. Four tobacco companies produced over 90 percent of the cigarettes. One percent of all financial institutions controlled 46 percent of the nation's banking business. Even retail merchandising, traditionally the domain of the small shopkeeper, reflected the trend. The A & P food chain expanded from 400 stores in 1912 to 17,500 in 1928. The Woolworth chain of five-and-ten-cent stores experienced similar growth.

Most large manufacturers, aware that bad public relations resulting from the unbridled use of monopolistic power outweighed any immediate economic gain, sought stability and "fair" prices rather than the maximum profit possible at the moment. "Regulated" competition was the order of the day, dominance by a few large manufacturers the typical situation. The trade association movement flourished; producers formed voluntary organizations to exchange information, discuss policies toward government and the public, and "administer" prices in their industry. Usually the largest corporation, such as U.S. Steel in the iron and steel business, became the "price leader," its competitors, some themselves giants, following slavishly.

The success of the trade associations depended in part on the attitude of the federal government, for such organizations might well have been attacked under the antitrust laws. Their defenders, including President Harding, argued that the associations made business more efficient and prevented violent fluctuations of prices and production. Secretary of Commerce Hoover put the facilities of his department at the disposal of the associations. "We are passing from a period of extremely individualistic action into a period of associational activities," Hoover stated. After Coolidge became president, the Antitrust Division of the Justice

Department itself encouraged the trade associations to cooperate in ways that had previously been considered violations of the Sherman Anti-Trust Act.

Even more important to the trade associations were the good times. With profits high and markets expanding, the most powerful producers could afford to share the bounty with smaller, less efficient competitors.

The weakest element in the economy was agriculture. Farm prices slumped and farmers' costs mounted. Besides having to purchase expensive machinery in order to compete, farmers were confronted by high foreign tariffs and in some cases quotas on the importation of foodstuffs. As crop yields per acre rose, chiefly because of the increased use of chemical fertilizers, agricultural prices fell further.

Despite the efforts of the farm bloc, the government did little to improve the situation. President Harding opposed direct aid to agriculture as a matter of principle. "Every farmer is a captain of industry," he declared. "The elimination of competition among them would be impossible without sacrificing that fine individualism that still keeps the farm the real reservoir from which the nation draws so many of the finest elements of its citizenship." During his administration Congress strengthened the laws regulating railroad rates and grain exchanges and made it easier for farmers to borrow money, but it did nothing directly to increase agricultural income. Nor did the high tariffs on agricultural produce have much effect. Being forced to sell their surpluses abroad, farmers found that world prices depressed domestic prices despite the tariff wall.

Thus the unprecedented prosperity rested on unstable foundations. The problem was mainly one of maldistribution of resources. Productive capacity raced ahead of buying power. Too large a share of the profits was going into too few pockets. The 27,000 families with the highest annual incomes in 1929 received as much money as the 11 million with annual incomes of under $1500, the minimum sum required at that time to maintain a family decently. High earnings and low taxes permitted huge sums to pile up in the hands of individuals who did not invest the money productively. A good deal of it went into stock market speculation, which led to the "big bull market" and eventually to the Great Depression.

The Stock Market Crash of 1929

In the spring of 1928, prices on the New York Stock Exchange, already at a historic high, began to surge ahead. As the presidential campaign gathered momentum, the market increased its upward pace, stimulated by the candidates' efforts to outdo each other in praising the marvels of the American economic system. "Glamour" stocks skyrocketed—Radio Corporation of America rose from under 100 to 400 between March and November. A few conservative brokers expressed alarm, warning that most stocks were grossly overpriced. The majority scoffed at such talk. "Be a bull on America," they urged. "Never sell the United States short."

During the first half of 1929 stock prices climbed still higher. A mania for speculation swept the country, thousands of small investors putting their savings in common stocks. Then, in September the market wavered. Amid volatile fluctuations stock averages eased downward. Most analysts contended that the stock exchange was "digesting" previous gains. A Harvard economist expressed the prevailing view when he said that stock prices had reached a "permanently high plateau" and would soon resume their advance.

On October 24 a wave of selling sent prices spinning. Nearly 13 million shares changed hands—a record. Bankers and politicians rallied to check the decline, as they had during the Panic of 1907. J. P. Morgan Jr. rivaled the efforts of his father in that earlier crisis. President Hoover assured the people that "the business of the country . . . is on a sound and prosperous basis." But on October 29, the bottom seemed to drop out. More than 16 million shares were sold, prices plummeting. The boom was over.

Hoover and the Depression

The collapse of the stock market did not cause the Depression; stocks rallied late in the year, and business activity did not begin to decline significantly until the spring of 1930. The Great Depression was a worldwide phenomenon caused chiefly by economic imbalances resulting from the chaos of the Great War. In the United States too much wealth had fallen into too few hands, with the result that consumers were unable to buy all the goods produced. The trouble came to a head mainly because of the easy-credit policies of the Federal Reserve Board and the Mellon tax structure, which favored the rich. Its effects were so profound and prolonged because the politicians (and for that matter the professional economists) did not fully understand what was happening or what to do about it.

The chronic problem of underconsumption operated to speed the downward spiral. Unable to rid themselves of mounting inventories, manufacturers closed plants and laid off workers, thereby causing demand to shrink further. Automobile output fell from 4.5 million units in 1929 to 1.1 million in 1932. When Ford closed his Detroit plants in 1931, some 75,000 workers lost their jobs, and the decline in auto production affected a host of suppliers and middlemen as well.

The financial system cracked under the strain. More than 1,300 banks closed their doors in 1930, 3,700 more during the next two years. Each failure deprived thousands of persons of funds that might have been used to buy goods; when the Bank of the United States in New York City became insolvent in December 1930, 400,000 depositors found their savings immobilized. And of course the industrial depression worsened the depression in agriculture by further reducing the demand for American foodstuffs. Every economic indicator reflected the collapse. New investments declined from $10 billion in 1929 to $1 billion in 1932, and the national income fell from over $80 billion to under $50 billion in the same brief period. Unemployment, under 1 million at the height of the boom, rose to at least 13 million.

President Hoover was an intelligent man, experienced in business matters and knowledgeable in economics. His program for ending the Depression evolved gradually. At first he called on businessmen to maintain prices and wages. The government should cut taxes in order to increase consumers' spendable income, institute public works programs to stimulate production and create jobs for the unemployed, lower interest rates to make it easier for businesses to borrow in order to expand, and make loans to banks and industrial corporations threatened with collapse and to homeowners unable to meet mortgage payments. The president also proposed measures making it easier for farmers to borrow money, and he suggested that the government should support cooperative farm marketing schemes designed to solve the problem of overproduction. He called for an expansion of state and local relief programs and urged all who could afford it to give more to charity. Above all he tried to restore public confidence. The economy was basically healthy; the Depression was only a minor downturn; prosperity was "just around the corner."

Although Hoover's plans were theoretically sound, they failed to check the economic slide, in part because of curious limitations in his conception of how they should be implemented. He placed far too much reliance on his powers of persuasion and the willingness of citizens to act in the public interest without legal compulsion. He urged manufacturers to maintain wages and keep their factories in operation, but the manufacturers, under the harsh pressure of economic realities, soon slashed wages and curtailed output sharply. He permitted the Federal Farm Board (created under the Agricultural Marketing Act of 1929) to establish semipublic stabilization corporations with authority to buy up surplus wheat and cotton, but he refused to countenance crop or acreage controls. The stabilization corporations poured out hundreds of millions of dollars without checking falling agricultural prices because farmers increased production faster than the corporations could buy up the excess for disposal abroad.

Hoover resisted proposals to shift responsibility from state and local agencies to the federal government, despite the fact—soon obvious—that they lacked the resources to cope with the emergency. By 1932 the federal government, with Hoover's approval, was spending $500 million a year on public works projects, but because of the decline in state and municipal construction, the total public outlay fell nearly $1 billion below what it had been in 1930. More serious was his refusal, on constitutional grounds, to allow federal funds to be used for the relief of individuals. State and municipal agencies and private charities must take care of the needy.

Unfortunately the Depression was drying up the sources of private charities just as the demands on these organizations were expanding. State and municipal agencies were swamped just when their capacities to tax and borrow were shrinking. By 1932 more than 40,600 Boston families were on relief (compared with 7,400 families in 1929); in Chicago 700,000 persons—40 percent of the workforce—were unemployed. Only the national government possessed the power and the credit to deal adequately with the crisis.

Yet Hoover would not act. He set up a committee to coordinate local relief activities but insisted on preserving what he called "the principles of individual and local responsibility." For the federal government to take over relief would "lead to the super-state where every man becomes the servant of the state and real liberty is lost."

WHAT CAUSED THE GREAT DEPRESSION?

Walter Thompson, pictured below, saw his assets evaporate during the stock market collapse of 1929, forcing him to sell this snappy roadster. Like countless others, he was befuddled by what caused so much wealth to evaporate.

The first historian of the Depression wrote about it before it happened, or so some claimed. In the *Communist Manifesto* (1848) Karl Marx and Friedrich Engels had predicted that advanced industrial capitalism would lead to overproduction, wars of imperial expansion, and worsening economic depressions. The Great Depression after 1929 lent credibility to the Marxist explanation. As the Depression persisted through the decade, more historians embraced the Marxist paradigm.

But the economic revival following World War II indicated that either Marx was wrong or that capitalistic industrialism had not yet matured. Most historians now looked elsewhere for the cause of the Depression.

In 1954 economist John K. Galbraith focused on a mania for speculative investment in stocks, aggravated by easy credit policies. Other historians blamed federal policies, such as the high Smoot-Hawley tariff and the Federal Reserve's untimely constriction of credit immediately after the crash. Such measures made things worse, but none were of such a magnitude to have plunged the nation into a depression. Robert Sobel (1968) saw "no causal relationship between the events of late October 1929 and the great depression."

John Garraty (1986) showed that the Great Depression affected much of the world simultaneously. Government policies in many nations contributed to global collapse, but no one nation or policy caused it.

John K. Galbraith, *The Great Crash* (1954), Robert Sobel, *The Great Bull Market* (1968), Peter Temin, *Did Monetary Forces Cause the Great Depression?* (1976), John A. Garraty, *The Great Depression* (1986).

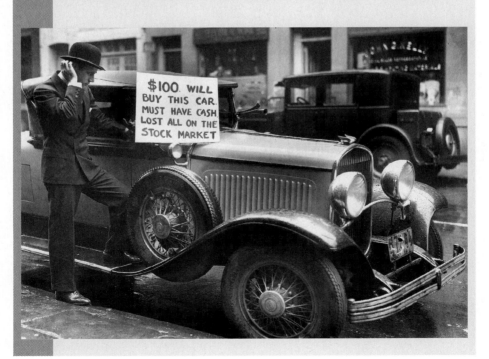

As time passed and the Depression worsened, Hoover put more stress on the importance of balancing the federal budget, reasoning that since citizens had to live within their limited means in hard times, the government should set a good example. This policy was counterproductive; by reducing its expenditures the government made the Depression worse, which reduced federal revenue further. By June 1931 the budget was nearly $500 million in the red.

Hoover understood the value of pumping money into a stagnant economy. He might have made a virtue of necessity. The difficulty lay in the fact that nearly all "informed" opinion believed that a balanced budget was essential to recovery. The most prestigious economists insisted on it; so did business leaders, labor leaders, and even most socialists. In 1932, when the House of Representatives refused to vote a tax increase, the Democratic Speaker compelled reconsideration of the bill by asking those "who do not want to balance the budget to rise." Not a single member did so. As late as 1939 a public opinion poll revealed that over 60 percent of the people (even 57.5 percent of the unemployed) favored reducing government expenditures to balance the budget. When Hoover said, "prosperity cannot be restored by raids on the public Treasury," he was mistaken, but it is equally wrong to criticize him for failing to understand what almost no one understood in the 1930s.

Much of the contemporary criticism of Hoover and a good deal of that heaped on him by later historians was unfair. Yet his record as president shows that he was too rigidly wedded to a particular theory of government to cope effectively with the problems of the day. Since these problems were in a sense insoluble—no one possessed enough knowledge to understand entirely what was wrong or enough authority to enforce corrective measures—flexibility and a willingness to experiment were essential to any program aimed at restoring prosperity. Hoover lacked these qualities. He was his own worst enemy, being too uncompromising to get on well with the politicians and too aloof to win the confidence and affection of ordinary people. He had too much faith in himself and his plans. When he failed to achieve the results he anticipated, he attracted, despite his devotion to duty and his concern for the welfare of the country, not sympathy but scorn.

The Economy Hits Bottom

During the spring of 1932, as the economy sounded the depths, thousands of Americans faced starvation. In Philadelphia during an 11-day period when no relief funds were available, hundreds of families existed on stale bread, thin soup, and garbage. In the nation as a whole, only about one-quarter of the unemployed were receiving any public aid. In Birmingham, Alabama, landlords in poor districts gave up trying to collect rents, preferring, one Alabama congressman told a Senate committee, "to have somebody living there free of charge rather than to have the house . . . burned up for fuel [by scavengers]." Many people were evicted, and they often gathered in ramshackle communities constructed of packing boxes, rusty sheet metal, and similar refuse on swamps, garbage dumps, and other wasteland. People began to call these places "Hoovervilles."

Evicted from their homes, many unemployed gravitated to vacant industrial property, where they erected hovels from scraps of lumber, tarpaper, and cardboard. This shantytown is on the outskirts of Seattle.

Thousands of tramps roamed the countryside begging and scavenging for food. At the same time, food prices fell so low that farmers burned corn for fuel. In Iowa and Nebraska farmers organized "farm holiday" movements, refusing to ship their crops to market in protest against the 31-cent-a-bushel corn and 38-cent wheat. They blocked roads and rail lines, dumped milk, overturned trucks, and established picket lines to enforce their boycott. The world seemed to have been turned upside down. Professor Felix Frankfurter of the Harvard Law School remarked only half humorously that henceforth the terms B.C. and A.D. would mean "Before Crash" and "After Depression."

The national mood ranged from apathy to resentment. In 1931 federal immigration agents and local groups in the Southwest began rounding up Mexican Americans and deporting them. Some of those returned to Mexico had entered the United States illegally; others had come in properly. Unemployed Mexicans were ejected because they might become public charges, those with jobs because they were presumably taking bread from the mouths of citizens. "Capitalism is dying," the socialist theologian Reinhold Niebuhr remarked in 1932, "and . . . it ought to die."

In June and July 1932, 20,000 World War veterans marched on Washington to demand immediate payment of their "adjusted compensation" bonuses. When Congress rejected their appeal, some 2,000 refused to leave, settling in a jerrybuilt camp of shacks and tents at Anacostia Flats, a swamp bordering the Potomac River.

In 1932, thousands of "bonus army" marchers camped outside the U.S. Capitol seeking federal assistance.

President Hoover, alarmed, charged incorrectly that the "Bonus Army" was largely composed of criminals and radicals and sent troops into the Flats to disperse it with bayonets, tear gas, and tanks. The task was accomplished amid much confusion; fortunately no one was killed. The protest had been aimless and not entirely justified, yet the spectacle of the United States government chasing unarmed veterans with tanks appalled the nation.

The unprecedented severity of the Depression led some persons to favor radical economic and political changes. The disparity between the lots of the rich and the poor, always a challenge to democracy, became more striking and engendered considerable bitterness. "Unless something is done to provide employment," two labor leaders warned Hoover, "disorder . . . is sure to arise. . . . There is a growing demand that the entire business and social structure be changed because of the general dissatisfaction with the present system."

The Communist party gained few converts among farmers and industrial workers, but a considerable number of intellectuals, alienated by the trends of the 1920s, responded positively to the communists' emphasis on economic planning and the total mobilization of the state to achieve social goals. Even the cracker-barrel humorist Will Rogers was impressed by reports of the absence of serious unemployment in Russia. "All roads lead to Moscow," the former muckraker Lincoln Steffens wrote.

The Depression and Its Victims

The Depression affected the families of the jobless in many ways. It caused a dramatic drop in the birthrate, from 27.7 per thousand population in 1920 to 18.4 per thousand in the early 1930s, the lowest in American history. Sometimes it strengthened family ties. Some unemployed men spent more time with their children and helped their wives with cooking and housework. Others, however, became impatient when their children demanded attention, refused to help around the house, sulked, or took to drink.

The influence of wives in families struck by unemployment tended to increase, and in this respect women suffered less psychologically from the Depression. They were usually too busy trying to make ends meet to become apathetic. But the way they used this influence varied. Some wives were sympathetic, others scornful, when the "breadwinner" came home with empty hands. When the wife of an unemployed man managed to find a job, the result could be either gratitude and pride or bitter resentment on the man's part, resentment or a sense of liberation on the woman's.

Children often caused strains in families. Parental authority declined when there was less money available to supply children's needs. Some youngsters became angry when their allowance was cut or when told they could not have something they particularly wanted. Some adolescents found part-time jobs to help out. Others refused to go to school. If there is any generalization about the effects of the Depression on family relations it is probably an obvious one—where relationships were close and loving they became stronger, where they were not, the results could be disastrous.

The Election of 1932

As the end of his term approached, President Hoover seemed to grow daily more petulant and pessimistic. The Depression, coming after 12 years of Republican rule, probably ensured a Democratic victory in any case, but his attitude as the election neared alienated many voters and turned defeat into rout.

Confident of victory, the Democrats chose Governor Franklin Delano Roosevelt of New York as their presidential candidate. Roosevelt owed his nomination chiefly to his success as governor. Under his administration, New York had led the nation in providing relief for the needy and had enacted an impressive program of old-age pensions, unemployment insurance, and conservation and public power projects. In 1928, while Hoover was carrying New York against Smith by a wide margin, Roosevelt won election by 25,000 votes. In 1930 he swept the state by a 700,000-vote majority, double the previous record. He also had the advantage of the Roosevelt name (he was a distant cousin of the inimitable TR), and his sunny, magnetic personality contrasted favorably with that of the glum and colorless Hoover.

Two boys, barefoot, at a clinic in Arkansas. In 1914 a Rockefeller Foundation study determined that hookworm, which caused debilitating anemia in the rural South, commonly entered the body through the feet. Although Arkansas legislators denounced the study as a plot to make its children buy northern shoes, the Rockefeller Foundation persisted in the campaign, which was backed by federal health officials in the 1930s.

Roosevelt was far from being a radical. Although he had supported the League of Nations while campaigning for the vice presidency in 1920, during the 1920s he had not seriously challenged the basic tenets of Coolidge prosperity. He never had much difficulty adjusting his views to prevailing attitudes. For a time he even served as head of the American Construction Council, a trade association. Indeed, his life before the Depression gave little indication that he understood the aspirations of ordinary people or had any deep commitment to social reform.

Roosevelt was born to wealth and social status in Dutchess County, New York, in 1882. Pampered in childhood by a doting yet domineering mother, he was educated at the exclusive Groton School and then at Harvard. Ambition as much as the desire to render public service motivated his career in politics; even after an attack of polio in 1921 had badly crippled both his legs, he refused to abandon his hopes for high office. During the 1920s he was a hardworking member of the liberal wing of his party. He supported Smith for president in 1924 and 1928.

To some observers Roosevelt seemed rather a lightweight intellectually. When he ran for the vice presidency, the *Chicago Tribune* commented: "If he is Theodore Roosevelt, Elihu Root is Gene Debs, and Bryan is a brewer." Twelve years later many critics judged him too irresolute, too amiable, too eager to please all factions to be a forceful leader. Herbert Hoover thought he was "ignorant but well-meaning," and the political analyst Walter Lippmann, in a now-famous observation, called him "a pleasant man who, without any important qualifications for the job, would very much like to be President."

Despite his physical handicap—he could walk only a few steps, and then only with the aid of steel braces and two canes—Roosevelt was a marvelous campaigner. He traveled back and forth across the country, radiating confidence and

A vigorous-looking Franklin D. Roosevelt campaigning for the presidency in 1932. His vice-presidential running mate, John N. Garner, and the conveniently placed post allowed the handicapped candidate to stand when greeting voters along the way.

good humor even when directing his sharpest barbs at the Republicans. Like every great political leader, he took as much from the people as he gave them, understanding the causes of their confusion and sensing their needs. "I have looked into the faces of thousands of Americans," he told a friend. "They have the frightened look of lost children. . . They are saying: 'We're caught in something we don't understand; perhaps this fellow can help us out.'"

Roosevelt soaked up information and ideas from a thousand sources—from professors like Raymond Moley and Rexford Tugwell of Columbia, from politicians like the Texan vice-presidential candidate, John N. Garner, from social workers, businessmen, and lawyers. To those seeking specific answers to the questions of the day, he was seldom satisfying. On such vital matters as farm policy, the tariff, and government spending, he equivocated, contradicted himself, or remained silent.

Roosevelt called for a "re-appraisal of values," a "New Deal." Instead of adhering to conventional limits on the extent of federal power, the government should do whatever was necessary to protect the unfortunate and advance the public good. Lacking concrete answers, Roosevelt advocated a point of view rather than a plan: "The country needs bold, persistent experimentation. It is common sense to take a method and try it. If it fails, admit it frankly and try another. But above all, try something."

The popularity of this approach was demonstrated in November. Hoover, who had lost only eight states in 1928, won only six, all in the Northeast, in 1932. Roosevelt amassed 22.8 million votes to Hoover's 15.8 million and carried the Electoral College, 472 to 59.

During the interval between the election and Roosevelt's inauguration in March 1933, the Great Depression reached its lowest point. The holdover "lame duck" Congress, last of its kind, proved incapable of effective action.[2] President Hoover, perhaps understandably, hesitated to institute changes without the cooperation of his successor. Roosevelt, for equally plausible reasons, refused to accept responsibility before assuming power officially. The nation, curiously apathetic in the face of so much suffering, drifted aimlessly, like a sailboat in a flat calm.

Milestones

1921–1922	Washington Conference tries to slow arms race
1923	President Harding dies; Coolidge becomes president
	Teapot Dome and other Harding scandals are exposed
1924	Dawes Plan restructures German reparations payments
	National Origins Act establishes immigration quotas
	Coolidge is elected president
1928	Fifteen nations sign Kellogg-Briand Pact to "outlaw" war
	Herbert Hoover is elected president
1929	New York Stock Exchange crash ends big bull market; Great Depression begins
	Young Plan further reduces German reparations
1930	Clark Memorandum renounces Roosevelt Corollary to Monroe Doctrine
	Hawley-Smoot tariff raises duties on foreign manufactures
	Ten-year Dust Bowl begins in South and Midwest
1931	Japan invades Manchuria
	Hoover imposes moratorium on war debts
1932	Federal troops disperse Bonus Marchers in Washington, D.C.
	Reconstruction Finance Corporation (RFC) lends to banks, railroads, insurance companies
	Franklin Delano Roosevelt is elected president
1933	Japan withdraws from League of Nations

---

[2]*The Twentieth Amendment (1933) provided for convening new Congresses in January instead of the following December. It also advanced the date of the president's inauguration from March 4 to January 20.*

CHAPTER 26

The New Deal: 1933–1941

OF THE $2.4 TRILLION THE U.S. TREASURY RECEIVED IN 2006, about a third ($745 billion) came from payments to the Social Security system made by employees and employers. The Social Security Administration in turn sent monthly payments to elderly persons and provided for their medical care. It also sent checks to the children (under 18) of deceased and retired workers and to disabled workers and their children. In 2006, 49 million Americans received $555 billion. The $190 billion surplus of payments over expenditures was added to the Social Security Trust Fund, pushing it over 2 trillion dollars.

But some claim that Social Security will run out of money before they reach retirement age. In 2005 President George W. Bush warned that within thirteen years beneficiaries will receive more than is paid into the system. "And every year thereafter," he added, "the gap grows wider." By 2042, Social Security will be "bust." He proposed that workers be allowed to put a third of their Social Security (FICA) taxes into private investment accounts.

The American Association of Retired Persons (AARP), among others, disputed Bush's prediction. It insisted that Social Security was fundamentally sound unless payroll taxes were diverted into private retirement accounts. Polls show that two-thirds of Americans want to retain the existing Social Security system.

But many young people are skeptical. According to an AARP poll, only 31 percent of those between the ages of 18 and 39 believe that Social Security will be available to them on retirement. Protests have sprouted on college campuses. In 2007 students at Mount Holyoke College held a "Social Insecurity Bake Sale": Freshmen were charged $2 a cookie while seniors got them for free. Ann Coulter, a conservative pundit, went so far as to denounce Social Security as an elaborate fraud that "would have landed its innovators in a secure federal prison" had they not been government officials.

President Franklin D. Roosevelt signed the Social Security Act in 1935, the cornerstone of his "New Deal" to counteract the Great Depression. Other New Deal initiatives sought to put the unemployed to work on government projects; to use federal funds to help farmers by raising the price of agricultural products; to reorganize banks; and to alter federal regulation of corporations.

These measures generated opposition. Conservatives regarded much of the New Deal as an unconstitutional infringement of private rights; populists and Marxists denounced the New Deal as a band-aid that failed to address the root causes of poverty. Through it all, however, Roosevelt won the allegiance of voters who regarded him almost as an economic savior and the New Deal as gospel.

The Hundred Days

As the date of Franklin Roosevelt's inauguration approached, the banking system completely disintegrated. Starting in the rural West and spreading to major cities like Detroit and Baltimore, a financial panic swept the land. Depositors lined up before the doors of even the soundest institutions, desperate to withdraw their savings. Hundreds of banks were forced to close. In February, to check the panic, the governor of Michigan declared a "bank holiday," shutting every bank in the state for eight days. Maryland, Kentucky, California, and a number of other states followed suit; by inauguration day four-fifths of the states had suspended all banking operations.

Something drastic had to be done. The most conservative business leaders were as ready for government intervention as the most advanced radicals. Partisanship, while not disappearing, was for once subordinated to broad national needs. A sign of this change came in February, even before Roosevelt took office, when Congress submitted to the states the Twenty-first Amendment, putting an

A 1933 banner celebrating the repeal of prohibition.

end to prohibition. Before the end of the year the necessary three-quarters of the states had ratified it, and the prohibition era was over.

But it was unquestionably Franklin D. Roosevelt who provided the spark that reenergized the American people. His inaugural address reassured the country and at the same time stirred it to action. "The only thing we have to fear is fear itself. . . This Nation asks for action, and action now. . . . I assume unhesitatingly the leadership of this great army of our people. . . ." Many such lines punctuated the brief address, which concluded with a stern pledge: "In the event that Congress shall fail . . . I shall not evade the clear course of duty that will then confront me. I shall ask the Congress for the one remaining instrument to meet the crisis—broad Executive power to wage a war against the emergency."

Roosevelt had the power and the will to act but no comprehensive plan of action. He and his eager congressional collaborators proceeded in a dozen directions at once, sometimes wisely, sometimes not, often at cross-purposes with themselves and one another. One of the first administration measures was the Economy Act, which reduced the salaries of federal employees by 15 percent and cut various veterans' benefits. Such belt-tightening measures could only make the Depression worse.

On March 5 Roosevelt declared a nationwide bank holiday and placed an embargo on the exportation of gold. To explain the complexities of the banking problem to the public, Roosevelt delivered the first of his "fireside chats" over a national radio network. "I want to talk for a few minutes with the people of the United States about banking," he explained. His warmth and steadiness reassured millions. A plan for reopening the banks under Treasury Department licenses was devised, and soon most of them were functioning again, public confidence in their solvency restored. This solved the problem, but it also determined that banks would remain private institutions. Reform, not revolutionary change, had been decided upon at the very start of Roosevelt's presidency.

In April Roosevelt took the country off the gold standard, hoping thereby to cause prices to rise. Before the session ended, Congress established the Federal Deposit Insurance Corporation (FDIC) to guarantee bank deposits. It also forced the separation of investment banking and commercial banking concerns while extending the power of the Federal Reserve Board over both types of institutions, and it created the Home Owners Loan Corporation (HOLC) to refinance mortgages and prevent foreclosures.[1]

The National Recovery Administration (NRA)

Problems of unemployment and industrial stagnation had high priority during the Hundred Days. Congress appropriated $500 million for relief of the needy, and it created the Civilian Conservation Corps to provide jobs for men between the ages of 18 and 25 in reforestation and other conservation projects. To stimulate industry,

---

[1]In 1934 this task was transferred to the new Securities and Exchange Commission, which was given broad authority over the activities of stock exchanges.

Congress passed one of its most controversial measures, the National Industrial Recovery Act (NIRA). Besides establishing the Public Works Administration with authority to spend $3.3 billion, this law permitted manufacturers to draw up industrywide codes of "fair business practices." Under the law producers could agree to raise prices and limit production without violating the antitrust laws. The law gave workers the protection of minimum wage and maximum hours regulations and guaranteed them the right "to organize and bargain collectively through representatives of their own choosing," an immense stimulus to the union movement.

The act created a government agency, the National Recovery Administration (NRA), to supervise the drafting and operation of the business codes. Drafting posed difficult problems, first because each industry insisted on tailoring the agreements to its special needs and second because most manufacturers were unwilling to accept all the provisions of Section 7a of the law, which guaranteed workers the right to unionize and bargain collectively. While thousands of employers agreed to the pledge "We Do Our Part" in order to receive the Blue Eagle symbol of NRA, many were more interested in the monopolistic aspects of the act than in boosting wages and encouraging unionization. In practice, the largest manufacturers in each industry drew up the codes.

The effects of the NIRA were both more and less than the designers of the system had intended. In a sense it tried to accomplish the impossible—to change the very nature of business ethics and control the everyday activities of millions of individual enterprises. At the practical level, it did not end the Depression. There was a brief upturn in the spring of 1933, but the expected revival of industry did not take place; in nearly every case the dominant producers in each industry used their power to raise prices and limit production rather than to hire more workers and increase output.

Labor leaders used the NIRA to persuade workers that Roosevelt wanted them to join unions—which was something of an overstatement. In 1935, because the craft-oriented AFL had displayed little enthusiasm for enrolling unskilled workers on an industrywide basis, John L. Lewis, together with officials of the garment trade unions, formed the Committee for Industrial Organization (CIO) and set out to rally workers in each of these mass-production industries into one union without regard for craft lines. Since a union containing all the workers in a factory was easier to organize and direct than separate craft unions, this was a far more effective way of unionizing factory labor. The AFL expelled these unions, however, and in 1938 the CIO became the Congress of Industrial Organizations. Soon it rivaled the AFL in size and importance.

The Agricultural Adjustment Administration (AAA)

Roosevelt was more concerned about the plight of the farmers than that of any other group because he believed that the nation was becoming overcommitted to industry. The Agricultural Adjustment Act of May 1933 combined compulsory restrictions on production with government subsidies to growers of wheat, cotton, tobacco, pork, and a few other staple crops. The money for these payments was raised by levying processing taxes on middlemen such as flour millers. The object was to lift agricultural prices to "parity" with industrial prices, the ratio in most cases being based on the levels of 1909–1914, when farmers had been reasonably prosperous. In return for withdrawing part of their land from cultivation, farmers received "rental" payments from the Agricultural Adjustment Administration (AAA).

Thereafter, limitation of acreage proved sufficient to raise some agricultural prices considerably. Tobacco growers benefited, and so did those who raised corn and hogs. The price of wheat also rose, though more because of bad harvests than because of the AAA program. But dairy farmers and cattlemen were hurt by the law, as were the railroads (which had less freight to haul) and, of course, consumers. Many farmers insisted that the NRA was raising the cost of manufactured goods more than the AAA was raising the prices they received for their crops. "While the farmer is losing his pants to his creditors," one Iowan complained, "NRA is rolling up his shirt. [Soon] we'll have a nudist colony."

A far more serious weakness of the program was its effect on tenant farmers and sharecroppers, many of whom lost their livelihoods when owners took land out of production to obtain AAA payments. In addition many landowners substituted machinery for labor. In the Cotton Belt farmers purchased more than 100,000 tractors during the 1930s. Each could do the work of several tenant or sharecropping families. Yet acreage restrictions and mortgage relief helped thousands of others. The law was a remarkable attempt to bring order to the chaotic agricultural economy.

The Dust Bowl

A protracted drought compounded the plight of the farmers, especially in dry sections of the Midwest. During the first third of the twentieth century, Midwestern farmers perfected dryland techniques. This entailed "dragging" the fields after rainfall to improve absorption; raking them repeatedly to eliminate water-devouring weeds; and plowing the soil deeply and frequently to allow rain to sink in quickly. The use of tractors, combines, plows and trucks during the 1920s made possible this intensive working of the fields. Farmers planted the driest areas in winter wheat, which required little moisture; in Nebraska and Iowa, most farmers planted corn.

Then came the dust storms. During the winter of 1933–1934, bitter cold killed off the winter wheat and heavy storms pulverized the soil. By March 1934, driving winds whipped across the Great Plains. In April storms from the Dakotas belched great clouds of dust through Nebraska and Kansas. In May, after the fields had been plowed, more windstorms scattered the seeds and topsoil.

The summer of 1934 was dry, especially in the Dakotas and western Kansas. These farmers were accustomed to dry weather, but the topsoil had been loosened through dryland farming. Strong winds scooped up the dried-out dirt and blew it in heaving clouds throughout the Plains. Dust, forced into people's lungs, induced "dust pneumonia," a respiratory ailment that sometimes proved fatal.

Photograph by Dorothea Lange of refugees from the "dust bowl" in Oklahoma, now living in Blythe, California (1936).

The winds devastated wheat and corn. Over 30 percent of the crops in much of North Dakota, South Dakota, Nebraska, Kansas, and the Oklahoma panhandle failed. Two years later, another drought produced similar results. Coming in the midst of the Great Depression, this second calamity proved more than many farmers could bear. Tens of thousands abandoned their farms.

The Tennessee Valley Authority (TVA)

Although Roosevelt could do little about the Midwestern droughts, he did propose a major initiative to alter the economic infrastructure of the upper South. During his first Hundred Days, he proposed a Tennessee Valley Authority (TVA) to implement a broad experiment in social planning. Besides expanding hydroelectric plants at Muscle Shoals, Alabama, and developing nitrate manufacturing in order to produce cheap fertilizers, he envisioned a coordinated program of soil conservation, reforestation, and industrialization.

Over the objections of private power companies, led by Wendell L. Willkie of the Commonwealth and Southern Corporation, Congress passed the TVA Act in May 1933. This law created a board authorized to build dams, power plants, and transmission lines and to sell fertilizers and electricity to individuals and local communities. The board could undertake flood control, soil conservation, and reforestation projects and improve the navigation of the river. Although the TVA never became the comprehensive regional planning organization some of its sponsors had anticipated, it improved the standard of living of millions of inhabitants of the valley. In addition to producing electricity and fertilizers and providing a "yardstick" whereby the efficiency—and thus the rates—of private power companies could be tested, it took on other functions ranging from the eradication of malaria to the development of recreational facilities.

The Unemployed

At least 9 million persons were still without work in 1934 and hundreds of thousands of them were in real need. Malcolm Little, later famous as the radical black leader, Malcolm X, recalled:

> By 1934, we really began to suffer. This was about the worst depression year, and no one we knew had enough to eat or live on. . . . There was a bakery where, for a nickel, a couple of us children would buy a tall flour sack of day-old bread and cookies. . . . But there were times when there wasn't even a nickel and we would be so hungry we were dizzy. My mother would boil a big pot of dandelion greens and we would eat that.

Yet the Democrats confounded the political experts, including their own, by increasing their already large majorities in both houses of Congress in the 1934 elections. All the evidence indicates that most of the jobless continued to support the administration. Their loyalty can best be explained by Roosevelt's unemployment policies.

In May 1933 Congress had established the Federal Emergency Relief Administration (FERA) and given it $500 million to be dispensed through state relief organizations. Roosevelt appointed Harry L. Hopkins, an eccentric but bril-

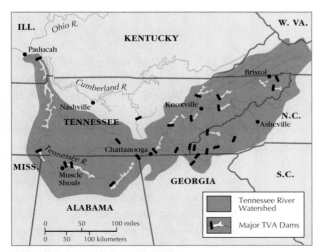

The Tennessee Valley Authority
Although the Tennessee Valley Authority (TVA) never fully became the regional planning organization its sponsors had anticipated, the TVA nevertheless was able to expand the hydroelectric plants at Muscle Shoals, Alabama, and build dams, power plants, and transmission lines to service the surrounding area.

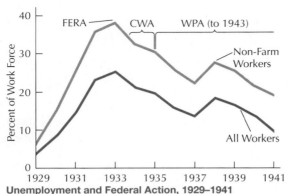

Unemployment and Federal Action, 1929–1941
Unemployment of non-farm workers reached nearly 40 percent by early 1933. The Federal Emergency Relief Act (FERA) and Civil Works Administration (CWA) (both in 1933) and the Works Progress Administration (WPA) (1935) put millions back to work.

liant and dedicated social worker, to direct the FERA. Hopkins insisted that the unemployed needed jobs, not handouts. In November he persuaded Roosevelt to create the Civil Works Administration (CWA) and swiftly put 4 million people to work building and repairing roads and public buildings, teaching, decorating the walls of post offices with murals, and utilizing their special skills in dozens of other ways.

The cost of this program frightened Roosevelt—Hopkins spent about $1 billion in less than five months—and he soon abolished the CWA. But an extensive public works program was continued throughout 1934 under the FERA. Despite charges that many of the projects were "boondoggles," thousands of roads, bridges, schools, and other structures were built or refurbished.

In May 1935 Roosevelt put Hopkins in charge of the Works Progress Administration (WPA). By the time this agency was disbanded in 1943 it had found employment for 8.5 million people. Besides building public works, the WPA made important cultural contributions. It developed the Federal Theatre Project, which put actors, directors, and stagehands to work; the Federal Writers' Project, which turned out valuable guidebooks, collected local lore, and published about 1,000 books and pamphlets; and the Federal Art Project, which employed painters and sculptors. In addition, the National Youth Administration created part-time jobs for more than 2 million high school and college students.

At no time during the New Deal years did unemployment fall below 10 percent of the workforce, and in some places it was much higher. Unemployment in Boston, for instance, ranged between 20 and 30 percent throughout the 1930s. WPA did not go far enough, chiefly because Roosevelt could not escape his fear of drastically unbalancing the budget. Halfway measures did not stimulate the economy. The president also hesitated to undertake projects that might compete with private enterprises. Yet his caution did him no good politically; the business interests he sought to placate were becoming increasingly hostile to the New Deal.

Literature During the Depression

Some American novelists found Soviet communism attractive and wrote "proletarian" novels in which ordinary workers were the heroes, and stylistic niceties gave way to the rough language of the street and the factory. Most of these books are of little artistic merit, and none achieved great commercial success. The best of the Depression writers avoided the party line, although they were critical of many aspects of American life.

One was John Dos Passos, author of the trilogy *U.S.A.* (1930–1936), a massive, intricately constructed work with an anticapitalist and deeply pessimistic point of view. Dos Passos's method was relentless, cold, and methodical—utterly realistic. He displayed no sympathy for his characters or their world. *U.S.A.* was a monument to the despair and anger of liberals confronted with the Depression. After the Depression, however, Dos Passos rapidly abandoned his radical views.

The novel that best portrayed the desperate plight of the millions impoverished by the Depression was John Steinbeck's *The Grapes of Wrath* (1939), which described the fate of the Joads, an Oklahoma farm family driven by drought and bad times to abandon their land and become migratory laborers in California. Steinbeck captured the patient bewilderment of the downtrodden, the brutality bred of fear that characterized their exploiters, and the furious resentments of the radicals of the 1930s. He depicted the parching blackness of the Oklahoma dust bowl, the grandeur of California, the backbreaking toil of the migrant fruit pickers, and the ultimate indignation of a people repeatedly degraded. "In the eyes of the hungry there is a growing wrath. In the souls of the people the grapes of wrath are filling and growing heavy, growing heavy for the vintage."

William Faulkner, among the finest American novelists of the era, responded in still another way. Born in 1897, within a year of Fitzgerald and Hemingway, he attained literary maturity only in the 1930s. Suddenly, between 1929 and 1932, he burst into prominence with four major novels: *The Sound and the Fury, As I Lay Dying, Sanctuary,* and *Light in August.*

No contemporary excelled him as a commentator on the multiple dilemmas of life. His characters are possessed, driven to pursue high ideals yet weighted down with awareness of their inadequacies and their sinfulness.

Three Extremists: Long, Coughlin, and Townsend

Roosevelt's moderation and the desperation of the poor roused extremists both on the left and on the right. The most formidable was Louisiana's Senator Huey Long, the "Kingfish." Raised on a farm in northern Louisiana, Long was successively a traveling salesman, a lawyer, state railroad commissioner, governor, and, after 1930, U.S. senator. By 1933 his rule in Louisiana was absolute. Long was certainly a

(text continues on page 732)

Cinderella Man

As *Cinderella Man* (2005) opens, boxer James J. Braddock (Russell Crowe) lands a thunderous right hook that sends his opponent sprawling to the canvas—a knockout. Braddock raises his hands in triumph. The crowd roars.

Later Braddock, in a dapper suit, emerges from Madison Square Garden and gets into a limousine with his agent, Joe Gould, who peels off a wad of bills—over $8,000— Braddock's winnings for the night. This is just the beginning, Gould says, because Braddock has a shot at the heavyweight title.

When Braddock arrives at his home in New Jersey, his wife, Mae (Renée Zellweger) leaps into his arms. "I'm so proud of you," she says. Three children pour out of the house and mob their father. Later, as Braddock prepares for bed, he sets his gold watch and thick wallet onto a polished wood dresser. The year is 1928. Abruptly, the scene dissolves. Slowly, a cheap, unfinished dresser comes into focus. The watch and wallet are gone. Braddock looks wearily around a squalid hovel. The children, on mattresses in shadows, cough and wheeze. The year is 1933. Braddock, like much of the nation, has fallen on hard times, his savings wiped out by the Depression. Worse, he broke his powerful right hand and, desperate for money, resumed boxing before it healed and he slipped out of contention. Things could hardly get worse.

But they do. During a bout in Mount Vernon, Braddock again breaks his hand but tries to finish the match in order to earn his $50 fee. The fans jeer and the boxing commission revokes his license. He tries to find work at the dockyards but is often turned away. The grocer refuses credit. The milkman stops deliveries. The power company shuts off the

Russell Crowe and Renée Zellweger in *Cinderella Man*.

gas and electricity. His children, underfed and chilled, become sick. Braddock returns to Madison Square Garden, hat in hand, and begs for money. He also applies and receives federal assistance—welfare—at $6.40 a week. By comparison, Cinderella had it easy.

Then Gould shows up with an extraordinary proposition. A huge, young bruiser and leading contender for the heavyweight title—"Corn" Griffin—had been scheduled to fight the next evening at Madison Square Garden, but his opponent has backed out. Rather than cancel the fight, Madison Square Garden has offered Braddock $250 to serve as Griffin's punching bag. Desperate for money, Braddock accepts.

What happens the next day—June 14, 1934—is the stuff of fairy tales. Braddock borrows boxing boots and heads to Madison Square Garden. When he enters the ring, his robe bears another boxer's name.

After the opening bell, Griffin, a thick-necked bull of a man, charges Braddock and hacks away at him. Braddock, sustained by raw courage, and a tough chin, survives the first two rounds. Then, in the third, he surprises Griffin with a monstrous hook, a knockout.

This shocking upset thrusts Braddock onto the list of contenders! He scores one upset after another until he faces Max Baer (Craig Bierko), the heavyweight champion whose fearsome right has killed two boxers. The manager of Madison Square Garden requires Braddock to sign a waiver absolving it of responsibility should Braddock also perish at Baer's hands. At a restaurant, Baer runs into Mae and warns her against letting her husband into the ring, adding that she's too pretty to become a widow. "Maybe I'd comfort you after he's gone," he says with a leer.

On June 13, 1935, the night of the fight, as Mae goes to church to pray, reporters speculate on whether Braddock can last a single round against the champ. The betting odds against Braddock are the worst in memory. But a movie named after a fairy tale must have a happy ending, and *Cinderella Man* comes through. After fifteen harrowing rounds, Braddock wins a unanimous decision. In 364 days, he has gone from impov-

Max Baer *(left)* and James J. Braddock in the heavyweight championship fight on June 13, 1935.

erished "bum" to heavyweight champion of the world.

"This is a true story," declared director Ron Howard. Yet fairy tales, by definition, are make-believe; and Hollywood, by reputation, believes in nothing as fervently as the dollar. Thus viewers are entitled to ask: Does *Cinderella Man* tell the actual story of James J. Braddock?

The surprising answer, given the implausibility of the plot, is yes, up to a point. And that point begins with the Baer-Braddock fight: Madison Square Garden did not warn Braddock of the danger of fighting Baer or oblige him to sign a waiver. Also, the fight was no slugfest. The *New York Times* dubbed it "one of the worst heavyweight championship contests" in boxing history. Reporters assumed that Baer failed to take the early rounds seriously, and realized too late that he was behind. But Baer was no unfeeling monster. He never teased Mae Braddock or gloated over killing two fighters in the ring. He even raised money for the first boxer's widow. Most interesting is the movie's error of omission. It makes no mention of the fact that Baer proudly trumpeted his Jewish ancestry. When he boxed, Baer had a large Star of David stitched onto his trunks, an image that appears in the movie once, briefly and from a distance.

Why did director Howard evade the truth about Baer? The likely answer is that Howard knew that fairy tales require villains as well as heroes. Cinderella Man Braddock looms larger for slaying the Big Bad Baer.

In fact, the real enemy was the Great Depression. Braddock understood this. When asked how he managed to turn his career around, he explained, "I was fighting for milk." Damon Runyon, the writer who first called Braddock "Cinderella Man," recognized that the boxer's story took on mythic proportions because it encapsulated the aspirations of an entire nation.

But the movie misses the point that many ethnic groups had their own boxing champions. After Braddock had upset Griffin, he fought Joe Louis, the Brown Bomber. While the movie rightly shows Irish Americans praying for their hero, it neglects the millions of African Americans who also gathered around radios, praying for Louis. Jewish fans, similarly, identified with Baer, cherishing his 1933 defeat of the German boxer, Max Schmeling, Hitler's favorite. When Braddock defeated Baer, many Jews were devastated.

In 1936, the *Chicago Defender*, an African American newspaper, wrote that history would be kind to Braddock. "Years from today you will read that Jim Braddock was the one champion who would not and did not draw the color line," it noted. But it concluded that Braddock did so for financial reasons, knowing that a fight with Joe Louis would "draw a purse benefiting a champion's appearance." When Louis defeated Braddock to win the heavyweight title, the fight at Chicago's Comiskey Park attracted the largest mixed crowd of blacks and whites in boxing history.

Madison Square Garden, aware of the ethnic appeal of boxing, worked hard to ensure that nearly every major immigrant group had someone to cheer for on fight night. Boxing promoters were among the first to learn that in sports, as in entertainment more generally, segregation did not pay.

Cinderella Man depicts, with considerable accuracy, a simple and good man's triumph over adversity. His story was, indeed, the stuff of myth. But in its earnest attempt to universalize Braddock's appeal, the movie obscures the ethnic divisions that characterized so much of American life during the first half of the twentieth century.

Questions for Discussion

■ Did the Depression encourage solidarity among Americans? Or did it exacerbate tensions by pitting different groups against each other in search of jobs?

Although Louisiana Senator Huey Long supported FDR in 1932, "the Kingfish" had changed his mind two years later, when this picture was taken. He opposed Roosevelt's large government bureaucracies, such as the National Recovery Administration (NRA), and sought more aggressive income redistribution. Also, he wanted to be president.

demagogue—yet the plight of all poor people concerned him deeply. More important, he tried to do something about it.

As a reformer, Long stood in the populist tradition; he hated bankers and "the interests." He believed that poor people, regardless of color, should have a chance to earn a decent living and get an education. His arguments were simplistic, patronizing, possibly insincere, but effective. "Don't say I'm working for niggers," he told one northern journalist. "I'm for the poor man—all poor men. Black and white, they all gotta have a chance. . . . 'Every Man a King'—that's my slogan."

By 1935 Long's "Share Our Wealth" movement had a membership of over 4.6 million. His program called for the confiscation of family fortunes of more than $5 million and a tax of 100 percent on incomes over $1 million a year, the money to be used to buy every family a "homestead" (a house, a car, and other necessities) and provide an annual family income of $2,000 to $3,000, plus old-age pensions, educational benefits, and veterans' pensions. As the 1936 election approached, he planned to organize a third party to split the liberal vote. He assumed that the Republicans would win the election and so botch the job of fighting the Depression that he could sweep the country in 1940.

Less powerful than Long but more widely influential was Father Charles E. Coughlin, the "Radio Priest." A genial Canadian of Irish lineage, Coughlin in 1926 began broadcasting a weekly religious message over station WJR in Detroit. His mellifluous voice and orotund rhetoric attracted a huge national audience, and the Depression gave him a secular cause. In 1933 he had been an eager New Dealer, but his dislike of New Deal financial policies—he believed that inflating the currency would end the Depression—and his need for ever more sensational ideas to hold his radio audience led him to turn against the New Deal. By 1935 he was calling Roosevelt a "great betrayer and liar."

Another rapidly growing movement alarmed the Democrats in 1934–1935: Dr. Francis E. Townsend's campaign for "old-age revolving pensions." Townsend, a retired California physician, colorless and low-keyed, had an oversimplified and therefore appealing "solution" to the nation's troubles. The pitiful state of thousands of elderly persons, whose job prospects were even dimmer than those of the mass of the unemployed, he found shocking. He advocated paying every person aged 60 years and over a pension of $200 a month, the only conditions being that the pensioners not hold jobs and that they spend the entire sum within 30 days. Their purchases, he argued, would stimulate production, thereby creating new jobs and revitalizing the economy. A stiff transactions tax, collected whenever any commodity changed hands, would pay for the program.

Economists quickly pointed out that with about 10 million persons eligible for the Townsend pensions, the cost would amount to $24 billion a year—roughly half the national income. But among the elderly the scheme proved extremely popular. Townsend Clubs, their proceedings conducted in the spirit of revivalist camp meetings, flourished everywhere, and the *Townsend National Weekly* reached a circulation of over 200,000. Although most Townsendites were anything but radical politically, their plan, like Long's Share Our Wealth scheme, would have revolutionized the distribution of wealth in the country. The movement marked the emergence of a new force in American society. With medical advances lengthening the average life span, the percentage of old people in the population was rising. The breakdown of close family ties in an increasingly mobile society now caused many of these citizens to be cast adrift to live out their last years poor, sick, idle, and alone.

Political imperatives had much to do with Roosevelt's responses, and the influence of Supreme Court Justice Louis Brandeis and his disciples, notably Felix Frankfurter, was great. They urged Roosevelt to abandon his probusiness programs, especially the NRA, and stress restoring competition and taxing corporations more heavily. The fact that most businessmen were turning away from him encouraged the president to accept this advice; so did the Supreme Court's decision in *Schechter* v. *United States* (May 1935), which declared the National Industrial Recovery Act unconstitutional. (The case involved the provisions of the NRA Live Poultry Code; the Court voided the act on the grounds that Congress had delegated too much legislative power to the code authorities and that the defendants, four brothers engaged in slaughtering chickens in New York City, were not engaged in interstate commerce.)

The Second New Deal

Existing laws had failed to end the Depression. Conservatives roundly denounced Roosevelt, and extremists were luring away some of his supporters. Voters, heartened by the partial success of early New Deal measures, were clamoring for further reforms. But the Supreme Court had declared many key New Deal measures unconstitutional. For these many reasons, Roosevelt, in June 1935, launched what historians call the Second New Deal.

There followed the "Second Hundred Days," one of the most productive periods in the history of American legislation. The National Labor Relations Act—commonly known as the Wagner Act—restored the labor guarantees wiped out by the *Schecter* decision. It gave workers the right to bargain collectively and prohibited employers from interfering with union organizational activities in their factories. A National Labor Relations Board (NLRB) was established to supervise plant elections and designate successful unions as official bargaining agents when a majority of the workers approved. It was difficult to force some big corporations to bargain "in good faith," as the law required, but the NLRB could conduct investigations of employer practices and issue cease and desist orders when "unfair" activities came to light.

Passage of the Social Security Act resulted in the issuance of nine-digit Social Security cards. This prompted banal jokes, such as this one, predicting that people's identity would be determined by that number rather than by their name.

The Social Security Act of August 1935 set up a system of old-age insurance, financed partly by a tax on wages (paid by workers) and partly by a tax on payrolls (paid by employers). It created a state-federal system of unemployment insurance, similarly financed. Liberal critics considered this social security system inadequate because it did not cover agricultural workers, domestics, self-employed persons, and some other groups particularly in need of its benefits. Health insurance was not included, and because the size of pensions depended on the amount earned, the lowest-paid workers could not count on much support after reaching 65. Yet the law was of major significance. Over the years the pension payments were increased and the classes of workers covered expanded.

The Rural Electrification Administration (REA), created by executive order, also began to function during this remarkable period. The REA lent money at low interest rates to utility companies and to farmer cooperatives interested in bringing electricity to rural areas. When the REA went into operation, only one farm in ten had electricity; by 1950 only one in ten did not.

Another important measure was the Wealth Tax Act of August 1935, which, while not the "soak the rich" measure both its supporters and its opponents claimed, raised taxes on large incomes considerably. Estate and gift taxes were also increased. Stiffer taxes on corporate profits reflected the Brandeis group's desire to penalize corporate giantism. Much of the opposition to other New Deal legislation arose from the fact that after these changes in the tax laws were made, the well-to-do had to bear a larger share of the cost of *all* government activities.

Whether the Second New Deal was more radical than the first depends largely on the vantage point from which it is considered. Measures like the Social Security Act had greater long-range effect on American life than the legislation of the First Hundred Days but were fundamentally less revolutionary than laws like the National Industrial Recovery Act and the Agricultural Adjustment Act, which attempted to establish a planned economy.

Herbert Hoover epitomized the attitude of conservatives when he called the New Deal "the most stupendous invasion of the whole spirit of Liberty that the nation has witnessed." Undoubtedly many opponents of the New Deal sincerely believed that it was undermining the foundations of American freedom. The cost of the New Deal also alarmed them. By 1936 some members of the administration had fallen under the influence of the British economist John Maynard Keynes, who argued that the world Depression could be conquered if governments would deliberately unbalance their budgets by reducing interest rates and taxes and by increasing expenditures to stimulate consumption and investment.

Roosevelt never accepted Keynes's theories; he conferred with the economist in 1934 but could not grasp the "rigmarole of figures" with which Keynes deluged him. Nevertheless the imperatives of the Depression forced him to spend more than the government was collecting in taxes; thus he adopted in part the Keynesian approach. Conservative businessmen considered him financially irresponsible, and the fact that deficit spending seemed to be good politics made them seethe with rage.

The Election of 1936

The election of 1936 loomed as a showdown. "America is in peril," the Republican platform declared. The GOP candidate, Governor Alfred M. Landon of Kansas, was a former follower of Theodore Roosevelt, a foe of the Ku Klux Klan in the 1920s, and a believer in government regulation of business. But he was a poor speaker, colorless, and handicapped by the reactionary views of many of his backers. Against the charm and political astuteness of Roosevelt, Landon's arguments—chiefly that he could administer the government more efficiently than the president—made little impression. He won the support of some anti-New Deal Democrats, among them two former presidential candidates, Al Smith and John W. Davis, but this was not enough.

On election day the country gave the president a tremendous vote of confidence. He carried every state but Maine and Vermont. The Republicans elected only eighty-nine members of the House of Representatives and their strength in the Senate fell to sixteen, an all-time low. In dozens of city and state elections, Democratic candidates also made large gains. Both Roosevelt's personality and his program had captivated the land. He seemed irresistible, the most powerfully entrenched president in the history of the United States.

Roosevelt did not win in 1936 because of the inadequacies of his foes. Having abandoned his efforts to hold the businessmen, whom he now denounced as "economic royalists," he appealed for the votes of workers and the underprivileged. The new labor unions gratefully poured thousands of dollars into the campaign to reelect him. Black voters switched to the Democrats in record numbers. Farmers liked Roosevelt because of his evident concern for their welfare. Countless elderly persons backed Roosevelt out of gratitude for the Social Security Act. Homeowners were grateful for his program guaranteeing mortgages—eventually about 20 percent of all urban private dwellings were refinanced by the Home Owners Loan Corporation—and for the Federal Housing Administration, which, beginning in 1934, made available low-cost, long-term loans for modernizing old buildings and constructing new ones.

Roosevelt Tries to Undermine the Supreme Court

On January 20, in his second inaugural address, Roosevelt spoke of the plight of millions of citizens "denied the greater part of what the very lowest standards of today call the necessities of life." A third of the nation, he added without exaggeration, was "ill-housed, ill-clad, ill-nourished." He interpreted his landslide victory as a mandate for further reforms, and with his prestige and his immense congressional majorities, nothing appeared to stand in his way. Nothing, that is, except the Supreme Court.

Throughout Roosevelt's first term the Court had stood almost immovable against increasing the scope of federal authority and broadening the general power of government, state as well as national, to cope with the exigencies of the Depression. Moreover, much of the early New Deal legislation, pushed through Congress at top speed during the Hundred Days, had been drafted without proper regard for the Constitution. Even liberal justices considered the National Industrial Recovery Act unconstitutional (the *Schecter* decision was unanimous).

In 1937 all the major measures of the Second Hundred Days appeared doomed. The Wagner Act had little chance of winning approval, experts predicted. Lawyers were advising employers to ignore the Social Security Act, so confident were they that the Court would declare it unconstitutional.

Faced with this situation, Roosevelt decided to ask Congress to shift the balance on the Court by increasing the number of justices, thinly disguising the purpose of his plan by making it part of a general reorganization of the judiciary. A member of the Court who reached the age of 70 would have the option of retiring at full pay. Should such a justice choose not to retire, the president was to appoint an additional justice, up to a maximum of six, to ease the burden of work for the aged jurists who remained on the bench.

Although polls showed the public fairly evenly divided on the "Court-packing" bill, the opposition was vocal and influential. To the expected denunciations of conservatives were added the complaints of liberals fearful that the principle of court packing might in the future be used to subvert civil liberties. What, Senator Norris asked, would have been the reaction if a man like Harding had proposed such a measure? Opposition in Congress was immediate and intense; many who had cheerfully supported every New Deal bill came out against the plan. The press denounced it, and so did most local bar associations.

For months Roosevelt stubbornly refused to concede defeat, but in July 1937, he had to yield. Minor administrative reforms of the judiciary were enacted, but the size of the Court remained unchanged.

The struggle did result in saving the legislation of the Second New Deal. Alarmed by the threat to the Court, a majority of the justices upheld key New Deal measures, such as the minimum wage, the Wagner Act, and the Social Security Act.

The New Deal Winds Down

The Court fight marked the beginning of the end of the New Deal. Social and economic developments contributed to its decline, and the final blow originated in the area of foreign affairs. With unemployment high, wages low, and workers relatively powerless against their employers, most Americans had liked New Deal labor legislation and sympathized with the industrial unions whose growth it stimulated. The NRA, the Wagner Act, and the CIO's organization of industries like steel and automobiles changed the power structure within the economy. What amounted to a revolution in the lives of wage earners had occurred. Aside from the obvious changes—higher wages, shorter hours, paid vacations, insurance of various kinds—unionization had meant fair methods of settling disputes about work practices and a measure of job security based on seniority for tens of thousands of workers. The CIO in particular had done much to increase the influence of labor in politics and to bring blacks and other minorities into the labor movement.

In 1937 a series of "sit-down strikes" broke out, beginning at the General Motors plant in Flint, Michigan. Striking workers barricaded themselves inside the factories; when police and strikebreakers tried to dislodge them, they drove them off with barrages of soda bottles, tools, spare parts, and crockery. The tolerant attitude of the Roosevelt administration ensured the strikers against government intervention. "It is illegal," Roosevelt said of the General Motors strike, "but shooting it out . . . [is not] the answer. . . . Why can't those fellows in General Motors meet with the committee of workers?" Fearful that all-out efforts to clear their plants would result in the destruction of expensive machinery, most employers capitulated to the workers' demands. All the automobile manufacturers but Henry Ford quickly came to terms with the United Automobile Workers.

The major steel companies, led by U.S. Steel, recognized the CIO and granted higher wages and a 40-hour week. The auto and steel unions alone boasted more than 725,000 members by late 1937; other CIO units conquered the rubber industry, the electrical industry, the textile industry, and many more.

While the sit-down strikes and the Court fight were going on, the New Deal suffered another heavy blow. Business conditions had been gradually improving since 1933. Heartened by the trend, Roosevelt, who had never fully grasped the importance of government spending in stimulating recovery, cut back sharply on the relief program in June 1937, with disastrous results. Between August and October the economy slipped downward like sand through a chute. Stock prices plummeted; unemployment rose by 2 million; industrial production slumped. This "Roosevelt recession" further damaged the president's reputation, and for many months he aggravated the situation by adopting an almost Hoover-like attitude. "Everything will work out all right if we just sit tight and keep quiet," he actually said.

While the president hesitated, rival theorists within his administration warred. The Keynesians clamored for stepped-up government spending. The conservatives, led by Treasury Secretary Henry Morgenthau Jr., advocated retrenchment. Perhaps confused by the conflict, Roosevelt seemed incapable of decisive action.

In April 1938 Roosevelt finally committed himself to heavy deficit spending. At his urging Congress passed a $3.75 billion public works bill. Two major pieces of legislation were also enacted at about this time. A new AAA program (February 1938) set marketing quotas and acreage limitations for growers of staples like wheat, cotton, and tobacco and authorized the Commodity Credit Corporation to lend money to farmers on their surplus crops.

The second measure, the Fair Labor Standards Act, abolished child labor and established a national minimum wage of 40 cents an hour and a maximum workweek of 40 hours, with time and a half for overtime. Although the law failed to cover many of the poorest-paid types of labor, its passage meant wage increases for 750,000 workers. In later years many more classes of workers were brought within its protection, and the minimum wage was repeatedly increased.

DID THE NEW DEAL SUCCEED?

Debating the Past

A swimming pool such as this one in Carbon Hill, Alabama, built with federal "New Deal" funds, can be found in many cities and in most towns and villages in the United States. The New Deal visibly changed the nation; but did it succeed?

Few issues have been more controversial. At the time and for decades afterward conservative historians such as Edgar E. Robinson (1955) denounced the New Deal as an economic failure that infringed on individual rights. Most liberals—foremost among them Arthur M. Schlesinger Jr. (1957–1960)—acknowledged that the New Deal did not end the Depression but it did restrain corporations and address the needs of most workers, farmers, and consumers. That such people benefited from its actions was proven by how many of them voted for FDR, time and again.

William Leuchtenburg (1963) approved of much of the New Deal, but claimed that it left share croppers, slum dwellers, and most blacks "outside of the new equilibrium." It was but a "halfway revolution." A few years later Barton Bernstein (1968) led the far left in a blistering attack: "The New Deal failed to solve the problem of depression, it failed to raise the impoverished, it failed to redistribute income, it failed to extend equality and generally countenanced racial discrimination and segregation." The New Deal, in short, was no revolution at all.

In subsequent decades historians were more inclined to assess the New Deal in light of what was possible at the time. David Kennedy (1999), while acknowledging the New Deal's many failures, was struck by the "the boldness of its vision." Its achievements were as tangible as the city halls and high schools it had built, the people it had put to work, and the democratic nation it had preserved in time of crisis.

Edgar E. Robinson, *The Roosevelt Leadership* (1955), Arthur M. Schlesinger Jr., *The Age of Roosevelt*, 3 volumes (1957–1960), William Leuchtenburg, *Franklin D. Roosevelt and the New Deal, 1932–1940* (1963), Barton Bernstein, *Toward a New Past* (1968), David M. Kennedy, *Freedom from Fear* (1999).

These measures further alienated conservatives without dramatically improving economic conditions. The resistance of many Democratic members of Congress to additional economic and social "experiments" hardened. As the 1938 elections approached, Roosevelt decided to go to the voters in an effort to strengthen party discipline and reenergize the New Deal. He singled out a number of conservative Democratic senators, notably Walter F. George of Georgia, Millard F. Tydings of Maryland, and "Cotton Ed" Smith of South Carolina, and tried to "purge" them by backing other Democrats in the primaries.

The purge failed. Southern voters liked Roosevelt but resented his interference in local politics. In the nation at large, the Republicans made important gains for the first time since Roosevelt had taken office. The Democrats maintained nominal control of both houses of Congress, but the conservative coalition, while unable to muster the votes necessary to do away with accomplished reforms, succeeded in blocking additional legislation.

Significance of the New Deal

After World War II broke out in 1939, the Great Depression was swept away on a wave of orders from the beleaguered European democracies. For this prosperity, Roosevelt received much undeserved credit. His New Deal had not returned the country to full employment. Despite the aid given to the jobless, the generation of workers born between 1900 and 1910 who entered the 1930s as unskilled laborers had their careers permanently stunted by the Depression. Far fewer rose to middle-class status than at any time since the 1830s and 1840s.

Roosevelt's fondness for establishing new agencies to deal with specific problems vastly increased the federal bureaucracy, indirectly added to the influence of lobbyists, and made it more difficult to monitor government activities. His cavalier attitude toward constitutional limitations on executive power, which he justified as being necessary in a national emergency, set in motion trends that so increased

The proliferation of federal agencies during the New Deal inspired cartoonists. In this example, Swift's Gulliver—the United States—is tied down by the Lilliputian Brain Trusters.

the prestige and authority of the presidency that the balance among the executive, legislative, and judicial branches was threatened.

Yet these are criticisms after the fact. By 1939 the country was committed to the idea that the federal government should accept responsibility for the national welfare and act to meet specific problems in every necessary way. What was most significant was not the proliferation of new agencies or the expansion of federal power. These were continuations of trends already a century old when the New Deal began. The importance of the "Roosevelt revolution" was that it removed the issue from politics. "Never again," the Republican presidential candidate was to say in 1952, "shall we allow a depression in the United States."

Because of New Deal decisions, many formerly unregulated areas of American life became subject to federal authority: the stock exchange, agricultural prices and production, labor relations, old-age pensions, relief of the needy. If the New Deal failed to end the Depression, it effected changes that have—so far, at least—prevented later economic declines from becoming catastrophes. By encouraging the growth of unions, the New Deal probably helped workers obtain a larger share of the profits of industry. By putting a floor under the income of many farmers, it checked the decline of agricultural living standards, though not that of the agricultural population. The social security program, with all its inadequacies, lessened the impact of bad times on an increasingly large proportion of the population and provided immense psychological benefits to all.

Women as New Dealers: The Network

Largely because of the influence of Eleanor Roosevelt and Molly Dewson, head of the Women's Division of the Democratic National Committee, the Roosevelt administration employed far more women in positions of importance than any earlier one. Secretary of Labor Frances Perkins, the first woman appointed to a Cabinet post, had been active in labor relations for more than 20 years, as secretary of the Consumers' League during the progressive period, as a factory inspector immediately after the war, and as chair of the New York State Industrial Commission. As secretary of labor she helped draft New Deal labor legislation and kept Roosevelt informed on various labor problems outside the government.

Through her newspaper column "My Day" and as a speaker on public issues, Eleanor Roosevelt became a major political force, especially in the area of civil rights, where the administration needed constant prodding.

She particularly identified with efforts to obtain better treatment for blacks, in and out of government. Her best-known action occurred in 1939 after the Daughters of the American Revolution (DAR) refused to permit the use of their Washington auditorium for a concert by the black contralto Marian Anderson. Eleanor Roosevelt resigned from the DAR in protest, and after the president arranged for Anderson to sing at the Lincoln Memorial, she persuaded a small army of dignitaries to sponsor the concert. An interracial crowd of 75,000 people

Eleanor Roosevelt dispensing soup to the needy. As a wealthy young socialite, she exhibited little interest in public matters. But after Eleanor discovered that Franklin was having an affair with her own social secretary, Lucy Mercer, Eleanor began to change. Her marriage, she confided to a friend, ceased to have any "fundamental love to draw on." Liberated and energized, she threw herself into social and political reform.

attended the performance. The *Chicago Defender*, an influential black newspaper, noted that the First Lady "stood like the Rock of Gibraltar against pernicious encroachments on the rights of minorities." (A disgruntled white Southerner made the same point differently: "She goes round telling the Negroes they are as good as anyone else.")

Blacks During the New Deal

The shift of black voters from the Republican to the Democratic party during the New Deal years was one of the most significant political turnarounds in American history. In 1932 when things were at their worst, fewer African Americans defected from the Republican party than the members of any other traditionally Republican group. Four years later, however, blacks voted for Roosevelt in overwhelming numbers.

Blacks supported the New Deal for the same reasons that whites did, but how the New Deal affected blacks in general and racial attitudes specifically are more complicated questions. Claiming that he dared not antagonize southern congressmen, whose votes he needed for his recovery programs, Roosevelt did nothing about civil rights before 1941 and relatively little thereafter. For the same reason, many southern white liberals hesitated to support racial integration for fear that other liberal causes could be injured as a result.

Many of the early New Deal programs treated blacks as second-class citizens. Blacks were often paid at lower rates than whites under NRA codes (and so joked that NRA stood for "Negro Run Around" and "Negroes Ruined Again"). The early farm programs shortchanged black tenants and sharecroppers. Blacks in the

Black sharecroppers evicted from their tenant farms were photographed by Arthur Rothstein along a Missouri road in 1939. Rothstein was one of a group of outstanding photographers who created a unique "sociological and economic survey" of the nation between 1936 and 1942 under the aegis of the Farm Security Administration. Dorothea Lange (p. 726) was another.

Civilian Conservation Corps were assigned to all-black camps. TVA developments were rigidly segregated, and almost no blacks got jobs in TVA offices. New Deal urban housing projects inadvertently but nonetheless effectively increased the concentration of blacks in particular neighborhoods. Because the Social Security Act excluded agricultural laborers and domestic servants, it did nothing for hundreds of thousands of poor black workers or for Mexican American farmhands in the Southwest. In 1939 unemployment was twice as high among blacks as among whites, and whites' wages were double the level of blacks' wages.

In the labor movement the new CIO unions accepted black members, a particularly significant move because these unions were organizing industries—steel, automobiles, and mining among others—that employed large numbers of blacks. Thus, while black Americans suffered horribly during the Depression, New Deal efforts to counteract its effects brought them some relief and a measure of hope. And this became increasingly true with the passage of time. During Roosevelt's second term, blacks found far less to criticize than had been the case earlier.

A New Deal for Indians

New Deal policy toward American Indians built on earlier trends but carried them further. During the Harding and Coolidge administrations more Indian land had passed into the hands of whites, and agents of the Bureau of Indian Affairs had tried to suppress elements of Indian culture they considered "pagan" or "lascivious." In 1924 Congress finally granted citizenship to all Indians, but most whites still generally believed that Indians should be treated as wards of the state.

Government policy took a new direction in 1933 when President Roosevelt named John Collier commissioner of Indian affairs. When he was appointed commissioner, the Depression had reduced perhaps a third of all Indians living on reservations to penury.

Collier favored a pluralistic approach, seeking to help the Indians preserve their ancient cultures but also (somewhat contradictorily) to help them earn more money and make use of modern medical advances and modern techniques of soil conservation. He was particularly eager to encourage the revival of tribal governments that could represent the Indians in dealings with the U.S. government.

In part because of Collier's urging, Congress passed the Indian Reorganization Act of 1934. This law did away with the Dawes Act allotment system and enabled Indians to establish tribal governments with powers like those of cities, and it encouraged Indians to return individually owned lands to tribal control. About 4 million of the 90 million acres of land lost under the allotment system were returned to the tribes.

New Deal Indian policy was controversial among Indians as well as among many white groups. Some critics charged Collier with trying to turn back the clock. Others attacked him as a segregationist and claimed that he was trying to restore "pagan" religious practices and convert the Indians to communism.

Collier resigned in 1945, and in the 1950s Congress "terminated" most government efforts aimed at preserving Indian cultures. Nevertheless, like so many of its programs, the New Deal's Indian policy was a bold effort to deal constructively with a long-standing national problem.

The Role of Roosevelt

How much of the credit for New Deal policies belongs personally to Franklin D. Roosevelt is debatable. He had little to do with many of the details and some of the broad principles behind the New Deal. His knowledge of economics was skimpy, his understanding of many social problems superficial, his political philosophy distressingly vague. The British leader Anthony Eden described him as "a conjurer, skillfully juggling with balls of dynamite, whose nature he failed to understand."

Nevertheless, every aspect of the New Deal bears the brand of Roosevelt's remarkable personality. Rexford Tugwell has left one of the best-balanced judgments of the president. "Roosevelt was not really very much at home with ideas," Tugwell explained. But he was always open to new facts, and something within him "forbade inaction when there was something to be done." Roosevelt constructed the coalition that made the program possible; his humanitarianism made it a reform movement of major significance. Although considered by many a terrible administrator because he encouraged rivalry among his subordinates, assigned different

Well-wishers greet the president at Warm Springs, Georgia, in 1933. Franklin's "first-class temperament" compensated for his "second-class intellect," Justice Oliver Wendell Holmes famously observed.

agencies overlapping responsibilities, failed to discharge many incompetents, and frequently put off making difficult decisions, he was in fact one of the most effective chief executives in the nation's history. His seemingly haphazard practice of dividing authority among competing administrators unleashed the energies and sparked the imaginations of his aides.

Like Andrew Jackson, Roosevelt maximized his role as leader of all the people. His informal biweekly press conferences kept the public in touch with developments and himself in tune with popular thinking. His "fireside chats" convinced millions that he was personally interested in each citizen's life and welfare, as in a way he was. At a time when the size and complexity of the government made it impossible for any one person to direct the nation's destiny, Roosevelt managed the minor miracle of personifying that government to 130 million people. Under Hoover, a single clerk was able to handle the routine mail that flowed into the office of the president from ordinary citizens. Under Roosevelt, the task required a staff of fifty.

While the New Deal was still evolving, contemporaries recognized Roosevelt's right to a place beside Washington, Jefferson, and Lincoln among the great presidents. Yet as his second term drew toward its close, some of his most important work still lay in the future.

The Triumph of Isolationism

The danger of another world war mounted steadily as Germany, Italy, and Japan repeatedly resorted to force to achieve their expansionist aims. In March 1935 Adolf Hitler instituted universal military training and denounced the settlement at Versailles. In May Benito Mussolini massed troops in Italian Somaliland in Africa, using a trivial border clash as a pretext for threatening the ancient kingdom of Ethiopia.

Congress responded by passing the Neutrality Act of 1935, which forbade the sale of munitions to all belligerents whenever the president should proclaim that a state of war existed. Americans who took passage on belligerent ships after such a proclamation had been issued would do so at their own risk. Roosevelt would have preferred a discretionary embargo or no new legislation at all, but he dared not rouse the ire of the isolationists by vetoing the bill.

In October 1935 Italy invaded Ethiopia and Roosevelt invoked the new neutrality law. Secretary of State Cordell Hull asked American exporters to support a "moral embargo" on the sale of oil and other products not covered by the act. His plea was ignored; oil shipments to Italy tripled between October and January. Italy quickly overran and annexed Ethiopia. In February 1936 Congress passed a second neutrality act forbidding all loans to belligerents.

Then, in the summer of 1936, civil war broke out in Spain. The rebels, led by the reactionary General Francisco Franco and strongly backed by Italy and Germany, sought to overthrow the somewhat leftist Spanish Republic. Here, clearly, was a clash between democracy and fascism, and the neutrality laws did not apply to civil wars. However, Roosevelt now became more fearful of involvement than some isolationists. The president believed that American interference might cause the conflict in Spain to become a global war, and he was wary of antagonizing the substantial number of American Catholics who were sympathetic to the Franco regime. At his urging Congress passed another neutrality act broadening the arms embargo to cover civil wars.

Isolationism now reached its peak. A public opinion poll revealed in March 1937 that 94 percent of the people thought American policy should be directed at keeping out of all foreign wars rather than trying to prevent wars from breaking out. In April Congress passed still another neutrality law. It continued the embargo on munitions and loans, forbade Americans to travel on belligerent ships, and gave the president discretionary authority to place the sale of other goods to belligerents on a cash-and-carry basis. This played into the hands of the aggressors. While German planes and cannons were turning the tide in Spain, the United States was denying the hard-pressed Spanish loyalists even a case of cartridges.

In January 1938, the House narrowly defeated the Ludlow amendment, which would have prohibited Congress from declaring war without the prior approval of the nation's voters.

"With every surrender the prospects of a European war grow darker," Claude G. Bowers, the American ambassador to Spain, warned. The *New York Herald*

Tribune pointed out that the neutrality legislation was literally reactionary—designed to keep the United States out of the war of 1914–1918, not the conflict looming on the horizon. President Roosevelt, in part because of domestic problems such as the Supreme Court packing struggle and the wave of sit-down strikes, and in part because of his own vacillation, seemed to have lost control over the formulation of American foreign policy. The American people, like wild creatures before a forest fire, were rushing in blind panic from the conflagration.

War Again in Europe

There were limits beyond which Americans would not go. In July 1937 the Japanese resumed their conquest of China, pressing ahead on a broad front. Roosevelt believed that invoking the neutrality law would only help the well-armed Japanese. Taking advantage of the fact that neither side had formally declared war, he allowed the shipment of arms and supplies to both sides.

Then the president went further. Speaking in Chicago in October, he condemned nations—he mentioned none by name—who were "creating a state of international anarchy and instability from which there is no escape through mere isolation or neutrality." The way to deal with "the epidemic of world lawlessness" was to "quarantine" it. Evidently Roosevelt had no specific plan in mind; nevertheless the "quarantine speech" produced a windy burst of isolationist rhetoric that forced him to back down. "It's a terrible thing," he said, "to look over your shoulder when you are trying to lead—and to find no one there."

Roosevelt came gradually to the conclusion that resisting aggression was more important than keeping out of war, but when he did, the need to keep the country united led him at times to be less than candid in his public statements. Hitler's annexation of Austria in March 1938 caused him deep concern. The Nazis' vicious anti-Semitism had caused many of Germany's 500,000 Jewish citizens to seek refuge abroad. Now 190,000 Austrian Jews were under Nazi control. When Roosevelt learned that the Germans were burning synagogues, expelling Jewish children from schools, and otherwise mistreating innocent people, he said that he "could scarcely believe that such things could occur." But public opinion opposed changing the immigration law so that more refugees could be admitted, and the president did nothing.

In September 1938 Hitler demanded that Czechoslovakia cede the German-speaking Sudetenland to the Reich. British Prime Minister Neville Chamberlain and French Premier Edouard Daladier, in a conference with Hitler at Munich, yielded to Hitler's threats and promises and persuaded the Czechs to surrender the region. Roosevelt failed again to speak out. But when the Nazis seized the rest of Czechoslovakia in March 1939, Roosevelt called for "methods short of war" to demonstrate America's determination to check the fascists.

When Hitler threatened Poland in the spring of 1939, demanding the free city of Danzig and the Polish Corridor separating East Prussia from the rest of

Germany, and when Mussolini invaded Albania, Roosevelt urged Congress to repeal the 1937 neutrality act so that the United States could sell arms to Britain and France in the event of war. Congress refused. "Captain," Vice President Garner told Roosevelt after counting noses in the Senate, "you haven't got the votes," and the president did not press the issue.

In August 1939 Germany and the Soviet Union signed a nonaggression pact, prelude to their joint assault on Poland. On September 1 Hitler's troops invaded Poland, at last provoking Great Britain and France to declare war. Roosevelt immediately asked Congress to repeal the arms embargo. In November, in a vote that followed party lines closely, the Democratic majority pushed through a law permitting the sale of arms and other contraband on a cash-and-carry basis. Short-term loans were authorized, but American vessels were forbidden to carry any products to the belligerents. Since the Allies controlled the seas, cash-and-carry gave them a tremendous advantage.

The German attack on Poland effected a basic change in American thinking. Keeping out of the war remained an almost universal hope, but preventing a Nazi victory became the ultimate, if not always conscious, objective of many citizens. In Roosevelt's case it was perfectly conscious, although he dared not express his feelings candidly because of isolationist strength in Congress and the country. He moved slowly, responding to rather than directing the course of events.

Cash-and-carry did not stop the Nazis. Poland fell in less than a month; then, after a winter lull that cynics called the "phony war," Hitler loosed his armored divisions. Between April 9 and June 22 he taught the world the awful meaning of *Blitzkrieg*—lightning war. Denmark, Norway, the Netherlands, Belgium, and France were successively overwhelmed. The British army, pinned against the sea at Dunkirk, saved itself from annihilation only by fleeing across the English Channel. After the French submitted to his harsh terms on June 22, Hitler controlled nearly all of western Europe.

Roosevelt responded to these disasters in a number of ways. In the fall of 1939, reacting to warnings from Albert Einstein and other scientists that the Germans were trying to develop an atomic bomb, he committed federal funds to a top-secret atomic bomb program, which came to be known as the Manhattan Project. Even as the British and French were falling back, he sold them, without legal authority, surplus government arms. When Italy entered the war against France, the president called the invasion a stab in the back. During the first five months of 1940 he asked Congress to appropriate over $4 billion for national defense. To strengthen national unity he named Henry L. Stimson secretary of war[2] and another Republican, Frank Knox, secretary of the navy.

After the fall of France, Hitler attempted to bomb and starve the British into submission. The epic air battles over England during the summer of 1940 ended in a decisive defeat for the Nazis, but the Royal Navy, which had only about 100 destroyers, could not control German submarine attacks on shipping. Far more

---

[2]*Stimson had held this post from 1911 to 1913 in the Taft Cabinet!*

destroyers were needed. In this desperate hour, Prime Minister Winston Churchill, who had replaced Chamberlain in May 1940, asked Roosevelt for fifty old American destroyers to fill the gap.

The navy had 240 destroyers in commission and more than fifty under construction. But direct loan or sale of the vessels would have violated both international and American laws. Any attempt to obtain new legislation would have roused fears that the United States was going down the path that had led it into World War I. Long delay if not outright defeat would have resulted. Roosevelt therefore arranged to "trade" the destroyers for six British naval bases in the Caribbean. In addition, Great Britain leased bases in Bermuda and Newfoundland to the United States.

The destroyers-for-bases deal was a masterful achievement. It helped save Great Britain, and at the same time it circumvented isolationist prejudices since the president could present it as a shrewd bargain that bolstered America's defenses. A string of island bastions in the Atlantic was more valuable than 50 old destroyers.

Lines were hardening throughout the world. In September 1940, despite last-ditch isolationist resistance, Congress enacted the first peacetime draft in American history. Some 1.2 million draftees were summoned for one year of service, and 800,000 reservists were called to active duty. That same month Japan signed a mutual-assistance pact with Germany and Italy. This Rome-Berlin-Tokyo coalition—the Axis Powers—fused the conflicts in Europe and Asia, turning the struggle into a global war.

A Third Term for FDR

In the midst of these events the 1940 presidential election took place. Why Roosevelt decided to run for a third term is a much-debated question. Partisanship had something to do with it, for no other Democrat seemed so likely to carry the country. Nor would the president have been human had he not been tempted to hold on to power, especially in such critical times. His conviction that no one else could keep a rein on the isolationists was probably decisive. In any case, he was easily renominated. Vice President Garner, who had become disenchanted with Roosevelt and the New Deal, did not seek a third term; at Roosevelt's dictation, the party chose Secretary of Agriculture Henry A. Wallace to replace him.

By using concern about the European war to justify running for a tradition-breaking third term, Roosevelt brought down on his head the hatred of conservative Republicans and the isolationists of both major parties, just when they thought they would be rid of him. The Republicans nominated the darkest of dark horses, Wendell L. Willkie of Indiana, the utility magnate who had led the fight against the TVA in 1933.

Despite his political inexperience and Wall Street connections, Willkie made an appealing candidate. He was an energetic, charming, openhearted man. His rough-hewn, rural manner (one Democrat called him "a simple, barefoot Wall Street lawyer") won him wide support in farm districts. Willkie had difficulty, however, finding issues on which to oppose Roosevelt. Good times were at last returning. The New Deal reforms were too popular and too much in line with his own thinking to invite attack. He believed as strongly as the president that America could no longer ignore the Nazi threat.

In the end Willkie focused his campaign on Roosevelt's conduct of foreign relations. While rejecting the isolationist position, Willkie charged that Roosevelt intended to make the United States a participant in the war. "If you reelect him," he told one audience, "you may expect war in April 1941," to which Roosevelt retorted (disingenuously, since he knew he was not a free agent in the situation), "I have said this before, but I shall say it again and again and again: Your boys are not going to be sent into any foreign wars." In November Roosevelt carried the country handily, though by a smaller majority than in 1932 or 1936. The popular vote was 27 million to 22 million, the electoral count 449 to 82.

The Undeclared War

The election encouraged Roosevelt to act more boldly. When Prime Minister Churchill informed him that the cash-and-carry system would no longer suffice because Great Britain was rapidly exhausting its financial resources, he decided at once to provide the British with whatever they needed. Instead of proposing to lend them money, a step certain to rouse memories of the vexatious war debt controversies, he devised the lend-lease program, one of his most ingenious and imaginative creations.

First he delivered a "fireside chat" that stressed the evil intentions of the Nazis and the dangers that a German victory would create for America. Aiding Britain should be looked at simply as a form of self-defense. "As planes and ships and guns and shells are produced," he said, American defense experts would decide "how much shall be sent abroad and how much shall remain at home." When the radio talk provoked a favorable public response, Roosevelt went to Congress in January 1941 with a plan calling for the expenditure of $7 billion for war materials that the president could sell, lend, lease, exchange, or transfer to any country whose defense he deemed vital to that of the United States After two months of debate, Congress gave him what he had asked for.

Although the wording of the Lend-Lease Act obscured its immediate purpose, the saving of Great Britain, the president was frank in explaining his plan. He did not minimize the dangers involved, yet his mastery of practical politics was never more in evidence. To counter Irish American prejudices against the English, he pointed out that the Irish Republic would surely fall under Nazi domination if Hitler won the war. He coupled his demand for heavy military expenditures with his enunciation of the idealistic "Four Freedoms"—freedom of speech, freedom of religion, freedom from want, and freedom from fear—for which, he said, the war was being fought.

After the enactment of lend-lease, aid short of war was no longer seriously debated. The American navy began to patrol the North Atlantic, shadowing German submarines and radioing their locations to British warships and planes. In April 1941 U.S. forces occupied Greenland; in May the president declared a state of unlimited national emergency. After Hitler invaded the Soviet Union in June, Roosevelt moved slowly, for anti-Soviet feeling in the United States was intense.[3] But it was obviously to the nation's advantage to help any country that was resisting Hitler's armies. In November, $1 billion in lend-lease aid was put at the disposal of the Soviet Union.

Meanwhile, Iceland was occupied in July 1941, and the draft law was extended in August—by the margin of a single vote in the House of Representatives. In September the German submarine *U–652* fired a torpedo at the destroyer *Greer* in the North Atlantic. The *Greer*, which had provoked the attack by tracking *U–652* and flashing its position to a British plane, avoided the torpedo and dropped nineteen depth charges in an effort to sink the submarine.

Roosevelt (nothing he ever did provided more ammunition for his critics) announced that the *Greer* had been innocently "carrying mail to Iceland." He called the U-boats "the rattlesnakes of the Atlantic" and ordered the navy to "shoot on sight" any German craft in the waters south and west of Iceland and to convoy merchant vessels as far as that island. After the sinking of the destroyer *Reuben James* on October 30, Congress voted to allow the arming of American merchant ships and to permit them to carry cargoes to Allied ports. For all practical purposes, though not yet officially, the United States had gone to war.

Milestones

1933	FDR becomes president
	Hitler is elected German chancellor
	FDR proclaims Good Neighbor Policy
	Banking Act gives FDR broad powers
	Civilian Conservation Corps (CCC) employs 250,000 young men
	Federal Emergency Relief Act (FERA) funds relief programs
	Agricultural Adjustment Act (AAA) seeks relief for farmers
	Tennessee Valley Authority (TVA) plans dams and power plants
	National Industrial Recovery Act (NIRA) establishes Public Works Administration (PWA) and National Recovery Administration (NRA)

[3]During the 1930s the Soviet Union took a far firmer stand against the fascists than any other power, but after joining Hitler in swallowing up Poland, it attacked and defeated Finland during the winter of 1939–1940 and annexed the Baltic states. These acts virtually destroyed the small communist movement in the United States.

Milestones

1933	Banking Act establishes Federal Deposit Insurance Corporation (FDIC)
	Civil Works Administration puts 4 million to work
	Twenty-first Amendment ends prohibition
1934	Indian Reorganization Act gives tribes more autonomy
	Securities and Exchange Commission (SEC) regulates stocks and bonds
	Federal Communications Commission (FCC) regulates interstate and foreign communication
	Federal Housing Administration (FHA) gives housing loans
1935	Emergency Relief Appropriation Act creates Works Project Administration (WPA)
	Rural Electrification Administration brings electricity to farms
	Supreme Court rules NIRA unconstitutional in *Schechter* v. *United States*
	National Labor Relations Act (Wagner-Connery) encourages unionization
	Social Security Act guarantees pensions and other benefits
	Neutrality Act forbids wartime arms sales to belligerents
	Italy invades and annexes Ethiopia
	Walter Millis publishes isolationist *The Road to War: America, 1914–1917*
1936	FDR is reelected in record landslide
	Supreme Court declares AAA unconstitutional
1937	Roosevelt tries to pack Supreme Court
	Japanese in China seize Beijing, Shanghai, Nanking
1938	Fair Labor Standards Act abolishes child labor, sets minimum wage
	House of Representatives defeats Ludlow (isolationist) Amendment
	Britain and France appease Hitler at Munich
1939	Germany invades Poland; World War II begins
1940	Hitler conquers Denmark, Norway, the Netherlands, Belgium, France
	FDR is reelected to third term
	Axis powers sign Rome-Berlin-Tokyo pact
	Isolationists form America First Committee
1941	Lend-Lease Act helps Britain

CHAPTER 27

War and Peace

In AUGUST 1945, JAPAN SURRENDERED, ENDING WORLD WAR II. IN August 2005, President George W. Bush gave a speech at the San Diego naval base to honor the 400,000 Americans who had died during that war in an effort to defeat "tyranny and terror." "Today," Bush continued, American soldiers serving in Afghanistan and Iraq are "every bit as selfless and dedicated to liberty as the generations that came before them."

But by 2007 critics were chafing at a lack of national commitment to the war in Iraq. "Marines are at war," one general complained, "America is at the mall." The *Seattle Times* observed that although the Iraq war had gone on longer than World War II, "life for most Americans has clicked along without personal loss or even higher federal taxes."

Bush explained that he had not wanted to allow terrorists to disrupt American lives: "One thing we want is for people to feel like their life's moving on, that they're able to make a living and send their kids to college and put more money on the table," he noted.

Such remarks, however, underscored how different the Iraq war was from World War II, a monstrous global conflict among advanced industrial nations. Of every five American males between the ages of 20 and 25, four served in World War II. At the beginning of World War II, 4 million Americans paid income tax; by its end, 43 million did so. Over 85 million Americans—half the nation's population—spent $185 billion to buy war bonds. Food and gasoline were rationed. World War II required the mobilization of the entire nation.

World War II transformed society, too. In the absence of so many young men, women assumed new roles and worked at different types of jobs. Minorities, African Americans and Hispanics especially, found new opportunities even as they encountered persistent discrimination. Americans of Japanese extraction were relocated against their will to isolated camps. Technological change—culminating in the atom bomb—transformed everyone's lives. It was a war unlike any other.

The Road to Pearl Harbor

Neither the United States nor Japan wanted war. Roosevelt considered Germany by far the more dangerous enemy and was alarmed by the possibility of engaging in a two-front war. In the spring of 1941 Secretary of State Hull conferred in Washington with the Japanese ambassador, Kichisaburo Nomura, in an effort to resolve their differences. Hull showed little appreciation of the political and military situation in East Asia. He demanded that Japan withdraw from China and promise not to attack the Dutch and French colonies in Southeast Asia.

Japan might well have accepted limited annexations in the area in return for the removal of American trade restrictions, but Hull seemed bent on converting the Japanese to pacifism by exhortation. He insisted on total withdrawal, to which even the moderates in Japan would not agree. When Hitler invaded the Soviet Union, thereby removing the threat of Russian intervention in East Asia, Japan decided to occupy French Indochina even at the risk of war with the United States. Roosevelt retaliated (July 1941) by freezing Japanese assets in the United States and clamping an embargo on oil. He hoped that the Japanese war machine, deprived of American oil, would grind to a halt.

Now the ultranationalist war party in Japan assumed control. Nomura was instructed to tell Hull that Japan would refrain from further expansion if the United States and Great Britain would cut off all aid to China and lift the economic blockade. Japan promised to pull out of Indochina once "a just peace" had been established with China. When the United States rejected these demands, the Japanese prepared to assault the Dutch East Indies, British Malaya, and the Philippines. To

Japan's surprise attack on Pearl Harbor on December 7, 1941, killed more than 2,400 American servicemen and thrust the United States into World War II. President Roosevelt asked Congress for a declaration of war the next day, calling the attack "a date that will live in infamy."

immobilize the U.S. Pacific fleet, they planned a surprise aerial raid on the Hawaiian naval base at Pearl Harbor.

An American cryptanalyst, Colonel William F. Friedman, had cracked the Japanese diplomatic code: the Japanese were making plans to attack in early December. But in the hectic rush of events, both military and civilian authorities failed to make effective use of the information collected. They expected the blow to fall somewhere in East Asia, possibly the Philippines.

The garrison at Pearl Harbor was alerted against "a surprise aggressive move in any direction." The commanders there, Admiral Husband E. Kimmel and General Walter C. Short, believing an attack impossible, took precautions only against Japanese sabotage. Thus when planes from Japanese aircraft carriers swooped down upon Pearl Harbor on the morning of December 7, 1941, they found easy targets. In less than two hours they reduced the Pacific fleet to a smoking ruin: two battleships destroyed, six others heavily battered, nearly a dozen lesser vessels put out of action. More than 150 planes were wrecked; over 2,400 soldiers and sailors were killed and 1,100 wounded.

On December 8 Congress declared war on Japan. Formal war with Germany and Italy was still not inevitable—isolationists were far more ready to resist the "yellow peril" in Asia than to fight in Europe. The Axis powers, however, honored their treaty obligations to Japan and on December 11 declared war on the United States. America was now fully engaged in another great war, World War II. (The Great War fought by the previous generation was now identified as World War I.)

Mobilizing the Home Front

Roosevelt was an inspiring war leader but not a very good administrator. Any honest account of the war on the home front must reveal glaring examples of confusion, inefficiency, and pointless bickering. The squabbling and waste characteristic of the early New Deal period made relatively little difference—what mattered then was raising the nation's spirits and keeping people occupied; efficiency was less than essential, however desirable. But in wartime, the nation's fate, perhaps that of the entire free world, depended on delivering weapons and supplies to the battlefronts.

The confusion attending economic mobilization can easily be overstressed. Nearly all of Roosevelt's basic decisions were sensible and humane: to pay a large part of the cost of the war by collecting taxes rather than by borrowing and to base taxation on ability to pay; to ration scarce raw materials and consumer goods; to regulate prices and wages. If these decisions were not always translated into action with perfect effectiveness, they operated in the direction of efficiency and the public good.

Roosevelt's greatest accomplishment was his inspiring of industrialists, workers, and farmers with a sense of national purpose. In this respect his function duplicated his earlier role in fighting the Depression, and he performed it with even greater success.

The tremendous economic expansion can be seen in the official production statistics. In 1939 the United States was still mired in the Great Depression. The gross national product amounted to about $91.3 billion. In 1945, after allowing for changes in the price level, it was $166.6 billion. More specifically, manufacturing output nearly doubled and agricultural output rose 22 percent. In 1939 the United States turned out fewer than 6,000 airplanes, in 1944 more than 96,000. Shipyards produced 237,000 tons of vessels in 1939, 10 million tons in 1943.

Wartime experience proved that the Keynesian economists were correct in saying that government spending would spark economic growth. About 8 million people were unemployed in June 1940. After Pearl Harbor, unemployment virtually disappeared, and by 1945 the civilian workforce had increased by nearly 7 million. Military mobilization had begun well before December 1941, by which time 1.6 million men were already under arms. Economic mobilization proceeded much more slowly, mainly because the president refused to centralize authority. For months after Pearl Harbor various civilian agencies squabbled with the military over everything from the allocation of scarce raw materials to the technical specifications of weapons. Roosevelt refused to settle these conflicts.

The War Economy

Yet by early 1943 the nation's economic machinery had been converted to a wartime footing and was functioning effectively. Supreme Court Justice James F. Byrnes resigned from the Court to become a sort of "economic czar." His Office of War Mobilization had complete control over priorities and prices. Rents, food prices, and wages were strictly regulated, and items in short supply were rationed to consumers. While wages and prices had soared during 1942, after April 1943 they leveled off. Thereafter the cost of living scarcely changed until controls were lifted after the war.

Expanded industrial production together with conscription caused a labor shortage that increased the bargaining power of workers. At the same time, the national emergency required some limitation on the workers' right to take advantage of this power. After Pearl Harbor Roosevelt created a National War Labor Board (NWLB) to arbitrate disputes and stabilize wage rates, and he banned all changes in wages without NWLB approval.

Prosperity and stiffer government controls added significantly to the strength of organized labor; indeed, the war had more to do with institutionalizing industrywide collective bargaining than the New Deal. As workers recognized the benefits of union membership, they flocked into the organizations. Strikes declined sharply, but some crippling work stoppages did occur. In May 1943, after John L. Lewis's United Mine Workers walked out of the pits, the government seized the coal mines. This strike led Congress to pass, over Roosevelt's veto, the Smith-Connally War Labor Disputes Act, which gave the president the power to take over any war plant threatened by a strike and outlawed strikes against seized plants.

The federal government spent twice as much money between 1941 and 1945 as in its entire previous history. This made heavy borrowing necessary. The national debt, which stood at less than $49 billion in 1941, increased by more than that amount each year between 1942 and 1945 and totaled nearly $260 billion when the war ended. However, more than 40 percent of the total was met by taxation, a far larger proportion than in any earlier war.

This policy helped to check inflation by siphoning off money that would otherwise have competed for scarce consumer goods. Heavy excise taxes on amusements and luxuries further discouraged spending, as did the government's war bond campaigns, which persuaded patriotic citizens to lend part of their income to Uncle Sam. High taxes on incomes (up to 94 percent) and on excess profits (95 percent), together with a limit of $25,000 a year after taxes on salaries, convinced people that no one was profiting inordinately from the war effort.

The income tax, which had never before touched the mass of white-collar and industrial workers, was extended downward until nearly everyone had to pay it. To collect efficiently the relatively small sums paid by most persons, Congress adopted the payroll-deduction system proposed by Beardsley Ruml, chairman of the Federal Reserve Bank of New York. Employers withheld the taxes owed by workers from their paychecks and turned the money over to the government.

The steeply graduated tax rates, combined with a general increase in the income of workers and farmers, effected a substantial shift in the distribution of wealth in the United States. The poor became richer, while the rich, if not actually poorer, collected a smaller proportion of the national income. The wealthiest 1 percent of the population had received 13.4 percent of the national income in 1935 and 11.5 percent in 1941. In 1944 this group received 6.7 percent.

War and Social Change

Enormous social effects stemmed from this shift, but World War II altered the patterns of American life in so many ways that it would be wrong to ascribe the transformations to any single source. Never was the population more fluid. The millions who put on uniforms found themselves transported first to training camps in every section of the country and then to battlefields scattered from Europe and Africa to the far reaches of the Pacific. Burgeoning new defense plants, influenced by a government policy of locating them in "uncongested areas," drew other millions to places like Hanford, Washington, and Oak Ridge, Tennessee, where great atomic energy installations were constructed, and to the aircraft factories of California and other states. As in earlier periods the trend was from east to west and from the rural south to northern cities. The population of California increased by more than 50 percent in the 1940s, that of other far western states almost as much.

During the war the marriage rate rose steeply, from 75 per thousand adult women in 1939 to 118 in 1946. A kind of backlog existed because many people had been forced to put off marrying and having children for financial reasons during

"above and beyond the call of duty"

DORIE MILLER
*Received the Navy Cross
at Pearl Harbor, May 27, 1942*

A poster commemorating Doris "Dorie" Miller, a mess attendant aboard the USS *West Virginia* at Pearl Harbor. Before the ship sank, Miller manned an antiaircraft machine gun and shot down several Japanese planes. He won the Navy Cross for courage, the first awarded to an African American.

the Great Depression. Now wartime prosperity put an end to that problem at the same time that large numbers of young couples were feeling the need to put down roots before the husbands went off to risk death in distant lands. The population of the United States had increased by only 3 million during the Depression decade of the 1930s; during the next *five* years it rose by 6.5 million.

Minorities in Time of War: Blacks, Hispanics, and Indians

The war affected black Americans in many ways. Several factors operated to improve their lot. One was their own growing tendency to demand fair treatment. Another was the reaction of Americans to Hitler's barbaric treatment of millions of Jews, an outgrowth of his doctrine of "Aryan" superiority. These barbarities compelled millions of white citizens to reexamine their views about race. If the nation expected African Americans to risk their lives for the common good, how could it continue to treat them as second-class citizens? Black leaders pointed out the inconsistency between fighting for democracy abroad and ignoring it at home. "We want democracy in Alabama," the NAACP announced, and this argument too had some effect on white thinking.

Blacks in the armed forces were treated more fairly than they had been in World War I. They were enlisted for the first time in the air force and the marines, and they were given more responsible positions in the army and navy. The army commissioned its first black general. Some 600 black pilots won their wings.

Altogether about a million served, about half of them overseas. The extensive and honorable performance of these units could not be ignored by the white majority.

However, segregation in the armed services was maintained. In some cases German prisoners of war were seated in front of black American soldiers at camp movies. Such practices led frequently to rioting and even to local mutinies among black recruits. The navy continued to confine black and Hispanic sailors to demeaning, noncombat tasks, and black soldiers were often provided with inferior recreational facilities and otherwise mistreated in and around army camps, especially those in the South. In 1943 William Hastie, a former New Dealer who was serving as an adviser on racial matters to Secretary of War Stimson, resigned in protest because of the "reactionary policies and discriminatory practices of the Army and Air Forces in matters affecting Negroes." The NAACP, which increased its membership from 50,000 in 1940 to almost 405,000 in 1946, adopted a more militant stance than in World War I. Discrimination in defense plants seemed far less tolerable than it had in 1917–1918.

Prejudice and mistreatment did not cease. In areas around defense plants white resentment of the black "invasion" mounted. By 1943, 50,000 new blacks had crowded into Detroit. A wave of strikes disrupted production at U.S. Rubber and several former automobile plants where white workers laid down their tools to protest the hiring of blacks. In June a race riot marked by looting and bloody fighting raged for three days. By the time federal troops restored order, twenty-five blacks and nine whites had been killed. Rioting also erupted in New York and many other cities.

In Los Angeles the attacks were upon Hispanic residents. Wartime employment needs resulted in a reversal of the Depression policy of forcing Mexicans out of the Southwest, and many thousands flocked north in search of work. Most had to accept menial jobs. But work was plentiful, and they, as well as resident Spanish-speaking Americans, experienced rising living standards. A larger proportion of Mexican American men served in the armed forces than the national average.

The willingness of white leaders to tolerate attacks on blacks and Hispanics at a time when national unity was so necessary was particularly frustrating. For example, blood plasma from blacks and whites was kept separately even though the two "varieties" were indistinguishable and the process of storing plasma had been devised by a black doctor, Charles Drew.

Blacks became increasingly embittered. Roy Wilkins, head of the NAACP, put it this way in 1942: "No Negro leader with a constituency can face his members today and ask full support for the war in the light of the atmosphere the government has created." Many black newspaper editors were so critical of the administration that conservatives demanded they be indicted for sedition.

The war also affected Native American communities. The wartime drive for national unity led to a reaction against the New Deal policy of encouraging Indians to preserve their ancient cultures and develop self-governing communities. There was even talk of going back to the allotment system and trying to assimilate Indians into the larger society. John Collier resigned as commissioner of Indian affairs in disgust in 1945. In fact, the war encouraged assimilation in several ways. More than 24,000

Indians served in the armed forces, an experience that brought them in contact with new people, new places, and new ideas. Many thousands more left the reservations to work in defense industries in cities all over the country.

Internment of the Japanese

Although World War II affected the American people far more drastically than had World War I, it produced much less intolerance and fewer examples of the repression of individual freedom of opinion. People seemed able to distinguish between Italian fascism and Italian Americans and between the government of Nazi Germany and Americans of German descent in a way that had escaped their parents. The nation's 100,000 conscientious objectors, too, met with little hostility.

The relatively tolerant treatment accorded most people makes the nation's policies toward American citizens of Japanese extraction all the more difficult to comprehend. Generals on the west coast were understandably unnerved by the Japanese attack on Pearl Harbor and warned that people of Japanese descent might engage in sabotage or espionage for Japan. "The Japanese race is an enemy race," General John L. Dewitt claimed. The 112,000 Americans of Japanese ancestry, the majority of them native-born citizens, were "potential enemies." "The very fact that no sabotage has taken place to date," Dewitt observed, "is a disturbing and confirming indication that such action will be taken." This is like arguing that the driver with a perfect record is all the more likely to have an accident at any moment. Secretary of War Stimson proposed the relocation of the west coast people of Japanese extraction, including American citizens, to internment camps in

Japanese Relocation from the West Coast, 1942–1945

A Japanese girl in California, tagged and awaiting deportation.

Wyoming, Arizona, and other interior states. President Roosevelt concurred but weakly suggested: "Be as responsible as you can."

The Japanese were properly indignant but also baffled, in some cases hurt more than angry. "We didn't feel Japanese. We felt American," one woman, the mother of three small children, recalled many years later. Some Japanese Americans refused to submit to military authorities. Gordon Hirabayashi, an American citizen and senior at the University of Washington, refused to report for transportation to an internment camp. After being convicted and sentenced to prison, he decided to appeal. Previous Supreme Courts had ruled that the government could deprive Americans of their freedoms during war only when the "military necessity" was compelling. By the time the Supreme Court ruled on his and similar cases, the Japanese military had been thrown back in the Pacific; no invasion was even conceivable. Yet the justices worried that if they declared the internment policy to be unconstitutional, they would appear "out of step" with the nation, as Justice Felix Frankfurter put it. In June 1943, the Court upheld the conviction of Hirabayashi. Finally, in *Ex parte Endo*, it forbade the internment of loyal Japanese American citizens. Unfortunately the latter decision was not handed down until December 1944.

Women's Contribution to the War Effort

With economic activity on the rise and millions of men going off to war, a sudden need for more women workers developed. The trends of the 1920s—more women workers and more of them married—soon accelerated. By 1944, 6.5 million addi-

Entitled "Rosie the Riveter Steps Out" (1943), this cartoon depicts women's exodus from farm life for seemingly lucrative work in defense plants. Although "Rosie" is told to "come right back" after the war, the viewer may have doubts.

tional women had entered the workforce, and at the peak of war production in 1945, more than 19 million women were employed, many of them in well-paying industrial jobs. Additional thousands were serving in the armed forces: 100,000 in the Women's Auxiliary Army Corps, others in navy, marine, and air corps auxiliaries.

At first there was considerable resistance to what was happening. About one husband in three objected in principle to his wife taking a job. Many employers in so-called heavy industry and in other fields traditionally dominated by men doubted that women could handle such tasks.

These attitudes lost force in the face of the escalating demand for labor. That employers usually did not have to pay women as much as men made them attractive, as did the fact that they were not subject to the draft. A breakthrough occurred when the big Detroit automobile manufacturers agreed to employ women on their wartime production lines. Soon women were working not only as riveters and cab drivers but also as welders, as machine tool operators, and in dozens of other occupations formerly the exclusive domain of men.

Black women workers had a particularly difficult time, employers often hesitating to hire them because they were black, black men looking down on them because they were women. But the need for willing hands was infinite. Sybil Lewis of Sapula, Oklahoma, went to Los Angeles and found a job as a waitress in a black restaurant. Then she responded to a notice of a training program at Lockheed Aircraft, took the course, and became a riveter making airplane gas tanks. When an unfriendly foreman gave her a less attractive assignment, she moved on to Douglas Aircraft. By 1943 she was working as a welder in a shipyard.

The war also affected the lives of women who did not take jobs. Families by the tens and hundreds of thousands pulled up stakes and moved to the centers of war production, such as Detroit and southern California. Housing was always in short supply in these areas, and while the men went off to the familiar surroundings of yard and factory, their wives had to cope with cramped quarters, ration books, the absence of friends and relatives, the problems encountered by their children in strange schools and playgrounds, and in some situations even with outdoor toilets. With so many people living among strangers and in unstable circumstances it is not surprising that crime, juvenile delinquency, and prostitution increased, as indeed they did in other parts of the country too.

Housewives also had to deal with shortages, ration books, and other inconveniences during the war. In addition most took on other duties and bore other burdens, such as tending "victory gardens" and preserving their harvests, using crowded public transportation when there was no gas for the family car, mending and patching old clothes when new ones were unavailable, participating in salvage drives, and doing volunteer work for hospitals, the Red Cross, or various civil defense and servicemen's centers.

Allied Strategy: Europe First

Only days after Pearl Harbor, British Prime Minister Churchill and his military chiefs met in Washington with Roosevelt and his advisers. In every quarter of the globe, disaster threatened. The Japanese were gobbling up East Asia. Hitler's armies, checked outside Leningrad and Moscow, were preparing for a massive attack in the direction of Stalingrad, on the Volga River. German divisions under General Erwin Rommel were beginning a drive across North Africa toward the Suez Canal. U-boats were taking a heavy toll in the North Atlantic. British and American leaders believed that eventually they could muster enough force to smash their enemies, but whether the troops already in action could hold out until this force arrived was an open question.

The decision of the strategists was to concentrate first against the Germans. Japan's conquests were in remote and, from the Allied point of view, relatively unimportant regions. If the Soviet Union surrendered, Hitler could throw all of German might against Great Britain. If it were defeated, Hitler's position in Europe might prove impregnable.

But how to strike at Hitler? American leaders wanted a second front in France, at least by 1943, and the Soviets, with their backs to the wall and bearing the full weight of the German war machine, heartily agreed. Churchill, however, was more concerned with protecting Britain's overseas possessions than with easing the pressure on the Soviet Union. He advocated instead air bombardment of German industry combined with an attempt to drive the Germans out of North Africa, and his argument carried the day.

During the summer of 1942 Allied planes began to bomb German cities. In a crescendo through 1943 and 1944, British and American bombers pulverized the centers of Nazi might. While air attacks did not destroy the German army's capacity to fight, they hampered war production, tangled communications, and brought the war home to the German people in awesome fashion.

In November 1942 an Allied army commanded by General Dwight D. Eisenhower struck at French North Africa. After the fall of France, the Nazis had set up a puppet regime in those parts of France not occupied by their troops, with headquarters at Vichy in central France. This collaborationist Vichy government controlled French North Africa. But the North African commandant, Admiral Jean Darlan, agreed to switch sides when Eisenhower's forces landed. After a brief show of resistance, the French surrendered.

The Allies were willing to do business with Darlan despite his record as a collaborationist. This angered General Charles de Gaulle, who had organized a government in exile immediately after the collapse of France and who considered himself the true representative of the French people. Many Americans agreed with de Gaulle, but the arrangement with Darlan paid large dividends. Eisenhower was able to press forward quickly against the Germans. In February 1943 at Kasserine Pass in the desert south of Tunis, American tanks met Rommel's Afrika Korps. The battle ended in a standoff, but with British troops closing in from their Egyptian bases to the east, the Germans were soon trapped and crushed. In May, after Rommel had been recalled to Germany, his army surrendered.

In July 1943, while air attacks on Germany continued and the Russians slowly pushed the Germans back from the gates of Stalingrad, the Allies invaded Sicily from Africa. In September they advanced to the Italian mainland. Mussolini had already fallen from power and his successor surrendered. However, the German troops in Italy threw up an almost impregnable defense across the rugged Italian peninsula. The Anglo American army inched forward, paying heavily for every advance. Monte Cassino, halfway between Naples and Rome, did not fall until May 1944, the capital itself not until June; months of hard fighting remained before the country was cleared of Germans. The Italian campaign was an Allied disappointment even though it weakened the enemy.

Germany Overwhelmed

By the time the Allies had taken Rome, the mighty army needed to invade France had been collected in England under Eisenhower's command. On D-day, June 6,

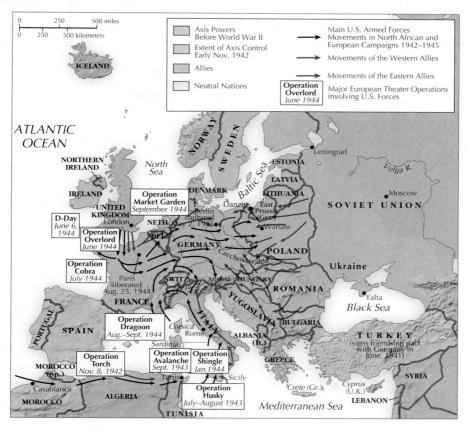

Map legend:

Axis Powers Before World War II

Extent of Axis Control Early Nov. 1942

Allies

Neutral Nations

Main U.S. Armed Forces Movements in North African and European Campaigns 1942–1945

Movements of the Western Allies

Movements of the Eastern Allies

Operation Overlord June 1944 — Major European Theater Operations involving U.S. Forces

0   250   500 miles
0   250   500 kilometers

ICELAND

ATLANTIC OCEAN

NORTHERN IRELAND

North Sea

IRELAND

Operation Market Garden September 1944

UNITED KINGDOM

D-Day June 6, 1944

Operation Overlord June 1944

London

NETH. May 2, 1945

BEL.

Operation Cobra July 1944

Paris liberated Aug. 25, 1944

FRANCE

Operation Dragoon Aug.–Sept. 1944

SPAIN

PORTUGAL

Operation Torch Nov. 8, 1942

MOROCCO (Sp.)

Casablanca

MOROCCO

ALGERIA

Corsica

Sardinia

Operation Avalanche Sept. 1943

Operation Shingle Jan.1944

Tunis

Operation Husky July–August 1943

TUNISIA

NORWAY

SWEDEN

DENMARK

Baltic Sea

Danzig

Berlin Captured

GERMANY

Czechoslovakia

SWITZ.

Austria

HUNGARY

ITALY

Rome

ALBANIA (It.)

Sicily

Mediterranean Sea

ESTONIA

LATVIA

LITHUANIA

East Prussia

Warsaw

POLAND

YUGOSLAVIA

ROMANIA

BULGARIA

GREECE

Crete (Gr.)

Leningrad

Volga R.

Moscow

SOVIET UNION

Ukraine

Yalta

Black Sea

TURKEY (signs friendship pact with Germany in June, 1941)

Cyprus (U.K.)

SYRIA

LEBANON

The Liberation of Europe

1944, the assault forces stormed ashore at five points along the coast of Normandy, supported by a great armada and thousands of planes and paratroops. Against fierce but ill-coordinated German resistance, they established a beachhead: Within a few weeks a million troops were on French soil. (See the feature essay, Re-Viewing the Past: "Saving Private Ryan," pp. 766–767.)

Thereafter victory was assured, though nearly a year of hard fighting lay ahead. In August the American Third Army under General George S. Patton, an eccentric but brilliant field commander, erupted southward into Brittany and then veered east toward Paris. Another Allied army invaded France from the Mediterranean in mid-August and advanced rapidly north. Free French troops were given the honor of liberating Paris on August 25. Belgium was cleared by British and Canadian units a few days later. By mid-September the Allies were fighting on the edge of Germany itself.

(text continues on page 74)

Saving Private Ryan

Steven Spielberg's *Saving Private Ryan* (1998), starring Tom Hanks, has been widely praised as the most realistic combat movie ever made. This judgment is based chiefly on its re-creation of the June 6, 1944, Allied assault on Omaha Beach during the invasion of Normandy. The camera focuses on Hanks, rain dripping from helmet, huddled in a crowded landing vessel. Explosions rumble in the distance. The ship plows through heavy seas toward a blackened brow of land. Around him, men vomit. Explosions become louder and sharper. Nearby ships strike mines and blow up; others are obliterated by shellfire. Hanks's landing craft lurches to avoid the mayhem. Like hail against a tin roof, gunfire riddles the landing craft. Some of the men are hit, and the others hunch lower, still vomiting. A deafening din envelops the ship as its bow opens. A curtain of bullets cuts down the men in front. Hanks and several others leap into the sea, but the ship has stopped far short of the beach. They sink. As bullets tear through the water, ripping into those still submerged, Hanks struggles to the surface. He swims, weaponless, toward the beach.

He has crossed the threshold of hell, and over the next 15 minutes viewers descend with him the rest of the way.

Saving Private Ryan differs from other combat films not in the graphic horror of the bloodshed, but in its randomness. The audience expects Hanks to survive the opening scenes of the movie in which he stars, and he does. But all other bets are off: a valiant exploit, a kind gesture, a handsome face—none influences the grim lottery of battle. When huge armies converge, hurling high explosives and steel at each other, one's chances of survival are unaffected by ethics or aesthetics.

But having made this point with heart-pounding emphasis, the movie subverts it. Hanks, unnerved and dispirited, initially hunkers down in the relative safety of the seawall. But then he does his job, rallying his men. They blast a hole through obstacles, crawl toward the concrete fortifications above, penetrate trench defenses, blow up

bunkers, and seize the hill. Many perish in the effort; Hanks, an infantry captain, is among the survivors.

Then comes a new mission, which occupies the remainder of the movie. George C. Marshall, U.S. Army Chief of Staff, has learned of a Mrs. Ryan who has been notified on a single day that three of her sons were killed in action. Her fourth son, James, a private in the 101st Airborne, has just parachuted into Normandy behind German lines. Marshall orders that he be returned to safety. This mission is given to Hanks and the eight surviving members of his platoon. They march inland, encounter snipers, ambushes, and, in the final scenes, a large detachment of German armored vehicles. But they also find Private Ryan (played by Matt Damon).

Along the way, the movie asks many provocative questions, such as whether war improves those who fight. "I think this is all good for me, sir," one earnest soldier confides to Hanks. "Really," Hanks says with a faint smile, "how is that?" The soldier cites Ralph Waldo Emerson: "War educates the senses. Calls into action the will. Perfects the physical constitution." "Emerson had a way of finding the bright side," Hanks deadpans, and the movie endorses his cynicism.

Except in one sense, and that may be all that matters: Hanks and his men have repeatedly demonstrated a willingness to give up their lives for others. Indeed, the movie's central dilemma concerns the moral arithmetic of sacrifice. Is it right to risk eight men to save one? To send a thousand men to near certain death in an initial assault to improve the chances of those that follow? To make one generation endure hell so that another may have freedom? The movie provides no ready answers. But in nearly the final scene it does issue a challenge. Hanks, mortally wounded, is lying amidst the corpses of his platoon, and he beckons to Ryan, who is unhurt. "Earn this," Hanks says, vaguely gesturing to the others.

Saving Private Ryan was part of a wave of nostalgic appreciation during the 1990s for

Tom Hanks, Matt Damon, and Edward Burns in *Saving Private Ryan*.

Actual photograph of American troops approaching code-named Omaha Beach at Normandy.

the generation that had won World War II. A spate of books, movies, and TV documentaries were other expressions of this phenomenon. On accepting the Oscar for his film, Spielberg thanked his father, a World War II vet, "for showing me that there is honor in looking back and respecting the past."

But respect for the past entails getting it right, and the movie makes some significant errors and omissions. For one, it suggests that the men huddled at the base of the seawall blew up the concrete bunkers on their own. This was not possible. In fact, commanders of destroyers took their ships close to the beaches and fired countless heavy shells into the fortifications, allowing the infantry to move up the hills.

The movie also shows the German soldiers as uniformly expert and professional. But the German army had been decimated by losses in the Soviet Union. The army manning the Normandy defenses included many units composed mostly of old men, boys, or conscripted soldiers from Poland or the Soviet Union. Many surrendered as soon as they encountered American soldiers.

Of the movie's implausible elements, the premise that the U.S. Army high command ordered a special mission to pluck a grieving mother's son from danger was based on fact. A real Mrs. Niland received telegrams on the same day informing her that three of her sons had been killed in action. Her fourth son, "Fritz," had parachuted into Normandy with the 101st Airborne. The army did in fact snatch him from the front line and return him to safety.

Saving Private Ryan captures the effect of war on soldiers. Many men at Omaha Beach, like those depicted in the movie, were shattered by the experience. One private, nearly hit by a shell, recalled that he burst into tears. "My buddies got me behind a burned-out craft, where I cried for what seemed like hours. I cried until tears would no longer come. To this day I've never shed another." Other men confessed that, after the terror of a firefight, they shot Germans who had raised their arms in surrender. "In my opinion any enemy shot during this intense action had waited too long to surrender," one G.I. declared.

Yet through it all, some men, like the captain portrayed by Hanks, drew heroism from some unfathomed depths of the soul. One real soldier at Omaha Beach remembered "a captain and two lieutenants who demonstrated courage beyond belief as they struggled to bring order to the chaos around them."

Saving Private Ryan is not a fully accurate representation of the attack on Omaha Beach, but it depicts—realistically and memorably—how soldiers conferred meaning on the heedless calculus of modern warfare.

Questions for Discussion

■ Do generals have the right to order some men to near certain death in order to save others? Do soldiers have the right to disobey such orders? Why or why not?

The front now stretched from the Netherlands along the borders of Belgium, Luxembourg, and France all the way to Switzerland. If the Allies had mounted a massive assault at any one point, as the British commander, Field Marshal Bernard Montgomery, urged, the struggle might have been brought to a quick conclusion. Although the two armies were roughly equal in size, the Allies had complete control of the air and twenty times as many tanks as the foe. The pressure of the advancing Russians on the eastern front made it difficult for the Germans to reinforce their troops in the west. But General Eisenhower believed a concentrated attack too risky. He prepared instead for a general advance.

While he was regrouping, the Germans on December 16 launched a counterattack, planned by Hitler himself, against the Allied center in the Ardennes Forest. The Germans hoped to break through to the Belgian port of Antwerp, thereby splitting the Allied armies in two. The plan was foolhardy and therefore unexpected, and it almost succeeded. The Germans drove a salient ("the bulge") about 50 miles into Belgium. But once the element of surprise had been overcome, their chance of breaking through to the sea was lost. Eisenhower concentrated first on preventing them from broadening the break in his lines and then on blunting the point of their advance. By late January 1945 the old line had been reestablished.

The Battle of the Bulge cost the United States 77,000 casualties and delayed Eisenhower's offensive, but it exhausted the Germans' last reserves. The Allies then pressed forward to the Rhine, winning a bridgehead on the far bank of the river on March 7. Thereafter, one German city fell almost daily. With the Soviets racing westward against crumbling resistance, the end could not be long delayed. In April, American and Soviet forces made contact at the Elbe River. A few days later, with Soviet shells reducing his capital to rubble, Hitler, by then probably insane, took his own life in his Berlin air raid shelter. On May 8 Germany surrendered.

As the Americans drove swiftly forward in the late stages of the war, they began to overrun Nazi concentration camps where millions of Jews had been murdered. The Americans were horrified by what they discovered, but they should not have been surprised. Word of this holocaust, in which no less than 12 million people, half of them Jews, were slaughtered, had reached the United States much earlier. At first the news had been dismissed as propaganda, then discounted as grossly exaggerated. Hitler was known to hate Jews and to have persecuted them, but that he could order the murder of millions of innocent people, even children, seemed beyond belief. By 1943, however, the truth could not be denied.

Little could be done about those already in the camps, but there were thousands of refugees in occupied Europe who might have been spirited to safety. President Roosevelt declined to make the effort; he refused to bomb the Auschwitz death camp in Poland or the rail lines used to bring victims to its gas chambers on the grounds that the destruction of German soldiers and military equipment took precedence over any other objective. Thus, when American journalists entered the camps with the advancing troops, saw the heaps of still-unburied corpses, and talked with the emaciated survivors, their reports caused a storm of protest in America.

The Naval War in the Pacific

Defeating Germany first had not meant abandoning the Pacific region entirely to the Japanese. While armies were being trained and matériel accumulated for the European struggle, much of the available American strength was diverted to maintaining vital communications in East Asia and preventing further Japanese expansion.

The navy's aircraft carriers had escaped destruction at Pearl Harbor, a stroke of immense good fortune because, without most tacticians realizing it, the airplane had revolutionized naval warfare. Commanders discovered that carrier-based planes were far more effective against warships than the heaviest naval artillery because of their greater range and more concentrated firepower. Battleships made excellent gun platforms from which to pound shore installations and support land operations, but against other vessels aircraft were of prime importance.

This truth was demonstrated in May 1942 in the Battle of the Coral Sea. Having captured an empire in a few months without the loss of any warship larger than a destroyer, the Japanese believed the war already won. This led them to overextend themselves.

The Coral Sea lies northeast of Australia and south of New Guinea and the Solomon Islands. Japanese mastery of these waters would cut Australia off from Hawaii and thus from American aid. Admiral Isoroku Yamamoto had dispatched a large fleet of troopships screened by many warships to attack Port Moresby, on the

On February 13 and 14, 1945, British and American forces firebombed Dresden, the cultural capital of Germany. Some 35,000 perished. The purpose of the raid was to terrorize and demoralize the German people; the city's few war industries were not even targeted. This photograph was taken more than a year after the bombing.

Once into Germany the Third Army advanced so quickly in the spring of 1945 that it came upon military installations almost without warning. The photograph here is of General Dwight D. Eisenhower inspecting the condition of the concentration camp at Gotha, Germany, where slain inmates had been left unburied by their fleeing captors.

southern New Guinea coast. On May 7–8 planes from the American carriers *Lexington* and *Yorktown* struck the convoy's screen, sinking a small carrier and damaging a large one. Superficially, the battle seemed a victory for the Japanese, for their planes mortally wounded the *Lexington* and sank two other ships, but the troop transports had been forced to turn back—Port Moresby was saved. Although large numbers of cruisers and destroyers took part in the action, none came within sight or gun range of an enemy ship. All the destruction was wrought by carrier aircraft.

Encouraged by the Coral Sea "victory," Yamamoto decided to force the American fleet into a showdown battle by assaulting the Midway Islands, west of Hawaii. His armada never reached its destination. Between June 4 and 7 control of the central Pacific was decided entirely by airpower. American dive bombers sent four large Japanese carriers to the bottom. About 300 Japanese planes were destroyed. The United States lost only the *Yorktown* and a destroyer. Thereafter the initiative in the Pacific war shifted to the Americans, but victory came slowly and at painful cost.

American land forces were under the command of Douglas MacArthur, a brilliant but egocentric general whose judgment was sometimes distorted by his

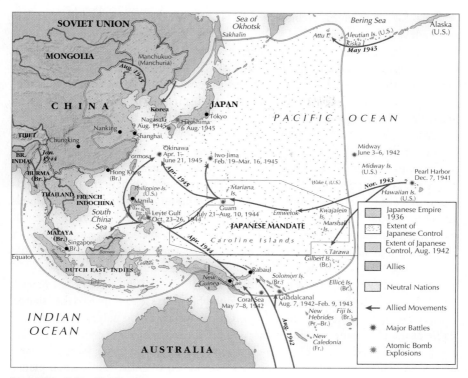

World War II, Pacific Theater

intense concern for his own reputation. MacArthur was in command of American troops in the Philippine Islands when the Japanese struck in December 1941. After his heroic but hopeless defense of Manila and the Bataan peninsula, President Roosevelt had him evacuated by PT boat to escape capture; those under MacArthur's command endured horrific conditions as prisoners of Japan.

Thereafter MacArthur was obsessed with the idea of personally leading an American army back to the Philippines. Although many strategists believed that the islands should be bypassed in the drive on the Japanese homeland, in the end MacArthur convinced the Joint Chiefs of Staff, who determined strategy. Two separate drives were undertaken, one from New Guinea toward the Philippines under MacArthur, the other through the central Pacific toward Tokyo under Admiral Chester W. Nimitz.

Island Hopping

Before commencing this two-pronged advance, the Americans had to eject the Japanese from the Solomon Islands in order to protect Australia from a flank attack. Beginning in August 1942, a series of land, sea, and air battles raged around

Guadalcanal Island in this archipelago. Once again American airpower was decisive, although the bravery and skill of the ground forces that actually won the island must not be underemphasized. American pilots, better trained and with tougher planes than the Japanese, had a relatively easier task. They inflicted losses five to six times heavier on the enemy than they sustained themselves. Japanese airpower disintegrated progressively during the long battle, and this in turn helped the fleet to take a heavy toll on the Japanese navy. By February 1943 Guadalcanal had been secured.

In the autumn of 1943 the American drives toward Japan and the Philippines got under way at last. In the central Pacific campaign the Guadalcanal action was repeated on a smaller but equally bloody scale from Tarawa in the Gilbert Islands to Kwajelein and Eniwetok in the Marshalls. The Japanese soldiers on these islands fought for every foot of ground. They had to be blasted and burned from tunnels and concrete pillboxes with hand grenades, flamethrowers, and dynamite. They almost never surrendered. But Admiral Nimitz's forces were in every case victorious. By midsummer of 1944 this arm of the American advance had taken Saipan and Guam in the Marianas. Now land-based bombers were within range of Tokyo.

Meanwhile, MacArthur was leapfrogging along the New Guinea coast toward the Philippines. In October 1944 he made good his promise to return to the islands, landing on Leyte, south of Luzon. Two great naval clashes in Philippine waters, the Battle of the Philippine Sea (June 1944) and the Battle for Leyte Gulf (October 1944), completed the destruction of Japan's sea power and reduced its air force to a band of fanatical suicide pilots called *kamikazes*, who tried to crash bomb-laden planes into American warships and airstrips. The *kamikazes* caused much damage but could not turn the tide. In February 1945 MacArthur liberated Manila.

The end was now inevitable. B-29 Superfortress bombers from the Marianas rained high explosives and firebombs on Japan. The islands of Iwo Jima and Okinawa, only a few hundred miles from Tokyo, fell to the Americans in March and June 1945. But such was the tenacity of the Japanese soldiers that it seemed possible that it would take another year of fighting and a million more American casualties to subdue the main Japanese islands.

Building the Atom Bomb

At this point came the most controversial decision of the entire war, and it was made by a newcomer on the world scene. In November 1944 Roosevelt had been elected to a fourth term, easily defeating Thomas E. Dewey. Instead of renominating Henry A. Wallace for vice president, whom conservatives considered too radical, the Democratic convention had nominated Senator Harry S Truman of Missouri, a reliable party man well liked by professional politicians. Then, in April 1945, President Roosevelt died of a cerebral hemorrhage. Thus it was Truman, a man painfully conscious of his limitations yet equally aware of the power and responsibility of his office, who had to decide what to do when, in July 1945, American scientists placed in his hands a new and awful weapon, the atomic bomb.

SHOULD THE UNITED STATES HAVE USED ATOMIC BOMBS AGAINST JAPAN?

Robert J. C. Butow's (1954) analysis of Japanese sources proved that the devastation of Hiroshima and Nagasaki had led to Japan's surrender. If there had been no atom bomb, the United States would probably have been forced to invade the islands. According to military estimates cited at the time, an invasion would have resulted in a half million American casualties. Biographers such as David McCullough (1992) and Alonzo L. Hamby (1995) agreed that, given public and congressional opinion, Truman had little choice but to end the war as quickly as possible and with the fewest American casualties.

But Gar Alperovitz (1965), writing when the United States was mired in a global struggle against the Soviet Union, proposed that Truman had been influenced more by a desire to intimidate Stalin than to force the surrender of Japan. This position was strengthened by subsequently declassified documents indicating that few U.S. military analysts anticipated losses as high as those re-

ported in Butow and other sources. John W. Dower (1986) discovered evidence in Japanese sources that the Soviet declaration of war, which came in the wake of Hiroshima, shattered the confidence of the Japanese high command as much as the atomic bombs. Soviet entry alone might have ended the war. The American rush to use atomic weapons against Japan was due to "sheer visceral hatred" of the Japanese, Dower insisted.

The revisionist hypothesis—that Japan might have surrendered without the atomic bombs—is belied by exhaustive last-ditch Japanese preparations for defending the home islands. Whether this information justifies this first—and to date, only—use of these weapons of mass destruction will forever remain a source of debate.

Robert J. C. Butow, *Japan's Decision to Surrender* (1954), Alonzo L. Hamby, *Man of the People* (1995), David McCullough, *Truman* (1992), Gar Alperovitz, *Atomic Diplomacy* (1965), and *The Decision to Use the Atomic Bomb and the Architecture of an American Myth* (1995), John W. Dower, *War Without Mercy* (1986), and Martin J. Sherwin, *A World Destroyed* (1975).

After Roosevelt had responded to Albert Einstein's warning in 1939, government-sponsored atomic research had proceeded rapidly, especially after the establishment of the so-called Manhattan Project in May 1943. The manufacture of the element plutonium at Hanford, Washington, and of uranium 235 at Oak Ridge, Tennessee, continued, along with the design and construction of a transportable atomic bomb at Los Alamos, New Mexico, under the direction of J. Robert Oppenheimer. Almost $2 billion was spent before a successful bomb was exploded at Alamogordo, in the New Mexican desert, on July 16, 1945. As that first mushroom cloud formed over the desert, Oppenheimer recalled the prophetic words of the *Bhagavad Gita:* "I am become death, the shatterer of worlds."

Should a bomb with the destructive force of 20,000 tons of TNT be employed against Japan? By striking a major city, its dreadful power could be demonstrated convincingly, yet doing so would bring death to tens of thousands of Japanese civilians. Many of the scientists who had made the bomb now argued against its use. Others suggested alerting the Japanese and then staging a demonstration explosion at sea, but that idea was discarded because of concern that the bomb might fail to explode.

Truman was torn between his awareness that the bomb was "the most terrible thing ever discovered" and his hope that using it "would bring the war to an end." The bomb might cause a revolution in Japan, might lead the emperor to intervene, might even persuade the military to give up. Considering the thousands of Americans who would surely die in any conventional invasion of Japan and, on a less humane level, influenced by a desire to end the Pacific war before the Soviet Union could intervene effectively and thus claim a role in the peacemaking, the president chose to go ahead. The moral soundness of Truman's decision has been debated ever since.

On August 6 the Superfortress *Enola Gay* dropped an atomic bomb on Hiroshima, killing about 78,000 persons (including twenty American prisoners of war) and injuring nearly 100,000 more out of a population of 344,000. Over 96 percent of the buildings in the city were destroyed or damaged. Three days later, while the stunned Japanese still hesitated, a second atomic bomb, the only other one that had so far been assembled, blasted Nagasaki. This second drop was less defensible morally, but it had the desired result. On August 15 Japan surrendered.

Thus ended the greatest war in history. Its cost was beyond calculation. No accurate count could be made even of the dead; we know only that the total was in the neighborhood of 20 million. As in World War I, American casualties—291,000 battle deaths and 671,000 wounded—were smaller than those of the other major belligerents. About 7.5 million Soviets died in battle, 3.5 million Germans, 1.2 million Japanese, and 2.2 million Chinese; Britain and France, despite much smaller populations, suffered losses almost as large as did the United States. And far more than in World War I, American resources, human and material, had made victory possible.

No one could account the war a benefit to humanity, but in the late summer of 1945 the future looked bright. Fascism was dead. The successful wartime diplomatic dealings of Roosevelt, Churchill, and the Soviet dictator, Joseph Stalin, encouraged many to hope that the communists were ready to cooperate in rebuilding Europe. In the United States isolationism had disappeared; the message of Wendell Willkie's best-selling *One World*, written after a globe-circling tour made by the 1940 Republican presidential candidate at the behest of President Roosevelt in 1942, appeared to have been absorbed by the majority of the people.

Out of the death and destruction had come technological developments that seemed to herald a better world as well as a peaceful one. Enormous advances in the design of airplanes and the development of radar (which some authorities think was more important than any weapons system in winning the war) were about to revolutionize travel and the transportation of goods. Improvements in surgery and other medical advances gave promise of saving millions of lives, and the development of penicillin and other antibiotics, which had greatly reduced the death rate among troops, would perhaps banish all infectious diseases.

Above all, there was the power of the atom. The force that seared Hiroshima and Nagasaki could be harnessed to serve peaceful needs, the scientists promised, with results that might free humanity forever from poverty and toil. The period of reconstruction would be prolonged, but with all the great powers adhering to the new United Nations charter, drafted at San Francisco in June 1945, international cooperation could be counted on to ease the burdens of the victims of war and help the poor and underdeveloped parts of the world toward economic and political independence. Such at least was the hope of millions in the victorious summer of 1945.

Wartime Diplomacy

That hope was not to be realized, in large part because of a conflict that developed between the Soviet Union and the western Allies. During the war Americans with as different points of view as General Douglas MacArthur and Vice President Henry A. Wallace took strongly pro-Soviet positions, and American newspapers and magazines published many laudatory articles about Russia. These views were naive, to say the least, but the United States and the Soviet Union agreed emphatically on the need to defeat Hitler. The Soviets repeatedly expressed a willingness to cooperate with the Allies in dealing with postwar problems. The Soviet Union was one of the twenty-six signers of the Declaration of the United Nations (January 1942), in which the Allies promised to eschew territorial aggrandizement after the war, to respect the right of all peoples to determine their own form of government, to work for freer trade and international economic cooperation, and to force the disarmament of the aggressor nations.[1]

Between August and October 1944, Allied representatives met at Dumbarton Oaks, outside Washington, to plan a new league of nations. The chief Soviet delegate, Andrei A. Gromyko, opposed limiting the use of the veto by the great powers on the future United Nations (UN) Security Council, but he did not take a deliberately obstructionist position. At a conference held at Yalta in the Crimea in February 1945, Stalin joined Roosevelt and Churchill in the call for a meeting in April at San Francisco to draft a charter for the UN.

The UN charter drafted at the fifty-nation San Francisco Conference gave each UN member a seat in the General Assembly, a body designed for discussion rather than action. The locus of authority in the new organization resided in the Security

---

[1]These were the principles first laid down in the so-called Atlantic Charter, drafted by Roosevelt and Churchill at a meeting on the USS Augusta off Newfoundland in August 1941.

Council, "the castle of the great powers." This consisted of five permanent members (the United States, the Soviet Union, Great Britain, France, and China) and six others elected for two-year terms.

The Security Council was charged with responsibility for maintaining world peace, but any great power could block UN action whenever it wished to do so. The United States insisted on this veto power as strongly as the Soviet Union did. In effect the charter paid lip service to the Wilsonian ideal of a powerful international police force, but it incorporated the limitations that Henry Cabot Lodge had proposed in his 1919 reservation to Article X of the League Covenant, which relieved the United States from the obligation of enforcing collective security without the approval of Congress.

Allied Suspicion of Stalin

Long before the war in Europe ended, however, the Allies had clashed over important policy matters. Since later world tensions developed from decisions made at this time, an understanding of the disagreements is essential for evaluating several decades of history.

Much depends on one's view of the postwar Soviet system. If the Soviet government under Stalin was bent on world domination, events fall readily into one pattern of interpretation. If, having at enormous cost endured an unprovoked assault by the Nazis, it was seeking only to protect itself against the possibility of another invasion, these events are best explained differently.

It is clear, however, that the Soviets resented the British-American delay in opening up a second front. They were fighting for survival against the full power of the German armies; any invasion, even an unsuccessful one, would have relieved some of the pressure. Roosevelt and Churchill would not move until they were ready, and Stalin had to accept their decision. At the same time, Stalin never concealed his determination to protect his country from future attack by extending its western frontier after the war. He warned the Allies repeatedly that he would not tolerate any unfriendly government along the western boundary of the Soviet Union.

Most Allied leaders, including Roosevelt, admitted privately during the war that the Soviet Union would annex territory and possess preponderant power in Eastern Europe after the defeat of Germany, but they never said this publicly. They believed that free governments could somehow be created in countries like Poland and Bulgaria that the Soviets would trust enough to leave to their own devices. "The Poles," Winston Churchill said early in 1945, "will have their future in their own hands, with the single limitation that they must honestly follow . . . a policy friendly to Russia. This is surely reasonable."

However reasonable, Churchill's statement was impractical. The Polish question was a terribly difficult one. The war, after all, had been triggered by the German attack on Poland; the British in particular felt a moral obligation to restore that nation to its prewar independence. During the war a Polish government in exile was set up in London, and its leaders were determined—especially after the discovery in 1943 of the murder of some 5,000 Polish officers several years earlier at Katyn, in Russia, presumably by the Soviet secret police—to make no concessions to Soviet territorial demands. Public opinion in Poland (and indeed in all the states along Russia's western frontier) was not so much anti-Soviet as anti-Russian. Yet the Soviet Union's legitimate interests (to say nothing of its power in the area) could not be ignored.

Yalta and Potsdam

At the Yalta Conference, Roosevelt and Churchill agreed to Soviet annexation of large sections of eastern Poland. In return they demanded that free elections be held in Poland itself. "I want this election to be . . . beyond question," Roosevelt told Stalin. "It should be like Caesar's wife." In a feeble attempt at a joke he added: "I did not know her but they said she was pure." Stalin agreed, almost certainly without intending to keep his promise. The elections were never held; Poland was run by a pro-Soviet puppet regime.

Stalin apparently could not understand why the Allies were so concerned about the fate of a small country remote from their strategic spheres. That they professed to be concerned seemed to him an indication that they had some secret, devious purpose. He could see no difference (and "revisionist" American historians agree with him) between the Soviet Union's dominating Poland and maintaining a government there that did not reflect the wishes of a majority of the Polish people and the United States's dominating many Latin American nations and supporting

Churchill, Roosevelt, and Stalin photographed at the weeklong Yalta conference in February 1945. By April 1945, Roosevelt was dead.

unpopular regimes within them. Roosevelt, however, was worried about the political effects that Soviet control of Poland might have in the United States. Polish Americans would be furious if the United States allowed the Soviets to control their homeland.

But had Roosevelt described the difficulties to the Poles and the rest of the American people more frankly, their reaction might have been less angry. In any case, when he realized that Stalin was going to act as he pleased, Roosevelt was furious. "We can't do business with Stalin," he said shortly before his death in April 1945. "He has broken every one of the promises he made at Yalta." In July 1945, following the surrender of Germany, the new president, Harry Truman, met with Stalin and Churchill at Potsdam, outside Berlin.[2] They agreed to try the Nazi leaders as war criminals, made plans for exacting reparations from Germany, and confirmed the division of the country into four zones to be occupied separately by American, Soviet, British, and French troops. Berlin, deep in the Soviet zone, had itself been split into four sectors. Stalin rejected all arguments that he loosen his hold on Eastern Europe, and Truman (who received news of the successful testing of the atom bomb while at Potsdam) made no concessions. But he was impressed by Stalin. The dictator was "smart as hell," he wrote in his diary. "Stalin was an SOB," the plainspoken president explained to some officers while returning to the United States from Potsdam on the cruiser *Augusta*. Then he added: "Of course he thinks I'm one too."

On both sides suspicions were mounting, positions hardening. Yet all the advantages seemed to be with the United States. Was this not, as Henry Luce, the publisher of *Time* had declared, "the American century," an era when American power and American ideals would shape the course of events the world over? Besides its army, navy, and air force and its immense industrial potential, alone among the nations the United States possessed the atomic bomb. When Stalin's actions made it clear that he intended to control Eastern Europe and to exert influence elsewhere in the world, most Americans first reacted somewhat in the manner of a mastiff being worried by a yapping terrier: Their resentment was tempered by amazement. It took time for them to realize that the war had caused a fundamental change in international politics. The United States might be the strongest country in the world, but the western European nations, victor and vanquished alike, were reduced to their own and America's surprise to the status of second-class powers. The Soviet Union, on the other hand, had gained more influence than it had held under the czars and regained the territory it had lost as a result of World War I and the communist revolution.

---

[2]*Clement R. Attlee replaced Churchill during the conference after his Labour party won the British elections.*

1941	Japan attacks Pearl Harbor
	Roosevelt and Churchill draft Atlantic Charter
1942	Executive Order 9066 sends Japanese Americans to relocation camps
	Japanese take Philippines
	Carrier-based planes dominate Battle of Coral Sea
	U.S. airpower takes control of central Pacific at Battle of Midway
	U.S. troops invade North Africa
1943	Oppenheimer directs Manhattan Project to make atom bomb
	Allies invade Italy
1944	Allies invade Normandy, France (D-Day)
	Battle of the Bulge exhausts German reserves
1945	Roosevelt, Churchill, and Stalin meet at Yalta Conference
	Fifty nations draft UN Charter at San Francisco
	Roosevelt dies; Truman becomes president
	Germany surrenders (V-E Day)
	United States tests atom bomb at Alamogordo, New Mexico
	Truman, Churchill, Stalin meet at Potsdam
	United States drops atom bombs on Hiroshima and Nagasaki, Japan
	Japan surrenders (V-J Day)

28 | CHAPTER

The American Century

THE SCHOLASTIC APTITUDE TEST (SAT)—OR THE SIMILAR ACT TEST
—is an obligatory rite of passage for college-bound Americans today. But few are
aware that, like so much of modern American society, the SAT was a product of
World War II. In April 1943, the military sought to determine which of the nation's
young men were best suited to become officers or take on other specialized tasks;
to that end, it administered an aptitude test, the Army-Navy College Qualifying
Test, to 316,000 male high school seniors, half of the male seniors in the country.
At the time, James Bryant Conant, president of Harvard and chairman of the
agency that spearheaded the Manhattan Project, lauded the tests and proposed that
they be used to determine who should be admitted to the nation's elite colleges
and universities. In 1948, the Army-Navy test evolved into the SAT, administered by
the Educational Testing Service (ETS) for the College Board.

World War II influenced postwar America in countless other ways, including
innovations in technology. For example, the 1955 Chevy Nomad was the brainchild
of Edward Cole, who designed the engine of the M-5 tank in 1941. Cole applied his
wartime insights in engine design to the V-8 that powered the Chevy. "Gun sights"
and a jet airplane as a hood ornament highlighted the car's link to the war. It became one of the most popular cars ever made.

After World War II, the United States did not convert to peace so much as in-
ternalize the lessons learned during war. One was the obligation of defending
democracy throughout the world. This had been the goal of *Time* publisher Henry
Luce, who in 1941 had predicted the nation's preeminent role in what would be
known as the "American century."

But Luce did not envision what transpired during the fifteen years after 1945.
The revolution in armaments following the atom bomb gave rise to more weapons
of unimaginable destructiveness. The Soviet Union and Communist China sup-

planted Nazi Germany and Japan as formidable challenges to American democracy. War erupted in Korea and, again, American troops fought far from American soil. The advance of communism abroad precipitated fears about hidden enemies at home. The military budget ballooned.

President Dwight D. Eisenhower grew increasingly alarmed by the social consequences of Luce's vision. In his final speech before leaving office in 1961, Eisenhower warned Americans of the "grave implications" resulting from "the conjunction of an immense military establishment and a large arms industry." What Eisenhower called the "military-industrial complex" potentially endangered "the very structure of our society." Could the nation mount a worldwide defense of democracy without endangering that democracy at home?

Truman Becomes President

In late 1945 most Americans were probably more concerned with what was happening at home than with foreign developments, and no one was more aware of this than Harry Truman. When he received the news of Roosevelt's death, he claimed that he felt as though "the moon, the stars, and all the planets" had suddenly fallen upon him. Although he could not have been quite as surprised as he indicated (Roosevelt was known to have been in extremely poor health), he was acutely conscious of his own limitations.

Truman was born in Missouri in 1884. After his service in a World War I artillery unit, he opened a men's clothing store in Kansas City. The store failed in the postwar depression. Truman then became a minor cog in the political machine of Democratic boss Tom Pendergast. In 1934 Truman was elected to the U.S. Senate, where he proved to be a loyal but obscure New Dealer. He first attracted national attention during World War II when his "watchdog" committee on defense spending, working with devotion and efficiency, saved the government immense sums. This led to his nomination and election as vice president.

As president, Truman sought to carry on in the Roosevelt tradition. Curiously, he was at the same time humble and cocky, even brash—both idealistic and cold-bloodedly political. He adopted liberal objectives only to pursue them sometimes by rash, even repressive means. Too often he insulted opponents instead of convincing or appeasing them. Complications tended to confuse him, in which case he either dug in his heels or struck out blindly, usually with unfortunate results. On balance, however, he was a strong and in many ways a successful president.

The Postwar Economy

Nearly all the postwar leaders were worried by the possibility of a serious depression, and nearly all accepted the necessity of employing federal authority to stabilize the economy and speed national development. The Great Depression and the huge government expenditures made necessary by the war had proven the theories of John Maynard Keynes. Democrats and Republicans alike were convinced that it was possible to prevent sharp swings in the business cycle and therefore to do away with serious unemployment by monetary and fiscal manipulation.

When World War II ended, nearly everyone wanted to demobilize the armed forces, remove wartime controls, and reduce taxes. Yet everyone also hoped to prevent any sudden economic dislocation, to check inflation, and to make sure that goods in short supply were fairly distributed. Neither the politicians nor the public could reconcile these conflicting objectives. Labor wanted price controls retained but wage controls lifted; industrialists wished to raise prices and keep the lid on wages. Farmers wanted subsidies but opposed price controls and the extension of social security benefits to agricultural workers. In this difficult situation President Truman failed to win either the confidence of the people or the support of Congress.

Yet the country weathered the reconversion period with remarkable ease. The pent-up demand for houses, automobiles, clothing, washing machines, and countless other products, backed by the war-enforced savings of millions, kept factories operating at capacity. But when the veterans returned (more than 60,000 of them accompanied by foreign brides), few went without work for long. Because of the boom, the demand for labor was large and growing. In addition, the government made an unprecedented educational opportunity available to veterans. Instead of a general bonus, which would have stimulated consumption and inflation, in 1944 Congress passed the GI Bill of Rights, which made subsidies available to veterans so they could continue their educations, learn new trades, or start new businesses. Nearly 8 million veterans took advantage of the education and training grants, greatly to their long-term advantage, and thus to the country's.

Cutting taxes and removing price controls did cause a period of rapid inflation. Food prices rose more than 25 percent between 1945 and 1947, which led to demands for higher wages and a wave of strikes—nearly 5,000 in 1946 alone. Inflation and labor unrest helped the Republicans to win control of both houses of Congress in 1946 for the first time since the 1920s.

This was the climate when in June 1947 the new Congress passed the Taft-Hartley Act over the veto of President Truman. The measure outlawed the closed shop (a provision written into many labor contracts requiring new workers to join the union before they could be employed). Most important, it authorized the president to seek court injunctions to prevent strikes that in his opinion endangered the national interest. The injunctions would hold for 80 days—a "cooling-off" period during which a presidential fact-finding board could investigate and make recommendations. If the dispute remained unresolved after 80 days, the president was to recommend "appropriate action" to Congress.

The Taft-Hartley Act made the task of unionizing unorganized industries more difficult, but it did not seriously hamper existing unions. Although it outlawed the closed shop, it permitted union shop contracts, which forced new workers to join the union after accepting employment.

The Containment Policy

Although postwar economic recovery went more smoothly than most expected, foreign policy issues vexed the Truman presidency. Repeatedly Stalin made it clear that he had no intention of even consulting with Western leaders about his domination of Eastern Europe, and he seemed intent on extending his power deep into war-devastated central Europe. The Soviet Union also controlled Outer Mongolia, parts of Manchuria, and northern Korea, and it had annexed the Kurile Islands and regained the southern half of Sakhalin Island from Japan. It was fomenting trouble in Iran. By January 1946 Truman had decided to stop "babying" the Russians. "Only one language do they understand," he noted in a memorandum. "How many [military] divisions have you?"

Truman's problem—and it would bedevil American policymakers for years—was that Stalin had far more divisions than anyone else. Truman, a seasoned politician, had swiftly responded to the postwar clamor to "bring the boys home." In the two years following the surrender of Japan, the armed forces of the United States had dwindled from 6 million to 1.5 million. Stalin, who kept domestic foes out of office by shooting them, ignored domestic pressure to demobilize the Red Army, estimated by U.S. intelligence at twice the size of the American army.

Stalin and the Red Army evoked the image of Hitler's troops pouring across the north European plains. Like Hitler, Stalin was a cruel dictator who championed an ideology of world conquest. Averill Harriman, American ambassador to the Soviet Union, warned that communist ideology exerted an "outward thrust" more dangerous than Nazism. George Kennan, a scholarly foreign officer who also had served in Moscow, called for a policy of "long-term, patient but firm and vigilant containment" of the Soviet Union.

A Turning Point in Greece

The strategy of containment began to take shape early in 1947 as a result of a crisis in Greece. Greek communists, waging a guerrilla war against the monarchy, were receiving aid from communist Yugoslavia and Bulgaria. Great Britain had been assisting the monarchists but could no longer afford this drain on its resources. In February 1947 the British informed President Truman that they would cut off aid to Greece.

The British predicament forced American policymakers to confront the fact that their European allies had not been able to rebuild their war-weakened economies. The communist "Iron Curtain" (a phrase coined by Winston Churchill) seemed about to close down on another nation. Policymakers ignored the fact that the Soviet Union was actually discouraging the rebels out of fear of American intervention in the area. As Undersecretary of State Dean Acheson put it, the "corruption" of Greece might "infect" the entire Middle East and then spread through Asia Minor and Egypt and to Italy and France.

Truman therefore asked Congress to approve what became known as the Truman Doctrine. If Greece or Turkey fell to the communists, he said, all of the Middle East might be lost. To prevent this "unspeakable tragedy," he asked for $400 million in military and economic aid to Greece and Turkey. "It must be the policy of the United States to support free peoples who are resisting attempted subjugation by armed minorities or by outside pressures," he said.

By exaggerating the consequences of inaction and by justifying his request on ideological grounds, Truman obtained his objective. The result was the establishment of a right-wing, military-dominated government in Greece. In addition, by not limiting his request to the specific problem posed by the situation in Greece, Truman caused considerable concern in many countries.

The threat to Western Europe certainly loomed large in 1947. With the region, in the words of Winston Churchill (the great phrase-maker of the era), "a rubble-heap, a charnel house, a breeding-ground of pestilence and hate," the entire continent seemed in danger of falling into communist hands without the Soviet Union raising a finger.

The Marshall Plan and the Lesson of History

In a 1946 speech entitled "The Lesson of History," George C. Marshall, army chief of staff during World War II, reminded Americans that their isolationism had contributed to Hitler's unchecked early aggression. This time, Marshall noted, the people of the United States must be prepared to act against foreign aggressors. In 1947 Marshall was named secretary of state. He outlined an extraordinary plan by which the United States would finance the reconstruction of the European economy. "Hunger, poverty, desperation, and chaos" were the real enemies of freedom and democracy, Marshall said. The need was to restore "the confidence of the European people in the economic future of their own countries." Even the Soviet Union and Soviet-bloc nations would be eligible for American aid.

The European powers eagerly seized upon Marshall's suggestion. They set up a sixteen-nation Committee for European Economic Cooperation, which soon submitted plans calling for up to $22.4 billion in American assistance.

The Soviet Union and its European satellites were tempted by the offer of aid and sent representatives to the initial planning meetings. But Stalin grew anxious that his satellite states, attracted by American money, would be drawn into the American orbit. He recalled his delegates and demanded that Eastern European nations do likewise. Those who hesitated were ordered to report to the Kremlin. "I went to Moscow as the Foreign Minister of an independent sovereign state," Jan Masaryk of Czechoslovakia commented bitterly. "I returned as a lackey of the Soviet government."

In February 1948 a communist coup took over the Czechoslovak government; Masaryk fell (or more likely was pushed) out a window to his death. These

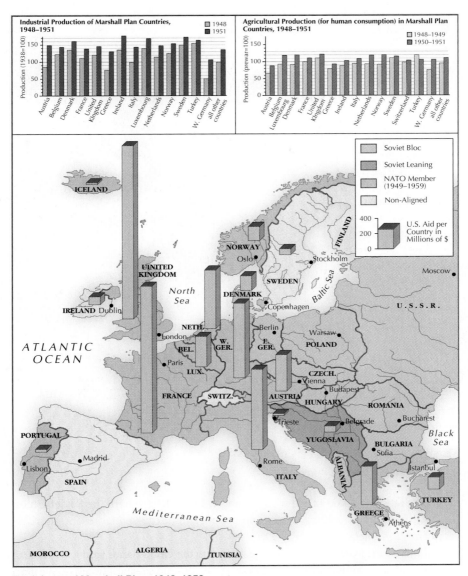

Industrial Production of Marshall Plan Countries, 1948–1951

☐ 1948   ■ 1951

Agricultural Production (for human consumption) in Marshall Plan Countries, 1948–1951

☐ 1948–1949   ■ 1950–1951

Soviet Bloc
Soviet Leaning
NATO Member (1949–1959)
Non-Aligned

U.S. Aid per Country in Millions of $

Recipients of Marshall Plan, 1948–1952

strong-arm tactics brought to mind the Nazi takeover of Czechoslovakia a decade earlier and helped persuade Congress to appropriate over $13 billion for the Marshall aid program. Results exceeded all expectations. By 1951 Western Europe was booming.

But Europe was now divided in two. In the West, where American-influenced governments were elected, private property was respected if often taxed heavily,

Air Relief to Berlin, 1948–1949

and corporations gained influence and power. In the East, where the Soviet Union imposed its will and political system on client states, deep-seated resentment festered among subject peoples.

In March 1948 Great Britain, France, Belgium, the Netherlands, and Luxembourg signed an alliance aimed at social, cultural, and economic collaboration. The Western nations abandoned their understandable but counterproductive policy of crushing Germany economically. They announced plans for creating a single West German Republic with a large degree of autonomy.

In June 1948 the Soviet Union retaliated by closing off surface access to Berlin from the west. For a time it seemed that the Allies must either fight their way into the city or abandon it to the communists. Unwilling to adopt either alternative, Truman decided to fly supplies to the capital from Frankfurt, Hanover, and Hamburg. American C-47 and C-54 transports shuttled back and forth in fair weather and foul, carrying enough food, fuel, and other goods necessary to maintain more than 2 million West Berliners. The Berlin airlift put the Soviets in an un-

In June 1948 the Soviet Union cut off all water and road traffic into West Berlin. Truman's plan to airlift food and fuel to provision 2.5 million people seemed impossible, but during the 15 months of the Berlin crisis, planes such as this one, landing every four minutes, delivered nearly 2.5 million tons of supplies.

comfortable position; if they were determined to keep supplies from West Berlin, they would have to start the fighting. They were not prepared to do so. In May 1949 they lifted the blockade.

The Election of 1948

In the spring of 1948 President Truman's fortunes were at low ebb. Public opinion polls suggested that a majority of the people considered him incompetent or worse. The Republicans seemed so sure to win the 1948 presidential election that many prominent Democrats began to talk of denying Truman the nomination. Two of FDR's sons came out for General Eisenhower as the Democratic candidate. Governor Dewey, who again won the Republican nomination, ran confidently (even complacently), certain that he would carry the country.

Truman's position seemed hopeless because he had alienated both southern conservatives and northern liberals. The Southerners were particularly distressed because in 1946 the president had established a Committee on Civil Rights, which had recommended antilynching and anti-poll tax legislation and the creation of a permanent Fair Employment Practices Commission. When the Democratic convention adopted a strong civil rights plank, the southern delegates walked out. Southern conservatives then founded the States' Rights ("Dixiecrat") party and nominated J. Strom Thurmond of South Carolina for president.

As for the liberals, in 1947 a group that believed Truman's containment policy a threat to world peace organized a new Progressive party and nominated former

In 1948 the strongly Republican *Chicago Daily Tribune* printed its post-election headlines before all the returns were in. For Truman, it was the perfect climax to his hard-won victory.

Vice President Henry A. Wallace. With two minor candidates sure to cut into the Democratic vote, the president's chances seemed minuscule.

Promising to "give 'em hell," Truman launched an aggressive whistle-stop campaign. Traveling by rail, he made several hundred informal but hard-hitting speeches. He excoriated the "do-nothing" Republican Congress, which had rejected his program and passed the Taft-Hartley Act, and he warned labor, farmers, and consumers that if Dewey won, Republican "gluttons of privilege" would do away with all the gains of the New Deal years.

Millions were moved by Truman's arguments and by his courageous fight against great odds. The success of the Berlin airlift during the presidential campaign helped him considerably, as did disaffection among normally Republican midwestern farmers. The Progressive party fell increasingly into the hands of communist sympathizers, driving away many liberals who might otherwise have supported Wallace. Dewey's smug, lackluster speeches failed to attract independents.

The president reinvigorated the New Deal coalition and won an amazing upset victory on election day. He collected 24.1 million votes to Dewey's 21.9 million, the two minor candidates being held to about 2.3 million. In the Electoral College his margin was a thumping 303 to 189.

Truman's victory encouraged him to press forward with what he called his Fair Deal program. He urged Congress to raise the minimum wage, fund an ambitious public housing program, develop a national health insurance system, and repeal the Taft-Hartley Act. However, relatively little of Truman's Fair Deal was enacted into law. Congress approved a federal housing program and measures increasing the minimum wage and social security benefits, but these were merely extensions of New Deal legislation.

Containing Communism Abroad

During Truman's second term the confrontation between the United States and the Soviet Union dominated the headlines. To strengthen ties with the European democracies, in April 1949 the North Atlantic Treaty was signed in Washington. The United States, Great Britain, France, Italy, Belgium, the Netherlands, Luxembourg, Denmark, Norway, Portugal, Iceland, and Canada[1] agreed "that an armed attack against one or more of them in Europe or North America shall be considered an attack against them all" and that in the event of such an attack each would take "individually and in concert with the other Parties, such action as it deems necessary, including the use of armed force." The pact established the North Atlantic Treaty Organization (NATO).

In September 1949 the Soviet Union detonated an atomic bomb. Truman had expressed doubts that the Soviets could build such sophisticated weapons. But when the explosion was confirmed, he called for rapid expansion of the American nuclear arsenal. He also asked his advisers to determine whether the United States should develop a new weapon thousands of times more destructive than atomic bombs. The "super" or hydrogen bomb would replicate the fusion process on the surface of the sun. The Atomic Energy Commission argued that there was no military use for hydrogen bombs, which would destroy hundreds of square miles as well as precipitate a dangerous arms race with the Soviet Union. The Joint Chiefs of Staff disagreed. Even if the hydrogen bomb could not be used in battle, they argued, its mere existence would intimidate enemies; and, the military men added, the Soviets would themselves build a hydrogen bomb whether or not the United States did so. (Unbeknownst to American leaders, Stalin was already developing a hydrogen bomb.) On January 31, 1950, Truman publicly announced that "though none wants to use it" he had no choice but to proceed with a hydrogen bomb.

In Asia the effort to contain communism in China failed utterly. Civil war erupted following Japan's surrender. By the end of 1949 the communists under Mao Zedong had crushed the Nationalists under Chiang Kai-shek (sometimes spelled Jiang Jieshi). The remnants of Chiang Kai-shek's forces fled to the island of Formosa, now called Taiwan. The "loss" of China to communism strengthened right-wing elements in the Republican party. They charged that Truman had not backed the Nationalists strongly enough and that he had stupidly underestimated Mao's dedication to the cause of world revolution.

Despite a superficial plausibility, neither charge made much sense. American opinion would not have supported military intervention, and such intervention unquestionably would have alienated the Chinese people. That *any* American action could have changed the outcome in China is unlikely. The United States probably gave the Nationalists too much aid rather than too little.

Containment had relied on American money, materials, and know-how, but not on American soldiers. In early 1950, Truman proposed to pare the budget by

---

[1]In 1952, Greece and Turkey joined the alliance, and in 1954, West Germany.

further reducing the nation's armed forces. Truman also called for a thorough review of the concept of containment. Dean Acheson, who recently had succeeded George Marshall as secretary of state, supervised the study. In March, it was submitted to the National Security Council, assigned a numerical designation (NSC-68), classified top secret, and sent to the nation's military and diplomatic leaders for review.

NSC-68 called for an enormous military expansion. The Soviet Union, it declared, was engaged in a worldwide assault on freedom: "A defeat of free institutions anywhere is a defeat everywhere." Instead of relying on other nations, the United States itself must develop sufficient military forces to stop communism from spreading *anywhere in the world*. Military spending therefore had to be increased by a staggering 350 percent to nearly $50 billion. If the Soviet Union failed to keep up with the American armed forces, it would no longer pose a threat, and if it attempted to match the high levels of American military spending, its less efficient economic system would collapse from the strain.

The document was submitted to Truman on April 7, 1950. He was initially cool to the idea and appalled by its cost. He had planned to cut $1 billion from the $14 billion military budget. Within a few months, however, events in Korea changed his mind.

Hot War in Korea

After World War II the province of Korea was taken from Japan and divided at 38° north latitude into the Democratic People's Republic in the north, backed by the Soviet Union, and the Republic of Korea in the south, backed by the United States and the UN. Both powers withdrew their troops from the peninsula. The Soviets left behind a well-armed local force, but the Republic of Korea's army was small and ill trained. In June 1950, when North Korean armored divisions, led by 150 Soviet-made tanks, rumbled across the 38th parallel, the South Koreans were unable to stop them.

Truman was at his family home in Independence, Missouri, when Acheson telephoned with the news of the North Korean attack. "Dean," Truman explained, "we've got to stop the sons of bitches no matter what." Truman hastened to Washington. On the flight, he recalled how the communists in Korea were acting "just as Hitler, Mussolini, and the Japanese had acted ten, fifteen, and twenty years earlier." "If this were allowed to go unchallenged," he concluded, "it would mean a third world war, just as similar incidents had brought on the Second World War." With the backing of the UN Security Council (but without asking Congress to declare war), he sent American planes into battle.[2] Ground troops soon followed. Truman also ordered the adoption of NSC-68 "as soon as feasible."

---

[2]*The Soviet Union, which could have vetoed this action, was at the moment boycotting the Security Council because the UN had refused to give the Mao Zedong regime China's seat on that body.*

DID TRUMAN NEEDLESSLY EXACERBATE RELATIONS WITH THE SOVIET UNION?

Debating the Past

Here Stalin applauds Soviet military might. Historian Thomas A. Bailey (1950), like most Americans at the time, blamed Stalin's takeover of Eastern Europe and his threats elsewhere for the onset of the Cold War. In his view, Truman was right to contain Stalin.

But as the Cold War intensified and its costs mounted, historians looked more critically at Truman's actions. William Appleman Williams (1959) proposed that Truman, like American policymakers before him, had promoted worldwide containment of the Soviet Union chiefly to advance American economic interests abroad. Michael Hogan (1987) more subtly argued that the Marshall Plan put corporations at the center of the reconstruction of Europe. Walter La Feber (1967) and other revisionists found Truman's actions and rhetoric needlessly provocative.

John Lewis Gaddis (1972, 1982) rejected the contention that Truman was motivated by economic considerations. Truman's goal, rather, was to cobble together a military coalition of independent allies capable of containing the Soviet Union militarily.

Historians focused on Truman because little was known of Stalin's thinking. But as Soviet archives opened up following the collapse of the Soviet Union, Gaddis revised his views. In *Now We Know* (1997), he emphasized Stalin's commitment to communist ideology. Truman had not goaded him into these beliefs. Thomas Mastny (1996) attributed the despot's behavior to his insecurity rather than his belief in communist ideology.

Thomas A. Bailey, *America Faces Russia* (1950), William Appleman Williams, *The Tragedy of American Diplomacy* (1959), Walter La Feber, *America, Russia and the Cold War* (1967), Michael Hogan, *Marshall Plan* (1987), John Lewis Gaddis, *The United States and the Origins of the Cold War* (1972), *Strategies of Containment* (1982), and *Now We Know* (1997), and Thomas Mastny, *The Cold War and Soviet Insecurity* (1996).

Nominally the Korean War was a struggle between the invaders and the United Nations. General MacArthur, placed in command, flew the blue UN flag over his headquarters, and sixteen nations supplied troops for his army. However, more than 90 percent of the forces were American. At first the North Koreans pushed them back rapidly, but in September a front was stabilized around the port of Pusan, at the southern tip of Korea. Then MacArthur executed a brilliant amphibious maneuver, striking at the west coast city of Inchon, about 50 miles south of the 38th parallel. Outflanked, the North Koreans retreated in disorder. By October the battlefront had moved north of the 1945 boundary.

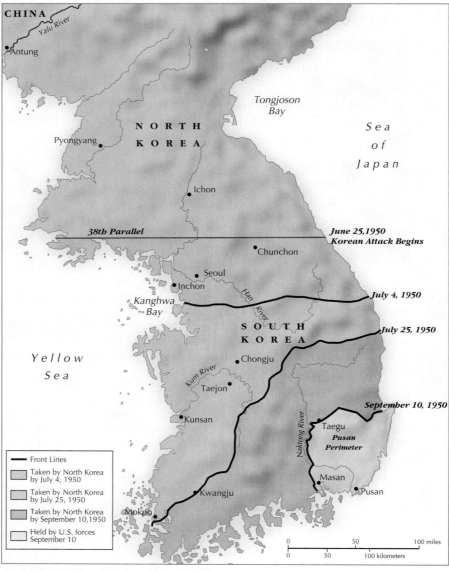

North Korean Offensive, June–August 1950

General MacArthur now proposed the conquest of North Korea, even if it meant bombing "privileged sanctuaries" on the Chinese side of the Korean border. Less sanguine military officials balked at taking on China but urged occupying North Korea to protect the future security of the south. A few of Truman's civilian advisers, the most important being George Kennan, opposed advancing beyond the 38th parallel, fearing intervention not only by the Red Chinese but also by the Soviets.

The Chinese counteroffensive of November 1950 caught the Americans by surprise and cut off many units. Here, a U.S. Marine rests during the retreat that winter.

Truman authorized MacArthur to advance as far as the Yalu River, the boundary between North Korea and China. It was an unfortunate decision, an example of how power, once unleashed, so often gets out of hand. As the advance progressed, ominous reports came from north of the Yalu. Foreign Minister Chou En-lai warned that the Chinese would not "supinely" tolerate seeing their neighbors being "savagely invaded by imperialists." Chinese "volunteers" began to turn up among the captives taken by UN units.

Alarmed, Truman flew to Wake Island, in the Pacific, to confer with MacArthur, but the general, who had a low opinion of Asian soldiers, assured him that the Chinese would not dare to intervene. If they did, he added, his army would crush them easily; the war would be over by Christmas.

Seldom has a general miscalculated so badly. Ignoring intelligence reports and dividing his advancing units recklessly, he drove toward the Yalu. Suddenly, on November 26, thirty-three Chinese divisions, hidden in the interior mountains of Korea, smashed through the center of MacArthur's lines. Overnight a triumphant advance became a bloody, disorganized retreat. MacArthur now spoke of the "bottomless well of Chinese manpower" and justified his earlier confidence by claiming that he was fighting "an entirely new war."

The UN army rallied south of the 38th parallel, and MacArthur then urged that he be permitted to bomb Chinese installations north of the Yalu. He also suggested a naval blockade of the coast of China and the use of Chinese Nationalist troops. When Truman rejected these proposals on the ground that they would lead to a third world war, MacArthur, who tended to ignore the larger political aspects of the conflict, attempted to rouse Congress and the public against the president by openly criticizing administration policy. Truman ordered him to be silent, and when the general persisted, he removed him from command.

At first the Korean "police action" had been popular in the United States, but as the months passed and the casualties mounted, many citizens became disillusioned and angry. To Americans accustomed to triumph and fond of oversimplifying complex questions, containment seemed, as its costs in blood and dollars mounted, a monumentally frustrating policy. Military men backed the president almost unanimously. General Omar N. Bradley, chairman of the Joint Chiefs of Staff, said that a showdown with communist China "would involve us in the wrong war, at the wrong place, at the wrong time and with the wrong enemy." In June 1951 the communists agreed to discuss an armistice in Korea, although the negotiations dragged on interminably. The war was unresolved when Truman left office: by the time it was over, it had produced 157,000 American casualties, including 54,200 dead.

If the Korean War persuaded Truman to adopt NSC-68, it also exposed the failings of the policy. By conceiving of communism as a monolithic force it tended to make it so, driving Red China and the Soviet Union into each other's arms. By committing American military forces to potential trouble spots throughout the world, it increased the likelihood they would prevail in none.

The Communist Issue at Home

The Korean War highlighted the paradox that, at the pinnacle of its power, the influence of the United States in world affairs was declining. Its monopoly on nuclear weapons had been lost. China had passed into the communist orbit. Elsewhere in Asia and throughout Africa, new nations, formerly colonial possessions of the Western powers, were adopting a "neutralist" position in the Cold War. Despite the billions poured into armaments and foreign aid, national security seemed far from ensured.

Internal as well as external dangers loomed. Alarming examples of communist espionage in Canada, in Great Britain, and in the United States itself convinced many citizens that clever conspirators were everywhere at work undermining American security. Both the Republicans and conservative Democratic critics of Truman's domestic policies were charging that he was "soft" on communists.

There were never more than 100,000 communists in the United States, and party membership plummeted after the start of the Cold War. However, the possibility that a handful of spies could do enormous damage fueled a kind of panic that could be used for partisan purposes. In 1947, hoping to defuse the communists-in-government issue by being more zealous in pursuit of spies than his critics, Truman established a Loyalty Review Board to check up on government employees. The program made even sympathy for a long list of vaguely defined "totalitarian" or "subversive" organizations grounds for dismissal. During the following 10 years about 2,700 government workers were discharged, only a relative handful of them for legitimate reasons. A much larger number resigned.

In 1948 Whittaker Chambers, an editor of *Time* who had formerly been a communist, charged that Alger Hiss, president of the Carnegie Endowment for International Peace and a former State Department official, had been a communist in the 1930s. Hiss denied the charge and sued Chambers for libel. Chambers then produced microfilms purporting to show that Hiss had copied classified documents for dispatch to Moscow. Hiss could not be indicted for espionage because of the statute of limitations; instead he was charged with perjury. His first trial resulted in a hung jury; his second, ending in January 1950, in conviction and a five-year jail term.

If a distinguished official such as Hiss had been disloyal, anything seemed possible. The case fed the fears of those who believed in the existence of a powerful communist underground in the United States. The disclosure in February 1950 that a British scientist, Klaus Fuchs, had betrayed atomic secrets to the Soviets heightened these fears, as did the arrest and conviction of his American associate, Harry Gold, and two other Americans, Julius and Ethel Rosenberg, on the same charge.

Although they were not major spies and the information they revealed was not crucial, the Rosenbergs were executed, to the consternation of many liberals in the United States and elsewhere. However, information gathered by other spies had speeded the Soviet development of nuclear weapons. This fact encouraged some Republicans to press the communists-in-government issue hard.

McCarthyism

In February 1950 an obscure senator, Joseph R. McCarthy of Wisconsin, introduced this theme in a speech to the even less well-known Ohio County Republican Women's Club of Wheeling, West Virginia. "The reason we find ourselves in a position of impotency," he stated, "is not because our only powerful potential enemy has sent men to invade our shores, but rather because of the traitorous actions of those who have been treated so well by this nation." The State Department, he added, was "infested" with communists. "I have here in my hand a list of 205—a list of names that were known to the Secretary of State as being members of the Communist Party and who nevertheless are still working and shaping . . . policy."[3]

---

[3]*McCarthy was speaking from rough notes, and no one made an accurate record of his words. The exact number mentioned has long been in dispute. On other occasions he said there were fifty-seven and eighty-one "card-carrying" communists in the State Department.*

McCarthy was totally unscrupulous. The "big lie" was his most effective weapon: The enormity of his charges and the status of his targets convinced thousands that there must be some truth in what he was saying. Nevertheless, his crude tactics would have failed if the public had not been so worried about communism. The worries were caused by the reality of Soviet military power, the attack on Korea, the loss of the nuclear monopoly, and the stories about spies, some of them true.

Dwight D. Eisenhower

As the 1952 presidential election approached, Truman's popularity was again at low ebb. Senator McCarthy attacked him relentlessly for his handling of the Korean conflict and his "mistreatment" of General MacArthur. In choosing their candidate, the Republicans passed over the twice-defeated Dewey and their most prominent leader, Senator Robert A. Taft of Ohio, an outspoken conservative, and nominated General Dwight D. Eisenhower.

Eisenhower's popularity did not grow merely out of his achievements in World War II. Although a West Pointer (class of 1915), he struck most persons as anything

Many critics lampooned Eisenhower for his banal amusements. A popular bumper sticker read: "BEN HOGAN [a famous golfer] FOR PRESIDENT. IF WE'RE GOING TO HAVE A GOLFER FOR PRESIDENT, LET'S HAVE A GOOD ONE." Others have viewed Eisenhower's passion for golf as characteristic of his presidential style: methodical, prudent, and, when in the rough, disarmingly shrewd.

but warlike. After the bristly, combative Truman, his genial personality and evident desire to avoid controversy proved widely appealing. In his reluctance to seek political office, Eisenhower reminded the country of George Washington, whereas his seeming ignorance of current political issues was no more a handicap to his campaign than the similar ignorance of Jackson and Grant in their times. People "liked Ike" because his management of the Allied armies suggested that he would be equally competent as head of the complex federal government. His promise during the campaign to go to Korea if elected to try to bring the war to an end was a political masterstroke.

The Democrats nominated Governor Adlai E. Stevenson of Illinois, whose grandfather had been vice president under Grover Cleveland. Stevenson's unpretentiousness was appealing, and his witty, urbane speeches captivated intellectuals. In retrospect, however, it is clear that he had no chance of defeating the popular Eisenhower. Eisenhower received almost 34 million votes to Stevenson's 27 million, and in the Electoral College his margin was 442 to 89.

Eisenhower was unwilling to do away with existing social and economic legislation or to cut back on military expenditures. Some economists claimed that he reacted too slowly in dealing with business recessions and that he showed insufficient concern for speeding the rate of national economic growth. Yet he adopted an almost Keynesian approach to economic problems; that is, he tried to check downturns in the business cycle by stimulating the economy.

Eisenhower approved the extension of social security to an additional 10 million persons; created a new Department of Health, Education, and Welfare; began the St. Lawrence Seaway project; and in 1955 came out for federal support of education and a highway construction act that eventually produced a 40,000-mile network of superhighways covering every state in the Union. His somewhat doctrinaire belief in decentralization and private enterprise reduced the effectiveness of his social welfare measures, but on balance, he proved to be an excellent politician. He knew how to be flexible without compromising his basic values.

The Eisenhower-Dulles Foreign Policy

The American people, troubled and uncertain over the stalemate in Korea, counted on Eisenhower to find a way to employ the nation's immense strength constructively. The new president shared the general feeling that a change of tactics in foreign affairs was needed. He counted on his secretary of state to solve the practical problems.

His choice, John Foster Dulles, was a lawyer with considerable diplomatic experience. He had been an outspoken critic of Truman's foreign policy. In a May 1952 article in *Life* entitled "A Policy of Boldness," he argued that global military containment was both expensive and ineffective. Instead of waiting for the communist powers to make a move and then "containing" them, the United States should put more emphasis on nuclear bombs and less on conventional weapons. Such a "new look" military would be cheaper to maintain than a force of conventional weapons and a large standing army, and it would prevent the United States from being caught up in "local" conflicts like the Korean War. The nation's military forces, spearheaded by its formidable nuclear arsenal, would serve as "a deterrent of war instead of a mere means of waging war after we got into it."

Korea offered the first test of his views. After Eisenhower's post-election trip to Korea failed to bring an end to the war, Dulles signaled his willingness to use tactical nuclear weapons in Korea by showily transferring nuclear warheads from the United States mainland to bomber units stationed in East Asia. He also issued a calculatedly vague warning about tough new measures. Several weeks later, in July 1953, the Chinese signed an armistice that ended hostilities but left Korea divided. The administration interpreted the softening of the Chinese position as proof that the nuclear threat had worked. (Dulles was apparently mistaken about the effectiveness of his Korean gambit. In recent years, Chinese officials have said that they were unaware of the American nuclear threats.)

Emboldened by his evident triumph, Dulles again brandished the nation's nuclear threats. Chiang Kai-shek had stationed 90,000 soldiers—one-third of his army—in Quemoy and Matsu, two small islands located a few miles from mainland China. In 1954 the Chinese communists began shelling the islands, presumably in preparation to invade them. Chiang appealed for American protection, warning that loss of the islands would bring about the collapse of Nationalist China. Dulles concurred that the consequences throughout East Asia would be "catastrophic." At a press conference in 1955 Eisenhower announced his willingness to use nuclear weapons to defend the islands, "just exactly as you would use a bullet or anything else." The Chinese communists backed down.

Massive retaliation succeeded, further, in reducing the defense budget. The reliance on a nuclear threat allowed Eisenhower to pare another half million men from the armed forces, saving $4 billion annually. On balance, however, Dulles's strategy was flawed, and many of his schemes were preposterous. Above all, massive retaliation made little sense when the Soviet Union possessed nuclear weapons as powerful as those of the United States.

McCarthy Self-Destructs

Although the State Department was now controlled by Dulles, a hard-line anticommunist, Senator McCarthy continued his attacks on the department. In 1953 television newscaster Edwin R. Murrow cast doubt on McCarthy's methods; soon he and McCarthy were pummeling each other on the air. (See Re-Viewing the Past, "Good Night, and Good Luck," pp. 800–801.) Finally, McCarthy overreached himself. Early in 1954 he turned his guns on the army, accusing Pentagon officials of trying to blackmail his committee. The resulting Army-McCarthy hearings, televised before the country, proved the senator's undoing. For weeks his dark scowl, his blind combativeness, and his disregard for every human value stood exposed for millions to

Senator Joe McCarthy and his aide Roy Cohn *(left)* listen to testimony at the Army-McCarthy hearings in April 1954. Cohn, a tough, young lawyer who had made a reputation prosecuting suspected communists in Manhattan, intimidated some people by threatening to make public their homosexuality; yet he was himself a homosexual who steadfastly denied it. In 1986 he died of AIDS. Tony Kushner's Pulitzer Prize–winning play *Angels in America* (1993) told Cohn's story.

see. When the hearings ended in June 1954 after some million words of testimony, his spell had been broken.

The Senate, with President Eisenhower, who despised McCarthy but considered it beneath his dignity as president to "get into the gutter with that guy," applying pressure behind the scenes, at last moved to censure the senator in December 1954. This reproof completed the destruction of his influence. Although he continued to issue statements and wild charges, the country no longer listened. In 1957 he died of cirrhosis of the liver.

Asian Policy After Korea

Shortly after an armistice was finally arranged in Korea in July 1953, new trouble erupted far to the south in the former French colony of Indochina. Nationalist rebels led by the communist Ho Chi Minh had been harassing the French in Vietnam, one of the three puppet kingdoms (the others were Laos and Cambodia) fashioned by France in Indochina after the defeat of the Japanese. When China recognized the rebels, who were known as the Vietminh, and supplied them with arms, President Truman countered with economic and military assistance to the French, and President Eisenhower continued and expanded this assistance.

Good Night, and Good Luck

Good Night, and Good Luck (2005), directed by George Clooney, highlights the struggle between Edward R. Murrow, the nation's first prominent television broadcaster, and Joseph McCarthy, the Wisconsin Senator who led a crusade against communist subversion. Their battle, which raged from October 1953 through April 1954, was fought on five episodes of *See It Now*, Murrow's Tuesday evening television show. The movie's title was taken from Murrow's sign-off for the program.

The first skirmish was over Milo Radulovich, a lieutenant whom the Air Force dismissed as a security risk because his father, an immigrant, had subscribed to a Serbian-language newspaper that supported Marshall Tito, the Communist dictator of Yugoslavia. Murrow's documentary, "The Case against Lt. Milo Radulovich" (October 1953), asserted that the officer had been treated unfairly. "We believe the son shall not bear the iniquity of the father," Murrow concluded, "Even though that iniquity be proved and in this case it was not."

In February 1954 McCarthy counterattacked indirectly. His head of staff informed CBS that "Murrow was on the Soviet payroll in 1934." Murrow's defense of Radulovich, the staffer added, was further reason to doubt the broadcaster's loyalty to the nation.

Murrow decided to strike publicly at McCarthy. On March 9, 1954, Murrow aired "A Report on Senator Joseph R. McCarthy." The show featured unflattering news footage showing McCarthy browbeating witnesses and chortling at the foibles of presidents and generals—interspersed with Murrow's inci-

sive commentary: "We cannot defend freedom abroad by deserting it at home."

The following week, *See It Now* focused on McCarthy's interrogation of Anne Lee Moss, a black woman who worked as a code clerk at the Pentagon. McCarthy and his staff cited unnamed accusers who claimed that Moss had secretly belonged to the Communist party. Without affirming her innocence, Murrow concluded that Moss "had the right to meet her accusers face to face."

McCarthy demanded equal time and CBS granted it. On April 6, *See It Now* ran McCarthy's verbose rebuttal on the advance of communism during the twentieth century. He called Murrow "the leader and the cleverest of the jackal pack" who promoted communism, adding that Murrow had "sponsored a Communist school in Moscow" and had belonged to the Industrial Workers of the World—"a terrorist organization."

Murrow flatly denied the charges. He explained that in 1934 he had worked at the Institute of International Education to promote study abroad; of the nearly 100 seminars he arranged, a couple were to be held at Moscow University, run by the Soviet state.

Opinion turned against McCarthy. Within seven months, the Senate censured him for abusing his position. Murrow's victory, the movie shows, was bittersweet: CBS, unnerved by being thrust into a political firestorm, retreated from hard-hitting journalism and instead broadcast mindless amusements.

Clooney's movie is structured around the above episodes, and holds to the historical record with singular tenacity. Whenever David Strathairn, the actor who plays Murrow, is shown on *See It Now*, for example, he uses Murrow's exact words. And Clooney did not cast an actor to play McCarthy, choosing instead to show only archival footage. "Nobody was going to be able to play McCarthy without getting nailed for overacting," Clooney later explained.

Although *Good Night, and Good Luck* at times resembles a documentary rather than a Hollywood film, the movie advances several historical arguments that warrant closer examination. The movie asserts that

Edward R. Murrow *(right)* talking with *See It Now* producer Fred Friendly (1955).

David Strathairn *(right)* as Murrow, and George Clooney as Friendly. (Clooney also directed the movie.)

McCarthyism was a witch hunt, a phrase that surfaces repeatedly in the movie. Clooney himself praised Arthur Miller's *The Crucible*, a play about the Salem witch trials that indicted McCarthyism by implication. (See Re-Viewing the Past in Chapter 2.) A witch hunt, at least among modern sensibilities, is fraudulent if one assumes that witches do not exist. But the fact is that some Americans *did* spy for the Soviet Union; the movie made no mention of Julius Rosenberg, a Soviet spy who was executed just four months before the Radulovich episode, or of Alger Hiss, who was in prison on espionage-related charges during the Murrow-McCarthy episode.

The movie also credits Murrow with bringing down McCarthy. "McCarthy was untouchable until Murrow stepped up," Clooney claimed. That Murrow, an early master of the medium, used television to hurt McCarthy is indisputable. But others hit the Wisconsin senator with body blows. A few hours before Murrow's show on McCarthy, for example, Senator Ralph Flanders of Vermont denounced McCarthy on the Senate floor: "He dons war paint; he goes into his war dance; he emits his war whoops; he goes forth to battle and proudly returns with the scalp of a pink Army dentist." Some scholars maintain that McCarthy's demise was caused when the army, with Eisenhower's support, went after McCarthy. On March 11, 1954, the army released transcripts showing that McCarthy had used his influence to extort special treatment for his staff. The fatal blow to McCarthy, such scholars claim, came not from Murrow but from Joseph Welch, head attorney for the army: "Have you no sense of decency, sir, at long last?" Welch asked McCarthy in a famous exchange.

The movie's most important debate, however, is less about McCarthy and Murrow

than about the role of television journalism in American life. *Good Night, and Good Luck* opens with Murrow's speech to broadcasters in 1958. Television, he complains, "is being used to distract, delude, amuse and insulate us." The movie closes with Murrow's call for the television industry to educate and inform the American people. "Otherwise," he intoned, "it is merely wires and lights in a box."

Murrow was speaking from painful experience. In 1955 Alcoa, which sponsored *See It Now* to burnish its corporate image, sought a larger audience to sell a new product—aluminum foil. That same year, CBS's new quiz show, *The $64,000 Question*, became a smash hit. *See It Now* was moved out of prime time; in 1958, it was canceled.

By ending on this note, the movie implicitly calls on television to emulate Murrow's crusading brand of journalism. But Murrow himself was ambivalent. Years before his encounter with McCarthy, Murrow had insisted that broadcast journalists refrain from taking sides. "I favor some such device as radio and TV stations ringing a bell every time a newscaster is about to inject his own views," he said. But with the Radulovich show, Murrow abandoned this standard. The *New York Times* observed that the Radulovich episode "marked perhaps the first time that a major network . . . consented to a program taking a vigorous editorial stand in a matter of national importance and controversy." Murrow demonstrated that reporters could wield tremendous power. *Good Night, and Good Luck* raises several important questions. Clooney's resolute answers can be fairly debated, but one issue is beyond dispute. The popular actor could have made more money with a fluffy romantic comedy; but, as Murrow asked in 1958, what's the point if it's all "merely wires and lights in a box"?

Questions for Discussion

- Do you think that television journalists wield more influence than newspaper reporters?
- Are journalists morally obliged to report a story in a neutral way even if they believe that one side is right and the other wrong? Why or why not?

Early in 1954 Ho Chi Minh's troops trapped and besieged a French army in the remote stronghold of Dien Bien Phu. In May the 20,000-man garrison surrendered. In July France, Great Britain, the Soviet Union, and China signed an agreement dividing Vietnam along the 17th parallel. France withdrew from the area. The northern sector became the Democratic Republic of Vietnam, controlled by Ho Chi Minh; the southern remained in the hands of the emperor, Bao Dai. An election to settle the future of all Vietnam was scheduled for 1956.

When it seemed likely that the communists would win that election, Ngo Dinh Diem, a conservative anticommunist, overthrew Bao Dai and became president of South Vietnam. The United States supplied his government liberally with aid. The planned election was never held, and Vietnam remained divided.

Dulles responded to the diplomatic setback in Vietnam by establishing the Southeast Asia Treaty Organization (SEATO), but only three Asian nations—the Philippine Republic, which was granted independence in 1947, Thailand, and Pakistan—joined this alliance.[4]

Israel and the Middle East

The slaughter of six million European Jews by the Nazis strengthened Jewish claims to a homeland and intensified pressure to allow hundreds of thousands of Jewish refugees to immigrate to Palestine, which was governed by Great Britain according to a League of Nations mandate. But the influx of Jewish settlers, and their calls for creation of a Jewish state (Israel), provoked Palestinian and Arab leaders. Fighting broke out. President Truman angered Arab leaders by endorsing the partition of the region into an Israeli and a Palestinian state. In 1947, the United Nations voted for partition and on May 14, 1948, the State of Israel was established. Within hours, Truman recognized its sovereignty.

Then Arab armies from Egypt, Jordan, Iraq, Syria, and Lebanon attacked Israel. Although badly outnumbered, the Israelis were better organized and better armed than the Arabs and drove them off with relative ease. With them departed nearly a million local Arabs, thereby creating a desperate refugee problem in nearby countries.

President Truman had consistently placed support for Israel before other considerations in the Middle East, partly because of the conviction that survivors of the Nazi holocaust were entitled to a country of their own and partly because of the political importance of the Jewish vote in the United States. Dulles and Eisenhower tried to restore balance by deemphasizing American support of Israel. They hoped to mollify the Arabs. Of increasing importance to the United States were the seas of oil that lay beneath the Middle East's deserts. Iran, Iraq, Kuwait, and Saudi Arabia sat upon nearly 60 percent of the world's known reserves. Gas-hungry Americans could ill-afford to alienate the Arab world.

---

[4]*The other signatories were Great Britain, France, the United States, Australia, and New Zealand.*

In 1952 a revolution in Egypt had overthrown the dissolute King Farouk. Colonel Gamal Abdel Nasser emerged as the strongman of Egypt. When Eisenhower refused to sell Egypt arms, Nasser drifted toward the communist orbit and nationalized the Suez Canal. The British, in conjunction with the French and without consulting the United States, decided to take back the canal by force. The Israelis, alarmed by repeated Arab hit-and-run raids, also attacked Egypt.

Events moved swiftly. Israeli armored columns crushed the Egyptian army in the Sinai Peninsula in a matter of days. Then Nikita Khrushchev, who had become First Secretary of the Communist party of the Soviet Union following Stalin's death in 1953, threatened to send "volunteers" to Egypt and launch atomic missiles against France and Great Britain if they did not withdraw. Eisenhower also demanded that the invaders pull out of Egypt. In London large crowds demonstrated against their own government. On November 6, only nine days after the first Israeli units had invaded Egypt, Prime Minister Anthony Eden, haggard and shaken, announced a cease-fire. Israel withdrew its troops. The crisis subsided as rapidly as it had arisen.

The United States had won a measure of respect in the Arab countries, but at what cost? Its major allies had been humiliated. Their ill-timed attack had enabled the Soviet Union to recover much of the prestige it had lost as a result of its brutal suppression of a Hungarian revolt that had broken out a week before the Suez fiasco.

Eisenhower and Khrushchev

In 1956 Eisenhower was reelected, defeating Adlai Stevenson even more decisively than he had in 1952. Despite evident satisfaction with their leader, however, the American people were in a sober mood. Hopes of pushing back the Soviet Union with clever stratagems and moral fervor were fading. Although the United States detonated the first hydrogen bomb in November 1952, the Soviets followed suit within six months. The Cold War between the superpowers had become yet more chilling.

The United States had far more air force bases, bombers, and radar installations than the Soviet Union. But this advantage disappeared in the exhaust cloud of a Soviet rocket, launched on October 4, 1957, that carried a 184-pound capsule named *Sputnik* far above the atmosphere into earth orbit. Soon, American policymakers knew, Soviet missiles capable of reaching American soil would be tipped with nuclear warheads. The nation's far-flung network of bomber defenses had become obsolete, and with it the strategy of massive retaliation.

Several weeks later Khrushchev rubbed hard at the rawest sore in the American psyche: the anguished memory of Pearl Harbor. In an interview with publisher William Randolph Hearst Jr., Khrushchev blustered that the Soviet Union could launch ten or twenty intercontinental missiles with nuclear warheads "tomorrow." He boasted that the American military was no match for the Soviet behemoth. This was nonsense and Eisenhower knew it. Yet to point out the weaknesses of the Soviet

Vice President Richard M. Nixon and Soviet leader Nikita Khrushchev engaged in their "kitchen debate" over the future of capitalism at a Moscow trade fair in 1959. Although this encounter did little to advance United States–Soviet relations, it established Nixon's credentials as a tough negotiator.

military—to call Khrushchev's bluff—was potentially to goad the unstable Soviet leader to rash action. While critics at home flayed Eisenhower for allowing a "missile gap" with the Soviet Union, the president testily reassured the American people that they had little to fear, but otherwise remained silent. In September 1960, however, Khrushchev told the United Nations that the Soviet Union was turning out nuclear missiles "like sausages from an automatic machine."

Latin America Aroused

Events in Latin America compounded Eisenhower's difficulties. During World War II the United States, needing Latin American raw materials, had supplied its southern neighbors liberally with economic aid. In the period following victory a hemispheric mutual defense pact was signed at Rio de Janeiro in September 1947, and the following year the Organization of American States (OAS) came into being. In the OAS, decisions were reached by a two-thirds vote; the United States had neither a veto nor any special position.

But as the Cold War progressed, the United States neglected Latin American questions. Economic problems plagued the region, and in most nations reactionary governments reigned. Radical Latin Americans accused the United States of supporting cliques of wealthy tyrants, whereas conservatives blamed insufficient American economic aid for the plight of the poor.

Eisenhower, eager to improve relations, stepped up economic assistance. Resistance to communism nonetheless continued to receive first priority. In 1954 the government of Jacobo Arbenz Guzman in Guatemala began to import Soviet weapons. The United States promptly dispatched arms to neighboring Honduras. Within a month an army led by an exiled Guatemalan officer marched into the country from Honduras and overthrew Arbenz. Elsewhere in Latin America, Eisenhower, as Truman had before him, continued to support regimes that were kept in power by the local military.

The depth of Latin American resentment of the United States became clear in the spring of 1958, when Vice President Nixon made what was supposed to be a goodwill tour of South America. Everywhere he was met with hostility. In Lima, Peru, he was mobbed; in Caracas, Venezuela, students pelted him with eggs and stones. He abandoned the remainder of his trip. For the first time the American people gained some inkling of Latin American opinion and the social and economic troubles that lay behind it.

Events in Cuba demonstrated that there was no easy solution to Latin American problems. In 1959 a revolutionary movement headed by Fidel Castro overthrew Fulgencio Batista, one of the most noxious of the Latin American dictators. Eisenhower recognized the Castro government at once, but the Cuban leader soon began to criticize the United States in highly colored speeches. Castro confiscated American property, suppressed civil liberties, and entered into close relations with the Soviet Union. After he negotiated a trade agreement with the Soviet Union in February 1960, which enabled the Russians to obtain Cuban sugar at bargain rates, the United States retaliated by prohibiting the importation of Cuban sugar into America.

Khrushchev then announced that if the United States intervened in Cuba, he would defend the country with atomic weapons. "The Monroe Doctrine has outlived its time," Khrushchev warned. Shortly before the end of his second term, Eisenhower broke off diplomatic relations with Cuba.

The Politics of Civil Rights

During Eisenhower's presidency a major change occurred in the legal status of American blacks. Eisenhower had relatively little to do with this change, which was part of a broad shift in attitudes toward the rights of minorities in democracies. After 1945 the question of racial equality took on special importance because of the ideological competition with communism. Evidence of color prejudice in the United States damaged the nation's image, particularly in Asia and Africa, where the United States and the Soviet Union were competing for influence. An awareness of foreign criticism of American racial attitudes, along with resentment that almost a century after the Emancipation Proclamation they were still second-class citizens, produced a growing militancy among American blacks. At the same time, fears of communist subversion in the United States led to the repression of the rights of many white citizens. Even before McCarthy's fateful Wheeling speech, Congress contemplated a crackdown on suspected communists. In 1950, over Truman's veto, it passed an Internal Security Act (better known as the McCarran Act), which required every "communist-front organization" to register with the attorney general. Members of such organizations were barred from defense work and from traveling abroad. The law even provided for construction of internment camps in the event of a national emergency.

Under Eisenhower, while the McCarthy hysteria reached its peak and declined, the government compiled a spotty record on civil rights. The search for subversive federal employees continued. The refusal to grant security clearance to Oppenheimer, one of the fathers of the atomic bomb, on the grounds that he had associated with communists and communist sympathizers, was the most glaring instance of the administration's catering to anticommunist extremists, for it was based on the supposition that Oppenheimer could be denied access to discoveries he had helped to make possible. Eisenhower completed the integration of the armed forces begun by Truman, but he was temperamentally incapable of a frontal assault on the racial problem. This was done by the Supreme Court, which interjected itself into the civil rights controversy in dramatic fashion in 1954.

Under pressure of litigation sponsored by the NAACP, the Court had been gradually undermining the "separate but equal" principle laid down in *Plessy* v. *Ferguson* in 1896, at least insofar as it applied to higher education. In 1938 it ordered the University of Missouri law school to admit a black student because no law school for blacks existed in the state. This decision gradually forced some southern states to admit blacks to advanced programs. "You can't build a cyclotron for one student," the president of the University of Oklahoma confessed when the Court, in 1948, ordered Oklahoma to provide equal facilities. Two years later, when Texas actually attempted to create a separate law school for a single black applicant, the Court ruled that truly equal education could not be provided under such circumstances.

In 1953 President Eisenhower appointed California's Governor Earl Warren chief justice of the U.S. Supreme Court. Convinced that the Court must take the offensive in the cause of civil rights, Warren succeeded in welding his associates into a unit on this question. In 1954 an NAACP-sponsored case, *Brown* v. *Board of Education of Topeka*, came up for decision. The NAACP lawyer, Thurgood Marshall, challenging the "separate but equal" doctrine, submitted a mass of sociological evidence to show that the mere fact of segregation made equal education impossible and did serious psychological damage to both black and white children. Speaking for a unanimous Court, Warren reversed the *Plessy* decision. "In the field of public education, the doctrine of 'separate but equal' has no place," he declared. "Separate educational facilities are inherently unequal." The next year the Court ordered the states to end segregation "with all deliberate speed."

Despite these decisions, few districts in the southern and border states tried to integrate their schools. Many white Southerners who deplored the way blacks were treated in the region nonetheless opposed integrating the schools. As late as September 1956, barely 700 of the South's 10,000 school districts had been desegregated. The region became more alienated from the rest of the nation than at any time since Reconstruction.

White citizens' councils dedicated to all-out opposition sprang up throughout the South. When the school board of Clinton, Tennessee, integrated the local high school in September 1956, a mob rioted in protest, shouting "Kill the niggers!" and destroying the property of blacks. The school was kept open with the help of the National Guard until segregationists blew up the building with dynamite. In

Angry jeers from whites rain down on Elizabeth Eckford, one of the first black students to arrive for registration at Little Rock's Central High School in 1957. State troops turned black students away from the school until President Eisenhower overruled the state decision and called in the National Guard to enforce integration.

Virginia the governor announced a plan for "massive resistance" to integration that denied state aid to local school systems that wished to desegregate. When the University of Alabama admitted a single black woman in 1956, riots broke out. University officials forced the student to withdraw temporarily and then expelled her when she complained more forcefully than they deemed proper.

President Eisenhower thought equality for blacks could not be obtained by government edict. He said that the Court's ruling must be obeyed, but he did little to discourage southern resistance to desegregation. "I am convinced that the Supreme Court decision set back progress in the South at least fifteen years," he remarked to one of his advisers. "The fellow who tries to tell me you can do these things by force is just plain nuts."

However, in 1957 events compelled him to act. When the school board of Little Rock, Arkansas, opened Central High School to a handful of black students, the governor of the state, Orval M. Faubus, called out the National Guard to prevent them from attending. Unruly crowds taunted the students and their parents. Eisenhower could not ignore the direct flouting of federal authority. After the mayor of Little Rock sent him a telegram saying, in part, "situation is out of control and police cannot disperse the mob," he dispatched 1,000 paratroopers to Little Rock and summoned 10,000 National Guardsmen to federal duty, thus removing them from Faubus's control. The black students then began to attend class. A token force of soldiers was stationed at Central High for the entire school year to protect them.

The Election of 1960

As the end of his second term approached, Eisenhower somewhat reluctantly endorsed Vice President Richard Nixon as the Republican candidate to succeed him. Nixon had originally skyrocketed to national prominence by exploiting the public fear of communist subversion. "Traitors in the high councils of our government," he charged in 1950, "have made sure that the deck is stacked on the Soviet side of the diplomatic tables." In 1947 he was an obscure young congressman from California; in 1950 he won a seat in the Senate; two years later Eisenhower chose him as his running mate.

The Democrats nominated Senator John F. Kennedy of Massachusetts. His chief rival for the nomination, Lyndon B. Johnson of Texas, the Senate majority leader, became his running mate. Kennedy was the son of Joseph P. Kennedy, a wealthy businessman who had served as ambassador to Great Britain under Franklin Roosevelt. An indifferent student at Harvard, Kennedy in his junior year—1939—traveled with his father to Europe. When Hitler attacked Poland a few months later, Kennedy had the topic for his senior thesis: "Appeasement at Munich," in which he chastised British and American leaders in the 1920s and 1930s for a lack of foresight and resolve. Published in 1940 as *Why England Slept*, the book received favorable reviews and was briefly a best seller. During World War II, Kennedy served in the Pacific, captaining a torpedo boat. When the boat was sliced in two by a Japanese destroyer, Kennedy showed personal courage in rescuing his men. Besides wealth, intelligence, good looks, and charm, Kennedy had the advantage of his Irish-Catholic ancestry, a particularly valuable asset in heavily Catholic Massachusetts. After three terms in the House, he moved on to the Senate in 1952.

After his landslide reelection in 1958, only Kennedy's religion seemed to limit his political future. No Catholic had ever been elected president, and the defeat of Alfred E. Smith in 1928 had convinced most students of politics (including Smith) that none ever would be elected. Nevertheless, influenced by Kennedy's victories in the Wisconsin and West Virginia primaries—the latter establishing him as an effective campaigner in a predominantly Protestant region—the Democratic convention nominated him.

Kennedy had not been a particularly liberal congressman. He was not involved in the civil rights movement (which was not a major issue in the presidential campaign). He enthusiastically endorsed the Cold War and indicted the Eisenhower administration for falling behind the Soviet Union in the race to build missiles. He admitted frankly that he liked Senator Joseph McCarthy and thought that "he may have something" in his campaign against supposed communists in government. However, as a presidential candidate, he sought to appear more forward-looking. He stressed his youth and "vigor" (a favorite word) and promised to open a "New Frontier" for the country. Nixon ran on the Eisenhower record, which he promised to extend in liberal directions.

A series of television debates between the candidates helped Kennedy by enabling him to demonstrate his maturity and mastery of the issues. Although both candidates laudably avoided it, the religious issue was important. His Catholicism helped Kennedy in eastern urban areas but injured him in many farm districts and throughout the West. Kennedy's victory, 303 to 219 in the Electoral College, was paper-thin in the popular vote, 34,227,000 to 34,109,000.

Milestones

1944	Congress provides subsidies to veterans in GI Bill of Rights
1947	Taft-Hartley Act regulates unions and labor disputes
	Truman announces Truman Doctrine to stop communism's spread
1948	Marshall Plan provides funds to rebuild Europe
	Harry S Truman is elected president
	State of Israel is created as Jewish homeland; Arabs declare war
1948–1949	United States supplies West Berlin during Berlin airlift
1949	North Atlantic Treaty Organization (NATO) formed
	USSR detonates atom bomb
1950	North Korea invades South Korea
	NSC-68 calls for massive military buildup
	Alger Hiss is convicted of perjury
	McCarran Act restricts "subversive" activity
	Senator Joseph McCarthy charges that the State Department is riddled with communists
	UN counterattack in Korea is driven back by Red Chinese army
1952	Dwight D. Eisenhower is elected president
1953	John Foster Dulles institutes nuclear-based foreign policy
	Korean War ends with armistice
1954	Senate holds Army-McCarthy hearings
	United States helps overthrow Arbenz in Guatemala
	French are defeated after siege of Dien Bien Phu
	Supreme Court orders school desegregation in *Brown* v. *Board of Education of Topeka*
1956	Egypt nationalizes Suez Canal in Suez Crisis
	Eisenhower is reelected president
1957	National Guard enforces desegregation of Central High School in Little Rock, Arkansas
1959	Fidel Castro overthrows Fulgencio Batista, takes power in Cuba
1960	John F. Kennedy is first Roman Catholic to be elected president

From Camelot to Watergate

I N 2007 NIELSEN MEDIA RESEARCH REPORTED THAT COLLEGE students spend three and a half hours a day "tuned in to television," about an hour less than most other Americans. Among Nielsen's findings: college students constitute a significant share of the after-midnight television audience; college men prefer sporting events; and college women, *Desperate Housewives* and *Grey's Anatomy*.

The Nielsen report is carefully worded: Students are "tuned in" to television, not watching it. Other studies have shown that when the television set is on, college students are occupied with other activities, such as playing video games—nearly two hours a day—or checking e-mail, searching Facebook, doing research for papers, or performing other Internet activities. Still, television remains an important, if declining, force in American life.

Television broadcasting began in 1946, and the decade of the 1950s witnessed an increase of from 5 million households with TVs to 55 million. But it was during the years from 1960 to 1975 that television moved to the center of public life. John F. Kennedy, a master of the medium, likely won the presidency because of his strong performance in his televised debates with Richard Nixon. Kennedy's years in office were highlighted by unforgettable television images: Soviet missiles and launching pads in Cuba; civil rights protesters being harassed and beaten; Buddhist monks setting themselves afire in Vietnam; and public grief following the assassination of Kennedy in Dallas.

Lyndon Johnson, Kennedy's successor, articulated his vision for a "Great Society" on television and saw it come undone as race riots set the nation's ghettos aflame. Disturbing footage of the Vietnam War unsettled viewers, as did the images of antiwar protesters in pitched battles with police.

Richard Nixon was elected president in 1968 in part because he had learned how to present himself on television. And the decade ended with a televised extravaganza of extraterrestrial proportions: the landing of an American on the moon in 1969. The collapse of the Nixon presidency following the burglary at the Watergate complex was played out on television, culminating in the Senate Watergate hearings and the House Judiciary Committee's deliberations recommending Nixon's impeachment. Through it all, Americans were glued to their TV sets.

Kennedy in Camelot

Having lampooned the Eisenhower administration as stodgy and unimaginative, President Kennedy made a show of his style and wit. He flouted convention by naming Robert, his younger brother, attorney general: "I can't see that it's wrong to give him a little legal experience before he goes out to practice law." Kennedy also prided himself on being a man of letters, winner of a Pulitzer Prize for *Profiles in Courage*. He quoted Robert Frost and Dante. He played and replayed recordings of Winston Churchill, hoping to imprint the great orator's sonorous cadences on his own flat Bostonian vowels. At the instigation of his elegant wife, Jacqueline, Kennedy surrounded himself with the finest intellects at glittering White House galas to honor Nobel Prize winners and celebrated artists.

Kennedy's youthful senior staff boasted impressive scholarly credentials. His national security adviser, McGeorge Bundy, had been dean of the faculty at Harvard (and the first undergraduate at Yale to receive perfect scores in three college entrance examinations). Secretary of Defense Robert McNamara also had taught at Harvard before becoming the first non–family member to head the Ford Motor Company. The administration constituted, as journalist David Halberstam observed later, and somewhat ruefully, "the best and the brightest."

The Cuban Crises

"The torch has been passed to a new generation of Americans," Kennedy declared in his inaugural address. Their chief task was to stop the spread of communism. Whereas Eisenhower had relied on the nation's nuclear arsenal to intimidate the Kremlin, Kennedy proposed to challenge communist aggression whenever and wherever it occurred. "We shall pay any price, bear any burden, meet any hardship, support any friend, oppose any foe to assure the survival and the success of liberty," Kennedy intoned. A new breed of cold warrior, Kennedy called on young men and women to serve in the Peace Corps, an organization that he created to mobilize American idealism and technical skills to help developing nations. His was a call for commitment—and action.

Fidel Castro, leader of Communist Cuba, visiting with students in 1961. Despite JFK's efforts to assassinate him and remove him from power, Castro was still in office in 2007.

Perhaps seduced by his own rhetoric, Kennedy blundered almost immediately. Anti-Castro exiles were eager to organize an invasion of their homeland, reasoning that the Cuban people would rise up against Castro and communism as soon as "democratic" forces provided the necessary leadership. Under Eisenhower the CIA had begun training some 2,000 Cuban exiles in Nicaragua. Kennedy was of two minds about the proposed invasion. Some in his administration opposed it strongly, but his closest advisers, including his brother Robert, urged him to give his approval. In the end he did.

The invaders, 1,400 strong, struck in April 1961. They landed at the Bay of Pigs, on Cuba's southern coast. But the Cuban people failed to flock to their lines, and soon Castro's army pinned the invaders down and forced them to surrender. Because American involvement could not be disguised, the affair exposed the United States to all the criticism that a straightforward assault would have produced, without accomplishing the overthrow of Castro. Worse, it made Kennedy appear impulsive as well as unprincipled. Castro tightened his connections with the Soviet Union.

In June, Kennedy met with Soviet Premier Khrushchev in Vienna. Furious over the invasion of Cuba, Khrushchev blustered about grabbing West Berlin. In August, he abruptly closed the border between East and West Berlin and erected a wall of concrete blocks and barbed wire across the city to stop the flow of East Germans into the noncommunist zone. At the same time, the Soviets resumed nuclear testing. Khrushchev ordered detonation of a series of gigantic hydrogen bombs, including one with a power 3,000 times that of the bomb that had devastated Hiroshima.

Kennedy followed suit: He announced plans to build thousands of nuclear missiles, known as Minutemen, capable of hitting targets on the other side of the world. He expanded the space program, vowing that an American would land on the moon within ten years. The president called on Congress to pass a large increase in military spending.

In 1962 Khrushchev precipitated the most dangerous confrontation of the Cold War. To forestall the anticipated American invasion of Cuba, he moved tanks, heavy bombers, and 42,000 Soviet troops and technicians to the island. But his most fateful step was to sneak several dozen guided nuclear missiles into the country and begin constructing launching pads for them. Although the range of these missiles was far less than that of the American Minutemen, if fired from Cuba the Soviet missiles could have delivered nuclear warheads to most of the eastern United States.

On October 14 American spy planes spotted the launching pads and missiles. The president faced a dreadful decision. After the Bay of Pigs fiasco, he could not again appear to back down to the communists. But if he invaded Cuba or bombed the Soviet bases and missile sites, Khrushchev would likely seize West Berlin or bomb U.S. missile sites in Turkey. Either action might lead to a full-scale nuclear war and millions of deaths.

On October 22 Kennedy went on television to address the nation. The Soviet buildup was "a deliberately provocative and unjustified change in the status quo." He ordered the American navy to stop and search all vessels headed for Cuba and to turn back any containing "offensive" weapons. Kennedy called on Khrushchev to dismantle the missile bases and remove from the island all weapons capable of striking the United States. Any Cuban-based nuclear attack would result, he warned, in "a full retaliatory response upon the Soviet Union."

For days, while the world held its breath, Soviet ships steamed toward Cuba and work on the missile bases continued. Then Khrushchev backed down. He recalled the ships, withdrew the missiles, and reduced his military establishment in Cuba to modest proportions. Kennedy then lifted the blockade. He also promised not to invade Cuba, thus ensuring Castro's survival; Kennedy also agreed to withdraw U.S. missiles from Turkey, though this latter concession was not made public at the time.

Immediately the president was hailed for his steady nerve and consummate statesmanship; the Cuban missile crisis was widely regarded as his finest hour. Yet in retrospect it appears that he may have overreacted to the missiles in Cuba. The Soviet nuclear threat had been exaggerated. After *Sputnik*, the Soviet long-range missile program flopped, though this was not known at the time. By the summer of 1962 a "missile gap" existed, but it was overwhelmingly in favor of the United

MISSILE ERECTOR
CABLE
MISSILE SHELTER TENT
TRACKED PRIME MOVERS
OXIDIZER TANK TRAILERS
FUEL TANK TRAILERS

This photograph, taken by an American U–2 spy plane and released during the Cuban missile crisis, shows the installation of liquid-fueled Soviet missiles. Khrushchev expected that the missiles could be kept secret. "Our military specialists informed us that strategic missiles can be reliably concealed in the palm forests of Cuba," one of Khrushchev's advisers recalled. Khrushchev, who assumed that the missiles would be harder to spot if they were in a horizontal position, ordered that they be placed in an upright position only at night. This was a mistake: The U–2 was easily able to detect the missiles in their horizontal position.

States, whose nuclear missiles outnumbered those of the Soviet Union by a ratio of 17 to 1. Khrushchev's decision to put medium-range missiles in Cuba signified Soviet weakness rather than impending aggression.

Both Kennedy and Khrushchev were sobered by the missile crisis; afterward neither spoke so glibly about superpower confrontation. They agreed to the installation of a telephone "hot line" between the White House and the Kremlin, so that in any future crisis leaders of the two nations could communicate instantly. They also signed a treaty outlawing nuclear testing in the atmosphere. But Khrushchev's bluff had been called—a public humiliation from which he would never recover. Within two years, hard-liners in the Kremlin forced him out of office. His successor, Leonid Brezhnev, was an old-style Stalinist who inaugurated an intensive program of long-range missile development. The nuclear arms race moved to new terrain, uncertain and unimaginably dangerous.

The Vietnam War

After the French withdrew from Vietnam in 1954, the Vietnamese people were supposed to determine their own future. But Ngo Dinh Diem, the U.S.-backed leader in the south, feared that he would be defeated by Ho Chi Minh, a well-known nationalist and leader of the communist Viet Minh. Diem canceled the election scheduled for 1956. With Eisenhower's help, he attempted to build a new nation in the south. The United States sent weapons and a handful of American military "advisers" to help Diem equip and train a South Vietnamese army. Ho decided to ignore Diem and consolidate his rule in the north. Those Viet Minh units that remained in the south—they soon came to be known as Vietcong—were instructed to form secret cells and bide their time. During the late 1950s they gained in strength and militancy.

In May 1959 Ho decided that the time had come to overthrow Diem. Vietcong guerrillas infiltrated thousands of villages, ambushed South Vietnamese convoys, and assassinated government officials. Soon the Vietcong controlled large sections of the countryside, some almost within sight of the capital city of Saigon.

By the time Kennedy took office, Diem's government was tottering. As a senator, Kennedy had endorsed Diem and the attempt to build a noncommunist South Vietnam. He called it the "cornerstone of the Free World in Southeast Asia, the keystone in the arch, the finger in the dike." After the Bay of Pigs debacle, furthermore, Kennedy worried that his credibility with Khrushchev had been damaged. "If he thinks I'm inexperienced and have no guts," he told an aide, "we won't get anywhere with him. So we have to act." Vietnam, he added, "looks like the place."

Kennedy sharply increased the American military and economic commitment to South Vietnam. At the end of 1961 there were 3,200 American military personnel in the country; within two years, there were more than 16,000, and 120 American soldiers had been killed. Despite the expanded effort, by the summer of 1963 Diem's regime was in ruins. An ardent Catholic, he cracked down on the Buddhists, who, joined by students, protested his repression. Thousands were arrested, and some were shot. In protest, several Buddhist monks became martyrs by setting themselves on fire in public.

Unable to persuade Diem to moderate his policies, Kennedy sent word to dissident Vietnamese generals of his willingness to support them if they ousted Diem. On November 1 several of these generals surrounded the presidential palace with troops and tanks, seized Diem, and killed him. Kennedy, though appalled by Diem's death, recognized the new junta.

"We Shall Overcome": The Civil Rights Movement

Kennedy initially approached the race question with exceeding caution. His razor-thin victory had depended on the votes both of African Americans in northern cities and white Democrats in the Deep South. As president, his visible support for one group would alienate the other. So Kennedy temporized, urging leaders on both sides to show restraint. This proved impossible.

During and after World War II, like a glacier, slowly but with massive force, a demand for change had developed in the South. Its roots lay in southern industrialization; in the shift from small sharecropping holdings to large commercial farms; in the vast wartime expenditures of the federal government on aircraft factories and army bases in the region; in the impact of the GI Bill on southern colleges and universities; and in the gradual development of a southern black middle class.

This change first came to national attention during the Eisenhower administration in the rigidly segregated city of Montgomery, Alabama. On Friday, December 1, 1955, Rosa Parks, a seamstress at the Montgomery Fair department store, boarded a bus on her way home from her job. She dutifully took a seat toward the rear as custom and law required. As white workers and shoppers filled the forward section, the driver ordered her to give up her place to a white passenger. Parks, who was also secretary of the Montgomery NAACP chapter, refused. She had decided, she later recalled, that "I would have to know once and for all what rights I had as a human being and a citizen."

She was arrested. Over the weekend, Montgomery's black leaders organized a boycott. "Don't ride the bus . . . Monday," their mimeographed notice ran. "If you work, take a cab, or share a ride, or walk." Monday dawned bitterly cold, but the boycott was a total success.

Most Montgomery blacks could not afford to miss a single day's wages, so the protracted struggle to get to work was difficult to maintain. Black-owned taxis reduced their rates sharply, and when the city declared this illegal, car pools were quickly organized. Few African Americans owned cars. Although nearly everyone who did volunteered, there were never more than 350 cars available to the more than 10,000 people who needed rides to their jobs and back every day. Nevertheless, the boycott went on.

Late in February the Montgomery authorities obtained indictments of 115 leaders of the boycott, but this move backfired because it focused national attention on the situation. A young clergyman, the Reverend Dr. Martin Luther King Jr., was emerging as the leader of the boycott. A gifted speaker, he became an overnight celebrity. Money poured in from all over the country to support the movement. The boycott lasted for over a year. Finally the Supreme Court declared the local law enforcing racial separation unconstitutional: Montgomery had to desegregate its public transportation system.

This success encouraged blacks elsewhere in the South to band together against segregation. A new organization founded in 1957, the Southern Christian Leadership Conference (SCLC), headed by King, moved to the forefront of the civil rights movement. Other organizations joined the struggle, notably the Congress of Racial Equality (CORE), which had been founded in 1942.

In February 1960 four African American college students in Greensboro, North Carolina, sat down at a lunch counter at a Woolworth's store. "We do not serve Negroes," they were told. They returned with more and more demonstrators. By the end of the week over a thousand protesters descended on Woolworth's

This "sit-in" tactic was not new. CORE had staged sit-ins in Chicago restaurants back in 1943. But the Greensboro students sparked a national movement; students in dozens of other southern towns and cities copied their example. Within a

This Greyhound bus carried freedom riders—whites and blacks who fought segregation by intentionally violating segregation policies. When a mob of whites from Anniston, Alabama, learned of this, they descended on the bus, slashed its tires, and piled into dozens of cars to chase it as it pulled away. As the bus was racing along Highway 78, the tires went flat. After the bus stopped, someone tossed a firebomb through the back window. As the riders got out of the bus, they were beaten. This photograph was shown that evening on wire services throughout the world.

fortnight more than fifty sit-ins were in progress in southern cities. By the end of 1961 over 70,000 people had participated in such demonstrations. Still another new organization, the Student Nonviolent Coordinating Committee (SNCC), was founded by black college students in 1960 to provide a focus for the sit-in movement and to conduct voter registration drives in the South, actions that more than any other roused the fury of southern segregationists.

In May 1961 black and white foes of segregation organized a "freedom ride" to test the effectiveness of federal regulations prohibiting discrimination in interstate transportation. Boarding two buses in Washington, an integrated group of thirteen volunteers took off across the South toward New Orleans. In Alabama they ran into trouble. At Anniston racists set fire to one of the buses, and in Birmingham the students were assaulted by a mob. But violence did not stop the freedom riders. Other groups followed, many deliberately seeking arrest to test local segregation ordinances. The resultant court cases repeatedly broke down legal racial barriers throughout the South.

This protracted struggle eventually yielded practical and moral benefits for southern whites as well as blacks. Gradually all but the most unwavering defenders of segregation changed their attitudes. But this took time, and many blacks were unwilling to wait.

Some blacks, contemptuous of white prejudices, were urging their fellows to reject "American" society and all it stood for. In the North, black nationalism became a potent force. Elijah Muhammad, leader of the Black Muslim movement, loathed whites so intensely that he demanded that a part of the United States be set aside exclusively for blacks. He urged his followers to be industrious, thrifty, and abstemious—and to view all whites with suspicion and hatred.

"This white government has ruled us and given us plenty hell, but the time has arrived that you taste a little of your own hell," Muhammad said. "There are many of my poor black ignorant brothers . . . preaching the ignorant and lying stuff that you should love your enemy. What fool can love his enemy?" Another important Black Muslim, Malcolm X, put it this way in a 1960 speech: "For the white man to ask the black man if he hates him is just like the rapist asking the raped, or the wolf asking the sheep, 'Do you hate me?'" "If someone puts a hand on you," he advised blacks on another occasion, "send him to the cemetery."

President Kennedy reluctantly began to give his support to a modest civil rights bill. When this measure ran into stiff opposition in Congress, blacks organized a demonstration in Washington, attended by 200,000 people. At this gathering, King delivered his "I Have a Dream" address, looking forward to a time when racial prejudice no longer existed and people of all religions and colors could join hands and say, "Free at last! Free at last!" Kennedy sympathized with the Washington gathering but feared it would make passage of the civil rights bill more difficult rather than easier. As in other areas, he was not a forceful advocate of his own proposals.

Tragedy in Dallas: JFK Assassinated

Through it all, Kennedy retained his hold on public opinion. In the fall of 1963 most observers believed he easily would win a second term. Then, while visiting Dallas, Texas, on November 22, he was shot in the head by an assassin, Lee Harvey Oswald, and died almost instantly. One measure of Kennedy's hold on the public imagination was the outpouring of grief that attended his death. Kennedy had given hope to people who had none.

Kennedy's assassination precipitated an extraordinary series of events. Oswald had fired on the president with a rifle from an upper story of a warehouse. No one saw him pull the trigger. He was apprehended largely because he panicked and killed a policeman across town later in the day. He denied his guilt, but a mass of evidence connected him with the assassination of the president. Before he could be brought to trial, however, he was himself murdered by Jack Ruby, the owner of a Dallas nightclub. The incident took place in full view of television cameras, while Oswald was being transferred from one place of detention to another.

Each day brought new revelations. Oswald had defected briefly to the Soviet Union in 1959, then had returned to the United States and formed a pro-Castro organization in New Orleans. Many concluded that some nefarious conspiracy lay at

JFK and Jacqueline Kennedy riding in a motorcade in Dallas, November 22, 1963. Several minutes later, Kennedy was shot and killed.

the root of the tragedy. Oswald, the argument ran, was a pawn—either of communists or anticommunists (the conspiracy theories lost none of their appeal for being contradictory)—whose murder was designed to shield from exposure the masterminds who had engineered the assassination. A special commission headed by Chief Justice Earl Warren was convened to analyze the evidence. After a lengthy investigation, it concluded that Oswald had acted alone.

Instead of dampening charges of conspiracy, the report of the Warren Commission provoked new doubts. As word leaked out about earlier CIA assassination attempts against Castro, the failure of the Warren Report even to mention them made the commission suspect. In fact, there is little solid evidence to suggest that Oswald was part of a wider conspiracy. But the decision of the Warren Comission to protect CIA secrets engendered skepticism toward the Commission—and the U.S. government.

Lyndon Baines Johnson

John F. Kennedy's death made Lyndon B. Johnson president. From 1949 until his election as vice president, Johnson had been a senator from Texas and, for most of that time, Senate Democratic leader. He could be heavy-handed or subtle, and also devious, domineering, persistent, and obliging. Many people swore by him; few had the fortitude to swear at him.

Johnson, who had consciously modeled his career after that of Franklin D. Roosevelt, considered social welfare legislation his specialty. The contrast with Kennedy could not have been sharper. In his inaugural address, Kennedy had made no mention of domestic issues. Kennedy's plans for federal aid for education, urban renewal, a higher minimum wage, and medical care for the aged were blocked in Congress by Republicans and southern Democrats. The same coalition also defeated his chief economic initiative—a broad tax cut to stimulate the economy. But Kennedy had reacted to these defeats mildly, almost wistfully. He thought the machinery of the federal government was cumbersome and ineffective.

Johnson knew how to make it work. On becoming president, he pushed hard for Kennedy's programs. "Civil righters are going to have to wear sneakers to keep up with me," he boasted. Bills long buried in committee sailed through Congress. Early in 1964 Kennedy's tax cut was passed. A few months later, an expanded version of another Kennedy proposal became law as the Civil Rights Act of 1964.

The Great Society

The much-strengthened Civil Rights Act outlawed discrimination by employers against blacks and also against women. It broke down legal barriers to black voting in the southern states and outlawed racial segregation of all sorts in places of public accommodation, such as movie theaters, hotels, and restaurants. In addition, unlike presidents Eisenhower and Kennedy, Johnson made sure that the government enforced civil rights legislation.

Johnson's success in steering the Civil Rights Act through Congress confirmed his belief that he could be a reformer in the tradition of Franklin Roosevelt. He declared war on poverty and set out to create a "great society" in which poverty no longer would exist. The primary objective of Johnson's war on poverty was to give poor people the opportunity to improve themselves.

The Economic Opportunity Act of 1964 created a mixture of programs, among them a Job Corps similar to the New Deal Civilian Conservation Corps; a community action program to finance local antipoverty efforts; and a system for training the unskilled unemployed and for lending money to small businesses in poor areas. The programs combined the progressive concept of government aid for those in need with the conservative idea of individual responsibility.

Buttressed by his legislative triumphs, Johnson sought election as president in his own right in 1964. He achieved this ambition in unparalleled fashion. His championing of civil rights won him the almost unanimous support of blacks; his tax policy attracted the well-to-do and the business interests; his war on poverty held the allegiance of labor and other traditionally Democratic groups. His down-home southern antecedents counterbalanced his liberalism on the race question in the eyes of many white Southerners.

LBJ as Texas cowboy, a masculine image he assiduously cultivated. Biographers have suggested that Johnson was torn between the expectations of his father, a crude local politician who flouted polite society, and those of his mother, a refined woman who insisted that her son read poetry and practice the violin. Johnson later told biographer Doris Kearns Goodwin that he persisted in Vietnam because he worried that critics would accuse him of being "an unmanly man. A man without a spine."

The Republicans played into his hands by nominating the conservative Senator Barry M. Goldwater of Arizona, whose objective in Congress had been "not to pass laws but to repeal them." As a presidential candidate he favored such laissez-faire policies as cutting back on the social security system and doing away with the Tennessee Valley Authority. A large majority of voters found Goldwater out-of-date on economic questions and dangerously aggressive on foreign affairs.

In November, Johnson won a sweeping victory, collecting over 61 percent of the popular vote and carrying the whole country except Goldwater's Arizona and five states in the Deep South, where many conservatives were voting more against Johnson's civil rights policies than in favor of Goldwater.

Quickly Johnson pressed ahead with his Great Society program. In January 1965 he proposed a compulsory hospital insurance system, known as Medicare, for all persons over the age of 65. As amended by Congress, the Medicare Act consisted of Part A, hospital insurance for the retired (funded by increased Social Security taxes), and a voluntary plan, Part B, covering doctors' bills (paid for in part by the government). The law also provided for grants to the states to help pay the medical expenses of poor people, even those below the retirement age of 65. This part of the system was called Medicaid. Before the passage of the Medicare Act, about half of Americans over 65 years old had had no medical insurance.

Next, Congress passed the Elementary and Secondary Education Act in 1965, which supplied federal funds to school districts. Head Start, a program for poor preschoolers, was designed to prepare them for elementary school. It also incidentally improved the children's health by providing medical examinations and nutritious meals.

Still another important reform was the Voting Rights Act of 1965, pressed through Congress by President Johnson after more brutal repressions of civil rights demonstrators in the South. This law provided for federal intervention to protect black registration and voting in six southern states. It applied to state and local as well as federal elections.

On balance, the achievements of the Great Society were far below what President Johnson had promised and his supporters had envisioned. The same, of course, can be said of most ambitious reform programs—of Reconstruction; of the Progressive movement; certainly of the New Deal, to which Johnson had contributed as a young man. Despite his long political experience, Johnson tried to accomplish too many things too quickly. He relied too heavily on the techniques of political manipulation. Perhaps he was carried away by his unexpected power—that he would ever become president must have seemed to a man of his political acumen most unlikely after he failed to win the nomination in 1960. He seized too avidly this opportunity to make history. Without the crisis atmosphere that had appeared to justify hasty experimentation during the New Deal years, the public judged the results of the Great Society and the president who had shaped it skeptically.

Johnson Escalates the War

After Diem's assassination, the situation in South Vietnam continued to deteriorate. One military coup followed another, and political instability aggravated military incapacity. President Johnson nevertheless felt that he had no choice but to prop up the South Vietnamese regime. "If I don't go in now," he told an adviser, "they'll be all over me in Congress. They won't be talking about my civil rights bill, or education, or beautification. No sir, they'll push Vietnam up my ass every time."

Johnson decided to punish North Vietnam directly for prosecuting the war in the south. In early 1964 he secretly ordered American warships to escort the South Vietnamese navy on missions far into the Gulf of Tonkin; the South Vietnamese attacked North Vietnamese ships and port facilities and landed commandos in North Vietnam. After one such mission, American destroyers were fired on by North Vietnamese gunboats. Several nights later during a heavy storm, American ships reported that they were being fired on, though the enemy was never spotted. Using this Tonkin "incident" as pretext, Johnson demanded, and in an air of crisis obtained, an authorization from Congress to "repel any armed attack against the forces of the United States and to prevent further aggression." With this blank check, known as the Gulf of Tonkin Resolution, and buttressed by his sweeping defeat of Goldwater in the 1964 presidential election, Johnson authorized air attacks in North Vietnam. By the summer of 1965, American bombers were conducting some 5,000 raids each month.

But the hail of bombs on North Vietnam had little effect on the struggle in the south. If the war was to be won, American soldiers—lots of them—would have to do much of the fighting themselves.

In July 1965 Johnson ordered the first of several huge increases in American ground forces in Vietnam. By the end of 1965, 184,000 Americans were in the field; a year later, 385,000; after another year, 485,000. By the middle of 1968 the number exceeded 538,000. Each increase was met by corresponding increases from the other side. The Soviet Union and China sent no combat troops, but stepped up their aid, and thousands of North Vietnamese regulars filtered across the 17th parallel to fight with the Vietcong guerrillas.

The new American strategy was not to seize any particular battlefield or terrain as in all previous wars, but to kill as many of the enemy as possible through bloody "search and destroy" operations. As the scope of the action broadened, the number of American casualties rose. The United States was engaged in a full-scale war, one that Congress never declared.

Opposition to the War

Some Americans claimed that the struggle between the South Vietnamese government and the Vietcong was a civil war in which the United States should not meddle. They stressed the repressive character of the South Vietnamese government as proof that the war was not a contest between democracy and communism. They objected to the massive aerial bombings (more explosives were dropped on Vietnam between 1964 and 1968 than on Germany and Japan combined in World War II), to the use of napalm bombs and defoliants such as Agent Orange that were sprayed on forests and crops and that wreaked havoc among noncombatants, and to the killing of civilians by American troops. Above all, opponents of the war deplored the heavy loss of life—over 40,000 American dead by 1970, and hundreds of thousands of Vietnamese.

The cost of the war came to exceed $20 billion a year. But in large part because so many people objected to the war, Johnson refused to ask Congress to raise taxes to pay for it. The resulting deficits forced the government to borrow huge sums, caused interest rates to soar, and pushed prices higher.

The Election of 1968

Gradually the opponents of the war gained numbers and strength. They began to include some of the president's advisers. By late 1967 McNamara, who had methodically tracked kill ratios, troop replacement rates, and nearly every other conceivable statistic, concluded that "the figures didn't add up" and the war could not be won. Deeply despondent, he resigned.

Opposition to the war was especially vehement on college campuses, some students objecting because they thought the United States had no business intervening in the Vietnam conflict, others because they feared being drafted, still others because so many students obtained educational deferments, while young men who were unable to attend college were conscripted.

Then, in November 1967, Eugene McCarthy, a low-keyed, introspective senator from Minnesota, announced his candidacy for the 1968 Democratic presidential nomination. Opposition to the war was his issue.

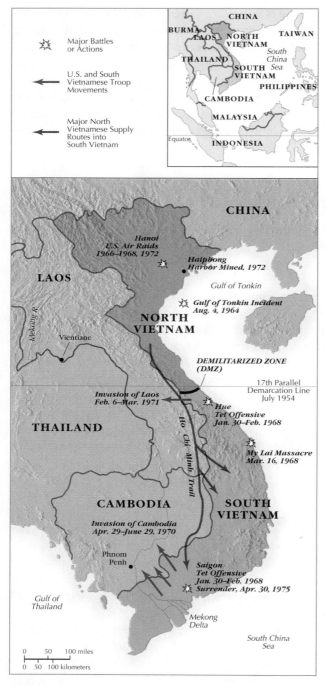

Southeast Asia, 1954–1975

WOULD JFK HAVE SENT A HALF-MILLION AMERICAN TROOPS TO VIETNAM?

In the summer of 1963, Buddhist monks immolated themselves to protest Diem's repression. Several months later, Diem was ousted in a coup and JFK was assassinated. Within two years, President Johnson raised American troop levels in Vietnam to 300,000 and, by 1967, to half a million.

Many historians believe that if Kennedy had lived, he too would have sent more troops to Vietnam. Journalist David Halberstam (1969) emphasized that the same foreign policy advisers who guided Kennedy did so for Johnson, too. These men—Robert McNamara, McGeorge Bundy, and others—were, in Halberstam's mordantly ironic phrase, "the best and the brightest." Larry Berman (1982, 1989) showed that because Johnson was inexperienced in foreign policy, he had little choice but to listen to JFK's team. Lloyd C. Gardner (1995) and Brian Van De Mark (1991) emphasized the continuity—or rigidity—of American policymaking throughout the period. David Barrett (1993) described how Johnson wanted a way out of "that bitch of a war" but could not find one.

Those who have championed Kennedy's reputation insisted that JFK would have left Vietnam earlier. Arthur M. Schlesinger Jr. (1978) explained that while Kennedy publicly endorsed the war, he was "secretly wondering how to get out." Schlesinger's thesis received unwanted support from filmmaker Oliver Stone's movie, *JFK* (1991). The movie hypothesized that Kennedy was assassinated by pro-war hawks in the military who feared the president would pull American troops out of Vietnam. The following year John M. Newman (1992) provided a historical brief for the movie.

But if Kennedy was looking for an excuse to get out of the war, why didn't he withdraw in response to Diem's persecution of the Buddhists? His decision to support a coup to replace Diem seemingly committed the United States to helping Diem's successors.

David Halberstam, *The Best and the Brightest* (1969), Larry Berman, *Planning a Tragedy* (1982) and *Lyndon Johnson's War* (1989), Brian Van De Mark, *Into the Quagmire* (1991), Lloyd C. Gardner, *Pay Any Price* (1995), David Barrett, *Uncertain Warriors* (1993), Arthur M. Schlesinger Jr., *Robert Kennedy and His Times* (1978), John M. Newman, *JFK and Vietnam* (1992).

Suddenly, early in 1968, on the heels of this announcement, North Vietnamese and Vietcong forces launched a general offensive to correspond with their Lunar New Year (called Tet). Striking thirty-nine of the forty-four provincial capitals, many other towns and cities, and every American base, they caused chaos throughout South Vietnam. They held Hué, the old capital of the country, for weeks. To root them out of Saigon the Americans had to level large sections of the city. Elsewhere the destruction was total, an irony highlighted by the remark of an American officer after the recapture of the village of Ben Tre: "It became necessary to destroy the town to save it."

The Tet offensive was essentially a series of raids; the communists did not expect to hold the cities indefinitely, and they did not. Their losses were enormous. Nevertheless the psychological impact in South Vietnam and in the United States made Tet a clear victory for the North. American pollsters reported an enormous shift of public opinion against further escalation of the fighting. When Westmoreland described Tet as a communist defeat and yet requested an additional 206,000 troops, McCarthy, who was campaigning in the New Hampshire primary, suddenly became a formidable figure. Thousands of students and other volunteers flocked to the state to ring doorbells on his behalf. On primary election day he polled 42 percent of the Democratic vote.

The political situation was confused. Before the primary, former attorney general Robert F. Kennedy, brother of the slain president, had refused either to seek the Democratic nomination or to support McCarthy, although he disliked Johnson intensely and was opposed to his policy in Vietnam. After McCarthy's success, he announced his candidacy.

Confronting this division in the ranks, President Johnson realized he could no longer hope to be an effective president. In a surprising televised announcement, he withdrew from the race. Vice President Hubert H. Humphrey then announced his candidacy, and Johnson threw the weight of his administration behind him.

Kennedy carried the primaries in Indiana and Nebraska. McCarthy won in Wisconsin and Oregon. In the climactic contest in California, Kennedy won by a small margin. However, immediately after his victory speech in a Los Angeles hotel, he was assassinated by Sirhan Sirhan, an Arab nationalist who had been incensed by Kennedy's support of Israel. In effect, Kennedy's death ensured the nomination of Humphrey.

The contest for the Republican nomination was far less dramatic, although its outcome, the nomination of Richard M. Nixon, would have been hard to predict a few years earlier. After his loss to Kennedy in 1960, Nixon ran unsuccessfully for governor of California in 1962, then moved to New York City and joined a prominent law firm. But he remained active in Republican affairs. In 1964 he had campaigned hard for Goldwater. When no other Republican developed extensive support as the 1968 election approached, Nixon entered the race, swept the primaries, and won an easy first-ballot victory at the Republican convention.

Nixon then astounded the country and dismayed liberals by choosing Governor Spiro T. Agnew of Maryland as his running mate. Agnew was a political unknown. ("Spiro who?" jokesters asked.) Nixon chose him primarily to attract southern votes.

Placating the South seemed necessary because Governor George C. Wallace of Alabama was making a determined bid to win enough electoral votes for his American Independent party to prevent any candidate from obtaining a majority. Wallace was flagrantly antiblack and anti-intellectual. Nixon's choice of Agnew appeared to be an effort to contend with Wallace for conservative voters in the South.

This Republican strategy heightened the tension surrounding the Democratic convention, which met in Chicago in late August. Humphrey delegates controlled the convention. The vice president had a solid liberal record on domestic issues, but he had supported Johnson's Vietnam policy with equal solidity. Those who could not stomach the Nixon-Agnew ticket and who opposed the war faced a difficult choice. Several thousand activists, representing a dozen groups and advocating tactics ranging from orderly demonstrations to civil disobedience to indiscriminate violence, descended on Chicago to put pressure on the delegates to repudiate the Johnson Vietnam policy.

In the tense atmosphere that resulted, the party hierarchy overreacted. The mayor of Chicago, Richard J. Daley, whose ability to "influence" election results in a manner favorable to Democrats had often been demonstrated, ringed the convention with policemen to protect it from disruption. This was a reasonable precaution in itself. Inside the building the delegates nominated Humphrey and adopted a war plank satisfactory to Johnson. Outside, however, provoked by the abusive language and violent behavior of radical demonstrators, the police tore into the protesters, in novelist Norman Mailer's graphic phrase, "like a chain saw cutting into wood," while millions watched on television in fascinated horror.

At first the mayhem in Chicago seemed to benefit Nixon by strengthening the convictions of many voters that the tougher treatment of criminals and dissenters

Riot police clubbing antiwar demonstrators outside the 1968 Democratic national convention in Chicago.

that he and Agnew were calling for was necessary. Those who were critical of the Chicago police tended to blame Humphrey, whom Mayor Daley supported.

Nixon campaigned at a deliberate, dignified pace. He made relatively few public appearances, relying instead on carefully arranged television interviews and taped commercials. He stressed firm enforcement of the law and his desire "to bring us together." As for Vietnam, he would "end the war and win the peace," by just what means he did not say.

The Democratic campaign was badly organized. Humphrey was subjected to merciless heckling from antiwar audiences. He seemed far behind in the early stages. Black voters and the urban poor had no practical choice but to vote Democratic. Gradually Humphrey gained ground, and on election day the popular vote was close: Nixon slightly less than 31.8 million, Humphrey nearly 31.3 million. Nixon's Electoral College margin, however, was substantial—301 to 191. The remaining forty-six electoral votes went to Wallace, whose 9.9 million votes came to 13.5 percent of the total. Together, Nixon and Wallace received 57 percent of the popular vote. Nevertheless, the Democrats retained control of both houses of Congress.

Nixon as President: "Vietnamizing" the War

In office, Nixon first proposed a phased withdrawal of all non–South Vietnamese troops, to be followed by an internationally supervised election in South Vietnam. The North Vietnamese rejected this scheme and insisted that the United States withdraw its forces unconditionally. If the United States could not prevail with a half million American troops, how, the North Vietnamese negotiator asked Henry Kissinger, the American negotiator, "can you succeed when you let your puppet troops do the fighting?" That question, Kissinger later admitted, "tormented" him.

The intransigence of the North Vietnamese left the president in a difficult position. Nixon could not compel the foe to end a war it had begun against the French nearly a quarter of a century earlier, and every passing day added to the strength of antiwar sentiment, which, as it expressed itself in ever more emphatic terms, in turn led to deeper divisions in the country. Yet Nixon could not face up to the consequences of ending the war on the communists' terms.

The president responded to the dilemma by trying to build up the South Vietnamese armed forces so that American troops could pull out without South Vietnam being overrun by the communists. He shipped so many planes to the Vietnamese that they came to have the fourth-largest air force in the world. The trouble with this strategy, called Vietnamization, was that for 15 years the United States had been trying without success to make the South Vietnamese capable of defending themselves.

For a while, events appeared to vindicate Nixon's position. A gradual slowing of military activity in Vietnam had reduced American casualties. Troop withdrawals continued in an orderly fashion. A new lottery system for drafting men for military duty eliminated some of the inequities in the selective service law.

But the war continued. Early in 1970 reports that an American unit had massacred civilians, including dozens of women and children, in a Vietnamese hamlet known as My Lai revived the controversy over the purposes of the war and its corrosive effects on those who were fighting it. The American people, it seemed, were being torn apart by the war: one from another according to each one's interpretation of events; many within themselves as they tried to balance the war's horrors against their pride, their abhorrence of communism, and their unwillingness to turn their backs on their elected leader.

The Cambodian "Incursion"

Late in April 1970 Nixon announced that Vietnamization was proceeding more rapidly than he had hoped, that communist power was weakening, and that within a year another 150,000 American soldiers would be extracted from Vietnam. A week later he announced that military intelligence had indicated that the enemy was consolidating its "sanctuaries" in neutral Cambodia and that he was therefore dispatching thousands of American troops to destroy these bases. (American planes had been bombing enemy sites in Cambodia for some time, although this fact was not revealed to the public until 1973.)

Nixon's shocking announcement triggered many campus demonstrations. One college where feeling ran high was Kent State University in Ohio. For several days students there clashed with local police; they broke windows and caused other damage to property. When the governor of Ohio called out the National Guard, angry students showered the soldiers with stones. During a noontime protest on May 4 the guardsmen, who were poorly trained in crowd control, suddenly opened fire. Four students were killed, two of them women who were merely passing by on their way to class.

The Viet Cong were initially terrified of what they called "angleworms," helicopters that swooped from the sky belching fire and rockets. The Viet Cong soon learned to aim two-thirds the distance of the fuselage ahead, so that the helicopter would fly into their bullets. Hundreds of helicopters were shot down by small arms fire.

While the nation reeled from this shock, two students at Jackson State University were killed by Mississippi state policemen. A wave of student strikes followed, closing down hundreds of colleges, including many that had seen no previous unrest. Moderate students by the tens of thousands had joined with the radicals.

The almost universal condemnation of the invasion and of the way it had been planned shook Nixon hard. He backtracked, pulling American ground troops out of Cambodia quickly. But he did not change his Vietnam policy, and in fact Cambodia apparently stiffened his determination. As American ground troops were withdrawn, he stepped up air attacks.

The balance of forces remained in uneasy equilibrium through 1971. But late in March 1972 the North Vietnamese again mounted a series of assaults throughout South Vietnam. Nixon responded with heavier bombing, and he ordered the approaches to Haiphong and other North Vietnamese ports sown with mines to cut off the communists' supplies.

Détente with Communism

But in the midst of these aggressive actions, Nixon and his National Security Adviser, Henry Kissinger, devised a bold diplomatic offensive, executed in nearly complete secrecy—from even the State and Defense departments! Nixon and Kissinger made an effective though not always harmonious team.

Abandoning a lifetime of treating communism as a single worldwide conspiracy that had to be contained at all costs, Nixon decided to deal with China and the Soviet Union as separate powers and, as he put it, to "live together and work together" with both. Nixon and Kissinger called the new policy *détente*, a French term meaning "the relaxation of tensions between governments." But *détente* was not an

National Guardsmen firing into a crowd of antiwar protesters at Kent State University killed four students and injured eleven others. The shootings triggered massive demonstrations and protests across the nation.

President and Mrs. Nixon dining with Chinese communist officials in Beijing in February 1972. Even Nixon's harshest critics conceded that his initiative in reopening United States–China relations was a diplomatic masterstroke.

expression of friendship so much as an acknowledgment that for decades the policy of containment had driven China and the Soviet Union closer together.

First Nixon sent Kissinger secretly to China and the Soviet Union to prepare the way for summit meetings with the communist leaders. Both the Chinese and the Soviets agreed to the meetings. Then, in February 1972, Nixon and Kissinger, accompanied by a small army of reporters and television crews, flew to Beijing. After much dining, sightseeing, posing for photographers, and consultation with Chinese officials, Nixon agreed to promote economic and cultural exchanges and supported the admission of communist China to the United Nations. (Since the founding of the United Nations, the United States had recognized only the Republic of China—Taiwan.) As a result, exports to communist China increased substantially, reaching $4 billion in 1980. Among other American products, the Chinese were introduced to Coca-Cola, marketed under a name meaning "tasty happiness," and other American products. Nixon's visit, ending more than 20 years of adamant American refusal to accept the reality of the Chinese revolution, marked a dramatic reversal; as such it was hailed throughout the world.

By the summer of 1972, with the presidential election looming in the fall, Kissinger redoubled his efforts to negotiate an end to the Vietnam war. By October he and the North Vietnamese had hammered out a settlement calling for a cease-fire, the return of American prisoners of war, and the withdrawal of United States forces from Vietnam. Shortly before the presidential election Kissinger announced that peace was "at hand."

Nixon in Triumph

A few days later President Nixon was reelected, defeating the Democratic candidate, Senator George McGovern of South Dakota, in a landslide—521 electoral votes to 17. McGovern carried only Massachusetts and the District of Columbia. McGovern's campaign had been hampered by his tendency to advance poorly thought-out proposals, such as his scheme for funneling money directly to the poor, and by his rather bumbling, low-key oratorical style. The campaign marked the historical breakdown of the coalition that Franklin D. Roosevelt had fashioned and on which he and his Democratic successors, particularly Truman and Johnson, had ridden to power. Of that coalition, only African Americans voted solidly for McGovern.

Suddenly Nixon loomed as one of the most powerful and successful presidents in American history. His tough-minded but flexible handling of foreign policy questions, even his harsh Vietnamese policy, suggested decisiveness and self-confidence, qualities he had often seemed to lack in his earlier career. His willingness, despite his long history as a militant cold warrior, to negotiate with the communist nations indicated a new flexibility and creativity. His landslide victory appeared to demonstrate that a large majority of the people approved of his way of tackling the major problems of the times.

But Kissinger's agreement with the North Vietnamese came apart when Nguyen Van Thieu, the South Vietnamese president, refused to sign it. Thieu claimed that the agreement, by permitting communist troops to remain in the south, would ensure his ultimate defeat. To Kissinger's chagrin, Nixon sided with Thieu and resumed the bombing of North Vietnam in December 1972, this time sending the mighty B-52s directly over Hanoi and other cities. The destruction they caused was great, but their effectiveness as a means of forcing concessions from the North Vietnamese was at best debatable, and in these strikes for the first time the United States lost large numbers of the big strategic bombers.

In January 1973 a settlement was finally reached. As with the October "agreement," the North Vietnamese retained control of large sections of the south, and they promised to release American prisoners of war within 60 days. Thieu assented this time, largely because Nixon secretly pledged that the United States would "respond with full force" if North Vietnam resumed its offensive. Within several months most prisoners of war were released, and the last American troops were pulled out of Vietnam. More than 57,000 Americans had died in the long war, and over 300,000 more had been wounded. Nearly a million communist soldiers and 185,000 South Vietnamese soldiers were reported killed.

Domestic Policy Under Nixon

When Nixon became president in 1969, the major economic problem he faced was inflation. This was caused primarily by the heavy military expenditures and easy-money policies of the Johnson administration. Nixon cut federal spending and balanced the 1969 budget, while the Federal Reserve Board forced up interest rates to slow the expansion of the money supply. When prices continued to rise, uneasiness mounted and labor unions demanded large wage increases.

In 1970 Congress passed a law giving the president power to regulate prices and wages. Nixon originally opposed this legislation, but in the summer of 1971 he changed his mind and announced a 90-day price and wage freeze. Then he set up a pay board and a price commission with authority to limit wage and price increases when the freeze ended. These controls did not check inflation completely—and they angered union leaders, who felt that labor was being shortchanged—but they did slow the upward spiral.

In handling other domestic issues, the president was less firm. Like President Kennedy he was primarily interested in foreign affairs. He supported a bold plan for a "minimum income" for poor families, but dropped it when it alarmed his conservative supporters and got nowhere in Congress. But when a groundswell of public support for conserving natural resources and checking pollution led Congress to pass bills creating the Environmental Protection Agency (EPA) and the Clean Air Act of 1970, he signed them cheerfully.

Primarily he was concerned with his own political standing. Hoping to strengthen the Republican party in the South, he checked further federal efforts to force school desegregation on reluctant local districts, and he set out to add what he called "strict constructionists" to the Supreme Court, which he believed had swung too far to the left in such areas as race relations and the rights of persons accused of committing crimes. He also proposed mostly conservatives to fill vacancies in the Supreme Court.

After his triumphant reelection and the withdrawal of the last American troops from Vietnam, Nixon resolved to change the direction in which the nation had been moving for decades. He sought, on the one hand, to strengthen the power of the presidency vis-à-vis Congress and, on the other, to decentralize the administration by encouraging state and local management of government programs. He announced that he intended to reduce the interference of the federal government in the affairs of individuals. People should be more self-reliant, he said, and he denounced what he called "permissiveness." Overconcern for the interests of blacks and other minorities must end. Criminals should be punished "without pity." No person or group should be coddled by the state.

The Watergate Break-In

On March 19, 1973, James McCord, a former agent of the Federal Bureau of Investigation accused of burglary, wrote a letter to the judge presiding at his trial. His act precipitated a series of disclosures that first disrupted and then destroyed the Nixon administration.

McCord had been employed during the 1972 presidential campaign as a security officer of the Committee to Re-elect the President (CREEP). At about 1 A.M. on

June 17, 1972, he and four other men had broken into Democratic party headquarters at the Watergate, a complex of apartments and offices in Washington. The burglars were members of an unofficial CREEP surveillance group known as "the plumbers." Nixon, who was obsessed by a need to conceal information about his administration, had formed the group after the Pentagon Papers, a confidential report on government policy in Vietnam, had been leaked to the press. The "plumbers" had been caught rifling files and installing electronic eavesdropping devices.

Two other Republican campaign officials were soon implicated in the affair. Their arrest aroused suspicions that the Republican party was behind the break-in. Nixon denied it. "I can say categorically," he announced on June 22, "that no one on the White House staff, no one in this Administration presently employed, was involved in this very bizarre incident."

Most people evidently took the president at his word. He was far ahead in the polls and seemed so sure to win re-election that it was hard to believe he would stoop to burglary to discover what the Democrats were up to. In any case, the affair did not materially affect the election. When brought to trial early in 1973, most of the Watergate burglars pleaded guilty.

McCord, who did not, was convicted by the jury. Before Judge John J. Sirica imposed sentences on the culprits, however, McCord wrote his letter. High Republican officials had known about the burglary in advance and had paid the defendants "hush money" to keep their connection secret, McCord claimed. Perjury had been committed during the trial.

The truth of McCord's charges swiftly became apparent. The head of CREEP, Jeb Stuart Magruder, and President Nixon's lawyer, John W. Dean III, admitted their involvement. Most of Nixon's closest advisers were implicated and forced to resign. This raised the question of the president's personal connection with the scandals. This he steadfastly denied. He insisted that he would investigate the Watergate affair thoroughly and see that the guilty were punished. He refused, however, to allow investigators to examine White House documents, on grounds of executive privilege, which he continued to assert in very broad terms.

In the teeth of Nixon's denials, John Dean, testifying under oath, stated flatly and in circumstantial detail that the president had been closely involved in the Watergate cover-up. Dean had been a persuasive witness, but many people were reluctant to believe that a president could lie so cold-bloodedly to the entire country. Therefore, when it came out during later hearings of the Senate committee investigating the Watergate scandal that the president had systematically made secret tape recordings of White House conversations and telephone calls, the disclosure caused a sensation. It seemed obvious that these tapes would settle the question of Nixon's involvement once and for all. Again Nixon refused to allow access to the evidence.

One result of the scandals and of Nixon's attitude was a precipitous decline in his standing in public opinion polls. Calls for his resignation, even for impeachment, began to be heard. Yielding to pressure, he agreed to the appointment of an

Garry Trudeau and his politically biting cartoon strip "Doonesbury" enlivened the Vietnam and Watergate years. "Doonesbury" became the first cartoon strip to win a Pulitzer Prize. (Ron Ziegler was President Nixon's press secretary.)

"independent" special prosecutor to investigate the Watergate affair, and he promised the appointee, Professor Archibald Cox of Harvard Law School, full cooperation.

Cox swiftly aroused the president's ire by seeking access to White House records, including the tapes. When Nixon refused to turn over the tapes, Cox obtained a subpoena from Judge Sirica ordering him to do so. The administration appealed this decision and lost in the appellate court. Then, while the case was headed for the Supreme Court, Nixon ordered the new attorney general, Elliot Richardson, to dismiss Cox. Both Richardson, who had promised the Senate during his confirmation hearings that the special prosecutor would have a free hand, and his chief assistant resigned rather than do as the president directed. The third-ranking officer of the Justice Department carried out Nixon's order.

These events of Saturday, October 20, promptly dubbed the Saturday Night Massacre, caused an outburst of public indignation. Congress was bombarded by thousands of letters and telegrams demanding the president's impeachment. The House Judiciary Committee began an investigation to see if enough evidence for impeachment existed. (The House of Representatives must vote to indict federal officials for impeachment; the actual impeachment trial is conducted by the Senate.)

More Troubles for Nixon

The nation had never before experienced such a series of morale-shattering crises. While the seemingly unending complications of Watergate were unfolding during 1973, a number of unrelated disasters struck. First, pushed by a shortage of grain resulting from massive Soviet purchases authorized by détente policy, food prices shot up—wheat from $1.45 a bushel to over $5.00.

Then Vice President Agnew (defender of law and order, foe of permissiveness) was accused of income tax fraud and of having accepted bribes while serving as Baltimore county executive and governor of Maryland. To escape a jail term Agnew admitted in October that he had been guilty of tax evasion and resigned as vice president.

Acting according to the procedures for presidential and vice-presidential succession of the Twenty-fifth Amendment, adopted in 1967, President Nixon nominated Representative Gerald R. Ford of Michigan as vice president, and he was confirmed by Congress. Ford had served continuously in Congress since 1949 and as minority leader since 1964. His positions on public issues were close to Nixon's; he was an internationalist in foreign affairs and a conservative and convinced Republican partisan on domestic issues.

Not long after the Agnew fiasco, Nixon, responding to charges that he had paid almost no income taxes during his presidency, published his 1969 to 1972 returns. They showed that he had paid only about $1,600 in two years during which his income had exceeded half a million dollars. Although Nixon claimed that his returns were perfectly legal—he had taken huge deductions for the gift of some of his vice presidential papers to the National Archives—the legality, to say nothing of the propriety, of his actions was questionable. Combined with charges that millions of dollars of public funds had been spent on improvements for his private residences in California and Florida, the tax issue further eroded his reputation, so much so that he felt obliged during a televised press conference to assure the audience: "I am not a crook."

The Judgment on Watergate: "Expletive Deleted"

In March 1974 a grand jury indicted Nixon's top advisers, including former attorney general John Mitchell, for conspiring to block the Watergate investigation and other crimes. The jurors also named Nixon an "unindicted co-conspirator." Judge Sirica thereupon turned over the jury's evidence against Nixon to the House Judiciary Committee. Then both the Internal Revenue Service (IRS) and a joint congressional committee announced that most of his deductions had been unjustified. The IRS assessed him nearly half a million dollars in taxes and interest, which he agreed to pay.

In an effort to check the mounting criticism, late in April Nixon released edited transcripts of the tapes he had turned over to the court the previous November. In addition to much incriminating evidence, the transcripts provided the public with a fascinating and shocking view of how the president conducted himself in private. In conversations he seemed confused, indecisive, and lacking in any concern for the public interest. His repeated use of foul language, so out of keeping with his public image, offended millions. The phrase "expletive deleted," inserted in place of words considered too vulgar for publication in family newspapers, overnight became a catchword.

The publication of the transcripts led even some of Nixon's strongest supporters to demand that he resign. And once the Judiciary Committee obtained the actual tapes, it became clear that the White House transcripts were in crucial respects inaccurate. Much material prejudicial to the president's case had been suppressed. Yet impeaching a president seemed so drastic a step that many people felt more direct proof of Nixon's involvement in the cover-up was necessary.

In the summer of 1974—after so many months of alarms and crises—the Watergate drama reached its climax. The Judiciary Committee, following months of study of the evidence behind closed doors, decided to conduct its deliberations in open session. While millions watched on television, thirty-eight members of the House of Representatives debated the charges. The discussions revealed both the thoroughness of the investigation and the soul-searching efforts of the representatives to render an impartial judgment. Three articles of impeachment were adopted. They charged the president with obstructing justice, misusing the powers of his office, and failing to obey the committee's subpoenas. Except in the case of the last article, many of the Republicans on the committee joined with the Democrats in voting aye, a clear indication that the full House would vote to impeach.

On the eve of the debates, the Supreme Court had ruled unanimously that the president must turn over the sixty-four subpoenaed tapes to the special prosecutor. Executive privilege had its place, the Court stated, but no person, not even a president, could "withhold evidence that is demonstrably relevant in a criminal trial." For reasons that soon became obvious, Nixon seriously considered defying the Court. Only when convinced that to do so would make his impeachment and conviction certain did he agree to comply.

The sixty-four subpoenaed tapes had to be transcribed and analyzed. When they were, Nixon's fate was sealed. Three recorded conversations between the president and a key aide just after the Watergate break-in proved conclusively that Nixon had tried to obstruct justice by engaging the CIA in an effort to persuade the FBI not to follow up leads in the case on the spurious grounds that national security was involved.

When the House Judiciary Committee members read the new transcripts, all the Republican members who had voted against the impeachment articles reversed themselves. Republican leaders told the president categorically that the House would impeach him and that no more than a handful of senators would vote for acquittal.

On August 8 Nixon announced his resignation. "Dear Mr. Secretary," his terse official letter to Secretary of State Kissinger ran, "I hereby resign the Office of President of the United States. Sincerely, Richard Nixon." The resignation took effect at noon on August 9, when Gerald Ford was sworn in as president. "Our long national nightmare is over," Ford declared.

Within weeks of taking office, Ford pardoned Nixon for whatever crimes he had committed in office, even any, if such existed, as had yet come to light. Not many Americans wanted to see the ex-president lodged in jail, but pardoning him seemed both illogical and incomprehensible when Nixon had admitted no guilt and had not yet been officially charged with any crime. (Nixon's instant acceptance of the pardon while claiming to have done no wrong was also illogical but not incomprehensible.)

Milestones

1942	Pacifists found Congress of Racial Equality (CORE)
1955–1956	Martin Luther King Jr. leads Montgomery, Alabama, bus boycott
1957	Southern Christian Leadership Conference (SCLC) is founded in Atlanta
1960	Black college students found Student Nonviolent Coordinating Committee (SNCC)
1961	CIA-trained Cuban exiles launch disastrous Bay of Pigs invasion
	John F. Kennedy founds Peace Corps
	Freedom riders integrate buses in South
1962	Soviet Premier Khrushchev precipitates Cuban missile crisis
1963	United States supports coup to oust President Ngo Dinh Diem of South Vietnam
	Martin Luther King Jr. leads March on Washington
	Lee Harvey Oswald assassinates President Kennedy; Lyndon Johnson becomes president
1964	Congress endorses Vietnam escalation in Gulf of Tonkin Resolution
	Lyndon Johnson is elected president, begins Great Society program
	Congress passes historic Civil Rights Act
1965	Congress's Medicare Act pays some medical costs for senior citizens and the poor
	Congress funds education with Elementary and Secondary Education Act
1968	Communists strike all over South Vietnam in Tet Offensive
	Lyndon Johnson withdraws as candidate for reelection
	Richard Nixon is elected president
1969	Nixon announces "Vietnamization" of war
1970	Nixon announces "incursion" into Cambodia

	Antiwar student protesters are killed at Kent State and Jackson State universities
	Congress passes Clean Air Act and creates Environmental Protection Agency (EPA)
1972	Nixon's "plumbers" burglarize Democratic national headquarters at Watergate complex
	Nixon and Kissinger visit China and Soviet Union
	Nixon is reelected in landslide
1973	House Judiciary Committee begins impeachment hearings against Nixon
	Vice President Spiro Agnew resigns; Gerald Ford is appointed vice president
	Last American troops leave Vietnam
	Nixon fires Watergate special prosecutor Archibald Cox (Saturday Night Massacre)
1974	Supreme Court orders release of Nixon's White House tapes
	Nixon resigns; Gerald Ford becomes president and pardons Nixon

Society in Flux

IN 2003, THE MOST RECENT YEAR THAT HAS BEEN ANALYZED BY federal researchers, 10,300 Americans between the ages of 16 and 24 were killed in motor vehicle crashes—the leading cause of death for young people. Next came homicide (5,233), suicide (3,825), and accidental poisoning (1,973). Among all age groups, traffic accidents killed 43,340 and injured nearly 3 million.

But it could be worse—and was. During the decade of the 1970s, a half million Americans perished in traffic accidents—over 50,000 per year. Highway officials note that traffic fatalities in recent years have declined despite the fact that far more Americans nowadays have cars and drive greater distances than a generation ago. National speed limits, mandatory use of seat belts, and improved automobile and highway design are credited for the reduction in fatalities.

Yet the gruesome facts remain. Since Henry Ford rolled out the Model-T, more than 3.5 million Americans have died on the nation's roads and highways. The 54,589 fatalities in 1972 alone—a record—exceeded total American deaths in the Korean War. Today, more Americans die in traffic accidents each month than perished in the terrorist attacks on September 11, 2001.

Most Americans regard the carnage on the highways with stoicism. During the past half century, Americans have lived much of their lives in automobiles—traveling to work or school, shopping, and meeting friends. The United States has become a "society in flux" in part because Americans are literally in motion so much of the time.

Suburbs have sprawled far into the countryside, connected to the cities by webs of concrete. For novelists, artists, and songwriters, the automobile has served as metaphor for speed and power, freedom and self-reliance, affluence and romance. Cars have simultaneously symbolized middle-class conformity—parents and kids in a station wagon—and countercultural rebellion—Jack Kerouac's sexual and drug-laced antics On the Road (1957). The automobile promoted the sexual revolution by providing courting couples with a refuge from parental supervision.

Perhaps no social gulf is greater than that separating those who can afford automobiles from those who cannot. Many of the important battles of the civil rights movement turned on issues of public transportation—such as the freedom riders and school busing to desegregate schools. The race riots of the 1960s suggested that, for many African Americans, the nation's ghettos, lacking decent public transportation, had become prisons.

A Society on the Move

During the booming 1920s, when the car became an instrument of mass transportation, about 31 million autos were produced by American factories. During the 1950s, 58 million rolled off the assembly lines; during the 1960s, 77 million.

The new cars were heavier and more powerful than their predecessors. Gasoline consumption first touched 15 billion gallons in 1931; it soared to 35 billion gallons in 1950 and to 92 billion in 1970. A new business, the motel industry (the word, typically American, was a combination of *motor* and *hotel*) developed to service the millions of tourists and business travelers who burned all this fuel.

From 1940 to 1980, highway expenditures in terms of constant dollars nearly doubled. Much of this money was provided by the federal government for construction of interstate highways. Eisenhower justified the National Interstate and Defense Highway Act of 1956, the largest public works project in the nation's history to that point, on the grounds of defense: If an enemy nation invaded the United States, the interstate highways would promote mobilization. The new roads did far more than facilitate long-distance travel; they accelerated the shift of population to the suburbs and the consequent decline of inner-city districts.

Although commercial air travel had existed in the 1930s and had profited from wartime technical advances in military aircraft, it truly came of age when the first jetliner—the Boeing 707, built in Seattle, Washington—went into service in 1958. Almost immediately jets came to dominate long-distance travel, while railroad passenger service and transatlantic liners declined in importance.

The Advent of Television

Another important postwar change was the advent of television as a means of mass communication. By 1961 there were 55 million sets in operation, and by the mid-1960s orbiting government and commercial satellites were relaying pictures from one continent to another instantly.

Television combined the immediacy of radio with the visual impact of films, and it displayed most of the strengths and weaknesses of both in exaggerated form. It swiftly became indispensable to the political system, both for its coverage of public events and as a vehicle for political advertising.

Television also brought sports events before the viewer vividly, attracting enormous audiences and producing so much money in advertising revenue that the economics of professional sports was revolutionized. Team franchises were bought and sold for huge sums, and ordinary players commanded salaries in the hundreds of thousands, stars in the millions.

Some excellent drama was presented, especially on the National Educational Television network, along with many filmed documentaries. However, Newton Minow of the Federal Communications Commission (FCC) called the programming offered by most television stations a "vast wasteland." The lion's share of television time was devoted to uninspired and vulgar serials, routine variety shows, giveaway and quiz programs designed to reveal and revel in the ignorance of the average citizen, and reruns of old movies cut to fit rigid time periods and repeatedly interrupted at climactic points by commercials. Most sets had poor acoustic qualities, which made them inferior instruments for listening to music. Yet children found television fascinating, remaining transfixed before the screen when—their elders said—they should have been out of doors or curled up with a book.

At Home and Work

Family life was changing in complicated ways. Sometimes men and women devised entirely new ways of raising families and reconciling the demands of work and marriage; at other times, they looked resolutely to the past for guidance as to their own lives.

In 1946, more than 10 percent of all single females over the age of 14 in the country got married. Government policies buttressed the inclinations of the people: to encourage taxpayers to have children, the federal government granted income tax deductions for dependents. The birthrate soared.

The period was marked by a cultural reaffirmation of domesticity. A 1947 survey by the *Woman's Home Companion* found that among possible careers, its readers favored nursing, clerical work, retailing, and teaching because these jobs offered the best preparation for women's "prime objective": marriage. Popular magazines like the *Ladies' Home Journal*, full of articles such as "Keep Those Home Fires Burning—With Hobbies" and "See How to Knit a Baby Blanket," showed college-educated women how to make a "career" of home management and child development.

Scholars mostly agreed that women belonged at home. In 1947 psychoanalyst Marynia Farnham explained that the female reproductive organs predisposed women to the protective and nurturing tasks of child rearing; women who pursued careers in the competitive world of business would forever be at odds with their bodies. Dr. Benjamin Spock, whose *Common Sense Guide to Baby and Child Care* first appeared in 1946 and sold 24 million copies during the next quarter century, insisted that a mother's most important job was to shore up her children's sense of self by providing continuous support and affection. Women who worked outside the home necessarily "neglected" their children. The child who was "mildly neglected," Spock added, was apt to grow up "mildly disturbed."

Art historian Karal Ann Marling observed in *As Seen on TV* (1994) that the TV set originally functioned as a kind of picture, such as would be hung over the mantelpiece. This 1950s American living room illustrates the point: pictures have been arranged above the television, but the family is looking at the TV, riveted by the antics of a clown.

Although men assumed prominent roles in some domestic rituals, such as presiding over the backyard barbecue or carving the holiday turkey, their chief responsibility was to earn enough money to sustain the family. This was considerably easier than in the past. From 1949 through 1975, unemployment never exceeded 7 percent, and during the mid-1960s it fell well below 4 percent. For those who had lived during the Depression the dominant social fact of the postwar era was the availability of work.

But the *character* of work was changing in unsettling ways. The Second World War accelerated the growth of giant corporations, whose complex, global operations were built on mountains of paper. Regiments of managers ran the systems, and vast armies of clerical workers processed the expanded flow of information. In 1870, 1 in 160 workers was employed in clerical work; by 1950, that figure was 1 in 8. One-fifth of all employees of manufacturing firms worked in offices.

The growth of suburbs gave a geographic dimension to the changing roles of husbands and wives. In the postwar years the federal government encouraged single-family home construction by allowing homeowners to deduct mortgage interest from their income taxes and by making low-cost mortgages available through the Federal Housing Administration.

New suburbs appeared almost like mushrooms after a spring rain. With their streets named after flowers or pleasant emotional states (the large postwar suburb of Levittown, near Philadelphia, featured Friendly Lane, Graceful Lane, Good Lane, and Shelter Lane), the suburbs were to function as havens for work-weary men.

In fact, the suburban world was unreal even for many of the women who in-habited it. More women were leaving the home during the day to find work in the burgeoning clerical and service sector. In 1940, only 1 in 4 civilian employees was female, one-third of them married. Three decades later, 4 in 10 paid employees were women, two-thirds of them married. Perhaps 20 million women—after re-turning home from work, fixing dinner, putting the children to bed, and doing a load of laundry—collapsed in front of the television set and watched domestic heroines such as Donna Reed vacuuming the house in high heels and pearls, mak-ing clothes and cakes from scratch, soothing the fragile psyches of her husband and children, and otherwise living a fantasy that accorded with the idealized image of female domesticity.

The Growing Middle Class

Another postwar change was the marked broadening of the middle class. In 1947 only 5.7 million American families had what might be considered middle-class in-comes—enough to provide something for leisure, entertainment, and cultural ac-tivities as well as for life's necessities. By the early 1960s more than 12 million fam-ilies, about a third of the population, had such incomes.

As blue-collar workers invaded the middle class by the tens of thousands, they moved to suburbs previously reserved for junior executives, shopkeepers, and the like. They shed their work clothes for business suits. They took up golf. In sum, they adopted values and attitudes commensurate with their new status—which helps explain the growing conservatism of labor unions. During the Great Depression, when they were underdogs of sorts, the unions fought for social jus-tice. In the 1960s many union workers seemed more interested in preserving their gains against the ravages of inflation and taxation than in reforming society.

Religion in Changing Times

Sociologists and other commentators on contemporary affairs found in the expan-sion of the middle class another explanation of the tendency of the country to glo-rify the conformist. They attributed to this expansion the blurring of party lines in politics, the national obsession with moderation and consensus, the complacency of so many Americans, and their tendency, for example, to be more interested in the social aspects of churchgoing than in the moral and philosophical aspects of religion.

Organized religion traditionally deals with eternal values, but it is always influ-enced by social, cultural, and economic developments. Never had this been truer in America than in the decades after World War II. All the major faiths, despite their differences, were affected. Immediately after the war the prosperity and buoyant optimism of the period led to an expansion of religious activity. The Catholic

Martin Luther King Jr. at the Antioch Baptist Church, 1966. As a student at Crozer Theological Seminary, King excelled at homiletics—the art of preaching. His deep, booming voice and pronounced gestures helped inspire the civil rights movement. "He's damn good," President Kennedy remarked after seeing him on television. King's powerful persona helped bring religion directly into public life.

Church alone built over a thousand new schools and more than a hundred hospitals along with countless new churches. By 1950 the Southern Baptists had enrolled nearly 300,000 new members and built some 500 churches.

But while most faiths prospered materially, the faithful tended to accept the world as it was. In *Catholic, Protestant, Jew* (1955), Will Herberg argued that ethnic differences between people of different backgrounds were becoming less important, and as a result, religious toleration was becoming routine. President Eisenhower lent authority to this argument when he said: "Our government makes no sense unless it is founded on a deeply felt religious faith—and I don't care what it is."

Church and state were by law and the Constitution separate institutions, but on Flag Day in 1954 Eisenhower signed a law that added the phrase "one nation under God" to the Pledge of Allegiance. The next year, Congress added "In God We Trust" to the nation's currency. New Deal welfare legislation took on a large part of a burden previously borne by church groups.

The civil rights movement and the war in Vietnam had important religious implications. Many militant blacks (Malcolm X is an early example) converted to the Muslim faith because of its lack of racial bias. Among those in the public eye who became Muslims were the heavyweight champion boxer Cassius Clay, who changed his name to Muhammad Ali, and Lew Alcindor, a basketball star who became Kareem Abdul Jabbar.

Nearly all religious groups played significant roles in the fight for racial justice that erupted after the Supreme Court outlawed segregation. Priests, ministers, and rabbis joined in antiwar demonstrations. The Reverend Martin Luther King Jr.'s nonviolent approach was essentially religious, his oratory deeply felt, passionate, but always dignified and controlled.

The enormous outpouring produced by King's March on Washington in 1963 was swelled by many prominent religious leaders, and their example put pressure on both church hierarchies and ordinary members to become civil rights activists. Shocking photographs of police dogs being used to "subdue" demonstrating Catholic nuns in the Deep South converted uncounted thousands to the struggle.

All the social changes of the period had religious ramifications. Feminists objected to male domination of most Christian churches and called for the ordination of female ministers and priests; some religious leaders supported the feminists, but conservatives rejected their ideas out of hand. Every aspect of the sexual revolution, from the practice of couples living together openly outside of marriage to the tolerance of homosexuality and pornography to the legalization of contraception and abortion, caused shock waves in the religious community. The Roman Catholic insistence that the clergy remain celibate resulted in a decline in the number of young Catholics becoming priests and nuns. This dealt a crippling blow to the parochial school system, which depended heavily on the clergy for teachers.

Radio and television had more direct effects on organized religion. The "Radio Priest" of the New Deal era, Father Charles Coughlin, was the prototype of a new kind of clergyman that flourished in the postwar period. The airwaves enabled rhetorically skilled preachers to reach millions with emotionally charged messages on religious topics and also on political and social questions. The most successful in the postwar years were the leaders of evangelical Protestant sects, and by the 1960s they had mastered television. Whereas most postwar revivalists, the most famous being Billy Graham, stressed interdenominational cooperation, in the 1970s a more militant, fundamentalist type emerged. Television preachers founded their own churches and educational institutions, supported by direct appeals to viewers.

In the mid-1980s a number of scandals involving prominent televangelists caused disillusionment and widespread defections. On the other hand, the rapid spread of cable television during this time greatly increased the number of available channels, enabling scores of new evangelists to reach out to viewers. Although most of them placed considerable emphasis on biblical authority, Americans had never before been exposed to such a wide range of religious messages and interpretations. Contributions poured into countless charities and missionary activities.

Regular ministers worried that the direct appeal of the televangelists and the convenience of worshiping in the living room would empty the churches. But this did not happen. In 1989, membership in all churches and synagogues surpassed 148 million, an increase of 60 million during the previous four decades. (The total population during the period increased by nearly 100 million.) Membership in the

Roman Catholic Church more than doubled, largely due to a large influx of Hispanic immigrants. In 1990 two-thirds of all Americans reported that they belonged to a church, the highest percentage by far among the major industrial nations of the West.

The Perils of Progress

The many changes of the era help explain why President Johnson warned in his inaugural address, "We have no promise from God that our greatness will endure." Looking at American society more broadly, two dilemmas seem to have emerged. One was that progress was often self-defeating. Reforms and innovations instituted with the best of motives often made things worse rather than better. Instances of this dilemma, large and small, are so numerous as to defy summary. DDT, a powerful chemical developed to kill insects that were spreading disease and destroying valuable food crops, proved to have lethal effects on birds and fish— and perhaps indirectly on human beings. Goods manufactured to make life fuller and happier (automobiles, detergents, electric power) produced waste products that disfigured the land and polluted air and water. Cities built to bring culture and employment to millions became pestholes of poverty and depravity.

The second dilemma was that modern industrial society placed an enormous premium on social cooperation, at the same time undermining the individual citizen's sense of being essential to the proper functioning of society. The economy was as complicated as a fine watch; a breakdown in any one sector swiftly spread to other sectors. Yet specialization had progressed so far that individual workers had little sense of the importance of their personal contributions and thus felt little responsibility for the smooth functioning of the whole. Effective democratic government required that all voters be knowledgeable and concerned, but few could feel that their individual voices had any effect on elections or public policies. The exhaust fumes of millions of automobiles poisoned the air, but it was difficult to expect the single motorist to inconvenience himself by leaving his car in the garage when his restraint would have no measurable effect on total pollution. "One person just can't feel that she's doing anything," a frustrated teenager wrote. "I can use soap instead of detergent . . . but what good do I feel I'm doing when there are people next door having a party with plastic spoons and paper plates?"

These dilemmas produced a paradox. The United States was the most powerful nation in the world, its people the best educated, the richest, and probably the most energetic. American society was technologically advanced and dynamic; American traditional values were idealistic, humane, democratic. Yet the nation seemed incapable of mobilizing its resources intelligently to confront the most obvious challenges, its citizens unable to achieve much personal happiness or identification with their fellows, the society helpless in trying to live up to its most universally accepted ideals.

New Racial Turmoil

The persistence of grave social inequalities jolted the nation from its complacency. President Johnson and most of those who supported his policies expected that the 1964 Civil Rights Act, the Economic Opportunity Act, Medicare and Medicaid, and the other elements in the war on poverty would produce an era of racial peace and genuine social harmony—the Great Society that everyone wanted. The change that occurred in the thinking of the black radical Malcolm X seemed a straw in the wind. In 1964 Malcolm left the Muslims and founded his own Organization of Afro-American Unity. While continuing to stress black self-help and the militant defense of black rights, he now saw the fight for racial equality as part of a larger struggle for all human rights. "What we do . . . helps all people everywhere who are fighting against oppression," he said. Yet as in so many other aspects of modern life, progress itself created new difficulties. Early in 1965 Black Muslim fanatics, furious at his defection, assassinated Malcolm X while he was making a speech in favor of racial harmony.

The assassination was an act of vengeance, not of social protest. More significant was the fact that official white recognition of past injustices was making blacks more insistent that all discrimination end. The very process of righting some past wrongs gave African Americans the strength to fight more vigorously. Black militancy, building steadily during the war and the postwar years, had long been ignored by the white majority; in the mid-1960s it burst forth so powerfully that the most smug and obtuse white citizens had to accept its existence.

Even Martin Luther King Jr., the herald of nonviolent resistance, became more aggressive. "We are not asking, we are demanding the ballot," he said in January 1965. A few weeks after Malcolm's death, King led a march from Selma, Alabama, to Montgomery as part of a campaign to force Alabama authorities to allow blacks to register to vote. King chose Selma because the county in which it was located had a black majority but only 325 registered black voters. He expected the authorities to react brutally, thus attracting public sympathy for the marchers, and he was not disappointed. His marchers were assaulted by state policemen who wielded clubs and tossed canisters of tear gas. Liberal opinion was shocked as never before. Thousands of people descended on Selma to demonstrate their support for the black cause.

The Student Nonviolent Coordinating Committee (SNCC), which had been born out of the struggle for racial integration, had become by the mid-1960s a radical organization openly scornful of integration and interracial cooperation. Many students had been radicalized by the threats and open violence they had experienced while trying to register rural blacks and organize schools for black children and by the foot-dragging of the Kennedy administration in working for racial justice. The slogan of the radicals was "Black Power," an expression that was given national currency by Stokely Carmichael, chairman of SNCC. Carmichael, a West Indian by birth, had grown up in Harlem. He had worked ceaselessly for black rights in the South, and as a result he had spent considerable time in southern jails, often on such trumped-up charges as pitching a tent on the grounds of a black school. Although willing to work with black moderates such as King, he was adamantly opposed to cooperating with whites of any stripe. "The time for white involvement in the fight for equality has ended," Carmichael announced in 1966. "If we are to proceed toward true liberation, we must set ourselves off from white people." "Integration is a subterfuge for the maintenance of white supremacy," Carmichael said on another occasion. Blacks should have their own schools, their own businesses, their own political parties, their own (African) culture.

Black Power caught on swiftly among militants. This troubled white liberals, who feared that Black Power would antagonize white conservatives. They argued that since blacks made up only about 11 percent of the population, any attempt to obtain racial justice through the use of naked power was sure to fail.

Meanwhile, black anger erupted in a series of destructive urban riots. The most important occurred in Watts, a ghetto of Los Angeles, in August 1965. A trivial incident brought thousands into the streets. The neighborhood almost literally exploded: For six days Watts was swept by fire, looting, and bloody fighting between local residents and nearly 15,000 National Guardsmen, called up to assist the police. The following two summers saw similar outbursts in scores of cities.

Then, in April 1968, Martin Luther King Jr. was murdered in Memphis, Tennessee, by a white man, James Earl Ray. Blacks in more than a hundred cities unleashed their anger in outbursts of burning and looting. Whites were shocked and profoundly depressed. The death of King appeared to destroy the hope that his peaceful appeal to reason and right could solve the problems of racism.

Public fear and puzzlement led to many investigations of the causes of the riots, the most important being that of the commission headed by Governor Otto Kerner of Illinois, which President Johnson had appointed after the 1967 riots. The conclusions of most of the studies were complex but fairly clear. Race riots had a long history in the United States, but earlier troubles usually began with attacks by whites that led to black counterattacks. Riots of the Watts type were begun by blacks. Although much white-owned property was destroyed, the fighting was mostly between blacks and law enforcement officers trying to control them.

The rioters were expressing frustration and despair; their resentment was directed more at the social system than at individuals. As the Kerner Commission put it, the basic cause was the "white racism" that deprived blacks of access to good jobs, crowded them into slums, and eroded all hope of escape from such misery. Ghettoes bred crime and depravity—as slums always have—and the complacent refusal of whites to invest enough money and energy to help ghetto residents, or even to acknowledge that the black poor deserved help, made the modern slum unbearable. While the ghettoes expanded, middle-class whites tended more and more to flee to the suburbs or to call on the police "to maintain law and order," a euphemism for cracking down hard on deviant black behavior no matter how obvious the connection between that behavior and the slum environment.

The victims of racism employed violence not so much to force change as to obtain psychic release; it was a way of getting rid of what they could not stomach, a kind of vomiting. Thus the riots concentrated in the ghettos themselves, smashing, Samson-like, the source of degradation even when this meant self-destruction. When fires broke out in black districts, the firefighters who tried to extinguish them were often showered with bottles and bricks and sometimes shot at, while above the roar of the flames and the hiss of steam rose the apocalyptic chant, "Burn, baby, burn!"

Middle-class city residents often resented what seemed the "favoritism" of the federal government and state and local administrations, which sought through affirmative action to provide blacks with economic opportunities and social benefits. Efforts to desegregate ghetto schools by busing children out of their local neighborhoods were a particularly bitter cause of conflict. These developments caused a powerful white backlash. People already subjected to the pressures caused by inflation, specialization, and rapid change, and worried by rising urban crime rates and welfare costs, found black radicalism infuriating.

Native-Born Ethnics

The struggles of blacks for equality went hand in hand with the struggles of those of Mexican descent, principally in the Southwest. After World War I, thousands of immigrants from Mexico flocked into that part of the country, mingling with the far larger native-born Hispanic population. They could do so legally because the restrictive immigration legislation of the 1920s did not apply to Western Hemisphere nations. When the Great Depression struck, Mexican Americans were the first to suffer—about half a million Hispanics who were not citizens were either deported or "persuaded" to return to Mexico. But during World War II and again between 1948 and 1965, federal legislation encouraged the importation of *braceros* (temporary farm workers). Many other Mexicans entered the country illegally. The latter were known as *mojados*, or "wetbacks," because they often slipped over the border by swimming across the Rio Grande.

Many of these Mexicans and other Spanish-speaking people, including the thousands from the territory of Puerto Rico who could immigrate to the mainland legally in unlimited numbers, settled in the big cities, where low-paying but usually steady work was available. They lived in slums called *barrios*, as segregated, crowded, and crime-ridden as the ghettos of the blacks.

Spanish-speaking residents of the Southwest, native- and foreign-born, and to a lesser degree those in the big eastern cities, were for a time largely apolitical; they tended to remain close-knit and insular. But in the 1960s a new spirit of resistance arose. Leaders of the new movement called themselves Chicanos. The Chicanos demanded better schools for their children and easier access to higher education. They urged friends and relatives to take pride in their traditions and culture, to demand their rights, and to organize themselves politically. One Chicano nationalist group tried to secede from New Mexico, an act that brought it into confrontation with the army.

The Mexican American founder of the National Farm Workers Association and later head of the United Farm Workers Organizing Committee, César Chávez successfully organized migrant workers throughout California in the early 1960s and later led a nationwide boycott against California grape producers.

The Chicano leader with the widest influence was César Chávez, who concentrated on what superficially was a more limited goal—organizing migrant farm workers into unions. Chávez grew up in migrant camps in California; he had no schooling beyond the seventh grade. After serving in the navy during World War II, he went to work for the Community Service Organization (CSO), a group seeking to raise the political consciousness of the poor and to develop self-help programs for them. Chávez became general director of the CSO but resigned in 1962 because he felt it was not devoting enough attention to the plight of migrant workers. He then founded the National Farm Workers' Association, later known as the United Farm Workers Organizing Committee.

The struggles of black people for equal treatment in the 1950s and 1960s radicalized many Indians. These militants referred to themselves as Native Americans, not Indians. They used the term *Red Power* as blacks spoke of Black Power and called their more conservative colleagues "Uncle Tomahawks." The National Indian Youth Council and later the American Indian Movement (AIM) demanded the return of lands taken illegally from their ancestors. They called for self-determination and a concerted effort to revive tribal cultures, even the use of the mind-altering controlled substance peyote in religious ceremonies,[1] and they organized a Pan-Indian movement to advance the cause. Paradoxically, this policy brought them into conflict with traditionalist Indians devoted to local autonomy. (At least forty Indian languages are still spoken.)

Some AIM leaders sought total separation from the United States; they envisaged setting up states within states, such as the Cherokees had established in Georgia in Jacksonian days. In 1973 radicals occupied the town of Wounded Knee, South Dakota (site of one of the most disgraceful massacres of Indians in the nineteenth century), and held it at gunpoint for weeks.

While traditionalists resisted the militants, liberal white opinion proved to be generally sympathetic. In 1975 Congress passed the Indian Self-Determination Act,

---

[1]*The California Supreme Court upheld the right to use peyote in this way in* People v. Woody *(1964).*

which gave individual tribes much greater control over such matters as education, welfare programs, and law enforcement. The act specifically recognized the government's obligation to ensure "maximum Indian participation" in the management of federal policy in these areas.

Militant ethnic pride characterized the behavior of other racial minorities and of many white Americans too. Blacks donned dashikis and other African garments and wore their hair in natural "Afro" styles. Italian Americans, Polish Americans, and descendants of other "new immigrant" groups eagerly studied their history in order to preserve their culture and where necessary revive dying traditions. The American "melting pot," some historians now argued, had not amalgamated the immigrant strains as completely as had been thought. Ethnic diversity became for some an end to be desired, despite the possibility that differences might as easily inspire conflict as harmonious adjustment.

The color line was broken in major league baseball by Jackie Robinson in 1947, and soon all professional sports were open to black athletes. Whereas the reign of black heavyweight boxing champion Jack Johnson (1908–1915) had inspired an open search for a "white hope" to depose him, and whereas the next black champion, Joe Louis (1937–1949), had been accepted by whites because he "knew his place" and was "well behaved," champion Muhammad Ali was a hero to both white and black boxing fans despite his often bizarre behavior, his militant advocacy of racial equality, and his adoption of the Muslim religion.

Their achievements and advances aside, African Americans had found real self-awareness. The attitude of mind that ran from the lonely Denmark Vesey to Frederick Douglass and to W. E. B. Du Bois had become the black consensus.

Rethinking Public Education

Young people were in the forefront of the fight for the rights of minorities. In a time of uncertainty and discontent, full of conflict and dilemma, youth was affected more strongly than the older generations, and it reacted more forcefully. No institution escaped its criticisms, not even the vaunted educational system, which many students claimed poorly suited their needs. This was still another paradox of modern life, for American public education was probably the most comprehensive in the world.

After World War I, under the impact of Freudian psychology, the emphasis in elementary education shifted from using the schools as instruments of social change, as John Dewey had recommended, to using them to promote the emotional development of the students. "Child-centered" educators played down academic achievement in favor of "adjustment." The change probably stimulated the students' imaginations and may possibly have improved their psychological well-being, but observers soon noted that the system produced poor work habits and fuzzy thinking and fostered plain ignorance. Although "educationists" insisted that they were not abandoning traditional academic subjects, they surely de-emphasized them.

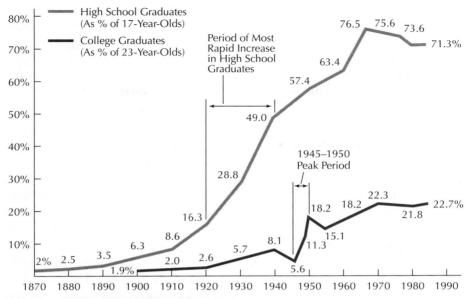

High School and College Graduates, 1870–1983

Lyndon Johnson's Elementary and Secondary Education Act, passed in 1965, was a landmark in the century-long expansion of high school education and directly influenced college education in the United States. The most rapid increase in high school graduates occurred between 1920 and 1940, but the number of graduates as a percentage of all people aged 17 was greatest in 1967. The peak period for college graduates, 1945 to 1950, reflects the GI Bill after World War II.

The demands of society for rigorous intellectual achievement made this distortion of progressive education increasingly less satisfactory. Following World War II, critics began a concerted assault on the system. The leader of the attack was James B. Conant, former president of Harvard. His book *The American High School Today* (1959) sold nearly half a million copies, and his later studies of teacher education and the special problems of urban schools also attracted wide attention.

Conant flayed the schools for their failure to teach English grammar and composition effectively, for neglecting foreign languages, and for ignoring the needs of both the brightest and the dullest students. He insisted that teachers' colleges should place subject matter above educational methodology in their curricula.

The success of the Soviet Union in launching the first *Sputnik* in 1957 increased the influence of critics like Conant because it dealt a healthy blow to American overconfidence. To match the Soviet achievement, the United States needed thousands of engineers and scientists, and the schools were not turning out enough graduates prepared to study science and engineering at the college level. Suddenly the schools were under enormous pressure, for with more and more young people desiring to go to college, the colleges were raising their admission standards. The traditionalists thus gained the initiative, academic subjects a revived prestige. The National Defense Education Act of 1958 supplied a powerful stimulus by allocating funds for upgrading work in the sciences, foreign languages, and other subjects and for expanding guidance services and experimenting with television and other new teaching devices. States encouraged small schools to consolidate into larger units; high schools became larger, as Conant proposed, allowing greater specialization among faculty and more college-level classes. Not until the large high schools were built did administrators perceive that many students, especially from disadvantaged minority groups, felt lost in them.

The post-*Sputnik* stress on academic achievement profoundly affected higher education too. Critics demanded that secondary schools and colleges raise their standards and place more stress on the sciences. Prestige institutions such as Harvard, Yale, Columbia, Stanford, and a dozen other colleges and universities, raised their entrance requirements. By the mid-1960s, the children of the baby boom generation were flocking to the nation's high schools and colleges. Population growth and the demands of society for specialized intellectual skills were causing educational institutions to burst at the seams. Enrollments had risen rapidly after World War II, mostly because of the GI Bill; by 1950 there were 2.3 million students in American colleges and universities. Forty years later there were about 14 million. To bridge the gap between high school and college, two-year community colleges proliferated. Almost unknown before 1920, there were about 1,300 two-year colleges by 1980, nearly all of them publicly financed. Enrollment in these institutions rose from 1.3 million in the mid-1960s to 5.2 million in 1990.

Students in Revolt

For a time after World War II, the expansion of higher education took place with remarkable smoothness. The veterans, more mature and eager to make up for lost time, concentrated on their studies, and younger students tended to follow their lead. But in the 1960s the mood changed. The members of this college generation had grown up during the postwar prosperity and had been trained by teachers who were, by and large, New Deal liberals. They had been told that government was supposed to regulate the economy in the general interest, help the weak against the strong, and protect the liberties of all. It seemed to many students not to be performing these functions.

Modern industrial society, with its "soul-less" corporations and its almost equally unfeeling human bureaucracies, provided these young people with material comforts and social advantages, but it made them feel insignificant and powerless. Their advantages also made them feel guilty when they thought about the millions of Americans who did not have them. The persistence of poverty in a country as rich as the United States was intolerable, and racial prejudice both stupid and evil. Yet the government seemed incapable of attacking these disgraceful conditions head-on. Still worse in their eyes, the response of their elders to McCarthyism appeared contemptible—craven cowardice of the worst sort—and

"Alma mater," outside Low Memorial Hall of Columbia University, looks on sedately as SDS leader Mark Rudd denounces the school. Later, Rudd and other radicals climbed these stairs and ordered administrators to vacate the building. The students then occupied the buildings. New York City police subsequently threw the students out.

dangerous. In the age of the atom, rabid anticommunism might end in nuclear war.

All these influences were encapsulated in a manifesto put forth by a small group of students at a meeting of Students for a Democratic Society (SDS), held at Port Huron, Michigan, in 1962. "We are the people of this generation . . . looking uncomfortably to the world we inherit," the Port Huron Statement began. Their main concerns were racial bigotry, the bomb, and the "disturbing paradoxes" associated with these concerns. How could an American reconcile the contradictions between the idea that "all men are created equal" with "the facts of Negro life in the South and the big cities of the North" and between the declared peaceful intentions of the government and its huge "economic and military investments in the Cold War?" Too many people and too many institutions, concentrating on preserving what they own and can command, had "closed their minds to the future."

SDS grew rapidly, powered by rising college enrollments, protest against the escalation of the war in Vietnam, and a seemingly unending list of local campus issues. Radical students generally had little tolerance for injustice, and their dissatisfaction often found expression in public protests. The first great student outburst convulsed the University of California at Berkeley in the fall of 1964. Angry students, many veterans of the 1964 fight for black rights in the South, staged sit-down strikes in university buildings to protest the prohibition of political canvassing on the campus. This Free Speech Movement disrupted the institution over a period of weeks. Hundreds were arrested; the state legislature threatened reprisals; the faculty became involved in the controversy; and the crisis led to the resignation of the president of the University of California, Clark Kerr.

On campus after campus in the late 1960s students organized sit-ins and employed other disruptive tactics. Frequently professors and administrators played into the radicals' hands, being so offended by their methods and manners that they refused to recognize the legitimacy of some of their demands.

Equally significant in altering the students' mood was the frustration that so many of them felt with traditional aspects of college life. Regulations that students had formerly merely grumbled about evoked determined, even violent opposition. Dissidents denounced rules that restricted their personal lives, such as prohibitions on the use of alcohol and the banning of members of the opposite sex from dormitories. They complained that required courses inhibited their intellectual development. They demanded a share in the government of their institutions, long the private preserve of administrators and professors.

Beyond their specific complaints, the radicals refused to put up with anything they considered wrong. The knotty social problems that made their elders gravitate toward moderation led these students to become intransigent absolutists. The line between right and wrong became as sharply defined as the edge of a ruler. Racial prejudice was evil: it must be eradicated. War in a nuclear age was insane: armies must be disbanded. Poverty amid plenty was an abomination: end poverty now. To the counsel that evil can be eliminated only gradually, that misguided persons must be persuaded to mend their ways, that compromise was the path to true progress, they responded with scorn. Extremists among them, observing the weaknesses of American civilization, adopted a nihilistic position—the only way to deal with a "rotten" society was to destroy it.

The Counterculture

Some young people, known generally as hippies, were so "turned off" by the modern world that they retreated from it, finding refuge in communes, drugs, and mystical religions, often wandering aimlessly from place to place. During the 1960s and 1970s groups of them could be found in every big city in the United States and Europe. Some hippies, like the poet Allen Ginsberg, one of their elder statesmen, and the novelist Ken Kesey, were genuinely creative people. Ginsberg's dark, desperate masterpiece "Howl," written apparently while under the influence of drugs in 1955, was perhaps the most widely read poem of the postwar era, certainly a work of major literary significance. "Howl" begins: "I saw the best minds of my generation destroyed by madness, starving hysterical naked," and goes on to describe the wanderings and searchings of these "angelheaded hipsters," a "lost battalion of platonic conversationalists . . . seeking jazz or sex or soup" in Houston, "whoring in Colorado," and "investigating the F.B.I. in beards and shorts" in California, all the while denouncing "the narcotic tobacco haze of Capitalism." "Howl" ends with

Ginsberg's indignant, almost frantic assault on that "sphinx of cement and aluminum," the fire god Moloch, the devourer of children.

Most hippies resembled the radicals in their political and social opinions. They were disgusted by the dishonesty and sordid antics of so many of the politicians, horrified by the brutality of Vietnam, appalled by racism, contemptuous of the smugness they encountered in colleges and universities. They believed in conservation, freedom of expression, tolerance, and peace.

But they rejected activism, being almost totally apolitical. Theirs was a world of folk songs and blaring acid rock music, of "be-ins," casual sex, and drugs. Their slogan, "Make love, not war" was more a general pacifist pronouncement than a specific criticism of events in Vietnam, although Vietnam surely had a great deal to do with their underlying pessimism. Indeed, with them passivity was a philosophy, almost a principle. At rock concerts they listened where earlier generations had danced. Hallucinogenic drugs heightened users' "experiences" while they were in fact in a stupor. Timothy Leary, a Harvard psychologist who became known as the "Johnny Appleseed of LSD," advised them to "Tune in, turn on, drop out." Another hippie slogan, "Do your own thing," will work in social situations only if no one does anything. Their communes were a far cry from the busy centers of social experimentation of the pre–Civil War Age of Reform.

The Sexual Revolution

Young people made the most striking contribution to the revolution that took place in the late 1960s in public attitudes toward sexual relationships. Here change came with startling swiftness. Almost overnight (it seemed in retrospect) conventional ideas about premarital sex, contraception and abortion, homosexuality, pornography, and a host of related matters were openly challenged. Probably the behavior of the majority of Americans did not alter radically, but the majority's beliefs and practices were no longer automatically acknowledged as the only valid ones. It became possible for individuals to espouse different values and to behave differently with at least relative impunity. Actions that in one decade would have led to social ostracism or even to imprisonment were in the next decade accepted almost as a matter of course.

The causes of this revolution were complex and interrelated; one change led to others. More efficient methods of contraception, especially the birth control pill, and antibiotics that cured venereal disease removed the two principal practical arguments against sex outside of marriage; with these barriers down, many people found their moral attitudes changing. Almost concurrently, Alfred C. Kinsey's *Sexual Behavior in the Human Male* (1948), based on thousands of confidential interviews with persons from many walks of life, claimed that half of American men engaged in homosexual activities before adolescence; that 90 percent had masturbated; that between 30 and 45 percent had adulterous sexual relations; that 70 percent had patronized prostitutes; and that 17 percent of farm boys had had sexual

Debating the Past

DID MASS CULTURE MAKE LIFE SHALLOW?

At the 1969 Woodstock festival in New York, a half million young people came together to commune with each other through the medium of rock music. Did mass-produced culture—pop music, movies, TV, consumer products—render life superficial or did it deepen life by allowing many to share similar experiences?

For much of the twentieth century, intellectuals had sniffed at the low-brow cultural products of the mass media: Elvis Presley and rap, western films and fast-food restaurants, television sit-coms and Disneyland. A group of European Marxists known as the "Frankfurt school," many of whom had fled to the United States to escape Nazi persecution, maintained that when popular culture was transformed into a mass-marketed consumer item, it became debased. Worse, mass culture was a form of mindless escapism that distracted people from meaningful political action.

But during the 1960s and 1970s, historians began to look at mass culture and consumption in a different way. Historians of women, minorities, workers, and other marginalized groups decided that it was not enough to recount such peoples' struggles against oppression: it was equally important to explain how they lived and what they thought. Warren Susman (1984), Robin D. Kelley (1994), Kathy Peiss (1998), and others embraced popular culture—even mass culture—because the people they studied did so, too. Lizabeth Cohen (2003) added that the triumph of mass culture did not mean that Americans had abandoned politics. On the contrary, the United States became a "Consumer Republic" ruled by "citizen consumers."

Warren Susman, *Culture as History* (1984), Robin D. Kelley, *Race Rebels* (1994), Kathy Peiss, *Hope in a Jar* (1998), Lizabeth Cohen, *A Consumers' Republic* (2003). For the Frankfurt school, see Theodor Adorno, *Culture Industry* (1991) and Christopher Lasch, *The Culture of Narcissism* (1979). Walter Benjamin, *Complete Correspondence* (1999), argued in this correspondence with Adorno that mass-produced culture could free culture from the snob fetishism of high culture.

relations with animals. Kinsey's data emphasized the diversity of sexual urges, and the foolishness of societal attempts to prescribe narrow standards of morality.

Sexual Behavior in the Human Male shocked many people, although social scientists pointed out that a large sample was not necessarily representative. When he published *Sexual Behavior in the Human Female* in 1958, a book that demonstrated

On June 26, 1994, thousands carry a mile-long rainbow banner in New York City commemorating the twenty-fifth anniversary of the 1969 Stonewall protests in Greenwich Village that inaugurated the gay rights movement.

that the sexual practices of women were as varied as those of men, Kinsey was subjected to a storm of abuse and deprived of the foundation support that had financed his research. (In 1997 historian James H. Jones challenged Kinsey's claims to scientific objectivity. Jones found that Kinsey and some of his researchers organized, participated in, and even filmed all manner of sexual activities involving interview subjects, prostitutes, colleagues, and spouses.)

That the sexual revolution in its many aspects served useful functions was beyond dispute. Reducing irrational fears and inhibitions was liberating for many persons of both sexes, and it tended to help young people form permanent associations on the basis of deeper feelings than their sexual drives. Women surely profited from the new freedom, just as a greater sharing of family duties by husbands and fathers opened men's lives to many new satisfactions. Homosexuals began openly to admit their feelings and to demand that heterosexual society cease to harass and discriminate against them.

But like other changes, the sexual revolution produced new problems, and some of its results were at best ambiguous. For young people, sexual freedom could be very unsettling; sometimes it generated social pressures that propelled them into relationships they were not yet prepared to handle, with grave psychological results. Equally perplexing was the rise in the number of illegitimate births. Easy cures did not eliminate venereal disease; on the contrary, the relaxation of sexual taboos produced what public health officials called a veritable epidemic of gonorrhea, a frightening increase in the incidence of syphilis, and the emergence of a new disease, acquired immunodeficiency syndrome (AIDS).

Exercising the right to advocate and practice previously forbidden activities involved subjecting people who found those activities offensive—still a large proportion of the population—to embarrassment and even to acute emotional distress. To some people pornography seemed ethically wrong, and to most feminists it seemed degrading to women. Abortion raised difficult legal and moral questions, which exacerbated already serious social conflicts. Clearly, however, the sexual revolution was not about to end, nor the direction of change to be reversed.

Women's Liberation

Sexual freedom also contributed to the revival of the women's rights movement. For one thing, freedom involved a more drastic revolution for women than for men. Effective methods of contraception obviously affected women more directly than men, and the new attitudes heightened women's awareness of the way the old sexual standards and patterns of family living had restricted their entire existence. In fact the two movements interacted with each other in innumerable ways, some clear, others obscure. Concern for better job opportunities and for equal pay for equal work, for example, fed the demand for day-care centers for children.

Still another cause of the new drive for women's rights was concern for improving the treatment of minorities. Participation in and the mere observation of the civil rights movement encouraged American women—as it frequently had in earlier times—to speak out more forcefully for their own rights. Just as white people had callously demeaned and dominated black people until forced to desist by the victims of their prejudice, so, feminists argued, they were being demeaned and dominated by a male-oriented society and must fight back.

One of the leaders of the new women's movement was Betty Friedan, an activist journalist in the labor movement who presented herself publicly as an unhappy housewife. In *The Feminine Mystique* (1963), Friedan argued that advertisers, popular magazines, and other opinion-shaping forces were undermining the capacity of women to use their intelligence and their talents creatively by a pervasive and not very subtle form of brainwashing designed to convince them of the virtues of domesticity. This Friedan deplored. She argued that without understanding why, thousands of women living supposedly happy lives were experiencing vague but persistent feelings of anger and discomfort. "The only way for a woman . . . to know herself as a person is by creative work of her own," she wrote. A "problem that had no name" was stifling women's potential.

The Feminine Mystique was what later came to be known as "consciousness raising" for thousands of women. Over a million copies were quickly sold. Back in 1922 a committee of physicians and social scientists had queried a thousand middle-class women about their personal lives. To the question: "Is your married life a

Bella Abzug—in white hat—campaigns for the Equal Rights Amendment (1980) in New York City. "The woman's place is in the house—the House of Representatives," Abzug famously declared in her successful campaign to be elected to that body in 1970.

happy one?" only 116 had answered no. But after her book came out, Friedan was deluged by hundreds of letters from women who had thought that their unease and depression despite their "happy" family life were both unique and unreasonable. Many now determined to expand their horizons by taking jobs or resuming their education.

Friedan had assumed that if able women acted with determination, employers would recognize their abilities and stop discriminating against them. This did not happen. In 1966 she and other feminists founded the National Organization for Women (NOW). Copying the tactics of black activists, NOW called for equal employment opportunities and equal pay as civil rights. "The time has come for a new movement toward true equality for all women in America and toward a fully equal partnership of the sexes," the leaders announced. "The silken curtain of prejudice and discrimination against women" in government, industry, the professions, religion, education, "and every other field of importance" must be drawn back. In 1967 NOW came out for an equal rights amendment to the Constitution, for changes in the divorce laws, and for the legalization of abortion, the right of "control of one's body."

Some radical feminists advocated raising children in communal centers and doing away with marriage as a legal institution. Others described marriage as "legalized rape." Some rejected heterosexuality as a matter of principle.

Abortion rights advocate Inga Coulter of Harrisburg, Pennsylvania, and antiabortion advocate Elizabeth McGee of Washington express opposing views during demonstrations outside the U.S. Supreme Court building in 1993.

The militants attacked all aspects of the standard image of the female sex. Avoiding the error of the progressive era reformers, who had fought for the vote by stressing the supposed purity and high moral character of women, they insisted on total equality. Clichés such as "the fair sex" and "the weaker sex" made them see red. They demanded that men bear as much of the burden of caring for their children, cooking, and housework as women traditionally did. They took courses in self-defense to be able to protect themselves from muggers, rapists, and casual mashers. They denounced the use of masculine words like *chairman* (favoring *chairperson*) and of such terms as *mankind* and *men* to designate people in general. They substituted *Ms.* for both *Miss* and *Mrs.* on the grounds that the language drew no such distinction between unmarried and married men.

Few people escaped being affected by the women's movement. The presence of women in new roles—as television commentators, airline pilots, police officers—did not prove that a large-scale shift in employment patterns had taken place. Yet even the most unregenerate male seemed to recognize that the balance of power and influence between the sexes had been altered. The sexual revolution was not about to end, the direction of change in gender relationships not to be reversed.

Many people in the vanguard of change thought they could catch a glimpse, in the not too distant future, of an egalitarian, tolerant, and fulfilling world. But it is hard to see clearly when one is moving, and American society in the 1960s was in flux. Many soon learned that change begets change, and not always what one expects.

1946	Dr. Benjamin Spock publishes *Common Sense Guide to Baby and Child Care*
1948	Alfred C. Kinsey publishes *Sexual Behavior in the Human Male*
1955	Allen Ginsberg publishes "Howl"
1956	Federal Highway Act plans superhighway network
1957	Soviets launch *Sputnik*
1958	Congress passes National Defense Education Act
	Alfred C. Kinsey publishes *Sexual Behavior in the Human Female*
1959	James B. Conant attacks American education system in *The American High School*
1962	Students for a Democratic Society (SDS) issues Port Huron Statement
1963	Betty Friedan publishes *The Feminine Mystique*
1964	Free Speech Movement disrupts University of California at Berkeley
1965	Black Muslim fanatics assassinate Malcolm X
	César Chávez organizes boycott to support grape pickers
1965–1968	Riots rock black ghettos
1966	National Organization for Women (NOW) is founded
1969	A half million attend Woodstock Festival in New York
	Stonewall riots in New York City mark public assertion of rights of homosexuals
1973	Supreme Court legalizes abortion in *Roe* v. *Wade*
1975	Congress gives tribes more autonomy in Indian Self-Determination Act

Running on Empty: The Nation Transformed

EVERY YEAR SINCE 1966, THE UCLA SCHOOL OF EDUCATION HAS surveyed nearly a quarter of a million first-year college students. The data show that in some ways students have not changed much. Then, as now, the great majority regard themselves as "middle-of-the-road" in politics. They also continue to overestimate their academic worth: More than two-thirds consider themselves to be among the top 10 percent of their peers academically.

But the past 40 years have witnessed an astonishing reversal in life goals. In the late 1960s and early 1970s, about three-fourths of first-year college students affirmed that "acquiring a meaningful philosophy of life" was "essential" or "very important." Only a third attached similar importance to "being well off financially." But by 2006, the percentages had been reversed: Now three-fourths of entering college students believed that "being well off financially" was "essential" or "very important" while only 40 percent thought it equally important to acquire "a meaningful philosophy of life." (The figures do not add up to 100 percent because respondents could give opinions for more than one statement.) College students today are far more likely to seek wealth—and not a meaningful life—than was true a generation ago.

One explanation is that the college students in the late 1960s grew up during a period of unprecedented economic growth. They could ponder life's meaning because they worried little about finding a well-paying job. But that security was soon jolted by a massive economic upheaval.

The first tremor came from the Middle East when Arab nations, angered by President Nixon's support of Israel during the 1973 war, cut off the supply of oil to the West. Rising prices and falling demand crippled the nation's manufacturers. Presidents Gerald Ford and Jimmy Carter failed to halt the nation's slide into a deep and protracted recession. Two aftershocks buried the Carter presidency. Islamic revolutionaries in Iran seized and held more than fifty American embassy employees for over a year; and the Soviet Union invaded Afghanistan, a dangerous escalation of Cold War tensions.

Ronald Reagan, Carter's successor as president, had promised to "get the nation moving again" and restore its international position. To the delight of his supporters and amazement of his critics, the economy, though staggered by massive layoffs and deficits, somehow found new sources of strength and the Soviet Union, just as mysteriously, crumbled completely.

The Oil Crisis

While most Americans watched, transfixed, as the events of Watergate interred the Nixon presidency, few were aware that a battle on the other side of the world was about to transform their lives. On October 6, 1973, the eve of Yom Kippur, the Jewish Day of Atonement, Egypt and Syria attacked the state of Israel. Six years earlier Israel had trounced the Egyptians with humiliating ease and taken possession of the Sinai peninsula and the West Bank of the Jordan River, an area including Jerusalem. But now Egypt's armored divisions roared into the Sinai and threatened to slice Israel in half; Syrian troops advanced against Israel farther north. Israeli Prime Minister Golda Meir pleaded with President Nixon for additional arms and aircraft. He responded vigorously, promising that "every last goddamn airplane" be sent to Israel. "We are going to be condemned by the Arabs one way or the other," Nixon concluded. The United States immediately airlifted scores of fighter planes and other desperately needed matériel to Israel. The Israelis recrossed the Suez Canal, cut Egyptian supply lines, and forced Egypt's president, Anwar Sadat, to capitulate. But the Arab world aimed its biggest weapon squarely at the United States: It cut off oil shipments to the West.

Deprived of Middle Eastern oil, the American economy sputtered. The price of oil rose to $12 a barrel, up from $3. This sent prices soaring for nearly everything else. Homes were heated with oil, factories were powered by it, utility plants used it to generate electricity, and farm produce was shipped to markets on gas-fueled trucks. Nylon and other synthetic fibers as well as paints, insecticides, fertilizers, and many plastic products were based on petrochemicals. Above all else, oil was refined into gasoline. By the time of the Yom Kippur War, American car owners were driving more than a trillion miles a year, the major reason why the United States, formerly a major oil exporter, imported one-third of its oil. The Arab oil embargo pushed up gas prices; service stations intermittently ran out of gasoline; long lines formed at those that remained open.

In the spring of 1974, Henry Kissinger negotiated an agreement that required Israel's withdrawal from some territory occupied since the 1967 war; the Arab

After the Arab oil embargo, gasoline was rationed in the United States. To help ensure that all drivers had enough gasoline to get to work, customers were limited to buying 10 gallons at a time.

nations then lifted the oil embargo. But the principal oil-exporting nations—Venezuela, Saudi Arabia, Kuwait, Iraq, and Iran—had learned a valuable lesson: if they limited production, they could drive up the price of oil. After the embargo had ended, their cartel, the Organization of Petroleum Exporting Countries (OPEC), announced another price increase. Gasoline prices doubled overnight.

American automakers who had scoffed at bulbous Volkswagen "bugs" and tiny Japanese "boxes" now winced as these foreign competitors claimed the new market for small, fuel-efficient, front-wheel-drive cars. American auto companies were unable to respond to this challenge because their contracts with the United Automobile Workers (UAW) linked wages to consumer prices, which had floated upward with the price of oil. As production costs rose, manufacturers needed to sell more of their behemoth models, loaded with expensive options such as air conditioning, power windows, and stereo systems. They could not profitably sell the small cars the public craved. (In 1982, when Ford belatedly entered the front-wheel drive market, it lost $40 on each car sold.) Because the automobile industry stimulated so many other industries—steel, vinyl, glass, rubber—the nation's manufacturing sector was soon in trouble.

Ford as President

Gerald Ford replaced Nixon as president in the summer of 1974, just as the economy was beginning to deteriorate. At first, the country greeted the accession of Gerald Ford to the presidency with a collective sigh of relief. Most observers considered Ford unimaginative, certainly not brilliant. But he was hardworking, and—most important under the circumstances—his record was untouched by scandal.

Ford identified inflation as the chief economic culprit and asked patriotic citizens to signify their willingness to fight it by wearing WIN (Whip Inflation Now) buttons. Almost immediately the economy entered a precipitous slump. Production fell and the unemployment rate rose to above 9 percent, about twice the postwar average. The president was forced to ask for tax cuts and other measures aimed at stimulating business activity. This made inflation worse and did little to promote employment. The economic problems were difficult, and Ford was handicapped by the fact that the Democrats had solid control of Congress, but his performance was at best inept.

The Fall of South Vietnam

Depressing news about the economy was compounded by unsettling events in Vietnam. In January 1975, after two years of a bloody "cease fire" (Hanoi charged Saigon with 301,000 violations; and Saigon charged its adversary with 35,673), North Vietnam initiated a two-year plan to conquer South Vietnam by striking just south of the 17th parallel. Dispirited and incompetently led, the South Vietnamese fell back, then fled headlong, and finally dissolved with a rapidity that astonished their attackers.

Ford had always supported the Vietnam War. As the military situation deteriorated, he urged Congress to pour more arms into the South to stem the North

The rapid collapse of the South Vietnamese army in 1975 caught many by surprise. Here evacuees form a line on the roof of the U.S. embassy in Saigon, hoping to crowd into the last helicopters leaving the country before the North Vietnamese took over.

Vietnamese advance. The legislators flatly refused to do so, and on May 1, 1975 the Viet Cong and North Vietnamese entered Saigon, which they renamed Ho Chi Minh City. The long Vietnam War was finally over.

Ford Versus Carter

Ford's uninspiring record on the economy and foreign policy suggested that he would be vulnerable in 1976. That year the Democrats chose James Earl Carter, a former governor of Georgia, as their candidate. Carter's rise from almost total obscurity was even more spectacular than that of George McGovern in 1972 and was made possible by the same forces: television, the democratization of the delegate-selection process, and the absence of a dominant leader among the Democrats.

Carter had been a naval officer and a substantial peanut farmer and warehouse owner before entering politics. He was elected governor of Georgia in 1970. While governor he won something of a reputation as a southern public official who treated black citizens fairly. (He hung a portrait of Martin Luther King Jr. in his office.) Carter's political style was informal—he preferred to be called Jimmy. During the campaign for delegates he turned his inexperience in national politics to advantage, emphasizing his lack of connection with the Washington establishment rather than apologizing for it. He repeatedly called attention to his integrity and deep religious faith. "I'll never lie to you," he promised voters, a pledge that no candidate would have bothered to make before Nixon's disgrace. He won the Democratic nomination easily.

Carter sought to make the election a referendum on morality. After Watergate, an atmosphere of scandal permeated Washington, and aspiring journalists and congressmen trained their sights on Kissinger, who remained secretary of state after Nixon's resignation. The most significant of the allegations was his meddling in the affairs of Chile, which in 1970 was on the verge of electing Salvadore Allende, a Marxist, as president. "I don't see why we need to stand by and watch a country go communist due to the irresponsibility of its people," Kissinger had quipped. After Allende's election, Kissinger called on the CIA to "destabilize" Allende's regime. In 1973, Allende was murdered in a military coup and his government toppled. Carter promised an administration of "constant decency" in contrast to Kissinger's penchant for secret diplomacy and Machiavellian skullduggery.

Ford was opposed in the Republican campaign by ex-governor Ronald Reagan of California, a movie actor turned politician who was the darling of the Republican right wing. Reagan was an excellent speaker, whereas Ford proved somewhat bumbling on the stump. Reagan, too, hammered away at Kissinger, citing his "immoral" détente with Communist China. At Reagan's insistence, the Republican platform denounced "secret agreements, hidden from our people"—another jab at Kissinger.

Both Republican candidates gathered substantial blocs of delegates, but Ford staved off the Reagan challenge. That he did not win easily, possessed as he was of the advantage of incumbency, made his chances of election in November appear slim.

When the final contest began, both candidates were vague with respect to issues, a situation that hurt Carter particularly because he had made so much of honesty and straight talk. Ford stressed the need to control inflation, Carter to attack high unemployment. The election was memorable chiefly for its gaffes: Carter's admission to *Playboy* that he had "lusted after women in my heart" and Ford's declaration in a televised debate, "There is no Soviet domination in Eastern Europe." Voters were left to choose between Carter's seeming ignorance of human frailty and Ford's human frailty of seeming ignorant.

With both candidates stumbling toward the finish line, pundits predicted an extremely close contest, and they were right: Carter won, 297 electoral votes to 241, having carried most of the South, including Texas, and a few large industrial states. He also ran well in districts dominated by labor union members. The wish of the public to punish the party of Richard Nixon probably was a further reason for his victory.

The Carter Presidency

Carter shone brightly in comparison with Nixon, and he seemed more forward-looking and imaginative than Ford. He tried to give a tone of democratic simplicity and moral fervor to his administration. After delivering his inaugural address he walked with his wife Rosalynn and their small daughter Amy in the parade from the Capitol to the White House instead of riding in a limousine. He enrolled Amy, a fourth-grader, in a largely black Washington public school. Soon after taking office he held a "call-in"; for two hours he answered questions phoned in by people from all over the country.

A National Malaise

In a heralded television speech Carter complained that "a moral and spiritual crisis" had sapped people's energies and undermined civic pride: "We've learned that piling up material goods cannot fill the emptiness of lives which have no confidence or purpose." Critics responded that the nation needed a president rather than a preacher, and that sermons on the emptiness of consumption rang hollow to those who had lost their jobs or whose paychecks had been shrunk by inflation.

The economic downturn, though triggered by the energy shortage, had more fundamental causes. In the prosperous postwar decades, many companies had become too big and complacent, more attuned to the demands of the corporate bureaucracy than the needs of customers. Workers' boredom lowered productivity. Absenteeism at General Motors and Ford doubled during the 1960s. On an average day in 1970, 5 percent of GM's workforce was missing without explanation, and on Mondays and Fridays 10 percent failed to show up. That year Lee Iacocca, the president of Ford, was unnerved by employee attitudes during his visit to a plant at

Wixcom, Indiana: "I see some young guy who's going full-time to school at Wayne State, his mind is elsewhere, and he doesn't give a shit what he builds, he doesn't care and he isn't involved in his job. We can't change a man like that anymore." Incapable of eliminating slipshod work in Ford plants, Iacocca recommended that dealers improve their repair shops.

Younger workers were growing impatient too with aging union leaders and a system that welded salary increases to seniority. Increasingly the young rejected the postwar accord in which organized labor essentially ceded control of the workplace in return for cost-of-living increases and job security.

Union membership slipped badly from the high point of the mid-1950s, when over one in three nonagricultural workers belonged to unions; by 1978, the proportion had declined to one in four, and by 1990, one in six. During the 1940s and 1950s, most workers voted to join a union, pay dues, and have the organization bargain for them. By 1978, however, union organizers were losing three-fourths of their campaigns to represent workers; and many workers who belonged to unions were opting to get out. Every year, 800 more union shops voted to rescind their affiliation.

Stagflation: The Weird Economy

Recessions are part of the natural business cycle: when economies overheat, they eventually cool down. But the economic crisis after 1973 was unsettling because, for the first time in the nation's history, the rising tide of unemployment had failed to extinguish inflation. Millions of workers lost their jobs, yet wages and prices continued to rise. The term "stagflation" (a combination of stagnation and inflation) was coined to describe this anomaly. In 1971 an inflation rate of 5 percent had so alarmed President Nixon that he had imposed a price freeze. By 1975 inflation had soared to 11 percent and by 1979, it peaked at a whopping 13 percent; unemployment ranged from 6 to 10 percent, nearly twice the usual postwar level.

Congress raised the minimum wage to help low-paid workers cope with inflation. It pegged social security payments to the cost of living index in an effort to protect retirees. Thereafter, when prices rose, social security payments went up automatically. The poor and the pensioners got some immediate relief, but the laws made balancing the federal budget more difficult and the increased spending power of the recipients caused further upward pressure on prices. During the decade, social welfare spending more than doubled. The federal deficit soared from $8.7 billion in 1970 to $72.7 billion in 1980. The price spiral seemed unstoppable.

The federal government made matters worse in several ways. Wages and salaries rose in response to inflation, but taxes went up more rapidly because larger dollar incomes put people in higher tax brackets. This "bracket creep" caused resentment and frustration among middle-class families. There were "taxpayer revolts" as many people turned against long-accepted but expensive government

An abandoned steel mill at Youngstown, Ohio, in 1986. The sign *(right)* reads: "Free Wood at Your Own Risk." The backbone of American industry throughout the twentieth century, midwestern steel sharply declined in the 1970s and all but collapsed during the 1980s.

programs for aiding the poor. Federal borrowing to cover the deficit pushed up interest rates and increased the costs of all businesses that had to borrow.

Soaring mortgage rates made it more difficult to sell homes. The housing slump meant unemployment for thousands of carpenters, bricklayers, and other construction workers and bankruptcy for many builders. Double-digit interest rates also hurt small businesses seeking to expand. Savings and loan institutions were especially hard-hit because they were saddled with countless mortgages made when rates were as low as 4 and 5 percent. Now they had to pay much more than that to hold deposits and offer even higher rates to attract new money.

Families Under Stress: Defeat of the Equal Rights Amendment

Bad as inflation was in the mid-1970s, it got worse in 1979 when further instability in the Middle East nearly tripled the price of oil, which now reached $34 a barrel. This sent gasoline far over the $1 a gallon price barrier many had thought inconceivable. Within months Ford stock, at 32 in 1978, plummeted to 16; its credit rating with Standard and Poor's fell from AAA to an ignominious BBB. Chrysler, the third largest automaker, tottered near bankruptcy and then fell over the edge, saved in mid-fall only by a $1.2 billion federal loan guarantee. From 1978 to 1982, the jobs of one in three autoworkers were eliminated.

Failure of the Equal Rights Amendment, 1972–1982

In 1972, Congress approved the Equal Rights Amendment. For it to become part of the Constitution, three-fourths of the states—thirty-eight—had to ratify it. By the end of the year, twenty-two states had ratified. But then Phyllis Schlafly's campaign against ERA began to take hold. Only eight ratified in 1973, and three in 1974. By the fall of 1978, only thirty-five states had ratified. Congress voted to extend the ratification deadline for four years but failed to win enough states; in the meantime, some states that had ratified rescinded their vote, an action of uncertain legality. Opposition to ERA was focused in the South and in the Rocky Mountain states.

For the millions of young women whose gender consciousness had been shaped by Betty Friedan and other feminists, the recession struck at the worst possible time. Those who had anticipated a scamper up the corporate ladder discovered that the lower rungs were the first to be cut during recession. Many abandoned the idea of a career and settled for low-paying, dead-end jobs in the clerical or service sector. Yet some women, especially those who were well-educated, achieved strong gains during the 1970s: female lawyers jumped from 5 to 12 percent of the profession; and accountants, from 25 to 33 percent.

Just when the feminist movement required a united fight to gain legal parity with men, women increasingly were divided: into an intellectual and professional elite, eager to prove their merits on the job in fair competition with men; and an underpaid and ill-used underclass, vulnerable to the vagaries of a recessionary economy and to the dictates of (mostly male) bosses.

One casualty was the Equal Rights Amendment (ERA), which would make it unconstitutional to deny equal rights "on account of sex." First proposed by the National Woman's party in 1923, the ERA got nowhere. The National Organization for Women (NOW) revived the measure in the 1960s. The House of Representatives approved the ERA in 1971 and the Senate in 1972. By the end of

1972, twenty-two states had ratified the amendment, sixteen short of the three-fourths needed for the ERA to become part of the constitution.

In 1973 Phyllis Schlafly, a former vice president of the National Federation of Republican Women and publisher of a conservative newsletter, spearheaded a nationwide campaign against the ERA. She argued that it would subject young women to the military draft, deprive divorced women of alimony and child custody, and make married women legally responsible for providing 50 percent of household income. Although most polls indicated that a majority of voters supported the ERA, Schlafly's words struck a responsive chord among anxious housewives and low-wage-earning women who doubted they could survive the recessionary economy on their own. The ratification campaign lost momentum and stalled, falling just three states short.

Cold War or Détente?

"It is a new world," Carter declared in his first speech on foreign affairs. In contrast to the shadowy dealings and sly gambits of the Nixon-Kissinger years, he based his foreign policy on "constant decency." He announced that he would deal with other nations in a fair and humane way, putting the defense of "basic human rights" before all other concerns. He then cut off aid to Chile and Argentina because of human rights violations. He also negotiated treaties with Panama that provided for the gradual transfer of the Panama Canal to that nation and guaranteed the canal's neutrality. But he said little about what was going on in a long list of other nations whose citizens' rights were being repressed.

In 1979 another Strategic Arms Limitation Treaty (SALT II) was signed with the Soviet Union, but the following winter the Soviet Union sent troops into Afghanistan to overthrow the government there. Carter denounced the invasion and warned the Soviets that he would use force if they invaded any of the countries bordering the Persian Gulf. He withdrew the SALT treaty, which he had sent to the Senate for ratification. He also refused to allow American athletes to compete in the 1980 Olympic games, which were held in Moscow. Zbigniew Brzezinski, Carter's national security adviser, regarded the Soviet invasion as an opportunity. "Now we can give the USSR its own Vietnam war," he wrote to Carter. Soon the United States was secretly funneling money and arms to Afghan militias that were resisting the Soviets.

Carter's one striking diplomatic achievement was the so-called Camp David Accords negotiated by Israel and Egypt. In September 1978 President Anwar Sadat of Egypt and Prime Minister Menachem Begin of Israel came to the United States at Carter's invitation to seek a peace treaty ending the state of war that had existed between their two countries for many years.

For two weeks they conferred at Camp David, the presidential retreat outside the capital, and Carter's mediation had much to do with their successful negotiations. In the treaty Israel promised to withdraw from territory captured from Egypt during the 1967 Israeli-Egypt war. Egypt in turn recognized Israel as a nation, the first Arab country to do so. Peace ensured an uninterrupted supply of Arab oil to the United States. The Camp David Accords were the first and, as it turned out, the last significant agreement between Israel and a major Arab state.

The Iran Crisis: Origins

At this point a dramatic shift in the Middle East thrust Carter into the spotlight as never before. On November 4, 1979, about 400 armed Muslim militants broke into the American embassy compound in Tehran, Iran, and took everyone within the walls captive.

The seizure had roots that ran far back in Iranian history. During World War II, Great Britain, the Soviet Union, and later the United States occupied Iran and forced its pro-German shah into exile, replacing him with his 22-year-old son, Muhammad Reza Pahlavi. But in the early 1950s power shifted to prime minister Muhammad Mossadegh, a leftist who sought to finance social reform by nationalizing the mostly American-owned Anglo-Iranian Oil Company.

In 1953, the Iranian army, backed by the CIA, arrested Mossadegh and put the young Pahlavi in power. The fall of Mossadegh ensured a steady flow of cheap oil, but it turned most Iranians against the United States and Shah Pahlavi. Because his American-supplied army and his American-trained secret police kept the shah in power, his opponents hated the United States almost as much as they hated their autocratic ruler.

Throughout 1977, riots and demonstrations convulsed Iran. When soldiers fired on protesters, the bloodshed caused more unrest, and that unrest, more bloodshed. Over 10,000 civilians were killed; many times that number were wounded. In 1978 the whole country seemed to rise against the shah. Finally, in January 1979, he was forced to flee. A revolutionary government headed by a religious leader, the Ayatollah Ruhollah Khomeini, assumed power.

Khomeini denounced the United States, the "Great Satan," whose support of the shah, he said, had caused the Iranian people untold suffering. When President Carter allowed the shah to come to the United States for medical treatment for cancer, militants in Tehran seized the American embassy.

The Iran Crisis: Carter's Dilemma

The militants announced that the Americans at the embassy would be held hostage until the United States returned the shah to Iran for trial as a traitor. They also demanded that the shah's vast wealth be confiscated and surrendered to the Iranian government. President Carter rejected these demands. Instead Carter froze Iranian assets in the United States and banned trade with Iran until the hostages were freed.

A stalemate developed. Months passed. Even after the shah, who was terminally ill, left the United States for Panama, the Iranians remained adamant. The crisis produced a remarkable emotional response in the United States. For the first time since the Vietnam war the entire country agreed on something.

Nevertheless the hostages languished in Iran. In April 1980 Carter finally ordered a team of marine commandos flown into Iran in Sea Stallion helicopters in a desperate attempt to free the hostages. The raid was a fiasco. Several helicopters broke down when their rotors sucked sand into the engines. While the other helicopters were gathered at a desert rendezvous south of Tehran, Carter called off the attempt. In the confusion of a night departure there was a crash and eight commandos were killed. The Iranians made political capital of the incident, gleefully displaying on television the wrecked aircraft and captured American equipment. The stalemate continued. When the shah died in exile in Egypt in July 1980, the Iranians made no move to release the hostages.

The Election of 1980

Despite the failure of the raid and the persistence of stagflation, Carter had more than enough delegates at the Democratic convention to win nomination on the first ballot. His Republican opponent in the campaign that followed was Ronald Reagan. At age 69, Reagan was the oldest person ever nominated for president by a major party. However, his age was not a serious handicap in the campaign; he was physically trim and vigorous and seemed no older than most other prominent politicians.

Reagan had grown up a New Deal Democrat, but during and immediately after World War II he became disillusioned with liberalism. As president of the Screen Actors Guild he attacked the influence of communists in the movie industry. After his movie career ended (he always insisted that he had not been typed as "the nice guy who didn't get the girl"), Reagan did publicity for General Electric until 1960, then worked for various conservative causes. Reagan won the undying loyalty of supporters of the Vietnam War, as well as the permanent enmity of the left, by proposing that the United States "level North Vietnam, pave it, paint stripes on it, and make a parking lot out of it." In 1966 he ran for governor of California and struck a responsive chord by attacking the counterculture. "Hippies," he quipped, "act like Tarzan, look like Jane, and smell like Cheetah." He won the election and was easily reelected in 1970.

Both Carter and Reagan spent much of the 1980 campaign explaining why the other was unsuited to be president. Carter defended his record, though without much conviction. Reagan denounced criminals, drug addicts, and all varieties of immorality and spoke in support of patriotism, religion, family life, and other "old-fashioned" virtues. This won him the enthusiastic backing of fundamentalist religious sects and other conservative groups. He also called for increased spending on defense, and he promised to transfer some functions of the federal government

Iranian militants in Tehran burning the American flag. Such demonstrations attracted millions and helped establish the revolutionary regime's legitimacy among its own people. The alternative means of creating legitimacy, by holding elections, was often rejected on theological (and pragmatic) grounds by rulers in the Middle East.

to the states and to cut taxes. He insisted at the same time that the budget could be balanced and inflation sharply reduced.

Reagan's tendency to depend on popular magazine articles, half-remembered conversations, and other informal sources for his economic "facts" reflected a mental imprecision that alarmed his critics, but his sunny disposition and his easy-going style compared favorably with Carter, who seemed tight-lipped and tense even when flashing his habitual toothy smile. A television debate between Carter and Reagan pointed up their personal differences, but Reagan's question to the audience: "Are you better off now than you were four years ago?" had more effect on the election than any policy he said he would pursue.

On election day the voting was light, but Reagan received 8 million more votes than Carter. Dissatisfaction with the economy and the unresolved hostage crisis seem to have determined the result. The Republicans also gained control of the Senate and cut deeply into the Democratic majority in the House of Representatives.

Carter devoted his last weeks in office to the continuing hostage crisis. War had broken out between Iran and Iraq in September. The Iraqi president, Saddam Hussein, had hoped to exploit the chaos following the downfall of the shah to seize oil-rich territory in Iran. Early Iraqi victories prompted the Iranians to free the hostages in return for the release of Iranian assets that had been frozen in the United States. After 444 days in captivity, the 52 hostages were set free on January 20, the day Reagan was inaugurated.

Ronald Reagan astride a horse—a familiar photo opportunity for presidents. (Recall the similar picture of LBJ, p. 821). But Reagan was an amiable cowboy; his smile and sense of humor were his most disarming weapons. In 1966 just after the election, when reporters asked him what sort of governor he would be, Reagan, a former actor, answered, "I don't know. I've never played a governor." Three months into his presidency, moments after he was seriously wounded in an assassination attempt, he took his wife's hand. "Honey," he said, "I forgot to duck." While being wheeled into the operating room, he quipped to the surgeons, "I hope you are all Republicans."

Reagan as President

Reagan hoped to change the direction in which the country was moving. He demanded steep reductions in federal spending and the deficit, to be accomplished by cutting social expenditures, such as welfare, food stamps, and student loans, and by turning many functions of the federal government over to the states. The marketplace, not federal bureaucratic regulations, should govern most economic decisions.

He asked Congress to lower income taxes by 30 percent. When critics objected that this would increase the deficit, the president and his advisers reasoned that the tax cut would leave people with more money, which they would invest in productive ways. The new investment would generate more goods and jobs—and, ultimately, taxes for the federal government. This scheme became known as Reaganomics.

Helped by the votes of conservative Democrats, Reagan won congressional approval of the Budget Reconciliation Act, which reduced government expenditures on domestic programs by $39 billion. But Congress resisted reducing the politically popular "entitlement" programs, such as Social Security and Medicare, which accounted for about half of the budget.

Many of Reagan's advisers urged him to reduce the military budget to bring the government's income more nearly in line with its outlays. Instead, reviving the containment policy wholeheartedly, the president insisted that the military buildup was necessary because of the threat posed by the Soviet Union, which he called an "evil empire." In particular, he sought to expand and improve the nation's nuclear arsenal. He made no secret of his wish to create so formidable a nuclear force that the Soviets would have to back down in any confrontation.

In Central America he sought the overthrow of the left-wing government of Nicaragua and the defeat of communist rebels in El Salvador. He even used American troops to overthrow a Cuban-backed regime on the tiny Caribbean island of Grenada. When criticized for opposing leftist regimes while backing rightist dictators, Jeane Kirkpatrick, U.S. ambassador to the United Nations, explained that "rightist authoritarian regimes can be transformed peacefully into democracies, but totalitarian Marxist ones cannot."

Four More Years

Being a sitting president with an extraordinarily high standing in public opinion polls, Reagan was nominated for a second term at the 1984 Republican convention without opposition. The Democratic nomination went to Walter Mondale of Minnesota, who had been vice president under Carter. Mondale electrified the country by choosing Representative Geraldine Ferraro of New York as his running mate. An Italian American and a Catholic, Ferraro was expected to appeal to conservative Democrats who had supported Reagan in 1980 and to win the votes of many Republican women.

Reagan began the campaign with several important advantages. He was especially popular among religious fundamentalists and other social conservatives, and these groups were increasingly vocal. President Nixon had spoken of a "silent majority." By 1980 the kind of people he was referring to were no longer silent. Fundamentalist television preachers were almost all fervent Reaganites and the most successful of them were collecting tens of millions of dollars annually in contributions from viewers. One of these, the Reverend Jerry Falwell, founded the Moral Majority and set out to create a new political movement. "Americans are sick and tired of the way the amoral liberals are trying to corrupt our nation," Falwell announced in 1979.

During the first Reagan administration, the Moral Majority had become a powerful political force. Falwell was against drugs, the "coddling" of criminals, homosexuality, communism, and abortion, all things that Reagan also disliked. While not openly antiblack, Falwell disapproved of forced busing to integrate schools and a number of other government policies designed to help blacks and other minorities. Of course, Walter Mondale was also against many of the things that Falwell and his followers denounced, but Reagan was against them all. In addition, Reagan was in favor of government aid to private schools run by church groups, something dear to the Moral Majority despite the constitutional principle of separation of church and state.

But the Moral Majority, despite its name, was far from being an actual majority. Reagan's support was much more broadly based. Thousands of working people and an enormous percentage of white Southerners, types that had been solidly Democratic during the New Deal and beyond, now voted Republican. The president's personality was another important plus—voters continued to admire his informal yet firm style and his stress on patriotism and other "old-fashioned" virtues.

The tendency of voters to support a sitting president when the economy was on the rise was still another advantage. Unemployment fell to 7 percent, investment finally picked up, and inflation remained low. Interest rates were moving down slowly but steadily.

From the start Mondale emphasized the difficulties that he saw ahead for the nation. The president's economic policies, he said, hurt the poor, women, and minorities. Mondale also tried to focus attention on the huge increase in the federal deficit that Reagan's policies had produced. These were conventional campaign tactics. But Mondale, in a daring move, announced that he would *raise* taxes if elected. This promise, most unusual for a person running for office, was an attempt to counter his reputation for political caution.

Most polls showed Reagan far in the lead when the campaign began, and this remained true throughout the contest. Nothing Mondale or Ferraro did or said affected the president's popularity. Bad news, even his own mistakes, had so little effect on Reagan's standing that people began to call him "the Teflon president." On election day he got nearly 60 percent of the popular vote and lost only in Minnesota, Mondale's home state, and in the District of Columbia. Reagan's Electoral College margin was overwhelming, 525 to 13.

Of all the elements in the Democratic New Deal coalition, only African Americans, who voted solidly for Mondale, remained loyal. The Democratic strategy of nominating a woman for vice president was a failure; far more women voted for Reagan than for the Mondale-Ferraro ticket.

Reagan's triumph, like the two landslide victories of Dwight Eisenhower in the 1950s, was a personal one. The Republicans made only minor gains in the House of Representatives and actually lost two seats in the Senate.

"The Reagan Revolution"

Reagan's agenda for his second term closely resembled that of his first. In foreign affairs, he ran into continuing congressional resistance to his requests for military support for his anticommunist crusade. This was particularly true after Mikhail S. Gorbachev became the Soviet premier in March 1985. Gorbachev seemed far more moderate and flexible than his predecessors. He began to encourage political debate and criticism in the Soviet Union—the policy known as *glasnost* (openness)—and he sought to stimulate the stagnant Soviet economy by decentralizing administration and rewarding individual enterprise *(perestroika)*.

Gorbachev also announced that he would continue to honor the unratified SALT II agreement, whereas Reagan, arguing that the Soviet Union had not respected the limits laid down in the pact, seemed bent on pushing ahead with the expansion and modernization of America's nuclear arsenal. Reagan sought funds to develop an elaborate system of missile defenses. He referred to it as the Strategic Defense Initiative (SDI), although it was popularly known as Star Wars, a reference to the 1977 George Lucas film. SDI would consist of a network of computer-controlled space stations that would detect oncoming enemy missiles and attempt to destroy them.

When the president realized that the Soviets were eager for an agreement to limit nuclear weapons, he ceased referring to the Soviet Union as an "evil empire." In October 1986 he met with Gorbachev in Iceland in search of an agreement on arms control. The chief sticking point was SDI, which Gorbachev denounced as "space strike" weaponry that might be used to wipe out Soviet cities. Gorbachev proposed instead the elimination of all nuclear weapons—including SDI. Reagan, however, was determined to push Star Wars, and the summit collapsed.

Reagan pressed ahead with the Star Wars defense-in-space system. Congress, however, balked at the enormous cost of Star Wars. Costs aside, the idea of relying for national defense on the complex technology involved in controlling machines in outer space suffered a further setback in 1986, when the space shuttle *Challenger* exploded shortly after takeoff, killing its seven-member crew. This disaster put a stop to the program until the cause had been discovered. In 1989 the shuttles began to fly again.

Reagan's basic domestic objectives—to reduce the scope of federal activity, particularly in the social welfare area; to lower income taxes; and to increase the strength of the armed forces—remained constant. Despite the tax cuts already made, congressional leaders of both parties agreed to the Income Tax Act of 1986, which reduced the top levy on personal incomes from 50 percent to 28 percent and the tax on corporate profits from 46 percent to 34 percent.

Reagan advanced another of his objectives more gradually. This was his appointment of conservatives to federal judgeships, including Sandra Day O'Connor, the first woman named to the Supreme Court. By 1988 Reagan had appointed three Supreme Court justices and well over half the members of the federal judiciary.

Change and Uncertainty

But if the "Reagan revolution" seemed to have triumphed, powerful countering forces were at work that no individual or party could effectively control. For one

DID REAGAN END THE COLD WAR?

In 1983 President Ronald Reagan denounced the Soviet Union as an "evil empire." In that same speech he made a prophecy that few took seriously at the time: The "last pages" in the history of communism "even now are being written." Six years later, when the Berlin wall came down (shown here), the Soviet empire was over. Within a few years, the Soviet Union itself had disintegrated.

Many credited Reagan with having won the Cold War. Caspar Weinberger, secretary of defense, explained that the Reagan administration had had a "secret campaign" to undermine the Soviet economy. Others credited Reagan's massive arms buildup with causing the Soviet economy to collapse from exhaustion. On the other hand, historian William E. Pemberton (1997) doubted whether Reagan had any coherent foreign policy at the outset; his chief contribution to winning the Cold War was resisting the advice of skeptical hardliners and accepting the conciliatory overtures of Mikhail Gorbachev, the Soviet premier.

Arthur M. Schlesinger Jr. and John Lewis Gaddis (1992) saw the victory as a long-term and largely bipartisan team effort dating from the Truman presidency. Robert M. Gates (1996), intelligence director under George H. W. Bush, and later defense secretary under George W. Bush (2007), said that Bush and his four predecessors in the presidency had ground down the Soviet opposition.

On the left, some scholars insisted that there had been no winner in a protracted dispute that had led to such chaos throughout the Third World. The United States, burdened with massive deficits, was not in much better shape. Others maintained that Reagan was fortunate to be the American president when a new generation of leaders, foremost among them Gorbachev, came to power in the Soviet Union.

For now, perhaps the last word can be that of George Smiley, the anti-Soviet spymaster created by novelist John le Carré (1991): "We won. Not that the victory matters a damn. And perhaps we didn't win anyway. Perhaps they just lost."

Peter Schweizer, *Victory* (1994), William E. Pemberton, *Exit with Honor* (1997), Robert M. Gates, *From the Shadows* (1996), Dana Allin, *Cold War Illusions* (1998); Schlesinger and Gaddis are cited in Michael J. Hogan, ed., *The End of the Cold War* (1992), and John le Carré, *The Secret Pilgrim* (1991).

thing, the makeup of the American people, always in a state of flux, was changing at a rate approaching that of the early 1900s when the "new" immigration had been at its peak. In the 1970s, after the Immigration Act of 1965 had put an end to the national-origins concept, more than 4 million immigrants entered the country, and the vast majority of these newcomers came from Asia and Latin America. This trend continued; of the 643,000 who arrived in 1988, more than 550,000 were from these two regions. More than 111,000 of the immigrants came from the Philippines, Korea, Vietnam, and other parts of the Pacific Rim and East Asia. In addition, uncounted thousands entered the United States illegally, most crossing the long, sparsely settled border with Mexico. The nation's Hispanic population increased by 53 percent during the 1980s.

Some of the new immigrants were refugees from repressive regimes in Vietnam, Cuba, Haiti, and Central America, and nearly all were poor. Most tended, like their predecessors, to crowd together in ethnic neighborhoods. Spanish could be heard more often than English in large sections of Los Angeles, New York, Miami, and many other cities.

No strong demand for immigration restriction developed, perhaps because so many Americans were descendents of immigrants, and because the immigrants did work that needed to be done. However, conservatives found it appalling that so many people could enter the country illegally, and even Americans sympathetic to the so-called undocumented aliens agreed that control was desirable. Finally, in 1986, Congress passed a law offering amnesty to illegal immigrants long resident in the country and penalizing employers who hired illegal immigrants in the future. Many persons legalized their status under the new law, but the influx of illegal immigrants continued. Problems developed because some employers refused to hire anyone with a foreign accent on the grounds that they might be "illegals" bearing false papers.

AIDS

During the 1980s, the nation confronted its most serious health crisis in decades. In the late 1970s, world health officials had spotted the outbreak of yet another viral epidemic in central Africa; but no one noticed that this virus had mutated into a more lethal strain and was spreading to Europe and North America. On June 5, 1981, the Centers for Disease Control (CDC) alerted American health officials to an outbreak of a rare bacterial infection in Los Angeles. What made the outbreak distinctive was that this particular infection, usually found in infants or older people with fragile immune systems, had struck five healthy young men. All were homosexuals. Within months, all died.

By 1982 the CDC decided to call this new disease acquired immunodeficiency syndrome (AIDS). They learned that AIDS was caused by the human immunodeficiency virus (HIV), a lethal retro virus that destroys the body's defenses against infection, making victims susceptible to many diseases. HIV spreads when an

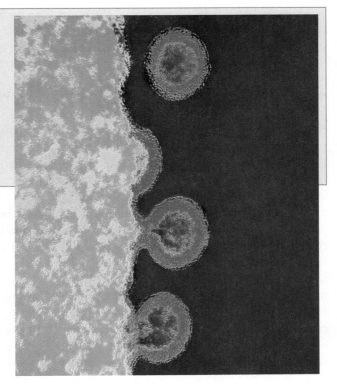

In this electron microscopic photograph, four human immunodeficiency virus (HIV) cells, in different stages of budding, are emerging from an infected T-lymphocyte human blood cell (pink). The HIV cell that has broken free includes RNA (green—the cell's genetic code) and it will reinfect other T-cells. T-cells are part of the body's immune system.

infected person's body fluids come in contact with someone else's. By the end of 1982, the CDC had documented 900 cases of AIDS; the disease was increasing exponentially. Soon HIV contaminated some of the nation's blood banks, and some recipients of transfusions came down with AIDS. In June 1983, when the federal budget approached $1 trillion, Congress finally voted $12 million for AIDS research and treatment.

Not until 1985, when the square-jawed romantic actor Rock Hudson confirmed that he was dying of AIDS, did the subject command widespread public attention. President Reagan, an old friend of Hudson's, publicly acknowledged that the disease constituted a grave health crisis. Congress approved Reagan's call for a substantial increase in AIDS funding. But Reagan's appeal was belated and insufficient. By then, nearly 21,000 Americans had died; by 1999, the total number of AIDS-related deaths approached 400,000.

The AIDS epidemic affected public policy and private behavior. A nationwide educational campaign urged "safe" sex, especially the use of condoms, which by 1990 were distributed free in many high schools. Fear of the disease, and of those who suffered from it, exacerbated many people's homophobia. But the AIDS epidemic also forced most people to confront homosexuality directly and perhaps for the first time, and thus contributed to a deeper understanding of the complexity of human nature. After Hudson's revelation, for example, the *New York Times* commenced using "gay" and "lesbian," the terms then preferred by the people so identified, instead of "homosexual." Gay and lesbian organizations, the vanguard in the initial war against AIDS, continued to fight for social acceptance and legal rights.

The New Merger Movement

The Reagan years witnessed a mad frenzy of corporate mergers. The person most responsible was Michael Milken, a shrewd stockbroker of the firm of Drexel Burnham Lambert. Milken specialized in selling "junk bonds," the debt offerings of companies whose existing debts were already high. He persuaded hundreds of savings and loan associations, insurance companies, pension funds, and other big investors to buy these junk bonds, which, though risky, offered unusually high interest rates. The success of his initial ventures prompted Milken to approach smaller companies, invite them to issue huge numbers of junk bonds, and use the proceeds to acquire larger firms.

In 1985 Ronald Perelman, an aggressive entrepreneur, employed this strategy to perfection. He had recently obtained control of Pantry Pride, a small supermarket chain with a net worth of about $145 million, and sought to acquire Revlon, a $2 billion cosmetics and health care conglomerate. With Milken's help, he sold $1.5 billion in Pantry Pride bonds ("junk," because the debt so greatly exceeded the company's worth) and used that capital to buy Revlon. He then paid off the Pantry Pride bonds by selling huge chunks of Revlon and amalgamated the remainder of the company into Pantry Pride. The bond purchasers profited handsomely from the high return on the junk bonds, and Perelman made a fortune on the acquisition and reorganization of Revlon. That same year the R. J. Reynolds Tobacco Company purchased the food conglomerate Nabisco for $4.9 billion. Three years later this new giant, RJR Nabisco, was itself taken over by Kohlberg, Kravis, Roberts and Company for $24.9 billion.

During the frenzied decade of the 1980s, one-fifth of the Fortune 500 companies were taken over, merged, or forced to go private; in all, some 25,000 mergers and acquisitions were successfully undertaken; their total value was nearly a half-trillion dollars. To make their companies less tempting to cash-hungry raiders, many corporations took on whopping debts or acquired unprofitable companies. By the late 1980s, many American corporations were wallowing in red ink. Debt payments were gobbling up 50 percent of the nation's corporate pretax earnings.

"A Job for Life": Layoffs Hit Home

Most corporations coped with the debt in two ways: they sold assets, such as factories, offices, and warehouses; or they cut costs through layoffs. U.S. Steel, whose rusting mills desperately needed an infusion of capital, instead spent $5 billion to acquire Marathon Oil of Ohio; that decision meant that nearly 100,000 steelworkers lost their jobs. No firm was immune, nor any worker secure. "A job for life" had long been IBM's unofficial but endlessly repeated slogan. As late as 1985, it ran an advertisement to reassure employees: "Jobs may come and go—But people shouldn't." Yet during the next nine years a crippled IBM eliminated 80,000 jobs and more than a third of its workforce. During the 1980s, the total number of employees who worked for the Fortune 500 companies declined by three million; nearly one-third of all positions in middle management were eliminated. Millions of "organization men" (about one-third of whom now were women) were laid off as the organizations themselves "downsized," the corporate euphemism for wholesale firings.

Many of the jobs went abroad, where labor costs were lower and unions nonexistent. In 1980 Xerox of America, realizing that it could no longer compete with its more efficient Japanese subsidiary, transferred contracts to Japan and laid off tens of thousands of American workers. In 1984 Nike moved sewing operations to Indonesia, where it could hire female workers for a mere 14 cents an hour. In 1986 the chassis for the Mustang, the symbol of American automotive style, was built by Mazda in Hiroshima, Japan.

Towering mountains of private corporate debt nearly were overshadowed by the Everest of public debt held by the federal government itself. Reagan's insistence on a sharp cut in personal taxes and a substantial increase in military expenditures produced huge—and growing—annual federal deficits. When Reagan took office, the total federal debt was $900 million; eight years later, it exceeded $2.5 *trillion*. "No one imagined how bad the outcome would be," explained David Stockman, Reagan's budget director. "It got away from us."

A "Bipolar" Economy, a Fractured Society

Although weighed down by debt, the economy did not crash through the floor, as many expected. In 1982 it began to gain strength and by the late 1980s it was growing at a rate unparalleled since the halcyon days of the 1960s. Despite the ominous, persistent increase in corporate layoffs, the stock market soared. Prices were coming down—traditionally evidence of slackening demand—yet the volume of business was growing!

Although few perceived it at the time, the economy was undergoing a transformation of historic dimensions. Much as the depression after 1893 had strengthened the nation's economy by wiping out thousands of inefficient steel and machinery firms in New England and the Northeast, facilitating the rise of heavy industry and manufacturing in Michigan, Ohio, Pennsylvania, and Illinois, the seismic economic upheavals of the 20 years after 1973 toppled many of the factories that had triumphed in the early twentieth century, but gave rise to new ones. As weeds grew in the parking lots of the factories of the "Rust Belt" of the Midwest, new technology industries sprouted in the "Silicon Valley" of California, along Route 128 outside of Boston, and in booming cities such as Seattle, Washington, and Austin, Texas.

By the end of the Reagan era, the economy consisted of two separate and increasingly unequal components: a battered sector of traditional heavy industry, characterized by declining wages and diminishing job opportunities; and an advancing high-tech and service sector dominated by aggressive, innovative, and individualistic entrepreneurs. The older corporations that survived the shakeout of the 1980s were leaner and better equipped to compete in expanding global markets.

Yet American society was becoming as fractured as the "bipolar" economy from which it drew sustenance. The Reagan tax cuts had disproportionately benefited the wealthy, as had the extraordinary rise of the stock market. Conversely, the economic transformation struck low- or semiskilled wage earners hardest; at the same time, the Reagan administration's shifting of much of the burden of social welfare onto state and local governments reduced benefits to those who lost jobs or could not find work in the strange new economy dominated by information services and bewildering new technologies. At the end of Reagan's second term the standard of living of the poorest fifth of the population (40 million people) was 9 percent lower than it had been in 1979, while that of the wealthiest fifth had risen about 20 percent.

The Iran-Contra Arms Deal

The Reagan administration was generally credited with the nation's successes, and absolved of its failures. The effectiveness of the administration was finally compromised by two self-inflicted wounds involving American policy in Central America and the Middle East.

The Central American problem resulted from a revolution in Nicaragua, where in 1979 leftist rebels had overthrown the dictatorial regime of Anastasio Somoza. Because the victorious Sandinista government was supported by both Cuba and the Soviet Union, President Reagan was determined to force it from power. He backed anti-Sandinista elements in Nicaragua known as the Contras and in 1981 persuaded Congress to provide these "freedom fighters" with arms.

But the Contras made little progress, and many Americans feared that aiding them would lead, as it had in Vietnam, to the use of American troops in the fighting. In October 1984 Congress banned further military aid to the rebels. The President then sought to persuade other countries and private American groups to help the Contras (as he put it) keep "body and soul together."

In the Middle East, the war between Iran and Iraq continued to rage. If either won decisively, it could control the flow of Middle Eastern oil. The United States therefore preferred a stalemate. Thus when Iran gained the advantage, Reagan provided $500 million a year in credits to Saddam Hussein's Iraq. In early 1986, however, Reagan authorized the secret sale of American weapons directly to the Iranians in return for their help in releasing Americans held hostage to Islamic fundamentalists elsewhere in the Middle East.

"Mistakes were made," a cartoon in the *Washington Post*, 1986, which pointedly contrasts President Reagan with Teddy Roosevelt, Franklin D. Roosevelt, and Harry S Truman.

The arms sale was arranged by Marine Colonel Oliver North, an aide of Reagan's national security adviser. North, who was already in charge of the administration's effort to supply the Nicaraguan Contras indirectly, used $12 million of the profit from the Iranian sales to provide weapons for the Contras, in plain violation of the congressional ban on such aid.

News of the sales to Iran and of the use of the profits to supply the Contras came to light in November 1986 and of course caused a sensation. Colonel North was fired from his job with the security council, a special prosecutor was appointed to investigate the affair, and both a presidential committee and a joint congressional committee also began investigations. Reagan insisted that he knew nothing about the aid to the Contras. Critics pointed out that if he was telling the truth it was almost as bad since that meant that he had not been able to control his own administration.

Reagan was not an able administrator; the Iran-Contra and financial scandals of his administration did not stick to him because he was seldom close enough to the action to get splattered by it. Reagan articulated, simply and persuasively, a handful of concepts—the "evil" character of Soviet communism, the need to get government off people's backs—and in so doing created a political climate conducive to change. Reagan was directly responsible for neither of the great transformations of the late twentieth century—the collapse of the Soviet Union and the restructuring of American corporations. Yet his actions and, indeed, his failures to act indisputably influenced them. His decision to increase military spending and undertake the fantastically expensive SDI ("Star Wars") forced Gorbachev to seek an accommodation with the United States. Reagan's tax cuts precipitated unimaginably large federal deficits, and deregulation unloosed a sordid pack of predators who preyed on the economy. Yet the ensuing Darwinian chaos strengthened those corporations that survived and gave them the muscle to prevail in emerging global markets. "We are the change," Reagan declared in his farewell address. What he had done, exactly, he did not say. Yet the statement, however roseate, vague, and self-congratulatory, was not untrue.

During the preceding 15 years, the American nation, like the automobiles that stretched for blocks in line to buy gasoline during the oil embargo, had been running on empty. The federal government was deeply in debt. Corporations had exhausted their cash reserves. Workers lived in fear of the layoff or bank foreclosure notice. Gone were the fanciful expressions of an earlier era—long and wide-bodied chassis, roaring V-8 engines, sweeping tail fins, chromium grills like the jaws of a barracuda. Most cars had become simple boxes, trimmed with plastic, whose efficient four-cylinder engines thrummed steadily.

The nation's aspirations, like its cars, had become smaller, more sensible. Politicians muted their rhetoric, rarely issuing grandiose declarations of war against some intractable foe of humanity. Corporate executives spoke of "downsizing" firms rather than building them into empires. Freshmen entered college hoping to get a degree that would help them to make money rather than to find meaning in their lives. And the American people increasingly hunkered down in their own private spaces, which they locked up and wired with alarms.

1973	Israel, aided by United States, defeats Egypt and Syria
1973–1974	Arabs impose oil embargo
1974–1976	Gerald Ford serves as president after Nixon's resignation
1975	Vietnam War ends when South Vietnam falls
1976	Jimmy Carter is elected president
1978	Egypt and Israel sign Camp David Accords
1979	Jerry Falwell founds the Moral Majority
	Muslim militants seize U.S. Embassy in Tehran, Iran
1980	Soviet troops invade Afghanistan
	U.S. rescue mission in Iran fails
	Ronald Reagan is elected president
1980s	Entrepreneurs' merger movement leads to huge corporate debt
1981	Iran releases U.S. hostages
	Reagan appoints Sandra Day O'Connor to Supreme Court
1981–1988	War persists between Iran and Iraq
1982	Centers for Disease Control (CDC) identify new disease, AIDS
1984	Reagan is reelected president
1985	Mikhail Gorbachev becomes head of the Soviet Union
	Reagan secretly sells arms to Iran to finance Nicaraguan Contras
1986	Space shuttle *Challenger* explosion kills crew of seven

32 CHAPTER

Misdemeanors and High Crimes

IN FEBRUARY 2007 A DERANGED STUDENT AT VIRGINIA TECH bought a .22 caliber Walther P22 pistol on the Internet. On March 13, he went to a local store, showed his driver's license and several other sources of identification, and bought a Glock 19 rapid-fire semiautomatic pistol. Later that week he acquired ammunition from online vendors and from Wal-Mart and Dick's Sporting Goods. On April 8, he made a videotape of himself delivering a hate-and-obscenity-laced diatribe against "rich kids," "snobs," and "brats." Early the morning of April 16, he got dressed, applied acne cream to his face, went to another dorm, and shot and killed a female student and the resident advisor. He returned to his dorm, reloaded his guns, drove to the Blacksburg Post Office, and mailed the video to NBC headquarters in New York. He went back to campus, entered Norris Hall, an engineering building, chained all three entry doors closed, climbed the stairs to the second floor, and walked up and down the hallway, taking aim at students and teachers and shooting them. Then he put a pistol to his head and committed suicide. The shooting spree at Norris lasted less than 10 minutes: He shot over sixty people, killing thirty-three.

The massacre at Virginia Tech was the worst mass killing in recent American history. But it recalled scores of similar shootings. On October 2, 2006, a 32-year-old truck driver took a dozen Amish schoolgirls hostage and shot and killed six of them. A week earlier, in two separate incidents, a gunman took six girls hostage at Platte Canyon High School in Bailey, Colorado, and shot and killed one; and a 15-year-old student at Weston High School in Cazenovia, Wisconsin, shot and killed his principal. On April 20, 1999, two teenagers wearing trench coats and armed with automatic weapons went on a rampage at Columbine High School in Littleton, Colorado. Before shooting themselves to death, they killed twelve students and a teacher and wounded more than thirty.

Each year, about 14,000 Americans are killed with guns. Each shooting ignites a heated debate. Proponents of gun control deplore the easy access to such lethal weapons. The National Rifle Association and other defenders of the right to bear arms, affirmed by the Second Amendment to the Constitution, blame criminals for the mayhem. They say that law-abiding citizens need guns to defend themselves from such evildoers.

With the collapse of the Soviet Union and the revival of the U.S. economy in the late 1980s, crime had emerged as the nation's main political issue. The initial focus was on street crime and a popular culture that seemed to condone it. But other types of crime soon crowded into the headlines: the looting of the savings and loans by financial manipulators; the impeachment (but not conviction) of President Bill Clinton on charges of "high crimes and misdemeanors"; the arrest and trial of O. J. Simpson, a football celebrity who was accused of murdering his former wife; and then arguably the greatest crime committed on the mainland United States—the terrorist attack on September 11, 2001. Punishing those responsible, and preventing others from committing similar crimes, defined the new national agenda.

The Election of 1988

The issues that had dominated American politics for over a decade—the Soviet threat, the energy crisis, stagflation—were gone. The presidential election of 1988 initially lacked focus. The selection of Vice President George H. W. Bush for the Republican nomination was a foregone conclusion. Bush, the son of a Connecticut senator, had attended an elite private school and Yale. He served as a pilot during World War II and then settled in Texas, where he worked in the family's oil business and became active in Republican politics. From 1971 to 1973 he served as ambassador to the UN and from 1976 to 1977 as director of the CIA. As Republican presidential hopeful, he trumpeted his experience as vice president; but when the Reagan administration was tarnished by the Iran-Contra scandal, Bush claimed that he had been "out of the loop" and thus free of the scandal. When testimony proved otherwise, he dithered.

The Democratic race was far more complicated but scarcely more inspiring. So many lackluster candidates entered the field that wits called them "the seven dwarfs." Governor Michael Dukakis of Massachusetts, stressing his record as an efficient manager, accumulated delegates steadily. During one debate, however, another Democratic hopeful, Senator Albert Gore of Tennessee, accused Dukakis of handing out "weekend passes for convicted criminals." This referred to a policy, adopted by Massachusetts and many other states, of granting brief furloughs to convicts with satisfactory prison records. Dukakis brushed aside the accusation and went on to win the nomination.

But Lee Atwater, campaign manager for Bush, discovered that during one such furlough Willie Horton, an African American who was serving time in a

Massachusetts prison for rape and assault, had stabbed and raped a Maryland woman. "If I can make Willie Horton a household name," Atwater predicted, "we'll win the election." Atwater produced and aired a television advertisement showing prisoners, many of them black, streaming through a revolving door. After describing Horton's record, a voice intoned: "Dukakis wants to do for America what he's done for Massachusetts." The ad struck a responsive chord among white voters. Dukakis's attempts to shift the focus away from race and crime failed.

The presidential campaign became, in effect, a referendum on violent crime in which Dukakis failed the toughness test. Bush won 54 percent of the vote and carried the Electoral College, 426 to 112.

Crime and Punishment

The "law and order" movement had been initiated by Nixon in the late 1960s, but many of its goals were achieved during the next two decades. Responding to widespread calls for a crackdown on crime, elected officials hired more police, passed tougher laws, and built additional prisons.

The shift toward capital punishment was symptomatic. During the 1960s only a handful of criminals were executed. When the Supreme Court ruled in 1972 in the *Furman* decision that jury-imposed capital punishment was racially biased and thus unconstitutional, the matter seemed moot: no criminal had been executed since 1967. But many states, responding to a public demand for tough legislation against criminals, rewrote capital punishment statutes in light of the *Furman* decision, depriving juries of discretion in sentencing. The Supreme Court upheld these laws and capital punishment resumed in 1976. Since then, over a thousand convicts have been executed.

Another manifestation of the crackdown on crime was the increase in the nation's prison population. From 1973 to 1980 the number of convicts tripled, and during the 1980s it doubled again. The growth in the nation's prison population during the early 1990s required the construction of a new 1,000-bed prison every week. In 1995 California spent twice as much on prisons as on its huge university system. By 2007, the United States incarcerated more people than any country in the world, except perhaps Communist China, which did not disclose such information.

"Crack" and Urban Gangs

Several factors intensified the problem of violent crime, especially in the inner cities. One was a shift in drug use. During the 1960s marijuana had become commonly available, especially on college campuses; this was followed by cocaine, which was far more powerful and addictive but so expensive that few could afford it.

During the 1980s growers of coca leaves in Peru and Bolivia greatly expanded production. Drug traffickers in Colombia devised sophisticated systems to trans-

A teenage boy in a Texas jail; most prisons did not allow shoes or belts, which might be fashioned into weapons. During the 1990s, about nineteen out of twenty prison inmates were male. The great majority had been first arrested during their late teens and early twenties. In 1990 six in ten federal inmates had been convicted of drug charges.

port cocaine to the United States. The price of cocaine dropped from $120 an ounce in 1981 to $50 in 1988.

Still more important was the proliferation of a cocaine-based compound called "crack" because it crackled when smoked. Crack was sold in $10 vials. Many users found that it gave an intense spasm of pleasure that overrode all other desires.

The lucrative crack trade led to bitter turf wars in the inner cities; dealers hired neighborhood youths, organized them into gangs, armed them with automatic weapons, and told them to drive competitors away. The term "drive-by shooting" entered the vocabulary. A survey of Los Angeles County in the early 1990s found that more than 150,000 young people belonged to 1,000 gangs. Violence had become a fact of life. In 1985, before crack had seized hold of the inner city, there were 147 murders in Washington, D.C.; in 1991, the figure skyrocketed to 482.

Black on black murder had become an important cause of death for African Americans in their twenties. In 1988 Monsta' Kody Scott, who at age 11 pumped shotgun blasts into rival gang members, returned after prison to his Los Angeles neighborhood. He was horrified: gangs no longer merely shot their rivals but "sprayed" them with automatic weapons, 75 rounds to a clip, or blew them away with small rockets. By 2006, 30 percent of African American men in their twenties were in prison, or on probation or parole. The recurrent refrain of rap performers—that America was a prison—had become, for many, an everyday reality.

George H. W. Bush as President

In 1989 President Bush, having attacked Dukakis for being soft on crime, named a "drug czar" to coordinate various bureaucracies, increased federal funding of local police, and spent $2.5 billion to stop the flow of illegal drugs into the nation. Although the campaign generated plenty of arrests, drugs continued to pour in: as one dealer or trafficker was arrested, another took his place.

Bush worked to shed the tough image he had cultivated during the campaign. In his inaugural address he said that he hoped to "make kinder the face of the nation and gentler the face of the world." He also displayed a more traditional command of the workings of government and the details of current events than his predecessor. At the same time he pleased right-wing Reagan loyalists by his opposition to abortion and gun control, and by calling for a constitutional amendment prohibiting the burning of the American flag. His standing in the polls soared.

The Collapse of Communism in Eastern Europe

One reason for this was the bumper crop of good news from abroad. The reforms instituted in the Soviet Union by Gorbachev led to demands from its Eastern European satellites for similar liberalization. Gorbachev responded by announcing that the Soviet Union would not use force to keep communist governments in power in these nations. Swiftly the people of Poland, Hungary, Czechoslovakia, Bulgaria, Romania, East Germany, and the Baltics did away with the repressive regimes that had ruled them throughout the postwar era. Except in Romania, where the dictator Nicolae Ceausescu was executed, all these fundamental changes were carried out peacefully.

Almost overnight the international political climate changed. Soviet-style communism had been discredited. The Warsaw Pact was no longer a significant force. A Soviet attack anywhere was almost unthinkable. The Cold War was over.

President Bush profited from these developments immensely. He expressed moral support for the new governments (and in some cases provided modest financial assistance) but he refrained from embarrassing the Soviets.

In 1989 President Bush sent troops to Panama to overthrow General Manuel Noriega, who had refused to yield power when his figurehead presidential candidate lost a national election. Noriega was under indictment in the United States for drug trafficking. After temporarily seeking refuge in the Vatican embassy in Panama, he surrendered to the American forces and was taken to the United States, where he was tried, convicted, and imprisoned.

The following labels and features appear on the map:

1	SLOVENIA
2	CROATIA
3	BOSNIA AND HERZEGOVINA
4	MACEDONIA
5	MONTENEGRO
6	KOSOVO
7	SERBIA

Lithuania declares independence, 1990.

Latvia and Estonia begin process of separation from Soviet Union, 1990.

Soviet Union. Dissolves, 1991; Russia and 10 former Soviet republics form Commonwealth of Independent States.

Germany. Berlin Wall breached, 1989; East and West Germany reunited, 1990.

Poland. Solidarity Party sweeps elections, 1989.

Czechoslovakia. Communist leadership ousted, 1989; country divided into Czech Republic and Slovakia, 1993.

Communist regimes collapse, 1989.

Yugoslavia. Nation disintegrates, 1991–1992.

Former Soviet Bloc

The Collapse of Communism in Eastern Europe

Meanwhile, in the summer of 1991, civil war broke out in Yugoslavia as Croatia and Slovenia sought independence from the Serbian-dominated central government. This conflict soon became a religious war, pitting Serb and Croatian Christians against Bosnian Muslims. In the Soviet Union, nationalist and anticommunist groups demanded more local control of their affairs. President Gorbachev, who opposed this breakup, sought compromise, backing a draft treaty that would increase local autonomy and further privatize the Soviet economy.

In August, however, before this treaty could be ratified, hard-line communists attempted a coup. They arrested Gorbachev, who was vacationing in the Crimea, and ordered tanks into Moscow. But Boris Yeltsin, the anticommunist president of the Russian Republic, defied the rebels and roused the people of Moscow. The coup swiftly collapsed. Its leaders were arrested, the Communist party was officially disbanded, and the Soviet Union itself was replaced by a federation of states, of which Russia, led by Yeltsin, was the most important. Gorbachev, who had begun the process of liberation, found himself without a job.

The War in the Persian Gulf

Although Reagan had provided economic assistance to Saddam Hussein of Iraq to prevent Iran from winning the Iran-Iraq war, few in the administration were enthusiastic about the Iraqi dictator. For years Saddam had been crushing the Kurds, an ethnic minority in northern Iraq that sought independence. In 1987 the U.S. State Department reported on his "widespread destruction and bulldozing of

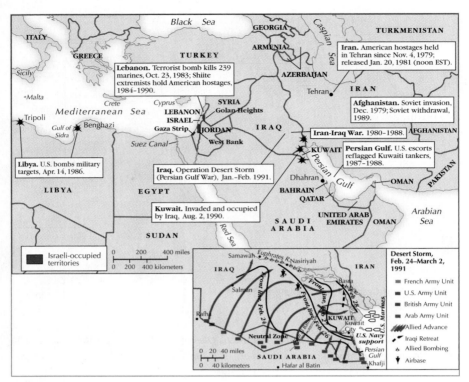

The Middle East

Kurdish villages." In March 1988, after Kurdish rebels had supported an Iranian advance into Iraq near Halabja, a mostly Kurdish city, Saddam's troops dropped mustard gas, sarin, and other chemical weapons on the city. Some 5,000 civilians died.

Worse was to come. In 1988, after the Iran-Iraq war had ended in a stalemate, Saddam intensified his war on the Kurds. In August 1990, he launched an all-out attack on Iraq's tiny neighbor to the south, the oil-rich sheikdom of Kuwait. Saddam hoped to swallow up Kuwait, thus increasing Iraq's already large oil reserves to about 25 percent of the world's total. His soldiers overran Kuwait swiftly, then systematically carried off everything of value they could bring back to Iraq. Within a week Saddam annexed Kuwait and massed troops along the border of neighboring Saudi Arabia.

The Saudis and the Kuwaitis turned to the United States and other nations for help, and it was quickly given. In a matter of days the UN applied trade sanctions against Iraq, and at the invitation of Saudi Arabia, the United States (along with Great Britain, France, Italy, Egypt, and Syria) moved troops to Saudi bases. Islamist fundamentalists opposed the presence of non-Muslim troops on Saudi soil; but the Saudi ruling family overruled them, fearing an Iraqi invasion.

By November, Bush had increased the American troops in the area from 180,000 to more than 500,000. In late November the UN took the fateful step of

As the routed Iraqi army fled Kuwait, it ignited (literally) an ecological disaster by setting fire to the Kuwaiti oil fields. Here American soldiers advance past a burning oil well; it took many months before all the wells could be extinguished.

authorizing the use of this force if Saddam did not withdraw from Kuwait by January 15, 1991. He flatly refused to do so.

Congress voted to use force to dislodge Saddam. On January 17, the Americans unleashed an enormous air attack, directed by General Norman Schwarzkopf. This air assault went on for nearly a month, and it reduced much of Iraq to rubble. The Iraqi forces, aside from firing a number of Scud missiles at Israel and Saudi Arabia and setting fire to hundreds of Kuwaiti oil wells, simply endured the rain of destruction that fell on them daily.

On February 23 Bush issued an ultimatum to Saddam: Pull out of Kuwait or face an invasion. When Saddam ignored the deadline, UN troops, more than 200,000 strong, struck. Bush called the assault "Desert Storm." Between February 24 and February 27 they retook Kuwait, killing tens of thousands of Iraqis in the process and capturing still larger numbers. Some 4,000 Iraqi tanks and enormous quantities of other military equipment were destroyed.

Bush then stopped the attack, and Saddam agreed to UN terms that included paying reparations to Kuwait and allowing UN inspectors to determine whether Iraq was developing atomic and biological weapons. Polls indicated that about 90 percent of the American people approved both the president's management of the war and his overall performance as chief executive. These were the highest presidential approval ratings ever recorded.

President Bush and indeed most observers expected Saddam to be driven from power in disgrace by his own people. Indeed, Bush publicly urged the Iraqis to do so. The Kurds in northern Iraq and pro-Iranian Muslims in the south then took up arms, but Saddam used the remnants of his army to crush them. He also refused repeatedly to carry out the terms of the peace agreement, chiefly by hindering the UN inspections for weapons of mass destruction. This led critics to argue that Bush should not have stopped the fighting until Baghdad, the Iraqi capital, had been captured and Saddam's army destroyed.

The Deficit Worsens

The huge cost of the Persian Gulf War exacerbated the federal deficit. Candidate Bush had promised not to raise taxes, saying in a phrase he would later regret: "Read my lips: No new taxes." As President he recommitted himself to that objective; in fact he even proposed reducing the tax on capital gains. But like his conservative predecessor, Bush could not control the deficit. Congress obstinately resisted closing local military bases or cutting funding for favored defense contractors. Reducing nonmilitary expenditures, especially popular entitlement programs such as Medicare and Social Security, also proved nearly impossible.

The deficit for 1992 hit $290 billion. Bush had no choice but to join with Congress in raising the top income tax rate from 28 percent to 31 percent and levying higher taxes on gasoline, liquor, expensive automobiles, and certain other luxuries. This damaged his credibility and angered conservative Republicans. "Read my lips," critics muttered: "No more Bush."

Enter Bill Clinton

William (Bill) Clinton was born William Jefferson Blythe IV, but his father died in a car accident before he was born. Though his stepfather was abusive and an alcoholic, at age 15 Bill legally took his stepfather's name. He graduated from Georgetown, won a Rhodes scholarship to study at Oxford University, and graduated from Yale Law School. He returned to Arkansas and was soon elected state attorney general.

In 1977 Clinton and his wife, Hillary Rodham, joined with James McDougal, a banker, to secure a loan to build vacation homes in the Ozarks. But the development, which they named Whitewater, eventually became insolvent. McDougal illegally covered the debts with a loan from a savings and loan company he had acquired. In 1989 the savings and loan failed, costing the federal government $60 million to reimburse depositors. In 1992 federal investigators claimed that the Clintons had been "potential beneficiaries" of McDougal's illegal activities.

By this time Clinton, now governor of Arkansas, was campaigning in the New Hampshire primary for the Democratic nomination for president. Few voters could make much sense of this tangled web of fiduciary finagling, nor did they have much opportunity to do so: Another, far more explosive story threatened to sink the Clinton campaign. It came out that Clinton had for many years engaged in an extramarital affair with one Gennifer Flowers; Clinton's standing in the polls tumbled.

Hillary Rodham Clinton appeared with her husband on CBS's *60 Minutes* to address the allegations. Bill Clinton indignantly denied Flowers's statements but then issued an earnest if ambiguous appeal for forgiveness. "I have acknowledged causing pain in my marriage," he said. "I think most Americans will know what we're saying; they'll get it." Clinton was right, early evidence of his ability to address the American people directly, but on his own—carefully worded—terms. He finished second in New Hampshire, captured most of the remaining primaries, and won the Democratic nomination with ease. His choice of running mate—Senator Al Gore of Tennessee, a Vietnam veteran, family man, and environmentalist—helped the ticket considerably.

The Election of 1992

While Clinton tiptoed through a minefield of personal scandal, President Bush rested secure in the belief that, after crushing Saddam's forces in the Gulf War, the 1992 election campaign would be little more than a victory lap. But he encountered unexpectedly stiff opposition within the Republican party. Patrick Buchanan, an outspoken conservative, did well enough to alarm White House strategists. Then Ross Perot, a billionaire Texan, announced his independent candidacy. Perot charged that both major parties were out of touch with "the people." He promised to spend $100 million of his own money on his campaign. Perot's platform had both conservative and liberal planks. He would "take the shackles off of American business," avoid raising taxes, and cut government spending by "getting rid of waste." He also supported gun control, backed a woman's right to have an abortion, promised to get rid of political action committees, and called for an all-out effort to "restructure" the health care system.

Polls quickly revealed that Perot was popular in California, Texas, and other key states that Bush was counting on winning easily. At the Republican convention in August, Bush was nominated without opposition.

Clinton accused Bush of failing to deal effectively with the lingering economic recession, which had worsened during the summer. Clinton promised to undertake public works projects, to encourage private investment, and to improve the nation's education and health insurance systems. Bush played down the seriousness of the recession, but his jaunty comments offended those who had lost their jobs.

On election day, more than 100 million citizens voted. About 44 million voted for Clinton, 38 million for Bush, and 20 million for Perot. Clinton was elected with 370 electoral votes to Bush's 168. Perot did not win any electoral votes.

Clinton as President

One reason for Clinton's success was his expressed intention to change health insurance and the welfare system, and to bring the budget deficit under control. His solid knowledge of public issues was impressive, and he created a general impression of mastery and self-confidence.

Young Bill Clinton *(left)* shakes hands with President John F. Kennedy. "The torch has been passed to a new generation of Americans," Kennedy had declared in his inaugural. "Ask not what your country can do for you—ask what you can do for your country," JFK added. Thirty years later, Clinton's inaugural echoed Kennedy's: "Today, a generation raised in the shadows of the Cold War assumes new responsibilities," Clinton declared. "I challenge a new generation of young Americans to a season of service."

Clinton had promised to end the ban on gays and lesbians in the armed services, but when the Joint Chiefs of the armed forces and a number of important members of Congress objected, he settled for a policy known as "don't ask, don't tell," meaning that such persons would be allowed to enlist only if they did not openly proclaim their sexual orientation. When relatively minor objections were raised to a number of his important appointments, he tended to back down rather than stand behind his choices.

In July 1993 Clinton used his executive authority to strengthen the Supreme Court majority in favor of upholding the landmark case of *Roe* v. *Wade*. The majority included three conservative justices who had been appointed by Reagan and Bush. Clinton appointed Ruth Bader Ginsberg, a judge known to believe that abortion was constitutional. Clinton also indicated that he would veto any bill limiting abortion rights. He also reversed important Bush policies by signing a revived family leave bill into law and by authorizing the use of fetal tissue for research purposes.

The first major test of the president's will came when he submitted his first budget to Congress. He hoped to reduce the deficit by roughly $500 billion in five years, half by spending cuts, half by new taxes. The proposal for a tax increase roused a storm of protest. A number of congressional Democrats refused to go along with Clinton's budget, and since the Republicans in Congress voted solidly against any increase in taxes, the president was forced to accept major changes. Even so, the final bill passed by the narrowest of margins. Clinton rightly claimed a victory.

He then turned to his long-awaited proposal to reform the nation's expensive and incomplete health insurance system. A committee headed by his wife had been working for months with no indication that a plan acceptable to the medical profession, the health insurance industry, and ordinary citizens was likely to come from its deliberations. The plan that finally emerged seemed even more complicated and quite possibly more costly than the existing system. It never came to a vote in Congress.

Emergence of the Republican Majority

The Whitewater scandal, which Clinton had managed to brush aside during the campaign, gnawed at his presidency. Public pressure forced Attorney General Janet Reno to appoint a special prosecutor. She named Kenneth W. Starr, a Republican lawyer, to investigate Whitewater and other alleged misdeeds of the Clintons.

More troubles followed. Paula Corbin Jones, a State of Arkansas employee, charged that Clinton, while governor, had invited her to his hotel room and asked her to engage in oral sex. Clinton's attorney denied the accusation and sought to have the case dismissed on the grounds that a president could not be sued while in office. The case commenced a tortuous route through the courts.

Eager to take advantage of Clinton's troubles, Republicans looked to the 1994 congressional elections. Led by congressman Newt Gingrich of Georgia, they offered voters an ambitious program to stimulate the economy by reducing both the federal debt and the federal income tax. This would turn many of the functions of the federal government over to the states or to private enterprise. Federally administered welfare programs were to be replaced by block grants to the states. Many measures protecting the environment, such as those making businesses responsible for cleaning up their waste, were to be repealed.

On election day, the Republicans gained control of both houses of Congress. Under the firm direction of Gingrich, now Speaker, the House approved nearly all of the provisions of this "Contract with America." This appalled Clinton, who vetoed the 1995 budget drafted by the Republicans. When neither side agreed to a compromise, the government briefly ran out of money and shut down all but essential services.

The Election of 1996

Clinton was renominated for a second term without opposition. A number of Republicans competed in their primaries, but after a slow start Bob Dole of Kansas, the Senate majority leader, won the nomination. Dole had been a senator for more than 30 years, but despite his experience he was a poor campaigner, stiff and monotone. His main proposal was a steep reduction of the deficit and a 15 percent income tax cut. Pressed to explain how this could be done without drastic cuts in popular social programs, especially Social Security and Medicare, he gave a distressingly vague reply. Clinton, a charismatic campaigner, also promised to reduce the deficit, but by a lesser amount, so as to be able to spend more on education, the environment, and social welfare needs. He stressed preparing for the twenty-first century and took, in general, an optimistic view of the economy.

On election day Clinton won an impressive victory, sweeping the Northeast, all the Midwest except Indiana, the upper Mississippi Valley, and the Far West. He divided the South with Dole, who carried a band of states running north from Texas. Clinton's Electoral College margin was substantial, 379 to 159. The Republicans, however, retained control of both houses of Congress. Many retained, as well, an unquenchable hatred of Clinton.

Clinton Impeached

Although President Clinton steadfastly denied allegations of womanizing, in January 1998 a judge ordered him to testify in the lawsuit Paula Corbin Jones had filed against him. Jones, who sought to strengthen her suit by showing that Clinton had a history of propositioning women, also subpoenaed a former White House intern. Her name was Monica Lewinsky.

Lewinsky and Clinton were separately asked if they had had an affair, and each denied the charge. When word of their alleged relationship was leaked to the press, Clinton declared in a TV news conference: "I did not have sexual relations with that woman, Miss Lewinsky." Hillary Clinton denounced the allegations as part of a "vast right-wing conspiracy" against her husband.

Unbeknown to the Clintons, however, Lewinsky had been confiding to Linda Tripp, a former White House employee. Tripp had secretly tape-recorded some 20 hours of their conversations. Tripp turned these tapes over to special prosecutor Starr, whose investigations of the Clintons' roles in the Whitewater scandal had broadened into a more general inquiry. In the tapes Lewinsky provided intimate details of repeated sexual encounters with the president. Clinton and Lewinsky appeared to have lied under oath. Starr threatened to indict Lewinsky for perjury. In return for immunity from prosecution, she repudiated her earlier testimony and admitted that she had engaged in sexual relations with the president and that he and his aides had encouraged her to give misleading testimony in the Jones case.

When called in August to testify on videotape before the Starr grand jury, Clinton conceded that he had engaged in "inappropriate intimate contact" with Lewinsky. But he insisted, "I have not had sex with her as I defined it." When pressed to supply his own definition, he responded with legalistic obfuscation: "My understanding of this definition is it covers contact by the person being deposed with the enumerated areas, if the contact is done with an intent to arouse or gratify." Because Clinton had not intended to arouse or gratify Lewinsky, he had not "had sex" with her. He allowed that this definition was "rather strange."

More legalisms followed. When asked if he had ever been alone with her, he responded, "It depends on how you define alone." When asked if his lawyer had been correct when he had assured the judge in January that "there is absolutely no

A seemingly anonymous well-wisher from the crowd greets President Bill Clinton. When Clinton was later investigated for having an affair with Monica Lewinsky, a former White House intern, this photograph of the two surfaced. Clinton's lack of discretion struck many as self-destructive.

sex of any kind," Clinton said that the statement was not untrue because "it depends on what the meaning of the word 'is' is."

Clinton's testimony infuriated Starr, who made public Lewinsky's humiliatingly detailed testimony and announced that Clinton's deceptive testimony warranted consideration by the House of Representatives for impeachment.

But throughout Clinton's legal battles, opinion polls suggested that two in three Americans approved of his performance as president. Buoyed by the vibrant economy, most Americans blamed the scandal on the intrusive Starr nearly as much as the evasive Clinton. The November election proved disastrous for the Republicans, who nearly lost their majority in the House.

Clinton's troubles, however, were by no means over. Republican leaders in the House impeached Clinton on the grounds that he had committed perjury and had obstructed justice by inducing Lewinsky and others to give false testimony in the Jones case. The vote closely followed party lines.

The impeachment trial in the Senate began in January 1999. Chief Justice William Rehnquist presided. The Republicans numbered 55, enough to control the proceedings but twelve short of the two-thirds necessary to convict the president and remove him from office. Democrats, while publicly critical of Clinton's behavior, maintained that his indiscretions did not constitute "high crimes and misdemeanors" as specified in the Constitution for removal from office. They prevailed. The article accusing Clinton of perjury was defeated by a vote of 55 to 45; on the article alleging obstruction of justice, the vote was 50 to 50. Clinton remained president.

Clinton's Legacy

One reason why Clinton survived was the health of the economy. Few wanted to rock the ship of state when it was stuffed with cash. Until the final months, the Clinton years coincided with the longest economic boom in the nation's history.

Clinton deserves considerable credit for the remarkable prosperity of the era. By reducing the federal deficit, interest rates came down, spurring investment and economic growth. By August 1998 unemployment had fallen to 4.5 percent, the lowest level since the 1960s; inflation had eased to a minuscule 1 percent, the lowest level since the 1950s. In 1998 the federal government operated at its first surplus since 1969. Then, as the economy soared during the next two years, so did government income. In the 2000 fiscal year, the surplus hit $237 billion.

Clinton also promoted globalization of the economy. He successfully promoted the North American Free Trade Agreement to reduce restrictions on trade. During the last half of the 1990s, the United States led all industrial nations in the rate of growth of its real gross domestic product. But the new global economy harmed many. Some union leaders bitterly asked how their members could compete against convict labor in China or sweatshop workers in Indonesia or Malaysia. Others complained that the emphasis on worldwide economic growth was generating an environmental calamity. International protests against the World Trade Organization culminated in the disruption of its 2000 meeting in Seattle, when thousands of protesters went on a rampage, setting fires and looting stores.

Clinton's record in foreign affairs was mixed. In 1993 he failed in an effort to assemble an international force to prevent "ethnic cleansing" by Serbian troops against Muslims in Bosnia, formerly part of Yugoslavia. That same year a U.S. initiative to Somalia, an African nation wracked by civil war and famine, ended in failure when a Somali warlord ambushed and killed fifteen American commandos. "Operation Restore Hope," as it was called, did not do so. In 1999 critics predicted another debacle when Clinton proposed a NATO effort to prevent General Slobodan Milosevic of Yugoslavia from crushing the predominantly Muslim province of Kosovo, which was attempting to secede. But after several months of intense NATO bombing of Serbia, Milosevic withdrew from Kosovo. Within a year, he was forced out of office and into prison, awaiting trial for war crimes before a UN tribunal.

Whatever the successes and shortcomings of his administration, the Clinton presidency will always be linked to his relationship with a White House intern and the impeachment proceedings that ensued. Though by no means the first president to stray from matrimonial propriety, Clinton's behavior, in an era when the media thrived on scandal and crime, was symptomatic of an almost willful self-destructiveness.

A Racial Divide

The decade of the 1990s had an unusually sharp edge, as politicians increasingly accused each other of crimes and sexual misbehavior. Contributing to the harsh tone of the era was the arrest and spectacular murder trial of O. J. Simpson, a former star football running back for the University of Southern California and the Buffalo Bills. Simpson, who was black, was accused of stabbing his estranged wife and another man. Both of them were white. After a tempestuous nine-month trial, Simpson was acquitted.

To many whites, Simpson was another violent black male, while to many African Americans, he was but another innocent black abused by a prejudiced criminal justice system. According to polls, 85 percent of blacks agreed with the "not guilty" verdict of the first Simpson trial, while only 34 percent of whites did. For the most part, neither race could understand the other's reasoning.

Many concluded that the cultural chasm between whites and blacks was widening. In 1992 Supreme Court justice Thurgood Marshall observed that educated Americans of each race appeared to have "given up on integration." After the Simpson trial Louis Farrakhan, leader of the black separatist Nation of Islam, called on African American men to express their solidarity by participating in a "Million Man March" on Washington, D.C. Many black leaders, including Jesse Jackson, embraced it. On October 16, 1995, the demonstration attracted perhaps a half million marchers, far more than had participated in Martin Luther King Jr.'s "March on Washington" in 1963. But where King welcomed the whites in the audience and declared, "We cannot walk alone," Farrakhan called for "a more perfect union" of the multitude of black men gathered before him.

The persistence of inequality was one reason for the new separatism. In 1972 the incomes of black families were one-third less than those of white families; this was virtually unchanged 20 years later.

A significant casualty of the changing tone of race relations was "affirmative action," which gave minorities preference in hiring and college admissions. Initially justified on the grounds that the legacy of slavery and the persistence of racism put blacks at an unfair disadvantage in finding jobs or gaining admission to college, affirmative action programs spread during the 1970s and 1980s. But in July 1995 the Regents of the University of California ordered an end to affirmative action. This decision touched off protests throughout the university system. The protests, however, drew attention to the issue and the following year California voters approved Proposition 209, which abolished racial and gender preferences in all government hiring and education. The U.S. Supreme Court let the law stand. Other states enacted similar laws.

The overt racism of an earlier era, enforced by custom and law, had become socially unacceptable and often explicitly illegal. But as the British writer Godfrey Hodgson observed, Americans in the 1990s appeared to be moving toward "a kind of voluntary apartheid" in which blacks and whites preferred to keep their distance. In 1997, when President Clinton went to Little Rock to celebrate the fortieth anniversary of the desegregation of Central High School, he commented on the deterioration in race relations. The formerly all-white school was now mostly black, as were all public schools in Little Rock. "For the first time since the 1950s, our schools in America are resegregating," he noted.

Violence and Popular Culture

Popular culture often bridged the racial divide. But many observers noted the increasingly violent tone of popular culture, especially in youth-focused movies, pop songs, video and computer games, and TV shows. Such entertainment, they contended, romanticized an increasingly bloody culture of crime and violence. They cited as proof the intense violence of the movie industry, pointing out that in *Public Enemy*, reputedly the most violent film of the 1930s, and *Death Wish*, a controversial vigilante fantasy of 1974, the body count reached eight. But three movies released during the late 1980s—*Robocop*, *Die Hard*, and *Rambo III*—each produced a death tally of 60 or more, nearly one every two minutes. Television imitated the movies as the networks crammed violent crime shows into prime time. In 1991 an exhaustive survey found that by the age of 18, the average viewer had witnessed some 40,000 murders on TV.

Popular music also acquired a new edge. In 1981 Warner Brothers launched a television channel featuring pop songs set to video. Music TV (MTV) was an instant success; within three years, some 24 million tuned in every day. Michael Jackson's video extravaganza, *Thriller* (1984), transformed the genre. Its surreal images, disjointed editing, and frenzied music set a new standard. Pop music acquired a harder beat and more explicit lyrics. In 1988 the American Academy of Pediatrics expressed concern that teenagers on the average spent two hours a day watching rock videos. Over half featured violence and three-fourths contained sexually suggestive material.

A new sound called "rap" then emerged from the ghetto and spread by means of radio, cassettes, and CDs. Rap consisted of unpredictably metered lyrics set against an exaggeratedly heavy downbeat. Rap performers did not play musical instruments or sing songs so much as convey, in words and gestures, an attitude of raw rage.

The appeal of rap quickly spread beyond black audiences. When Dr. Dre (Andrew Young), founder of a gangsta rap group and head of a record firm, discovered that whites bought more rap CDs than blacks, he promoted the career of a young white rapper, Eminem. Born Marshall Bruce Mathers III, Eminem attracted attention with songs such as "Murder, Murder," "Kill You," "Drug Ballad," and "Criminal" in which he bashed women, gays, his wife, and nearly everyone else. His lyrics were of such surpassing offensiveness that he became an overnight celebrity and instant millionaire. His fans, whom he treated with scorn, were delighted by the universality of his contempt. The list of those suing him included his mother.

Most consumers of pop violence in the 1990s and early years of the 2000s had little difficulty distinguishing between cultural fantasies and everyday life. But for those who had grown up in ghettos where gangs ruled the streets and where friends and relatives were commonly swallowed up by the criminal justice system, the culture of violence seemed to legitimate the meanness of everyday life. Moreover, violence and criminality were becoming so much a part of popular culture, and popular culture of adolescent life, that some retreated wholly to imaginative worlds conjured by movies, video and computer games, TV, and pop music. To them, the world of parents and teachers seemed duller and less responsive—less *real*—than the one inside their heads. Whether this helped explain the spate of school shootings was endlessly debated during the 1990s, and continues to be debated today.

The Economic Boom and the Internet

Since the 1950s, youthful consumers had long been an important part of the economy. But a significant part of the prosperity of the 1990s came from new technologies such as cellular phones and genetic engineering. The most important was the development of a revolutionary form of communication: the Internet. Developed in the 1970s by U.S. military and academic institutions to coordinate research, the Internet initially proved an awkward means of linking information. Data in one computer did not readily relate to that elsewhere. The Internet was a communication system that lacked a common language.

That was remedied in the early 1990s by Tim Berners-Lee, a British physicist working at a research institute in Switzerland. He devised the software that became the grammar—the "protocols"—of the Internet "language." With this language, the internet became the World Wide Web (WWW), a conduit for a stream of electronic impulses flowing among hundreds of millions of computers.

The number of Web sites increased exponentially. In 1995 Bill Gates's Microsoft entered the picture with its Windows operating system, which made the computer easy to use. Rather than drown in the coming deluge, Microsoft seized control of it. It competed with Netscape by creating a Web browser—Microsoft Internet Explorer—and embedded its software in the Windows 95 bundle. This provoked howls of protest from Netscape as well as from other service providers: America Online, CompuServe, and Prodigy. Microsoft, they complained, was threatening to monopolize access to and use of the Internet. (A federal judge concurred, ordering that Microsoft be broken up; his ruling was overturned on appeal in 2001.)

In the meantime, Jeff Bezos dreamed of using the Internet to sell books. In 1995 his company, Amazon.com, sold its first book. Within six years, its annual sales approached $3 billion and its stock soared. Bezos became one of the richest men in the nation.

If Bezos could use the Web for selling books, others imagined they could sell everything from pet food to pornography. (eBay, an Internet auction house, had an online catalog consisting of three million items.) Many start-up companies (dot-coms, in the argot of the day) consisted of little more than the hopes of the founders. "Venture capitalists," independent investors seeking to fund emerging "tech" companies, sensed a glittering new economic frontier somewhere down the Internet superhighway, and they poured billions into start-up dot-coms. In 1999 some 200 Internet companies "went public," selling shares in the major stock exchanges. They raised $20 billion easily. NASDAQ, the exchange that specialized in tech companies, saw the value of its stocks skyrocket, its index more than doubling between October 1999 and March 2000. The prices of dot-com stocks kept on climbing though few generated profits; some lacked any revenue whatsoever.

In the spring of 2000, with the stock market still surging, a selling wave hit the tech stocks and spilled over to other companies. Stock prices plummeted. Within six months NASDAQ lost nearly half its value. In all, some $2 trillion in stocks and stock funds disappeared. As the 2000 election approached, many feared that the economy was nearing a recession.

The 2000 Election: George W. Bush Wins by One Vote

During the 2000 campaign, Vice President Al Gore secured the Democratic nomination and chose as running mate Senator Joseph Lieberman of Connecticut, an orthodox Jew and outspoken critic of Clinton during the impeachment proceedings.

The leading contender was George W. Bush, son of former President Bush. Like his father, Bush graduated from Yale and worked in the family oil business. He headed a group that bought the Texas Rangers baseball team. Although some doubted Bush's abilities, his visible success with the Rangers catapulted him into Texas politics. An effective and personable campaigner, he was elected governor in 1994. Six years later he defeated Senator John McCain of Arizona in a battle for the Republican nomination for president. Bush selected as running mate Richard Cheney, who had served as defense secretary in his father's administration.

Consumer activist and environmentalist Ralph Nader also entered the presidential race, running on the Green party ticket. This worried Gore, author of *Earth in the Balance;* he had hoped to carry the environmentalist vote.

Gore, though knowledgeable, seemed stiff, and he occasionally indulged in self-serving bombast, as when he claimed to have "invented" the Internet. Bush's principal offense was against the English language. "Rarely is the question asked," he once declaimed, "Is our children learning?" However exaggerated or garbled their message, the candidates spent a record $1 billion in getting it to the voters.

Having been inundated with advertisements, many on election night breathed a sigh of relief that the election was finally over. They were wrong. By midnight it appeared that Bush had 246 electoral votes, and Gore, 267, with 270 necessary to win; but Florida, with 25 electoral votes, had not been decided. As returns trickled in, the television networks reversed themselves and declared Florida—and the election—"too close to call." Bush's lead there was 1,784 out of nearly 6 million cast.

After a machine recount, Bush's margin in Florida was reduced to several hundred votes, with Democrats complaining that a punch-card ballot used in some communities was confusing, depriving Gore of thousands of votes; worse, the machines routinely failed to count incompletely punched ballots. Gore's lawyers demanded that the ballots in several predominantly Democratic counties be counted by hand. Republicans countered that Democrats had no right to change voting procedures after the election. They demanded that the hand recounts cease.

The entire election ended up in the courts. On December 12, more than a month after the election, the Supreme Court ruled by a 5 to 4 vote that the selective hand recounts violated the Constitution's guarantee of equal protection. Bush's margin would stand.

Nationwide, Gore received 51 million votes, Bush, 50.5 million. Nader, who did not win any electoral votes, received nearly 3 million.

The New Terrorism Intensifies

After the fall of the Soviet Union, American military might seemed unassailable. Military dictators who had been kept afloat by the Soviets or the Americans—and often from both simultaneously—now were obliged to seek the support of the people they had long ruled. This further destabilized the Middle East. The military leaders of Egypt and hereditary rulers of Saudi Arabia, for example, sought to retain the support of Islamic clerics while refraining from accepting an Islamic theocracy—direct rule by Islamic rulers. Such leaders cultivated popular support by denouncing Israel, which refused to return land seized from Palestine in the 1967 war. The United States encouraged Israel to trade that land for peace. But few Israelis believed the promises of Arab leaders who had steadfastly called for the annihilation of Israel and had trained and funded terrorism. Insofar as Israel relied ultimately on American support, the Arab rage was increasingly directed at the United States and American soldiers stationed abroad.

During these years, Islamist terrorists emerged throughout the Middle East, usually in response to the repression of radical Islamic clerics. In 1998 a new figure surfaced from among such groups: Osama bin Laden, the son of a Saudi oil billionaire. In 1998, bin Laden published a *fatwa*—a religious edict—to Islamic peoples throughout the world: "To kill Americans and their allies, both civil and military, is an individual duty of every Muslim who is able ..." By now, bin Laden was protected by an extremist Islamic group, the Taliban, which ruled Afghanistan. Six months later, bin Laden's terrorist organization—al-Qaeda—had perpetrated the bombings of the U.S. embassies in Nairobi and Dar es-Salaam in Africa. Worse was to follow.

September 11, 2001

At 8:40 on the morning of September 11, 2001, Madeline Amy Sweeney, an attendant on American Airlines Flight 11, placed a cell phone call from the galley of the plane to her supervisor in Boston. In a whisper, she said that four Arab men had slashed the throats of two attendants, forced their way into the cockpit, and taken over the plane. She gave him their seat numbers so that their identities could be

A second jetliner approaches the South Tower of the World Trade Center on September 11, 2001. The North Tower had already been hit and was engulfed in flames and smoke.

determined from the passenger log. The supervisor asked if she knew where the plane was headed. She looked out the window and noted that it was descending rapidly. "I see water and buildings." Then she paused: "Oh my God." The water was the Hudson River, and the buildings were the skyscrapers of lower Manhattan, foremost among them the 110-story twin towers of the World Trade Center.

The hijackers pushed the throttle to full, and the Boeing 767 was traveling at 500 miles per hour at 8:46 when it slammed into the 96th floor of the north tower. A fireball, fed by 10,000 gallons of jet fuel, instantly engulfed eight or nine stories.

Fifteen minutes later a second airliner came into view over Manhattan harbor, banked sharply, and plowed into the 80th floor of the south tower.

At 9:30 the White House received word that another hijacked airliner was barreling toward Washington, D.C. Secret Service agents rushed Vice President Richard Cheney to an emergency command bunker far below the White House. At 9:35 the airliner plunged into the Pentagon and burst into flames. Cheney telephoned President Bush, who was in Sarasota, Florida. The nation was under attack. Bush authorized the Air Force to shoot down any other hijacked airliners. A few minutes later a fourth hijacked airliner crashed into a field in Pennsylvania after passengers had declared their intention—again by cell phone—to retake the plane.

While television viewers absorbed these shocks, they watched as the upper floors of the World Trade Center towers blackened, like charred matches. At 9:59, the south tower collapsed, followed by the north tower a half hour later, pulverizing millions of tons of concrete and glass and enveloping lower Manhattan in choking dust. Nearly three thousand lay dead in the mountain of rubble; several hundred more perished at the Pentagon and in the crash of the airliner in Pennsylvania.

Teams of four or five Arabic-speaking men had hijacked each of the planes. Several of the hijackers were quickly linked to the al-Qaeda terrorist network run by Osama bin Laden, who had previously been indicted (but not captured) for the 1998 bombing of U.S. embassies in East Africa and the 2000 attack on the USS *Cole*. Bin Laden operated with impunity in Afghanistan.

That evening President Bush addressed the nation. He spoke simply and with force. "We will find these people," he said of the terrorists. "They will pay." Any government harboring the terrorists—an obvious reference to the Taliban—would be held equally responsible for the attack. Bin Laden, in a video recorded from an undisclosed location, denied involvement in the attack but praised those who carried it out.

Several weeks later, Bush declared that bin Laden would be taken "dead or alive." The president also offered a $25 million reward for his death or capture, an evocation of swift frontier justice that suited the national mood. Within the United States, thousands of Arabs were rounded up and detained; those with visa and immigration violations were imprisoned.

Then more trouble arrived at the capital, this time in the mail. Several letters addressed to government officials included threatening messages and a white powder consisting of billions of anthrax spores, which could prove fatal if touched or inhaled. Thousands of government employees took antibiotics as a precaution, but some spores had seeped out of the envelopes and killed a half dozen postal workers and mail recipients.

Bush responded to these multiple threats by creating a Cabinet position, the Office of Homeland Security, and naming Pennsylvania governor Tom Ridge to direct it. Repeatedly Ridge issued vague warnings of imminent terrorist attacks. How exactly Americans were to protect themselves, he did not say.

America Fights Back: War in Afghanistan

Bush had declared "war on terror," but it was to be a battle unlike any the nation had ever fought. Al-Qaeda had secret terrorist cells in many countries. Bin Laden was ensconced in remote Afghanistan, protected by thousands of Taliban soldiers who had inflicted heavy losses on Soviet invaders in the 1980s. (At the time, the United States had provided bin Laden and the Taliban with money and weapons.)

Bush's challenge was all the greater because of his own stated opposition to ill-defined and far-flung military operations. He had chastised the Clinton-Gore administration for "extending our troops all around the world." He underscored his reticence for such ventures by naming Colin Powell secretary of state. Powell, who had been sobered by his experiences in Vietnam, maintained that U.S. troops should only be deployed when their political objective was clear, military advantage overwhelming, and means of disengaging secure. This became known as the Powell doctrine, and Bush had endorsed it during the campaign. But the proposed war against terror adhered to none of its precepts. Now such scruples did not matter; the president had little choice but to fight.

Powell urged European, Asian, and even Islamic states to crack down on terrorist cells in their countries and to provide assistance in the U.S. military campaign against the Taliban; he also persuaded anti-Taliban factions within Afghanistan to join forces to topple the regime. On September 20 Bush ordered the Taliban to surrender bin Laden and top al-Qaeda leaders; when the Taliban refused, Bush unloosed missiles and warplanes against Taliban installations and defenses, much like the campaign that had ended Serbian aggression against ethnic Muslims in Kosovo.

For several weeks, Taliban soldiers cowered in bunkers as bombs thudded nearby; but they defended their positions when anti-Taliban forces attacked. Then small teams of elite American soldiers, armed with hand-held computers and satellite-linked navigational devices, joined with anti-Taliban contingents, marking Taliban positions with laser spotters and communicating with high-altitude bombers. These planes, circling at 30,000 feet, dropped electronically guided bombs on Taliban troops with uncanny (but not infallible) accuracy. Within weeks the Taliban were driven from power. Only one American soldier was killed by hostile fire. The United States had won the first battles in the war against terror.

The Second Iraq War

In January 2002, after the Taliban had been crushed, President Bush declared that he would not "wait on events while dangers gather." The United States would take "preemptive actions"—war—against regimes that threatened it. Bush identified Iran, North Korea, and Iraq as an "axis of evil" that warranted special scrutiny. Immediately after the terrorist attacks on September 11, 2001, he secretly initiated plans to attack Iraq, ruled by Saddam Hussein.

Secretary of State Colin Powell advised Bush not to attack Iraq. If Saddam were driven from power, Powell warned, Bush would become "the proud owner of 25 million people—you'll own it all." Vice President Dick Cheney, Defense Secretary Donald Rumsfeld, and others in the administration insisted that the Iraqis would welcome liberation and embrace democracy. A free Iraq, they added, would stimulate democratic reforms throughout the Middle East, as had happened in eastern Europe following the collapse of the Soviet Union. Bush agreed.

The Joint Chiefs of Staff proposed an invasion force numbering a half-million troops, as had been hurled against Saddam in 1991. Rumsfeld insisted on a smaller, faster, and cheaper force of 125,000, and his views prevailed.

In September, Bush sought congressional support. "The Iraqi regime possesses chemical and biological weapons," he declared, adding that Saddam also sought nuclear weapons. Congress voted overwhelmingly for the war appropriation.

Bush then called on the United Nations to join in the attack on Saddam. That Saddam had used chemical weapons during the Iran-Iraq war and also against the Kurds was beyond dispute; but following Saddam's defeat in 1991, UN inspectors had destroyed thousands of tons of chemical weapons and they doubted that more such weapons had been stockpiled. Bush saw this as proof that Saddam had hoodwinked the inspectors. Then Powell, like Adlai Stevenson during the Cuban missile crisis in 1962, presented classified U.S. intelligence to the United Nations. Saddam, he said, had indeed been building and stockpiling weapons of mass destruction. The UN Security Council ordered Saddam to cooperate with UN inspectors and warned of "serious consequences" if he refused to do so.

When the Security Council delayed taking action against Saddam, Bush decided to form a coalition on his own to oust the Iraqi leader. He was joined by Great Britain, Italy, Spain and a few other countries.

On March 20, 2003, American missiles and bombs pounded Saddam's defenses. The "Shock and Awe" campaign to liberate Iraq had begun. Two immense armored columns roared across the Kuwaiti border into Iraq, passing burned-out

President George W. Bush aboard the USS *Abraham Lincoln* on May 1, 2004. "Major combat operations in Iraq have ended," he declared. But in the months to come, American casualties mounted as some Iraqis resisted occupation by the United States. By that fall, more than 1,000 United States soldiers had been killed in the Iraq war.

Iraqi tanks from the first Gulf War. British forces moved along the coast toward the oil port of Basra. Television reporters, perched atop Humvees and armored personnel carriers, provided live coverage. Iraqi resistance was ineffective. The first night, American units advanced deep into Iraq, halfway to Baghdad.

On April 4, the U.S. army seized the Baghdad International Airport. The next morning, some 800 American soldiers in tanks and armored vehicles raced down Highway 8 and blasted their way into downtown Baghdad. Some Iraqis poured into the streets to celebrate; others looted government buildings, museums, stores, and hospitals. Saddam disappeared and his government evaporated. By mid-April, the Pentagon declared that major combat operations had come to an end.

But Iraq was in chaos. There were too few U.S. troops to preserve order. Islamist radicals, enraged by the American occupation of Iraq, increasingly joined with Saddam's supporters in attacking occupation forces. The insurgents rammed trucks filled with explosives into police stations, wired cell phones to artillery shells and detonated them as Americans approached, and sabotaged oil pipelines and power generators.

2004: Bush Wins a Second Term

The war in Iraq became the main issue of the presidential campaign. In December 2003, when American soldiers captured Saddam in an underground bunker, Bush's approval rating soared.

By January Senator John Kerry of Massachusetts was gaining in the polls. The son of a diplomat and a graduate of Yale, Kerry appeared accomplished and steady. He had commanded a patrol boat during the Vietnam War and was decorated for courage under fire. By April, Kerry had won the Democratic nomination. He chose Senator John Edwards of North Carolina, a wealthy trial lawyer, as his running mate.

In Iraq, the situation had deteriorated further. In April the *60 Minutes* news program revealed that American captors had tortured Iraqi captives in the Abu Ghraib prison. Photographs of American soldiers, including women, taunting naked Muslim men fueled the insurgency. Casualties mounted. The cost of the occupation spiraled upward. More damaging politically was the failure to find any Iraqi weapons of mass destruction.

At the Democratic convention in July, Kerry emphasized his military background. "I am John Kerry, and I am reporting for duty," he said in his acceptance speech. "As president," Kerry declared, "I will fight a smarter, more effective war on terror." He criticized Bush for attacking Iraq before capturing Osama bin Laden, who remained at large. He also criticized Bush for not sending enough troops to preserve order and rebuild Iraq, and for initiating war with insufficient international support.

Republicans pounced on Kerry's war record. Vietnam veterans challenged his heroism, others his leadership. Many seized on the fact that in 1971 Kerry had told a

A U.S. soldier taunting an Iraqi prisoner at Abu Ghraib prison. U.S. Major General Antonio M. Taguba reported on many such instances of "sadistic, blatant, and wanton criminal abuses." At least one prisoner died while being interrogated. The commander of the prison was dismissed, and criminal charges were filed against some of the soldiers.

congressional committee that the Vietnam War was wrong and immoral. How, they asked, could an antiwar activist lead the nation in time of war?

Republicans also portrayed Kerry as opportunistic. If Kerry and Edwards thought the war was a mistake, why did they vote for the original war resolution in the Senate? Kerry became entangled in long-winded explanations. "I actually voted for the $87 billion before I voted against it," he said on one occasion. Bush gleefully seized on this "flip-flop" and dubbed Kerry "Flipper." During a debate with Bush, Kerry conceded that he had "made a mistake" in explaining his position on Iraq. "But the president made a mistake in invading Iraq. Which is worse?"

Bush mobilized conservatives and religious fundamentalists by proposing a constitutional amendment that would define marriage as the union between a man and a woman. Kerry endorsed gay rights but endlessly qualified earlier statements in support of same-sex marriage.

No wartime president had ever lost a reelection campaign. Many voters preferred Bush's simple nostrums, even if flawed, to Kerry's complicated (and sometimes contradictory) approach. "You know where I stand," Bush had declared at nearly every campaign stop, and in the end a majority of voters stood with him. The election, one of the most divisive in recent decades, brought twelve million more voters to the polls than in 2000. Kerry received 57 million votes, three million more than Ronald Reagan in his 1984 landslide. But Bush got over 60 million, a record. He also prevailed in the Electoral College, 286 to 252.

More Trouble in Asia

Although his main goal was to win the wars in Iraq and Afghanistan, Bush became increasingly concerned over political stability elsewhere in Asia. When the radical Islamist regime in Iran acquired the technology to enrich the uranium necessary for nuclear warheads, the United States raised objections with the United Nations and hinted at the use of force. Iran readily agreed to discussions but pushed ahead with its nuclear arms program.

In October 2006, while world leaders were focused on the Middle East and Iran, Kim Jong Il, the erratic leader of Communist North Korea (and son of Kim Il Sung), exploded that nation's first nuclear bomb. Fearing that North Korea might sell nuclear devices to terrorists or endanger its neighbors in East Asia, the United States persuaded the United Nations to impose economic sanctions against North Korea; this pushed North Korea to the negotiating table, but as had happened with Iran, talks dragged on without accomplishing much.

Concerns at Home

By the early 2000s, crime rates were dropping throughout the United States. Explanations varied. Some insisted that the "law and order" campaigns of the previous three decades had put the worst criminals in prison; others cited the general health of the economy.

But new types of "criminal behavior" remained at the center of national debate. In 2005, conservative congressmen proposed construction of a 2,000-mile fence along the border with Mexico to halt the flow of illegal immigrants into the United States. This provoked massive demonstrations among Hispanics in major cities throughout the United States. Politicians, who count heads, saw a lot of them; many legislators opposed the fence and called for liberalization of immigration laws.

Mexican workers hold placards at a rally for immigration reform on the National Mall in Washington, D.C., April 10, 2006.

Conservatives, however, voiced opposition, especially when Hispanic protesters carried Mexican flags. "If you want to fly the Mexican flag," observed Virgil Goode, a Republican Congressman from Virginia, "go to Mexico." In late 2006, Congress forged a compromise: the fence would be built, but its length reduced to 700 miles. In 2007, Congress deadlocked over whether to make it possible for illegal immigrants to gain U.S. citizenship.

Controversy roiled the nation's favorite pastime with accusations that baseball superstars had been using performance-enhancing—and illegal—steroids. In 2003, prosecutors launched an investigation against a San Francisco laboratory for concocting illegal steroids and selling them to the trainers of professional athletes. The next year, grand jury testimony in the case was leaked and published. (This violation of grand jury secrecy was also a crime!) The testimony indicated that baseball sluggers including Barry Bonds and Jason Giambi had likely used steroids. In 2005, after Oakland slugger José Canseco published a book claiming that many major leaguers used illegal steroids, Congress chided Major League Baseball for insufficient vigilance. The issue peaked in August 2007 when Bonds broke Hank Aaron's career record of 755 home runs.

If some new drugs enabled baseball players to hit more home runs, other kinds of controversial drugs and treatments held the promise of curing diseases. A potential advance along these lines emerged through stem cell research. Embryonic stem cells potentially generate every type of cell in the human body. Some scientists think it possible that transplanted stem cells might repair the damaged nerves of victims of Parkinson's disease or the dysfunctional pancreatic cells of diabetics. "Stem cells have already cured paralysis in animals," actor Christopher Reeve declared in 2004, a week before he died from complications of his long-term paralysis after a horse-riding accident. President Bush was among those who sought to limit embryonic stem-cell research because it entailed destruction of potential human life. In the absence of substantial federal support, universities, biotech firms, and states such as California and Connecticut funded stem cell research.

The health of the environment, which had preoccupied scientists and environmentalists for decades, also became a more urgent concern. In particular, global warming, though still a controversial issue, made steady gains in capturing national attention. In 1997, more than 140 nations, including the United States, meeting in Kyoto, Japan, signed an agreement to reduce emissions of carbon dioxide and other atmospheric pollutants. In 2001, President George W. Bush insisted that the Kyoto provisions would harm the U.S. economy; he withdrew the United States from the accords. But some states and municipalities, struggling to cope with smog and pollution, took matters into their own hands. In 2006 the mayors of over 200 U.S. cities signed a Climate Protection Agreement pledging to meet the Kyoto targets for greenhouse gas reductions by 2012. By 2007, Bush was calling for a more aggressive response as well, though he still opposed mandatory reductions.

Hurricane Katrina

Bush's interest in global warming had likely been stimulated by the ferocity of Hurricane Katrina, which swept across Florida and into the warm waters of the Gulf Coast in August 2005. State and federal officials ordered mandatory evacuation of the Louisiana coastline.

Millions fled in their cars, clogging the highways. But of the half million residents of New Orleans, 100,000 remained, many of them poor African Americans who lacked access to automobiles or who desperately awaited end-of-the month welfare or Social Security checks. As rain started to fall, some 10,000 people took refuge in the New Orleans Superdome stadium.

Early the next morning Katrina crashed ashore in full force. Within minutes, it destroyed nearly every building in Plaquemines Parish. By afternoon, the hurricane had moved north, dumping more water along the way, swelling the rivers, streams, and canals that emptied into the Gulf. Within hours, rising waters spilled over the banks and collapsed the canals. Then the levees at Lake Pontchartrain were breached, unloosing a torrent that flooded much of New Orleans.

Rural areas were hit equally hard. Waters rose so rapidly that thousands sought refuge on their roofs; many were drowned when rising waters trapped them in attics. At St. Rita's Nursing Home in St. Bernard Parish, water rose to the ceiling of the one-story building in 20 minutes. Frantic workers attempted to float bed-ridden elderly out of windows on mattresses; within an hour 35 were dead.

The aftermath of Hurricane Katrina in New Orleans. Many people took refuge in the Superdome and the Convention Center in downtown New Orleans, seen in the distance.

By that evening, much of New Orleans was underwater. Some 25,000 people crowded into the Superdome. Food and water grew scarce. Fights broke out. When officials locked the Superdome's doors, the thousands left outside went to the nearby Convention Center, surged past security guards, and took possession of the complex.

At first, no one comprehended the dimensions of the catastrophe. Communication systems failed. Over a million people had been displaced from their homes. In the heat and humidity, dead bodies, sewage, rotting food and plants, and factory effluents combined to form a fetid and toxic inland sea. The Convention Center, which soon housed 20,000, descended into anarchy. Throughout the storm-devastated region, looting became widespread; public order collapsed.

"Mr. President, we need your help," declared Louisiana Governor Kathleen Blanco. But TV crews arrived long before assistance from the Federal Emergency Management Agency (FEMA). Television viewers were outraged to see footage of the dead floating in pools of filth or abandoned in wheelchairs, and of people trapped in trees and on rooftops.

Yet Michael Chertoff, Secretary of Homeland Security which oversaw FEMA, expressed satisfaction with its efforts. "Considering the dire circumstances that we have in New Orleans, virtually a city that has been destroyed—things are going relatively well," he declared. By then, more than 1,300 people were dead.

Many shared in the blame. For decades, engineers had warned that the levees and canals in New Orleans could fail, but little was done to strengthen them. Environmentalists had complained of the overdevelopment and erosion of the coastal marshes and wetlands whose vegetation sponged up excess water, but their warnings, too, were mostly ignored. Officials in New Orleans had neglected to devise an evacuation plan for those without cars; worse, one-sixth of the police force abandoned the city before the storm struck. Mayor C. Ray Nagin inexplicably took refuge in the 27-story Hyatt; when he did venture down the stairs—the elevators ceased working when power failed—his statements were emotional and confused. In Washington, FEMA director Michael Brown was so worried about making a mistake that he failed to do much at all—the worse mistake possible. Bush erred in publicly complimenting the beleaguered FEMA director: "Brownie, you're doing a heck of a job," he said, a statement so obviously at variance with public perception that it became an instant joke. Within a week Brown was demoted; soon afterward he resigned.

Katrina was not the worst natural disaster in the nation's history. In 1900 a hurricane destroyed Galveston, then the largest city in Texas, killing 10,000. In 1906 an earthquake hit San Francisco, ignited hundreds of fires that burned 500 blocks of the city, and killed 700—a larger proportion of the population than perished in Katrina. But Katrina was disturbing quite apart from the terrible human toll: The hurricane pointed up the nation's vulnerability. How could the most powerful and prosperous nation in the world fail to respond promptly to the needs of its people? If Homeland Security could not get buses or water to New Orleans in a timely fashion, how could it protect the nation from determined terrorists or respond effectively should they mount another attack?

Iraq Insurgency Intensifies

Bush faltered during Katrina partly because he was distracted by Iraq. Ironically, the chaos left in the wake of Katrina in many ways paralleled the collapse of civil society in Iraq after Saddam. (A further irony: half of the Louisiana National Guard had been deployed to restore order in Iraq and thus were unavailable to restore order in Louisiana.) Iraq certainly needed all the help it could get. Insurgents blew up police stations and marketplaces, saboteurs destroyed power facilities and cut oil pipelines, and rival religious sects, tribes, warlords, and criminal gangs pushed the country toward anarchy.

While coalition forces attempted to halt the violence, political officials laid the foundations for a new Iraqi government. On June 28, 2004, the coalition transferred nominal authority to an Iraqi Governing Council whose chief task was to organize the election of a National Assembly to draft a constitution. As the date of the election neared—January 30, 2005—insurgents targeted polling places and warned voters to stay away. Nevertheless, nearly 8 million Iraqis went to the polls, almost two-thirds of the eligible voters.

The election, though fraught with irregularities, offered a glimpse of the democratic Iraq that Bush hoped would initiate a broader transformation of the Middle East. But the election also underscored the divisions within Iraq. In the north, the Kurdish majority won most of the seats; but they sought to form a Kurdish state and secede. In the south, the Shiites embraced a messianic strain of Islam and had strong ties to the radical Islamic clerics who ruled Iran. Iran, having fought Saddam's Iraq to a draw during the 1980s, had no wish to promote a strong and independent Iraq. The Sunnis, adherents of the version of Islam that prevailed in most of the Arab world from Saudi Arabia through North Africa, dominated the region around Baghdad. Saddam, himself a Sunni, had chosen Sunnis for most positions in his government. But the Sunnis constituted only 20 percent of Iraq's population; rather than participate in an election they would lose, Sunnis boycotted it and vowed to have nothing to do with the ensuing government. The post-Saddam Iraq was on the verge of fracturing into separate nations.

The Sunni boycott ensured that Shiites would dominate the new federal government, which quickly drafted a constitution. Article 2 embraced Islam as "the official religion of the state" and declared that no law could "contradict the undisputed rules of Islam." Article 15 held that "every Iraqi has the right to life and security and freedom." Yet Islam proscribed many types of behavior and expression, especially pertaining to women's rights. An explicitly Islamic state was incompatible with individual freedom. The Iraqi constitution, like so much of the new nation, attempted to reconcile the irreconcilable. Nevertheless, on October 15, 2005, Iraqi voters endorsed it by a 3 to 1 margin.

Complicating matters further was the decision by terrorists to wreck the new government by driving a deeper wedge between Sunnis and Shiites. On February 22, 2006, insurgents blew up the golden dome of the Askariya Mosque in Sammara, a Shiite shrine. Enraged Shiites attacked Sunni mosques and clerics, triggering an

A female U.S. soldier at the site of a bombing attack that killed another soldier on a convoy near Sammara, Iraq.

endless cycle of reprisals. Some Iraqi military and police officers formed extralegal death squads to eliminate Sunni leaders and terrorize their followers. Sunni militias responded in kind.

In the fall of 2006, an Iraqi tribunal convicted Saddam of killing 148 Shiites, the first of several planned trials to chronicle his regime's genocide. But on December 30, 2006 the Iraqi government dispatched Saddam to the gallows. Instead of marking the triumph of law over tyranny, the executioners resembled the Shiite death squads: Hangmen taunted Saddam and chanted the name of Muqtada Al Sadr, a Shiite cleric whose militias caused much of the chaos.

American officials groped their way through the bewildering labyrinth of Iraqi politics and religion. In principle, the United States sought to weaken and isolate Iran, yet the American insistence on democratizing Iraq ensured the electoral triumph of Iraqi Shiites who had already allied with their Iranian neighbors. Conversely, American policymakers encouraged the Shiite-dominated Iraqi government to bring Sunnis into the administration. But many Shiites thought this absurd: Since Sunnis were behind the insurgency, why should Sunnis be brought into the government? For their part, most Sunni leaders believed that, as a distinct minority, they would derive little benefit from any role in a democratic Iraq. They blamed the United States for putting the Shiites in power.

U.S. policies offended everyone. Often the only apparent issue uniting Iraqi factions was their condemnation of the presence of "infidel" troops in Iraq. Yet thoughtful Iraqis conceded that in the absence of American soldiers, Iraq would likely fracture, plunging the country into full-scale civil war and perhaps setting the entire Middle East ablaze. Bush decided to persist.

Attacks on security forces and civilians intensified. In 2003, about thirty attacks occurred each day; but by 2005, this had increased to seventy and by the fall of

2006, to more than one hundred. Casualties mounted. As the 2006 U.S. congressional elections approached, the war cost $2 billion a week; the annual U.S. deficit soared to a half trillion dollars. Democrats, most of whom had voted for the war initially, increasingly withdrew their support for the war. Some Republicans, too, defected from the president's position.

When the midterm votes were counted, the Republicans were decisively defeated. Democrats gained thirty-one seats in the House of Representatives and five seats in the Senate; they now controlled Congress—and the budget. Several days after the election Bush dismissed Defense Secretary Rumsfeld, acknowledging voter "displeasure with the lack of progress in Iraq." But the president vowed to remain. "America's going to stand with you," Bush promised Iraqi leaders.

Democrats named Nancy Pelosi Speaker of the House of Representatives, the first woman to hold that position. Insofar as the speaker follows the vice president in chain of succession, Pelosi became the highest-ranking woman ever to hold office in the United States. In January 2007, when Bush called for a modest increase in troop levels in Iraq, Pelosi and the Democrats opposed the measure. The Democratic leadership in Congress voted to reduce funding for the war, actions Bush vetoed.

By the summer of 2007, attacks had increased to over 150 a day. The death toll of American military personnel approached 4,000. American troops had been in Iraq longer than their forefathers had fought in World War II. No end seemed in sight.

Button commemorating the choice of Nancy Pelosi of California as the new Speaker of the House in January 2007.

DO HISTORIANS EVER GET IT RIGHT?

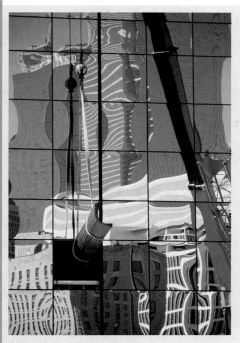

The Debating the Past essays in previous chapters have offered hundreds of interpretations, many of them contradictory. Why, if historians are looking at the same past, do they see it so differently?

Consider the photograph (*left*). It shows a cityscape as reflected on the many windows of a new skyscraper. Each pane of glass has its own angle of reflection, imposing unique distortions on the scene; note that one window—all black—is open, about to receive a pipe. Historians, too, look at the past from different perspectives, and sometimes crucial pieces of evidence are missing.

Well into the twentieth century, most historians believed that their collective labors—more research, more books—were leading to a composite picture that provided a fuller and clearer rendering of the past. But some recent historians have doubted whether their profession can sharpen the picture's focus, or whether a coherent vista of "the past" even existed. If our own lives are a jumble of motivations and confusions, how can one think it possible to paint a portrait of an entire people?

In an exhaustive study of the American Historical Association, Peter Novick (1988) further demonstrated that while historians have long championed objectivity in principle, their research has been riddled with bias. Ignorant of their cultural blinders, historians grope for historical truths they can never see.

By undercutting their profession's claims of "truth," Novick's book made historians more susceptible to an idea that was sweeping through literature departments. Known as "deconstruction" or "textualism" and derived from French philosopher Jacques Derrida, it held that "there is nothing outside the text." (Or, to use the metaphor of the photograph, there is nothing beyond the reflections.) No one could reasonably claim to know what a novelist meant by any novel, or what any statesman or historical figure meant by the words he or she spoke or wrote. By extension, no historian can explain what any historical record meant to the people of the times it reflected. Inspired by such observations, Robert F. Berkhofer Jr. (1995) repudiated the very idea of a grand historical narrative, partly because readers would interpret that narrative in their own ways. Raising Berkhofer's contention at the end of a book that purports to provide just such a narrative may seem perverse. But his point contains an obvious truth: Readers of any work of history, this one included, will make of it what they will.

Peter Novick, *That Noble Dream* (1988), Robert F. Berkhofer Jr., *Beyond the Great Story* (1995), Jacques Derrida, *Deconstruction in a Nutshell* (1997).

The Persistent Past and Imponderable Future

This book affirms the connectedness of time. Although we inhabit the shores of the present, the waves of the past, originating far in the distance, continuously touch our lives. Sometimes they ebb and flow so gently we can scarcely perceive them, and sometimes they form huge breakers that come crashing down on us.

The introductions at the beginning of each chapter have illuminated these points of intersection. The most obvious illustration of the persistence of the past is the existence of the American nation itself. But sometimes we forget how subtly decisions that were debated over two centuries ago influence our lives. The past is never truly past. It radiates through time. It affects our lives, just as what we do today will influence the future. By connecting to the past, we understand our own lives better; and we perhaps understand as well the difficulties of making predictions about the future.

Just about everything that happens in one part of the modern world is in some way related to everything else that is going on. Far too many things are happening for anyone to sort out which is going to have what effect on tomorrow's events, let alone those that occur a year from now. "Then" (whether tomorrow or next year) historians will be able to study those particular events and puzzle out their chief causes—but not "now."

Yet "now" is where we happen to be, and thus this book, so full of events and their causes and results, must end inconclusively. No one knows what will happen next. But not knowing what will happen is one reason why life is so interesting.

Milestones

1988	Republican George H. W. Bush elected president
1989	Gorbachev allows Eastern European nations to establish independent democratic governments
1990	Iraq invades Kuwait
	Germany is reunited
1991	UN Forces, led by the United States, drive Iraqi forces from Kuwait
	Soviet Union is dissolved; Boris Yeltsin becomes president of Russia
1992	Democrat Bill Clinton elected president
1993	Ruth Bader Ginsberg becomes second woman associate justice of the Supreme Court
	Bomb explodes in parking garage of World Trade Center in New York, killing six and injuring 1,000
1994	Republicans win control of both houses of Congress
	Congress defeats Clinton's health care reform plan
1995	Terrorist bomb destroys Alfred P. Murrah Federal Building in Oklahoma City, killing 169

1996	Democrat Bill Clinton is reelected president, Republicans retain control of Congress.
	Measure revamping federal welfare system is passed by Congress and signed by President Clinton
1998	Clinton is impeached by House of Representatives
1999	Clinton is acquitted by Senate and remains president
	NATO troops, including Americans, are sent to Kosovo to stop Serbian "Ethnic Cleansing"
	Gun violence in schools escalates; twelve die at Columbine High School in Colorado
2000	Republican George W. Bush becomes president when Supreme Court halts Florida recounts
2001	Terrorists fly airliners into World Trade Center in New York and into Pentagon in Washington, D.C.; third hijacked airliner crashes in Pennsylvania when passengers storm hijackers
	United States attacks and defeats Taliban in Afghanistan
2002	President Bush prepares for war as he accuses Saddam Hussein of Iraq of developing weapons of mass destruction
2003	U.S. and United Kingdom attack and defeat Iraq and capture Saddam Hussein
	Hostilities persist in Iraq
2004	George W. Bush is reelected president
2005	Bush appoints Condoleeza Rice Secretary of State, the first African American woman in that position
	Hurricane Katrina devastates New Orleans and Gulf Coast region
2007	Democrat Nancy Pelosi becomes first woman Speaker of the House
	Deranged student kills thirty-three at Virginia Tech

The Declaration of Independence

The Constitution of the United States of America

Amendments to the Constitution

Supplementary Reading

Present-Day United States

Present-Day World

For additional reference material, including suggested websites, go to www.longmanamericanhistory.com

The Declaration of Independence

In Congress, July 4, 1776

The Unanimous Declaration
of the Thirteen United States of America,

When, in the course of human events, it becomes necessary for one people to dissolve the political bonds which have connected them with another, and to assume, among the powers of the earth, the separate and equal station to which the laws of nature and of nature's God entitle them, a decent respect to the opinions of mankind requires that they should declare the causes which impel them to the separation.

We hold these truths to be self-evident: That all men are created equal; that they are endowed by their Creator with certain unalienable rights; that among these are life, liberty, and the pursuit of happiness; that, to secure these rights, governments are instituted among men, deriving their just powers from the consent of the governed; that whenever any form of government becomes destructive of these ends, it is the right of the people to alter or to abolish it, and to institute new government, laying its foundation on such principles, and organizing its powers in such form, as to them shall seem most likely to effect their safety and happiness. Prudence, indeed, will dictate that governments long established should not be changed for light and transient causes; and accordingly all experience hath shown that mankind are more disposed to suffer, while evils are sufferable, than to right themselves by abolishing the forms to which they are accustomed. But when a long train of abuses and usurpations, pursuing invariably the same object, evinces a design to reduce them under absolute despotism, it is their right, it is their duty, to throw off such government, and to provide new guards for their future security. Such has been the patient sufferance of these colonies; and such is now the necessity which constrains them to alter their former systems of government. The history of the present King of Great Britain is a history of repeated injuries and usurpations, all having in direct object the establishment of an absolute tyranny over these states. To prove this, let facts be submitted to a candid world.

He has refused his assent to laws, the most wholesome and necessary for the public good.

He has forbidden his governors to pass laws of immediate and pressing importance, unless suspended in their operation till his assent should be obtained; and, when so suspended, he has utterly neglected to attend to them.

He has refused to pass other laws for the accommodation of large districts of people, unless those people would relinquish the right of representation in the legislature, a right inestimable to them, and formidable to tyrants only.

He has called together legislative bodies at places unusual, uncomfortable, and distant from the depository of their public records, for the sole purpose of fatiguing them into compliance with his measures.

He has dissolved representative houses repeatedly, for opposing, with manly firmness, his invasions on the rights of the people.

He has refused for a long time, after such dissolutions, to cause others to be elected; whereby the legislative powers, incapable of annihilation, have returned to the people at large for their exercise; the state remaining, in the mean time, exposed to all the dangers of invasions from without and convulsions within.

He has endeavored to prevent the population of these states; for that purpose obstructing the laws for naturalization of foreigners; refusing to pass others to encourage their migration hither, and raising the conditions of new appropriations of lands.

He has obstructed the administration of justice, by refusing his assent to laws for establishing judiciary powers.

He has made judges dependent on his will alone, for the tenure of their offices, and the amount and payment of their salaries.

He has erected a multitude of new offices, and sent hither swarms of officers to harass our people and eat out their substance.

He has kept among us, in times of peace, standing armies, without the consent of our legislatures.

He has affected to render the military independent of, and superior to, the civil power.

He has combined with others to subject us to a jurisdiction foreign to our constitution, and unacknowledged by our laws, giving his assent to their acts of pretended legislation:

For quartering large bodies of armed troops among us;

For protecting them, by a mock trial, from punishment for any murder which they should commit on the inhabitants of these states;

For cutting off our trade with all parts of the world;

For imposing taxes on us without our consent;

For depriving us, in many cases, of the benefits of trial by jury;

For transporting us beyond seas, to be tried for pretended offenses;

For abolishing the free system of English laws in a neighboring province, establishing therein an arbitrary government, and enlarging its boundaries, so as to render it at once an example and fit instrument for introducing the same absolute rule into these colonies;

For taking away our charters, abolishing our most valuable laws, and altering fundamentally the forms of our governments;

For suspending our own legislatures, and declaring themselves invested with power to legislate for us in all cases whatsoever.

He has abdicated government here, by declaring us out of his protection and waging war against us.

He has plundered our seas, ravaged our coasts, burned our towns, and destroyed the lives of our people.

He is at this time transporting large armies of foreign mercenaries to complete the works of death, desolation, and tyranny already begun with circumstances of cruelty and perfidy scarcely paralleled in the most barbarous ages, and totally unworthy the head of a civilized nation.

He has constrained our fellow-citizens, taken captive on the high seas, to bear arms against their country, to become the executioners of their friends and brethren, or to fall themselves by their hands.

He has excited domestic insurrection among us, and has endeavored to bring on the inhabitants of our frontiers the merciless Indian savages, whose known rule of warfare is an undistinguished destruction of all ages, sexes, and conditions.

In every stage of these oppressions we have petitioned for redress in the most humble terms; our repeated petitions have been answered only by repeated injury. A prince, whose character is thus marked by every act which may define a tyrant, is unfit to be the ruler of a free people.

Nor have we been wanting in our attentions to our British brethren. We have warned them, from time to time, of attempts by their legislature to extend an unwarrantable jurisdiction over us. We have reminded them of the circumstances of our emigration and settlement here. We have appealed to their native justice and magnanimity; and we have conjured them, by the ties of our common kindred, to disavow these usurpations, which would inevitably interrupt our connections and correspondence. They, too, have been deaf to the voice of justice and of consanguinity. We must, therefore, acquiesce in the necessity which denounces our separation, and hold them, as we hold the rest of mankind, enemies in war, in peace friends.

We, therefore, the representatives of the United States of America, in General Congress assembled, appealing to the Supreme Judge of the world for the rectitude of our intentions, do, in the name and by the authority of the good people of these colonies, solemnly publish and declare, that these United Colonies are, and of right ought to be, FREE AND INDEPENDENT STATES; that they are absolved from all allegiance to the British crown, and that all political connection between them and the state of Great Britain is, and ought to be, totally dissolved; and that, as free and independent states, they have full power to levy war, conclude peace, contract alliances, establish commerce, and do all other acts and things which independent states may of right do. And for the support of this declaration, with a firm reliance on the protection of Divine Providence, we mutually pledge to each other our lives, our fortunes, and our sacred honor.

JOHN HANCOCK

Button Gwinnett
Lyman Hall
Geo. Walton
Wm. Hooper
Joseph Hewes
John Penn
Edward Rutledge
Thos. Heyward, Junr.
Thomas Lynch, Junr.
Arthur Middleton
Samuel Chase
Wm. Paca
Thos. Stone
Charles Carroll of
  Carrollton
George Wythe
Richard Henry Lee
Th. Jefferson
Benj. Harrison

Thos. Nelson, Jr
Francis Lightfoot Lee
Carter Braxton
Robt. Morris
Benjamin Rush
Benja. Franklin
John Morton
Geo. Clymer
Jas. Smith
Geo. Taylor
James Wilson
Geo. Ross
Caesar Rodney
Geo. Read
Tho. M'Kean
Wm. Floyd
Phil. Livingston
Frans. Lewis
Lewis Morris

Richd. Stockton
Jno. Witherspoon
Fras. Hopkinson
John Hart
Abra. Clark
Josiah Bartlett
Wm. Whipple
Saml. Adams
John Adams
Robt. Treat Paine
Eldbridge Gerry
Step. Hopkins
William Ellery
Roger Sherman
Sam'el Huntington
Wm. Williams
Oliver Wolcott
Matthew Thornton

The Constitution of the United States of America

PREAMBLE

We the People of the United States, in Order to form a more perfect Union, establish Justice, insure domestic Tranquility, provide for the common defence, promote the general Welfare, and secure the Blessings of Liberty to ourselves and our Posterity, do ordain and establish this Constitution for the United States of America.

ARTICLE 1

Section 1

All legislative Powers herein granted shall be vested in a Congress of the United States, which shall consist of a Senate and House of Representatives.

Section 2

The House of Representatives shall be composed of Members chosen every second Year by the People of the several States, and the Electors in each State shall have the Qualifications requisite for Electors of the most numerous Branch of the State Legislature.

No Person shall be a Representative who shall not have attained to the Age of twenty five Years, and been seven Years a Citizen of the United States, and who shall not, when elected, be an inhabitant of that State in which he shall be chosen.

Representatives and direct Taxes shall be apportioned among the several States which may be included within this Union, according to their respective Numbers, *which shall be determined by adding to the whole Number of free Persons, including those bound to Service for a Term of Years, and excluding Indians not taxed, three fifths of all other Persons.** The actual Enumeration shall be made within three Years after the first Meeting of the Congress of the United States, and within every subsequent Term of ten Years, in such Manner as they shall by Law direct. The Number of Representatives shall not exceed one for every thirty Thousand, but each State shall have at Least one Representative; *and until such enumeration shall be made, the State of New Hampshire shall be entitled to chuse three, Massachusetts eight, Rhode-Island and Providence Plantations one, Connecticut five, New York six, New Jersey four, Pennsylvania eight, Delaware one, Maryland six, Virginia ten, North Carolina five, South Carolina five, and Georgia three.*

When vacancies happen in the Representation from any State, the Executive Authority thereof shall issue Writs of Election to fill such Vacancies.

The House of Representatives shall chuse their Speaker and other Officers; and shall have the sole Power of Impeachment.

Section 3

The Senate of the United States shall be composed of two Senators from each State, *chosen by the Legislature thereof,* for six Years; and each Senator shall have one Vote.

Immediately after they shall be assembled in Consequence of the first Election, they shall be divided as equally as may be into three Classes. The Seats of the Senators of the first Class shall be vacated at the Expiration of the second Year, of the second Class at the Expiration of the fourth Year, and of the third Class at the Expiration of the sixth Year so that one third may be chosen every second Year; and if Vacancies

---

Passages no longer in effect are printed in italic type.

happen by Resignation, or otherwise, during the Recess of the Legislature of any state, the Executive thereof may make temporary Appointments until the next Meeting of the Legislature, which shall then fill such Vacancies.

No Person shall be a Senator who shall not have attained to the Age of thirty Years, and been nine Years a Citizen of the United States, and who shall not, when elected, be an Inhabitant of that State for which he shall be chosen.

The Vice President of the United States shall be President of the Senate, but shall have no Vote, unless they be equally divided.

The Senate shall chuse their other Officers, and also a President *pro tempore,* in the Absence of the Vice President, or when he shall exercise the Office of President of the United States.

The Senate shall have the sole Power to try all Impeachments. When sitting for that Purpose, they shall be on Oath or Affirmation. When the President of the United States is tried the Chief Justice shall preside: And no Person shall be convicted without the Concurrence of two thirds of the Members present.

Judgment in Cases of Impeachment shall not extend further than to removal from Office, and disqualification to hold and enjoy any Office of honor, Trust or Profit under the United States: but the Party convicted shall nevertheless be liable and subject to Indictment, Trial, Judgment and Punishment, according to Law.

Section 4

The Times, Places and Manner of holding Elections for Senators and Representatives, shall be prescribed in each State by the Legislature thereof; but the Congress may at any time by Law make or alter such Regulations, except as to the Places of chusing Senators.

The Congress shall assemble at least once in every Year, *and such Meeting shall be on the first Monday in December, unless they shall by Law appoint a different Day.*

Section 5

Each House shall be the Judge of the Elections, Returns and Qualifications of its own Members, and a Majority of each shall constitute a Quorum to do Business; but a smaller Number may adjourn from day to day, and may be authorized to compel the Attendance of absent Members, in such Manner, and under such Penalties as each House may provide.

Each House may determine the Rules of its Proceedings, punish its Members for disorderly Behaviour, and, with the Concurrence of two thirds, expel a Member.

Each House shall keep a Journal of its Proceedings, and from time to time publish the same, excepting such Parts as may in their Judgment require Secrecy; and the Yeas and Nays of the Members of either House on any question shall, at the Desire of one fifth of those Present, be entered on the Journal.

Neither House, during the Session of Congress, shall, without the Consent of the other, adjourn for more than three days, nor to any other Place than that in which the two Houses shall be sitting.

Section 6

The Senators and Representatives shall receive a Compensation for their Services, to be ascertained by Law, and paid out of the Treasury of the United States. They shall in all Cases, except Treason, Felony and Breach of the Peace, be privileged from Arrest during their Attendance at the Session of their respective Houses, and in going to and returning from the same; and for any Speech or Debate in either House, they shall not be questioned in any other Place.

No Senator or Representative shall, during the Time for which he was elected, be appointed to any civil Office under the Authority of the United States, which shall have been created, or the Emoluments whereof shall have been encreased during such time, and no Person holding any Office under the United States, shall be a Member of either House during his Continuance in Office.

Section 7

All Bills for raising Revenue shall originate in the House of Representatives; but the Senate may propose or concur with Amendments as on other Bills.

Every Bill which shall have passed the House of Representatives and the Senate, shall, before it become a Law, be presented to the President of the United States; If he approve he shall sign it, but if not he shall return it, with his Objections to the House in which it shall have originated, who shall enter the Objections at large on their Journal, and proceed to reconsider it. If after such Reconsideration two thirds of that House shall agree to pass the Bill, it shall be sent, together with the Objections, to the other House, by which it shall likewise be reconsidered, and if approved by two thirds of that House, it shall become a Law. But in all such Cases the Votes of both Houses shall be determined by Yeas and Nays, and the Names of the Persons voting for and against the Bill shall be entered on the Journal of each House respectively. If any Bill shall not be returned by the President within ten Days (Sundays excepted) after it shall have been presented to him, the Same shall be a Law, in like Manner as if he had signed it, unless the Congress by their Adjournment prevent its Return, in which Case it shall not be a Law.

Every Order, Resolution, or Vote to which the Concurrence of the Senate and House of Representatives may be necessary (except on a question of Adjournment) shall be presented to the President of the United States; and before the Same shall take Effect, shall be approved by him, or being disapproved by him, shall be repassed by two thirds of the Senate and House of Representatives, according to the Rules and Limitations prescribed in the Case of a Bill.

Section 8

The Congress shall have Power To lay and collect Taxes, Duties, Imposts and Excises, to pay the Debts and provide for the common Defence and general Welfare of the United States; but all Duties, Imposts and Excises shall be uniform throughout the United States;

To borrow Money on the credit of the United States;

To regulate Commerce with foreign Nations, and among the several States, and with the Indian Tribes;

To establish an uniform Rule of Naturalization, and uniform Laws on the subject of Bankruptcies throughout the United States;

To coin Money, regulate the Value thereof, and of foreign Coin, and fix the Standard of Weights and Measures;

To provide for the Punishment of counterfeiting the Securities and current Coin of the United States;

To establish Post Offices and post Roads;

To promote the Progress of Science and useful Arts, by securing for limited Times to Authors and Inventors the exclusive Right to their respective Writings and Discoveries;

To constitute Tribunals inferior to the supreme Court;

To define and punish Piracies and Felonies committed on the high Seas, and Offences against the Law of Nations;

To declare War, grant Letters of Marque and Reprisal, and make Rules concerning Captures on Land and Water;

To raise and support Armies, but no Appropriation of Money to that Use shall be for a longer Term than two Years;

To provide and maintain a Navy;

To make Rules for the Government and Regulation of the land and naval Forces;

To provide for calling forth the Militia to execute the Laws of the Union, suppress Insurrections and repel Invasions;

To provide for organizing, arming, and disciplining, the Militia, and for governing such Part of them as may be employed in the Service of the United States, reserving to the States respectively, the Appointment of the Officers, and the Authority of training the Militia according to the discipline prescribed by Congress;

To exercise exclusive Legislation in all Cases whatsoever, over such District (not exceeding ten Miles square) as may, by Cession of particular States, and the Acceptance of Congress, become the Seat of the Government of the United States, and to exercise like Authority over all Places purchased by the Consent of the Legislature of the State in which the Same shall be, for the Erection of Forts, Magazines, Arsenals, dock-Yards, and other needful Buildings;—And

To make all Laws which shall be necessary and proper for carrying into Execution the foregoing Powers, and all other Powers vested by this Constitution in the Government of the United States, or in any Department or Officer thereof.

Section 9

The Migration or Importation of such Persons as any of the States now existing shall think proper to admit, shall not be prohibited by the Congress prior to the Year one thousand eight hundred and eight, but a Tax or duty may be imposed on such Importation, not exceeding ten dollars for each Person.

The Privilege of the Writ of Habeas Corpus shall not be suspended, unless when in Cases of Rebellion or Invasion the public Safety may require it.

No Bill of Attainder or ex post facto Law shall be passed.

No Capitation, or other direct, Tax shall be laid, unless in Proportion to the Census or Enumeration herein before directed to be taken.

No Tax or Duty shall be laid on Articles exported from any State.

No Preference shall be given by any Regulation of Commerce or Revenue to the Ports of one State over those of another: nor shall Vessels bound to, or from, one State, be obliged to enter, clear, or pay Duties in another.

No Money shall be drawn from the Treasury, but in Consequence of Appropriations made by Law; and a regular Statement and Account of the Receipts and Expenditures of all public Money shall be published from time to time.

No Title of Nobility shall be granted by the United States: And no Person holding any Office of Profit or Trust under them, shall, without the Consent of the Congress, accept of any present, Emolument, Office, or Title, of any kind whatever, from any King, Prince, or foreign State.

Section 10

No State shall enter into any Treaty, Alliance, or Confederation; grant Letters of Marque and Reprisal; coin Money; emit Bills of Credit; make any Thing but gold and silver Coin a Tender in Payment of Debts; pass any Bill of Attainder, ex post facto Law, or Law impairing the obligation of Contracts, or grant any Title of Nobility.

No State shall, without the Consent of the Congress, lay any Imposts or Duties on Imports or Exports, except what may be absolutely necessary for executing its inspection Laws: and the net Produce of all Duties and Imposts, laid by any State on Imports or Exports, shall be for the Use of the Treasury of the United States; and all such Laws shall be subject to the Revision and Controul of the Congress.

No State shall, without the Consent of Congress, lay any Duty of Tonnage, keep Troops, or Ships of War in time of Peace, enter into any Agreement or Compact with another State, or with a foreign Power, or engage in War, unless actually invaded, or in such imminent Danger as will not admit of delay.

ARTICLE II

Section 1

The executive Power shall be vested in a President of the United States of America. He shall hold his Office during the Term of four Years, and, together with the Vice President, chosen for the same Term, be elected, as follows:

Each State shall appoint, in such Manner as the Legislature thereof may direct, a Number of Electors, equal to the whole Number of Senators and Representatives to which the State may be entitled in the Congress: but no Senator or Representative, or Person holding an Office of Trust or Profit under the United States, shall be appointed an Elector.

The Electors shall meet in their respective States, and vote by Ballot for two Persons, of whom one at least shall not be an Inhabitant of the same State with themselves. And they shall make a List of all the

Persons voted for, and of the Number of Votes for each; which List they shall sign and certify, and transmit sealed to the Seat of the Government of the United States, directed to the President of the Senate. The President of the Senate shall, in the Presence of the Senate and House of Representatives, open all the Certificates, and the Votes shall then be counted. The Person having the greatest Number of Votes shall be the President, if such Number be a Majority of the whole number of Electors appointed; and if there be more than one who have such Majority, and have an equal Number of Votes, then the House of Representatives shall immediately chuse by Ballot one of them for President; and if no Person have a Majority, then from the five highest on the List the said House shall in like Manner chuse the President. But in chusing the President, the Votes shall be taken by States, the Representation from each State having one Vote; A quorum for this Purpose shall consist of a Member or Members from two thirds of the States, and a Majority of all the States shall be necessary to a Choice. In every Case, after the Choice of the President, the Person having the greatest Number of Votes of the Electors shall be the Vice President. But if there should remain two or more who have equal Votes, the Senate shall chuse from them by Ballot the Vice President.

The Congress may determine the time of chusing the Electors, and the Day on which they shall give their Votes; which Day shall be the same throughout the United States.

No person except a natural born Citizen, or a Citizen of the United States, at the time of the Adoption of this Constitution, shall be eligible to the Office of President; neither shall any Person be eligible to that Office who shall not have attained to the Age of thirty five Years, and been fourteen Years a Resident within the United States.

In Case of the Removal of the President from Office, or of his Death, Resignation, or Inability to discharge the Powers and Duties of the said Office, the Same shall devolve on the Vice President, and the Congress may by Law provide for the Case of Removal, Death, Resignation or Inability, both of the President and Vice President, declaring what Officer shall then act as President, and such Officer shall act accordingly, until the Disability be removed, or a President shall be elected.

The President shall, at stated Times, receive for his Services, a Compensation, which shall neither be encreased nor diminished during the Period for which he shall have been elected, and he shall not receive within that period any other Emolument from the United States, or any of them.

Before he enter on the Execution of his Office, he shall take the following Oath or Affirmation:— "I do solemnly swear (or affirm) that I will faithfully execute the Office of President of the United States, and will to the best of my Ability, preserve, protect and defend the Constitution of the United States."

Section 2

The President shall be Commander in Chief of the Army and Navy of the United States, and of the Militia of the several States, when called into the actual Service of the United States; he may require the Opinion, in writing, of the principal Officer in each of the executive Departments, upon any Subject relating to the Duties of their respective Offices, and he shall have Power to grant Reprieves and Pardons for Offences against the United States, except in Cases of Impeachment.

He shall have Power, by and with the Advice and Consent of the Senate, to make Treaties, provided two thirds of the Senators present concur; and he shall nominate, and by and with the Advice and Consent of the Senate, shall appoint Ambassadors, other public Ministers and Consuls, Judges of the supreme Court, and all other Officers of the United States, whose Appointments are not herein otherwise provided for, and which shall be established by Law: but the Congress may by Law vest the Appointment of such inferior Officers, as they think proper in the President alone, in the Courts of Law, or in the Heads of Departments.

The President shall have Power to fill up all Vacancies that may happen during the Recess of the Senate, by granting Commissions which shall expire at the End of their next Session.

Section 3

He shall from time to time give to the Congress Information of the State of the Union, and recommend to their Consideration such Measures as he shall judge necessary and expedient; he may, on extraordinary Occasions, convene both Houses, or either of them, and in Case of disagreement between them, with Respect to the Time of Adjournment, he may adjourn them to such Time as he shall think proper; he shall receive Ambassadors and other public Ministers; he shall take Care that the Laws be faithfully executed, and shall Commission all the officers of the United States.

Section 4

The President, Vice President and all civil Officers of the United States, shall be removed from Office on Impeachment for, and Conviction of, Treason, Bribery or other high Crimes and Misdemeanors.

ARTICLE III

Section 1

The judicial Power of the United States, shall be vested in one supreme Court, and in such inferior Courts as the Congress may from time to time ordain and establish. The Judges, both of the supreme and inferior Courts, shall hold their offices during good Behaviour, and shall, at stated Times, receive for their Services, a Compensation, which shall not be diminished during their Continuance in Office.

Section 2

The judicial Power shall extend to all Cases, in Law and Equity, arising under this Constitution, the Laws of the United States, and Treaties made, or which shall be made, under their Authority;—to all Cases affecting Ambassadors, other public Ministers and Consuls;—to all Cases of admiralty and maritime Jurisdiction;—to Controversies to which the United States shall be a Party;—to Controversies between two or more States;—*between a State and Citizens of another State;*—between Citizens of different States;—between Citizens of the same State claiming Lands under Grants of different States, and between a State, or the Citizens thereof, and foreign States, Citizens or Subjects.

In all Cases affecting Ambassadors, other public Ministers and Consuls, and those in which a State shall be Party, the supreme Court shall have original Jurisdiction. In all the other Cases before mentioned, the supreme Court shall have appellate Jurisdiction, both as to Law and Fact, with such Exceptions, and under such Regulations as the Congress shall make.

The Trial of all Crimes, except in Cases of Impeachment, shall be by Jury; and such Trial shall be held in the State where the said Crimes shall have been committed, but when not committed within any State, the Trial shall be at such Place or Places as the Congress may by Law have directed.

Section 3

Treason against the United States, shall consist only in levying War against them, or in adhering to their Enemies, giving them Aid and Comfort. No person shall be convicted of Treason unless on the Testimony of two Witnesses to the same overt Act, or on Confession in open Court.

The Congress shall have Power to declare the Punishment of Treason, but no Attainder of Treason shall work Corruption of Blood, or Forfeiture except during the Life of the Person attainted.

ARTICLE IV

Section 1

Full Faith and Credit shall be given in each State to the public Acts, Records, and judicial Proceedings of every other State. And the Congress may by general Laws prescribe the Manner in which such Acts, Records and Proceedings shall be proved, and the Effect thereof.

Section 2

The Citizens of each State shall be entitled to all Privileges and Immunities of Citizens in the several States.

A Person charged in any State with Treason, Felony, or other Crime, who shall flee from Justice, and be found in another State, shall on Demand of the executive Authority of the State from which he fled, be delivered up, to be removed to the State having Jurisdiction of the Crime.

No Person held to Service or Labour in one State, under the Laws thereof, escaping into another, shall, in Consequence of any Law or Regulation therein, be discharged from such Service or Labour, but shall be delivered up on Claim of the Party to whom such Service or Labour may be due.

Section 3

New States may be admitted by the Congress into this Union; but no new State shall be formed or erected within the Jurisdiction of any other State; nor any State be formed by the Junction of two or more States, or Parts of States, without the Consent of the Legislatures of the States concerned as well as of the Congress.

The Congress shall have Power to dispose of and make all needful Rules and Regulations respecting the Territory or other Property belonging to the United States; and nothing in this Constitution shall be so construed as to Prejudice any Claims of the United States, or of any particular States.

Section 4

The United States shall guarantee to every State in this Union a Republican Form of Government, and shall protect each of them against Invasion; and on Application of the Legislature, or of the Executive (when the Legislature cannot be convened) against domestic violence.

ARTICLE V

The Congress, whenever two thirds of both Houses shall deem it necessary, shall propose Amendments to this Constitution, or, on the Application of the Legislatures of two thirds of the several States, shall call a Convention for proposing Amendments, which, in either Case, shall be valid to all Intents and Purposes, as Part of this Constitution, when ratified by the Legislatures of three fourths of the several States, or by Conventions in three fourths thereof, as the one or the other Mode of Ratification may be proposed by the Congress; Provided *that no Amendment which may be made prior to the Year One thousand eight hundred and eight shall in any Manner affect the first and fourth Clauses in the Ninth Section of the first Article;* and that no State, without its Consent, shall be deprived of its equal Suffrage in the Senate.

ARTICLE VI

All Debts contracted and Engagements entered into, before the Adoption of this Constitution, shall be as valid against the United States under this Constitution, as under the Confederation.

This Constitution, and Laws of the United States which shall be made in Pursuance thereof; and all Treaties made, or which shall be made, under the Authority of the United States, shall be the supreme Law of the Land; and the Judges in every State shall be bound thereby, any Thing in the Constitution or Laws of any State to the Contrary notwithstanding.

The Senators and Representatives before mentioned, and the Members of the several State Legislatures, and all executive and Judicial Officers, both of the United States and of the several States, shall be bound by Oath or Affirmation, to support this Constitution; but no religious Test shall ever be required as a Qualification to any Office of public Trust under the United States.

ARTICLE VII

The Ratification of the Conventions of nine States, shall be sufficient for the Establishment of this Constitution between the States so ratifying the Same.

Done in Convention by the Unanimous Consent of the States present the Seventeenth Day of September in the Year of our Lord one thousand seven hundred and Eighty seven and of the Independence of the United States of America the Twelfth.[*] IN WITNESS whereof We have hereunto subscribed our Names,

GEORGE WASHINGTON
President and Deputy from Virginia

Delaware
GEORGE READ
GUNNING BEDFORD, JR.
JOHN DICKINSON
RICHARD BASSETT
JACOB BROOM

Maryland
JAMES MCHENRY
DANIEL OF ST. THOMAS JENIFER
DANIEL CARROLL

Virginia
JOHN BLAIR
JAMES MADISON, JR.

North Carolina
WILLIAM BLOUNT
RICHARD DOBBS SPRAIGHT
HUGH WILLIAMSON

South Carolina
JOHN RUTLEDGE
CHARLES COTESWORTH PINCKNEY
CHARLES PINCKNEY
PIERCE BUTLER

Georgia
WILLIAM FEW
ABRAHAM BALDWIN

New Hampshire
JOHN LANGDON
NICHOLAS GILMAN

Massachusetts
NATHANIEL GORHAM
RUFUS KING

Connecticut
WILLIAM SAMUEL JOHNSON
ROGER SHERMAN

New York
ALEXANDER HAMILTON

New Jersey
WILLIAM LIVINGSTON
DAVID BREARLEY
WILLIAM PATERSON
JONATHAN DAYTON

Pennsylvania
BENJAMIN FRANKLIN
THOMAS MIFFLIN
ROBERT MORRIS
GEORGE CLYMER
THOMAS FITZSIMONS
JARED INGERSOLL
JAMES WILSON
GOUVERNEUR MORRIS

---

[*]*The Constitution was submitted on September 17, 1787, by the Constitutional Convention, was ratified by the Convention of several states at various dates up to May 29, 1790, and became effective on March 4, 1789.*

Amendments to the Constitution

AMENDMENT I

Congress shall make no law respecting an establishment of religion, or prohibiting the free exercise thereof; or abridging the freedom of speech, or of the press; or the right of the people peaceably to assemble, and to petition the Government for a redress of grievances.

AMENDMENT II

A well regulated Militia being necessary to the security of a free State, the right of the people to keep and bear Arms, shall not be infringed.

AMENDMENT III

No Soldier shall, in time of peace be quartered in any house, without the consent of the Owner, nor in time of war, but in a manner to be prescribed by law.

AMENDMENT IV

The right of the people to be secure in their persons, houses, papers, and effects, against unreasonable searches and seizures, shall not be violated, and no Warrants shall issue, but upon probable cause, supported by Oath or affirmation, and particularly describing the place to be searched, and the persons or things to be seized.

AMENDMENT V

No person shall be held to answer for a capital, or otherwise infamous crime, unless on a presentment or indictment of a Grand Jury, except in cases arising in the land or naval forces, or in the Militia, when in actual service in time of War or public danger; nor shall any person be subject for the same offense to be twice put in jeopardy of life or limb; nor shall be compelled in any criminal case to be a witness against himself, nor be deprived of life, liberty, or property, without due process of law; nor shall private property be taken for public use, without just compensation.

AMENDMENT VI

In all criminal prosecutions, the accused shall enjoy the right to a speedy and public trial, by an impartial jury of the State and district wherein the crime shall have been committed, which district shall have been previously ascertained by law, and to be informed of the nature and cause of the accusation; to be confronted with the witnesses against him; to have compulsory process for obtaining witnesses in his favor, and to have the Assistance of Counsel for his defence.

AMENDMENT VII

In Suits at common law, where the value in controversy shall exceed twenty dollars, the right of trial by jury shall be preserved, and no fact tried by a jury, shall be otherwise re-examined in any Court of the United States, than according to the rules of the common law.

AMENDMENT VIII

Excessive bail shall not be required, nor excessive fines imposed, nor cruel and unusual punishments inflicted.

AMENDMENT IX

The enumeration in the Constitution, of certain rights, shall not be construed to deny or disparage others retained by the people.

AMENDMENT X*

The powers not delegated to the United States by the Constitution, nor prohibited by it to the States, are reserved to the States respectively, or to the people.

AMENDMENT XI
[ADOPTED 1798]

The Judicial power of the United States shall not be construed to extend to any suit in law or equity, commenced or prosecuted against one of the United States by Citizens of another State, or by Citizens or Subjects of any Foreign State.

AMENDMENT XII
[ADOPTED 1804]

The Electors shall meet in their respective states, and vote by ballot for President and Vice President, one of whom, at least, shall not be an inhabitant of the same state with themselves; they shall name in their ballots the person voted for as President, and in distinct ballots the person voted for as Vice President, and they shall make distinct lists of all persons voted for as President, and of all persons voted for as Vice President, and of the number of votes for each, which lists they shall sign and certify, and transmit sealed to the seat of the government of the United States, directed to the President of the Senate;—The President of the Senate shall, in the presence of the Senate and House of Representatives, open all the certificates and the votes shall then be counted;—The person having the greatest number of votes for President, shall be the President, if such number be a majority of the whole number of Electors appointed; and if no person have such majority, then from the persons having the highest numbers not exceeding three on the list of those voted for as President, the House of Representatives shall choose immediately, by ballot, the President. But in choosing the President, the votes shall be taken by states, the representation from each state having one vote; a quorum for this purpose shall consist of a member or members from two-thirds of the states, and a majority of all the states shall be necessary to a choice. And if the House of Representatives shall not choose a President whenever the right of choice shall devolve upon them, before *the fourth day of March* next following, then the Vice President shall act as President, as in the case of the death or other constitutional disability of the President.—The person having the greatest number of votes as Vice President, shall be the Vice President, if such number be a majority of the whole number of Electors appointed, and if no person have a majority, then from the two highest numbers on the list, the Senate shall choose the Vice President; a quorum for the purpose shall consist of two-thirds of the whole number of Senators, and a majority of the whole number shall be necessary to a choice. But no person constitutionally ineligible to the office of President shall be eligible to that of Vice President of the United States.

AMENDMENT XIII
[ADOPTED 1865]

Section 1

Neither slavery nor involuntary servitude, except as a punishment for crime whereof the party shall have been duly convicted, shall exist within the United States, or any place subject to their jurisdiction.

The first ten amendments (the Bill of Rights) were ratified, and their adoption was certified, on December 15, 1791.

Section 2

Congress shall have power to enforce this article by appropriate legislation.

AMENDMENT XIV
[ADOPTED 1868]

Section 1

All persons born or naturalized in the United States, and subject to the jurisdiction thereof, are citizens of the United States and of the State wherein they reside. No State shall make or enforce any law which shall abridge the privileges or immunities of citizens of the United States; nor shall any State deprive any person of life, liberty, or property, without due process of law; nor deny to any person within its jurisdiction the equal protection of the laws.

Section 2

Representatives shall be apportioned among the several States according to their respective numbers, counting the whole number of persons in each State, excluding Indians not taxed. But when the right to vote at any election for the choice of electors for President and Vice President of the United States, Representatives in Congress, the Executive and Judicial officers of a State, or the members of the Legislature thereof, is denied to any of the male inhabitants of such State, being twenty-one years of age, and citizens of the United States, or in any way abridged, except for participation in rebellion, or other crime, the basis of representation therein shall be reduced in the proportion which the number of such male citizens shall bear to the whole number of male citizens twenty-one years of age in such State.

Section 3

No person shall be a Senator or Representative in Congress, or elector of President and Vice President, or hold any office, civil or military, under the United States, or under any State, who, having previously taken an oath, as a member of Congress, or as an officer of the United States, or as a member of any State legislature, or as an executive or judicial officer of any State, to support the Constitution of the United States, shall have engaged in insurrection or rebellion against the same, or given aid or comfort to the enemies thereof. But Congress may by a vote of two-thirds of each House, remove such disability.

Section 4

The validity of the public debt of the United States, authorized by law, including debts incurred for payment of pensions and bounties for services in suppressing insurrection or rebellion, shall not be questioned. But neither the United States nor any State shall assume or pay any debt or obligation incurred in aid of insurrection or rebellion against the United States, or any claim for the loss or emancipation of any slave; but all such debts, obligations and claims shall be held illegal and void.

Section 5

The Congress shall have power to enforce, by appropriate legislation, the provisions of this article.

AMENDMENT XV
[ADOPTED 1870]

Section 1

The right of citizens of the United States to vote shall not be denied or abridged by the United States or by any State on account of race, color, or previous condition of servitude.

Section 2

The Congress shall have power to enforce this article by appropriate legislation.

AMENDMENT XVI
[ADOPTED 1913]

The Congress shall have power to lay and collect taxes on incomes, from whatever source derived, without apportionment among the several States, and without regard to any census or enumeration.

AMENDMENT XVII
[ADOPTED 1913]

The Senate of the United States shall be composed of two Senators from each State, elected by the people thereof, for six years; and each Senator shall have one vote. The electors in each State shall have the qualifications requisite for electors of the most numerous branch of the State legislatures.

When vacancies happen in the representation of any State in the Senate, the executive authority of such State shall issue writs of election to fill such vacancies: *Provided,* That the legislature of any State may empower the executive thereof to make temporary appointments until the people fill the vacancies by election as the legislature may direct.

This amendment shall not be so construed as to affect the election or term of any Senator chosen before it becomes valid as part of the Constitution.

AMENDMENT XVIII
[ADOPTED 1919, REPEALED 1933]

Section 1

After one year from the ratification of this article the manufacture, sale, or transportation of intoxicating liqours within, the importation thereof into, or the exportation thereof from the United States and all territory subject to the jurisdiction thereof for beverage purposes is hereby prohibited.

Section 2

The Congress and the several States shall have concurrent power to enforce this article by appropriate legislation.

Section 3

This article shall be inoperative unless it shall have been ratified as an amendment to the Constitution by the legislatures of the several States, as provided in the Constitution, within seven years from the date of the submission hereof to the States by the Congress.

AMENDMENT XIX
[ADOPTED 1920]

The right of citizens of the United States to vote shall not be denied or abridged by the United States or by any State on account of sex.

Congress shall have power to enforce this article by appropriate legislation.

AMENDMENT XX
[ADOPTED 1933]

Section 1

The terms of the President and Vice President shall end at noon on the 20th day of January, and the terms of Senators and Representatives at noon on the 3d day of January, of the years in which such terms would have ended if this article had not been ratified and the terms of their successors shall then begin.

Section 2

The Congress shall assemble at least once in every year, and such meeting shall begin at noon on the 3d day of January, unless they shall by law appoint a different day.

Section 3

If, at the time fixed for the beginning of the term of the President, the President elect shall have died, the Vice President elect shall become President. If a President shall not have been chosen before the time fixed for the beginning of his term, or if the President elect shall have failed to qualify, then the Vice President elect shall act as President until a President shall have qualified; and the Congress may by law provide for the case wherein neither a President elect nor a Vice President elect shall have qualified, declaring who shall then act as President, or the manner in which one who is to act shall be selected, and such person shall act accordingly until a President or Vice President shall have qualified.

Section 4

The Congress may by law provide for the case of the death of any of the persons from whom the House of Representatives may choose a President whenever the right of choice shall have devolved upon them, and for the case of the death of any of the persons from whom the Senate may choose a Vice President whenever the right of choice shall have devolved upon them.

Section 5

Sections 1 and 2 shall take effect on the 15th day of October following the ratification of this article.

Section 6

This article shall be inoperative unless it shall have been ratified as an amendment to the Constitution by the legislatures of three fourths of the several States within seven years from the date of its submission.

AMENDMENT XXI
[ADOPTED 1933]

Section 1

The eighteenth article of amendment to the Constitution of the United States is hereby repealed.

Section 2

The transportation or importation into any State, Territory, or possession of the United States for delivery or use therein of intoxicating liquors in violation of the laws thereof, is hereby prohibited.

Section 3

This article shall be inoperative unless it shall have been ratified as an amendment to the Constitution by conventions in the several States, as provided in the Constitution, within seven years from the date of the submission hereof to the States by the Congress.

AMENDMENT XXII
[ADOPTED 1951]

Section 1

No person shall be elected to the office of the President more than twice, and no person who has held the office of President, or acted as President, for more than two years of a term to which some other person was elected President shall be elected to the office of the President more than once. But this Article shall not apply to any person holding the office of President when this Article was proposed by the Congress, and shall not prevent any person who may be holding the office of President, or acting as President, during the term within which this Article becomes operative from holding the office of President or acting as President during the remainder of such term.

Section 2

This article shall be inoperative unless it shall have been ratified as an amendment to the Constitution by the legislatures of three-fourths of the several States within seven years from the date of its submission to the States by the Congress.

AMENDMENT XXIII
[ADOPTED 1961]

Section 1

The District constituting the seat of Government of the United States shall appoint in such manner as the Congress shall direct:

A number of electors of President and Vice President equal to the whole number of Senators and Representatives in Congress to which the District would be entitled if it were a State, but in no event more than the least populous State; they shall be in addition to those appointed by the States, but they shall be considered, for the purposes of the election of President and Vice President, to be electors appointed by a State; and they shall meet in the District and perform such duties as provided by the twelfth article of amendment.

Section 2

The Congress shall have power to enforce this article by appropriate legislation.

AMENDMENT XXIV
[ADOPTED 1964]

Section 1

The right of citizens of the United States to vote in any primary or other election for President or Vice President, for electors for President or Vice President, or for Senator or Representative in Congress, shall not be denied or abridged by the United States or any state by reason of failure to pay any poll tax or other tax.

Section 2

The Congress shall have the power to enforce this article by appropriate legislation.

AMENDMENT XXV
[ADOPTED 1967]

Section 1

In case of the removal of the President from office or his death or resignation, the Vice President shall become President.

Section 2

Whenever there is a vacancy in the office of the Vice President, the President shall nominate a Vice President who shall take the office upon confirmation by a majority vote of both houses of Congress.

Section 3

Whenever the President transmits to the President pro tempore of the Senate and the Speaker of the House of Representatives his written declaration that he is unable to discharge the powers and duties of his office, and until he transmits to them a written declaration to the contrary, such powers and duties shall be discharged by the Vice President as Acting President.

Section 4

Whenever the Vice President and a majority of either the principal officers of the executive departments or of such other body as Congress may by law provide, transmit to the President pro tempore of the Senate and the Speaker of the House of Representatives their written declaration that the President is unable to discharge the powers and duties of his office, the Vice President shall immediately assume the powers and duties of the office as Acting President.

Thereafter, when the President transmits to the President pro tempore of the Senate and the Speaker of the House of Representatives his written declaration that no inability exists, he shall resume the powers and duties of his office unless the Vice President and a majority of either the principal officers of the executive department or of such other body as Congress may by law provide, transmit within four days to the President pro tempore of the Senate and the Speaker of the House of Representatives their written declaration that the President is unable to discharge the powers and duties of his office. Thereupon Congress shall decide the issue, assembling within 48 hours for that purpose if not in session. If the Congress, within 21 days after receipt of the latter written declaration, or, if Congress is not in session, within 21 days after Congress is required to assemble, determines by two-thirds vote of both houses that the President is unable to discharge the powers and duties of his office, the Vice President shall continue to discharge the same as Acting President; otherwise, the President shall resume the powers and duties of his office.

Amendment XXVI
[Adopted 1971]

Section 1

The right of citizens of the United States, who are 18 years of age or older, to vote shall not be denied or abridged by the United States or any state on account of age.

Section 2

The Congress shall have the power to enforce this article by appropriate legislation.

Amendment XXVII
[Adopted 1992]

No law, varying the compensation for the services of the Senators and Representatives shall take effect, until an election of Representatives shall have intervened.

Supplementary Reading

PROLOGUE BEGINNINGS

During the 1990s the prehistoric era in North America has witnessed an explosion of interest, especially among archaeologists. A global perspective, focusing on geography as a causal force, is outlined in Jared Diamond, *Guns, Germs, and Steel* (1997). Another readable summary is Charles C. Mann, *1491* (2006). David Hurst Thomas, *Exploring Native North America* (2000), provides detailed analyses of representative archaeological sites.

A good survey of the first peoples of North America is David J. Meltzer, *Search for the First Americans* (1993). The "overkill hypothesis" is developed in Paul Martin and Richard Klein, eds., *Quaternary Extinctions* (1984). The best survey on the southwestern peoples is Linda S. Cordell, *Prehistory of the Southwest* (1997). See also J. J. Brody, *The Anasazi* (1990), David Roberts, *In Search of the Old Ones: Exploring the Anasazi World of the Southwest* (1995), R. Gwinn Vivian, *The Chacoan Prehistory of the San Juan Basin* (1990), John P. Andrews and Todd W. Bostwick, *Desert Farmers at the River's Edge: The Hohokam and Pueblo Grande* (1997), and, on early agriculture, R. G. Matson, *The Origins of Southwestern Agriculture* (1991). For a study of Hopewell peoples, see Bruce D. Smith, *Rivers of Change* (1992).

On the Mississippian societies, see Thomas E. Emerson, *Cahokia and the Archaeology of Power* (1997), Thomas E. Emerson and R. Barry Lewis, eds., *Cahokia and the Hinterlands: Middle Mississippian Cultures of the Midwest* (1991), Biloine W. Young and Robert Fowler, *Cahokia, The Great Native American Metropolis* (2000), Timothy Pauketat, *The Ascent of Chiefs: Cahokia and Mississippian Politics in Native North America* (1994), and Robert A. Birmingham and Leslie Eisenberg, *Indian Mounds of Wisconsin* (2000). For early peoples elsewhere, see Vance T. Holliday, *Paleoindian Geoarchaeology of the Southern High Plains* (1997) and Ruth Kirk and Richard D. Daugherty, *Hunters of the Whale* (1974), for the Makah of the Northwest.

For an overview of political structures, see Robert D. Drennan, *Chiefdoms in the Americas* (1987). That warfare was a product of gender tensions is explored in Bruce G. Trigger, *Natives and Newcomers* (1985). The contention that the early peoples of North America lived in perfect harmony with nature is rebutted in Shepard Krech, *The Ecological Indian* (1999). Another common assumption, based on Native American folklore, of the essentially peaceful character of Southwestern peoples has been challenged by recent studies such as Glen E. Rice and Steven A. Leblanc, eds., *Deadly Landscapes: Case Studies in Prehistoric Southwestern Warfare* (2001), and Tim D. White, *Prehistoric Cannibalism at Mancos* (1992). In *Eve's Seed: Biology, the Sexes and the Course of History* (2001), Robert S. McElvaine argues that men enshrined raids and warfare in response to women's increasingly important economic role in farming activities.

CHAPTER 1 ALIEN ENCOUNTERS: EUROPE IN THE AMERICAS

For a study of Columbus, see Miles Davidson, *Columbus Then and Now* (1997). David Stannard, *American Holocaust* (1992), and Kirkpatrick Sale, *The Conquest of Paradise* (1990), are highly critical of Columbus. The history of Spanish colonization in the Southwest is treated in David J. Weber, *The Spanish Frontier in North America* (1992) and, in the Southeast, in Paul E. Hoffman, *A New Andalucia and a Way to the Orient* (1991) and *Florida's Frontiers* (2002). Ned Blackhawk, *Violence over the Land* (2006), summarizes recent research on the cycle of violence attending colonization and slave raiding in the Southwest. For an imaginative attempt to reconstruct the Native American response, see Ramon Guitierrez, *When Jesus Came, The Corn Mothers Went Away* (1991).

Accounts of the English background of colonization can be found in Nicholas Canny, ed., *The Oxford History of the British Empire: The Origins of Empire* (1998). On French colonization, see William J. Eccles, *The French in North America, 1500–1765* (1998), Carl J. Ekberg, *French Roots in the Illinois Country* (1998), and Carole Blackburn, *Harvest of Souls* (2000), which focuses on the Jesuit Missionaries.

Contemporary scholarship on Indian-colonist relations focuses on their interactions. Important studies in that vein include Richard White, *Indians, Empires and Republics in the Great Lakes Region, 1650–1815* (1991), James Merrell, *Into the American Woods: Negotiators on the Pennsylvania Frontier* (1999), Jill Lepore, *Name of War: King Philip's War and the Origins of American Identity* (1999), and Karen Kupperman, *Indians and English: Facing Off in Early America* (2000).

The impact of the Europeans is discussed in the Debating the Past (p. 26). See also Alfred W. Crosby, *Ecological Imperialism: The Biological Expansion of Europe, 900–1900* (1993) and, though it deals with a later period, Robert Boyd, *The Coming of the Spirit of Pestilence: Introduced Infectious Diseases and Population Decline among Northwest Coast Indians* (1999). Joyce E. Chaplin, *Subject Matter: Technology, the Body, and Science on the Anglo-American Frontier, 1500–1676* (2001), argues that Europeans did not assume that they were racially superior until they saw how readily native peoples died of diseases.

For a general study of American slave trade, see David Eltis, *The Rise of African Slavery in the Americas* (2000). General surveys of slavery include Ira Berlin, *Many Thousands Gone* (1998), and Peter Kolchin, *American Slavery, 1619–1877* (1993).

On Virginia, see David H. Fischer and James C. Kelly, *Bound Away: Virginia and the Westward Movement* (2000), and Edmund S. Morgan, *American Slavery, American Freedom* (1975). Jack P. Greene, *Pursuits of Happiness* (1988), argues for the centrality of the Chesapeake in the formation of American identity. On Roanoke, see Ivor Noel Hume, *The Virginia Adventure* (1994). See also Everett Emerson, *Captain John Smith* (1993). For Maryland, consult Gloria T. Main, *Tobacco Colony* (1982), and A. C. Land, *Colonial Maryland* (1981); for Carolina, see Roger Ekirch, *Poor Carolina* (1981).

For the middle colonies, see Michael Kammen, *Colonial New York* (1975) and Donna Merwick, *Possessing Albany, 1630–1710: The Dutch and English Experiences* (1990). In addition to Merrell, see Mary Geiter, *William Penn* (2000);

On New England, Edmund Morgan's *The Puritan Dilemma: The Story of John Winthrop* (1958), long a classic, has been superseded by Francis J. Bremer, *John Winthrop: America's Forgotten Founding Father* (2003). The dispute over Anne Hutchinson has been enlivened by Michael P. Winship, *Making Heretics: Militant Protestantism and Free Grace in Massachusetts, 1636–1641* (2002), who notes that few at the time accused Hutchinson of antinomianism; see also his *Anne Hutchinson* (2005). Louise A. Breen, *Transgressing the Bounds: Subversive Enterprises among the Puritan Elite in Massachusetts, 1630–1692* (2001), draws a connection between religious dissenters such as Hutchinson and economic entrepreneurship. For Rhode Island, see Edwin S. Gaustad, *Liberty of Conscience: Roger Williams in America* (1991). William Bradford's classic, *Of Plymouth Plantation,* is also well worth sampling.

CHAPTER 2 AMERICAN SOCIETY IN THE MAKING

Among general interpretations, D. J. Boorstin's *The Americans: The Colonial Experience* (1958), emphasizes the modern aspects of colonial society; Jon Butler's *Becoming America: The Revolution before 1776* (2000) similarly and more broadly emphasizes the rapid evolution of colonial society. Alan Kulikoff, *From British Peasants to Colonial American Farmers* (2000), underscores the importance of land in defining American life. Alan Taylor, *American Colonies* (2001), emphasizes the links between European and American societies.

On economic conditions, see John J. McCusker and Russell R. Menard, eds., *The Economy of British America, 1607–1789* (1991). For the economic growth of colonial New England, see Margaret Ellen Newell, *From Dependency to Independence* (1998). On the chronologically and geographically uneven development of slavery in America, consult Ira Berlin, *Generations of Captivity: A History of African-American Slaves* (2003), and *Many Thousands Gone* (1998). See also Philip D. Morgan, *Slave Counterpoint* (1998) and P. D. Curtin, *The Rise and Fall of the Plantation Complex* (1990). Alan Gallay, *The Indian Slave Trade* (2002) uncovers an issue that has long been overlooked.

On life in the colonial South, see T. W. Tate and David Ammerman, eds., *The Chesapeake in the Seventeenth Century* (1979), Allan Kulikoff, *Tobacco and Slaves* (1986), D. B. and A. H. Rutman, *A Place in Time* (1984), and Timothy H. Breen and Stephen Innes, *"Myne Owne Ground": Race and Freedom on Virginia's Eastern Shore* (1980).

Family and community life are surveyed in D. F. Hawke, *Everyday Life in Early America* (1988), and Edmund S. Morgan, *The Puritan Family* (1966). The places of women and children are effectively presented in Laurel T. Ulrich, *Good Wives: Image and Reality in the Lives of Women in Northern New England* (1982), and Philip Greven, *The Protestant Temperament: Patterns of Child-Rearing, Religious Experience, and the Self in Early America* (1980). Richard Godbeer, *Sexual Revolution in Early America* (2002), corrects the stereotype of the puritans as sexually repressive.

The works of Perry Miller remain the starting point for any serious study of the cultural life of colonial New England. Among them, *Errand into the Wilderness* (1956) provides a good introduction. More recent studies, most of which modify Miller's judgments, include D. D. Hall, *Worlds of Wonder, Days of Judgment* (1989), and Patricia U. Bonomi, *Under the Cope of Heaven* (1986). Some recent scholarship contends that Puritan practices complemented economic development: for example, John Frederick Martin, *Profits in the Wilderness* (1991), Stephen Innes, *Creating the Commonwealth* (1995), and Mark A. Peterson, *The Price of Redemption* (1997).

Larry D. Gragg, *The Salem Witch Crisis* (1992) provides a narrative account. Paul Boyer and Stephen Nissenbaum, *Salem Possessed* (1974), argue that the episode grew out of tensions between different factions within the community. Mary Beth Norton, *In the Devil's Snare: The Salem Witchcraft Crisis of 1692* (2002), views the crisis as a response to fear of Indians. The subject is considered more generally in John Demos, *Entertaining Satan: Witchcraft and the Culture of Early New England* (1982). On women and witchcraft, see Elizabeth Reis, *Damned Women* (1997), Elaine G. Breslaw, *Tituba, Reluctant Witch of Salem* (1996), and Carol F. Karlsen, *The Devil in the Shape of a Woman* (1987).

For an engaging overview of the ideology of gender authority in the seventeenth century, see Mary Beth Norton, *Founding Mothers and Fathers* (1996). On women and religion in New England, see also Susan Juster, *Disorderly Women* (1994). Karin Wolf, *Not All Wives* (2000), describes the range of women's activities in Philadelphia. For the role of women in Virginia, see Kathleen M. Brown, *Good Wives, Nasty Wenches and Anxious Patriarchs* (1996).

Educational and intellectual developments are treated in Bernard Bailyn, *Education in the Forming of American Society* (1960), and L. A. Cremin, *American Education: The Colonial Experience* (1970).

In the past decade there has been a profusion of studies on the interrelationship between settlers and Indians: Jane T. Merritt, *At the Crossroads: Indians and Empire on a Mid-Atlantic Frontier* (2003), Richard White, *The Middle Ground* (1991), Daniel K. Richter, *Ordeal of the Longhouse* (1992), Daniel H. Usner, *Indians, Settlers, and Slaves in a Frontier Exchange Economy* (1992), Colin G. Calloway, *New Worlds for All: Indians, Europeans, and the Remaking of Early America* (1997), Karen O. Kupperman, *Indians and English* (2001), and James F. Brooks, *Captives and Cousins* (2002).

CHAPTER 3 AMERICA IN THE BRITISH EMPIRE

A full analysis of the British imperial system can be found in the early volumes of L. H. Gipson's *British Empire Before the American Revolution* (1936–1968). See also James A. Henretta, *The Evolution of American Society* (1973), and Michael Kammen, *Empire and Interest* (1974). Jack P. Greene, *Peripheries and Center* (1989), describes how the colonists extended their control of political affairs. On colonial trade and the mercantilist system, see J. J. McCusker and R. R. Menard, *The Economy of British America* (1985), and P. J. Marshall, ed., *The Oxford History of the British Empire: The Eighteenth Century* (1998).

On the Great Awakening, Richard Bushman, *From Puritan to Yankee* (1967) emphasizes psychosocial factors while Frank Lambert, *Inventing the "Great Awakening"* (1999) focuses on the intersection of religion and economics. Catherine A. Brekus, *Strangers and Pilgrims: Female Preaching in America* (1998) addresses a long-neglected subject. See also P. U. Bonami, *Under the Cope of Heaven: Religion, Society, and Politics in Colonial America* (1986). For the Enlightenment, see H. F. May, *The Enlightenment in America* (1976); also Joyce E. Chaplin, *The First Scientific American: Benjamin Franklin and the Pursuit of Genius* (2006) and I. Bernard Cohen, *Science and the Founding Fathers* (1995). Fred Anderson, *The Crucible of War* (2000) is a readable and thorough narrative of the Great War for the Empire; see also his *A People's Army: Massachusetts Soldiers and Society in the Seven Years' War* (1984).

On the causes of the Revolution, see Pauline Maier, *From Resistance to Revolution* (1972), Edmund S. Morgan, *The Birth of the Republic* (1977), and Edward Countryman, *The American Revolution* (1985). Valuable local studies include T. H. Breen, *Tobacco Culture* (1985), on Virginia; Countryman's *A People in Revolution* (1989), on New York; and T. M. Doerflinger, *A Vigorous Spirit of Enterprise* (1986), on Philadelphia.

Bernard Bailyn's *The Ideological Origins of the American Revolution* (1967) and *The Origins of American Politics* (1968) are brilliant analyses of the political thinking and political structure of eighteenth-century America. Other seminal works include Gordon S. Wood, *The Radicalism of the American Revolution* (1992), and Edmund S. Morgan, *Inventing the People: The Rise of Popular Sovereignty in England and America* (1988). See also Pauline Maier, *The Old Revolutionaries* (1980). On Benjamin Franklin, in addition to Chapin (above), see two good recent biographies, by Edmund Morgan (2002) and Walter Isaacson (2003).

The full story of Eunice Williams/Gannenstenhawi is brilliantly told in John Demos, *The Unredeemed Captive* (1994); for the Indian perspective of the same event, see Evan Haefeli and Kevin Sweeney, *Captors and Captives: The 1704 French and Indian Raid on Deerfield* (2003).

CHAPTER 4 THE AMERICAN REVOLUTION

Good brief surveys of the Revolutionary years are Edward Countryman, *The American Revolution* (1985), and E. S. Morgan, *The Birth of the Republic* (1977). David McCullough, *1776* (2005) provides a gripping account of that pivotal year. David Hackett Fischer's account of the battle of Lexington and Concord in *Paul Revere's Ride* (1994) shows why the colonists won the war; his *Washington's Crossing* (2004) outlines the importance of the New Jersey campaign. See also John W. Shy, *A People Numerous and Armed* (1990).

For a short biography of Washington, see James MacGregor Burns and Susan Dunn, *George Washington* (2004). Longer biographies include Richard Norton Smith, *Patriarch: George Washington and the New American Nation* (1993), and Henry Wiencek, *Imperfect God: George Washington, His Slaves, and the Creator of America* (2003). John E. Ferling, *Setting the World Ablaze* (2000) and his *A Leap in the Dark* (2003) provide a good overview of how Washington, Jefferson, and John Adams interacted. See also Joseph Ellis, *Founding Brothers: The Revolutionary Generation* (2000), and David McCullough *John Adams* (2001).

On the broader context of the Revolution, see Lester Langley, *The Americas in the Age of Revolution, 1750–1850* (1996); Eliga Gould emphasizes the continuity in America of British political culture, *The Persistence of Empire* (2000).

On the Continental Congress and the Articles of Confederation, see Jackson T. Main, *The Sovereign States* (1973) and Jack N. Rakove, *The Beginnings of National Politics* (1979). P. S. Onuf, *Statehood and Union* (1987), deals with the Northwest Ordinance. Eric Foner, *Tom Paine and Revolutionary America* (1976), is an excellent brief biography. James K. Martin makes a case for his subject in *Benedict Arnold, Revolutionary Hero* (1997).

The classic study of the Declaration of Independence is C. L. Becker, *The Declaration of Independence* (1922); for contemporary analysis see Pauline Maier, *American Scripture* (1997), and Jay Fliegelman, *Declaring Independence* (1993).

The early history of the state governments is covered in W. P. Adams, *The First American Constitutions* (1980). Edward Countryman, *A People in Revolution* (1982), deals with conditions in New York; for Maryland, see Jean B. Lee, *The Price of Nationhood* (1994). The development of political and social ideas, before, during, and after the Revolution, is admirably described and analyzed in G. S. Wood, *The Creation of the American Republic* (1969) and *The Radicalism of the American Revolution* (1992).

The effects of the Revolution on slavery are treated in W. D. Jordan, *White over Black* (1968), and on the Indians, in Colin G. Calloway, *The American Revolution in Indian Country* (1995). For an account of Indians, debtors, and slaves in Virginia, see Woody Holton, *Forced Founders* (1999). L. K. Kerber, *Women of the Republic* (1980), M. B. Norton, *Liberty's Daughters* (1980), and Joy Day Buel and Richard Buel, *The Way of Duty* (1984) discuss the effects of the Revolution on women and the family.

CHAPTER 5 THE FEDERALIST ERA: NATIONALISM TRIUMPHANT

On the Constitution, in addition to the works cited in the Debating the Past (p. 168), see Reginald Horsman, *The New Republic* (2000), a good brief survey. Bernard Bailyn, *To Begin the World Anew* (2003) shows how the founders embraced ambiguity. For Madison's role, see Lance Banning, *The Sacred Fire of Liberty* (1995), Drew R. McCoy, *The Last of the Fathers* (1989), and Gary Rosen, *American Compact* (1999). On Hamilton, Ronald Chernow, *Alexander Hamilton* (2004) offers a balanced account while Richard Brookhiser's brief *Alexander Hamilton, American* (1999) is more partisan. See also Karl-Friedrich Walling, *Republican Empire: Alexander Hamilton on War and Free Government* (1999). The *Federalist Papers* of Hamilton, Madison, and Jay, available in many editions, are essential for the arguments of the supporters of the new government. For the Bill of Rights, consult Bernard Schwartz, *The Great Rights of Mankind* (1977).

For Washington, in addition to the works cited in the previous chapter, see Alexander De Conde, *Entangling Alliance: Politics and Diplomacy Under George Washington* (1958), Harry Ammon, *The Genet Mission* (1973), two volumes by S. F. Bemis, *Jay's Treaty* (1923) and *Pinckney's Treaty* (1926), Alexander De Conde, *The Quasi-War* (1966), and William Stinchcombe, *The XYZ Affair* (1980). On economic development, see E. J. Ferguson, *The Power of the Purse* (1968), and C. P. Nettels, *The Emergence of a National Economy* (1962), which puts this subject in the broader perspective of the period 1775–1815. On the radical western movements, see D. P. Szatmary, *Shays' Rebellion* (1980), and Thomas P. Slaughter, *The Whiskey Rebellion* (1986).

John Patrick Diggins, *John Adams* (2003) is a useful brief biography. Excellent full-length biographies include Joseph J. Ellis, *Passionate Sage* (1993), and David McCullough, *John Adams* (2001). Stanley Elkins and Eric McKitrick, *The Age of Federalism* (1993), and James Roger Sharp, *American Politics in the Early Republic* (1993), provide detailed accounts of the politics of this period. For the Alien and Sedition Acts, see J. M. Smith, *Freedom's Fetters* (1956), and L. W. Levy, *Freedom of Speech and Press in Early American History* (1963). Paul Nagel's collective biography, *The Adams Women* (1987), provides a superb account of a remarkable family.

CHAPTER 6 JEFFERSONIAN DEMOCRACY

No student interested in Jefferson's political and social philosophy should miss sampling his writings. A useful compilation is Merrill D. Peterson, ed., *Thomas Jefferson* (1984). The contradictory components of Jefferson's life and mind are best analyzed in Joseph Ellis, *American Sphinx: The Character of Thomas Jefferson.* See also Peter Onuf, *The Mind of Thomas Jefferson* (2007), and Christopher Hitchens, *Thomas Jefferson* (2005). On the issue of indebtedness, see Herbert Sloan, *Principle and Interest: Thomas Jefferson and the Problem of Debt* (1995), and Bruce H. Mann, *Republic of Debtors: Bankruptcy in the Age of American Independence* (2002).

For the election of 1800, see Bernard A. Weisberger, *America Afire* (2000). Arnold Rogow, *Fatal Friendship* (1998), describes the relationship of Hamilton and Burr; on Jefferson and Burr see Joseph Whelan, *Jefferson's Vendetta: The Pursuit of Aaron Burr and the Judiciary* (2005). See also Joanne B. Freeman, *Affairs of Honor* (2001) on politics and dueling more generally. On Jefferson and John Marshall see R. Kent Newmyer, *John Marshall and the Heroic Age of the Supreme Court* (2001). A useful monograph is Anthony F. C. Wallace, *Jefferson and the Indians* (1999).

Thomas Fleming, *The Louisiana Purchase* (2003) is a brief, clear account; Jon Kukla, *A Wilderness So Immense: The Louisiana Purchase and the Destiny of America* (2003) argues that the region was acquired chiefly as a place for resettling Indians. Thomas P. Slaughter, *Exploring Lewis and Clark* (2003) is a scholarly examination of the explorers' writings.

CHAPTER 7 NATIONAL GROWING PAINS

On Madison, see Lance Banning, *Sacred Fire of Liberty* (1995), Jack N. Rakove, *James Madison and the Creation of the American Republic* (2007), and Richard Labunski, *James Madison and the Struggle for the Bill of Rights* (2006). On the War of 1812 from the American perspective, see A. J. Langguth, *Union, 1812* (2006). For the political issues, see Richard Buel, Jr., *America on the Brink* (2005). For accounts of key figures, see Winston Groom, *Patriotic Fire* (2006), about Andrew Jackson and the Battle of New Orleans, Allison Robert, *Stephen Decatur* (2005), and David C. Skaggs, *Oliver Hazard Perry* (2006).

For the postwar diplomatic settlements and the Era of Good Feelings, see James Lewis, *The American Union and the Problem of Neighborhood: The United States and the Collapse of the Spanish Empire, 1783–1829* (1998), George Dangerfield, *The Era of Good Feelings* (1952), and Harry Ammon, *James Monroe: The Quest for National Identity* (1971), and on his famous doctrine, Ernest May, *The Making of the Monroe Doctrine* (1976).

Merrill D. Peterson, *The Great Triumvirate* (1987), is an interesting study of Clay, Calhoun, and Webster. Other biographies of statesmen of the period include Paul C. Nagel, *John Quincy Adams* (1997), Robert Remini, *Daniel Webster* (1997), Irving Bartlett, *John C. Calhoun* (1993), Maurice Baxter, *Henry Clay and the American System* (1995), and C. C. Mooney, *William H. Crawford* (1974). On the Missouri Compromise, see Glover Moore, *The Missouri Controversy* (1953). See also P. C. Nagel, *One Nation Indivisible* (1965).

On Indians, in addition to the works cited in Debating the Past (p. 223) see John Sugden, *Tecumseh* (1998), R. David Edmonds, *The Potawatomis* (1978), and Michael N. McConnell, *A Country Between: The Upper Ohio Valley and Its Peoples* (1992).

CHAPTER 8 TOWARD A NATIONAL ECONOMY

On the consumer revolution, see especially Richard Bushman, *The Refinement of America* (1992). In addition to the works cited in Debating the Past (p. 269) on the market revolution, see Melvyn Stokes and Stephen Conway, eds., *The Market Revolution in America* (1996), and Christopher Clark, *The Roots* of *Rural Capitalism: Western Massachusetts, 1780–1860* (1991). See also Laurel Thatcher Ulrich, *The Age of Homespun* (2001).

On the industrial revolution in America, see A. D. Chandler, Jr., *The Visible Hand: The Managerial Revolution in American Business* (1977). On the role of inventors, see Carroll Pursell, *The Machine in America* (1995), and B. M. Tucker, *Samuel Slater and the Origins of the American Textile Industry* (1984).

The growth of cities in the Jacksonian era can be traced in Richard C. Wade, *The Urban Frontier* (1957), and Howard Chudacoff, *The Evolution of American Urban Society* (1981). Allen F. Davis and Mark Halle, eds., *The Peoples of Philadelphia* (1973), Oscar Handlin, *Boston's Immigrants* (1968 ed.), and P. R. Knights, *The Plain People of Boston* (1971), deal with individual cities.

Important new works on slavery include Steven Deyle, *Carry Me Back: The Domestic Trade in Slavery* (2005), Robert H. Gudmestad, *Troublesome Commerce* (2003), and Erskine Clarke, *Dwelling Place, Plantation Epic* (2005).

On immigration and ethnicity, see P. T. Knoble, *Paddy and the Republic* (1986), J. P. Dolan, *Immigrant Church: New York's Irish and German Catholics* (1982), and Stephan Thernstrom, ed., *Harvard Encyclopedia of American Ethnic Groups* (1980).

On changes in the nature of work, consult Paul Johnson, *A Shopkeeper's Millennium* (1978), Sean Wilentz, *Chants Democratic* (1984), Bruce Laurie, *Artisans into Workers* (1989), Norman Ware, *The Industrial Worker* (1990), and Anthony F. C. Wallace, *Rockdale* (1978); on women in the early factories, see Mary Blewett, *Men, Women, and Work* (1988), and Thomas Dublin, *Women at Work* (1979).

Peter L. Bernstein, *The Wedding of the Waters* (2005) is a thorough account of the Erie Canal; see also Evan Cornog describes the origins and impact of the Erie Canal in *The Birth of Empire* (1998). On canal building, consult R. E. Shaw, *Canals for a Nation* (1990). Two works by Carter Goodrich, *Government Promotion of American Canals and Railroads* (1960) and *Canals and American Economic Development* (1961), describe the role of government aid in canal construction authoritatively. John Lauritz Larson, *Internal Improvement: National Public Works and the Promise of Popular Government in the Early United States* (2001), blames Andrew Jackson for the abandonment of public support for transportation infrastructure.

R. Kent Newmyer, *John Marshall and the Heroic Age of the Supreme Court* (2001) is strongly supportive of Marshall's actions; see also G. Edward White, *The Marshall Court and Cultural Change* (1991), as well as the sources cited in previous chapters.

CHAPTER 9 JACKSONIAN DEMOCRACY

The nature of Jacksonian democracy was analyzed brilliantly by Alexis de Tocqueville, *Democracy in America* (1835–1840). Other commentaries by foreigners throw much light on Jacksonian democracy. See especially, in addition to Tocqueville, Frances Trollope, *Domestic Manners of the Americans* (1832), Michel Chevalier, *Society, Manners and Politics in the United States* (1961), Harriet Martineau, *Retrospect of Western Travel* (1838) and *Society in America* (1837), and F. J. Grund, *Aristocracy in America* (1859).

In addition to the works on Jackson cited in Debating the Past (p. 295), see Bray Hammond, *Banks and Politics in America from the Revolution to the Civil War* (1957), and J. M. McFaul, *The Politics of Jacksonian Finance* (1972). Peter Temin, *The Jacksonian Economy* (1969) minimizes the effects of Jackson's policies on economic conditions. Jill Norgren, *The Cherokee Cases* (1996) is critical of Jackson's policies toward Indians; Robert Remini is more supportive in *Andrew Jackson and His Indian Wars* (2001). For recent accounts of Indian resistance to removal, see Patricia W. Wickman *Osceola's Legacy* (2006), and Kerry Trask, *Black Hawk* (2006).

On the transformation of political parties, see Richard P. McCormick, *The Second American Party System* (1966), and Michael Holt, *The Rise and Fall of the American Whig Party* (1999), which focuses on variations at the state level. Gerald Leonard, *The Invention of Party Politics* (2002) provides a detailed study of Illinois.

On the nullification controversy, see R. E. Ellis, *The Union at Risk* (1987), and William W. Freehling, *The Road to Disunion* (1990), which stresses the close relationship between the nullifiers and the slavery issue.

For the Van Buren administration, see Ted Widmer, *Martin Van Buren* (2005), and Joel H. Silbey, *Martin Van Buren and the Emergency of American Popular Politics* (2002).

Louis Masur's *1831, Year of Eclipse* (2001), provides an interesting perspective on that pivotal year.

CHAPTER 10 THE MAKING OF MIDDLE-CLASS AMERICA

On Tocqueville and his views of America, see Alexis de Tocqueville, *Democracy in America*, J. P. Mayer, ed. (1966 edition), and also Andre Jardin, *Alexis de Tocqueville* (1988). For an analysis of the middle class, see Stuart M. Blumin, *The Emergence of the Middle Class* (1989).

On the changing place of the family and the changes within it, see Mary P. Ryan, *Cradle of the Middle Class: The Family in Oneida, New York* (1981), Catherine E. Kelly, *In the New England Fashion: Reshaping Women's Lives in the Nineteenth Century* (1999), Nancy Cott, *The Bonds of Womanhood* (1977), and Carl Degler, *At Odds: Women and Family in America from the Revolution to the Present* (1980).

Fertility and the frontier is examined in Yasukichi Yasuba, *Birth Rates of the White Population in the U.S., 1800–1860* (1962), and John Modell, "Family and Fertility on the Indiana Frontier, 1820," in *American Quarterly* (1971).

The Second Great Awakening has been examined both as a religious and as a social phenomenon. Still useful is Whitney Cross, *The Burned-Over District* (1950), but see also Paul E. Johnson, *A Shopkeeper's Millennium* (1978). Mark A. Noll, *America's God: From Jonathan Edwards to Abraham Lincoln* (2002), provides a broader study of the religious dimension of reform movements. For the Shakers, see Stephen J. Stein, *The Shaker Experience in America* (1992). Richard Bushman, *Joseph Smith and the Beginnings of Mormonism* (1984), provides a good introduction to the subject. For a broader study see Leonard J. Arrington, *The Mormon Experience* (1992).

For the origins of feminism, see Nancy Cott, *The Grounding of Modern Feminism* (1987), Ellen C. DuBois, *Feminism and Suffrage: The Emergence of an Independent Women's Movement in America, 1848–1869* (1978), and Linda K. Kerber, *No Constitutional Right to Be Ladies* (1998). Bruce Dorsey, *Reforming Men and Women* (2002) shows how men often initiated reforms but women took control of them.

Accounts of the temperance movement include Barbara L. Epstein, *The Politics of Domesticity* (1981), and W. J. Rorabaugh, *The Alcoholic Republic* (1979).

For a general study of the context of abolitionism, see Richard S. Newman, *The Transformation of American Abolitionism* (2002). For sharply contrasting views of the abolitionist movement, see Stanley Elkins, *Slavery* (1975), and Lewis Perry and Michael Fellman, eds., *Anti-Slavery Reconsidered* (1979). Women's role in the movement is discussed in Julie Roy Jeffrey, *The Great Silent Army of Abolitionism* (1998).

The persistence of slavery in the North, a topic that is often overlooked, is examined in Joanne P. Melish, *Disowning Slavery* (1998). Biographical accounts include John L. Thomas, *The Liberator: William Lloyd Garrison* (1963), Gerda Lerner, *The Grimké Sisters from South Carolina* (1967), and Nathan Huggins, *Slave and Citizen: The Life of Frederick Douglass* (1980).

On Lydia Maria Child, see Carolyn L. Karcher, *The First Woman in the Republic: A Cultural Biography of Lydia Maria Child* (1994), Charles Capper, *Margaret Fuller* (1992), Elizabeth Griffith, *In Her Own Rights: The Life of Elizabeth Cady Stanton* (1984), and Kathryn K. Sklar, *Catharine Beecher* (1973), are solid biographies of important women in the era.

For Emerson and Thoreau, see the biographies by Robert D. Richardson, *Emerson: The Mind on Fire* (1995), and *Henry Thoreau: The Life of the Mind* (1986). For Poe, the biography by Kenneth Silverman (1991) is excellent. David S. Reynold's *Walt Whitman's America* (1995) examines the poet's relation to other trends in American life. See also Hershel Parker, *Herman Melville: 1819–1851* (1996) and *Herman Melville: 1851–1891* (2002).

On the cultural life of the South, see Bertram Wyatt-Brown, *Hearts of Darkness* (2003), and Drew Faust, *A Sacred Circle* (1977).

On education see Lawrence A. Cremin, *American Education: The National Experience* (1980), and C. F. Kaestle, *Pillars of the Republic* (1983). Jill Lepore, *A Is For American* (2002) is also useful.

CHAPTER 11 WESTWARD EXPANSION

For John Tyler, perhaps the least examined of the presidents, see Edgar Crapol, *John Tyler* (2006), and Dan Monroe, *The Republican Vision of John Tyler* (2003). For an overview of the politics of the era, see David P. Currie, *Constitution in Congress: Democrats and Whigs, 1829–1861* (2005); on the Whigs, see Michael F. Holt, *The Rise and Fall of the American Whig Party* (1999), and Daniel Walker Howe, *The Political Culture of the American Whigs* (1979).

On the debate over annexation of Texas, see Joel H. Silbey, *Storm over Texas: The Annexation Controversy and the Road to Civil War* (2005).

The course of western development is treated in R. A. Billington and Martin Ridge, *The Far Western Frontier* (1982). Important recent studies of the California gold rush include Malcolm J. Rohrbough, *Days of Gold* (1997), and Susan Lee Johnson, *Roaring Camp: The Social World of the California Gold Rush* (2000). On the effects of the settling of the Great Plains, see Elliott West, *The Contested Plains: Indians, Goldseekers and the Rush to Colorado* (1998) and J. D. Unruh, *The Plains Across* (1979). Francis Parkman's classic account, *The Oregon Trail* (1849), is absorbing.

For Polk, see two recent short biographies: Samuel W. Haynes, *James K. Polk* (2006), and John Siegenthaler, *James K. Polk* (2004). William Dusinberre, *Slavemaster President: The Double Career of James Polk* (2003), is sharply critical.

On the Mexican-American War, see Richard Bruce Winders, *Mr. Polk's Army* (1997), R. W. Johannsen, *To the Halls of the Montezumas* (1987), and K. J. Bauer, *The Mexican War* (1974). J. H. Schroeder, *Mr. Polk's War* (1973), discusses American opposition to the conflict. See also Randolph B. Campbell, *Sam Houston and the American Southwest* (2007). Randy Roberts and James S. Olson, *A Line in the Sand: The Alamo in Blood and Memory* (2001), is an accessible account.

For the Compromise of 1850, see John C. Waugh, *On the Brink of Civil War* (2003), and David M. Potter, *The Impending Crisis, 1848–1861* (1976). See also Robert Remini, *Daniel Webster: The Man and His Time* (1997), and Irving H. Bartlett, *John C. Calhoun* (1993).

Chapter 12 The Sections Go Their Ways

Most of the volumes dealing with economic developments mentioned in earlier chapters continue to be useful for this period. On the Panic of 1857, see J. L. Huston, *The Panic of 1857 and the Coming of the Civil War* (1987). For a useful comparative study, see John Majewski, *A House Dividing: Economic Development in Pennsylvania and Virginia before the Civil War* (2000). On the economy of the South, see Gavin Wright, *The Political Economy of the Cotton South* (1978), and Michael Tadman, *Speculators and Slaves* (1989).

On slavery, in addition to the essential works listed in Debating the Past (p. 357), see Brenda Stevenson, *Life in Black and White* (1996), and Walter Johnson, *Soul by Soul: Life Inside the Antebellum Slave Market* (1999), which focuses on New Orleans. Recent evidence of slave resistance is documented in John Hope Franklin and Loren Schweninger, *Runaway Slaves* (1999), David Robertson, *Denmark Vesey* (1999), and Douglas R. Egerton, *Gabriel's Rebellion* (1993). An earlier study is Eugene D. Genovese, *From Rebellion to Revolution* (1979).

Excellent regional studies include Peter Coclanis, *The Shadow of a Dream* (1989), for South Carolina, as well as Charles E. Joyner, *Down by the Riverside: A South Carolina Slave Community* (1984), and Ann Patton Malone, *Sweet Chariot: Slave Family and Household Structure in Nineteenth-Century Louisiana* (1992).

Among specialized volumes, Bertram Wyatt-Brown, *Southern Honor* (1982), and Ira Berlin, *Slaves Without Masters* (1975), are important. Richard C. Wade, *Slavery in the Cities* (1964), contends that urban life eroded slavery, while Robert Starobin, *Industrial Slavery in the Old South* (1970), found that the institution could be adapted to industrial purposes. Most local studies take an intermediate position; see, for example, Midori Takagi, *"Rearing Wolves to Our Own Destruction": Slavery in Richmond, Virginia, 1782–1865* (1999).

Irish emigration is the subject of Tim Pat Coogan's expansive *Wherever Green Is Worn* (2000), and Edward Laxton, *The Famine Ships* (1997), as well as the scholarly collection edited by Arthur Gribben, *The Great Famine and the Irish Diaspora in America* (1999). J. Matthew Gallman, *Receiving Erin's Children* (2000), examines the arrival of Irish famine emigrants in Philadelphia. Although fewer sources on German emigration are available in English, see Marianne Wokeck, *Trade in Strangers* (1999).

On the New England shoe industry and labor organization, see Mary Blewett, *Men, Women and Work* (1988); for a more general study see her *Constant Turmoil: The Politics of Industrial Life in Nineteenth Century New England* (2000). For workingmen's political activities, Edward Pessen's *Most Uncommon Jacksonians* (1967) remains valuable.

Chapter 13 The Coming of the Civil War

On the origins of the Civil War, in addition to the Debating the Past (p. 381), David M. Potter, *The Impending Crisis* (1976), remains useful. See also Don E. Fehrenbacher, *Sectional Crisis and Southern Constitutionalism* (1995), and Marshall De Rosa, *The Politics of Dissolution* (1998). In *States' Rights and the Union* (2000), as in his other works, Forrest McDonald affirms the South's right to secede. David Brion Davis, *Inhuman Bondage* (2006), provides a sweeping survey of the rise and fall of slavery. William A. Link, *Roots of Secession: Slavery and Politics in Antebellum Virginia* (2003), is a useful state study.

On slave resistance, see especially John Hope Franklin and Loren Schweninger, *Runaway Slaves* (1999), William Dusinberre, *Them Dark Days: Slavery in the American Rice Swamps* (1996), and Steven Weisenburger, *Modern Medea: A Family Story of Slavery and Child-Murder from the Old South* (1998).

On abolitionism in the north, see Sandra Petrulionis, *To Set this World Aright* (2006). Everyone should read Harriet Beecher Stowe's *Uncle Tom's Cabin*. Joan Hedrick's biography, *Harriet Beecher Stowe* (1994), is excellent.

For the foreign policy of the 1850s, see C. H. Brown, *Agents of Manifest Destiny* (1980), and P. B. Wiley and Korogi Ichiro, *Yankees in the Land of the Gods* (1990), which focuses on American involvement in Japan.

On Stephen A. Douglas, see James L. Huston, *Stephen A. Douglas* (2007). Sumner's role in the deepening crisis is brilliantly discussed in David H. Donald, *Charles Sumner and the Coming of the Civil War* (1960), and *Charles Sumner and the Rights of Man* (1970); a more recent, brief study is Frederick J. Blue, *Charles Sumner and the Conscience of the North* (1994). Jean Baker, *James Buchanan* (2004), is solid and concise. On Dred Scott, see Paul Finkelman, *Dred Scott v. Sandford* (1997).

For Lincoln's own well-crafted words, see Abraham Lincoln, *Selections* (2 vols., 1989). On his use of words, see Douglas L. Wilson, *Lincoln's Sword* (2006). Excellent biographies of Lincoln include David H. Donald, *Lincoln* (1995), and Mark Neely, *The Last Best Hope on Earth* (1993). Lincoln's early struggles are thoughtfully examined in Douglas L. Wilson, *Honor's Voice: The Transformation of Abraham Lincoln* (1998). W. E. Gienapp, *The Origins of the Republican Party* (1987), and Eric Foner, *Free Soil, Free Labor, Free Men* (1970), are excellent analyses of Republican ideas and policies. Allen Guelzo, *Lincoln's Emancipation Proclamation* (2004), is also useful.

John Brown remains controversial. Recent works include David S. Reynolds, *John Brown, Abolitionist* (2005), which is sympathetic, and Evan Carton, *Patriotic Treason* (2006), which is less so. See also James Oakes, *Radical and the Republican* (2007), on Frederick Douglass and Lincoln.

CHAPTER 14 THE WAR TO SAVE THE UNION

The best survey of the Civil War period is James M. McPherson, *Battle Cry of Freedom* (1988), but see also Russell F. Weigley, *A Great Civil War* (2000).

On the precipitating events of the war, see Maury Klein, *Days of Defiance: Sumter, Secession and the Coming of the Civil War* (1997), and Wallace Hettle, *The Peculiar Democracy: Southern Democrats in Peace and Civil War* (2001).

For Lincoln, in addition to books mentioned in previous chapters, see Richard Cawardine, *Lincoln* (2006), William Marvel, *Mr. Lincoln Goes to War* (2006), and Philip Paludan, *The Presidency of Abraham Lincoln* (1994). Mark E. Neely, *The Fate of Liberty* (1991), examines Lincoln's position on civil liberties. Frank Klement, *The Limits of Dissent* (1998), focuses on Clement Vallandigham. For the movement to make abolition a war aim and the reaction to it, see Michael Vorenberg, *Final Freedom* (2001).

On economic issues, see Heather Cox Richardson, *The Greatest Nation on Earth: Republican Economy Policies during the Civil War* (1997), and Bray Hammond, *Sovereignty and an Empty Purse: Banks and Politics in the Civil War* (1970).

On African Americans in the Union army, see Joseph T. Glatthaar, *Forged in Battle: The Civil War Alliance of Black Soldiers and White Officers* (1990); Peter Burchard, *One Gallant Rush* (1965), recounts the story of Robert Gould Shaw and the Massachusetts 54th. See also Martin H. Blatt, *Hope & Glory: Essays on the Legacy of the 54th Massachusetts Regiment* (2001).

For aspects of economic and social history, see Philip S. Paludan, *"A People's Contest": The Union at War* (1988). Edward L. Ayers, *In the Presence of Mine Enemies* (2003), examines the effect of the war on various communities. For women and the war, see Drew Gilpin Faust, *Mothers of Invention* (1997), Judith Ann Giesberg, *Civil War Sisterhood: The U.S. Sanitary Commission and Women's Politics in Transition* (2000), and Laura Edwards, *Scarlett Doesn't Live Here Anymore* (2000). Elizabeth Young considers the literary heritage of women and the war in *Disarming the Nation: Women's Writing and the American Civil War* (1999). See also Iver Bernstein, *The New York City Draft Riots* (1990).

For the Confederacy, see Gary W. Gallagher, *The Confederate War* (1997). See also his edited collection, *Lee the Soldier* (1996). On divisions within the Confederacy, see William W. Freehling, *The South vs. The South: How Anti-Confederate Southerners Shaped the Course of the Civil War* (2001). Important biographies include William Cooper, *Jefferson Davis, American* (2000). See also Mark Grimsley and Brooks D. Simpson, eds., *Collapse of the Confederacy* (2001), and Steven V. Ash, *When the Yankees Came: Conflict and Chaos in the Occupied South* (1995).

Gerald F. Linderman, *Embattled Courage* (1988), argues that the soldiers on both sides grew disillusioned with the fighting; the persistence of the initial ideals is a theme in James McPherson, *What They Fought For, 1861–1865* (1994), and Reid Mitchell, *The Vacant Chair* (1993). Bertram Wyatt-Brown,

The Shaping of Southern Culture: Honor, Grace and War, 1760s–1880s (2001), contends that while soldiers on both sides used the same rhetoric to defend their cause, they had different notions of what terms such as "honor" meant.

Among the biographies of Civil War generals, northern and southern, the following are especially noteworthy: Brooks D. Simpson, *Ulysses S. Grant: Triumph over Adversity, 1822–1865* (2000), Jean E. Smith, *Grant* (2001), William S. McFeely, *Grant* (1981), Michael Fellman, *The Making of Robert E. Lee* (2000), Douglass S. Freeman, *R. E. Lee* (1934–1935), James I. Robertson, *Stonewall Jackson* (1997), Stephen W. Sears, *George B. McClellan* (1988), Stanley P. Hirshson, *The White Tecumseh: A Biography of William T. Sherman* (1997), and Chester G. Hearn, *Admiral David Glasgow Farragut* (1998).

The diplomacy of the Civil War period is covered in two works by Howard Jones, *Union in Peril* (1992), on British intervention, and *Abraham Lincoln and a New Birth of Freedom* (1999), on issues of slavery. See also John Taylor, *William Henry Seward* (1991).

John C. Waugh, *Reelecting Lincoln* (1997) considers the election of 1864. The assassination of Lincoln and its aftermath is the subject of Jay Winik, *April 1865: The Month That Saved America* (2001).

The legacy of the Civil War is thoughtfully examined in David W. Blight, *Race and Reunion: The Civil War in American Memory* (2001), and Tony Horwitz, *Confederates in the Attic: Dispatches from the Unfinished Civil War* (1998).

CHAPTER 15 RECONSTRUCTION AND THE SOUTH

Lincoln's ideas about Reconstruction are analyzed in William C. Harris, *With Charity for All* (1997), and in many of the Lincoln volumes mentioned in earlier chapters. Hans Trefousse, *Andrew Johnson: A Biography* (1989), is a balanced account. See also Brooks D. Simpson, *The Reconstruction Presidents* (2001), and Howard B. Means, *The Avenger Takes His Place* (2006), an account of Johnson's pivotal struggle with the Radical Republicans.

A number of biographies provide information helpful in understanding the Radicals. The most important are Hans Trefousse, *Thaddeus Stevens* (1997), and David Donald, *Charles Sumner and the Rights of Man* (1970). J. M. McPherson, *The Struggle for Equality: Abolitionists and the Negro in the Civil War and Reconstruction* (1964), is also valuable. See also W. E. Nelson, *The Fourteenth Amendment* (1988).

Conditions in the South during Reconstruction are discussed in Edward Ayers, *The Promise of the New South* (1992). The Freedmen's Bureau is examined in Paul Cimbala, *Under the Guardianship of the Nation* (1997). See also R. H. Abbott, *The Republican Party and the South* (1986), Michael Perman, *Reunion Without Compromise* (1973), H. N. Rabinowitz, *Race Relations in the Urban South* (1978), J. L. Roark, *Masters Without Slaves* (1977), and Leon Litwack, *Been in the Storm Too Long* (1979). For recent general studies, see Don E. Fehrenbacher, *The Slaveholding Republic* (2001), and Pamela Brandwein, *Reconstructing Reconstruction* (1999). Daniel Stowell's *Rebuilding Zion* (1998) explores the religious dimensions of Reconstruction.

Of state studies see, for Virginia, Jane E. Dailey, *Before Jim Crow* (2000); for South Carolina, Julie Saville, *The Work of Reconstruction* (1994), and Thomas Holt, *Black over White: Negro Political Leadership in South Carolina* (1977); for Texas, Randolph B. Campbell, *Grass-Roots Reconstruction in Texas* (1997); and for Mississippi, Nicholas Lemann, *Redemption: The Last Battle of the Civil War* (2006). Much recent work on the Ku Klux Klan similarly focuses on particular states: see Lou F. Williams, *The Great South Carolina Ku Klux Klan Trials* (1996), Glenn Feldman, *Politics, Society and the Klan in Alabama* (1999), and Noel Fisher, *War at Every Door* (1997), which examines East Tennessee.

On the economic and social effects of Reconstruction, see G. D. Jaynes, *Branches Without Roots: Genesis of the Black Working Class* (1986), R. L. Ransom and Richard Sutch, *One Kind of Freedom: The Economic Consequences of Emancipation* (1977), Robert Higgs, *Competition and Coercion* (1977), and C. F. Oubre, *Forty Acres and a Mule* (1978). The ambiguities of dependence and independence as they relate to racial and gender issues are explored in Laura F. Edwards, *Gendered Strife and Confusion* (1997), and Amy Dru Stanley, *From Bondage to Contract* (1998).

Recent works on Grant include Josiah Bunting III, *Ulysses S. Grant* (2004), and Jean Edwards Smith, *Grant* (2001), though W. S. McFeely, *Grant* (1981) remains valuable.

David W. Blight, *Race and Reunion* (2001) considers the Civil War and Reconstruction in a deeper historical perspective.

CHAPTER 16 CONQUEST OF THE WEST

Recent historians of the West do not regard it as a frontier to be settled, but as a region where white settlers and Native American peoples converged, to the destruction of the latter's way of life. For the older view, see Frederick Jackson Turner's *The Frontier in American History* (1920), which has been updated in R. A. Billington and Martin Ridge, *Westward Expansion* (1982). For a summary of the newer interpretation, see Gregory H. Nobles, *American Frontiers* (1997). See also Patricia Nelson Limerick, *The Legacy of Conquest* (1987), Richard White, *"It's Your Misfortune and None of My Own"* (1991), and Elliott West, *Contested Plains: Indians, Goldseekers, and the Rush to Colorado* (1998).

The economic, political, and legal ideas current in this period are covered in David M. Wrobel, *Promised Lands* (2002), and Patricia Limerick, *Something in the Soil: Legacies and Reckonings in the New West* (2000).

On government policy and white attitudes toward Indians, see Robert F. Berkhofer, Jr., *The White Man's Indian* (1978), Robert Wooster, *The Military and U.S. Indian Policy* (1988), and Andrew C. Isenberg, *The Destruction of the Bison* (2000).

Two superb recent studies, in addition to Elliott West, cited above, have transformed our understanding of the California gold rush: Susan Lee Johnson, *Roaring Camp: The Social World of the California Gold Rush* (2000), and Malcolm J. Rohrbough, *Days of Gold: The California Gold Rush and the American Nation* (1997). For women on the frontier, see Deborah Lawrence, *Writing the Trail: Women's Narratives* (2006), John Mack Faragher, *Women and Men on the Overland Trail* (1979), and Sandra L. Myres, *Westering Women and the Frontier Experience* (1982).

For a compelling account of the development of transcontinental railroads see David Haward Bain, *Empire Express: Building the First Transcontinental Railroad* (1999).

On cattle ranching on the Plains, a good account is Lewis Atherton, *The Cattle Kings* (1961), but see also Don Worcester, *The Chisholm Trail* (1980).

Chapter 17 An Industrial Giant

In addition to the works cited in Debating the Past (p. 500), see David Haward Bain, *Empire* Express (1999) on the construction of the transcontinental railroads. On railroad regulation, see Steven Usselman, *Regulating Railroad Innovation* (2002). On the ways that technology transformed the way people understood daily life, see David E. Nye, *Electrifying America* (1990), and Jill Jonnes, *Empires of Light* (2003). Sven Beckert, *The Monied Metropolis: New York City and the Consolidation of the American Bourgeoisie, 1850–1896* (2001), outlines the special significance of that city in the nation's economic development and cultural mores.

The nation's expansive economy in the 1990s sparked interest in the leading businessmen and inventors a century earlier. For a detailed study of the key investment figure, see Jean Strouse, *Morgan: American Financier* (1999). Other useful works include Harold C. Livesay, *Andrew Carnegie and the Rise of Big Business* (2007); Michael P. Malone, *James J. Hill* (1996); Ron Chernow, *Titan* (1998), on John D. Rockefeller and the oil industry; James A. Mackey, *Alexander Graham Bell: A Life* (1997); and Martin V. Melosi, *Thomas A. Edison and the Modernization of America* (2007).

For the radical critics, see John L. Thomas, *Alternative Americas: Henry George, Edward Bellamy, Henry Demarest Lloyd* (1983), and also the radicals' own writings.

On the growth of unions see David Montgomery, *Beyond Equality* (1967), Leon Fink, *Workingmen's Democracy: The Knights of Labor and American Politics* (1983), and Nick Salvatore, *Eugene V. Debs* (1982). Jo Ann Argersinger, *Making the Amalgamated* (1999), describes the relation of gender and ethnicity in the rise of the clothing workers' union in Baltimore. Robert E. Weird, *Knights Unhorsed* (2000), blames internal dissension for the Knights' rapid decline. Lawrence Blickman, *A Living Wage* (1997), insists that labor radicalism persisted even after unionized workers won steady wages. The important strikes and labor violence of the period are covered in David O. Stowell, *Streets, Railroads, and the Great Strike of 1877* (1999), Susan Hirsch, *After the Strike* (2003) on Pullman, Paul Avrich, *The Haymarket Tragedy* (1984), and Carl S. Smith, *Urban Disorder and the Shape of Belief* (1995). On the challenge confronting the unions, see David Montgomery, *The Fall of the House of Labor* (1987).

Chapter 18 American Society in the Industrial Age

Henry Adams, *The Education of Henry Adams* (1918), is a fascinating if highly personal view of the period, and James Bryce, *The American Commonwealth* (1888), while primarily a political analysis, contains a great deal of information about social conditions. For two classic accounts of the settlement house movement, see Jane Addams, *Twenty Years at Hull House* (1910), and Lillian Wald, *The House on Henry Street* (1915). Addams's own life is the subject of two recent biographies: Jean Bethke Elshtain, *Jane Addams and the Dream of American Democracy* (2002), and Victoria Bissel Brown, *The Education of Jane Addams* (2004).

On the public character of nineteenth-century life, see Mary P. Ryan, *Civic Wars* (1997). On communities more generally, Robert Wiebe's *The Search for Order* (1967) shows how corporate and administrative bureaucracies overspread the nation, while Alan Trachtenberg, *The Incorporation of America* (1982), considers the cultural implications of Wiebe's insight. See also Gunther Barth, *City People* (1980).

On middle-class life and culture, see John Kasson, *Rudeness and Civility* (1990), Karen Halttunen, *Confidence Men and Painted Women* (1982), Burton Bledstein, *The Culture of Professionalism* (1976), and Mark C. Carnes, *Secret Ritual and Manhood in Victorian America* (1989). Karen Lystra, *Searching the Heart* (1989), emphasizes the close character of marriage, and Peter Gay, *The Bourgeois Experience* (1984–1997), argues that the middle classes throughout the Western world were not prudes. On contraception see Janet F. Brodie, *Contraception and Abortion in Nineteenth-Century America* (1994). On issues of consumption see Daniel Horowitz, *The Morality of Spending* (1985), William Leach, *Land of Desire: Merchants, Power, and the Rise of a New American Culture* (1993), and Elaine S. Abelson, *When Ladies' Go A-Thieving* (1989).

A broad survey on issues of disease is Gerald N. Grob, *The Deadly Truth: A History of Disease in America* (2002).

On working-class culture, Keith Peiss, *Cheap Amusements: Working Women and Leisure in Turn-of-the-Century New York* (1986), and Roy Rosenzweig, *Eight Hours for What We Will* (1983), are excellent. Kenneth T. Jackson, *Crabgrass Frontier* (1985), is a pioneering history of suburban development, and Jon C. Teaford, *The Metropolitan Revolution* (2007), gives weight to the accomplishments of the cities as well as to their inadequacies.

On the early development of intercollegiate sports, see Ronald A. Smith, *Sports and Freedom: The Rise of Big-Time College Athletics* (1988); on sports and modernization, see Melvin L. Adelman, *A Sporting Time* (1986), and Allen Guttmann, *From Ritual to Record* (1978).

CHAPTER 19 INTELLECTUAL AND CULTURAL TRENDS

The best overviews on intellectual trends include Louis Menand, *The Metaphysical Club* (2001), John Patrick Diggins, *The Promise of Pragmatism* (1994), and Jackson Lears, *No Place for Grace: Antimodernism and the Transformation of American Culture, 1880–1920* (1981). Gail Bederman, *Manliness and Civilization* (1995), is also stimulating.

On the impact of Darwin on late nineteenth-century America, see Richard Hofstadter's *Social Darwinism in American Thought* (1955), though his view has been substantially modified. See Robert C. Bannister, *Social Darwinism* (1979), Carl Degler, *In Search of Human Nature: The Decline and Revival of Darwinism in American Social Thought* (1991), and Paul Crook, *Darwinism, War and History* (1994). James Turner, *Without God, Without Creed: The Origins of Unbelief in America* (1996), contends that Darwinism promoted skepticism.

Thorstein Veblen, *The Higher Learning in America* (1918), is full of provocative opinions. Stimulating modern studies include Kim Townsend, *Manhood at Harvard* (1996), William McNeill, *Hutchins' University* (1992), on the University of Chicago, and Robert McCaughey, *Stand, Columbia* (2004), and George Marsden, *The Soul of the American University* (1994).

On law and the social sciences, see Morton Horwitz, *The Transformation of American Law, 1870–1960* (1992), and Dorothy Ross, *The Origins of American Social Science* (1991). For various figures, see Robert D. Richardson, *William James: In the Maelstrom of American Modernism* (2006), and William Gale, *The Philosophy of William James* (2005); Jay Martin, *Education of John Dewey* (2002), and Jerome Popp, *Evolution's First Philosopher* (2007), also on Dewey; Garry Wills, *Henry Adams and the Making of America* (2005).

On women, see Rosalind Rosenberg, *Beyond Separate Spheres: Intellectual Roots of Modern Feminism* (1982), and Regina Morantz-Sanchez, *Sympathy and Science: Women Physicians in American Medicine* (1985). See also Jane Hunter, *How Young Ladies Became Girls: The Victorian Origins of American Girlhood* (2003).

On Twain, see Everett Emerson, *Mark Twain: A Literary Life* (1999). On other leading figures, see Susan Goodman, *William Dean Howells* (2005); Leon Edel, *Henry James* (1985); and Edward Chalfant, *Better in Darkness* (1994), also on James; William McFeely, *Portrait: The Life of Thomas Eakins* (2007), and more generally, Kathleen Pyne, *Art and the Higher Life: Painting and Evolutionary Thought in Late Nineteenth-Century America* (1996).

A recent interpretation of the Chautauqua movement is John E. Tapia, *Circuit Chautauqua* (1997). On journalism, see especially David Nasaw, *The Chief: The Life of William Randolph Hearst* (2000), and Denis Brian, *Pulitzer: A Life* (2001).

Chapter 20 Politics: Local, State, and National

There are several superb analyses of the political system of the period written by men who studied it firsthand: James Bryce, *The American Commonwealth* (1888), and Woodrow Wilson, *Congressional Government* (1886). On the evolution of political parties, see Paul Kleppner, *The Third Electoral System, 1853–1892* (1979), and Michael E. McGerr, *The Decline of Popular Politics* (1986).

C. Vann Woodward, *Origins of the New South* (1951), is an important regional study. Following in Woodward's path are Heather Cox Richardson, *The Death of Reconstruction* (2001), and Michael Perman, *Struggle for Mastery: Disfranchisement in the South, 1888–1908* (2001), who focus on the 1890s as the pivotal decade for the defeat of Reconstruction. Samuel C. Hyde Jr., examines the tension between the old planting elite of the South and plain folk in *Pistols and Politics* (1996). Steven Hahn's *Nation Under Our Feet* (2003), is a superb study of black political struggles in the South for several generations after Reconstruction.

Among biographies of political leaders, the following are especially worth consulting: Ari Hoogenboom, *Rutherford B. Hayes* (1995), Ira Rutkin *James A. Garfield* (2006), Zachary Karabell, *Chester A. Arthur* (2004), H. Paul Jeffers, *An Honest President* (2000), on Cleveland, also Henry Graff, *Grover Cleveland* (2002), Charles W. Calhoun, *Benjamin Harrison* (2005), Michael Kazin, *Godly Hero: The Life of William Jennings Bryan* (2006), H. Wayne Morgan, *William McKinley and His Era* (2003), and Kevin Phillips, *William McKinley* (2003). See also Stephen D. Kantrowitz, *Ben Tillman and the Reconstruction of White Supremacy* (2000).

Populism has been the subject of intensive study. Richard Hofstadter, *The Age of Reform* (1955), takes a dim view of populism as a reform movement; Lawrence Goodwyn, *Democratic Promise: The Populist Movement in America* (1976), calls it "a people's movement of mass democratic aspiration." Elizabeth Sanders, *Roots of Reform* (1999), champions the farmers' political efforts, a position amplified by Gene Clanton, *Congressional Populism and the Crisis of the 1890s* (1998). Peter Argersinger, *The Limits of Agrarian Radicalism: Western Populism and American Politics* (1995), Sheldon Hackney, *Populism to Progressivism in Alabama* (1969), and Steven Hahn, *The Roots of Southern Populism* (1983), are more than local studies. Michael Kazin, *The Populist Persuasion* (1994), insists on the enduring legacy of the movement.

See also Gretchen Ritter, *Goldbugs and Greenbacks* (1997), and Ross Evans Paulson, *Liberty, Equality and Justice: Civil Rights, Women's Rights and the Regulation of Business, 1865–1932* (1997).

Chapter 21 The Age of Reform

The Progressive Era is surveyed in Michael McGerr, *A Fierce Discontent: The Rise and Fall of the Progressive Movement in America, 1870–1920* (2003), and David Traxel, *Crusader Nation: The United States in Peace and the Great War* (2006). Two recent scholars examine American progressivism in the context of reform movements elsewhere: Daniel T. Rodgers, *Atlantic Crossings: Social Politics in a Progressive Age* (1998), and Alan Dawley, *Changing the World: American Progressives in War and Revolution* (2003). The works cited in the Debating the Past feature (p. 597) are also essential.

The role of muckraking journalism is explored in David Nasaw, *The Chief: The Life of William Randolph Hearst* (2000). See also Louise K. Knight, *Citizen: Jane Addams* (2005).

For regional studies, see Dewey W. Grantham, *The South in Modern America* (1994), Nancy Unger, *Fighting Bob La Follette* (2000), and Bernard A. Weisberger, *The La Follettes of Wisconsin* (1994). Kenneth Finegold, *Experts and Politicians* (1995), compares the struggles between urban machines and reformers in New York, Cleveland, and Chicago. James J. Connolly, *The Triumph of Ethnic Progressivism* (1998), examines the political dynamics in Boston. J. Anthony Lukas, *Big Trouble* (1997), provides a detailed account of labor strife in Idaho and Colorado. Chuck Chalberg, *Emma Goldman* (2007), is accessible.

On the woman suffrage campaign, see Jean Baker, *Sisters: The Lives of America's Suffragists* (2005), Margaret Finnegan, *Selling Suffrage: Consumer Culture and Votes for Women* (1999), Ellen Carol DuBois, *Harriot Stanton Blanch and the Winning of Woman Suffrage* (1997), and Gayle Gullett, *Becoming Citizens: The Emergence and Development of the California Women's Movement, 1880–1911* (2000). Other useful works include Lynn D. Gordon, *Gender and Higher Education in the Progressive Era* (1990), Robyn Muncy, *Creating a Female Dominion in American Reform, 1890–1935* (1991), and Paula Baker, *The Moral Frameworks of Public Life: Gender, Politics and the State in Rural New York, 1870–1930* (1991).

Books treating special aspects of progressivism include Edward A. Purcell, *Brandeis and the Progressive Constitution* (2000), Tony Freyer, *Regulating Big Business: Antitrust in Great Britain and*

America, 1880–1990 (1992), James Weinstein, *The Corporate Ideal and the Liberal State* (1981), and Naomi Lamoreaux, *The Great Merger Movement in American Business, 1895–1940* (1985).

On African Americans, see David Levering Lewis, *W. E. B. DuBois: Biography of a Race, 1868–1919* (1993), and *W. E. B. DuBois: The Fight for Equality, 1919–1963* (2000).

H. W. Brands, *TR* (1997), and Kathleen Dalton, *Theodore Roosevelt: A Strenuous Life* (2003), offer concise narratives. Edmund Morris's *Theodore Rex* (2001) is engaging. An interesting critique of Roosevelt's environmental policies can be found in Karl Jacoby, *Crimes Against Nature* (2001). James Chace, *1912: Wilson, Roosevelt, Taft, and Debs—the Election that Changed the Country* (2004), describes that pivotal event.

The standard multi-volume biography of Wilson is Arthur S. Link, *Wilson* (1947–1965). Recent works include H. W. Brands, *Woodrow Wilson* (2003). See also David Steigerwald, *Wilsonian Idealism in America* (1996).

CHAPTER 22 FROM ISOLATION TO EMPIRE

Contemporary attitudes are reflected in Josiah Strong, *Our Country* (1885), and Alfred T. Mahan, *The Influence of Sea Power Upon History* (1890), which provides the clearest presentation of Mahan's thesis.

For post–Civil War diplomatic history the works cited in Debating the Past (p. 617) are essential. William Zimmermann, *First Great Triumph: How Five Americans Made Their Country a World Power* (2003), is an accessible study of the convergence of Theodore Roosevelt, John Hay, A. T. Mahan, Elihu Root, and Henry Cabot Lodge. See also Thomas D. Schoonover, *The United States in Central America* (1991), and David Healy, *U.S. Expansionism: The Imperialist Urge in the 1890's* (1970). Emily S. Rosenberg, *Financial Missionaries to the World: The Politics and Culture of Dollar Diplomacy, 1900–1930* (1999), shows how cultural and economic forces intersected to promote expansionism.

On Hawaiian annexation, see Merze Tate, *The United States and the Hawaiian Kingdom* (1965). On the Spanish-American War, see Paul T. McCartney, *Power and Progress: American National Identity, the War of 1898, and the Rise of American Imperialism* (2006), and John L. Offner, *An Unwanted War: The Diplomacy of the United States and Spain over Cuba, 1895–1898* (1992). John Lawrence Tone, *War and Genocide in Cuba: 1895–1898* (2006), is sharply critical.

For colonial problems in the Philippines, see Stuart Creighton Miller, *"Benevolent Assimilation": The American Conquest of the Philippines, 1899–1903* (1982), and H. W. Brands, *Bound to Empire: The United States and the Philippines* (1992). Barthelomew Sparrow, *The Insular Cases and the Emergence of American Empire* (2006), examines the role of the Court in American expansionist policy. On the Caribbean, see Thomas O'Brien, *The Revolutionary Mission: American Enterprise in Latin America, 1900–1945* (1996). David McCullough, *The Path Between the Seas* (1977), is excellent on the history of the Panama Canal.

CHAPTER 23 WOODROW WILSON AND THE GREAT WAR

On the American involvement with Mexico, see Eileen Welsome, *The General and the Jaguar: Pershing's Hunt for Pancho Villa* (2006), and Joseph A. Stout, *Border Conflict: Villistas, Carrancistas, and the Punitive Expedition, 1915–1920* (1999).

On Woodrow Wilson, in addition to the works discussed in previous chapters and in *Debating the Past* (p. 666), see H. W. Brands, *Woodrow Wilson* (2003), and, less critical, Arthur S. Link: *Woodrow Wilson and the Progressive Era* (1954), and *Wilson the Diplomatist* (1957).

The war on the home front is covered in David M. Kennedy, *Over Here: The First World War and American Society* (1980). Paul A. C. Koistinen, *Mobilizing for Modern War* (1997), examines the emergence of business and military ties during the war.

On American military participation, see Mark Meigs, *Optimism at Armageddon* (1997), and Gene Smith, *Until the Trumpet Sounds* (1998), on Pershing. On African-Americans and the war, see Mark Ellis, *Race, War and Surveillance* (2001), and Stephen L. Harris, *Harlem's Hell-Fighters* (2003). See also Herbert A. Johnson, *Wingless Eagle: U.S. Army Aviation through World War* (2001). Women's role with the AEF is examined in Susan Zeiger, *In Uncle Sam's Service* (1999).

On the peace settlement, in addition to the biographies of Wilson, consult Thomas J. Knock, *The War to End All Wars: Woodrow Wilson and the Quest for a New World Order* (1992), A. J. Mayer, *Politics and Diplomacy of Peacemaking* (1967), and John M. Cooper, *Breaking the Heart of the World* (2001).

On labor, see David Montgomery, *The Fall of the House of Labor: The Workplace, the State, and American Labor Activism, 1865–1921* (1987). For a detailed study of organized labor in the South, see Bryant Simon, *A Fabric of Defeat* (1998). Kathleen Kennedy, *Disloyal Mothers and Scurrilous Citizens*

(1999), examines the intersection of war, gender, and free speech. On radicalism and the red scare, see R. K. Murray, *The Red Scare* (1955), Stanley Coben, *A. Mitchell Palmer* (1963), David Brody, *The Steel Strike of 1919* (1965), and E. Anthony Lukas, *Big Trouble* (1997), on labor disturbances in the Far West. On the Spanish influenza epidemic, see John Barry, *Great Influenza* (2004), and Gina Kolata, *Flu: The Story of the Great Influenza Pandemic of 1918 and the Search for the Virus That Caused It* (1999).

CHAPTER 24 POSTWAR SOCIETY AND CULTURE: CHANGE AND ADJUSTMENT

In addition to the works cited in Debating the Past (p. 676), Ann Douglas, *Terrible Honesty: Mongrel Manhattan in the 1920s* (1995), emphasizes the positive aspects of urban life, and Stanley Coben, *Rebellion Against Victorianism* (1991), emphasizes its elements of change. David Goldberg's survey, *Discontented America* (1999), focuses on divisions of race, ethnicity, and class.

Nativism and immigration restriction are covered in Desmond King, *Making Americans* (2000). On changes in the family, see Steven Mintz and Susan Kellogg, *Domestic Revolutions* (1988); on other social trends, John D'Emilio and Estelle Freedman, *Intimate Matters* (1988), and Paula Fass, *The Damned and the Beautiful* (1977).

The "new" woman is discussed in Nancy F. Cott, *The Grounding of Modern Feminism* (1987), William Chafe, *The American Woman* (1972), Ellen Chesler, *Woman of Valor* (1992) (on Margaret Sanger and the birth control movement), Dorothy M. Brown, *Setting a Course: American Women in the 1920s* (1987), and Nancy Woloch, *Women and the American Experience* (1971). Peter N. Stearns, *Anxious Parents* (2003) is a survey of childrearing advice, with special emphasis on the early twentieth century.

On the evolution of celebrity in popular culture, see Charles L. Ponce de Leon, *Self-Exposure: Human-Interest Journalism and the Emergence of Celebrity in America, 1890–1940* (2002). On Hollywood, see Steven J. Ross, *Working-Class Hollywood: Silent Film and the Shaping of Class in America* (1998). On radio, see Hugh R. Slotten, *Radio and Television Regulation: Broadcast Technology in the United States* (2000). On the rise of consumer credit, see Lendol Calder, *Financing the American Dream* (1999).

Fundamentalism is treated in Joel A. Carpenter, *Revive Us Again: The Reawakening of American Fundamentalism* (1997); the Scopes trial in Edward J. Larson, *Summer for the Gods: The Scopes Trial and America's Continuing Debate over Science and Religion* (1997), and Paul Conkin, *When All the Gods Trembled* (1998). On prohibition, see Stanley Walker, *The Night Club Era* (1999). On the Klan, consult Nancy MacLean, *Behind the Mask of Chivalry: The Making of the Second Ku Klux Klan* (1994), and Jim Ruiz, *The Black Hood of the Ku Klux Klan* (1998).

Francis Russell, *Tragedy in Dedham* (1962), casts doubt on the innocence of Sacco and Vanzetti; see also Paul Avrich, *Sacco and Vanzetti: The Anarchist Background* (1991).

Milton C. Sernetet, *Bound for the Promised Land* (1997), emphasizes the religious dimensions of the black migration to the North. Alfred L. Brophy, *Reconstructing the Dreamland: The Tulsa Riot of 1921* (2002), is useful on that important episode. On blacks in Harlem, see Gilbert Osofsky, *Harlem: The Making of a Ghetto* (1965). The Harlem Renaissance is the subject of Steven Watson, *The Harlem Renaissance* (1995), and J. Martin Favor, *Authentic Blackness* (1999). Eric Porter, *What Is This Thing Called Jazz?* (2002), explores the connections between music and intellectual life.

The literature of the period is analyzed in Nathan Miller, *New World Coming: The 1920s and the Making of Modern America* (2003). See Jeffrey Meyers, *Scott Fitzgerald: A Biography* (1994), and also his *Hemingway: A Biography* (1999); also Carlos H. Baker, *Hemingway* (1956); on Mencken, William R. Manchester, *Disturber of the Peace* (1951); on Lewis, Mark Schorer, *Sinclair Lewis* (1961); on Wharton, R. W. B. Lewis, *Edith Wharton* (1975), and Shari Benstock, *No Gifts from Chance* (1994).

On Henry Ford, see Douglas Brinkley, *Wheels for the World* (2004); Clarence Hooker, *Life in the Shadows of the Crystal Palace 1910–1927* (1997), illuminates the role of labor at Ford. On the early history of General Motors, see David Farber, *Sloan Rules: Alfred P. Sloan and the Triumph of General Motors* (2002). On women and cars, see Virginia Scharff, *Taking the Wheel* (1991). Beth Bailey, *From Front Porch to Back Seat* (1988), considers the ramifications of the automobile on courtship.

On Lindbergh and early aviation, see Walter L. Hixon, *Charles A. Lindbergh: Lone Eagle* (2006).

CHAPTER 25 THE NEW ERA: 1921–1933

The political history of the 1920s is surveyed in Michael Parrish, *Anxious Decades: America in Prosperity and Depression, 1920–1941* (1992), and Geoffrey Parret, *America in the Twenties* (1982).

Robert K. Murray, *The Harding Era* (2000), relates the embattled president to his times. John Dean's *Warren G. Harding* (2004) is interesting in that the author was himself convicted of crimes connected with the Watergate burglary during the Nixon administration. See also David Greenberg, *Calvin Coolidge* (2007), and Robert Ferrell, *The Presidency of Calvin Coolidge* (1998). On Hoover, see Martin L. Fausold, *The Presidency of Herbert Hoover* (1985), and a narrower monograph, Kendrick A. Clements, *Hoover, Conservatives and Consumerism* (2000).

Barry Eichengreen, *Golden Fetters: The Gold Standard and the Great Depression* (1992), considers an important issue; Maury Klein, *Rainbow's End* (2001), examines the stock market crash of 1929. See also the works cited in the Debating the Past feature (p. 713).

Stephen Kneeshaw, *The Pursuit of Peace* (1991), examines the Kellogg-Briand pact. See also Manfred Jonas, *Isolationism in America, 1935–1941* (1990) and Charles De Benedetti, *Origins of the Modern Peace Movement* (1978).

CHAPTER 26 THE NEW DEAL: 1933–1941

The most important surveys of the New Deal are listed in the Debating the Past (p. 739). Jonathan Alter, *Defining Moment: FDR's Hundred Days and the Triumph of Hope* (2006), is an accessible introduction to that formative period. See also R. Alan Lawson, *Commonwealth of Hope* (2005), Maxwell Bloomfield, *Peaceful Revolution* (2000), Ronald Edsforth, *The New Deal* (2000), and Alan Brinkley, *Liberalism and Its Discontents* (1998). Robert Shogan, *Backlash: The Killing of the New Deal* (2006), recounts the mounting opposition of the late 1930s.

Of the many biographies of Roosevelt, Allan Winkler, *Franklin D. Roosevelt and the Making of Modern America* (2006), is concise; for longer studies, see Geoffrey Ward, *A First-Class Temperament: The Emergence of Franklin Roosevelt* (1989). On Eleanor Roosevelt, see Blanche W. Cook, *Eleanor Roosevelt* (1992–1999), and J. William T. Youngs, *Eleanor Roosevelt* (2006).

On the New Deal and agriculture, see David E. Hamilton, *From New Day to New Deal: American Farm Policy from Hoover to Roosevelt, 1928–1933* (1991); Donald Worster, *Dust Bowl* (2004), analyzes the calamity while Timothy Egan, *Worst Hard Time* (2006), describes its consequences in personal terms. Sarah T. Phillips, *This Land, This Nation* (2007), addresses the impact of the New Deal on farmers with a focus on conservation issues.

On the New Deal and economic policy, see William J. Barber, *Designs within Disorder* (1996), Morton Keller, *Regulating the New Economy: Public Policy and Economic Change in America* (1990) and *Regulating a New Society: Public Policy and Social Change in America, 1900–1933* (1994).

On workers and the New Deal, see Edwin Amenta, *Bold Relief: Institutional Politics and the Origins of Modern Social Policy* (1998), Gery Gerstle, *Working-Class Americanism: The Politics of Labor in a Textile City 1914–1960* (1989), Vicki Ruiz, *Cannery Women, Cannery Lives: Mexican Women, Unionization, and the California Food Processing Industry, 1930–1950* (1987), Lizabeth Cohen, *Making a New Deal: Industrial Workers in Chicago, 1919–1939* (1990), and Melvyn Dubofsky, *The State and Labor in Modern America* (1994). Bruce Nelson, *Divided We Stand: American Workers and the Struggle for Black Equality* (2001), describes a cleavage within the labor movement over racial issues. On the relation of private pensions and social security, see Jennifer Klein, *For All These Rights: Business, Labor, and the Shaping of America's Public-Private Welfare State* (2003).

On constitutional questions, see William E. Leuchtenburg, *The Supreme Court Reborn: The Constitutional Revolution in the Age of Roosevelt* (1995).

For the activities of the radical fringe, consult Michael Denning, *The Cultural Front: The Laboring of American Culture in the Twentieth Century* (1996), Donald R. McCoy, *Angry Voices: Left-of-Center Politics in the New Deal Era* (1958), and D. H. Bennett, *Demagogues in the Depression* (1969). On blacks during the 1930s, see Raymond Wolters, *Negroes and the Great Depression* (1970), Nancy J. Weiss, *Farewell to the Party of Lincoln* (1983), and Harvard Sitkoff, *A New Deal for Blacks* (1978).

On women and gender, apart from the works cited above, see Suzanne Mettler, *Dividing Citizens* (1998), Landon Storrs, *Civilizing Capitalism* (2000), Susan Ware, *Beyond Suffrage: Women in the New Deal* (1981), and *Partner and I* (1987), a life of Molly Dewson. Also Linda Gordon, *Pitied But Not Entitled: Single Mothers and the History of Welfare* (1994), and Susan Ware, *Holding Their Own: American Women in the 1930s* (1982). On New Deal Indian policy, see Kenneth R. Philip, *Termination Revisited: American Indians on the Trail to Self-Determination, 1933–1953* (1999).

On isolationism and the events leading to Pearl Harbor, see Justus D. Doenecke, *Storm on the Horizon: The Challenge to American Intervention, 1939–1941* (2000), and David Reynolds, *From Munich to Pearl Harbor: Roosevelt's America and the Origins of the Second World War* (2001).

On James J. Braddock, see Michael C. De Lisa, *Cinderella Man* (2005).

CHAPTER 27 WAR AND PEACE

The best history of the worldwide events leading to the Japanese attack on Pearl Harbor is Waldo Heinrichs, *Threshold of War* (1988), but for more detail see Akira Iriye, *Pearl Harbor and the Coming of the Pacific War* (1999), and Michael S. Stackman, *Target: Pearl Harbor* (1990). Charles C. Tansill, *Back Door to War* (1952), and Charles A. Beard, *President Roosevelt and the Coming of the War* (1948), are interesting interpretations by isolationists. Useful overviews include David M. Kennedy, *Freedom from Fear: The American People in Depression and War* (1999), Murray Williamson and Allan R. Millett, *A War to Be Won* (2000), and Warren F. Kimball, *Forged in War: Roosevelt, Churchill and the Second World War* (1997). Mark A. Stoler, *Allies and Adversaries* (2000), focuses on the Joint Chiefs of Staff. Thomas S. Fleming, *The New Dealers' War* (2001), is critical of Roosevelt.

Alan Schom, *Eagle and the Rising Sun* (2004), chronicles the war in the Pacific from 1941–1943. On aerial warfare, see Williamson Murray, *War in the Air, 1914–1945* (1999), and Geoffrey Peret, *Winged Victory* (1993); see also Michael S. Sherry, *The Rise of American Airpower* (1987). Paul Fussell, *Wartime: Understanding and Behavior in the Second World War* (1989), provides a realistic rendering of the carnage and chaos of modern warfare; Gerald F. Linderman, *The World Within War: America's Combat Experience in World War II* (1997), contends that the spectacle of war offers little sustenance to soldiers. The term "the greatest generation" is from Tom Brokaw's 1998 book by that title.

For a general, brief overview of the home front, see Lewis A. Erenberg and Susan E. Hirsch, *The War in American Culture: Society and Consciousness During World War II* (1996), Doris Kearns Goodwin, *No Ordinary Time* (1995), and Steven Mintz and Susan Kellogg, *Domestic Revolutions* (1988). The effects of the war on women are described in Margaret Paton-Walsh, *Our War Too* (2002), D'Ann Campbell, *Women at War with America* (1984), Karen Anderson, *Wartime Women* (1981), and Susan M. Hartmann, *The Home Front and Beyond* (1982). William M. Tuttle Jr., "*Daddy's Gone To War*": *The Second World War in the Lives of America's Children* (1993), offers an interesting perspective. The impact of the war on radical politics is examined in Bill V. Mullen, *Popular Fronts: Chicago and African-American Cultural Politics, 1935–46* (1999).

African American participation is the subject of Maggie M. Morehouse, *Fighting in the Jim Crow Army* (2002), Nat Brandt, *Harlem at War* (1996), Neil A. Wynn, *The Afro-American and the Second World War* (1993), and Dominic J. Capeci, Jr., *Race Relations in Wartime Detroit* (1984). See also Maggie Rivas-Rodriguz, ed., *Mexican-Americans and World War II* (2007). On the Japanese internment, see Greg Robinson, *By Order of the President: FDR and the Internment of Japanese Americans* (2001).

Major biographies include Carlo D'Este, *Eisenhower: A Soldier's Life* (2002), Geoffrey Perret, *Eisenhower* (1999), and Ed Cray, *General of the Army: George C. Marshall* (1990).

Richard Rhodes, *The Making of the Atom Bomb* (1986), is superb. For the relationship among key Manhattan Project scientists, see Gregg Herken, *Brotherhood of the Bomb* (2002).

CHAPTER 28 THE AMERICAN CENTURY

General surveys include William Chafe, *The Unfinished Journey* (1986), James T. Patterson, *Grand Expectations: Postwar America, 1945–1974* (1996), David Halberstam, *The Fifties* (1993), H. W. Brands, *The Devil We Knew: Americans and the Cold War* (1993), John Patrick Diggins, *The Proud Decades, 1941–1960* (1989), and Michael S. Sherry, *In the Shadow of War* (1995).

The evolution of American policy toward nuclear weapons is debated in Gar Alperovitz, *Atomic Diplomacy: Hiroshima and Potsdam* (1985), Gregg Herken, *The Winning Weapon: The Atomic Bomb in the Cold War* (1982), and Melvyn P. Leffler, *A Preponderance of Power: National Security, the Truman Administration, and the Cold War* (1992). An accessible overview is Richard Rhodes, *Dark Sun: The Making of the Hydrogen Bomb* (1995).

The 1948 election is described in Gary Donaldson, *Truman Defeats Dewey* (1999). On the origins of the shift of the South away from the Democrats, see Kari Frederickson, *The Dixiecrat Revolt and the End of the Solid South, 1932–1968* (2001). On the cultural effects of the Cold War, see Elaine Tyler May, *Homeward Bound: American Families in the Cold War* (1988), and Paul Boyer, *By the Bomb's Early Light* (1986).

In addition to works cited in the previous chapter, see Donald R. McCoy, *The Presidency of Harry S Truman* (1984). David McCullough's *Truman* (1992), is accessible and sympathetic; Alonzo L. Hamby's *Man of the People: A Life of Harry S Truman* (1995), is scholarly and analytical.

Truman's foreign policy and the origins of the Cold War are examined in the Debating the Past feature for this chapter (p. 791). See also Robert L. Beisher, *Dean Acheson: A Life in the Cold War* (2006), and Michael J. Hogan, *The Marshall Plan* (1987). Roger C. Miller, *To Save a City: The Berlin Airlift* (2000), is a succinct account. See also John Lukas, *George Kennan* (2007).

The origins of the Korean War are now becoming clearer. In two volumes Bruce Cummings, *The Origins of the Korean War* (1981, 1990), emphasizes that the struggle was, at the outset, a civil war; William Stueck, *The Korean War: An International History* (1995), focuses on miscalculations by Stalin and Mao Zedong. For other perspectives, see Paul G. Pierpaoli Jr., *Truman and Korea* (1999), and Stanley Sandler, *The Korean War* (1999). On MacArthur, see Geoffrey Perret, *Old Soldiers Never Die* (1996).

On McCarthyism, see Tom Wicker, *Shooting Star: The Brief Arc of Joseph McCarthy* (2006). Ellen Schrecker, *Many Are the Crimes: McCarthyism in America* (1998), argues that the phenomenon was broader than McCarthy and became institutionalized in the FBI under J. Edgar Hoover. For different views of McCarthy himself, see Thomas C. Reeves, *Life and Times of Joe McCarthy* (1997), and Arthur Herman, *Joseph McCarthy* (2000). On the Hiss case, see Allen Weinsten, *Perjury: The Hiss-Chambers Case* (1978), and Sam Tanenhaus, *Whittaker Chambers* (1997). George Clooney, *Good Night, and Good Luck* (2006), includes the actor-director's thoughts on his movie about Edward R. Murrow and McCarthy, as well as the screenplay itself.

On the early history of the Civil Rights movement, see Mark Tushnet, *Making Civil Rights Law* (1994), and *Making Constitutional Law: Thurgood Marshall and the Supreme Court* (1997). The first volume of Taylor Branch's superb biography of Martin Luther King Jr., *Parting the Waters* (1988), covers 1959 through 1963. Thomas Borstelmann, *The Cold War and the Color Line* (2001), and Mary Dudziak, *Cold War Civil Rights* (2000), show how the civil rights movement became embroiled in foreign policy issues, especially with respect to African nations.

Recent (and increasingly positive) assessments of Dwight D. Eisenhower include Robert Bowie and Richard Immerman, *Waging Peace: How Eisenhower Shaped an Enduring Cold War Strategy* (1998), Craig Campbell, *Destroying the Village: Eisenhower and Thermonuclear War* (1998), and Ray Takeyh, *The Origins of the Eisenhower Doctrine* (2000) on Suez. See also Richard H. Immerman, *John Foster Dulles* (1999).

Chapter 29 From Camelot to Watergate

On Kennedy, consult Robert Dallek, *Unfinished Life: John F. Kennedy, 1917–1963* (2003), Richard Reeves, *President Kennedy* (1992), and James Giglio, *The Presidency of John F. Kennedy* (1991). Barbara Leaming, *Jack Kennedy* (2006), focuses on the person rather than the presidency. On Kennedy's foreign policy, see Lawrence Freedman, *Kennedy's Wars* (2000), and William Taubman, *Khrushchev* (2003). The Kennedy style can be "heard" in Ernest R. May and Philip D. Zelikow, eds., *The Kennedy Tapes: Inside the White House During the Cuban Missile Crisis* (1997). Also on the Cuban missile crisis, see Sheldon M. Stern, *The Week the World Stood Still* (2005). Gerald Posner, *Case Closed: Lee Harvey Oswald and the Assassination of JFK* (1994), debunks the conspiracy theorists.

Robert Caro, *The Years of Lyndon B. Johnson: The Path to Power* (1982) and *Means of Ascent* (1990), are extremely critical; Robert Dallek, *Lone Star Rising: Lyndon Johnson and His Times, 1908–1960* (1991) and *Flawed Giant: Lyndon B. Johnson, 1960–1973* (1998), are more balanced. Michael Beschloss, ed., *Taking Charge: The Johnson White House Tapes, 1963–1969* (1997), provides a verbatim, previously secret, account.

For civil rights, in addition to works cited in the previous chapter, consult Taylor Branch's second and third volumes in his trilogy on Martin Luther King Jr., *Pillar of Fire* (1998) and *At Canaan's Edge* (2006). Diane McWhorter, *Carry Me Home* (2001), provides a gripping account of the civil rights struggle in Birmingham, Alabama. Raymond Arsenault, *Freedom Riders: 1961* (2006), examines that important movement. Nicholas Lemann, *The Promised Land: The Great Black Migration and How It Changed America* (1991), is also indispensable. Malcolm X, *Autobiography*, is a classic account of black alienation, but see also Robert Terrill, *Malcolm X* (2006). Joseph E. Peniel, *Waiting 'til the Midnight Hour* (2006), examines the Black Power movement. James T. Patterson, *Brown v. Board of Education* (2001), provides a thorough account of that Supreme Court decision.

For a concise biography of Nixon, see Herbert H. Parmet, *Richard M. Nixon* (2006). See also Richard Reeves, *Richard Nixon: Alone in the White House* (2001), and Joan Hoff, *Nixon Reconsidered* (1994). Allen J. Matusow, *Nixon's Economy* (1998), is excellent. Dean J. Kotlowski, *Nixon's Civil Rights* (2001), argues that Nixon's actions—if not his rhetoric—were mostly supportive; J. Brooks Flippen, *Nixon and the Environment* (2000), makes a similar point about Nixon and environmental issues.

Henry Kissinger's memoirs, *White House Years* (1979) and *Years of Upheaval* (1982), are important though, like most such works, self-serving. See also Christopher Hitchens, *The Trial of Henry Kissinger* (2001).

The literature on the war in Vietnam is enormous. See David E. Kaiser, *American Tragedy: Kennedy, Johnson and the Origins of the Vietnam War* (2000), Lawrence Freedman, *Kennedy's Wars: Berlin, Cuba, Laos, and Vietnam* (2000), A. J. Langguth, *Our Vietnam: The War: 1954–1975* (2000), and Robert D. Schulzinger, *A Time for War* (1997). Neil Sheehan, *A Bright and Shining Lie* (1988), an account of the war from one American adviser's perspective, provides the best explanation of why the war could not be won. See also Lloyd C. Gardner, *Pay Any Price: Lyndon Johnson and the Wars for Vietnam* (1995).

For the antiwar movement, see Robert Buzzanco, *Masters of War: Military Dissent and Politics in the Vietnam Era* (1996), Rhodri Jeffreys-Jones, *Peace Now!* (1999), and Mary Hershberger, *Traveling to Vietnam: American Peace Activists and the War* (1998) on the ending of the war. See also Michael S. Foley, *Confronting the War Machine: Draft Resistance during the Vietnam War* (2003).

The best analysis of the Watergate affair is Stanley I. Kutler, *The Wars of Watergate* (1990) and *Abuse of Power* (1997), but see also Carl Bernstein and Robert Woodward, *All the President's Men* (1974) and *Final Days* (1976), and John W. Dean, *Blind Ambition* (1976). On Ford's elevation to the presidency, see James Cannon, *Time and Chance* (2001).

CHAPTER 30 SOCIETY IN FLUX

Kenneth T. Jackson, *Crabgrass Frontier* (1985), is indispensable on the evolution of the suburbs. On Jackson's argument that home ownership contributed to political conservativism, see Becky M. Nicolaides, *My Blue Heaven: Life and Politics in the Working-Class Suburbs of Los Angeles, 1920–1965* (2002). Elaine Tyler May, *Homeward Bound: American Families in the Cold War* (1988), locates the rise of a conservative ideological mindset within the home. The environmental consequences of suburbanization are the subject of Adam Rome, *The Bulldozer in the Countryside* (2001). For the cities, see Robert M. Fogelson, *Downtown: Its Rise and Fall, 1880–1950* (2001).

On the effects of the automobile, see Jane H. Kay's history/manifesto, *Asphalt Nation* (1997), and Virginia Scharff's *Taking the Wheel: Women and the Coming of the Motor Age* (1992).

For a favorable account of New Left of the 1960s, by a former leader of the SDS, see Todd Gitlin, *The Sixties: Years of Hope, Days of Rage* (1987). Maurice Isserman and Michael Kazin, *America Divided: The Civil War of the 1960s* (2000), though sympathetic to the New Left, note that conservatives emerged from the decade victorious. David Burner, *Making Peace with the Sixties* (1996), argues that the New Left unwisely abandoned its Old Left origins, and thus slipped into self-destructive hedonism. Peter Collier and David Horowitz, *Destructive Generation: Second Thoughts about the '60s* (1989), contend that the decade's "hedonism" and "revolutionary passion" culminated in "tragic consequences." See also Roger Kimball, *The Long March: How the Cultural Revolution of the 1960s Changed America* (2000), Dominick Cavallo, *A Faction of the Past: The Sixties in American History* (1999), and David Farber, *Chicago 68* (1988). Ellen Fitzpatrick, *History's Memory: Writing America's Past, 1880–1980* (2002), is especially critical of historians of this period for neglecting their scholarly forebears.

For television, see Mary Ann Watson, *The Expanding Vista: American Television in the Kennedy Years* (1994), and two books by James L. Baughman, *The Republic of Mass Culture: Journalism, Filmmaking, and Broadcasting in America Since 1941* (2006), and *Same Time, Same Station: Creating American Television* (2007). On cultural issues, see Karal Ann Marling, *As Seen on TV: The Visual Culture of Everyday Life in the 1950s* (1994), and Josh Ozersky, *Archie Bunker's America: TV in an Era of Change* (2003).

On black radicalism, in addition to works cited in the previous chapter, see the first person accounts by Malcolm X, *Autobiography* (1966), Stokely Carmichael and C. V. Hamilton, *Black Power* (1967), and Eldridge Cleaver, *Soul on Ice* (1967). Modern studies include Robert Terrill, *Malcolm X* (2006), and, on the Black Power movement, Joseph Peniel, *Waiting 'til the Midnight Hour* (2006). Taylor Branch's three-volume biography of Martin Luther King Jr.—*Parting the Waters: 1954–1963* (1988), *Pillar of Fire: America in the King Years, 1963–1965* (1998), and *At Canaan's Edge* (1965–1968)—is a modern classic. The neglected role of women in the civil rights movement is addressed in Chana Kai Lee, *For Freedom's Sake: The Life of Fannie Lou Hamer* (1999), and Carolyn Wedin, *Inheritors of the Spirit: Mary White Ovington and the Founding of NAACP* (1998).

Ronald Takaki, *A Different Mirror: A History of Multicultural History* (1993), provides an overview of the contemporary immigrant experience. Rodolfo Acuna, *Occupied America: A History of Chicanos* (2000), Manuel Gonzales, *Mexicanos: A History of Mexicans in the United States* (1999), and Ernesto Vigil, *The Crusade for Justice* (1999) provide surveys of broad trends of Chicano history in the United States. See especially Dan La Botz, *César Chavez and La Causa* (2006). John W. Sayer, *Ghost Dancing the Law* (1997), examines the legal issues surrounding the Native American protests at Wounded Knee. See also Kenneth S. Stern, *Loud Hawk: The United States Against the American Indian Movement* (1994).

The literature on the women's movement is voluminous. Betty Friedan's *The Feminine Mystique* (1963), is essential, though her account must be modified in light of Daniel Horowitz, *Betty Friedan and the Making of The Feminine Mystique* (1998). Susan Oliver, *Betty Friedan: The Personal Is Political* (2007), is a concise account. On abortion, Rickie Solinger, *Wake Up Little Suzie: Single Pregnancy and Race before* Roe *v.* Wade (1992), considers the situation before 1973. On the *Roe* v. *Wade* decision itself, see Laurence H. Tribe, *Abortion: The Clash of Absolutes* (1990), and Linda Gordon, *Moral Property of Women: A History of Birth Control Politics in America* (2002). Andrea Tone, *Devices and Desires: A History of Contraceptives in America* (2001) is useful on contraception more generally.

James H. Jones, *Alfred C. Kinsey: A Public/Private Life* (1997), finds that Kinsey's odd behavior discredits his scholarship; Jonathan Gathorne-Hardy, *Alfred C. Kinsey: Sex the Measure of All Things* (1998), is less critical. On sexual trends more generally, see Beth Bailey, *Sex in the Heartland* (1999), on Kansas in the 1960s and 1970s.

The early history of the AIDS crisis is movingly told in Randy Shilts, *And the Band Played On* (1987). See also Elizabeth Fee and Daniel M. Fox, eds., *AIDS: The Making of a Chronic Disease* (1992).

CHAPTER 31 RUNNING ON EMPTY: THE NATION TRANSFORMED

Bruce J. Schulman, *The Seventies* (2001), surveys that decade, as Haynes Johnson, *Sleepwalking through History* (1992) does for the 1980s. James T. Patterson surveys a somewhat broader period in *Restless Giant: The United States from Watergate to Bush v. Gore* (2004). On Gerald Ford, the definitive account is Yanek Mieczkowski, *Gerald Ford and the Challenges of the 1970s* (2005).

Peter G. Bourne, *Jimmy Carter* (1997), relates his subject's life and policies. W. Carl Biven, *Jimmy Carter's Economy* (2002), examines that critical issue. Donald Spencer, *The Carter Implosion: Jimmy Carter and the Amateur Style of Diplomacy* (1988), contains its thesis in the title; Robert A. Strong, *Working the World: Jimmy Carter and the Making of American Foreign Policy* (2000), defends Carter's record.

On Reagan, in addition to the works cited in Debating the Past (p. 881), see two recent studies: Michael Schaller, *Right Turn: American Life in the Reagan-Bush Era* (2007), and John Patrick Diggins, *Ronald Reagan: Fate, Freedom, and the Making of History* (2007). Although Edmund Morris's *Dutch: A Memoir* (1999), which includes fictional characters and footnotes, is not what it purports to be, it nevertheless offers interesting observations. David A. Stockman, *The Triumph of Politics* (1986), contains a frank discussion of administration fiscal policies. Reagan's foreign policy remains controversial. Especially useful is Jack F. Matlock, *Reagan and Gorbachev* (2004). Peter Schweizer, *Victory: The Reagan Administration's Secret Strategy That Hastened the Collapse of the Soviet Union* (1994), summarizes its achievements; Frances FitzGerald, *Way Out There in the Blue: Reagan, Star Wars and the End of the Cold War* (2000), is sharply critical. See also Jay Winik, *On the Brink* (1996).

The early history of the AIDS crisis is movingly told in Randy Shilts, *And the Band Played On* (1987); see also Elizabeth Fee and Daniel M. Fox, eds., *AIDS: The Making of a Chronic Disease* (1992). John-Manual Andriote examines its impact on gays themselves in *Victory Deferred: How AIDS Changed Gay Life in America* (1999).

On the transformation of the economy, see Robert M. Collins, *More: The Politics of Economic Growth in Postwar America* (2000), Daniel Yergin, *The Prize: The Epic Quest for Oil, Money and Power* (1991), and Barry Bluestone and Bennett Harrison, *The Deindustrializing of America* (1982).

CHAPTER 32 MISDEMEANORS AND HIGH CRIMES

Haynes Johnson, *Divided We Fall: Gambling with History in the Nineties* (1994), notwithstanding its expansive title, discusses the first few years of the 1990s; for the end of the Cold War see Michael R. Beschloss and Strobe Talbot, *At the Highest Levels: The Inside Story of the End of the Cold War*, and John Lewis Gaddis, *The United States and the End of the Cold War* (1992).

David Courtwright, *Violent Land: Single Men and Social Disorder from the Frontier to the Inner City* (1996), argues that much of the nation's crime has come from single males; for a cultural analysis of the infatuation with aggression, see Richard Slotkin, *Gunfighter Nation: The Myth of the Frontier in Twentieth-Century America* (1992). Bruce Jacobs, *Dealing Crack* (1999), provides a case study of the drug problem.

On the Reagan and Bush administrations, see Michael Schaller, *Right Turn: American Life in the Reagan/Bush Era* (2007). For Bush see Tom Wicker, *George Herbert Walker Bush* (2004), and John R. Greene, *The Presidency of George Bush* (2000). Gary R. Hess provides a thoughtful comparison on war-making processes in *Presidential Decisions for War: Korea, Vietnam and the Persian Gulf* (2001).

On Clinton prior to his move to the White House, see David Marannis, *First in His Class: A Biography of Bill Clinton* (1995). On the presidential years, see John F. Harris, *Survivor: Bill Clinton in the White House* (2005), as well as Clinton's memoir, *My Life* (2004). The *Starr Report* (1998), though hastily released and published, constituted the evidentiary base and set the tone for the subsequent impeachment debate. See also Richard A. Posner, *An Affair of State: The Investigation, Impeachment, and Trial of President Clinton* (1999). On foreign policy, see David Halberstam, *War in a Time of Peace: Bush, Clinton and the Generals* (2001).

On the advance of conservatism, see Godfrey Hodgson, *The World Turned Rightside Up: A History of the Conservative Ascendancy in America* (1996). On the defeat of the ERA, see Mary Francis Berry, *Why ERA Failed* (1986), and Donald G. Mathews and Jane Sherron De Hart, *Sex, Gender, and the Politics of E.R.A.* (1990).

On race and ethnicity, see David A. Hollinger, *Postethnic America: Beyond Multiculturalism* (1995), Andrew Hacker, *Two Nations: Black and White, Separate, Hostile, Unequal* (1992), and Stephen Thernstrom and Abigail Thernstrom, *America in Black and White: One Nation, Indivisible* (1997).

John Cassidy, *Dot.con* (2002), surveys the Internet economy. For a history of the Internet, see Janet Abbate, *Inventing the Internet* (1999). On the 2000 election, see David A. Kaplan, *The Accidental President* (2001), and Richard Posner, *Breaking the Deadlock* (2001).

The literature on terrorism is expanding rapidly. *The 9/11 Commission* Report (2004) is a detailed assessment of multiple failures in intelligence and security. Lawrence Wright, *The Looming Tower: Al Qaeda and the Road to 9/11* (2006), is indispensable. Douglas Little, *American Orientalism: The United States and the Middle East since 1945* (2002), provides a useful overview of American policies, while Thomas L. Friedman, *From Beirut to Jerusalem* (1989) offers a thoughtful analysis of the complex problems of the region. See also George Packer, *The Assassin's Gate: The United States in Iraq* (2005).

Bob Woodward's three books provide the best account of George W. Bush after the terrorist attack of September 11, 2001. *Bush at War* (2002) applauds his leadership immediately after 9/11; *Plan of Attack* (2004), more critical, details Bush's campaign to oust Saddam Hussein of Iraq; *State of Denial* (2006) maintains that Bush was incapable of accepting that the war was failing.

Recent works on immigration include Gary Hytuck and Kristine Zentgraf, *America Transformed* (2008), and Reed Ueda and Mary Water, ed., *New Americans* (2007). On the effects of globalization on children, see Paula Fass, *Children of a New World* (2007).

In *Game of Shadows* (2006), Mark Fainaru-Wada and Lance Williams, reporters for the *San Francisco Chronicle*, leaked secret grand jury testimony and broke the scandal of steroid use in organized sports.

On global warming and climate change, see Ann Rappaport and Sarah Creighton, *Degrees that Matter* (2007). Al Gore, the Democratic candidate for President in 2000, published an influential polemic, *An Inconvenient Truth* (2006), which was made into a movie by that title. On Hurricane Katrina, Doug Brinkley, *The Great Deluge* (2006), is definitive.

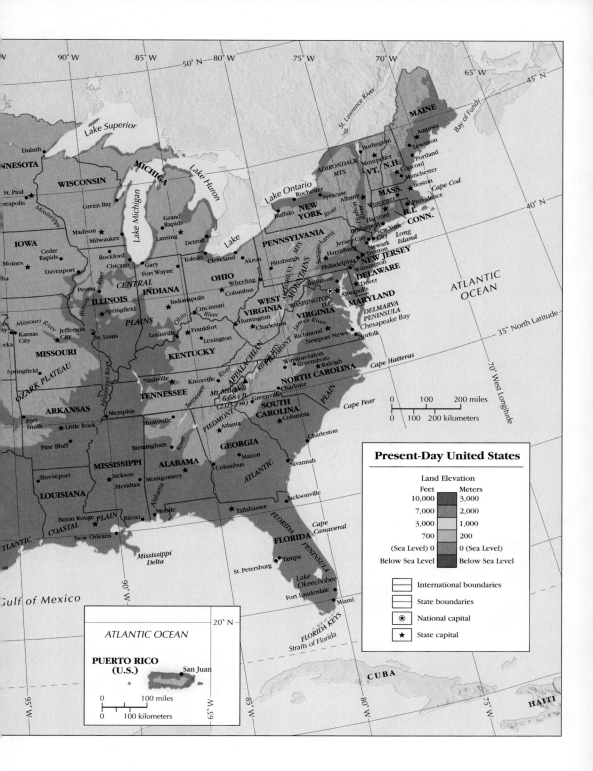

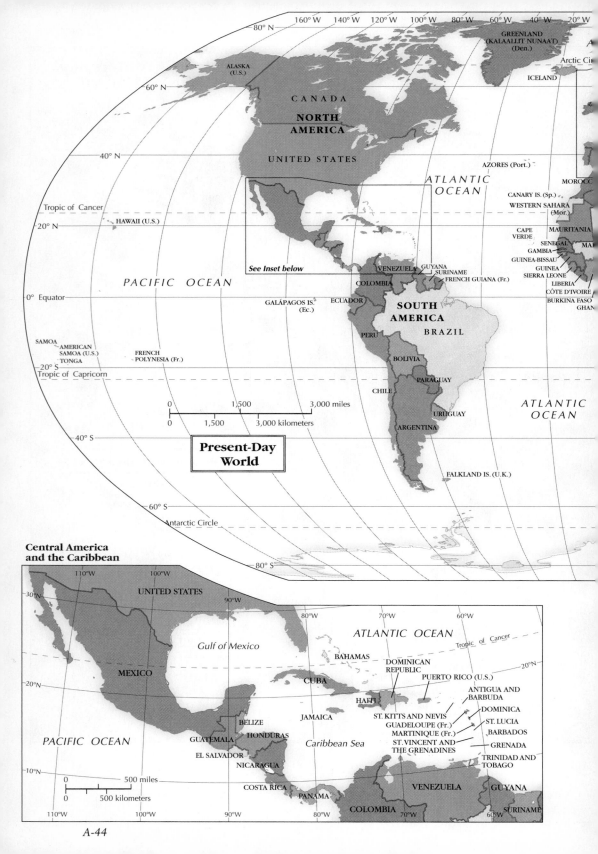

160° W 140° W 120° W 100° W 80° W 60° W 40° W 20° W

80° N

GREENLAND
(KALAALLIT NUNAAT)
(Den.)

Arctic Cir

ALASKA
(U.S.)

ICELAND

60° N

C A N A D A

NORTH
AMERICA

40° N

UNITED STATES

AZORES (Port.)

ATLANTIC
OCEAN

MOROCC

CANARY IS. (Sp.)

WESTERN SAHARA
(Mor.)

Tropic of Cancer

20° N

HAWAII (U.S.)

CAPE
VERDE

MAURITANIA

SENEGAL   MA
GAMBIA
GUINEA-BISSAU
GUINEA
SIERRA LEONE
LIBERIA
CÔTE D'IVOIRE
BURKINA FASO
GHAN

See Inset below

VENEZUELA GUYANA
           SURINAME
           FRENCH GUIANA (Fr.)
COLOMBIA

P A C I F I C   O C E A N

0° Equator

GALÁPAGOS IS.
(Ec.)

ECUADOR

SOUTH
AMERICA

BRAZIL

PERU

SAMOA

AMERICAN
SAMOA (U.S.)
TONGA

FRENCH
POLYNESIA (Fr.)

BOLIVIA

20° S

Tropic of Capricorn

PARAGUAY

CHILE

ATLANTIC
OCEAN

0   1,500   3,000 miles

0   1,500   3,000 kilometers

URUGUAY

ARGENTINA

40° S

**Present-Day
World**

FALKLAND IS. (U.K.)

60° S

Antarctic Circle

80° S

**Central America
and the Caribbean**

110°W   100°W

30°N

UNITED STATES

90°W   80°W   70°W   60°W

ATLANTIC OCEAN

Tropic of Cancer

Gulf of Mexico

BAHAMAS

DOMINICAN
REPUBLIC

20°N

MEXICO

20°N

PUERTO RICO (U.S.)

CUBA

ANTIGUA AND
BARBUDA

HAITI

DOMINICA

BELIZE

JAMAICA

ST. KITTS AND NEVIS
GUADELOUPE (Fr.)
MARTINIQUE (Fr.)
ST. VINCENT AND
THE GRENADINES

ST. LUCIA

BARBADOS

GRENADA

PACIFIC OCEAN

GUATEMALA
HONDURAS

Caribbean Sea

EL SALVADOR

10°N

NICARAGUA

TRINIDAD AND
TOBAGO

0   500 miles

0   500 kilometers

COSTA RICA

PANAMA

VENEZUELA

GUYANA

110°W   100°W   90°W

COLOMBIA

80°W   70°W

SURINAME

60°W

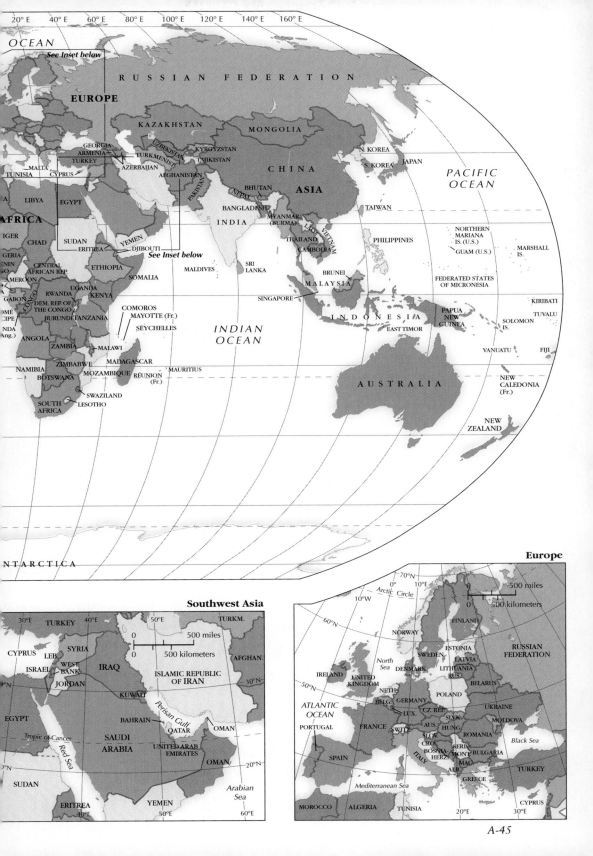

20° E   40° E   60° E   80° E   100° E   120° E   140° E   160° E

OCEAN

See Inset below

EUROPE

RUSSIAN FEDERATION

KAZAKHSTAN

MONGOLIA

GEORGIA
ARMENIA
TURKEY
AZERBAIJAN

UZBEKISTAN
KYRGYZSTAN
TURKMENISTAN
TAJIKISTAN

N. KOREA
S. KOREA   JAPAN

MALTA
TUNISIA
CYPRUS

AFGHANISTAN

CHINA

ASIA

PACIFIC OCEAN

LIBYA
EGYPT

AFRICA

SUDAN
ERITREA
YEMEN
DJIBOUTI

PAKISTAN
NEPAL
BHUTAN
BANGLADESH

INDIA

MYANMAR
(BURMA)
THAILAND
LAOS
VIETNAM
CAMBODIA

TAIWAN

NORTHERN
MARIANA
IS. (U.S.)
GUAM (U.S.)

MARSHALL
IS.

IGER
CHAD

CENTRAL
AFRICAN REP.
CAMEROON
ETHIOPIA

SOMALIA

See Inset below

MALDIVES

SRI
LANKA

PHILIPPINES

FEDERATED STATES
OF MICRONESIA

GERIA
NIN
GO
GABON
RWANDA
UGANDA
KENYA

BRUNEI

MALAYSIA

KIRIBATI

OMÉ
CIPE
NDA
Ang.)

DEM. REP. OF
THE CONGO
BURUNDI TANZANIA

COMOROS
MAYOTTE (Fr.)

SEYCHELLES

SINGAPORE

INDONESIA

EAST TIMOR

PAPUA
NEW
GUINEA

SOLOMON
IS.

TUVALU

ANGOLA
ZAMBIA
MALAWI

*INDIAN
OCEAN*

VANUATU

FIJI

NAMIBIA
ZIMBABWE
BOTSWANA
MOZAMBIQUE
MADAGASCAR
RÉUNION
(Fr.)

MAURITIUS

AUSTRALIA

NEW
CALEDONIA
(Fr.)

SOUTH
AFRICA
SWAZILAND
LESOTHO

NEW
ZEALAND

NTARCTICA

Southwest Asia

30°E   TURKEY   40°E   50°E   TURKM.

CYPRUS   LEB.
SYRIA
ISRAEL   WEST
BANK
JORDAN

IRAQ

AFGHAN.

ISLAMIC REPUBLIC
OF IRAN

0   500 miles
0   500 kilometers

30°N

EGYPT

KUWAIT

Persian Gulf

BAHRAIN
QATAR

OMAN

SAUDI
ARABIA

UNITED ARAB
EMIRATES

OMAN

20°N

Tropic of Cancer

Red Sea

SUDAN

ERITREA
40°E

YEMEN
50°E

Arabian
Sea

60°E

Europe

70°N
0°   10°E
Arctic Circle
10°W
60°N

0   500 miles
0   500 kilometers

FINLAND

NORWAY

ESTONIA
SWEDEN   LATVIA

RUSSIAN
FEDERATION

North
Sea
DENMARK
LITHUANIA
RUS.

IRELAND
UNITED
KINGDOM
NETH.
BELG.
GERMANY
LUX.
CZ. REP.
POLAND

BELARUS

50°N

*ATLANTIC
OCEAN*

PORTUGAL
FRANCE
SWITZ.
AUS.
SLOV.
SLVK.
HUNG.
CRO.
BOSNIA-
HERZ.
SERB.
MONT.
MAC.
ALB.

UKRAINE

MOLDOVA

ROMANIA

BULGARIA

Black Sea

SPAIN
ITALY

GREECE

TURKEY

Mediterranean Sea

CYPRUS

MOROCCO
ALGERIA
TUNISIA
20°E

30°E

A-45

C-1

CHAPTER 4   128 Concord Museum, Concord, MA. 132 The Granger Collection, New York. 133 William Walcott, *Pulling Down the Statue of George III at Bowling Green* (detail), c. 1857. Lafayette College Art Collection, Easton, PA. 135 The Granger Collection, New York. 139 The Pierpont Morgan Library/Art Resource, New York. 146 The Granger Collection, New York. 148 Photofest. 149 (top) Sir Joshua Reynolds, *Colonel Banastre Tarleton* (detail), 1782, National Gallery, London. 156 New York State Historical Association, Cooperstown, NY. 159 Alex Maclean/Landslides Aerial Photography.

CHAPTER 5   165 National Portrait Gallery, Smithsonian Institution/Art Resource, New York. 167 Creative Eye/Mira.com. 168 www.picturehistory.com. 170 Gilbert Stuart, *James Madison*, c. 1820. Mead Art Museum, Amherst College. Bequest of Herbert L. Pratt, Class of 1895 (1945.82). 177 © Collection of the New-York Historical Society (neg. No. 1371). 184 Frederick Kemmelmeyer, *Washington Reviewing the Western Army at Ft. Cumberland, October 18th, 1794* (detail), 1800. Courtesy, Winterthur Museum. 188 www.Picturehistory.com. 190 The Granger Collection.

CHAPTER 6   198 (left) © Paul Rocheleau Photography. 198 (right) Courtesy of the Massachusetts Historical Society. 204 Private Collection/Bridgeman Art Library. 205 Chicago Historical Society, G1932.0018. 207 Photo by Vincent Colabella Photography/Courtesy JP Morgan Chase Archives. 209 Clark Family Collection, William Clark Papers Voorhis #2/Missouri Historical Society, St. Louis. 211 National Maritime Museum, London. 214 Collection of the New-York Historical Society, (Neg. No. 7278).

CHAPTER 7   221 (left) Private collection. 221 (right) Library of Congress. 223 Getty Images. 225 Jacob Maentel, *General Schumacker*, c. 1812, Gift of Edgar William and Bernice Chrysler Garbisch, © 2003 Board of Trustees, National Gallery of Art, Washington, DC. 227 The Mariners' Museum, Newport News, VA. 230 The Granger Collection, New York. 235 (left) Courtesy of the National Park Service. 235 (right) Lee Snider/Photo Images/CORBIS. 244 Chicago Historical Society. 245 Hood Museum of Art, Dartmouth College, Hanover, New Hampshire, Gift of George C. Shattuck, Class of 1803. 247 National Portrait Gallery, Smithsonian Institution/Art Resource, New York.

CHAPTER 8   251 © 1992 Paul Rocheleau Photography. 255 The Granger Collection, New York. 260 © Bettmann/CORBIS. 265 Museum of Fine Arts, Boston, MA. 269 White House Historical Association (White House Collection). 270 New York Public Library/Art Resource, NY. 273 Boston Athenaeum.

CHAPTER 9   279 The Hermitage, Nashville, TN. 282 Memphis Brooks Museum of Art, Memphis, TN, Memphis Park Commission. 285 The Granger Collection, New York. 291 The Granger Collection, New York. 295 Library of Congress. 298 National Museum of American History/Smithsonian Institution, Washington, DC.

CHAPTER 10   303 Museum of Fine Arts, Boston, MA. Gift of Maxim Karolik for the M. and M. Karolik Collection. 305 Courtesy of the New Bedford Whaling Museum. 306 Gerry Images. 308 Prints and Photographs Collection, Library of Congress. 310 (left) Courtesy of

American Correctional Association. 310 (right) French-Made at the Rihouet Factory, PA. Philadelphia Museum of Art. Gift of Mrs. John Penn Brock, 1964. 315 National Portrait Gallery, Washington, DC/Art Resource, New York. 317 National Portrait Gallery, Washington, DC/Smithsonian Institution/Art Resource, New York. 320 © Bettmann/CORBIS. 323 National Archives. 325 Museum of Fine Arts, Boston, MA.

CHAPTER 11   329 Chicago Historical Society, (ICHi-12725)/Photo by J. M. Edwards and E. Anthony. 333 Kansas State Historical Society, Topeka, KS. 338 Beinecke Rare Book and Manuscript Library/Yale University Collection of Western Americana. 341 The Granger Collection, New York. 346 Courtesy of the California State Library.

CHAPTER 12   351 National Archives. 357 Missouri Historical Society. 361 The Granger Collection, New York. 363 Newcomb Art Gallery, Tulane University, (detail). 367 The Granger Collection, New York.

CHAPTER 13   375 The Granger Collection, New York. 376 Library of Congress. 378 By courtesy of the Trustees of the Boston Public Library. 381 The Granger Collection, New York. 386 CORBIS. 390 (left) Photo by Alexander Hesler/Chicago Historical Society. 390 (right) Library of Congress. 393 Kansas State Historical Society, Topeka, KS. 395 The Granger Collection, New York.

CHAPTER 14   404 Cook Collection, Valentine Museum, Richmond, VA. 405 The Museum of the Confederacy, Richmond, Virginia/Copy Photography by Katherine Wetzel. 406 Library of Congress. 421 (center left) Courtesy of the Massachusetts Historical Society. 421 (far left) Photofest. 421 (center right) Courtesy of the Massachusetts Historical Society, Luis F. Emilio Collection. 421 (far right) Everett Collection. 425 Library of Congress. 426 Library of Congress. 428 The Granger Collection, New York. 429 Library of Congress. 432 Library of Congress.

CHAPTER 15   439 www.picturehistory.com. 447 The Granger Collection, New York. 449 Library of Congress. 451 The Granger Collection, New York. 455 The Granger Collection, New York. 464 Colorado Historical Society.

CHAPTER 16   467 Burton Historical Collection, Detroit Public Library. 470 Bettmann/CORBIS. 475 Superstock, Inc. 479 Nebraska State Historical Society.

CHAPTER 17   485 Tony Aruza/CORBIS. 489 Library of Congress. 495 © Collection of the New-York Historical Society. 500 (left) The Baltimore Company. 500 (right) www .picturehistory.com. 504 Bettmann/CORBIS. 506 The Granger Collection, New York.

CHAPTER 18   520 The Granger Collection, New York. 522 Library of Congress. 524 National Park Service, Statue of Liberty Monument. 527 Culver Pictures, Inc. 529 Bettmann/CORBIS. 532 Alice Kellogg Tyler, *Portrait of Jane Addams*, 1893. Chicago Historical Society, (P & S -1971.0140).

CHAPTER 19   537 Michael Mc Closkey/Alamy. 538 Smith College Archives, Smith College, Northampton, MA. 543 Nebraska State Historical Society, Solomon Butcher Collection. 547 Bettmann/CORBIS. 549 (left) Photofest. 549 (right) Brown Brothers, Inc. 551 The Image Works.

CHAPTER 20   556 The Granger Collection, New York. 561 Culver Pictures, Inc. 563 Private Collection. 566 The Granger Collection, New York. 571 Kansas State Historical Society, Topeka, KS. 573 Kansas State Historical Society, Topeka, KS. 576 Culver Pictures, Inc. 578 © CORBIS.

CHAPTER 21   583 Culver Pictures, Inc. 585 The Library of Congress. 589 Courtesy of the Fogg Art Museum, Harvard University Museums, on deposit from the Carpenter Center for the Visuals Arts. 591 Culver Pictures, Inc. 595 National Museum of American History, Smithsonian Institution. 597 Library of Congress. 601 The Granger Collection, New York. 605 Brown Brothers, Inc. 609 National Portrait Gallery, Smithsonian Institution/Art Resource, New York.

CHAPTER 22   617 (bottom) Killie Family Papers/Presbyterian Historical Society, Presbyterian Church, U. S. A. 617 (top) Private Collection/Bridgeman Art Library. 618 Taxi/Getty Images. 622 The Granger Collection, New York. 623 Library of Congress. 625 The Granger Collection, New York. 629 © Bettmann/CORBIS. 637 Library of Congress.

CHAPTER 23   643 Imperial War Museum, London, UK. 645 Brown Brothers, Inc. 652 Photoworld/FPG/Getty Images. 654 Courtesy of the Hagley Museum and Library. 655 Library of Congress. 663 The Granger Collection, New York. 666 (left) Library of Congress. 666 (right) Library of Congress. 667 Chicago Historical Society.

CHAPTER 24   672 Culver Pictures, Inc. 676 Getty Images. 677 Bettmann/CORBIS. 678 The Kobal Collection. 679 (left) DN00767511 Chicago Daily News Collection, Chicago Historical Society. 679 (right) DN0076798 Chicago Daily News Collection, Chicago Historical Society. 681 Culver Pictures, Inc. 683 Bettmann/CORBIS. 685 Bettmann/COR-BIS. 687 Kansas State Historical Society, Topeka, KS. 691 Hulton Archive/Getty Images. 693 Culver Pictures, Inc.

CHAPTER 25   698 Culver Pictures, Inc. 701 Culver Pictures, Inc. 705 Getty Images. 707 AP/Wide World Photos. 708 Bettmann/CORBIS. 713 Bettmann/CORBIS. 715 University of Washington Libraries, Special Collections. 716 Library of Congress. 718 FDR Library. 719 Bettmann/CORBIS.

CHAPTER 26   722 The Granger Collection, New York. 726 The Granger Collection, New York. 730 The Everett Collection. 731 Hulton Archive/Getty Images. 732 AP/Wide World Photos. 734 The Granger Collection, New York. 739 W. C. Pryor/National Archives. 740 William Gropper/*Vanity Fair*/Conde Nast Publications, Inc. 742 Bettmann/CORBIS. 743 Library of Congress. 745 Bettmann/CORBIS.

CHAPTER 27   754 Superstock, Inc. 758 Library of Congress. 761 Library of Congress. 762 The Granger Collection, New York. 767 (left) Photofest. 767 (right) Bettmann/CORBIS. 769 Bettmann/CORBIS. 770 Culver Pictures, Inc. 773 © CORBIS. 777 The Granger Collection, New York.

CHAPTER 28   787 AP/Wide World Photos. 788 © Bettmann/CORBIS. 791 Sovfoto/Eastfoto. 793 Bettmann/CORBIS. 796 Bettmann/CORBIS. 799 Bettmann/CORBIS. 800 Hulton Archive/Getty Images. 801 The Everett Collection. 804 © Elliot Erwitt/Magnum Photos, Inc. (detail). 807 Bettmann/CORBIS.

CHAPTER 29   812 Time & Life Pictures/Getty Images. 814 Bettmann/CORBIS. 817 AP/Wide World Photos. 819 Bettmann/CORBIS. 825 AP/Wide World Photos. 827 Jeroboam. 829 Time & Life Pictures/Getty Images. 830 Getty Images. 831 Magnum Photos, Inc. 835 © 1997 G. P. Trudeau. Reprinted with permission of Universal Press Syndicate. All rights reserved.

CHAPTER 30   843 © Harold M. Lambert/Superstock, Inc. 845 Magnum Photos, Inc. 851 Time & Life Pictures/Getty Images. 855 Getty Images. 858 © H. Diltz/CORBIS. 859 AP/Wide World Photos. 861 Bettmann/CORBIS. 862 AP/Wide World Photos.

CHAPTER 31   866 Stock Boston. 867 Bettmann/CORBIS. 871 Liaison/Getty Images. 876 © Sipa Press. 877 Ronald Reagan Library. 881 AP/Wide World Photos. 883 NIBSC/Photo Researchers, Inc. 887 Library of Congress © 1986 by Herblock in the *Washington Post*.

CHAPTER 32   893 Bob Daemmrich/The Image Works. 897 AP/Wide World Photos. 900 Getty Images. 903 Getty Images. 910 AP/Wide World Photos. 913 AP/Wide World Photos. 915 AFP/Getty Images. 916 AP/Wide World Photos, Inc. 918 Vincent LaForetReuters/CORBIS.

Note: Italicized letters *f* and *m* following page numbers indicate figures (photos, illustrations, and graphs) and maps respectively.

A & P food chain, 709
AAA. *See* Agricultural Adjustment Administration
Aaron, Hank, 917
AARP. *See* American Association of Retired Persons
Abilene, Kansas, 470*f*, 476–477
Abolitionist movement, 313–316; antislavery societies in, 314, 445; Civil War and, 402, 414–416; Emerson on, 319; and fugitive slaves, 378; and Kansas-Nebraska Act, 377–378; and Mexican War, 341; Whigs in, 378; and women's rights movement, 316–317
Abortion, 857, 862*f*, 900
Abraham Lincoln (ship), 913*f*
Abu Ghraib prison, 914*f*
Abzug, Bella, 861*f*
Accidents, on-the-job, 589–590
Acculturation, of slaves, 64
Acheson, Dean, 783, 790
ACLU. *See* American Civil Liberties Union
Acquired immunodeficiency syndrome (AIDS), 860, 882–884, 883*f*
ACT Test, 780
Acushnet (ship), 322
Adams, Abigail, 156, 156*f*
Adams, Charles Francis, 409
Adams, Charles Francis, Jr., 498
Adams, Henry, 205, 498, 533, 542, 555, 595
Adams, James Truslow, 94*f*
Adams, Jane, 541
Adams, John, 188*f*; and alcohol consumption, 312; on Anglo-French relations, 101; at Boston Massacre, 119; and confederation, 166; in Continental Congress, 129; death of, 248; and Declaration of Independence, 131, 132, 134; domestic policy of, 190–191; in 1800 presidential election, 195–196; European furnishings adopted by, 251; foreign policy of, 189–190; and Jefferson, 134, 239; and judiciary, 201;

Kentucky and Virginia Resolves and, 191–192; in Peace of Paris, 146; in Revolutionary War, 124, 136; on riots, 114; in 1796 presidential election, 188; and social reform, 156; taxation and, 86; as vice president, 173; women and, 156
Adams, John Quincy: in 1824 presidential election, 245–246; in 1828 presidential election, 278, 299; at Ghent negotiations, 231; on Jackson, 277, 281; as Jeffersonian, 200; on Missouri Compromise, 244; opinion of colleagues, 239; presidency of, 246; as secretary of state, 236–238
Adams, Samuel, 119*f*; in Continental Congress, 129; as revolutionary agitator, 118, 119, 121, 128
Addams, Jane: as anti-imperialist, 628; and NAACP, 610; and settlement house movement, 532–533, 532*f*; on women, 592; and World War I, 651
Adena communities, 6
Adkins v. *Children's Hospital,* 677
Administration of Justice Act (1774), 122–123
Adobe bricks, 56*f*
Advertising: in post–World War I period, 681*f*, 682, 693*f*; on television, 841–842; for tobacco, 60*f*
AEF. *See* American Expeditionary Force
Affirmative action, 850, 905
Afghanistan, 911–912; bin Laden in, 909; Bush (George W.) and, 753; in late 20th-century, 896*m*; nation-building in, 613; Soviet invasion of, 865, 873; Taliban in, 909; U.S. retaliation against, 911–912
AFL. *See* American Federation of Labor
Africa: agriculture in, 13; Barbary pirates from, 202; colonization by freed slaves in, 565; colonization of freed slaves in, 261–262, 313–314; embassy bombings in, 911; exploration voyages to, 19; Neolithic revolution in, 13; population growth in, 13; slave trade from, 58, 59*m*, 355–356; in World War II, 763, 764, 765*m*

African Americans. *See* Black Americans
African Methodist Church, 261–262
Afro-American League, 565
Age (newspaper), 565
The Age of Innocence (Wharton), 689
Age of Reason, 98
Agnew, Spiro T., 826, 836
Agricultural Adjustment Act (1933), 724–725, 735
Agricultural Adjustment Administration (AAA), 724–725, 735
Agricultural Marketing Act (1929), 712
Agriculture: colonial, 49, 58–63, 76, 80; European *vs.* Indian, 48; Farm Loan Act and, 647; in Great Depression, 711, 712, 714–715, 725–726; in mid-19th century, 351, 368*m*; in middle colonies, 80; New Deal policies for, 724–725; in New England, 76; in 19th century, 483; and Panic of 1857, 370; on plantations, 352; in post–Civil War South, 450–452, 451*f*, 452*f*; post–World War I, 710; prehistoric, 4, 7–9, 12, 13; railroads and, 366–368, 472; in South, 57–58, 59–61, 450–452, 451*f*, 452*f*; in West, 369, 472; in World War I, 650, 659
Aguilera, Christina, 162
Aguinaldo, Emilio, 624, 629, 629*f*
Aid. *See* Foreign aid
AIDS. *See* Acquired immunodeficiency syndrome
AIM. *See* American Indian Movement
Air travel, 695–696, 841
Airplane(s): early development of, 695–696; industry, 695–696; terrorism and, 909–911, 910*f*; in World War I, 695; in World War II, 769, 770
Aix-la-Chapelle, Treaty of (1748), 101
Al Sadr, Muqtada, 921
Alabama: bus boycott in, 816; civil rights movement in, 816, 817, 817*f*, 848; cotton in, 260, 289; iron industry in, 487; mound builders in, 11; slavery in, 353*m*
Alabama (ship), 409
Alamo, 330–331
Alaska: passage to, 2; purchase of, 613
Albania, 748
Albany Plan (1754), 97, 106–107
Albemarle settlement, 44
Alcindor, Lew (Abdul-Jabbar, Kareem), 845
Alcohol consumption: colonial, 311–313; 19th-century, 311–313, 527; post–World War I, 686; present, 670–671. *See also* Prohibition; Temperance movement
Alcoholism, 311–312
Alcorn, John L., 445
Alcorn University, 447*f*
Aldrich, Nelson, 555

Alexander, Francis, 245*f*
Alexander VI, Pope, 21, 22
Algonquin Indians, 48, 101
Ali, Muhammad, 845, 852
Alien Act (1798), 191, 199
Alien and Sedition Acts (1798), 190–191
Alien Enemies Act (1798), 190
Allan, John, 320
Allen, Frederick Lewis, 676*f*
Allen, Joan, 78
Allen, Richard, 261
Allende, Salvadore, 868
Alliance movement, 570–573
Allied Powers (World War I), 643, 706–707
Allied Powers (World War II): in European theater, 763–765, 765*m*, 768; trade with, 750
Allison, Alexander, 623*f*
Almshouses, 309
Alperovitz, Gar, 773*f*
al-Qaeda terrorist network, 909, 911, 912
Amalgamated Association of Iron and Steel Workers, 507, 521
Amalgamated Copper, 582
Amana Community, 307, 308
Amazon.com, 907
Amendments, constitutional, 176, A-14—A-20. *See also specific amendments*
America (ship), 225
America Online (AOL), 907
American Academy of Arts and Sciences, 550
American Academy of Pediatrics, 906
American Airlines Flight 11, 909
American Anti-Slavery Society, 445
American Association of Retired Persons (AARP), 721
American Birth Control League, 675
American Civil Liberties Union (ACLU): and curfews on teenagers, 510; and Scopes trial, 684
American Colonization Society, 262
The American Commonwealth (Bryce), 613
American Economic Association, 498
American empire, 106–108
American Expeditionary Force (AEF), 656
American Federation of Labor (AFL), 505; CIO and, 724; in early 20th century, 586; and unskilled workers, 724; women and, 677
The American High School Today (Conant), 853
American Historical Association, 923*f*
American identity, shaping of, 52–53, 84–85
American Independent party, 827
American Indian(s). *See* Indian Americans
American Indian Movement (AIM), 851
American League, 528
American Legion, 700

American Museum of Natural History, 526

American party. *See* Know-Nothing (American) party

American Philosophical Society, 99

American Political Economy (Bowen), 497

American Railway Union, 508

American Revolution, 126–160, 132*f,* 133*f*; balance of forces in, 134–136; beginning of, 122–124, 126–127; early defeats in, 137–138; events leading to, 111–118; financing of, 127, 150–151; heroes of, 160; New England in, 127–128; and social reform, 153–155; South in, 142–143, 144*m*; taxation and, 86–87; and unification process, 145–147, 157–158; uniqueness of, 134; and women, 155–157

"The American Scholar" (Emerson), 319

American Steel and Wire Company, 492

American Sugar Refining Company, 503

American System, 248

American Telephone and Telegraph (AT&T), 488

American Temperance Union, 312

American Tin Plate Company, 492

American Tobacco Company, 596

American Woman Suffrage Association, 591

Ames, Fisher, 187

Amherst, Jeffrey, 104, 108*f*

Amish school, hostage shooting at, 890

Amusement parks, 529*f*

Anaconda Mining, 469

Anaconda Plan, 406

Anarchists: and Haymarket Square bombing, 505, 506*f*; post–World War I persecution of, 667–668, 688

Anasazi civilization, 8, 8*f,* 13

Anderson, Alexander, 214*f*

Anderson, Marian, 741–742

Anderson, Robert, 402

Andersonville prison, 437

Andover, Massachusetts, 73*f*

André, John, 143

Andrew Jackson (ship), 362

Andros, Edmund, 72

Angell, James B., 538

Angels in America (Kushner), 799*f*

Angleworms, 829*f*

Anglican church, 34, 66

Anglo-African (newspaper), 417

Anglo-American relations: and administration costs of empire, 106; Burr conspiracy and, 209–211; in Civil War, 409; colonial controversies in, 115–118; imperial controls, tightening of, 108–110; impressment policy and, 212–213; in late 19th century, 614–616, 619–621; Latin American diplomacy and, 619–621; and Oregon border, 336–337; Panama Canal and, 375; Peace of

Paris and, 145–147; post-Revolutionary, 163–164, 181–182, 184–185; post-War of 1812, 234; trade and, 91–92, 362–363; in World War I, 642–644. *See also* American Revolution; War of 1812

Anglo-French War (1793), 181–182

Anglo-Iranian Oil Company, 874

Animals, domestication of, 13

Annan, Beulah, 678*f,* 679*f*

Annapolis group, and Philadelphia Convention, 166

Annenberg Public Policy Center, 697

Anthem, 228–229

Anthony, Susan B., 318, 591, 592

Antietam, Battle of, 413–414, 413*m*

Anti-Federalists, 172

Anti-imperialists, 627–628

Anti-Semitism: in Nazi Germany, 747; in post–World War I period, 673

Antislavery societies, 314, 445

Antitrust Division, of Justice Department, 709–710

Antitrust legislation: Supreme Court on, 503, 575, 596; Wilson and, 606–607. *See also specific laws*

Antitrust legislation, Roosevelt (Theodore) and, 596

AOL. *See* America Online

Apache Indians, 54, 466

Apathy, political, 276

Appalachian Mountains, 84–85; divide, 109*m,* 110; foothills, 56–57

"Appeal of the Independent Democrats," 378

Appeal to the Coloured Citizens of the World (Walker), 314

Appleby, Joyce, 168*f*

Applied Christianity (Gladden), 531

Appomattox Court House, 430, 431*m*

Arapaho Indians, 463

Arbenz Guzman, Jacobo, 804

Archaic period, 4

Argall, Samuel, 100

Argentina, 873

Arizona, territorial organization of, 471

Arkansas: desegregation in, 807, 807*f*; progressive reform in, 587; readmission to Union, 442; secession and, 396, 398*m,* 402; territory, 242, 243, 243*m*

Armfield, John, 352

Arminianism, 34, 97

Army: blacks in, 417, 655–656, 758*f,* 759; in Civil War, 417; Continental, 129, 135*f*; late 19th-century, 615; McCarthy and, 798–799, 800*f*–801*f*; in Mexican War, 338*f*; in Spanish-American War, 624–626; in War of 1812, 225*f*; women in, 762; in World War I, 649, 655–656, 656–657; in World War II, 756, 758–759, 758*f,* 771*m*

Army-McCarthy hearings, 798–799, 799*f,* 800*f*–801*f*
Army-Navy College Qualifying Test, 780
Arnold, Benedict, 135, 140, 143; in Saratoga Campaign, 141*m*
Arnum, Charles, 421*f*
Arthur, Chester A., 560, 564
Articles of Confederation, 150; copyright laws and, 162–163; dissatisfaction with, 163; inadequacies of, 163–164; need for revision of, 165; United States under, 151*m*
As I Lay Dying (Faulkner), 729
As Seen On TV (Marling), 843*f*
Ashburton, Lord, 330
Ashcan School artists, 585*f*
Ashiriya Mosque, 920–921
Asia: exploration voyages to, 19–20; prehistoric migration from, 2. *See also* Far East; *specific countries*
Assembly line, 694
Astor, John Jacob, 334, 548*f*
Astor, Mrs. John Jacob, 549*f*
Asylums, 309, 311
Atchison, David R., 377, 382
Atchison, Topeka, and Santa Fe Railroad, 473, 477*m*
Athletics. *See* Sports
Atkins, John, 467
Atlanta, Georgia, in Civil War, 429*f*
Atlanta Compromise (1895), 567
Atlantic and Pacific Railroad, 477*m*
Atlantic Coast Line, 485
Atlantic Monthly (magazine), 416, 542, 545, 552, 584
Atlantic seaboard: English colonies of, 67*m*; European settlements along, 84–85
Atmospheric pollution, 917
Atomic bomb: Soviet development of, 789; United Nations on, 789; U.S. development of, 748, 753; in World War II, 748, 753, 772–775, 773*f. See also* Nuclear weapons
Atomic Energy Commission, 789
AT&T. *See* American Telephone and Telegraph
Attack and Die (McWhiney, Jamieson), 444*f*
Atwater, Lee, 891–892
Auburn prison system, 311
Augusta (ship), 778
Auschwitz death camp, 768
Austin, Stephen F., 330
Australia, in World War II, 769–770
Austria-Hungary, after World War I, 658
Authority, colonial attitude toward, 61–62
Autobiography (Van Buren), 296
Automobile, impact of, 692–694, 693*f,* 840–841
Automobile accidents, 840–841

Automobile industry: Ford and, 694–695; in Great Depression, 711; in New Deal period, 738; in oil crisis, 866, 871; post–World War I, 692–694, 709; post–World War II, 841, 869–870; strikes in, 738; unionization of, 738
Awakening. *See* Great Awakening
"Axis of evil," 912
Axis Powers (World War II), 754–755, 765*m*
Aztalan, 11
Aztec empire, 47; destruction of, 21, 26*f*

Babbitt (Lewis), 689
Babcock, Orville E., 454
Bache, Benjamin, 188*f*
Back country, 56, 66–68
Bacon, Nathaniel, 62
Bacon's Rebellion, 61–62
Baer, George F., 597
Baer, Max, 730*f*–731*f*
Baghdad International Airport, capture of, 914
Bailey, Colorado, hostage shooting at, 890
Bailey, Thomas A., 791*f*
Bailyn, Bernard, 168*f*
Bainbridge, William, 224
Baker, John "Home Run," 683
Baker, Newton D., 653
Balance of trade, concept of, 89–90
Balboa, Vasco Nuñez de, 21
Ballinger, Richard A., 601–602
Baltimore, Lord. *See* Calvert *entries*
Baltimore, Maryland: in Civil War, 419; foreign trade in, 362; infrastructure of, 523; in War of 1812, 228, 230
Baltimore and Ohio Railroad, 364, 392, 507, 537
Baltimore Evening Sun (newspaper), 685
Baltimore Sun (newspaper), 552, 577
Bancroft, George, 295*f*
Bank notes. *See* Currency
Bank of the United States: Biddle and, 282–283; creation of, 179; Jackson and, 282–286, 291–292; Maryland attempts to tax, 272; opposition to, 179; plan for, 329–330; second, 240–241; success of, 180
Bank robbery, 697
Bank(s) and banking: during Civil War, 407, 424; Federal Reserve system of, 606; Great Depression and, 711–712, 722–723; Hamiltonian reforms and, 179–180; investment banking, 369, 723; under Jackson, 282–286, 292; in post–World War I period, 709; Revolutionary War and, 150–151; under Van Buren, 296; War of 1812 and, 240–241; under Wilson, 606
Bao Dai, 802

Baptism, 70
Baptists, fundamentalism and, 684
Barbados, 44, 90
Barbary pirates, war with, 201–202
Barbed wire, 478–480, 479*f*
Baring Brothers Bank, 574
Barnard, Henry, 324, 517
Barnard College, 538, 549*f*
Barnburners, 344
Barnstorming, 695
Barrett, David, 825*f*
Barrios, 850
Barron, James, 214
Barton, Bruce, 692
Barton, Clara, 426
Bartram, John, 99
Baseball: integration of, 852; in late 19th-century, 528–529; in post–World War I period, 683; steroid scandal and, 917
Bases-for-destroyers deal, 749
Basketball, 528, 529
Batista, Fulgencio, 805
Batteries, 488
The Battle of Sand Creek (Lindneux), 464*f*
Battles. *See under specific geographic locations*
Bay of Pigs invasion, 812
Bayard, Thomas, daughter of, 592
Beard, Charles, 381*f*
Beard, Charles A., 168*f*
Beard, George M., 534
Beard, Mary, 381*f*
Beaumont, Gustave de, 301, 311
Beauregard, Pierre G. T., 406
Becker, Carl, 132*f*
Beecher, Catharine, 303
Beecher, Lyman, 304
Beer, patriotic names of, 126
Begin, Manachem, 873
Beijing, China, 617*f*
Belgian Relief Commission, 650
Belgium, in World War II, 768
Belknap, William W., 454
Bell, Alexander Graham, 488, 561*f*
Bell, John, 395, 396*m*
Bellamy, Edward, 499–500, 531, 534
Ben Hur (Wallace), 544
Benton, Thomas Hart, 338, 343, 347
Bering, Vitus, 236
Bering Strait, 2
Berkeley, John, 45–46
Berkeley, William, 61–62, 61*f*
Berkhofer, Robert E., 923*f*
Berkman, Alexander, 508
Berlin, Germany: in Cuban missile crisis, 812–813; division into east and west, 786–787, 786*m,* 812–813; in Potsdam agreement, 778; reunification of, 881*f*

Berlin airlift, 786–787, 786*m,* 787*f*
Berlin Decree (1806), 211, 220, 224
Berlin Wall, 786*m*; destruction of, 881*f*
Berman, Larry, 825*f*
Berners-Lee, Tim, 907
Bernstein, Barton, 739*f*
Bessemer, Henry, 487
Bessemer process, 487, 492
Beyond the Lines (Brown), 386*f*
Bezos, Jeff, 907
Bible: Darwin's theory of evolution and, 547; King James version, 34
Bicycling, 528, 530
Biddle, Nicholas, 283–286, 292
Bifocal spectacles, invention of, 100
Big Bonanza, 469
Bill of Rights, 176, 385–387
"Billy Budd, Foretopman" (Melville), 322
Biltmore mansion, 500*f*
bin Laden, Osama, 909, 911, 912
Bingham, George Caleb, 269*f*
Birch, William Russel, 190*f*
Birchbark canoe, 49
Birmingham, Alabama: in Great Depression, 714; iron industry in, 487
Birth control: in post–World War I period, 675–680; and sexual revolution, 857
Birth of a Nation, The (film), 446*f,* 680
Birthrate: in Great Depression, 717; in New England colonies, 69; in 19th century, 256, 303, 511; prehistoric, 9–10
Bison. *See* Buffalo
Black Americans: affirmative action and, 850, 905; and African colonization plans, 261–262, 314, 565; after Reconstruction, 564–565; in antislavery societies, 314; as campus radicals, 855; in Civil War, 417; in colonial South, 63–65, 64*f*; crime and, 893–894; in Democratic Party, 736, 742–743; Du Bois and, 608–611; in early 20th century, 608–611; education for, 437, 446*f,* 448, 449*f,* 565, 566*f,* 608, 806–807, 850, 905; in 1868 presidential election, 444; Emancipation Proclamation and, 414–416; gold rush and, 345; in government, 445–448; Hurricane Katrina and, 918–919; Industrial Revolution and, 253; inferiority thesis about, 197; Irish immigrants and, 359–360; Klan persecution of, 452–453, 686–687; Know-Nothing party and, 379; in late 19th-century, 564–567; in late 20th century, 905; literature of, 691–692; Long and, 732; lynchings of, 608, 656; migration of, 654–656, 690–692; in military, 417, 655–656, 758–759, 758*f*; New Deal and, 736, 742–743; in North, 263, 654–656;

Black Americans *(continued)*
in Populist party, 572–573; in post–World War I period, 690–692; in post–World War II period, 805–807; prejudice against, 63–64, 197, 359–360, 608–611, 758–759; progressivism and, 608; racial pride among, 852; rap music by, 906; as Reconstruction-era legislators, 445–448, 447*f*; in Republican party, 445–448, 557, 736, 742–743; Revolutionary War and, 154; Roosevelt (Franklin) and, 736; Simpson trial and, 904–905; in War of 1812, 226; white violence against, 453; women, 449–450; in World War I, 655*f*; World War I and, 654–656; in World War II, 753, 758–759. *See also* Black suffrage; Civil rights movement; Segregation; Slave(s); Slavery

Black Belt, 260, 353*m*

Black Codes, 439, 440

Black Hand, 642

Black Hawk, 289

Black Hills Indian reservation, 465, 469, 483

Black militancy, 608–611; in 1950s, 805; in 1960s, 848–850; after World War I, 690–692; and racial pride, 852

Black Muslims, 818, 845, 848

Black nationalism, 261–262, 314, 565, 690–692, 818

Black Power, 848–849

Black separatism, 565, 690–692, 818, 848–849

Black Star Line Steamship Company, 690

Black suffrage: civil rights movement and, 848; and 1848 presidential election, 444; Fifteenth Amendment and, 444–445; Fourteenth Amendment and, 441; under Johnson (Lyndon), 810, 820, 821–822; in mid-1960s, 848–850; Populist party and, 572–573; resistance to, 452–453, 564–565

Blackfoot Indians, 462

Blackwell, Elizabeth, 425–426

Bladensburg, Battle of, 228

Blaine, James G.: in 1876 presidential election, 455; in 1884 presidential election, 562

Blanco, Kathleen, 919

Bland-Allison Silver Purchase Act (1890), 574, 575

"Bleeding Kansas," 372, 380–382, 383*m*

Blennerhassett Island, 210

Blind people, education for, 309, 311

Bliss, William D. P., 531

Blitzkrieg, 748

Bloody shirt issue, 557

Blount, James H., 618

Blythe, California, 726*f*

Board of Indian Commissioners, 465

Board of Trade, 89

Bodnar, John, 524*f*

Boeing, William E., 696

Boeing Air Transport, 696

Boise, Idaho, immigrants in, 350

Bok, Edward W., 704

Bonds, Barry, 917

Bonsack cigarette-rolling machine, 483

"Bonus Army," 715–716, 716*f*

Book(s). *See* Publishing

Book of Mormon, 307

Boorstin, Daniel, 73*f*, 168*f*

Booth, John Wilkes, 436

Bootleggers, 686

Borah, William E., 663

Border issues: with Canada, 234, 330; colonial, 100–104; Ghent Treaty and resolution of, 234; with Indians, 464–466; with Mexico, 328, 917; post–Revolutionary, 163–164, 180–181; present-day, with Mexico, 328; with Texas, 331; and War of 1812, 220

Bosnia, 904; immigrants from, 350

"Boss Tweed," 568*f*

Boston, Massachusetts: Anthony Burns's arrest in, 379; civic culture of, 527; colonial, 68, 77; founding of, 37; in Great Depression, 712, 728; 1919 steel strike in, 666; settlement houses in, 532; shipping decline in, 362

Boston (ship), 618

Boston Associates, 253; and Waltham System, 255

Boston Guardian (newspaper), 611

Boston Herald (newspaper), 577

Boston Manufacturing Company, 253

Boston Massacre, 118–119, 120*f*

Boston Port Act (1774), 122, 123

Boston Symphony, 527

Boston Tea Party, 121–122

Boundary disputes. *See* Border issues

Bouquet, Henry, 108*f*

Bowen, Francis, 497

Bower, John, 230*f*

Bowers, Claude G., 746

Bowie, Jim, 331

Boxer Rebellion, 633

Boxing, 528, 730*f*–731*f*, 852

Boyer, Paul, 73*f*

Bozeman Trail, 463

Braceros, 850

Bracket creep, 870

Braddock, Edward, 104

Braddock, James J., 730–731, 730f
Bradford, William, 35, 36, 39, 79
Bradley, Joseph P., 456
Bradley, Omar N., 794
Bradstreet, Anne, 69
Braille, Louis, 309
Brandegee, Frank, 698f
Brandeis, Louis D.: appointment to Supreme Court, 646–647; influence on Roosevelt (Franklin), 733; on working hour legislation, 590
Brandywine, Battle of, 140
Braudel, Fernand, 73f
Breckinridge, John, 394–396, 396m
Breweries, 126
Brewster, William, 35
Brezhnev, Leonid, 814
Briand, Aristide, 704
Britain. See Anglo-American relations; Great Britain
British Guiana, 620–621
Brock, Isaac, 226
Broderick, Matthew, 420, 421f
Brooklyn Bridge, 526
Brooks, N. C., 614
Brooks, Preston S., 384, 408
Brown, John, 372, 393f; at Harper's Ferry, 392–393; in Kansas, 382, 393f
Brown, Joseph E., 445
Brown, Joshua, 386f
Brown, Michael, 919
Brown, Moses, 252
Brown University: founding of, 96; reform at, 326
Brown v. Board of Education of Topeka, 806
Bruce, Blanche K., 447f
Bryan, William Jennings: in 1896 presidential election, 576f, 577, 578m; in fundamentalist movement, 684–685; in 1900 presidential election, 629; in 1908 presidential election, 600; and Philippines, annexation of, 628–629; and Scopes trial, 684–685
Bryan-Chamorro Treaty (1914), 641
Bryce, James, 568f, 584, 613
Bryn Mawr College, 538
Brzezinski, Zbigniew, 873
Buchanan, James, 375, 384–385; and Douglas, 376, 387; and Dred Scott decision, 385, 387; in 1852 presidential election, 376; in 1856 presidential election, 384–385; and Lecompton constitution, 387; and secession, 398
Buchanan, Patrick, 899
Buddhists, in Vietnam, 810, 815, 825f
Budget, federal, balancing of: and Carter, 871; and Clinton, 900; and Hoover, 714

Budget deficit: under Bush (George H. W.), 898; under Carter, 871; under Clinton, 899, 904; under Reagan, 877, 885
Budget Reconciliation Act (1981), 877–878
Buena Vista, 338
Buenker, John, 568f
Buffalo, 467f; destruction of, 466, 467f; Plains Indians and, 462
Buffalo Bill, 467f
Buffalo County, South Dakota, 460
Bulgaria: and Greek civil war, 783; liberalization of, 894
Bulge, Battle of the, 768
Bull Run, Battle of, 405–407; Second, 413–414
Bulwer, Henry Lytton, 375
Bunau-Varilla, Philippe, 635, 636
Bundy, McGeorge, 811, 825f
Bunker Hill, Battle of, 129–130
Bunyan, John, 584
Bureau of Colored Troops, 417
Bureau of Corporations, 596, 606
Bureau of Indian Affairs, 743–744
Bureaucracy, federal, New Deal and, 738. See also Civil service
Burgoyne, John, 139–140
Burk, John Daly, 190
Burke, Edmund, 122, 127
Burlingame Treaty (1868), 461
Burnett, Frances Hodgson, 544
Burns, Anthony, 378f, 379
Burns, Edward, 767f
Burnside, Ambrose E., 418–419
Burr, Aaron: attempted secession of Federalists and, 206; conspiracy of, 209–211; duel with Hamilton, 206, 207f; in 1800 presidential election, 195–196
Bush, George H. W., 891, 892; Cold War and, 881f; deficit under, 898; foreign policy of, 894–898; Iran-Contra arms deal and, 891; in 1988 presidential election, 891–892; in 1992 presidential election, 899; and Persian Gulf War, 896–898; presidency of, 894
Bush, George W. (Jr.), 328; Afghanistan and, 753; Iraq and, 753; isolationism and, 613; and Kyoto Protocol, 917; military under, 753; Patriot Act (2001) and, 640–641; and Second Iraq War, 912–914, 913f, 920–922; Social Security and, 721; stem cell research and, 917; taxation under, 753; terrorism and, 763; in 2000 presidential election, 908–909; 2001 terrorist attacks and, 910–911; in 2004 presidential election, 914–916
Bushman, Richard, 251f
Bushnell, Horace, 304

Business: after Reconstruction, 454; after World War I, 692–694, 709–710; big, ambivalence toward, 496–498; Marshall Court and, 272; and military, alliance between, 649; in political campaigns, 578. *See also* Commerce; Corporations; Monopolies

Business codes, in New Deal, 723–724, 733

Business regulation, 501–502; under Coolidge, 700, 702, 709–710; under Harding, 699–700, 709–710; in New Deal, 723–724, 733; progressivism and, 582, 584; under Reagan, 877; under Roosevelt (Theodore), 596, 598–600; under Wilson, 606–607, 649; in World War I, 649; in World War II, 757

Butcher, S. D., 479*f*

Butler, Andrew P., 383–384

Butow, Robert J. C., 773*f*

Byrd, William, II, 66

Byrnes, James F., 756

Cabeza de Vaca, Alvar Núñez, 23

Cabinet: of Harrison (William Henry), 329; of Jackson, 285; of Lincoln, 401; of Pierce, 377; of Tyler, 329–330; of Washington, 175

Cables, transoceanic, 552

Cahokia, 10–12, 11*f,* 53

Calamity Jane, 469

Caldwell, as cattle town, 470*f*

Calhoun, John C., 247*f,* 336; and Bank of United States, 285; and Compromise of 1850, 347; in 1824 presidential election, 244–245; in 1836 presidential election, 296; in 1844 presidential election, 336; Jackson and, animosity between, 286–287; in nullification crisis, 291; as secretary of state, 331; *South Carolina Exposition and Protest,* 247–248; and tariff question, 247–248; and Texas question, 331, 332, 336; and Whig party, 294, 296; and Wilmot Proviso, 343

Califano, Joseph A., 670

California: affirmative action in, 905; Chinese immigration and, 461, 462; free blacks in, 345; gold rush in, 342, 344–345, 346*f*; immigrants in, post–Civil War, 461; Indians in, 55–56; in Mexican War, 339; mission settlements in, 55–56, 56*f*; prisons in, 892; Reagan governorship in, 875, 877*f*; Republic of, 339; settlement of, 334; slavery in, 346–349; Spain's claim to, 55; statehood for, 348; stem cell research in, 917; in Treaty of Guadalupe Hidalgo, 340–341; woman suffrage in, 592

California Jack, 469

Callender, James, 191

Calloway, Colin, 132*f*

Calvert, Cecilius (Lord Baltimore), 43–44, 43*f*

Calvert, George (Lord Baltimore), 43–44

Calvin, John, 14

Calvinism, 301, 304–305

Cambodia: immigrants from, 350; in Vietnam war, 824*m,* 829–830

Cameron, James, 548*f*

Camp, Walter, 682

Camp David Accords, 873–874

Campaigns. *See* Political campaigns

Canada: American appetites toward, 222; border issues with, 234; British conquest of, 104, 105; exploration of, 44; and fugitive slaves, 373; in Revolutionary War, 135; settlement of, 44; in War of 1812, 226–228; Webster–Ashburton Treaty and, 330

Canal(s), 267–270, 271*m*; across Central American isthmus, 375; and commerce, 364; competition with railroads, 364, 369

Canal Zone. *See* Panama Canal

Canning, 483

Canning, George, 237

Canseco, José, 917

Cape Horn, 362

Capital investment, in early 19th century, 258

Capital punishment, 892

Capitalism: churches and, 531; Marxist critics of, 501; progressivism and, 585, 586

Capone, Alphonse "Scarface Al," 686

Car. *See* Automobile

Carbon dioxide emissions, 917

Carbon Hill, Alabama, 739*f*

Caribbean: post–World War I relations with, 705; Spanish-American War in, 626*m*; U.S. expansionism in, 630–632, 632*m*; U.S. interest in, 375. *See also specific countries*

Carlyle, Thomas, 245*f,* 318

Carmichael, Stokely, 848–849

Carnegie, Andrew, 492–493, 500*f,* 605*f*; as anti-imperialist, 627; as businessman, 492–493; defense of big business by, 498; as example of social mobility, 516–517; philanthropy of, 492, 498, 551; on Sherman Act, 503; and unions, 507

Carnegie Endowment for International Peace, 704, 795

Carnegie Steel Company, 492, 493

Carolinas: colonial, 67*m*; settlement of, 44. *See also* North Carolina; South Carolina

Carpetbaggers, 445

Carranza, Venustiano, 642

Carter, Amy, 869

Carter, Jimmy, 372; economy under, 865, 870–871; foreign policy of, 873–875; hostage crisis and, 874–875, 876; in 1976 presidential election, 868–869; in 1980 presidential election, 875–876; presidency of, 869

Carter, Robert "King," 65

Carter, Rosalynn, 869

Carteret, George, 45–46

Carver, George Washington, 566*f*

CASA (National Center on Addiction and Substance Abuse), 670

Cash-and-carry system, 748

Casinos, on Indian reservations, 460

"The Cask of Amontillado" (Poe), 320

Cass, Lewis, 343, 344, 376

Castlereagh, Lord, 224

Castro, Fidel, 805, 812–814, 812*f,* 818–819

Catholic, Protestant, Jew (Herberg), 845

Catholics and Catholic Church: California missions of, 334; in cities, late 19th-century, 530–531; in civil rights movement, 844–845; in Civil War draft riots, 416; colonization activities, 56*f*; and Coughlin, 732–733; Indians and, 47, 54, 55–56; and Irish immigrants, 257; Know-Nothing party and, 379; Ku Klux Klan and, 686–687; in Maryland colony, 43–44; in mid-20th century, 844–846; in 1928 presidential election, 687, 708; in 1960 presidential election, 808–809; Oregon missionaries from, 334; and Spanish civil war, 746; temperance movement and, 312–313; in Vietnam, 815

Catt, Carrie Chapman, 677

Cattle drives, 476–477; Western trails, 477*m*

Cattle ranching, 476–480

Cattle towns, in West, 470*f*

Cavities, dental, 9

Cazenovia, Wisconsin, school shooting at, 890

CDC. *See* Centers for Disease Control

Ceasar's Column (Donnelly), 572

Ceausescu, Nicolae, 894

"The Celebrated Jumping Frog of Calaveras County" (Twain), 544

Centers for Disease Control (CDC), 882–883

Central America: Anglo-American relations and, 375. *See also* Latin America; *specific countries*

Central government: Bill of Rights and, 176; constitutional provisions for, 169–171;

formation of, 147, 148, 150; Philadelphia Convention and debates on, 166–188

Central Intelligence Agency (CIA): Allende regime and, 868; in Cuban missile crisis, 812; in Iran, 874; and Warren Report, 819; and Watergate scandal, 837

Central Pacific Railroad, 473, 475*f,* 477*m,* 555; and Union Pacific, competition between, 474–475

Central Powers (World War I), 643

The Century (magazine), 552, 565

Cerro Gordo, 339

Cervera, Pascual, 625

Chaco Canyon, 8, 12

Challenger (space shuttle), 880

Chamberlain, John, 597*f*

Chamberlain, Neville, 747

Chambers, Whittaker, 795

Champion of the Seas (ship), 362

Champlain Canal, 268

Chancellorsville, Battle of, 418*m,* 419

Chandler, Alfred D., Jr., 369, 500*f*, 504*f*

Channing, Edward, 444*f*

Charbonneau, Toussaint, 207

Charity, by churches, 530–531

Charles I (King of England), 37, 43, 72

Charles II (King of England), 45, 72

Charles River Bridge case, 274

Charleston, South Carolina: in Revolutionary War, 142; settlement of, 44; slavery in, 290, 351

Charleston Mercury, 290

Chase, Salmon P., 443; 1864 nomination of, 428; in Lincoln's Cabinet, 401, 407

Chase, Samuel, 201

Chattanooga, Tennessee, in Civil War, 423, 429*f*

Chauncy, George, 676*f*

Chávez, César, 851, 851*f*

Checks and balances, 171

Chemical weapons, in Middle East, 896

Cheney, Dick, 17, 908, 910, 912

Cherokee Indians, forced removal of, 287–289, 288*m*

Chertoff, Michael, 919

Chesapeake (ship), 213–214

Chesapeake and Ohio Railroad, 485

Chesapeake Bay, in War of 1812, 228

Chesapeake colonies, 42–44, 56, 57; agriculture in, 59–61; slavery in, 58, 63–65. *See also* Maryland; Virginia

Chevalier, Michel, 282

Cheves, Langdon, 240, 282–283

Cheyenne Indians, 462, 463; massacre of, 463, 464*f*

Chiang Kai-shek, 705, 789, 798

Chicago, Illinois: blacks in, 654; in Great Depression, 712; Haymarket Square bombing, 505, 506*f*; immigrants in, 521–522; infrastructure of, 523; meat industry in, 599; 1968 Democratic convention in, 827–828; Pullman strike in, 508; railroads and, 364, 365*m*, 368–369; settlement houses in, 532; in War of 1812, 226
Chicago (film), 678–679*f*
Chicago Chronicle (newspaper), 577
Chicago Daily Tribune (newspaper), 788*f*
Chicago Defender (newspaper), 742
Chicago River, 523
Chicago Tribune (newspaper), 718
Chicano movement, 850–851
Chickamauga, Battle of, 423
Child, David, 316
Child, Lydia Maria, 316, 453
Child labor: in early 20th century, 582; in late 18th to early 19th century, 252, 254, 255*f*; legislation on, 589; in mid-19th century, 360–361; progressivism and, 582, 589; Wilson and, 647; World War I and, 653
Children: colonial, 69–70, 69*f*; *genizaros*, 54; Great Depression and, 717; in late 19th-century, 511–512; in mid-19th century family, 302–303; in post–World War I period, 673; prehistoric, 9–10; Puritan notion of, 69–70, 69*f*; television and, 842. *See also* Education
Chile, 873
China: communism in, rise of, 789; détente and, 830–831, 831*f*; immigration from, 461, 462, 518; Japan and, 633, 641, 703, 705–706, 705*f*, 747; and Korean War, 792–794, 793*f*, 798; 19th-century relations with, 616; Open Door policy and, 633–634, 703; post–World War I, 703; post–World War II, 780–781, 789
Chinese Exclusion Act (1882), 461
Chinese Americans, in American West, 461, 462, 474, 475*f*
Chinook Indians, 209*f*
Chippendale, Thomas, 251
Chisholm Trail, 477
Chivington, Colonel J. M., 463, 464*f*
Choctaw Indians, 288–289
Chou En-lai, 793
Christian Commission, 426
Christian Socialists, 531
Christianity: American identity and, 52; and colonization activities, 47, 56*f*; expansionism and, 615; and exploration voyages, 21–24; and Islam, cultural gap between,

17–18; in mid-20th century, 844–847. *See also specific denominations*
Chrysler Corporation: in late 20th century, 871; in post–World War I period, 709
Chubbock, Emily, 254
Church(es): and big business, 531; in civil rights movement, 844–847; membership in, restrictions on, 38, 70–71; in mid-20th century, 844–847; mission San Diego de Alcalá, 56*f*; and state, separation of, 153; and urban problems, 530–531; women in, 846. *See also* Religion(s); *specific denominations*
Church of England. *See* Anglican church
Churchill, Winston: on Iron Curtain, 783, 784; post–World War II diplomacy of, 775, 777, 777*f*; in World War II, 749, 763
CIA. *See* Central Intelligence Agency
Cigarettes, 452, 483, 709
Cincinnati Red Stockings, 528
Cinderella Man (film), 730–731, 730*f*
CIO. *See* Congress of Industrial Organizations
Cities: automobiles and, 692–694; black migration to, 654–656, 690–692; city manager system in, 586–587; corruption in, 554–555, 567–569, 586–587; entertainment in, 526–530; of Eurasia, 14; geographic mobility in, 516–517; housing in, late 19th-century, 523, 525; immigrants in, 517, 520, 521, 523, 525; Indian, 10–13; infrastructure of, 523, 525; modernization of, 525–526; 19th-century life in, 510–511; political bosses in, 567–569; population growth in, 301*f*, 673–674; in post–World War I period, 673–674; prehistoric, 10–13; progressive reforms in, 586–587; railroads and, 368–369; and rural areas, conflicts between, 684–686; shopping malls and, 510–511; in South, 355; in West, 461. *See also* Ghettos; Slums; Urbanization
Citizenship: American identity and, 52; Dred Scott decision on, 385; Fourteenth Amendment definition of, 441; for immigrants, 522, 917
City manager system, 586–587
"Civil Disobedience" (Thoreau), 320
Civil liberties: in Civil War, 408; imperial encroachment on, 111–118; Patriot Act (2001) and, 640–641; in post–World War I red scare, 667–668; in World War I, 651–652
Civil rights: Eisenhower and, 805–807; Johnson (Lyndon) and, 810, 820, 848; Kennedy and, 810, 815–818; progressivism and, 607–608; Truman and, 787

Civil Rights Act(s): of 1866, 440; of 1964, 820

Civil rights movement, 810, 815–818; militancy in, 848–850; religious impacts of, 844–847; and women's rights movement, 860–862

Civil service: corruption in, 446f; under Grant, 454–455; under Harrison (Benjamin), 563; under Jackson, 280–281; late 19th-century reform of, 558–559, 561; in post-Reconstruction South, 447–448; spoils system and, 280–281

Civil Service Act (1883), 577, 578

Civil Service Commission, 561, 563

Civil War: Antietam, 412–414, 413m; blockade on South, 406, 408–409; Bull Run, Battle of, 405–407, 413–414; casualties of, 410, 433f; draft riots in, 416; economy during, 423–424; economy immediately prior to, 370–371; and Emancipation Proclamation, 414–416; end of, 429, 430–431, 433; events leading to, 381f; financing of, 407, 408–409; Fort Sumter, 401–402; Gettysburg campaign, 418, 418m, 419; Glory (film), 420–421, 420f–421f; Great Britain and, 409; isolationism after, 613; opposition to, 408; Peninsula campaign, 412, 413m; politics during, 407–408; results of, 430–431, 433, 444f; Shiloh, Battle of, 409–410, 411m; South's defeat in, reasons for, 444f; veterans' pensions and, 557; Vicksburg, siege of, 422–423; women in, 424–426, 425f, 426f

Civil Works Administration (CWA), 728, 729f

Civilian Conservation Corps, 723, 743

Civilization, concept of, 480

Clark, J. Reuben, 705

Clark, Jonas, 537

Clark, William, expedition of, 207–209, 208m, 209f

Clark Memorandum (1930), 705

Clark University, 537

Clarke, Edward Y., 687

Class structure: in 1896 presidential election, 579; Industrial Revolution and, 253–254; post-Revolutionary, 154. See also Middle class; Working class

Clay, Cassius (Ali, Muhammed), 845, 852

Clay, Henry, 244f, 246, 339; alcohol consumption of, 312; American System of, 248; and Bank of United States, 284–286, 329–330; and Compromise of 1850, 346–349, 373; in 1824 presidential election, 245–246; in 1832 presidential election, 282; in 1840 presidential election, 297, 329–330; in 1844 presidential election, 331, 335–336; and Missouri Compromise, 244; in nullification crisis, 291; railroad system and, 370; and Texas annexation, 331, 336; and Tyler (John), 329–330; and War of 1812, 225; and Whig party, 294, 329–330

Clayton, John M., 375

Clayton Antitrust Act (1914), 606–607

Clayton-Bulwer Treaty (1850), 619–620, 635

Clean Air Act (1970), 833

"Clear and present danger" doctrine, 652

Clemenceau, Georges, 660

Clemens, Samuel L. See Twain, Mark

Clergy, in colonial period, 98

Clermont (ship), 267

Cleveland, Frances Folsom, 563f

Cleveland, Grover, 561–563, 563f; on blacks, 564; and Cuban revolution, 621; in 1884 presidential election, 561–562; in 1888 presidential election, 563; in 1892 presidential election, 573; on 1896 presidential election, 577; first term of, 562–563; foreign policy of, 620; and Hawaii, 618–619; and immigration, 521; presidency of, 561–563; and silver coinage controversy, 575–576; and strikes, 507, 508

Cleveland, Ohio, 270; oil industry in, 493; progressivism in, 586

Clews, Elsie, 549f

Climate change, 1–2

Climate Protection Agreement (2006), 917

Clinton, Bill, 898–899, 900f; economy under, 901, 903–904; foreign policy of, 904; Gore and, 908; impeachment of, 891, 902–903, 903f; legacy of, 903–904; in 1992 presidential election, 899; in 1996 presidential election, 901–902; presidency of, 899–901, 903–904; on race relations, 905; Whitewater and, 898, 901

Clinton, DeWitt, 268

Clinton, George, 173, 209

Clinton, Henry, 140, 142, 145

Clinton, Hillary Rodham, 898, 899, 900–901

Clipper ships, 362–363

Clooney, George, 800f–801f

Clothes, in colonial South, 65

Clovis hunters, 2, 4

Coal, 358; in factory system, 358; in 19th-century, 257, 358; post–Civil War extraction of, 451, 487; post–World War I decline, 709; strike of 1902, 596–598

Coalition forces, in Iraq, 920
Cobb, Howell, 421
Coca-Cola, 831
Cocaine, 892–893
Cochran, Thomas C., 500*f*
Cochrane, Alexander, 228
Cockburn, George, 228
Cody, William F. (Buffalo Bill), 467*f*
Coercive Acts (1774), 122–123
Coeur d'Alene, Idaho, 508
Cohen, Lizabeth, 858*f*
Cohn, Roy, 799*f*
Coinage Act (1873), 574
Coit, Stanton, 532
Cold Harbor, 427, 431*m*
Cold War: containment policy and, 783,
    789–790, 803–804; Cuban missile crisis
    in, 810, 811–814, 814*f*; domestic reper-
    cussions of, 794–796; end of, 881*f*, 894,
    895*m*; Far East conflicts in, 799, 802;
    Latin American conflicts in, 804–805;
    Middle East conflicts in, 802–803; nu-
    clear weapons in, 789, 797–798,
    803–804; Reagan and, 881*f*; U.S.–Soviet
    relations during, 803–804
Cole, Arthur, 381*f*
Cole, Edward, 780
Cole (ship), bombing of, 911
Coleridge, Samuel Taylor, 318
College Board, 780
College of New Jersey, 96. *See also*
    Princeton University
College of Philadelphia, 98
College of Rhode Island, 96. *See also* Brown
    University
College of William and Mary, 66
Colleges and universities: admission tests
    for, 780; affirmative action at, 905; in
    colonial era, 66, 96, 98–99; expansion of,
    536–539, 853*f*, 854; football in, 529,
    535; gambling at, 697; integration of,
    806–807; Jews at, 673; in late 19th cen-
    tury, 536–539; in mid-19th century, 324,
    325–326; post–World War II reforms at,
    853–854; present-day alcohol use at,
    670–671; sports at, 529; student radicals
    at, 854–856; and Vietnam war protests,
    823, 829–830; women in, 325, 326,
    538–539, 538*f*. *See also specific institutions*
Collier, John, 744, 760
Collins, Ellen, 526
Colombia: drug trade in, 892–893; loss of
    Panama, 635–637
Colonialism. *See* Expansionism
Colonies: agriculture in, 49, 58–63, 76, 80;
    alcohol consumption in, 311–313; chil-
    dren in, 69–70, 69*f*; economy in, 63,

76–77, 80, 82; education in, 66, 96,
    98–99; family in, 57, 65–66; government
    in, 36–38, 37–38, 71–72, 74, 87–89;
    growth of, 108; hardships in, 31, 57;
    homes in, 65–66; imperial control of,
    tightening of, 108–110; and Indians, in-
    teraction with, 31–32, 48, 49–50,
    101–102, 106, 108*f*, 223*f*; intellectual life
    in, 98–100; middle, 45–47, 77, 80–84;
    northern, 67*m*, 68–77; proprietary,
    42–43; religion in, 40, 43–44, 66, 68–71,
    73*f*, 80, 93–96, 97–98; resistance move-
    ment in, 111–122; revolts in, 61–62, 68,
    113–115; royal influence in, 87–89;
    southern, 42–44, 57–68; taxation in,
    86–87, 109–118; trade in, 44, 76–77,
    92*f*, 117–118; urban growth in, 77; wars
    for, 101–102; witchhunt in, 74–76, 75*f*,
    78–79; women in, 40, 57, 65, 69–70
Colonists, and economic gain, 94*f*
Colonization, by freed slaves,
    261–262–262, 314, 565
Colorado: gold rush in, 469; Indian Wars in,
    463, 464*f*; massacre of Indians at Sand
    Creek (1864), 463, 464*f*; progressive re-
    form in, 588; territorial organization of,
    471; woman suffrage in, 592
Colored Alliance, 572
"Colored Rule in a Reconstructed (?) State"
    (Nast), 446*f*
Columbia River, 334–335, 336
Columbia University, 98, 670; quotas on
    Jews at, 673; student radicals at, 855*f*
Columbian Centinel, 239
Columbian Exchange, 49
Columbine High School (Colorado), 890
Columbus, Christopher, 14, 18–22, 23, 476
Comanche Indians, 54
Commager, Henry Steele, 676*f*
Commerce. *See* Business; Corporations;
    Monopolies; Trade
Commerce and Labor, Department of, 595
Commerce Court, 601
Commercial and Financial Chronicle (newspa-
    per), 551
Committee for European Economic
    Cooperation, 784
Committee for Industrial Organization
    (CIO), 724. *See also* Congress of
    Industrial Organizations
Committee on Civil Rights, 787
Committee on Public Information (CPI),
    651
Committee to Re-elect the President
    (CREEP), 833–834, 836
Commodity Credit Corporation, 738
Common school movement, 324

Common Sense (Paine), 131, 154, 155
Common Sense Guide to Baby and Child Care (Spock), 842
Commonwealth and Southern Corporation, 726
Communist Manifesto (Marx), 713*f*
Communists and communism: after World War I, 658, 665; Cold War domestic fears of, 781, 794–796, 800*f*–801*f,* 805–806; collapse of, in Eastern Europe, 894–895, 895*m;* détente and, 830–831; in Great Depression, 716; and red scare, 665–668. *See also* Containment policy
Communitarians, 306–309
Community colleges, 854
Community Service Organization (CSO), 851
Compromise of 1850, 346–349, 348*m,* 373, 376–377
Compromise of 1877, 457–458, 457*f,* 560
CompuServe, 907
Comstock Act (1873), 675
Comstock Lode, 469
Conant, James Bryant, 780, 853
Concentration camps, in World War II, 768
"Concentration" policy, Plains Indians and, 463, 464
Concessions and Agreements of 1677, 46
Concord, Battle of, 128, 128*f*
Concord, Massachusetts, literary figures in, 318–320
Conestoga Indians, 84
Coney Island, 529*f*
Confederate States of America: casualties of, 410, 433*f;* creation of, 396, 398; economic effects of war on, 423–424; finance in, 409; foreign policy of, 409; military forces of, 403–405, 403*f,* 404*f,* 406*f;* at start of Civil War, 402–404; strategy after Bull Run, 408
Confiscation Act (1862), 415
Congregationalists, 304
Congress, U.S.: blacks in, 445–448, 447*f;* in 1852 presidential election, 376; first achievements of, 176; in late 19th century, 555–556, 563–564; post–Civil War debates in, 437–441; progressive reforms of, 592–594; and Reconstruction, 438, 439–440, 443–444. *See also* Congressional elections; House of Representatives; Senate
Congress of Industrial Organizations (CIO): blacks in, 743; contributions to labor movement, 737–738; formation of, 724
Congress of Racial Equality (CORE), 816
Congress of Verona (1822), 236

Congressional elections: of 1852, 376; of 1854, 380; of 1858, 388, 389–401; of 1866, 442; of 1874, 455; of 1890, 564; of 1892, 572; of 1894, 575; of 1936, 735; of 1994, 901
Congressional Government (Wilson), 605
Congressional Medal of Honor, to black soldiers, 417, 655
Congressional Union, 592
Connecticut: colonial government of, 87; in presidential politics, 559; ratification of Constitution by, 172, 174*m;* settlement of, 41; stem cell research in, 917
A Connecticut Yankee in King Arthur's Court (Twain), 545
Conquistadores, 22–23
Conscription. *See* Draft
Conscription Act (1863), 415–416
Conservation: under Nixon, 833; under Roosevelt (Theodore), 600; under Taft, 601–602
Constitution(s): British, 152–153; colonial, 46; Confederate, 404–405; definitions of, 116–117; state, in post-Reconstruction era, 438, 442–443; state republican, 152–153, 155; U.S. (*See* Constitution, U.S.)
Constitution, U.S.: alternative interpretations of, 179–180; amendments to, 176, A-14–A-20; attempt to revise, 231; framing of, 166–171; ideas shaping, 168*f;* interpretations of, 191; and political parties, 182–183; ratification of, 171–173, 177*f;* slavery and, 169–170, 313–314, 314–315, 343; text of, A-6–A-13. *See also specific amendments*
Constitution (ship), 224
Constitutional Union party, 395, 396*m*
Consumerism: drop in, and Great Depression, 711; in post–World War I period, 692–694
Consumers' League, 590, 741
Containment policy, 783, 789–790, 803–804, 878
Continental Army, 129; female soldier in, 135*f*
Continental Congress(es): First, 123–124; Olive Branch Petition by, 130; and Peace of Paris, 147; Second, 129
Continental Divide, and Oregon Trail, 334, 335*m*
Continental System, Napoleon's, 224
Contraception. *See* Birth control
Contract(s): *Charles River Bridge* case, 274; Marshall Court on, 272
Contract with America, 901
Contras, 886–888

Convention Center, New Orleans, 919
Convention method, 155
Convention of 1800, 192
Convention of 1818, 235
Conyers, John, 435
Coolidge, Calvin, 698, 701*f*; Boston steel strike and, 666; economic policies of, 700, 702, 709–710; foreign policy of, 702–707; on Hoover, 708*f*; in 1924 presidential election, 702; in 1928 presidential election, 707–709; presidency of, 701–702; on war, 704
Cooper, Peter, 558
Cooper, Thomas, 191
Cooper, William, 438*f*
The Cooperative Commonwealth (Gronlund), 501
Copley, John Singleton, 119*f*
Copperheads, 408, 439
Copyright laws, 162–163
Coral Sea, Battle of, 769–770
CORE. *See* Congress of Racial Equality
Corinth, Mississippi, 410
Corn, 49, 76; diffusion of, 9; early cultivation of, 7–9, 7*f*; in mid-19th century, 368*m*; and population growth, 9–10; tooth decay and, 9
Corn Mother symbolism, 8
Corn Tassel, 289
Cornell University, 547, 570*f*
Corning, Erastus, 364
Cornwallis, General, 142–145; surrender of, 146*f*
Coronado, Francisco Vásquez de, 23
Corporations: capital investment and, 258; mergers of, 582, 583, 884; *vs.* trusts, 494–496. *See also* Business; Commerce
Corruption: in city government, 567–569, 586–587; in civil service, post-Reconstruction, 446*f*, 558; in Grant administration, 454–455; in Harding administration, 700–701; progressive reforms and, 586–587; in Reconstruction governments, 446*f*; urban, 554–555
Cortés, Hernán, 21, 22
Cosby, William, 83
Cosmetics, advertising, in post–World War I period, 681*f*
Cotton: and Cherokee Indians, 287; and Civil War, 403, 409, 424; exportation of, 362; in late 19th century, 570; in mid-19th century, 351; in post–Civil War South, 450–451, 451*f*, 452, 452*f*; as pre–Civil War export, 362; and slavery, 261–262, 262*f*, 263*f*, 351–352, 353*m*; in South, 259–261, 351–352, 450–451, 451*f*, 452, 452*f*; and Texas annexation, 330

Cotton gin, 259–260, 260*f*
Cotton States International Exposition, 566
Coughlin, Charles E., 732–733, 846
Coulter, Ann, 721
Council for New England, 36, 43
Counterculture, 840, 856–857
Courts, colonial, 38
Courtship, in 1920s, 674
Cowboys, 470*f*
Cowpens, Battle of, 143, 148
Cowperthewaite, Samuel, 310*f*
Cox, Archibald, 835
Cox, James M., 668
Coxey, Jacob S., 575
CPI. *See* Committee on Public Information
Crack cocaine, 893
Crane, Stephen, 546, 689
Craven, Avery, 381*f*
Crawford, William H., 245–246
Crazy Horse, 465
Creek Indians, in War of 1812, 232, 234
Creel, George, 651
CREEP. *See* Committee to Re-elect the President
Crescent City. *See* New Orleans, Louisiana
Crèvecoeur, Hector St. John de, 81; and American identity, 52
Crime: bank robbery, 697; in colonial times, 71–72, 77; copyright infringement, 162; drug use and, 892–894; in early 21st-century, 890–891, 916–917; immigrants blamed for, 520*f*; in late 19th century, 525; in late 20th century, 890–891, 892, 893*f*, 906–907; in 1988 presidential election, 891–892; in prohibition era, 686; and rehabilitation movement, 309, 312; in Revolutionary War period, 154; tax evasion, 86
"The Crime Against Kansas" (Sumner), 383
The Crisis (journal), 610, 611, 656, 690, 691
Croatia, 895
Crocker, Charles, 474
Crockett, Davy, 331
Croghan, George, 102
Croker, Richard, 569
Cromwell, Oliver, 72
Crop-lien system, 450–452, 451*f*
Croquet, 530
Crow Creek Indian Reservation, South Dakota, 460
Crowe, Russell, 730*f*
Crown Point, 128
The Crucible (film), 78–79
The Crucible (Miller), 801*f*
Crude oil, 487
CSO. *See* Community Service Organization

Cuba, 617*f*, 622*f*; annexation of, 391; attempted purchase of, 375; Bay of Pigs invasion of, 812; as colony, 638; Columbus in, 20; 1868 revolt in, 621–624; Guantanamo Bay sold by, 637; isolationism and, 614; missile crisis in, 810, 811–814, 814*f*, 913; and Nicaraguan Sandinistas, 886; 19th-century expansionism and, 614; 1959 revolution in, 805; protectorate relations with, 630–631, 705; slavery in, 621; Spanish control of, 104, 105; Spanish-American war and, 624–626; struggle for independence from Spain, 621–624; U.S. interests in, 621–624, 637

Cuffe, Pauls, 261

Culture(s): American *vs.* Iraqi, 17–18; European *vs.* Indian, misunderstandings between, 48–49; gay, post–World War I, 674; Indian, 22–23; in 19th-century cities, 526–530; Works Progress Administration and, 728. *See also* Intellectual life; Literature; Popular culture

Cumming, Kate, 424–425

Curfew, on teenagers, 510

Currency, 282–283; and early 19th-century speculation, 291–292; late 19th-century reform of, 558; Revolutionary War and, 150; silver *vs.* gold, 574, 579

Curry, John Stewart, 393*f*

Custer, George A., 465

Custer County, Nebraska, 543*f*

"Custer's Last Stand," 465–466

Cutler, Timothy, 96

CWA. *See* Civil Works Administration

Czechoslovakia: communist coup in, 784–785; creation of, 661; German aggression in, 747; liberalization of, 894; Marshall plan and, 784–785

Czolgosz, Leon, 594

D-day, 764–765, 765*m*

Dakotas: Alliance movement in, 571, 572; Dust Bowl in, 725–726; population in late 19th century, 570

Daley, Richard J., 827–828

Dallas, Alexander J., 240–241

Damon, Matt, 767*f*

DAR. *See* Daughters of the American Revolution

Dar Es Salaam, Tanzania, 909

Darlan, Jean, 764

Darrow, Clarence, 684–685

Dartmouth (ship), 121

Dartmouth College, 96, 272, 274

Dartmouth College v. *Woodward,* 272

Darwin, Charles, 497, 536

Darwinism, 536; academic theories of, 540; and feminism, 592; and immigration, 521; and intellectual life, late 19th century, 540, 547; religious fundamentalism and, 684–685

Das Kapital (Marx), 501, 509

Dating, in post–World War I period, 674

Daugherty, Harry M., 699, 700, 701

Daughters of the American Revolution (DAR), 741

Davidson, Julia, 425

Davis, Jefferson, 391, 405, 405*f*; after Civil War, 436; and Compromise of 1850, 405; as Confederate president, 398, 405, 444*f*; in Pierce cabinet, 377, 405; strategy after Bull Run, 408

Davis, John W., 702, 736

Davis, Stephen, 405

Dawes, Henry L., 467

Dawes Act (1887), 744

Dawes Plan (1924), 707

Dawes Severalty Act (1887), 466–467

The Dawn (journal), 531

"The Day of Doom" (Wigglesworth), 71

Day-Lewis, Daniel, 78

DDT, 847

de Gaulle, Charles, 764

De Leon, Daniel, 586

De Lesseps, Ferdinand, 620

de Lôme, Dupuy, 622

De Mille, Cecil B., 679*f*

de Soto, Hernando, 23

Dead Indian Land Act (1902), 608

Deadwood Dick, 469

Deaf, schools for, 309

Dean, John W., III, 834

Deane, Silas, 141

Dearborn, Henry, 226

Dearborn, Michigan, 350

Death penalty, 892

Death Wish (film), 906

Debates, televised political, 372

Debs, Eugene V., 508, 509; imprisonment of, 652; Margaret Sanger and, 675; in 1900 presidential election, 586; in 1904 presidential election, 586; in 1912 presidential election, 604*m,* 605

Debt: corporate, 885; personal, present-day, 194. *See also* National debt

Decatur, Stephen, 202, 224

Declaration of Independence, 130–134, 167*f*; and racial equality, 439; and slavery, 153–154; social change and, 154–155; text of, A-3–A-5; and women's rights, 155, 316

Declaration of Sentiments, 317, 317*f*

Declaration of the Causes and Necessity of Taking Up Arms, 130
Declaratory Act, 116–117, 118
Dedham, Massachusetts, 73*f*
Deere, John, 367
Deficit. *See* Budget deficit
Deflation, in late 19th century, 489, 558, 574
Defoe, Daniel, 90
Deism, 98
Deladier, Edouard, 747
Delaware: ethnic groups in, 80; ratification of Constitution by, 172, 174*m*; separation from Pennsylvania, 88; settlement of, 45
Delaware and Hudson Canal, 268
Delaware Indians, 104
Democracy: economic concentration and, 482; education for, 324–325; frontier and, 542, 543*f*; individualism and, 542; intrafamily, 673; Jacksonian, 277–278, 280; Jeffersonian, 197, 199, 216–217, 277; late 19th-century academic studies of, 542; monopolies and, 508–509; Philadelphia Convention and, 166; in Puritan settlements, 38, 71–72
Democracy (Adams), 555
Democracy in America (Tocqueville), 301–302; on Indian removals, 288–289
Democratic National Convention: of 1835, 296; of 1844, 335; of 1852, 377; of 1860, 393; of 1868, 444; of 1896, 576–577; of 1916, 647; of 1968, 827–828
Democratic party: in 1840 election, 297–299; in 1844 election, 335–336; in 1848 election, 344; in 1852 election, 377; in 1856 election, 384–385; in 1860 election, 393–394, 396*m*; in 1864 election, 428; in 1868 election, 444; in 1872 election, 455; in 1874 congressional election, 455; in 1876 election, 455–457; in 1896 election, 577, 578*m*; in 1912 election, 604*m*; in 1916 election, 647; in 1924 election, 702; in 1928 election, 707–709; Alliance movement and, 571; beginnings of, 279, 293; blacks in, 736, 742–743; Buchanan-Douglas split and, 387; Civil War and, 407–408; and emancipation, 415; extremists' threat to, 732; Free Soil split with, 343; and Kansas territory, 382; and Kansas-Nebraska Act, 377; in late 19th century, 556, 558, 559; and League of Nations, 662–665; in post–Civil War North, 453–454; prohibition and, 686; Second Iraq War and, 922
Democratic Republicans. *See* Republicans (Democratic)
Demos, John, 73*f*

Dempsey, Jack, 682
Denby, Edwin, 700
Denmark, in World War II, 748
Department(s), government. *See specific departments*
Department stores, 461, 496, 513, 514*f*, 525
Depression(s), economic: of 1819, 240; of 1830s, 297; of 1890s, 489, 574–577; and War of 1812, 222. *See also* Great Depression
Derrida, Jacques, 923*f*
Descartes, René, 98
Desert Land Act (1877), 478
Desert Storm, 896*m*
Desperate Housewives (television show), 810
Détente: Carter and, 873–874; Nixon and, 830–831, 831*f*
Detroit, Michigan: blacks in, 654; progressivism in, 586; settlement of, 53; in War of 1812, 226
Dewey, George, 624, 629*f*
Dewey, John, 543*f*; and educational reform, 541, 852; and NAACP, 610; pragmatism and, 550
Dewey, Thomas E.: in 1944 presidential election, 772; in 1948 presidential election, 787, 788*f*; in 1952 presidential election, 796
Dewitt, John, 760
Dewson, Molly, 741
Diabetes, 917
Dias, Bartholomeu, 19
Díaz, Adolfo, 641
DiCaprio, Leonardo, 548*f*, 549*f*
Dickens, Charles, 310*f*; on Howe's school for blind, 309; on Waltham system, 256
Dickinson, John, 118, 130, 147
Die Hard (film), 906
Dien Bien Phu, 802
Dinwiddie, Robert, 102
Diplomacy: attempted purchase of Cuba and, 375; Indian nations and, 462–463; Louisiana Purchase and, 203–205; Peace of Paris and, 145–147; in World War II, 775–776. *See also* Foreign policy
Direct primary system, 587–588
Disabled people, 309, 311
Discipline and Punish (Foucault), 310*f*
Discounts, railroads and, 490
Discovery (ship), 31
Discovery of America, 18–19
Disease(s): after 1250, 12; animal domestication and, 14; in colonies, 62; European, and Indians, 25, 26*f*, 56; in Great Depression, 718*f*; sexually transmitted, 860
District of Columbia. *See* Washington, D.C.

Diversity, political, in middle colonies, 82–84

Divorce, 673

Dix, Dorothea, 311, 312

Dixiecrats, 787

Dobyns, Henry, 26f

Dodd, C. T., 495

Dodge City, as cattle town, 470f

Doheny, Edward L., 700

Dole, Bob, 901–902

Dollar diplomacy, 637, 641; in Latin America, 638

Dominican Republic: attempt to annex, 614; dollar diplomacy in, 638; as U.S. protectorate, 632–633, 705

Dominion of New England, 72, 74, 88

Donnelly, Ignatius, 572, 573

Doonesbury (comic strip), 835f

Dorchester Heights, 135

Dos Passos, John, 729

Dostoevsky, Fyodor, 546

Dot-coms, 907–908

Douglas, Stephen A., 376–377, 376f, 383; in 1858 senatorial campaign, 388, 389–401; and Compromise of 1850, 349, 376–377; debates with Lincoln, 37, 389–401, 395f; in 1852 presidential election, 376; in 1860 presidential election, 393–396, 396m; in 1869 presidential campaign, 395f; and Kansas, 387; and Nebraska Territory, 378–379; politics of, 376–377

Douglass, Frederick, 314–315, 315f, 852; on black soldiers, 417; on Emancipation Proclamation, 416–417; on Hayes, 564; on Lincoln, 416–417

Dow, Neal, 313

Dower, John W., 773f

Downsizing, 884–885

Dr. Dre (Andrew Young), 906

Draft: in Civil War, 416, 523; in World War I, 649, 652, 655; in World War II, 749

Drake, Edwin L., 487

Drake, Francis, 25

Drake, Sir Francis, 89

Dred Scott decision (1857), 372, 385–387, 390, 391

Dreiser, Theodore, 546

Dresden, Germany, 769f

Drew, Charles, 759

Drexel Burnham Lambert, 884

Drought, cattle ranching and, 480

Drugs: beneficial new treatments, 917; in counterculture, 857; and crime, 892–894; illegal use in baseball, 917

Du Bois, W. E. B., 446f, 608–611, 609f, 852; The Crisis, 610, 611, 656, 690, 691; on integration vs. separatism, 690; on Washington (Booker T.), 609–610; on Wilson, 611, 656; on World War I, 656

Duane, William J., 285

Dukakis, Michael, 891–892

Dulles, John Foster, 797–798; McCarthyism and, 798

Dumbarton Oaks, 775

Dunning, William A., on Reconstruction, 446f

Dust Bowl, 725–726, 726f

Dwight, Timothy, 304

E pluribus unum, 672

Early, Jubal, 428

Earth in the Balance (Gore), 908

Earthenware, Anasazi, 8f

East Chelmsford, Massachusetts, 253

East Florida: American interests in, 236; creation of, 110

East Germany, 786m, 894

East India Company, 121

East Saint Louis, Illinois, 1917 riot in, 654

Eastern Europe: communism in, fall of, 894–895, 895m; immigrants from, 519, 521, 673; Marshall plan and, 785–786; post–World War II, 776–777; Soviet domination of, 783, 784–787

Eastern State Penitentiary, 310f

Eastern Trunk Line Association, 486

Eastman, George B., 483–484

Eaton, John, 287, 312

Eaton, Peggy, 287

eBay, 907

Eckford, Elizabeth, 807f

Economic aid. See Foreign aid

Economic gain, and the colonists, 94f

Economic mobility, late 19th-century, 516–518

Economic Opportunity Act (1964), 820

Economics: under Bush, G. W., 917; classical school of, 539; government regulation of, 496–498; institutionalist school of, 539; Keynesian, 735, 756, 782; Marshall's national view of, 272; progressive reform of, 590; of slavery, 351–353; study of, late 19th-century, 539, 540

Economy, 359; Carter and, 865, 870–871; in Civil War, 423–424; Clinton and, 901, 902, 903–904; colonial, 63, 76–77, 80, 82; in Era of Good Feelings, 238–239; expansionism and, 637; Ford and, 865, 867; globalization of, 903–904; government regulation of, 496–498, 501–502; in Great Depression, 711–717; Hamiltonian reforms and, 176–180; immigrants and, 360; industrial growth and,

Economy (continued)
359; in late 19th century, 483–484, 489–491; in mid-19th century, 351; national vs. local, politics and, 555; New Deal and, 723–724, 735, 740–741; of New England, colonial, 76–77; Nixon and, 832–833, 870; oil crisis and, 864–866; post–Civil War, 448–451, 454; post-Revolutionary, 164; post–World War I, 692–694, 709–710; post–World War II, 781–782; pre-Civil War, 370–371; railroads and, 366–369, 484–486; Reagan and, 865, 877–878, 879, 884–886; southern, 63, 448–451; Wal-Mart and, 482; in World War I, 648–650; in World War II, 756–757

Economy Act (1933), 723
Eden, Anthony, 744, 803
Ederle, Gertrude, 683
Edison, Thomas A., 488, 489f, 534
Edison Illuminating Company, 488
Education: for blacks, 437, 446f, 448, 449f, 565, 566f, 608, 806–807, 850, 905; colonial, 66; common school movement in, 324; for democracy, 324–325; desegregation of, 806–807; for disabled people, 309, 311; Enlightenment and, 87, 98–99; Great Awakening and, 96; Great Society programs for, 821; for Indians, 608; for Japanese Americans, 634; in late 19th-century, 517–518, 536–539; level of public participation and, 581–582; and mobility, 517–518; post-Revolutionary, 157; post–World War I, 684–685, 852; post–World War II, 852–854; present-day alcohol use and, 670–671; progressive, 540–541; religious fundamentalism and, 684–685; southern, colonial, 66; testing and, 780; 20th-century expansion of, 853f, 854; for women, 325, 326, 538–539; for World War II veterans, 782, 853f, 854; young voters and, 581. See also Colleges and universities; Teachers
Educational Testing Service (ETS), 780
Edwards, John, 914
Edwards, Jonathan, 96–97, 206
Egypt: Camp David Accords and, 874; Suez Canal crisis and, 803; in Yom Kippur War, 865
Eighteenth Amendment, 653, 670–671, 686
Eight-hour work day, 505
Eighty Years and More (Stanton), 317
Einstein, Albert, 748, 773
Eisenhower, Dwight D., 796f; and civil rights, 805–807; and Cuba, 805; foreign policy of, 797–798, 799, 802;

Khrushchev and, 803–804; and Latin America, 804; military-industrial complex and, 781; in 1952 presidential election, 796–797; presidency of, 796–797; and Vietnam, 799, 802; in World War II, 764–765, 768, 770f
"El Dorado," 89
El Salvador, 878
Elderly: insurance for, 733; Townsend's campaign for, 733
Elections: congressional (See Congressional elections); in Iraq (2005), 920; presidential (See Presidential election[s])
Elective system, in higher education, 536–537, 539
Electoral college: constitutional provisions for, 171, 456–457; in early 19th century, 276, 278; in 1876 presidential election, 456, 457f; in 1952 presidential election, 797; in 1960 presidential election, 809; separation of balloting for president and vice-president, 195; in 2000 presidential election, 908; in 2004 presidential election, 915
Electricity: development of, 488; New Deal and, 726–727, 727m, 735; in post–World War I period, 692; in rural areas, 735
Elementary and Secondary Education Act (1965), 821, 853f
Elements of Political Economy (Wayland), 326
Eliot, Charles W., 536, 628
Elizabeth I (Queen of England), 29, 30, 30f, 34
Elk Hills oil reserve, 700
Elkhorn Ranch, 478, 480
Elkins, Stanley, 357f
Elkins Railroad Act (1903), 595
Elliot, Robert Brown, 447f
Ely, Richard T., 498, 540
Emancipation, 154, 402. See also Abolitionist movement
Emancipation Proclamation, 414–417
Embargo Act (1807), 213–215, 214f, 215f
Embassy bombings, in Africa, 909, 911
Emerson, John, 385
Emerson, Ralph Waldo, 319–320, 392, 393f; Hawthorne on, 321; on Lincoln, 511; Melville on, 322; on war, 766f; on Whigs, 294, 296; Whitman on, 322
Eminem (Marshall Mathers III), 906
Engels, Friedrich, 713f
England. See Anglo-American relations; Great Britain
England, Church of. See Anglican church
English Channel, 683
Enlightenment, 97–98; European, 87, 98
Enola Gay (plane), 774

Entail, 153

Entertainment: in colonial South, 66; in late 19th century, 526–530. *See also* Sports

"Enumerated" cargos, tax on, 86

Environment, global warming and, 1, 917

Environmental protection. *See* Conservation

Environmental Protection Agency (EPA), 833

Environmentalists, 919

Equal rights. *See* Women's rights movement

Equal rights amendment (ERA), 680, 861, 872–873; failure of, 872*m*

Equality: in families, 302–303; idea of, 154; social, 440; and woman suffrage, 592, 680. *See also* Racial equality

Equitable Life Company, 496

ERA. *See* Equal rights amendment

Era of Good Feelings, 238–239, 564

Ericson, Leif, 15

Erie, Lake. *See* Lake Erie

Erie Canal, 270, 368; commerce over, 364; construction of, 268; and petroleum industry, 493; and the Second Great Awakening, 304

Erie Railroad, 364, 493

Espionage Act (1917), 640, 651–652

Essex (ship), 212

Essex Junto, 206

Esteban, 23

Ethiopia, Italian invasion of, 746

Ethnic cleansing, in Bosnia, 904

Ethnic diversity: in colonial times, 80–82; desirability of, 852

Ethnic pride, 852

Etowah, Mississippi, 11–12

Eugenicists, 675

Eurasia: diseases in, 14; Neolithic revolution in, 13

Europe: and American identity, 52–53; invasion of America by, 18; in late 19th-century foreign policy, 614–616; Marshall plan and, 784–787; medieval, 14–15; population growth in, 14–15; post–World War I, 657–659, 661*m*; post–World War II, 786*m*; pre–World War I, 660*m*; quest for gold, 50*f*; in World War II, 747–749, 763–765, 765*m,* 768. *See also* Eastern Europe; *specific countries*

"Evil empire," 881*f*

Evolution, theory of, 547, 684–685. *See also* Darwinism

Ex parte Endo (1944), 761

Examination of a Witch (Matteson), 75*f*

Excise tax, 181

Exclusion Act (1882), 521

Expansionism, Soviet Union, 777–778, 783, 865

Expansionism, U.S., 627, 637, 638; in Caribbean, 630–632, 632*m*; in Cuba, 621–624, 630–631; domestic opposition to, 627–628; 1867–1901, 619*m*; late 19th-century, 614–616, 627; in Latin America, 615, 619–621, 634–638; under Madison, 222; and Open Door policy, 633–634; origins of, 614–616; in Pacific region, 616–619, 627; and Panama Canal, 619–620, 634–638; under Polk, 336–337; and slavery, 342–344

Exploration voyages, 18–24

Exports. *See* Trade

Extremists, in Great Depression years, 729, 732–733

Factories: first, 252–253; Industrial Revolution and, 252–253; mid-19th century, 360; in mid-19th century, 358; post–World War I, 692–694; Waltham System, 254–255; women in, 254–256

Fair, James G. "Bonanza," 555

Fair Employment Practices Commission, 787

Fair Labor Standards Act, 738

Fall, Albert B., 699, 700

Fallen Timbers, Battle of, 183, 185, 207

Falwell, Jerry, 878–879

Family life: in 1940s, 842–844; during Civil War, 426*f*; colonial, 57, 65–66; of freedmen, 450; in Great Depression, 717; in late 19th century, 511–512; in mid-19th century, 300, 302–303, 303*f*; of pioneers, 332–333, 334; post–World War I, 673; present-day, 300; of slaves, 352; working-class, 673; in World War II, 757–758, 761–763

Far East, policy toward: late 19th to early 20th century, 616–619, 633–634; post–Korean War, 799, 802; post–World War I, 703. *See also* Asia; *specific countries*

Faragher, John Mack, 333*f*

A Farewell to Arms (Hemingway), 689

Farm bloc, 710

Farm Loan Act (1916), 647

Farm Security Administration, 743*f*

Farmer-Paellman, Deadria, 435

Farmers, 514–516; in late 19th century, 472; 19th-century, 295*f*; in politics, 570–573. *See also* Agriculture

Farmers Alliance, 570

Farnham, Marynia, 842

Farouk (King of Egypt), 803

Farragut, David, 410

Farrakhan, Louis, 905

Fatwa, 909

Faubus, Orval M., 807

Faulkner, William, 729
FCC. *See* Federal Communications Commission
FDIC. *See* Federal Deposit Insurance Corporation
Federal Art Project, 728
Federal Communications Commission (FCC), 682, 842
Federal Deposit Insurance Corporation (FDIC), 723
Federal Emergency Management Agency (FEMA), 919
Federal Emergency Relief Act (FERA), 727–728, 729*f*
Federal Farm Board, 712
Federal government. *See* Central government
Federal Housing Administration (FHA), 736, 843
Federal Reserve Act (1913), 606
Federal Reserve Board: creation of, 606; New Deal and, 723; in post–World War I period, 692, 700
Federal Steel Company, 492
Federal Theatre Project, 728
Federal Trade Commission (FTC), 606
Federal Writers' Project, 728
Federalist Papers (Hamilton, Madison, and Jay), 173, 178
Federalists, 172; contributions of, 196–197; discredited, 206–207; in 1800 presidential election, 195, 196; formation of party, 183; and Republicans, rivalry of, 186; secession attempt by, 206; in 1796 presidential election, 187–189; War of 1812 and, 231–232, 233–234; XYZ Affair and, 189
Female Missionary Society, 305
The Feminine Mystique (Friedan), 860–861
Feminism. *See* Women's rights movement
Fenno, John, 183
FERA. *See* Federal Emergency Relief Act
Ferraro, Geraldine, 878, 879
Fertility, geographic gradient of. *See* Birthrate
Fetterman, W. J., 463
FHA. *See* Federal Housing Administration
Fiction. *See* Literature
Field, Erastus Salisbury, 303*f*
Field, Marshall, 496
Fifteenth Amendment, 444–445, 564
Fifth Amendment, and slavery, 313, 385
Figsby, Captain, 212
Fillmore, Millard: and Compromise of 1850, 348; in 1852 presidential election, 376, 377; in 1856 presidential election, 384–385

Films, 680–681, 905–906. *See also specific films*
Finger Lakes, New York State, 1
Finney, Charles Grandison, 305, 312, 314
Fireside chats, Roosevelt's, 723, 745, 750
First Amendment, 510
Fischer, David Hackett, 73*f*, 148
Fish, trade in, 76–77
Fiske, John, 615
Fitzgerald, F. Scott, 688–689, 729
Fitzpatrick, Thomas, 462
Five Nations, 101
Five-Power Treaty (1921), 703
Flag, American, 157–158
Flanagan, Kimberly, 510
Flanders, Ralph, 801*f*
Flatboats, 267, 269*f*
Fletcher, Henry, 511
Florida: acquisition from Spain, 235–236, 237*m*; American interests in, 222; British control of, 105; division into East and West, 110; returned to Spain, 147; Seminoles in, 288; Spanish exploration of, 23; in 2000 presidential election, 908
Florida (ship), 409
Florida State University, 671
Flowers, Gennifer, 898
Flying Cloud (ship), 362
Foner, Eric, on Reconstruction, 446*f*
Food: canning factories and, 483; in colonial New England, 76; in colonial South, 65; in Great Depression, 712, 714–715; in late 19th century, 483; safety legislation for, 599; in World War I, 650
Food chains, 709
Football, 529; college, 529, 535; in post–World War I period, 682; rise of, 535–536
Foote, Roxanna, 254
Foraker Act (1900), 630
Foran Act (1885), 519
Forbes, Charles R., 699
Force Acts (1870–1871), 453
Force Bill, 291, 292
Ford, Gerald R.: economy under, 865; in 1976 presidential election, 868–869; Nixon's resignation and, 838; presidency of, 866–867; as vice president, 836
Ford, Henry, 694–695
Ford Motor Company, 350; assembly lines at, 694; in early 20th century, 694–695; in late 20th century, 866, 871; in post–World War I period, 709
Foreign affairs, sectionalism and, 374–375
Foreign aid: to Latin America, 804, 873; Marshall plan and, 784–787; 1948–1984, 785*f*; Truman Doctrine and, 784

Foreign Debt Commission, 706–707
Foreign policy: under Adams (John), 189–190; under Bush (George H. W.), 894–898; under Carter, 873–875; under Cleveland, 620–621; under Clinton, 904; of Confederacy, 409; under Coolidge, 702–707; dollar diplomacy in, 637, 641; 1867–1901, 619m; under Eisenhower, 797–798, 799, 802; Good Neighbor policy, 704–705; under Grant, 614, 619; under Harding, 702–707; under Hoover, 705; under Jefferson, 202, 213; under Kennedy, 811–815; "large," 615; late 19th-century, 614–616; under Madison, 219–220; under McKinley, 616, 617, 621–624, 627, 630, 635; missionary diplomacy in, 641–642; neutrality in, 642–644, 647–648, 746–747; under Nixon, 828–831; Open Door policy, 633–634, 703; under Reagan, 878, 879–880; under Roosevelt (Franklin), 746–749; under Roosevelt (Theodore), 632–633, 634; under Taft, 637; under Truman, 783, 789–790, 799, 802; War of 1812 and, 233–234; under Washington, 181–182, 184–186; under Wilson, 641–642. See also Diplomacy; Expansionism; Isolationism
Formosa. See Taiwan
Fort Bridger, 334
Fort de Chartres, 53
Fort Dearborn, 226
Fort Donelson, 410
Fort Duquesne, 103, 104
Fort Henry, 410
Fort Laramie, 334
Fort Laramie, Wyoming, 462, 464
Fort Le Boeuf, 102
Fort McHenry, 228, 230f
Fort Michilimackinac, 226
Fort Necessity, 103
Fort Niagara: in French and Indian War, 104; in War of 1812, 226, 227
Fort Orange, 45
Fort Pickens, Florida, 402
Fort Pillow, 417
Fort Pitt, 104
Fort Presque Isle, 102
Fort Sumter, 143, 402
Fort Ticonderoga, 128
Fort Vancouver, 334
Fort Venango, 102
Fort Wagner, 420, 421
Fortune, T. Thomas, 565
49th parallel, 336–337
Fosse, Bob, 679f
Foster, William Z., 666

Foucault, Michel, 310f
Founding Fathers, 166–168, 168f; presence in present-day life, 126–127
Fourier, Charles, 308–309
Fourierism, 308–309
Four-Power Treaty, 703
Fourteen Points, plan of Woodrow Wilson, 658–662
Fourteenth Amendment, 440–441, 442
Fox Indians, 288
Foxwoods Casino, Connecticut, 460
Framers of the Constitution. See Founding fathers
France: Adams administration and, 189–190; in American Revolution, 140–141, 145–147; colonial wars of, 100–104; exploration and colonization by, 44–45, 53–54, 107m; exploration voyages by, 20m; in French and Indian War, 103–104; in Indochina, 799, 802; and Louisiana Purchase, 202–207; and Mexico, 613; in Paris Peace Conference, 660–662; in Revolutionary War, 145m; Revolutionary War financing and, 150; Suez Canal crisis and, 803; and World War I, 644–645, 656–657; in World War II, 747, 748, 764, 765; in XYZ Affair, 189–190, 190f
Franciscan friars, 47, 56f
Franco, Francisco, 746
Frank Leslie's Illustrated Newspaper, 386f
Frankfurt school, 858f
Frankfurter, Felix, 650, 715, 733, 761
Franklin, Benjamin, 99f; as colonial agent, 89, 115; on colonial growth, 108; in Continental Congress, 129; and Declaration of Independence, 131; Deism and, 98; and French Treaty, 141; intellectual life of, 99, 100; as national hero, 160; in Peace of Paris, 146; in Pennsylvania politics, 84; prejudices of, 81; and religion, 95, 98; as scientist, 100; on taxes, 109; and unification, 157
Franklin, Isaac, 352
Franklin stove, 100
Franz Ferdinand (Archduke of Austria), 642
Frasch, Herman, 487
Fraser River, Canada, 469
Fredericksburg, Battle of, 418, 418m
Free Soil party: Brown and, 382; in 1848 presidential election, 344; in 1856 presidential election, 384; formation of, 344; in Kansas, 387; and Kansas-Nebraska Act, 378; and Republican party, 380
Free Speech Movement, 856
Freedmen: in California, 345; economic hardships of, 448–452; education for,

Freedmen *(continued)*
446*f*, 448, 449*f*, 565; family life of, 449–450; and Fugitive Slave Act, 373, 378*f*; in post-Reconstruction South, 446*f*; in pre–Civil War South, 356–357; Radical Republicans and, 440–441; southern mistreatment of, 440, 442; white backlash against, 452–453. *See also* Reconstruction
Freedmen's Bureau, 440, 448, 449*f*
Freedom of speech, suppression in World War I, 651–652
Freedom Riders, 817*f*
Freedom rides, 817
Freeman, Morgan, 420
Freeman, Thomas (explorer), 208
Freeport Doctrine, 390, 391, 394
Frelinghuysen, Theodore, 94
Frémont, John C., 339, 384, 385
French and Indian War, 103–104, 105*m*, 107–108
French Revolution, 181–182; American reaction to, 183; Jefferson and, 199; and Second Great Awakening, 304
French Treaty (1778), 141–142, 181
Freneau, Philip, 183
Freudian psychology, 852
Frey, Sylvia R., 132*f*
Frick, Henry Clay, 508
Friedan, Betty, 860–861, 872
Friedman, William F., 755
Friendly, Fred, 800*f*
Frontier: concept of, 480; and democracy, 542, 543*f*. *See also* West
Front-porch campaigns, 578
FTC. *See* Federal Trade Commission
Fuchs, Klaus, 795
Fugitive Slave Act (1793), 348; amendment of, 348; 1850 amendment of, 372, 373, 378*f*; Harriet Beecher Stowe and, 374
Fuller, Margaret, 316
Fulton, Robert, 267
Fundamental Orders, 41
Fundamentalism: in 1980s politics, 878–879; in post–World War I period, 684–685, 685*f*
Funerals, colonial, 66
Fur trade: colonial, 50; contention over, 100–101; in Pacific West, 334
Furman decision, 892

Gabriel (slave), 261
Gaddis, John Lewis, 791*f*, 881*f*
Gadsden, Christopher, 129
Gaertner, Belva, 678*f*, 679*f*
Gage, Thomas, 127, 128, 129
Galbraith, John K., 713*f*

Galilei, Galileo, 98
Gallatin, Albert, 219–220
Gallaudet, Thomas, 309
Galloway, Joseph, 123
Galveston, Texas, 586, 919; Hurricane (1900), 919
Gálvez, José de, 143
Gambling: on Indian reservations, 460; present-day, 697–698; stock market and, 697–698
Gangs: late 20th-century, 892–894; in prohibition era, 686
Gangsta rap, 906
GAR. *See* Grand Army of the Republic
Gardner, Chris, 250
Gardner, Lloyd C., 825*f*
Garfield, James A., 442, 445, 560, 564; assassination of, 560, 561*f*; in Compromise of 1877, 458; in 1880 presidential election, 560; on Fifteenth Amendment, 445; on Indian Bureau, 465; on post–Civil War South, 442
Garland, Hamlin, 546
Garner, John N., 719, 719*f*, 748, 749
Garraty, John, 713*f*
Garrison, William Lloyd, 341; in abolitionist movement, 313–315, 315*f*; on Mexican War, 341; in women's movement, 318
Garvey, Marcus, 690, 691*f*
Gary, Elbert H., 596
"Gas and water" socialism, 587
Gasoline, 487, 841, 864–866, 866*f*, 871
Gaspee (patrol boat), 120
Gates, Horatio, 140, 142
Gates, Robert M., 881*f*
Gazette of the United States, 183
Geddes, Eric, 659
General Intelligence Division, of Justice Department, 667
General Motors (GM): 1937 strike at, 738; in post–World War I period, 709; post–World War II malaise at, 869; *vs.* Ford, 695
Genet, Edmond Charles, 181–182
Genizaros, 54
Genoa, Italy, 14
Genocide, under Saddam Hussein, 921
Genovese, Eugene D., 357*f*
Gentility, 251–252
Gentlemen's Agreement (1907), 607, 634
Geographic mobility: in late 19th century, 516–518. *See also* Migration
George, Henry, 498, 540
George, Walter F., 740
George II (King of England), 104
George III (King of England), 107, 122, 127, 130, 131, 133, 146*f*

Georgia: Alliance movement in, 571; in Civil War, 423, 427–429; colleges in, 326; colonial, 67m; cotton in, 259, 289; founding of, 66; Indian removals in, 287–289; progressive reform in, 587; ratification of Constitution by, 172, 174m; readmission to Union, 442; in Revolutionary War, 142–143

Georgia Female College, 326

Gere, Richard, 678f

German Americans, 256–257, 519; Know-Nothing party and, 379; temperance movement and, 312–313; World War I and, 643–644, 651

Germany: division into East and West, 786m; under Hitler, 746–749; immigration from, 519, 519f; post–World War I debts and aid to, 706–707, 706f; post–World War II treatment of, 776; re-unification of, 881f; universities in, 537; in World War I, 644–646, 648, 648f, 656–657; World War I peace settlement and, 659, 660–662, 661–662; in World War II, 746–749, 763–765, 768, 769f, 770f

Geronimo, 466

Gerry, Elbridge, 189

Gettysburg, Battle of, 418, 418m, 419

Ghent, Treaty of (1814), 230, 232, 234

Ghettos: compensating advantages of, 690–691; formation after World War I, 690. See also Slums

GI Bill of Rights, 782, 853f, 854

Giambi, Jason, 917

Giant Steamboats on the Levee at New Orleans (Sebron), 363f

Gibbons, Thomas, 273

Gibbons v. Ogden, 273

Gibson, Mel, 148, 148f

Gienapp, William, 381f

Gila River Indian Reservation, Arizona, 460

Gilded Age, 542

Gilman, Daniel Coit, 537

Gilman Hall, 537f

Gingrich, Newt, 901

Ginsberg, Allen, 856–857

Ginsberg, Ruth Bader, 900

Gladden, Washington, 531

Glasnost, 880

Glidden, Joseph F., 479

Global warming, 1, 917

Globalization: of economy, 903–904; economy and, 904

Glorieta Pass, Battle of, 409

Glorious Revolution, 72, 88, 117

Glory (film), 420–421, 420f–421f

GM. See General Motors

GNP. See Gross national product

Godey's Ladies Book (magazine), 303

Godoy, Manuel de "the Prince of Peace," 185

"God's Controversy with New England" (Wigglesworth), 71

Godspeed (ship), 31

Godwin, Parke, 308

Gold: colonial trade in, 89; as currency, 558; European desire for, 50f

Gold, Harry, 795

Gold rush: in California, 342, 344–345, 346f; effect on Indians, 344–345, 462, 463, 465; in post-Reconstruction era, 468–471

Gold standard, 574, 579; withdrawal from, 723

Goldman, Emma, 675

Goldwater, Barry M., 821

Golf, 527

Goliad, Texas, 331

Gompers, Samuel, 505–506, 627

Good, Sarah, 74

Good Housekeeping (magazine), 483

Good Neighbor policy, 704–705

Good Night, and Good Luck (film), 800–801

Goode, Virgil, 917

Goodnight, Charles, 476

Goodwin, Doris Kearns, 821f

Gorbachev, Mikhail S., 879–880, 881f, 895

Gordon-Reed, Annette, 198f

Gore, Al: isolationism and, 613; in 1988 presidential election, 891; in 1992 presidential election, 899; in 2000 presidential election, 908–909

Gorges, Ferdinando, 36, 41

Gouge, William, 240

Gough, John B., 312

Gould, Jay, 485, 504, 504f, 597f

Government(s): balanced, 115; colonial, 36–38, 37–38, 71–72, 74, 87–89; economic regulation by, 496–498, 501–502; Jacksonian spoils system and, 280–281; Marshall Court and, 271–274; post–Civil War, 564; progressivism and, 582–584; railroad financing by, 366; Reconstruction and, 443–444; self-reliance and, 319–320; state, 438, 444–445; state republican, 152–153; state vs. federal laws of, 272, 290–291; transcendentalism on, 318. See also Business regulation; Central government; Civil service

Governor(s): colonial, 87–89; state republican, 152–153

Graham, Billy, 846

Grand Army of the Republic, 557

Grange, Harold "Red," 682

Granger laws, 501

Granger movement, 501, 515
Grant, James, 127
Grant, Ulysses S., 422; at Appomattox Court House, 430; in 1868 presidential election, 444; 1872 campaign poster, 455f; in 1872 presidential election, 455; on Fifteenth Amendment, 445; foreign policy of, 614, 619; presidency of, 454–455, 465; at Shiloh, 410; at Vicksburg, 422–423; at Wilderness, 426–427, 431m
Grant, William, 212
The Grapes of Wrath (Steinbeck), 729
Grasse, François de, 143, 145
Graves, Thomas, 144
Gray, Robert, 334
Great Awakening, 87, 93–96, 97, 530; Second, 303–305
Great Britain: Civil War and, 409–410; Civil War and Protectorate in, 72; colonial system of, 87–89, 107m; colonial trade of, 92f; colonial wars of, 100–104; colonization by, 31, 35–41; exploration by, 27–28; exploration voyages by, 20m; French and Indian War victories, 105m; Glorious Revolution in, 72, 117; Greek crisis of 1947 and, 783–784; immigration from, 519; Latin America and, 237–238, 619–621; migration from, 38f; and Napoleon, standoff with, 211–212, 220; and Netherlands, rivalry with, 45, 91; and Panama Canal, 619–620, 635; religious movements in, 34; and Revolutionary War, 126–160, 134–136, 139f; settlements by, 38f; and Spain, rivalry with, 27; Suez Canal crisis and, 803; and Texas, Republic of, 331–332; trade with, 362–363; and Venezuela, 620–621; in War of 1812, 227, 228, 229m; World War I and, 643–646, 660–662; World War II and, 748–749, 750–751, 761–762, 764, 765, 768. See also Anglo-American relations
Great Compromise, 169
Great Depression, 697–698, 710–717; and blacks, 742–743; causes of, 713f; Hoover's policies for, 711–717; literature in, 729; origins of, 710; psychological effects of, 717; stock market crash of 1929 and, 710–711; World War II and, 756–757. See also New Deal
Great Eastern (ship), 518
The Great Gatsby (Fitzgerald), 688–689
Great Lakes, 1, 231, 234, 270
"Great Men and Their Environment" (James), 550

Great migration, of blacks to North, 654–656, 690–692
Great Migration (1630s), 37
Great Northern Railroad, 476, 477m
The Great Plains (Webb), 480
Great Society, 810, 820–822
The Great Train Robbery (film), 680
Greece: civil war in, 783–784; immigrants from, 522; Truman Doctrine and, 784
Greeley, Horace: and 1872 presidential election, 454; on emancipation, 402; Fourierists and, 308; and Log Cabin, 298; and New York Tribune, 308, 360, 454
Green Bay Packers (football team), 535
Green party, 908
Green Spring faction, 61
Greenback Labor party, 558
Greenbacks, 407, 558, 575
Greene, Catherine, 259
Greene, Jack, 94f
Greene, Nathanael, 143, 259
Greenhouse gas emissions, 917
Greenland, in World War II, 751
Greensboro, North Carolina, Woolworth's sit-in, 816
Greenville, Treaty of (1795), 185
Greer (ship), 751
Grenada, 878
Grenville, George, 110–111, 112, 116
Greven, Philip, 73f, 94f
Grey's Anatomy (television show), 810
Griffith, D. W., 446f, 680
Griffith, Ernest S., 570f
Grimké, Angelina, 316
Grimké, Sarah, 316
Grocery stores, 709
Gromyko, Andrei A., 775
Gronlund, Laurence, 501
Gross national product (GNP), World War II and, 756
Guadalcanal Island, battles around, 772
Guadalupe Hidalgo, Treaty of, 340–341
Guam, 626; as colony, 638
Guanahani island, 18
Guangzhou, China, 617f
Guantanamo base, as colony, 638
Guantanamo Bay, 637
Guatemala, 804
Guerrière (ship), 224
Guerrilla warfare, 463, 464
Guiteau, Charles J., 560
Gulf of Mexico, Hurricane Katrina and, 918–919
Gulf of Tonkin Resolution, 822
Gulf War, 895–898, 896m, 897f
Gutman, Herbert, 357f

Haiti: dollar diplomacy in, 638; 1930s withdrawal from, 705; occupation of Hispaniola (Santo Domingo), 203; 1790 slave revolt in, 260–261
Halberstam, David, 825*f*
Hale, John, 78–79
Hale, Sarah, 303
Half-Way Covenant, 71
Halifax (ship), 214
Halleck, Henry W., 413, 422
Hamby, Alonzo L., 773*f*
Hamilton, Alexander: and Bank of the United States, 272–273; on blacks, 197; and confederation, 166, 168; and Constitution, 173, 177*f*; on cotton, 259; duel with Burr, 206, 207*f*; and 1800 presidential election, 195–196; *Federalist Papers,* 173, 178; and Federalist party, 183, 186; financial reforms of, 176–180; personality of, 177–178; political theories of, 197, 199; *Report on Manufactures,* 180; *Report on the Public Credit,* 178; in 1796 presidential election, 188; in Washington administration, 175, 176–180; XYZ Affair and, 189
Hamlet, James, 373
Hammond, Bray, 283
Hammond, James H., 391, 403
Hampton, Wade, 564
Hancock, John, 128
Handlin, Oscar, 524*f*
Hanks, Tom, 766*f*–767*f*
Hanna, Marcus Alonzo, 577–578, 580
Harding, Chester, 273*f*
Harding, Warren G., 698*f,* 701*f*; agricultural policies of, 710; and business, 699–700, 709; death of, 701; foreign policy of, 702–707; in 1920 presidential election, 668; presidency of, 698–701; scandals under, 698, 700–701
Harlan, John Marshall, 565
Harlem Renaissance, 691
Harmar, Josiah, 180
Harper, William Rainey, 535, 537
Harper's Ferry, Virginia: in Civil War, 414; John Brown's raid on, 392–393
Harper's Weekly (magazine), 446*f,* 545, 552, 565
Harriman, Averill, 783
Harris, Katherine, 333*f*
Harrisburg, Pennsylvania, in Civil War, 419
Harrison, Benjamin, 297–299, 563; in 1888 presidential election, 563; in 1892 presidential election, 573; on foreign affairs, 613; presidency of, 563–564
Harrison, William Henry: cabinet of, 329; death of, 299; in 1836 presidential election, 294, 296; in 1840 presidential election, 298–299, 298*f*; and Indian relations, 220–221; in War of 1812, 226
Hartford, founding of, 41
Hartford Convention, 231–232
Harvard Encyclopedia of American Ethnic Groups (Handlin, Schlesinger), 524*f*
Harvard University, 98; elective system at, 536–537, 539; football at, 529, 535; James (William) at, 550; in 19th century, 326, 536–537, 539; quotas on Jews at, 673; reform of, late 19th-century, 536–537, 539; and Washington (Booker T.), 566
Hastie, William, 759
Hattaway, Herman, 444*f*
Havemeyer, Henry O., 497
Hawaii, as colony, 638
Hawaiian Islands: attempts to annex, 616–619, 618*f*; 19th-century expansionism and, 616–619
Hawley, Joseph, 97
Hawthorn, Nathaniel, 542
Hawthorne, Nathaniel, 73*f,* 321
Hay, John, 633, 635
Hayes, Rutherford B., 559–560; in 1876 presidential election, 455–457, 457*f,* 559–560; presidency of, 560; and railroad strike, 507; and southern blacks, 560, 564
Haymarket Square bombing, 505, 506*f,* 507
Hayne, Robert Y., 290
Haywood, "Big Bill," 586, 675
A Hazard of New Fortunes (Howells), 545
Head Start program, 821
Health, Education, and Welfare, Department of, 797
Health insurance, 653, 821, 900–901
Hearst, William Randolph, 552, 622
Helicopters, in Vietnam war, 829*f*
Hemings, Eston, 194*f*
Hemings, Madison, 194*f*
Hemings, Sally, 194*f,* 197
Hemingway, Ernest, 689, 729
Henry, Patrick, 112–113; and Constitution, 172; in Continental Congress, 129
Henry Street Settlement (New York), 532
Hepburn Act (1906), 599
Herbart, Johann Friedrich, 540
Herberg, Will, 845
Herrán, Tomás, 635
Hesler, Alexander, 390*f*
Hewitt, Abram S., 500–501
Hickok, Wild Bill, 469
Higginson, Thomas Wentworth, 392
High Plains, farming in, 515–516
Higham, John, 676*f*
The Higher Learning in America (Veblen), 539

Highway system, interstate, 841
Hijacking. *See* Terrorism
Hill, David B., 577
Hill, James J., 476, 485, 597*f*
Hillsborough, Lord, 118
Hippies, 856–857
Hirabayashi, Gordon, 761
Hiroshima, 773*f,* 774
Hispanic Americans: civil rights for,
    850–851; gold rush and, 344–345; immi-
    grants, present-day, 350; in World War II,
    753, 759
Hispaniola (Santo Domingo): slave revolt of
    1790 in, 260–261; slave uprising in,
    203–204, 204*f*
Hiss, Alger, 795, 801*f*
History, late 19th-century study of, 539,
    542
History of the United States During the
    Administrations of Jefferson and Madison
    (Adams), 542
Hitler, Adolf: aggression in Europe,
    746–749, 751; Japanese invasion of China
    and, 706; pre-war actions of, 746,
    747–748; in World War II, 763–764, 768
HIV. *See* Human immunodeficiency virus
Ho Chi Minh, 799, 802, 814–815
Ho Chi Minh City, 868
Hoar, George Frisbie, 502, 627, 628
Hobbes, Thomas, 57, 166
Hodgson, Godfrey, 905
Hoe, Richard, 551
Hofstadter, Richard, 295*f,* 597*f,* 676*f*
Hogan, Ben, 796*f*
Hogan, Greg, Jr., 697
Hogan, Michael, 791*f*
Hohokam peoples, 7–9
HOLC. *See* Home Owners Loan
    Corporation
Hollywood, California, 680
Holmes, Oliver Wendell, Jr., 652, 667,
    745*f*
Holocaust, 768, 770*f*
Holt, Charles, 191
Holt, Michael, 381*f*
Home(s). *See* Housing
Home Buildings, 526
Home Owners Loan Corporation (HOLC),
    723, 736
Homeland Security, Office of, 911, 919
Homer, Winslow, 420
Homestake Mining, 469
Homestead Act (1862), 424, 448–449,
    471–472
Homestead steel plant, 507
Homestead steel strike (1892), 507
Homicides, in cattle towns, 470*f*

Homosexuals: AIDS and, 883–884; and gay
    culture, in post–World War I period, 674,
    676*f*; same-sex marriage and, 915;
    Stonewall protests and, 859*f*; sexual revo-
    lution and, 859
Honduras, 804
Hooker, Joseph, 418*m,* 419
Hooker, Thomas, 41
Hookworm, 718*f*
Hoover, Herbert, 698, 708*f*; as Commerce
    Secretary, 698; economic policies of, 706,
    707–708; as food administrator in World
    War I, 650; foreign policy of, 706; foreign
    policy under, 705; in Harding administra-
    tion, 699, 710; in 1928 presidential elec-
    tion, 707–709; 1929 stock market crash
    and, 710–711; in 1932 presidential elec-
    tion, 717, 718; on prohibition, 686; on
    Roosevelt (Franklin), 718
Hoover, J. Edgar, 667
"Hoovervilles," 714
Hopewell mound builders, 6
Hopi Indians, 460
Hopkins, Esek, 130
Hopkins, Harry L., 727–728
Hopkins, Johns, 537
Hopkins, Mark, 474
Horse(s): racing of, 528; reintroduction of,
    21*f*
Horse Creek, 462
Horsecars, 525
Horton, Willie, 891–892
Hostage situations, 890
House of Burgesses, 113
House of Representatives, U.S.: constitu-
    tional provisions for, 170; in late 19th-
    century, 555
The House of the Seven Gables (Hawthorne),
    321
Housing: in colonial South, 65–66; in late
    19th-century cities, 523, 525; in late
    20th century, 871; New Deal and, 736,
    743
Houston, Sam, 331
"How to Make Our Ideas Clear" (Peirce),
    550
Howard, Ron, 731*f*
Howard, Simeon, 153
Howe, Richard, 135
Howe, Samuel Gridley, 309
Howe, William, 130, 135, 137, 139, 142
Howe sewing machine, Lynn strike and,
    361*f*
Howells, William Dean, 545–546, 610, 628
"Howl" (Ginsberg), 856–857
Huckleberry Finn (Twain), 545
Hudson, Henry, 45

Hudson, Rock, 883–884
Hudson's Bay Company, 337
Huerta, Victoriano, 641–642
Hughes, Charles Evans: in Harding administration, 699, 702; in 1916 presidential election, 647
Hughes, Langston, 691
Hull, Cordell, 746, 754
Hull, Isaac, 224
Hull, William, 226
Hull House (Chicago), 532
Human immunodeficiency virus (HIV), 882–883, 883f
Hume, David, 98
Hummel, Jeffrey, 444f
Humphrey, Hubert H., 826
Hundred Days, 722–723; Second, 734–735
Hungary: liberalization of, 894; 1956 revolt in, 803
Hunter, Robert, 83
Hunting, prehistoric, 2–4
Huntington, Collis P., 474
Huron Indians, 50, 101
Hurricane Katrina (2005), 1, 918–919
Hussein, Saddam, 876, 886, 895–898; capture of, 914; convicted of murder, 921; in Second Iraq War, 912–914; Sunnis and, 920
Hutcheson, Francis, 98
Hutchinson, Anne, 39–41
Hutchinson, Thomas, 113, 114, 120, 121
Hyde, Henry B., 496
Hydroelectric plants, 726–727
Hydrogen bomb, 789, 803

"I Have a Dream" (King), 818
Iacocca, Lee, 869–870
IBM. See International Business Machines
Ibsen, Henrik, 546
ICC. See Interstate Commerce Commission
Ice sheets, 1
Iceland: Reagan-Gorbachev summit in, 880; in World War II, 751
Idaho: gold rush in, 469; silver miners' strike in, 507; territorial organization of, 471; woman suffrage in, 592
Identity, American, shaping of, 52–53, 84–85
Il, Kim Jong, 916
Illinois: agriculture in, railroads and, 366–368; colleges in, 537–538; Granger movement in, 501; in presidential politics, 559
Illinois Central Railroad, 366–368, 472, 473
Immigrants: assimilation of, 524f; in cities, 517, 520, 521, 522f, 523, 525; in Dearborn, Michigan, 350; ethnic pride among, 852; in Great Depression, 715; illegal, 882, 916–917; Know-Nothing party and, 379; Ku Klux Klan and, 686–687; old vs. new, 520–521; origin of word, 360; in post–World War I period, 667, 667f, 671–673, 672f; prejudice by and against, 360, 686–687; progressivism and, 585, 607; railroads and, 474, 486; society's ills blamed on, 520f; transatlantic travel by, 363–364, 518–519; World War I and, 643; World War II and, 760–761. See also specific nationalities
Immigration: in 16th and 17th centuries, 18, 37; Alien and Sedition Acts, 190–191; Atlantic seaboard and, 84–85; in 18th-century, 80–82, 190–191; illegal immigrants, present-day, 328; Industrial Revolution and, 254; industrialization and, 360; land lure and, 57–58; from Mexico, 328; National Origins Act and, 672; nativism and, 520–521, 522–523; in 19th century, 256–257, 360, 461–462, 483, 518–519, 519f; post–World War I, 671–673; pre–World War II, 747; quota system for, 671–673; restrictions on, 461, 519, 521, 634, 671–673; in 20th-century, 519, 519f, 671–673, 882; to West, 461–462
Immigration Act (1965), 882
Immigration reform, 916–917, 916f
Immigration Restriction League, 521
Impeachment: Clinton and, 891, 902–903, 903f; Johnson and, 443–444; Nixon and, 811, 837
Imperialism. See Expansionism
Import(s). See Trade
Import duties. See Tariff(s)
Impressment, 212–213
Inca empire, 21
Income tax: under Carter, 870–871; in Civil War, 408, 575; in early 21st-century, 86; and Nixon administration, 836; under Reagan, 877, 880; Supreme Court on, 575; in World War I, 651; in World War II, 757
Income Tax Act (1986), 880
Incorporation laws. See Corporations
Independence: divisiveness over, 136–137; evolution of doctrine, 238; implications of, 130–131; war for, 127 (See also American Revolution)
Independence Hall, Philadelphia, 167f
Independent Treasury Act (1840), 297, 329
Indian Americans: ancient communities of, 4–7, 5f; in California, 55–56, 334, 344–345; casinos owned by, 460–461; in Civil War, 409; and colonies, interaction

Indian Americans (continued)
with, 31–32, 47–50, 84, 101–102, 106, 108f, 223f; cultures of, 22–23; destruction of tribal life of, 466–468; disease and, 25, 26f; European invasion and, 18, 21–25, 31, 47–49, 84; and Europeans, misunderstandings between, 48–49; forced migrations of, 287–289, 288m; in French and Indian War, 103–104; gold rush and, 344–345, 462, 465; interaction with settlers, 223f; Jesuits and, 55–56; land loss by, 468m; Lewis and Clark expedition and, 208–209; liberation movement under Tecumseh, 220–221; militant movements by, mid-20th century, 851–852; New Deal and, 743–744; origin of name, 20; and pioneers, 332, 334; population decline among, 25; post-Revolutionary relations with, 180–181, 183–184, 185–186, 223f; poverty among, 460; Proclamation of 1763 and, 109m, 110; progressivism and, 607–608; reservations of, 460–461, 464, 465; unemployment among, 460; urban centers of, 10–13; in War of 1812, 226–227, 232; wars with, late 19th century, 464–466; western tribes, plight of, 461; in World War II, 759–760. See also specific tribes
Indian Bureau, 465
Indian Gaming Regulatory Act (1988), 460
Indian lands, loss of, 468m
Indian Reorganization Act (1934), 744
Indian Ring, 465
Indian Self-Determination Act (1975), 851–852
Indian Territory (Oklahoma), 288m, 462, 464
Indiana: Ku Klux Klan in, 687, 687f; in presidential politics, 559; "Washington" townships in, 126
Indiana Territory, 187m; formation of, 186; relations with Indians, 220–221
Indigo cultivation, 63
Individualism, 543f; and democracy, 542; frontier and, 542, 543f; self-reliance and, 319–320; in transcendentalism, 318
Indochina: post-Korean War, 799, 802; in World War II, 754–755
Industrial combinations. See Monopolies
Industrial Revolution: factories and, 252–253; technology of, 252–253; working class during, 252–254
Industrial Workers of the World (IWW), 586, 665, 800f
Industrial-military complex, development in World War I, 649

Industry and industrialization: Civil War and, 424–425; consolidation of, 582, 583, 709–710; discontent with, 533–534; in early 19th century, 257–258; in early 20th century, 709–710; and education, 517–518; and immigrants, 360, 518–519; inventions in, 359; in late 19th century, 483–484; New Deal and, 723–724, 735; in North, 358–359; in post–World War I period, 692–694, 709–710; in Progressive Era, 582, 583; and workers, 512–513; in World War I, 648–650; in World War II, 755–756. See also Manufacturing; specific industries
Inflation: Carter and, 870–871; during Civil War, 407, 423, 424; colonial wars and, 101; Ford and, 867; in late 19th century, 558; Nixon and, 832–833, 870; post-Revolutionary, 164
The Influence of Sea Power Upon History (Mahan), 615–616
The Influence of Sea Power Upon the French Revolution and Empire (Mahan), 615–616
Ingersoll, Jared, 113
The Innocents Abroad (Twain), 544
Inquiry into the Effects of Ardent Spirits (1784), 312
Institutions, 19th-century, 309, 311, 312
Insurance: health, 653, 821, 900–901; life, 496, 589–590; old-age, 733, 735; unemployment, 735
Intellectual life: colonial, 98–100; in late 19th century, 536; late 19th-century, 536–539. See also Culture(s); Literature
Intellectual property, 162–163
Intellectuals: alienation of, post–World War I, 688–690; and Communist party, in Great Depression, 716
Interior, Department of the, 465
Internal improvements: federal, 265–266, 366–368, 369; railroads as, 366–368, 369; turnpikes as, 265–266; under Van Buren, 296
Internal Security Act, 805
International Business Machines (IBM), 885
International Harvester Company, 582
Internet, 907–908
Internment, of Japanese Americans, 753, 760m, 761f
Interstate commerce, federal control of, 273–274
Interstate Commerce Act (1887), 502, 582
Interstate Commerce Commission (ICC): under Coolidge, 700; establishment of, 502; under Harding, 700; under Roosevelt (Theodore), 595, 599; under Taft, 601

Interstate highway system, 841. *See also* Road(s)

Intolerable Acts, 123

Inventions, copyright protection and, 162–163

Investment banking, 369, 723

Iowa: progressive reform in, 587; public colleges in, 324; "Washington" townships in, 126

IRA. *See* Individual retirement account

Iran, 876*f*; Americans in Iraqi war and, 921; hostage crisis in, 874–875, 876; in late 20th century, 896*m*; nuclear weapons in, 915–916; post–World War II, 874–875; Soviet Union and, 783

Iran-Contra arms deal, 886–888, 891

Iran-Iraq War, 895–896

Iraq: American military death toll in, 922; Bush (George W.) and, 753; Carter and, 876; invasion of (2003), 17; in late 20th-century, 896*m*; in Persian Gulf War, 895–898, 897*f*; Reagan and, 886; in Second Iraq War, 912–914, 920–922; Sunni and Shiite sects in, 920, 921

Iraqi Governing Council, 920

Irish Americans, 256–257; in American West, 474; and blacks, 360; in Civil War draft riots, 416; Know-Nothing party and, 379; temperance movement and, 312–313; as textile mill workers, 256–257, 360; World War II and, 750

Iron Act (1750), 91

Iron Curtain, 783, 786*m*

Iron industry, 257; after Civil War, 451; Industrial Revolution and, 257; in late 19th century, 486–487; monopoly in, 491–493; railroads and, 369; in South, 358

Iroquois, 12–13, 54, 101

The Irrepressible Conflict (Cole), 381*f*

Isaacs, Jason, 148*f*

Isabella (Queen of Spain), 19

Islam: and Christianity, cultural gap between, 17–18; *fatwa* and, 909; Sunni and Shiite sects in, 920

Isolationism: after the Civil War, 613; and Bush (George W.), 613; and Gore, 613; under Harding and Coolidge, 702–703, 705–706; late 19th-century, 614–616; and League of Nations ratification debate, 663; pre–World War II, 749; Wilson's attempt to break with, 659

Israel: Camp David Accords and, 873–874; Suez canal crisis and, 803; terrorism and, 909; in Yom Kippur War, 864–866

Italian Americans, 519, 522

Italy: after World War I, 660–662; Jews in, 14; in Paris Peace Conference, 660–662;

pre–World War II aggression of, 746, 748; revolutions in, 14; in World War II, 748, 749, 764

Iwo Jima, 771*m*, 772

IWW. *See* Industrial Workers of the World

J. Edgar Thomson Steel Works, 492

J. P. Morgan and Company, 488, 508

J. Walter Thompson advertising agency, 681*f*

Jabbar, Kareem Al, 845

Jackson, Andrew, 279*f*, 280, 281–282, 282*f*; and Bank of United States, 282–287, 291–292; cabinet of, 285; and Calhoun, animosity between, 287; cartoon of, 285*f*; democratic principles of, 277–278, 280; in 1824 presidential election, 245–246; in 1828 presidential election, 276, 278–279; in 1832 presidential election, 282; farmers and, 295*f*; Florida campaign of, 235–236; as Hero of New Orleans, 233–234; inauguration of, 277, 279; Indian resettlement by, 287–289, 288*m*; nullification crisis and, 289–292; personality of, 279, 280, 281–282, 293, 294; presidency of, 280–293; spoils system of, 280–281; and tariff question, 247; and Texas annexation, 331; *vs.* Jeffersonian democracy, 277, 281; in War of 1812, 232, 260

Jackson, Michael, 906

Jackson, Rachel, 279, 279*f*, 280

Jackson, Thomas J. "Stonewall," 406, 412, 414, 419

Jackson State University, 830

Jacksonians (Democrats), and party system, 278–279, 293–294

Jamaica, in War of 1812, 227, 229, 231

James, Henry, 546, 547*f*

James, Jesse, 470*f*

James, Thomas, 114

James, William, 547*f*, 550

James (Duke of York), 45

James I (King of England), 30–31, 34, 37, 59

James II (King of England), 72, 83, 88; Dominion of, 88

Jamestown, Virginia: Bacon's Rebellion and, 61–62; lessons of, 57–58; settlement of, 31–32; slavery in, 58

Jamieson, Perry D., 444*f*

Japan: atomic bomb and, 772–775, 773*f*; and China, 633, 641, 703, 705–706, 705*f*, 747; early 20th-century relations with, 633–634, 641; Pearl Harbor attack by, 754*f*, 755; Perry's expedition to, 616; post–World War I relations with, 703; in World War II, 749, 753, 754–755, 769–772

Japanese Americans: exclusion of, 607, 634; internment of, 753, 760*m*, 761*f*; segregation of, 634

Java (ship), 224

Jay, John: in Anglo-American War, 182; as chief justice, 175; and Constitution, 171; *Federalist Papers,* 173; in negotiations with Britain, 184–185; and Peace of Paris, 146

Jay Treaty, 184–185

Jazz, 691

Jazz Age, 671, 674–675

The Jazz Singer (film), 681

Jefferson, Field, 194*f*

Jefferson, Randolph, 194*f*

Jefferson, Thomas, 146*f*; and Adams (John), 134, 239; Alien and Sedition Acts and, 191; architecture and, 194*f*; and Burr affair, 210; in Continental Congress, 129; copyright laws and, 162; death of, 248; debt and, 194, 217; and Declaration of Independence, 131–132; democratic principles of, 197, 199, 216–217, 278; on education, 324; in 1800 presidential election, 195–196; in 1804 presidential election, 200; Embargo Act of, 213–215; foreign policy of, 202, 213; ginger beer and, 126; government debt and, 217; home of, 194*f*; intellectual life of, 100; and judiciary, 200–202; Kentucky and Virginia Resolves and, 191–192; land ordinances and, 158; on Missouri Compromise, 244; on Monroe, 239; on Napoleon, 224; in Peace of Paris, 146; personal debt and, 194; political theories of, 197, 199–200; popularity of, 216–217; prejudices of, 197; presidency of, 196–200; progeny of, 194*f*; and Republican party, 182–183, 186; in 1796 presidential election, 188; on Shays's Rebellion, 165; on slaves, 358; and social reform, 153; *vs.* Jackson, 277, 282; in Washington administration, 175, 178–179, 180; western policies of, 202–207, 207–209

Jeffrey, Julie Roy, 333*f*

Jenkins, Frederick "Shadrach," 373

Jerry (slave), 373

Jesuit priests, Indian life and, 55–56

Jews: Holocaust and, 768, 770*f*; immigration of, 520, 522, 673, 747; in Israel, 802–803; Ku Klux Klan and, 686–687; in Nazi Europe, 747, 768; in post–World War I period, 673; prejudice against, 673, 747; as Supreme Court justices, 647

JFK (film), 825*f*

Jiang Jieshi. *See* Chiang Kai-shek

Job Corps, 820

John II (King of Portugal), 19

Johns Hopkins University, 537, 537*f,* 540, 542

Johnson, Andrew, 438–439, 438*f,* 555; Civil War promise to freed slaves, 436; 1864 nomination of, 428; Fourteenth Amendment and, 441; impeachment of, 443–444; and Reconstruction, 438–441, 443–444

Johnson, Hiram, 647

Johnson, Jack, 852

Johnson, Lyndon Baines, 819–823, 821*f*; civil rights under, 810, 820, 848; Great Society program of, 810, 820–822; in 1960 presidential election, 808; in 1964 presidential election, 820–821; in 1968 presidential election, 823, 826–828; presidency of, 820; on society, 847; Vietnam war under, 810, 822–823, 824*m*, 825*f*

Johnson, Richard Mentor: in 1840 presidential election, 298; in War of 1812, 226

Johnson, Samuel, 153

Johnson, Tom L., 586, 587

Johnson, William, 110

Johnston, Albert Sidney, 410

Johnston, Joseph E., 412, 427

Joint-stock companies, and colonization, 30–33

Jones, Archer, 444*f*

Jones, Iredell, 421

Jones, James H., 859

Jones, Mary Harris "Mother," 586

Jones, Paula Corbin, 901

Jones, Robert T. "Bobby," 682

Jordan, David Starr, 628

Jordon, Jesse, 162, 163

Joseph (Indian Chief), 466

Josephson, Matthew, 500*f*

Journalism: and Cuban revolution, 622; early 20th-century, 584; and Harlem Renaissance, 691; and political campaigns, 577; and political parties, 83, 183; in Progressive Era, 584; racism in, 565. *See also specific publications*

Joy, James F., 490

Judiciary: colonial, 87–88; constitutional provisions for, 171; Jefferson's attack on, 200–202. *See also* Supreme Court

Judiciary Act (1789), 175, 200–201

Judiciary Act (1801), 200

The Jungle (Sinclair), 599

Junk bonds, 884

Junto (club), 99; Essex Junto, 206

Justice Department: General Intelligence Division of, 667; and red scare, 667

Justice Department, Antitrust Division of, 709–710

Kalakaua (King of Hawaii), 618
Kalm, Peter, 80
Kalstedt, Harry, 678*f*
Kamikazes, 772
Kansas: Alliance movement in, 571, 572; creation of territory, 377–378; Dust Bowl in, 725–726; Lecompton constitution in, 387–388; population in late 19th century, 570; Populists in, 572, 573, 573*f*; progressive reform in, 587; settlement of, 380–383; slavery in, 377–383, 387–388
Kansas Indians, 463
Kansas Pacific Railroad, 476, 485
Kansas-Nebraska Act, 377–378
Kaskaskia, 53
Katrina (Hurricane), 1, 918–919
Katz, Michael B., 310*f*
Keating-Owen Child Labor Act (1916), 647
Kelley, Abby, 316
Kelley, Oliver H., 501
Kelley, Robin D., 858*f*
Kellogg, Frank B., 704
Kellogg-Briand Pact (1928), 704, 705
Kelly, William, 487
Kenna, "Hinky Dink," 567
Kennan, George, 666*f*, 783, 792
Kennan, George F., 617*f*
Kennedy, David M., 739*f*
Kennedy, Jacqueline, 811, 819*f*
Kennedy, John F., 372, 808–809, 900*f*; assassination of, 810, 818–819; and civil rights movement, 815–818; in Cuban missile crisis, 811–814; in 1960 presidential election, 808–809, 810; presidency of, 811; in Vietnam, 815; in World War II, 808
Kennedy, Joseph P., 808
Kennedy, Robert, 819*f*; assassination of, 826; as attorney general, 811; in Cuban missile crisis, 812; in 1968 presidential election, 826
Kent State University, 829, 830*f*
Kentucky, formation of, 186, 187*m*
Kentucky Resolution, 191–192
Keppler, Joseph, 556*f*
Kerber, Linda, 94*f*
Kerner, Otto, 849
Kerner Commission, 849
Kerosene, 487
Kerouac, Jack, 840
Kerr, Clark, 856
Kerry, John, in 2004 presidential election, 914–915
Kesey, Ken, 857
Key, David M., 458
Key, Francis Scott, 228–229
Key to Uncle Tom's Cabin (Stowe), 375*f*

Keynes, John Maynard, 735, 738, 756, 782
Khomeini, Ayatollah Ruhollah, 874
Khrushchev, Nikita, 803–803, 804*f*; in Cuban missile crisis, 812–814, 814*f*; Cuban revolution and, 805; Eisenhower and, 803–804; Kennedy and, 812–814; rise of, 803; Suez Canal crisis and, 803
Kimmel, Husband E., 755
Kinetoscope, 489*f*
King, Charles Bird, 247*f*
King, Martin Luther, Jr., 845*f*; approach to civil rights, 818, 846, 848, 905; assassination of, 849; in Montgomery bus boycott, 816; in SCLC, 816; writings and speeches of, 818
King George III (King of England), 154
King George's War, 101
King James Bible, 34
King William's War (1689–1697), 101
King's College, New York City, 98
Kingsley, Anna (Anta), 235*f*
Kingsley, Zephaniah, 235*f*
Kinsey, Alfred C., 857–859
Kirkpatrick, Jeane, 878
Kissinger, Henry, 838; and détente, 830–831; and Nixon's resignation, 837–838; and Vietnam, 828, 832; and Yom Kippur War, 865–866
Kitchen Debate, 804*f*
Klan. *See* Ku Klux Klan
Klumpke, Anna Elizabeth, 317*f*
Knights of Labor, 503–504, 572
Knights of Reliance, 570
Knights of the White Camelia, 452
Knowledge revolution, 551–552
Know-Nothing (American) party, 379–380
Knox, Henry, 748
Knox, Philander C., 596
Kodak camera, 484
Kohlberg, Kravis, Roberts and Company, 884
Kolko, Gabriel, 597*f*
Korea: division into North and South, 790–794, 792*m*; Soviet control of, 783; war between Japan and China over, 633
Korean War, 790–794, 792*m*, 793*f*, 797–798
Kosovo, 904
Kremer, "Honest George," 277
Ku Klux Klan, 452–453, 671; in *Birth of a Nation,* 680; post–World War I revival of, 686–687, 687*f*
Kuhn, Loeb (private bank), 491
Kulikoff, Alan, 94*f*
Kurds: in Iraq, 920; in late 20th century, 895–896, 897–898; in Second Iraq War, 913
Kurile Islands, 783

Kurz, Louis, 623*f*
Kushner, Tony, 799*f*
Kuwait, 895–898, 897*f*; in late 20th century, 896*m*; in Second Iraq War, 912, 913
Kyoto Protocol (1997), 917

La Feber, Walter, 791*f*
La Follette, Robert M., 587–588; in 1924 presidential election, 702; reforms of, 587–588
Labor. *See* Work
Labor legislation: in New Deal, 723–724, 734; post–World War II, 782; in World War II, 756
Labor unions: blacks and, 742–743; in early 19th century, 253, 361; in early 20th century, 585–586; and 1896 presidential election, 579; growth in 1930s, 738; Industrial Revolution and, 361; in late 19th century, 503–508; in mid-19th century, 361, 424; in mid-20th century, 844, 870; migrant workers in, 851; militancy of, late 19th-century, 506–508; New Deal and, 723–724, 734, 737–740; Nixon and, 833; post–World War II, 782, 870; progressivism and, 585; radicalism in, 586; red scare and, 665–666; Roosevelt (Franklin) and, 736, 737–738; Roosevelt (Theodore) and, 596–598; socialism and, 586; Wal-Mart and, 482; in World War I, 650; in World War II, 756. *See also* Strikes
Ladies' Home Journal, 704, 842
Lafayette, Marquis de, 142, 145, 165*f*
Laissez faire: challenges to, 502, 540; in post–World War I period, 702; progressive denunciation of, 584
Lake Champlain, 128; Plattsburg, Battle of, 230; Rush-Bagot Agreement and, 234
Lake Erie, Battle of, 226, 227*f*
Lake Ontario, Rush-Bagot Agreement and, 234
Lake Pontchartrain, Louisiana, 53, 918
Lake Shore and Michigan Southern Railroad, 484
Land: access to water and, 478, 479, 479*f*; classification of, 478; colonial, 57–58, 82; Indian, loss of, 468*m*; Indian attitude toward, 23, 48–49; Jeffersonian policy on, 202–207; late 19th-century, 472, 477–480; in medieval Europe, 15; post-Revolutionary issues regarding, 158–159; for railroads, 366, 473–476, 474, 486; in Reconstruction South, 448–452; sale of, 292; sectional controversy over, 241; and War of 1812, 222; in West, 472, 477–480, 478. *See also* Border issues; Territory

Land Ordinance (1785), 158–159, 159*f*
Land-grant railroads, 366
Land-grant system, railroads and, 473–474, 486
Land-grant universities, 538
Landon, Alfred M., 736
Lange, Dorothea, 726*f*
Laos, in Vietnam war, 824*m*
Large policy, 615
Lark (ship), 364
Larkin, Oliver, 273*f*
Las Casa, Bartolomé de, 22
Latin America: Cold War conflicts in, 804–805; dollar diplomacy in, 637, 638; early 20th-century policy toward, 634–638, 641–642; Good Neighbor policy toward, 704–705; Iran-Contra arms deal and, 886–888; late 19th-century policy toward, 615, 619–621, 630–632; post–World War I policy toward, 704–705; revolutions in, American response to, 237–238. *See also specific countries*
Latinos. *See* Hispanic Americans
Laud, William, 37
Laurens, Henry, 146
Law(s): colonies and, 87–88; federal *vs.* state, 272, 290–291. *See also specific laws*
Law, Walter, 678*f*
Lawrence (ship), 227*f*
Lawyers, colonial, 99
Layoffs, 884–885
Lazarus, Emma, 672, 672*f*
le Carré, John, 881*f*
League of Nations, 662, 663*f*; and Japanese invasion of China, 705–706; U.S. refusal to ratify, 662–665; *vs.* United Nations, 776
Leary, Timothy, 857
Lease, Mary Elizabeth, 571*f*
Leaves of Grass (Whitman), 320*f*, 323
Lebanon, in late 20th century, 896*m*
Leclerc, Charles, 203
Lecompton constitution, 387–388
Lee, Ann, 306
Lee, Arthur, 141
Lee, Higginson (private bank), 491
Lee, Richard Henry: and Constitution, 172; in Continental Congress, 129, 131
Lee, Robert E.: at Antietam, 413–414, 413*m*; at Appomattox Court House, 430; daughter of, 608; in folklore, 444*f*; at Gettysburg, 418, 418*m*, 419; at Harper's Ferry, 392; in Mexican War, 412; Peninsula battles of, 412, 413*m*; on secession, 398; at Wilderness, 426–427, 431*m*

Legislation. *See* Labor legislation; Law(s); *specific laws*
Legislature: colonial, 38, 87–89; debates on, Philadelphia Convention and, 169–170; state republican, 152–153. *See also* Congress
Lehigh University, 697
Leisler, Jacob, 83
"Leisler's Rebellion," 83
Leisure activities. *See* Entertainment; Sports
Lemon, James, 94*f*
Lend-Lease Act (1941), 750
Leopard (ship), 214
"The Lesson of History" (Marshall), 784
"Letters from a Farmer in Pennsylvania to the Inhabitants of the British Colonies" (Dickinson), 118
Leuchtenburg, William, 676*f,* 739*f*
Levees, destruction by Hurricane Katrina, 919
Lever Act (1917), 650
Lewinsky, Monica, 902–903, 903*f*
Lewis, John L., 724, 756
Lewis, Meriwether, expedition of, 207–209, 208*m*
Lewis, Sinclair, 689–690
Lewis and Clark expedition, 207–209, 208*m*
Lexington, Battle of, 128*f*
Lexington (ship), 770
Leyte Gulf, Battle for, 772
Liberal Republican party, 454, 582
Liberator (newspaper), 313, 314
Liberia, Republic of, 262
Liberties. *See* Civil liberties
Liberty and Victory Loan drives, 651
"Liberty Boys," 113
Liberty Party, 344
Libraries, 551
Libya, in late 20th century, 896*m*
Lieberman, Joseph, 908
Life (magazine), 797–798
Life expectancy, in colonies, 57
Life insurance business, 496, 589–590
Life on the Mississippi (Twain), 545
Light bulb, invention of, 488
Light in August (Faulkner), 729
Lightning rod, invention of, 100
Liliuokalani (Queen of Hawaii), 618
Lincoln, Abraham, 388–389, 390*f*; assassination of, 436; cabinet of, 401; civil liberties under, 408; in Civil War, 401–402, 408, 413, 414, 422; debates with Douglas, 372, 389–401, 395*f*; in 1860 presidential election, 394–396, 396*m*; in 1864 presidential election, 428, 430; 1869 presidential campaign, 395*f*; 1872 Grant campaign poster, 455*f*; on emanci-
pation, 402; and Emancipation Proclamation, 414–417; on Know-Nothing party, 380; and Mexican War, opposition to, 339, 389; as president-elect, 398, 401; and Reconstruction, 436, 437–439; on secession, 398, 401–402; on slavery, 389, 390, 391; on touring Civil War military hospital wards, 400; on wage labor, 362
Lincoln, Thomas, 388
Lindbergh, Charles A., 695–696
Lindgren, Elaine, 333*f*
Lindneux, Robert, 464*f*
Link, Arthur, 666*f*
Linotype, 552
Lippmann, Walter, 718
Literacy: and black suffrage, 564; and immigrants, 522; in New England, 353; in South, 353
Literature: in 1920s, 688–690; black, 691–692; of counterculture, 840, 856–857; in the Depression, 729; early 19th-century, 318–325; late 19th-century, 542–546; naturalism in, 546; realism in, 542, 544, 545–546; on slavery, 373–374; of West, 544–545
Little, Malcolm. *See* Malcolm X
Little Big Horn Casino, Montana, 460
Little Bighorn, 466
Little Lord Fauntleroy (Burnett), 544
Little Rock, Arkansas, desegregation in, 807, 807*f*
Little Rock and Fort Smith Railroad, 562
Little Turtle (Miami chief), 180
Littleton, Colorado, school shooting at, 890
Livingston, Robert R.: and Declaration of Independence, 131; and Louisiana Purchase, 203–207; and steam navigation, 267, 273
Lloyd, Henry Demarest, 493, 499, 584
Lloyd George, David, 660, 661
Locke, John, 98, 111, 166, 261
Lockheed, Haimes, 695
Lockheed, Malcolm, 695
Lockridge, Kenneth, 73*f*
Locofoco, 293
Locomotives, 486
Lodge, Henry Cabot, 535, 666*f*; and Harding, 699; and navy, 616; opposition to League of Nations, 662–665, 776; on Philippines, 627; reservations of, 666*f*; and Taft-Roosevelt dispute, 602
Lodge Reservations, 664, 665, 666*f*
Log Cabin (newspaper), 298
Log Cabin campaign, 298–299, 298*f*
Lombardi, Vince, 535
London Company, 31, 32, 43, 58, 59

Long, Huey, 729, 732, 732*f*, 733
Long Island, Battle of, 137, 138*f*
Longfellow, Henry Wadsworth, 542
Longstreet, James, 445
Looking Backward 2000–1887 (Bellamy), 499, 509, 531
Los Angeles, California: gangs in, 893; progressivism in, 585; socialism in, 585; Watts riots in (1965), 849
Los Angeles, in Mexican War, 339
Lott, Trent, 400
Loudoun, Lord, 108
Louis, Joe, 731, 852
Louis XVI (King of France), 141, 183
Louisiana: Long in, 729, 732; slave uprising in, 355
Louisiana National Guard, 920
Louisiana Purchase, 202–207; exploration of, 208–209, 208*m*; and population of New Orleans (1803), 205*f*
Louisville and Nashville Railroad, 485
Louverture, Toussaint "Black Napoleon," 203, 204*f*
Lovejoy, Elijah, 314
Loving, Oliver, 476
Low, Seth, 586, 587
Low country, 56
Lowden, Frank, 698
Lowell, Francis Cabot, 253
Lowell, Massachusetts, 253, 255–256; immigrants in, 350; textile industry in, 253, 255–256
Loyalists: post-Revolutionary War, 155; in Revolutionary War, 136–137, 142–143
Loyalty Review Board, 795
Lucas, Eliza. *See* Pinckney, Eliza Lucas
Lucas, George, 880
Lucayans, 22
Luce, Henry, 778, 780
Luce, Stephen B., 616
Luk, George, 585*f*
Luna Park, 529*f*
Lusitania (ship), 645*f*, 646, 648*f*
Luther, Martin, 14
Lyell, Charles, 358
Lynchings, 608, 656
Lynn, Massachusetts, strike by women in, 361*f*

MacArthur, Douglas: in Korean War, 791–794, 796; in World War II, 770–771, 772
Macdonough, Thomas, 230
Macedonian (ship), 224
Macomb, Alexander, 230
Macon, Nathaniel, 219
Macon's Bill No. 2, 219

Madagascar rice, 63
Madison, James: Alien and Sedition Acts and, 191; and American Colonization Society, 262; beer and, 126; and Bill of Rights, 176; and Constitution, 166, 169, 170*f*, 173; copyright laws and, 162; declaration of war, 220; in 1808 presidential election, 219; *Federalist Papers,* 173; and Hamiltonian reforms, 178; inaugural address of, 219; in Jefferson administration, 200–201, 213, 215; Kentucky and Virginia Resolves and, 191–192; land policies of, 221–222; and political parties, 182–183; in War of 1812, 226, 228
Madness and Civilization (Foucault), 310*f*
Magazines, 552, 565, 584. *See also individual magazines by name*
Magellan, Ferdinand, 21
Maggie, A Girl of the Streets (Crane), 546
Magón, Ricardo Flores, 652
Magruder, Jeb Stuart, 834
Mahan, Alfred Thayer, 615–616
Mailer, Norman, 827
Main Street (Lewis), 689
Maine: colonial, 41; statehood for, 243; temperance movement in, 313
Maine (ship), 622–624, 623*f*
Mainline Canal, 270
Malaria, 14
Malcolm X, 727, 818, 845, 848
Mall of America, Minneapolis, Minnesota, 510
Malone, Dumas, 194*f*
Mammals: extinction of, 2–4; prehistoric, 2–4
Mammoth(s), woolly, 2–4
Mammoth Oil Company, 700
The Man Nobody Knows (Barton), 692
Manassas. *See* Bull Run, battle of
Manchuria, Japan and, 633–634, 703, 705–706, 705*f*
Manchuria, Soviet control of, 783
Manhattan Island, 45, 523
Manhattan Project, 773
Manifest destiny, 332, 334, 374, 615
Mann, Horace, 324, 517
Mann-Elkins Act (1910), 601
Manufacturing: assembly line impact on, 694; during Civil War, 407; colonial, 63, 91, 117; in early 19th century, 257–258; in Great Depression, 712; innovations in, 358, 692–694; in late 19th century, 483–484, 486–488, 614–615; and Marshall Court, 272; in mid 19th century, 351, 358, 406–407; northern, 358–359; in post–Civil War South, 451; post-Revolutionary, 157; post–World War

I, 692–694, 709; royal restrictions on, 91;
   southern, 358, 451; in World War I, 649;
   in World War II, 755–756
Mao Zedong, 789
Marathon Oil, 884–885
Marbury, William, 200
Marbury v. Madison, 200–201
Marchand, Roland, 676*f*
Marcy, William L., 278, 377
Marijuana, 892
Marion, Francis "Swamp Fox," 143
Marion Star (newspaper), 698
Marling, Karal Ann, 843*f*
Marriage: in 19th century, 303–304, 307,
   511–512; among slaves, 352, 354; in
   colonial South, 66; companionate, 673; in
   New France, 53; post–World War I, 673,
   675; same-sex, 915; in World War II,
   757–758, 760
Marshall, George C., 766*f,* 784
Marshall, James W., 342
Marshall, John, 273*f*; in Adams administra-
   tion, 189; and American Colonization
   Society, 262; as chief justice, 200–201,
   210, 271–274; death of, 274; and Indian
   rulings, 289; and Jackson's inauguration,
   277; in *Marbury v. Madison,* 201
Marshall, Thurgood, 806, 905
Marshall Plan, 784–787, 785*m,* 791*f*
Marx, Karl, 438, 501, 509, 713*f*
Marxism, 501
Mary I (Queen of England), 34
Mary II (Queen of England), 72
Maryland: Articles of Confederation and,
   150; colonial, 67*m*; colonial life in, 57;
   politics in, 83; ratification of Constitution
   by, 172, 174*m*; settlement of, 43–44; slav-
   ery in, 58; in War of 1812, 227, 228
Masaryk, Jan, 784–785
Mashantucket Pequot Tribe, 460
Mason, George, 152
Mason, James M., 347
Mason, John, 36, 41
Mason, John Y., 375
Massace, at Sand Creek, Colorado (1864),
   463, 464*f*
Massachusetts: and Coercive Acts, 122–123;
   colonial, 72, 74; common school move-
   ment in, 324; mobility in, 517; post-
   Revolutionary violence in, 165; ratifica-
   tion of Constitution by, 172, 174*m*; in
   Revolutionary War, 127–128; settlement
   of, 35–41
Massachusetts 54th, 417, 420, 420*f*–421*f,*
   421
Massachusetts Anti-Slavery Society, 314
Massachusetts Bay Company, 37

Massachusetts Circular Letter, 118
Massachusetts General Court, 38, 40, 113,
   231
Massachusetts Government Act (1774), 123
Massachusetts Militia, 135*f*
Massachusetts Patriots, 127, 128; and
   Boston Tea Party, 121–122
The Masses (magazine), 652
Mastny, Thomas, 791*f*
Matamoros, 338
Materialism, late 19th century, 534, 536
Mather, Cotton, 69–70, 76, 78
Mather, Increase, 49, 75
Mathers, Marshall Bruce, III, 906
Matteson, T. H., 75*f*
Maximilian (Archduke of Austria), 613
Mayflower (ship), 35
Mayflower Compact, 36
Mayhew, Jonathan, 112
Maysville Road, 287
Mazda, 885
McAdoo, William G., 649, 702
McCain, John, 908
McCarran Act, 805
McCarthy, Eugene, 826
McCarthy, Joseph R., 795–796, 798–799,
   799*f,* 800–801, 805–806
McCarthyism, 795–796, 798–799,
   800*f*–801*f,* 805–806
McClellan, George B., 406–407, 411–412;
   at Antietam, 413–414; 1864 nomination
   of, 428; Peninsula campaign, 412, 413*m*
McClure, S. S., 584
McClure's (magazine), 584
McColl, Ada, 333*f*
McCord, James, 833–834
McCormick, Cyrus Hall, 367
McCormick Harvesting Machine Company,
   505
McCoy, Joseph G., 476, 477
McCulloch, John W., 272
McCulloch v. Maryland, 272, 274, 282–283,
   284
McCullough, David, 773*f*
McDougal, James, 898
McDowell, Irvin, 406
McGovern, George, 832
McKay, Donald, 362
McKinley, William, 557, 579–580; assassina-
   tion of, 594; and Cuba, 621–624, 630; in
   1896 presidential election, 576,
   577–579, 578*m*; and expansionism, 627,
   630; foreign policy of, 616, 617,
   621–624, 627, 630, 635; in 1900 presi-
   dential election, 630; and Philippines, an-
   nexation of, 628
McKinley Tariff Act (1890), 618

McLane, Louis, 285
McNamara, Robert, 811, 825*f*
McTeague (Norris), 546
McWhiney, Grady, 444*f*
Meade, George G., 418*m,* 422
Measles, 26*f*
Meat packing industry, 599
Medicaid, 821
Medicare, 821, 878
Medicare Act (1965), 821
Medicine Lodge Creek, 464
Medieval society, 14–15
Melampus (ship), 214
Mellon, Andrew: in Coolidge administra-
    tion, 702; on Great Depression, 711; in
    Harding administration, 699–700; taxa-
    tion program of, 699–700, 711; on World
    War I debts, 706
Melville, Herman, 321–322, 560
Mencken, H. L., 523, 685
Menlo Park, New Jersey, 488
Mentally ill patients, 311, 312
Mercantilism, 89–90; effects of, 92–93;
    post-Revolutionary, 164
Mercer, Lucy, 742*f*
Merchant marine: Anglo-French War and,
    181–182; British impressment policy and,
    211–212; Embargo Act and, 214–215;
    Napoleonic wars and, 211–212, 220; in
    War of 1812, 225
Mergenthaler, Ottmar, 552
Mergers, 582, 583, 884
Merrell, James, 46*f,* 223*f*
Merrimack (ship), 411
Merrimack Manufacturing Company, 255
Merritt, Jane T., 223*f*
Merry, Anthony, 210
Mesabi region, 487
Methodists: fundamentalism and, 684; and
    Oregon missionaries, 334; in Second
    Great Awakening, 304
Metropolitan Health Board (New York
    City), 523
Metropolitan Museum of Art, 526
Metropolitan Opera, 526
Mexican War, 337–342, 338*f,* 340*m;* opposi-
    tion to, 320, 339, 389; Texas annexation
    and, 337; Treaty of Guadalupe Hidalgo,
    340–341
Mexican Americans: civil rights for,
    850–851; deportation in Great
    Depression, 715, 850; immigration re-
    form and, 916–917, 916*f*
Mexico: and California, 334; cattle in, 476;
    current border, 328; dollar diplomacy in,
    638; expansionism and, 337–338, 613;
    French protectorate over, 613; missionary

diplomacy in, 641–642; post–World War
    I relations with, 704; Spanish conquest of,
    21; and Texas, 330
Mexico City, in Mexican War, 339–341
Miami Dolphins (football team), 535
Miami Indians, 180
Michigan: banks in, 722; colleges in, 324,
    538
Michigan Central Railroad, 484
Michigan State University, 538
Michigan Technological University, 162
Microsoft Internet Explorer, 907
Middle class: in mid-20th century, 844; in
    19th century, 302–303, 303*f,* 511–512;
    in post–World War I period, 673; and
    prohibition, 686
Middle colonies, 45–47, 67*m,* 77, 80–84;
    agriculture in, 80; economy of, 82; het-
    erogeneity of, 80–82; politics in, 82–84;
    religious awakening in, 93–96
Middle East: Camp David Accords and,
    873–874; Cold War conflicts in,
    802–803; hostages in, Iran-Contra arms
    deal and, 886–888; Israel and, 802–803;
    in late 20th century, 896*m;* Truman on,
    783–784. *See also specific countries*
Midway, Battle at, 770
Midway Islands: acquisition of, 614; in
    World War II, 770
Migrant labor system, reform of, 851
Migration: by blacks, 654–656, 690; colo-
    nial, 38, 38*f;* gold rush and, 344–345;
    prehistoric, 2; World War I and, 654–656;
    World War II and, 757. *See also*
    Geographic mobility
Milan Decree (1807), 211, 220, 224
Militant movements, by minorities,
    608–611, 690–692, 848–852
Military: in Afghanistan, 912; blacks in, 417,
    655–656, 758–759, 758*f;* under Bush
    (George W.), 753; Cold War expansion
    of, 781, 790; death toll in Iraq, 922; un-
    der Eisenhower, 797–798; in *Glory* (film),
    420–421, 420*f*–421*f;* in Iraq, 17, 920,
    921*f,* 922; post–World War II demobiliza-
    tion of, 783; under Reagan, 878; in
    Second Iraq War, 913–914; women in,
    762; World War II mobilization, 755–756.
    See also Army; Navy
Military bases: bases-for-destroyers deal,
    749; overseas, importance of, 615–616
Military-industrial complex, Eisenhower
    and, 781
Milken, Michael, 884
Miller, Arthur, 78, 79, 801*f*
Miller, Doris "Dorie," 758*f*
Miller, Perry, 71, 73*f*

Miller, Phineas, 259–260
Miller, William, 500*f*
Million Man March, 905
Milosevic, Slobodan, 904
Mimeograph, 488
Minimum wage, New Deal legislation on, 724
Mining, in West, 477*m*
Mining industry: late 19th-century boom in, 468–471; 1902 coal strike and, 596–598; strikes against, 507
Mining towns, 469, 471
Minneapolis, Minnesota, 510
Minnesota: Alliance movement in, 572; Populist party in, 573; progressive reform in, 587
Minorities: rights for, progressivism and, 607–611; in World War II, 753, 758–760. *See also specific groups*
Minow, Newton, 842
Minuit, Peter, 45
Minute Men, 127
Minutemen missiles, 813
Mission settlements, 54, 334; in California, 55, 56*f*
Missionary diplomacy, 641–642
Mississippi: Black Code in, 440; black suffrage in, 453, 564; cotton in, 260, 289; formation of territory, 186, 187*m*; progressive reform in, 587; slaves in, 351
Mississippi River: Civil War, 422; in Civil War, 410, 411*m*; commerce and, 264; New France and, 53; post-Revolutionary trade and, 163; railroads and, 370; steamboats and, 267; and trade, 364
Mississippi Valley: agriculture in, 367; in mid-19th century agriculture in, 368*m*; in Panic of 1857, 370; slavery in, 353*m*; and trade, 264, 267, 364, 367
Mississippian mound builders, 6*f*, 11–12
Missouri Compromise, 241–245, 243*m*, 313–314, 377–378; Dred Scott decision and, 385; proposed extension of, 343; repeal of, 379
Missouri Pacific Railroad, 476, 485, 504, 504*f*
Mitchell, John, 836
Mitchell, John P., 586
Mobility: late 19th-century, 516–518. *See also* Migration
Mobilization: in World War I, 648–650; in World War II, 755–756
Moby Dick (Melville), 321
Model A Ford, 695
Model G airplane, 695
Model T Ford, 694, 695
"A Modelle of Christian Charity" (Winthrop), 37–38

Moderate Republicans: after Civil War, 439; during Civil War, 408
Mogollon peoples, 7–9
Mojados, 850
Molasses Act (1733), 93
Moley, Raymond, 719
Mondale, Walter, 878, 879
Monetary policy: gold *vs.* silver in, 574; New Deal and, 723–724. *See also* Currency
Money, paper, 286; Bank of United States and, 282–283; during Civil War, 407, 409; Revolutionary War and, 150
Money Trust, 508
Moneymaker, Chris, 697
Mongolia, Outer, 783
Monitor (ship), 411
Monkey Trial, 684–685
Monopolies, 483, 489–496; attacks on, 496–503, 584; and democracy, 508–509; and economic system of 1920s, 709–710; progressive attacks on, 584, 590; Roosevelt's (Theodore) attacks on, 596. *See also* Trust(s)
Monroe, James: and American Colonization Society, 262; and Era of Good Feelings, 238–239; and Louisiana Purchase, 203; and Monroe Doctrine, 236–238; presidency of, 235–240
Monroe Doctrine, 236–238, 620; Khrushchev on, 805; Roosevelt Corollary to, 632, 705; Venezuela crisis and, 620
Montana: gold rush in, 469; territorial organization of, 471
Montcalm, Louis Joseph de, 104
Monte Cassino, 764
Monterey, California, 55; in Mexican War, 339
Montesquieu, Charles-Louis de Secondat, 98, 166
Montgomery, Alabama, 485*f*; civil rights movement in, 816, 848
Montgomery, Richard, 135
Monticello, 194*f*
Montojo, Admiral, 624
Moody, Dwight L., 530
Moore, Joseph, and family, 303*f*
Moral Majority, 878–879
Morgan, Daniel, 143
Morgan, Edmund, 94*f*, 132*f*
Morgan, J. Pierpont, 491, 492, 508, 575, 597*f*, 598
Morganizations, 491
Morgenthau, Jr., Henry, 738
Morison, Samuel Eliot, 676*f*
Mormon Trail, 335*m*
Mormons, 307–309, 308*f*

Morrill Land Grant Act (1862), 424, 536, 538
Morris, Lewis, 83, 88*f*
Morris, Robert, Revolutionary War financing and, 150–151
Moss, Anne Lee, 800*f*
Motel industry, 841
Motion picture industry, 489*f*
Motion pictures, 680–681
Motion-picture projector, 488
Mott, Lucretia, 316, 317
Mound builders, 6, 6*f*, 10, 11–12
Moundville, Alabama, 11–12
Mount Holyoke College, 538
Moussa, Amr, 400
Movies, 680–681, 905–906; first, 489*f*. *See also specific movies*
Moving assembly line, 694
MTV, 906
Muckrakers, 584
Mugwumps, 582
Muhammad, Elijah, 818
Mulberry Grove (plantation), 259
Muller v. *Oregon,* 590
Mulligan letters, 562
Municipal socialism, 585
Munn v. *Illinois,* 501
Munsey, Frank, 603
"The Murders in the Rue Morgue" (Poe), 320
Murrow, Edward R., 798, 800–801
Musaddig, Muhammad, 874
Muscle Shoals, Alabama, 726, 727*m*
Museum of Fine Arts (Boston), 527
Music: in 1920s, 691; in 1990s, 906; copyright infringement, 162; MTV and, 906; popular, 906; rap, 906
Muslims, Black, 818, 845, 848
Mussolini, Benito, 746, 764
Mutual Life, 496
My Lai massacre, 829
Myres, Sandra L., 333*f*

NAACP. *See* National Association for the Advancement of Colored People
Nabisco, 884
Nader, Ralph, 908
Nagasaki, 773*f*, 774
Nagin, C. Ray, 919
Nairobi, Kenya, 909
Naismith, James, 529
Napoleon Bonaparte: abdication of, 227; and America, threat to, 224; and Britain, stand-off with, 211–212; and Convention of 1800, 192; and Louisiana Purchase, 202–207
Narrative of the Life of Frederick Douglass (Douglass), 315

Narváez, Pánfilo de, 23
Nash, Gary B., 132*f*
Nashville (ship), 635
Nasser, Gamal Abdel, 803
Nast, Thomas, 446*f*
Nation, founding of, 134
The Nation (magazine), 545, 689
National Academy of Science, 359
National American Woman Suffrage Association (NAWSA), 592
National Association for the Advancement of Colored People (NAACP), 816; civil rights litigation by, 806; founding of, 610
National Broadcasting Company, 682
National Center on Addiction and Substance Abuse (CASA), 670
National Child Labor Committee, 589
National debt: Hamiltonian reforms to reduce, 178; under Jefferson, 199; under Reagan, 885; in World War I, 650–651
National Defense Education Act (1958), 854
National Democrats, 577
National Educational Television, 842
National Farm Workers' Association, 851, 851*f*
National Federation of Republican Women, 873
National Football League, 682
National Gazette, 183
National Grange of the Patrons of Husbandry, 501, 515; Populists and, 573
National Greenback party, 558
National identity, development of, 93
National Indian Youth Council, 851
National Industrial Recovery Act (NIRA), 723–724, 734, 735
National Institution for the Promotion of Science (1840), 359
National Labor Relations (Wagner) Act (1935), 734
National Labor Relations Board (NLRB), 734
National Labor Union, 503
National League, 528
National Organization for Women (NOW), 861, 872
National Origins Act (1921), 672
National Recovery Administration (NRA), 723–724, 733
National Republican party, 294
National Rifle Association, 881
National Road, 245, 266, 339
National Security Council (NSC), 790
National Trades Union, 361
National Tube Company, 492
National Union party, 428
National War Labor Board (NWLB), 756

National Women's Party (NWP), 680, 872

Nationalism: after Civil War, 453–454; after Revolutionary War, 157–158; after World War I, 661; black, 261–262, 314, 565, 690–692, 818; and immigrants, 359; New, 602, 604; railroads and, 370

Nation-building, in Afghanistan, 613

Native Americans. *See* Indian Americans

Nativism, 520–521, 522–523. *See also* Know-Nothing (American) party

NATO. *See* North Atlantic Treaty Organization

Natural disasters, 1, 919

Naturalism, in literature, 546

Naturalization Act (1798), 190, 199

Nature, in romanticism, 318

Nauvoo, Illinois, 307, 308*f*

Nauvoo Legion, 307

Navajo Indians, 460

Naval Affairs Committee, 616

Naval War College, 616

Naval War of 1812 (Roosevelt), 594

Navigation. *See* Merchant marine; Navy; Ships and Shipbuilding

Navigation Acts, 91–92, 111

Navy: bases-for-destroyers deal, 749; blacks in, 759; buildup in 1920s, 703; in Civil War, 406, 410; in Cuban missile crisis, 813; Jeffersonian policy and, 214; in late 19th century, 615–616; in Mexican War, 339, 340*m*; in Revolutionary War, 143–144; in Spanish-American War, 624, 625*f*; in War of 1812, 224–225; in World War I, 656; before World War II, 749, 751; in World War II, 769–772; in XYZ Affair, 189

Navy Department, creation of, 189

Nazi Germany. *See* Germany; Hitler

Nebraska: Alliance movement in, 572; population in late 19th century, 570; progressive reform in, 588; territorial organization of, 377–378

Nebraska Land and Cattle Company, 478

Neighborhood Guild, 532

Nelson, Horatio, 211, 211*f*

Neolithic revolution, 13

Nesmith, John, 335

Netherlands: and England, rivalry with, 45, 91, 101; exploration and colonization by, 45; exploration voyages by, 20*m*; in World War II, 748

Netscape, 907

Neutrality, in foreign policy: in World War I, 643–646, 647–648; in World War II, 746–747

Neutrality Act (1935), 746

Nevada: gold rush in, 469; territorial organization of, 471

New Amsterdam, 45

New Bedford, whaling in, 362

New Deal, 719; agricultural policies of, 724–725, 735; and blacks, 736, 742–743; critique of, 739, 740–741; extremists and, 729, 732–733; and Indian Americans, 743–744; industrial policies of, 723–724, 733; influences on, 733; Keynesian economics and, 735; labor unions and, 723–724, 734, 737–740; monetary policies of, 723–724; opposition to, 729, 732–733, 735; Roosevelt's role in, 744–745; Second, 734–735; significance of, 740–741; slowing down of, 737–740; social insurance program of, 735; success of, 739*f*; and Supreme Court, 733, 736–737; unemployment policies of, 727–728, 729*f*, 735; utility policies of, 726–727, 735; and women, 741–742

New England: colonial, 35–41, 67*m*, 68–77; Dominion of, 72, 74, 88; and Kansas, slavery in, 380; literacy in, 353; and Mexican War, opposition to, 339; and Republican party formation, 379; in Revolutionary War, 127–128; romanticism in, 318; in Second Great Awakening, 303–305; shipping line in, 362; slavery in, 58; in War of 1812, 231; whaling in, 362

New England Anti-Slavery Society, 313–314

New England colonies, 67*m*

New England Emigrant Aid Society, 381–382

"New era," 692, 698, 707

New France, 53–54, 84–85

New Freedom policy, 605–607, 620, 649

New Hampshire: colonial, 41; ratification of Constitution by, 172, 174*m*

New Harmony, Indiana, 308

New Jersey: College of, 96; ethnic groups in, 80; in presidential politics, 559; progressive reform in, 588; ratification of Constitution by, 172, 174*m*; settlement of, 45–46

New Mexico: Compromise of 1850 and, 347, 348, 348*m*; in Mexican War, 339; prehistoric hunting in, 2–4; Spanish settlement in, 23–24, 54–55, 55*m*; in Treaty of Guadalupe Hidalgo, 340–341

New Nationalism policy, 602, 604

"New Negro," 690–692

New Netherland, 41

New Orleans, Louisiana: in 1803, 205*f*; foreign trade in, 362; French settlement of, 53; geostrategic importance of, 202;

New Orleans, Louisiana: *(continued)*
Hurricane Katrina devastates, 1,
918–919, 918*f*; jazz in, 691; slavery in,
351; Spanish control of, 105; steamboats
and, 267; in War of 1812, 232–233
New Panama Canal Company, 635
New Spain, 54–55, 55*m*, 84–85
New Sweden, 45
New York, Port of, 560
New York (state): Articles of Confederation
and, 151*m*; and Erie Canal, 267–269; eth-
nic groups in, 80; politics in, 83; in presi-
dential politics, 559; progressivism in,
587–588; prosperity in, 82; ratification of
Constitution by, 173, 174*m*, 177*f*;
Roosevelt (Franklin) and, 717; settlement
of, 45
New York Anti-Slavery Society, 314
New York Associated Press, 552
New York Central Railroad, 365, 366, 484,
490, 493, 516
New York City: blacks in, 654, 690–691;
Broadway in (1835), 270*f*; canals and,
268, 270; civic culture in, 526; as commercial center, 268–270, 270*f*; draft riots
in, 416, 523; foreign trade in, 362;
Harlem Renaissance in, 691; immigrants
in, 517, 521–522; infrastructure of, 523,
525; mobility in, 517; naming of, 45;
newspaper circulation in, 554; 19th-cen-
tury life in, 510–511; politics in, early
20th century, 567, 568–569; progressivism in, 586, 587; in Revolutionary War,
135–136, 137, 138*f*; settlement houses
in, 532; transportation in, 525; Triangle
shirtwaist factory fire in, 589; Tweed
Ring in, 455, 569; 2001 World Trade
Center attacks in, 909–911; woman suf-
frage in, 592; World Trade Center attacks
in, 910*f*
New York Custom House, 558
New York Evening Post (newspaper), 308
New York Herald (newspaper), 552
New York Infirmary for Women and
Children, 425
New York Journal (newspaper), 552, 622
New York Life, 496
New York Pike, 266
New York Sun (newspaper), 552, 598
New York Times (newspaper), 488, 801*f*,
883–884
New York Tribune (newspaper), 308, 360, 455,
552
New York Weekly Journal, 83
New York World (newspaper), 552, 577, 622
New York Yankees, 683, 683*f*
Newburyport, Massachusetts, 517

Newlands Act (1902), 595
Newman, John M., 825*f*
Newspapers: on blacks after
Reconstruction, 565; late 19th-century,
552, 554; and political campaigns, 577;
printing press and, 551–552; readership
decline in late 20th century, 554
Newton, Isaac, 98
Nez Percé Indians, 466
Ngo Dinh Diem, 802, 814–815, 825*f*
Nguyen Van Thieu, 832
Niagara movement, 610
Nicaragua: dollar diplomacy in, 637–638; in
Iran-Contra arms deal, 886; as possible
canal zone, 635; Reagan and, 878; U.S.
protectorate over, 637–638, 641, 705
Nickelodeons, 680
Niebuhr, Reinhold, 715
Nielsen Media Research, 810
Nievelt, Joseph, 162, 163
Nike, 885
Nimitz, Chester W., 771, 772
Niña (ship), 19
Nine-Power Treaty, 703, 705
Nineteenth Amendment, 677; effects of pas-
sage, 677; ratification of, 592; and
women's equality, 653
NIRA. *See* National Industrial Recovery Act
Nissenbaum, Stephen, 73*f*
Nixon, Pat, 831*f*
Nixon, Richard M., 372, 808–809; and dé-
tente, 830–831, 831*f*; domestic policy of,
832–833; economic policy of, 832–833,
870; Khrushchev and, 804*f*; in Latin
America, 805; in 1960 presidential elec-
tion, 808–809, 810–811; in 1968 presi-
dential election, 826–828; in 1972 presi-
dential election, 832, 833; resignation of,
837–838; as vice president, 804*f*, 805;
Vietnam war under, 828–830, 832;
Watergate and, 811, 833–835, 836–838;
and Yom Kippur War, 864–866
NLRB. *See* National Labor Relations Board
Nomura, Kichisaburo, 754
Non-Intercourse Act, 215, 219
Noriega, Manuel, 894
Normalcy, 699
Normandy beach, 765, 765*m*
Norris, Frank, 546
Norris Hall, Virginia Tech, shooting at, 890
North: black migration to, 654–656, 690;
blacks in, early 19th century, 263; in 1860
presidential election, 393–396, 396*m*; and
Fugitive Slave Act, 373; Harper's Ferry
raid and, 392; Kansas-Nebraska Act and,
378; manufacturing in, 358–359; in mid-
19th century agriculture in, 368*m*;

pre–Civil War economy of, 396; railroads and, 369, 370; and Texas annexation, 331. *See also* New England; Union

North, Lord, 121, 123, 124, 142

North, Oliver, 887

North Africa, in World War II, 763, 764, 765*m*

North Atlantic, in World War II, 749, 751

North Atlantic Treaty, 789

North Atlantic Treaty Organization (NATO), 789, 904

North Carolina: civil rights movement in, 816; colonial, 63, 67*m*; ratification of Constitution by, 173, 174*m*; secession and, 396, 398*m*, 402; separation from South Carolina, 44, 88

North Dakota: Alliance movement in, 571; Dust Bowl in, 725–726; farming in, 515; population in late 19th century, 570; sod house in, 515*f*

North Korea, 790–794, 792*m*; nuclear weapons in, 916

North River Steam Boat (ship), 267

Northern Pacific Railroad, 465, 473, 477*m*, 485

Northern Securities Company, 598

Northwest Ordinance (1787), 158, 242

Northwest Territory, 151*m*

Norton, Mary Beth, 94*f*, 132*f*

Norway, in World War II, 748

Novick, Peter, 923*f*

NOW. *See* National Organization for Women

Now We Know (Gaddis), 791*f*

Noyes, John Humphrey, 307

NRA. *See* National Recovery Administration

NSC. *See* National Security Council

NSC-68 (classified document), 790, 794

Nuclear weapons: in Cold War, 789, 797–798, 803–804; in Cuban missile crisis, 813, 814*f*; as deterrent, 789, 797–798, 803–804; in Iran and North Korea, 915–916; reduction of, 830–831, 880; Soviet development of, 789; in World War II, 772–775

Nueces River, 337

Nullification, 289–292

Nursing, 513, 539

NWLB. *See* National War Labor Board

OAS. *See* Organization of American States

Oberlin Institute, 326

Occupational patterns, mid-19th century, 302

Ocean commerce, 362–364

O'Connell, Daniel, 360

O'Connor, Sandra Day, 880

"Of Mr. Booker T. Washington and Others" (Du Bois), 609–610

Of Plymouth Plantation (Bradford), 36

Office of Homeland Security, 911

Office of War Mobilization, 756

Office workers, 514

Ogden, Aaron, 273

Ogden, Utah, 475, 477*m*

Oglala Sioux Indians, 463

Oglethorpe, James, 68

Ohio: canals in, 270; colleges in, 538; in presidential politics, 559; steel industry in, 871*f*

Ohio and Erie Canal, 270

Ohio Company, 102

Ohio Country: conflicts over, 102–103, 106, 180–181; Indian liberation movement in, 220–221

"Ohio Gang," 699, 700

Ohio State Journal (newspaper), 545

Ohio State University, 538

Oil: crisis of 1973, 864–866; in Middle East, 802, 871, 886; in Persian Gulf War, 895–898, 897*f*; scandal under Harding, 700; in World War II, 754

Oil industry, 487–488, 493–496, 498

Okinawa, 771*m*, 772

Oklahoma: desegregation in, 806; Dust Bowl in, 725–726; Indians in, 462, 464

Old Guard, of Republican party, 602

Old National Road, 266

Old Spanish Trail, 335*m*

Old-age insurance, 878; Social Security, 735; Townsend's campaign for, 733

Olds, Ransom E., 694

Olive Branch Petition, 130

Olney, Richard, 620–621

Olympic games, 873

Omaha, Nebraska, immigrants in, 350

Omaha beach, 765*f*

Omoo (Melville), 322

"On the Present Collegiate System" (Wayland), 326

On the Road (Kerouac), 840

One World (Willkie), 774

Oneida Community, 307, 308

Oneida County Female Missionary Society, 305

Onís, Luis de, 236

Only Yesterday (Allen), 676*f*

OPEC. *See* Organization of Petroleum Exporting Countries

Open Door policy, 617*f*, 633–634, 703

Open-range ranching, 477–478; end of, 480

Operation Restore Hope, 904

Oppenheimer, J. Robert, 774; McCarthyism and, 806

Orders in Council, 211, 220, 222
Oregon: gold rush and, 345; initiative system in, 588; Polk and, 336–337; progressive reform in, 587, 588, 590; settlement of, 334–335
Oregon (ship), 625*f*, 635
Oregon Trail, 334, 335*m*
O'Reilly, Bill, 400
Organization of Afro-American Unity, 848
Organization of American States (OAS), 804
Organization of Petroleum Exporting Countries (OPEC), 866
Organized crime, immigrants blamed for, 520*f*
Orient. *See* Asia; Far East
Oriental products, and exploration voyages, 19
The Origin of Species (Darwin), 497
Orlando, Vittorio, 660, 661
Orphanages, rise of, 309
Orphans, in early 20th century, 589*f*
Osborne, Sarah, 74
Osceola, 289
Ostend Manifesto, 375
O'Sullivan, John L., 332
Oswald, Lee Harvey, 818–819
Otis, James, 111, 116–117
Our American Cousin (play), 436
Our Country (Strong), 615
Outer Mongolia, 783
"Overkill" hypothesis, 3
Overland Trail, women pioneers on, 333*f*
Owen, Robert, 308
Owsley, Frank L., 444*f*
Oxbow Route, 335*m*

Pacific Coast: manifest destiny and, 332; San Francisco and, 461; settlement of, 334, 335*m*; Treaty of Guadalupe Hidalgo and, 340–341
Pacific Fur Company, 334
Pacific Railway Act (1862), 424, 473
Pacific region: American expansionism in, 616–619, 627; in World War II, 769–772, 771*m* (*See also specific countries*)
Padrone system, 519
Pahlavi, Muhammad Reza (Shah of Iran), 874
Paine, Thomas, 131, 136
Pakenham, Edward, 232–233
Pakenham, Richard, 336
Palace Car factory, 508
Pale Faces, 452
Palestinian Arabs, 802–803
Palmer, A. Mitchell, 667
Palo Alto, 338

Pan African Conferences, 690
Panama: independence from Colombia for, 635–637; Noriega in, 894
Panama Canal, 375, 619–620, 634–638, 637*f*; transfer to Panama, 873; Zone, 632*m*, 636, 636*m*
Panama Canal Zone, as colony, 638
Pan-American Petroleum Company, 700
Panic(s): of 1819, 241; of 1837, 292, 296, 361; of 1857, 361, 371; of 1873, 454; of 1933, 722
Pan-Indian movement, 851
Pantry Pride, 884
Paris, liberation of, 765
Paris, Peace of (1783), 145–147
Paris, Treaty of (1763), 105–106
Paris Peace Conference (1919), 659–662
Park(s), amusement, 529*f*
Parker, Alton B., 598
Parker, Dorothy, 701*f*
Parkinson's disease, 917
Parkman, Francis, 105
Parks, Rosa, 816
Parris, Samuel, 74
Paterson, William, 169
The Path I Trod (Powderly), 504
The Patriot (film), 148–149, 148*f*, 149*f*
Patriot Act (2001), 640–641
Patriotism, 248
Patriots, *vs.* Loyalists, 137
Patronage, 558. *See also* Civil service; Spoils system
Patrons of Husbandry, 501
Patton, George S., 765
Pasturage land, 478
Paul, Alice, 592, 680
Pauncefote, Lord, 635
Pawtucket Falls, Rhode Island, 252
"Paxton Boys," 84
Peace Corps, 811
Peace Democrats, 408
Peace movement(s), in post–World War I period, 704
Pearl Harbor, 618, 754*f*, 755, 758*f*, 803
Peffer, William A., 572
Peirce, Charles S., 550
Peiss, Kathy, 676*f*, 858*f*
Pell-mell policy, 199, 216–217, 277–278
Pelosi, Nancy, 922, 922*f*
Pemberton, John C., 423
Pemberton, William, 881*f*
Pendergast, Tom, 781
Pendleton Act (1883), 561
Pendleton Civil Service Act (1883), 577, 578
Peninsula campaign, 412, 413*m*
Penn, William, 46*f*, 47, 82–83

Pennsylvania: Delaware separation from, 88; ethnic groups in, 80; hijacked plane crash in, 910, 911; "Paxton Boys" uprising in, 84; politics in, 82–83; prosperity in, 82; ratification of Constitution by, 172, 174*m*; settlement of, 47; whiskey tax in, opposition to, 181, 183, 184*f*
Pennsylvania Railroad, 365, 484, 492
Pensions, Social Security, 735
Pensions, Townsend, 733
Pensions, veterans', 557
Pentagon, 2001 terrorist attack on, 910, 911
Pentagon Papers, 834
People's party. *See* Populist party
Perelman, Ronald, 884
Perestroika, 880
Performance-enhancing drugs, illegal use in baseball, 917
Perkins, Frances, 741
Perkins, George W., 603
Perkins Institution, 309
Perot, Ross, 899
Perry, Matthew C., 616
Perry, Oliver Hazard, 226, 227*f*
Pershing, John J., 642, 656
Persian Gulf War, 895–898, 896*m*, 897*f*
Peru, Nixon's visit to, 805
Peru, Spanish conquest of, 21
Pessen, Edward, 295*f*
Petersburg, siege of, 427, 431*m*
Peterson, Merrill, 194*f*
Petroleum industry, 487–488, 493–496, 498. *See also* Oil
Phee, Molly, 17
Philadelphia, Pennsylvania: colonial, 82; foreign trade in, 362; in Great Depression, 714; immigrants in, 522; in Revolutionary War, 142
Philadelphia (frigate), 190*f*, 202
Philadelphia Aurora, 188*f*
Philadelphia Constitutional Convention (1787), 166–171
Philadelphia prison system, 311
Philadelphia Public Ledger (newspaper), 552
Philippine Commission, 600
Philippine Islands: annexation by U.S., 627; as colony, 638; insurrection against U.S., 629–630; isolationism and, 614; Roosevelt (Theodore) on, 634; Spanish control of, 105; Spanish-American War and, 624, 627, 628; Taft as governor of, 600; in World War II, 754, 771, 772
Philippine Sea, Battle of, 772
Phillips, Ulrich Bonnell, 357*f*
Philosophy, Benjamin Franklin and, 99
Philosophy, pragmatic school, 547, 550–551

Phips, Mary, 75
Phips, William, 75
Phonograph, 488
Physicians, in colonial period, 99
Pickering, John, 201
Pickering, Timothy, 206
Pickett, George E., 419
Pierce, Franklin: and Anthony Burns's arrest, 379; Cuba and, 375; in 1852 presidential election, 377; and Kansas territory, 377, 382; and Kansas-Nebraska Act, 377; presidency of, 377–378
Pierrepont, Edwards, 453
Pike, Lt. Zebulon (explorer), 208–209
Pikes Peak, 469
Pilgrim(s), 35–36
Pilgrim's Progress (Bunyan), 584
Pinchot, Gifford, 601–602
Pinckney, Charles, 65
Pinckney, Charles (son), 189, 200
Pinckney, Eliza Lucas, 63, 65
Pinckney, Henry L., 290
Pinckney, Thomas, 185, 188
Pinckney's Treaty, 185
Pine Ridge Indian Reservation, South Dakota, 460
Pinkerton detectives, 508, 572
Pinta (ship), 18, 19
Pioneers, 263–265, 332–334, 369–370
"The Pit and the Pendulum" (Poe), 320
Pitt, William, 104
Pittsburgh, Pennsylvania: as iron and steel capital, 487; origins of, 104
Pizarro, Francisco, 21
Plagues, 14
Plains Indians, 462–463; ascendancy of, 54; culture of, 462; massacre of, at Sand Creek (1864), 463, 464*f*; wars with, 464–466
Plantations, 352, 448–449
Plaquemines Parish, Louisiana, 918
Plastics, 847
Platt Amendment (1900), 631
Platte Canyon High School (Colorado), hostage shooting at, 890
Plattsburg, Battle of, 230
Playboy (magazine), 869
Plessy v. *Ferguson,* 564–565, 806
Plow, steel, 367
Plymouth, Massachusetts, settlement of, 35–36, 35*f*, 73*f*
Plymouth Company, 36
Pocahontas, 31, 32, 33*f*
Poe, Edgar Allan, 320–321, 320*f*
Poe, Edgar Allen, 542
Poetry. *See* Literature
Poker, online gambling and, 697

Poker Alice, 469
Poland: creation of, 661; immigrants from, 522; liberalization of, 894; post–World War II, 777–778; in World War II, 747–748
"A Policy of Boldness" (Dulles), 797–798
Political apathy, 276
Political campaigns, 395f; business involvement in, 578; changing nature of, 577–579; in late 19th century, 554–555, 559; rise of, 276, 278–279, 298; and television ads, 372; television and, 810–811, 841, 868
Political debates, televised, 372
Political parties: and blacks, affiliation of, 557, 742–743; early 19th-century, 278–279, 293; early 20th-century, 708–709; late 19th-century, 557–559; mid-19th century, 379–380; national conventions of, 277; rise of, 182–183; second system of, 278, 292–293; structure of, 278; workingmen's, 361. See also specific parties
Politics: change in party system, 381f; city, 567–569; during Civil War, 407–408; democratization of, 277–278; diversity of, 82–84; economy and, 555; farmers in, 570–573; late 19th-century, 557–559; in middle colonies, 82–84; and perceived apathy, 276–277; progressive reforms of, 586–588; television as source of information about, 372; youth participation in, 581–582
Polk, James K., 336–337; in 1844 presidential election, 336; on gold strike, 344; and Mexican War, 337–342; and Oregon boundary, 336–337; presidency of, 336–337
Poll taxes, 564
Pollock v. Farmers' Loan and Trust Company, 575
Pollution, atmospheric, 917
Polo, Marco, 18
Polygamy, 308
Ponce de León, Juan, 23
Pond's Company, 681f
Pontiac (Ottawa chief), 108f, 110
Poor Richard's Almanack, 160
Pop music, 906
Pope, John, 413–414
Popular culture: early 20th-century, 680–682; late 19th-century, 536; violence and, 891, 905–907
Popular Science Monthly (magazine), 540
Popular sovereignty, and slavery, 344, 377, 380, 383, 386
Population: of New Orleans (1803), 205f; urban vs. rural density, 522

Population decline: among Indians, 25; in rural areas, 301f
Population growth: after 800 A.D., 9–10; among slaves, 354; colonial, 108; in Eurasia, 13; in Europe, 14–15; 19th-century, 239, 242–243, 256–257, 301f; 20th-century, 757–758; urban, 301f, 673–674; in World War II, 757–758
Populist movement, 570–573
Populist party, 571f, 572–573, 573f; in 1896 presidential election, 577, 579; formation of, 572
Port(s), trade concentration at, 362
Port Hudson, 422
Port Huron Statement, 855
Port of New York, 560
Portugal: exploration activities of, 19, 21; exploration voyages by, 20m; Jews in, 14
Potsdam conference, 778
Pottawatomie Creek, 382, 393
Pottery. See Earthenware
Pound, Ezra, 688
Poverty: among Indian Americans, 460; Johnson's war on, 820; Long on, 729, 732, 733; in 19th century, 516; in Progressive Era, 582–583; and race riots, 848–849; in 20th century, 820; urban, 530–531, 582–583
Poverty Point, 6
Powderly, Terence V., 504, 516
Powell, Colin, 911–912; Second Iraq War and, 912, 913
Powell, John Wesley, 478
Powell doctrine, 912
Powhatan Indians, 32–33
Pownall, Thomas, 106
Pragmatism, 547, 547f, 550–551
Preble, Edward, 202
Precious metals, search for. See Gold rush
Predestination, 34
Prehistoric era, 1–4
Prejudice. See Racial prejudice
Presbyterians, 80, 96, 334
Presidency: constitutional provisions for, 170–171, 195; late 19th-century, 559–564; Reconstruction and, 436, 444
President (ship), 301
Presidential election(s): constitutional provisions for, 171; of 1796, 187–189; of 1800, 195–196; of 1804, 200; of 1808, 219; of 1816, 236, 239; of 1824, 244–246, 277; of 1828, 276, 278–279; of 1832, 282; of 1840, 298–299, 298f, 329–330; of 1844, 331, 335–336; of 1848, 343; of 1852, 377; of 1856, 384–385; of 1860, 372–373, 393–396, 396m; of 1864, 428, 429; of 1868, 444; of

1872, 455; of 1876, 455–457, 558, 560; of 1880, 560; of 1884, 556, 561–562; of 1888, 563; of 1892, 556, 573; of 1896, 577, 578*m,* 621; of 1900, 586, 629, 630; of 1904, 586; of 1908, 600; of 1912, 603–605, 604*m,* 611; of 1916, 646–647; of 1920, 668–669, 698; of 1924, 702; of 1928, 687, 707–709, 808–809; of 1932, 717–720; of 1936, 736; of 1940, 749–750; of 1944, 772; of 1948, 787–788; of 1952, 796–797; of 1960, 808–809, 810–811; of 1964, 820–821, 822; of 1968, 823, 826–828; of 1972, 832; of 1976, 868–869; of 1980, 875–876; of 1984, 878–879; of 1988, 891–892; of 1992, 899; of 1996, 901–902; of 2000, 908–909; of 2004, 914–915

Presley, Elvis, 858*f*

"Press gangs," 212–213

Prevost, George, 230

Price, Birch & Company, 351*f*

Primary system, direct, 587–588

Princeton, Battle of, 138*f,* 139

Princeton (ship), 331

Princeton University: football at, 529; founding of, 96; Wilson at, 605, 605*f*

Princip, Gavrilo, 642

Principles of Psychology (James), 550

Pring, Martin, 49

Printing press, 551–552

Printing process, development of, 14–15

Prisons: Civil War, 437; creation of, 309; in Iraq, 914, 914*f;* late 20th-century, 892, 893*f;* 19th-century, 309, 311; Tocqueville and Beaumont on, 309

Privy Council, 88

Prize fighting. *See* Boxing

Proclamation of 1763, 109*m,* 110

"Proclamation to the People of South Carolina" (Jackson), 290

Prodigy, 907

Profiles in Courage (Kennedy), 811

Progress, perils of, 847

Progress and Poverty (George), 498–499

Progressive education, 540–541, 852–854

Progressive party: in 1912 presidential election, 603–604, 604*m;* in 1916 presidential election, 646–647; in 1924 presidential election, 702; in 1948 presidential election, 787–788; youth participation in, 581–582

Progressivism: in Mexico, 642; minority rights and, 607–611; muckraking journalists and, 584; 1912 presidential election and, 604–605; political reforms, 586–594; prohibition and, 686; radical,

586; Roosevelt (Theodore) and, 598, 600, 602; roots of, 582–584; social reforms, 588–590; in states, 587–588; Taft and, 600–601, 602; urban reforms, 586–587; *vs.* socialism, 585; Wilson and, 607; woman suffrage and, 590–592; World War I and, 643, 652–653

Prohibition, 686; end of, 721, 722*f;* present-day comparisons to, 670–671; during World War I, 653, 686

Promontory, Utah, 474–475, 477*m*

Propaganda, in World War I, 651–652

Property, private: *genizaros and,* 54; Indian attitude toward, 23, 48–49, 50; and slavery, 261, 346–347; tax on, 499

Proposition 209, 905

Proprietary colonies, 42–43

Prospectors, 344–345

Prosperity, 82

Prostitution: colonial, 77; World War I and, 653

Protectionism, under Adams (John Quincy) administration, 246–247. *See also* Tariff(s)

Protestant Reformation, 14

Protestants: in cities, 530; in colonies, 43; temperance movement and, 312–313

Providence, founding of, 40

Psychology, 550; Freudian, 852

Public Enemy (film), 906

Public libraries, 551

Public space, shopping malls as, 510–511

Public utilities. *See* Utilities

Public Works Administration, 724

Publishing, 551–552; 15th-century, 14–15; 19th-century, 358, 552; printing press and, 551–552; printing process and, 14–15. *See also* Journalism

Puebla, 339

Pueblo Bonito, 8

Pueblo Indians, 54

Puerto Rico, 626, 630, 632*m;* as colony, 638

Pugh, George E., 394

Pulitzer, Joseph, 552, 622

Pullman, George, 486, 508

Pullman strike, 508, 575

Purdue University, 52

Pure Food and Drug Act (1906), 599

Puritans: anticommercial bias of, 76; cemetery of, 39*f;* church membership among, 38, 70–71; dissenters among, 39–41; government according to, 71–72; origins of, 34; settlements, 73*f;* women, 69–70, 74–76, 79*f*

"The Purloined Letter" (Poe), 320

The Pursuit of Happyness (film), 250

Putnam, Ann, 74

Quadroon ball, 301
Quakers, 46–47; banning of, 71; political disputes and, 83–84; on slavery, 65
Quartering Act, 115
Quebec, Canada, 44, 110; in Revolutionary War, 135
Queen Anne's War, 101
Queen's College, founding of, 96
Quincy, Josiah, 222
Quitrents, 72
Quota system: in education, 673; in immigration, 671–673
QWERTY keyboard, 551*f*

R. J. Reynolds Tobacco Company, 884
Race relations: Civil War and, 407; new separatism in, 905
Race riots, 759, 810; of 1877, 461; of 1960s, 849–850; reasons for, 848–849
Racial equality: after World War II, 805–807; black militants and, 848–850; churches in fight for, 844–847; Declaration of Independence and, 439; Reconstruction-era debates on, 439–441; status of, in late 20th century, 905; Supreme Court on, 564–565; Washington (Booker T.) and, 565–567
Racial prejudice: in 19th century, 359–360; among progressives, 607–608; in biology textbooks, 685; in early 20th century, 608–611; against immigrants, 359; against Indian Americans, 607–608; against Japanese, 607; against Jews, 673, 747; 1960s student revolts and, 854–856; in post–World War I period, 685; and slavery, 63–64; in World War II, 758–760. *See also* Ku Klux Klan
Racial pride, 852
Racial segregation. *See* Segregation
Radical(s), post–World War I persecution of, 665–668
Radical feminism, 680, 861–862
Radical progressivism, 586
Radical Republicans: and black rights, 439–441, 444–445; during Civil War, 408, 428; Civil War promise to freed slaves, 436; and Fifteenth Amendment, 444–445; and Johnson impeachment, 443–444; and southern readmission, 437, 439, 440–441
Radical students, in 1960s, 854–856
Radio: and religion, 846; rise of, 681–682; sports on, 682
Radio Corporation of America, 710
Radulovich, Milo, 800*f*–801*f*
Rafts, 267
Rahim, Sheik, 17

Railroad(s), 369; and agriculture, 366–368, 472; as big business, 484–486; cattle and, 476–477; Chinese labor and, 461, 475*f*; in Civil War, 429*f*; competition between, 474–475; discounts and rebates given by, 490; and economy, 366–369, 484–486; financing of, 365–366; and Indians, 465, 466; integrated system for, 484–485; land-grant system and, 473–474; in mid-19th century commerce, 364–365; monopoly in, 489–491; 19th-century, 297; regulation of, 501–502, 601; sectional conflict over, 365*m*, 366, 369–370; in South, 364–365, 365*m*, 447; strikes against, 504, 508; under Taft, 601; in West, 369, 370, 473–476, 477*m*; in World War I, 649. *See also* Transcontinental railroads
Railroad Administration, 649
Rain-in-the-Face, 465
A Rainy Day in Camp (Homer), 420
Rakove, Jack, 168*f*
Raleigh, Sir Walter, 29
Raleigh, Walter, 59
Rambo III (film), 906
Ranching, 476–480; barbed wire and, 478–480, 479*f*; open-range, 477–478, 480
Randall, James G., 381*f*
Randolph, Edmund, 169, 175
Randolph, John (of Roanoke), 215, 245
Rap music, 906
Rapp, George, 309
Raulston, John, 685
"The Raven" (Poe), 321
Ray, James Earl, 849
Raynell, John, 118
REA. *See* Rural Electrification Administration
Reading Railroad, 597
Reagan, Ronald, 372, 877*f*; on AIDS, 883; assignation attempt on, 877*f*; Cold War and, 881*f*; economy under, 865, 877–878, 879, 884–886; first term of, 877–879; foreign policy of, 878, 879–880; Iran-Contra and, 886–888; in 1976 presidential election, 868; in 1980 presidential election, 875–876; in 1984 presidential election, 878–879; presidency of, 886–888, 887*f*; second term of, 879–880
Realism, in late 19th century literature, 542, 544, 545–546
Reapers: horse-pulled, 367*f*; mechanical, 367–368
Reason, Age of, romanticism and, 318
Rebates, railroads and, 490

Recession, economic: under Carter, 870–871. *See also* Inflation

Reconstruction: black legislators in, 445–448, 447*f*; economic conditions of, 448–452; end of, 458; Fifteenth Amendment in, 444–445; Fourteenth Amendment in, 441–442, 443; historians on, 446*f*; Johnson and, 439–441; Lincoln and, 436, 437–439; Radical Republicans and, 437–441; white backlash against, 452–454

Reconstruction Acts, 442–443

Recreation. *See* Entertainment

Red Army, 783

The Red Badge of Courage (Crane), 546

Red Cloud (Indian chief), 463

Red Power, 851

Red scare, 665–668, 667*f*

Reeve, Christopher, 917

Referendums, 588

Reform: in antebellum period, 310*f*; of civil service, 558–559, 561; Civil War and, 511; for disabled people, treatment of, 309, 311; economic, 498–501; of education, 324–325, 540–541; financial, 558; in mid-19th century, 300; pragmatism and, 550; Revolutionary War and, 153–155; temperance movement, 311–313; through education, 540–541; through experimental communities, 306–309; in World War I, 652–653. *See also* New Deal; *specific movements*

Regional conflict. *See* Sectionalism

Regulators, 68

Rehnquist, William, 903

Reign of Terror, 183, 216

Reiss, Winold, 609*f*

Relativism, pragmatism and, 547, 550–551

Religion(s): colonial, 43–44, 66, 68–71, 73*f*, 80, 93–96, 97–98; in early 20th century, 684–685; Enlightenment and, 87, 97–98; and evolution, theory of, 547; fundamentalism in, 684–685, 878–879; Great Awakening, 87, 93–96, 97, 530; Indian, 22–23; in mid-20th century, 844–847; post-Revolutionary reforms and, 153; prehistoric, 8, 10; Second Great Awakening, 304–305; of slaves, 354; television and, 847, 878; temperance movement and, 311–313. *See also* Church(es); *specific denominations*

Remington company, 484

Remini, Robert, 295*f*

Reno, Janet, 901

Rensselaer Polytechnic Institute, 162

Rensselaerswyck, 45

Report on Manufactures (Hamilton), 180, 259

Report on the Lands of the Arid Region of the United States (Powell), 478

Report on the Public Credit (Hamilton), 178

Representation: conflicting definitions of, 116–117; democratization and, 278; post–Civil War, 439–440; taxation without, 111–112; Thirteenth Amendment and, 438–439; virtual *vs.* actual, 111–112, 152–153

The Repressible Conflict (Craven), 381*f*

Republic of California, 339

Republican National Convention: of 1856, 389; of 1860, 394; of 1868, 444; of 1880, 560; of 1912, 602–603

Republican party (GOP): in 1856 election, 384–385; in 1858 congressional election, 389–391; in 1860 election, 394, 395–396, 396*m*; in 1864 election, 428; in 1866 congressional election, 442; in 1868 election, 444; in 1874 congressional election, 455; in 1876 election, 455–457, 560; in 1880 election, 560; in 1884 election, 562; in 1890 congressional election, 564; in 1896 election, 576, 577, 578*m*, 579; in 1912 election, 602–603, 604*m*; in 1920 election, 668–669, 698; in 1924 election, 702; in 1928 election, 707–709; in 1936 election, 736; in 1940 election, 749–750; in 1994 congressional election, 901; Alliance movement and, 571, 572; beginnings of, 380; and black suffrage, 444–445; blacks in, 445–448, 557, 736, 742–743; Civil War and, 407–408; and communists-in-government issue, 794; Dred Scott decision and, 387; and emancipation, 415; emergence of, 381*f*; under Grant, 454–455; Jefferson and, 182–183; and Kansas territory, 382; in late 19th-century, 557–559; and League of Nations, 662–665; Old Guard-progressive split under Taft, 602; Reconstruction and, 437, 439–441, 443–444; Second Iraq War and, 922; in South, 455

Republicans (Democratic): in 1800 presidential election, 195; and Federalists, rivalry with, 186; in 1796 presidential election, 187–189; strengthening of, Jefferson and, 216–217; XYZ Affair and, 189–190

Requerimiento, 22

Resaca de la Palma, in Mexican War, 338

Resistance movement, colonial, 111–122

Retail sales, 482

Reuben James (ship), 751

Revels, Hiram, 447*f*

Revere, Paul, 120*f*, 128

Revlon, 884

Revolution of 1800, 197

Revolutionary War. *See* American Revolution

Rhode Island: College of, 96; colonial, 87; founding of, 40; ratification of Constitution by, 173, 174*m*

Rhymes, Busta, 162

Rice, in mid-19th century, 368*m*

Rice cultivation: colonial, 63; diffusion of, 13; and slavery, 289

Richardson, Henry Hobson, 485*f*

Richmond, Virginia: in Civil War, 411–412, 429, 431*m*; trolley line in, 525–526

Richmond and West Point Terminal Company, 485

Richmond Times (newspaper), 577

Richter, Daniel K., 223*f*

Ridge, Tom, 911

Rights. *See* Civil rights

The Rights of the British Colonies Asserted and Proved (Otis), 111

Riis, Jacob, 522*f*

Rike's Department Store, 514*f*

Rio Grande River, 337, 340

Riots: draft, 416, 523; Stamp Act and, 113–115. *See also* Race riots

The Rise of Silas Lapham (Howells), 545

Riverboats, 363

RJR Nabisco, 884

Road(s), 271*m*; early, 264–265; highway construction, 265–266; interstate highway system of, 841; National Road, 244, 266, 339; in post–World War I period, 693

Roanoke Island, settlement of, 29, 30

Roaring Twenties, 676*f*, 678*f*

Robards, Lewis, 279, 279*f*

Robber Barons, 483

Robinson, Edgar E., 739*f*

Robinson, Jackie, 852

Robinson, John, 35

Robocop (film), 906

Roby, Peter, 535

Rochambeau, Comte de, 144

Rockefeller, John D., 493–495, 495*f*, 498, 501, 537, 666

Rockefeller Foundation, 718*f*

Rockefeller National City Bank, 508

Rocky Mountain Fur Company, 462

Rocky Mountain Husbandman, 480

Rocky Mountains: gold rush in, 468–471; and Oregon Trail, 334; states, ERA failure in, 872*m*

Roderigue Hortalez et Cie., 141

Rodgers, Daniel, 597*f*

Rodney, George, 144

Roe v. *Wade,* 900

Roebling, John A., 526

Rogers, Will, 716

Rolfe, John, 32

Roman Catholicism. *See* Catholics and Catholic Church

Romania, 894

Romanticism, 301, 318, 542

Rome, in World War II, 764

Rommel, Erwin, 763

Roosevelt, Eleanor, 741–742, 742*f*

Roosevelt, Franklin Delano, 295*f*, 717–720, 745*f*; assessment of, 744–745; and blacks, 742–743; conservative opposition to, 735; critique of policies, 739, 740–741; death of, 772, 781; extremist opposition to, 729, 732–733; foreign policy of, 746–749; inaugural addresses of, 736; and labor unions, 736, 737–738; as New York governor, 717; in 1932 presidential election, 717–720, 719*f*; in 1936 presidential election, 736; in 1940 presidential election, 749–750; in 1944 presidential election, 772; philosophy of, 719; Reagan compared with, 887*f*; *vs.* Supreme Court, 736–737; women in administration of, 741–742; and World War II, before U.S. entry, 746–749; in World War II, 755–756, 768; at Yalta, 777–778, 777*f*. *See also* New Deal

Roosevelt, Theodore, 478, 594–600; on 1896 presidential campaign, 578, 579; and blacks, 610–611; at Civil Service Commission, 563; conservation efforts of, 600; at Elkhorn Ranch, 480; foreign policy of, 632–633, 634; on Harrison (Benjamin), 563; on Indians, 608; leftward shift of, 600; in McKinley administration, 616; and Monroe Doctrine, 632; on muckrakers, 584; and navy, 616; New Nationalism policy of, 602, 604; 1902 coal strike and, 596–598; in 1912 presidential election, 602–604, 604*m*, 610–611; in 1916 presidential election, 646, 647; and Panama Canal, 635–637; on patronage, 559; on politics, 569; presidency of, 598–600; Reagan compared with, 887*f*; and Rough Riders, 625; in Spanish-American War, 624; and Taft, 601*f*, 602–604; trustbusting by, 596

Roosevelt Corollary, 632–633, 705

Root, Elihu, 632, 636–637

Rosebud Indian Reservation, South Dakota, 460

Rosenberg, Ethel, 795

Rosenberg, Julius, 795, 801*f*

Rosie the Riveter Steps Out (cartoon), 762*f*

Ross, Kary, 510

Ross, Robert, 228

Rothman, David J., 310*f*

Rothstein, Arthur, 743*f*
Rough Riders, 625
Royal African Company, 58
Ruby, Jack, 818
Rudd, Mark, 855*f*
Rugby, 529
Rule of War (1756), 211–212
Ruml, Beardsley, 757
Rumsfeld, Donald, 912; dismissal of, 922
Rural areas: and cities, conflicts between, 684–686; electricity brought to, 735; population decline in, 301*f*; population in, 511
Rural Electrification Administration (REA), 735
Rush, Benjamin, 312
Rush-Bagot Agreement of 1817, 234
Russert, Tim, 17
Russia: Alaska sold by, 614; exploration and colonization by, 107*m*; Germany and, nonaggression pact between, 748; immigrants from, 519, 522; and Manchuria, 633–634; territorial claims of, 236–237. *See also* Soviet Union
Russian Revolution (1917), 648
Rutgers University, 96, 529
Ruth, Babe, 683, 683*f*
Ryan, Mary, 310*f*
Ryan, Paddy, 528
Ryder, Winona, 72*f*, 78
Ryswick, Peace of (1697), 101

Saban, Nick, 535
Sac Indians, 288
Sacajawea, 207
Sacco, Nicola, 688
Sacco-Vanzetti case, 688
Sacramento Valley: gold discovered in, 342; in Mexican War, 339
Sadat, Anwar, 873
Sahara Desert, 14
Saigon, fall of, 867–868, 867*f*
Sailing packets, 362
Saint Domingue. *See* Hispaniola
Sakhalin Islands, 783
Salem, Massachusetts, 39, 73*f*, 74–76, 78–79
Saloons, 527, 686
SALT. *See* Strategic Arms Limitation Treaty
Saltillo, Mexico, 338*f*
Salutary neglect, policy of, 93, 109
Salvation Army, 530
Same-sex marriage, 915
Sammara, Iraq, 920–921
Samoan Islands, 618
Sampson, Deborah, 135*f*
Sampson, William T., 626

Samuel Adams Brewery, 126
San Antonio, Texas: settlement of, 54; in Texas rebellion, 330
San Carlos Indian Reservation, Arizona, 460
San Diego, California, 55; in Mexican War, 339
San Diego de Alcalá (mission church), 56*f*
San Francisco, California, 55; commercial importance of, 461; earthquake (1906), 919; gold miners and, 344–345; immigrants in, 461, 634; in late 19th century, 461; in Mexican War, 339; missions in, 334
San Francisco Conference, 775–776
San Ildefonso, Treaty of, 203
San Jacinto River, 331
San Lorenzo, Treaty of, 185
San Salvador, 18, 22
Sanborn, Franklin B., 392
Sanctuary (Faulkner), 729
Sand Creek, Colorado, 463; massacre of Indians at (1864), 463, 464*f*
Sandinistas, 886
Sanger, Margaret, 675, 677, 677*f*
Sanitary Commission, 426
Santa Anna, Antonio López de, 330–331
Santa Barbara, California, 55
Santa Fe Trail, 335*m*
Santa Maria (ship), 19
Santo Domingo. *See* Hispaniola
Saratoga, Battle of, 139–142, 139*f*, 141*m*
Saratoga Campaign, 141*m*
Saturday Night Live (TV show), 482
Saturday Night Massacre, 835
Saudi Arabia, and Persian Gulf War, 895–898
Savannah, Georgia: in Civil War, 429; founding of, 68; in Revolutionary War, 142
Saving Private Ryan (film), 766*f*–767*f*
Sawyer, Philetus, 555
Scalawags, 445
Scandinavia: exploration and colonization by, 45; exploration voyages by, 20*m*
The Scarlet Letter (Hawthorne), 73*f*, 321
Schecter v. United States, 733, 737
Schenck v. United States, 652
Schlafly, Phyllis, 872*m*, 873
Schlesinger, Arthur, Sr., 132*f*
Schlesinger, Arthur M., Jr., 295*f*, 524*f*, 739*f*, 825*f*, 881*f*
Schley, Winfield Scott, 626
Scholastic Aptitude Test (SAT), 780
School(s): naming after Founding Fathers, 126. *See also* Colleges and universities; Education
The School and Society (Dewey), 541
School shootings, 890–891, 907
Schultz, Stanley K., 310*f*

Schuyler, Philip, 140, 177
Schwarzkopf, Norman, 897
Science: colonial, 99–100; Louisiana Purchase exploration and, 208–209; in public education, 517; and religion, 547, 550
Scientific method, 539
Scientific shop management, 694
SCLC. *See* Southern Christian Leadership Conference
Scobey, "Ed," 699
Scopes, John T., 684–685
Scopes trial, 684–685
Scott, Dred, 385–386, 386*f*
Scott, Emmett J., 656
Scott, Harriet, 385, 386*f*
Scott, Monsta' Kody, 893
Scott, Thomas A., 484
Scott, Winfield, 338, 339–340; in Civil War, 404; in 1852 presidential election, 377; in Mexican War, 339–340
Scribner's (magazine), 565
Scripps, Edward W., 552
SDI. *See* Strategic defense initiative
SDS. *See* Students for a Democratic Society
Sea Captains Carousing in Surinam (Greenwood), 90*f*
Sea Nymph (ship), 212
Sea power, importance of, 615–616
Seasoning time, 62
SEATO. *See* Southeast Asia Treaty Organization
Seattle, Washington, during Great Depression, 715*f*
Seattle Times (newspaper), 753
Sebron, Hippolyte, 363*f*
Secession, 396–398, 398*m*; arguments for and against, 401–412; early movement toward, 290–291; readmission after, 437–439, 442–443, 443*m*
Second Bull Run, Battle of, 413–414
Second Great Awakening, 304–305
Second Hundred Days, 734–735
Second Iraq War, 753, 912–914; casualties in, 913*f*
Second New Deal, 734–735
Second Treatise on Government (Locke), 111
Secrecy, at Philadelphia Convention, 167–168, 167*f*
Sectionalism: as binding force, 248; foreign affairs and, 374–375; Fugitive Slave Act and, 373; under Jackson, 289–291; under Monroe, 240–242; railroads and, 365*m*, 366, 369–370
Secure Fence Act (2006), 328
Sedalia, Missouri, 476

Sedentary communities, 5–7
Sedition Act (1798), 191, 199, 201
Sedition Act (1918), 640, 651–652
Segregation, 806–807; in education, end of, 806–807, 849; of Japanese Americans, 634; in military, 656, 758–760; in post–World War I period, 690–692; in Progressive Era, 608; psychological effects of, 806–807; and race riots, 849; in schools, 564; in sports, end of, 852; Supreme Court on, 564–565, 806, 816; voluntary, 905; Washington (Booker T.) on, 566; under Wilson, 611. *See also* Civil rights
Self-determination principle, in Civil War, 402
Self-sufficency, colonial, 89–90
Sellers, Charles, 269*f*
Selma, Alabama, 848
Seminole Indians, 235, 289
Semmes, Raphael, 412
Senate, U.S.: caning in, 384; constitutional provisions for, 170; in late 19th century, 555–556, 556*f*; opposition to League of Nations by, 662–665
Seneca Falls Convention, 317
Separate but equal doctrine, 806
Separate spheres, 303
Separatism, black, 565, 690, 818, 848–849, 905
Separatists, 35
September 11, 2001, 909–911
Servants: *vs.* "help," 278; white, *vs.* slaves, 58
Settlement houses, 531–533, 541, 582
Seven Pines, Battle of, 412, 413*m*
Seven Years' War, 104
Severalty Act (1887), 466–467
Sewall, Arthur, 577
Seward, William H., 347, 381*f*, 391, 394, 614; in Lincoln's cabinet, 401
Sexual behavior: AIDS and, 883; in colonial era, 79; in 19th century, 306, 307, 308, 511; in post–World War I period, 674, 675–680; sexual revolution and, 857–860
Sexual Behavior in the Human Female (Kinsey), 859
Sexual Behavior in the Human Male (Kinsey), 858–859
Sexually transmitted diseases (STDs), 860
Seymour, Horatio, 444
Shafter, William, 625
Shakers, 306–307, 306*f*, 308
Shakespeare, William, 33, 322
The Shame of the Cities (Steffens), 570*f*
Share Our Wealth movement, 732, 733
Share tenancy, 450

Sharecropping: in Great Depression, 725, 743*f*; in post-Reconstruction South, 450–452, 451*f*
Sharpsburg. *See* Antietam, Battle of
Shaw, Robert Gould, 420–421, 421*f*
Shawnee Indians, 220–221
Shays, Daniel, 164–165, 165*f*
Shays's Rebellion, 164–165
Shenandoah Valley, in Civil War, 412
Sheridan, Philip, 464
Sherman, Roger, 131, 169
Sherman, William Tecumseh, 426, 427–430, 429*f*, 465; Civil War promise to freed slaves, 436
Sherman Antitrust Act (1890), 502–503; failure of, 582; Roosevelt (Theodore) administration and, 596, 598; Supreme Court on, 503, 575; Taft's use of, 601; unions and, 509
Sherman Silver Purchase Act (1890), 575
Sherman's March, 429–430
Shiite Muslims, 400; in Iraq, 920, 921
Shiloh, Battle of, 409–410, 411*m*
Shinngass (Delaware chieftain), 104
Ships and Shipbuilding: colonial, 92; in early 19th century, 211, 211*f*, 362–363; Navigation Acts and, 92
"Shock and Awe" campaign, in Second Iraq War, 913–914
Shop management, scientific, 692
Shopping malls, 510
Short, Walter C., 755
Shoshone Indians, 207
Shurtlieff, Robert (assumed name of Deborah Sampson), 135*f*
Sierra Leone, 154, 261
"The Significance of the Frontier in American History" (Turner), 542
Silver: colonial trade in, 89; as currency, 558, 574; in West, 468–471
Silver Purchase Act (1890), 574, 575
Simmons, William J., 686
Simpson, O. J., 891, 904–905
Simpson, "Sockless Jerry," 572
Sinclair, Harry F., 700
Sinclair, Upton, 599
Single tax, 499
"Sinners in the Hands of an Angry God" (Edwards), 97
Sioux Indians, 462–463, 466
Sirhan Sirhan, 826
Sirica, John J., 834, 836
Sit-in protests, 816–817
Sitting Bull, 465
60 Minutes (television show), 899, 914
The $64,000 Question (television show), 801*f*

Slater, Samuel, 252–253
Slave(s): acculturation of, 64; in early colonies, 84, 85; in exploration voyages, 22; Hispanola revolt of, 203–204, 204*f*; Indian, 24, 54; rebellions by, 261–262, 290, 355–356; relationships with owners, 354, 355, 357*f*; runaway, 373, 378; seizing in North, 373
Slave trade, 59*m*, 351*f*; illegal, 263, 355–356; in mid-19th century, 351–353; revival of, 391; in South Carolina, 262; in Virginia, 262; in Washington, D.C., 346, 348
Slavery: beginnings in America, 58; Civil War promise to freed slaves, 436; colonial solidarity and, 62; in colonial South, 63–65, 64*f*; Compromise of 1850 and, 346–349, 348*m*; Confiscation Act and, 415; Constitution and, 169–170, 313–314, 314–315, 343; cotton and, 261–262, 262*f*, 263*f*, 351–352, 353*m*; in Cuba, 621; Declaration of Independence and, 133; Dred Scott decision and, 385–387; economics of, 351–353; in 1848 presidential election, 343; in 1860 presidential election, 394, 396*m*; Emancipation Proclamation and, 414–416; and family life, 352; Fugitive Slave Act and, 348, 373; and immigration, 328; legacy of, 435; literature on, 373–374; Missouri annexation and, 242–245; and party system change, 376, 379–380; on plantations, 352; post-Revolutionary denunciation of, 153; present-day compensation for, 435; psychological effects of, 356–357, 357*f*; Republican party on, 380; rice cultivation and, 289; sectional controversy over, 241–242, 289–291; sociology of, 353–356; Texas annexation and, 336; in West, 342–344, 346–349; Wilmot Proviso and, 343. *See also* Abolitionist movement; Missouri Compromise
Slidell, John, 391
Sloat, John D., 339, 340*m*
Slovenia, 895
Slums: churches and, 530–531; in 19th century, 522*f*, 523, 525; and race riots, 848–849; schools in, 541; settlement houses in, 531–533, 541; in 20th century, 582–583
Smallpox, 26, 26*f*
Smiley, George (fictional spymaster), 881*f*
Smith, Adam, 93, 497
Smith, Alfred E.: Ku Klux Klan and, 687; in 1924 presidential election, 702; in 1928 presidential election, 687, 708, 808

Smith, "Cotton Ed," 740
Smith, Hyrum, 308*f*
Smith, John, 31–32, 36
Smith, Joseph, 307, 308*f*
Smith, Samuel, 228
Smith, Will, 250
Smith College, 538, 538*f*
Smoot-Hawley tariff, 713*f*
Smuggling, in colonial era, 86
Snake River, and Oregon Trail, 334
Snake River Valley, gold rush in, 469
Snaketown, 8, 12
SNCC. *See* Student Nonviolent Coordinating
   Committee
Sobel, Robert, 713*f*
Social change: post-Revolutionary,
   154–155; in World War II, 757–758
Social Darwinism, 497. *See also* Darwinism
Social equality, 440
Social feminism, 680
Social Gospel, 531, 584
Social mobility, 512, 516–518
Social reforms. *See* Progressivism; Reform
Social science, 539–540
Social Security, 721–722, 735, 878
Social Security Act (1935), 734*f,* 735, 736
Social workers: and progressivism,
   582–583; women as, 539
Socialism: in early 20th century, 585–586;
   "gas and water," 587; immigrants blamed
   for, 520*f*; and labor movement, 501,
   585–586, 665; in late 19th century,
   499–501, 531; municipal, 585; and pro-
   gressivism, 585; World War I and,
   651–652
Socialist Labor party, 501
Socialist party: in 1912 presidential election,
   604*m,* 605; in Progressive Era, 585–586;
   youth participation in, 581–582
Society of Christian Socialists, 531
Society of Cincinnati, 154
Society of St. Vincent de Paul, 530
Sociology, 540
Sod house, 515*f*
Solomon Islands, 769, 771
Somalia, 904
Somoza, Anastasio, 886
"Song of Myself" (Whitman), 323
Sonoma, in Mexican War, 339
Sons of Liberty, 113, 201
Soto, Hernando de, 23, 25
Soulé, Pierre, 375
The Sound and the Fury (Faulkner), 729
South: agriculture in, 351, 450–452, 451*f,*
   452*f*; alliance with West, 289; blacks in,
   355, 356–357, 564–565; cities in, 355;
   civil rights movement in, 815–818; col-

leges in, 326; colonial, 42–44, 57–68,
   67*m*; cotton in, 258–260, 351–352, 451,
   451*f,* 452, 452*f*; desegregation in,
   806–807; economy after Civil War,
   448–450; economy before Civil War, 396;
   economy in mid-19th century, 351–353;
   in 1860 presidential election, 393–396,
   396*m*; ERA failure in, 872*m*; Harper's
   Ferry raid and, 392; literacy in, 353; manufacturing in, 358; in mid-19th century
   agriculture in, 368*m*; origin of concept,
   57, 62; in Panic of 1857, 370; railroads
   in, 364, 365*m,* 370, 448; readmission to
   Union, 437–439, 442–443, 443*m*; in
   Revolutionary War, 142–143, 144*m*; secession by, 396–398, 398*m*; segregation
   in, 564–565, 806–807; solidarity principle of, 62; troop withdrawal from, 458;
   and Truman, 787. *See also* Confederate
   States of America; Reconstruction;
   Slavery
South America. *See* Latin America; *specific
   countries*
South Carolina: Alliance movement in, 571;
   black politicians in, 447–448; colonial,
   63, 67*m*; cotton in, 259, 289; and nullifi-
   cation, 289–292; ratification of
   Constitution by, 172, 174*m*; in
   Revolutionary War, 143; secession by,
   396; separation from North Carolina, 44,
   88; slave trade in, 262; slavery in,
   289–291, 355, 356
South Carolina Exposition and Protest
   (Calhoun), 247–248
South Carolina Negro Act of 1740, 63–64
South Dakota: Alliance movement in, 571,
   572; Dust Bowl in, 725–726; population
   in late 19th century, 570
South End House (Boston), 532
South Korea, 790–794, 792*m*
South Park (TV cartoon), 482
South Sea Bubble, 284
Southeast Asia Treaty Organization
   (SEATO), 802
Southern Alliance, 571
Southern Christian Leadership Conference
   (SCLC), 816
Southern Pacific Railroad, 473, 477*m*
Sovereignty: conflicting definitions of, 117;
   of Indian nations, 483; popular, and slav-
   ery, 344, 377, 380, 382, 386
Soviet Union: atomic bomb developed by,
   789; and Berlin blockade, 785*f*; breakup
   of, 891, 895; Carter and, 873; contain-
   ment policy and, 783, 789–790; Cuba
   and, relations between, 810, 813–814; in
   Cuban missile crisis, 810, 813–814, 814*f*;

détente and, 830–831; disintegration of, 881*f*; expansionism of, 777–778, 783, 865; Greek crisis of 1947 and, 783; under Khrushchev, 803–804; Marshall plan and, 784–787; post–World War II, 775–778, 780–781; Reagan and, 865, 878, 879–880; and Sandinista government, 886; spies working for, 794–796, 800*f*–801*f*; Suez Canal crisis and, 803; in World War II, 748, 751, 754, 761–762, 775–777, 776. *See also* Russia

Space program, 811, 813, 880

Spain: American colonies of, 21–24, 47, 55*f*, 107*m*; in American Revolution, 141, 147; attempted purchase of Cuba from, 375; California claim by, 55; civil war in, 746; colonial wars of, 100–104; Cuban struggle for independence from, 621–624; and England, rivalry with, 27–28; exploration voyages by, 20*m*, 21–23; and Florida surrender, 235–236; Indian slaves and, 54; Jews in, 14; and Louisiana Purchase, 202–203; post-Revolutionary relations with, 163, 185; and quest for gold and silver, 89; southwestern settlement by, 54, 56; Transcontinental Treaty with, 235–236, 237*m*, 330

Spanish-American War, 624–626, 626*m*

Speakeasies, 686

Specie Circular, 292–293

Speech, freedom of, suppression in World War I, 651–652

Spencer, Herbert, 540, 550

Spices, and exploration voyages, 19

Spielberg, Steven, 766*f*, 767*f*

Spinning machines, 255*f*

Spirit of St. Louis (airplane), 695–696

Spock, Benjamin, 842

Spoils system, 280–281. *See also* Civil service; Patronage

Sports, 852; college, 529; in early 20th century, 682–683; in late 19th century, 527–530; on television, 842; women in, 530

Spotsylvania Court House, 427, 431*m*

Sprague, Frank J., 525

Springer v. *United States,* 575

Sputnik, 803, 853–854

Squanto (Tisquantum), 36

Square-riggers, 362

St. Bernard Parish, Louisiana, 918

St. Clair, Arthur, 180

St. Lawrence Seaway project, 797

St. Leger, Barry, 139–140; in Saratoga Campaign, 141*m*

St. Louis Post-Dispatch (newspaper), 552

St. Rita's Nursing Home, New Orleans, 918

Stagflation, 870–871

Stalin, Joseph, 791*f*; Marshall plan and, 784; post–World War II expansion by, 777–778, 783; support for, in United States, 776; in World War II, 775; at Yalta, 777–778, 777*f*

Stamp Act (1765), 112–114, 113*f*, 117, 132*f*; protests against, 113*f*; riots following, 113–115

Stamp Act Congress, 118

Stampp, Kenneth, 357*f*; on Reconstruction, 446*f*

Standard of living: of 19th-century industrial workers, 360; under Reagan, 885–886

Standard Oil Company, 493–496, 495*f*; attacks on, 499, 584

Stanford, Leland, 474, 475*f*, 555

Stanford, Mrs. Leland, 539

Stanford University, 539

Stanton, Edwin M., 417, 443

Stanton, Elizabeth Cady, 317–318, 317*f*, 444, 591, 592

"The Star Spangled Banner" (Key), 228–229, 230*f*

Star Wars (film), 880

Star Wars (strategic defense initiative), 880

Starr, Kenneth W., 901, 902–903

State(s): and church, separation of, 153; constitutions of, 152–153, 155, 442–443; direct primary system in, 587–588; ERA failure in, 872*m*; governments of, 152–153; laws of, *vs.* federal laws, 272, 290–291; progressive political reforms in, 587–588; progressive social reforms in, 588–590; rights of, 283, 294, 296, 396, 397; "ten percent," 436–438; woman suffrage in, 592, 593*m*. *See also* individual states by name; specific states

The State (Wilson), 605

State Department: communists in, 795–796, 798; Open Door policy and, 703; under Taft, 637

States' Rights party, 787

Status revolution, 584

Statute of Religious Liberty (1786), 153

STDs. *See* Sexually transmitted diseases

Steam: and industry, 358–359; replacement by electricity, 488

Steamboats, 267, 269*f*; and interstate commerce, 273–274; and ocean commerce, 363

Stearns, George L., 392

Steel industry: labor organization in, 666; in late 19th century, 486–487, 614–615; in late 20th century, 873*f*; monopoly in, 491–493; railroads and, 487; strikes against, 507–508, 666; in World War I, 651

Steffens, Lincoln, 570*f*, 584, 586, 628, 716
Stein, Gertrude, 689
Steinbeck, John, 729
Stem cell research, 917
Stephens, Alexander H., 439, 444
Stephens, Uriah S., 503–504
Stephenson, David C., 687
Steroids, illegal use in baseball, 917
Stevens, John, 267
Stevens, Thaddeus, 408, 437, 438, 444, 448–449
Stevenson, Adlai E., 797, 803, 913
Stewart, Alexander T., 496, 513
Stimson, Henry L., 706, 759
Stimson Doctrine, 706
Stock market: in 1980s, 885–886; collapse of 1929, 697–698; Internet companies in, 907–908; New Deal controls over, 723. *See also* Panic(s)
Stockman, David, 885
Stockton, Robert F., 340*m*
Stoddard, Solomon, 96, 97
Stone, Harlan Fiske, 701
Stone, Oliver, 825*f*
Store clerks, 514
Stowe, Harriet Beecher, 254, 372, 373–374, 375*f*; on teaching, 324
Strasser, Adolph, 505
Strategic Arms Limitation Treaty (SALT), SALT II, 873, 880
Strategic defense initiative (SDI), 880
Stratification, social. *See* Class structure
Strauss, Levi, 461
Street names, 126
Streetcars, 525–526, 527*f*, 528
Strikes: in coal industry, 596–598; by female textile workers, 256; government reaction to, 575; Industrial Revolution and, 253; IWW and, 586; by migrant workers, 851; in New Deal period, 738; in post–World War I period, 665–666; in steel industry, 507–508; unions and, 504–505, 506–508; by women shoemakers (1860), 361*f*
Strong, Josiah, 615
Student Nonviolent Coordinating Committee (SNCC), 817, 848–849
Students: aspirations of, 864; 1960s radicals, 854–856
Students for a Democratic Society (SDS), 855
Submarine warfare, 648*f*; in World War I, 645–646, 645*f*, 647–648, 656; in World War II, 751
Suburbs: late 19th-century migration to, 526, 527*f*; post–World War II growth of, 840, 843–844; trolley cars and, 525–526, 527*f*

Sudan, immigrants from, 350
Sudetenland crisis, 747
Suez Canal crisis, 803
Suffrage. *See* Black suffrage; Woman suffrage
Sugar: colonial trade in, 90; Cuban, 621, 805; Hawaiian, 616–617, 618*f*; in post–Civil War South, 452*f*; trade during Napoleonic wars, 212
Sugar Act (1764), 110–111
Sugar Trust, 503, 575
Sullivan, "Big Tim," 567–568
Sullivan, John L., 528
"A Summary View of the Rights of British America" (Jefferson), 129
Summit Tunnel, 474
Sumner, Charles, 383–384, 408, 437, 444
Sumner, William Graham, 497
Sumter, Thomas, 143
The Sun Also Rises (Hemingway), 689
Sung, Kim Il, 916
Sunni Muslims, 400; in Iraq, 920, 921
Superdome, New Orleans, 919
The Suppression of the African Slave Trade (Du Bois), 609
Supreme Court, U.S.: on affirmative action, 905; on antitrust legislation, 503, 575, 596; on blacks after Reconstruction, 564–565; Brandeis appointed to, 646–647; and business regulation, 501, 502, 503, 734; on capital punishment, 892; on child labor, 589; on civil liberties, 652; on civil rights, 806; clear and present danger doctrine, 652; Clinton appointments to, 900; on colonial rights, 630; Dred Scott decision by, 385–387, 390, 391; establishment of, 175; on free speech, 652; Hamilton's reforms and, 180; on Indian tribes, standing of, 289; on Japanese internment, 761; Marshall Court, 271–274; on monopolies, 596; and New Deal, 734, 736–737; on oil scandal under Harding, 700; powers of, establishment of, 201; Reagan appointments to, 880; on segregation, 564–565, 806, 816; on 2000 presidential election, 909; on Watergate investigation, 836, 837; on working hour legislation, 590, 677
Susan Constant (ship), 31
Susman, Warren, 858*f*
Sweden, colonization by, 45
Sweeney, Madeline Amy, 909
Syria, in Yom Kippur War, 865

Taft, Robert A., 796
Taft, William Howard, 600–603; break with Roosevelt, 601*f*, 602–603; foreign policy

of, 637; in 1908 presidential election, 600; in 1912 presidential election, 603–604, 604*m*; as Philippines governor, 600, 630; presidency of, 600–603
Taft-Hartley Act, 782, 788
Taguba, Antonio M., 914*f*
Taiwan, 789
Taliban, 909, 911, 912
Talleyrand, Charles Maurice de, 189, 191, 192, 204–205
Tallmadge, James, 242
Tammany Hall, 569, 592
Taney, Roger B., 274; Dred Scott decision, 385–386; as secretary of treasury, 286, 292
Tappan, Arthur, 314
Tappan, Lewis, 314
Tar-and-feathering, 122*f*
Tarbell, Ida, 584
Tariff(s), 218–219; of Abominations, 219, 247; under Adams (John Quincy), 247–248; under Cleveland, 562–563; and 1824 presidential election, 244–245; under Harrison (Benjamin), 563; under Jackson, 289–291; in late 19th century, 483, 557–558; post–Civil War, 454; present-day example, 218; on Puerto Rican products, 630; as sectional issue, 289–291; slavery and, 290–291; under Taft, 601; under Van Buren, 296; under Wilson, 606
Tariff Act (1789), 176
Tarleton, Banastre, 143, 149, 149*f*
Tarrytown, New York, 135*f*
Taxation: under Bush (George H. W.), 898; under Bush (George W.), 753; on cargos, 86; during Civil War, 407, 408, 409; colonial, 109–118; in early 21st-century, 86; and Great Depression, 711, 712; Hamiltonian reforms and, 176, 181, 183, 184*f*; under Harding, 699–700; Mellon's program of, 699–700, 711; post-Revolutionary, 164; pre-Revolutionary resistance to, 86–87; of property, 499; under Reagan, 877, 880; without representation, 111–112; in World War I, 651, 659; in World War II, 757. *See also* Income tax
Taylor, Alan, 73*f*
Taylor, George Rogers, 269*f*
Taylor, Zachary: and Compromise of 1850, 347; death of, 347–348; in 1848 presidential election, 343–344; and gold rush, 344, 345; in Mexican War, 337–339; and slavery, 345, 347–348
Tea Act crisis, 121–122
Tea pots: ceramics for, 113*f*; imported, 251*f*

Tea tax, 119–122
Teachers: college, 326, 539; in common school movement, 324; in progressive education, 541; women as, 324, 513, 539
Teaford, Jon, 568*f*
Teapot Dome scandal, 700
Technology: in Civil War, 410; impact of, 753, 780; in Industrial Revolution, 251–253; Internet, 907–908; in 19th-century industry, 358–359; receptivity to, 358–359
Tecumseh, 221*f*; death of, 298; in Indian liberation movement, 220–221; in War of 1812, 226–227
"Teddy's Bears," 595*f*
Teenagers, curfews imposed on, 510
Telegraph: Edison and, 488; and news gathering, 552; and railroads, 486
Telephone industry, 488
Television, 841–842; journalism and, 800*f*–801*f*; political campaigns and, 372, 800*f*–801*f*, 868; and religion, 846, 878; violence on, 906
Teller, Henry M., 576
Teller Amendment, 627
Temperance movement: in 19th century, 311–313; and prohibition, 686
"Ten percent plan," 436–438
Tenancy, share, 450
Tenement housing, 522*f*, 523, 525, 526
Tennent, William, 94
Tennessee: Alliance movement in, 571; and cotton, 260; desegregation in, 806; evolution taught in schools of, 684–685; formation of, 186, 187*m*; secession and, 396, 398*m*, 402
Tennessee Coal and Iron Company, 603
Tennessee Valley Authority (TVA), 726–727, 727*m*, 743
Tennis, 527, 530
Tenskwatawa ("The Prophet"), 220, 221*f*
Tenth Amendment, 176
Tenure of Office Act, 443
Tepees, 462
Territorial Enterprise (newspaper), 544
Territory, U.S.: under Articles of Confederation, 151*m*; in early 19th century, 237*m*; in late 18th century, 187*m*
Terrorism, 909; in 1990s, 909; after fall of Soviet Union, 909; Bush (George W.) and, 763; in Iran-Contra arms deal, 886; in post-Reconstruction South, 453; in post–World War I period, 666–667; of September 11, 2001, 909–911; Sunni *vs.* Shiite, 920–921; 2001 World Trade Center attacks, 891, 909–911, 910*f*; U.S. war against, 911–912

Terry, Alfred H., 465

Tet offensive, 826

Texas: Alliance movement in, 570, 571; annexation of, 330–332, 336; cattle in, 476; and Compromise of 1850, 347, 348; cotton in, 330; desegregation of education in, 806; farming in, 515; independence of, 330–332; in Mexican War, 337, 340–341; Republic of, 330; Spanish settlement in, 54; statehood for, 336

Texas Hold'em (online poker game), 697

Texas longhorn cattle, 476

Textbooks, post–World War I, 685

Textile industry: after Civil War, 452; cotton, 251–253, 255f, 452; immigrants and, 360; in post–World War I period, 709; in South, 358; Triangle shirtwaist factory fire, 589; women in, 513

Thames, Battle of, 226

Thayer, Timothy (assumed name of Deborah Sampson), 135f

Thernstrom, Stephen, 524f

Thirteenth Amendment: ratification of, 438–439; and representation, 438–439; southern transgressions of, 440

This Side of Paradise (Fitzgerald), 688–689

Thomas, Emory, 444f

Thomas, Jesse B., 243

Thompson, Frederic, 529f

Thompson, Walter, 713f

Thomson Steel Works, 492

Thoreau, Henry David, 319–320, 392, 534, 542

Thornton, Russell, 26f

Thorpe, Jim, 682

Three-fifths Compromise, 170, 439

Thriller (music video), 906

Thumper, Clod, 354

Thurmond, J. Strom, 787

Tidewater colonies, 56, 57, 60

Tilden, Samuel J., 456, 457, 457f, 491

Tilden, William "Big Bill," 682

Tillman, "Pitchfork Ben," 627

Time (magazine), 778, 780, 795

Time Piece (newspaper), 190

Tippecanoe, Battle of, 221, 297

Tisquantum. See Squanto

Titanic (film), 548f

Tituba, 74, 75

Tobacco, 452, 483; advertisement for, 60f; colonial cultivation of, 43, 59–61; discovery of, 32; in mid-19th century, 368m; in post–Civil War South, 451, 451f; in post–World War I period, 709

Tocqueville, Alexis de: in America, 301–302; on families, 302; on Indian removals, 288–289; on Jackson, 293; on prisons, 311

Toledo, Ohio, 586, 587

Toleration Act (1649), 43, 66

Tolstoy, Leo Nikolayevich, 546

Tompkins, Sally, 424–425

Tonkin incident, 822

Tontine, 496

Tooth decay, corn and, 9

Tordesillas, Treaty of (1494), 21

Tories. See Loyalists

Torture, of Iraqi prisoners, 914, 914f

Tourists, and destruction of buffalo, 467f

Towns: cattle, 470f; colonial, 73f, 77; mining, 469, 471; Puritan, 73f

Townsend, Francis E., 733

Townsend National Weekly, 733

Townshend, Charles, 117

Townshend duties, 117–118

Toynbee Hall, 532

Trade: after War of 1812, 233; with Allies, in World War II, 748, 750; cash-and-carry, 748, 750; colonial, 44, 76–77, 92f, 117–118; in early 19th century, 257–258; Embargo Act and, 213–215, 215f; embargoes on, in 1930s, 746, 748; and exploration voyages, 19; Hamilton and, 177f; Indians use of wampum for, 50f; lend-lease program, 750; Napoleonic wars and, 211–212, 219–220; New France and, 53; in 19th century, 362–363, 614–615; post-Revolutionary, 164; royal restrictions on, 91–93; tax on cargos, 86; transportation improvements and, 362–364; in 20th century, 614–615; and World War I, 644–646. See also Fur trade; Slave trade; Tariff(s)

Trade associations: New Deal and, 724; in post–World War I period, 709–710

Trade unions. See Labor unions

Trafalgar, Battle of, 211, 211f

Trail of Tears, 288m, 289

Transatlantic travel: in late 19th century, 518; in mid-19th century, 362–364

Transcendentalism, 318, 322

Transcontinental railroads, 473–476, 477m; competition between, 474–475; land-grant system and, 473–474; Pacific Railway Act and, 424, 473; plans for, 473–476; as trunk lines, 485

Transcontinental Treaty (1819), 235–236, 237m, 330

Transoceanic cables, 552

Transportation: freight, 486; highway construction, 264–266; and immigration, 518–519; immigration and, 350–351; in late 19th-century cities, 525–526; in mid-20th century, 840–841; railroad competition and, 490; and trade, 362–364; by water, 269f. See also specific modes

Travis, William B., 330

A Treatise on Domestic Economy for the Use of Young Ladies (Beecher), 303
Trench warfare, in Civil War, 426–427, 428*f*
Trenton, Battle of, 138*f,* 139, 239
Triana, Roderigo de, 18
Triangle shirtwaist factory fire, 589
Triangular trade, 77
Tripoli, war with, 202
Tripp, Linda, 902
Trolley cars, 525–526. *See also* Streetcars
Trotter, William Monroe, 611
Trudeau, Garry, 835*f*
"True Sons of Freedom," 655*f*
True-Blooded Yankee (ship), 225
Truman, Harry S, 781; atomic bomb and, 772, 774; and communists in government, 794–795; economic policies of, 782; foreign policy of, 783, 789–790, 799, 802; and Israel, 802; and Korean War, 790–794; in 1944 presidential election, 772; in 1948 presidential election, 787–788, 788*f*; at Potsdam, 778; presidency of, 781; Reagan compared with, 887*f*
Truman Doctrine, 784
Trumbull, John, 132*f,* 146*f*
Trunk lines, 365*m,* 369, 485–486
Trust(s), 494–496, 556*f,* 596–599; progressivism and, 582; Roosevelt (Theodore) and, 596. *See also* Antitrust legislation
Tuberculosis, 26*f*
Tucker, Stephen, 551
Tugwell, Rexford, 719, 744
Tunney, "Gentlemen Gene," 682
Turkey, Truman Doctrine and, 784
Turner, Frederick Jackson, 223*f,* 333*f,* 542, 543*f,* 615
Turner, Henry M., 565
Turner, Nat, 290, 355
Turnpikes, 265–266
Tuskegee Institute, 566, 566*f*
TVA. *See* Tennessee Valley Authority
Twain, Mark, 544–545, 628, 689
Tweed, William Marcy, 569
Tweed Ring (New York City), 456, 569
Twelfth Amendment, 195
Twenty-fifth Amendment, 836
Twenty-first Amendment, 722–723
Twenty-One Demands (1915), 641
Twice-told Tales (Hawthorne), 321
Tydings, Millard F., 740
Tyler, Alice Kellog, 532*f*
Tyler, Elizabeth, 687
Tyler, John, 329, 329*f*; in 1840 presidential election, 298–299; and Henry Clay, 329–330; and Texas question, 330, 331, 336
Typee (Melville), 322

Typewriter, first, 551*f*
Typewriters, 484
"Typewriters," 514

U-652 (submarine), 751
UAW. *See* United Automobile Workers
U-boat campaigns, 648*f*; in World War I, 645–646, 645*f,* 647–648, 656; in World War II, 751
Uganda Railroad, 614–615
UMW. *See* United Mine Workers
UN. *See* United Nations
Uncle Tomahawk, 851
Uncle Tom's Cabin (Stowe), 254, 372, 373–374, 375*f*
Underwood Tariff (1913), 606
Unemployment, 513; among Indian Americans, 460; under Clinton, 904; in Great Depression, 711, 712, 716–717, 742–743; insurance, 735; in late 19th-century, 513, 575; New Deal programs for, 727–728, 729*f,* 735; post–World War II, 782; psychological effects of, 717; in World War II, 756
The Unheralded Triumph (Teaford), 568*f*
Unicorn (ship), 212
Unification: Articles of Confederation and, 148, 150; factors for, 118; Revolutionary War and, 145–147, 157–158; sectionalism and, 248
Union, in Civil War: casualties of, 410, 433*f*; economic effects of war on, 423–424; military forces of, 403–405, 403*f,* 406*f*; at start of Civil War, 402–404
Union(s), labor. *See* Labor unions
Union Bank of Baltimore, 285
Union Cattle Company of Wyoming, 478
Union League of America, 452
Union of Russian Workers, 667
Union Pacific Railroad, 466, 467*f,* 473–476, 477*m,* 484, 504*f*; and Central Pacific, competition between, 474–475
Union Railroad Station, Montgomery, Alabama, 485*f*
Unitarianism, 318
United Aircraft and Transport, 696
United Automobile Workers (UAW): 1937 strike by, 738; in oil crisis, 866
United Farm Workers' Organizing Committee, 851*f*
United Fruit Company, 638
United Kingdom. *See* Anglo-American relations; Great Britain
United Mine Workers (UMW), 756; 1902 coal strike and, 596–598
United Nations (UN): charter, 775–776; Declaration of, 775–776; in Korean War, 790–794; nuclear weapons and, 789; and

United Nations (UN) *(continued)*
Persian Gulf War, 896–898; and Second
Iraq War, 913; Suez Canal crisis and, 803
United Nations Security Council: formation
of, 775–776; and Korean War, 790
United States: present-day, A-42*m*–A-43*m*;
recognition of, 141, 145–147
United States (ship), 224
United States v. *E. C. Knight Company,* 503,
575
Universal Negro Improvement Association,
690
Universities. *See* Colleges and universities;
specific institutions
University of Alabama, 535, 807
University of California, 855–856, 905
University of Chicago, 535, 537, 541
University of Connecticut health Center,
697
University of Hawaii, 670
University of Illinois, 538
University of Michigan, 538
University of Missouri law school, 806
University of Oklahoma, 806
University of Pennsylvania, 98, 697
Upshur, Abel P., 331
Urban areas. *See* Cities; Towns
Urbanization: colonies and, 77; highway
construction, 264–265; Jefferson's opin-
ion of, 199
U.S. Census (2000), 460
U.S. Steel, 492, 494*f,* 503; formation of,
582; layoffs at, 884–885; in Taft adminis-
tration, 602–603; in World War I, 651
U.S.A. (Dos Passos), 729
USS *Cole,* bombing of, 911
Utah: Compromise of 1850 and, 348, 348*m*;
Mormons in, 307–308; woman suffrage
in, 592
Ute Indians, 54
Utica, New York: and New York Anti-
Slavery Society, 314; Second Great
Awakening in, 304, 305; temperance
movement in, 312
Utica and Schenectady Railroad, 366
Utilities, New Deal and, 726–727, 735. *See
also* Electricity
Utrecht, Treaty of (1713), 101

Vaca, Alvar Núñez Cabeza de, 23
Vallandigham, Clement L., 408
Van Buren, Martin: in 1832 presidential
election, 296; in 1836 presidential election, 296; in 1840 presidential election,
297–299; in 1844 presidential election,
331, 335–336; in 1848 presidential election, 344; Jackson and, 285, 286; on

Jackson and nullification crisis, 290; presi-
dency of, 296; split with Democratic
party, 344; Tariff of Abominations and,
247; and Texas annexation, 331, 336
Van De Mark, Brian, 825*f*
Van Rensselaer, Kiliaen, 45
Vancouver Island, 337
Vanderbilt, "Commodore" Cornelius, 273,
484, 500*f*
Vanderbilt, William, 500*f,* 516
Vanzetti, Bartolomeo, 688
Varieties of Religious Experience (James), 550
Vassar College, 538, 681*f*
Veblen, Thorstein, 539
Venezuela: border dispute with British
Guiana, 620–621; Nixon's visit to, 805
Venture capitalists, 907
Vera Cruz, in Mexican War, 339
Vergennes, Comte de, 141, 146
Versailles Treaty (1919), 660–662
Vesey, Denmark, 290, 355, 356, 852
Veterans: benefits under Harding, 700; 1932
protest in Washington, 715–716; of
World War II, 782, 853*f,* 854
Veterans Bureau, 699
Vetoes, presidential: by Jackson, 282,
284–286, 287; by Johnson (Andrew), 440
Vicksburg campaign, 410, 411*m,* 422–423
Vietcong, 815, 826, 829*f*
Vietminh, 799
Vietnam: division of, 802; French in, 799,
802
Vietnam War: costs of, 823, 832–833; end
of, 867–868; under Johnson, 822–823,
824*m,* 825*f;* under Kennedy, 815; under
Nixon, 828–830, 832; opposition to,
810, 823, 828–830; Saigon, fall of,
867–868, 867*f;* in 2004 presidential elec-
tion, 914–915
Vietnamization, 828–829
Villa, Francisco "Pancho," 642
Villard, Henry, 485
Villard, Oswald Garrison, 610
Violence: in cattle towns, 470*f;* popular culture and, 891, 905–907
Virgin Islands, 632*m*
Virginia: and American Colonization Society,
261–262; Articles of Confederation and,
151*m;* Bacon's Rebellion in, 61–62; colonial, 43, 57, 67*m;* and cotton, 260; naming
of, 29; politics in, 83; ratification of
Constitution by, 172, 174*m;* in
Revolutionary War, 143; secession and,
396, 398*m,* 402; settlement of, 30–33;
slave revolt in, 355; slave trade in, 263;
slavery in, 58, 352; Spanish settlements in,
23; tobacco cultivation in, 59–61

Virginia City, Nevada, 469
Virginia Militia, First, 404*f*
Virginia Resolution, 191–192
Virginia Tech, shooting at, 890
Visible saints, 38, 40, 70–71
Vocational public schools, 517
Voltaire (François Marie Arouet), 98
Volunteerism, 581
Voting: in Jacksonian era, 277–278; in late
   19th century, 554–555; by youth, educa-
   tion and, 581. *See also* Black suffrage;
   Woman suffrage
Voting Rights Act (1965), 821–822

Wabash and Erie Canal, 270
Wachovia Bank, robbery at, 697
Wade, Ben, 438
Wade-Davis bill, 437–438
Wage, minimum. *See* Minimum wage
Wagner Act (1935), 734
Wald, Lillian, 532
Walden (Thoreau), 320
Walden Pond, 320
Walker, David, 314
Walker, Robert J., 387
Wallace, George C., 827
Wallace, Henry A.: in 1940 presidential
   election, 749; in 1944 presidential elec-
   tion, 772; in 1948 presidential election,
   788; on Soviet Union, 775
Wallace, Henry C., 699
Wallace, Lew, 544
Wal-Mart, 482
Walpole, Robert, 93, 109
Walsh, Thomas J., 700
Waltham, Massachusetts, 253, 255
Waltham System, 255–256
Wampum, 50*f*
Wanamaker, John, 496
Wanghia, Treaty of (1844), 616
War Department, 656
War Hawks, 222
War Industries Board (WIB), 649
War Labor Policies Board, 650
War Mobilization, Office of, 756
War of 1812, 224–228, 229*m*; aftermath to,
   230, 233–236; American forces in, 225*f*;
   Battle of New Orleans, 232–233; British
   offensive in, 227, 228, 229*m*; events lead-
   ing to, 220–221; resistance to, 222
War of the Austrian Succession
   (1740–1748), 101
War of the Spanish Succession (1702–1713),
   101
Warfare, Indian *vs.* European, 24, 48
*The Warfare of Science with Theology in
   Christendom* (White), 547

Warm Springs, Georgia, 745*f*
Warner, Susan, 542
Warren, Earl, 806, 819
Warren Commission, 819
Warsaw Pact, 894
Washington, Booker T., 565–567, 608, 611
Washington, D.C.: Compromise of 1850
   and, 347; immigration rally in, 916*f*;
   March on (1963), 818, 847, 905; Million
   Man March in (1995), 905; slave trade in,
   347, 348; 2001 terrorist attack on, 910,
   911; in War of 1812, 227, 228–230,
   230–232
Washington, Denzel, 420, 421*f*
Washington, George, 154; on American independence, 141; beer and, 126; and Bill
   of Rights, 176; cabinet of, 175; and confederation, 163, 166; in Continental
   Congress, 129; 1872 Grant campaign
   poster, 455*f*; election for president, 166,
   173–174; foreign policy of, 181–182,
   184–186; in French and Indian War,
   102–103; Jackson compared to, 280; law
   enforcement by, 183, 184*f*; as national
   hero, 160; presidency of, 174–175, 180;
   on Proclamation of 1763, 110; retirement
   of, 186; in Revolutionary War, 128, 136,
   137–139, 145; on Shays's Rebellion, 165;
   and social reform, 153; towns and institu-
   tions named after, 126; in XYZ Affair, 189
Washington, Lewis, 392
Washington Globe (newspaper), 293
Washingtonians, 311–313
Water, transportation by, 267–268,
   362–364
Water rights, in West, 478
Watergate scandal, 811, 833–835, 836–838
Watkins, Maurine, 678*f*, 679*f*
Watson, Harry, 269*f*
Watson, Tom, 572, 573, 577
Watts riots (1965), 849
Wayland, Francis, 326
Wayne, "Mad Anthony," 184, 207
Wealth: attacks on, 498–501; Long's Share
   Our Wealth plan and, 732, 733;
   Townsend's pension plan and, 733; World
   War II and, 757
Wealth Against Commonwealth (Lloyd), 499,
   509
Wealth of Nations (Smith), 497
Wealth Tax Act (1935), 735
Weapons: Civil War, 410, 428*f*; European,
   Indians acquire, 54; Indian *vs.*
   European/American, 49, 464; interna-
   tional sale of, 746, 748, 886; medieval,
   15; prehistoric, 2, 4. *See also specific types*
Weaver, James B., 572, 573, 574

Webb, Walter Prescott, 480

Webster, Daniel, 245, 245*f*, 329; alcohol consumption of, 312; and Bank of United States controversy, 284–286; and Compromise of 1850, 347, 349; in 1836 presidential election, 294, 296; in 1840 presidential election, 298, 299; on tariff question, 245, 247; as Tyler's secretary of state, 331; on Van Buren, 297

Webster–Ashburton Treaty, 330

Wedgewood, Josiah, 251

Weehawken, New Jersey, 206

A Week on the Concord and Merrimack Rivers (Thoreau), 320

Weinberger, Caspar, 881*f*

Weinstein, Edwin, 666*f*

Welch, Joseph, 801*f*

Weld, Theodore Dwight, 314, 316

Wellesley College, 538

Wellington, Duke of, 230, 231, 233, 340

Wells Fargo, 461

Wesley, John, 94

West, 369; agriculture in, 472; canals and, 267–269; cattle ranching in, 476–480; cattle towns in, 470*f*; cattle trails in, 477*m*; Civil War in, 409–410; classification of land in, 478; colleges in, 326; conquest of, 460–480; Erie Canal and, 268, 270; and expansionism, 615; frontier violence and, 470; Indian land and life in (late 19th century), 461; Indian wars in, 464–466; Jeffersonian policy on, 202–207, 207–209; land bonanza in, 471–472; literature of, 544–545; manifest destiny and, 332; mineral wealth of, 468–471; mining in, 477*m*; during Monroe mandate, 239, 240; Plains Indians in, 462–463; post–Civil War, 461–462; post-Revolutionary development, 158–159, 159*f*, 181; railroads and, 369, 370, 473–476, 477*m*; settlement of, 186, 263–265, 332–334, 461–462; slavery in, 342–344, 346–349; and southern alliance, 289; transportation and, 263–265

West, Benjamin, 46*f*, 146*f*

West Florida: acquisition by U.S., 235–236; creation of, 110

West Germany, 786*m*

West Indies: colonial trade with, 44, 77, 90; exploration voyages to, 18; French interests in, 203; sugar trade, 212

West Virginia, secession and, 398*m*

Western Europe. *See* Europe

Western Territories, development of, 158–159, 159*f*

Western Traffic Association, 486

Western Union Company, 486, 488, 504*f*

Westinghouse, George, 486

Westmoreland, William C., 826

Weston High School (Wisconsin), hostage shooting at, 890

Weyler, Valeriano, 621–622

Whaling, 362

Wharton, Edith, 689

Wheat: Civil War and, 451; diffusion of cultivation, 13; in late 19th century, 518, 570; mechanical reaper and, 367–368; in mid-19th century, 368*m*, 370; in West, 472

Whig party, 379–380; beginnings of, 294, 296; and Constitutional Union party, 395; demise of, 381*f*; divisions in, 377; in 1840 presidential election, 297–299, 329–330; in 1844 presidential election, 335–336; in 1848 presidential election, 343–344; in 1852 presidential election, 377; and Kansas-Nebraska Act, 377; in Mexican War, 337–338; and Republican party, 380; split with Tyler, 329–330

Whip Inflation Now (WIN) buttons, 867

Whipple, E. P., on Whitman, 323*f*

Whiskey Ring affair, 454–455

Whiskey Tax, 181, 183, 199

White, Alfred T., 526

White, Andrew D., 547, 568*f*

White, Hugh Lawson, 294, 296

White, Richard, 223*f*, 543*f*

White House, destruction in War of 1812, 228

Whitefield, George, 95, 95*f*, 96, 97, 530

Whitewater, 898, 901

Whitman, Walt, 322–323, 323*f*, 533

Whitney, Eli, 259–260, 260*f*

Why England Slept (Kennedy), 808

WIB. *See* War Industries Board

Wichita, as cattle town, 470*f*

The Wide, Wide World (Warner), 542

Wigglesworth, Michael, 71

Wilderness, Battle of, 426–427, 431*m*

Wilderness Road, 266

Wilkins, Roy, 759

Wilkinson, James, 210

Willamette Valley, 334, 337

William (ship), 212

William of Orange, 72

William Penn's Treaty with the Indians (West), 46*f*

Williams, Roger, 39–41

Williams, William A., 617*f*

Williams, William Appleman, 791*f*

Williamsburg, Virginia, 66

Williamson, Joel, on Reconstruction, 446*f*

Willkie, Wendell L., 726, 749–750, 774

Wills, Helen, 683

Wilmot, David, 343, 415
Wilmot Proviso, 343, 347, 415
Wilson, John, 40
Wilson, Woodrow, 512, 605–607; and blacks, 611, 656; deteriorating health of, 664, 665, 666*f*; financial reforms of, 606–607; foreign policy of, 641–642; and League of Nations, 662–665, 663*f*, 668–669; and minority rights, 607; New Freedom program of, 605–607, 620, 649; in 1912 presidential election, 603–605, 604*m*, 611; in 1916 presidential election, 646–647; in 1920 presidential election, 668–669; in Paris Peace Conference, 659–662; postwar peace negotiations of, 659–662; *vs.* Senate, 662–665; World War I policies of, 640–641, 644, 646–647, 649–651
Wimbledon, 683
Winder, William H., 228
Windows operating system, 907
Winning of the West (Roosevelt), 594
Winslet, Kate, 548*f*, 549*f*
Winstanley, William, 188*f*
Winthrop, John (governor), 37–38, 76, 93
Wirt, William, 289
Wirz, Henry, 437
Wisconsin, progressivism in, 587–588, 590
Witchhunt, 74–76, 75*f*, 78–79
Wolfe, James, 104, 107–108
Wollaston, John, 95*f*
Woman suffrage movement: after World War I, 677, 680; Fifteenth Amendment and, 444; Fourteenth Amendment and, 441–442; in late 19th century, 590–592; in Progressive Era, 590–592, 591*f*; racial prejudice in, 608; and states, 592, 593*m*; World War I and, 653–654
Woman's Home Companion, 842
Women: advertising aimed at, 681*f*; black, 450; in Civil War, 424–426, 425*f*, 426*f*; in colleges, 324, 325, 326; in colonies, 40, 57, 65, 69–70; and dating, in post–World War I period, 674; education for, higher, 325, 326, 538–539, 538*f*; and Fifteenth Amendment, 444; and Fourteenth Amendment, 441–442; in Great Depression, 717; in late 19th century, 512; Lynn strike by, 361*f*; in mid-19th century, 300, 302–303, 303*f*; in military, 762; New Deal and, 741–742; in New France, 53; pioneer, 332–333, 334; in post–World War I period, 673, 674; progressivism and, 582, 590; Puritan, 69–70, 74–76, 79*f*; Revolutionary War and, 155–157; Second Great Awakening and, 304–305; in settlement house movement, 532–533; in sports, 530; as teachers, 324; World War I and, 653–654, 654*f*; World War II and, 753, 761–763. *See also* Working women
Women in the Nineteenth Century (Fuller), 316
Women's Auxiliary Army Corps, 762
Women's rights movement, 316–318; in 1960s, 860–862, 861*f*; abolitionist movement and, 316–317; higher education and, 538–539; in 19th century, 590–592; 1970s recession and, 872–873; in post–World War I period, 674, 675–680; World War I and, 653–654. *See also* Woman suffrage movement
Wood, Gordon, 122*f*
Wood, John E., 338*f*
Woodrow Wilson Foundation, 704
Woods, Robert A., 532
Woodstock, 858*f*
Wool Act (1699), 91
Woolworth chain, 709, 816
Woolworth sit-in, 816
Wordsworth, William, 318
Work: in colonial South, 66; in early 19th-century, 253–256; in early 20th century, 673; Industrial Revolution and, 253–254; in late 19th century, 512–513; in mid-19th century, 302, 359, 360–361; in mid-20th century, 820; post–World War II changes in, 782; in World War I, 650–651. *See also* Labor legislation
Workers: immigrants as, 256–257, 359–360, 520–521; industrial growth and, 360–361; Industrial Revolution and, 253–254; in late 19th century, 512–513; layoffs of, 884–885; migrant, 851; in post–World War I period, 673; in post–World War II period, 869–870; progressivism and, 583, 585–586; World War I and, 650–651; World War II and, 756, 761–763
Worker's compensation, 589
Working class, attitudes of, 516
Working women: in Civil War, 424–426; in early 19th century, 255–256; in early 20th century, 582, 590; in late 19th century, 513–514; in late 20th century, 860, 872–873; in mid-19th century, 302–303, 360, 361; in post–World War I period, 673, 675–680; World War I and, 654*f*; in World War II, 753, 761–763
Works Progress Administration (WPA), 728, 729*f*
World, present-day, A-44*m*–A-45*m*
World Anti-Slavery Convention (1840), 316
World Series, 528

World Trade Center, 2001 terrorist attack on, 909–911, 910*f*
World Trade Organization (WTO), 904
World War I: aftermath of, 657–659, 661*m*; Allied Powers in, 643; blacks and, 654–656; casualties in, 658*f*; Central Powers in, 643; civil liberty restrictions in, 651–652; economic impact of, 648–650; financing of, 650–651; mobilization for, 648–650; opposition to, 651–652; outbreak of, 642–644; peace settlement following, 659–662; propaganda in, 651–652; sea warfare in, 644–646, 647–648, 648*f*, 656; social reforms during, 652–653; U.S. entry into, 647–648; U.S. military engagements in, 656–657; U.S. neutrality in, 643–646, 647–648; Western Front in, 657*m*; women and, 653–654, 654*f*; workers in, 650–651
World War II: Allied strategy in, 763–765, 768; atomic bomb in, 772–775; costs of, 774–775; diplomacy in, 775–776; economy during, 756–757; European theater of, 763–765, 765*m*, 768; minorities in, 753, 758–760; in North Atlantic, 749, 751; outbreak of, 746–749; Pacific theater of, 769–772, 771*m*; Pearl Harbor in, 754*f*, 755; social change in, 757–758; turning point in, 764–765, 778; U.S. entry into, 754–755; before U.S. entry, 746–749; women in, 753, 761–763
World Wide Web (WWW), 907
Wormley Hotel, 458
Worster, Donald, 543*f*
Wounded Knee, South Dakota, 851
WPA. *See* Works Progress Administration
Wright, Chauncey, 550
Wright, Orville, 695
Wright, Wilbur, 695
WTO. *See* World Trade Organization
WWW. *See* World Wide Web
Wyoming, woman suffrage in, 592

Xerox of America, 885
XYZ Affair, 189–190, 190*f*

Yale University, 98; football at, 529; Great Awakening and, 96; in 19th century, 325, 326; quotas on Jews at, 673
Yalta Conference (1945), 777–778
Yamamoto, Isoroku, 769–770
Yancey, William L., 391, 394
Yankee Stadium, 683*f*
Yeltsin, Boris, 895
YMCA, 530
Yom Kippur War, 864–866
Yorktown, Battle of, 144*m*, 145; Cornwallis's surrender at, 145*m*, 146*f*
Yorktown (ship), 770
Yorktown Campaign, in Revolutionary War, 145*m*
Youmans, Edward L., 540
Young, Andrew (Dr. Dre), 906
Young, Brigham, 307–308
"Young America" movement, 374–376; Stephen Douglas in, 376
Young people: curfews imposed on, 510; participation in politics, 581–582; in post–World War I period, 674–675
Young Plan (1929), 707
Youngstown, Ohio, steel industry in, 871*f*
Ypres, Third Battle of, 643*f*
Yugoslavia: civil war in, 895; and Greek civil war, 783

Zellweger, Renée, 678*f*, 730*f*
Zenger, John Peter, 83
Zeta-Jones, Catherine, 678*f*
Ziegler, Ron, 835*f*
Zola, Emile, 546
Zouave units, 404, 405
Zuckerman, Paul, 73*f*
Zwick, Edward, 420